# America Past and Present,
## Seventh Edition, Primary Source Edition
### Volume I

## It has everything students need to master the course!

A rich text with a clear, relevant, and balanced presentation of the social, economic, and cultural issues in the United States. A wealth of original primary source documents (at the end of this text) help make the material come alive by supporting the chapter content. Accompanying *Document Analysis* questions encourage students to delve deeper into the documents and explore how they relate to the events of the time. Documents are organized to correlate with chapter material.

Would you like even more primary source documents?

**myhistorylab**™
Where it's a good time to connect to the past!

## FREE when bundled with this book!

All of the primary source documents in this text plus hundreds more at no additional cost can be found on Longman's exclusive Web site—

www.ablongman.com/myhistorylab

*MyHistoryLab also contains a wealth of other resources including:*

• **Images** (photos, cartoons, and artwork), **maps** (including interactive maps), and **audio and video clips** (with historical music and historical and political video clips from the last century).

• **The electronic textbook** (eBook) with multimedia icons that link to exciting resources, expanding upon the key topics students encounter as they read through the text.

• **An integrated quizzing and testing program**—including pre-tests, post-tests, and chapter exams—to help students identify areas of strength and weakness.

• **"The History Bookshelf"** where fifty of the most commonly assigned works like Thomas Paine's *Common Sense*, *The Autobiography of Benjamin Franklin*, or *The Narrative of the Life of Frederick Douglass, An American Slave* can be read, downloaded, or printed.

*Professors get a wealth of instructor resources including a course management system, test bank, instructor's manual, PowerPoint® presentations, and more.*

**Go to www.myhistorylab.com, or read more about this exciting new Web site on the insert included in this textbook.**

# America

## Past and Present

### Volume I: To 1877

PRIMARY SOURCE EDITION

# America

## Past and Present

**Volume I To 1877**
**Seventh Edition**

**ROBERT A. DIVINE**
University of Texas

**T. H. BREEN**
Northwestern University

**GEORGE M. FREDRICKSON**
Stanford University

**R. HAL WILLIAMS**
Southern Methodist University

**ARIELA J. GROSS**
University of Southern California

**H. W. BRANDS**
Texas A&M University

PEARSON
Longman

New York   San Francisco   Boston
London   Toronto   Sydney   Tokyo   Singapore   Madrid
Mexico City   Munich   Paris   Cape Town   Hong Kong   Montreal

Executive Editor: Michael Boezi
Development Manager: Betty Slack
Development Editor: Karen Helfrich
Executive Marketing Manager: Sue Westmoreland
Supplements Editor: Kristi Olson
Project Coordination, Text Design, and Electronic Page Makeup: Elm Street Publishing Services, Inc.
Senior Design Manager/Cover Designer: Nancy Danahy
Cover and Frontispiece Image: Sarah Ann Wilson, American, unknown, United States, New York or New Jersey.
    Bedcover known as "Album Quilt." Inscription: Sarah Ann Wilson Aug, 1854. Needlework, 217.1 x 255.8 cm.
    Restricted gift of Mrs. David W. Grainger, 1999.509. Photographed by Gail Specht. Reproduction: The Art
    Institute of Chicago. All rights reserved.
Art Studio: Maps.com and Burmar Technical Corporation
Photo Research: Photosearch, Inc.
Manufacturing Manager: Mary Fischer
Printer and Binder: Quebecor World/Versailles
Cover Printer: The Lehigh Press, Inc.

For permission to use copyrighted material, grateful acknowledgment is made to the following copyright holders
and to those on pp. C1–C3, which are hereby made part of this copyright page.

Library of Congress Cataloging-in-Publication Data

America, past and present / Robert A. Divine . . . [et al.].—7th ed.
    p. cm.
Includes bibliographical references and index.
ISBN 0-321-18309-6 (set)—ISBN 0-321-18308-8 (v. 1)—ISBN
0-321-18307-X (v. 2)
  1. United States—History.   I. Divine, Robert A.
E178.1.A4894 2004
973—dc22

                                                                                    2003026058

Please visit our website at http://www.ablongman.com/divine

ISBN 0-321-36570-4 (Primary Source Edition, Complete Edition)
ISBN 0-321-36569-0 (Primary Source Edition, Volume I)
ISBN 0-321-36568-2 (Primary Source Edition, Volume II)

1 2 3 4 5 6 7 8 9 10—QWV—08 07 06 05

# Brief Contents

# Detailed Contents

## CHAPTER 7
## Democracy in Distress: The Violence of Party Politics, 1788–1800    190

## CHAPTER 8
## Republican Ascendancy: The Jeffersonian Vision    218

## CHAPTER 9
## Nation Building and Nationalism    246

## CHAPTER 10
# The Triumph of White Men's Democracy   272

## CHAPTER 11
# Slaves and Masters   300

## CHAPTER 12
# The Pursuit of Perfection   328

## CHAPTER 13
# An Age of Expansionism   358

# Maps

# Figures and Tables

## FIGURES

## TABLES

# Features

## Feature Essays

## Law and Society Essays

## A Look at the Past

# Preface

The seventh edition of *America Past and Present* is a major revision that strives to achieve the shared goal of the previous editions: to present a clear, relevant, and balanced history of the United States as an unfolding story of national development, from the days of the earliest inhabitants to the present. We emphasize the story because we strongly believe in the value of historical narrative in providing a vivid sense of the past. In each chapter, we seek to blend the excitement and drama of the American experience with insights about the social, economic, and cultural issues that underlie it.

## REVISIONS FOR THE SEVENTH EDITION

In this edition, we have reviewed each chapter carefully to take account of recent scholarly work, to offer new perspectives, and to sharpen the analysis and the prose. In many cases, we have adopted the suggestions offered by those who used the previous editions in their classrooms.

Throughout this edition, as in previous editions, we pay particular attention to the roles that women and minority groups have played in the development of American society and the American nation. These people appear throughout the text, not as witnesses to the historical narrative but as principal actors in its evolution. New and expanded material in this edition includes the following:

- Chapter 1, ecological transformation and the impact of the environment on human encounters during the contact era.
- Chapter 6, new opening vignette highlighting the search for balance between public morality and private freedom in the new republic; additional coverage of treaties and western lands after the Revolutionary War.
- Chapter 7, scientific debate and the spirit of nationalism in the post–revolutionary era.
- Chapter 9, expanded discussion of treaties negotiated with Great Britain following the War of 1812.
- Chapter 11, revised and reorganized to enhance and emphasize coverage of the lives and lifestyles of slaves and their experience of slavery.

- Chapter 12, expanded discussion of black abolitionists and women's rights reformers.
- Chapter 16, restructured and revised to devote greater attention to lives of former slaves during Reconstruction; includes new sections on Black Codes and Jim Crow laws.
- Chapter 17, new opening vignette exploring a Native American's experience of conquest and exploitation of the American West.
- Chapter 26, new opening vignette highlighting personal experiences of hardship during the Great Depression; revised discussion of the stock market crash of 1929.
- Chapter 29, expanded discussion of early civil rights leaders.
- Chapter 31, shifts in the labor movement in the 1970s, including the rise of public employee unions; the changing American family at the turn of the century.
- Chapter 33, revised and restructured to concentrate on the shifting economy of the 1990s to the present and the role of government policy in shaping American economy; updated with new discussion of foreign policy and homeland defense post–September 11, including new sections on the war on terrorism and war in Iraq.

## APPROACH AND THEMES

As the title suggests, our book is a blend of the traditional and the new. The strong narrative emphasis and chronological organization are traditional; the incorporation of the many fresh insights that historians have gained from social sciences in the past quarter century is new. We have used significant incidents and episodes to reflect the dilemmas, the choices, and the decisions made by the people as well as by their leaders. After discussion of the colonial period, most of the chapters examine shorter time periods, usually about a decade, permitting us to view major political and public events as points of reference and orientation around which social themes are integrated. This approach gives unity and direction to the text.

In recounting the story of the American past, we see a nation in flux. The early Africans and Europeans developed complex agrarian folkways that blended Old World customs and New World experiences; as cultural identities evolved, the idea of political independence became more acceptable. People who had been subjects of the British crown created a system of government that challenged later Americans to work out the full implications of theories of social and economic equality.

The growing sectional rift between the North and South, revolving around divergent models of economic growth and conflicting social values, culminated in civil war. In the post–Civil War period, the development of a more industrialized economy severely tested the values of an agrarian society, engendering a Populist reform movement. In the early twentieth century, Progressive reformers sought to infuse the industrial order with social justice. World War I demonstrated the extent of American power in the world. The Great Depression and World War II tested the resiliency of the maturing American nation. The Cold War ushered in an era of crises, foreign and domestic, that revealed both the strengths and the weaknesses of modern America. Although the Cold War ended with the break-up of the Soviet Union in the early 1990s, new threats to world peace in Africa, the Balkans, and the Middle East, and attacks on the World Trade Center and the Pentagon on September 11, 2001, led to the war on terrorism rather than to a new era of peace and tranquility.

Our story of American history goes beyond the major events that have helped to shape the nation—the wars fought, the presidents elected, the legislation enacted, the treaties signed. The impact of change on human lives adds a vital dimension to our understanding of history. How did the American Revolution affect the lives of ordinary citizens? What was it like for both blacks and whites to live in a plantation society? How did the shift from an agrarian to an industrial economy affect both men and women? What impact has technology, in the form of the automobile and the computer, had on patterns of life in the twentieth century? Our narrative explores these issues as well.

Our commitment is not to any particular ideology or point of view; rather, we hope to challenge our readers to rediscover the fascination of the American past and reach their own conclusions about its significance in their lives. At the same time, we have not avoided controversial issues; instead, we have tried to offer reasoned judgments on such morally charged subjects as the nature of slavery and the advent of nuclear weapons. We believe that while history rarely repeats itself, the story of the American past is relevant to the problems and dilemmas facing the nation today, and we have therefore sought to stress themes and ideas that continue to shape our national culture.

## STRUCTURE AND FEATURES

The structure and features of the book are intended to stimulate student interest and to reinforce learning. Each chapter begins with a vignette that introduces the chapter themes and previews the topics to be discussed. The chapter chronology serves as a summary of the key events covered in the chapter. The recommended readings and suggested Web sites at the end of each chapter are sources students can consult for further information on many topics. The feature essay in each chapter offers an examination of a high-interest topic related to the chapters themes and topics. Key terms, highlighted in boldface type in the chapter text, are defined in the new end-of-text glossary, pp. G1–G13.

### Feature Essays

There are eight new "Feature Essays" in the seventh edition, four of them focusing on aspects of peoples' relationships with and impact on the natural world throughout American history. The new essays are:

- Chapter 7, "Defense of Superiority: Science in the Service of Nationalism in the Early Republic"
- Chapter 8, "Barbary Pirates and American Captives: The Nation's First Hostage Crisis"
- Chapter 9, "Confronting New Land"
- Chapter 11, "Harriet Jacobs and Maria Norcom: Women of Southern Households"
- Chapter 18, "Chicago's 'Second Nature'"
- Chapter 19, "Ellis Island: Isle of Hope, Isle of Tears"
- Chapter 31, "Three Mile Island and Chernobyl: The Promise and Peril of Nuclear Power"
- Chapter 33, "The Dot.com Boom and Bust"

### Law and Society Essays

Nine "Law and Society" essays appear in the text. Each of these essays focuses on a significant legal case or legal problem in American history and includes a discussion of the background of the case, excerpts from the trial transcript or other relevant primary source material, and coverage of the case in the news media of the period. The introductory section establishes the context for the case and the concluding paragraphs of each essay invite students to explore the legal contest from the perspective of social/cultural historians. New discussion questions are included to spark class discussion. The seventh edition includes two new "Law and Society" essays:

- Chapter 12, "The Legal Rights of Married Women: Reforming the Law of Coverture"
- Chapter 25, "The Scopes "Monkey" Trial: Contesting Cultural Differences"

### Visual Program

The extensive full-color map program has been improved with several new and revised maps. Each map includes a caption to help students identify the purpose and significance of the map. New charts, graphs, and tables—many with a capsulized format for convenient review of factual information—relate to social and economic change. The rich, full-color illustration program, bearing directly on the narrative, advances and expands the themes, provides elaboration and contrast, tells more of the story, and generally adds another dimension of learning. "Look at the Past" photographs are illustrations of artifacts that present students with a material record of America's past.

Captions invite them to consider the historical significance of the artifacts and make connections with similar materials they encounter today.

## AUTHOR RESPONSIBILITY

Although this book is a joint effort, each author took primary responsibility for writing one section. T. H. Breen contributed the first eight chapters, going from the earliest Native American period to the second decade of the nineteenth century. George M. Fredrickson wrote Chapters 9 through 16, carrying the narrative through the Reconstruction era. Ariela J. Gross revised Chapters 11 and 16 and contributed the Law and Society feature in Chapter 12. R. Hal Williams was responsible for Chapters 17 through 24, focusing on the industrial transformation, urbanization, and the events culminating in World War I. The final nine chapters, bringing the story through the Great Depression, World War II, and the Cold War and its aftermath, were the work of H. W. Brands, especially Chapters 25 through 27, and Robert A. Divine, primarily Chapters 28 through 33. Each contributor reviewed and revised the work of his or her colleagues and helped shape the material into its final form.

# Supplements

## For Qualified College Adopters: Instructor Supplements

### Instructor's Resource Manual

Prepared by James Walsh of Central Connecticut State University, each chapter of this resource manual contains interpretative essays, anecdotes and references to biographical or primary sources, and a comprehensive summary of the text. ISBN: 0-321-21724-1.

### Test Bank

Prepared by Denise Wright of University of Georgia, this test bank contains over 1,200 multiple-choice, true/false, matching, and completion questions. ISBN: 0-321-21721-7.

### TestGen-EQ Computerized Testing System

This flexible, easy-to-master computerized test bank on a dual-platform CD includes all of the items in the printed test bank and allows instructors to select specific questions, edit existing questions, and add their own items to create exams. Tests can be printed in several different fonts and formats and can include figures such as graphs and tables. ISBN: 0-321-21720-9.

### History Digital Media Archive CD-ROM

The Digital Media Archive CD-ROM contains electronic images and interactive and static maps, along with media elements such as video. These media assets are fully customizable and ready for classroom presentation or easy downloading into your PowerPoint™ presentations or any other presentation software. ISBN: 0-321-14976-9.

### Digital Media Archive, Updated Second Edition

Now on two CD-ROMs and with added content, this encyclopedic collection contains dozens of narrated vignettes and videos as well as hundreds of photos and illustrations ready for use in your own PowerPoint™ presentations, course web sites, or on-line courses. Free to qualified college adopters.

### Companion Web Site, www.ablongman.com/divine

Instructors can take advantage of the Companion Web Site that supports this text. The instructor section of the Web site includes teaching links and links to downloadable versions of all print supplements.

### PowerPoint™ Presentations

These presentations contain an average of 15 PowerPoint™ slides for each chapter. These slides may include key points and terms for a lecture on the chapter as well as four-color slides of all maps, graphs, and charts within a particular chapter. The presentations are available for download at www.ablongman.com/suppscentral.

### CourseCompass™, www.ablongman.com/coursecompass

Combines the strength of the content from *America Past and Present*, Seventh Edition, with state-of-the-art eLearning tools. CourseCompass™ is an easy-to-use on-line course management system that allows professors to tailor content and functionality to meet individual course needs. Every CourseCompass™ course includes a range of pre-loaded content—all designed to help students master core course objectives. Organized by era, CourseCompass™ allows you to access maps, map exercises, and primary sources as well as test questions from the print test bank and the full text of several of our best-selling supplements. The *America Past and Present* CourseCompass™ site is available at no additional charge for students whose professor has requested that a student Access Kit be bundled with the text.

### BlackBoard and WebCT

Longman's extensive American history content is available in these two major course management platforms: BlackBoard and WebCT. All quickly and easily customizable for use with *America Past and Present*, Seventh Edition, the content includes multiple primary sources, maps, and map exercises. Book-specific testing is simply uploaded.

### The History Place Premium Web Site, www.ushistoryplace.com

Available at no additional cost when requested as a bundle component by the professor, the site offers extraordinary breadth and depth, featuring unmatched interactive maps, timelines, and activities; hundreds of source documents, images, and audio clips; and much more.

### Comprehensive American History Transparency Set

This collection includes more than 200 four-color American history map transparencies on subjects ranging from the first Native Americans to the end of the Cold War, covering wars, social trends, elections, immigration, and demographics. ISBN: 0-673-97211-9.

### Text-specific Transparency Set

A set of four-color transparency acetates showing maps from the text. ISBN: 0-321-21719-5.

### Video Lecture Launchers

Prepared by Mark Newman, University of Illinois at Chicago, these video lecture launchers (each two to five minutes in duration) cover key issues in American history from 1877 to the present. The launchers are accompanied by an Instructor's Manual. ISBN: 0-321-01869-9.

## For Students

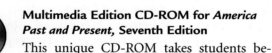

### Multimedia Edition CD-ROM for *America Past and Present*, Seventh Edition

This unique CD-ROM takes students beyond the printed page, offering them a complete multimedia learning experience. It contains the full annotatable textbook on CD-ROM, with contextually placed media—audio, video, interactive maps, photos, figures, Web links, and practice tests—that link students to additional content directly related to key concepts in the text. The CD also contains the Study Guide, map workbooks, a primary source reader, and more than a dozen supplementary books most often assigned in American history courses. Free to qualified college adopters when packaged with the text. ISBN: 0-321-23474-4.

### Study Guide and Practice Tests

Prepared by Jennifer Lynn Gross of Jacksonville State University and John Walker Davis of University of Georgia. Each of the two-volume study guides begins with an introductory essay, "Skills for Studying and Learning History." Each chapter contains a summary, learning objectives, identification list, map exercises, glossary, and multiple-choice, completion, and essay questions, and new critical thinking exercises involving primary sources. Volume One: ISBN: 0-321-21286-X; Volume Two: ISBN: 0-321-21722-5.

### Longman American History Atlas

A four-color reference tool and visual guide to American history that includes almost 100 maps and covers the full scope of history. Atlas overhead transparencies available to qualified college adopters. $3.00 when bundled. ISBN: 0-321-00486-8.

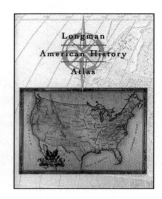

### *Mapping America: A Guide to Historical Geography,* Second Edition

A two-volume workbook by Ken L. Weatherbie, Del Mar College, that presents the basic geography of the United States and helps students place the history of the United States into spatial perspective. Free to qualified college adopters when bundled. Volume One: ISBN: 0-321-00487-6; Volume Two: ISBN: 0-321-00488-4.

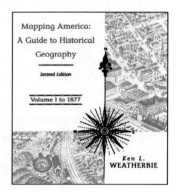

### *Mapping American History*

A workbook created by Gerald A. Danzer for use in conjunction with *Discovering American History Through Maps and Views* and designed to teach students to interpret and analyze cartographic materials as historical documents. Free to qualified college adopters when bundled. ISBN: 0-673-53768-4.

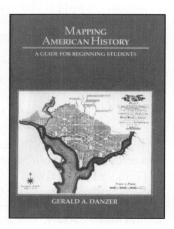

### Companion Web Site for *America Past and Present,* Seventh Edition, www.ablongman.com/divine

The Companion Web Site provides a wealth of resources for students using the text. Students can access chapter summaries, interactive practice test questions, and Web links for every chapter. The Web site is a comprehensive on-line study guide for students.

### Research Navigator Guide

This guidebook includes exercises and tips on how to use the Internet. It also includes an access code for Research Navigator™—the easiest way for students to start a research assignment or research paper. Research Navigator™ is composed of three exclusive databases of credible and reliable source material including EBSCO's ContentSelect™ Academic Journal Database, New York Times Search by Subject Archive, and "Best of the Web" Link Library. This comprehensive site also includes a detailed help section. ISBN: 0-205-40838-9.

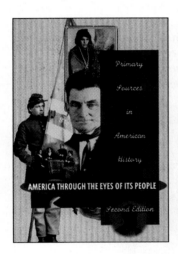

### America Through the Eyes of Its People, Second Edition

A comprehensive anthology that makes primary sources widely available in an inexpensive format, balancing social and political history and providing up-to-date narrative material. Free to qualified college adopters when bundled. ISBN: 0-673-97738-2.

### Sources of the African American Past, Second Edition

Edited by Roy Finkenbine, University of Detroit at Mercy, this collection of primary sources covers key themes in the African American experience from the West African background to the present. Balanced between political and social history, it offers a vivid snapshot of the lives of African Americans in different historical periods and includes documents representing women and different regions of the United States. Available to qualified college adopters at a minimum cost when bundled with the text. ISBN: 0-321-16216-1.

### Women and the National Experience, Second Edition

Edited by Ellen Skinner, Pace University, this primary source reader contains both classic and unusual documents describing the history of women in the United States. The documents provide dramatic evidence that outspoken women attained a public voice and participated in the development of national events and policies long before they could vote. Chronologically organized and balanced between social and political history, this reader offers a striking picture of the lives of women across American history. Available to qualified college adopters at a minimum cost when bundled with the text. ISBN: 0-321-00555-4.

### Reading the American West

Edited by Mitchel Roth, Sam Houston State University, this primary source reader uses letters, diary excerpts, speeches, interviews, and newspaper articles to let students experience how historians research and how history is written. Every document is accompanied by a contextual headnote and study questions. The book is divided into chapters with extensive introductions. Available to qualified college adopters at a minimum cost when bundled with the text. ISBN: 0-321-04409-6.

### A Short Guide to Writing About History, Fifth Edition

Richard Marius, Harvard University, Melvin E. Page Eastern Tennessee University. This engaging and practical text helps students get beyond merely compiling dates and facts; it teaches them how to incorporate their own ideas into their papers and to tell a story about history that interests them and their peers. Covering both brief essays and the documented resource paper, the text explores the writing and researching processes, different modes of historical writing including argument, and concludes with guidelines for improving style. ISBN: 0-321-22716-6.

### Constructing the American Past, Fifth Edition

Compiled and edited by Elliot Gorn and Randy Roberts of Purdue University, this popular two-volume reader consists of a variety of primary sources, grouped around central themes in American history. Each chapter focuses on a particular problem in American history, providing students with several points of view from which to examine the historical evidence. Introductions and study questions prompt students to participate in interpreting the past and challenge them to understand the problems in relation to the big picture of American history. Volume One ISBN: 0-321-21642-3; Volume Two ISBN: 0-321-21641-5.

### From These Beginnings: A Biographical Approach to American History, Seventh Edition

Written by Roderick Nash of the University of California, Santa Barbara, and Gregory Graves of California State University, Northridge, this collection of biographical essays takes a look at the lives of famous men and women whose contributions helped create a nation and a society. Each biography offers students a uniquely personal and provocative glimpse into the lives of these Americans and shows how their experiences are linked to historical events. Volume One ISBN: 0-321-21640-7; Volume Two ISBN: 0-321-21639-3.

### American Experiences: Readings in American History, Sixth Edition

This two-volume collection of secondary readings, compiled and edited by Randy Roberts of Purdue University and James Olson of Sam Houston State University, contains articles that emphasize social history in order to illuminate important aspects of America's past. *American Experiences* addresses the complexity and richness of the nation's past by focusing on the people themselves—how they coped with, adjusted to, or rebelled against America. The readings examine people as they worked and played, fought and loved, lived and died. Volume One ISBN: 0-321-21644-X; Volume Two ISBN: 0-321-21643-1.

### American History in a Box

This unique primary source reader offers students the opportunity to experience written documents, visual materials, material culture artifacts, and maps in order to learn firsthand what history is and what historians actually do. It was written and put together by Julie Roy Jeffrey and Peter Frederick; Volume One (to 1877) ISBN: 0-321-30005-2; Volume Two (since 1865) ISBN: 0-321-03006-0.

### The History Place Premium Web Site, www.ushistoryplace.com

Available at no additional cost when requested as a bundle component by the professor, the site is a continually updated American history Web site of extraordinary breadth and depth, which features unmatched interactive maps, timelines, and activities; hundreds of source documents, images, and audio clips; and much more.

### The Library of American Biography Series

Each of the interpretative biographies in this series focuses on a figure whose actions and ideas significantly influenced the course of American history and national life. Brief and inexpensive, they are ideal for any American history survey course. Available to qualified college adopters at a discount when bundled with this text.

## Penguin Books

The partnership between Penguin-Putnam USA and Longman Publishers offers students a discount on many titles when you bundle them with any Longman survey. Among these include

- Frederick Douglass, *Narrative of the Life of Frederick Douglass*
- L. Jesse Lemisch (Editor), *Benjamin Franklin: The Autobiography & Other Writings*
- Upton Sinclair, *The Jungle*
- Harriet Beecher Stowe, *Uncle Tom's Cabin*

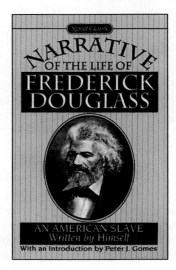

# Acknowledgments

The authors acknowledge with special gratitude the contribution of Professor Jeanne Whitney of Salisbury State University for her work in selecting many of the featured "Look at the Past" illustrations and writing the informative and thought-provoking captions to accompany these photos. We are also most grateful to our consultants and reviewers whose thoughtful and constructive work contributed greatly to this edition. Their many helpful suggestions led to significant improvements in the final product.

Elizabeth Ansnes, *San Jose State University*

Donald Scott Barton, *East Central University*

Chad Berry, *Maryville College*

Kent Blaser, *Wayne State College*

Eric J. Bolsterli, *University of Texas at Arlington*

Kathleen S. Carter, *High Point University*

Yvonne Sutton Cornelius, *Nashville State Community College*

Edward R. Crowther, *Adams State University*

Roger P. Davis, *University of Nebraska at Kearney*

Patricia Norred Derr, *Kutztown University*

Wallace Hettle, *University of Northern Iowa*

Virginia G. Jelatis, *Western Illinois University*

Sandra Wagner-Wright, *University of Hawaii at Hilo*

This book owes much to the many conscientious historians who reviewed previous editions and offered valuable suggestions that led to many improvements in the text. We acknowledge with gratitude the contributions of the following:

Frank W. Abbott, *University of Houston*

Joseph L. Adams, *St. Louis Community College at Meramec*

Frank Alduino, *Anne Arundel Community College*

Kenneth G. Alfers, *Mountain View College*

Thomas Archdeacon, *University of Wisconsin*

James Axtell, *College of William and Mary*

Kenneth R. Bain, *Northwestern University*

James Banks, *Cuyahoga Community College*

Lois W. Banner, *Hamilton College*

David Bernstein, *California State University, Long Beach*

James D. Border, *Berkshire Community College*

Alexander O. Boulton, *Villa Julie College*

Mary C. Brennan, *Ohio State University*

Blanche Brick, *Blinn College*

Daniel Patrick Brown, *Moorpark College*

Thomas Camfield, *Sam Houston State University*

Clayborne Carson, *Stanford University*

Kathleen S. Carter, *High Point University*

Raphael Cassimere, Jr., *University of New Orleans*

Francis Coan, *Central Connecticut State University*

Charles L. Cohen, *University of Wisconsin*

Jerald Combs, *San Francisco State University*

John Cooper, *University of Wisconsin*

Nancy F. Cott, *Yale University*

Virginia Crane, *University of Wisconsin, Oshkosh*

James C. Curtis, *University of Delaware*

Bruce J. Dierenfield, *Canisius College*

Charles Douglass, *Florida Community College at Jacksonville*

Thomas Dublin, *State University of New York at Binghamton*

Perry R. Duis, *University of Illinois at Chicago*

Richard Ellis, *State University of New York at Buffalo*

John P. Farr, *Chattanooga State Technical Community College*

James E. Fell, Jr., *University of Colorado, Denver*

Eric Foner, *Columbia University*

Stephen Foster, *Northern Illinois University*

William W. Freehling, *Johns Hopkins University*

Fred E. Freidel, *Bellevue Community College*

Richard Frey, *Southern Oregon State College*

Gary W. Gallagher, *Pennsylvania State University*

Sara E. Gallaway, *Oxnard College*

Don R. Gerlach, *University of Akron*

August W. Giebelhaus, *Georgia Institute of Technology*

Louis S. Gomolak, *Southwest Texas State University*

Lewis L. Gould, *University of Texas*

Lawrence Grear, *Langston University*

Richard C. Haney, *University of Wisconsin, Whitewater*

George Harrison, *Jones County Junior College*

Edward F. Hass, *Wright State University*

Tim Heinrichs, *Bellevue Community College*

Mary Ann Heiss, *Kent State University*

Kenneth E. Hendrickson, *Sam Houston State University*

Sondra Herman, *De Anza Community College*

Anne Hickling, *San Jose City College*

James Hollingsworth, *Pasco-Hernando Community College*

Ranford Hopkins, *Moorpark College*

Brian Hosmer, *University of Delaware*

John R. Howe, *University of Minnesota*

Nathan I. Huggins, *Harvard University*

Susan Hult, *Houston Community College*

James A. Hurst, *Northwest Missouri State University*

Wallace S. Hutcheon, *Northern Virginia Community College*

Robert M. Ireland, *University of Kentucky*

Carol E. Jenson, *University of Wisconsin, La Crosse*

Juli A. Jones, *St. Charles County Community College*

Robert R. Jones, *University of Southwestern Louisiana*

John Kelley, *Shawnee State Community College*

Richard S. Kirkendall, *University of Washington*

I. E. Kirkpatrick, *Tyler Junior College*

Fred Koestler, *Tarleton State University*

Lawrence F. Kohl, *University of Alabama*

Steven Lawson, *Rutgers University*

Edward Lee, *Winthrop University*

Kathy Long, *Chattanooga State Technical Community College*

Henry Louis, *Kansas City Kansas Community College*

Warren Mackey, *Chattanooga State Technical Community College*

Thomas R. Mandeville, *Clinton Community College*

Karen Marcotte, *Palo Alto College*

Herbert F. Margulies, *University of Hawaii*

Myron Marty, *National Endowment for the Humanities*

Robert C. McMath, Jr., *Georgia Institute of Technology*

T. Ronald Melton, *Brewton-Parker College*

James H. Merrell, *Vassar College*

Joseph C. Miller, *University of Virginia*

William G. Morris, *Midland College*

Harmon Mothershead, *Northwest Missouri State University*

Timothy Moy, *University of New Mexico*

Peter Murray, *Methodist College*

John M. Murrin, *Princeton University*

John K. Nelson, *University of North Carolina*

Roger L. Nichols, *University of Arizona*

Elizabeth R. Osborne, *Indiana University–Purdue University at Indianapolis*

Elliot Pasternack, *Middlesex County College*

J'Nell L. Pate, *Tarrant County Junior College*

Michael Perman, *University of Illinois, Chicago*

Charles A. Pilant, *Cumberland College*

Nora Ramirez, *San Antonio Community College*

Marlette Rebhorn, *Austin Community College*

Douglas W. Richmond, *University of Texas, Arlington*

Andrew W. Robertson, *Louisiana State University*

David Sandoval, *University of Southern Colorado*

Howard Schonberger, *University of Maine*

Ingrid Winther Scobie, *Texas Women's University*

Rebecca S. Shoemaker, *Indiana State University*

Kathryn Kish Sklar, *State University of New York at Binghamton*

Allan Spetter, *Wright State University*

Cherry L. Spruill, *Indiana University–Purdue University at Indianapolis*

Mark J. Stegmaier, *Cameron University*

George G. Suggs, Jr., *Southeast Missouri State University*

H. Micheal Tarver, *McNeese State University*

Paul F. Taylor, *Augusta College*

Michael E. Thompson, *South Seattle Community College*

George Torok, *El Paso Community College*

Clyde D. Tyson, *Niagara County Community College*

Nancy C. Unger, *San Francisco State University*

Richard Vanderpool, *Umpqua Community College*

Donna L. VanRaaphorst, *Cuyahoga Community College*

Russell Veeder, *Dickinson State University*

Daniel C. Vogt, *Jackson State University*

Forrest A. Walker, *Eastern New Mexico State University*

James P. Walsh, *Central Connecticut State University*

Ronald Walters, *Johns Hopkins University*

Marli Weiner, *University of Maine*

Frank Wetta, *Galveston Community College*

James C. Williams, *De Anza College*

James M. Woods, *Georgia Southern University*

David Yancey, *San Jose City College*

Rosemarie Zagarri, *Catholic University*

Robert F. Zeidel, *University of Wisconsin, Stout*

The staff at Longman continued its generous support and assistance for our efforts. We thank Acquisitions Editor Ashley Dodge for her attention, support, and thoughtful guidance throughout this revision; Development Manager Betty Slack and Development Editor Karen Helfrich, who helped us augment and enhance the appeal of the text; and Executive Marketing Manager Sue Westmoreland, who worked zealously to convey the message and vision of the authors to the Longman sales force and to the marketplace. Production Manager Douglas Bell, Cover Design Manager/Cover Designer Nancy Danahy, and Project Editor Heather Johnson and the staff at Elm Street Publishing Services put the finishing touches on this new edition and deftly guided it through the many phases of production.

Finally, each author received aid and encouragement from many colleagues, friends, and family members. Bob Divine extends special thanks to Mitch Lerner for research assistance and editorial suggestions. T. H. Breen thanks Bradley S. Schlager, Seth Cotlar, Timothy Hall, Christopher Hodson, and Patrick Griffin for their help with this edition. George Fredrickson acknowledges with gratitude the research and assistance of Jared Farmer. Hal Williams extends thanks to Carole S. Cohen, Jacqueline Bradley, Lisa R. Henry, and Susan Harper-Bisso for their help with revisions for this edition. Ariela Gross extends thanks to Lori Martinez, John Acevedo, and especially Stephen Andrews for invaluable help with this edition.

*The Authors*

# About the Authors

## ROBERT A. DIVINE

Robert A. Divine, George W. Littlefield Professor Emeritus in American History at the University of Texas at Austin, received his Ph.D. from Yale University in 1954. A specialist in American diplomatic history, he taught from 1954 to 1996 at the University of  Texas, where he was honored by both the student association and the graduate school for teaching excellence. His extensive published work includes *The Illusion of Neutrality* (1962); *Second Chance: The Triumph of Internationalism in America During World War II* (1967); and *Blowing on the Wind* (1978). His most recent work is *Perpetual War for Perpetual Peace* (2000), a comparative analysis of twentieth-century American wars. He is also the author of *Eisenhower and the Cold War* (1981) and editor of three volumes of essays on the presidency of Lyndon Johnson. His book, *The Sputnik Challenge* (1993), won the Eugene E. Emme Astronautical Literature Award for 1993. He has been a fellow at the Center for Advanced Study in the Behavioral Sciences and has given the Albert Shaw Lectures in Diplomatic History at Johns Hopkins University.

## T. H. BREEN

T. H. Breen, William Smith Mason Professor of American History at Northwestern University, received his Ph.D. from Yale University in 1968. He has taught at Northwestern since 1970. Breen's major books include *The Character of the Good Ruler: A Study of Puritan*  *Political Ideas in New England* (1974); *Puritans and Adventurers: Change and Persistence in Early America* (1980); *Tobacco Culture: The Mentality of the Great Tidewater Planters on the Eve of Revolution* (1985); and, with Stephen Innes of the University of Virginia, *"Myne Owne Ground": Race and Freedom on Virginia's Eastern Shore* (1980). His *Imagining the Past* (1989) won the 1990

Historic Preservation Book Award. His most recent book is *Common Goods: Revolutionary Markets on the Eve of American Independence* (2003). In addition to receiving several awards for outstanding teaching at Northwestern, Breen has been the recipient of research grants from the American Council of Learned Societies, the Guggenheim Foundation, the Institute for Advanced Study (Princeton), the National Humanities Center, and the Huntington Library. For his article "Narrative of Commercial Life: Consumption, Ideology, and Community on the Eve of the American Revolution," which appeared in the July 1993 issue of *William and Mary Quarterly*, Breen received an award from the National Society, Daughters of Colonial Wars, for best article published in the quarterly in 1993 and the Douglass Adair Memorial Prize for best article published in the quarterly during the 1988–1993 period. He has served as the Fowler Hamilton Fellow at Christ Church, Oxford University (1987–1988), the Pitt Professor of American History and Institutions, Cambridge University (1990–1991), and the Harmsworth Professor of American History at Oxford University (2000–2001). He is currently working on an opera based on an essay he wrote on the wrongful execution of an African American in 1768.

## GEORGE M. FREDRICKSON

George M. Fredrickson is Edgar E. Robinson Professor Emeritus of United States History at Stanford University. He is the author or editor of several books, including *The Inner Civil War* (1965), *The Black Image in the White Mind* (1971), and *White Supremacy:*  *A Comparative Study in American and South African History* (1981), which won both the Ralph Waldo Emerson Award from Phi Beta Kappa and the Merle Curti Award from the Organization of American Historians. His most recent books are *Black Liberation: A Comparative History of Black Ideologies in the United States and South Africa* (1995); *The Comparative Imagination: Racism, Nationalism, and Social Movements* (1997); and *Racism: A Short History* (2002). He received his A.B. and Ph.D. from Harvard and has been the recipient of a Guggenheim Fellowship, two National Endowment for the Humanities Senior Fellowships, and a fellowship from the Center for Advanced Studies in the Behavioral Sciences. Before coming to Stanford in 1984, he taught at Northwestern. He has also served as Fulbright lecturer in American History at Moscow University and as the Harmsworth Professor of American History at Oxford. He served as president of the Organization of American Historians in 1997–1998.

## R. HAL WILLIAMS

R. Hal Williams is professor of history at Southern Methodist University. He received his A.B. from Princeton University in 1963 and his Ph.D. from Yale University in 1968. His books include *The Democratic Party and California Politics, 1880–1896* (1973);
*Years of Decision: American Politics in the 1890s* (1978); and *The Manhattan Project: A Documentary Introduction to the Atomic Age* (1990). A specialist in American political history, he taught at Yale University from 1968 to 1975 and came to SMU in 1975 as chair of the Department of History. From 1980 to 1988, he served as dean of Dedman College, the school of humanities and sciences, at SMU. In 1980, he was a visiting professor at University College, Oxford University. Williams has received grants from the American Philosophical Society and the National Endowment for the Humanities, and he has served on the Texas Committee for the Humanities. He is currently working on a biography of James G. Blaine, the late-nineteenth-century speaker of the House, secretary of state, and Republican presidential candidate.

## ARIELA J. GROSS

Ariela J. Gross is professor of law and history at the University of Southern California. She received her B.A. from Harvard University, her J.D. from Stanford Law School, and her Ph.D. from Stanford University. She is the author of *Double Character:*
*Slavery and Mastery in the Antebellum Southern Courtroom* (2000) and numerous law review articles and book chapters. Her current work in progress, a history of racial identity on trial in the United States to be published by Farrar, Straus & Giroux, is supported by fellowships from the Guggenheim Foundation, the National Endowment for the Humanities, and the American Council for Learned Societies.

## H. W. BRANDS

H. W. Brands is University Distinguished Professor and Melbern G. Glasscock Chair in American History at Texas A&M University, where he has taught since 1987. He is the author of numerous works of history and international affairs, including *The Devil We*
*Knew: Americans and the Cold War* (1993), *What America Owes the World: The Struggle for the Soul of Foreign Policy* (1998), *Into the Labyrinth: The United States and the Middle East* (1994), *The Reckless Decade: America in the 1890s* (1995), *TR: The Last Romantic* (a biography of Theodore Roosevelt) (1997), *The First American: The Life and Times of Benjamin Franklin* (2000), *The Strange Death of American Liberalism* (2001), *The Age of Gold: The California Gold Rush and the New American Dream* (2002), and *Woodrow Wilson* (2003). His writing has received critical and popular acclaim; *The First American* was a finalist for the Pulitzer Prize and a national best-seller. He lectures frequently across North America and in Europe. His essays and reviews have appeared in the *New York Times*, the *Wall Street Journal*, the *Washington Post*, the *Los Angeles Times*, and *Atlantic Monthly*. He is a regular guest on radio and television, and has participated in several historical documentary films.

# America

## Past and Present

Europeans imagined a New World that often bore little relation to reality. This early engraving depicts the coast of North America as a dangerous place where hostile Indians, navigational hazards, and sea monsters greeted English sailors. ❖

# New World Encounters

## *Clash of Cultures: Interpreting Murder in Early Maryland*

New World conquest sparked unexpected, often embarrassing contests over the alleged superiority of European culture. Not surprisingly, the colonizers insisted they brought the benefits of civilization to the primitive and savage peoples of North America. Native Americans never shared this perspective, voicing a strong preference for their own values and institutions. In early seventeenth-century Maryland the struggle over cultural superiority turned dramatically on how best to punish the crime of murder, an issue about which both Native Americans and Europeans had firm opinions.

The actual events that occurred at Captain William Claiborne's trading post in 1635 may never be known. Surviving records indicate that several young Native American males identified as Wicomesses apparently traveled to Claiborne's on business, but to their great annoyance, they found the proprietor entertaining Susquehannocks, their most hated enemies. The situation deteriorated rapidly after the Susquehannocks ridiculed the Wicomesses, "whereat some of Claiborne's people that saw it, did laugh." Unwilling to endure public humiliation, the Wicomesses later ambushed the Susquehannocks, killing five, and then returned to the trading post where they murdered three Englishmen.

Wicomess leaders realized immediately that something had to be done. They dispatched a trusted messenger to inform the governor of Maryland that they intended "to offer satisfaction for the harm ... done to the English." The murder of the Susquehannocks was another matter, best addressed by the Native Americans themselves. The governor praised the Wicomesses for coming forward, announcing that "I expect that those men, who have done this outrage, should be delivered unto me, to do with them as I shall think fit."

The Wicomess spokesman was dumbfounded. The governor surely did not understand basic Native American legal procedure. "It is the manner amongst us Indians, that if any such like accident happens," he explained, "we do redeem the life of a man that is so slain with a 100 Arms length of *Roanoke* (which is a sort of Beads that they make, and use for money.)" The governor's demand for prisoners seemed doubly impertinent, "since you [English settlers] are here strangers, and coming into our Country, you should rather conform your selves to the Customs of our Country, than impose yours upon us." At this point the governor hastily ended the conversation, perhaps uncomfortably aware that if the legal tables had been turned and the murders committed in England, he would be the one loudly defending "the Customs of our Country."

EUROPEANS SAILING IN THE WAKE of Admiral Christopher Columbus constructed a narrative of superiority that survived long after the Wicomesses had been dispersed—a fate that befell them in the late seventeenth century. The story recounted first in Europe and then in the United States depicted heroic adventures, missionaries, and soldiers sharing Western civilization with the peoples of the New World and opening a vast virgin land to economic development. The familiar tale celebrated material progress, the inevitable spread of European values, and the taming of frontiers.

It was a history crafted by the victors—usually by white leaders such as Maryland's governor—and by the children of the victors to explain how they had come to inherit the land.

This narrative of events no longer provides an adequate explanation for European conquest and settlement. It is not so much wrong as partisan, incomplete, even offensive. History recounted from the perspective of the victors inevitably silences the voices of the victims, the peoples who, in the victors' view, foolishly resisted economic and technological progress. Heroic tales of the advance of Western values only serve to deflect modern attention away from the rich cultural and racial diversity that characterized North American societies for a very long time. More disturbing, traditional tales of European conquest also obscure the sufferings of the millions of Native Americans who perished, as well as the huge numbers of Africans sold in the New World as slaves.

By placing these complex, often unsettling, experiences within an interpretive framework of *creative adaptations*—rather than of *exploration* or *settlement*—we go a long way toward recapturing the full human dimensions of conquest and resistance. While the New World often witnessed tragic violence and systematic betrayal, it allowed ordinary people of three different races and many different ethnic identities opportunities to shape their own lives as best they could within diverse, often hostile environments.

It should be remembered that neither the Native Americans nor the Africans were passive victims of European exploitation. Within their own families and communities they made choices, sometimes rebelling, sometimes accommodating, but always trying to make sense in terms of their own cultures of what was happening to them. Of course, that was precisely what the Wicomess messenger tried to tell the governor of Maryland.

## NATIVE AMERICAN HISTORIES BEFORE CONQUEST

As almost any Native American could have informed the first European adventurers, the peopling of America did not begin in 1492. In fact, although Spanish invaders such as Columbus proclaimed the discovery of a "New World," they really brought into contact three worlds—Europe, Africa, and America—that in the fifteenth century were already old. Indeed, the first migrants reached the North American continent some fifteen to twenty thousand years ago. The precise dating of this great human trek remains a hotly contested topic. Although some archaeologists maintain that settlement began as early as thirty thousand years ago, the scientific evidence in support of this thesis currently is not persuasive. However this debate eventually resolves itself, no one doubts that Native Americans have recorded a very long history in North America. Their social and cultural development over the period was as complex as any encountered in the so-called Old World.

Environmental conditions played a major part in the story. Twenty thousand years ago the earth's climate was considerably colder than it is today. Huge glaciers, often more than a mile thick, extended as far south as the present states of Illinois and Ohio and covered broad sections of western Canada. Much of the world's moisture was transformed into ice, and the oceans dropped hundreds of feet below their current levels. The receding waters created a land bridge connecting Asia and North America, a region now submerged beneath the Bering Sea that modern archaeologists named Beringia.

Even at the height of the last Ice Age, much of the far North remained free of glaciers. Small bands of spear-throwing Paleo-Indians pursued giant mammals (megafauna)—woolly mammoths and mastodons, for example—across the vast tundra of Beringia. These hunters were the first human beings to set foot on a vast, uninhabited continent. Because these migrations took place over a long period of time and involved small, independent bands of highly nomadic people, the Paleo-Indians never developed a sense of common identity. Each group focused on its own immediate survival, adjusting to the opportunities presented by various microenvironments.

The material culture of the Paleo-Indians differed little from that of other Stone Age peoples found in Asia, Africa, and Europe. In terms of human health, however, something occurred on the Beringian tundra that forever altered the history of Native Americans. For reasons that remain obscure, the members of these small migrating groups stopped hosting a number of communicative diseases—smallpox and measles being the deadliest—and although Native Americans experienced illnesses such as tuberculosis, they no longer suffered the major epidemics that under normal conditions would have killed a large percentage of their population every year. The physical isolation of the various bands may have protected them from the spread of contagious disease. Another theory notes that epidemics have frequently been associated with prolonged contact with domestic animals such as cattle and pigs. Since the Paleo-Indians did not domesticate animals, not even horses, they may have avoided the microbes that caused virulent European and African

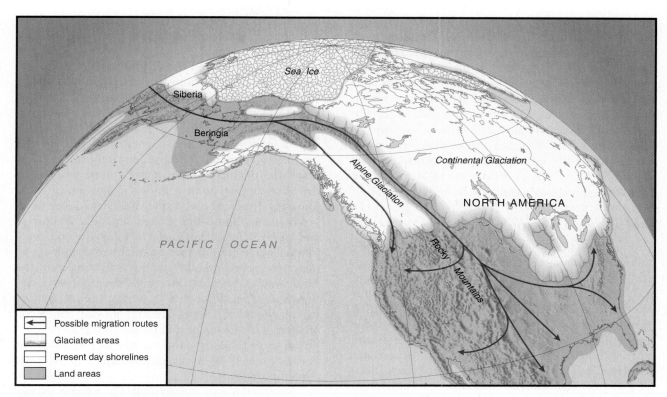

**ROUTES OF THE FIRST AMERICANS**    *The peopling of North America began about 20,000 years ago, during an Ice Age, and continued for many millennia. Land bridges created by lower sea levels during glaciation formed a tundra coastal plain over what is now the Bering Strait, between Asia and North America.* ❖

diseases. Whatever the explanation for this curious epidemiological record, Native Americans lost inherited immunities that later might have protected them from many contagious germs. Thus, when they first came into contact with Europeans and Africans, Native Americans had no defense against the great killers of the Early Modern world.

## The Environmental Challenge: Food, Climate, and Culture

Some twelve thousand years ago global warming substantially reduced the glaciers, allowing nomadic hunters to pour into the heart of the North American continent. Within just a few thousand years, Native Americans had journeyed from Colorado to the southern tip of South America. Blessed with a seemingly inexhaustible supply of meat, the early migrants experienced rapid population growth. As archaeologists have discovered, however, the sudden expansion of human population coincided with the loss of scores of large mammals, many of them the spear-throwers' favorite sources of food. The animals that died out during this period included mammoths and mastodons; camels and, amazingly, horses were eradicated from the land.

The peoples of the Great Plains did not obtain horses until the Spanish reintroduced them in the New World in 1547. Some archaeologists have suggested that the early Paleo-Indian hunters bear responsibility for the mass extinction of so many animals. It is more probable that climatic warming, which transformed well-watered regions into arid territories, put the large mammals under severe stress, and the early humans simply contributed to an ecological process over which they ultimately had little control.

The Indian peoples adjusted to the changing environmental conditions. As they dispersed across the North American continent, they developed new food sources, at first smaller mammals and fish, nuts and berries, and then about five thousand years ago, they discovered how to cultivate certain plants. Knowledge of maize (corn), squash, and beans spread north from central Mexico. The peoples living in the Southwest acquired cultivation skills long before the bands living along the Atlantic Coast. The shift to basic crops—a transformation that is sometimes termed the **Agricultural Revolution**—profoundly altered Native American societies. The availability of a more reliable store of food helped liberate nomadic groups from the insecurities of hunting and gathering. It was during this period that Native Americans began to produce ceramics, a valuable technology for the storage of grain. The vegetable harvest made possible the establishment of permanent villages, that often were governed by clearly defined hierarchies of elders and kings, and as the food supply increased, the Native American population greatly expanded, especially around urban centers in the Southwest and in the Mississippi Valley. Although the evidence is patchy, scholars currently estimate that approximately four million Native Americans lived north of Mexico at the time of the initial encounter with Europeans.

## Mysterious Disappearances

Several magnificent sites in North America provide powerful testimony to the cultural and social achievements of native peoples during the final two thousand years before European conquest. One of the more impressive is Chaco Canyon on the San Juan River in present-day New Mexico. The massive pueblo was the center of Anasazi culture, serving both political and religious functions, and it is estimated that its complex structures may have housed as many as fifteen thousand people. The Anasazis sustained their agriculture through a huge, technologically sophisticated network of irrigation canals that carried water long distances. They also constructed a transportation system con-

necting Chaco Canyon by road to more than seventy outlying villages. Some of the highways were almost a hundred miles long.

During this period equally impressive urban centers developed throughout the Ohio and Mississippi Valleys. In present-day southern Ohio, the Adena and Hopewell peoples—names assigned by archaeologists to distinguish differences in material culture—built large ceremonial mounds, where they buried the families of local elites. Approximately a thousand years after the birth of Christ, the groups gave way to the Mississippian culture, a loose collection of communities dispersed along the Mississippi River from Louisiana to Illinois that shared similar technologies and beliefs. Cahokia, a huge fortification and ceremonial site in Illinois that originally rose high above the river, represented the greatest achievement of the Mississippian peoples. Covering almost twenty acres, Cahokia once supported a population of almost twenty-thousand, a city rivaling in size many encountered in late medieval Europe. As one archaeologist observed, Cahokia was "as spectacular as any of the magnificent Mexican civilizations that were its contemporaries."

Recent research reveals that the various Native American peoples did not live in isolated communities. To be sure, over the millennia they developed many different cultural and social practices, reflecting the specific constraints of local ecologies. More than three hundred separate languages had evolved in North America before European conquest. But members of the groups traded goods over extremely long distances. Burial mounds found in the Ohio Valley, for example, have yielded obsidian from western Wyoming, shells from Florida, mica quarried in North Carolina and Tennessee, and copper found near Lake Superior.

Yet however advanced the Native American cultures of the southwest and Mississippi Valley may have been, both cultures disappeared mysteriously just before the arrival of the Europeans. No one knows what events brought down the great city of Cahokia or persuaded the Anasazis to abandon Chaco Canyon. Some scholars have suggested that climatic changes coupled with continuing population growth put too much pressure on food supplies; others insist that chronic warfare destabilized the social order. It has even been argued that diseases carried to the New World by the first European adventurers ravaged the cultures. About one point modern commentators are in full agreement: The breakdown of Mississippian culture caused smaller bands to disperse, construct new identities, and establish different political structures. They were the peoples who first encountered the Europeans along the Atlantic Coast and who seemed to the newcomers to have

The center of the Anasazi culture was Chaco Canyon. Pueblo Bonita was the largest of Chaco's twelve towns. The pueblo rose five stories high on walls made of adobe and faced with sandstone slabs. More than 650 living quarters and storage rooms surrounded the central plaza. Roads extending some four hundred miles linked Pueblo Bonita to outlying pueblos. ❖

lived in the same places and followed the same patterns of behavior since the dawn of time.

## Aztec Dominance

The stability resulting from the Agricultural Revolution allowed the Indians of Mexico and Central America to structure their societies in more complex ways. Like the Incas who lived in what is now known as Peru, the Mayan and Toltec peoples of Central Mexico built vast cities, formed government bureaucracies that dominated large tributary populations, and developed hieroglyphic writing as well as an accurate solar calendar. Their cities, which housed several hundred thousand people, greatly impressed the Spanish conquerors. Bernal Díaz del Castillo reported, "When we saw all those [Aztec] towns and villages built in the water, and other great towns on dry land, and that straight and level causeway leading to Mexico, we were astounded. . . . Indeed, some of our soldiers asked whether it was not all a dream."

Not long before Columbus began his first voyage across the Atlantic, the Aztecs, an aggressive, warlike people, swept through the Valley of Mexico, conquering the great cities that their enemies had constructed. Aztec warriors ruled by force, reducing defeated rivals to tributary status. In 1519, the Aztecs' main ceremonial center, Tenochtitlán, contained as many as 250,000 people as compared with only 50,000 in Seville, the port from which the early Spaniards had sailed. Elaborate human sacrifice associated with Huitzilopochtli, the Aztec sun god, horrified Europeans, who apparently did not find the savagery of their own civilization so objectionable. The Aztec ritual killings were connected to the agricul-

*Aztec human sacrifice depicted in the* Codex Magliabechiano, *a sixteenth-century Spanish account of the lives of the native Mexicans. The ritual sacrifices performed by Aztec priests were associated with worship of the sun god—each offering was considered a sacred debt payment.* ❖

### ❖ A Look at the Past ❖

**Effigy Jar**
Clay effigy jars suggest the complexity of Mississippian society. Members of the culture built large earthen temple mounds, practiced elaborate burials, and made clay jars depicting the faces of respected dead members. What do these customs, particularly the effigy jars, reveal about the Mississippian attitude toward death?

tural cycle, and the Indians believed the blood of their victims possessed extraordinary fertility powers. A fragment of an Aztec song-poem captures the indomitable spirit that once pervaded this militant culture:

> Proud of itself
> is the city of Mexico-Tenochtitlán.
> Here no one fears to die in war.
> This is our glory. . . .
>
> Who could conquer Tenochtitlán?
> Who could shake the foundation of heaven?

## Eastern Woodland Cultures

In the northeast region along the Atlantic coast, the Indians did not practice intensive agriculture. These peoples, numbering less than a million at the time of conquest, generally supplemented farming with seasonal hunting and gathering. Most belonged to what ethnographers term the Eastern Woodland Cultures. Small bands formed villages during the warm summer months. The women cultivated maize and other crops while the men hunted and fished. During the winter, difficulties associated with feeding so many people forced the communities to disperse. Each family lived off the land as best it could.

Seventeenth-century English settlers were most likely to have encountered the Algonquian-speaking peoples who occupied much of the territory along the Atlantic coast from North Carolina to Maine. Included in this large linguistic family were the Powhatans of Tidewater Virginia, the Narragansetts of Rhode Island, and the Abenakis of northern New England.

Despite common linguistic roots, however, the scattered Algonquian communities would have found communication extremely difficult. They had developed very different dialects. A sixteenth-century Narragansett, for example, would have found it hard to comprehend a Powhatan. The major groups of the Southeast, such as the Creeks, belonged to a separate language group (Muskogean); the Indians of the eastern Great Lakes region and upper St. Lawrence Valley generally spoke Iroquoian dialects.

Linguistic ties had little effect on Indian politics. Algonquian groups who lived in different regions, exploited different resources, and spoke different dialects did not develop strong ties of mutual identity, and when their own interests were involved, they were more than willing to ally themselves with Europeans

or "foreign" Indians against other Algonquian speakers. Divisions among Indian groups would in time facilitate European conquest. Local Native American peoples greatly outnumbered the first settlers, and had the Europeans not forged alliances with the Indians, they could not so easily have gained a foothold on the continent.

However divided the Indians of eastern North America may have been, they shared many cultural values and assumptions. Most Native Americans, for example, defined their place in society through kinship. Such personal bonds determined the character of economic and political relations. The farming bands living in areas eventually claimed by England were often matrilineal, which meant in effect that the women owned the planting fields and houses, maintained tribal customs, and had a role in tribal government. Among the native communities of Canada and the northern Great Lakes, patrilineal forms were much more common. In these groups, the men owned the hunting grounds that the family needed to survive.

Eastern Woodland communities organized diplomacy, trade, and war around reciprocal relationships that impressed Europeans as being extraordinarily egalitarian, even democratic. Chains of native author-

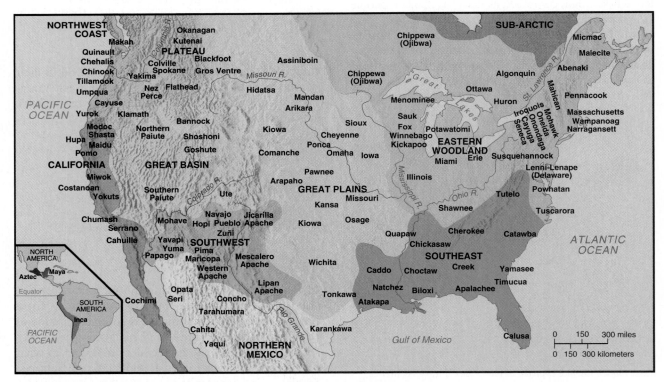

**THE FIRST AMERICANS: LOCATION OF MAJOR INDIAN GROUPS AND CULTURE AREAS IN THE 1600s** *Native Americans had complex social structures, religious systems, and a sophisticated agricultural technology when they came into initial contact with Europeans.* ❖

ity were loosely structured. Native leaders were such renowned public speakers because persuasive rhetoric was often their only effective source of power. It required considerable oratorical skills for an Indian leader to persuade independent-minded warriors to support a certain policy.

Before the arrival of the white settlers, Indian wars were seldom very lethal. Young warriors attacked neighboring bands largely to exact revenge for a previous insult or the death of a relative, or to secure captives. Fatalities, when they did occur, sparked cycles of revenge. Some captives were tortured to death; others were adopted into the community as replacements for fallen relatives.

# A WORLD TRANSFORMED

The arrival of large numbers of white men and women on the North American continent profoundly altered Native American cultures. Change did not occur at the same rates in all places. Indian villages located on the Atlantic coast came under severe pressure almost immediately; inland groups had more time to adjust. Wherever they lived, however, Indians discovered that conquest strained traditional ways of life, and as daily patterns of experience changed almost beyond recognition, native peoples had to devise new answers, new responses, and new ways to survive in physical and social environments that eroded tradition. Historian James Merrell reminded us the Indians found themselves living in a world that from their perspective was just as "new" as that which greeted the European invaders.

## Cultural Negotiations

Native Americans were not passive victims of geopolitical forces beyond their control. So long as they remained healthy, they held their own in the early exchanges, and although they eagerly accepted certain trade goods, they generally resisted other aspects of European cultures. The earliest recorded contacts between Indians and explorers suggest curiosity and surprise rather than hostility. A Southeastern Indian who encountered Hernando de Soto in 1540 expressed awe (at least that is what a Spanish witness recorded): "The things that seldom happen bring astonishment. Think, then, what must be the effect on me and mine, the sight of you and your people, whom we have at no time seen . . . things so altogether new, as to strike awe and terror to our hearts."

What Indians desired most was peaceful trade. The earliest French explorers reported that natives waved from shore, urging the Europeans to exchange metal items for beaver skins. In fact, the Indians did not perceive themselves at a disadvantage in these dealings. They could readily see the technological advantage of guns over bows and arrows. Metal knives made daily tasks much easier. And to acquire such goods they gave up pelts, which to them seemed in abundant supply. "The English have no sense," one Indian informed a French priest. "They give us twenty knives like this for one Beaver skin." Another native announced that "the Beaver does everything perfectly well: it makes kettles, hatchets, swords, knives, bread . . . in short, it makes everything." The man who recorded these observations reminded French readers—in case they had missed the point—that the Indian was "making sport of us Europeans."

Trading sessions along the eastern frontier were really cultural seminars. The Europeans tried to make sense out of Indian customs, and although they may have called the natives "savages," they quickly discovered that the Indians drove hard bargains. They demanded gifts; they set the time and place of trade.

The Indians used the occasions to study the newcomers. They formed opinions about the Europeans, some flattering, some less so, but they never concluded from their observations that Indian culture was inferior to that of the colonizers. They regarded the beards worn by European men as particularly revolting. As an eighteenth-century Englishman said of the Iroquois, "They seem always to have Looked upon themselves as far Superior to the rest of Mankind and accordingly Call themselves *Ongwehoenwe*, i.e., Men Surpassing all other men."

For Europeans, communicating with the Indians was always an ordeal. The invaders reported having gained deep insight into Native American cultures through sign languages. How much accurate information explorers and traders took from these crude improvised exchanges is a matter of conjecture. In a letter written in 1493, Columbus expressed frustration: "I did not understand those people nor they me, except for what common sense dictated, although they were saddened and I much more so, because I wanted to have good information concerning everything."

In the absence of meaningful conversation, Europeans often concluded that the Indians held them in high regard, perhaps seeing the newcomers as gods. Such one-sided encounters involved a good deal of projection, a mental process of translating alien sounds and gestures into messages that Europeans wanted to hear. Sometimes the adventurers did not even try to communicate, assuming from superficial observation—as did the sixteenth-century explorer Giovanni da Verrazzano—"that they have no religion, and that they live in absolute freedom, and that everything they do proceeds from Ignorance."

Ethnocentric Europeans tried repeatedly to "civilize" the Indians. In practice that meant persuading natives to dress like the colonists, attend white schools, live in permanent structures, and, most important, accept Christianity. The Indians listened more or less patiently, but in the end, they usually rejected European values. One South Carolina trader explained that when Indians were asked to become more English, they said no, "for they thought it hard, that we should desire them to change their manners and customs, since they did not desire us to turn Indians."

To be sure, some Indians were strongly attracted to Christianity, but most paid it lip service or found it irrelevant to their needs. As one Huron told a French priest, "It would be useless for me to repent having sinned, seeing that I never have sinned." Another Huron announced that he did not fear punishment after death since "we cannot tell whether everything that appears faulty to Men, is so in the Eyes of God."

Among some Indian groups, gender figured significantly in a person's willingness to convert to Christianity. Native men who traded animal skins for European goods had more frequent contact with the whites, and they proved more receptive to the arguments of missionaries. But native women jealously guarded traditional culture, a system that often sanctioned polygamy—a husband having several wives—and gave women substantial authority over the distribution of food within the village. French Jesuits seemed especially eager to undermine the independence of Native American women. Among other demands, missionaries insisted on monogamous marriages, an institution based on Christian values but that made little sense in Indian societies where constant warfare killed off large numbers of young males and increasingly left native women without sufficient marriage partners.

The white settlers' educational system proved no more successful than their religion was in winning cultural converts. Young Indian scholars deserted stuffy classrooms at the first chance. In 1744, Virginia offered several Iroquois boys a free education at the College of William and Mary. The Iroquois leaders rejected the invitation because they found that boys who had gone to college "were absolutely good for nothing being neither acquainted with the true methods of killing deer, catching Beaver, or surprising an enemy."

Even matrimony seldom eroded the Indians' attachment to their own customs. When Native Americans and whites married—unions the English found less desirable than did the French or Spanish—the European partner usually elected to live among the Indians. Impatient settlers who regarded the Indians simply as an obstruction to progress sometimes developed more coercive methods, such as enslavement, to achieve cultural conversion. Again, from the white perspective, the results were disappointing. Indian slaves ran away or died. In either case, they did not become Europeans.

## Threats to Survival: Trade and Disease

Over time, cooperative encounters between the Native Americans and Europeans became less frequent. The Europeans found it almost impossible to understand the Indians' relation to the land and other natural resources. English planters cleared the forests and fenced the fields and, in the process, radically altered the ecological systems on which the Indians depended. The European system of land use inevitably reduced the supply of deer and other animals essential to traditional native cultures.

Dependency also came in more subtle forms. The Indians welcomed European commerce, but like so many consumers throughout recorded history, they discovered that the objects they most coveted inevitably brought them into debt. To pay for the trade goods, the Indians hunted more aggressively and even further reduced the population of fur-bearing mammals.

Commerce eroded Indian independence in other ways. After several disastrous wars—the Yamasee War in South Carolina (1715), for example—the natives learned that demonstrations of force usually resulted in the suspension of normal trade, on which the Indians had grown quite dependent for guns and ammunition, among other things. A hardened English businessman made the point quite bluntly. When asked if the Catawbas would harm his traders, he responded that "the danger would be . . . little from them, because they are too fond of our trade to lose it for the pleasure of shedding a little English blood."

It was disease, however, that ultimately destroyed the cultural integrity of many North American tribes. European adventurers exposed the Indians to bacteria and viruses against which they possessed no natural immunity. Smallpox, measles, and influenza decimated the Native American population. Other diseases such as alcoholism took a terrible toll.

Within a generation of initial contact with Europeans, the Caribs, who gave the Caribbean its name, were virtually extinct. The decimation of Native American peoples was an aspect of ecological transformation known as the **Columbian Exchange.** European conquerors exposed the Indians to several new fatal diseases; the Indians introduced the invaders to marvelous plants such as corn and potatoes, which altered the course of European history. (See the Feature Essay, "The Columbian Exchange: Ecological Revolution," pp. 12–13.)

The Algonquian communities of New England experienced appalling rates of death. One Massachusetts colonist reported in 1630 that the Indian peoples of his region "above twelve years since were swept away by a great & grievous Plague . . . so that there are verie few left to inhabit the Country." Settlers possessed no knowledge of germ theory—it was not formulated until the mid-nineteenth century—and speculated that a Christian God had providentially cleared the wilderness of heathens.

Historical demographers now estimate that some tribes suffered a 90 to 95 percent population loss within the first century of European contact. The death of so many Indians decreased the supply of indigenous laborers, who were needed by the Europeans to work the mines and to grow staple crops such as sugar and tobacco. The decimation of native populations may have persuaded colonists throughout the New World to seek a substitute labor force in Africa. Indeed, the enslavement of blacks has been described as an effort by Europeans to "repopulate" the New World.

Indians who survived the epidemics often found that the fabric of traditional culture had come unraveled. The enormity of the death toll and the agony that accompanied it called traditional religious beliefs and practices into question. The survivors lost not only members of their families, but also elders who might have told them how properly to bury the dead and give spiritual comfort to the living.

Some native peoples, such as the Iroquois, who lived a long way from the coast and thus had more time to adjust to the challenge, withstood the crisis better than did those who immediately confronted the Europeans and Africans. Refugee Indians from the hardest hit eastern communities were absorbed into healthier western groups. However horrific the crisis may have been, it demonstrated powerfully just how much the environment—a source of opportunity as well as devastation—shaped human encounters throughout the New World.

## WEST AFRICA: ANCIENT AND COMPLEX SOCIETIES

During the era of the European slave trade, roughly from the late fifteenth through the mid-nineteenth centuries, a number of enduring myths about sub-Saharan West Africa were propagated. Even today, commentators claim that the people who inhabited this region four hundred years ago were isolated from the rest of the world and had a simple, self-sufficient economy. Indeed, some scholars still depict the vast region stretching from the Senegal River south to modern Angola as a single cultural unit, as if at one time all the men and women living there must have shared a common set of African political, religious, and social values.

Sub-Saharan West Africa defies such easy generalizations. The first Portuguese who explored the African coast during the fifteenth century encountered a great variety of political and religious cultures. Many hundreds of years earlier, Africans living in this region had come into contact with Islam, the religion founded by the Prophet Muhammad during the seventh century. Islam spread slowly from Arabia into West Africa. Not until A.D. 1030 did a kingdom located in the Senegal Valley accept the Muslim religion. Many other West Africans, such as those in ancient Ghana, resisted Islam and continued to observe traditional religions.

As Muslim traders from North Africa and the Middle East brought a new religion to parts of West Africa, they expanded sophisticated trade networks that linked the villagers of Senegambia with urban centers in northwest Africa, Morocco, Tunisia, and Cyrenaica. Great camel caravans regularly crossed the Sahara carrying trade goods that were exchanged for gold and slaves. Sub-Saharan Africa's well-developed links with Islam surprised a French priest who in 1686 observed African pilgrims going "to visit Mecca to visit Mahomet's tomb, although they are eleven or twelve hundred leagues distance from it."

West Africans spoke many languages and organized themselves into diverse political systems. Several populous states, sometimes termed "empires," exercised loose control over large areas. Ancient African empires such as Ghana were vulnerable to external attack as well as internal rebellion, and the oral and written histories of this region record the rise and fall of several large kingdoms. When European traders first arrived, the list of major states would have included Mali, Benin, and Kongo. Many other Africans lived in what are known as stateless societies, really largely autonomous communities organized around lineage structures. In these respects, African and Native American cultures had much in common.

Whatever the form of government, men and women constructed their primary social identity within well-defined lineage groups, which consisted of persons claiming descent from a common ancestor. Disputes among members of lineage groups were generally settled by clan elders. The senior leaders allocated economic and human resources. They determined who received land and who might take a wife—critical decisions because within the villages of West Africa, women and children cultivated the fields. The communities were economically self-sufficient. Not only were they able to grow enough food to feed themselves, but they also produced trade goods, such as iron, kola, and gum.

The first Europeans to reach the West African coast by sail were the Portuguese. Strong winds and

# THE COLUMBIAN EXCHANGE

## Ecological Revolution

Modern Americans often speak of the degradation of the global environment in apocalyptic terms, as if the current generation confronts a unique challenge in world history. No doubt, many chemical compounds produced during the twentieth century have proved far more toxic than their inventors ever imagined. But contemporary concerns about the future of the planet should not cause us to lose sight of the historical sweep of these problems. We are certainly not the first society to experience a massive ecological transformation caused by the inevitable intervention of human beings into the processes of nature. Recapturing an earlier moment of environmental history—known as the Columbian Exchange—reminds us that the moral dimensions of change are often a matter of perspective. What one group proclaims as providential progress may strike others as utter disaster.

The first major "ecological revolution" occurred as a direct result of New World exploration during the fifteenth and sixteenth centuries. The earliest explorers had expected America to be an extension of Europe, a place inhabited by familiar plants and animals. They were surprised. The exotic flora of the New World, sketched here from sixteenth-century drawings, included the food staple maize and the succulent pineapple. Equally strange to European eyes were buffalo, rattlesnakes, catfish, and the peculiar absence of horses and cattle. No domestic animal was common to both sides of the Atlantic except the dog. And perhaps the most striking difference was between the people themselves. Both Native Americans and Europeans found each other to be the most exotic people they had ever encountered.

The most immediate biological consequence of contact between the people of Europe, Africa, and the New World was the transfer of disease. Within a year of Columbus's return from the Caribbean, syphilis appeared in Europe for the first time and became identified as the American disease, even though as we now know, it came originally from West Africa. By 1505, syphilis had spread all the way to China.

The effect of Old World diseases in the Americas was catastrophic. Native Americans had little natural immunity to common African and European diseases because America remained biologically isolated after the reimmersion of the Bering land bridge. When they were exposed to influenza, typhus, measles, and especially smallpox, they died by the millions. Indeed, European exploration of America set off the worst demographic disaster in world history. Within fifty years of the first contact, epidemics had virtually exterminated the native population of Hispaniola and devastated the densely populated Valley of Mexico.

Also unsettling but by no means as destructive was the transfer of plants and animals from the Old World to the New. Spanish colonizers carried sugar

As Native Americans were exposed to common Old World diseases, particularly smallpox, they died by the millions. ❖

Two examples of Old World–New World species exchange. Maize (corn) became a European dietary staple in the centuries after contact with America, while the Old World dandelion stepped off invaders' ships in the crusted mud of English or Spanish boots and spread far beyond the newcomers' initial cultural dominions, becoming today's most familiar "weed." ❖

crop—reintroduced the potato into Massachusetts Bay in 1718. And in West Africa, corn gradually replaced traditional animal feeds of low yield.

These sweeping changes in agriculture and diet helped reshape the Old World economies. Partly because of the rich new sources of nutrition from America, the population of Europe, which had long been relatively stable, nearly doubled in the eighteenth century. Even as cities swelled and industries flourished, European farmers were able to feed the growing population. In many ways, the seeds and plants of the New World were far more valuable in Western economic development than all the silver of Mexico and Peru.

and bananas across the Atlantic, and in time these crops transformed the economies of Latin America. Even more spectacular was the success of European animals in America. During the sixteenth century, pigs, sheep, and cattle arrived as passengers on European ships, and in the fertile New World environment, they multiplied more rapidly than they had in Europe. Some animals survived shipwrecks. On Sable Island, a small, desolate island off the coast of Nova Scotia, one can still see the small, longhaired cattle, the successors of the earliest cattle transported to America. Other animals escaped from the ranches of New Spain, generating new breeds such as the fabled Texas longhorn.

No European animal more profoundly affected Native American life than the horse. Once common in North America, the horse mysteriously disappeared from the continent sometime during the last Ice Age. The early Spanish explorers reintroduced the horse to North America, and the sight of this large, powerful animal at first terrified the Indians. Mounted conquistadores discovered that if they could not frighten Indian foes into submission, they could simply outmaneuver them on horseback. The Native Americans of the Southwest quickly adapted the horse to their own use. Sedentary farmers acquired new hunting skills, and soon the Indians were

riding across the Great Plains in pursuit of buffalo. The Comanche, Apache, Sioux, and Blackfoot tribes—just to name a few—became dependent on the horse. Mounted Indian warriors galloped into battle, unaware that it was their white adversaries who had brought the horse to America.

Equally dramatic was the effect of American crops on European and African societies. From his first trip to the New World, Columbus brought back a plant that revolutionized the diets of both humans and animals— maize. During the next century, American beans, squash, and sweet potatoes appeared on European tables. The pepper and tomato, other New World discoveries, added a distinctive flavor to Mediterranean cooking. Despite strong prohibitions on the use of tobacco (in Russia, a user might have his nose amputated), European demand for tobacco grew astronomically during the seventeenth century. The potato caught on more slowly in Europe because of a widespread fear that root crops caused disease. The most rapid acceptance of the white potato came in Ireland, where it became a diet staple in the 1600s. Irish immigrants—unaware of the genealogy of this native American

*Embarcadero de los Cavallos.*

Europeans brought animals such as domestic cattle and horses to the New World. The reintroduction of the horse to North America, where it had once thrived and then disappeared, had a profound impact on Native Americans. ❖

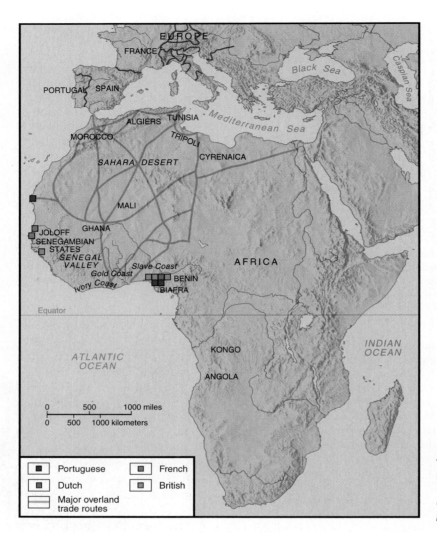

**TRADE ROUTES IN AFRICA** *African trade routes were well established by the late 1600s. Trade restrictions—and a deadly disease environment—confined European settlements primarily to coastal regions.* ❖

currents along the Atlantic coast moved southward, which meant a ship could sail with the wind from Portugal to West Africa without difficulty. The problem was returning. Advances in maritime technology allowed the Portuguese to overcome these difficulties. By constructing a new type of ship, one uniting European hull design with lateen (triangular) sails from the Middle East, Portuguese caravels were able to navigate successfully against African winds and currents. During the fifteenth century, Portuguese sailors discovered that by sailing far to the west, often as far as the Azores, they could, on their return trips to Europe, catch a reliable westerly wind. Columbus was evidently familiar with the technique. Before attempting to cross the Atlantic Ocean, he sailed to the Gold Coast, and on the way, he undoubtedly studied the wind patterns that would carry his famed caravels to the New World and back again.

The Portuguese journeyed to Africa in search of gold and slaves. Mali and Joloff officials were willing partners in this commerce but insisted that Europeans

respect trade regulations established by Africans. They required the Europeans to pay tolls and other fees and restricted the foreign traders to conducting their business in small forts or castles located at the mouths of the major rivers. Local merchants acquired some slaves and gold in the interior and transported them to the coast, where they were exchanged for European manufactures. Transactions were calculated in terms of local African currencies: A slave would be offered to a European trader for so many bars of iron or ounces of gold.

European slave traders accepted these terms largely because they had no other choice. The African states fielded formidable armies, and outsiders soon discovered they could not impose their will on the region simply by demonstrations of force. Moreover, local diseases proved so lethal for Europeans—six out of ten of whom would die within a single year's stay in Africa—that they were happy to avoid dangerous trips to the interior. The slaves were usually men and women taken captive during wars; others were victims of judicial practices designed specifically to supply the growing American

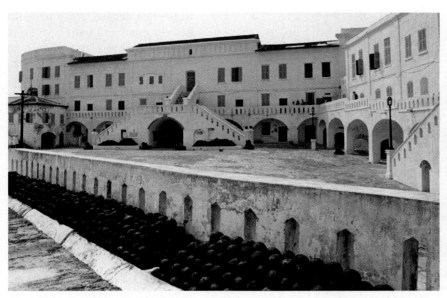

*Local African rulers allowed European traders to build compounds along the West African coast. Constructed to expedite the slave trade, each of these so-called "slave factories" served a different European interest. Cape Coast Castle, which changed hands several times as rival nations fought for its control, became one of the largest slave trading posts in the world after the British captured and reinforced it in 1665. ❖*

market. By 1650, most West African slaves were destined for the New World rather than the Middle East.

Even before Europeans colonized the New World, the Portuguese were purchasing almost a thousand slaves a year on the West African coast. The slaves were frequently forced to work on the sugar plantations of Madeira (Portuguese) and the Canaries (Spanish), Atlantic islands on which Europeans experimented with forms of unfree labor that would later be more fully and more ruthlessly established in the American colonies. It is currently estimated that approximately 10.7 million Africans were taken to the New World as slaves. The figure for the eighteenth century alone is about 5.5 million, of which more than one-third came from West Central Africa. The Bight of Benin, the Bight of Biafra, and the Gold Coast supplied most of the others.

The peopling of the New World is usually seen as a story of European migrations. But in fact, during every year between 1650 and 1831, more Africans than Europeans came to the Americas. As historian Davis Eltis wrote, "In terms of immigration alone ... America was an extension of Africa rather than Europe until late in the nineteenth century."

## EUROPE ON THE EVE OF CONQUEST

In ancient times, the West possessed a mythical appeal to people living along the shores of the Mediterranean Sea. Classical writers speculated about the fate of

Atlantis, a fabled Western civilization that was said to have sunk beneath the ocean. Fallen Greek heroes allegedly spent eternity in an uncharted western paradise. But because the ships of Greece and Rome were ill designed to sail the open ocean, the lands to the west remained the stuff of legend and fantasy. In the fifth century, an intrepid Irish monk, St. Brendan, reported finding enchanted islands far out in the Atlantic. He even claimed to have met a talking whale named Jasconius, who allowed the famished voyager to cook a meal on his back.

In the tenth century, Scandinavian seafarers known as Norsemen or Vikings actually established settlements in the New World, but almost a thousand years passed before they received credit for their accomplishment. In the year 984, a band of Vikings led by Eric the Red sailed west from Iceland to a large island in the North Atlantic. Eric, who possessed a fine sense of public relations, named the island Greenland, reasoning that others would more willingly colonize the icebound region "if the country had a good name." A few years later, Eric's son Leif founded a small settlement he named Vinland at a location in northern Newfoundland now called L'Anse aux Meadows. At the time, the Norse voyages went unnoticed by other Europeans. The hostility of Native Americans, poor lines of communication, climatic cooling, and political upheavals in Scandinavia made maintenance of these distant outposts impossible. At the time of his first voyage in 1492, Columbus seemed to have been unaware of these earlier exploits.

### Building New Nation-States

At the time of the Viking settlement, other Europeans were unprepared to sponsor transatlantic exploration. Nor would they be in a position to do so for several more centuries. Medieval kingdoms were loosely organized, and until the early fifteenth century, fierce provincial loyalties, widespread ignorance of classical learning, and dreadful plagues such as the Black Death discouraged people from thinking expansively about the world beyond their own immediate communities.

In the fifteenth century, however, these conditions began to change. Europe became more prosperous, political authority was more centralized, and the **Renaissance** fostered a more expansive outlook

*Materials excavated at L'Anse aux Meadows, on the northernmost tip of Newfoundland, provide evidence of a Viking settlement in North America. Using the materials excavated at the site, archaeologists have reconstructed the typically Norse dwellings, which had turf walls and roofs, wooden doors and doorframes.* ❖

among literate people in the arts and sciences, the Renaissance encouraged—first in Italy and later throughout Europe—bold new creative thinking which challenged the orthodoxies of the Middle Ages. A major element in the shift was the slow but steady growth of population after 1450. Historians are uncertain about the cause of the increase—after all, neither the quality of medicine nor sanitation improved much—but the result was a substantial rise in the price of land, since there were more mouths to feed. Landlords profited from these trends, and as their income expanded, they demanded more of the luxury items, such as spices, silks, and jewels, that came from distant Asian ports. Economic prosperity created powerful new incentives for exploration and trade.

This period also witnessed the centralization of political authority under a group of rulers whom historians refer to collectively as the New Monarchs. Before the mid-fifteenth century, feudal nobles dominated small districts throughout Europe. Conceding only nominal allegiance to larger territorial leaders, the local barons taxed the peasants and waged war pretty much as they pleased. They also dispensed what passed for justice. The New Monarchs challenged the nobles' autonomy. The changes that accompanied the challenges came slowly, and in many areas violently, but the results altered traditional political relationships between the nobility and the crown, and between the citizen and the state. The New Monarchs of Europe recruited armies and supported these expensive organizations with revenues from national taxes. They created effective national courts. While these monarchs

were often despotic, they personified the emergent nation-states of Europe and brought a measure of peace to local communities weary of chronic feudal war.

The story was the same throughout most of western Europe. The Tudors of England, represented by Henry VII (r. 1485–1509), ended a long civil war known as the War of the Roses. Louis XI, the French monarch (r. 1461–1483), strengthened royal authority by reorganizing state finances. The political unification of Spain began in 1469 with the marriage of Ferdinand of Aragon and Isabella of Castile, setting off a nation-building process that involved driving both the Jews and Muslims out of Spain. These strong-willed monarchs forged nations out of groups of independent kingdoms. If political centralization had not occurred, the major European countries could not possibly have generated the financial and military resources necessary for worldwide exploration.

A final prerequisite to exploration was reliable technical knowledge. Ptolemy (second century A.D.) and other ancient geographers had mapped the known world and had even demonstrated that the world was round. During the Middle Ages, however, Europeans lost effective contact with classical tradition. Within Arab societies, the old learning had survived, indeed flourished, and when Europeans eventually rediscovered the classical texts during the Renaissance, they drew heavily on the work of Arab scholars. This "new" learning generated great intellectual curiosity about the globe and about the world that existed beyond the Mediterranean.

The invention of printing from movable type by Johann Gutenberg in the 1440s greatly facilitated the spread of technical knowledge. Indeed, printing sparked a communications revolution whose impact on the lives of ordinary people was as far-reaching as that caused by telephones, television, and computers in modern times. Sea captains published their findings as quickly as they could engage a printer, and by the beginning of the sixteenth century, a small, though growing, number of educated readers throughout Europe were well informed about the exploration of the New World. The printing press invited Europeans to imagine exciting opportunities that they had hardly perceived when the Vikings sailed the North Atlantic.

This 1507 map of the world drawn by Martin Waldseemüller incorporated data from the voyages of Italian adventurer Amerigo Vespucci, who asserted that the New World was a separate continent. Waldseemüller gave Vespucci more credit than he deserved and named the continent "America," rather than Columbia in honor of Christopher Columbus ✤

# IMAGINING A NEW WORLD

By 1500, centralization of political authority and advances in geographic knowledge brought Spain to the first rank as a world power. In the early fifteenth century, though, Spain consisted of several autonomous kingdoms. It lacked rich natural resources and possessed few good seaports. In fact, there was little about this land to suggest its people would take the lead in conquering and colonizing the New World.

By the end of the century, however, Spain suddenly came alive with creative energy. The union of Ferdinand and Isabella sparked a drive for political consolidation that, because of the monarchs' fervid Catholicism, took on the characteristics of a religious crusade. Spurred by the militant faith of their monarchs, the armies of Castile and Aragon waged holy war—known as the *Reconquista*—against the independent states in southern Spain that earlier had been captured by Muslims. In 1492, the Moorish (Islamic) kingdom of Granada fell, and, for the first time in centuries, the entire Iberian peninsula was united under Christian rulers. Spanish authorities showed no tolerance for people who rejected the Catholic faith.

During the Reconquista, thousands of Jews and Moors were driven from the country. Indeed, Columbus undoubtedly encountered such refugees as he was preparing for his famous voyage. From this volatile social and political environment came the **conquistadores,** men eager for personal glory and material gain, uncompromising in matters of religion, and unswerving in their loyalty to the crown. They were prepared to employ fire and sword in any cause sanctioned by God and king, and these adventurers carried European culture to the most populous regions of the New World.

Long before Spaniards ever reached the West Indies, they conquered the indigenous peoples of the Canary Islands, a strategically located archipelago in the eastern Atlantic. The harsh labor systems the Spanish developed in the Canaries served as models of subjugation in America. Indeed, the Spanish experience paralleled that of the English in Ireland (see "English Conquest of Ireland," p. 25). An early-fifteenth-century Spanish chronicle described the Canary natives as "miscreants . . . [who] do not acknowledge their creator and live in part like beasts." Many islanders quickly died of disease; others were killed in battle or enslaved. The new Spanish landholders introduced sugar, a labor-intensive plantation crop. The landowners forced slaves captured in Africa to provide the labor. This oppressive process was driven by dreams of great wealth, and would be repeated many times by European colonists through the centuries.

## Myths and Reality

If it had not been for Christopher Columbus (Cristoforo Colombo), of course, Spain might never have gained an American empire. Little is known about his early life. Born in Genoa in 1451 of humble parentage, Columbus soon devoured the classical learning that had so recently been rediscovered and made available in printed form. He mastered geography, and—perhaps while sailing the coast of West Africa—he became obsessed with the idea of voyaging west across the Atlantic Ocean to reach Cathay, as China was then known.

In 1484, Columbus presented his plan to the king of Portugal. However, while the Portuguese were just as interested as Columbus in reaching Cathay, they elected to voyage around the continent of Africa instead of following the route suggested by Columbus. They suspected that Columbus had substantially underestimated the circumference of the earth and that for all his enthusiasm, he would almost certainly starve before reaching Asia. The Portuguese decision eventually paid off quite handsomely. In 1498, one of their captains, Vasco da Gama, returned from the coast of India carrying a fortune in spices and other luxury goods.

Undaunted by rejection, Columbus petitioned Isabella and Ferdinand for financial backing. They were initially no more interested in his grand design than the Portuguese had been. But time was on Columbus's side. Spain's aggressive New Monarchs envied the success of their neighbor, Portugal. Columbus boldly played on the rivalry between the countries, talking of wealth and empire. Indeed, for a person with little success or apparent support, he was supremely confident. One contemporary reported that when Columbus "made up his mind, he was as sure he would discover what he did discover, and find what he did find, as if he held it in a chamber under lock and key."

Columbus's stubborn lobbying on behalf of the "Enterprise of the Indies" gradually wore down opposition in the Spanish court, and the two sovereigns provided him with a small fleet that contained two of the most famous caravels ever constructed, the *Niña* and the *Pinta,* as well as the square-rigged *nao Santa Maria.* The indomitable admiral set sail for Cathay in August 1492, the year of Spain's unification.

Educated Europeans of the fifteenth century knew the world was round. No one seriously believed that Columbus and his crew would tumble off the edge of the earth. The concern was with size, not shape. Columbus estimated the distance to the mainland of Asia to be about 3,000 nautical miles, a voyage his small ships would have no difficulty completing. The actual distance is 10,600 nautical miles, however, and had the New World not been in his way, he and his crew would have run out of food and water long before they reached China, as the Portuguese had predicted.

After stopping in the Canary Islands to refit the ships, Columbus continued his westward voyage in early September. When the tiny Spanish fleet sighted an island in the Bahamas after only thirty-three days at sea, the admiral concluded he had reached Asia. Since his mathematical calculations had obviously been correct, he assumed he would soon encounter the Chinese. It never occurred to Columbus that he had stumbled upon a new world. He assured his men, his patrons, and perhaps himself that the islands were indeed part of the fabled "Indies." Or if not the Indies themselves, then they were surely an extension of the great Asian landmass. He searched for the splendid cities Marco Polo had described, but instead of meeting wealthy Chinese, Columbus encountered Native Americans, whom he appropriately, if mistakenly, called "Indians."

After his first voyage of discovery, Columbus returned to the New World three more times. But despite his considerable courage and ingenuity, he could never find the treasure his financial supporters in Spain angrily demanded. Columbus died in 1506 a frustrated but wealthy entrepreneur, unaware that he had reached a previously unknown continent separating Asia from Europe. The final disgrace came in December 1500 when an ambitious falsifier, Amerigo Vespucci, published a sensational account of his travels across the Atlantic that convinced German mapmakers he had proved America was distinct from Asia. Before the misconception could be corrected, the name *America* gained general acceptance throughout Europe.

Only two years after Columbus's first voyage, Spain and Portugal almost went to war over the anticipated treasure of Asia. Pope Alexander VI negotiated a settlement that pleased both kingdoms. Portugal wanted to exclude the Spanish from the west coast of Africa and, what was more important, from Columbus's new route to "India." Spain insisted on maintaining complete control over lands discovered by Columbus, which then still were regarded as extensions of China. The **Treaty of Tordesillas** (1494) divided the entire world along a line located 270 leagues west of the Azores. Any new lands discovered west of the line belonged to Spain. At the time, no European had ever seen Brazil, which turned out to be on Portugal's side of the line. (To this day, Brazilians speak Portuguese.) The treaty failed to discourage future English, Dutch, and French adventurers from trying their luck in the New World.

## The Conquistadores: Faith and Greed

Spain's new discoveries unleashed a horde of conquistadores on the Caribbean. These independent adventurers carved out small settlements on Cuba, Hispaniola, Jamaica, and Puerto Rico in the 1490s and early 1500s. They were not interested in creating a permanent society in the New World. Rather, they came for instant wealth, preferably in gold, and were not squeamish about the means they used to obtain it. Bernal Díaz, one of the first Spaniards to migrate to the region, explained he had traveled to America "to serve God and His Majesty, to give light to those who were in darkness, and to grow rich, as all men desire to do." In less than two decades, the Indians who had inhabited the Caribbean islands had been exterminated, victims of exploitation and disease.

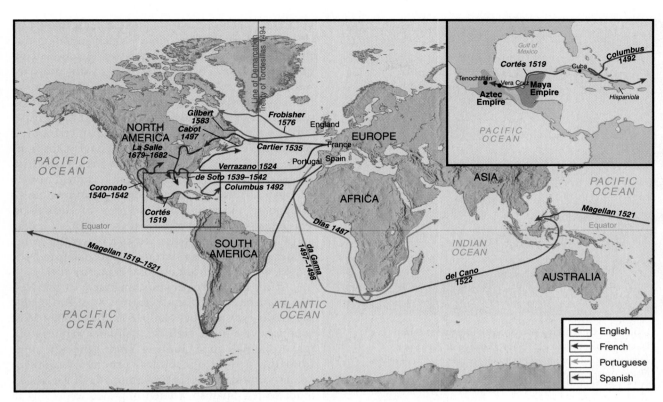

**VOYAGES OF EUROPEAN EXPLORATION**    *The routes of the major voyagers to the New World and Asia. Early explorers established land claims for the competing European states.* ❖

For a quarter century, the conquistadores concentrated their energies on the major islands that Columbus had discovered. Rumors of fabulous wealth in Mexico, however, aroused the interest of many Spaniards, including Hernán Cortés, a minor government functionary in Cuba. Like so many members of his class, he dreamed of glory, military adventure, and riches that would transform him from an ambitious court clerk into an honored *hidalgo*. On November 18, 1518, Cortés and a small army left Cuba to verify the stories of Mexico's treasure. Events soon demonstrated that Cortés was a leader of extraordinary ability.

His adversary was the legendary Aztec emperor, Montezuma. The confrontation between the two powerful personalities is one of the more dramatic of early American history. A fear of competition from rival conquistadores coupled with a burning desire to conquer a vast new empire drove Cortés forward. Determined to push his men through any obstacle, he scuttled the ships that had carried them to Mexico in order to prevent them from retreating. Cortés led his band of six hundred followers across rugged mountains and on the way gathered allies from among the Tlaxcalans, a tributary people eager to free themselves from Aztec domination.

In matters of war, Cortés possessed obvious technological superiority over the Aztecs. The sound of gunfire initially frightened the Indians. Moreover, Aztec troops had never seen horses, much less armored horses carrying sword-wielding Spaniards. But these elements would have counted for little had Cortés not also gained a psychological advantage over his opponents. At first, Montezuma thought that the Spaniards were gods, representatives of the fearful plumed serpent, Quetzalcoatl. Instead of resisting immediately, the emperor hesitated. When Montezuma's resolve hardened, it was too late. Cortés's victory in Mexico, coupled with other conquests in South America, transformed Spain, at least temporarily, into the wealthiest state in Europe.

## From Plunder to Settlement

Following the conquest of Mexico, renamed New Spain, the Spanish crown confronted a difficult problem. Ambitious conquistadores, interested chiefly in their own wealth and glory, had to be brought under royal authority, a task easier imagined than accomplished. Adventurers like Cortés were stubbornly independent, quick to take offense, and thousands of miles away from the seat of imperial government.

The crown found a partial solution in the **encomienda system.** The monarch rewarded the leaders of the conquest with Indian villages. The people who

Indian Slaves Working at a Spanish Sugar Plantation on the
Island of Hispaniola *(1595) by Theodore de Bry. Some
contemporaries condemned the brutal Spanish treatment of the
Native Americans.* ❖

lived in the settlements provided the *encomenderos* with
labor tribute in exchange for legal protection and religious guidance. The system, of course, cruelly exploited
Indian laborers. One historian concluded, "The first encomenderos, without known exception, understood
Spanish authority as provision for unlimited personal
opportunism." Cortés alone was granted the services of
more than twenty-three thousand Indian workers. The
encomienda system made the colonizers more dependent on the king, for it was he who legitimized their title. In the words of one scholar, the new economic
structure helped to transform "a frontier of plunder
into a frontier of settlement."

Spain's rulers attempted to maintain tight personal control over their American possessions. The
volume of correspondence between the two conti-
nents, much of it concerning mundane matters, was
staggering. All documents were duplicated several
times by hand. Because the trip to Madrid took many
months, a year often passed before receipt of an answer to a simple request. But somehow the cumber-
some system worked. In Mexico, officials appointed in
Spain established a rigid hierarchical order, directing
the affairs of the countryside from urban centers.

The Spanish also brought Catholicism to the New
World. The Dominicans and Franciscans, the two
largest religious orders, established Indian missions
throughout New Spain. Some friars tried to protect the
Native Americans from the worst forms of exploitation. One courageous Dominican, Fra Bartolomé de

las Casas, published an eloquent defense of Indian
rights, *Historia de las Indias,* which among other
things questioned the legitimacy of European conquest of the New World. Las Casas's work provoked
heated debate in Spain, and while the crown had no
intention of repudiating the vast American empire, it
did initiate certain reforms designed to bring greater
"love and moderation" to Spanish-Indian relations. It
is impossible to ascertain how many converts the friars
made. In 1531, however, a newly converted Christian
reported a vision of the Virgin, a dark-skinned woman
of obvious Indian ancestry, who became known
throughout the region as the Virgin of Guadalupe.
This figure—the result of a creative blending of Indian
and European cultures—served as a powerful symbol
of Mexican nationalism in the wars for independence
fought against Spain almost three centuries later.

About 250,000 Spaniards migrated to the New
World during the sixteenth century. Another 200,000
made the journey between 1600 and 1650. Most
colonists were single males in their late twenties seeking economic opportunities. They generally came
from the poorest agricultural regions of southern
Spain—almost 40 percent migrating from Andalusia.
Since so few Spanish women migrated, especially in
the sixteenth century, the men often married Indians
and blacks, unions which produced *mestizos* and *mulattos.* The frequency of interracial marriage indicated
that, among other things, the people of New Spain
were more tolerant of racial differences than were the
English who settled in North America. For the people
of New Spain, social standing was affected as much, or
more, by economic worth as it was by color. Persons
born in the New World, even those of Spanish parentage (*criollos*), were regarded as socially inferior to natives of the mother country (*peninsulares*).

Spain claimed far more of the New World than it
could possibly manage. Spain's rulers regarded the
American colonies primarily as a source of precious
metal, and between 1500 and 1650, an estimated 200
tons of gold and 16,000 tons of silver were shipped
back to the Spanish treasury in Madrid. This great
wealth, however, proved a mixed blessing. The sudden
acquisition of so much money stimulated a horrendous inflation that hurt ordinary Spaniards. They were
hurt further by long, debilitating European wars
funded by American gold and silver. Moreover, instead
of developing its own industry, Spain became dependent on the annual shipment of bullion from America,
and in 1603, one insightful Spaniard declared, "The
New World conquered by you, has conquered you in
its turn." This somewhat weakened, although still formidable, empire would eventually extend its territorial
claims north to California and the Southwest (see
Chapter 4).

*The Virgin of Guadalupe is perhaps the best-known religious symbol of Mexico. The image reflects the sixteenth-century encounter between Europeans and Indians. The Virgin Mary was already an important religious figure among the Spanish when they arrived in America. Like the Indian Juan Diego to whom she is said to have appeared and offered hope, comfort, and protection, the Virgin is dark-skinned. This 1531 representation shows her clothed in a robe adorned with stars and surrounded by a crown of sunrays. Each year hundreds of thousands of people visit the shrine of the Virgin at Tepeyac, outside Mexico City.* ❖

## THE FRENCH CLAIM CANADA

French interest in the New World developed slowly. More than three decades after Columbus's discovery, King Francis I sponsored the unsuccessful efforts of Giovanni da Verrazzano to find a short water route to China, via a northwest passage around or through North America. In 1534, the king sent Jacques Cartier on a similar quest. The rocky, barren coast of Labrador depressed the explorer. He grumbled, "I am rather inclined to believe that this is the land God gave to Cain."

Discovery of a large, promising waterway the following year raised Cartier's spirits. He reconnoitered the Gulf of Saint Lawrence, traveling up the magnificent river as far as modern Montreal. Despite his high expectations, however, Cartier got no closer to China, and discouraged by the harsh winters, he headed home in 1542. Not until sixty-five years later did Samuel de Champlain resettle this region for France. He founded Quebec in 1608.

As was the case with other colonial powers, the French declared they had migrated to the New World in search of wealth as well as in hopes of converting the Indians to Christianity. As it turned out, these economic and spiritual goals required full cooperation between the French and the Native Americans. In contrast to the English settlers, who established independent farms and who regarded the Indians at best as obstacles in the path of civilization, the French viewed the natives as necessary economic partners. Furs were Canada's most valuable export, and to obtain the pelts of beaver and other animals, the French were absolutely dependent on Indian hunters and trappers. French traders lived among the Indians, often taking native wives and studying local cultures.

Frenchmen known as *coureurs de bois* (forest runners), following Canada's great river networks, paddled deep into the heart of the continent in search of fresh sources of furs. Some intrepid traders penetrated beyond the Great Lakes into the Mississippi Valley. In 1673, Père Jacques Marquette journeyed down the Mississippi River, and nine years later, Sieur de La Salle traveled all the way to the Gulf of Mexico. In the early eighteenth century, the French established small settlements in Louisiana, the most important being New Orleans. The spreading French influence worried English colonists living along the Atlantic coast, for it appeared the French were about to cut them off from the trans-Appalachian west.

Catholic missionaries also depended on Indian cooperation. Canadian priests were drawn from two orders, the Jesuits and the Recollects, and although measuring their success in the New World is difficult, it seems they converted more Indians to Christianity than did their English Protestant counterparts to the south. Like the fur traders, the missionaries lived among the Indians and learned to speak their languages.

The French dream of a vast American empire suffered from serious flaws. The crown remained largely indifferent to Canadian affairs. Royal officials stationed in New France received limited and sporadic support from Paris. An even greater problem was the decision to settle what seemed to many rural peasants and urban artisans a cold, inhospitable land. Throughout the colonial period, Canada's European population remained small. A census of 1663

*A French* coureur de bois, *or forest runner, is shown equipped with a rifle, a pipe, and snowshoes to track new sources of fur in the wilderness of New France.* ❖

recorded a mere 3035 French residents. By 1700, the figure had reached only 15,000. Moreover, because of the colony's geography, all exports and imports had to go through Quebec. It was relatively easy, therefore, for crown officials to control that traffic, usually by awarding fur-trading monopolies to court favorites. Such practices created political tensions and hindered economic growth.

# THE ENGLISH ENTER THE COMPETITION

The first English visit to North America remains shrouded in mystery. Fishermen working out of Bristol and other western English ports may have landed in Nova Scotia and Newfoundland as early as the 1480s. The codfish of the Grand Banks undoubtedly drew vessels of all nations, and during the summer months some sailors probably dried and salted their catches on Canada's convenient shores. John Cabot (Giovanni Caboto), a Venetian sea captain,

completed the first recorded transatlantic voyage by an English vessel in 1497, while attempting to find a northwest passage to Asia.

Cabot died during a second attempt to find a direct route to Cathay in 1498. Although Sebastian Cabot continued his father's explorations in the Hudson Bay region in 1508–1509, England's interest in the New World waned. For the next three-quarters of a century, the English people were preoccupied with more pressing domestic and religious concerns. When curiosity about the New World revived, however, Cabot's voyages established England's belated claim to American territory.

## Birth of English Protestantism

At the time of Cabot's death, England was not prepared to compete with Spain and Portugal for the riches of the Orient. Although Henry VII, the first Tudor monarch, brought peace to England after a bitter civil war, the country still contained too many "over-mighty subjects," powerful local magnates who maintained armed retainers and who often paid little attention to royal authority. Henry possessed no standing army; his small navy intimidated no one. To be sure, the Tudors gave nominal allegiance to the pope in Rome, but unlike the rulers of Spain, they were not crusaders for Catholicism.

A complex web of international diplomacy also worked against England's early entry into New World colonization. In 1509, to cement an alliance between Spain and England, the future Henry VIII married Catherine of Aragon. As a result of this marital arrangement, English merchants enjoyed limited rights to trade in Spain's American colonies, but any attempt by England at independent colonization would have threatened those rights and jeopardized the alliance.

By the end of the sixteenth century, however, conditions within England had changed dramatically, in part as a result of the **Protestant Reformation.** As they did, the English began to consider their former ally, Spain, to be the greatest threat to English aspirations. Tudor monarchs, especially Henry VIII (r. 1509–1547) and his daughter Elizabeth I (r. 1558–1603), developed a strong central administration, while England became more and more a Protestant society. The merger of English Protestantism and English nationalism affected all aspects of public life. It helped propel England into a central role in European affairs and was crucial in creating a powerful sense of an English identity among all classes of people.

Popular anticlericalism helped spark religious reformation in England. Although they observed traditional Catholic ritual, the English people had long resented paying monies to a pope who lived in far-off Rome. Early in the sixteenth century, criticism of the clergy grew increasingly vocal. Cardinal Thomas Wolsey, the most powerful prelate in England, flaunted his immense wealth and unwittingly became a symbol of spiritual corruption. Parish priests were objects of ridicule. Poorly educated men for the most part, they seemed theologically ignorant and perpetually grasping. Anticlericalism did not run as deep in England as it had in Martin Luther's Germany, but by the late 1520s, the Catholic Church could no longer take for granted the allegiance of the great mass of the population. The people's growing anger is central to an understanding of the English Reformation. Put simply, if ordinary men and women throughout the kingdom had not accepted separation from Rome, then Henry VIII could not have forced them to leave the church.

The catalyst for Protestant Reformation in England was the king's desire to rid himself of his wife, Catherine of Aragon, who happened to be the daughter of the former king of Spain. Their marriage had produced a daughter, Mary, but, as the years passed, no son. The need for a male heir obsessed Henry. He and his counselors assumed a female ruler could not maintain domestic peace and England would fall once again into civil war. The answer seemed to be remarriage. Henry petitioned Pope Clement VII for a divorce (technically, an annulment), but the Spanish had other ideas. Unwilling to tolerate the public humiliation of Catherine, they forced the pope to procrastinate. In 1527, time ran out. The passionate Henry fell in love with Anne Boleyn, who later bore him a daughter, Elizabeth. The king decided to divorce Catherine with or without papal consent.

The final break with Rome came swiftly. Between 1529 and 1536, the king, acting through Parliament, severed all ties with the pope, seized church lands, and dissolved many of the monasteries. In March 1534, the Act of Supremacy boldly announced, "The King's Majesty justly and rightfully is supreme head of the Church of England." The entire process, which one historian termed a "state reformation," was conducted with impressive efficiency. Land formerly owned by the Catholic Church passed quickly into private hands, and within a short period, property holders throughout England had acquired a vested interest in Protestantism. Beyond breaking with the papacy, Henry showed little enthusiasm for theological change. Many Catholic ceremonies survived.

The split with Rome, however, opened the door to increasingly radical religious ideas. The year 1539 saw the publication of the first Bible in English. Before then the Scripture had been available only in Latin, the language of an educated elite. For the first time in English history, ordinary people could read the word of God in the vernacular. It was a liberating experience that persuaded some men and women that Henry had not sufficiently reformed the English church.

With Henry's death in 1547, England entered a period of acute political and religious instability. Edward VI, Henry's young son by his third wife, Jane Seymour, came to the throne, but he was still a child and sickly besides. Militant Protestants took advantage of the political uncertainty, insisting the Church of England remove every trace of its Catholic origins. With the death of young Edward in 1553, these ambitious efforts came to a sudden halt. Henry's eldest daughter, Mary, next ascended the throne. Fiercely loyal to the Catholic faith of her mother, Catherine of Aragon, Mary I vowed to return England to the pope.

However misguided were the queen's plans, she possessed her father's iron will. Hundreds of Protestants were executed; others scurried off to the safety of Geneva and Frankfurt, where they absorbed the most radical Calvinist doctrines of the day. When Mary died in 1558 and was succeeded by Elizabeth, the "Marian exiles" flocked back to England, more eager than ever to rid the Tudor church of Catholicism. Mary had inadvertently advanced the cause of Calvinism by creating so many Protestant martyrs, reformers burned for their faith and now celebrated in the woodcuts of the most popular book of the period, John Foxe's *Acts and Monuments,* commonly known as the *Book of Martyrs* (1563). The Marian exiles served as the leaders of the Elizabethan church, an institution that remained fundamentally Calvinist until the end of the sixteenth century.

## Militant Protestantism

By the time Mary Tudor came to the throne, the vast popular movement known as the Reformation had swept across northern and central Europe, and as much as any of the later great political revolutions, it had begun to transform the character of the modern world. The Reformation started in Germany when, in 1517, a relatively obscure German monk, Martin Luther, publicly challenged the central tenets of Roman Catholicism. Within a few years, the religious unity of Europe was permanently shattered. The Reformation divided kingdoms, sparked bloody wars, and unleashed an extraordinary flood of religious publication.

Luther's message was straightforward, one ordinary people could easily comprehend. God spoke through the Bible, Luther maintained, not through the pope or priests. Scripture taught that women and men were saved by faith alone. Pilgrimages, fasts, alms, indulgences—none of the traditional ritual

*John Foxe's* Book of Martyrs *(1563), depicting the sufferings of English dissenters executed under the Catholic queen Mary. It provided powerful propaganda for the advance of the Protestant faith. ❖*

observances could assure salvation. The institutional structure of Catholicism was challenged as Luther's radical ideas spread rapidly across northern Germany and Scandinavia.

After Luther, other Protestant theologians—religious thinkers who would determine the course of religious reform in England, Scotland, and the early American colonies—mounted an even more strident attack on Catholicism. The most influential of these was John Calvin, a lawyer turned theologian, who lived most of his adult life in the Swiss city of Geneva. Calvin stressed God's omnipotence over human affairs. The Lord, he maintained, chose some persons for "election," the gift of salvation, while condemning others to eternal damnation. A man or woman could do nothing to alter this decision.

Common sense suggests that such a bleak doctrine—known as predestination—might lead to fatalism or hedonism. After all, why not enjoy the world's pleasures to the fullest if such actions have no effect on God's judgment? But many sixteenth-century Europeans did not share modern notions of what constitutes common sense. Indeed, Calvinists were constantly "up and doing," searching for signs that they had received God's gift of grace. The uncertainty of their eternal state proved a powerful psychological spur, for as long as people did not know whether they were scheduled for heaven or hell, they worked diligently to demonstrate that they possessed at least the seeds of grace.

John Calvin's *Institutes of the Christian Religion* (1536) contained a powerful statement of the new faith, and his teachings spawned religious movements in most northern European countries. In France, the reformed Protestants were known as Huguenots. In Scotland, people of Calvinist persuasion founded the Presbyterian Church. And in seventeenth-century England and America, most of those who put Calvin's teachings into practice were called Puritans.

## Woman in Power

Queen Elizabeth demonstrated that Henry and his advisers had been mistaken about the capabilities of female rulers. She was a woman of such talent that modern biographers find little to criticize in her decisions. She governed the English people from 1558 to 1603, an intellectually exciting period during which some of her subjects took the first halting steps toward colonizing the New World.

Elizabeth recognized her most urgent duty as queen was to end the religious turmoil that had divided the country for a generation. She had no desire to restore Catholicism. After all, the pope openly referred to her as a woman of illegitimate birth. Nor did she want to re-create the church exactly as it had been in the final years of her father's reign. Rather, Elizabeth established a unique institution, Catholic in much of its ceremony and government but clearly Protestant in doctrine. Under her so-called Elizabethan settlement, the queen assumed the title "Supreme Head of the Church." Some churchmen who had studied with Calvin in Geneva urged her to drop immediately all Catholic rituals, but she ignored these strident reformers. The young queen understood she could not rule effectively without the full support of her people, and as the examples of Edward and Mary before her demonstrated, neither radical change nor widespread persecution gained a monarch lasting popularity.

The state of England's religion was not simply a domestic concern. One scholar aptly termed this period of European history "the Age of Religious Wars." Catholicism and Protestantism influenced the way ordinary men and women across the continent interpreted the experiences of everyday life. Religion shaped political and economic activities. Protestant leaders, for example, purged the English calendar of the many saints' days that had punctuated the agricultural year in Catholic countries. The Reformation certainly had a profound impact on the economic development of Calvinist countries. Max Weber, a brilliant German sociologist of the early twentieth century, argued in his *Protestant Ethic and Spirit of Capitalism* that a gnawing sense of self-doubt created by the doctrine of "predestination" drove Calvinists to extraordinary diligence. They generated large profits not because they wanted to become rich, but because they wanted to be doing the Lord's work, to show they might be among God's "elect."

Indeed, it is helpful to view Protestantism and Catholicism as warring ideologies, bundles of deeply held beliefs that divided countries and families much as communism and capitalism did during the late twentieth century. The confrontations between the two faiths affected Elizabeth's entire reign. Soon after she became queen, Pope Pius V excommunicated her, and in his papal bull *Regnans in Exelsis* (1570), he stripped Elizabeth of her "pretended title to the kingdom." Spain, the most fervently Catholic state in Europe, vowed to restore England to the "true" faith, and Catholic militants constantly plotted to overthrow the Tudor monarchy.

### Religion, War, and Nationalism

Slowly, but steadily, English Protestantism and English national identity merged. A loyal English subject in the late sixteenth century loved the queen, supported the Church of England, and hated Catholics, especially those who happened to live in Spain. Elizabeth herself came to symbolize this militant new chauvinism. Her subjects adored the Virgin Queen, and they applauded when her famed "Sea Dogs"—dashing figures such as Sir Francis Drake and Sir John Hawkins—seized Spanish treasure ships in American waters. The English

sailors' raids were little more than piracy, but in this undeclared state of war, such instances of harassment passed for national victories. There seemed to be no reason patriotic Elizabethans should not share in the wealth of the New World. With each engagement, each threat, each plot, English nationalism took deeper root. By the 1570s, it had become obvious the English people were driven by powerful ideological forces similar to those that had moved the Spanish subjects of Isabella and Ferdinand almost a century earlier.

In the mid-1580s, Philip II, who had united the empires of Spain and Portugal in 1580, decided that England's arrogantly Protestant queen could be tolerated no longer. He ordered the construction of a mighty fleet, hundreds of transport vessels designed to carry Spain's finest infantry across the English channel. When one of Philip's lieutenants viewed the Armada at Lisbon in May 1588, he described it as *la felicissima armada,* the invincible fleet. The king believed that with the support of England's oppressed Catholics, Spanish troops would sweep Elizabeth from power.

It was a grand scheme; it was an even grander failure. In 1588, a smaller, more maneuverable English navy dispersed Philip's Armada, and severe storms finished it off. Spanish hopes for Catholic England lay wrecked along the rocky coasts of Scotland and Ireland. English Protestants interpreted victory in providential terms: "God breathed and they were scattered."

## IRISH REHEARSAL FOR AMERICAN SETTLEMENT

After the defeat of the Armada, it seemed as if England had fulfilled the prerequisites for American colonization. Before they crossed the Atlantic, however, English settlers moved to Ireland. Their experiences there powerfully shaped how later migrants would view the New World. It was on this island that enterprising Englishmen first learned to subdue a foreign population and to seize its lands. When Elizabeth assumed the throne, Ireland's one million inhabitants were scattered across the countryside. There were few villages, most of which were located along the coast. To the English eye, the Irish people seemed wild and barbaric. They were also fiercely independent and difficult to control. The English dominated a small region around Dublin by force of arms, but much of Ireland's territory remained in the hands of Gaelic-speaking Catholics who presumably lived beyond the reach of civilization.

### English Conquest of Ireland

During the 1560s and 1570s, various enterprising English people decided that considerable fortunes could be made in Ireland. There were substantial risks, of course, not the least of which was the resistance of the Irish. Nevertheless, private "projectors" sponsored English settlements, and, in turn, these colonists forced the Irish either into tenancy or off the land altogether. It was during this period that semimilitary colonies were planted in Ulster and Munster.

As one might expect, colonization produced severe cultural strains. The English settlers, however humble their origins, felt superior to the Irish. After all, the English people had championed the Protestant religion. They had constructed a complex market economy and created a powerful nation-state. To the English settlers, the Irish appeared to be lazy, licentious, superstitious, even stupid. English settlers ridiculed unfamiliar local customs, and it is not surprising that even educated representatives of the two cultures found communication almost impossible. English colonists, for example, criticized the pastoral farming methods prevalent in sixteenth-century Ireland. It seemed perversely wasteful for the Irish to be forever moving about, since as any English person could see, such practices retarded the development of towns. Sir John Davies, a leading English colonizer, declared that if the Irish were left to themselves, they would "never (to the end of the world) build houses, make townships or villages or manure or improve the land *as it ought to be*." Such stubborn inefficiency—surely (the English reasoned) the Irish must have known better—became the standard English justification for the seizure of large tracts of land.

### English Brutality

English ethnocentrism was relatively benign so long as the Irish accepted the subservient roles the colonizers assigned them. But when they rebelled against the invaders, something they did with great frequency, English condescension turned to violence. Resistance smacked of disrespect and, moreover, to ensure the safety of the English, it had to be crushed. The brutality of Sir Humphrey Gilbert in Ireland would have made even the most insensitive Spanish conquistador uneasy. Gilbert was a talented man who wrote treatises on geography, explored the coast of North America, and entertained Queen Elizabeth with witty conversation. But as a colonizer in a strange land—in what some historians now call England's "permissive frontier"—he tolerated no opposition.

In 1569, he was appointed military governor of Munster, and when the Irish in his district rose up, he executed everyone he could catch, "mane, woman and childe." Gilbert's excesses would never have been permitted in England no matter how serious the rebellion. He cut off the heads of many enemy soldiers killed in battle, and in the words of one contemporary,

Gilbert laid his macabre trophies "on the ground by each side of the way leading to his tent, so that none should come into his tent for any cause but commonly he must pass through a lane of heads." Such behavior was not only unprecedented, it was also calamitous. Instead of bringing peace and security, it helped generate a hatred so deep that Ireland remains divided to this day.

The Irish experiments served as models for later English colonies in the New World, just as the Canary Island plantations had done for Spain. Indeed, one modern Irish scholar argues that "English colonization in Virginia was a logical continuation of the Elizabethan conquest of Ireland." English adventurers in the New World commonly compared Native Americans with the "wild" Irish, a kind of ethnocentric shorthand that equated all alien races. This mental process was a central element in the transfer of English culture to America. The English, like the Spanish and the French, did not perceive America in objective terms. Instead, they saw an America they had already constructed in their imaginations, and the people and objects that greeted them on the other side of the Atlantic were forced into Old World categories, one of which was "Irish."

## AN UNPROMISING BEGINNING: MYSTERY AT ROANOKE

By the 1570s, English interest in the New World had revived. An increasing number of wealthy gentlemen were in an expansive mood, ready to challenge Spain and reap the profits of Asia and America. Yet the adventurers who directed Elizabethan expeditions were only dimly aware of Cabot's voyages, and their sole experience in settling distant outposts was in Ireland. Over the last three decades of the sixteenth century, English adventurers made almost every mistake one could possibly imagine. They did, however, acquire valuable information about winds and currents, supplies and finance.

Sir Walter Ralegh's experience provided all English colonizers with a sobering example of the difficulties that awaited them in America. In 1584, he dispatched two captains to the coast of present-day North Carolina to claim land granted to him by Elizabeth. The men returned with glowing reports, no doubt aimed in part at potential financial backers. "The soile," declared Captain Arthur Barlow, "is the most plentifull, sweete, fruitfull, and wholesome of all the world."

Ralegh diplomatically renamed this marvelous region Virginia, in honor of his patron, the Virgin Queen. Indeed, highly gendered vocabulary figured prominently in the European conquest of the New World. As historian Kathleen M. Brown explains,

*John White depicted fishing techniques practiced by the Algonquian Indians of the present-day Carolinas. In the canoe, dip nets and multipronged spears are used. In the background, Indians stab at fish with long spears. At left, a weir traps fish by taking advantage of the river current's natural force.* ❖

## CHRONOLOGY

| | |
|---|---|
| 24,000– 17,000 B.C. | Indians cross the Bering Strait into North America |
| 2000– 1500 B.C. | Agricultural Revolution transforms Native American life |
| A.D. 1001 | Norsemen establish a small settlement in Vinland (Newfoundland) |
| 1030 | Death of War Jaabi (king of Takrur), first Muslim ruler in West Africa |
| 1450 | Gutenberg perfects movable type |
| 1469 | Marriage of Isabella and Ferdinand leads to the unification of Spain |
| 1481 | Portuguese build castle at Elmina on the Gold Coast of Africa |
| 1492 | Columbus lands at San Salvador |
| 1497 | Cabot leads first English exploration of North America |
| 1498 | Vasco da Gama of Portugal reaches India by sailing around Africa |
| 1502 | Montezuma becomes emperor of the Aztecs |
| 1506 | Columbus dies in Spain after four voyages to America |
| 1517 | Martin Luther's protest sparks Reformation in Germany |
| 1521 | Cortés defeats the Aztecs at Tenochtitlán |
| 1529–1536 | Henry VIII provokes English Reformation |
| 1534 | Cartier claims Canada for France |
| 1536 | Calvin's *Institutes* published |
| 1540 | Coronado explores the Southwest for Spain |
| 1558 | Elizabeth I becomes queen of England |
| 1585 | First Roanoke settlement established on coast of North Carolina |
| 1588 | Spanish Armada defeated by the English |
| 1608 | Champlain founds Quebec |

"Associations of the land with virgin innocence reinforced the notion that Virginia had been saved from the Spaniard's lust to be conquered by the chaste English." Elizabeth encouraged Ralegh in private conversation but rejected his persistent requests for money. With rumors of war in the air, she did not want to alienate Philip II unnecessarily by sponsoring a colony on land long ago claimed by Spain.

Ralegh finally raised the funds for his adventure, but his enterprise seemed ill-fated from the start. Despite careful planning, everything went wrong. The settlement was poorly situated. Located inside the Outer Banks—perhaps to avoid detection by the Spanish—the Roanoke colony proved extremely difficult to reach. Even experienced navigators feared the treacherous currents and storms off Cape Hatteras. Sir Richard Grenville, the leader of the expedition, added to the colonists' troubles by destroying an entire Indian village in retaliation for the suspected theft of a silver cup.

Grenville hurried back to England in the autumn of 1585, leaving the colonists to fend for themselves. Although they coped quite well, a peculiar series of accidents transformed Ralegh's settlement into a ghost town. In the spring of 1586, Sir Francis Drake was returning from a Caribbean voyage and decided to visit Roanoke. Since an anticipated shipment of supplies was overdue, the colonists climbed aboard Drake's ships and went home.

In 1587, Ralegh launched a second colony. This time he placed in charge John White, a veteran administrator and talented artist, who a few years earlier had produced a magnificent sketchbook of the Algonquian Indians who lived near Roanoke. Once again, Ralegh's luck turned sour. The Spanish Armada severed communication between England and America. Every available English vessel was pressed into military service, and between 1587 and 1590, no ship visited the Roanoke colonists. When rescuers eventually reached the island, they found the village deserted. The fate of the "lost" colonists remains a mystery. The best guess is that they were absorbed by neighboring groups of natives, some from as far as the southern shore of the James River.

## CONCLUSION:
## CAMPAIGN TO SELL AMERICA

Had it not been for Richard Hakluyt, the Younger, who publicized explorers' accounts of the New World, the dream of American colonization might have died in England. Hakluyt, a supremely industrious man, never saw America. Nevertheless, his vision of the New World powerfully shaped English public opinion. He interviewed captains and sailors upon their return from distant voyages and carefully collected their stories in a massive book titled *The Principall Navigations, Voyages, and Discoveries of the English Nation* (1589).

The work appeared to be a straightforward description of what these sailors had seen across the sea. That was its strength. In reality, Hakluyt edited each piece so it would drive home the book's central point: England needed American colonies. Indeed, they were essential to the nation's prosperity and independence. In Hakluyt's America, there were no losers. "The earth bringeth fourth all things in aboundance, as in the first creations without toil or labour," he wrote of Virginia. His blend of piety, patriotism, and self-interest proved immensely popular, and his *Voyages* went through many editions.

As a salesperson for the New World, Hakluyt was as misleading as he was successful. He failed to appreciate, or purposely ignored, the rich cultural diversity of the Native Americans and the varied backgrounds of the Europeans. He said not a word about the sufferings of Africans in America. Instead, he and many other polemicists for colonization led the ordinary English men and women who traveled to America to expect nothing less than a paradise on earth. This European perspective on the resources of the New World invited continuous human suffering and ecological disaster.

## RECOMMENDED READING

The histories of three different peoples coming together for the first time in the New World has sparked innovative scholarship. Many interdisciplinary works explore diverse patterns of cultural adaptation. Some of the best titles bring fresh insights to the Native Americans' response to radical environmental and social change. Among these are Inga Clendinnen, *Aztecs: An Interpretation* (1991); James H. Merrell, *The Indians' New World: Catawbas and Their Neighbors From European Contact Through the Era of Removal* (1989); and James F. Brooks, *Captives and Cousins: Slavery, Kinship and Community in the Southwest Borderlands* (2002). Other broad-ranging volumes examine how early European invaders imagined the New World and how they translated what they thought they had seen into a familiar and unthreatening language: Stephen Greenblatt, *Marvelous Possessions: The Wonder of the New World* (1991), and Anthony Pagden, *European Encounters with the New World: From Renaissance to Romanticism* (1992). The impact of the environment—a major theme of this chapter—is the topic of three pioneering investigations: A. W. Crosby, *The Columbian Voyages, The Columbian Exchange, and Their Historians* (1987); William Cronon, *Changes in the Land: Indians, Colonists, and the Ecology of New England* (1983); and Shepard Krech III, *The Ecological Indian: Myth and History* (1999). The best overview of the European response to the Conquest is John H. Elliott, *The Old World and New, 1492–1650* (1970). For the Irish experience one should consult Nicholas Canny, *Making Ireland British 1580–1650* (2001). Two outstanding interpretations of the English Reformation are Ethan H. Shagan, *Popular Politics and the English Reformation* (2003) and Eamon Duffy, *The Stripping of the Altars: Traditional Religion in England 1400–1580* (1992). Books that offer boldly original interpretations of the Conquest are Kirkpatrick Sale, *The Conquest of Paradise: Christopher Columbus and the Columbian Legacy* (1990); and Kathleen M. Brown, *Good Wives, Nasty Wenches, and Anxious Patriarchs: Gender, Race, and Power in Colonial Virginia* (1996).

**For a list of additional titles related to this chapter's topics, please see** http://www.ablongman.com/divine.

# SUGGESTED WEB SITES

### Vikings in the New World

http://emuseum.mnsu.edu/prehistory/vikings/vikhome.html
This site explores the history of some of the earliest European visitors to America.

### Sir Francis Drake

http://www.mcn.org/2/oseeler/drake.htm
This comprehensive site covers much of Drake's life and voyages.

### Ancient Mesoamerican Civilizations

http://www.angelfire.com/ca/humanorigins/index.html
Kevin L. Callahan of the University of Minnesota Department of Anthropology maintains this page that supplies information regarding Mesoamerican civilizations with well-organized essays and photos.

### National Museum of the American Indian

http://www.si.edu/nmai
The Smithsonian Institution maintains the site, providing information about the museum. The museum is dedicated to everything about Native Americans.

### 1492: An Ongoing Voyage

http://www.loc.gov/exhibits/1492
An exhibit of the Library of Congress, Washington, D.C. With brief essays and images about early civilizations and contact in the Americas.

### Cahokia Mounds

http://medicine.wustl.edu/~mckinney/cahokia/cahokia.html
The Cahokia Mounds State Historical Site gives information about a fascinating pre-Columbian culture in North America.

### The Computerized Information Retrieval System on Columbus and the Age of Discovery

http://muweb.millersv.edu/~columbus/
The History Department and Academic Computing Services of Millersville University, Pennsylvania, provide this text retrieval system containing more than 1000 text articles from various magazines, journals, newspapers, speeches, official calendars, and other sources relating to various encounter themes.

### Mexico Pre-Columbian History

http://www.mexonline.com/precolum.htm
This site "provides information on the Aztecs, Maya, Mexica, Olmecs, Toltec, Zapotecs and other pre-European cultures, as well as information on museums, archeology, language, and education."

### White Oak Fur Post

http://www.whiteoak.org/
This site documents an eighteenth-century fur trading post among the Indians in what would become Minnesota.

### La Salle Shipwreck Project

http://www.thc.state.tx.us/belle/lasbelle.html
Texas Historical Commission site about the archaeological dig to recover the ship of one of America's famous early explorers.

### The Discoverers' Web

http://www.win.tue.nl/cs/fm/engels/discovery/
Andre Engels maintains this complete collection of information on the various efforts at exploration.

Map of New York City presented to James, Duke of York (the future James II), shortly after the English captured New Amsterdam from the Dutch in 1664. ❖

# New World Experiments: England's Seventeenth-Century Colonies

## *Profit and Piety: Competing Visions for English Settlement*

In the spring of 1644, John Winthrop, governor of Massachusetts Bay, learned that Native Americans had overrun the scattered tobacco plantations of Virginia, killing as many as five hundred colonists. Winthrop never thought much of the Chesapeake settlements. He regarded the people who had migrated to that part of America as grossly materialistic, and because Virginia had recently expelled several Puritan ministers, Winthrop decided the hostilities were God's way of punishing the tobacco planters for their worldliness. "It was observable," he related, "that this massacre came upon them soon after they had driven out the godly ministers we had sent to them." When Virginians appealed to Massachusetts for military supplies, they received a cool reception. "We were weakly provided ourselves," Winthrop explained, "and so could not afford them any help of that kind."

In 1675, the tables turned. Native Americans declared all-out war against the New Englanders, and soon reports of the destruction of Puritan communities were circulating in Virginia. "The Indians in New England have burned Considerable Villages," wrote one leading tobacco planter, "and have made them [the New Englanders] desert more than one hundred and fifty miles of those places they had formerly seated."

Sir William Berkeley, Virginia's royal governor, was not displeased by news of New England's adversity. He and his friends held the Puritans in contempt. Indeed, the New Englanders reminded them of the religious fanatics who had provoked civil war in England and who in 1649 had executed Charles I. During this particular crisis, Berkeley noted that he might have shown more pity for the beleaguered New Englanders "had they deserved it of the King." The governor, sounding like a Puritan himself, described the warring Indians as the "Instruments" with which God intended "to destroy the King's Enemies." For good measure, Virginia outlawed the export of foodstuffs to their embattled northern neighbors.

SUCH EXTRAORDINARY DISUNITY in the colonies—not to mention lack of compassion—comes as a surprise to anyone searching for the roots of modern nationalism in this early period. English colonization in the seventeenth century did not spring from a desire to build a centralized empire in the New World similar to that of Spain or France. Instead, the English crown awarded colonial charters to a wide variety of entrepreneurs, religious idealists, and aristocratic adventurers who established separate and profoundly different colonies. Not only did New Englanders have little in common with the earliest Virginians and Carolinians, but they were often divided among themselves.

Migration itself helps to explain this striking competition and diversity. At different times, different colonies appealed to different sorts of people. Men and women moved to the New World for various reasons, and as economic, political, and religious conditions changed on both sides of the Atlantic during the course of the seventeenth century, so too did patterns of English migration.

# BREAKING AWAY

English people in the early decades of the seventeenth century experienced what seemed to them an accelerating pace of social change. What was most evident was the rapid growth of population. Between 1580 and 1650, a period during which many men and women elected to journey to the New World, the population of England expanded from about 3.5 million to more than 5 million. Among other things, the expansion strained the nation's agrarian economy. Competition for food and land drove up prices, and people desperate for work took to the roads. Those migrants, many of them drawn into the orbit of London by tales of opportunity, frightened the traditional leaders of English society. To the propertied class, the wandering poor represented a threat to good order, and, particularly during the early decades of the seventeenth century, landholders urged local magistrates throughout the kingdom to enforce the laws against vagrancy.

Even by modern standards, the English population of this period was quite mobile. To be sure, most men and women lived out their days rooted in the tiny country villages of their birth. A growing number of English people, however, were migrant laborers who took seasonal work. Many others relocated from the countryside to London, already a city of several hundred thousand inhabitants by the early seventeenth century. Because health conditions in London were poor, a large number of the new arrivals quickly died, and had their places not been taken by other migrants from the rural villages, the population of London would almost certainly have decreased.

Other, more exotic destinations also beckoned. A large number of English settlers migrated to Ireland, while lucrative employment and religious freedom attracted people to Holland. The Pilgrims, people who separated themselves from the established Church of England, initially hoped to make a new life in Leyden. The migrations within Europe serve as reminders that ordinary people had choices. A person who was upset about the state of the Church of England or who had lost a livelihood did not have to move to America. That some men and women consciously selected this much more dangerous and expensive journey set them apart from their contemporaries.

English colonists crossed the Atlantic for many reasons. Some wanted to institute a purer form of worship, more closely based on their interpretation of Scripture. Others dreamed of owning land and improving their social position. A few came to the New World to escape bad marriages, jail terms, or the dreary prospect of lifelong poverty. Since most seventeenth-century migrants, especially those who transferred to the Chesapeake colonies, left almost no records of their previous lives in England, it is futile to try to isolate a single cause or explanation for their decision to leave home.

In the absence of detailed personal information, historians usually have assumed that poverty, or the fear of soon falling into poverty, drove people across the Atlantic. No doubt economic considerations figured heavily in the final decision. But so too did religion, and it was not uncommon for the poor of early modern England to be among those demanding the most radical ecclesiastical reform. As a recent historian of seventeenth-century migration concluded, "Individuals left for a variety of motives, some idealistic, others practical, some simple, others complex, many perhaps contradictory and imperfectly understood by the migrants themselves."

Whatever their reasons for crossing the ocean, English migrants to America in this period left a nation wracked by recurrent, often violent political and religious controversy. During the 1620s, autocratic Stuart monarchs—James I (r. 1603–1625) and his son Charles I (r. 1625–1649)—who succeeded Queen Elizabeth on the English throne fought constantly with the elected members of Parliament. At stake were rival notions of constitutional and representative government.

Many royal policies—the granting of lucrative commercial monopolies to court favorites, for example—fueled popular discontent, but the crown's hostility to far-reaching religious reform sparked the most vocal protest. Throughout the kingdom, Puritans became adamant in their demand for radical purification of ritual.

Tensions grew so severe that in 1629, Charles attempted to rule the country without Parliament's assistance. The autocratic strategy backfired. When Charles finally was forced to recall Parliament in 1640 because he was running out of money, Parliament demanded major constitutional reforms. Militant Puritans, supported by many members of Parliament, insisted on restructuring the church—abolishing the office of bishop was high on their list. In this angry political atmosphere, Charles took up arms against the supporters of Parliament. The confrontation between Royalists and Parliamentarians set off a long and bloody conflict, known as the English Civil War. In 1649, the victorious Parliamentarians beheaded Charles, and for almost a decade, Oliver Cromwell, a skilled general and committed Puritan, governed England as Lord Protector.

In 1660, following Cromwell's death from natural causes, the Stuarts returned to the English throne. During a period known as the Restoration, neither Charles II (r. 1660–1685) nor James II (r. 1685–1688)—both sons of Charles I—was able to establish genuine political stability. When the authoritarian James lifted some of the restrictions governing Catholics, a Protestant nation rose up in what the

**THE STUART MONARCHS**

English people called the **Glorious Revolution** (1688) and sent James into permanent exile.

The Glorious Revolution altered the course of English political history and, therefore, that of the American colonies as well. The monarchs who followed James II surrendered some of the prerogative powers that had destabilized English politics for almost a century. The crown was still a potent force in the political life of the nation, but never again would an English king or queen attempt to govern without Parliament.

Such political events, coupled with periodic economic recession and religious repression, determined, in large measure, the direction and flow of migration to America. During times of political turmoil, religious persecution, and economic insecurity, men and women thought more seriously about transferring to the New World than they did during periods of peace and prosperity. Obviously, people who moved to America at different times came from different social and political environments. A person who emigrated to Pennsylvania in the 1680s, for example, left an England unlike the one that a Virginian in 1607 or a Bay Colonist in 1630 might have known. Moreover, the young men and women who migrated to London in search of work and who then, in their frustration and poverty, decided to move to the Chesapeake carried a very different set of memories from those people who moved directly to New England from the small rural villages of their homeland.

Regardless of the exact timing of departure, English settlers brought with them ideas and assumptions that helped them make sense of their everyday experiences in an unfamiliar environment. Their values were tested and sometimes transformed in the New World, but they were seldom destroyed. Settlement involved a complex process of adjustment. The colonists developed different subcultures in America, and in each it is possible to trace the interaction between the settlers' values and the physical elements, such as the climate, crops, and soil, of their new surroundings. The Chesapeake, the New England colonies, the Middle Colonies, and the Southern Colonies formed distinct regional identities that have survived to the present day.

## THE CHESAPEAKE: DREAMS OF WEALTH

After the Roanoke debacle in 1590, English interest in American settlement declined, and only a few aging visionaries such as Richard Hakluyt kept alive the dream of colonies in the New World. These advocates argued that the North American mainland contained resources of incalculable value. An innovative group, they insisted, might reap great profits and at the same time supply England with raw materials that it would otherwise be forced to purchase from European rivals: Holland, France, and Spain.

Moreover, any enterprise that annoyed Catholic Spain or revealed its weakness in America seemed a desirable end in itself to patriotic English Protestants. Anti-Catholicism and hatred of Spain became an integral part of English national identity during this period, and unless one appreciates just how deeply those sentiments ran in the popular mind, one cannot fully understand why ordinary people who had no direct financial stake in the New World so generously supported English efforts to colonize America. Soon after James I ascended to the throne, adventurers were given an opportunity to put their theories into practice in the colonies of Virginia and Maryland, an area known as the Chesapeake, or somewhat later, as the Tobacco Coast.

### Entrepreneurs in Virginia

During Elizabeth's reign, the major obstacle to successful colonization of the New World had been raising money. No single person, no matter how rich or well connected, could underwrite the vast expenses a New World settlement required. The solution to this financial problem was the **joint-stock company,** a business organization in which scores of people could invest without fear of bankruptcy. A merchant or landowner could purchase a share of stock at a stated price, and at the end of several years the investor could anticipate recovering the initial amount plus a portion of whatever profits the company had made. Joint-stock ventures sprang up like mushrooms. Affluent English citizens, and even some of more modest fortunes, rushed to invest in the companies and, as a result, some projects were able to amass large amounts of capital, enough certainly to launch a new colony in Virginia.

On April 10, 1606, James issued the first Virginia charter. The document authorized the London Company to establish plantations in Virginia. The London Company was an ambitious business venture. Its leader, Sir Thomas Smith, was reputedly London's wealthiest merchant. Smith and his partners gained possession of the territory lying between present-day North Carolina and the Hudson River. These were generous but vague boundaries, to be sure, but the Virginia Company—as the London Company soon called itself—set out immediately to find the treasures Hakluyt had promised.

In December 1606, the *Susan Constant,* the *Godspeed,* and the *Discovery* sailed for America. The ships carried 104 men and boys who had been instructed to establish a fortified outpost some hundred miles up a large navigable river. The natural beauty and economic potential of the region was apparent to everyone. A voyager on the expedition reported seeing "faire meaddowes and goodly tall trees, with such fresh waters running through the woods, as almost ravished [us] at first sight."

The leaders of the colony selected—without consulting resident Native Americans—what the Europeans considered a promising location more than thirty miles from the mouth of the James River. A marshy peninsula jutting out into the river became the site for one of America's most unsuccessful villages, Jamestown. Modern historians have criticized the choice, for the low-lying ground proved to be a disease-ridden death trap; even the drinking water was contaminated with salt. But the first Virginians were neither stupid nor suicidal. Jamestown seemed the ideal place to build a fort, since surprise attack by Spaniards or Native Americans rather than sickness appeared the more serious threat in the early months of settlement.

Almost immediately, dispirited colonists began quarreling. The adventurers were not prepared for the challenges that confronted them in America. Part of the problem was cultural. Most of them had grown up in a depressed agricultural economy that could not provide full-time employment for all who wanted it. In England, laborers shared what little work was available. One man, for example, might perform a certain chore while others simply watched. Later, the men who had been idle were given an opportunity to work for an hour or two. This labor system may have been appropriate for England, but in Virginia it nearly destroyed the colony. Adventurers sat around Jamestown while other men performed crucial agricultural tasks. It made little sense, of course, to share work in an environment in which people were starving because too little labor was expended on the planting and harvesting of crops. Not surprisingly, some modern historians—those who assumed all workers should put in an eight-hour day—branded the early Virginians as lazy, irresponsible beings who preferred to play while others labored. In point of fact, however, the first settlers were merely attempting to replicate a traditional work experience.

Avarice exacerbated the problems. The adventurers had traveled to the New World in search of the sort of instant wealth they imagined the Spaniards to have found in Mexico and Peru. Published tales of rubies and diamonds lying on the beach probably inflamed their expectations. Even when it must have been apparent that such expectations were unfounded, the first settlers often behaved in Virginia as if they fully expected to

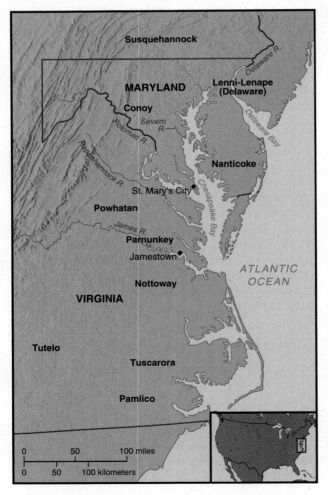

**CHESAPEAKE COLONIES, 1640** *The many deep rivers flowing into the Chesapeake Bay provided scattered English planters with a convenient transportation system, linking them directly to European markets.* ❖

## ❖ A Look at the Past ❖

### Armor

The earliest English settlers to Virginia may have come with insufficient food and too few practical tools, but they did supply themselves with arms and armor. Armor like this breastplate recovered from James Fort reveals how carefully the settlers prepared in advance for military combat. Could the imagined enemy have been other Europeans such as the Spanish? If so, why might they have attacked Jamestown during its infancy? Would such heavy armor have offered much protection against the weapons of Powhatan's warriors?

various beautiful women. Because of his reputation for boasting, historians have discounted Smith's account of life in early Virginia. Recent scholarship, however, has affirmed the truthfulness of his curious story. In Virginia, Smith brought order out of anarchy. While members of the council in Jamestown debated petty politics, he traded with the local Indians for food, mapped the Chesapeake Bay, and may even have been rescued from execution by a young Indian girl, Pocahontas. In the fall of 1608, he seized control of the ruling council and instituted a tough military discipline. Under Smith, no one enjoyed special privilege. Individuals whom he forced to work came to hate him. But he managed to keep them alive, no small achievement in such a deadly environment.

Leaders of the Virginia Company in London recognized the need to reform the entire enterprise. After all, they had spent considerable sums and had received nothing in return. In 1609, the company directors obtained a new charter from the king, which completely reorganized the Virginia government. Henceforth all commercial and political decisions affecting the colonists rested with the company, a fact that had not been made sufficiently clear in the 1606 charter. Moreover, in an effort to raise scarce capital, the original partners opened the joint-stock company to the

become rich. Instead of cooperating for the common good—guarding or farming, for example—individuals pursued personal interests. They searched for gold when they might have helped plant corn. No one was willing to take orders, and those who were supposed to govern the colony looked after their private welfare while disease, war, and starvation ravaged the settlement.

### Spinning Out of Control

Virginia might have gone the way of Roanoke had it not been for Captain John Smith. By any standard, he was a resourceful man. Before coming to Jamestown, he had traveled throughout Europe and fought with the Hungarian army against the Turks—and, if Smith is to be believed, he was saved from certain death by

*Pocahontas bore little relation to the person caricatured in modern film. She married John Rolfe, a settler who pioneered the cultivation of tobacco as a cash crop. She converted to Christianity, taking the name Rebeka. This portrait, painted during a visit to London, shows her in European court dress.* ❖

general public. For a little more than £12—approximately one year's wages for an unskilled English laborer—a person or group of persons could purchase a stake in Virginia. It was anticipated that in 1616 the profits from the colony would be distributed among the shareholders. The company sponsored a publicity campaign; pamphlets and sermons extolled the colony's potential and exhorted patriotic English citizens to invest in the enterprise.

The burst of energy came to nothing. Bad luck and poor planning plagued the Virginia Company. A vessel carrying additional settlers and supplies went aground in Bermuda, and while this misadventure did little to help the people at Jamestown, it provided Shakespeare with the idea for *The Tempest*. The governor, Lord De La Warr, added to the confusion by postponing his departure for America. Even the indomitable Captain Smith suffered a gunpowder accident and was forced to return to England.

Between 1609 and 1611, the remaining Virginia settlers lacked capable leadership, and perhaps as a result, they lacked food. The terrible winter of 1609–1610 was termed the "starving time." A few desperate colonists were driven to cannibalism, an ironic situation since early explorers had assumed that only Native Americans would eat human flesh. In England, Smith heard that one colonist had killed his wife, powdered [salted] her, and "had eaten part of her before it was known; for which he was executed." The captain, who possessed a droll sense of humor, observed, "Now, whether she was better roasted, broiled, or carbonadoed [sliced], I know not, but such a dish as powdered wife I never heard of." Other people simply lost the will to live.

The presence of so many Native Americans heightened the danger. The first colonists found themselves living—or attempting to live—in territory controlled by what was probably the most powerful Indian confederation east of the Mississippi River. Under the leadership of their *werowance*, Powhatan, these Indians had by 1608 created a loose association of some thirty tribes, and when Captain John Smith arrived to lead several hundred adventurers, the Powhatans (named for their king) numbered some 14,000 people, of whom 3200 were warriors. These people hoped initially to enlist the Europeans as allies against native enemies. When it became clear that the two groups, holding such different notions about labor and property and about the exploitation of the natural environment, could not coexist in peace, the Powhatans tried to drive the invaders out of Virginia, once in 1622 and again in 1644. The failure of the second campaign ended in the complete destruction of the Powhatan empire.

In June 1610, the settlers who had survived despite starvation and conflicts with the Indians actually abandoned Virginia. Through a stroke of luck, however, they encountered De La Warr just as they commenced their voyage down the James River. The governor and the deputy governors who succeeded him, Sir Thomas Gates and Sir Thomas Dale, ruled by martial law. The new colonists, many of them male and female servants employed by the company, were marched to work by the beat of the drum. Such methods saved the colony but could not make it flourish. In 1616, company shareholders received no profits. Their only reward was the right to a piece of unsurveyed land located three thousand miles from London.

*In 1608, Powhatan, the father of Pocahontas, gave this shell-decorated ceremonial cloak to Captain Christopher Newport. During the seventeenth century, this beautiful Native American artifact was given to Oxford University, where it can still be seen today.* ❖

## "Stinking Weed"

The economic solution to Virginia's problems grew in the vacant lots of Jamestown. Only Indians bothered to cultivate tobacco until John Rolfe, a settler who achieved notoriety by marrying Pocahontas, realized this local weed might be a valuable export. Rolfe experimented with the crop, eventually growing in Virginia a milder variety that had been developed in the West Indies and was more appealing to European smokers.

*This tobacco label advertises Virginia's valuable export—tobacco. Despite King James's initial attitude toward the "stinking weed," once the government saw that tobacco made a profit, it dropped its moral criticism of the American crop.* ❖

Virginians suddenly possessed a means to make money. Tobacco proved relatively easy to grow, and settlers who had avoided work now threw themselves into its production with single-minded diligence. In 1617, one observer found that Jamestown's "streets and all other spare places [are] planted with tobacco . . . the Colony dispersed all about planting tobacco." Although King James I originally considered smoking immoral and unhealthy, he changed his mind when the duties he collected on tobacco imports began to mount. He was neither the first nor the last ruler who decided a vice that generates revenue is not really so bad.

The company sponsored another ambitious effort to transform Virginia into a profitable enterprise. In 1618, Sir Edwin Sandys (pronounced Sands) led a faction of stockholders that began to pump life into the dying organization by instituting a series of sweeping reforms and eventually ousting Sir Thomas Smith and his friends. Sandys wanted private investors to develop their own estates in Virginia. Before 1618, there had been little incentive to do so, but by relaxing Dale's martial law and promising an elective representative assembly called the **House of Burgesses,** Sandys thought he could make the colony more attractive to wealthy speculators.

Even more important was Sandys's method for distributing land. Colonists who covered their own transportation cost to America were guaranteed a **headright,** a 50-acre lot for which they paid only a small annual rent. Adventurers were granted additional headrights for each servant they brought to the colony. This procedure allowed prosperous planters to build up huge estates while they also acquired dependent laborers. This land system persisted long after the company's collapse.

So too did the notion that the wealth of a few justified the exploitation of many others.

Sandys had only just begun. He also urged the settlers to diversify their economy. Tobacco alone, he argued, was not a sufficient base. He envisioned colonists busily producing iron and tar, silk and glass, sugar and cotton. There was no end to his suggestions. He scoured Europe for skilled artisans and exotic plant cuttings. To finance such a huge project, Sandys relied on a lottery, a game of chance that promised a continuous flow of capital into the company's treasury. The final element in the grand scheme was people. Sandys sent new English settlers by the thousand to Jamestown, ordinary men and women swept up by the same hopes that had carried the colonists of 1607 to the New World.

## Time of Reckoning

Between 1619 and 1622, colonists arrived in Virginia in record number. Company records reveal that during this short period, 3570 individuals were sent to the colony. People seldom moved to Virginia in families. Although the first women arrived in Jamestown in 1608, most emigrants were single males in their teens or early twenties who came to the New World as indentured servants. In exchange for transportation across the Atlantic, they agreed to serve a master for a stated number of years. The length of service depended in part on the age of the servant. The younger the servant, the longer he or she served. In return, the master promised to give the laborers proper care and, at the conclusion of their contracts, to provide them with tools and clothes according to "the custom of the country."

Powerful Virginians corrupted the system. Poor servants wanted to establish independent tobacco farms. As they discovered, however, headrights were awarded not to the newly freed servant, but to the great planter who had borne the cost of the servant's transportation to the New World and paid for food and clothing during the indenture. And even though **indentured servants** were promised land at the moment of freedom, they were most often cheated, becoming members of a growing, disaffected landless class in seventeenth-century Virginia.

Whenever possible, planters in Virginia purchased able-bodied workers, in other words, persons (preferably male) capable of performing hard agricultural labor. This preference dramatically skewed the colony's sex ratio. In the early decades, men outnumbered women by as much as six to one. As one historian, Edmund S. Morgan, observed, "Women were scarcer than corn or liquor in Virginia and fetched a higher price." Such gender imbalance meant that even if a male servant lived to the end of his indenture—an unlikely prospect—he could not realistically expect to start a family of his own. Moreover, despite apparent legal safeguards, masters could treat dependent workers as they pleased; after all, these people were legally considered property. Servants were sold, traded, even gambled away in games of chance. It does not require much imagination to see that a society that tolerated such an exploitative labor system might later embrace slavery.

Most Virginians then did not live long enough to worry about marriage. Death was omnipresent. Indeed, extraordinarily high mortality was a major reason the Chesapeake colonies developed so differently from those of New England. On the eve of the 1618 reforms, Virginia's population stood at approximately 700. The company sent at least 3000 more people, but by 1622 only 1240 were still alive. "It Consequentilie followes," declared one angry shareholder, "that we had then lost 3000 persons within those 3 yeares." The major killers were contagious diseases. Salt in the water supply also took a toll. And on Good Friday, March 22, 1622, the Powhatans slew 347 Europeans in a well-coordinated surprise attack.

No one knows for certain what effect such a horrendous mortality rate had on the men and women who survived. At the very least, it must have created a sense of impermanence, a desire to escape Virginia with a little money before sickness or violence ended the adventure. The settlers who drank to excess aboard the tavern ships anchored in the James River described the colony "not as a place of Habitacion but only of a short sojourninge."

## Corruption and Reform

On both sides of the Atlantic, people wondered who should be blamed. Why had so many colonists died in a land so rich in potential? The burden of responsibility lay in large measure with the Virginia Company. Sandys and his supporters were in too great a hurry to make a profit. Settlers were shipped to America, but neither housing nor food awaited them in Jamestown. Weakened by the long sea voyage, they quickly succumbed to contagious disease.

Company officials in Virginia also bore a share of guilt. They were so eager to line their own pockets that they consistently failed to provide for the common good. Various governors and their councilors grabbed up the indentured servants and sent them to their own private plantations to cultivate tobacco, and, as the 1622 surprise attack demonstrated, officials ignored the colony's crumbling defenses. Jamestown took on all the most unattractive characteristics of a boomtown. There was no shared sense of purpose, no common ideology, except perhaps unrestrained self-advancement, to keep the society from splintering into highly individualistic, competitive fragments.

The company's scandalous mismanagement embarrassed the king, and in 1624, he dissolved the bankrupt enterprise and transformed Virginia into a royal colony. The crown appointed a governor and a council. No provision was made, however, for continuing the local representative assembly, an institution the Stuarts heartily opposed. The House of Burgesses had first convened in 1619. While elections to the Burgesses were hardly democratic, the assembly did provide wealthy planters with a voice in government. Even without the king's authorization, the representatives gathered annually after 1629, and in 1639, Charles recognized the body's existence.

He had no choice. The colonists who served on the council or in the assembly were strong-willed, ambitious men. They had no intention of surrendering control over local affairs. Since Charles was having political troubles of his own and lived three thousand

A reconstruction of a free white planter's house from the late seventeenth-century Chesapeake. Even well-to-do colonists lived in structures that seemed by English standards quite primitive. ❖

miles from Jamestown, he usually allowed the Virginians to have their own way. In 1634, the assembly divided the colony into eight counties. In each one, a group of appointed justices of the peace—the wealthy planters of the area—convened as a court of law as well as a governing body. The "county court" was the most important institution of local government in Virginia, and long after the American Revolution, it served as a center for social, political, and commercial activities.

Changes in government had little impact on the character of daily life in Virginia. The planters continued to grow tobacco, ignoring advice to diversify, and as the Indians were killed, made into tributaries, or pushed north and south, Virginians took up large tracts of land along the colony's many navigable rivers. The focus of their lives was the isolated plantation, a small cluster of buildings housing the planter's family and dependent workers. These were modest wooden structures. Not until the eighteenth century did the Chesapeake gentry build the great Georgian mansions that still attract tourists. The dispersed pattern of settlement retarded the development of institutions such as schools and churches. Besides Jamestown there were no population centers, and as late as 1705, Robert Beverley, a leading planter, reported that Virginia did not have a single place "that may reasonably bear the Name of a Town."

## Maryland: A Troubled Refuge for Catholics

By the end of the seventeenth century, Maryland society looked remarkably like that of its Chesapeake neighbor, Virginia. At the time of first settlement in 1634, however, no one would have predicted that Maryland, a colony wholly owned by a Catholic nobleman, would have survived, much less become a flourishing tobacco colony.

The driving force behind the founding of Maryland was Sir George Calvert, later Lord Baltimore. Calvert, a talented and well-educated man, enjoyed the patronage of James I. He was awarded lucrative positions in the government, the most important being the king's secretary of state. In 1625, Calvert shocked almost everyone by publicly declaring his Catholicism; in this fiercely anti-Catholic society, persons who openly supported the Church of Rome were immediately stripped of civil office. Although forced to resign as secretary of state, Calvert retained the crown's favor.

Before resigning, Calvert sponsored a settlement on the coast of Newfoundland, but after visiting the place, the proprietor concluded that no English person, whatever his or her religion, would transfer to a place where the "ayre [is] so intolerably cold." He turned his attention to the Chesapeake, and on June 30, 1632, Charles I granted George Calvert's son,

Cecilius, a charter for a colony to be located north of Virginia. The boundaries of the settlement, named Maryland in honor of Charles's queen, were so vaguely defined that they generated legal controversies not fully resolved until the mid-eighteenth century when Charles Mason and Jeremiah Dixon surveyed their famous line between Pennsylvania and Maryland.

Cecilius, the second Lord Baltimore, wanted to create a sanctuary for England's persecuted Catholics. He also intended to make money. Without Protestant settlers, it seemed unlikely Maryland would prosper, and Cecilius instructed his brother Leonard, the colony's governor, to do nothing that might frighten off hypersensitive Protestants. The governor was ordered to "cause all Acts of the Roman Catholic Religion to be done as privately as may be and . . . [to] instruct all Roman Catholics to be silent upon all occasions of discourse concerning matters of Religion." On March 25, 1634, the *Ark and Dove,* carrying about 150 settlers, landed safely, and within days, the governor purchased from the Yaocomico Indians a village that became St. Mary's City, the capital of Maryland.

The colony's charter was an odd document, a throwback to an earlier feudal age. It transformed Baltimore into a "palatine lord," a proprietor with almost royal powers. Settlers swore an oath of allegiance not to the king of England but to Lord Baltimore. In England, such practices had long ago passed into obsolescence. As the proprietor, Lord Baltimore owned outright almost 6 million acres; he possessed absolute authority over anyone living in his domain.

On paper, at least, everyone in Maryland was assigned a place in an elaborate social hierarchy. Members of a colonial ruling class, persons who purchased 6000 acres from Baltimore, were called lords of the manor. These landed aristocrats were permitted to establish local courts of law. People holding less acreage enjoyed fewer privileges, particularly in government. Baltimore figured that land sales and rents would adequately finance the entire venture.

Baltimore's feudal system never took root in Chesapeake soil. People simply refused to play the social roles the lord proprietor had assigned. These tensions affected the operation of Maryland's government. Baltimore assumed that his brother, acting as his deputy in America, and a small appointed council of local aristocrats would pass necessary laws and carry out routine administration. When an elected assembly first convened in 1635, Baltimore allowed the delegates to discuss only those acts he had prepared. The members of the assembly bridled at such restrictions, insisting on exercising traditional parliamentary privileges. Neither side gained a clear victory in the assembly, and for almost twenty-five years, legislative squabbling contributed to the widespread political instability that almost destroyed Maryland.

*Cecilius Calvert, the second Lord Baltimore, insisted that Maryland tolerate all Christian religions, including Catholicism, something no other colony was willing to do. The young slave in the background reminds us who did the hard labor in the Chesapeake Colonies.* ❖

The colony drew both Protestants and Catholics, and the two groups might have lived in harmony had civil war not broken out in England. When Cromwell and the Puritan faction executed Charles, transforming England briefly into a republic, it seemed Baltimore might lose his colony. To head off such an event and to placate Maryland's restless Protestants, in 1649, the proprietor drafted the famous "Act concerning Religion," which extended toleration to all individuals who accepted the divinity of Christ. At a time when European rulers regularly persecuted people for their religious beliefs, Baltimore championed liberty of conscience.

However laudable the act may have been, it did not heal religious divisions in Maryland, and when local Puritans seized the colony's government, they promptly repealed the act. For almost two decades, vigilantes roamed the countryside, and during the "Plundering Time" (1644–1646), one armed group temporarily drove Leonard Calvert out of Maryland. In 1655, civil war flared again.

In this troubled sanctuary, ordinary planters and their workers cultivated tobacco on plantations dispersed along riverfronts. In 1678, Baltimore complained that he could not find fifty houses in a space of thirty miles. Tobacco affected almost every aspect of local culture. "In Virginia and Maryland," one Calvert explained, "Tobacco, as our Staple, is our all, and indeed leaves no room for anything Else." A steady stream of indentured servants supplied the plantations with dependent laborers—until they were replaced by African slaves at the end of the seventeenth century.

Europeans sacrificed much by coming to the Chesapeake. For most of the century, their standard of living was primitive when compared with that of people of the same social class who had remained in England. Two-thirds of the planters, for example, lived in houses of only two rooms and of a type associated with the poorest classes in contemporary English society.

## REFORMING ENGLAND IN AMERICA

The Pilgrims enjoy almost mythic status in American history. These brave refugees crossed the cold Atlantic in search of religious liberty, signed a democratic compact aboard the *Mayflower,* landed at Plymouth Rock, and gave us our Thanksgiving Day. As with most legends, this one contains only a core of truth.

The Pilgrims were not crusaders who set out to change the world. Rather, they were humble English farmers. Their story began in the early 1600s in Scrooby Manor, a small community located approximately 150 miles north of London. Many people living in this area believed the Church of England retained too many traces of its Catholic origin. To support such a corrupt institution was like winking at the devil. Its very rituals compromised God's true believers, and so, in the early years of the reign of James I, the Scrooby congregation formally left the established state church. Like others who followed this logic, they were called Separatists. Since English statute required citizens to attend Anglican services, the Scrooby Separatists moved to Holland in 1608–1609 rather than compromise.

The Netherlands provided the Separatists with a good home—too good. The members of the little church feared they were losing their distinct identity; their children were becoming Dutch. In 1617, therefore, a portion of the original Scrooby congregation vowed to sail to America. Included in this group was William Bradford, a wonderfully literate man who wrote *Of Plymouth Plantation,* one of the first and certainly most poignant accounts of an early American settlement.

Poverty presented the major obstacle to the Pilgrims' plans. They petitioned for a land patent from the Virginia Company of London. At the same time, they looked for someone willing to underwrite the staggering costs of colonization. The negotiations went well, or so it seemed. After stopping in England to take on supplies and laborers, the Pilgrims set off for America in 1620 aboard the *Mayflower,* armed with a patent to settle in Virginia and indebted to a group of English investors who were only marginally interested in religious reform.

Because of an error in navigation, the Pilgrims landed not in Virginia but in New England. The patent for which they had worked so diligently had no validity in the region. In fact, the crown had granted New England to another company. Without a patent, the colonists possessed no authorization to form a civil government, a serious matter since some sailors who were not Pilgrims threatened mutiny. To preserve the struggling community from anarchy, 41 men signed an agreement known as the **Mayflower Compact** to "covenant and combine our selves together into a civil body politick."

Although later praised for its democratic character, the Mayflower Compact could not ward off disease and hunger. During the first months in Plymouth, death claimed approximately half of the 102 people who had initially set out from England. Moreover, debts contracted in England severely burdened the new colony. To their credit, the Pilgrims honored their financial obligations, but it took almost twenty years to satisfy the English investors. Without Bradford, whom they elected as governor, the settlers might have allowed adversity to overwhelm them. Through strength of will and self-sacrifice, however, Bradford persuaded frightened men and women that they could survive in America.

Bradford had a lot of help. Almost anyone who has heard of the Plymouth Colony knows of Squanto, a Patuxt Indian who welcomed the first Pilgrims in excellent English. In 1614 unscrupulous adventurers kidnapped Squanto and sold him in Spain as a slave. Somehow this resourceful man escaped bondage, making his way to London, where a group of merchants who owned land in Newfoundland taught him to speak English. They apparently hoped that he would deliver moving public testimonials about the desirability of moving to the New World. In any case, Squanto returned to the Plymouth area just before the Pilgrims arrived. Squanto joined Massasoit, a local Native American leader, in teaching the Pilgrims much

about hunting and agriculture, a debt that Bradford freely acknowledged. Although evidence for the so-called "First Thanksgiving" is extremely sketchy, it is certain that without Native American support the Europeans would have starved.

In time, the Pilgrims replicated the humble little farm communities they had once known in England. They formed Separatist congregations to their liking; the population slowly increased. The settlers experimented with commercial fishing and the fur trade, but the efforts never generated substantial income. Most families relied on mixed husbandry, grain, and livestock. Because Plymouth offered only limited economic prospects, it attracted only a trickle of new settlers. In 1691, the colony was absorbed into its larger and more prosperous neighbor, Massachusetts Bay.

## "The Great Migration"

In the early decades of the seventeenth century, an extraordinary spirit of religious reform burst forth in England, and before it had burned itself out, Puritanism had transformed the face of England and America. Modern historians have difficulty comprehending this powerful spiritual movement. Some consider the **Puritans** rather neurotic individuals who condemned liquor and sex, dressed in drab clothes, and minded their neighbors' business.

The crude caricature is based on a profound misunderstanding of the actual nature of this broad popular movement. The seventeenth-century Puritans were more like today's radical political reformers, men and women committed to far-reaching institutional change, than like naive do-gooders or narrow fundamentalists. To their enemies, of course, the Puritans were irritants, always pointing out civil and ecclesiastical imperfections and urging everyone to try to fulfill the commands of Scripture. A great many people, however, shared their vision, and not only did they found several American colonies, but they also sparked the English Civil War, an event that generated bold new thinking about republican government and popular sovereignty.

The Puritans were products of the Protestant Reformation. They accepted a Calvinist notion that an omnipotent God predestined some people to salvation and damned others throughout eternity (see Chapter 1). But instead of waiting passively for Judgment Day, the Puritans examined themselves for signs of grace, for hints that God had in fact placed them among his "elect." A member of this select group, they argued, would try to live according to Scripture, to battle sin and eradicate corruption.

For the Puritans, the logic of everyday life was clear. If the Church of England contained unscriptural elements—clerical vestments, for example—then they must be eliminated. If the pope in Rome was in league with the Antichrist, then Protestant kings had better not form alliances with Catholic states. If God condemned licentiousness and intoxication, then local officials should punish whores and drunks. There was nothing improper about an occasional beer or passionate physical love within marriage, but when sex and drink became ends in themselves, the Puritans thought England's ministers and magistrates should speak out. Persons of this temperament were more combative than the Pilgrims had been. They wanted to purify the Church of England from within, and before the 1630s at least, separatism held little appeal for them.

From the Puritan perspective, the early Stuarts, James I and Charles I, seemed unconcerned about the spiritual state of the nation. James tolerated corruption within his own court; he condoned gross public extravagance. His foreign policy appeased European Catholic powers. At one time, he even tried to marry his son to a Catholic princess. Neither king showed interest in purifying the Anglican Church. In fact, Charles assisted the rapid advance of William Laud, a bishop who represented everything the Puritans detested. Laud defended church ceremonies that they found obnoxious. He persecuted Puritan ministers, forcing them either to conform to his theology or lose their licenses to preach. As long as Parliament met, Puritan voters in the various boroughs and countries throughout England elected men sympathetic to their point of view. These outspoken representatives criticized royal policies and hounded Laud. Because of their defiance, Charles decided in 1629 to rule England without Parliament and four years later named Laud archbishop of Canterbury. The last doors of reform slammed shut. The corruption remained.

John Winthrop, the future governor of Massachusetts Bay, was caught up in these events. Little about his background suggested such an auspicious future. He owned a small manor in Suffolk, one that never produced sufficient income to support his growing family. He dabbled in law. But the core of Winthrop's life was his faith in God, a faith so intense his contemporaries immediately identified him as a Puritan. The Lord, he concluded, was displeased with England. Time for reform was running out. In May 1629, he wrote to his wife, "I am verily perswaded God will bring some heavye Affliction upon this lande, and that speedylye." He was, however, confident that the Lord would "provide a shelter and a hidinge place for us."

Other Puritans, some wealthier and politically better connected than Winthrop, reached similar conclusions about England's future. They turned their attention to the possibility of establishing a colony in America, and on March 4, 1629, their Massachusetts Bay Company obtained a charter directly from the

*Voters in Massachusetts who were called "freemen" reelected John Winthrop governor many times, an indication of his success in translating Puritan values into practical policy. ❖*

king. Charles and his advisers apparently thought the Massachusetts Bay Company was a commercial venture no different from the dozens of other joint-stock companies that had recently sprung into existence.

Winthrop and his associates knew better. On August 26, 1629, twelve of them met secretly and signed the Cambridge Agreement. They pledged to be "ready in our persons and with such of our severall familyes as are to go with us . . . to embark for the said plantation by the first of March next." There was one loophole. The charters of most joint-stock companies designated a specific place where business meetings were to be held. For reasons not entirely clear—a timely bribe is a good guess—the charter of the Massachusetts Bay Company did not contain this standard clause. It could hold meetings anywhere the stockholders, called "freemen," desired, even America, and if they were in America, the king and his archbishop could not easily interfere in their affairs.

## "A City on a Hill"

The Winthrop fleet departed England in March 1630. By the end of the first year, almost 2,000 people had arrived in Massachusetts Bay, and before the "Great Migration" concluded in the early 1640s, more than

16,000 men and women had arrived in the new Puritan colony.

A great deal is known about the background of these particular settlers. A large percentage of them originated in an area northeast of London called East Anglia, a region in which Puritan ideas had taken deep root. London, Kent, and the West Country also contributed to the stream of emigrants. In some instances, entire villages were reestablished across the Atlantic. Many Bay Colonists had worked as farmers in England, but a surprisingly large number came from industrial centers, such as Norwich, where cloth was manufactured for the export trade.

Whatever their backgrounds, they moved to Massachusetts as nuclear families, fathers, mothers, and their dependent children, a form of migration strikingly different from the one that peopled Virginia and Maryland. Moreover, because the settlers had already formed families in England, the colony's sex ratio was more balanced than that found in the Chesapeake colonies. Finally, and perhaps more significantly, once they had arrived in Massachusetts, these men and women survived. Indeed, their life expectancy compares favorably to that of modern Americans. Many factors help explain this phenomenon—clean drinking water and a healthy climate, for example. While the Puritans could not have planned to live longer than did colonists in other parts of the New World, this remarkable accident reduced the emotional shock of long-distance migration.

The first settlers possessed another source of strength and stability. They were bound together by a common sense of purpose. God, they insisted, had formed a special covenant with the people of Massachusetts Bay. On his part, the Lord expected them to live according to Scripture, to reform the church, in other words, to create an Old Testament "city on a hill" that would stand as a beacon of righteousness for the rest of the Christian world. If they fulfilled their side of the bargain, the settlers could anticipate peace and prosperity. No one, not even the lowliest servant, was excused from this divine covenant, for as Winthrop stated, "Wee must be knitt together in this worke as one man." Even as the first ships were leaving England, John Cotton, a popular Puritan minister, urged the emigrants to go forth "with a publicke spirit, looking not on your owne things only, but also on the things of others." Many people throughout the ages have espoused such communal rhetoric, but these particular men and women went about the business of forming a new colony as if they truly intended to transform a religious vision into social reality.

In ecclesiastical affairs, the colonists proceeded by what one founder called "experimental footsteps."

They arrived in Massachusetts Bay without a precise plan for their church. Although the rituals and ceremonies enforced by Laud had no place in Massachusetts, the American Puritans refused to separate formally from the Church of England. In this matter, they thought the Pilgrims had made a serious mistake. After all, what was the point of reforming an institution if the reformers were no longer part of it?

The Bay Colonists gradually came to accept a highly innovative form of church government known as Congregationalism. Under the system, each village church was independent of outside interference. The American Puritans, of course, wanted nothing of bishops. The people (the "saints") were the church, and as a body, they pledged to uphold God's law. In the Salem Church, for example, the members

*One early Puritan meetinghouse was called the Old Ship Meetinghouse in Hingham, Massachusetts. Its name derives from its interior design, which resembles the hull of a ship. The oldest wooden church in the United States, it could accommodate about seven hundred people, nearly the entire population of seventeenth-century Hingham. Members of the congregation would have sat on backless wooden benches in the unheated building, listening to the preacher address them, not from an altar but from an undecorated square speaking box. ❖*

*Built in 1668, the house at 54 Turner Street in Salem, Massachusetts, is the oldest surviving seventeenth-century wooden mansion in New England. It was later made famous by Nathaniel Hawthorne as the "House of the Seven Gables," so called for its steeply pitched gable roofs.* ❖

church members were compelled to attend regular religious services. Perhaps because of the homogeneity of the colony's population, however, the loose polity of the Congregational churches held together for the entire colonial period.

Some aspects of community religiosity in early Massachusetts may, of course, strike modern Americans as morbid. Ministers expected people convicted of capital crimes to offer a full public confession of their sins just before their own execution. Such rituals reinforced everyday moral values by reminding ordinary men and women—those who listened to the confession—of the fatal consequences awaiting those who ignored the teachings of Scripture. (See the Feature Essay, "Capital Punishment in Early America," pp. 46–47.)

In creating a civil government, the Bay Colonists faced a particularly difficult challenge. Their charter allowed the investors in a joint-stock company to set up a business organization. When the settlers arrived in America, however, company leaders—men like Winthrop—moved quickly to transform the commercial structure into a colonial government. An early step in this direction took place on May 18, 1631, when the category of "freeman" was extended to all adult males who had become members of a Congregational church. This decision greatly expanded the franchise of Massachusetts Bay, and historians estimate that during the 1630s, at least 40 percent of the colony's adult males could vote in elections. While this percentage may seem low by modern or even Jacksonian standards, it was higher than anything the emigrants would have known in England. The freemen voted annually for a governor, a group of magistrates called the Court of Assistants, and after 1634, deputies who represented the interests of the individual towns. Even military officers were elected every year in Massachusetts Bay.

Two popular misconceptions about this government should be dispelled. It was neither a democracy nor a theocracy. The magistrates elected in Massachusetts did not believe they represented the voters, much less the whole populace. They ruled in the name of the electorate, but their responsibility as rulers was to God. In 1638, Winthrop warned against overly democratic forms, since "the best part [of the people] is always the least, and of that best part the wiser is always the lesser." And second, the Congregational ministers possessed no formal political authority in Massachusetts Bay. They could not

covenanted "with the Lord and with one another and do bind ourselves in the presence of God to walk together in all his ways."

Simply because a person happened to live in a certain community did not mean he or she automatically belonged to the local church. The churches of Massachusetts were voluntary institutions, and in order to join one a man or woman had to provide testimony—a confession of faith—before neighbors who had already been admitted as full members. It was a demanding process. Whatever the personal strains, however, most men and women in early Massachusetts aspired to full membership, which entitled them to the sacraments, and gave some of them responsibility for choosing ministers, disciplining backsliders, and determining difficult questions of theology. Although women and blacks could not vote for ministers, they did become members of the Congregational churches. Over the course of the seventeenth century, women made up an increasingly large share of the membership.

There were limits on Congregational autonomy, to be sure, and colonial magistrates sometimes ferreted out heretical beliefs. Those who did not become even hold civil office, and it was not unusual for the voters to ignore the recommendations of a respected minister such as John Cotton.

In New England, the town became the center of public life. In other regions of British America where the county was the focus of local government, people did not experience the same density of social and institutional interaction. In Massachusetts, groups of men and women voluntarily covenanted together to observe common goals. The community constructed a meetinghouse where religious services and town meetings were held. This powerful sense of shared purpose—something that later Americans have greatly admired—should not obscure the fact that the founders of New England towns also had a keen eye for personal profit. Seventeenth-century records reveal that speculators often made a good deal of money from selling "shares" in village lands. But acquisitiveness never got out of control, and recent studies have shown that entrepreneurial practices rarely disturbed the peace of the Puritan communities. Inhabitants generally received land sufficient to build a house to support a family. Although villagers escaped the kind of feudal dues collected in other parts of America, they were expected to contribute to the minister's salary, pay local and colony taxes, and serve in the militia.

## Limits of Religious Dissent

The European settlers of Massachusetts Bay managed to live in peace—at least with each other. This was a remarkable achievement considering the chronic instability that plagued other colonies at this time. The Bay Colonists disagreed over many issues, sometimes vociferously; whole towns disputed with neighboring villages over common boundaries. But the people inevitably relied on the civil courts to mediate differences. They believed in a rule of law, and in 1648 the colonial legislature, called the General Court, drew up the *Lawes and Liberties,* the first alphabetized code of law printed in English. This is a document of fundamental importance in American constitutional history. In clear prose, it explained to ordinary colonists their rights and responsibilities as citizens of the commonwealth. The code engendered public trust in government and discouraged magistrates from the arbitrary exercise of authority.

The Puritans never supported the concept of religious toleration. They transferred to the New World to preserve *their own* freedom of worship; about religious freedom of those deemed heretics, they expressed little concern. The most serious challenges to Puritan orthodoxy in Massachusetts Bay came from two brilliantly charismatic individuals. The first, Roger Williams, arrived in 1631 and immediately attracted a body of loyal followers. Indeed, everyone seemed to have liked Williams as a person.

Williams's *religious ideas,* however, created controversy. He preached extreme separatism. The Bay Colonists, he exclaimed, were impure in the sight of the Lord so long as they remained even nominal members of the Church of England. Moreover, he questioned the validity of the colony's charter, since the king had not first purchased the land from the Indians, a view that threatened the integrity of the entire colonial experiment. Williams also insisted that the civil rulers of Massachusetts had no business punishing settlers for their religious beliefs. It was God's responsibility, not men's, to monitor people's consciences. The Bay magistrates were prepared neither to tolerate heresy nor to accede to Williams's other demands, and in 1636, after attempts to reach a compromise had failed, they banished him from the colony. Williams worked out the logic of his ideas in Providence, a village he founded in what would become Rhode Island.

The magistrates of Massachusetts Bay rightly concluded that the second individual, Anne Hutchinson, posed an even graver threat to the peace of the commonwealth. This extremely intelligent woman, her husband William, and her children followed John Cotton to the New World in 1634. Even contemporaries found her religious ideas, usually termed **Antinomianism,** somewhat confusing.

Whatever her thoughts, Hutchinson shared them with other Bostonians, many of them women. Her outspoken views scandalized orthodox leaders of church and state. She suggested that all but two ministers in the colony had lost touch with the "Holy Spirit" and were preaching a doctrine in the Congregational churches that was little better than that of Archbishop Laud. When authorities demanded she explain her unusual opinions, she suggested that she experienced divine inspiration independently of either the Bible or the clergy. In other words, Hutchinson's teachings could not be tested by Scripture, a position that seemed dangerously subjective. Indeed, Hutchinson's theology called the very foundation of Massachusetts Bay into question. Without clear, external standards, one person's truth was as valid as anyone else's, and from Winthrop's perspective, Hutchinson's teachings invited civil and religious anarchy. But her challenge to authority was not simply theological. As a woman, her aggressive speech sparked a deeply misogynist response from the colony's male leaders.

When this woman described Congregational ministers—some of them the leading divines of Boston—as unconverted men, the General Court intervened. For two very tense days in 1637, the ministers and magistrates of Massachusetts Bay cross-examined

# CAPITAL PUNISHMENT IN EARLY AMERICA

## A Kind of Moral Theater?

Public executions, however ghoulish they might appear to modern Americans, were not unusual events in colonial society. Indeed, they represented what one historian has described as a kind of theater or ritual performance, often drawing thousands of spectators.

Esther Rodgers, aged 21, was hanged in Ipswich, Massachusetts, in July 1701. A local court had convicted her of murdering her own infant, a child fathered out of wedlock. The condemned woman played to perfection the role society had assigned. According to a minister who witnessed her last moments, "the manner of her Entertaining DEATH" astonished the crowd of four or five thousand people who crowded around the gallows.

Rodgers's "Composure of Spirit, Cheerfulness of Countenance, pleasantness of Speech, and a sort of Complaisantness in Carriage towards the Ministers . . . melted the hearts of all that were within seeing or hearing, into Tears of affection."

Various members of a community, including the condemned criminals, accepted socially sanctioned roles in these public spectacles. It was important that the order of events be correct. Usually the felon—a person allegedly hardened by a life of sin—maintained his or her innocence during the trial. Following conviction, however, such persons often confessed. A minister recorded the full story, and on the day of the execution, he delivered a formal sermon

attended by colonists who had sometimes traveled more than fifty miles just to see the hanging. Before they died, the criminals spoke directly to the spectators, and within a very short time, these last words along with the minister's execution sermon appeared in pamphlets.

Clergymen played a central role in these public dramas. They engaged in what today we might call criminal sociology. Why, they asked, had the condemned man or woman come to such a tragic end? What lessons could be drawn from a close study of their lives? Not surprisingly, the answer to these questions involved sin. Long before the condemned person had contemplated murder or some equally heinous act, he or she had engaged in seemingly petty vices—disobedience to parents, pride, lying, profanity, irreligion, drunkenness—a range of ungodly behavior that inevitably led the unwary sinner to more serious transgressions. Seen from this perspective, of course, average colonists became potential murderers or rapists, and only by resisting small temptations could they ever hope to avoid the fate of poor Esther Rodgers.

The ministers paid special attention to the young people in the audience, in other words, to those persons who seemed most likely to experiment with vice. Standing next to the condemned criminals, clergymen of New England thundered out their warnings. In 1674, for example, the famous Puritan divine Increase Mather observed that when "Children shall rebel against their Parents, their wickedness

Mr. Richard Mather.

This primitive woodcut depicts the Reverend Richard Mather, one of early New England's most influential Puritan ministers. ❖

*The Wages of Sin;*
OR,
Robbery juftly Rewarded:
A
P O E M;
Occafioned by the untimely Death of
**Richard Wilfon,**
Who was Executed on *Bofton* Neck, for Burglary,
On *Thurfday* the 19th of *October*, 1732.

**T**His Day from Goal muft *Wilfon* be conveyed in a Cart, By Guards unto the Gallows-Tree, to die as his Defert.

Here we may fee what Men for Stealth and Robbing muft endure; And what the Gain of ill got Wealth will in the End procure.

is excessively great. And such Children do usually die *before their Time.*" Lest the boys and girls missed his point, Mather added, "[It] is greatly to be observed that most of those that die upon the Gallows do confess that they have been guilty of disobedience to Parents."

In 1713, Cotton Mather, Increase's son, delivered an execution sermon specifically designed to strike terror in the hearts of the young. Look, he said, pointing to a felon about to die, "[Here] is a poor Young man before you, that is just *going to the Dead.* God this day is holding up a *Young man* in Chains, that all the *Young People* of New England, may . . . be withheld from Sinning."

The execution ritual reaffirmed the traditional moral order; rebellion against elders was rebellion against God. The ministers knew the adolescents before them would probably not end their days as murderers or rapists. But by making a spectacle of an extreme case, by transforming the execution into a public drama, they hoped to discourage lesser vices.

Without the cooperation of the condemned, the execution lost much of its social meaning. Most men and women—people about to be hanged and without hope of clemency—not only voluntarily confessed to a host of moral failings, but also admonished

the crowds to avoid a life of sin. Esther Rodgers ended her life with these words: "I beg of all to have Care. Be Obedient to your Parents and Masters; Run not at Nights, especially on Sabbath Nights, Refrain bad Company for the Lord's Sake. . . . " Her moving performance made for a "good" execution. James Morgan, a convicted murderer, also fulfilled everyone's expectations. "Have a care of that Sin of Drunkenness," he warned the citizens of Boston in 1686, "for that is a sin that leads to all manner of sins and wickedness." And just before he died, Morgan cried out, "I am going out of this World; O take warning by me, and beg God to keep you from this Sin which hath been my ruine."

Although the ministers may have encouraged the public displays of penance—they may have even suggested the actual wording—there is no reason to doubt the criminals' sincerity. They too shared the religious values of the seventeenth century, and however far from the accepted norms they may have strayed, they desired in some small way to win favor in the sight of the Lord. As the Reverend William Cooper observed in 1733, "It may be [that] there is no Place in the World, where such Pains are taken with condemned Criminals to prepare them for their Death; that in *the Destruction of the Flesh, the Spirit may*

*be saved in the Day of the Lord Jesus.*" Standing on the gallows, men and women rarely expressed even a hint of bitterness. In fact, they frequently praised their judges, noting that the magistrates had merely carried out God's will.

Soon after the execution, colonial printers issued pamphlets containing the execution sermon, the criminal's dying confession, and, in some cases, a lurid woodcut depicting an individual about to hang. These works sold quite well. The account of James Morgan's execution went through several editions. Others bore provocative titles such as *The Wicked Man's Portion* and *Death The Certain Wages of Sin.* The most ambitious production was Cotton Mather's *Pillars of Salt. An HISTORY OF SOME CRIMINALS Executed in this Land; for Capital Crimes. With some of their Dying Speeches; Collected and Published, For the WARNING of such as Live in Destructive Courses of Ungodliness* (1699). What effect the execution rituals had upon colonial Americans—spectators as well as readers—is impossible to judge. Some may have reformed their evil ways; for others, the theater of punishment may have involved no more than an "Entertaining DEATH."

Hutchinson; in this intense theological debate, she more than held her own. She knew as much about the Bible as did her inquisitors.

Hutchinson defied the ministers and magistrates to demonstrate exactly where she had gone wrong. Just when it appeared Hutchinson had outmaneuvered— indeed, thoroughly embarrassed—her opponents, she let down her guard, declaring forcefully that what she knew of God came "by an immediate revelation. . . . By the voice of his own spirit to my soul." Here was what her accusers had suspected all along but could not prove. She had confessed in open court that the Spirit can live without the Moral Law. This Antinomian statement fulfilled the worst fears of the Bay rulers, and they were relieved to exile Hutchinson and her followers to Rhode Island.

## Mobility and Division

Massachusetts Bay spawned four new colonies, three of which survived to the American Revolution. New Hampshire became a separate colony in 1677. Its population grew very slowly, and for much of the colonial

**NEW ENGLAND COLONIES, 1650** *The early settlers quickly carved up New England. New Haven briefly flourished as a separate colony before being taken over by Connecticut in 1662. Long Island later became part of New York; Plymouth was absorbed into Massachusetts, and in 1677 New Hampshire became a separate colony.* ❖

period, New Hampshire remained economically dependent on Massachusetts, its commercial neighbor to the south.

Far more people were drawn to the fertile lands of the Connecticut River Valley. In 1636, settlers founded the villages of Hartford, Windsor, and Wethersfield. No one forced these men and women to leave Massachusetts, and in their new surroundings, they created a society that looked much like the one they had known in the Bay Colony. Through his writings, Thomas Hooker, Connecticut's most prominent minister, helped all New Englanders define Congregational church polity. Puritans on both sides of the Atlantic read Hooker's beautifully crafted works. In 1639, representatives from the Connecticut towns passed the Fundamental Orders, a blueprint for civil government, and in 1662, Charles II awarded the colony a charter of its own.

In 1638, another group, led by Theophilus Eaton and the Reverend John Davenport, settled New Haven and several adjoining towns along Long Island Sound. These emigrants, many of whom had come from London, lived briefly in Massachusetts Bay but then insisted on forming a Puritan commonwealth of their own, one that established a closer relationship between church and state than the Bay Colonists had allowed. The New Haven colony never prospered, and in 1662, it was absorbed into Connecticut.

Rhode Island experienced a wholly different history. From the beginning, it drew people of a highly independent turn of mind, and according to one Dutch visitor, Rhode Island was "the receptacle of all sorts of riff-raff people. . . . All the cranks of New-England retire thither." This description, of course, was an exaggeration. Roger Williams founded Providence in 1636; two years later, Anne Hutchinson took her followers to Portsmouth. Other groups settled around Narragansett Bay. Not surprisingly, these men and women appreciated the need for toleration. No one was persecuted in Rhode Island for his or her religious beliefs.

One might have thought the separate Rhode Island communities would cooperate for the common good. They did not. Villagers fought over land and schemed with outside speculators to divide the tiny colony into even smaller pieces. In 1644, Parliament issued a patent for the "Providence Plantations," and in 1663, the Rhode Islanders obtained a royal charter. These successes did not calm political turmoil. For most of the seventeenth century, colonywide government existed in name only. Despite their constant bickering, however, the settlers of Rhode Island built up a profitable commerce in agricultural goods.

# DIVERSITY IN THE MIDDLE COLONIES

New York, New Jersey, Pennsylvania, and Delaware were settled for quite different reasons. William Penn, for example, envisioned a Quaker sanctuary; the Duke of York worried chiefly about his own income. Despite the founders' intentions, however, some common characteristics emerged. Each colony developed a strikingly heterogeneous population, men and women of different ethnic and religious backgrounds. This cultural diversity became a major influence on the economic, political, and ecclesiastical institutions of the Middle Colonies. The raucous, partisan public life of the Middle Colonies foreshadowed later American society.

## Anglo-Dutch Rivalry on the Hudson

By the early decades of the seventeenth century, the Dutch had established themselves as Europe's most aggressive traders. Holland—a small, loosely federated nation—possessed the world's largest merchant fleet. Its ships vied for the commerce of Asia, Africa, and

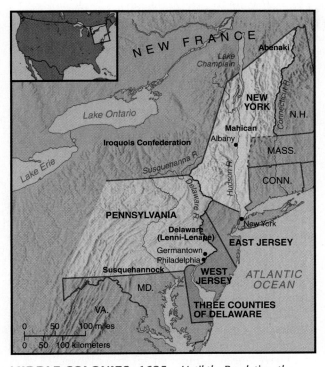

**MIDDLE COLONIES, 1685** *Until the Revolution, the Iroquois blocked European expansion into Western New York. The Jerseys and Pennsylvania initially attracted English and Irish Quakers, who were soon joined by thousands of Protestant Irish and Germans.* ❖

America. Dutch rivalry with Spain, a fading though still formidable power, was in large measure responsible for the settlement of New Netherland. While searching for the elusive Northwest Passage in 1609, Henry Hudson, an English explorer employed by a Dutch company, sailed up the river that now bears his name. Further voyages led to the establishment of trading posts in New Netherland, although permanent settlement did not occur until 1624. The area also seemed an excellent base from which to attack Spain's colonies in the New World.

The directors of the Dutch West India Company sponsored two small outposts, Fort Orange (Albany) located well up the Hudson River and New Amsterdam (New York City) on Manhattan Island. The first Dutch settlers were not actually colonists. Rather, they were salaried employees, and their superiors in Holland expected them to spend most of their time gathering animal furs. They did not receive land for their troubles. Needless to say, this arrangement attracted relatively few Dutch immigrants.

The colony's population may have been small, only 270 in 1628, but it contained an extraordinary ethnic mix. One visitor to New Amsterdam in 1644 maintained he had heard "eighteen different languages" spoken in the city. Even if this report was exaggerated, there is no doubt the Dutch colony drew English, Finns, Germans, and Swedes. By the 1640s, a sizable community of free blacks (probably former slaves who had gained their freedom through self-purchase) had developed in New Amsterdam, adding African tongues to the cacophony of languages. The colony's culture was further fragmented by New England Puritans who left Massachusetts and Connecticut to stake out farms on eastern Long Island.

New Netherland lacked capable leadership. The company sent a number of director-generals to oversee judicial and political affairs. Without exception, these men were temperamentally unsuited to govern an American colony. They adopted autocratic procedures, lined their own pockets, and, in one case, blundered into a war that needlessly killed scores of Indians and settlers. The company made no provision for an elected assembly. As much as they were able, the scattered inhabitants living along the Hudson River ignored company directives. They felt no loyalty to the trading company that had treated them so shabbily. Long Island Puritans complained bitterly about the absence of representative institutions. The Dutch system has aptly been described as "unstable pluralism."

In August 1664, the Dutch lost their tenuous hold on New Netherland. The English crown, eager to score an easy victory over a commercial rival, dispatched a

*Dutch colonization in the first half of the seventeenth century extended from New Amsterdam (New York City) up the Hudson River to Fort Orange (Albany). Another important settlement was at Wiltwyck (Kingston), where traces of colonization are still evident in the architecture. This stone building, known as the Hoffman House, displays several characteristics of early American-Dutch housing, including rubble construction, a front porch, and shuttered windows.* ❖

fleet of warships to New Amsterdam. The commander of this force, Colonel Richard Nicolls, ordered the colonists to surrender. The last director-general, a colorful character named Peter Stuyvesant (1647–1664), rushed wildly about the city urging the settlers to resist the English. But no one obeyed. Even the Dutch remained deaf to Stuyvesant's appeals. They accepted the Articles of Capitulation, a generous agreement that allowed Dutch nationals to remain in the province and to retain their property.

Charles II had already granted his brother, James, the Duke of York, a charter for the newly captured territory and much else besides. The duke became absolute proprietor over Maine, Martha's Vineyard, Nantucket, Long Island, and the rest of New York all the way to Delaware Bay. The king perhaps wanted to encircle New England's potentially disloyal Puritan population, but whatever his aims may have been, he created a bureaucratic nightmare.

During the English Civil War, the duke had acquired a thorough aversion to representative government. After all, Parliament had executed the duke's fa-

ther, Charles I, and raised up Oliver Cromwell. The new proprietor had no intention of letting such a participatory system take root in New York. "I cannot *but* suspect," the duke announced, that an assembly "would be of dangerous consequence." The Long Islanders felt betrayed. In part to appease these outspoken critics, Governor Nicolls—one of the few competent administrators to serve in the Middle Colonies—drew up in March 1665 a legal code known as the Duke's Laws. It guaranteed religious toleration and created local governments.

There was no provision, however, for an elected assembly or, for that matter, for democratic town meetings. The legal code disappointed the Puritan migrants on Long Island, and when the duke's officers attempted to collect taxes, these people protested that they were "inslav'd under an Arbitrary Power."

The Dutch kept silent. For several decades they remained a large unassimilated ethnic group. They continued to speak their own language, worship in their own churches (Dutch Reformed Calvinist), and eye their English neighbors with suspicion. In fact, the colony seemed little different from what it had been under the Dutch West India Company: a loose collection of independent communities ruled by an ineffectual central government.

## Confusion in New Jersey

Only three months after receiving a charter for New York, the Duke of York made a terrible mistake—something this stubborn, humorless man was prone to do. As a gift to two courtiers who had served Charles during the English Civil War, the duke awarded the land lying between the Hudson and Delaware rivers to John, Lord Berkeley, and Sir George Carteret. This colony was named New Jersey in honor of Carteret's birthplace, the Isle of Jersey in the English Channel. When Nicolls heard what the duke had done, he exploded. In his estimation, this fertile region contained the "most improveable" land in all New York, and to give it away so casually seemed the height of folly.

The duke's impulsive act bred confusion. Soon it was not clear who owned what in New Jersey. Before Nicolls had learned of James's decision, the governor had allowed migrants from New England to take up farms west of the Hudson River. He promised the settlers an opportunity to establish an elected assembly, a headright system, and liberty of conscience. In exchange for these privileges, Nicolls asked only that they pay a small annual quitrent to the duke. The new proprietors, Berkeley and Carteret, recruited colonists on similar terms. They assumed, of course, that they would receive the rent money.

The result was chaos. Some colonists insisted that Nicolls had authorized their assembly. Others, equally insistent, claimed that Berkeley and Carteret had done so. Both sides were wrong. Neither the proprietors nor Nicolls possessed any legal right whatsoever to set up a colonial government. James could transfer land to favorite courtiers, but no matter how many times the land changed hands, the government remained his personal responsibility. Knowledge of the law failed to quiet the controversy. Through it all, the duke showed not the slightest interest in the peace and welfare of the people of New Jersey.

Berkeley grew tired of the venture. It generated headaches rather than income, and in 1674, he sold his proprietary rights to a group of surprisingly quarrelsome Quakers. The sale necessitated the division of the colony into two separate governments known as East and West Jersey. Neither half prospered. Carteret and his heirs tried unsuccessfully to turn a profit in East Jersey. In 1677, the Quaker proprietors of West Jersey issued a remarkable democratic plan of government, the Laws, Concessions, and Agreements. But they fought among themselves with such intensity that not

even William Penn could bring tranquility to their affairs. Penn wisely turned his attention to the unclaimed territory across the Delaware River. The West Jersey proprietors went bankrupt, and in 1702, the crown reunited the two Jerseys into a single royal colony.

In 1700, the population of New Jersey stood at approximately fourteen thousand. Largely because it lacked a good deepwater harbor, the colony never developed a commercial center to rival New York City or Philadelphia. Its residents lived on scattered, often isolated farms; villages of more than a few hundred people were rare. Visitors commented on the diversity of the settlers. There were colonists from almost every European nation. Congregationalists, Presbyterians, Quakers, Baptists, Anabaptists, and Anglicans somehow managed to live together peacefully in New Jersey.

## QUAKERS IN AMERICA

The founding of Pennsylvania cannot be separated from the history of the Quaker movement. Believers in an extreme form of Antinomianism, the **Quakers** saw no need for a learned ministry, since one person's interpretation of Scripture was as valid as anyone else's. This radical religious sect, a product of the social upheaval in England during the Civil War, gained its name from the derogatory term that English authorities sometimes used to describe those who "tremble at the word of the Lord." The name persisted even though the Quakers preferred being called Professors of the Light or, more commonly, Friends.

### Quaker Beliefs and Practice

By the time the Stuarts regained the throne in 1660, the Quakers had developed strong support throughout England. One person responsible for their remarkable success was George Fox (1624–1691), a poor shoemaker whose own spiritual anxieties sparked a powerful new religious message that pushed beyond traditional reformed Protestantism. According to Fox, he experienced despair "so that I had nothing outwardly to help me . . . [but] then, I heard a voice which said, 'There is one, even Christ Jesus, that can speak to thy condition.'" Throughout his life, Fox and his growing number of followers gave testimony to the working of the Holy Spirit. Indeed, they informed ordinary men and women that if only they would look, they too would discover they possessed an "Inner Light." This was a wonderfully liberating invitation, especially for persons of lower-class origin. With the Lord's personal assistance, they could attain greater spiritual perfection on earth. Gone was the stigma of original sin; discarded was the notion of eternal predestination. Everyone could be saved.

Quakers practiced humility in their daily lives. They wore simple clothes and employed old-fashioned forms of address that set them apart from their neighbors. Friends refused to honor worldly position and accomplishment or to swear oaths in courts of law. They were also pacifists. According to Fox, all persons were equal in the sight of the Lord, a belief that generally annoyed people of rank and achievement.

Moreover, the Quakers never kept their thoughts to themselves. They preached conversion constantly, spreading the "Truth" throughout England, Ireland, and America. The Friends played important roles in the early history of New Jersey, Rhode Island, and North Carolina, as well as Pennsylvania. In some places, the "publishers of Truth" wore out their welcome. English authorities harassed the Quakers. Thousands, including Fox himself, were jailed, and in Massachusetts Bay between 1659 and 1661, Puritan magistrates ordered several Friends put to death. Such measures proved counterproductive, for persecution only inspired the martyred Quakers to redouble their efforts.

## Penn's "Holy Experiment"

William Penn lived according to the Inner Light, a commitment that led eventually to the founding of Pennsylvania. Penn possessed a curiously complex personality. He was an athletic person who threw himself into intellectual pursuits. He was a bold visionary capable of making pragmatic decisions. He came from an aristocratic family and yet spent his entire adult life involved with a religious movement associated with the lower class.

Penn's father had served with some distinction in the English navy. Through luck and skill, he acquired a considerable estate in Ireland, and as a wealthy landowner, he naturally hoped his son would be a favorite at the Stuart court. He befriended the king, the Duke of York, and several other powerful Restoration figures. But William disappointed his father. He was expelled from Oxford University for holding unorthodox religious views. Not even a grand tour through Europe could dissuade the young man from joining the Society of Friends. His political connections and driving intellect quickly propelled him to a position of prominence within the struggling sect. Penn wrote at least forty-two books testifying to his deep attachment to Quaker principles. Even two years in an English jail could not weaken his faith.

Precisely when Penn's thoughts turned to America is not known. He was briefly involved with the West Jersey proprietorship. This venture may have suggested the possibility of an even larger enterprise. In any case, Penn negotiated in 1681 one of the more impressive

*Penn's plan for Philadelphia shows the city laid out where the Scool Kill (Schuylkill) and Delaware rivers parallel each other. Four of the five public squares were intended to be parks while the fifth (at the center) was designated for public buildings. Today, it is the site of Philadelphia's city hall. ❖*

land deals in the history of American real estate. Charles II awarded Penn a charter making him the sole proprietor of a vast area called Pennsylvania (literally, "Penn's woods"). The name embarrassed the modest Penn, but he knew better than to look the royal gift horse in the mouth.

Why the king bestowed such generosity on a leading Quaker who had recently been released from prison remains a mystery. Perhaps Charles wanted to repay an old debt to Penn's father. The monarch may have regarded the colony as a means of ridding England of its troublesome Quaker population, or, quite simply, he may have liked Penn. In 1682, the new proprietor purchased from the Duke of York the so-called Three Lower Counties that eventually became Delaware. This astute move guaranteed that Pennsylvania would have access to the Atlantic and determined even before Philadelphia had been established that it would become a commercial center.

Penn lost no time in launching his "Holy Experiment." In 1682, he set forth his ideas in an unusual document known as the Frame of Government. The charter gave Penn the right to create any form of government he desired, and his imagination ran wild. His plan blended traditional notions about the privileges of a landed aristocracy with quite daring concepts of personal liberty. Penn guaranteed that settlers would enjoy among other things liberty of conscience, freedom from persecution, no taxation without representation, and due process of law.

In designing his government, Penn drew heavily on the writings of James Harrington (1611–1677). This English political philosopher argued that no government could ever be stable unless it reflected the actual distribution of landed property within society. Both the rich and poor had to have a voice in political affairs; neither should be able to overrule the legitimate interests of the other class. The Frame of Government envisioned a governor appointed by the proprietor, a 72-member Provincial Council responsible for initiating legislation, and a 200-person Assembly that could accept or reject the bills presented to it. Penn apparently thought the Council would be filled by the colony's richest landholders, or in the words of the Frame, "persons of most note for their wisdom, virtue and ability." The governor and Council were charged with the routine administration of justice. Smaller landowners spoke through the Assembly. It was a clumsy structure, and in America the entire edifice crumbled under its own weight.

## Settling Pennsylvania

Penn promoted his colony aggressively throughout England, Ireland, and Germany. He had no choice.

His only source of revenue was the sale of land and the collection of quitrents. Penn commissioned pamphlets in several languages extolling the quality of Pennsylvania's rich farmland. The response was overwhelming. People poured into Philadelphia and the surrounding area. In 1685 alone, eight thousand immigrants arrived. Most of the settlers were Irish, Welsh, and English Quakers, and they generally moved to America as families. But Penn opened the door to men and women of all nations. He asserted that the people of Pennsylvania "are a collection of divers nations in Europe, as French, Dutch, Germans, Swedes, Danes, Finns, Scotch, Irish, and English."

The settlers were by no means all Quakers. The founder of Germantown, Francis Daniel Pastorius, called the vessel that brought him to the New World a "Noah's Ark" of religions, and within his own household, there were servants who subscribed "to the Roman [Catholic], to the Lutheran, to the Calvinistic, to the Anabaptist, and to the Anglican church, and only one Quaker." Ethnic and religious diversity were crucial in the development of Pennsylvania's public institutions, and its politics took on a quarrelsome quality absent in more homogeneous colonies such as Virginia and Massachusetts.

Penn himself emigrated to America in 1682. His stay, however, was unexpectedly short and unhappy. The Council and Assembly—reduced now to more manageable size—fought over the right to initiate legislation. Wealthy Quaker merchants, most of them residents of Philadelphia, dominated the Council. By contrast, the Assembly included men from rural settlements and the Three Lower Counties who showed no concern for the Holy Experiment.

Penn did not see his colony again until 1699. During his absence, much had changed. The settlement had prospered. Its agricultural products, especially its excellent wheat, were in demand throughout the Atlantic world. Despite this economic success, however, the population remained deeply divided. Even the Quakers had briefly split into hostile factions. Penn's handpicked governors had failed to win general support for the proprietor's policies, and one of them exclaimed in anger that each Quaker "prays for his neighbor on First Days and then preys on him the other six." As the seventeenth century closed, few colonists still shared the founder's desire to create a godly, paternalistic society.

In 1701, legal challenges in England again forced Penn to depart for the mother country. Just before he sailed, Penn signed the Charter of Liberties, a new frame of government that established a unicameral or one-house legislature (the only one in colonial America) and gave the representatives the right to initiate bills. Penn also allowed the Assembly to conduct its business without proprietary interference. The charter provided for the political separation of the Three Lower Counties (Delaware) from Pennsylvania, something people living in the area had demanded for years. This hastily drafted document served as Pennsylvania's constitution until the American Revolution.

His experience in America must have depressed Penn, now both old and sick. In England, Penn was imprisoned for debts incurred by dishonest colonial agents, and in 1718, Pennsylvania's founder died a broken man.

## PLANTING THE CAROLINAS

In some ways, Carolina society looked much like the one that had developed in Virginia and Maryland. In both areas, white planters forced African slaves to produce staple crops for a world market. But such superficial similarities masked substantial regional differences. In fact, "the South"—certainly the fabled solid South of the early nineteenth century—did not exist during the colonial period. The Carolinas, joined much later by Georgia, stood apart from their northern neighbors. As a historian of colonial Carolina explained, "the southern colonies were never a cohesive section in the same way that New England was. The great diversity of population groups . . . discouraged southern sectionalism."

### Proprietors of the Carolinas

Carolina was a product of the Restoration of the Stuarts to the English throne. Court favorites who had followed the Stuarts into exile during the Civil War demanded tangible rewards for their loyalty. New York and New Jersey were obvious plums. So too was Carolina. Sir John Colleton, a successful English planter returned from Barbados, organized a group of eight powerful courtiers who styled themselves the True and Absolute Lords Proprietors of Carolina. On March 24, 1663, the king granted these proprietors a charter to the vast territory between Virginia and Florida and running west as far as the "South Seas."

The failure of similar ventures in the New World taught the Carolina proprietors valuable lessons. Unlike the first Virginians, for example, this group did not expect instant wealth. Rather, the proprietors reasoned that they would obtain a steady source of income from rents. What they needed, of course, were settlers to pay those rents. Recruitment turned out to be no easy task. Economic and social conditions in the mother country improved considerably after its civil war, and English people were no longer so willing to transfer to the New World. Even if they had shown interest, the cost of transporting settlers across the Atlantic seemed prohibitively expensive. The proprietors concluded, therefore, that with the proper incentives—a generous land policy, for example—they could attract men and women from established American colonies and thereby save themselves a great deal of money. Unfortunately for the men who owned Carolina, such people were not easily persuaded. They had begun to take for granted certain rights and privileges, and as the price of settlement, they demanded a representative assembly, liberty of conscience, and a liberal headright system.

The Carolina proprietors divided their grant into three distinct jurisdictions, anticipating no doubt that

Bridgetown, Barbados, was a thriving Caribbean trading port in the seventeenth century, as depicted in this engraving from 1695. But overcrowding, tropical disease, and a series of natural disasters drove many merchants to emigrate. A popular destination for Barbadians was colonial Carolina, particularly the Port Royal area in present-day South Carolina. ❖

these areas would become the centers of settlement. The first region, called Albemarle, abutted Virginia. As the earlier ill-fated Roanoke colonists had discovered, the region lacked a good deepwater port. Nevertheless, it attracted a number of dissatisfied Virginians who drifted south in search of fresh land. Farther south, the mouth of the Cape Fear River seemed a second likely site for development. And third, within the present state of South Carolina, the Port Royal region contained a maze of fertile islands and meandering tidal streams.

Colleton and his associates waited for the money to roll in, but to their dismay, no one seemed particularly interested in moving to the Carolina frontier. A tiny settlement at Port Royal failed. One group of New Englanders briefly considered taking up land in the Cape Fear area, but these people were so disappointed by what they saw that they departed, leaving behind only a sign that "tended not only to the disparagement of the Land . . . but also to the great discouragement of all those that should hereafter come into these parts to settle." By this time, a majority of surviving proprietors had given up on Carolina.

## The Barbadian Connection

Anthony Ashley Cooper, later Earl of Shaftesbury, was the exception. In 1669, he persuaded the remaining Carolinian proprietors to invest their own capital in the colony. Without such financial support, Ashley recognized, the project would surely fail. Once he received sufficient funds, this energetic organizer dispatched three hundred English colonists to Port Royal under the command of Joseph West. The fleet put in briefly at Barbados to pick up additional recruits, and in March 1670, after being punished by Atlantic gales that destroyed one ship, the expedition arrived at its destination. Only one hundred people were still alive. The unhappy settlers did not remain long at Port Royal, an unappealing, low-lying place badly exposed to Spanish attack. They moved northward, locating eventually along the more secure Ashley River. Later the colony's administrative center, Charles Town (it did not become Charleston until 1783) was established at the junction of the Ashley and Cooper rivers.

Ashley also wanted to bring order to the new society. With assistance from John Locke, the famous English philosopher (1632–1704), Ashley devised the Fundamental Constitutions of Carolina. Like Penn, Ashley had been influenced by the writings of Harrington. The constitutions created a local aristocracy consisting of proprietors and lesser nobles called *landgraves* and *cassiques,* terms as inappropriate to the realities of the New World as was the idea of creating a hereditary landed elite. Persons who purchased vast tracts of land automatically received a title and the

right to sit in the Council of Nobles, a body designed to administer justice, oversee civil affairs, and initiate legislation. A parliament in which smaller landowners had a voice could accept or reject bills drafted by the council. The very poor were excluded from political life altogether. Ashley thought his scheme maintained the proper "Balance of Government" between aristocracy and democracy, a concept central to Harrington's philosophy. Not surprisingly, the constitutions had little impact on the actual structure of government.

Before 1680, almost half the men and women who settled in the Port Royal area came from Barbados. This small Caribbean island, which produced an annual fortune in sugar, depended on slave labor. By the third quarter of the seventeenth century, Barbados had become overpopulated. Wealthy families could not provide their sons and daughters with sufficient land to maintain social status, and as the crisis intensified, Barbadians looked to Carolina for relief.

These migrants, many of whom were quite rich, traveled to Carolina both as individuals and family groups. Some even brought gangs of slaves with them to the American mainland. The Barbadians carved out plantations on the tributaries of the Cooper River and established themselves immediately as the colony's most powerful political faction. "So it was," wrote historian Richard Dunn, "that these Caribbean pioneers helped to create on the North American coast a slave-based plantation society closer in temper to the islands they fled from than to any other mainland English settlement."

Much of the planters' time was taken up with the search for a profitable crop. The early settlers experimented with a number of plants: tobacco, cotton, silk, and grapes. The most successful items turned out to be beef, skins, and naval stores (especially tar used to maintain ocean vessels). By the 1680s, some Carolinians had built up great herds of cattle—seven or eight hundred head in some cases. Traders who dealt with Indians brought back thousands of deerskins from the interior, and they often returned with Indian slaves as well. These commercial resources together with tar and turpentine enjoyed a good market. It was not until the 1690s that the planters came to appreciate fully the value of rice, but once they had done so, it quickly became the colony's main staple.

Proprietary Carolina was in a constant political uproar. Factions vied for special privilege. The Barbadian settlers, known locally as the Goose Creek Men, resisted the proprietors' policies at every turn. A large community of French Huguenots located in Craven County distrusted the Barbadians. The proprietors—an ineffectual group following the death of Shaftesbury—appointed a series of utterly incompetent governors who only made things worse. One visitor observed that "the Inhabitants of Carolina should be as free from Oppression as any [people] in the Universe . . . if their own Differences amongst themselves do not occasion the contrary." By the end of the century, the Commons House of Assembly had assumed the right to initiate legislation. In 1719, the colonists overthrew the last proprietary governor, and in 1729, the king created separate royal governments for North and South Carolina.

## THE FOUNDING OF GEORGIA

The early history of Georgia was strikingly different from that of Britain's other mainland colonies. Its settlement was really an act of aggression against Spain, a country that had as good a claim to this area as did the English. During the eighteenth century, the two nations were often at war (see Chapter 4), and South Carolinians worried that the Spaniards moving up from bases in Florida would occupy the disputed territory between Florida and the Carolina grant.

The colony owed its existence primarily to James Oglethorpe, a British general and member of Parliament who believed that he could thwart Spanish designs on the area south of Charles Town while at the same time providing a fresh start for London's worthy poor, saving them from debtors' prison. Although Oglethorpe envisioned Georgia as an

### ENGLAND'S PRINCIPAL MAINLAND COLONIES

| Name | Original Purpose | Date of Founding | Principal Founder | Major Export | Estimated Population ca. 1700 |
|---|---|---|---|---|---|
| Virginia | Commercial venture | 1607 | Captain John Smith | Tobacco | 64,560 |
| New Amsterdam (New York) | Commercial venture | 1613 (made English colony, 1664) | Peter Stuyvesant, Duke of York | Furs, grain | 19,107 |
| Plymouth | Refuge for English Separatists | 1620 (absorbed by Massachusetts, 1691) | William Bradford | Grain | Included with Massachusetts |
| New Hampshire | Commercial venture | 1623 | John Mason | Wood, naval stores | 4,958 |
| Massachusetts | Refuge for English Puritans | 1628 | John Winthrop | Grain, wood | 55,941 |
| Maryland | Refuge for English Catholics | 1634 | Lord Baltimore (George Calvert) | Tobacco | 34,100 |
| Connecticut | Expansion of Massachusetts | 1635 | Thomas Hooker | Grain | 25,970 |
| Rhode Island | Refuge for dissenters from Massachusetts | 1636 | Roger Williams | Grain | 5,894 |
| New Sweden (Delaware) | Commercial venture | 1638 (included in Penn grant, 1681; given separate assembly, 1703) | Peter Minuit, William Penn | Grain | 2,470 |
| North Carolina | Commercial venture | 1663 | Anthony Ashley Cooper | Wood, naval stores, tobacco | 10,720 |
| South Carolina | Commercial venture | 1663 | Anthony Ashley Cooper | Naval stores, rice, indigo | 5,720 |
| New Jersey | Consolidation of new English territory, Quaker settlement | 1664 | Sir George Carteret | Grain | 14,010 |
| Pennsylvania | Refuge for English Quakers | 1681 | William Penn | Grain | 18,950 |
| Georgia | Discourage Spanish expansion; charity | 1733 | James Oglethorpe | Rice, wood, naval stores | 5,200 (in 1750) |

**Sources:** U.S. Bureau of the Census, *Historical Statistics of the United States: Colonial Times to 1970*, Washington, D.C., 1975; John J. McCusker and Russell R. Menard, *The Economy of British America, 1607–1789*, Chapel Hill, 1985.

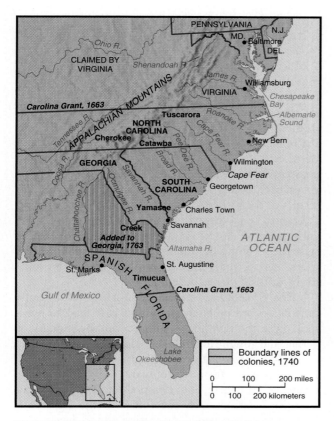

**THE CAROLINAS AND GEORGIA**  *Caribbean sugar planters migrated to the Goose Creek area where, with knowledge supplied by African slaves, they eventually mastered rice cultivation. Poor harbors in North Carolina retarded the spread of European settlement in that region.* ❖

asylum as well as a garrison, the military aspects of his proposal were especially appealing to the leaders of the British government. In 1732, the king granted Oglethorpe and a board of trustees a charter for a new colony to be located between the Savannah and Altamaha rivers and from "sea to sea." The trustees living in the mother country were given complete control over Georgia politics, a condition the settlers soon found intolerable.

During the first years of colonization, Georgia fared no better than had earlier utopian experiments. The poor people of England showed little desire to move to an inclement frontier, and the trustees, in their turn, provided little incentive for emigration. Each colonist received only 50 acres. Another 50 acres could be added for each servant transported to Georgia, but in no case could a settler amass more than 500 acres. Moreover, land could be passed only to an eldest son, and if a planter had no sons at the time of his death, the holding reverted to the trustees. Slavery was prohibited. So too was rum.

Almost as soon as they arrived in Georgia, the settlers complained. The colonists demanded slaves,

pointing out to the trustees that unless the new planters possessed an unfree labor force, they could not compete economically with their South Carolina neighbors. The settlers also wanted a voice in local government. In 1738, 121 people living in Savannah petitioned for fundamental reforms in the colony's constitution. Oglethorpe responded angrily, "The idle ones are indeed for Negroes. If the petition is countenanced, the province is ruined." The settlers did not

## CHRONOLOGY

| | |
|---|---|
| **1607** | First English settlers arrive at Jamestown |
| **1608–1609** | Scrooby congregation (Pilgrims) leaves England for Holland |
| **1609–1611** | "Starving time" in Virginia threatens survival of the colonists |
| **1616–1618** | Plague destroys Native American populations of coastal New England |
| **1619** | Virginia assembly, called House of Burgesses, meets for the first time  ❖  First slaves sold at Jamestown |
| **1620** | Pilgrims sign the Mayflower Compact |
| **1622** | Surprise Indian attack devastates Virginia |
| **1624** | Dutch investors create permanent settlements along Hudson River  ❖  James I, king of England, dissolves Virginia Company |
| **1625** | Charles I ascends English throne |
| **1630** | John Winthrop transfers Massachusetts Bay charter to New England |
| **1634** | Colony of Maryland is founded |
| **1636** | Harvard College is established  ❖  Puritan settlers found Hartford and other Connecticut Valley towns |
| **1638** | Anne Hutchinson exiled to Rhode Island  ❖  Theophilus Eaton and John Davenport lead settlers to New Haven Colony |
| **1639** | Connecticut towns accept Fundamental Orders |
| **1644** | Second major Indian attack in Virginia |
| **1649** | Charles I executed during English Civil War |
| **1660** | Stuarts restored to the English throne |
| **1663** | Rhode Island obtains royal charter  ❖  Proprietors receive charter for Carolina |
| **1664** | English soldiers conquer New Netherland |
| **1677** | New Hampshire becomes a royal colony |
| **1681** | William Penn granted patent for his "Holy Experiment" |
| **1702** | East and West Jersey unite to form single colony |
| **1732** | James Oglethorpe receives charter for Georgia |

give up. In 1741, they again petitioned Oglethorpe, this time addressing him as "our Perpetual Dictator."

While the colonists grumbled about various restrictions, Oglethorpe tried and failed to capture the Spanish fortress at Saint Augustine (1740). This personal disappointment coupled with the growing popular unrest destroyed his interest in Georgia. The trustees were forced to compromise their principles. In 1738, they eliminated all restrictions on the amount of land a man could own; they allowed women to inherit land. In 1750, they permitted the settlers to import slaves. Soon Georgians could drink rum. In 1751, the trustees returned Georgia to the king, undoubtedly relieved to be free of what had become a hard-drinking, slave-owning plantation society much like that in South Carolina. The king authorized an assembly in 1751, but even with these social and political changes, Georgia attracted very few new settlers.

## CONCLUSION: LIVING WITH DIVERSITY

Long after he had returned from his adventures in Virginia, Captain John Smith reflected on the difficulty of establishing colonies in the New World. It was a task for which most people were not temperamentally suited. "It requires," Smith counseled, "all the best parts of art, judgment, courage, honesty, constancy, diligence, and industry, [even] to do neere well." On another occasion, Charles I warned Lord Baltimore that new settlements "commonly have rugged and laborious beginnings."

Over the course of the seventeenth century, women and men had followed leaders such as Baltimore, Smith, Winthrop, Bradford, Penn, and Berkeley to the New World in anticipation of creating a successful new society. Some people were religious visionaries; others were hardheaded businessmen. The results of their efforts, their struggles to survive in an often hostile environment, and their interactions with various Native American groups yielded a spectrum of settlements along the Atlantic coast, ranging from the quasi-feudalism of South Carolina to the Puritan commonwealth of Massachusetts Bay.

The diversity of early English colonization must be emphasized precisely because it is so easy to overlook. Even though the colonists eventually banded together and fought for independence, persistent differences separated New Englanders from Virginians, Pennsylvanians from Carolinians. The interpretive challenge, of course, is to comprehend how European colonists managed over the course of the eighteenth century to overcome fragmentation and to develop the capacity to imagine themselves a nation.

## RECOMMENDED READING

The literature of seventeenth-century English settlement in North America is immense. To comprehend better the diversity of American colonial experience, it is wise to start with the society from which the settlers migrated. Two good introductions to England's participation in an Atlantic World are David Armitage and Michael J. Braddick, eds., *The British Atlantic World, 1500–1800* (2002) and Nicholas Canny, ed., *The Oxford History of the British Empire, vol. 1, The Origins of Empire: English Overseas Enterprise from the Beginning to the Close of the Seventeenth Century* (1998). The best single work on Puritanism remains Perry Miller, *The New England Mind: From Colony to Province* (1956). David D. Hall explores popular religious practice in New England in *Worlds of Wonder, Days of Judgment: Popular Religious Belief in Early New England* (1989). Also valuable is Michael P. Winship, *Making Heretics: Militant Protestantism and Free Grace in Massachusetts, 1636–1641* (2002). On the challenge of creating new social and political institutions in early Massachusetts, see Kenneth A. Lockridge, *A New England Town: The First Hundred Years* (1970). Two brilliantly original studies of the founding of Virginia are Edmund S. Morgan, *American Slavery, American Freedom: The Ordeal of Colonial Virginia* (1975) and Kathleen M. Brown, *Good*

*Wives, Nasty Wenches, and Anxious Patriarchs: Gender, Race, and Power in Colonial Virginia* (1996). T. H. Breen compares the development of seventeenth-century New England and the Chesapeake in *Puritans and Adventurers: Change and Persistence in Early America* (1980). The forces that drove migration to the New World during this period are the subject of David Cressy's *Coming Over: Migration and Communication Between England and New England in the Seventeenth Century* (1987) and James Horn's, *Adapting to a New World: English Society in the Seventeenth-Century Chesapeake* (1994). On the rituals of public execution, see Daniel A. Cohen, *Pillars of Salt, Monuments of Grace: New England Crime Literature and the Origins of American Popular Culture, 1674–1860* (1993). Useful investigations of the founding of New York and Pennsylvania are Gary B. Nash, *Quakers and Politics: Pennsylvania 1681–1726* (1968); Richard S. Dunn and Mary Maples Dunn, eds., *The World of William Penn* (1986); and Joyce D. Goodfriend, *Before the Melting Pot: Society and Culture in Colonial New York City, 1664–1730* (1995).

**For a list of additional titles related to this chapter's topics, please see** http://www.ablongman.com/divine.

# SUGGESTED WEB SITES

### The Plymouth Colony Archive Project at the University of Virginia

http://etext.virginia.edu/users/deetz
This site contains comprehensive and fairly extensive information about late seventeenth-century Plymouth Colony.

### Jamestown Rediscovery

http://www.apva.org
This site mounted by the Association for the Preservation of Virginia Antiquity has excellent material on archaeological excavations at Jamestown.

### Georgia Before Oglethorpe

http://www.spanishflorida.net/gboindex.htm
This resources guide informs about Native American Georgia in the seventeenth century.

### William Penn, Visionary Proprietor

http://xroads.virginia.edu/~CAP/PENN/pnhome.html
William Penn had an interesting life, and this site is a good introduction to the man and some of his achievements.

### LVA Colonial Records Project—Index of digital facsimiles of documents on early Virginia.

http://eagle.vsla.edu/colonial/
This site contains numerous early documents, but it is unguided and a little difficult to use.

The Mason Children: David, Joanna, and Abigail, *c.1670, an early portrait of three children from a wealthy Massachusetts Bay Colony family. The artist lavished attention on the details of the children's clothing and the objects they hold, marks of their social status and prosperity.* ❖

# Putting Down Roots: Opportunity and Oppression in Colonial Society

## *Families in an Atlantic Empire*

The Witherspoon family moved from Great Britain to the South Carolina backcountry early in the eighteenth century. Although otherwise indistinguishable from the thousands of other ordinary families that put down roots in English America, the Witherspoons were made historical figures by the candid account of pioneer life produced by their son, Robert, who was only a small child at the time of their arrival.

The Witherspoons' initial reaction to the New World—at least, that of the mother and children—was utter despondence. "My mother and us children were still in expectation that we were coming to an agreeable place," Robert confessed, "but when we arrived and saw nothing but a wilderness and instead of a fine timbered house, nothing but a very mean dirt house, our spirits quite sunk." For many years, the Witherspoons feared they would be killed by Indians, become lost in the woods, or be bitten by snakes.

The Witherspoons managed to survive the early difficult years on the Black River. To be sure, the Carolina backcountry did not look very much like the world they had left behind. The discrepancy, however, apparently did not greatly discourage Robert's father. He had a vision of what the Black River settlement might become. "My father," Robert recounted, "gave us all the comfort he [could] by telling us we would get all these trees cut down and in a short time [there] would be plenty of inhabitants, [and] that we could see from house to house."

ROBERT WITHERSPOON'S ACCOUNT REMINDS US just how much the early history of colonial America was an intimate story of families, and not, as some commentators would have us believe, of individuals. Neither the peopling of the Atlantic frontier, the cutting down of the forests, nor the creation of new communities where one could see from "house to house" was a process that involved what we would today recognize as state policy. Men and women made significant decisions about the character of their lives within families. It was within this primary social unit that most colonists earned their livelihoods, educated their children, defined gender, sustained religious tradition, and nursed each other in sickness. In short, the family was the source of their societal and cultural identities.

Early colonial families did not exist in isolation. They were part of larger societies. As we have already discovered, the character of the first English settlements in the New World varied substantially (see Chapter 2). During much of the seventeenth century, these initial differences grew stronger as each region responded to different environmental conditions and developed its own traditions. The various local societies in which families like the Witherspoons put down roots reflected several critical elements: supply of labor, abundance of land, unusual demographic patterns, and commercial ties with European markets. In the Chesapeake, for example, an economy based almost entirely on a single staple—tobacco—created an insatiable demand for indentured servants and black slaves. In Massachusetts Bay, the extraordinary longevity of the founders generated a level of social and political stability that Virginians and Marylanders did not attain until the very end of the seventeenth century.

By 1660, it seemed regional differences had undermined the idea of a unified English empire in America. During the reign of Charles II, however, a trend toward cultural convergence began. Although subcultures had evolved in strikingly different directions, countervailing forces such as common language and religion gradually pulled English American settlers together. Parliament took advantage of this trend and began to establish a uniform set of rules for the expanding American empire. The process was slow and uneven, often sparking violent colonial resistance. By the end of the seventeenth century, however, England had made significant progress toward transforming New World provinces into an empire that produced needed raw materials and purchased manufactured goods. If a person was black and enslaved, however, he or she was more apt to experience oppression rather than opportunity in British America.

## SOURCES OF STABILITY: NEW ENGLAND COLONIES OF THE SEVENTEENTH CENTURY

Seventeenth-century New Englanders successfully replicated in America a traditional social order they had known in England. The transfer of a familiar way of life to the New World seemed less difficult for these Puritan migrants than it did for the many English men and women who settled in the Chesapeake colonies. Their contrasting experiences, fundamental to an understanding of the development of both cultures, can be explained, at least in part, by the extraordinary strength and resilience of New England families.

### Immigrant Families and New Social Order

Early New Englanders believed God ordained the family for human benefit. It was essential to the maintenance of social order, since outside the family, men and women succumbed to carnal temptation. Such people had no one to sustain them or remind them of Scripture. "Without Family care," declared the Reverend Benjamin Wadsworth, "the labour of Magistrates and Ministers for Reformation and Propagating Religion, is likely to be in great measure unsuccessful."

The godly family, at least in theory, was ruled by a patriarch, father to his children, husband to his wife, the source of authority and object of unquestioned obedience. The wife shared responsibility for the raising of children, but in decisions of importance, especially those related to property, she was expected to defer to her spouse.

The New Englanders' concern about the character of the godly family is not surprising. This institution played a central role in shaping their society. In contrast to those who migrated to the colonies of Virginia and Maryland, New Englanders crossed the Atlantic within nuclear families. That is, they moved within established units consisting of a father, mother, and their dependent children rather than as single youths and adults. People who migrated to America within families preserved local English customs more fully than did the youths who traveled to other parts of the continent as single men and women. The comforting presence of immediate family members reduced the shock of adjusting to a strange environment three thousand miles from home. Even in the 1630s, the ratio of men to women in New England was fairly well balanced, about three males for every two females. Persons who had not already married in England before coming to the New World could expect to form nuclear families of their own.

The great migration of the 1630s and early 1640s brought approximately 20,000 persons to New England. After 1642, the English Civil War reduced the flood of people moving to Massachusetts Bay to a trickle. Nevertheless, by the end of the century, the population of New England had reached almost 120,000, an amazing increase considering the small number of original immigrants. Historians have been hard pressed to explain this striking rate of growth. Some have suggested that New Englanders married very young, thus giving couples extra years in which to produce large families. Other scholars have maintained that New England women must have been more fertile than their Old World counterparts.

Neither demographic theory adequately explains how so few migrants produced such a large population so rapidly. Early New England marriage patterns, for example, did not differ substantially from those recorded in seventeenth-century England. The average age for men at first marriage was the mid-twenties.

Wives were slightly younger than their husbands, the average age being about 22. There is no evidence that New Englanders favored child brides. Nor, for that matter, were Puritan families unusually large by European standards of the period.

The explanation for the region's impressive growth turned out to be survival rather than fertility. Put simply, people who, under normal conditions, would have died in contemporary Europe lived in New England. Indeed, the life expectancy of seventeenth-century settlers was not very different from our own. Males who survived infancy might have expected to see their seventieth birthday. Twenty percent of the men of the first generation reached the age of eighty. The figures for women were only slightly lower. Why the early settlers lived so long is not entirely clear. No doubt, pure drinking water, a cool climate that retarded the spread of fatal contagious disease, and a dispersed population promoted general good health.

Longer life altered family relations. New England males lived not only to see their own children reach adulthood but also to witness the birth of grandchildren. One historian, John Murrin, has suggested that New Englanders "invented" grandparents. In other words, this society produced real patriarchs, males of recognized seniority and standing. This may have been one of the first societies in recorded history in which a person could reasonably anticipate knowing his or her grandchildren, a demographic surprise that con-

tributed to social stability. The traditions of particular families and communities literally remained alive in the memories of the colony's oldest citizens.

## Commonwealth of Families

The life cycle of the seventeenth-century New England family began with marriage. Young men and women generally initiated courtships. If parents exercised a voice in such matters, it was to discourage union with a person of unsound moral character. Puritan ministers advised single people to choose godly partners, warning:

> The Wretch that is alone to Mannon Wed,
> May chance to find a Satan in the bed.

In this highly religious society, there was not much chance that young people would stray far from shared community values. The overwhelming majority of the region's population married, for in New England, the single life was not only morally suspect but also physically difficult.

A couple without land could not support an independent and growing family in these agrarian communities. While men generally brought farmland to the marriage, prospective brides were expected to provide a dowry worth approximately one-half what the bridegroom offered. Women often contributed money or household goods.

*African Americans often appeared in the formal portraits of elite white families. This eighteenth-century overmantle (oil on wood) depicts the Potter family of Rhode Island with a black child. In the northern colonies, most slaves worked as house and body servants.* ❖

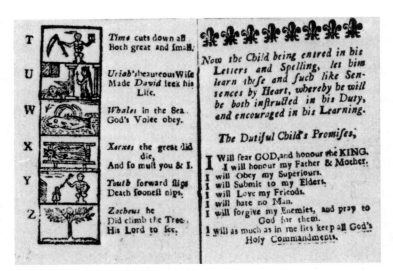

*New England parents took seriously their responsibility for the spiritual welfare of their children. To seek the word of God, young people had to learn to read. The New-England Primer, shown here, was their primary vehicle.* ❖

The household was primarily a place of work—very demanding work. The primary goal, of course, was to clear enough land to feed the family. Additional cultivation allowed the farmer to produce a surplus that could then be sold or bartered, and since agrarian families required items that could not be manufactured at home—metal tools, for example—they usually grew more than they consumed. Early American farmers were not economically self-sufficient; the belief that they were is a popular misconception.

During the seventeenth century, men and women generally lived in the communities of their parents and grandparents. New Englanders usually managed to fall in love with a neighbor, and most marriages took place between men and women living less than 13 miles apart. Moving to a more fertile region might have increased their earnings, but such thoughts seldom occurred to early New Englanders. Religious values, a sense of common purpose, and the importance of family reinforced traditional communal ties.

Towns, in fact, were collections of families, not individuals. Over time, these families intermarried, so the community became an elaborate kinship network. Social historians have discovered that in many New England towns, the original founders dominated local politics and economic affairs for several generations. Not surprisingly, newcomers who were not absorbed into the family system tended to move away from the village with greater frequency than did the sons and daughters of the established lineage groups.

Congregational churches were also built on a family foundation. During the earliest years of settlement, the churches accepted persons who could demonstrate they were among God's "elect." Members were drawn from a broad social spectrum. Once the excitement of establishing a new society had passed, however, New Englanders began to focus more attention on the spiritual welfare of their own families. This quite normal parental concern precipitated a major ecclesiastical crisis. The problem was the status of the children within a gathered church. Sons and daughters of full church members regularly received baptism, usually as infants, but as these people grew to adulthood, they often failed to provide testimony of their own "election." Moreover, they wanted their own children to be baptized. A church synod—a gathering of Congregational ministers—responded to this generational crisis by adopting the so-called Half-Way Covenant (1662). The compromise allowed the grandchildren of persons in full communion to be baptized even though their parents could not demonstrate conversion. Congregational ministers assumed that "God cast the line of election in the loins of godly parents." Because of the New Englanders' growing obsession with family—termed *tribalism* by some historians—the Congregational churches by the end of the seventeenth century were increasingly turning inward, addressing the spiritual needs of particular lineage groups rather than reaching out to the larger Christian community.

Colonists regarded education as primarily a family responsibility. Parents were supposed to instruct children in the principles of Christianity, and so it was necessary to teach boys and girls how to read. In 1642, the Massachusetts General Court reminded the Bay Colonists of their obligation to catechize their families. Five years later, the legislature ordered towns containing at least fifteen families to open an elementary school supported by local taxes. Villages of a hundred or more families had to maintain more advanced grammar schools, which taught a basic knowledge of Latin. At least eleven schools were operating in 1647, and despite their expense, new schools were established throughout the century.

This family-based education system worked. A large majority of the region's adult males could read and write, an accomplishment not achieved in the Chesapeake colonies for another century. The literacy rate for women was somewhat lower, but by the standards of the period, it was still impressive. A printing press operated in Cambridge as early as 1639. *The New-England Primer,* first published in 1690 in Boston by Benjamin Harris, taught children the alphabet as well as the Lord's Prayer. This primer announced:

> He who ne'er learns his ABC,
> forever will a blockhead be.
> But he who to his book's inclined,
> will soon a golden treasure find.

The best-seller of seventeenth-century New England was Rev. Michael Wigglesworth's *The Day of Doom* (1662), a poem of 224 stanzas describing in terrifying detail the fate of sinners on Judgment Day. In words that even young readers could comprehend, Wigglesworth wrote of these unfortunate souls:

> They cry, no, no: Alas! and wo!
> Our Courage all is gone:
> Our hardiness (fool hardiness)
> Hath us undone, undone.

Many New Englanders memorized the entire poem.

After 1638, young men could attend Harvard College, the first institution of higher learning founded in England's mainland colonies. The school was originally intended to train ministers, and of the 465 students who graduated during the seventeenth century, more than half became Congregational divines. Harvard had a demanding curriculum. The boys read logic, rhetoric, divinity, and several ancient languages, including Hebrew. Yale College followed Harvard's lead, admitting its first students in 1702.

## Women's Lives in Puritan New England

The role of women in the agrarian societies north of the Chesapeake is a controversial subject among colonial historians. Some scholars point out that common law as well as English custom treated women as inferior to men. Other historians, however, depict the colonial period as a "golden age" for women. According to this interpretation, wives worked alongside their husbands. They were not divorced from meaningful, productive labor. They certainly were not transformed into the frail, dependent beings allegedly much admired by middle-class males of the nineteenth century. Both views provide insights into the lives of early American women, but neither fully recaptures their community experiences.

To be sure, women worked on family farms. They did not, however, necessarily do the same jobs that men performed. Women usually handled separate tasks, including cooking, washing, clothes making, dairying, and gardening. Their production of food was absolutely essential to the survival of most households. Sometimes wives—and the overwhelming majority of adult seventeenth-century women were married—raised poultry, and by selling surplus birds they achieved some economic independence. When people in one New England community chided a man for allowing his wife to peddle her fowl, he responded, "I meddle not with the geese nor turkeys for they are hers." In fact, during this period women were often described as "deputy husbands," a label that drew attention to their dependence on family patriarchs as well as to their roles as decision makers.

Women also joined churches in greater number than men. Within a few years of founding, many New England congregations contained two female members for every male, a process historians describe as the "feminization of colonial religion." Contemporaries offered different explanations for the gender shift. Cotton Mather, the leading Congregational minister of Massachusetts Bay, argued that God had created "far more *godly Women*" than men. Others thought that the life-threatening experience of childbirth gave women a deeper appreciation of religion. The Quakers gave women an even larger role in religious affairs, which may help to explain the popularity of this sect among ordinary women.

In political and legal matters, society sharply curtailed the rights of colonial women. According to English common law, a wife exercised no control over property. She could not, for example, sell land, although if her husband decided to dispose of their holdings, he was free to do so without her permission. Divorce was extremely difficult to obtain in any colony before the American Revolution. Indeed, a person married to a cruel or irresponsible spouse had little recourse but to run away or accept the unhappy situation.

Yet most women were neither prosperous entrepreneurs nor abject slaves. Surviving letters indicate that men and women generally accommodated themselves to the gender roles they thought God had ordained. One of early America's most creative poets, Anne Bradstreet, wrote movingly of the fulfillment she had found with her husband. In a piece titled "To my Dear and loving Husband," Bradstreet declared:

> If ever two were one, then surely we.
>   If ever man were lov'd by wife, then thee;
> If ever wife was happy in a man,
>   Compare with me ye women if you can.

Although Puritan couples worried that the affection they felt for a husband or a wife might turn their thoughts away from God's perfect love, this was a danger they were willing to risk.

## Social Hierarchy in New England

During the seventeenth century, the New England colonies attracted neither noblemen nor paupers. The absence of these social groups meant that the American social structure seemed incomplete by contemporary European standards. The settlers were not displeased that the poor remained in the Old World. The lack of very rich persons—and in this period great wealth frequently accompanied noble title—was quite another matter. According to the prevailing hierarchical view of the structure of society, well-placed individuals were natural rulers, people intended by God to exercise political authority over the rank and file. Migration forced the colonists, however, to choose their rulers from men of more modest status. One minister told a Plymouth congregation that since its members were "not furnished with any persons of *special eminency above the rest,* to be chosen by you into office of government," they would have to make due with neighbors, "not beholding in them the *ordinariness of their persons.*"

The colonists gradually sorted themselves out into distinct social groupings. Persons who would never have been "natural rulers" in England became provincial gentry in the various northern colonies. It helped, of course, if an individual possessed wealth and education, but these attributes alone could not guarantee a newcomer would be accepted into the local ruling elite, at least not during the early decades of settlement. In Massachusetts and Connecticut, Puritan voters expected their leaders to join Congregational churches and defend orthodox religion.

The Winthrops, Dudleys, and Pynchons—just to cite a few of the more prominent families—fulfilled these expectations, and in public affairs they assumed

## ❖ A Look at the Past ❖

### Freake Portraits

Bright colors, lace, embroidery, and other lavish details on the clothing John and Elizabeth Freake wore for their portraits, painted by an anonymous artist in the 1670s, refute the notion that Puritans wore only somber clothes. The Freakes's attire also reveals attitudes about children and gender roles. Elizabeth is holding her son, dressed in a gown as both male and female babies were at the time. Note how similar their gowns are; her son's is nearly a miniature version of Elizabeth's. If babies wore miniaturized adult clothing, what does that suggest about the lives of children? Was childhood a distinctive developmental stage to be relished? Why are we surprised by the splendor of the Freake's dress?

dominant roles. They took their responsibilities quite seriously and certainly did not look kindly on anyone who spoke of their "ordinariness." A colonist who jokingly called a Puritan magistrate a "just ass" found himself in deep trouble with civil authorities.

The problem was that while most New Englanders accepted a hierarchical view of society, they disagreed over their assigned places. Both Massachusetts Bay and Connecticut passed sumptuary laws—statutes that limited the wearing of fine apparel to the wealthy and prominent—to curb the pretensions of those of lower status. Yet such restraints could not prevent some people from rising and others from falling within the social order.

Governor John Winthrop provided a marvelous description of the unplanned social mobility that occurred in early New England. During the 1640s, he recorded in his diary the story of a master who could not afford to pay a servant's wages. To meet this obligation, the master sold a pair of oxen, but the transaction barely covered the cost of keeping the servant. In desperation, the master asked the employee, a man of lower social status, "How shall I do . . . when all my cattle are gone?" The servant replied, "You shall then serve me, so you may have your cattle again." In the margin of his diary next to this account, Winthrop scribbled "insolent."

Most northern colonists were yeomen (independent farmers) who worked their own land. While few became rich in America, even fewer fell hopelessly into debt. Their daily lives, especially for those who settled New England, centered on scattered little communities where they participated in village meetings, church-related matters, and militia training. Possession of land gave agrarian families a sense of independence from external authority. As one man bragged to those who had stayed behind in England, "Here are no hard landlords to rack us with high rents or extorting fines. . . . Here every man may be master of his own labour and land . . . and if he have nothing but his hands he may set up his trade, and by industry grow rich."

## ✦ A Look at the Past ✦

### Gravestones

Seventeenth-century Puritan carvers transformed the production of gravestones into a distinctive folk art form. Each symbolic element in the design has a spiritual significance. Examine closely the two early New England headstones shown here, noting the details of the carvings as well as the dates. What elements do they have in common? What differences do you see? What do the ornate sculpture and the images on these gravestones suggest about Puritans' attitudes toward death? Do the differences in the two stones suggest any shift in attitudes toward death?

During the seventeenth century, this independence was balanced by an equally strong feeling of local identity. Not until the late eighteenth century, when many New Englanders left their familial villages in search of new land, did many northern yeomen place personal material ambition above traditional community bonds.

It was not unusual for northern colonists to work as servants at some point in their lives. This system of labor differed greatly from the pattern of servitude that developed in seventeenth-century Virginia and Maryland. New Englanders seldom recruited servants from the Old World. The forms of agriculture practiced in this region, mixed cereal and dairy farming, made employment of large gangs of dependent workers uneconomic. Rather, New England families placed their adolescent children in nearby homes. These young persons contracted for four or five years and seemed more like apprentices than servants. Servitude was not simply a means by which one group exploited another. It was a form of vocational training program in which the children of the rich as well as the poor participated.

By the end of the seventeenth century, the New England Puritans had developed a compelling story about their own history in the New World. The founders had been extraordinarily godly men and women, and in a heroic effort to establish a purer form of religion, pious families had passed "over the vast ocean into this vast and howling wilderness." Although the children and grandchildren of the first generation sometimes questioned their own ability to please the Lord, they recognized the mission to the New World had been a success: they were "as Prosperous as ever, there is Peace & Plenty, & the Country flourisheth."

# THE CHALLENGE OF THE CHESAPEAKE ENVIRONMENT

An entirely different regional society developed in England's Chesapeake colonies, Virginia and Maryland. This contrast with New England seems puzzling. After all, the two areas were founded at roughly the same time by men and women from the same mother country. In both regions, settlers spoke English, accepted Protestantism, and gave allegiance to one crown. And yet, to cite an obvious example, seventeenth-century Virginia looked nothing like Massachusetts Bay. In an effort to explain the difference, colonial historians have studied environmental conditions, labor systems, and agrarian economies. The most important reason for the distinctiveness of these early southern plantation societies, however, turned out to be the Chesapeake's death rate, a frighteningly high mortality that tore at the very fabric of traditional family life.

## Family Life at Risk

Unlike New England's settlers, the men and women who emigrated to the Chesapeake region did not move in family units. They traveled to the New World as young unmarried servants, youths cut off from the security of traditional kin relations. Although these immigrants came from a cross section of English society, most had been poor to middling farmers. It is now estimated that 70 to 85 percent of the white colonists who went to Virginia and Maryland during the seventeenth century were not free; that is, they owed four or five years' labor in exchange for the cost of passage to America. If the servant was under age 15, he or she had to serve a full seven years. The overwhelming majority of these laborers were males between the ages of 18 and 22. In fact, before 1640, the ratio of males to females stood at 6 to 1. This figure dropped to about 2½ to 1 by the end of the century, but the sex ratio in the Chesapeake was never as favorable as it had been in early Massachusetts.

Most immigrants to the Chesapeake region died soon after arriving. It is difficult to ascertain the exact cause of death in most cases, but malaria and other diseases took a frightful toll. Recent studies also indicate that drinking water contaminated with salt killed many colonists living in low-lying areas. Throughout the entire seventeenth century, high mortality rates had a profound effect on this society. Life expectancy for Chesapeake males was about 43, some ten to twenty years less than for men born in New England! For women, life was even shorter. A full 25 percent of all children died in infancy; another 25 percent did not see their twentieth birthdays. The survivors were often weak or ill, unable to perform hard physical labor.

These demographic conditions retarded normal population increase. Young women who might have become wives and mothers could not do so until they had completed their terms of servitude. They thus lost several reproductive years, and in a society in which so many children died in infancy, late marriage greatly restricted family size. Moreover, because of the unbalanced sex ratio, many adult males simply could not find wives. Migration not only cut them off from their English families but also deprived them of an opportunity to form new ones. Without a constant flow of immigrants, the population of Virginia and Maryland would have actually declined.

High mortality compressed the family life cycle into a few short years. One partner in a marriage usually died within seven years. Only one in three Chesapeake marriages survived as long as a decade.

Not only did children not meet grandparents—they often did not even know their own parents. Widows and widowers quickly remarried, bringing children by former unions into their new homes, and it was not uncommon for a child to grow up with persons to whom he or she bore no blood relation. The psychological effects of such experiences on Chesapeake settlers cannot be measured. People probably learned to cope with a high degree of personal insecurity. However they adjusted, it is clear family life in this region was vastly more impermanent than it was in the New England colonies during the same period.

Women were obviously in great demand in the early southern colonies. Some historians have argued that scarcity heightened the woman's bargaining power in the marriage market. If she was an immigrant, she did not have to worry about obtaining parental consent. She was on her own in the New World and free to select whomever she pleased. If a woman lacked beauty or strength, if she were a person of low moral standards, she could still be confident of finding an American husband. Such negotiations may have provided Chesapeake women with a means of improving their social status.

Nevertheless, liberation from some traditional restraints on seventeenth-century women must not be exaggerated. As servants, women were vulnerable to sexual exploitation by their masters. Moreover, in this unhealthy environment, childbearing was extremely dangerous, and women in the Chesapeake usually died twenty years earlier than their New England counterparts.

## The Structure of Planter Society

Colonists who managed somehow to survive grew tobacco—as much tobacco as they possibly could. This crop became the Chesapeake staple, and since it was relatively easy to cultivate, anyone with a few acres of cleared land could harvest leaves for export. Cultivation of tobacco did not, however, produce a society roughly equal in wealth and status. To the contrary, tobacco generated inequality. Some planters amassed large fortunes; others barely subsisted. Labor made the difference, for to succeed in this staple economy, one had to control the labor of other men and women. More workers in the fields meant larger harvests, and, of course, larger profits. Since free persons showed no interest in growing another man's tobacco, not even for wages, wealthy planters relied on white laborers who were not free, as well as on slaves. The social structure that developed in the seventeenth-century Chesapeake reflected a wild, often unscrupulous scramble to bring men and women of three races—black, white, and Indian—into various degrees of dependence.

Great planters dominated Chesapeake society. The group was small, only a trifling portion of the population of Virginia and Maryland. During the early decades of the seventeenth century, the composition of Chesapeake gentry was continually in flux. Some gentlemen died before they could establish a secure claim to high social status; others returned to England, thankful to have survived. Not until the 1650s did the family names of those who would become famous eighteenth-century gentry appear in the records. The first gentlemen were not—as genealogists sometimes discover to their dismay—dashing cavaliers who had fought in the English Civil War for King Charles I. Rather, such Chesapeake gentry as the Burwells, Byrds, Carters, and Masons consisted originally of the younger sons of English merchants and artisans.

These ambitious men arrived in America with capital. They invested immediately in laborers, and one way or another, they obtained huge tracts of the best tobacco-growing land. The members of this gentry were not technically aristocrats, for they did not possess titles that could be passed from generation to generation. They gave themselves military titles, sat as justices of the peace on the county courts, and directed local (Anglican) church affairs as members of the vestry. Over time, these gentry families intermarried so frequently that they created a vast network of cousins. During the eighteenth century, it was not uncommon to find a half dozen men with the same surname sitting simultaneously in the Virginia House of Burgesses.

Freemen formed the largest class in Chesapeake society. Their origins were strikingly different from those of the gentry, or for that matter, from those of New England's yeomen farmers. Chesapeake freemen traveled to the New World as **indentured servants** and, by sheer good fortune, managed to remain alive to the end of their contracts. If they had dreamed of becoming great planters, they were gravely disappointed. Most seventeenth-century freemen lived on the edge of poverty. Some freemen, of course, did better in America than they would have in contemporary England, but in both Virginia and Maryland, historians have found a sharp economic division separating the gentry from the rest of white society.

Below the freemen came indentured servants. Membership in this group was not demeaning; after all, servitude was a temporary status. But servitude in the Chesapeake colonies was not the benign institution it was in New England. Great planters purchased servants to grow tobacco. No one seemed overly concerned whether these laborers received decent food and clothes, much less whether they acquired trade skills. Young people, thousands of them, cut off from family ties, sick often to the point of death, unable to obtain normal sexual release, regarded their servitude

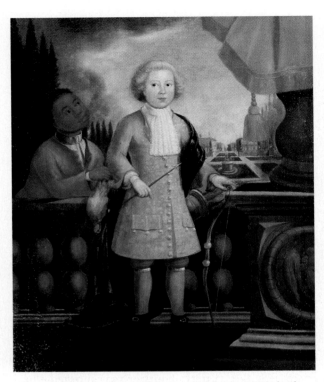

*This painting,* Henry Darnall III as a Child *(ca. 1710), by the German émigré painter Justus Engelhardt Kuhn depicts the son of a wealthy planter family in Maryland armed with a bow and arrow. To the left, an African American slave holds a dead bird. This is the earliest known depiction of an African American in a colonial American painting. The formal architecture and gardens in the background suggest an idealized European landscape and a connection to European culture that some members of the colonial gentry imagined for themselves.* ❖

as a form of slavery. Not surprisingly, the gentry worried that unhappy servants and impoverished freemen, what the planters called the "giddy multitude," would rebel at the slightest provocation, a fear that turned out to be fully justified.

The character of social mobility—and this observation applies only to whites—changed considerably during the seventeenth century. Until the 1680s, it was relatively easy for a newcomer who possessed capital to become a member of the planter elite. No one paid much attention to the reputation or social standing of one's English family.

Sometime after the 1680s, however—the precise date is impossible to establish—a dramatic demographic shift occurred. Although infant mortality remained high, life expectancy rates for those who survived childhood in the Chesapeake improved significantly, and for the first time in the history of Virginia and Maryland, important leadership positions went to men who had actually been born in America. This transition has been described by one political historian as the "emergence of a creole ma-

jority," in other words, as the rise of an indigenous ruling elite. Before this time, immigrant leaders had died without heirs or had returned as quickly as possible to England. The members of the new creole class took a greater interest in local government. Their activities helped give the tobacco colonies the kind of political and cultural stability that had eluded earlier generations of planter adventurers. Not surprisingly, it was during this period of demographic transition that creole leaders founded the College of William and Mary (1693) and authorized the construction of an impressive new capital called Williamsburg. These were changes that, in the words of one creole Virginian, provided the colony "with a sense of permanence and legitimacy . . . it had never before possessed."

The key to success in this creole society was ownership of slaves. Those planters who held more blacks could grow more tobacco and thus could acquire fresh capital needed to purchase additional laborers. Over time, the rich not only became richer; they also formed a distinct ruling elite that newcomers found increasingly difficult to enter.

Opportunities for advancement also decreased for freemen in the region. Studies of mid-seventeenth-century Maryland reveal that some servants managed to become moderately prosperous farmers and small officeholders. But as the gentry consolidated its hold on political and economic institutions, ordinary people discovered it was much harder to rise in Chesapeake society. Those men and women with more ambitious dreams headed for Pennsylvania, North Carolina, or western Virginia.

Social institutions that figured importantly in the daily experience of New Englanders were either weak or nonexistent in the Chesapeake colonies. In part, the sluggish development resulted from the continuation of high infant mortality rates. There was little incentive to build elementary schools, for example, if half the children would die before reaching adulthood. The great planters sent their sons to England or Scotland for their education, and even after the founding of the College of William and Mary in Virginia, the gentry continued to patronize English schools. As a result of this practice, higher education in the South languished for much of the colonial period.

Tobacco influenced the spread of other institutions in the region. Planters were scattered along the rivers, often separated from their nearest neighbors by miles of poor roads. Since the major tobacco growers traded directly with English merchants, they had no need for towns. Whatever items they required were either made on the plantation or imported from Europe. Other than the centers of colonial government, Jamestown (and later Williamsburg) and St. Mary's City (and later Annapolis), there were no vil-

*Undated, unsigned, and hidden on the back of another painting, the two-part painting* Virginian Luxuries *depicts a white man kissing a black woman and a white man whipping a black man. Indeed, the brutal system of slavery afforded slave owners such "luxuries" as rape and torture.* ❖

lages capable of sustaining a rich community life before the late eighteenth century. Seventeenth-century Virginia did not even possess a printing press. In fact, Governor Sir William Berkeley bragged in 1671, "There are no free schools, nor printing in Virginia, for learning has brought disobedience, and heresy . . . into the world, and printing had divulged them . . . God keep us from both!"

## RACE AND FREEDOM IN BRITISH AMERICA

Many people who landed in the colonies had no desire to come to the New World. They were Africans taken as slaves to cultivate rice, sugar, and tobacco. As the Native Americans were exterminated and the supply of white indentured servants dried up, European planters demanded ever more African laborers.

### Roots of Slavery

A great deal is known about the transfer of African peoples across the Atlantic. During the entire history of this human commerce, between the sixteenth and nineteenth centuries, slave traders carried almost eleven million blacks to the Americas. Most of these men and women were sold in Brazil or in the Caribbean. A relatively small number of Africans reached British North America, and of this group, the majority arrived after 1700. Because slaves performed hard physical labor, planters preferred purchasing young males. In many early slave communities, men outnumbered women by a ratio of two to one.

English colonists did not hesitate to enslave black people or, for that matter, Native Americans. While the institution of slavery had long before died out in the mother country, New World settlers quickly discovered how well this particular labor system operated in the Spanish and Portuguese colonies. The decision to bring African slaves to the colonies, therefore, was based primarily on economic considerations.

English masters, however, seldom justified the practice purely in terms of planter profits. Indeed, they adopted a quite different pattern of rhetoric. English writers associated blacks in Africa with heathen religion, barbarous behavior, sexual promiscuity—in fact, with evil itself. From such a racist perspective, the enslavement of Africans seemed unobjectionable. The planters maintained that if black slaves converted to Christianity, shedding their supposedly savage ways, they would benefit from their loss of freedom.

Africans first landed in Virginia in 1619 as a cargo of slaves stolen by a Dutch trader from a Spanish merchant ship in the Caribbean. For the next fifty years, the status of the colony's black people remained unclear. English settlers classified some black laborers as slaves for life, as chattel to be bought and sold at the master's will. But other Africans became servants, presumably for stated periods of time, and it was even possible for a few blacks to purchase their freedom. Several seventeenth-century Africans became successful Virginia planters. These rare exceptions in a long history of oppression remind modern Americans that once, long ago, it was possible to imagine a more open, less racially defined society. (See the Feature Essay, "Anthony Johnson, A Free Black Planter on Pungoteague Creek," pp. 74–75.)

One reason Virginia lawmakers tolerated such confusion was that the black population remained very small. By 1660, fewer than fifteen hundred people

**ORIGINS AND DESTINATIONS OF AFRICAN SLAVES, 1619–1760** *Although many African slaves were carried to Britain's North American colonies, far more slaves were sold in the Caribbean Sugar Colonies and Brazil, where because of horrific health conditions, the death rate far exceeded that of the British Mainland Colonies.* ❖

of African origin lived in the entire colony (compared to a white population of approximately twenty-six thousand), and it hardly seemed necessary for the legislature to draw up an elaborate slave code to control so few men and women. If the planters could have obtained more black laborers, they certainly would have done so. There is no evidence that the great planters preferred white indentured servants to black slaves. The problem was supply. During this period, slave traders sold their cargoes on Barbados or the other sugar islands of the West Indies, where they fetched higher prices than Virginians could afford. In fact, before 1680, most blacks who reached England's colonies on the North American mainland came from Barbados or through New Netherland rather than directly from Africa.

By the end of the seventeenth century, the legal status of Virginia's black people was no longer in doubt. They were slaves for life, and so were their children after them. This transformation reflected changes in the supply of Africans to British North America. After 1672, the Royal African Company was chartered to meet the colonial planters' demands for black laborers. Historian K. G. Davies terms this organization "the strongest and most effective of all European companies formed exclusively for the African trade." Between 1695 and 1709, more than

eleven thousand Africans were sold in Virginia alone; many others went to Maryland and the Carolinas. Although American merchants—most of them based in Rhode Island—entered the trade during the eighteenth century, the British continued to supply the bulk of the slaves to the mainland market for the entire colonial period.

The expanding black population apparently frightened white colonists, for as the number of Africans increased, lawmakers drew up ever stricter slave codes. It was during this period that racism, always a latent element in New World societies, was fully revealed. By 1700, slavery was unequivocally based on the color of a person's skin. Blacks fell into this status simply because they were black. A vicious pattern of discrimination had been set in motion. Even conversion to Christianity did not free the African from bondage. The white planter could deal with his black property as he alone saw fit, and one revolting Virginia statute excused masters who killed slaves, on the grounds that no rational person would purposely "destroy his own estate." Black women constantly had to fear sexual violation by a master or his sons. Children born to a slave woman became slaves regardless of the father's race. Unlike the Spanish colonies, where persons of lighter color enjoyed greater privileges in society, the English

This watercolor, Slave Deck of the Albanoz (1846), by naval officer Lieutenant Godfrey Meynell, shows slaves packed with cargo in the hold of a ship after being taken captive in West Africa. Because it was expected that many slaves would die en route, ship captains increased their profits by crowding even more slaves into the hold. ❖

colonies tolerated no mixing of the races. Mulattoes and pure Africans received the same treatment.

## Constructing African American Identities

The slave experience varied substantially from colony to colony. The daily life of a black person in South Carolina, for example, was quite different from that of an African American who happened to live in Pennsylvania or Massachusetts Bay. The size and density of the slave population determined in large measure how successfully blacks could maintain a separate cultural identity. In the lowlands of South Carolina during the eighteenth century, 60 percent of the population was black. The men and women were placed on large, isolated rice plantations, and their contact with whites was limited. In these areas blacks developed creole languages, which mixed the basic vocabulary of English with words borrowed from various African tongues. Until the end of the nineteenth century, one creole language, Gullah, was spoken on some of the Sea Islands along the Georgia–South Carolina coast. Slaves on the large rice plantations also were able to establish elaborate and enduring kinship networks that may have helped reduce the more dehumanizing aspects of bondage.

In the New England and Middle Colonies, and even in Virginia, African Americans made up a smaller percentage of the population: 40 percent in Virginia, 8 percent in Pennsylvania, and 3 percent in Massachusetts. In such environments, contact between blacks and whites was more frequent than in South Carolina and Georgia. These population patterns had a profound effect on northern and Chesapeake blacks, for while they escaped the physical drudgery of rice cultivation, they found the preservation of an independent African identity difficult. In northern cities, slaves working as domestics and living in the houses of their masters saw other blacks but had little opportunity to develop creole languages or reaffirm a common African past.

In eighteenth-century Virginia, native-born or creole blacks, people who had learned to cope with whites on a daily basis, looked with contempt on slaves who had just arrived from Africa. These "outlandish" Negroes, as they were called, were forced by blacks as well as whites to accept elements of English culture. It was especially important for newcomers to speak English. Consider, for example, the pain of young Olaudah Equiano, an African sold in Virginia in 1757. This 12-year-old slave declared, "I was now exceedingly miserable, and thought myself worse off than any . . . of my companions; for they could talk to each other [in English], but I had no person to speak to that I could understand. In this state I was constantly grieving and pining, and wishing for death."

Newly arrived men and women from Africa were far more likely to run away, assault their masters, and organize rebellion than were the creole slaves. The people described in colonial newspaper advertisements as "New Negroes" desperately tried to regain control over their lives. In 1770—just to cite one example—two young Africans, both recently sold in Virginia, "went off with several others, being persuaded that they could find their way back to their own Country."

Despite such wrenching experiences, black slaves creatively preserved elements of an African heritage. The process of establishing African American traditions involved an imaginative reshaping of African and European customs into something that was neither African nor European. It was African American. The

# ANTHONY JOHNSON

## A Free Black Planter on Pungoteague Creek

During the first decades of settlement, a larger proportion of Virginia's black population achieved freedom than at any time until the Civil War ended slavery. Despite considerable obstacles, these free black men and women—their number in these early years was quite small—formed families, acquired property, earned community respect, and helped establish a distinctive African American culture. One member of this group was Anthony Johnson, an immigrant who rose from slavery to prominence on Virginia's Eastern Shore.

Johnson came to Virginia aboard the English vessel *James* in 1621, just two years after the first blacks had arrived in the colony. As a slave known simply as "Antonio a Negro," Johnson found life a constant struggle for survival. Working in the tobacco fields of the Bennett plantation located on the south side of the James River, he endured long hours, poor rations, fearful epidemics, and haunting loneliness—conditions that, more often than not, brought an early death to slaves as well as indentured servants. Johnson, however, was a tough, intelligent, and lucky man.

Exactly how Johnson achieved freedom is not known. Early records reveal that while still living at the Bennett plantation, he took a wife, "Mary a Negro woman." Anthony was fortunate to find her. Because of an exceedingly unequal sex ratio in early Virginia, few males—regardless of color—had an opportunity to form families. Anthony and Mary reared at least four children. Even more re-

markable, in a society in which most unions were broken by death within a decade, their marriage lasted more than forty years.

Sometime during the 1630s, Anthony and Mary gained their freedom, perhaps with the help of someone named Johnson. Their bondage probably ended through self-purchase, an arrangement that allowed enterprising slaves to buy their liberty through labor. Later, again under unknown circumstances, the Johnsons migrated to Northampton County on the Eastern Shore of Virginia. During the 1640s, they acquired an estate of 250 acres on Pungoteague Creek, where they raised cattle, horses, and hogs and cultivated tobacco. To work these holdings, Anthony Johnson apparently relied on the labor of indentured servants and at least one black slave named Casor.

As the "patriarch of Pungoteague Creek," Johnson participated as fully as most whites in Northampton society. He traded with wealthy white landowners and apparently shared their assumptions about the sanctity of property and the legitimacy of slavery. When two white neighbors attempted to steal Casor, Johnson hauled them into court and forced them to return his laborer. On another occasion, Johnson appealed to the court for tax relief after an "unfortunate fire" destroyed much of his plantation.

The Johnsons also maintained close ties with other free blacks, such as Anthony Payne and Emmanuel Driggus, who had similarly attained freedom and prosperity through their own efforts. Johnson's strongest links

were with his family. Although his children lived in separate homes after reaching adulthood, his two sons laid out holdings in the 1650s adjacent to their father's plantation, and in times of crisis, parents and children participated in family conferences. These close bonds persisted even after the Johnson clan moved to Somerset County, Maryland, in the 1660s, and Anthony Johnson's subsequent death. When he purchased land in Somerset in 1677, Johnson's grandson, a third-generation free black colonist, named his plantation Angola, perhaps in memory of his grandfather's African homeland.

Interpreting Johnson's remarkable life has proved surprisingly difficult. An earlier generation of historians considered Johnson a curiosity, a sort of black Englishman who did not fit neatly into familiar racial categories. Even some recent writers, concerned about tracing the roots of slavery and prejudice in the United States, have paid scant attention to Johnson and the other free blacks on the Eastern Shore.

Most historians would now agree that Johnson's life illustrated the complexity of race relations in early Virginia. His surprising progression from slave to slaveholder and his easy participation in the world of the white gentry and in a network of black friendships and family ties demonstrated that relations among blacks and whites conformed to no single pattern in the fluid society of mid-seventeenth-century Virginia. Rather, they took a variety of forms—conflict, cooperation, exploitation, accommodation—depending on the goals, status, experience, and environment of the participants. Race was only a single factor—and by no means the decisive one—shaping relations among colonists.

The opportunities that had been available to Anthony Johnson and other Virginia blacks, however, disappeared during the last quarter of the seventeenth century. A growing reliance on slave labor rather than white indentured servitude brought about a rapid increase in the black population of Virginia and an accompanying curtailment of civil liberties on racial grounds. The rise of a group of great planters who dominated the colonial economy soon drove free black farmers into poverty. No longer did they enjoy the security, as had one black farmer in the 1640s, of having "myne owne ground and I will work when I please and play when I please." It is not surprising that after 1706, a time when Virginia's experiment in a genuinely multiracial free society was all but over, the Johnson family disappeared from the colonial records. When modern Americans discuss the history of race relations in the United States, they might consider the factors that allowed some of the first blacks who settled in America to achieve economic and social success.

A few months after Anthony Johnson died in 1670, a Virginia court ruled that because "he was a Negro and by consequence an alien," the 250 acres of land that he had owned should revert to England. Shown here is a portion of the court document with that decree. ❖

*A public notice announces a slave auction to be held at the Charles Town wharf (1769).* ❖

slaves accepted Christianity, but they did so on their own terms—terms their masters seldom fully understood. Blacks transformed Christianity into an expression of religious feeling in which an African element remained vibrant. In music and folk art, they gave voice to a cultural identity that even the most degrading conditions could not eradicate.

A major turning point in the history of African American people occurred during the early decades of the eighteenth century. At this time, blacks living in England's mainland colonies began to reproduce successfully. The number of live births exceeded deaths, and from that date, the expansion of the African American population owed more to natural increase than to the importation of new slaves. Even though thousands of new Africans arrived each year, the creole population was always much larger than that of the immigrant blacks. This demographic shift did not take place in the Caribbean or South American colonies until a much later date. Historians believe that North American blacks enjoyed a healthier climate and better diet than did other New World slaves.

Although mainland blacks lived longer than the blacks of Jamaica or Barbados, they were, after all, still slaves. They protested their debasement in many ways, some in individual acts of violence, others in organized revolt. The most serious slave rebellion of the colonial period was the Stono Uprising, which took place in September 1739. One hundred fifty South Carolina blacks rose up and, seizing guns and ammunition, murdered several white planters. "With Colours displayed, and two Drums beating," they marched toward Spanish Florida, where they had been promised freedom. The local militia soon overtook the rebellious slaves and killed most of them. Although the uprising was short-lived, such incidents helped persuade whites everywhere that their own blacks might secretly be planning bloody revolt. When a white servant woman in New York City announced in 1741 that blacks intended to burn the town, authorities executed 34 suspected arsonists (30 blacks and 4 whites) and dispatched 72 others either to the West Indies or to Madeira off the north coast of Africa. While the level of interracial violence in colonial society was quite low, everyone recognized that the blacks—in the words of one Virginia governor—longed "to Shake off the fetters of Slavery."

Even within the constraints of slavery, African Americans sometimes found opportunities that afforded a degree of personal freedom. Recent scholarship has discovered, for example, that during the eighteenth century a large number of black men became mariners. It is now estimated that by 1803, African Americans held at least 18 percent of all jobs open to American seamen, and although the number of positions may have been fewer before the Revolution, black colonial sailors—many of them slaves—sought work on sailing vessels to escape the drudgery of life on rice or tobacco plantations. These African American seamen connected black communities scattered throughout the Caribbean and along the mainland coast, bringing news about distant rebellions and spreading radical political ideologies to slaves who might otherwise not have known much about the transforming events of the eighteenth century.

## RISE OF A COMMERCIAL EMPIRE

In 1661, John Norton, a respected Congregational minister, delivered a remarkable sermon before the assembled legislators of Massachusetts Bay. "It is not a Gospel-spirit to be against Kings," Norton lectured, "'tis neither Gospel nor English Spirit for any of us to be against the Government by Kings, Lords and Commons." It was as if after some thirty years of vir-

Old Plantation, *a watercolor by an unknown artist (about 1800), shows that African customs survived plantation slavery. The man and women in the center dance (possibly to celebrate a wedding) to the music of drum and banjo. Instruments, turbans, and scarves reflect a distinctive African American culture in the New World.* ❖

tual freedom, the American Puritans had to be reminded of the political ties that bound them to England. As Norton sensed, however, the times were changing. The newly restored Stuart monarchy was beginning to establish rules for the entire empire, and the planters of the Chesapeake as well as the Puritans of New England would soon discover they were not as independent as they had imagined.

Until the middle of the seventeenth century, English political leaders largely ignored the American colonists. Private companies and aristocratic proprietors had created these societies, some for profit, others for religious sanctuary, but in no case did the crown provide financial or military assistance. After the Restoration of Charles II in 1660, intervention replaced indifference. Englishmen of various sorts—courtiers, merchants, parliamentarians—concluded that the colonists should be brought more tightly under the control of the mother country. The regulatory policies that evolved during this period formed a framework for an empire that survived with only minor adjustment until 1765.

## Response to Economic Competition

The famous eighteenth-century Scottish economist Adam Smith coined the term *mercantilist system* to describe Great Britain's commercial regulations, and ever since, his phrase has appeared in history books. An advocate of free trade, Smith argued that it made no sense for European states to exclude commercial competitors from their own colonial markets. More trade increased general prosperity. Smith's specific term, however, is misleading. **Mercantilism** suggests that

English policymakers during the reign of Charles II had developed a well-integrated set of ideas about the nature of international commerce and a carefully planned set of mercantilist government policies to implement them.

They did nothing of the sort. Administrators responded to particular problems, usually on an individual basis. In 1668, Charles informed his sister, "The thing which is nearest the heart of the nation is trade and all that belongs to it." National interest alone, however, did not shape public policy. Instead, the needs of several powerful interest groups led to the rise of English commercial regulation.

Each group looked to colonial commerce to solve a different problem. For his part, the king wanted money. For their part, English merchants were eager to exclude Dutch rivals from lucrative American markets and needed government assistance to compete successfully with the Dutch, even in Virginia or Massachusetts Bay. From the perspective of the landed gentry who sat in Parliament, England needed a stronger navy, and that in turn meant expansion of the domestic shipbuilding industry. And almost everyone agreed England should establish a more favorable balance of trade, that is, increase exports, decrease imports, and grow richer at the expense of other European states. None of these ideas was particularly innovative, but taken together they provided a blueprint for England's first empire.

## Regulating Colonial Trade

After some legislation in that direction during the Commonwealth, Parliament passed a Navigation Act in 1660. The statute was the most important piece of imperial legislation drafted before the American Revolution. Colonists from New Hampshire to Georgia paid close attention to the details of this statute, which stated (1) that no ship could trade in the colonies unless it had been constructed in either England or America and carried a crew that was at least 75 percent English (for these purposes, colonists counted as Englishmen), and (2) that certain **enumerated goods** of great value that were not produced in England—tobacco, sugar, cotton, indigo, dyewoods, ginger—could be transported from the colonies only to an English or another colonial port. In 1704, Parliament added rice and molasses to the enumerated list; in 1705, rosins, tars, and turpentines needed for shipbuilding were included.

The act of 1660 was masterfully conceived. It encouraged the development of domestic shipbuilding and prohibited European rivals from obtaining enumerated goods anywhere except in England. Since the Americans had to pay import duties in England (for this purpose colonists did not count as Englishmen) on such items as sugar and tobacco, the legislation also provided the crown with another source of income.

In 1663, Parliament passed a second Navigation Act known as the Staple Act, which stated that, with a few noted exceptions, nothing could be imported into America unless it had first been transshipped through England, a process that greatly added to the price ultimately paid by colonial consumers.

The **Navigation Acts** attempted to eliminate the Dutch, against whom the English fought three wars in this period (1652–1654, 1664–1667, and 1672–1674), as the intermediaries of American commerce. Just as English merchants were celebrating their victory, however, an unanticipated rival appeared on the scene: New England merchant ships sailed out of Boston, Salem, and Newport to become formidable world competitors in maritime commerce.

During the 1660s, the colonists showed little enthusiasm for the new imperial regulations. Reaction to the Navigation Acts varied from region to region. Virginians bitterly protested them. The collection of English customs on tobacco greatly reduced the colonial planters' profits. Moreover, the exclusion of the Dutch from the trade meant that growers often had to sell their crops at artificially low prices. The Navigation Acts hit the small planters especially hard, for they were least able to absorb increased production costs. Even though the governor of Virginia lobbied on the planters' behalf, the crown turned a deaf ear. By 1670, import duties on tobacco accounted for almost £100,000, a sum the king could scarcely do without.

At first, New Englanders simply ignored the commercial regulations. Indeed, one Massachusetts merchant reported in 1664 that Boston entertained "near one hundred sail of ships, this year, of ours and strangers." The strangers, of course, were the Dutch, who had no intention of obeying the Navigation Acts so long as they could reach colonial ports. Some New England merchants found clever ways to circumvent the Navigation Acts. These crafty traders picked up cargoes of enumerated goods such as sugar or tobacco, sailed to another colonial port (thereby technically fulfilling the letter of the law), and then made directly for Holland or France. Along the way they paid no customs.

To plug the loophole, Parliament passed the Navigation Act of 1673. This statute established a plantation duty, a sum of money equal to normal English customs duties to be collected on enumerated products at the various colonial ports. New Englanders could now sail wherever they pleased within the empire, but they could not escape paying customs. Parliament also extended the jurisdiction of the London Customs Commissioners to America. And in 1675, as part of the new imperial firmness, the Privy Council formed a powerful subcommittee, the Lords of Trade, whose members monitored colonial affairs.

Despite these legal reforms, serious obstacles impeded the execution of imperial policy. The customs service did not have enough effective agents in American ports to enforce the Navigation Acts fully, and some men sent from the mother country did more harm than good. Edward Randolph, head of the imperial customs service in New England, was such a person. He was dispatched to Boston in 1676 to gather information about the conduct of colonial trade. His behavior was so obnoxious, his reports about New Englanders so condescending, that he became the most hated man in late-seventeenth-century Massachusetts.

Parliament passed the last major piece of imperial legislation in 1696. Among other things, the statute tightened enforcement procedures, putting pressure specifically on the colonial governors to keep England's competitors out of American ports. The act of 1696 also expanded the American customs service and for the first time set up vice-admiralty courts in the colonies. This decision eventually rankled the colonists. Established to settle disputes that occurred at sea, vice-admiralty courts required neither juries nor oral cross-examination, both traditional elements of the common law. But they were effective and sometimes even popular for resolving maritime questions quickly enough to send the ships to sea again with little delay. The year 1696 witnessed one other significant change in the imperial system. William III replaced the ineffective Lords of Trade with a body of policy advisers that came to be known as the Board of Trade. This group was expected to monitor colonial affairs closely and to provide government officials with the best available advice on commercial and other problems. For several decades, at least, it energetically carried out its responsibilities.

The members of Parliament believed these reforms would belatedly compel the colonists to accept the Navigation Acts, and in large measure they were correct. By 1700, American goods transshipped through the mother country accounted for a quarter of all English exports, an indication the colonists found it profitable to obey the commercial regulations. In fact, during the eighteenth century, smuggling from Europe to America dried up almost completely.

## COLONIAL FACTIONS SPARK POLITICAL REVOLT, 1676–1691

The Navigation Acts created an illusion of unity. English administrators superimposed a system of commercial regulation on a number of different, often unstable American colonies and called it an empire. But these statutes did not remove long-standing differences. Within each society, men and women struggled to bring order out of disorder, to establish stable ruling elites, to diffuse ethnic and racial tensions, and to cope with population pressures that imperial planners only dimly understood. During the final decades of the seventeenth century, these efforts sometimes sparked revolt.

First, the Virginians rebelled, and then a few years later, political violence swept through Maryland, New York, and Massachusetts Bay, England's most populous mainland colonies. Historians once interpreted these events as rehearsals for the American Revolution, or even for Jacksonian democracy. They perceived the rebels as frontier democrats, rising in protest against an entrenched aristocracy.

Recent research suggests, however, that this view seriously misconstrued the character of these late-seventeenth-century rebellions. The uprisings certainly did not involve confrontations between ordinary people and their rulers. Indeed, the events were not in any modern sense of the word ideological. In each colony, the local gentry split into factions, usually the "outs" versus the "ins," and each side proclaimed its political legitimacy.

### Civil War in Virginia: Bacon's Rebellion

After 1660, the Virginia economy suffered a prolonged depression. Returns from tobacco had not been good for some time, and the Navigation Acts reduced profits even further. Into this unhappy environment came thousands of indentured servants, people drawn to Virginia, as the governor explained, "in hope of bettering their condition in a Growing Country."

The reality bore little relation to their dreams. A hurricane destroyed one entire tobacco crop, and in 1667, Dutch warships captured the tobacco fleet just as it was about to sail for England. Indentured servants complained about lack of food and clothing. No wonder that Virginia's governor, Sir William Berkeley, despaired of ever ruling "a People where six parts of seven at least are Poor, Endebted, Discontented and Armed." In 1670, he and the House of Burgesses disfranchised all landless freemen, persons they regarded as troublemakers, but the threat of social violence remained.

Enter Nathaniel Bacon. This ambitious young man arrived in Virginia in 1674. He came from a respectable English family and set himself up immediately as a substantial planter. But he wanted more. Bacon envied the government patronage monopolized by Berkeley's cronies, a group known locally as the Green Spring faction. When Bacon attempted to obtain a license to engage in the fur trade, he was rebuffed. This lucrative commerce was reserved for the governor's friends. If Bacon had been willing to wait, he probably would have been accepted into the ruling clique, but as subsequent events would demonstrate, Bacon was not a man of patience.

Events beyond Bacon's control thrust him suddenly into the center of Virginia politics. In 1675, Indians reacting to white encroachment attacked several outlying plantations, killing a few colonists, and Virginians expected the governor to send an army to retaliate. Instead, early in 1676, Berkeley called for the construction of a line of defensive forts, a plan that seemed to the settlers both expensive and ineffective. Indeed, the strategy raised embarrassing questions. Was Berkeley protecting his own fur monopoly? Was he planning to reward his friends with contracts to build useless forts?

While people speculated about such matters, Bacon stepped forward. He boldly offered to lead a volunteer army against the Indians at no cost to the hard-pressed Virginia taxpayers. All he demanded was an official commission from Berkeley giving him military command and the right to attack other Indians, not just the hostile Susquehannocks. The governor steadfastly refused. With some justification, Berkeley regarded his upstart rival as a fanatic on the subject of Indians. The governor saw no reason to exterminate peaceful tribes simply to avenge the death of a few white settlers.

What followed would have been comic had not so many people died. Bacon thundered against the governor's treachery; Berkeley labeled Bacon a traitor. Both men appealed to the populace for support. On several occasions, Bacon marched his followers to the frontier, but they either failed to find the enemy or, worse, massacred friendly Indians. At one point, Bacon burned Jamestown to the ground, forcing the governor to flee to the colony's Eastern Shore. Bacon's bumbling lieutenants chased Berkeley across Chesapeake Bay only to be captured themselves. Thereupon, the governor mounted a new campaign.

As **Bacon's Rebellion** dragged on, it became increasingly apparent that Bacon and his gentry supporters had only the vaguest notion of what they were trying to achieve. The members of the planter elite never seemed fully to appreciate that the rank-and-file soldiers, often black slaves and poor white servants, had serious, legitimate grievances against Berkeley's corrupt government and were demanding substantial reforms, not just a share in the governor's fur monopoly.

Although women had not been allowed to vote in colony elections, they made their political views clear enough during the rebellion. Some were apparently more violent than others. Sarah Glendon, for example, agitated so aggressively in support of Bacon that Berkeley later refused to grant her a pardon. Another outspoken rebel, Lydia Chiesman, defended her husband before Governor Berkeley, noting that the man would not have joined Bacon's forces had she not persuaded him to do so. "Therefore," Lydia Chiesman concluded, ". . . since what her husband had done, was by her meanes, and so, by consequence, she most guilty, that she might be hanged and he pardoned."

When Charles II learned of the fighting in Virginia, he dispatched a thousand regular soldiers to Jamestown. By the time they arrived, Berkeley had regained full control over the colony's government. In October 1676, Bacon died after a brief illness, and within a few months, his band of rebel followers had dispersed.

Berkeley, now an old and embittered man, was recalled to England in 1677. His successors, especially Lord Culpeper (1680–1683) and Lord Howard of Effingham (1683–1689), seemed interested primarily in enriching themselves at the expense of the Virginia planters. Their self-serving policies, coupled with the memory of near anarchy, helped heal divisions within the Virginia ruling class. For almost a century, in fact, the local gentry formed a united front against greedy royal appointees.

## The Glorious Revolution in the Bay Colony

During John Winthrop's lifetime, Massachusetts settlers developed an inflated sense of their independence from the mother country. After 1660, however, it became difficult even to pretend that the Puritan colony was a separate state. Royal officials such as Edward Randolph demanded full compliance with the Navigation Acts. Moreover, the growth of commerce attracted new merchants to the Bay Colony, men who were Anglicans rather than Congregationalists and who maintained close business contacts in London. These persons complained loudly of Puritan intolerance. The Anglican faction was never large, but its presence, coupled with Randolph's unceasing demands, divided Bay leaders. A few Puritan ministers and magistrates regarded compromise with England as treason, a breaking of the Lord's covenant. Other spokesmen, recognizing the changing political realities within the empire, urged a more moderate course.

In 1675, in the midst of this ongoing political crisis, the Indians dealt the New Englanders a terrible setback. Metacomet, a Wampanoag chief the whites called King Philip, declared war against the colonists. The powerful Narragansetts, whose lands the settlers had long coveted, joined Metacomet, and in little more than a year of fighting, the Indians destroyed scores of frontier villages, killed hundreds of colonists, and disrupted the entire regional economy. More than one thousand Indians and New Englanders died in the conflict. The war left the people of Massachusetts

*Metacomet, the Wampanoag chief known to the English colonists as King Philip, led Native Americans in a major war designed to remove the Europeans from New England.* ❖

deeply in debt and more than ever uncertain of their future. As in other parts of colonial America, the defeated Indians were forced off their lands, compelled by events to become either refugees or economically marginal figures in white society.

In 1684, the debate over the Bay Colony's relation to the mother country ended abruptly. The Court of Chancery, sitting in London and acting on a petition from the king, annulled the charter of the Massachusetts Bay Company. In one stroke of a pen, the patent that Winthrop had so lovingly carried to America in 1630, the foundation for a "city on a hill," was gone. The decision forced the most stubborn Puritans to recognize they were part of an empire run by people who did not share their particular religious vision.

James II, a monarch who disliked representative institutions—after all, Parliament, a representative assembly, had executed his father, Charles I—decided to restructure the government of the entire region in the Dominion of New England. In various stages from 1686 to 1689, the Dominion incorporated Massachusetts, Connecticut, Rhode Island, Plymouth, New York, New Jersey, and New Hampshire under a single appointed royal governor. For this demanding position, James selected Sir Edmund Andros (pronounced Andrews), a military veteran of tyrannical temperament. Andros ar-

rived in Boston in 1686, and within a matter of months he had alienated everyone: Puritans, moderates, and even Anglican merchants. Not only did Andros abolish elective assemblies, but he also enforced the Navigation Acts with such rigor that he brought about commercial depression. Andros declared normal town meetings illegal, collected taxes the people never approved, and packed the courts with supporters who detested the local population. Eighteenth-century historian and royal governor Thomas Hutchinson compared Andros unfavorably with the Roman tyrant Nero.

Early in 1689, news of the Glorious Revolution reached Boston. The previous fall, the ruling class of England had deposed James II, an admitted Catholic, and placed his Protestant daughter Mary and her husband, William of Orange, on the throne as joint monarchs (see the chart of the Stuart monarchs on p. 33). As part of the settlement, William and Mary accepted a Bill of Rights, a document stipulating the constitutional rights of all Englishmen. Almost immediately, the Bay Colonists overthrew the hated Andros regime. The New England version of the Glorious Revolution (April 18, 1689) was so popular that no one came to the governor's defense. Andros was jailed without a single shot having been fired. According to Cotton Mather, a leading Congregational minister, the

*William III and Mary II, joint monarchs of England after the Glorious Revolution of 1688. Mary ascended the throne when her father, James II, was deposed. Her husband William ruled Holland before accepting the English throne.* ❖

colonists were united by the "most Unanimous Resolution perhaps that was ever known to have Inspir'd any people."

However united as they may have been, the Bay Colonists could not take the crown's support for granted. William III could have declared the New Englanders rebels and summarily reinstated Andros. But thanks largely to the tireless lobbying of Increase Mather, Cotton's father, who pleaded the colonists' case in London, William abandoned the Dominion of New England, and in 1691, Massachusetts received a new royal charter. This document differed substantially from the company patent of 1629. The freemen no longer selected their governor. The choice now belonged to the king. Membership in the General Court was determined by annual election, and these representatives in turn chose the men who sat in the council or upper house, subject always to the governor's veto. Moreover, the franchise, restricted here as in other colonies to adult males, was determined on the basis of personal property rather than church membership, a change that brought Massachusetts into conformity with general English practice. On the local level, town government remained much as it had been in Winthrop's time.

## Contagion of Witchcraft

The instability of the Massachusetts government following Andros's arrest—what Reverend Samuel Willard described as "the short Anarchy accompanying our late Revolution"—allowed what under normal political conditions would have been an isolated, though ugly, local incident to expand into a major colonial crisis. Excessively fearful men and women living in Salem Village, a small, unprosperous farming community, nearly overwhelmed the new rulers of Massachusetts Bay.

Accusations of witchcraft were not uncommon in seventeenth-century New England. Puritans believed that an individual might make a compact with the devil, but during the first decades of settlement, authorities executed only about fifteen alleged witches. Sometimes villagers simply left suspected witches alone. Never before had fears of witchcraft plunged an entire community into panic.

The terror in Salem Village began in late 1691, when several adolescent girls began to behave in strange ways. They cried out for no apparent reason; they twitched on the ground. When concerned neighbors asked what caused their suffering, the girls announced they were victims of witches, seemingly innocent persons who lived in the community. The arrest of several alleged witches did not relieve the girls' "fits," nor did prayer solve the problem. Additional accusations were made, and at least one person confessed, providing a frightening description of the devil as "a thing all over hairy, all the face hairy, and a long nose." In June 1692, a special court convened and began to send men and women to the gallows. By the end of the summer, the court had hanged nineteen people; another was pressed to death. Many more suspects were in jail awaiting trial.

Then suddenly, the storm was over. Led by Increase Mather, a group of prominent Congregational ministers belatedly urged leniency and restraint. Especially

*The publication of Cotton Mather's* Memorable Providences, Relating to Witchcrafts and Possessions *(1689) contributed to the hysteria that resulted in the Salem witchcraft trials of the 1690s, but he did not take part in the trials. He is shown here surrounded by some of the forms a demon assumed in the "documented" case of an English family besieged by witches.* ❖

troubling to the clergymen was the court's decision to accept **spectral evidence**, that is, reports of dreams and visions in which the accused appeared as the devil's agent. Worried about convicting people on such dubious testimony, Mather declared, "It were better that ten suspected witches should escape, than that one innocent person should be condemned." The colonial government accepted the ministers' advice and convened a new court, which promptly acquitted, pardoned, or released the remaining suspects. After the Salem nightmare, witchcraft ceased to be a capital offense.

No one knows exactly what sparked the terror in Salem Village. The community had a history of religious discord, and during the 1680s, the people split into angry factions over the choice of a minister. Economic tensions played a part as well. Poorer, more traditional farmers accused members of prosperous, commercially oriented families of being witches. The underlying misogyny of the entire culture meant the victims were more often women than men. Terror of attack by Native Americans may also have played a part in this ugly affair. Indians in league with the French in Canada had recently raided nearby communities, killing people related to the families of the bewitched Salem girls, and significantly, during the trials some victims described the Devil as a "tawny man."

Whatever the ultimate social and psychological sources of this event may have been, jealousy and bitterness apparently festered to the point that adolescent girls who normally would have been disciplined were allowed to incite judicial murder. As so often happens in incidents like this one—the McCarthy hearings of the 1950s, for example—the accusers later came to their senses and apologized to the survivors for the needless suffering they had inflicted on the community. (For further discussion of the Salem witchcraft trials, see "Witches and the Law," pp. 86–90.)

## The Glorious Revolution in New York and Maryland

The Glorious Revolution in New York was more violent than it had been in Massachusetts Bay. Divisions within New York's ruling class ran deep and involved ethnic as well as religious differences. English newcomers and powerful Anglo-Dutch families who had recently risen to commercial prominence in New York City opposed the older Dutch elite.

Much like Nathaniel Bacon, Jacob Leisler was a man entangled in events beyond his control. Leisler, the son of a German minister, emigrated to New York in 1660 and through marriage aligned himself with the Dutch elite. While he achieved moderate prosperity as a merchant, Leisler resented the success of the Anglo-Dutch. When news of the Glorious Revolution reached New York City in May 1689, Leisler raised a group of militiamen and seized the local fort in the name of William and Mary. As leader of **Leisler's Rebellion**, he apparently expected an outpouring of popular support, but it was not forthcoming. His rivals waited, watching while Leisler desperately attempted to legitimize his actions. Through bluff and badgering, Leisler managed to hold the colony together, especially after French forces burned Schenectady (February 1690), but he never established a secure political base.

In March 1691, a new royal governor, Henry Sloughter, reached New York. He ordered Leisler to surrender his authority, but when Sloughter refused to prove he had been sent by William rather than by the deposed James, Leisler hesitated. The pause cost Leisler his life. Sloughter declared Leisler a rebel, and in a hasty trial, a court sentenced him and his chief lieutenant, Jacob Milbourne, to be hanged "by the Neck and being Alive their bodyes be Cutt downe to Earth and Their Bowells to be taken out and they being Alive, burnt before their faces. . . . " In 1695, Parliament officially pardoned Leisler, but he not being "Alive," the decision arrived a bit late. Long after his death, political factions calling themselves Leislerians and Anti-Leislerians struggled to dominate New York government. Indeed, in no other eighteenth-century colony was the level of bitter political rivalry so high.

During the last third of the seventeenth century, the colony of Maryland stumbled from one political crisis to another. Protestants in the colony's lower house resisted Lord Baltimore's Catholic friends in the upper house or council. When news of James's overthrow reached Maryland early in 1689, pent-up antiproprietary and anti-Catholic sentiment exploded. John Coode, a member of the assembly and an outspoken Protestant, formed a group called the Protestant Association, which in August forced Baltimore's governor, William Joseph, to resign.

Coode avoided Leisler's fatal mistakes. The Protestant Association, citing many wrongs suffered at the hands of local Catholics, petitioned the crown to transform Maryland into a royal colony. After reviewing the case, William accepted Coode's explanation, and in 1691, the king dispatched a royal governor to Maryland. A new assembly dominated by Protestants declared Anglicanism the established religion. Catholics were excluded from public office on the grounds that they might be in league with French Catholics in Canada. Lord Baltimore lost control of the colony's government, but he and his family did retain title to Maryland's undistributed lands. In 1715, the crown restored to full proprietorship the fourth Lord Baltimore, who had been raised a member of the Church of England, and Maryland remained in the hands of the Calvert family until 1776.

## CHRONOLOGY

| | |
|---|---|
| **1619** | First blacks arrive in Virginia |
| **1660** | Charles II is restored to the English throne ❖ First Navigation Act passed by Parliament |
| **1663** | Second Navigation (Staple) Act passed |
| **1673** | Plantation duty imposed to close loopholes in commercial regulations |
| **1675** | King Philip's (Metacomet's) War devastates New England |
| **1676** | Bacon's Rebellion threatens Governor Berkeley's government in Virginia |
| **1681** | William Penn receives charter for Pennsylvania |
| **1684** | Charter of the Massachusetts Bay Company revoked |
| **1685** | Duke of York becomes James II |
| **1686** | Dominion of New England established |
| **1688** | James II driven into exile during Glorious Revolution |
| **1689** | Rebellions break out in Massachusetts, New York, and Maryland |
| **1691** | Jacob Leisler executed |
| **1692** | Salem Village wracked by witch trials |
| **1696** | Parliament establishes Board of Trade |
| **1739** | Stono Uprising of South Carolina slaves terrifies white planters |

## CONCLUSION: LOCAL ASPIRATIONS WITHIN AN ATLANTIC EMPIRE

"It is no little Blessing of God," Cotton Mather announced proudly in 1700, "that we are part of the *English* nation." A half century earlier, John Winthrop would not have spoken these words, at least not with such enthusiasm. The two men were, of course, products of different political cultures. It was not so much that the character of Massachusetts society had changed. In fact, the Puritan families of 1700 were much like those of the founding generation. Rather, the difference was in England's attitude toward the colonies. Rulers living more than three thousand miles away now made political and economic demands that Mather's contemporaries could not ignore.

The creation of a new imperial system did not, however, erase profound sectional differences. By 1700, for example, the Chesapeake colonies were more, not less, committed to the cultivation of tobacco and slave labor. Although the separate regions were being pulled slowly into England's commercial orbit, they did not have much to do with each other. The elements that sparked a powerful sense of nationalism among colonists dispersed over a huge territory would not be evident for a very long time. It would be a mistake, therefore, to anticipate the coming of the American Revolution.

## RECOMMENDED READING

The most innovative research of chapters covered in this chapter explores the history of New World slavery during the period before the American Revolution. Much of this literature is boldly interdisciplinary, providing not only a fresh comparative interpretation of the creation and development of African American cultures in the New World, but also splendid insight into how imaginative scholars reconstruct the pasts of peoples who for a very long time have been denied a voice in mainstream histories. Among the more impressive contributions are Ira Berlin, *Many Thousands Gone: The First Two Centuries of Slavery in North America* (2000); Philip Morgan, *Slave Counterpoint: Black Culture in the Eighteenth-Century Chesapeaks and Lowcountry* (1998); and Robin Blackburn, *The Making of New World Slavery, 1492–1800* (1997). A pioneering work of high quality is Winthrop D. Jordan, *White Over Black: American Attitudes Toward the Negro, 1550–1812* (1968). Peter Wood provides an original interpretation of the evolution of race relations in *Black Majority: Negroes in Colonial South Carolina from 1670 Through the Stono Rebellion* (1974). The world of Anthony Johnson, the focus of the Feature Essay, is reconstructed in T. H. Breen and Stephen Innes, *"Myne Owne Ground": Race and Freedom on Virginia's Eastern Shore, 1640–1676* (1980). The most recent account of the Salem witch trials can be found in Mary Beth Norton, *In the Devil's Snare: The Salem Witchcraft Crisis of 1692* (2002). Richard Godbeer offers a solid account of the Puritans' intimate lives in *Sexual Revolution in Early America* (2002), but one should also consult Laurel T. Ulrich, *Good Wives: Image and Reality in the Lives of Women in Northern New England, 1650–1750* (1982), and a path-breaking essay by Lois G. Carr and Lorena Walsh, "The Planter's Wife: The Experience of White Women in Seventeenth-Century Maryland," *William and Mary Quarterly*, 3rd ser., 34 (1977): 542–571. A provocative discussion of cultural tensions within the British Empire can be found in Linda Colley, *Captives: The Story of Britain's Pursuit of Empire and How its Soldiers and Civilians Were Held Captive by the Dream of Global Supremacy, 1600–1850* (2002).

**For a list of additional titles related to this chapter's topics, please see** http://www.ablongman.com/divine.

# SUGGESTED WEB SITES

**DPLS Archive: Slave Movement During the 18th and 19th Centuries (Wisconsin)**

http://dpls.dacc.wisc.edu/slavedata/index.html

This site explores the slave ships and the slave trade that carried thousands of Africans to the New World.

**Excerpts from Slave Narratives**

http://vi.uh.edu/pages/mintz/primary.htm

Accounts of slavery from the seventeenth through nineteenth centuries speak volumes about the many impacts of slavery.

**Salem Witch Trials: Documentary Archive and Transcription Project**

http://www.iath.virginia.edu/salem/home.html

Extensive archive of the 1692 trials and life in late seventeenth-century Massachusetts.

**Colonial Documents**

http://www.yale.edu/lawweb/avalon/18th.htm

The key documents of the Colonial Era are reproduced here, as are some important documents from earlier and later periods in American history.

**LVA Colonial Records Project—Index of digital facsimiles of documents on early Virginia.**

http://eagle.vsla.edu/colonial/

This site contains numerous early documents, but it is unguided and a little difficult to use.

**Africans in America**

http://www.pbs.org/wgbh/aia/home.html

This PBS site contains images and documents recounting slavery in America.

# Witches and the Law

## A Problem of Evidence in 1692

The events that occurred at Salem Village in 1692 haunt modern memory. In popular American culture, the incident has come to represent our worst nightmare—a community-sanctioned witch hunt that ferrets out deviants in the name of law. What seems most unsettling about the incident is the failure of allegedly good men and women to bear witness against judicial terror. The ordeal of Salem Village links a distant colonial past with the infamous McCarthy hearings of the 1950s as well as other, more recent witch hunts. The story of this deeply troubled town challenges us to confront the possibility that we, too, might allow law and authority to become instruments of injustice.

The challenge in exploring law and society is how best to interpret the Salem trials. It would be easy to insist that Puritan magistrates were gross hypocrites, figures who consciously manipulated the law for their own hateful purposes. But such conclusions are simplistic; they fail to place the Salem nightmare in proper historical context. The participants in this intense social drama acted on a complex set of seventeenth-century assumptions—legal, religious, and scientific—and if judges and jurors wronged innocent people, they did so by the standards of a society very different from our own.

Few New Englanders doubted the existence of witches. For centuries, European communities had identified certain persons as agents of the devil, and when the Puritans migrated to America, they carried these beliefs with them. They recognized no conflict between rational religion and the possible existence of a satanic world populated by witches. Ordinary farmers regarded unusual events—the strange death of a farm animal, for example—as evidence of witchcraft. New England's intellectual leaders sustained popular superstition in impressive scientific publications. In his *Memorable Providences, Relating to Witchcrafts and Possessions* (1689), the Reverend Cotton Mather declared, "I am resolv'd . . . never to use . . . one grain of patience with any man that shall . . . impose upon me a Denial of Devils, or of Witches. I shall . . . count him down-right Impudent if he Assert the Non-Existence of things which we have had such palpable Convictions of."

Colonial New Englanders did more than talk and write about witches; as early as 1647, they executed several. Before the Salem outbreak, ninety-one people had been tried for witchcraft in Massachusetts and Connecticut, and eighteen of them were hanged (not burned as some historians have claimed). In addition, hundreds of people had accused neighbors of witchcraft, but for many reasons—usually lack of convincing evidence—they stopped short of taking such disputes before the court. These were isolated incidents. Before 1692, fear of witches had not sparked mass hysteria.

Salem Village was different. In this instance, charges of witchcraft shattered a community already deeply divided against itself. The predominantly agricultural Salem Village lay a few miles up the Ipswich Road from the bustling commercial port of Salem Town. The farmers of the Village envied their neighbors' prosperity. Even more, they resented the control that Town authorities exerted over the Village church and government. This tension found expression in numerous personal and family rivalries. In 1689, the congregation at Salem Village ordained the Reverend Samuel Parris, a troubled figure who provoked "disquietness" and "restlessness" and who fanned the factionalism that had long plagued the community.

The witchcraft crisis began suddenly in mid-January 1692, when two girls in the Parris household experienced violent convulsions and frightening visions. A local physician examined the afflicted children but found no "natural" cause for their condition. Soon anxious families raised the possibility of witchcraft, a move which set off a storm of accusations that did not abate until October. By that time, 19 people had died and more than 150 prisoners still awaited trial.

Although the witch hysteria affected everyone—men and women, rich and poor, farmers and merchants—the accusers and their targets were not evenly distributed among the population of Salem Village. Twenty of the thirty-four persons who claimed to have been bewitched were girls between the ages of 11 and 20. Women a full generation older than the accusers were most likely to be identified as witches; more than 40 percent of the accused fell into this category. Although men and women from many different backgrounds were accused, one widely shared characteristic was a history of socially unacceptable behavior. Sarah Good, for example, smoked a pipe and was known for cursing her enemies. John Aldin's accusers described him as "a bold fellow . . . who lies with Indian squaws . . . [and stands] with his hat on before the judges." Bridget Bishop ran a scandalous tavern and dressed in a particularly flashy, immodest manner. Those who testified against the supposed witches came from all classes, both genders, and every age group. Indeed, virtually the entire community was drawn into the ugly business of charge and countercharge, fear and betrayal.

New England's intellectual leaders—most of them Harvard-educated clergymen—tried to make sense out of reports coming out of Salem. Since the colonies did not yet have a newspaper, the reflections of these prominent figures significantly shaped how the entire society interpreted the frightening events of 1692. During the spring of that year, accusations of witchcraft mounted while magistrates interrogated everyone touched by the contagion.

Arriving from England in mid-May at the height of the witch hunt, the new royal governor of Massachusetts Bay, William Phips, appointed a special court of law (a court of "oyer and terminer") to try the cases at Salem Village. The seven judges he appointed all had previous experience in the colony's law courts. Phips wanted the trials to be as fair as possible and procedurally correct. A proper jury was impaneled. Despite precautions, however, the court itself soon succumbed to the frenzy. Chief judge and deputy governor William Stoughton, for example, staunchly believed the girls had been bewitched, and he had little doubt that "real" witches were responsible for the trouble at Salem Village. By contrast, Nathaniel Saltonstall was highly skeptical of the witchcraft charges. After witnessing the first round of executions, Saltonstall resigned from the court and turned to alcohol to persuade himself the court had not made a terrible mistake. Although the judges and jury may have felt ambivalent about what was happening, the law stated that persons convicted as witches must die.

This elegantly gabled house, built about 1675, stands at 310-1/2 Essex Street in Salem, Massachusetts. The residence of Jonathan Corwin, a magistrate for the court of oyer and terminer that heard the witchcraft cases in 1692, the structure became known as the Witch House. ❖

Everything turned on evidence. Confession offered the most reliable proof of witchcraft, and it occurred surprisingly often. We will never know what compelled people to confess. Some may have actually believed they had cast spells on their neighbors or had foretold the future. Many women, though believing themselves innocent, may have confessed because of guilt for impure thoughts that they had privately entertained. Perhaps the psychological strain of imprisonment, coupled with intense social scrutiny, convinced them they might have unwittingly entered into a contract with the devil. Regardless, the stories they told undoubtedly mortified those who heard them and fueled the growing frenzy. Imagine the reaction to Ann Foster's July 18 confession:

> Ann Foster . . . confessed that the devill in the shape of a black man appeared to her with [Martha] Carrier about six yeare since when they made her a witch and that she promised to serve the devill two years: upon which the Devill promised her prosperity and many things but never performed it, that she and Martha Carrier did both ride on a stick or pole when they went to the witch meeting at Salem Village and that the stick broak: as they were carried in the air above the tops of the trees and they fell but she did hang fast about the neck of [Martha] Carrier and were presently at the village, . . . she further saith that she heard some of the witches say that there was three hundred and five in the whole Country and that they would ruin that place the Village . . .

Most of the accused did not confess, however, forcing the judges to produce tangible evidence of witchcraft. The charge was difficult because the crime of bewitchment was, by nature, an invisible act. Earthly laws and magistrates had difficulty dealing with crimes that occurred in the spiritual world. In this situation, the beleaguered judges used a few customary tests. All witches supposedly had a "witch's teat," usually a flap of skin located anywhere on the body, from which they gave suck to the devil. The judges subjected almost every defendant to a humiliating physical examination in order to find such biological abnormalities. Witches could also be discovered by having them touch a girl in the midst of her torments. If the girl's fits ceased, then the person who touched her was assumed responsible for her agony. Since this form of evidence was immediately observable, judges relied on it heavily, oftentimes parading accused witches before the possessed girls waiting to see whose touch would calm them.

Had the terrible ordeal turned solely on unsightly warts, the trials might have ended without further note. But that did not happen. The judges allowed the jury to entertain a different sort of evidence, "spectral evidence," and it was this material that hanged people at Salem Village. New Englanders believed that witches worked by dispatching a specter, a phantom spirit, to torment their victims. This meant that witches had power over great distances; they were invisible. They entered people's dreams, and dozens of good New

A view of Gallows Hill at Salem. On this site, condemned witches were hanged. ❖

Englanders complained of having been bitten, pinched, or even choked by specters that looked a lot like their neighbors. The judges regularly accepted spectral testimony of the sort offered by 18-year-old John Cook:

> . . . one morning about sun rising as I was in bed . . . I saw [Bridget] Bishop . . . Standing in the chamber by the window and she looked on me & . . . presently struck me on the Side of the head w'ch did very much hurt me & then I Saw her goe Out under the End window at a little Creviss about So bigg as I Could thrust my hand into. I Saw her again the Same day . . . walke & Cross the roome & having at the time an apple in my hand it flew Out of my hand into my mothers lapp who stood Six or Eight foot distance from me & then She disappeared & though my mother & Severall others were in the Same room yet they affirmed they Saw her not.

As far as the witch hunters were concerned, Bridget Bishop had been caught in the act. To the modern observer, however, the problems with this kind of evidence seem obvious. First, how could one tell whether Cook was lying? The power of his story lay in its inability to be corroborated, for one could never check the authenticity of an intensely private dream or vision. The second problem was that persons accused of being witches had no defense against spectral testimony. When Captain John Aldin stood before his accusers, for example, they immediately fell to the ground, writhing in pain. When asked why he tormented the girls, Aldin firmly denied any wrongdoing, inquiring why the judges "suppose[d he had] no better things to do than to come to Salem to afflict these persons that I never knew or saw before." Aldin's defense did not carry much weight when set against the testimony of the suffering girls, and rather than conclude the accusers manifested a "lying spirit," the judges admitted all spectral evidence as incontestable proof of witchcraft.

Very early in the trials, a few people expressed doubts about the reliability of this particular form of evidence. Cotton Mather and other ministers, for example, issued a statement urging the judges to use spectral evidence with "a very critical and exquisite caution." Some feared the devil could assume the shape of innocent people. If this was the case, then the visions of the afflicted proved nothing but the devil's ability to deceive humans. In the absence of spectral evidence, the cases against most of the witches boiled down to little more than long-standing complaints against obnoxious neighbors. The fury of prosecution silenced the skeptical voices, however, and chief judge William Stoughton continued to accept dreams and visions as proof of witchcraft.

Fantastic testimony about flying witches and pinching specters lent an almost circuslike air to the proceedings at Salem. Before the judges and the members of the jury, the afflicted girls would fall to the ground, convulsing and screaming, claiming to see witches that remained invisible to the court. Hundreds of spectators sat horrified as Satan caused suffering before their own eyes. For seventeenth-century New Englanders who felt the presence of the spiritual world in their everyday lives, the courtroom at Salem offered the opportunity to witness the struggle between the forces of darkness and light. Because of the gravity of the situation, no one expected the judges to deal lightly with those who had sworn allegiance to the devil. Indeed, in the interest of obtaining a confession, the judges conducted harsh interrogations, usually assuming the guilt of the defendant. The intense psychological pressure inflicted on the defendants is revealed in the questioning of Sarah Good, a woman subsequently hanged as a witch:

**Judge:** Sarah Good, what evil spirit have you familiarity with?
**Good:** None.
**Judge:** Why do you hurt these children?
**Good:** I do not hurt them. I scorn it.
**Judge:** Who do you employ then to do it?
**Good:** I employ nobody.
**Judge:** Have you made a contract with the devil?
**Good:** No.
**Judge:** Sarah Good . . . why do you not tell us the truth? Why do you thus torment these poor children?
**Good:** I do not torment them.

Even the ministers who advised caution applauded the judges' "assiduous endeavors" and encouraged the "vigorous prosecution" of the witches. As the witch hysteria gained momentum, few people dared to defend the witches for fear of being accused themselves. The humble pleas of those who genuinely thought themselves innocent fell on the deaf ears of a community convinced of its own righteousness.

By late September, with nineteen people already executed, the emotional intensity that had sustained the witch hunt in its early stages began to ebb. For one thing, the accusations spun wildly out of control as the afflicted girls began naming unlikely candidates as witches: prominent ministers, a judge's mother-in-law, and even the governor's wife! Such accusations discredited the entire procedure by which the witches had been discovered. Also, although the jails could barely hold the 150 people still awaiting trial, the accusations kept coming. The terror was feeding on itself.

In mid-October, Governor Phips dismissed the original court and appointed a new one, this time bar-

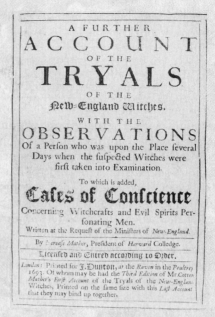

Title page of *A Further Account of the Tryals of the New England Witches* (1693), Increase Mather's reflection on the incidents at Salem Village. Mather's *Cases of Conscience Concerning Witchcrafts and Evil Spirits* is credited with helping end the witchcraft executions in Salem. ❖

ring spectral evidence. All remaining defendants were quickly acquitted, although, curiously enough, three women still confessed to having practiced witchcraft. In a letter to the king, Phips explained his decision to end the trials, claiming that "the people" had become "dissatisfied and disturbed." Men and women who had been so eager to purify the community of evil, to murder neighbors in the name of a higher good, now spoke of their fear of divine retribution. Perhaps the dying words of Sarah Good, uttered in response to the assistant minister of Salem Town, echoed in their ears: "I am no more a witch than you are a wizard, and if you take away my life, God will give you blood to drink."

Soon after the trials ended, the witch hunters quickly turned confessors. In 1706, Ann Putnam, one of the most prolific accusers, publicly asked for forgiveness: "I desire to be humbled before God. . . . It was a great delusion of Satan that deceived me in that time." Nine years earlier, the Salem jurors had issued a similar statement, asking the community to understand the particular pressures that compelled them to convict so many people:

We confess that we . . . were not capable to understand, nor able to withstand the mysterious delusions of the Powers of Darkness . . . ; but were for want of Knowledge in our selves, and better Information from others, prevailed with to take up with such

Evidence against the Accused, as on further consideration, and better Information, we justly fear was insufficient for the touching the Lives of any . . . whereby we fear we have been instrumental with others, tho Ignorantly and unwittingly, to bring upon our selves, and this People of the Lord, the Guilt of Innocent Blood.

The state never again executed citizens for witchcraft. The experience at Salem had taught New Englanders that, although witches may have existed, no human court could identify a witch beyond a reasonable doubt. The Reverend Increase Mather summed up the attitude of a post-Salem New England: "It were better that ten suspected witches should escape than that one innocent person should be condemned."

What triggered the tragic events of 1692 remains a mystery. Some historians view the witch hunt as a manifestation of Salem Village's socioeconomic troubles. This interpretation helps explain why the primary accusers came from the agrarian village while the alleged witches either resided in or were somehow connected to the market-oriented town. Perhaps the charge of witchcraft masked a deep resentment for their neighbors' monetary success and the new set of values that accompanied the market economy. Other historians believe the witch hunt reflected a deep ambivalence about gender roles in New England society. Young girls lashed out at older nonconforming women because they symbolized a freedom that was achievable within New England society, yet vehemently criticized. Facing the choice between becoming their husbands' servants or being free, the accusers may have expressed this cultural frustration in lethal ways. Terror of Indian attack may have exacerbated community fear. Some accusers described the devil as a "tawney man," a clear reference to Native Americans. These and many other factors contributed to the witch phenomenon.

Regardless of which interpretation one favors, one must acknowledge that Salem Village had indeed been possessed. The blame rests on the community as a whole, not just on a few vindictive judges. In 1697, another repentant witch hunter, the Reverend John Hale, tried to explain how well-meaning people had caused such harm:

I am abundantly satisfyed that those who were most concerned to act and judge in those matters, did not willingly depart from the rules of righteousness. But such was the darkness of that day, . . . that we walked in the clouds, and could not see our way.

Hale's words ring hollow. They came too late to do much good. As other communities have learned throughout the long history of this nation, it is easier to apologize after the fact than to stand up courageously against the first injustice.

## Questions for Discussion

- Do the interpretations for the Salem witch hunt provided by modern historians seem adequate to explain what happened in 1692? Why or why not?

- What could the people of Massachusetts Bay have done to halt the legal proceedings at an early stage?

- Since science and theology seemed to be on their side, can we hold the leading ministers and magistrates of the colony responsible for not halting the trials before so many executions had taken place? Should we judge their record by modern standards of evidence?

- Should the magistrates who sat in judgment at Salem have been tried later for incompetence or malfeasance? Or forced publicly to apologize for their actions?

- What can modern Americans learn from the events of 1692?

# Chapter 4

World commerce defined urban life in late colonial America. This engraving of a work originally done by William Burgis celebrates the impact of Anglo-American trade on mid-eighteenth-century Boston. ❖

# Experience of Empire: Eighteenth-Century America

## *Constructing an Anglo-American Identity: The Journal of William Byrd*

William Byrd II (1674–1744) was a type of British American one would not have encountered during the earliest years of settlement. This successful Tidewater planter was a product of a new, more cosmopolitan environment, and as an adult, Byrd seemed as much at home in London as in his native Virginia. In 1728, at the height of his political influence in Williamsburg, the capital of colonial Virginia, Byrd accepted a commission to help survey a disputed boundary between North Carolina and Virginia. During his long journey into the distant backcountry, Byrd kept a detailed journal, a satiric, often bawdy chronicle of daily events that is now regarded as a classic of early American literature.

On his trip into the wilderness, Byrd met many different people. No sooner had he departed a familiar world of tobacco plantations than he came across a self-styled "Hermit," an Englishman who apparently preferred the freedom of the woods to the constraints of society. "He has no other Habitation but a green Bower or Harbour," Byrd reported, "with a Female Domestick as wild & as dirty as himself."

As the boundary commissioners pushed farther into the backcountry, they encountered highly independent men and women of European descent, small frontier families that Byrd regarded as living no better than savages. He attributed their uncivilized behavior to a diet of too much pork. "The Truth of it is, these People live so much upon Swine's flesh . . . [that it] makes them . . . extremely hoggish in their Temper, & many of them seem to Grunt rather than Speak in their ordinary conversation." The wilderness journey also brought Byrd's party of surveyors into regular contact with Native Americans, whom he properly distinguished as Catawbas, Tuscaroras, Usherees, and Sapponis.

BYRD'S JOURNAL INVITES US TO VIEW the rapidly developing eighteenth-century backcountry from a fresh perspective. It was not a vast empty territory awaiting the arrival of European settlers. Maps often sustain this erroneous impression, depicting cities and towns, farms and plantations clustered along the Atlantic coast; they suggest a "line of settlement" steadily pushing outward into a huge blank area with no mark of civilization. The people Byrd met on his journey into the backcountry would not have understood such maps. After all, the empty space on the maps was their home. They experienced the frontier as populous zones of many cultures stretching from the English and French settlements in the north all the way to the Spanish borderlands in the far southwest.

The point is not to discount the significance of the older Atlantic settlements. During the eighteenth century, Britain's thirteen mainland colonies underwent a profound transformation. The population in the colonies grew at unprecedented rates.

*William Byrd II. Byrd's* History of the Dividing Line Run in the Year 1728 *contains a marvelously satirical account of the culture of poor country farmers in North Carolina.* ❖

German and Scots-Irish immigrants arrived in huge numbers. So too did African slaves.

Wherever they lived, colonial Americans of this period were less isolated from one another than colonists had been during most of the seventeenth century. Indeed, after 1690, men and women expanded their cultural horizons, becoming part of a larger Anglo-American empire. The change was striking. Colonists whose parents or grandparents had come to the New World to confront a "howling wilderness" now purchased imported European manufactures, read English journals, participated in imperial wars, and sought favors from a growing number of resident royal officials. No one—not even the inhabitants of the distant frontiers—could escape the influence of Britain. The cultural, economic, and political links connecting the colonists to the imperial center in London grew stronger with time.

This surprising development raises a difficult question for the modern historian. If the eighteenth-century colonists were so powerfully attracted to Great Britain, then why did they ever declare independence? The answer may well be that as the colonists became more British, they inevitably became more American as well. This was a development of major significance, for it helps to explain the appearance after midcentury of genuine nationalist sentiment. Political, commercial, and military links that brought the colonists into more frequent contact with Great Britain also made them more aware of other colonists. It was within an expanding, prosperous empire that they first began seriously to consider what it meant to be American.

## GROWTH AND DIVERSITY

The phenomenal growth of British America during the eighteenth century amazed Benjamin Franklin, one of the first persons to bring mathematical rigor to the study of demography. The population of the English colonies doubled approximately every twenty-five years, and, according to calculations Franklin made in 1751, if the expansion continued at such an extraordinary rate for another century or so, "the greatest Number of Englishmen will be on this Side [of] the water."

Accurate population data from the colonial period are extremely difficult to find. The first national census did not occur until 1790. Still, various sources surviving from prerevolutionary times indicate that the total white population of Britain's thirteen mainland colonies rose from about 250,000 in 1700 to 2,150,000 in 1770, an annual growth rate of 3 percent.

Few societies in recorded history have expanded so rapidly, and if the growth rate had not dropped sub-

stantially during the nineteenth and twentieth centuries, the current population of the United States would stand at well more than one billion people. Natural reproduction was responsible for most of the growth. More families bore children who in turn lived long enough to have children of their own. Because of this sudden expansion, the population of the late colonial period was strikingly young; approximately one-half of the populace at any given time was under age 16.

Not only was the total population increasing at a very rapid rate; it also was becoming more dispersed and heterogeneous. Each year witnessed the arrival of thousands of non-English Europeans. Unlike those seventeenth-century English settlers in search of religious sanctuary or instant wealth (see Chapter 2), the newcomers generally transferred in the hope of obtaining their own land and setting up as independent farmers. These people often traveled to the **backcountry,** a region stretching approximately eight hundred miles from western Pennsylvania to Georgia.

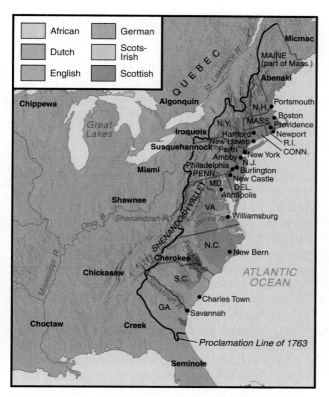

**DISTRIBUTION OF EUROPEAN AND AFRICAN IMMIGRANTS IN THE THIRTEEN COLONIES**
*A flood of non-English immigrants swept the British colonies between 1700 and 1775.* ❖

Although they planned to follow customs they had known in Europe, they found the challenge of surviving on the British frontier far more demanding than they had anticipated. They plunged into a complex, fluid, often violent society that included large numbers of Native Americans and African Americans as well as other Europeans.

## Scots-Irish Flee English Oppression

Non-English colonists poured into American ports throughout the eighteenth century, creating rich ethnic diversity in areas originally settled by Anglo-Saxons. The largest group of newcomers consisted of Scots-Irish. The experiences of these people in Great Britain influenced not only their decision to move to the New World but also their behavior once they arrived.

During the seventeenth century, English rulers thought they could thoroughly dominate Catholic Ireland by transporting thousands of lowland Scottish Presbyterians to the northern region of that war-torn country. The plan failed. English officials who were members of the Anglican Church discriminated against the Presbyterians. They passed laws that placed the Scots-Irish at a severe disadvantage when they traded in England; they taxed them at exorbitant rates.

After several poor harvests, many of the Scots-Irish elected to emigrate to America, where they hoped to find the freedom and prosperity that had been denied them in Ireland. "I have seen some of their letters to their friends here [Ireland]," one British agent reported in 1729, ". . . in which after they set forth and recommend the fruitfulness and commodities of the country [America], they tell them, that if they will but carry over a little money with them, they may for a small sum purchase considerable tracts of land." Often entire Presbyterian congregations followed charismatic ministers to the New World, intent on replicating a distinctive, fiercely independent culture on the frontier. It is estimated that 150,000 Scots-Irish migrated to the colonies before the Revolution.

Most Scots-Irish immigrants landed initially in Philadelphia, but instead of remaining in that city, they carved out farms on Pennsylvania's western frontier. The colony's proprietors welcomed the influx of new settlers, for it seemed they would form an ideal barrier between the Indians and the older, coastal communities. The Penn family soon had second thoughts, however. The Scots-Irish squatted on whatever land looked best, and when colony officials pointed out that large tracts had already been reserved, the immigrants retorted that "it was against the laws of God and nature that so much land should be idle when so many Christians wanted it to labour on and to raise their bread." Wherever they located, the Scots-Irish challenged established authority.

## Germans Search for a Better Life

A second large body of non-English settlers, more than 100,000 people, came from the upper Rhine Valley, the German Palatinate. Some of the migrants, especially those who relocated to America around the turn of the century, belonged to small pietistic Protestant sects whose religious views were somewhat similar to those of the Quakers. These Germans moved to the New World primarily in the hope of finding religious toleration. Under the guidance of Francis Daniel Pastorius (1651–1720), a group of Mennonites established in Pennsylvania a prosperous community known as Germantown.

By midcentury, however, the characteristics of the German migration had begun to change. Large numbers of Lutherans transferred to the Middle Colonies. Unlike members of the pietistic sects, these men and women were not in search of religious freedom. Rather, they traveled to the New World looking to better their material lives. The Lutheran Church in Germany initially tried to maintain control over the distant congregations, but even though the migrants themselves fiercely preserved many aspects of traditional German culture, they were eventually forced to accommodate to new social conditions. Henry Melchior Mühlenberg (1711–1787), a tireless leader, helped German Lutherans through a difficult cultural adjustment, and in 1748, Mühlenberg organized a meeting of local pastors and lay delegates that ordained ministers of their own choosing, an act of spiritual independence that has been called "the most important single event in American Lutheran history."

The German migrants—mistakenly called Pennsylvania Dutch because the English confused *deutsch* (meaning "German") with *Dutch* ("a person from Holland")—began reaching Philadelphia in large numbers after 1717, and by 1766, persons of German stock accounted for more than one-third of Pennsylvania's total population. Even their most vocal detractors admitted the Germans were the best farmers in the colony.

Ethnic differences in Pennsylvania bred disputes. The Scots-Irish as well as the Germans preferred to live with people of their own background, and they some-times fought to keep members of the other nationality out of their neighborhoods. The English were suspicious of both groups. They could not comprehend why the Germans insisted on speaking German in America. In 1753, for example, Franklin described these settlers as "the most stupid of their nation." He warned that "unless the stream of [German] importation could be turned from this to other colonies . . . they will soon outnumber us, . . . [and] all the advantages we have, will in my opinion, be not able to preserve our language, and even our government will become precarious." As Franklin's remarks suggest, the pressure on non-English colonists to accommodate to the dominant culture—in other words, to "Anglicize" their manners and behavior—was very great. In comparison to some of his contemporaries, Franklin seemed a moderate critic of the German and Scots-Irish settlers. Others threatened violence against the newcomers who refused to conform to English ways. (See the Feature Essay, "Learning to Live with Diversity in the Eighteenth Century: What Is an American?" pp. 100–101.)

Such prejudice may have persuaded members of both groups to search for new homes. After 1730, Germans and Scots-Irish pushed south from western Pennsylvania into the Shenandoah Valley, thousands of them settling in the backcountry of Virginia and the Carolinas. The Germans usually remained wherever they found unclaimed fertile land. By contrast, the Scots-Irish often moved two or three times, acquiring a reputation as a rootless people.

Wherever the newcomers settled, they often found themselves living beyond the effective authority of the various colonial governments. To be sure, backcountry residents petitioned for assistance during wars against the Indians, but most of the time they preferred to be left alone. These conditions heightened the importance of religious institutions within the small ethnic communities. Although the original stimulus for coming to America may have been a desire for economic independence and prosperity, backcountry families—especially the Scots-Irish—flocked to evangelical Protestant preachers, to Presbyterian, and later Baptist and Methodist ministers who not only fulfilled the settlers' spiritual needs but also gave scattered backcountry communities a pronounced moral character that survived long after the colonial period.

*This folk art painting from the cover of a clothes box depicts a well-dressed German-American farmer. The farmer's hat, his coat, and walking stick indicate that he enjoyed a middling to high status.* ❖

## Convict Settlers

Since the story of European migration tends to be upbeat—men and women engaged in a largely successful quest for a better material life—it often is forgotten that British courts compelled many people to come to America. Indeed, the African slaves were not the only large group of people coerced into moving to the New World. In 1718, Parliament passed the Transportation Act, allowing judges in England, Scotland, and Ireland to send convicted felons to the American colonies. Between 1718 and 1775, the courts shipped approximately fifty thousand convicts across the Atlantic. Some of these men and women may actually have been dangerous criminals, but the majority seem to have committed minor crimes against property. Although transported convicts—almost 75 percent of whom were young males—escaped the hangman, they found life difficult in the colonies. Eighty percent of them were sold in the Chesapeake colonies as indentured servants. At best they faced an uncertain future, and it is probably not surprising that few former convicts prospered in America.

British authorities lavished praise on this system. According to one writer, transportation drained "the Nation of its offensive Rubbish, without taking away their Lives." Although Americans purchased the convict servants, they expressed fear that these men and women would create a dangerous criminal class. In one irate essay, Benjamin Franklin asked his readers to consider just how the colonists might repay the leaders

of Great Britain for shipping so many felons to America. He suggested that rattlesnakes might be the appropriate gift. "I would propose to have them carefully distributed . . . ," Franklin wrote, "in the Gardens of all the Nobility and Gentry throughout the Nation; but particularly in the Gardens of the Prime Ministers, *the Lords of Trade* and *Members of Parliament*." The Revolution forced the British courts to redirect the flow of convicts to another part of the world; an indirect result of American independence was the founding of Australia by transported felons.

## Native Americans Stake Out a Middle Ground

In some histories of the colonial period, Native Americans make only a brief appearance, usually during the earliest years of conquest and settlement. After initial contact with the first European invaders, the Indians seem mysteriously to disappear from the central narrative of colonization, and it is not until the nineteenth century that they turn up again, this time to wage a last desperate battle against the encroachment of white society.

This obviously inadequate account slights one of the richer chapters of Native American history. During much of the seventeenth century, various Indian

*Elizabeth Canning, convicted of perjury, stands at the bar to receive her sentence from the London court. For her crime, she was sentenced to one month's imprisonment and transport for seven years to the American colonies.* ❖

groups who contested the English settlers for control of coastal lands suffered terribly, sometimes from war, but more often from the spread of contagious diseases such as smallpox. The two races found it very difficult to live in close proximity. As one Indian informed the members of the Maryland assembly in 1666, "Your hogs & Cattle injure Us, You come too near Us to live & drive Us from place to place. We can fly no farther; let us know where to live & how to be secured for the future from the Hogs & Cattle."

Against such odds the Indians managed to survive. By the eighteenth century, the site of the most intense and creative contact between the races had shifted to the cis-Mississippian west, that is, to the huge territory between the Appalachian Mountains and the Mississippi River, where several hundred thousand Native Americans made their homes.

Many Indians had only recently migrated to the area. The Delawares, for example, retreated to far western Pennsylvania and the Ohio Valley to escape almost continuous confrontation with advancing European invaders. Other Indians drifted west in less happy circumstances. They were refugees, the remnants of Native American groups who had lost so many people that they could no longer sustain an independent cultural identity. These survivors joined with other Indians to establish new multiethnic communities. In this respect, the Native American villages may not have seemed all that different from the mixed European settlements of the backcountry.

Stronger groups of Indians such as the Creek, Choctaw, Chickasaw, Cherokee, and Shawnee generally welcomed the refugees. Strangers were formally adopted to take the places of family members killed in battle or overcome by sickness, and it should be appreciated that many seemingly traditional Indian villages of the eighteenth century actually represented innovative responses to rapidly shifting external conditions. As historian Peter Wood explained, "Physically and linguistically diverse groups moved to form loosely organized confederacies, unions of mutual convenience, that effectively restrained interethnic hostilities."

The concept of a *middle ground*—a term that has only recently entered the interpretive vocabulary—helps us more fully to comprehend how eighteenth-century Indians held their own in the backcountry beyond the Appalachian Mountains. The Native Americans never intended to isolate themselves completely from European contact. They relied on white traders, French as well as English, to provide essential metal goods and weapons. The goal of the Indian confederacies was rather to maintain a strong independent voice in these commercial exchanges, whenever possible playing the French against the British, and so long as they had sufficient military strength—that is, large

numbers of healthy armed warriors—they compelled everyone who came to negotiate in the "middle ground" to give them proper respect. It would be incorrect, therefore, to characterize their relations with the Europeans as a stark choice between resistance or accommodation, between total war or abject surrender. Native Americans took advantage of rivals when possible; they compromised when necessary. It is best to imagine the Indians' middle ground as an open, dynamic process of creative interaction.

The Susquehannocks understood the rules of the middle ground. Indeed, they mastered the eighteenth-century language of commercial negotiation. When backcountry traders charged the Indians seemingly exorbitant prices for European goods, the angry Susquehannocks took their complaint to James Hamilton, the lieutenant governor of Pennsylvania. In fact, they forced Hamilton to give them a short lecture on international economics, an event that shows the Indians were fully capable of grasping the essential elements of modern capitalism. "You know we dont make the Goods ourselves," Hamilton whined, "they are made in England, and the Transporting them over the Seas is dangerous in time of War and very expensive, so that . . . their prices change, as the risque and demand for them is greater or less."

However desirable they may have appeared, European goods subtly eroded traditional structures of Native American authority. During the period of earliest encounter with white men, Indian leaders reinforced their own power by controlling the character and flow of commercial exchange. If a trader wanted a rich supply of animal skins, for example, he soon learned that he had better negotiate directly with a chief or tribal elder. But as the number of European traders operating within the "middle ground" expanded, ordinary Indians began to bargain on their own account, obtaining colorful and durable manufactured items without first consulting a Native American leader. Independent commercial dealings of this sort tended further to weaken the Indians' ability to resist organized white aggression. As John Stuart, a superintendent of Indian affairs, explained in 1761, "A modern Indian cannot subsist without Europeans; And would handle a Flint Ax or any other rude utensil used by his ancestors very awkwardly; So that what was only convenience at first is now become Necessity."

The survival of the middle ground depended ultimately on factors over which the Native Americans had little control. Imperial competition between France and Great Britain enhanced the Indians' bargaining position, but after the British defeated the French in 1763, the Indians no longer received the same solicitous attention as they had in earlier times. Keeping old allies happy seemed to the British a need-

*Tishcohan, chief of the Delaware tribe that lost much of its land in Thomas Penn's Walking Purchase of 1737, is shown here in a 1735 portrait by Gustavus Hesselius. Although treaties and agreements with European settlers were often detrimental to Native Americans, some alliances in the "middle ground" allowed the tribes to play off the French against the British. Alliances were often signified by tokens such as certificates, calumets (ceremonial pipes), wampum belts, and medals. ❖*

less expense. Moreover, contagious disease continued to take a fearful toll. In the southern backcountry between 1685 and 1790, the Indian population dropped an astounding 72 percent. In the Ohio Valley, the numbers suggest similar rates of decline. In fact, there is some evidence that British military officers practiced germ warfare against the Native Americans, giving them blankets contaminated by smallpox. Based on experience, the officers knew that personal belongings such as blankets taken from the sick were contaminated and, thus, that giving these items to the Indians would put them at risk. By the time the United States took control of this region, the middle ground itself had become a casualty of history.

## SPANISH BORDERLANDS OF THE EIGHTEENTH CENTURY

In many traditional histories of North America, the Spanish make only a brief appearance, usually as fifteenth-century conquistadors. But as soon as they have conquered Mexico, they are dropped from the story as if they had no serious part to play in the ongoing development of the continent. This is, of course, a skewed perspective that masks the roots of ethnic diversity in the United States. The Spanish empire did not disappear. Indeed, it continued to shape the character of borderlands societies well into the eighteenth century. As anyone who visits the modern American Southwest quickly discovers, Spanish administrators and priests—not to mention ordinary settlers—left a lasting imprint on the cultural landscape of this country.

Until 1821, when Mexico declared independence from Madrid, Spanish authorities struggled to control a vast northern frontier. During the eighteenth century, the Spanish empire in North America included widely dispersed settlements such as San Francisco, San Diego, Santa Fe, San Antonio, and St. Augustine. In these borderland communities, European colonists mixed with peoples of other races and backgrounds, forming multicultural societies. According to historian Ramón A. Gutiérrez, the Spanish provinces present a story of "the complex web of interactions between men and women, young

# LEARNING TO LIVE WITH DIVERSITY IN THE EIGHTEENTH CENTURY

## What Is an American?

Americans have had a hard time dealing with difference. It is only recently that some commentators have begun to describe social diversity as a positive good. For most of our history, attempts to define national identity have inevitably excluded members of minority groups or newcomers whose language and culture were not English. Over the past two centuries those in authority have devised various strategies for accommodating ethnic and racial diversity, some more successful than others, but all of them at any moment is likely to produce anger and violence as mutual understanding. These explosive issues first sparked public debate during the eighteenth century, long before Americans advocated independence.

The sudden arrival of thousands of men and women born in Ireland and Germany worried colonial leaders who assumed that being British meant that a person spoke English and accepted the basic traditions of English law and politics. Problems related to ethnic diversity seemed most pressing in the Middle Colonies such as Pennsylvania, for after the 1720s poor people from the German Palatinate and the area around Belfast flocked to America in search of economic opportunity. James Logan, the provincial secretary of Pennsylvania, sounded the alarm, warning those of English stock of the "foreigners" who threatened to transform the local culture. Because of the number of Germans entering the colony, Logan argued, "these colonies will in time be lost to the Crown." Although the Scots-Irish spoke English, they seemed even more menacing. These Protestant migrants who fled the north of Ireland to escape chronic poverty appeared intent on making "themselves Proprietors of the Province."

It might have been predicted that English colonists would have welcomed so many able workers, people who could pay taxes and defend the frontiers. But such was not the case. Benjamin Franklin, often depicted as a voice of reason, almost panicked when he contemplated the growing diversity. Why, he demanded, should the Germans be allowed "to swarm into our Settlements, and by herding together establish their Language and Manners to the Exclusion of ours? Why should Pennsylvania, founded by the English, become a Colony of *Aliens?*" In fact, Franklin predicted that "Instead of their Learning our Language, we must learn their's, or live as in a foreign Country." As in so many cultural confrontations of this sort, the representatives of the dominant group defined difference as a contest in which one either won or lost. Accommodation had little appeal for those so anxious to preserve the purity of their own heritage.

The question for people such as Franklin was how best to make the Germans and the Scots-Irish more like the English. It was thought that education might save the day. After all, the "foreigners" could be taught to accept a common set of values that obviously served as the foundation for society. Pennsylvania leaders contended that the standards rested ultimately on "the noble Privilege or Birth-Right of an *English Subject.*" As anyone could see,

Painted floral motifs adorn this 1790 pine schrank (wardrobe) from Lancaster County, Pennsylvania. Closets were rare in German homes in Pennsylvania so families stored all their clothing in such schränke. ❖

English identity meant developing a deep respect for the law, property, and institutions originally erected by migrants from England and their descendants. During the years of heaviest immigration, those who claimed to speak for the cultural mainstream, extolled the "sober and prudent conduct of the ancient Settlers and their Successors," in other words, those who understood that "the Rights and Privileges of this Colony, [rested] on the true basis of English *Liberty and Property.*" Some enthusiasts even encouraged the colonial legislature to pass laws for the encouragement of "Virtue, Sobriety, and Industry . . . [to] prevent an English Plantation from Being turned into a Colony of Aliens."

The key to preserving social order in face of growing diversity was Anglicization, a process of transforming Germans and Scots-Irish into people who at least seemed English. Success was just a matter of time. Strange languages, customs, and beliefs could be made to disappear under a veneer of Englishness. Thomas Penn, whose family actually owned Pennsylvania, predicted that the Germans would "certainly by degrees loose their attachment to their Language, and become English, and as they acquire property I dare prophecy will become good Subjects." Indeed, so confident was his brother John of the ability of the Germans to acculturate that he concluded "we ought by no Means to Debar their coming over," because "when settled these [people] will Esteem themselves Pennsylvanians." To accomplish this

goal, "Foreigners imported, should not be allowed to settle in large separate Districts . . . because for many Generations they may continue, as it were, a separate People in Language, Modes of Religion, Customs and Manners." The newcomers, therefore, were best "intermixed with the *British* settlers." But one had to be on guard. By "distinguishing themselves" from the dominant culture the members of these groups showed contempt for English traditions. After all, asked a colonial official, "How far is it consistent with the Peace, Honour or Security of an English Government that they, who . . . have had the utmost Protection, should upon Occasions, be thus nationally distinguished?"

All the advice apparently fell on deaf ears. The migrants failed to measure up to English standards, and differences came to be seen as rejection and hostility. To the chagrin of fully Anglicized Pennsylvanians, the German settlers could not be "restrained" from forming tight-knit ethnic communities. They refused to abandon the culture they had known in Europe. Moreover, they did not intermarry with those from other groups, established newspapers in their own language, and set up German-speaking schools. The Scots-Irish raised even more hackles. Although they had demonstrated their loyalty to the British crown in the Old World, they seemed in the New to "have little Honesty and less Sense." An unruly people, they squatted on lands owned by the Penn family or the Native Americans. What is more, they

showed no desire to mix with neighbors of different ethnicity. The Scots-Irish held that "no strangers should be admitted to settle within [their] Bounds," and instead of taking their legal disputes to the province's official courts—as any proper Englishman would do—they relied on church elders. To make matters worse for critics such as Franklin, they often reacted to minor insults with violence and were "generally rough" with the Indians. When some Scots-Irish murdered twenty Native Americans in 1763, Franklin called them "Christian white savages," while another colonial official dubbed them "the very scum of mankind."

As has been so often the case with cultural tensions of this sort, the various participants gradually reached an accommodation, often perhaps without even realizing how much they had adjusted to changing conditions. The "foreigners" did not in fact destroy Pennsylvania. Indeed, political leaders who identified themselves as English were soon soliciting the votes of the migrant population, and over time, it became clear that the colony's prosperity in the Atlantic World owed a lot to hard-working aliens. And on the eve of revolution, some Americans had come to realize that diversity was not all that objectionable. As one patriot who called himself "A Son of Liberty" observed in 1768, "It is true that the first emigrations were from *England;* but upon the whole, more settlers have come from *Ireland, Germany,* and other parts of *Europe,* than from *England.*"

The Donegal Presbyterian Church in Lancaster County, Pennsylvania, recalls the cultural heritage of the Scots-Irish settlers of the region. ❖

and old, rich and poor, slave and free, Spaniard and Indian, all of whom fundamentally depended on the other for their own self-definition."

## Conquering the Northern Frontier

Not until late in the sixteenth century did Spanish settlers, led by Juan de Oñate, establish European communities north of the Rio Grande. The Pueblos resisted the invasion of colonists, soldiers, and missionaries, and in a major rebellion in 1680 led by El Popé, the native peoples drove the whites completely out of New Mexico. "The heathen have conceived a mortal hatred for our holy faith and enmity for the Spanish nation," concluded one imperial bureaucrat. Not until 1692 were the Spanish able to reconquer this fiercely contested area. By then, Native American hostility coupled with the settlers' failure to find precious metal had cooled Spain's enthusiasm for the northern frontier.

Concern over French encroachment in the Southeast led Spain to colonize St. Augustine (Florida) in 1565. Although the enterprise never flourished, it claims attention as the first permanent European settlement established in what would become the United States, predating the founding of Jamestown and Plymouth by several decades. Pedro Menéndez de Avilés brought some fifteen hundred soldiers and settlers to St. Augustine, where they constructed an impressive fort, but the colony failed to attract additional Spanish migrants. "It is hard to get anyone to go to St. Augustine because of the horror with which Florida is painted," the governor of Cuba complained in 1673. "Only hoodlums and the mischievous go there from Cuba."

California never figured prominently in Spain's plans for the New World. Early explorers reported finding only impoverished Indians living along the Pacific coast. Adventurers saw no natural resources worth mentioning, and since the area proved extremely difficult to reach from Mexico City—the overland trip could take months—California received little attention. Fear that the Russians might seize the entire region belatedly sparked Spanish activity, however, and after 1769, two indomitable servants of empire, Fra Junípero Serra and Don Gaspar de Portolá, organized permanent missions and *presidios* (forts) at San Diego, Monterey, San Francisco, and Santa Barbara.

## Peoples of the Spanish Borderlands

In sharp contrast to the English frontier settlements of the eighteenth century, the Spanish outposts in North America grew very slowly. A few Catholic priests and imperial administrators traveled to the northern provinces, but the danger of Indian attack as well as a harsh physical environment discouraged ordinary colonists. The European migrants were overwhelmingly male, most of them soldiers in the pay of the empire. Although some colonists came directly from Spain, most had been born in other Spanish colonies such as Minorca, the Canaries, or New Spain, and because European women rarely appeared on the frontier, Spanish males formed relationships with Indian women, fathering large numbers of mestizos, children of mixed race.

As in other European frontiers of the eighteenth century, encounters with Spanish soldiers, priests, and traders altered Native American cultures. The experience here was quite different from that of the whites and Indians in the British backcountry. The Spanish exploited Native American labor, reducing entire Indian villages to servitude. Many Indians moved to the Spanish towns, and although they lived in close proximity to the Europeans—something rare in British America—they were consigned to the lowest social class, objects of European contempt. However much their material conditions changed, the Indians

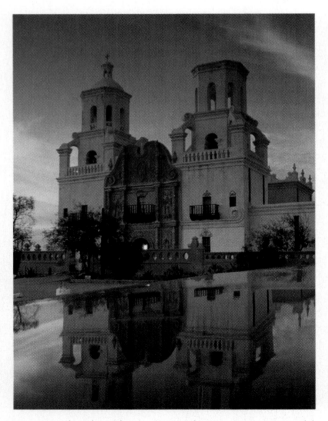

*Baroque-style eighteenth-century Spanish mission at San Xavier del Bac in present-day Arizona. Spanish missions dotted the frontier of northern New Spain from Florida to California.* ✦

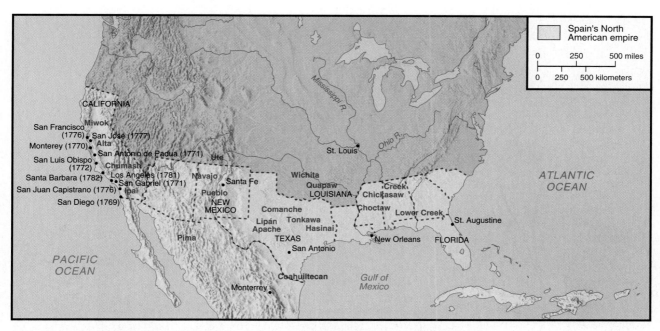

**THE SPANISH BORDERLANDS, CA. 1770** *In the late eighteenth century, Spain's North American empire extended across what is now the southern United States from Florida through Texas and New Mexico to California.* ❖

of the Southwest resisted strenuous efforts to convert them to Catholicism. The Pueblos maintained their own religious forms—often at great personal risk—and they sometimes murdered priests who became too intrusive. Angry Pueblos at Taos reportedly fed the hated Spanish friars corn tortillas containing urine and mouse meat.

The Spanish empire never had the resources necessary to secure the northern frontier fully. The small military posts were intended primarily to discourage other European powers such as France, Great Britain, and Russia from taking possession of territory claimed by Spain. It would be misleading, however, to stress the fragility of Spanish colonization. The urban design and public architecture of many southwestern cities still reflect the vision of the early Spanish settlers, and to a large extent, the old borderlands remain Spanish speaking to this day.

# THE IMPACT OF EUROPEAN IDEAS ON AMERICAN CULTURE

The character of the older, more established British colonies changed almost as rapidly as that of the backcountry. The rapid growth of an urban cosmopolitan culture impressed eighteenth-century commentators, and even though most Americans still lived on scattered farms, they had begun to participate aggressively in an exciting consumer marketplace that expanded their imaginative horizons.

## Provincial Cities

Considering the rate of population growth, it is surprising to discover how few eighteenth-century Americans lived in cities. Boston, Newport, New York, Philadelphia, and Charles Town—the five largest cities—contained only about 5 percent of the colonial population. In 1775, none had more than forty thousand persons. The explanation for the relatively slow development of colonial American cities lies in their highly specialized commercial character. Colonial port towns served as entrepôts, intermediary trade and shipping centers where bulk cargoes were broken up for inland distribution and where agricultural products were gathered for export. They did not support large-scale manufacturing. Indeed, the pool of free urban laborers was quite small, since the type of person who was forced to work for wages in Europe usually became a farmer in America.

Yet despite the limited urban population, cities profoundly influenced colonial culture. It was in the cities that Americans were exposed to and welcomed the latest English ideas. Wealthy colonists—merchants and lawyers—tried to emulate the culture of the mother country. They sponsored concerts and plays; they learned to dance. Women as well as men picked

This 1743 map of Boston depicts the port city as an active commercial and cultural center, with many wharves, buildings, churches, and meeting halls. ❖

up the new fashions quickly, and even though most of them had never been outside the colony of their birth, they sometimes appeared to be the products of London's best families.

It was in the cities, also, that wealthy merchants transformed commercial profits into architectural splendor, for, in their desire to outdo one another, they built grand homes of enduring beauty. Most of these buildings are described as Georgian because they were constructed during the reign of Britain's early Hanoverian kings, who all happened to be named George. Actually these homes were provincial copies of grand country houses of Great Britain. They drew their inspiration from the great Italian Renaissance architect Andrea Palladio (1508–1580), who had incorporated classical themes into a rigidly symmetrical form. Palladio's ideas were popularized in the colonies by James Gibbs, an Englishman whose *Book of Architecture* (1728) provided blueprints for the most spectacular homes of mid-eighteenth-century America.

Their owners filled the houses with fine furniture. Each city patronized certain skilled craftsmen, but the artisans of Philadelphia were known for producing magnificent copies of the works of Thomas Chippendale, Great Britain's most famous furniture designer. These developments gave American cities an elegance they had not possessed in the previous century. One foreign visitor noted of Philadelphia in 1748 that "its natural advantages, trade, riches and power, are by no means inferior to any, even of the most ancient towns of Europe." As this traveler understood, the cultural impact of the cities went far beyond the number of people who actually lived there.

## American Enlightenment

European historians often refer to the eighteenth century as an Age of Reason. During this period, a body of new, often radical, ideas swept through the salons and universities, altering the way that educated Europeans thought about God, nature, and society. This intellectual revolution, called the **Enlightenment,** involved the work of Europe's greatest minds, men such as Newton and Locke, Voltaire and Hume. The writings of these thinkers eventually reached the colonies, where they received a mixed reception. On the whole, the American Enlightenment was a rather tame affair compared to its European counterpart, for while the colonists welcomed experi-

### ✦ A Look at the Past ✦

#### Westover

By the mid-eighteenth century, a native-born elite took shape in Virginia and other colonies. Many wealthy Americans constructed estates to signify their status and power. Few were as grand as Westover in Virginia, probably built by William Byrd III, ca. 1750, but all "great houses" impressed visitors with their size and level of interior decoration. Such houses required vast sums of money as well as knowledge of the latest European styles to construct, maintain, and furnish. The funds needed to maintain these estates often came from the production of export crops such as tobacco and rice, crops cultivated by an unfree black labor force. What did the difference between great houses like Westover and the typical one-room dwellings suggest about eighteenth-century Virginia society? How did building large, elaborate, and fashionable houses contribute to cementing gentry power?

mental science, they defended the tenets of traditional Christianity.

Enlightenment thinkers shared basic assumptions. Philosophers of the Enlightenment replaced the concept of original sin with a much more optimistic view of human nature. A benevolent God, having set the universe in motion, gave human beings the power of reason to enable them to comprehend the orderly workings of his creation. Everything, even human society, operated according to these mechanical rules. The responsibility of right-thinking men and women, therefore, was to make certain that institutions such as church and state conformed to self-evident natural laws. It was possible—or so some of the *philosophes* claimed—to achieve perfection in this world. In fact, human suffering had come about only

because people had lost touch with the fundamental insights of reason.

For many Americans, the appeal of the Enlightenment was its focus on a search for useful knowledge, ideas, and inventions that would improve the quality of human life. What mattered was practical experimentation. A speech delivered in 1767 before the members of the American Society in Philadelphia reflected the new utilitarian spirit: "Knowledge is of little Use when confined to mere Speculation," the colonist explained, "But when speculative Truths are reduced to Practice, when Theories grounded upon Experiments . . . and the Arts of Living made more easy and comfortable . . . Knowledge then becomes really useful." The Enlightenment spawned scores of earnest scientific tinkerers, people who dutifully recorded changes in temperature, the appearance of strange plants and animals, and the details of astronomic phenomena. While these eighteenth-century Americans made few earth-shattering discoveries, they did encourage their countrymen, especially those who attended college, to apply reason to the solution of social and political problems.

## Benjamin Franklin

Benjamin Franklin (1706–1790) absorbed the new cosmopolitan culture. European thinkers regarded him as a genuine *philosophe,* a person of reason and science, a role that he self-consciously cultivated when he visited England and France in later life. Franklin had little formal education, but as a young man working in his brother's print shop, he managed to keep up with the latest intellectual currents. In his *Autobiography,* Franklin described the excitement of discovering a new British journal. It was like a breath of fresh air to a boy growing up in Puritan New England. "I met with an odd volume of *The Spectator,*" Franklin recounted; ". . . I had never before seen any of them. I bought it, read it over and over, and was much delighted with it. I thought the writing excellent, and wished if possible to imitate it."

Franklin's opportunity came in August 1721 when he and his brother founded the *New England Courant,* a weekly newspaper that satirized Boston's political and religious leaders in the manner of the contemporary British press. Writing under the name Silence Dogood, young Franklin asked his readers "Whether a Commonwealth suffers more by hypocritical Pretenders to Religion, or by the openly Profane?" Proper Bostonians were not prepared for a journal that one minister described as "full freighted with Nonesense, Unmanncrliness, Railery, Prophaneness, Immorality, Arrogance, Calumnies, Lyes, Contradictions, and what not, all tending to Quarrels and Divisions and to Debauch and Corrupt the Minds and Manners of New England." Franklin got the point; he left Massachusetts in 1723 in search of a less hostile intellectual environment.

After he had moved to Philadelphia, leaving behind an irritable brother as well as New England Puritanism, Franklin devoted himself to the pursuit of useful knowledge, ideas that would increase the happiness of his fellow Americans. Franklin never denied the existence of God. Rather, he pushed the Lord aside, making room for the free exercise of human reason. Franklin tinkered, experimented, and reformed. Almost everything he encountered in his daily life aroused his curiosity. His investigation of electricity brought him world fame, but Franklin was never satisfied with his work in this field until it yielded practical application. In 1756, he invented the lightning rod. He also designed a marvelously efficient stove that is still used today. In modern America, Franklin has become exactly what he would

*Benjamin Franklin (left) exemplified the scientific curiosity and search for practical knowledge characteristic of enlightenment thinkers of the eighteenth century. Franklin's experiments on electricity became world famous and inspired many others to study the effects of the strange force. The citizens shown above (right), eager to try out a new phenomenon, are rubbing metal rods together to produce static electricity.* ❖

have wanted to be, a symbol of material progress through human ingenuity.

Franklin energetically promoted the spread of reason. In Philadelphia, he organized groups that discussed the latest European literature, philosophy, and science. In 1727, for example, he "form'd most of my ingenious Acquaintances into a Club for mutual Improvement, which we call'd the Junto." Four years later Franklin took a leading part in the formation of the Library Company, a voluntary association that for the first time allowed people like him to pursue "useful knowledge." The members of these societies communicated with Americans living in other colonies, providing them not only with new information but also with models for their own clubs and associations. Such efforts broadened the intellectual horizons of many colonists, especially those who lived in cities.

## Economic Transformation

The colonial economy kept pace with the stunning growth in population. During the first three-quarters of the eighteenth century, the population increased at least tenfold, and yet even with so many additional people to feed and clothe, the per capita income did not decline. Indeed, with the exception of poor urban dwellers, such as sailors whose employment varied with the season, white Americans did quite well. An abundance of land and the extensive growth of agriculture accounted for their economic success. New farmers were able not only to provide for their families' well-being but also to sell their crops in European and West Indian markets. Each year, more Americans produced more tobacco, wheat, or rice—to cite just the major export crops—and by this means, they maintained a high level of individual prosperity without developing an industrial base.

At midcentury, colonial exports flowed along well-established routes. More than half of American goods produced for export went to Great Britain. The Navigation Acts (see Chapter 3) were still in effect, and "enumerated" items such as tobacco had to be landed first at a British port. Furs were added to the restricted list in 1722. The White Pines Acts passed in 1711, 1722, and 1729 forbade Americans from cutting white pine trees without a license. The purpose of this legislation was to reserve the best trees for the use of the Royal Navy. The Molasses Act of 1733—also called the Sugar Act—placed a heavy duty on molasses imported from foreign ports; the Hat and Felt Act of 1732 and the Iron Act of 1750 attempted to limit the production of colonial goods that competed with British exports.

These statutes might have created tensions between the colonists and the mother country had they been rigorously enforced. Crown officials, however, generally ignored the new laws. New England merchants imported molasses from French Caribbean islands without paying the full customs; ironmasters in the Middle Colonies continued to produce iron. Even without the Navigation Acts, however, a majority of colonial exports would have been sold on the English market. The emerging consumer society in Great Britain was beginning to create a new generation of buyers who possessed enough income to purchase American goods, especially sugar and tobacco. This rising demand was the major market force shaping the colonial economy.

Colonial merchants operating out of Boston, Newport, and Philadelphia also carried substantial tonnage to the West Indies. In 1768, this market accounted for 27 percent of all American exports. If there was a triangular trade that included the west coast of Africa, it does not seem to have been economically significant. Colonial ships carrying food sailed for the Caribbean and returned immediately to the Middle Colonies or New England with cargoes of molasses, sugar, and rum. In fact, recent research indicates that during the eighteenth century, trade with Africa involved less than 1 percent of all American exports. Slaves were transported directly to colonial ports where they were sold for cash or credit.

The West Indies played a vital role in preserving American credit in Europe. Without this source of income, colonists would not have been able to pay for the manufactured items they purchased in the mother country. To be sure, they exported American products in great quantity to Great Britain, but the value of the exports seldom equaled the cost of British goods shipped back to the colonists. To cover this small but recurrent deficit, colonial merchants relied on profits made in the West Indies.

## Birth of a Consumer Society

After midcentury, however, the balance of trade turned dramatically against the colonists. The reasons for this change were complex, but, in simplest terms, Americans began buying more English goods than their parents or grandparents had done. Between 1740 and 1770, English exports to the American colonies increased by an astounding 360 percent.

In part, this shift reflected a fundamental transformation in the British economy. Although the Industrial Revolution was still far in the future, the pace of the British economy picked up dramatically after 1690. Small factories produced certain goods more efficiently and more cheaply than the colonists could. The availability of these products altered the lives of most Americans, even those with modest incomes. Staffordshire china replaced crude earthenware; imported cloth replaced homespun. Franklin noted in

## ❖ A Look at the Past ❖

### Tea Set

A flood of British manufactured goods transformed the material culture of mid-eighteenth-century America. Some historians have called this dramatic change in the character of everyday life a "consumer revolution." Even ordinary men and women discovered that they could purchase colorful fabrics, fashionable ceramics, and other imported goods that they regarded as better made and more desirable than those produced in their own households. Decorative porcelain teapots, cups, and saucers, such as shown in this photograph of a 1770 English-made tea set, became part of a tea service, a domestic ritual that marked the arrival of a new cosmopolitan taste. Do you think that the mid-eighteenth-century flood of imported goods affected how the colonists felt about Great Britain? By copying English styles of dress, decoration, and behavior—drinking tea, for example—did the colonists strengthen their ties to the mother country? Do you think the availability of so many consumer items created class tensions between those Americans who could afford the latest imports and those who could not? How would colonists have known what items they were expected to purchase?

his *Autobiography* how changing consumer habits affected his life. For years, he had eaten his breakfast in an earthenware bowl with a pewter spoon, but one morning it was served "in a china bowl, with a spoon of silver." Franklin observed that "this was the first appearance of plate and china in our house which afterwards in the course of years, as our wealth increased, augmented gradually to several hundred pounds in value." In this manner, British industrialization undercut American handicraft and folk art.

To help Americans purchase manufactured goods, British merchants offered generous credit. Colonists deferred settlement by agreeing to pay interest on their debts. The temptation to acquire English finery blinded many people to hard economic realities. They gambled on the future, hoping bumper farm crops would reduce their dependence on the large merchant houses of London and Glasgow. Obviously, some persons lived within their means, but the aggregate American debt continued to grow. Colonial leaders tried various expedients to remain solvent—issuing paper money, for example—and while these efforts delayed a crisis, the balance-of-payments problem was clearly very serious.

The eighteenth century also saw a substantial increase in intercoastal trade. Southern planters sent tobacco and rice to New England and the Middle Colonies, where these staples were exchanged for meat and wheat as well as goods imported from Great Britain. By 1760, approximately 30 percent of the colonists' total tonnage capacity was involved in this extensive "coastwise" commerce. In addition, backcountry farmers in western Pennsylvania and the Shenandoah Valley carried their grain to market along an old Iroquois trail that became known as the Great Wagon Road, a rough, hilly highway that by the time of the Revolution stretched 735 miles along the Blue Ridge Mountains to Camden, South Carolina. Most of their produce was carried in long, gracefully designed Conestoga wagons. These vehicles—sometimes called the "wagons of empire"—had been invented by German immigrants living in the Conestoga River Valley in Lancaster County, Pennsylvania.

The shifting patterns of trade had immense effects on the development of an American culture. First, the flood of British imports eroded local and regional identities. Commerce helped to "Anglicize" American culture by exposing colonial consumers to a common range of British manufactured goods. Deep sectional differences remained, of course, but Americans from New Hampshire to Georgia were increasingly drawn into a sophisticated economic network centered in London. Second, the expanding coastal and overland trade brought colonists of different backgrounds into more frequent contact. Ships that sailed between New England and South Carolina, and between Virginia and Pennsylvania, provided dispersed Americans with a means to exchange ideas and experiences on a more regular basis. Mid-eighteenth-century printers, for example, established several dozen new journals; these were weekly newspapers that carried information not only about the mother country and world commerce but also about events in other colonies.

## RELIGIOUS REVIVALS IN PROVINCIAL SOCIETIES

A sudden, spontaneous series of Protestant revivals known as the **Great Awakening** had a profound impact on the lives of ordinary people. This unprece-

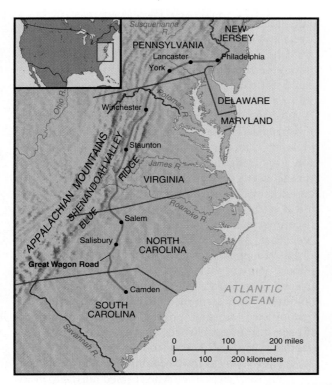

**THE GREAT WAGON ROAD**    *By the mid-eighteenth century, the Great Wagon road had become the major highway for the settlers in the Virginia and Carolina backcountry.* ❖

dented evangelical outpouring altered the course of American history. In our own time, of course, the force of religious revival has been witnessed in different regions throughout the world. It is no exaggeration to claim that a similar populist movement took place in mid-eighteenth-century America, and the new, highly personal appeal to a "new birth" in Christ caused men and women of all backgrounds to rethink basic assumptions about church and state, institutions and society.

## The Great Awakening

Only with hindsight does the Great Awakening seem a unified religious movement. Revivals occurred in different places at different times; the intensity of the events varied from region to region. The first signs of a spiritual awakening appeared in New England during the 1730s, but within a decade the revivals in this area had burned themselves out. It was not until the 1750s and 1760s that the Awakening made more than a superficial impact on the people of Virginia. The revivals were most important in Massachusetts, Connecticut, Rhode Island, Pennsylvania, New Jersey, and Virginia. Their effect on religion in New York, Delaware, and the Carolinas was marginal. No single religious denomination or sect monopolized the Awakening. In New

England, revivals shattered Congregational churches, and in the South, especially in Virginia, they had an impact on Presbyterians, Methodists, and Baptists. Moreover, there was nothing peculiarly American about the Great Awakening. Mid-eighteenth-century Europe experienced a similar burst of religious emotionalism.

Whatever their origins, the seeds of revival were generally sown on fertile ground. In the early decades of the century, many Americans—but especially New Englanders—complained that organized religion had lost vitality. They looked back at Winthrop's generation with nostalgia, assuming that common people at that time must have possessed greater piety than did later, more worldly colonists. Congregational ministers seemed obsessed with dull, scholastic matters; they no longer touched the heart. And in the Southern Colonies, there were simply not enough ordained ministers to tend to the religious needs of the population.

The Great Awakening arrived unexpectedly in Northampton, a small farm community in western Massachusetts, sparked by Jonathan Edwards, the local Congregational minister. Edwards accepted the traditional teachings of Calvinism (see Chapter 1), reminding his parishioners that their eternal fate had been determined by an omnipotent God, there was nothing they could do to save themselves, and they were totally dependent on the Lord's will. He thought his fellow ministers had grown soft. They left men and women with the mistaken impression that sinners might somehow avoid eternal damnation simply by performing good works. "How dismal will it be," Edwards told his complacent congregation, "when you are under these racking torments, to know assuredly that you never, never shall be delivered from them." Edwards was not exaggerating his message in an attempt to be dramatic. He spoke of God's omnipotence with such self-assurance that even people who had not thought deeply about religious matters were shaken by his words.

Why this uncompromising message set off several religious revivals during the mid-1730s is not known. Whatever the explanation for the popular response to Edwards's preaching, young people began flocking to the church. They experienced a searing conversion, a sense of "new birth" and utter dependence on God. "Surely," Edwards pronounced, "this is the Lord's doing, and it is marvelous in our eyes." The excitement spread, and evangelical ministers concluded that God must be preparing Americans, his chosen people, for the millennium. "What is now seen in America and especially in New England," Edwards explained, "may prove the dawn of that glorious day."

## The Voice of Popular Religion

Edwards was a brilliant theologian, but he did not possess the dynamic personality required to sustain the revival. That responsibility fell to George Whitefield, a young, inspiring preacher from England who toured the colonies from New Hampshire to Georgia. While Whitefield was not an original thinker, he was an extraordinarily effective public speaker. And like his friend Benjamin Franklin, he came to symbolize the powerful cultural forces that were transforming the Atlantic world. According to Edwards's wife, Sarah, it was wonderful to witness what a spell Whitefield "casts over an audience . . . I have seen upwards of a thousand people hang on his words with breathless silence, broken only by an occasional half-suppressed sob."

Whitefield's audiences came from all groups of American society: rich and poor, young and old, rural and urban. While Whitefield described himself as a Calvinist, he welcomed all Protestants. He spoke from any pulpit that was available. "Don't tell me you are a Baptist, an Independent, a Presbyterian, a dissenter," he thundered, "tell me you are a Christian, that is all I want."

Whitefield was a brilliant entrepreneur. Like Franklin, with whom he published many popular vol-

umes, the itinerant minister possessed an almost intuitive sense of how this burgeoning consumer society could be turned to his own advantage, and he embraced the latest merchandising techniques. He appreciated, for example, the power of the press in selling the revival, and he regularly promoted his own work in advertisements placed in British and American newspapers. The crowds flocked to hear Whitefield, while his critics grumbled about the commercialization of religion. One anonymous writer in Massachusetts noted that there was "a very wholesome law of the province to discourage Pedlars in Trade" and it seemed high time "to enact something for the discouragement of Pedlars in Divinity also."

Other American-born **itinerant preachers** followed Whitefield's example. The most famous was Gilbert Tennent, a Presbyterian of Scots-Irish background who had been educated in the Middle Colonies. His sermon "On the Danger of an Unconverted Ministry," printed in 1741, set off a storm of protest from established ministers who were understandably insulted. Lesser known revivalists traveled from town to town, colony to colony, challenging local clergymen who seemed hostile to evangelical religion. Men and women who thronged to hear the itinerants were called "New Lights," and during the 1740s and 1750s, many congregations split between defenders of the new emotional preaching and those who regarded the entire movement as dangerous nonsense.

Despite Whitefield's successes, many ministers remained suspicious of the itinerants and their methods. Some complaints may have amounted to little more than sour grapes. One "Old Light" spokesman labeled Tennent "a monster! impudent and noisy." He claimed Tennent told anxious Christians that "they were damned! damned! damned! This charmed them; and, in the most dreadful winter I ever saw, people wallowed in snow, night and day, for the benefit of his beastly brayings; and many ended their days under these fatigues." Charles Chauncy, minister of the prestigious First Church of Boston, raised much more troubling issues. How could the revivalists be certain God had sparked the Great Awakening? Perhaps the itinerants had relied too much on emotion? "Let us esteem those as friends of religion," Chauncy advised, " . . . who warn us of the danger of enthusiasm, and would put us on our guard, that we may not be led aside by it."

While Tennent did not condone the excesses of the Great Awakening, his attacks on formal learning invited the crude anti-intellectualism of such fanatics as James Davenport. This deranged

*The fervor of the Great Awakening was intensified by the eloquence of itinerant preachers such as George Whitefield, the most popular evangelical of the mid-eighteenth century.* ❖

revivalist traveled along the Connecticut coast in 1742 playing upon popular emotion. At night, under the light of smoky torches, he danced and stripped, shrieked and laughed. He also urged people to burn books written by authors who had not experienced the New Light as defined by Davenport. Like so many fanatics throughout history who have claimed a special knowledge of the "truth," Davenport later recanted and begged pardon for his disruptive behavior.

To concentrate on the bizarre activities of Davenport—as many critics of the Great Awakening have done—is to obscure the positive ways in which this vast revival changed American society. First, despite occasional anti-intellectual outbursts, the New Lights founded several important centers of higher learning. They wanted to train young men who would carry on the good works of Edwards, Whitefield, and Tennent. In 1746, New Light Presbyterians established the College of New Jersey, which later became Princeton University. Just before his death, Edwards was appointed its president. The evangelical minister Eleazar Wheelock launched Dartmouth (1769); other revivalists founded Brown (1764) and Rutgers (1766).

The Great Awakening also encouraged men and women who had been taught to remain silent before traditional figures of authority to speak up, to take an active role in their salvation. They could no longer rely on ministers or institutions. The individual alone stood before God. Knowing this, New Lights made religious choices that shattered the old harmony among Protestant sects, and in its place, they introduced a noisy, often bitterly fought competition. As one New Jersey Presbyterian explained, "There are so many particular *sects* and *Parties* among professed Christians . . . that we know not . . . in which of these different *paths,* to steer our course for *Heaven.*"

Expressive evangelicalism struck a particularly responsive chord among African Americans. Itinerant ministers frequently preached to large sympathetic audiences of slaves. Richard Allen (1760–1831), founder of the African Methodist Episcopal Church, reported he owed his freedom in part to a traveling Methodist minister who persuaded Allen's master of the sinfulness of slavery. Allen himself was converted, as were thousands of other black colonists. According to one historian, evangelical preaching "shared enough with traditional African styles and beliefs such as spirit possession and ecstatic expression . . . to allow for an interpenetration of African and Christian religious beliefs."

With religious contention came an awareness of a larger community, a union of fellow believers that extended beyond the boundaries of town and colony. In fact, evangelical religion was one of several forces at work during the mid-eighteenth century that brought scattered colonists into contact with one another for the first time. In this sense, the Great Awakening was a "national" event long before a nation actually existed.

People who had been touched by the Great Awakening shared an optimism about the future of America. With God's help, social and political progress was possible, and from this perspective, of course, the New Lights did not sound much different than the mildly rationalist American spokesmen of the Enlightenment. Both groups prepared the way for the development of a revolutionary mentality in colonial America.

# CLASH OF POLITICAL CULTURES

The political history of this period illuminates a growing tension within the empire. Americans of all regions repeatedly stated their desire to replicate British political institutions. Parliament, they claimed, provided a model for the American assemblies. They revered the English constitution. However, the more the colonists studied British political theory and practice—in other words, the more they attempted to become British—the more aware they became of major differences. By trying to copy Great Britain, they unwittingly discovered something about being American.

## The English Constitution

During the eighteenth century, political discussion began with the British constitution. It was the object of universal admiration. Unlike the U.S. Constitution of 1788, the British constitution was not a formal written document. It was something much more elusive. The English constitution found expression in a growing body of law, court decisions, and statutes, a sense of traditional political arrangements that people of all classes believed had evolved from the past, preserving life, liberty, and property. Eighteenth-century political commentators reluctantly admitted that the constitution had in fact changed. Historic confrontations between king and Parliament had generated new understandings about what the constitution did or did not allow. Nevertheless, almost everyone regarded change as dangerous and destabilizing, a threat to the political tradition that seemed to explain Britain's greatness.

In theory, the English constitution contained three distinct parts. The monarch was at the top, advised by handpicked court favorites. Next came the House of Lords, a body of 180 aristocrats who served with 26 Anglican bishops as the upper house of Parliament. And third was the House of Commons, composed of 558 members elected by various constituencies scattered throughout the realm.

Political theorists waxed eloquent on workings of the British constitution. Each of the three parts of government, it seemed, represented a separate socioeconomic interest: king, nobility, and common people. Acting alone, each body would run to excess, even tyranny, but operating within a mixed system, they automatically checked each other's ambitions for the common good. "Herein consists the excellence of the English government," explained the famed eighteenth-century jurist Sir William Blackstone, "that all parts of it form a mutual check upon each other." Unlike the delegates who wrote the Constitution of the United States, eighteenth-century Englishmen did not perceive their constitution as a balance of executive, legislative, and judicial branches.

## The Reality of British Politics

The reality of daily political life in Great Britain, however, bore little relation to theory. The three elements of the constitution did not, in fact, represent distinct socioeconomic groups. Men elected to the House of Commons often came from the same social background as those who served in the House of Lords. All represented the interests of Britain's landed elite. Moreover, there was no attempt to maintain strict constitutional separation. The king, for example, organized parliamentary associations, loose groups of political followers who sat in the House of Commons and who openly supported the monarch's policies in exchange for patronage or pension.

The claim that the members of the House of Commons represented all the people of England also seemed far-fetched. As of 1715, no more than 20 percent of Britain's adult males had the right to vote. Property qualifications or other restrictions often greatly reduced the number of eligible voters. In addition, the size of the electoral districts varied throughout the kingdom. In some boroughs, representatives to Parliament were chosen by several thousand voters. In many districts, however, a handful of electors controlled the result. These tiny, or "rotten," boroughs were an embarrassment. The Methodist leader John Wesley complained that Old Sarum, an almost uninhabited borough, "in spite of common sense, without house or inhabitant, still sends two members to the parliament." Since these districts were so small, a wealthy lord or ambitious politician could easily bribe or otherwise "influence" the entire constituency, something done regularly throughout the century.

Before 1760, few people spoke out against these constitutional abuses. The main exception was a group of radical publicists whom historians have labeled the Commonwealthmen. These writers decried the cor-

ruption of political life, noting that a nation that compromised civic virtue, that failed to stand vigilant against fawning courtiers and would-be despots, deserved to lose its liberty and property. The most famous Commonwealthmen were John Trenchard and Thomas Gordon, who penned a series of essays titled *Cato's Letters* between 1720 and 1723. If England's rulers were corrupt, they warned, then the people could not expect the balanced constitution to save them from tyranny. In one typical article, Trenchard and Gordon observed, "The Appitites . . . of Men, especially of Great Men, are carefully to be observed and stayed, or else they will never stay themselves. The Experience of every Age convinces us, that we must not judge of Men by what they ought to do, but by what they will do."

But however shrilly these writers protested, they won little support for political reforms. Most eighteenth-century Englishmen admitted there was more than a grain of truth in the commonwealth critique, but they were not willing to tamper with a system of government that had so recently survived a civil war and a Glorious Revolution. Americans, however, took Trenchard and Gordon to heart.

## Governing the Colonies: The American Experience

The colonists assumed—perhaps naively—that their own governments were modeled on the balanced constitution of Great Britain. They argued that within their political systems, the governor corresponded to the king and the governor's council to the House of Lords. The colonial assemblies were perceived as American reproductions of the House of Commons and were expected to preserve the interests of the people against those of the monarch and aristocracy. As the colonists discovered, however, general theories about a mixed constitution were even less relevant in America than they were in Britain.

By midcentury a majority of the mainland colonies had royal governors appointed by the crown. Many were career army officers who through luck, charm, or family connection had gained the ear of someone close to the king. These patronage posts did not generate income sufficient to interest the most powerful or talented personalities of the period, but they did draw middle-level bureaucrats who were ambitious, desperate, or both. It is perhaps not surprising that most governors decided simply not to "consider any Thing further than how to sit easy."

George Clinton, who served as New York's governor from 1743 to 1753, was probably typical of the men who hoped to "sit easy." Before coming to the colonies, Clinton had compiled an extraordinary record of ineptitude as a naval officer. He gained the governorship more as a means to get him out of England than as a sign of respect. When he arrived in New York City, Clinton ignored the colonists. "In a province given to hospitality," wrote one critic, "he [Clinton] erred by immuring himself in the fort, or retiring to a grotto in the country, where his time was spent with his bottle and a little trifling circle."

Whatever their demerits, royal governors in America possessed enormous powers. In fact, royal governors could do certain things in America that a king could not do in eighteenth-century Britain. Among these were the right to veto legislation and dismiss judges. The governors also served as military commanders in each province.

Political practice in America differed from the British model in another crucial respect. Royal governors were advised by a council, usually a body of about twelve wealthy colonists selected by the Board of Trade in London upon the recommendation of the governor. During the seventeenth century, the council had played an important role in colonial government, but its ability to exercise independent authority declined steadily over the course of the eighteenth century. Its members certainly did not represent a distinct aristocracy within American society.

If royal governors did not look like kings, nor American councils like the House of Lords, colonial assemblies bore little resemblance to the eighteenth-century House of Commons. The major difference was the size of the American franchise. In most colonies, adult white males who owned a small amount of land could vote in colonywide elections. One historian estimates that 95 percent of this group in Massachusetts were eligible to participate in elections. The number in Virginia was about 85 percent. These figures—much higher than those in contemporary England—have led some scholars to view the colonies as "middle-class democracies," societies run by moderately prosperous yeomen farmers who—in politics at least—exercised independent judgment. There were too many of them to bribe, no "rotten" boroughs, and when these people moved west, colonial assemblies usually created new electoral districts.

Colonial governments were not democracies in the modern sense of that term. Possessing the right to vote was one thing, exercising it quite another. Americans participated in elections when major issues were at stake—the formation of banks in mid-eighteenth-century Massachusetts, for example—but most of the time they were content to let members of the rural and urban gentry represent them in the assemblies. To be sure, unlike modern democracies, these colonial politics excluded women and nonwhites from voting. The point to remember, however, is that the power to expel legislative rascals was always present in America, and it was this political reality that kept autocratic gentlemen from straying too far from the will of the people.

## Colonial Assemblies

Elected members of the colonial assemblies believed that they had a special obligation to preserve colonial liberties. They perceived any attack on the legislature as an assault on the rights of Americans. The elected representatives brooked no criticism, and several colonial printers landed in jail because they criticized actions taken by a lower house.

So aggressive were these bodies in seizing privileges, determining procedures, and controlling money bills that some historians have described the political development of eighteenth-century America as "the rise of the assemblies." No doubt this is exaggerated, but the long series of imperial wars against the French, demanding large public expenditures, transformed the small, amateurish assemblies of the seventeenth century into the more professional, vigilant legislatures of the eighteenth.

This political system seemed designed to generate hostility. There was simply no reason for the colonial legislators to cooperate with appointed royal governors. Alexander Spotswood, Virginia's governor from 1710 to 1722, for example, attempted to institute a bold new land program backed by the crown. He tried persuasion and gifts and, when these failed, chicanery. But the members of the House of Burgesses refused to support a plan that did not suit their own interests. Before leaving office, Spotswood gave up trying to carry out royal policy in America. Instead, he allied himself with the local Virginia gentry who controlled the House as well as the Council, and because they awarded their new friend with large tracts of land, he became a wealthy man.

A few governors managed briefly to re-create in America the political culture of patronage, the system that eighteenth-century Englishmen took for granted. Most successful in this endeavor was William Shirley, who held office in Massachusetts from 1741 to 1757. The secret to his political successes in America was connection to people who held high office in Great Britain. But Shirley's practices—and those of men like him—clashed with the colonists' perception of politics. They really believed in the purity of the balanced constitution. They insisted on complete separation of executive and legislative authority. Therefore, when Americans suspected a governor, or even some of their own representatives, of employing patronage to influence government decisions, their protests seem to have been lifted directly from the pages of *Cato's Letters.*

A major source of shared political information was the weekly journal, a new and vigorous institution in American life. In New York and Massachusetts especially, weekly newspapers urged readers to preserve civic virtue, to exercise extreme vigilance against the spread of privileged power. In the first issue of the *Independent Reflector,* published in New York (November 30, 1752), the editor announced defiantly that no discouragement shall "deter me from vindicating the *civil and religious RIGHTS* of my Fellow-Creatures: From exposing the peculiar Deformity of publick *Vice,* and *Corruption;* and displaying the amiable Charms of Liberty, with the detestable Nature of *Slavery* and *Oppression.*" Through such journals, a pattern of political rhetoric that in Britain had gained only marginal respectability became after 1765 America's normal form of political discourse.

The rise of the assemblies shaped American culture in other, subtler ways. Over the course of the cen-

*Colonial newspapers were an important means of political participation. The masthead of this edition of* The Massachusetts Spy *declares its journalistic objectivity: "A Weekly, Political, and Commercial Paper; open to ALL Parties, but influenced by None."* ❖

tury, the language of the law became increasingly Anglicized. The Board of Trade, the Privy Council, and Parliament scrutinized court decisions and legislative actions from all thirteen mainland colonies. As a result, varying local legal practices that had been widespread during the seventeenth century became standardized. Indeed, according to one historian, the colonial legal system by 1750 "was substantially that of the mother country." Not surprisingly, many men who served in colonial assemblies were either lawyers or persons who had received legal training. When Americans from different regions met—as they frequently did in the years before the Revolution—they discovered that they shared a commitment to the preservation of the English common law.

As eighteenth-century political developments drew the colonists closer to the mother country, they also brought Americans a greater awareness of each other. As their horizons widened, they learned they operated within the same general imperial system, and the problems confronting the Massachusetts House of Representatives were not too different from those facing Virginia's House of Burgesses or South Carolina's Commons House. Like the revivalists and merchants—people who crossed old boundaries—colonial legislators laid the foundation for a larger cultural identity.

## CENTURY OF IMPERIAL WAR

The scope and character of warfare in the colonies changed radically during the eighteenth century. The founders of England's mainland colonies had engaged in intense local conflicts with the Indians, such as King Philip's War (1675–1676) in New England. But after 1690, the colonists were increasingly involved in hostilities that originated on the other side of the Atlantic, in rivalries between Great Britain and France over political and commercial ambitions. The external threat to security forced people in different colonies to devise unprecedented measures of military and political cooperation.

On paper, at least, the British colonies enjoyed military superiority over the settlements of New France. Louis XIV (r. 1643–1715) possessed an impressive army of 100,000 well-armed troops, but he dispatched few of them to the New World. He left the defense of Canada and the Mississippi Valley to the companies engaged in the fur trade. Meeting this challenge seemed almost impossible for the French outposts strung out along the St. Lawrence River and the Great Lakes. In 1754, New France contained only 75,000 inhabitants as compared to 1.2 million people living in Britain's mainland colonies.

For most of the century, the theoretical advantages enjoyed by the English colonists did them little

**NORTH AMERICA, 1750**
*By 1750, the French had established a chain of settlements southward through the heart of the continent from Quebec to New Orleans. The British saw this development as a threat to their own seaboard colonies, which were expanding westward.* ❖

good. While the British settlements possessed a larger and more prosperous population, they were divided into separate governments that sometimes seemed more suspicious of each other than of the French. When war came, French officers and Indian allies exploited these jealousies with considerable skill. Moreover, although the population of New France was comparatively small, it was concentrated along the St. Lawrence, so that while the French found it difficult to mount effective offensive operations against the English, they could easily mass the forces needed to defend Montreal and Quebec.

## King William's and Queen Anne's Wars

Colonial involvement in imperial war began in 1689, when England's new king, William III, declared war on Louis XIV. Europeans called this struggle the War of the League of Augsburg, but to the Americans, it was simply King William's War. Canadians commanded by the Comte de Frontenac raided the northern frontiers of New York and New England, and while they made

no territorial gains, they caused considerable suffering among the civilian populations of Massachusetts and New York.

The war ended with the Treaty of Ryswick (1697), but the colonists were drawn almost immediately into a new conflict. Queen Anne's War, known in Europe as the War of the Spanish Succession (1702–1713), was fought across a large geographic area. The bloody combat along the American frontier ended in 1713 when Great Britain and France signed the Treaty of Utrecht. European negotiators showed little interest in the military situation in the New World. Their major concern was preserving a balance of power among the European states. More than two decades of intense fighting had taken a heavy toll in North America, but neither French nor English colonists had much to show for their sacrifice.

After George I replaced Anne on the throne in 1714, parliamentary leaders were determined to preserve peace—mainly because of the rising cost of war. Yet on the American frontier, the hostilities continued with raids and reprisals. As people on both sides of this conflict now realized, the stakes of war were very high;

*Native Americans often depended on trade goods supplied by the British and sometimes adopted British dress. Here the Mohawk chief Theyanoguin, called King Hendrick by the British, wears a cloak he received from Queen Anne of England during a visit to London in 1710. During the Seven Years' War, Theyanoguin mobilized Mohawk support for the British.* ❖

they were fighting for control over the entire West, including the Mississippi Valley.

Both sides viewed this great contest in conspiratorial terms. From South Carolina to Massachusetts Bay, colonists believed the French planned to "encircle" the English settlements, to confine the English to a narrow strip of land along the Atlantic coast. The English noted that in 1682, La Salle had claimed for the king of France a territory—Louisiana—that included all the people and resources located on "streams and Rivers" flowing into the Mississippi River. To make good on their claim, the French constructed forts on the Chicago and Illinois rivers. In

1717, they established a military post two hundred miles up the Alabama River, well within striking distance of the Carolina frontier, and in 1718, they settled New Orleans. One New Yorker declared in 1715 that "it is impossible that we and the French can both inhabit this Continent in peace but that one nation must at last give way to the other."

On their part, the French suspected their rivals intended to seize all of North America. Land speculators and frontier traders pushed aggressively into territory claimed by the French and owned by the Native Americans. In 1716, one Frenchman urged his government to hasten the development of Louisiana, since "it is not difficult to guess that their [the British] purpose is to drive us entirely out . . . of North America."

To their great sorrow and eventual destruction, the original inhabitants of the frontier, the Native Americans, were swept up in this undeclared war. The Indians maneuvered to hold their own in the "middle ground." The Iroquois favored the British; the Algonquian peoples generally supported the French. But regardless of the groups to which they belonged, Indian warriors—acting independently and for their own strategic reasons—found themselves enmeshed in imperial policies set by distant European kings.

## King George's War and Its Aftermath

In 1743, the Americans were dragged once again into the imperial conflict. During King George's War (1743–1748), known in Europe as the War of the Austrian Succession, the colonists scored a magnificent victory over the French. Louisbourg, a gigantic fortress on Cape Breton Island, the easternmost promontory of Canada, guarded the approaches to the Gulf of St. Lawrence and Quebec. It was described as the Gibraltar of the New World. An army of New England troops under the command of William Pepperrell captured Louisbourg in June 1745, a feat that demonstrated the British colonists were able to fight and to mount effective joint operations.

The Americans, however, were in for a shock. When the war ended with the signing of the Treaty of Aix-la-Chapelle in 1748, the British government handed Louisbourg back to the French in exchange for concessions elsewhere. Such decisions exposed the deep and continuing ambivalence the colonists felt about participation in imperial wars. They were proud to support Great Britain, of course, but the Americans seldom fully understood why the wars were being fought, why certain tactics had been adopted, and why the British accepted treaty terms that so blatantly ignored colonial interests.

The French were not prepared to surrender an inch. But as they recognized, time was running against them. Not only were the English colonies growing more populous, but they also possessed a seemingly inexhaustible supply of manufactured goods to trade with the Indians. The French decided in the early 1750s, therefore, to seize the Ohio Valley before the Virginians could do so. They established forts throughout the region, the most formidable being Fort Duquesne, located at the strategic fork in the Ohio River and later renamed Pittsburgh.

Although France and England had not officially declared war, British officials advised the governor of Virginia to "repell force by force." The Virginians needed little encouragement. They were eager to make good their claim to the Ohio Valley, and in 1754, militia companies under the command of a promising young officer, George Washington, constructed Fort Necessity not far from Fort Duquesne. The plan failed. French and Indian troops overran the badly exposed outpost (July 3, 1754). Among other things, the humiliating setback revealed that a single colony could not defeat the French.

## Albany Congress and Braddock's Defeat

Benjamin Franklin, for one, appreciated the need for intercolonial cooperation. When British officials invited representatives from the Northern Colonies to Albany (June 1754) to discuss relations with the Iroquois, Franklin used the occasion to present a bold blueprint for colonial union. His so-called **Albany Plan** envisioned the formation of a Grand Council, made up of elected delegates from the various colonies, to oversee matters of common defense, western expansion, and Indian affairs. A President General appointed by the king would preside. Franklin's most daring suggestion involved taxation. He insisted the council be authorized to collect taxes to cover military expenditures.

*The first political cartoon to appear in an American newspaper was created by Benjamin Franklin in 1754 to emphasize the importance of the Albany Plan.* ❖

First reaction to the Albany Plan was enthusiastic. To take effect, however, it required the support of the separate colonial assemblies as well as Parliament. It received neither. The assemblies were jealous of their fiscal authority, and the English thought the scheme undermined the crown's power over American affairs.

In 1755, the Ohio Valley again became the scene of fierce fighting. Even though there was still no formal declaration of war, the British resolved to destroy Fort Duquesne, and to that end, they dispatched units of the regular army to America. In command was Major General Edward Braddock, an obese, humorless veteran who inspired neither fear nor respect. One colonist described Braddock as "very indolent, Slave to his passions, women & wine, as great an Epicure as could be in his eating, tho a brave man."

On July 9, Braddock led a joint force of twenty-five hundred British redcoats and colonists to

*This mid-eighteenth-century lithograph portrays colonial assault troops, under the command of William Pepperrell, establishing a beachhead at Freshwater Cove near Louisbourg. Pepperrell's troops went on to capture the French fortress at Louisbourg.* ❖

## A CENTURY OF CONFLICT: MAJOR WARS, 1689–1763

| Dates | European Name | American Name | Major Allies | Issues | Major American Battle | Treaty |
|---|---|---|---|---|---|---|
| 1689–1697 | War of the League of Augsburg | King William's War | Britain, Holland, Spain, their colonies, and Native American allies against France, its colonies, and Native American allies | Opposition to French bid for control of Europe | New England troops assault Quebec under Sir William Phips (1690) | Treaty of Ryswick (1697) |
| 1702–1713 | War of the Spanish Succession | Queen Anne's War | Britain, Holland, their colonies, and Native American allies against France, Spain, their colonies, and Native American allies | Austria and France hold rival claims to Spanish throne | Attack on Deerfield (1704) | Treaty of Utrecht (1713) |
| 1743–1748 | War of the Austrian Succession (War of Jenkin's Ear) | King George's War | Britain, its colonies, and Native American allies, and Austria against France, Spain, their Native American allies, and Prussia | Struggle among Britain, Spain, and France for control of New World territory; among France, Prussia, and Austria for control of central Europe | New England forces capture of Louisbourg under William Pepperrell (1745) | Treaty of Aix-la-Chapelle (1748) |
| 1756–1763 | Seven Years' War | French and Indian War | Britain, its colonies, and Native American allies against France, its colonies, and Native American allies | Struggle among Britain, Spain, and France for worldwide control of colonial markets and raw materials | British and Continental forces capture Quebec under Major General James Wolfe (1759) | Peace of Paris (1763) |

humiliating defeat. The French and Indians opened fire as Braddock's army waded across the Monongahela River, about eight miles from Fort Duquesne. Along a narrow road already congested with heavy wagons and confused men, Braddock ordered a counterattack, described by one of his officers as "without any form or order but that of a parcell of school boys coming out of s[c]hool." Nearly 70 percent of Braddock's troops were killed or wounded in western Pennsylvania. The general himself died in battle. The French, who suffered only light casualties, remained in firm control of the Ohio Valley.

The entire affair profoundly angered Washington, who fumed, "We have been most scandalously beaten by a trifling body of men." The British thought their allies the Iroquois might desert them after the embarrassing defeat. The Indians, however, took the news in stride, observing that "they were not at all surprised to hear it, as they [Braddock's redcoats] were men who had crossed the Great Water and were unacquainted with the arts of war among the Americans."

## Seven Years' War

Britain's imperial war effort had hit bottom. No one in England or America seemed to possess the leadership necessary to drive the French from the Mississippi Valley. The cabinet of George II (r. 1727–1760) lacked the will to organize and finance a sustained military campaign in the New World, and colonial assemblies balked every time Britain asked them to raise men and money. On May 18, 1756, the British officially declared war on the French, a conflict called the French and Indian War in America and the **Seven Years' War** in Europe.

Had it not been for William Pitt, the most powerful minister in George's cabinet, the military stalemate might have continued. This supremely self-confident Englishman believed he was the only person capable of saving the British empire, an opinion he publicly expressed. When he became effective head of the ministry in December 1756, Pitt had an opportunity to demonstrate his talents.

In the past, warfare on the European continent had worked mainly to France's advantage. Pitt saw no point in continuing to concentrate on Europe, and in 1757 he advanced a bold new imperial policy, one based on commercial assumptions. In Pitt's judgment, the critical confrontation would take place in North America, where Britain and France were struggling to control colonial markets and raw materials. Indeed, according to Pitt, America was "where England and Europe are to

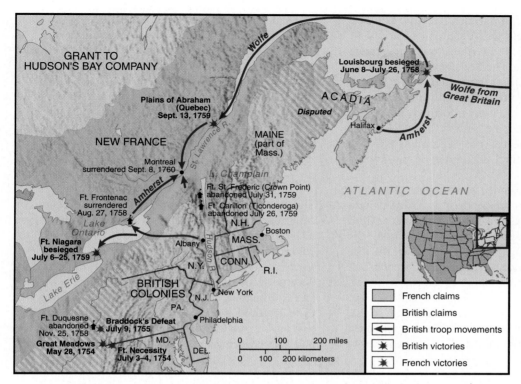

GRANT TO
HUDSON'S BAY COMPANY

Louisbourg besieged
June 8–July 26, 1758

Wolfe from
Great Britain

Plains of Abraham
(Quebec)
Sept. 13, 1759

ACADIA
*Disputed*

Halifax

Amherst

NEW FRANCE

MAINE
(part of
Mass.)

Montreal
surrendered Sept. 8, 1760

L. Champlain

ATLANTIC OCEAN

Ft. St. Frederic (Crown Point)
abandoned July 31, 1759

Ft. Frontenac
surrendered
Aug. 27, 1758

Ft. Carillon (Ticonderoga)
abandoned July 26, 1759

Lake
Ontario

N.H.

Ft. Niagara
besieged
July 6–25, 1759

Albany

MASS.

Boston

CONN.

Lake Erie

N.Y.

R.I.

BRITISH
COLONIES

N.J.

New York

PA.

Ft. Duquesne
abandoned
Nov. 25, 1758

Braddock's Defeat
July 9, 1755

Philadelphia

Great Meadows
May 28, 1754

Ft. Necessity
July 3–4, 1754

MD.

DEL.

| 0 | | 100 | | 200 miles |
| 0 | 100 | 200 kilometers | | |

French claims

British claims

British troop movements

British victories

French victories

**THE SEVEN YEARS' WAR, 1756–1763**    *Major battle sites. The conflict ended with Great Britain driving the French from mainland North America.* ❖

be fought for." He was determined, therefore, to expel the French from the continent, however great the cost.

To effect this ambitious scheme, Pitt took personal command of the army and navy. He mapped strategy. He even promoted young promising officers over the heads of their superiors. He also recognized that the success of the war effort could not depend on the generosity of the colonial assemblies. Great Britain would have to foot most of the bill. Pitt's military expenditures, of course, created an enormous national debt that would soon haunt both Britain and its colonies, but at the time, no one foresaw the fiscal consequences of victory in America.

To direct the grand campaign, Pitt selected two relatively obscure officers, Jeffrey Amherst and James Wolfe. It was a masterful choice, one that a less self-assured man than Pitt would never have risked. Both officers were young, talented, and ambitious, and on July 26, 1758, forces under their direction captured Louisbourg, the same fortress the colonists had taken a decade earlier!

This victory cut the Canadians' main supply line with France. The small population of New France could no longer meet the military demands placed on it.

As the situation became increasingly desperate, the French forts of the Ohio Valley and the Great Lakes began to fall. Duquesne was simply abandoned late in 1758 as French and Indian troops under the Marquis de Montcalm retreated toward Quebec and Montreal. During the summer of 1759, the French surrendered key forts at Ticonderoga, Crown Point, and Niagara.

The climax to a century of war came dramatically in September 1759. Wolfe, now a major general, assaulted Quebec with nine thousand men. But it was not simply force of arms that brought victory. Wolfe proceeded as if he were preparing to attack the city

*Powder horn illustrating New York battle scenes in the Seven Years' War, made by Samuel Davidson, May 27, 1765.* ❖

directly, but under cover of darkness, his troops scaled a cliff to dominate a less well defended position. At dawn on September 13, 1759, they took the French from the rear by surprise. The decisive action occurred on the Plains of Abraham, a bluff high above the St. Lawrence River. Both Wolfe and Montcalm were mortally wounded. When an aide informed Wolfe the French had been routed, he sighed, "Now, God be praised, I will die in peace." On September 8, 1760, Amherst accepted the final surrender of the French army at Montreal.

The Peace of Paris signed on February 10, 1763, almost fulfilled Pitt's grandiose dreams. Great Britain took possession of an empire that stretched around the globe. Only Guadeloupe and Martinique, the Caribbean sugar islands, were given back to the French. After a centurylong struggle, the French had been driven from the mainland of North America. Even Louisiana passed out of France's control into Spanish hands. The treaty gave Britain title to Canada, Florida, and all the land east of the Mississippi River. Moreover, with the stroke of a diplomat's pen, eighty

thousand French-speaking Canadians, most of them Catholics, became the subjects of George III.

The Americans were overjoyed. It was a time of good feelings and national pride. Together, the English and their colonial allies had thwarted the "Gallic peril." Samuel Davies, a Presbyterian who had brought the Great Awakening to Virginia, announced confidently that the long-awaited victory would inaugurate "a new heaven and a new earth."

## Perceptions of War

The Seven Years' War made a deep impression on American society. Even though Franklin's Albany Plan had failed, the military struggle had forced the colonists to cooperate on an unprecedented scale. It also drew them into closer contact with Britain. They became aware of being part of a great empire, military and commercial, but in the very process of waging war, they acquired a more intimate sense of an America that lay beyond the plantation and the village. Conflict had carried thousands of young men across colonial

**NORTH AMERICA AFTER 1763**    *The Peace of Paris (1763) redrew the map of North America. Great Britain received all the French holdings except a few islands in the Atlantic and some sugar-producing islands in the Caribbean.* ❖

boundaries, exposing them to a vast territory full of opportunities for a booming population. Moreover, the war trained a corps of American officers, people like George Washington, who learned from firsthand experience that the British were not invincible.

British officials later accused the Americans of ingratitude. England, they claimed, had sent troops and provided funds to liberate the colonists from the threat of French attack. The Americans, appreciative of the aid from England, cheered on the British but dragged their feet at every stage, refusing to pay the bills. These charges were later incorporated into a general argument justifying parliamentary taxation in America.

The British had a point. The colonists were, in fact, slow in providing the men and materials needed to fight the French. Nevertheless, they did make a significant contribution to the war effort, and it was perfectly reasonable for Americans to regard themselves at the very least as junior partners in the empire. After all, they had supplied almost twenty thousand soldiers and spent well over £2 million. In a single year, in fact, Massachusetts enlisted five thousand men out of an adult male population of about fifty thousand, a commitment that, in the words of one military historian, meant "the war was being waged on a scale comparable to the great wars of modern times." After making such a sacrifice—indeed, after demonstrating their loyalty to the mother country—the colonists would surely have been disturbed to learn that General James Wolfe, the hero of Quebec, had stated, "The Americans are in general the dirtiest, the most contemptible, cowardly dogs that you can conceive. There is no depending upon them in action. They fall down in their own dirt and desert in battalions, officers and all."

## CONCLUSION: RULE BRITANNIA?

James Thomson, an Englishman, understood the hold of empire on the popular imagination of the eighteenth century. In 1740, he composed words that British patriots have proudly sung for more than two centuries:

> Rule Britannia, rule the waves,
>   Britons never will be slaves.

Colonial Americans—at least, those of British background—joined the chorus. By midcentury they took their political and cultural cues from Great Britain. They fought its wars, purchased its consumer goods, flocked to hear its evangelical preachers, and read its many publications. Without question, the empire provided the colonists with a compelling source of identity.

## CHRONOLOGY

| | |
|---|---|
| **1680** | El Popé leads Pueblo revolt against the Spanish in New Mexico |
| **1689** | William and Mary accede to the English throne |
| **1706** | Birth of Benjamin Franklin |
| **1714** | George I of Hanover becomes monarch of Great Britain |
| **1732** | Colony of Georgia is established  ❖  Birth of George Washington |
| **1734–1736** | First expression of the Great Awakening at Northampton, Massachusetts |
| **1740** | George Whitefield electrifies listeners at Boston |
| **1745** | Colonial troops capture Louisbourg |
| **1748** | American Lutheran ministers ordained in Philadelphia |
| **1754** | Albany Congress meets |
| **1755** | Braddock is defeated by the French and Indians in western Pennsylvania |
| **1756** | Seven Years' War is formally declared |
| **1759** | British are victorious at Quebec; Wolfe and Montcalm are killed in battle |
| **1760** | George III becomes king of Great Britain |
| **1763** | Peace of Paris ending French and Indian War is signed |
| **1769** | Junípero Serra begins to build missions in California |
| **1821** | Mexico declares independence from Spain |

An editor justified the establishment of New Hampshire's first newspaper in precisely these terms. "By this Means," the publisher observed, "the spirited *Englishman*, the mountainous *Welshman*, the brave *Scotchman,* and *Irishman,* and the loyal *American,* may be firmly united and mutually RESOLVED to guard the glorious Throne of BRITANNIA . . . as *British Brothers,* in defending the Common Cause." Even new immigrants, the Germans, Scots-Irish, and Africans, who felt no political loyalty to Great Britain and no affinity to English culture, had to assimilate to some degree to the dominant English culture of the colonies.

Americans hailed Britannia. In 1763, they were the victors, the conquerors of the backcountry. In their moment of glory, the colonists assumed that Britain's rulers saw the Americans as "Brothers," as equal partners in the business of empire. Only slowly would they learn the British had a different perception. For them, "American" was a way of saying "not quite English."

# RECOMMENDED READING

The central theme of this chapter has been the re-integration of the American colonies into an increasingly powerful and prosperous British Empire. A good introduction to the imperial dimension of eighteenth-century experience is P. J. Marshall, ed., *The Oxford History of the British Empire, vol. 2, The Eighteenth Century* (1998). In *Britons: Forging the Nation, 1707–1837* (1992), Linda Colley provides an excellent discussion of the aggressive spirit of the British nationalism that the Americans came to celebrate. The arrival of new ethnic groups is examined in Eric Hinderaker and Peter C. Mancall, *At the Edge of Empire: The Backcountry in British North America* (2003); Patrick Griffin, *The People with No Name: Ulster's Presbyterians in a British Atlantic World, 1688–1763* (2001); Bernard Bailyn, *The Peopling of British North America: An Introduction* (1988); and Bernard Bailyn and Philip D. Morgan, eds., *Strangers Within the Realm: Cultural Margins of the First British Empire* (1991). Richard White has transformed how we think about Native American resistance during this period in *The Middle Ground: Indians, Empires, and Republics in the Great Lakes Region* (1991). Two other fine books explore the Indians' response to the expanding European empires: Timothy Shannon, *Indians and Colonists at the Crossroads of Empire:*

*The Albany Congress of 1754* (2000) and Gregory Evans Dowd, *War Under Heaven: Pontiac, The Indian Nations and the British Empire* (2002). The complex story of Spanish colonization of the Southwest is told masterfully in David J. Weber, *The Spanish Frontier in North America* (1992). Fred Anderson offers the most complete treatment of war and empire in *Crucible of War: The Seven Years' War and the Fate of Empire in British North America, 1754–1766* (2000). A splendid examination of Benjamin Franklin as a colonial voice of the Enlightenment is Edmund S. Morgan, *Benjamin Franklin* (2002). The extraordinary impact of evangelical religion on colonial life is addressed in Mark A. Noll, *America's God: From Jonathan Edwards to Abraham Lincoln* (2002); Frank Lambert, *"Pedlar of Divinity": George Whitefield and the Transatlantic Revivals, 1734–1770* (1994); and Timothy D. Hall, *Contested Boundaries: Itinerancy and the Reshaping of the Colonial Religious World* (1994). The cultural concerns of a rising Anglicized colonial middle class are analyzed in David S. Shields, *Civil Tongues and Polite Letters in British America* (1997).

**For a list of additional sites related to this chapter's topics, please see** http://www.ablongman.com/divine.

# SUGGESTED WEB SITES

### History Buff—American History Library

http://www.historybuff.com/library
Brief journalistic essays on newspaper coverage of sixteenth- to eighteenth-century American history.

### Benjamin Franklin Documentary History Web Site

http://www.english.udel.edu/lemay/franklin/
University of Delaware professor J. A. Leo Lemay tells the story of Franklin's varied life in seven parts on this intriguing site.

### Jonathan Edwards

http://www.jonathanedwards.com/
Speeches by this famous preacher of the Great Awakening are on this site.

### Religion and the Founding of the American Republic

http://lcweb.loc.gov/exhibits/religion/religion.html
This Library of Congress site is an on-line exhibit about religion and the creation of the United States.

### The French and Indian War

http://web.syr.edu/~laroux/
This site is about French soldiers who came to New France between 1755 and 1760 to fight in the French and Indian War.

### National Museum of the American Indian

http://www.si.edu/nmai
The Smithsonian Institution maintains this site, providing information about the museum. The museum is dedicated to everything about Native Americans.

### Smithsonian Institution: You Be the Historian

http://www.americanhistory.si.edu/hohr/springer
Part of the Smithsonian's on-line museum, this exhibit enables students to examine artifacts from the home of New Castle, Delaware, residents Thomas and Elizabeth Springer and interpret the lives of a late eighteenth-century American family.

### DoHistory, Harvard University Film Study Center

http://www.dohistory.org/
Focusing on the life of Martha Ballard, a late eighteenth-century New England woman, this site employs selections from her diary, excerpts from a book and film of her life, and other primary documents to enable students to conduct their own historical investigation.

The Battle of Bunker Hill *by Winthrop Chandler, also shows the Burning of Charles Town.* ❖

CHARLES TOWN

BOSTON

# The American Revolution: From Elite Protest to Popular Revolt, 1763–1783

## *Rethinking the Meaning of Social Equality*

During the American Revolution, a captured British officer spent some time at the plantation of Colonel Thomas Mann Randolph, a leader of Virginia's gentry. The Englishman described the arrival of three ordinary farmers who were members of the local militia. He characterized the militiamen as "peasants," for without asking their host's permission, the Americans drew chairs up to the fire, pulled off their muddy boots, and began spitting.

The British officer was appalled; after the farmers departed, he observed they had not shown Randolph proper deference. The colonel responded that such behavior had come to be expected, for "the spirit of independency" had been transformed into "equality." Indeed, every American who "bore arms" during the Revolution considered himself as good as his neighbors. "No doubt," Randolph remarked to the officer, "each of these men conceives himself, in every respect, my equal."

This chance encounter illuminates the character of the American Revolution. The initial stimulus for rebellion came from the gentry, from the rich and wellborn, who resented Parliament's efforts to curtail their rights within the British empire. They voiced their unhappiness in carefully reasoned statements and in speeches before elected assemblies. Passionate rhetoric made them uneasy.

But as these influential planters, wealthy merchants, and prominent clergymen discovered, the revolutionary movement generated a momentum that they could not control. As relations with Britain deteriorated, particularly after 1765, the traditional leaders of colonial society encouraged the ordinary folk to join the protest—as rioters, as petitioners, and finally, as soldiers. Newspapers, sermons, and pamphlets helped transform what had begun as a squabble among the gentry into a mass movement, and as Randolph learned, once the people had become involved in shaping the nation's destiny, they could never again be excluded.

HAD IT NOT BEEN FOR those pushy "peasant" militiamen in the various colonies, the British would have easily crushed American resistance. Although some accounts of the Revolution downplay the military side of the story, leaving the impression that a few famous "Founding Fathers" effortlessly carried the nation to independence, a more persuasive explanation must recognize the centrality of armed violence in achieving nationhood.

The American Revolution involved a massive military commitment. If common American soldiers had not been willing to stand up to seasoned British troops, to face the terror of the bayonet charge, independence would have remained a dream of intellectuals.

*Wahrhaffte Abbildung der Soldaten des Congreßes in Nordamericka, nach der Zeich- nung eines Deutschen Officiers. Die Mütze ist von Leder, mit der Aufschrift Congreß. Die gantze Kleidung von Zwillich überall mit weißen Frantzen besetzt, die Beinkleider gehen bis auf die Knochel herunter. Die Meisten laufen barfuß. Ihrre Feuer-gewehr sind mit sehr langen Bayonets versehen, welche Sie auch statt eines seiten gewehrs gebrauchen. C. B. Henning exc. Nürnberg.*

Proportionate to the population, a greater percentage of Americans died in military service during the Revolution than in any war in American history, with the exception of the Civil War. The concept of liberty so magnificently expressed in revolutionary pamphlets was not, therefore, simply an abstraction, an exclusive concern of political theorists such as Thomas Jefferson and John Adams. It also motivated ordinary folk—mud-covered Virginia militiamen, for example—to take up weapons and risk death. Those who survived the ordeal were never quite the same, for the very experience of fighting, of assuming responsibility in battle and perhaps even of taking the lives of British officers, gave dramatic new meaning to the idea of social equality.

*The colonial American military forces were drawn from all social classes. Some soldiers were poorly equipped. Although the militiamen depicted in this engraving have rifles and warm clothing, one is without shoes.❖*

## STRUCTURE OF COLONIAL SOCIETY

Colonists who were alive during the 1760s did not anticipate the coming of national independence. It is only from a modern perspective that we see how the events of this period would lead to the formation of the United States. The colonists, of course, did not know what the future would bring. They would probably have characterized these years as "postwar," as a time of heightened economic and political expectation following the successful conclusion of the Seven Years' War (see Chapter 4).

For many Americans, the period generated optimism. The population continued to grow. Indeed, in 1776, approximately 2.5 million people, black and white, were living in Great Britain's thirteen mainland colonies. The striking ethnic and racial diversity of these men and women amazed European visitors who apparently rated homogeneity more highly than did the Americans. In 1775, for example, a traveler corrected the impression in London that the "colonists are the offspring of Englishmen." To be sure, many families traced their roots to Great Britain, but one also encountered "French, Dutch, Germans innumerable, Indians, Africans, and a multitude of felons." He then asked rhetorically, "Is it possible to tell which are the most turbulent amongst such a mixture of people?"

The American population on the eve of Independence was also extraordinarily young, a fact of great importance in understanding the development of effective political resistance. Nearly 60 percent of the American people were under age 21. This is a fact of considerable significance. At any given time, most people in this society were small children, and many of the young men who fought the British during the Revolution either had not been born or had been infants during the Stamp Act crisis. Any explanation for the coming of independence, therefore, must take into account the continuing political mobilization of so many young people.

Postwar Americans also experienced a high level of prosperity. To be sure, some major port cities went through a difficult period as colonists who had been employed during the fighting were thrown out of work. Sailors and ship workers, for example, were especially vulnerable to layoffs of this sort. In general, however, white Americans did very well. The quality of their material lives was not substantially lower than that of the English. In 1774, the per capita wealth of the Americans—this figure includes blacks as well as whites—was £37.4. This sum exceeds the per capita wealth of many developing countries today. On the eve of revolution, £37.4 would have purchased about 310 bushels of wheat, 1600 pounds of rice, 11 cows, or 6 horses. A typical white family of five—a father, mother, and three dependent children—not only would have been able to afford decent food, clothing, and housing but also would have had money left over with which to purchase consumer goods. Even the poorest colonists seem to have benefited from a rising standard of living, and although they may not have done as well as their wealthier neighbors, they too wanted to preserve gains they had made.

Wealth, however, was not evenly distributed in this society. Regional variations were striking. The Southern Colonies enjoyed the highest levels of personal wealth in America, which can be explained in part by the ownership of slaves. More than 90 percent of America's unfree workers lived in the South, and they represented a huge capital investment. Even without including the slaves in these wealth estimates, the South did quite well. In terms of aggregate wealth, the Middle Colonies also scored impressively. In fact, only New England lagged noticeably behind, a reflection of its relative inability to produce large amounts of exports for a growing world market.

## Breakdown of Political Trust

Ultimate responsibility for preserving the empire fell to George III. When he became king of England in 1760, he was only 22 years of age. In public, contemporaries praised the new monarch. In private, however, they expressed grave reservations. The youth had led a sheltered, loveless life; his father, an irresponsible playboy, had died in 1751 before ascending the throne. Young George had not received a good education, and even though he demonstrated considerable mechanical ability, his grandfather, George II, thought his grandson dull-witted, an opinion widely shared. As one might expect, George grew up hating not only his grandfather but almost everyone associated with the reign of George II.

To hide his intellectual inadequacies, the new king adopted a pedantic habit of correcting people for small faults, a characteristic made all the more annoying by his obvious inability to grasp the larger implications of government policy. During a difficult period that demanded imagination, generosity, and wisdom, George muddled along as best he could.

The new monarch was determined to play an aggressive role in government. This decision caused considerable dismay among England's political leaders. For decades, a powerful, though loosely associated, group of men who called themselves **Whigs** had set policy and controlled patronage. George II had accepted this situation, and so long as the Whigs in Parliament did not meddle with his beloved army, the king had let them rule the nation.

In one stroke, George III destroyed this cozy relationship. He selected as his chief minister the Earl of Bute, a Scot whose chief qualification for office appeared to be his friendship with the young king. The Whigs who dominated Parliament were outraged. Bute had no ties with the members of the House of Commons; he owed them no favors. It seemed to the Whigs that with the appointment of Bute, George was trying to turn back the clock to the time before the Glorious Revolution, in other words, attempting to reestablish a personal Stuart monarchy free from traditional constitutional restraints. The Whigs blamed Bute for every wrong, real or imagined. George did not, in fact, harbor such arbitrary ambitions, but his actions threw customary political practices into doubt.

By 1763 Bute, despairing of public life, left office. His departure, however, neither restored the Whigs to

*Coat of Arms of George III, c.1760-1770. The royal coat of arms was evident in the American colonies as a representation of the British empire. After the early 1770s many dissatisfied colonists viewed it as emblematic of a monarchy that did not understand or care about their problems.* ❖

preeminence nor dampened the king's enthusiasm for domestic politics. Everyone agreed George had the right to select whomever he desired for cabinet posts, but until 1770, no one seemed able to please the monarch. Ministers came and went, often for no other reason than George's personal distaste. Because of this chronic instability, subministers (minor bureaucrats who directed routine colonial affairs) did not know what was expected of them. In the absence of clear long-range policy, some ministers made narrowly based decisions; others did nothing. Most devoted their energies to finding a political patron capable of satisfying the fickle king. Talent played little part in the scramble for office, and incompetent hacks were advanced as frequently as were men of vision. With such turbulence surrounding him, the king showed little interest in the American colonies.

The king, however, does not bear the sole responsibility for England's loss of empire. The members of Parliament who actually drafted the statutes that gradually drove a wedge between the colonies and Britain must share the blame, for they failed to provide innovative answers to the explosive constitutional issues of the day. The problem was not stupidity or even obstinacy, qualities found in equal measure among all peoples.

In part, the impasse resulted from sheer ignorance. Few Englishmen active in government had ever visited America. For those who attempted to follow colonial affairs, accurate information proved extremely difficult to obtain. Packet boats carrying passengers and mail sailed regularly between London and the various colonial ports, but the voyage across the Atlantic required at least four weeks. Furthermore, all correspondence was laboriously copied in longhand by overworked clerks serving in understaffed offices. One could not expect to receive from America an answer to a specific question in less than three months. As a result of the lag in communication between England and America, rumors sometimes passed for true accounts, and misunderstanding influenced the formulation of colonial policy.

But failure of communication alone was not to blame for the widening gap between the colonies and England. Even when complete information was available, the two sides were often unable to understand each other's positions. The central element in this Anglo-American debate was a concept known as **parliamentary sovereignty.** The English ruling classes viewed the role of Parliament from a historical perspective that most colonists never shared. They insisted that Parliament was the dominant element within the constitution. Indeed, this elective body protected rights and property from an arbitrary monarch. During the reign of the Stuarts, especially under Charles I (r. 1625–1649), the authority of Parliament had been challenged, and it was not until the Glorious Revolution of 1688 that the English crown formally recognized Parliament's supreme authority in matters such as taxation. Almost no one, including George III, would have dissented from a speech made in 1766 before the House of Commons, in which a representative declared, "The parliament hath, and must have, from the nature and essence of the constitution, has had, and ever will have a sovereign supreme power and jurisdiction over every part of the dominions of the state, *to make laws in all cases whatsoever.*"

Such a constitutional position did not leave much room for compromise. Most members of Parliament took a hard line on this issue. The notion of dividing or sharing sovereignty simply made no sense to the English ruling class. As Thomas Hutchinson, royal governor of Massachusetts, explained, no middle ground existed "between the supreme authority of Parliament and the total dependence of the colonies: it is impossible there should be two independent legislatures in one and the same state."

The logic of this argument seemed self-evident to the British. In fact, parliamentary leaders could never quite understand why the colonists were so difficult to persuade. In frustration, Lord Hillsborough, the British secretary of state, admonished the colonial agent for Connecticut, "It is essential to the constitution to preserve the supremacy of Parliament inviolate; and tell your friends in America . . . that it is as much

*Cartoons became a popular means of criticizing government during this period. Here, King George III watches as the kilted Lord Bute slaughters the goose America. A cabinet member holds a basket of golden eggs at rear. At front left, a dog relieves itself on a map of North America.* ❖

their interest to support the constitution and preserve the supremacy of Parliament as it is ours."

## No Taxation Without Representation: The American Perspective

Americans most emphatically did not see it in their "interest" to maintain the "supremacy of Parliament." The crisis in imperial relations forced the colonists first to define and then to defend principles deeply rooted in their own political culture. For more than a century, their ideas about the colonies' role within the British empire had remained a vague, untested bundle of assumptions about personal liberties, property rights, and representative institutions.

By 1763, however, certain fundamental American beliefs had become clear. From Massachusetts to Georgia, colonists aggressively defended the powers of the provincial assemblies. They drew on a rich legislative history of their own. Over the course of the century, the American assemblies had steadily expanded their authority over taxation and expenditure. Since no one in Britain bothered to clip their legislative wings, these provincial bodies assumed a major role in policymaking and routine administration. In other words, by midcentury the assemblies looked like American copies of Parliament. It seemed unreasonable, therefore, for the British suddenly to insist on the supremacy of Parliament, for as the legislators of Massachusetts observed in 1770, "This house has the same inherent rights in this province as the house of commons in Great Britain."

The constitutional debate turned ultimately on the meaning of representation itself. In 1764, a British official informed the colonists that even though they had not elected members to Parliament—indeed, even though they had had no direct contact with the current members—they were nevertheless "virtually" represented by that august body. The members of Parliament, he declared, represented the political interests of everyone who lived in the British empire. It did not really matter whether everyone had cast a vote.

The colonists ridiculed this notion of **virtual representation.** The only representatives the Americans recognized as legitimate were those actually chosen by the people for whom they spoke. On this crucial point they would not compromise. As John Adams insisted, a representative assembly should actually mirror its constituents: "It should think, feel, reason, and act like them." Since the members of Parliament could not possibly "think" like Americans, it followed logically they could not represent them. And if they were not genuine representatives, the members of Parliament— pretensions to sovereignty notwithstanding—had no business taxing the American people. Thus, in 1764

the Connecticut Assembly declared in bold letters, "NO LAW CAN BE MADE OR ABROGATED WITHOUT THE CONSENT OF THE PEOPLE BY THEIR REPRESENTATIVES."

## Ideas About Power and Virtue

The political ideology that had the greatest popular appeal among the colonists contained a strong moral component, one that British rulers and American **Loyalists** (people who sided with the king and Parliament during the Revolution) never fully understood. The origins of this highly religious perspective on civil government are difficult to locate with precision, but certainly, the Great Awakening created a general awareness of an obligation to conduct public as well as private affairs according to Scripture (see Chapter 4).

Americans expressed their political beliefs in a language they had borrowed from English writers. The person most frequently cited was John Locke, the influential seventeenth-century philosopher whose *Two Treatises of Government* (first published in 1690) seemed, to colonial readers at least, a brilliant description of what was in fact American political practice. Locke claimed that all people possessed natural and inalienable rights. In order to preserve these God-given rights—the rights of life, liberty, and property, for example—free men (the status of women in Locke's work was less clear) formed contracts. These agreements were the foundation of human society as well as civil government, and they required the consent of the people who were actually governed. There could be no coercion. Locke justified rebellion against arbitrary forms of government that were by their very nature unreasonable. Americans delighted in Locke's ability to unite traditional religious values with a spirited defense of popular government, and even when they did not fully understand his technical writings, they seldom missed a chance to quote from the works of "the Great Mr. Locke."

Colonial Americans also enthusiastically subscribed to the so-called Commonwealthman tradition, a body of political assumptions generally identified with two eighteenth-century English publicists, John Trenchard and Thomas Gordon (see Chapter 4). The writings of such figures—most of whom spent their lives in political opposition—helped persuade the colonists that *power* was extremely dangerous, a force that would surely destroy liberty unless it was countered by *virtue*. Persons who shared this highly charged moral outlook regarded bad policy as not simply the result of human error. Rather, it was an indication of sin and corruption.

Insistence on public virtue—sacrifice of self-interest to the public good—became the dominant theme of revolutionary political writing. American pamphleteers seldom took a dispassionate, legalistic approach to their analysis of power and liberty. More commonly, they exposed plots hatched by corrupt courtiers, such as the Earl of Bute. None of them—or their readers—had any doubt that Americans were more virtuous than were the people of England.

During the 1760s, however, popular writers were not certain how long the colonists could hold out against arbitrary taxation, standing armies, Anglican bishops—in other words, against a host of external threats designed to crush American liberty. In 1774, for example, the people of Farmington, Connecticut, declared that "the present ministry, being instigated by the devil and led by their wicked and corrupt hearts, have a design to take away our liberties and properties, and to enslave us forever." Indeed, these Connecticut farmers described Britain's leaders as "pimps and parasites." This highly emotional, conspiratorial rhetoric sometimes shocks modern readers who assume that America's revolutionary leaders were products of the Enlightenment, persons who relied solely on reason to solve social and political problems. Whatever the origins of their ideas may have been, the colonial pamphleteers successfully roused ordinary men and women to resist Britain with force of arms.

Colonial newspapers spread these ideas through a large dispersed population. A majority of adult white males—especially those in the Northern Colonies—were literate, and it is not surprising that the number of journals published in this country increased dramatically during the revolutionary period. For the first time in American history, persons living in various parts of the continent could closely follow events that occurred in distant American cities. Because of the availability of newspapers, the details of Bostonians' confrontations with British authorities were known throughout the colonies, and these shared political experiences drew Americans more closely together, making it possible—in the words of John Adams—for "Thirteen clocks . . . to strike together—a perfection of mechanism which no artist had ever before effected."

## ERODING THE BONDS OF EMPIRE

The Seven Years' War saddled Great Britain with a national debt so huge that more than half the annual national budget went to pay the interest on it. Almost everyone in government assumed that with the cessation of hostilities, the troops would be disbanded, thus saving a lot of money. George III had other plans. He insisted on keeping the largest peacetime army in British history on active duty, supposedly to protect Indians from predatory frontiersmen and to preserve order in the newly conquered territories of Florida and Quebec.

Maintaining such a force so far distant from the mother country fueled the budgetary crisis. The growing financial burden weighed heavily on restive English taxpayers and sent government leaders scurrying in search of new sources of revenue.

For their part, colonists doubted the value of this expensive army. Britain did not leave enough troops in America to maintain peace on the frontier effectively. The weakness of the army was dramatically demonstrated during the spring of 1763. The native peoples of the backcountry—the Senecas, Ottawas, Miamis, Creeks, and Cherokees—had begun discussing how they might turn back the tide of white settlement. The powerful spiritual leader Neolin, known as the Delaware Prophet and claiming vision from the "Master of Life," helped these Indians articulate their fear and anger. He urged them to restore their cultures to the "original state that they were in before the white people found out their country." If moral regeneration required violence, so be it. Neolin converted Pontiac, an Ottawa warrior, to the cause, and he, in turn, coordinated an uprising among the western Indians who had been French allies and who hated all British people—even those sent to protect them from land-grabbing colonists. The formidable Native American resistance was known as Pontiac's Rebellion. In May, Pontiac attacked Detroit; other Indians harassed the Pennsylvania and Virginia frontiers. At the end of the year, after his followers began deserting, Pontiac sued for peace. During even this brief outbreak, the British army proved unable to defend exposed colonial settlements, and several thousand people lost their lives.

From the perspective of the Native Americans who inhabited the Ohio Valley this was a period of almost unmitigated disaster. In fact, more than any other group, the Indians suffered as a direct result of imperial reorganization. The defeat of the French made it impossible for native peoples to play off one imperial power against European rivals (see Chapter 4), and the victorious British made it clear that they regarded their former Indian allies as little more than a nuisance. Diplomatic gifts stopped; humiliating restrictions were placed on trade. But even worse, Pontiac's rising unloosed vicious racism along the colonial frontier, and American colonists often used any excuse to attack local Indians, peaceful or not. Late in 1763 a group of vigilantes known as the Paxton Boys murdered a score of Christian Indians, women and children, living near Lancaster, Pennsylvania. White neighbors treated the killers as heroes, and the atrocity ended only after the Paxton Boys threatened to march on Philadelphia in search of administrators who dared to criticize such cold-blooded crimes. One of the administrators, Benjamin Franklin, observed sadly, "It grieves me to hear that our Frontier People are yet greater Barbarians than the Indians, and continue to murder them in time of Peace."

Whatever happened to the Indians, the colonists fully intended to settle the fertile region west of the Appalachian Mountains. After the British government issued the Proclamation of 1763, which prohibited governors from granting land beyond the headwaters of rivers flowing into the Atlantic, disappointed Americans viewed the army as an obstruction to legitimate economic development, a domestic police force that cost too much money.

## Paying Off the National Debt

The task of reducing England's debt fell to George Grenville, the rigid, somewhat unimaginative chancellor of the exchequer who replaced Bute in 1763 as the king's first minister. After carefully reviewing the state of Britain's finances, Grenville concluded that the colonists would have to contribute to the maintenance of the army. The first bill he steered through Parliament was the Revenue Act of 1764, known as the Sugar Act.

This legislation placed a new burden on the Navigation Acts that had governed the flow of colonial commerce for almost a century (see Chapter 3). Those acts had forced Americans to trade almost exclusively with Britain. The statutes were not, however, primarily intended as a means to raise money for the British government. The Sugar Act—and the acts that soon followed—redefined the relationship between America and Great Britain. Parliament now expected the colonies to generate revenue. The preamble of the Sugar Act proclaimed explicitly: "It is just and necessary that a revenue be raised . . . in America for defraying the expenses of defending, protecting, and securing the same." The purpose of the Sugar Act was to discourage smuggling, bribery, and other illegalities that prevented the Navigation Acts from being profitable. Parliament reduced the duty on molasses (set originally by the Molasses Act of 1733) from 6 to 3

**COLONIAL PRODUCTS AND TRADE**    *Although the American colonists produced many agricultural staples that were valuable to Britain, they were dependent on British manufactures such as cloth, metal goods, and ceramics.* ❖

pence per gallon. At so low a rate, Grenville reasoned, colonial merchants would have little incentive to bribe customs collectors. Much needed revenue would be diverted from the pockets of corrupt officials into the treasury so that it might be used to maintain the army.

Grenville had been too clever by half. The Americans immediately saw through his unconstitutional scheme. According to the members of the Rhode Island Assembly, the Sugar Act taxed the colonists in a manner "inconsistent with their rights and privileges as British subjects." James Otis, a fiery orator from Massachusetts, exclaimed the legislation deprived Americans of "the right of assessing their own taxes."

The act generated no violence. In fact, ordinary men and women were only marginally involved in the drafting of formal petitions. The protest was still confined to the members of the colonial assemblies, to the merchants, and to the well-to-do Americans who had personal interests in commerce.

## Popular Protest

Passage of the Stamp Act in 1765 transformed a debate among gentlemen into a mass political movement. The imperial crisis might have been avoided. Colonial agents had presented Grenville with alternative schemes for raising money in America. But Grenville was a stubborn man, and he had little fear of parliamentary opposition. The majority of the House of Commons assumed that Parliament possessed the right to tax the colonists, and when the chancellor of the exchequer announced a plan to squeeze £60,000 annually out of the Americans by requiring them to purchase special seals or stamps to validate legal documents, the members responded with enthusiasm. The Stamp Act was scheduled to go into effect on November 1, 1765, and in anticipation of brisk sales, Grenville appointed stamp distributors for every colony.

During discussion in Parliament, several members warned that the act would raise a storm of protest in the colonies. Colonel Isaac Barré, a veteran of the Seven Years' War, reminded his colleagues that the Americans were "sons of liberty" and would not surrender their rights without a fight. But Barré's appeal fell on deaf ears.

Word of the Stamp Act reached America in May, and it was soon clear that Barré

had gauged the colonists' response correctly. The most dramatic incident occurred in Virginia's House of Burgesses. Patrick Henry, young and eloquent, whom contemporaries compared in fervor to evangelical preachers, introduced five resolutions protesting the Stamp Act on the floor of the assembly. He timed his move carefully. It was late in the session; many of the more conservative burgesses had already departed for their plantations. Even then, Henry's resolves declaring that Virginians had the right to tax themselves as they alone saw fit passed by narrow margins. The fifth resolution, stricken almost immediately from the legislative records, announced that any attempt to collect stamp revenues in America was "illegal, unconstitutional, and unjust, and has a manifest tendency to destroy British as well as American liberty." Henry was carried away by the force of his own rhetoric. He reminded his fellow Virginians that Caesar had had his Brutus, Charles I his Cromwell, and he hoped that "some good American would stand up for his country"—but an astonished speaker of the house cut Henry off in mid-sentence, accusing him of treason.

The Virginia Resolves might have remained a local matter had it not been for the colonial press. Newspapers throughout America printed Henry's resolutions, but, perhaps because editors did not really know what had happened in Williamsburg, they reported that all five resolutions had received the burgesses' full support. Several journals even carried two resolves that Henry had not dared to introduce. A result of this misunderstanding, of course, was that the Virginians appeared to have taken an extremely radical position on the issue of the supremacy of Parliament, one that other Americans now trumpeted before their own assemblies. No wonder Francis Bernard, royal governor of Massachusetts, called the Virginia Resolves an "alarm bell."

Not to be outdone by Virginia, Massachusetts called a general meeting to protest Grenville's policy.

*The Stamp Act placed a tax on documents and printed matter—newspapers, marriage licenses, wills, deeds, even playing cards and dice. The stamps (like those shown here) varied in denomination. A tax stamp affixed to a legal document or bill of sale signified that the required tax had been paid.* ❖

Nine colonies sent representatives to the **Stamp Act Congress** that convened in New York City in October 1765. It was the first intercolonial gathering held since the abortive Albany Congress of 1754; if nothing else, the new congress provided leaders from different regions with an opportunity to discuss common problems. The delegates drafted petitions to the king and Parliament that restated the colonists' belief "that no taxes should be imposed on them, but with their own consent, given personally, or by their representatives." The tone of the meeting was restrained, even conciliatory. The congress studiously avoided any mention of independence or disloyalty to the crown.

Resistance to the Stamp Act soon spread from the assemblies to the streets. By taxing deeds, marriage licenses, and playing cards, the Stamp Act touched the lives of ordinary women and men. Anonymous artisans and seamen, angered by Parliament's apparent insensitivity and fearful that the statute would increase unemployment and poverty, organized mass protests in the major colonial ports.

Imperial politics played out on the streets of American cities as traditional rivalries between neighborhood youths and anti-Catholic sentiment suddenly was redirected against alleged parliamentary oppression. (See the Feature Essay, "Popular Resistance: Religion and Rebellion," pp. 136–137.) In Boston, the "Sons of Liberty" burned in effigy the local stamp distributor, Andrew Oliver, and when that action failed to bring about his resignation, they tore down one of his office buildings. Even after he resigned, the mob nearly demolished the elegant home of Oliver's close associate, Lieutenant Governor Thomas Hutchinson. The violence frightened colonial leaders, yet evidence suggests that they encouraged the lower classes to intimidate royal officials. Popular participation in these protests was an exciting experience for people who had traditionally deferred to their social betters. After 1765, it was impossible for either royal governors or patriot leaders to take for granted the support of ordinary men and women.

By November 1, 1765, stamp distributors in almost every American port had publicly resigned, and without distributors, the hated revenue stamps could not be sold. The courts soon reopened; most newspapers were published. Daily life in the colonies was undisturbed with one exception: The Sons of Liberty persuaded—some said coerced—colonial merchants to boycott British goods until Parliament repealed the Stamp Act. The merchants showed little enthusiasm for such tactics, but the threat of tar and feathers stimulated cooperation.

The boycott movement was in itself a masterful political innovation. Never before had a resistance movement organized itself so centrally around the market

## ❖ A Look at the Past ❖

### Stamp Act Teapot

Colonists could celebrate the repeal of the hated Stamp Act by purchasing goods decorated like this teapot. Because no manufacturers of fine ceramics existed in British America, this teapot came from England. As this piece indicates, English manufacturers readily produced goods suited to colonial tastes. British merchants and manufacturers had good reason to celebrate the repeal of the Stamp Act as it meant that colonists resumed purchasing English goods. What does this teapot suggest about the economic and cultural connections between England and the colonies? Why would some individuals in England regard parliamentary taxation as unfavorably as some colonists did?

decisions of ordinary consumers. The colonists depended on British imports—cloth, metal goods, and ceramics—and each year they imported more consumer goods than they could possibly afford. In this highly charged moral atmosphere, one in which ordinary people talked constantly of conspiracy and corruption, it is not surprising that Americans of different classes and backgrounds advocated a radical change in buying habits. Private acts suddenly became part of the public sphere. Personal excess threatened to contaminate the entire political community. This logic explains the power of an appeal made in a Boston newspaper: "Save your money and you can save your country."

The boycotts mobilized colonial women. They were excluded from voting and civil office, but such legal discrimination did not mean that women were not part of the broader political culture. Since wives and mothers spent their days involved with household chores, they assumed special responsibility to reform consumption, to root out luxury, and to promote frugality. Indeed, in this realm they possessed real power; they monitored the ideological commitment of the entire family. Throughout the colonies, women altered styles of dress, made homespun cloth, and shunned imported items on which Parliament had placed a tax.

## Failed Attempts to Save the Empire

What most Americans did not yet know—after all, communication with Britain required months—was that in July, Grenville had fallen from power. This unexpected shift came about not because the king thought Grenville's policies inept, but rather because George did not like the man. His replacement as first lord of the treasury, Lord Rockingham, was young, inexperienced, and terrified of public speaking, a serious handicap to launching a brilliant parliamentary career. The Rockinghamites—as his followers were called—envisioned a prosperous empire founded on an expanding commerce and local government under the gentle guidance of Parliament. In this unified structure, it seemed improbable that Parliament would ever be obliged to exercise control in a manner likely to offend the Americans. Rockingham wanted to repeal the Stamp Act, but because of the shakiness of his own political coalition, he could not announce such a decision until it enjoyed broad national support. He, therefore, urged merchants and manufacturers throughout England to petition Parliament for repeal of the act, claiming that the American boycott would soon drive them into bankruptcy and spark urban riots.

Grenville, now simply a member of Parliament, would tolerate no retreat on the issue of supremacy. He urged his colleagues in the House of Commons to be tough, to condemn "the outrageous tumults and insurrections which have been excited and carried on in North America." But William Pitt, the architect of victory in the Seven Years' War and a hero throughout America, eloquently defended the colonists' position, and after the Rockingham ministry gathered additional support from prominent figures such as Benjamin Franklin, who happened to be visiting England, Parliament felt strong enough to recommend repeal. On March 18, 1766, the House of Commons voted 275 to 167 to rescind the Stamp Act.

Lest its retreat on the Stamp Act be interpreted as weakness, the House of Commons passed the Declaratory Act (March 1766), a shrill defense of parliamentary supremacy over the Americans "in all cases whatsoever." The colonists' insistence on no taxation without representation failed to impress British rulers. England's merchants, supposedly America's allies, claimed sole responsibility for the Stamp Act repeal. The colonists had only complicated the task, the merchants lectured, and if the Americans knew what was good for them, they would keep quiet. To George Mason, a leading political figure in Virginia, such advice sounded patronizing. The British merchants seemed to be saying, "We have with infinite difficulty and fatigue got you excused this one time; pray be a good boy for the future, do what your papa and mama bid you, and hasten to return them your most grateful acknowledgements for condescending to let you keep what is your own." This, Mason snapped, was "ridiculous!"

The Stamp Act crisis also eroded the colonists' respect for imperial officeholders in America. Suddenly, these men—royal governors, customs collectors, military personnel—appeared alien, as if their interests were not those of the people over whom they exercised authority. One person who had been forced to resign the post of stamp distributor for South Carolina noted several years later, "The Stamp Act had introduc'd so much Party Rage, Faction, and Debate that the ancient Harmony, Generosity, and Urbanity for which these People were celebrated is destroyed, and at an End." Similar reports came from other colonies, and it is testimony to the Americans' lingering loyalty to the British crown and constitution that rebellion did not occur in 1765.

## Fueling the Crisis

Rockingham's ministry soon gave way to a government headed once again by William Pitt, who was now the Earl of Chatham. The aging Pitt suffered horribly from gout, and during his long absences from London, Charles Townshend, his chancellor of the exchequer, made important policy decisions. Townshend was an impetuous man whose mouth often outran his mind. During a parliamentary debate in January 1767, he surprised everyone by blithely announcing that he knew a way to obtain revenue from the Americans. The members of the House of Commons were so pleased with the news that they promptly voted to lower English land taxes, an action that threatened fiscal chaos.

A budgetary crisis forced Townshend to make good on his extraordinary boast. His scheme turned out to be a grab bag of duties on American imports of paper, glass, paint, lead, and tea, which collectively were known as the Townshend Revenue Acts (June–July 1767). He hoped to generate sufficient funds to pay the salaries of royal governors and other imperial officers, thus freeing them from dependence on the colonial assemblies.

The chancellor recognized that without tough instruments of enforcement, his duties would not produce the promised revenues. Therefore, he created an American Board of Customs Commissioners, a body based in Boston and supported by reorganized vice-admiralty courts located in Boston, Philadelphia, and

*The boycott movement drew many colonial women into popular politics. In this 1774 woodcut, a Daughter of Liberty stands ready to resist British oppression.* ❖

Charles Town. And for good measure, Townshend induced Parliament to order the governor of New York to veto all bills passed by that colony's assembly until it supplied resident British troops in accordance with the Quartering Act (May 1765) that required the colonies to house soldiers in barracks, taverns, and vacant buildings and to provide the army with firewood, candles, and beer, among other items. Many Americans regarded this as more taxation without representation, and in New York, at least, colonists refused to pay.

Colonists showed no more willingness to pay Townshend's duties than they had to buy Grenville's stamps. No congress was called; none was necessary. Recent events had taught people how to coordinate protest, and they moved to resist the unconstitutional revenue acts. In major ports, the Sons of Liberty organized boycotts of British goods. Protest often involved what one historian has termed "rituals of nonconsumption." In some large towns, these were moments of public moral reaffirmation. Men and women took oaths before neighbors promising not to purchase certain goods until Parliament repealed unconstitutional taxation. In Boston, ordinary people were encouraged to sign "Subscription Rolls." "The Selectmen strongly

recommend this Measure to Persons of *all ranks*," announced the *Boston Gazette,* "as the most honorable and effectual way of giving *public* Testimony of their Love to their Country, and of endeavouring to save it from ruin."

On February 11, 1768, the Massachusetts House of Representatives drafted a circular letter, a provocative appeal which it sent directly to the other colonial assemblies. The letter requested suggestions on how best to thwart the Townshend Acts; not surprisingly, legislators in other parts of America, busy with local matters, simply ignored this general appeal. But not Lord Hillsborough, England's secretary for American affairs. This rather mild attempt to create a united colonial front struck him as gross treason, and he ordered the Massachusetts representatives to rescind their "seditious paper." After considering Hillsborough's demand, the legislators voted 92 to 17 to defy him.

Suddenly, the circular letter became a cause célèbre. The royal governor of Massachusetts hastily dissolved the House of Representatives. That decision compelled the other colonies to demonstrate their support for Massachusetts. Assembly after assembly now felt obligated to take up the circular letter, an action Hillsborough had specifically forbidden. Assemblies in other colonies were dissolved, creating a much broader crisis of representative government. Throughout America, the number 92 (the number of legislators who voted against Hillsborough) immediately became a symbol of patriotism. In fact, Parliament's challenge had brought about the very results it most wanted to avoid: a foundation for intercolonial communication and a strengthening of conviction among the colonists of the righteousness of their position.

## Fatal Show of Force

In October 1768, British rulers made another mistake, one that raised tensions almost to the pitch they had reached during the Stamp Act riots. The issue at the heart of the trouble was the army. In part to save money and in part to intimidate colonial troublemakers, the ministry transferred four thousand regular troops from Nova Scotia and Ireland to Boston. Most of the army had already been withdrawn from the frontier to the seacoast to save revenue, thereby raising more acutely than ever the issue of why troops were in America at all. The armed strangers camped on the Boston Common, and when citizens passed the site, redcoats shouted obscenities. Sometimes, in accordance with martial law, an errant soldier was whipped within an inch of his life, a bloody sight that sickened Boston civilians. To make relations worse, redcoats—men who were ill treated and underpaid—competed

# POPULAR RESISTANCE

## Religion and Rebellion

No one knows exactly why men and women rebel against governments. Economic deprivation and political frustration contribute to unrest, but the spark that ignites popular passions, that causes ordinary people to risk their lives in battle, often arises from a society's most basic traditions and beliefs.

The American Revolution illustrates this complex process of revolt. The educated elite in the colonies may have found their inspiration in reading classical history or political pamphlets, but the ordinary people, those who protested British taxation in the streets and supported consumer boycotts, seem to have gained resolution from a deep Protestant tradition, a set of religious values recently reinforced during the Great Awakening (see Chapter 4). For these men and women, the American Revolution may have seemed a kind of morality play, a drama that transformed complicated issues of representation and sovereignty into a stark conflict between American good and British evil.

Even before colonial protests against British taxation led to bloodshed, religious passions helped draw thousands of people into the streets of Boston on Pope's Day, a traditional anti-Catholic holiday celebrated on November 5. (In England, the holiday was known as Guy Fawkes Day and commemorated exposure of the Gunpowder Plot of 1605, a conspiracy organized by English Catholics to blow up Parliament that was thwarted at the last minute.) For the holiday, Bostonians arranged elaborate processions, complete with effigies of the pope and the devil, which they burned at the climax of the festivities. Sometimes the annual celebration turned ugly, and rival gangs from the north and south ends of the city tried to disrupt each other's parades. During the Seven Years' War, the crowds grew increasingly unruly as the pageantry triggered an outpouring of emotions that sprang from the New Englanders' fervent commitment to the Reformation and their desire to rid Canada of Catholic domination.

The Pope's Day celebrations provided a model for demonstrations against the Stamp Act. The first public protest against the British law in Boston, on August 14, 1765, began with a rally under a large elm, the original colonial Liberty Tree. Hanging from its branches were effigies of Andrew Oliver, Boston's first stamp collector, and the devil, whose pitchforks menaced Oliver. A label attached to the effigy of Oliver read:

> Fair Freedom's glorious cause
>  I've meanly quitted
> For the sake of self;
> But ah! the Devil had me outwitted,
> And instead of *stamping* others,
>  I've *hang'd* myself.

As night fell, a diverse crowd of gentlemen, workers, and even a few women carried the effigies through the streets of Boston. After destroying a building owned by Oliver, they marched to Fort Hill, where "they made a burnt offering of the effigies for these sins of the people which had caused such heavy judgments as the Stamp Act, etc. to be laid upon them." This symbolic protest ended with a sort of conversion; in much the same way as anxious sinners renounced evil at evangelical meetings, Oliver announced publicly that he would resign as stamp collector.

Pope's Day celebrations—complete with burning effigies and pitched battles in the streets—provided the ordinary people of Boston with a model that they used in anti-British political demonstrations. ❖

The devil was a familiar feature in American political cartoons. In one famous illustration, published in 1774, the devil held a list of crimes committed by Governor Thomas Hutchinson of Massachusetts, as the viper of death prepared to punish the royal official for his sins. This gruesome imagery revealed that patriots thought of Hutchinson not only as a political opponent but also as a moral traitor. No one who saw the macabre figures could fail to appreciate the accompanying warning: "Let the destroyers of mankind behold and tremble!"

A similar message was at the heart of the patriot practice of tarring and feathering. Crowds in Boston usually reserved this humiliating punishment for informers who reported violations to the hated customs officers. The victim became the main actor in a public morality play, in which he was wheeled in a cart before jeering crowds and forced to repent. This spectacle recalled a verse often repeated on Pope's Day:

> See the informer how he stands
> If anyone now takes his part
> An enemy to all the Land
> He'll go to Hell without a cart.

Patriots regarded military traitors as the worst of sinners. When General Benedict Arnold, who had been a hero during the early stages of the war, went over to the British in 1780, Americans accused him of selling out to the devil. A huge parade held in Philadelphia included a two-faced Arnold riding in front of Satan. The devil held a bag of gold—presumably the source of Arnold's fall—and a pitchfork that he used to prod the traitor along the path to hell.

Revolutionary leaders also tapped long-standing Puritan hostility to the theater. Puritans and other strict Protestants indicted the theater for encouraging idleness, hypocrisy, deceit, and even effeminacy, since men usually played women's roles. But their greatest objection was that the stage appealed to those emotions and lusts that God-fearing men and women tried to restrain through knowledge of Scripture. Theaters, they believed, were nothing less than enemies of the church. "Those therefore who serve the Devill in Playes and Playhouses; it's impossible for them to serve the Lord in prayers and Churches," asserted one Puritan thinker.

Patriot leaders also considered the stage a rival for popular loyalties. In 1766, the Sons of Liberty in New York City demolished a theater. And in 1774, the First Continental Congress resolved to "discountenance and discourage every species of extravagance and dissipation especially . . . shews, plays and other expensive diversions and entertainments." Such proclamations helped to channel Protestant moral fervor into a commitment to the patriot cause.

During the war itself—when soldiers were actually fighting and dying—religion helped sustain patriotism. In 1775, for example, a company of Massachusetts soldiers on their way to Quebec camped briefly at Newburyport, where George Whitefield had been buried. Before the troops resumed their long march to Canada, some of them opened the minister's tomb and cut off small pieces of Whitefield's collar and wristband, an act that seems ghoulish only to those who do not fully comprehend the importance of religion in the lives of the common soldiers.

Religious symbol and ritual thus galvanized ordinary men and women by expressing in moral terms the issues that divided the colonies from England. The Great Awakening had prepared the colonists to view the contest in terms of American virtue and English vice, of God and the devil. By appealing to the strong Protestant tradition in the colonies, patriots mobilized the American people for revolution.

Traditional religious symbols enhanced the emotional impact of attacks on appointed British officials such as the hated Thomas Hutchinson of Massachusetts. ❖

Outrage over the Boston Massacre was fanned by propaganda, such as this etching by Paul Revere, which showed British redcoats firing on ordinary citizens. In subsequent editions, the blood spurting from the dying Americans became more conspicuous. ❖

seen as martyrs and were memorialized in extravagant terms. In one eulogy, Joseph Warren addressed the dead men's widows and children, dramatically re-creating the gruesome scene in King Street. "Behold thy murdered husband gasping on the ground," Warren cried, " . . . take heed, ye orphan babes, lest, whilst your streaming eyes are fixed upon the ghastly corpse, your feet slide on the stones bespattered with your father's brains." Apparently, to propagandists like Warren, it mattered little that the five civilians had been bachelors! Paul Revere's engraving of the massacre, appropriately splattered with blood, became an instant best-seller. Confronted with such intense reaction and with the possibility of massive armed resistance, crown officials wisely moved the army to an island in Boston Harbor.

At this critical moment, the king's new first minister restored a measure of tranquility. Lord North, congenial, well-meaning, but not very talented, became chancellor of the exchequer following Townshend's death in 1767. North was appointed the first minister in 1770, and for the next twelve years—indeed, throughout most of the American crisis—he managed to retain his office. His secret formula seems to have been an ability to get along with George III and to build an effective majority in Parliament.

One of North's first recommendations to Parliament was the repeal of the Townshend duties. Not only had these ill-conceived duties unnecessarily angered the colonists, but they also hurt English manufacturers. By taxing British exports such as glass and paint, Parliament had only encouraged the Americans to develop their own industries; thus, without much prodding, the House of Commons dropped all the Townshend duties—with the notable exception of tea. The tax on tea was retained not for revenue purposes, North insisted, but as a reminder that England's rulers still subscribed to the principles of the Declaratory Act. They would not compromise the supremacy of Parliament. In mid-1770, however, the matter of tea seemed trivial to most Americans. The colonists had drawn back from the precipice, a little frightened by

in their spare time for jobs with local dockworkers and artisans. Work was already in short supply, and the streets crackled with tension.

When colonists questioned why the army had been sent to a peaceful city, pamphleteers responded that it was there to further a conspiracy originally conceived by Bute to oppress Americans, to take away their liberties, to collect illegal revenues. Grenville, Hillsborough, Townshend: They were all, supposedly, part of the plot. Today such rhetoric may sound excessive, but to Americans who had absorbed the political theories of the Commonwealthmen, a pattern of tyranny seemed obvious.

Colonists had no difficulty interpreting the violence that erupted in Boston on March 5, 1770. In the gathering dusk of that afternoon, young boys and street toughs threw rocks and snowballs at soldiers in a small, isolated patrol outside the offices of the hated customs commissioners in King Street. The details of this incident are obscure, but it appears that as the mob grew and became more threatening, the soldiers panicked. In the confusion, the troops fired, leaving five Americans dead.

Pamphleteers promptly labeled the incident a massacre. The victims of this **Boston Massacre** were the events of the past two years, and desperately hoped to head off future confrontation with the British.

## Last Days of the Old Order, 1770–1773

For a short while, American colonists and British officials put aside their recent animosities. Like England's rulers, some colonial gentry were beginning to pull back from protest, especially violent confrontation with established authority, in fear that the lower orders were becoming too assertive. It was probably in this period that Loyalist Americans emerged as an identifiable group. Colonial merchants returned to familiar patterns of trade, pleased no doubt to end the local boycotts that had depressed the American economy. British goods flooded into colonial ports; the level of American indebtedness soared to new highs. In this period of apparent reconciliation, the people of Massachusetts—even of Boston—decided they could accept their new governor, Thomas Hutchinson. After all, he was one of their own, an American.

But appearances were deceiving. The bonds of imperial loyalty remained fragile, and even as Lord North attempted to win the colonists' trust, crown officials in America created new strains. Customs commissioners whom Townshend had appointed to collect his duties remained in the colonies long after his Revenue Acts had been repealed. If they had been honest, unobtrusive administrators, perhaps no one would have taken notice of their behavior. But the customs commissioners regularly abused their powers of search and seizure and in the process lined their own pockets. In Massachusetts, Rhode Island, and South Carolina—to cite the most notorious cases—these officials drove local citizens to distraction by enforcing the Navigation Acts with such rigor that a small boat could not cross Narragansett Bay with a load of firewood without first obtaining a sheaf of legal documents. One slip, no matter how minor, could bring confiscation of ship and cargo.

The commissioners were not only corrupt; they were also shortsighted. If they had restricted their extortion to the common folk, they might have avoided becoming a major American grievance. But they could not control their greed. Some customs officers harassed the wealthiest, most powerful men around, men such as John Hancock of Boston and Henry Laurens of Charles Town. The commissioners' actions drove some members of the colonial ruling class into opposition to the king's government. When in the summer of 1772 a group of disguised Rhode Islanders burned a customs vessel, the *Gaspee*, Americans cheered. A special royal commission sent to arrest the culprits discovered that not a single Rhode Islander had the slightest idea how the ship could have come to such an end.

Samuel Adams (1722–1803) refused to accept the notion that the repeal of the Townshend duties had secured American liberty. During the early 1770s, while colonial leaders turned to other matters, Adams kept the cause alive with a drumfire of publicity. He reminded the people of Boston that the tax on tea remained in force. He organized public anniversaries commemorating the repeal of the Stamp Act and the Boston Massacre. Adams was a genuine revolutionary, an ideologue filled with a burning sense of indignation at the real and alleged wrongs suffered by his countrymen. To his contemporaries, this man resembled a figure out of New England's Puritan past. He seemed obsessed with the preservation of public virtue. The American goal, he declared, was the creation of a "Christian Sparta," an ideal commonwealth in which vigilant citizens would constantly guard against the spread of corruption, degeneracy, and luxury.

With each new attempt by Parliament to assert its supremacy over the colonists, more and more Bostonians listened to what Adams had to say. He observed ominously that the British intended to use the tea revenue to pay judicial salaries, thus freeing the judges from dependence on the assembly. When in November 1772 Adams suggested the formation of a **committee of correspondence** to communicate grievances to villagers throughout Massachusetts, he

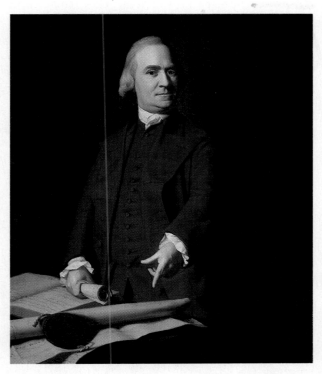

*Samuel Adams, seen here in a portrait by John Singleton Copley, was a fervid republican ideologue who urged the American colonists to defend their political virtue against British corruption.* ❖

received broad support. Americans living in other colonies soon copied his idea. It was a brilliant stroke. Adams developed a structure of political cooperation completely independent of royal government.

## The Final Provocation: The Boston Tea Party

In May 1773, Parliament passed the Tea Act, legislation the Americans might have welcomed. After all, it lowered the price for their favorite beverage. Parliament wanted to save one of Britain's largest businesses, the East India Company, from possible bankruptcy. This commercial giant imported Asian tea into England, where it was resold to wholesalers. The tea was also subject to heavy duties. The Company tried to pass these charges on to the consumers, but American tea drinkers preferred the cheaper leaves that were smuggled in from Holland.

The Tea Act changed the rules. Parliament not only allowed the Company to sell directly to American retailers, thus cutting out intermediaries, but also eliminated the duties paid in England. If all had gone according to plan, the agents of the East India Company in America would have undersold their competitors, including the Dutch smugglers, and with the new profits would have saved the business.

But Parliament's logic was flawed. First, since the tax on tea, collected in American ports, remained in effect, this new act seemed a devious scheme to win popular support for Parliament's right to tax the colonists without representation. Second, the act threatened to undercut powerful colonial merchants who did a good business trading in smuggled Dutch tea. Considering the American reaction, the British government might have been well advised to devise another plan to rescue the ailing company. In Philadelphia, and then at New York City, colonists turned back the tea ships before they could unload.

In Boston, however, the issue was not so easily resolved. Governor Hutchinson, a strong-willed man, would not permit the vessels to return to England. Local patriots would not let them unload. And so, crammed with the East India Company's tea, the ships sat in Boston Harbor waiting for the colonists to make up their minds. On the night of December 16, 1773, they did so in dramatic style. A group of men disguised as Mohawks boarded the ships and pitched 340 chests of tea worth £10,000 over the side. Whether Samuel Adams organized the famed Tea Party is not known. No doubt he and his allies were not taken by surprise. Even at the time, John Adams, Samuel's distant cousin, sensed the event would have far-reaching significance. "This Destruction of the Tea," he scribbled in his diary, "is so bold, so daring, so firm, intrepid, and inflexible, and it must have so important consequences, and so lasting, that I can't but consider it as an epocha in history."

*Colonists toss barrels of tea overboard while disguised as Mohawk Indians in a historic depiction of the Boston Tea Party of December 16, 1773. At right, a bottle of tea leaves preserved from the protest suggests that one participant or onlooker was mindful of the historical importance of the event.* ❖

## CHRONICLE OF COLONIAL–BRITISH TENSION

| Legislation | Date | Provisions | Colonial Reaction |
|---|---|---|---|
| **Sugar Act** | April 5, 1764 | Revised duties on sugar, coffee, tea, wine, other imports; expanded jurisdiction of vice-admiralty courts | Several assemblies protest taxation for revenue |
| **Stamp Act** | March 22, 1765; repealed March 18, 1766 | Printed documents (deeds, newspapers, marriage licenses, etc.) issued only on special stamped paper purchased from stamp distributors | Riots in cities; collectors forced to resign; Stamp Act Congress (October 1765) |
| **Quartering Act** | May 1765 | Colonists must supply British troops with housing, other items (candles, firewood, etc.) | Protest in assemblies; New York Assembly punished for failure to comply, 1767 |
| **Declaratory Act** | March 18, 1766 | Parliament declares its sovereignty over the colonies "in all cases whatsoever" | Ignored in celebration over repeal of the Stamp Act |
| **Townshend Revenue Acts** | June 26, 29, July 2, 1767; all repealed—except duty on tea, March 1770 | New duties on glass, lead, paper, paints, tea; customs collections tightened in America | Nonimportation of British goods; assemblies protest; newspapers attack British policy |
| **Tea Act** | May 10, 1773 | Parliament gives East India Company right to sell tea directly to Americans; some duties on tea reduced | Protests against favoritism shown to monopolistic company; tea destroyed in Boston (December 16, 1773) |
| **Coercive Acts (Intolerable Acts)** | March–June 1774 | Closes port of Boston; restructures Massachusetts government; restricts town meetings; troops quartered in Boston; British officials accused of crimes sent to England or Canada for trial | Boycott of British goods; First Continental Congress convenes (September 1774) |
| **Prohibitory Act** | December 22, 1775 | Declares British intention to coerce Americans into submission; embargo on American goods; American ships seized | Drives Continental Congress closer to decision for independence |

When news of the Tea Party reached London in January 1774, the North ministry was stunned. The people of Boston had treated parliamentary supremacy with utter contempt, and British rulers saw no humor whatsoever in the destruction of private property by subjects of the Crown dressed in costume. To quell such rebelliousness, Parliament passed a series of laws called the **Coercive Acts.** (In America, they were referred to as the Intolerable Acts.) The legislation (1) closed the port of Boston until the city fully compensated the East India Company for the lost tea; (2) restructured the Massachusetts government by transforming the upper house from an elective to an appointed body and restricting the number of legal town meetings to one a year; (3) allowed the royal governor to transfer British officials arrested for offenses committed in the line of duty to England, where there was little likelihood they would be convicted; and (4) authorized the army to quarter troops wherever they were needed, even if this required the compulsory requisition of uninhabited private buildings. George III enthusiastically supported this tough policy; he ap-

pointed General Thomas Gage to serve as the colony's new royal governor. Gage apparently won the king's favor by announcing that in America, "Nothing can be done but by forcible means."

The sweeping denial of constitutional liberties confirmed the colonists' worst fears. To men like Samuel Adams, it seemed as if Britain really intended to enslave the American people. Colonial moderates found their position shaken by the vindictiveness of the Coercive Acts. Edmund Burke, one of America's last friends in Parliament, noted sadly on the floor of Commons, that "this is the day, then, that you wish to go to war with all America, in order to conciliate that country to this."

In the midst of the constitutional crisis, Parliament announced plans to establish a new civil government for the Canadian province of Quebec (Quebec Act, June 22, 1774). This territory had been ruled by military authority following the Seven Years' War. The Quebec Act not only failed to create an elective assembly—an institution the Americans regarded as essential for the protection of liberty—but also awarded French Roman

Catholics a large voice in local political affairs. Moreover, since Quebec extended all the way south to the Ohio River and west to the Mississippi River, Americans concluded that Parliament wanted to deny the American settlers and traders in this fast-developing region their constitutional rights, a threat that affected all colonists, not just those of Massachusetts Bay.

If in 1774 the House of Commons thought it could isolate Boston from the rest of America, it was in for a rude surprise. Colonists living in other parts of the continent recognized immediately that the principles at stake in Boston affected all Americans. As one Virginian explained, "there were no Heats and Troubles in Virginia till the Blockade of Boston." Few persons advocated independence, but they could not remain passive while Boston was destroyed. They sent food and money and, during the fall of 1774, reflected more deeply than ever on what it meant to be a colonist in the British empire.

The sticking point remained—as it had been in 1765—the sovereignty of Parliament. No one in Britain could think of a way around this constitutional impasse. In 1773, Benjamin Franklin had offered a suggestion. "The Parliament," he observed, "has no right to make any law whatever, binding on the colonies . . . the king, and not the king, lords, and commons collectively, is their sovereign." But so long as it still seemed possible to coerce the Americans into obedience, to punish these errant children, Britain's rulers had little incentive to accept such a humiliating compromise.

## STEPS TOWARD INDEPENDENCE

During the summer of 1774, committees of correspondence analyzed the perilous situation in which the colonists found themselves. Something, of course, had to be done. But what? Would the Southern Colonies support resistance in New England? Would Pennsylvanians stand up to Parliament? Not surprisingly, the committees endorsed a call for a Continental Congress, a gathering of fifty-five elected delegates from twelve colonies (Georgia sent none but agreed to support the action taken). This **First Continental Congress** convened in Philadelphia on September 5. It included some of America's most articulate, respected leaders; among them were John Adams, Samuel Adams, Patrick Henry, Richard Henry Lee, Christopher Gadsden, and George Washington.

The delegates were strangers to one another. They knew little about the customs and values, the geography and economy of Britain's other provinces. As John Adams explained on September 18, "It has taken Us much Time to get acquainted with the Tempers, Views, Characters, and Designs of Persons and to let them into the Circumstances of our Province." During the early sessions of the Congress, the delegates eyed each other closely, trying to gain a sense of the strength and integrity of the men with whom they might commit treason.

Differences of opinion soon surfaced. Delegates from the Middle Colonies—Joseph Galloway of Pennsylvania, for example—wanted to proceed with caution, but Samuel Adams and other more radical members pushed the moderates toward confrontation. Boston's master politician engineered congressional commendation of the Suffolk Resolves, a bold statement drawn up in Suffolk County, Massachusetts, that encouraged forcible resistance of the Coercive Acts.

After this decision, the tone of the meeting was established. Moderate spokesmen introduced conciliatory measures, which received polite discussion but failed to win a majority vote. Just before returning to their homes (September 1774), the delegates created the "Association," an intercolonial agreement to halt all commerce with Britain until Parliament repealed the Intolerable Acts. This was a totally revolutionary decision. The Association authorized a vast network of local committees to enforce **nonimportation.** Violators were exposed, shamed, forced either to apologize publicly for their actions or to be shunned by all their patriot neighbors. In many of the communities, the committees *were* the government, distinguishing, in the words of James Madison, "Friends from Foes." George III sneered at these activities. "I am not sorry," he confided, "that the line of conduct seems now chalked out . . . the New England Governments are in a state of Rebellion, blows must decide whether they are to be subject to this country or independent."

### Shots Heard Around the World

The king was correct. Before Congress reconvened, "blows" fell at Lexington and Concord, two small farm villages in eastern Massachusetts. On the evening of April 18, 1775, General Gage dispatched troops from Boston to seize rebel supplies. Paul Revere, a renowned silversmith and active patriot, warned the colonists that the redcoats were coming. The militia of Lexington, a collection of ill-trained farmers, boys as well as old men, decided to stand on the village green on the following morning, April 19, as the British soldiers passed on the road to Concord. No one planned to fight, but in a moment of confusion, someone (probably a colonist) fired; the redcoats discharged a volley, and eight Americans lay dead.

Word of the incident spread rapidly, and by the time the British force reached its destination, the countryside swarmed with "minutemen," special com-

*This 1775 engraving by Amos Doolittle, an eyewitness, shows the American attack on the British regulars as they marched from Concord back to Boston. The minutemen fired from cover, killing and wounding many redcoats who expected little armed resistance.* ❖

panies of Massachusetts militia prepared to respond instantly to military emergencies. The redcoats found nothing of significance in Concord and so returned. The long march back to Boston turned into a rout. Lord Percy, a British officer who brought up reinforcements, remarked more in surprise than bitterness that "whoever looks upon them [the American soldiers] as an irregular mob, will find himself much mistaken." On June 17, colonial militiamen again held their own against seasoned troops at the battle of Bunker Hill (actually Breed's Hill). The British finally took the hill, but after this costly "victory" in which he suffered 40 percent casualties, Gage complained that the Americans had displayed "a conduct and spirit against us, they never showed against the French."

## Beginning "The World Over Again"

Members of the **Second Continental Congress** gathered in Philadelphia in May 1775. They faced an awesome responsibility. British government in the mainland colonies had almost ceased to function, and with Americans fighting redcoats, the country desperately needed strong central leadership. Slowly, often reluctantly, Congress took control of the war. The delegates formed a Continental Army and appointed George

Washington its commander, in part because he seemed to have greater military experience than anyone else available and in part because he looked like he should be commander in chief. The delegates were also eager to select someone who did not come from Massachusetts, a colony that seemed already to possess too much power in national councils. The members of Congress purchased military supplies and, to pay for them, issued paper money. But while they were assuming the powers of a sovereign government, the congressmen refused to declare independence. They debated and fretted, listened to the appeals of moderates who played on the colonists' remaining loyalty to Britain, and then did nothing.

Indecision drove men such as John Adams nearly mad. In one tirade against his timid colleagues, he exclaimed that they possessed "the vanity of the ape, the tameness of the ox, or the stupid servility of the ass." Haste, however, would have been a terrible mistake. While Adams and Richard Henry Lee of Virginia were willing to sever ties with Britain, many Americans were not convinced that such a step was either desirable or necessary. If Congress had moved too quickly, it might have become vulnerable to charges of extremism, in which case the rebellion would have seemed—and indeed, might have been—

more like an overthrow by a faction or clique than an expression of popular will.

The British government appeared intent on transforming colonial moderates into angry rebels. In December 1775, Parliament passed the Prohibitory Act, declaring war on American commerce. Until the colonists begged for pardon, they could not trade with the rest of the world. The British navy blockaded their ports and seized American ships on the high seas. Lord North also hired German mercenaries (the Russians drove too hard a bargain) to put down the rebellion. And in America, Virginia's royal governor Lord Dunmore further undermined the possibility of reconciliation by urging the colony's slaves to take up arms against their masters. Few did so, but the effort to stir up black rebellion infuriated the Virginia gentry.

Thomas Paine (1737–1809) pushed the colonists even closer to independence. Nothing in this man's background suggested he would write the most important pamphlet in American history. In England, Paine had tried and failed in a number of jobs, and exactly why he elected to move to America in 1774 is not clear. While still in England, Paine had the good fortune to meet Benjamin Franklin, who presented him with letters of introduction to the leading patriots of Pennsylvania. At the urging of his new American friends, Paine produced **Common Sense,** an essay that became an instant best-seller. In only three months, it sold more than 120,000 copies. Paine confirmed in forceful prose what the colonists had been thinking but had been unable to state in coherent form. "My motive and object in all my political works," he declared, " . . . have been to rescue man from tyranny and false systems of government, and enable him to be free."

*Common Sense* systematically stripped kingship of historical and theological justification. For centuries, the English had maintained the fiction that the monarch could do no wrong. When the government oppressed the people, the royal counselors received the blame. The crown was above suspicion. To this, Paine cried nonsense. Monarchs ruled by force. George III was simply a "royal brute," who by his arbitrary behavior had surrendered his claim to the colonists' obedience. The pamphlet also attacked the whole idea of a mixed and balanced constitution. Indeed, *Common Sense* was a powerful democratic manifesto.

Paine's greatest contribution to the revolutionary cause was persuading ordinary folk to sever their ties with Great Britain. It was not reasonable, he argued, to regard England as the mother country. "Europe, and not England," he explained, "is the parent country of America. This new world hath been the asylum for the persecuted lovers of civil and religious liberty from *every part* of Europe." No doubt that message made a deep impression on Pennsylvania's German population. The time had come for the colonists to form an independent republic. "We have it in our power," Paine wrote in one of his most moving statements, "to begin the world over again . . . the birthday of a new world is at hand."

On July 2, 1776, after a long and tedious debate, Congress finally voted for independence. The motion passed: twelve states for, none against (with New York abstaining). Thomas Jefferson, a young Virginia lawyer and planter who enjoyed a reputation as a graceful writer, drafted a formal declaration that was accepted with alterations two days later. Much of the Declaration of Independence consisted of a list of specific grievances against George III and his government. Like the skilled lawyer he was, Jefferson presented the evidence for independence. The document did not become famous for those passages. Long after the establishment of the new republic, the Declaration challenged Americans to make good on the principle that "all men are created equal." John Adams nicely expressed the patriots' fervor when he wrote on July 3, "Yesterday the greatest question was decided, which ever was debated in America, and a greater perhaps, never was or will be decided among men."

Many revolutionary leaders throughout the modern world—in Europe as in Asia—have echoed Adams's assessment. Of all the documents written during this period, including the Constitution, the Declaration remains the most powerful and radical invitation to Americans of all backgrounds to demand their equality and full rights as human beings.

*The message of Thomas Paine's pamphlet* Common Sense *(title page shown) was clear and direct. Paine's powerful argument called for "The Free and Independent States of America." He assured ordinary Americans not only that they could live without a king, but also that they would win the war.* ❖

*Congress Voting Independence, oil painting by Robert Edge Pine and Edward Savage, 1785. The committee appointed by Congress to draft a declaration of independence included (center, standing) John Adams, Roger Sherman, Robert Livingston, Thomas Jefferson, and (center foreground, seated) Benjamin Franklin. The committee members are shown submitting Jefferson's draft to the speaker.* ❖

# FIGHTING FOR INDEPENDENCE

Only fools and visionaries expressed optimism about America's prospects of winning independence in 1776. The Americans had taken on a formidable military power. The population of Britain was perhaps four times that of its former colonies. England also possessed a strong manufacturing base, a well-trained regular army supplemented by thousands of hired German troops (Hessians), and a navy that dominated the world's oceans. Many British officers had battlefield experience. They already knew what the Americans would slowly learn: Waging war requires discipline, money, and sacrifice.

The British government entered the conflict fully confident that it could beat the Americans. In 1776, Lord North and his colleagues regarded the war as a police action. They anticipated that a mere show of armed force would intimidate the upstart colonists. As soon as the rebels in Boston had been humbled, the British argued, people living in other colonies would desert the cause for independence. General Gage, for example, told the king that the colonists "will be Lions, whilst we are Lambs, . . . if we take a resolute part they will undoubtedly prove very weak." Since this advice confirmed George's views, he called Gage "an honest determined man."

As later events demonstrated, of course, Britain had become involved in an impossible military situation, in some ways analogous to that in which the United States would find itself in Vietnam some two hundred years later. Three separate elements neutral-

ized advantages held by the larger power over its adversary. First, the British had to transport men and supplies across the Atlantic, a logistic challenge of unprecedented complexity. Unreliable lines of communication broke down under the strain of war.

Second, America was too vast to be conquered by conventional military methods. Redcoats might gain control over the major port cities, but as long as the Continental Army remained intact, the rebellion continued. As Washington explained, "the possession of our Towns, while we have an Army in the field, will avail them little . . . It is our Arms, not defenceless Towns, they have to subdue." Even if England had recruited enough soldiers to occupy the entire country, it would still have lost the war. As one Loyalist instructed the king, "if all America becomes a garrison, she is not worth your attention." Britain could only win by crushing the American will to resist.

And third, British strategists never appreciated the depth of the Americans' commitment to a political ideology. In the wars of eighteenth-century Europe, such beliefs had seldom mattered. European troops before the French Revolution served because they were paid or because the military was a vocation, but most certainly not because they hoped to advance a set of constitutional principles. Americans were different. To be sure, some young men were drawn to the military by bounty money or by the desire to escape unhappy families. A few were drafted. But taking such people into account, one still encounters among the American troops a remarkable commitment to republican ideals. One French officer reported from the United States, "It

**THE AMERICAN REVOLUTION, 1775–1781** *The War for Independence ranged over a huge area. Battles were fought in the colonies, on the western frontier, and along the Gulf of Mexico. The major engagements of the first years of the war, from the spontaneous rising at Concord in 1775 to Washington's well-coordinated attack on Trenton in December 1776, were fought in the northern colonies. In the middle theater of war, Burgoyne's attempt in 1777 to cut off New England from the rest of the colonies failed when his army was defeated at Saratoga. Action in the final years of the war, from the battles at Camden, Kings Mountain, Cowpens, and Guilford Courthouse to the final victory at Yorktown, occurred in the southern theater of war.* ❖

is incredible that soldiers composed of men of every age, even of children of fifteen, of whites and blacks, almost naked, unpaid, and rather poorly fed, can march so well and withstand fire so steadfastly."

## Building a Professional Army

During the earliest months of rebellion, American soldiers—especially those of New England—suffered no lack of confidence. Indeed, they interpreted their courageous stands at Concord and Bunker Hill as evidence that brave yeomen farmers could lick British regulars on any battlefield. George Washington spent the first years of the war disabusing the colonists of this foolishness, for as he had learned during the French and Indian War, military success depended on endless drill, careful planning, and tough discipline—rigorous preparation that did not characterize the minutemen's methods.

Washington insisted on organizing a regular well-trained field army. Some advisers urged the commander in chief to wage a guerrilla war, one in which small partisan bands would sap Britain's will to rule Americans. But Washington rejected that course. He recognized that the Continental Army served not only as a fighting force but also as a symbol of the republican cause. Its very existence would sustain American hopes, and so long as the army survived, American agents could plausibly solicit foreign aid. This thinking shaped Washington's wartime strategy; he studiously avoided "general actions" in which the Continental Army might be destroyed. Critics complained about Washington's caution, but as they soon discovered, he understood better than they what independence required.

If the commander in chief was correct about the army, however, he failed to comprehend the political importance of the militia. These scattered, almost amateur, military units seldom altered the outcome of battle, but they did maintain control over large areas of the country not directly affected by the British army. Throughout the war, they compelled men and women who would rather have remained neutral to actively support the American effort. In 1777, for example, the militia of Farmington, Connecticut, visited a group of suspected Tories, as Loyalists were called, and after "educating" these people in the fundamentals of republican ideology, a militia spokesman announced, "They were indeed grossly ignorant of the true grounds of the present war with Great Britain . . . [but] They appeared to be penitent of their former conduct, [and] professed themselves convinced . . . that there was no such thing as remaining neuters." Without local political coercion, Washington's task would have been considerably more difficult.

For the half million African American colonists, most of them slaves, the fight for independence took on special poignancy. After all, they wanted to achieve personal as well as political freedom, and many African Americans supported those who seemed most likely to deliver them from bondage. As one historian explained, "the black soldier was likely to join the side that made him the quickest and best offer in terms of those 'unalienable rights' of which Mr. Jefferson had spoken." It is estimated that some five thousand African Americans took up arms to fight against the British. The Continental Army included two all-black units, one from Massachusetts and the other from Rhode Island. In 1778, the legislature of Rhode Island voted to free any slave who volunteered to serve, since, according to the lawmakers, history taught that "the wisest, the freest, and bravest nations . . . liberated their slaves, and enlisted them as soldiers to fight in defence of their country." In the South, especially in Georgia and South Carolina, more than ten thousand African Americans supported the British, and after the patriots had won the war, these men and women left the United States, relocating to Nova Scotia, Florida, and Jamaica, with some eventually resettling in Africa.

## Testing the American Will

After the embarrassing defeats in Massachusetts, the king appointed General Sir William Howe to replace the ill-fated Gage. British rulers now understood that a simple police action would not be sufficient to crush the American rebellion. Parliament authorized sending more than fifty thousand troops to the mainland colonies, and after evacuating Boston—an untenable strategic position—the British forces stormed ashore at Staten Island in New York Harbor on July 3, 1776. From this more central location, Howe believed he could cut the New Englanders off from the rest of America. He enjoyed the powerful support of the British navy under the command of his brother, Admiral Lord Richard Howe.

When Washington learned the British were planning to occupy New York City, he transferred many of his inexperienced soldiers to Long Island, where they suffered a major defeat (August 27, 1776). In a series of engagements disastrous for the Americans, Howe drove the Continental Army across the Hudson River into New Jersey. Because of his failure to take full advantage of the situation, however, General Howe lost what seemed in retrospect an excellent opportunity to annihilate Washington's entire army. Nevertheless, the Americans were on the run, and in the fall of 1776, contemporaries predicted the rebels would soon capitulate.

## "Times That Try Men's Souls"

Swift victories in New York and New Jersey persuaded General Howe that few Americans enthusiastically supported independence. He issued a general pardon, therefore, to anyone who would swear allegiance to George III. The results were encouraging. More than three thousand men and women who lived in areas occupied by the British army took the oath. This group included one intimidated signer of the Declaration of Independence. Howe perceived that a lasting peace in America would require his troops to treat "our enemies as if they might one day become our friends." A member of Lord North's cabinet grumbled that this was "a sentimental manner of making war," a shortsighted view considering England's experience in attempting to pacify the Irish. The pardon plan eventually failed not because Howe lacked toughness but because his soldiers and officers regarded loyal Americans as inferior provincials, an attitude that did little to promote good relations. In any case, as soon as the redcoats left a pardoned region, the rebel militia retaliated against those who had deserted the patriot cause.

In December 1776, Washington's bedraggled army retreated across the Delaware River into Pennsylvania. American prospects appeared bleaker than at any other time during the war. The Continental Army lacked basic supplies, and many men who had signed up for short-term enlistments prepared to go home. "These are the times that try men's souls," Paine wrote in a pamphlet titled *American Crisis*. "The summer soldier and the sunshine patriot will, in this crisis, shrink from the service of their country, but he that

stands it *now* deserves . . . love and thanks . . . " Before winter, Washington determined to attempt one last desperate stroke.

Howe played into Washington's hands. The British forces were dispersed in small garrisons across the state of New Jersey, and while the Americans could not possibly have defeated the combined British army, they did possess the capacity—with luck—to capture an exposed post. On the night of December 25, Continental soldiers slipped over the ice-filled Delaware River and at Trenton took nine hundred sleeping Hessian mercenaries by complete surprise.

Cheered by success, Washington returned a second time to Trenton, but on this occasion the Continental Army was not so fortunate. A large British force under Lord Cornwallis trapped the Americans. Instead of standing and fighting—really an impossible challenge—Washington secretly, by night, marched his little army around Cornwallis's left flank. On January 3, 1777, the Americans surprised a British garrison at Princeton. Washington then went into winter quarters. The British, fearful of losing more outposts, consolidated their troops, thus leaving much of the state in the hands of the patriot militia.

## Victory in a Year of Defeat

In 1777, England's chief military strategist, Lord George Germain, still perceived the war in conventional European terms. A large field army would somehow maneuver Washington's Continental troops into a decisive battle in which the British would enjoy a clear advantage. Complete victory over the Americans cer-

British defeat at the Battle of Princeton, *oil painting by William Mercer, ca. 1786–1790. The painting shows George Washington (left, on horseback) directing cannon fire with his sword. Often risking his own life, Washington led the American troops into battle. The artist's father was mortally wounded in the battle.* ❖

tainly seemed within England's grasp. Unfortunately for the men who advocated this plan, the Continental forces proved extremely elusive, and while one British army vainly tried to corner Washington in Pennsylvania, another was forced to surrender in the forests of upstate New York.

In the summer of 1777, General John Burgoyne, a dashing though overbearing officer, descended from Canada with a force of more than seven thousand troops. They intended to clear the Hudson Valley of rebel resistance; join Howe's army, which was to come up to Albany; and thereby cut New England off from the other states. Burgoyne fought in a grand style. Accompanied by a German band, thirty carts filled with the general's liquor and belongings, and two thousand dependents and camp followers, the British set out to thrash the Americans. The campaign was a disaster. Military units, mostly from New England, cut the enemy force apart in the deep woods north of Albany. At the battle of Bennington (August 16), the New Hampshire militia under Brigadier General John Stark overwhelmed a thousand German mercenaries. After this setback, Burgoyne's forces struggled forward, desperately hoping that Howe would rush to their rescue, but when it became clear that their situation at Saratoga was hopeless, the haughty Burgoyne was forced to surrender fifty-eight hundred men to the American General Horatio Gates (October 17).

Soon after Burgoyne left Canada, General Howe unexpectedly decided to move his main army from New York City to Philadelphia. Exactly what he hoped to achieve was not clear, even to Britain's rulers, and of course, when Burgoyne called for assistance, Howe was sitting in the new nation's capital still trying to devise a way to destroy the Continental Army. Howe's campaign began in late July. The British forces sailed to the head of the Chesapeake Bay and then marched north to Philadelphia. Washington's troops obstructed the enemy's progress, first at Brandywine Creek (September 11) and then at Paoli (September 20), but the outnumbered Americans could not stop the British from entering Philadelphia.

Anxious lest these defeats discourage Congress and the American people, Washington attempted one last battle before the onset of winter. In an engagement at Germantown (October 4), the Americans launched a major counterattack on a fog-covered battlefield, but just at the moment when success seemed assured, they broke off the fight. "When every thing gave the most flattering hopes of victory," Washington complained, "the troops began suddenly to retreat." Bad luck, confusion, and incompetence contributed to the failure. A discouraged Continental Army dug in at Valley Forge, twenty miles outside of Philadelphia, where camp diseases took twenty-five hundred American lives. In their misery, few American soldiers realized their situation was not nearly as desperate as it had been in 1776.

## The French Alliance

Even before the Americans declared their independence, agents of the government of Louis XVI began to explore ways to aid the colonists, not so much because the French monarchy favored the republican cause but because it hoped to embarrass the English. The French deeply resented the defeat they had sustained during the Seven Years' War. During the early months of the Revolution, the French covertly sent tons of essential military supplies to the Americans. The negotiations for these arms involved secret agents and fictitious trading companies, the type of clandestine operation more typical of modern times than of the eighteenth century. But when American representatives, Benjamin Franklin for one, pleaded for official recognition of American independence or for outright military alliance, the French advised patience. The international stakes were too great for the king openly to back a cause that had little chance of success.

The American victory at Saratoga convinced the French that the rebels had formidable forces and were serious in their resolve. Indeed, Lord North drew the same conclusion. When news of Saratoga reached London, North muttered, "This damned war." In private conversation, he expressed doubts about England's ability to win the contest, knowing the French would soon enter the fray.

In April 1778, North tried to avert a greatly expanded war by sending a peace commission to America. He instructed this group, headed by the Earl of Carlisle, to bargain with the Continental Congress "as if it were a legal body." If the colonists would agree to drop their demand for independence, they could turn the imperial calendar back to 1763. Parliament belatedly conceded the right of Americans to tax themselves, even to elect their own governors. It also promised to remove all British troops in times of peace. The proposal might have gained substantial support back in 1776. The war, however, had hardened American resolve; the Congress refused to deal with Carlisle.

In Paris, Franklin performed brilliantly. In meetings with French officials, he hinted that the Americans might accept a British peace initiative. If the French wanted the war to continue, if they really wanted to embarrass their old rival, then they had to do what the English refused: formally recognize the independence of the United States.

The stratagem paid off handsomely. On February 6, 1778, the French presented American representatives with two separate treaties. The first, called the Treaty of Amity and Commerce, established commercial relations between France and the United States. It tacitly accepted the existence of a new, independent republic. The Treaty of Alliance was even more generous, considering America's obvious military and economic weaknesses. In the event that France and England went to war (they did so on June 14, as everyone expected), the French agreed to reject "either Truce or Peace with Great Britain . . . until the independence of the United States shall have been formally or tacitly assured by the Treaty or Treaties that shall terminate the War." Even more amazing, France surrendered its claim to all territories formerly owned by Great Britain east of the Mississippi River. The Americans pledged they would not sign a separate peace with Britain without first informing their new ally. And in return, France made no claim to Canada, asking only for the right to take possession of certain British islands in the Caribbean. Never had Franklin worked his magic to greater effect.

French intervention instantly transformed British military strategy. What had been a colonial rebellion suddenly became a world conflict, a continuation of the great wars for empire of the late seventeenth century (see Chapter 4). Scarce military resources, especially newer fighting ships, had to be diverted from the American theater to guard the English Channel. In fact, there was talk in London of a possible French invasion. Although the threat of such an assault was not very great until 1779, the British did have cause for concern. The French navy posed a serious challenge to the overextended British fleet. By concentrating their warships in a specific area, the French could hold off or even defeat British squadrons, an advantage that would figure significantly in the American victory at Yorktown.

## The Final Campaign

British General Henry Clinton replaced Howe, who resigned after the battle of Saratoga. Clinton was a strangely complex individual. As a subordinate officer, he had impressed his superiors as imaginative but easily provoked to anger. When he took command of the British army, his resolute self-confidence suddenly dissolved. Perhaps he feared failure. Whatever the explanation for his vacillation, Clinton's record in America was little better than Howe's or Gage's.

Military strategists calculated that Britain's last chance of winning the war lay in the Southern Colonies, a region largely untouched in the early years of fighting. Intelligence reports reaching London indicated that Georgia and South Carolina contained a sizable body of Loyalists, men who would take up arms for the crown if only they received support and encouragement from the regular army. The southern strategy devised by Germain and Clinton in 1779 turned the war into a bitter guerrilla conflict, and during the last months of battle, British officers worried that their search for an easy victory had inadvertently opened a Pandora's box of uncontrollable partisan furies.

The southern campaign opened in the spring of 1780. Savannah had already fallen, and Clinton reckoned that if the British could take Charles Town, they would be able to control the entire South. A large fleet carrying nearly eight thousand redcoats reached South Carolina in February. Complacent Americans had allowed the city's fortifications to decay, and in a desper-

*French assistance on land and sea helped the Americans defeat the British in the American Revolution. In this French print of the battle at Yorktown, French ships block the entrance of Chesapeake Bay, preventing British vessels from resupplying their troops on land. Yorktown, which was unknown to the French artist who made this print, is depicted as a European walled city. ❖*

*During the Revolutionary War, Britain maintained prison ships in the harbors of New York City to hold American soldiers captured in battle. In this sketch, John Trumbull shows the squalid conditions aboard one floating jail off the shore of Brooklyn.* ❖

ate, last-minute effort to preserve Charles Town, General Benjamin Lincoln's forces dug trenches and reinforced walls, but to no avail. Clinton and his second in command, General Cornwallis, gradually encircled the city, and on May 12, Lincoln surrendered an American army of almost six thousand men.

The defeat took Congress by surprise, and without making proper preparations, it dispatched a second army to South Carolina under Horatio Gates, the hero of Saratoga. He too failed. At Camden, Cornwallis outmaneuvered the raw American recruits, capturing or killing 750 during the course of battle (August 16). Poor Gates galloped from the scene and did not stop until he reached Hillsboro, North Carolina, two hundred miles away.

Even at this early stage of the southern campaign, the dangers of partisan warfare had become evident. Tory raiders showed little interest in serving as regular soldiers in Cornwallis's army. They preferred night riding, indiscriminate plundering or murdering of neighbors against whom they harbored ancient grudges. The British had unleashed a horde of banditti across South Carolina. Men who genuinely supported independence or who had merely fallen victim to Loyalist guerrillas bided their time. They retreated westward, waiting for their enemies to make a mistake. Their chance came on October 7 at King's Mountain, North Carolina. In the most vicious fighting of the Revolution, the backwoodsmen decimated a force of British regulars and Tory raiders who had strayed too far from base. One witness reported that when a

British officer tried to surrender, he was summarily shot down by at least seven American soldiers.

Cornwallis, badly confused and poorly supplied, squandered his strength chasing American forces across the Carolinas. Whatever military strategy had compelled him to leave Charles Town had long since been abandoned, and in early 1781, Cornwallis informed Clinton, "Events alone can decide the future Steps." Events, however, did not run in the British favor. Congress sent General Nathanael Greene to the South with a new army. This young Rhode Islander was the most capable general on Washington's staff. Greene joined Daniel Morgan, leader of the famed Virginia Riflemen, and in a series of tactically brilliant engagements, they sapped the strength of Cornwallis's army, first at Cowpens, South Carolina (January 17, 1781), and later at Guilford Courthouse, North Carolina (March 15). Clinton fumed in New York City. In his estimation, the inept Cornwallis had left "two valuable colonies behind him to be overrun and conquered by the very army which he boasts to have completely routed but a week or two before."

Cornwallis pushed north into Virginia, planning apparently to establish a base of operations on the coast. He selected Yorktown, a sleepy tobacco market located on a peninsula bounded by the York and James rivers. Washington watched these maneuvers closely. The canny Virginia planter knew this territory intimately, and he sensed that Cornwallis had made a serious blunder. When Washington learned the French fleet could gain temporary dominance in the

Chesapeake Bay, he rushed south from New Jersey. With him marched thousands of well-trained French troops under the Comte de Rochambeau. All the pieces fell into place. The French admiral, the Comte de Grasse, cut Cornwallis off from the sea, while Washington and his lieutenants encircled the British on land. On October 19, 1781, Cornwallis surrendered his entire army of six thousand men. When Lord North heard of the defeat at Yorktown, he moaned, "Oh God! It is all over." The British still controlled New York City and Charles Town, but except for a few skirmishes, the fighting ended. The task of securing the independence of the United States was now in the hands of the diplomats.

## THE LOYALIST DILEMMA

The war lasted longer than anyone had predicted in 1776. While the nation won its independence, many Americans paid a terrible price. Indeed, a large number of men and women decided that however much they loved living in America, they could not accept the new government.

No one knows for certain how many Americans actually supported the crown during the Revolution. Some Loyalists undoubtedly kept silent and avoided making a public commitment that might have led to banishment or loss of property. But for many persons, neutrality proved impossible. Almost 100,000 men and women permanently left America. While a number of these exiles had served as imperial officeholders—Thomas Hutchinson, for example—in the main, they came from all ranks and backgrounds. A large number of humble farmers, more than 30,000, resettled in Canada. Others relocated to England, the West Indies, or Africa.

The political ideology of the Loyalists was not substantially different from that of their opponents. Like other Americans, they believed that men and women were entitled to life, liberty, and the pursuit of happiness. The Loyalists were also convinced that independence would destroy those values by promoting disorder. By turning their backs on Britain, a source of tradition and stability, the rebels seemed to have encouraged licentiousness, even anarchy in the streets. The Loyalists suspected that Patriot demands

**LOYALIST STRONGHOLDS**   *The highest concentration of Loyalists were in the colonies of New York, North Carolina, South Carolina, and Georgia, especially in the areas around port cities such as New York City, Wilmington, Charleston, and Savannah.* ❖

for freedom were self-serving, even hypocritical, for as Perserved Smith, a Loyalist from Ashfield, Massachusetts, observed, "Sons of liberty . . . did not deserve the name, for it was evident all they wanted was liberty from oppression that they might have liberty to oppress!"

The Loyalists were caught in a difficult squeeze. The British never quite trusted them. After all, they were Americans. During the early stages of the war, Loyalists organized militia companies and hoped to pacify large areas of the countryside with the support of the regular army. The British generals were unreliable partners, however, for no sooner had they called on loyal Americans to come forward than the redcoats marched away, leaving the Tories exposed to rebel retaliation. And in England, the exiles found themselves treated as second-class citizens. While many of them received monetary compensation for their sacrifice, they were never regarded as the equals of native-born English citizens. Not surprisingly, the Loyalist community in London was gradually transformed into a collection of bitter men and women who felt unwelcome on both sides of the Atlantic.

Americans who actively supported independence saw these people as traitors who deserved their fate of constant, often violent, harassment. In many states—but especially in New York—revolutionary governments confiscated Loyalist property. Other friends of the king received beatings, or as the rebels called them, "grand Toory [sic] rides." A few were even executed. According to one patriot, "A Tory is a thing whose head is in England, and its body in America, and its neck ought to be stretched."

Long after the victorious Americans turned their attentions to the business of building a new republic, Loyalists remembered a receding colonial past, a comfortable, ordered world that had been lost forever at Yorktown. Although many Loyalists eventually returned to their homes, a sizable number could not do so. For them, the sense of loss remained a heavy emotional burden. Perhaps the most poignant testimony came from a young mother living in exile in Nova Scotia. "I climbed to the top of Chipman's Hill and watched the sails disappear in the distance," she recounted, "and such a feeling of loneliness came over me that though I had not shed a tear through all the war I sat down on the damp moss with my baby on my lap and cried bitterly."

## WINNING THE PEACE

Congress appointed a skilled delegation to negotiate a peace treaty: Benjamin Franklin, John Adams, and John Jay. According to their official instructions, they were to insist only on the recognition of the independence of the United States. On other issues, Congress ordered its delegates to defer to the counsel of the French government.

But the political environment in Paris was much different from what the diplomats had been led to expect. The French had formed a military alliance with

| CHRONOLOGY | |
|---|---|
| **1763** | Peace of Paris ends the Seven Years' War |
| **1764** | Parliament passes Sugar Act to collect American revenue |
| **1765** | Stamp Act receives support of House of Commons (March) ❖ Stamp Act Congress meets in New York City (October) |
| **1766** | Stamp Act repealed the same day that Declaratory Act becomes law (March 18) |
| **1767** | Townshend Revenue Acts stir American anger (June–July) |
| **1768** | Massachusetts assembly refuses to rescind circular letter (February) |
| **1770** | Parliament repeals all Townshend duties except one on tea (March) ❖ British troops "massacre" Boston civilians (March) |
| **1772** | Samuel Adams forms committee of correspondence |
| **1773** | Lord North's government passes Tea Act (May) ❖ Bostonians hold Tea Party (December) |
| **1774** | Parliament punishes Boston with Coercive Acts (March–June) ❖ First Continental Congress convenes (September) |
| **1775** | Patriots take stand at Lexington and Concord (April) ❖ Second Continental Congress gathers (May) ❖ Americans hold their own at Bunker Hill (June) |
| **1776** | Congress votes for independence; Declaration of Independence is signed ❖ British defeat Washington at Long Island (August) ❖ Americans score victory at Trenton (December) |
| **1777** | General Burgoyne surrenders at Saratoga (October) |
| **1778** | French treaties recognize independence of the United States (February) |
| **1780** | British take Charles Town (May) |
| **1781** | Washington forces Cornwallis to surrender at Yorktown (October) |
| **1783** | Peace treaty signed (September) ❖ British evacuate New York City (November) |

Spain, and French officials announced that they could not consider the details of an American settlement until after the Spanish had recaptured Gibraltar from the British. The prospects for a Spanish victory were not good, and in any case, it was well known that Spain coveted the lands lying between the Appalachian Mountains and the Mississippi River. Indeed, there were even rumors afloat in Paris that the great European powers might intrigue to deny the United States its independence.

While the three American delegates publicly paid their respects to French officials, they secretly entered into negotiations with an English agent. The peacemakers drove a remarkable bargain, a much better one than Congress could have expected. The preliminary agreement signed on September 3, 1783, not only guaranteed the independence of the United States; it also transferred all the territory east of the Mississippi River, except Spanish Florida, to the new republic. The treaty established generous boundaries on the north and south and gave the Americans important fishing rights in the North Atlantic. In exchange, Congress promised to help British merchants collect debts contracted before the Revolution and compensate Loyalists whose lands had been confiscated by the various state governments. Even though the Americans negotiated separately with the British, they did not sign a separate peace. The preliminary treaty did not become effective until France reached its own agreement with Great Britain. Thus did the Americans

honor the French alliance. It is difficult to imagine how Franklin, Adams, and Jay could have negotiated a more favorable conclusion to the war. In the fall of 1783, the last redcoats sailed from New York City, ending 176 years of colonial rule.

## CONCLUSION: PRESERVING INDEPENDENCE

The American people had waged war against the most powerful nation in Europe and emerged victorious. The treaty marked the conclusion of a colonial rebellion, but it remained for the men and women who had resisted taxation without representation to work out the full implications of republicanism. What would be the shape of the new government? What powers would be delegated to the people, the states, the federal authorities? How far would the wealthy, well-born leaders of the rebellion be willing to extend political, social, and economic rights?

For many Americans the challenge of nation building appeared even more formidable than waging war against Great Britain. As Philadelphia physician Dr. Benjamin Rush explained, "There is nothing more common than to confound the terms of American Revolution with those of the late American war. The American war is over, but this is far from being the case with the American Revolution. On the contrary, nothing but the first act of the great drama is closed."

## RECOMMENDED READING

Several books have had a profound impact on how historians think about the ideas that energized the Revolution. In a moving narrative account, Edmund S. Morgan and Helen M. Morgan explore how Americans interpreted the first great imperial controversy: *The Stamp Act Crisis: Prologue to Revolution* (1953). In his classic study, *The Ideological Origins of the American Revolution* (1967), Bernard Bailyn maps an ideology of power that informed colonial protest. Gordon Wood extends this argument in *The Radicalism of the American Revolution* (1992). In *Marketplace of Revolution: How Consumer Politics Shaped American Independence* (2004), T. H. Breen attempts to integrate more fully the experiences of ordinary men and women into the analysis of popular mobilization. Alfred F. Young demonstrates that it is possible to write about revolution from the perspective of working class colonists in *The Shoemaker and the Tea Party: Memory and the American Revolution* (2000). Works that focus productively on popular mobilization in specific colonies include Rhys Isaac, *The Transformation of Virginia, 1740–1790* (1983); Robert A. Gross, *The Minutemen and Their World* (1976); Woody Holton, *Forced Founders: Indians, Debtors, Slaves and the Making of the American Revolution in Virginia* (1999); and T. H. Breen,

*Tobacco Culture: The Mentality of the Great Tidewater Planters on the Eve of Revolution* (1985). The tragedy that visited the Native Americans is examined in Colin C. Calloway, *American Revolution in Indian Country: Crisis and Diversity in Native American Communities* (1995) and Gregory Evans Dowd, *War Under Heaven: Pontiac, The Indian Nations and the British Empire* (2002). A useful study of the aspirations and disappointments of American women during this period is Linda Kerber, *Women of the Republic: Intellect and Ideology in Revolutionary America* (1980). Charles Royster investigates the changing attitudes of the American people about the Continental Army in *A Revolutionary People at War: The Continental Army and American Character, 1775–1783* (1979). Also valuable is John W. Shy, *A People Numerous and Armed: Reflections on the Military Struggle for American Independence*, rev. ed. (1990). Sidney Kaplan, *The Black Presence in the Era of the American Revolution* (1973), documents the hopes of African Americans during a period of radical political change.

**For a list of additional titles related to this chapter's topics, please see** http://www.ablongman.com/divine.

# SUGGESTED WEB SITES

### Canada History

http://www.civilization.ca/indexe.asp
Canada and the United States shared a colonial past but developed differently in the long run. This site is a part of the virtual museum of the Canadian Museum of Civilization Corporation.

### Georgia's Rare Map Collection

http://scarlett.libs.uga.edu/darchive/hargrett/maps/colamer.html
http://scarlett.libs.uga.edu/darchive/hargrett/maps/revamer.html
These two sites contain maps for Colonial and Revolutionary America.

### Maryland Loyalism and the American Revolution

http://users.erols.com/candidus/index.htm
This look at Maryland's loyalists promotes the author's book, but the site has good information about an underappreciated phenomenon, including loyalist songs and poems.

### The American Revolution

http://revolution.h-net.msu.edu/
This site accompanies the PBS series *Revolution* with essays and resource links.

*Francis Guy, Tontine Coffee House, 1797. The Tontine is the large building at left, on the corner of Wall and Water Streets in New York City, where merchants and traders met daily to transact business.* ❖

# The Republican Experiment

## *A New Political Morality*

In 1788, Lewis Hallam and John Henry petitioned the General Assembly of Pennsylvania to open a theater. Although a 1786 state law banned the performance of stage plays and other "disorderly sports," many Philadelphia leaders favored the request to hold "dramatic representations" in their city. A committee appointed to study the issue concluded that a theater would contribute to "the general refinement of manners and the polish of society." Some supporters even argued that the sooner the United States had a professional theater the sooner the young republic would escape the "foreign yoke" of British culture.

The Quakers of Philadelphia dismissed such claims out of hand. They warned that such "seminaries of lewdness and irreligion" would quickly undermine "the virtue of the people." They pointed out that "no sooner is a playhouse opened than it becomes surrounded with . . . brothels." Since Pennsylvania was already suffering from a "stagnation of commerce [and] a scarcity of money"—unmistakable signs of God's displeasure—it seemed unwise to risk divine punishment by encouraging new "hot-beds of vice."

Such rhetoric did not sit well with other citizens who interpreted the revolutionary experience from an entirely different perspective. At issue, they insisted, was not popular morality, but state censorship. If the government silenced the stage, then "the same authority . . . may, with equal justice, dictate the shape and texture of our dress, or the modes and ceremonies of our worship." Depriving those who wanted to see plays of an opportunity to do so, they argued, "will abridge the natural right of every freeman, to dispose of his time and money, according to his own tastes and dispositions."

THROUGHOUT POST–REVOLUTIONARY AMERICA everyday matters such as the opening of a new playhouse provoked passionate public debate. These divisions were symptomatic of a new, uncertain political culture struggling to find the proper balance between public morality and private freedom. During the long fight against Great Britain, Americans had defended individual rights. The problem was that the same people also believed that a republic that compromised its virtue could not long preserve liberty and independence.

In 1776, Thomas Paine had reminded ordinary men and women that "the sun never shined on a cause of greater worth. . . . 'Tis not the concern of a day, a year, or an age; posterity are virtually involved in the contest, and will be more or less affected, even to the end of time, by the proceedings now." During the 1780s Americans understood their responsibility not only to each other, but also to history. They worried, however, that they might not successfully meet the challenge. The dangers were manifest. Individual states seemed intent on looking out for local interests rather than the national welfare. Revolutionary leaders such as George Washington and James Madison concluded that the United States needed a strong central government to protect rights and property. Their creative quest for solutions brought forth a new and enduring constitution.

## DEFINING REPUBLICAN CULTURE

Today, the term *republican* no longer possesses the evocative power it did for most eighteenth-century Americans. For them, it defined an entire political culture. After all, they had done something that no other people had achieved for a very long time. They founded a national government without a monarch or aristocracy; in other words, a genuine republic. Making the new system work was a daunting task. Those Americans who read deeply in ancient and renaissance history knew that most republics had failed, often within a few years, only to be replaced by tyrants who cared not at all what ordinary people thought about the public good. To preserve their republic from such a fate, victorious revolutionaries such as Samuel Adams recast fundamental political values. For them, **republicanism** represented more than a particular form of government. It was a way of life, a core ideology, an uncompromising commitment to liberty and equality.

Adams and his contemporaries certainly believed that creating a new nation-state involved more than simply winning independence from Great Britain. More than did any other form of government, they insisted, a republic demanded an exceptionally high degree of public morality. If American citizens substituted "luxury, prodigality, and profligacy" for "prudence, virtue, and economy," then their revolution surely would have been in vain. Maintaining popular virtue was crucial to success. An innocent stage play, therefore, set off alarm bells. Such "foolish gratifications" seemed to compromise republican goals. It is not surprising that confronted by such temptations Adams thundered, "Rome, Athens, and all the cities of renown, whence came your fall?"

White Americans came out of the Revolution with an almost euphoric sense of the nation's special destiny. This expansive outlook, encountered among so many ordinary men and women, owed much to the spread of Protestant evangelicalism. However skeptical Jefferson and Franklin may have been about revealed religion, the great mass of American people subscribed to an almost utopian vision of the country's future. To this new republic, God had promised progress and prosperity. The signs were visible for everyone. "There is not upon the face of the earth a body of people more happy or rising into consequence with more rapid stride," one man announced in 1786, "than the Inhabitants of the United States of America. Population is increasing, new houses building, new lands clearing, new settlements forming, and new manufactures establishing with a rapidity beyond conception."

Such experience did not translate easily or smoothly into the creation of a strong central government. Modern Americans tend to take for granted the acceptance of the Constitution. Its merits seem self-evident largely because it has survived for two centuries. But in the early 1780s, no one could have predicted that the Constitution as we know it would have been written, much less ratified. It was equally possible that the Americans would have supported a weak confederation or perhaps allowed the various states and regions to go their separate ways.

In this uncertain political atmosphere, Americans divided sharply over the relative importance of *liberty* and *order*. The revolutionary experience had called into question the legitimacy of any form of special privilege. As one republican informed an aristocratic colleague in the South Carolina assembly, "the day is Arrived when *goodness,* and not *Wealth,* are the only *Criterions of greatness.*" A legislative leader in Pennsylvania put the point even more bluntly: "No man has a greater claim of special privilege for his $100,000 than I have for my $5." The man who passionately defended social equality for those of varying economic status, however, may still have resisted the extension of civil rights to women or blacks. Nevertheless, liberty was contagious, and Americans of all backgrounds began to make new demands on society and government. For them, the Revolution had suggested radical alternatives, and in many forums throughout the nation—especially in the elected state assemblies—they insisted on being heard.

In certain quarters, the celebration of liberty met with mixed response. Some Americans—often the very men who had resisted British tyranny—worried that the citizens of the new nation were caught up in a wild, destructive scramble for material wealth. Democratic excesses seemed to threaten order, to endanger the rights of property. Surely a republic could not long survive unless its citizens showed greater self-control. For people concerned about the loss of order, the state assemblies appeared to be the greatest source of instability. Popularly elected representatives lacked what men of property defined as real civic virtue, an ability to work for the common good rather than their private interests.

Working out the tensions between order and liberty, between property and equality, generated an outpouring of political genius. At other times in American history, persons of extraordinary talent have been drawn to theology, commerce, or science, but during the 1780s, the country's intellectual leaders—Thomas Jefferson, James Madison, Alexander Hamilton, and John Adams, among others—focused their creative energies on the problem of how republicans ought to govern themselves.

## LIVING IN THE SHADOW OF REVOLUTION

Revolution changed American society, often in ways no one had planned. This phenomenon is not surprising. The great revolutions of modern times produced radical transformations in French, Russian, and Chinese societies. By comparison, the immediate results of the American Revolution appear much tamer, less wrenching. Nevertheless, national independence compelled people to reevaluate hierarchical social relations that they had taken for granted during the colonial period. The faltering first steps of independence raised fundamental questions about the meaning of equality in American society, some of which remain as pressing today as during the 1780s.

### Social and Political Reform

Following the war, Americans aggressively ferreted out and, with republican fervor, denounced any traces of aristocratic pretense. As colonists, they had long resented the claims that certain Englishmen made to special privilege simply because of noble birth. Even so committed a republican as George Washington had to be reminded that artificial status was contrary to republican principles. In 1783, he and the officers who had served during the Revolution formed the Society of the Cincinnati, a hereditary organization in which membership passed from father to eldest son. The soldiers meant no harm; they simply wanted to maintain old friendships. But anxious republicans throughout America let out a howl of protest, and one South Carolina legislator, Aedanus Burke, warned that the Society intended to create "an hereditary peerage . . . [which would] undermine the Constitution and destroy civil liberty." After an embarrassed Washington called for appropriate reforms of the Society's bylaws, the Cincinnati crisis receded. The fear of privilege remained, however, and wealthy Americans dropped honorific titles such as "esquire." Lawyers of republican persuasion chided judges who had adopted the English custom of wearing great flowing wigs to court.

The appearance of equality was as important as its actual achievement. In fact, the distribution of wealth in postwar America was more uneven than it had been in the mid-eighteenth century. The sudden accumulation of large fortunes by new families made other Americans particularly sensitive to aristocratic display, for it seemed intolerable that a revolution waged against a monarchy should produce a class of persons legally, or even visibly, distinguished from their fellow citizens.

In an effort to root out the notion of a privileged class, states abolished laws of primogeniture and en-

*Questions of equality in the new republic extended to the rights of women. In this illustration, which appeared as the frontispiece in the 1792 issue of* The Lady's Magazine and Repository of Entertaining Knowledge, *the "Genius of the Ladies Magazine" and the "Genius of Emulation" (holding in her hand a laurel crown) present to Liberty a petition for the rights of woman. ❖*

tail. In colonial times, these laws allowed a landholder either to pass his entire estate to his eldest son or to declare that his property could never be divided, sold, or given away. Jefferson claimed that the repeal of these practices would eradicate "antient [sic] and future aristocracy; a foundation [has been] laid for a government truly republican." Jefferson may have exaggerated the social impact of this reform. But however many planters actually suffered from entail or primogeniture, the symbolism of the law counted as much as real social practice. Republican legislators wanted to cleanse traces of the former feudal order from the statute books.

Republican ferment also encouraged many states to lower property requirements for voting. After the break with Great Britain, such a step seemed logical. As one group of farmers declared, no man can be "free & independent" unless he possesses "a voice . . . in the choice of the most important Officers in the Legislature." Pennsylvania and Georgia allowed all white male taxpayers to participate in elections. Other states were less democratic, but with the exception of Massachusetts, they reduced property qualifications. The reforms, however, did not significantly expand the American electorate. Long before the Revolution, an overwhelming percentage of free white males had owned enough land to vote. In any case, during the 1780s, republican lawmakers were not prepared to experiment with universal manhood suffrage; John Adams observed that if the states pushed the reforms too far, "New claims will arise, women will demand a vote . . . and every man who has not a farthing, will demand an equal vote with any other."

The most important changes in voting patterns were the result of western migration. As Americans moved to the frontier, they received full political representation in their state legislatures, and because new districts tended to be poorer than established coastal settlements, their representatives seemed less cultured, less well trained than those sent by eastern voters. Moreover, western delegates resented traveling so far to attend legislative meetings, and they lobbied successfully to transfer state capitals to more convenient locations. During this period, Georgia moved the seat of its government from Savannah to Augusta, South Carolina from Charles Town to Columbia, North Carolina from New Bern to Raleigh, Virginia from Williamsburg to Richmond, New York from New York City to Albany, and New Hampshire from Portsmouth to Concord.

After gaining independence, Americans also reexamined the relation between church and state. Republican spokespersons such as Thomas Jefferson insisted that rulers had no right to interfere with the free expression of an individual's religious beliefs. As governor of Virginia, he strenuously advocated the disestablishment of the Anglican Church, an institution that had received tax monies and other benefits during the colonial period. Jefferson and his allies regarded such special privilege not only as a denial of religious freedom—after all, rival denominations did not receive tax money—but also as a vestige of aristocratic society.

In 1786, Virginia cut the last ties between church and state. Other southern states disestablished the Anglican Church, but in Massachusetts and New Hampshire, Congregational churches continued to enjoy special status. Moreover, while Americans championed toleration, they seldom favored philosophies that radically challenged Christian values.

## African Americans in the New Republic

Revolutionary fervor forced Americans to confront the most appalling contradiction to republican principles—slavery. The Quaker leader John Woolman (1720–1772) probably did more than any other white person of the era to remind people of the evils of this institution. A trip he took through the Southern Colonies as a young man forever impressed upon Woolman "the dark gloominess" of slavery. In a sermon, the outspoken humanitarian declared "that Men having Power too often misapplied it; that though we made Slaves of the Negroes, and the Turks made Slaves of the Christians, I believed that Liberty was the natural Right of all Men equally."

*A 1797 sketch by architect and engineer Benjamin Henry Latrobe depicting African Americans in Norfolk, Virginia, shaving and dressing in preparation for a Sunday afternoon. Latrobe's drawings of blacks in the American South offer valuable glimpses of daily life in the region.* ❖

During the revolutionary period, abolitionist sentiment spread. Both in private and in public, people began to criticize slavery in other than religious language. No doubt, the double standard of their own political rhetoric embarrassed many white Americans. They hotly demanded liberation from parliamentary enslavement at the same time that they held several hundred thousand blacks in permanent bondage.

By keeping the issue of slavery before the public through writing and petitioning, African Americans powerfully undermined arguments advanced in favor of human bondage. They demanded freedom, reminding white lawmakers that African American men and women had the same natural right to liberty as did other Americans. In 1779, for example, a group of African Americans living in Connecticut pointedly asked the members of the state assembly "whether it is consistent with the present Claims, of the United States, to hold so many Thousands, of the Race of Adam, our Common Father, in perpetual Slavery." In New Hampshire, nineteen persons who called themselves "natives of Africa" reminded local legislators that "private or public tyranny and slavery are alike detestable to minds conscious of the equal dignity of human nature."

The scientific accomplishments of Benjamin Banneker (1731–1806), Maryland's African American astronomer and mathematician, and the international fame of Phillis Wheatley (1753–1784), Boston's celebrated "African muse," made it increasingly difficult for white Americans to maintain credibly that African Americans could not hold their own in a free society. Wheatley's poems went through many editions, and after reading her work, the great French philosopher Voltaire rebuked a friend who had claimed "there never would be Negro poets." As Voltaire discovered, Wheatley "writes excellent verse in English." Banneker, like Wheatley, enjoyed a well-deserved reputation, in his case for contributions as a scientist. After receiving a copy of an almanac that Banneker had published in Philadelphia, Thomas Jefferson concluded "that nature has given to our black brethren, talents equal to those of the other colors of men."

In the northern states, there was no real economic justification for slavery, and white laborers, often recent European immigrants, resented having to compete in the workplace against slaves. This economic situation, combined with the acknowledgment of the double standard represented by slavery, contributed to the establishment of antislavery societies. In 1775, Franklin helped organize a group in Philadelphia called the Society for the Relief of Free Negroes, Unlawfully Held. John Jay, Alexander Hamilton, and other prominent New Yorkers founded

*This engraving of Phillis Wheatley appeared in her volume of verse,* Poems on Various Subjects, Religious and Moral *(1773), the first book published by an African American.* ❖

a Manumission Society in 1785. By 1792, antislavery societies were meeting from Virginia to Massachusetts, and in the northern states at least, these groups, working for the same ends as various Christian evangelicals, put slaveholders on the intellectual defensive for the first time in American history.

In several states north of Virginia, the abolition of slavery took a number of different forms. Even before achieving statehood, Vermont drafted a constitution (1777) that specifically prohibited slavery. In 1780, the Pennsylvania legislature passed a law effecting the gradual emancipation of slaves. Although the Massachusetts assembly refused to address the issue directly, the state courts took up the challenge and liberated the African Americans. (For further discussion of the end of slavery in Massachusetts, see "The Strange Ordeal of Quok Walker," pp. 186–189.) A judge ruled slavery unconstitutional in Massachusetts because it conflicted with a clause in the state bill of rights declaring "all men . . . free and equal." According to one enthusiast, this decision freed "a Grate number of Blacks . . . who . . . are held in a state of slavery within the bowels of a free and christian Country." By 1800, slavery was well on the road to extinction in the northern states.

These positive developments did not mean that white people accepted blacks as equals. In fact, in the very states that outlawed slavery, African Americans faced systematic discrimination. Free blacks were generally excluded from voting, juries, and militia duty—they were denied rights and responsibilities usually associated with full citizenship. They rarely enjoyed access to education, and in cities such as Philadelphia and New York, where African Americans went to look for work, they ended up living in segregated wards or neighborhoods. Even in the churches—institutions that had often spoken out against slavery—free African Americans were denied equal standing with white worshipers. Humiliations of this sort persuaded African Americans to form their own churches. In Philadelphia, Richard Allen, a former slave, founded the Bethel Church for Negro Methodists (1793) and later organized the African Methodist Episcopal Church (1814), an institution of great cultural as well as religious significance for nineteenth-century American blacks.

Even in the South, where African Americans made up a large percentage of the population, slavery disturbed thoughtful white republicans. Some planters simply freed their slaves, and by 1790, the number of free blacks living in Virginia was 12,766. By 1800, the

figure had reached 30,750. There is no question that this trend reflected the uneasiness among white masters. Richard Randolph, one of Virginia's wealthier planters, explained that he freed his slaves "to make restitution, as far as I am able, to an unfortunate race of bond-men, over whom my ancestors have usurped and exercised the most lawless and monstrous tyranny." George Washington also manumitted his slaves. To be sure, most southern slaveholders, especially those living in South Carolina and Georgia, rejected this course of action. Their economic well-being depended on slave labor. Perhaps more significant, however, is the fact that no southern leader during the era of republican experimentation defended slavery as a positive good. Such overtly racist rhetoric did not become part of the public discourse until the nineteenth century.

Despite promising starts in that direction, the southern states did not abolish slavery. The economic incentives to maintain a servile labor force, especially after the invention of the cotton gin in 1793 and the opening up of the Alabama and Mississippi frontier, overwhelmed the initial abolitionist impulse. An opportunity to translate the principles of the American Revolution into social practice had been lost, at least temporarily. Jefferson reported in 1805, "I have long since given up the expectation of any early provision for the extinction of slavery among us." Unlike some contemporary Virginians, the man who wrote the Declaration of Independence condoned slavery on his own plantation, even fathering several children by a woman who, since she was his slave, had little choice in the matter of her pregnancy.

## The Challenge of Women's Rights

The revolutionary experience accelerated changes in the way ordinary people viewed the family. At the beginning of the eighteenth century, fathers claimed authority over other members of their families simply on the grounds that they were fathers. As patriarchs, they demanded obedience. If they behaved like brutal despots, so be it; fathers could treat wives and children however they pleased. The English philosopher John Locke (1632–1704) powerfully undermined arguments of this sort. In his extremely popular treatise *Some Thoughts Concerning Education* (1693), Locke insisted that the mind was not formed at birth. The child learned from experience, and if the infant witnessed violent, arbitrary behavior, then the baby would become an abusive adult. As Locke warned parents, "If you punish him [the child] for what he sees you practice yourself, he will not think that Severity to proceed from Kindness in you careful to amend a Fault in him; but will be apt to interpret it, as Peevishness and Arbitrary Imperiousness of a Father."

*Born to slaves, Richard Allen became a zealous evangelical minister. Allen organized the African Methodist Episcopal Church in 1814.* ❖

Good eighteenth-century mothers and fathers—especially, fathers—condemned tyranny in the home.

At the time of the American Revolution few seriously accepted the notion that fathers—be they tyrannical kings or heads of ordinary families—enjoyed unlimited powers over women and children. Indeed, people in England as well as America increasingly described the family in terms of love and companionship. Instead of duties, they spoke of affection. This transformation in the way men and women viewed relations of power within the family was most evident in the popular novels of the period. Americans devoured *Pamela* and *Clarissa,* stories by the English writer Samuel Richardson about women who were the innocent victims of unreformed males, usually deceitful lovers and unforgiving fathers.

It was in this changing intellectual environment that American women began making new demands not only on their husbands but also on republican institutions. Abigail Adams, one of the generation's most articulate women, instructed her husband, John, as he set off for the opening of the Continental Congress: "I desire you would Remember the Ladies, and be more generous and favourable to them than your ancestors. Do not put such unlimited power into the hands of the Husbands." John responded in a condescending manner. The "Ladies" would have to wait until the country achieved independence. In 1777, Lucy Knox took an even stronger line with her husband, General Henry Knox. When he was about to return home from the army, she warned him, "I hope you will not consider yourself as commander in chief in your own house—but be convinced . . . that there is such a thing as equal command."

If Knox accepted Lucy's argument, he did so because she was a good republican wife and mother. In fact, women justified their assertiveness largely on the basis of political ideology. If survival of republics really depended on the virtue of their citizens, they argued, then it was the special responsibility of women as mothers to nurture the right values in their children and as wives to instruct their husbands in proper behavior. Contemporaries claimed that the woman who possessed "virtue and prudence" could easily "mold the taste, the manners, and the conduct of her admirers, according to her pleasure." In fact, "nothing short of a general reformation of manners would take place, were the ladies to use their power in discouraging our licentious manners."

Ill-educated women could not possibly fulfill these high expectations. Women required education that was at least comparable to what men received. Scores of female academies were established during this period to meet what many Americans, men as well as women, now regarded as a pressing social need. The schools may have received widespread encouragement

*Abigail Adams, wife of President John Adams, was a brilliant woman whose plea to limit the power of husbands gained little sympathetic attention. This portrait of her by Benjamin Blyth is from c. 1766.* ❖

precisely because they did not radically alter traditional gender roles. After all, the educated republican woman of the late eighteenth century did not pursue a career; she returned to the home, where she followed a familiar routine as wife and mother. The frustration of not being allowed to develop her talents may explain the bitterness of a graduation oration delivered by an otherwise obscure woman in 1793: "Our high and mighty Lords . . . have denied us the means of knowledge, and then reproached us for want of it. . . . They doom'd the sex to servile or frivolous employments, on purpose to degrade their minds, that they themselves might hold unrivall'd, the power and pre-eminence they had usurped."

During this period, women began to petition for divorce on new grounds. One case is particularly instructive concerning changing attitudes toward women and the family. In 1784, John Backus, an undistinguished Massachusetts silversmith, was hauled before a local court and asked why he beat his wife. He responded that "it was Partly owing to his Education for his father treated his mother in the same manner." The difference between Backus's case and his father's was that Backus's wife refused to tolerate such abuse, and she sued successfully for divorce. Studies of divorce patterns in Connecticut and Pennsylvania

*This needlepoint sampler extolling virtue and the value of an education was created in 1786 by Nabby Martin, a student at the Mary Balch School, an Academy for girls established in 1785 in Providence, Rhode Island. Many fine examples of needlework, an important part of girls' school curriculum in addition to academic subjects, came out of the Balch School.* ❖

show that after 1773, women divorced on about the same terms as men.

The war itself presented some women with fresh opportunities. In 1780, Ester DeBerdt Reed founded a large volunteer women's organization in Philadelphia—the first of its kind in the United States—that raised more than $300,000 for Washington's army. Other women ran family farms and businesses while their husbands fought the British. And in 1790, the New Jersey legislature explicitly allowed women who owned property to vote.

Despite these scattered gains, republican society still defined women's roles exclusively in terms of mother, wife, and homemaker. Other pursuits seemed unnatural, even threatening, and it is perhaps not surprising, therefore, that in 1807, New Jersey lawmakers—angry over a close election in which women voters apparently determined the result—repealed female suffrage in the interests of "safety, quiet, and good order and dignity of the state." Even

an allegedly progressive thinker such as Jefferson could not imagine allowing women to participate in serious politics. When in 1807 his secretary of the treasury, Albert Gallatin, called attention to the shortage of educated people to serve in government jobs and suggested recruiting women, Jefferson responded sharply: "The appointment of a woman to office is an innovation for which the public is not prepared, nor am I."

## Postponing Full Liberty

The Revolution did not bring about a massive restructuring of American society, at least not in the short term. Nevertheless, republicans such as Samuel Adams and Thomas Jefferson raised issues of immense significance for the later history of the United States. They insisted that equality, however narrowly defined, was an essential element of republican government. Even though they failed to abolish slavery, institute universal manhood suffrage, or apply equality to women, they vigorously articulated a set of assumptions about people's rights and liberties that challenged future generations of Americans to make good on the promise of the Revolution.

# THE STATES: EXPERIMENTS IN REPUBLICANISM

In May 1776, the Second Continental Congress invited the states to adopt constitutions. The old colonial charters filled with references to king and Parliament were clearly no longer adequate, and within a few years, most states had taken action. Rhode Island and Connecticut already enjoyed republican government by virtue of their unique seventeenth-century charters that allowed the voters to select both governors and legislators. Eleven other states plus Vermont created new political structures, and their deliberations reveal how Americans living in different regions and reacting to different social pressures defined fundamental republican principles.

Several constitutions were boldly experimental, and some states later rewrote documents that had been drafted in the first flush of independence. These early constitutions were provisional, but they nevertheless provided the framers of the federal Constitution of 1787 with invaluable insights into the strengths and weaknesses of government based on the will of the people.

## Blueprints for State Government

Despite disagreements over details, Americans who wrote the various state constitutions shared certain political assumptions. First, they insisted on preparing *written* documents. For many of them, of course, this seemed a natural step. As colonists, they had lived under royal charters, documents that described the workings of local government in detail. The Massachusetts Bay charter of 1629, for example (see Chapter 2), guaranteed that the Puritans would enjoy the rights of Englishmen even after they had moved to the New World. And in New England, Congregationalists drew up church covenants stating in clear contractual language the rights and responsibilities of the entire congregation.

However logical the decision to produce written documents may have seemed to the Americans, it represented a major break with English practice. Political philosophers in the mother country had long boasted of Britain's unwritten constitution, a collection of judicial reports and parliamentary statutes. But this highly vaunted system had not protected the colonists from oppression; hence, after declaring independence, Americans demanded that their state constitutions explicitly define the rights of the people as well as the power of their rulers.

## Natural Rights and the State Constitutions

The authors of the state constitutions believed men and women possessed certain **natural rights** over which government exercised no control whatsoever. So that future rulers—potential tyrants—would know the exact limits of authority, these fundamental rights were carefully spelled out. Indeed, the people of Massachusetts rejected the proposed state constitution of 1778 largely because it lacked a full statement of their basic rights. They demanded a guarantee of "rights of conscience, and . . . security of persons and property, which every member in the State hath a right to expect from the supreme power."

Eight state constitutions contained specific declarations of rights. The length and character of these lists varied, but, in general, they affirmed three fundamental freedoms: religion, speech, and press. They protected citizens from unlawful searches and seizures; they upheld trial by jury. George Mason, a shrewd political thinker who had written important revolutionary pamphlets, penned the most influential declaration of rights. It was appended to the Virginia Constitution of 1776, and the words were incorporated into other state constitutions as well as the famed Bill of Rights of the federal Constitution.

In almost every state, delegates to constitutional conventions drastically reduced the power of the governor. The constitutions of Pennsylvania and Georgia abolished the governor's office. In four other states, terms such as *president* were substituted for *governor*.

Even when those who designed the new state governments provided for a governor, they severely circumscribed his authority. He was allowed to make almost no political appointments, and while the state legislators closely monitored his activities, he possessed no veto over their decisions (Massachusetts being the lone exception). Most early constitutions lodged nearly all effective power in the legislature. This decision made good sense to men who had served under powerful royal governors during the late colonial period. These ambitious crown appointees had used executive patronage to influence members of the colonial assemblies, and as the Americans drafted their new republican constitutions, they were determined to bring their governors under tight control. In fact, the writers of the state constitutions were so fearful of the concentration of power in the hands of a single person, they failed to appreciate that elected governors—like the representatives themselves—were now the servants of a free people.

The legislature dominated early state government. The constitutions of Pennsylvania and Georgia provided for a unicameral, or one-house, system, and since any male taxpayer could cast a ballot in these states, their legislatures became the nation's most democratic. Other states authorized the creation of two houses, but even as they did so, some of the more demanding republicans wondered why America needed a senate or upper house at all. What social and economic interests, they asked, did that body represent that could not be more fully and directly voiced in the lower house? After all, America had just freed itself of an aristocracy. The two-house form survived the Revolution largely because it was familiar and because some persons had already begun to suspect that certain checks on the popular will, however arbitrary they might have appeared, were necessary to preserve minority rights.

## Power to the People

Massachusetts did not adopt a constitution until 1780, several years after the other states had done so. The experience of the people of Massachusetts is particularly significant because in their efforts to establish a workable system of republican government, they hit on a remarkable political innovation. After the rejection of two constitutions drafted by the state legislature, the responsibility fell to a specially elected convention of delegates whose sole purpose was the "formation of a new Constitution."

John Adams took a position of leadership at this convention and served as the chief architect of the governmental framework of Massachusetts. This framework included a house and senate, a popularly elected governor—who, unlike the chief executives of other states, possessed a veto over legislative bills—and property qualifications for officeholders as well as voters. The most striking aspect of the 1780 constitution, however, was the wording of its opening sentence: "We . . . the people of Massachusetts . . . agree upon, ordain, and establish." This powerful statement would be echoed in the federal Constitution. The Massachusetts experiment reminded Americans that ordinary officeholders could not be trusted to define fundamental rights. That important task required a convention of delegates who could legitimately claim to speak for the people.

In 1780, no one knew whether the state experiments would succeed. There was no question that a different type of person had begun to appear in public office, one who seemed, to the local gentry at least, a little poorer and less polished than they would have liked. When one Virginian surveyed the newly elected House of Burgesses in 1776, he discovered it was "composed of men not quite so well dressed, nor so politely educated, nor so highly born as some Assemblies I have formerly seen." This particular Virginian approved of such change, for he believed that "the People's men," however plain they might appear, possessed honesty and sincerity. They were, in fact, representative republicans, people who insisted they were anyone's equal in this burgeoning society.

Other Americans were less optimistic about the nation's immediate prospects. The health of a small republic depended entirely on the virtue of its people. If they or their elected officials succumbed to material temptation, if they failed to comprehend the moral dimensions of political power, or if personal liberty threatened the rights of property, then the state constitutions were no more than worthless pieces of paper. The risk of excess seemed great. In 1778, a group of New Englanders, fearful that unbridled freedom would create political anarchy, observed, "The idea of liberty has been held up in so dazzling colours that some of us may not be willing to submit to that subordination necessary in the freest states."

## STUMBLING TOWARD A NEW NATIONAL GOVERNMENT

When the Second Continental Congress convened in 1775, the delegates found themselves waging war in the name of a country that did not yet exist. As the military crisis deepened, Congress gradually—often reluctantly—assumed greater authority over national affairs, but everyone agreed such narrowly conceived measures were a poor substitute for a legally constituted government. The separate states could not possibly deal with the range of issues that now confronted the American people. Indeed, if independence meant anything in a world of sovereign nations, it implied the creation of a central authority capable of conducting war, borrowing money, regulating trade, and negotiating treaties.

### Articles of Confederation

The challenge of creating a viable central government proved more difficult than anyone anticipated. Congress appointed a committee to draw up a plan for confederation. John Dickinson, the lawyer who had written an important revolutionary pamphlet titled *Letters from a Farmer in Pennsylvania,* headed the committee. Dickinson envisioned the creation of a strong central government, and the report his committee presented on July 12, 1776, shocked delegates who assumed that the constitution would authorize a loose confederation of states. Dickinson's plan placed the western territories, land claimed by the separate states, under congressional control. In addition, Dickinson's committee called for equal state representation in Congress.

*John Dickinson, a highly respected lawyer, conceived a bold plan in 1776 for a strong central government, but the members of Congress saw it as a dangerous threat to the sovereignty of the states.* ❖

Since some states, such as Virginia and Massachusetts, were more populous than others, the plan fueled tensions between large and small states. Also unsettling was Dickinson's recommendation that taxes be paid to Congress on the basis of a state's total population, black as well as white, a formula that angered Southerners who did not think slaves should be counted. Indeed, even before the British evacuated Boston, Dickinson's committee raised many difficult political questions that would divide Americans for several decades.

Not surprisingly, the draft of the plan—the **Articles of Confederation**—that Congress finally approved in November 1777 bore little resemblance to Dickinson's original plan. The Articles jealously guarded the sovereignty of the states. The delegates who drafted the framework shared a general republican conviction that power—especially power so far removed from the people—was inherently dangerous and that the only way to preserve liberty was to place as many constraints as possible on federal authority.

The result was a government that many people regarded as powerless. The Articles provided for a single legislative body consisting of representatives selected annually by the state legislatures. Each state possessed a single vote in Congress. It could send as many as seven delegates, as few as two, but if they divided evenly on a certain issue, the state lost its vote. There was no independent executive and no veto over legislative decisions. The Articles also denied Congress the power of taxation, a serious oversight in time of war. The national government could obtain funds only by asking the states for contributions, called requisitions, but if a state failed to cooperate—and many did—Congress limped along without financial support. Amendments to this constitution required assent by all thirteen states. The authors of the new system expected the weak national government to handle foreign relations, military matters, Indian affairs, and interstate disputes. They most emphatically did not award Congress ownership of the lands west of the Appalachian Mountains.

The new constitution sent to the states for ratification encountered apathy and hostility. Most Americans were far more interested in local affairs than in the actions of Congress. When a British army marched through a state, creating a need for immediate military aid, people spoke positively about central government, but as soon as the threat had passed, they sang a different tune. During this period, even the slightest encroachment on state sovereignty rankled republicans who feared centralization would inevitably promote corruption.

## Western Land: Key to the First Constitution

The major bone of contention with the Articles, however, was the disposition of the vast, unsurveyed territory west of the Appalachians that everyone hoped the British would soon surrender. Although the region was claimed by the various states, most of it actually belonged to the Native Americans. In a series of land grabs that federal negotiators called treaties, the United States government took the land comprising much of modern Ohio, Indiana, Illinois, and Kentucky. Since the Indians had put their faith in the British during the war, they could do little to resist the humiliating treaty agreements at Fort McIntosh (1785), Fort Stanwix (1784), and Fort Finney (1786). As John Dickinson, then serving as the president of the Supreme Executive Council of Pennsylvania, told the Indians that since Great Britain has surrendered "the back country with all the forts . . . that they [the Indians] must now depend upon us for the preservation." If they dared to resist, "we will instantly turn upon them our armies . . . and extirpate them from the land where they were born and now live."

Some states, such as Virginia and Georgia, claimed land all the way from the Atlantic Ocean to the elusive "South Seas," in effect extending their boundaries to the Pacific coast by virtue of royal charters. State

**NORTHWEST TERRITORY**    *The U.S. government auctioned off the land in the Northwest Territory, the region defined by the Ohio River, the Great Lakes, and the Mississippi River. Proceeds from the sale of one section in each township were set aside for the creation and support of public schools.* ❖

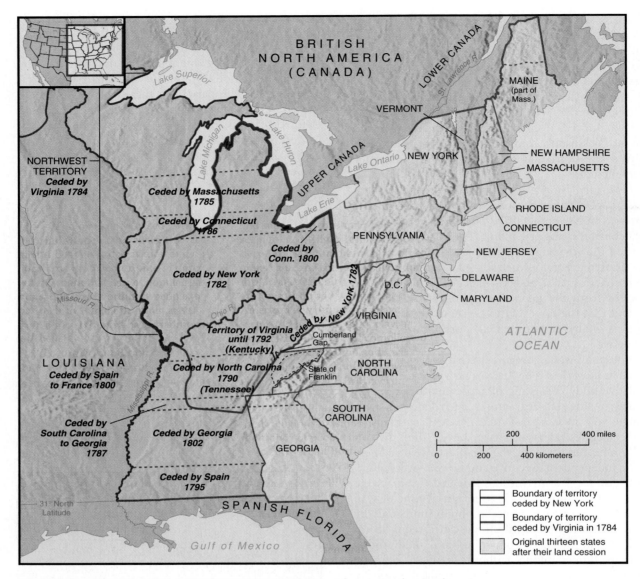

**WESTERN LAND CLAIMS CEDED BY THE STATES**   *After winning the war, the major issue facing the Continental Congress under the Articles of Confederation was mediating conflicting states' claims to rich western land. By 1802, the states had ceded all rights to the federal government.* ❖

legislators—their appetites whetted by aggressive land speculators—anticipated generating large revenues through land sales. Connecticut, New York, Pennsylvania, and North Carolina also announced intentions to seize blocks of western land.

Other states were not blessed with vague or ambiguous royal charters. The boundaries of Maryland, Delaware, and New Jersey had been established many years earlier, and it seemed as if people living in these states would be permanently cut off from the anticipated bounty. In protest, these "landless" states stubbornly refused to ratify the Articles of Confederation. Marylanders were particularly vociferous. All the states had made sacrifices for the common good during the

Revolution, they complained, and it appeared only fair that all states should profit from the fruits of victory, in this case, from the sale of western lands. Maryland's spokesmen feared that if Congress did not void Virginia's excessive claims to all of the Northwest Territory (the land west of Pennsylvania and north of the Ohio River) as well as to a large area south of the Ohio, beyond the Cumberland Gap, known as Kentucky, then Marylanders would desert their home state in search of cheap Virginia farms, leaving Maryland an underpopulated wasteland.

Virginians scoffed at the pleas for equity. They suspected that behind the Marylanders' statements of high purpose lay the greed of speculators. Private land companies had sprung up before the Revolution and purchased large tracts from the Indians in areas claimed by Virginia. Their agents petitioned Parliament to legitimize these questionable transactions. Their efforts failed. After the Declaration of Independence, however, the companies shifted the focus of their lobbying to Congress, particularly to the representatives of landless states like Maryland. By liberally distributing shares of stock, officials of the Indiana, Illinois, and Wabash companies gained powerful supporters such as Benjamin Franklin, Robert Morris, and Thomas Johnson, governor of Maryland. These activities encouraged Delaware and New Jersey to modify their demands and join the Confederation, while Maryland held out for five years. The leaders of Virginia, though, remained firm. Why, they asked, should Virginia surrender its historic claims to western lands to enrich a handful of selfish speculators?

The states resolved the bitter controversy in 1781 as much by accident as by design. Virginia agreed to cede its holdings north of the Ohio River to the Confederation on condition that Congress nullify the land companies' earlier purchases from the Indians. A practical consideration had softened Virginia's resolve. Republicans such as Jefferson worried about expanding their state beyond the mountains; with poor transportation links, it seemed impossible to govern such a large territory effectively from Richmond. The western settlers might even come to regard Virginia as a colonial power insensitive to their needs. Marylanders who dreamed of making fortunes on the land market grumbled, but when a British army appeared on their border, they prudently accepted the Articles (March 1, 1781). Congress required another three years to work out the details of the Virginia cession. Other landed states followed Virginia's example. These transfers established an important principle, for after 1781, it was agreed that the West belonged not to the separate states but to the United States. In this matter, at least, the national government now exercised full sovereignty.

No one greeted ratification of the Articles with much enthusiasm. When they thought about national politics at all, Americans concerned themselves primarily with winning independence. The new government gradually developed an administrative bureaucracy, and in 1781, it formally created the Departments of War, Foreign Affairs, and Finance. By far the most influential figure in the Confederation was Robert Morris (1734–1806), a freewheeling Philadelphia merchant who was appointed the first superintendent of finance. Although he was a brilliant manager, Morris's decisions as superintendent provoked controversy, indeed, deep suspicion. He hardly seemed a model republican. Morris mixed public

funds under his control with personal accounts, and he never lost an opportunity to make a profit. While such practices were not illegal, his apparent improprieties undermined his own political agenda. He desperately wanted to strengthen the central government, but highly vocal critics resisted, labeling Morris a "pecuniary dictator."

## Northwest Ordinance: The Confederation's Major Achievement

Whatever the weaknesses of Congress may have been, it did score one impressive triumph. Congressional action brought order to western settlement, especially in the Northwest Territory, and incorporated frontier Americans into an expanding federal system. In 1781, the prospects for success did not seem promising. For years, colonial authorities had ignored people who migrated far inland, sending neither money nor soldiers to protect them from Indian attack. Tensions between the seaboard colonies and the frontier regions had sometimes flared into violence. Disorders occurred in South Carolina in 1767, in North Carolina in 1769, and in Vermont in 1777. With thousands of men and women, most of them squatters, pouring across the Appalachian Mountains, Congress had to act quickly to avoid the past errors of royal and colonial authorities.

The initial attempt to deal with this explosive problem came in 1784. Jefferson, then serving as a member of Congress, drafted an ordinance that became the basis for later, more enduring legislation. Jefferson recommended carving ten new states out of the western lands located north of the Ohio River and recently ceded to the United States by Virginia. He specified that each new state establish a republican form of government. When the population of a territory equaled that of the smallest state already in the Confederation, the region could apply for full statehood. In the meantime, free white males could participate in local government, a democratic guarantee that frightened some of Jefferson's more conservative colleagues.

The impoverished Congress was eager to sell off the western territory as quickly as possible. After all, the frontier represented a source of income that did not depend on the unreliable generosity of the states. A second ordinance, passed in 1785 and called the Land Ordinance, established an orderly process for laying out new townships and marketing public lands.

The 1785 scheme possessed geometric elegance. Surveyors marked off townships, each running directly from east to west. These units, 6 miles square, were subdivided into 36 separate sections of 640 acres (1 square mile) each. (Roads and property boundaries established according to this grid pattern survived long

## LAND ORDINANCE OF 1785

**Grid pattern of a township**
36 sections of 640 acres (1 square mile each)

16    Income of one section reserved for the support of public education

A   Half-section    320 acres
B   Quarter-section    160 acres
C   Half-quarter section    80 acres
D   Quarter-quarter section    40 acres

after the Confederation had passed into history.) The government planned to auction off its holdings at prices of not less than $1 an acre. Congress set the minimum purchase at 640 acres, and near-worthless paper money was not accepted as payment. Section 16 was set aside for public education; the federal government reserved four other sections for its own use.

Public response disappointed Congress. Surveying the lands took far longer than anticipated, and few persons possessed enough hard currency to make even the minimum purchase. Finally, a solution to the problem came from Manasseh Cutler, a New England minister turned land speculator and congressional lobbyist, and his associates, who included several former officers of the Continental Army.

Cutler and his associates, representing the Ohio and Scioto companies, offered to purchase more than 6 million unsurveyed acres of land located in present-day southeastern Ohio by persuading Congress to accept, at full face value, government loan certificates that had been issued to soldiers during the Revolution. On the open market, the Ohio company could pick up the certificates for as little as 10 percent of their face value; thus, the company stood to make a fortune. Like so many other get-rich-quick schemes, however, this one failed to produce the anticipated millions. Unfortunately for Cutler and his friends, small homesteaders settled wherever they pleased, refusing to pay either government or speculators for the land.

Congress worried about the excess liberty on the frontier. In the 1780s, the West seemed to be filling up with people who by eastern standards were uncultured. Timothy Pickering, a New Englander, declared that "the emigrants to the frontier lands are the least worthy subjects in the United States. They are little less

savage than the Indians; and when possessed of the most fertile spots, for want of industry, live miserably." The charge was as old as the frontier itself. Indeed, seventeenth-century Englishmen had said the same things of the earliest Virginians. The lawless image stuck, however, and even a sober observer such as Washington insisted that the West crawled with "banditti." The Ordinance of 1784 placed the government of the territories in the hands of people about whom congressmen and speculators had second thoughts.

These various currents shaped the Ordinance of 1787, one of the final acts passed under the Confederation. The bill, also called the **Northwest Ordinance,** provided a new structure for government of the Northwest Territory. The plan authorized the creation of between three and five territories, each to be ruled by a governor, a secretary, and three judges appointed by Congress. When the population reached five thousand, voters who owned property could elect an assembly, but its decisions were subject to the governor's absolute veto. Once sixty thousand persons resided in a territory, they could write a constitution and petition for full statehood. While these procedures represented a retreat from Jefferson's original proposal, the Ordinance of 1787 contained several significant features. A bill of rights guaranteed the settlers the right to trial by jury, freedom of religion, and due process of law. In addition, the act outlawed slavery, a prohibition that freed the future states of Ohio, Indiana, Illinois, Michigan, and Wisconsin from the curse of human bondage.

By contrast, settlement south of the Ohio River received far less attention from Congress. Long before the end of the war, thousands of Americans streamed through the Cumberland Gap into a part of Virginia known as Kentucky. The most famous of these settlers was Daniel Boone. In 1775, the population of Kentucky was approximately one hundred; by 1784, it had jumped to thirty thousand. Speculators purchased large tracts from the Indians, planning to resell this acreage to settlers at handsome profits. In 1776, one land company asked Congress to reorganize the company's holdings into a new state called Transylvania. While nothing came of this self-serving request, another, even more aggressive group of speculators in 1784 carved the State of Franklin out of a section of present-day Tennessee, then claimed by North Carolina. Rival speculators prevented formal recognition of Franklin's government. By 1790, the entire region south of the Ohio River had been transformed into a crazy quilt of claims and counterclaims that generated lawsuits for many years to come.

# STRENGTHENING FEDERAL AUTHORITY

Despite its success in bringing order to the Northwest Territory, the Confederation increasingly came under heavy fire from critics who wanted a stronger central government. Complaints varied from region to region, from person to person, but most disappointment reflected economic frustration. Americans had assumed that peace would restore economic growth, but recovery following the Revolution was slow.

## The Nationalist Critique

Even before England signed a treaty with America, its merchants flooded American ports with consumer items and offered easy credit. Families that had postponed purchases of imported goods—either because of British blockade or personal hardship—now rushed to buy European finery.

This sudden renewal of trade with Great Britain on such a large scale strained the American economy. Gold and silver flowed back across the Atlantic, leaving the United States desperately short of hard currency. When large merchant houses called in their debts, ordinary American consumers often found themselves on the brink of bankruptcy. "The disagreeable state of our commerce," observed James Wilson, an advocate of strong national government, has been the result "of extravagant and injudicious importation.... We seemed to have forgot that to pay was as necessary in trade as to purchase."

To blame the Confederation alone for the economic depression would be unfair. Nevertheless, during the 1780s, many people agreed that a stronger central government could somehow have brought greater stability to the struggling economy. In their rush to acquire imported luxuries, Americans seemed to have deserted republican principles, and a weak Congress was helpless to restore national virtue.

Critics pointed to the government's inability to regulate trade. Whenever a northern congressman suggested restricting British access to American markets, southern representatives, who feared any controls on the export of tobacco or rice, bellowed in protest. Southerners anticipated that navigation acts written by the Confederation would put planters under the yoke of northern shipping interests.

The country's chronic fiscal instability increased public anxiety. While the war was still in progress, Congress printed well over $200 million in paper money, but because of extraordinarily high inflation, the rate of exchange for Continental bills soon declined to a fraction of their face value. In 1781, Congress, facing insolvency, turned to the states for help. They were asked to retire the depreciated currency. The situation was spinning out of control. Several states—pressed to pay their own war-related debts—not only recirculated the Continental bills but also issued nearly worthless money of their own.

A heavy burden of state and national debt compounded the general sense of economic crisis. Revolutionary soldiers had yet to be paid. Women and men who had loaned money and goods to the government clamored for reimbursement. Foreign creditors demanded interest on funds advanced during the Revolution. These pressures grew, but Congress was unable to respond. The Articles specifically prohibited Congress from taxing the American people. It required little imagination to see that the Confederation would soon default on its legal obligations unless something was done quickly.

In response, an aggressive group of men announced that they knew how to save the Confederation. The **nationalists**—persons such as Alexander Hamilton, James Madison, and Robert Morris—called for major constitutional reforms, the chief of which was an amendment allowing Congress to collect a 5 percent tax on imported goods sold in the states. Revenues generated by the proposed Impost of 1781 would be used by the Confederation to reduce the national debt. On this point the nationalists were adamant. They recognized that whoever paid the public debt would gain the public trust. If the states assumed the responsibility, then the country could easily fragment into separate republics. "A national debt," Hamilton explained in 1781, "if it is not excessive, will be to us a national blessing. It will be a powerful cement to our union." Twelve states accepted the Impost amendment, but Rhode Island—where local interests argued that the tax would make Congress "independent of their constituents"—resolutely refused to co-

## ❖ A Look at the Past ❖

### Paper Currency

Fighting the American Revolution cost a lot of money. The new government of the United States simply did not have sufficient gold and silver—called specie—to pay the troops and buy weapons. Pressed on all sides by creditors, the fledgling government issued huge quantities of paper money. The flood of Continental currency sparked massive inflation, as nearly worthless money chased a finite supply of consumer goods. Considering the threat of economic instability, should the Continental Congress have printed so much paper money? Did it have other realistic alternatives? What sorts of people in this society were most harmed by hyperinflation?

operate. One negative vote on this proposed constitutional change, and the taxing scheme was dead.

State leaders frankly thought the nationalists were up to no good. The "localists" were especially apprehensive of fiscal plans advanced by Robert Morris. His profiteering as superintendent of finance appeared a threat to the moral fiber of the young republic. Richard Henry Lee and Samuel Adams, men of impeccable patriotic credentials, decried Morris's efforts to create a national bank. Such an institution would bring forth a flock of

social parasites, the kind of people that Americans associated with corrupt monarchical government. One person declared that if an impost ever passed, Morris "will have all [the money] in his Pocket."

The nationalists regarded their opponents as economically naive. A country with the potential of the United States required a complex, centralized fiscal system. But for all their pretensions to realism, the nationalists of the early 1780s were politically inept. They underestimated the depth of republican fears, and in their rush to strengthen the Articles, they overplayed their hand.

A group of extreme nationalists even appealed to the army for support. To this day, no one knows the full story of the Newburgh Conspiracy of 1783. Officers of the Continental Army stationed at Newburgh, New York, worried that Congress would disband them without funding their pensions, began to lobby intensively for relief. In March, they scheduled general meetings to protest the weakness and duplicity of Congress. The officers' initial efforts were harmless enough, but frustrated nationalists such as Morris and Hamilton hoped that if the army exerted sufficient pressure on the government, perhaps even threatened a military takeover, then stubborn Americans might be compelled to amend the Articles.

The conspirators failed to take George Washington's integrity into account. No matter how much he wanted a strong central government, he would not tolerate insubordination by the military. Washington confronted the officers directly at Newburgh, intending to read a prepared statement. Fumbling with his glasses before his men, he commented, "Gentlemen, you must pardon me. I have grown gray in your service and now find myself growing blind." The unexpected vulnerability of this great soldier reduced the troops to tears, and in an instant, the rebellion was broken. Washington deserves credit for preserving civilian rule in this country.

In April 1783, Congress proposed a second impost, but it too failed to win unanimous ratification. Even a personal appeal by Washington could not save the amendment. As one opponent explained, if "permanent Funds are given to Congress, the aristocratic Influence, which predominates in more than a major part of the United States, will fully establish an arbitrary Government." With this defeat, nationalists gave up on the Confederation. Morris retired from government, and Madison returned to Virginia utterly depressed by what he had witnessed.

### Diplomatic Humiliation

In foreign affairs, Congress endured further embarrassment. It could not even enforce the provisions of its own peace treaty. American negotiators had promised Great Britain that its citizens could collect debts contracted before the Revolution. The states, however, dragged their heels, and several even passed laws obstructing the settlement of legitimate prewar claims. Congress was powerless to force compliance. The British responded to this apparent provocation by refusing to evacuate troops from posts located in the Northwest Territory. A strong national government would have driven the redcoats out, but without adequate funds, the weak Congress could not provide soldiers for such a mission.

Congress's postrevolutionary dealings with Spain were equally humiliating. That nation refused to accept the southern boundary of the United States established by the Treaty of Paris. Spain claimed sovereignty over much of the land located between Georgia and the Mississippi River, and its agents schemed with Indian tribes in this region to resist American expansion. On July 21, 1784, Spain fueled the controversy by closing the lower Mississippi River to citizens of the United States.

This unexpected decision devastated western farmers. Free use of the Mississippi was essential to the economic development of the entire Ohio Valley. Because of the prohibitively high cost of transporting freight for long distances over land, western settlers— and southern planters eyeing future opportunities in this area—demanded a secure water link with the world's markets. Their spokesmen in Congress denounced anyone who claimed that navigation of the Mississippi was a negotiable issue.

In 1786, a Spanish official, Don Diego de Gardoqui, opened talks with John Jay, a New Yorker appointed by Congress to obtain rights to navigation of the Mississippi. Jay soon discovered that Gardoqui would not compromise. After making little progress, Jay seized the initiative. If Gardoqui would allow American merchants to trade directly with Spain, thus opening up an important new market to ships from New England and the middle states, then the United States might forgo navigation of the Mississippi for twenty-five years. When southern delegates heard of Jay's concessions, they were outraged. It appeared to them as if representatives of northern commerce were ready to abandon the southern frontier. Angry congressmen accused New Englanders of attempting to divide the United States into separate confederations, for as one Virginian exclaimed, the proposed Spanish treaty "would weaken if not destroy the union by disaffecting the Southern States . . . to obtain a trivial commercial advantage." Congress wisely terminated the negotiations with Spain.

By the mid-1780s, the Confederation could claim several notable achievements. It designed an administrative system that lasted far longer than did the Articles. It also brought order out of the chaos of conflicting western land claims. Still, as anyone could see, the government was struggling. Congress met irregularly. Some states did not even bother to send delegates, and pressing issues often had to be postponed for lack of a quorum. The nation even lacked a permanent capital, and Congress drifted from Philadelphia to Princeton to Annapolis to New York City, prompting one humorist to suggest that the government purchase an air balloon. This newly invented device, he explained, would allow the members of Congress to "float along from one end of the continent to the other" and "suddenly pop down into any of the states they please."

## "HAVE WE FOUGHT FOR THIS?"

By 1785, the country seemed to have lost direction. The buoyant optimism that sustained revolutionary patriots had dissolved into pessimism and doubt. Many Americans, especially those who had provided leadership during the Revolution, agreed something had to be done. In 1786, Washington bitterly observed, "What astonishing changes a few years are capable of producing. Have we fought for this? Was it with these expectations that we launched into a sea of trouble, and have bravely struggled through the most threatening dangers?"

### The Genius of James Madison

The conviction of people such as Washington that the nation was indeed in a state of crisis reflected tensions within republican thought. To be sure, they supported open elections and the right of individuals to advance their own economic well-being, but when these elements seemed to undermine social and political order, they expressed the fear that perhaps liberty had been carried too far. The situation had changed quite rapidly. As recently as the 1770s, men of republican persuasion had insisted that the greatest threat to the American people was concentration of power in the hands of unscrupulous rulers. With this principle in mind, they transformed state governors into mere figureheads and weakened the Confederation in the name of popular liberties.

By the mid-1780s, persons of property and standing saw the problem in a different light. Recent experience suggested to them that ordinary citizens did not in fact possess sufficient virtue to sustain a republic. The states had been plagued not by executive tyranny but by an excess of democracy, by a failure of the majority to preserve the property rights of the minority, by an unrestrained individualism that promoted anarchy rather than good order.

Many state leaders did not seem particularly concerned about the fiscal health of the national government. Local presses churned out worthless currency, and in some states, assemblies passed laws impeding the collection of debt. In Rhode Island, the situation became absurd. State legislators made it illegal for merchants to reject Rhode Island money even though everyone knew it had no value. No wonder Governor William Livingston of New Jersey declared in 1787, "We do not exhibit the virtue that is necessary to support a republican government."

As Americans tried to interpret these experiences within a republican framework, they were checked by the most widely accepted political wisdom of the age. Baron de Montesquieu (1689–1755), a French political philosopher of immense international reputation and author of *The Spirit of the Laws* (1748), declared flatly that a republican government could not flourish in a large territory. The reasons were clear. If the people lost direct control over their representatives, they would fall prey to tyrants. Large distances allowed rulers to hide their corruption; physical separation presented aristocrats with opportunities to seize power.

In the United States, most learned men treated Montesquieu's theories as self-evident truths. His writings seemed to demonstrate the importance of preserving the sovereignty of the states, for however much these small republics abused the rights of property and ignored minority interests, it was plainly unscientific to maintain that a republic consisting of thirteen states, several million people, and thousands of acres of territory could long survive.

James Madison rejected Montesquieu's argument, and in so doing, he helped Americans to think of republican government in radical new ways. This soft-spoken, rather unprepossessing Virginian was the most brilliant American political thinker of his generation. One French official described Madison as "a man one must study a long time in order to make a fair appraisal." Those who listened carefully to what Madison had to say, however, soon recognized his genius for translating theory into practice.

Madison delved into the writings of a group of Scottish philosophers, the most prominent being David Hume (1711–1776), and from their works he concluded that Americans need not fear a greatly expanded republic. Madison perceived that "inconveniences of popular States contrary to prevailing Theory, are in proportion not to the extent, but to the narrowness of their limits." Indeed, it was in small states such as Rhode Island that legislative majorities tyrannized the propertied minority. In a large territory, Madison explained, "the Society becomes broken into a greater variety of interest, of pursuits, of passions, which check each other, whilst those who may

feel a common sentiment have less opportunity of communication and contact."

Madison did not, however, advocate a modern "interest-group" model of political behavior. The contending parties were incapable of working for the common good. They were too mired in their own local, selfish concerns. Rather, Madison thought competing factions would neutralize each other, leaving the business of running the central government to the ablest, most virtuous persons the nation could produce. In other words, Madison's federal system was not a small state writ large; it was something entirely different, a government based on the will of the people and yet detached from their narrowly based demands. This thinking formed the foundation of Madison's most famous political essay, *The Federalist* No. 10.

## Constitutional Reform

A concerted movement to overhaul the Articles of Confederation began in 1786, when Madison and his friends persuaded the Virginia assembly to recommend a convention to explore the creation of a unified system of "commercial regulations." Congress supported the idea. In September, delegates from five states arrived in Annapolis, Maryland, to discuss issues that extended far beyond commerce. The small turnout was disappointing, but the occasion provided strong nationalists with an opportunity to hatch an even bolder plan. The Annapolis delegates advised Congress to hold a second meeting in Philadelphia "to take into consideration the situation of the United States, to devise such further provisions as shall appear to them necessary to render the constitution of the Federal Government adequate to the exigencies of the Union." Whether staunch states' rights advocates in Congress knew what was afoot is not clear. In any case, Congress authorized a grand convention to gather in May 1787.

Events played into Madison's hands. Soon after the Annapolis meeting, an uprising known as **Shays's Rebellion,** involving several thousand impoverished farmers, shattered the peace of western Massachusetts. No matter how hard these men worked the soil, they always found themselves in debt to eastern creditors. They complained of high taxes, of high interest rates, and, most of all, of a state government insensitive to their problems. In 1786, Daniel Shays, a veteran of the battle of Bunker Hill, and his armed neighbors closed a county courthouse where creditors were suing to foreclose farm mortgages. At one point, the rural insurgents threatened to seize the federal arsenal located at Springfield. Congress did not have funds sufficient to support an army, and the arsenal might have fallen had not a group of wealthy Bostonians raised an army

*This 1787 woodcut portrays Daniel Shays with one of his chief officers, Jacob Shattucks. Shays led farmers in western Massachusetts in revolt against a state government that seemed insensitive to the needs of poor debtors. Their rebellion strengthened the demand for a strong new federal government. ❖*

many of whom had fought in the Revolution and served in the Congress of the Confederation. The majority were in their thirties or forties. The gathering included George Washington, James Madison, George Mason, Robert Morris, James Wilson, John Dickinson, Benjamin Franklin, and Alexander Hamilton, just to name some of the more prominent participants. Absent were John Adams and Thomas Jefferson, who were conducting diplomacy in Europe; Patrick Henry, a localist suspicious of strong central government, remained in Virginia, announcing he "smelled a rat."

As soon as the Constitutional Convention opened on May 25, the delegates made several procedural decisions of the utmost importance. First, they voted "that nothing spoken in the House be printed, or communicated without leave." The rule was stringently enforced. Sentries guarded the doorways to keep out uninvited visitors, windows stayed shut in the sweltering heat to prevent sound from either entering or leaving the chamber, and members were forbidden to copy the daily journal without official permission. As Madison explained, the secrecy rule saved "both the convention and the community from a thousand erroneous and perhaps mischievous reports." It also has made it extremely difficult for modern lawyers and judges to determine exactly what the delegates had in mind when they wrote the Constitution (see the Feature Essay "The Elusive Constitution: Search for Original Intent," pp. 178–179).

In a second procedural move, the delegates decided to vote by state, but, in order to avoid the kinds of problems that had plagued the Confederation, they ruled that key proposals needed the support of only a majority instead of the nine states required under the Articles.

of four thousand troops to put down the insurrection. The victors were in for a surprise. At the next general election, Massachusetts voters selected representatives sympathetic to Shays's demands, and a new liberal assembly reformed debtor law.

Nationalists throughout the United States were not so forgiving. From their perspective, Shays's Rebellion symbolized the breakdown of law and order that they had long predicted. "Great commotions are prevailing in Massachusetts," Madison wrote. "An appeal to the sword is exceedingly dreaded." The time had come for sensible people to speak up for a strong national government. The unrest in Massachusetts persuaded persons who might otherwise have ignored the Philadelphia meeting to participate in drafting a new constitution.

## The Philadelphia Convention

In the spring of 1787, fifty-five men representing twelve states traveled to Philadelphia. Rhode Island refused to take part in the proceedings, a decision that Madison attributed to its "wickedness and folly." Thomas Jefferson described the convention as an "assembly of demi-Gods," but this flattering depiction is misleading. However much modern Americans revere the Constitution, they should remember that the individuals who wrote it did not possess divine insight into the nature of government. They were practical people—lawyers, merchants, and planters—

## Inventing a Federal Republic

Madison understood that whoever sets the agenda controls the meeting. Even before all the delegates had arrived, he drew up a framework for a new federal system known as the **Virginia Plan.** Madison wisely persuaded Edmund Randolph, Virginia's popular governor, to present this scheme to the convention on May 29. Randolph claimed that the Virginia Plan merely revised sections of the Articles, but everyone, including Madison, knew better. "My ideas," Madison confessed, "strike . . . deeply at the old Confederation." He was determined to restrain the state assemblies, and in the original Virginia Plan, Madison gave the federal government power to veto state laws.

The Virginia Plan envisioned a national legislature consisting of two houses, one elected *directly* by the people, the other chosen by the first house from nominations made by the state assemblies. Representation in both houses was proportional to the state's population. The Virginia Plan also provided for an executive elected by Congress. Since most delegates at the Philadelphia convention sympathized with the nationalist position, Madison's blueprint for a strong federal government initially received broad support, and the Virginia Plan was referred to further study and debate. A group of men who allegedly had come together to reform the Confederation found themselves discussing the details of "a *national* Government . . . consisting of a *supreme* Legislature, Executive, and Judiciary."

The Virginia Plan had been pushed through the convention so fast that opponents hardly had an opportunity to present their objections. On June 15, they spoke up. William Paterson, a New Jersey lawyer, advanced the so-called **New Jersey Plan,** a scheme that retained the unicameral legislature in which each state possessed one vote and that at the same time gave Congress extensive new powers to tax and regulate trade. Paterson argued that these revisions, while more modest than Madison's plan, would have greater appeal for the American people. "I believe," he said, "that a little practical virtue is to be preferred to the finest theoretical principles, which cannot be carried into effect." The delegates listened politely and then soundly rejected the New Jersey Plan on June 19. Indeed, only New Jersey, New York, and Delaware voted in favor of Paterson's scheme.

Rejection of this framework did not resolve the most controversial issue before the convention. Paterson and others feared that under the Virginia Plan, small states would lose their separate identities. These delegates maintained that unless each state possessed an equal vote in Congress, the small states would find themselves at the mercy of their larger neighbors.

This argument outraged the delegates who favored a strong federal government. It awarded too much power to the states. "For whom [are we] forming a Government?" Wilson cried. "Is it for men, or for the imaginary beings called States?" It seemed absurd to claim that the 68,000 people of Rhode Island should have the same voice in Congress as Virginia's 747,000 inhabitants.

## Compromise Saves the Convention

The mood of the convention was tense. Hard work and frustration, coupled with Philadelphia's sweltering summer heat, frayed nerves, prompting some members to predict that the meeting would accomplish nothing of significance. But despite the growing pessimism, the gathering did not break up. The delegates desperately wanted to produce a constitution, and they refused to give up until they had explored every avenue of reconciliation. Perhaps cooler heads agreed with Washington: "To please all is impossible, and to attempt it would be vain. The only way, therefore, is . . . to form such a government as will bear the scrutinizing eye of criticism, and trust it to the good sense and patriotism of the people."

Mediation clearly offered the only way to overcome what Roger Sherman, a Connecticut delegate, called "a full stop." On July 2, a "grand committee" of one person from each state was elected by the convention to resolve persistent differences between the large and small states. Franklin, at age 81 the oldest delegate, served as chair. The two fiercest supporters of proportional representation based on population, Madison and Wilson, were left off the grand committee, a sure sign that the small states would salvage something from the compromise.

The committee recommended that the states be equally represented in the upper house of Congress, while representation was to be proportionate in the lower house. Only the lower house could initiate money bills. Franklin's committee also decided that one member of the lower house should be selected for every thirty thousand inhabitants of a state. Southern delegates insisted that this number include slaves. In the so-called three-fifths rule, the committee agreed that for the purpose of determining representation in the lower house, slaves would be counted, but not as much as free persons. For every five slaves, a congressional district received credit for three free voters, a deal that gave the South much greater power in the new government than it would have otherwise received. As with most compromise solutions, the one negotiated by Franklin's committee fully satisfied no one. It did, however, overcome a major impasse, and after the small states gained an assured voice in the upper house, the Senate, they cooperated enthusiastically in creating a strong central government.

## Compromising with Slavery

During the final days of August, a deeply disturbing issue came before the convention. It was a harbinger of the great sectional crisis of the nineteenth century. Many northern representatives detested the slave trade and wanted it to end immediately. They despised the three-fifths ruling that seemed to award slaveholders

# REVOLUTION OR REFORM?
## THE ARTICLES OF CONFEDERATION AND THE CONSTITUTION COMPARED

| Political Challenge | Articles of Confederation | Constitution |
| --- | --- | --- |
| Mode of ratification or amendment | Require confirmation by every state legislature | Requires confirmation by three-fourths of state conventions or legislatures |
| Number of houses in legislature | One | Two |
| Mode of representation | One to seven delegates represent each state; each state holds only one vote in Congress | Two senators represent each state in upper house; each senator holds one vote. One representative to lower house represents every 30,000 people (in 1788) in a state; each representative holds one vote |
| Mode of election and term of office | Delegates appointed annually by state legislatures | Senators chosen by state legislatures for six-year term (direct election after 1913); representatives chosen by vote of citizens for two-year term |
| Executive | No separate executive: delegates annually elect one of their number as president, who possesses no veto, no power to appoint officers or to conduct policy. Administrative functions of government theoretically carried out by Committee of States, practically by various single-headed departments | Separate executive branch: president elected by electoral college to four-year term; granted veto, power to conduct policy and to appoint ambassadors, judges, and officers of executive departments established by legislation |
| Judiciary | Most adjudication left to state and local courts; Congress is final court of appeal in disputes between states | Separate branch consisting of Supreme Court and inferior courts established by Congress to enforce federal law |
| Taxation | States alone can levy taxes; Congress funds the Common Treasury by making requisitions for state contributions | Federal government granted powers of taxation |
| Regulation of commerce | Congress regulates foreign commerce by treaty but holds no check on conflicting state regulations | Congress regulates foreign commerce by treaty; all state regulations must obtain congressional consent |

extra power in government simply because they owned slaves. "It seemed now to be pretty well understood," Madison jotted in his private notes, "that the real difference of interest lay, not between the large and small but between the N. and Southn. States. The institution of slavery and its consequences formed a line of discrimination."

Whenever northern delegates—and on this point they were by no means united—pushed too aggressively, Southerners threatened to bolt the convention, thereby destroying any hope of establishing a strong national government. Curiously, even recalcitrant Southerners avoided using the word *slavery*. They seemed embarrassed to call the institution by its true name, and in the Constitution itself, slaves were described as "other persons," "such persons," "persons held to Service or Labour," in other words, as everything but slaves.

A few northern delegates such as Roger Sherman of Connecticut sought at every turn to mollify the Southerners, especially the South Carolinians who

spoke so passionately about preserving slavery. Gouverneur Morris, a Pennsylvania representative, would have none of it. He regularly reminded the convention that "the inhabitant of Georgia and S.C. who goes to the Coast of Africa, and in defiance of the most sacred laws of humanity tears away his fellow creatures from their dearest connections and damns them to the most cruel bondage, shall have more votes in a Government instituted for the protection of the rights of mankind, than the Citizen of Pa. or N. Jersey."

Largely ignoring Morris's stinging attacks, the delegates reached an uneasy compromise on the continuation of the slave trade. Southerners feared that the new Congress would pass commercial regulations adversely affecting the planters—taxes on the export of rice and tobacco, for example. They demanded, therefore, that no trade laws be passed without a two-thirds majority of the federal legislature. They backed down on this point, however, in exchange for guarantees that Congress would not interfere with the slave trade until 1808 (see Chapter 8). The South even came away with

# THE ELUSIVE CONSTITUTION

## Search for Original Intent

Many prominent national leaders, alarmed at a perceived "judicial imperialism" in recent activist courts, have urged that judges interpret the Constitution strictly according to the "intent of the Framers." Arguing that a "jurisprudence of original intent" is the "only legitimate basis for constitutional decision making," *intentionalists* demand that judges measure decisions against a "demonstrable consensus among the Framers and ratifiers as to principles stated or implied in the Constitution."

Yet when one considers circumstances surrounding the Constitution's framing, demonstration of the Founders' intent proves elusive indeed. Delegates to the Constitutional Convention in Philadelphia in 1787 deliberately veiled the purpose of the convention in secrecy to avoid pressure by local constituencies who harbored deep suspicions concerning strong central government. Newspapers, barred from access to the convention, printed only occasional rumors. Delegates refused to speak or correspond with outsiders concerning the proceedings.

The strictness with which delegates observed the rule of secrecy not only restricted contemporary knowledge of what transpired but has also limited the number of sources in which subsequent generations may search for original intent. Only three members preserved complete accounts of convention debates. These records remained unpublished for more than thirty years, forcing the first generation of lawyers and federal judges to rely on the words of the Constitution alone for clues to the Framers' intent.

The publication of the three accounts did not necessarily make the delegates' intent more accessible. The *Journal, Acts and Proceedings of the Convention Assemblies in Philadelphia,* recorded by the convention secretary, William Jackson, provided only a chronological listing of motions, resolutions, and vote tallies. His unpublished manuscript of convention debates, which could have fleshed out the published *Journal's* "mere skeleton" of the proceedings, was lost.

The notes of New York delegate Robert Yates appeared in 1821 as *Secret Proceedings and Debates of the Convention Assembled at Philadelphia,* but the circumstances of their publication rendered them thoroughly unreliable. Their editor, the former French minister Citizen Edmond Genêt, attained notoriety in the 1790s when he violated American neutrality in the Anglo-French war by commissioning American privateers against British shipping. Genêt supported states' rights and popular government and manipulated Yates's notes to support his views. A comparison of *Secret Proceedings* with the two surviving pages of Yates's manuscript reveals that Genêt altered or deleted more than half the original text.

If the intent of the delegates survives anywhere, Madison's *Notes of Debates in the Federal Convention of 1787* provides its likeliest repository. The "father of the Constitution," as contemporaries called him, carefully preserved notes on convention proceedings and took every measure to ensure their accuracy. Recognizing his own limitations as a stenographer, Madison did not try to record everything said but sought manuscript copies of delegates' speeches that he incorporated into his notes at the end of each day. Madison also waited until the end of each day to record his own speeches, every one of which was extemporaneous, from memory. At the convention's end, he obtained a manuscript copy of secretary Jackson's notes, which he used to supplement and correct his own. Though Madison tinkered at times with his notes over the next thirty years, recent analysis has demonstrated that none of these minor corrections impaired the faithfulness of the text.

Yet in spite of the meticulous care that Madison lavished on his notes, they remain, at best, incomplete repositories of the Framers' original intent. Each day's notes contain only a few minutes of oral discourse, whereas actual delivery occupied between five and seven hours. Furthermore, written manuscripts of speeches may have approximated only roughly what the debaters actually said. Madison's speech on the benefits of a large republic, for example, occupies two closely reasoned pages in his notes. Yet others who took notes seem to have recorded a much shorter and far less impressive oral version. Such discrepancies raise important questions. How did the Framers understand the actual speeches on the convention floor? How did their understanding shape their intentions? How much of their intent is lost in the vast omissions?

These questions take on even greater significance when one considers that the Constitution was forged through a series of compromises among representatives whose interests and intentions differed widely. No delegate was completely satisfied, and the finished document permitted some functions none had intended. Madison himself complained, for example, that the principle of judicial review "was never intended and can never be proper."

Moreover, he thought it would be a mistake to search for the original intent of convention delegates. The delegates' intent could never possibly determine constitutional interpretation, he argued, for "the only authoritative intentions were those of the people of the States, as expressed thro' the Conventions which ratified the Constitution."

Yet the works most commonly cited from the time of state ratification raise problems with the application of

this principle as well. Stenographers who recorded the *Debates of the Several State Conventions on the Adoption of the Federal Constitution* did not possess skills adequate to their task, and Federalist partisans edited the speeches with abandon in order to promote their own views. Evidence also suggests that Jonathan Eliot, the journalist who published the debates in 1836, altered them further.

Given the limitations of sources most often cited by modern judges and lawyers, the original intent of most Framers remains as elusive today as it was for the first generation who had no access to those documents. The Constitution's often ambiguous wording, which furnished the sole guide to the Framers' intent in their day, remains the best recourse in our own.

*James Madison,* by Charles Willson Peale. Among the framers of the Constitution, Madison was the most effective advocate of a strong central government. ❖

The State House of Philadelphia in an engraving of 1776 by John McRae. After the Revolution and the drafting of the Constitution, the building became known as Independence Hall. During the hot summer of 1787, delegates kept the windows closed so that no one on the street could hear the debates. ❖

*Although the words* slave *and* slavery *do not appear in the U.S. Constitution, debate over slavery and the slave trade resulted in a compromise in which both institutions persisted in the new Republic. Not everyone was pleased with the compromise. The Library Company of Philadelphia commissioned this painting* Liberty Displaying the Arts and Sciences *(1792) by Samuel Jennings. The broken chain at the feet of the goddess Liberty is meant to demonstrate her opposition to slavery.* ❖

a clause assuring the return of fugitive slaves. "We have obtained," Charles Cotesworth Pinckney told the planters of South Carolina, "a right to recover our slaves in whatever part of America they may take refuge, which is a right we had not before."

Although these deals disappointed many Northerners, they conceded that establishing a strong national government was of greater immediate importance than ending the slave trade. "Great as the evil is," Madison wrote, "a dismemberment of the union would be worse."

## The Last Details

On July 26, the convention formed a Committee of Detail, a group that prepared a rough draft of the Constitution. After the committee completed its work—writing a document that still, after so many hours of debate, preserved the fundamental points of the Virginia Plan—the delegates reconsidered each article. The task required the better part of a month.

During these sessions, the members of the convention concluded that the president, as they now called the executive, should be selected by an electoral college, a body of prominent men in each state chosen by local voters. The number of "electoral" votes held by each state equaled its number of representatives and senators. This awkward device guaranteed that the president would not be indebted to the Congress for his office. Whoever received the second largest number

of votes in the electoral college automatically became vice president. In the event that no person received a majority of the votes, the election would be decided by the lower house—the House of Representatives—with each state casting a single vote. Delegates also armed the chief executive with veto power over legislation as well as the right to nominate judges. Both privileges, of course, would have been unthinkable a decade earlier, but the state experiments revealed the importance of having an independent executive to maintain a balanced system of republican government.

As the meeting was concluding, some delegates expressed concern about the absence in the Constitution of a bill of rights. Such declarations had been included in most state constitutions, and Virginians such as George Mason insisted that the states and their citizens needed explicit protection from possible excesses by the federal government. While many delegates sympathized with Mason's appeal, they noted that the hour was late and, in any case, that the proposed Constitution provided sufficient security for individual rights. During the hard battles over ratification, the delegates to the convention may have regretted passing over the issue so lightly.

## We, the People

The delegates adopted an ingenious procedure for ratification. Instead of submitting the Constitution to the various state legislatures, all of which had a vested interest in maintaining the status quo and most of which had two houses, either of which could block approval, they called for the election of thirteen state conventions especially chosen to review the new federal government. The delegates may have picked up this idea from the Massachusetts experiment of 1780. Moreover, the Constitution would take effect after the assent of only nine states. There was no danger, therefore, that the proposed system would fail simply because a single state like Rhode Island withheld approval.

The convention asked Gouverneur Morris of Pennsylvania, a delegate noted for his urbanity, to make final stylistic changes in the wording of the Constitution. When Morris examined the working draft, he discovered that it spoke of the collection of states forming a new government. This wording presented problems. Ratification required only nine states. No one knew whether all the states would accept the Constitution, and if not, which nine would. A strong possibility existed that several New England states would reject the document. Morris's brilliant phrase "We the People of the United States" eliminated this difficulty. The new nation was a republic of the people, not of the states.

On September 17, thirty-nine men signed the Constitution. A few members of the convention, like Mason, could not support the document. Others had already gone home. For more than three months, Madison had served as the convention's driving intellectual force. He now generously summarized the experience: "There never was an assembly of men, charged with a great and arduous trust, who were more pure in their motives, or more exclusively or anxiously devoted to the object committed to them."

# WHOSE CONSTITUTION? STRUGGLE FOR RATIFICATION

Supporters of the Constitution recognized that ratification would not be easy. After all, the convention had been authorized only to revise the Articles, but instead it produced a new plan that fundamentally altered relations between the states and the central government. The delegates dutifully dispatched copies of the Constitution to the Congress of Confederation, then meeting in New York City, and that powerless body referred the document to the separate states without any specific recommendation. The fight for ratification had begun.

## Federalists and Antifederalists

Proponents of the Constitution enjoyed great advantages over the unorganized opposition. In the contest for ratification, they took no chances. Their most as-

tute move was the adoption of the label **Federalist.** The term cleverly suggested that they stood for a confederation of states rather than for the creation of a supreme national authority. Critics of the Constitution, who tended to be somewhat poorer, less urban, and less well educated than their opponents, cried foul, but there was little they could do. They were stuck with the name **Antifederalist,** a misleading term that made their cause seem far more obstructionist than it actually was.

The Federalists recruited the most prominent public figures of the day. In every state convention, speakers favoring the Constitution were more polished and more fully prepared than were their opponents. In New York, the campaign to win ratification sparked publication of **The Federalist,** a brilliant series of essays written by Madison, Hamilton, and Jay during the fall and winter of 1787 and 1788. The nation's newspapers threw themselves overwhelmingly behind the new government. In fact, few journals even bothered to carry Antifederalist writings. In some states, the Federalists adopted tactics of questionable propriety in order to gain ratification. In Pennsylvania, for example, they achieved a legal quorum for a crucial vote by dragging several opposition delegates into the meeting from the streets. In New York, Hamilton intimidated upstate Antifederalists with threats that New York City would secede from the state unless the state ratified the Constitution.

In these battles, the Antifederalists articulated a political philosophy that had broad popular appeal. They spoke the language of the Commonwealthmen (see Chapter 4). Like the extreme republicans who drafted the first state constitutions, the Antifederalists were deeply suspicious of political power. During the debates over ratification, they warned that public officials, however selected, would be constantly scheming to expand their authority.

The preservation of individual liberty required constant vigilance. It seemed obvious that the larger the republic, the greater the opportunity for political corruption. Local voters could not possibly know what their representatives in a distant national capital were doing. The government outlined in the Constitution invited precisely the kinds of problems that Montesquieu had described in his famous essay, *The Spirit of the Laws.* "In so extensive a republic," one Antifederalist declared, "the great officers of government would soon become above the control of the people, and abuse their power."

Antifederalists demanded direct, personal contact with their representatives. They argued that elected officials should reflect the character of their constituents as closely as possible. It seemed unlikely that in large congressional districts, the people would be able to preserve such close ties with their representatives. According to the Antifederalists, the Constitution favored persons wealthy enough to have forged a reputation that extended beyond a single community. Samuel Chase told the members of the Maryland ratifying convention that under the new system, "the distance between the people and their representatives will be so great that there is no probability of a farmer or planter being chosen . . . only the *gentry,* the *rich,* and the well-born will be elected."

Federalist speakers mocked their opponents' localist perspective. The Constitution deserved general support precisely because it ensured that future Americans would be represented by "natural aristocrats," individuals possessing greater insights, skills, and training than did the ordinary citizen. These talented leaders, the Federalists insisted, could discern the interests of the entire population. They were not tied to the selfish needs of local communities. "The little demagogue of a petty parish or county will find his importance annihilated [under the Constitution] and

his intrigues useless," predicted Charles Cotesworth Pinckney, a South Carolina Federalist.

Historians have generally accepted the Federalist critique. It would be a mistake, however, to see the Antifederalists as "losers" or as persons who could not comprehend social and economic change. Although their rhetoric echoed an older moral view of political culture, they accepted more easily than did many Federalists a liberal marketplace in which ordinary citizens competed as equals with the rich and well-born. They believed the public good was best served by allowing individuals like themselves to pursue their own private interests. That is what they had been doing on the local level during the 1780s, and they resented the imposition of elite controls over their affairs. Although the Antifederalists lost the battle over ratification, their ideas about political economy later found many champions in the age of Andrew Jackson.

The Constitution drew support from many different types of people. In fact, historians have been unable to discover sharp correlations between wealth

**RATIFICATION OF THE CONSTITUTION**   *Advocates of the new Constitution called themselves Federalists, and those who opposed its ratification were known as Antifederalists.* ❖

and occupation on the one hand and attitudes toward the proposed system of central government on the other. In general, Federalists lived in more commercialized areas than did their opponents. In the cities, artisans as well as merchants called for ratification, while those farmers who were only marginally involved in commercial agriculture frequently voted Antifederalist.

Despite passionate pleas from Patrick Henry and other Antifederalists, most state conventions quickly adopted the Constitution. Delaware acted first (December 7, 1787), and within eight months of the Philadelphia meeting, eight of the nine states required to launch the government had ratified the document. The contests in Virginia (June 1788) and New York (July 1788) generated bitter debate, but they too joined the union, leaving only North Carolina and Rhode Island outside the United States. Eventually (November 21, 1789, and May 29, 1790), even these states ratified the Constitution. Still, the vote had been very close. The Constitution was ratified in New York by a tally of 30 to 27, in Massachusetts by 187 to 168, and in Virginia by 89 to 79. A swing of a few votes in several key states could have defeated the new government.

While the state conventions sparked angry rhetoric, Americans soon closed ranks behind the Constitution. An Antifederalist who represented one Massachusetts village explained that "he had opposed the adoption of this Constitution; but that he had been overruled . . . by a majority of wise and understanding men [and that now] he should endeavor to sow the seeds of union and peace among the people he represented."

## CHRONOLOGY

| | |
|---|---|
| **1776** | Second Continental Congress authorizes colonies to create republican government (May) ❖ Eight states draft new constitutions; two others already enjoy republican government by virtue of former colonial charters |
| **1777** | Congress accepts Articles of Confederation after long debate (November) |
| **1780** | Massachusetts finally ratifies state constitution |
| **1781** | States ratify Articles of Confederation following settlement of Virginia's western land claims ❖ British army surrenders at Yorktown (October) |
| **1782** | States fail to ratify proposed Impost tax |
| **1783** | Newburgh Conspiracy thwarted (March) ❖ Society of the Cincinnati raises a storm of criticism ❖ Treaty of peace signed with Great Britain (September) |
| **1785** | Land Ordinance for Northwest Territory passed by Congress |
| **1786** | Jay-Gardoqui negotiations over Mississippi navigation anger southern states ❖ Annapolis Convention suggests second meeting to revise the Articles of Confederation (September) ❖ Shays's Rebellion frightens American leaders |
| **1787– 1788** | The federal Constitution is ratified by all states except North Carolina and Rhode Island |
| **1791** | Bill of Rights (first ten amendments to the Constitution) ratified by states |

## Adding the Bill of Rights

The first ten amendments to the Constitution are the major legacy of the Antifederalist argument. In almost every state convention, opponents of the Constitution pointed to the need for greater protection of individual liberties, rights that people presumably had possessed in a state of nature. "It is necessary," wrote one Antifederalist, "that the sober and industrious part of the community should be defended from the rapacity and violence of the vicious and idle. A bill of rights, therefore, ought to set forth the purposes for which the compact is made, and serves to secure the minority against the usurpation and tyranny of the majority." The list of fundamental rights varied from state to state, but most Antifederalists demanded specific guarantees for jury trial and freedom of religion. They wanted prohibitions against cruel and unusual punishments. There was also considerable, though not universal, support for freedom of speech and freedom of the press.

Madison and others regarded the proposals with little enthusiasm. In *The Federalist* No. 84, Hamilton bluntly reminded the American people that "the constitution is itself . . . a BILL OF RIGHTS." But after the adoption of the Constitution had been assured, Madison moderated his stand. If nothing else, passage of a bill of rights would appease able men such as George Mason and Edmund Randolph, who might otherwise remain alienated from the new federal system. "We have in this way something to gain," Madison concluded, "and if we proceed with caution, nothing to lose."

The crucial consideration was caution. A number of people throughout the nation advocated calling a second constitutional convention, one that would take Antifederalist criticism into account. Madison wanted

*Patrick Henry and George Mason tirelessly pressed for a bill of rights to be added to the Constitution. They feared that without specific protections, the language of the document might be twisted to tyrannical ends. The Bill of Rights, composed of the first ten amendments to the Constitution, was added in 1789 after long and contentious debate.* ❖

to avoid such a meeting, and he feared that some members of the first Congress might use a bill of rights as an excuse to revise the entire Constitution or to promote a second convention.

Madison carefully reviewed these recommendations as well as the various declarations of rights that had appeared in the early state constitutions, and on June 8, 1789, he placed before the House of Representatives a set of amendments designed to protect individual rights from government interference. Madison told the members of Congress that the greatest dangers to popular liberties came from "the majority [operating] against the minority." A committee compressed and revised his original ideas into ten amendments that were ratified and became known collectively as the **Bill of Rights**. For many modern Americans these amendments are the most important section of the Constitution. Madison had hoped that additions would be inserted into the text of the Constitution at the appropriate places, not tacked onto the end, but he was overruled.

The Bill of Rights protected the freedoms of assembly, speech, religion, and the press; guaranteed speedy trial by an impartial jury; preserved the people's right to bear arms; and prohibited unreasonable searches. Other amendments dealt with legal procedure. Some opponents of the Constitution urged Congress to provide greater safeguards for states' rights, but Madison had no intention of backing away from a strong central government. Only the Tenth Amendment addressed the states' relation to the federal system. This crucial article, designed to calm Antifederalist fears, specified that those "powers not delegated to the United States by the Constitution, nor prohibited by it to the States, are reserved to the States respectively, or to the people."

On September 25, 1789, the Bill of Rights passed both houses of Congress, and by December 15, 1791, the amendments had been ratified by three-fourths of the states. Madison was justly proud of his achievement. He had effectively secured individual rights without undermining the Constitution. When he asked his friend Jefferson for his opinion of the Bill of Rights, Jefferson responded with typical republican candor: "I like [it] . . . as far as it goes; but I should have been for going further."

## CONCLUSION: SUCCESS DEPENDS ON THE PEOPLE

By 1789, one phase of American political experimentation had come to an end. During these years, the people gradually, often haltingly, learned that in a republican society, they themselves were sovereign. They could no longer blame the failure of government on inept monarchs or greedy aristocrats. They bore a great responsibility. Americans had demanded a government of the people only to discover during the 1780s that in some situations, the people could not be trusted with power, majorities could tyrannize minorities, and the best of governments could abuse individual rights.

Contemporaries had difficulty deciding just what had been accomplished. A writer in the *Pennsylvania Packet* thought the American people had preserved order. "The year 1776 is celebrated," the newspaper observed, "for a revolution in favor of liberty. The year 1787 . . . will be celebrated with equal joy, for a revolution in favor of Government." But some aging patriots grumbled that perhaps order had been achieved at too high a price. In 1788, Richard Henry Lee remarked, "Tis really astonishing that the same people, who have just emerged from a long and cruel war in defense of liberty, should now agree to fix an elective despotism upon themselves and their posterity."

But most Americans probably would have accepted Franklin's optimistic assessment. As he watched the delegates to the Philadelphia convention come forward to sign the Constitution, he noted that there was a sun carved on the back of George Washington's chair. "I have," the aged philosopher noted, " . . . often in the course of the session . . . looked at [the sun] behind the President without being able to tell whether it was rising or setting; but now at length I have the happiness to know that it is a rising and not a setting sun."

# RECOMMENDED READING

The best way to comprehend the major issues debated at the Philadelphia Convention and then later at the separate state ratifying conventions is to examine the key documents of the period. One could do no better than reading James Madison, *Journal of the Federal Constitution* (reprinted in many modern editions), our only detailed account of what actually occurred during the closed debates in Philadelphia. A good introduction to the contest between the Federalists and Antifederalists over ratification is Bernard Bailyn, ed., *The Debate on the Constitution: Federalist and Antifederalist Speeches, Articles, and Letters During the Struggle Over Ratification* (1993). Gordon S. Wood analyzes late-eighteenth-century republican political thought in *The Creation of the American Republic, 1776–1787* (1969). Three recent titles interpret the complex political experience of the 1780s: Jack N. Rakove, *The Beginnings of National Politics: An Interpretive History of the Continental Congress* (1979) and *Original Meanings: Politics and Ideas in the Making of the Constitution* (1996); and Peter Onuf, *Statehood and Union: A History of the Northwest Ordinance* (1987). For a thoughtful investigation of the many different meanings of "republicanism,"

see Richard Beeman et al., eds., *Beyond Confederation: Origins of the Constitution and American National Identity* (1987) and Daniel T. Rodgers, "Republicanism: The Career of a Concept," *Journal of American History*, Vol. 79 (June 1992), 1–38. On the expectations of African Americans and women during this period, see the final sections of Winthrop Jordan, *White Over Black: American Attitudes Toward the Negro, 1550–1812* (1968); T. H. Breen, "Making History: The Force of Public Opinion and the Last Years of Slavery in Revolutionary Massachusetts," in Ronald Hoffman, et al., eds., *Through a Glass Darkly: Reflections on Personal Identity in Early America* (1997), 67–95; and Ronald Hoffman and Peter J. Albert, eds., *Women in the Age of the American Revolution* (1990). The Newburgh Conspiracy is explored in Richard H. Kohn, *Eagle and Sword: The Federalists and the Creation of the Military Establishment in America, 1783–1802* (1975). On Shays's Rebellion, see Robert A. Gross, ed., *In Debt to Shays: The Bicentennial of an Agrarian Rebellion* (1993).

**For a list of additional titles related to this chapter's topics, please see** http://www.ablongman.com/divine.

# SUGGESTED WEB SITES

### The Leslie Brock Center for the Study of Colonial Currency

http://etext.lib.virginia.edu/users/brock
This site includes both useful primary and secondary documents on early American currency.

### Northwest Territory Alliance

http://www.nwta.com/main.html
This Revolutionary Era reenactment organization site contains several links and is an interesting look at historical reenactment.

### Independence Hall National Historical Park

http://www.nps.gov/inde/visit.html
This site includes images and historical accounts of Independence Hall and other Philadelphia buildings closely associated with the nation's founding.

### Biographies of the Founding Fathers

http://www.colonialhall.com/
This site provides interesting information about the men who signed the Declaration of Independence and includes a trivia section.

### The Federalist Papers

http://www.law.emory.edu/FEDERAL/federalist/
This site is a collection of the most important Federalist Papers, a series of documents designed to convince people to support the new Constitution and the Federalist party.

### The Constitution and the Amendments

http://www.law.emory.edu/FEDERAL/usconst.html
A searchable site to the Constitution, especially useful for its information about the Bill of Rights and other constitutional amendments.

### Documents from the Continental Congress and the Constitutional Convention, 1774–1789

http://memory.loc.gov/ammem/bdsds/bdsdhome.html
The Continental Congress Broadside Collection (253 titles) and the Constitutional Convention Broadside Collection (21 titles) contain 274 documents relating to the work of Congress and the drafting and ratification of the Constitution. Items include extracts of the journals of Congress, resolutions, proclamations, committee reports, treaties, and early printed versions of the United States Constitution and the Declaration of Independence. Most broadsides are one page long; others range from one to twenty-eight pages.

# THE STRANGE ORDEAL OF QUOK WALKER

## Slavery on Trial in Revolutionary Massachusetts

Revolutionary Americans bitterly denounced what they saw as Britain's plan to enslave a free people. If the conspiracy succeeded, ordinary men and women would be stripped of fundamental human rights. Throughout the colonies, gifted political thinkers such as John Adams, John Dickinson, and Thomas Jefferson condemned the plot against liberty, and in the words of the Declaration of Independence, the members of the Continental Congress dismissed George III as "unfit to be the ruler of a free people."

Such strident rhetoric raised an embarrassing problem, one that contemporary Americans, black as well as white, fully appreciated. The cause of freedom that mobilized so many patriots obviously excluded the hundreds of thousands of African Americans who had endured real slavery in every colony from Georgia to New Hampshire. Did they not, contemporaries asked, possess the same human rights as did white citizens? Was it not profoundly hypocritical to demand political freedom—"life, liberty, and the pursuit of happiness"—while every state in the new republic sanctioned racial slavery? As Abigail Adams observed to her husband, John, in 1774, "It always appeared a most iniquitous scheme to me to fight ourselves for what we are daily robbing and plundering from those who have as good a right to freedom as we have."

African Americans shared Abigail Adams's concern. During this period, they responded to the call of freedom in various ways. Some circulated petitions advocating the abolition of slavery. Others refused to wait for lawmakers and, at considerable personal risk, proclaimed their own independence from bondage. One such person was Quok Walker, a Massachusetts slave who accepted the egalitarian rhetoric of the Revolution at face value. By demanding that he be paid a fair wage for his labor, he announced that he now regarded himself as a free man. Had Walker served a less obstinate master, a person who might perhaps have acceded to the force of ideological change, this black man might have slipped unnoticed from the pages of history. Had Walker shown less courage, he might have compromised his own freedom. But that is not what occurred. The obstinate master fought to preserve his investment in a human being. When Walker courageously resisted, the entire matter came before the courts of Massachusetts Bay.

Quok Walker was born in 1753, probably in Africa soon after slave traders had captured his mother. At the age of 9 months, he was sold at public auction to a man who lived in Worcester, Massachusetts. The bill of sale listed "a certain negro man named Mingo, about twenty Years of Age, and also one negro wench named Dinah, about nineteen years of age, with child Quako." Presumably Mingo and Dinah were Quok's parents. The slave trader described the baby as "All sound & well." Following the death of his original owner a decade later, Quok Walker became the property of the man's widow. When she remarried, Walker found himself included in the new husband's estate. This man, Nathaniel Jennison, had a reputation as a harsh master. Walker spent the next fifteen years working on Jennison's farm in a small central Massachusetts village known today as Barre. In an isolated rural community that always had a very small black population, Jennison seems to have owned twelve other slaves.

Walker took control of his own life one spring day in 1781. Claiming that his "old master said [he] should be free at twenty-one," the 28-year-old Walker deserted Jennison's farm. Instead of leaving Barre—after all, other members of his family still lived in the town—

Walker offered his services for a reasonable wage to a pair of neighboring farmers, John and Seth Caldwell. Short of help during the planting season, they hired Walker, treating him like any other free laborer. Why Walker chose this precise moment to desert Jennison is not clear. Perhaps brutality was involved. An unexpected opportunity to escape may suddenly have presented itself. And surely the radical political ideas that were transforming the character of Massachusetts society played a part in Walker's decision. Somehow he had learned of a recently drafted state constitution which boldly announced that "all men are born free and equal." Walker probably interpreted these words as an invitation to judge for himself who would purchase his labor and at what rate, a right of free contract that white men in New England had long taken for granted.

Jennison rejected this line of reasoning. After searching for several weeks, he finally tracked Walker down. Jennison severely punished the fugitive. He beat Walker "about his head" and then dragged him back to his own farm, where he bound Walker and locked him in a shed. A writ presented in a later civil suit captured the horror of the event. Jennison, the court paper observed, "with force & arms . . . did make an assault, and then and there with force & arms aforesaid, seized the said Quok and threw him down and struck him several violent blows upon his back and arms with the handle of a whip."

By refusing to accept Walker's self-proclaimed emancipation and confining him, Jennison apparently believed he was acting like any slave owner who had been challenged by an insolent bondsman. Intent on forcing Walker to work on the same terms as he had before, Jennison probably thought that he had successfully concluded the matter. The next move, however, belonged to Walker.

Walker asked for and received the assistance of two young antislavery lawyers, Levi Lincoln and Caleb Strong. These recent Harvard graduates would later enjoy distinguished careers in politics and the law. On Walker's behalf, they filed civil suit against Jennison in the Worcester Inferior Court of Common Pleas, claiming damages for the assault and confinement their client had endured. Jennison could not believe what was happening. He testified in court that his actions represented the "necessary corrections" that any unruly slave could expect. Lincoln and Strong responded that no man had the right to impose such cruel treatment upon another, even if that man or woman was a slave. And although the lawyers attempted to introduce arguments concerning the legitimacy of slavery in Massachusetts, the local judges did not give Lincoln and Strong the latitude to do so. As a result, the initial

Slave owners considered slaves property and marked them as such. This branding iron was used to mark a slave with the owner's initials. ❖

case turned more on the facts of the assault itself than on the constitutional question of slavery.

Jennison was a tenacious adversary. Even as the original assault case made its way through the Worcester court, he filed suit against John and Seth Caldwell, the farmers in whose fields Walker had found employment as a free laborer. The very wording of Jennison's complaint suggests the possibility that he suspected—perhaps through the currents he detected in legal and popular opinion—that his and other slave owners' human property might soon become free men and women. Jennison claimed that the Caldwells had "unlawfully solicited & seduced [his] *servant*," not that they had stolen or absconded with his slave. Using the term servant redefined Jennison's relationship in regard to Walker from that of owner to employer. In this way, Jennison attempted to exclude the issue of constitutionality of slavery from the legal proceedings.

At this moment, the various moves and countermoves in the state courts became extremely complex. But whatever legal strategies came into play, the heart of the contest remained an African's right to freedom. Through it all, Walker repeatedly swore that he was "a free man, and not the proper slave of the said Nathaniel [Jennison]." Although the issues were clear enough to Walker, he learned a hard lesson about the workings of the law. It follows its own logic, however strange that may seem to outsiders. The Inferior Court of Common Pleas ruled for Walker in his complaint against Jennison, agreeing that he "was not the proper

Negro slave of the defendant" and therefore the assault represented a clear violation of Walker's civil rights. Damages against Jennison amounted to £50, a sizable sum in revolutionary Massachusetts. But Jennison also won a victory. In his case against the Caldwells, the judges ruled in favor of Jennison, awarding him £25 to compensate for the difficulty of "reclaiming and reducing his servant to his business and services, [the Caldwells] knowing [the] said Negro to be the plaintiff's servant."

Whether the judges reached their verdicts with the larger question of the constitutionality of slavery in mind remains unclear. The members of the inferior court did not explain their decisions. The judges in Walker's suit, headed by the respected Justice Moses Gill, may have been persuaded by Walker's claim to previous manumission and may have ruled solely on the issue of assault and battery. The very fact that a slave had won such a verdict, however, clipped away at the moral and legal standing of slavery in Massachusetts. The losing defendants in each case, Jennison and the Caldwells, appealed to the Supreme Judicial Court of Massachusetts, and in those arguments the matter of slavery clearly dominated the proceedings. And it was in this forum that one man's protest against injustice acquired larger significance in the great story of human emancipation.

Even before Walker's case reached final resolution, it raised difficult questions concerning relations between the law and society in revolutionary Massachusetts. To describe Walker as a passive figure in this legal narrative would be a serious mistake. To be sure, the creation of a new republican government transformed how everyone in this state defined concepts such as freedom and equality. The explosive ideological climate shaped the character of public opinion, and this in turn affected how judges and lawyers applied the law on specific controversies. But if Walker had not declared himself a free man and resisted Jennison's tyrannical designs, the case of *Walker* v. *Jennison* would never have come before the state courts. By bearing witness against bondage, Walker became an agent for constitutional change. Timing was critical. Walker's ordeal would surely have ended in tragedy had his lawsuit not coincided with a profound shift in popular thinking about slavery.

Walker was not alone. Other slaves seized on the doctrine of natural rights and human equality. Felix Cuff of Waltham, Massachusetts, for example, fled his master along with several other slaves in 1781. When the master gathered a posse to track the fugitives down, Cuff sued the entire group for rioting. The white community refused to support the slave owner, and Cuff won. Still another Massachusetts slave, Elizabeth Freeman, known as Mumbet, put her case

before the state courts at about the same time as Quok Walker. Her master's wife had wounded the black woman during a domestic argument, and Freeman cited the "insult and outrage" as the major reason she deserted the household. Claiming her liberty under the Massachusetts Declaration of Rights, she enlisted the assistance of a local lawyer to sue for manumission. When asked how she had arrived at her conviction that the law had already declared her free, she answered, "While waiting table, [she] heard gentlemen talking . . . that all people were born free and equal." And after "thinking about it," Freeman announced that she belonged "among them." A white jury concluded that the wording of the state constitution sustained her claim to equal humanity, and Mumbet spent the rest of her days working for wages in a household that treated her with respect.

However significant these cases may have been, it was Walker who made constitutional history. In the review of *Walker* v. *Jennison,* the Supreme Judicial Court allowed Levi Lincoln, who still represented Walker, to argue far beyond the specific evidence of Jennison's assault upon his client. Lincoln mounted a comprehensive attack on the intellectual and legal structures that had so long bolstered the institution of chattel slavery. Lincoln insisted upon Walker's human right as a man naturally and inalienably "free and equal," a phrase taken directly from the state's Declaration of Rights. Walker had "common origins, was descended from a common parent, clothed in the same kind of flesh, breathed the same breath of life," as did Jennison or any other man. Discounting Jennison's claim that slavery was an accepted local custom, Lincoln argued that "customs . . . against reason and right, are void." Lincoln challenged the judges to choose between possible interpretations of a flawed statute and "a higher law, the law of God."

Jennison's defense stubbornly resisted the argument of human equality. His attorneys contended that the sense of "free and equal" as Walker and Lincoln had construed it was "very different from what the people apprehended at the time the [state constitution] was established." They declared that the document would never have been ratified had the people understood that it would abolish slavery. Jennison's lawyer also implied that such a liberal reading would not be well received in the southern states and that the unity of the new republic would be seriously damaged if the Massachusetts court ruled in favor of Walker. In one last desperate attempt to hold on to his human property, Jennison maintained that slaveholders fed and cared for their aged slaves and that without such paternalism, African Americans would soon perish. At an earlier time, such self-serving arguments might have swayed the judges. But the Revolution had radi-

A portrait of Elizabeth Freeman at about age 70, painted in 1811 by Susan Sedgwick, a member of the family who helped her win her freedom. Freeman worked as a housekeeper for the Sedgwick family for many years. She is buried in the Sedgwick family plot in Stockbridge, Massachusetts. ❖

and appeals that were pending, concluding wisely that no court was prepared any longer to define human beings as property. Although they endured discrimination, African Americans had broken the chains of slavery and now received wages for their work. Defiant to the end, Jennison went to court once again, this time demanding to be relieved of "his obligation to support" his "remaining slaves." The judges did not even bother to comment on the merits of the request. Walker lived out his remaining days in rural Barre, an African slave who had successfully fought for freedom in the New World.

Quok Walker's courage did not bring down the institution of slavery in the American South. In that region for a very long time, many whites mouthed similar arguments to those that Jennison had advanced before a Massachusetts court. Even the United States Constitution compromised on the issue of slavery, making a mockery of the declaration that "all men are created equal." But Walker's story should not be dismissed as an insignificant chapter in the history of resistance to racial injustice. He demonstrated that a determined individual can stand up for civil rights. Although the nation's courts have often turned a deaf ear to appeals for social equality, they have sometimes—especially in the late twentieth century—done more to protect civil rights than have the other branches of government. Occasionally, all that it takes to gain a hearing is the righteousness of a person like Quok Walker.

cally transformed how the law defined equality, at least in Massachusetts, and it was Walker, not Jennison, who better understood the character of the new republican society.

The court of appeals upheld the verdict against Jennison in Walker's civil suit. Jennison's lawyers failed to file proper documents with the court in his action against the Caldwells, and that verdict was overturned. Perhaps Jennison's attorneys sensed a losing battle and decided to cut their losses. Jennison later sought through legislative petition to reenter his appeal in his case against the Caldwells, but the state senate refused his request. Later that year, a criminal court at Worcester indicted Jennison on charges of "assault, battery, and false imprisonment." A jury of white men found him guilty of those offenses, and the local judges sentenced him to pay a stiff fine plus court costs. In all three actions Jennison lost, and in the words of a contemporary observer, the Reverend Jeremy Belknap, these decisions dealt "a mortal wound to slavery in Massachusetts."

After the disposition of *Walker* v. *Jennison*, slaveholders throughout the state dropped other suits

## Questions for Discussion

- Why do you think Quok Walker equated a wage-paying job with freedom?

- Why did it take a brutal beating before the white people of Walker's community bore witness against the institution of slavery?

- Although the leaders of the Revolution protested against their own "slavery" to the British Parliament, they were slow to appreciate the need to liberate African Americans from bondage in the new republic. How can we explain the Founding Fathers' seeming hypocrasy?

- Why have modern Americans so often assumed that whites "gave" freedom to the African Americans?

- What arguments did Jennison use to persuade the judges? If he had employed different arguments do you think he would have won the case?

- Do you think that Quok Walker saw himself as a heroic figure in the fight for civil rights?

Well-wishers spread flowers in front of George Washington as he rides through Trenton on his way from Virginia to New York for his inauguration as the first president of the United States in 1789. ❖

# Democracy in Distress: The Violence of Party Politics, 1788–1800

## *Force of Public Opinion*

While presiding over the first meeting of the U.S. Senate in 1789, Vice President John Adams called the senators' attention to a pressing procedural question: How would they address George Washington, the newly elected president? Adams insisted that Washington deserved an impressive title, a designation lending dignity and weight to his office. The vice president warned the senators that if they called Washington simply "president of the United States," the "common people of foreign countries [as well as] the sailors and soldiers [would] despise him to all eternity." Adams recommended "His Highness, the President of the United States, and Protector of their Liberties," but some senators favored "His Elective Majesty" or "His Excellency."

Adams's initiative caught many persons, including Washington, completely by surprise. They regarded the entire debate as ridiculous. James Madison, a member of the House of Representatives, announced that pretentious European titles were ill suited to the "genius of the people" and "the nature of our Government." Thomas Jefferson, who was then residing in Paris, could not comprehend what motivated the vice president, and in private correspondence, he repeated Benjamin Franklin's judgment that Adams "means well for his Country, is always an honest Man, often a wise one, but sometimes, and in some things, absolutely out of his senses." When the senators learned that their efforts embarrassed Washington, they dropped the topic. The leader of the new republic would be called president of the United States. One wag, however, dubbed the portly Adams "His Rotundity."

THE COMIC-OPERA QUALITY of the debate about how to address Washington should not obscure the participants' serious concern about setting government policy. The members of the first Congress could not take the survival of republican government for granted. All of them, of course, wanted to secure the Revolution. The recently ratified Constitution transferred sovereignty from the states to the people, a bold and unprecedented decision that many Americans feared would generate chronic instability. Translating constitutional abstractions into practical legislation would have been difficult, even under the most favorable conditions. But these were especially trying times. Great Britain and France, rivals in a century of war, put nearly unbearable pressures on the leaders of the new republic and, in the process, made foreign policy a bitterly divisive issue.

Although no one welcomed them, political parties gradually took shape during this period. Neither the Jeffersonians (also called the Republicans) nor the Federalists—as the two major groups were called—doubted that the United States would one day become a great commercial power. They differed, however, on how best to manage the transition from an agrarian household economy to an international system of trade and industry. The Federalists encouraged rapid integration of the United States into a world economy, but however enthusiastic they were about capitalism, they did not trust the people or local government to do the job effectively. A modern economy, they insisted, required strong national institutions that would be directed by a social elite who understood the financial challenge and who would work in the best interests of the people.

Such claims frightened persons who came to identify themselves as Jeffersonians. Strong financial institutions, they thought, had corrupted the government of Great Britain from which they had just separated themselves. They searched for alternative ways to accommodate the needs of commerce and industry. Unlike the Federalists, the Jeffersonians put their faith in the people, defined for the most part politically as white yeoman farmers. The Jeffersonians insisted that ordinary entrepreneurs, if they could be freed from intrusive government regulations, could be trusted to resist greed and crass materialism and to sustain the virtue of the republic.

During the 1790s, former allies were surprised to discover themselves at odds over such basic political issues. One person—Hamilton, for example—would stake out a position. Another, such as Jefferson or Madison, would respond, perhaps speaking a little more extravagantly than a specific issue demanded, goaded by the rhetorical nature of public debate. The first in turn would rebut passionately the new position. By the middle of the decade, this dialectic had almost spun out of control, taking the young republic to the brink of political violence.

Leaders of every persuasion had to learn to live with "public opinion." The revolutionary elite had invited the people to participate in government, but the gentlemen assumed that ordinary voters would automatically defer to their social betters. Instead, the Founders discovered they had created a rough-and-tumble political culture, a robust public sphere of cheap newspapers and street demonstrations. The newly empowered "public" followed the great debates of the period through articles they read in hundreds of highly partisan journals and magazines.

Just as television did in the twentieth century, print journalism opened politics to a large audience that previously might have been indifferent to the activities of elected officials. By the time John Adams left the presidency in 1800, he had learned this lesson well. The ordinary workers and farmers of the United States, feisty individuals who thought they were as good as anyone else and who were not afraid to let their political opinions be known, were not likely to let their president become an "Elective Majesty."

## PRINCIPLE AND PRAGMATISM: ESTABLISHING A NEW GOVERNMENT

In 1788, George Washington enjoyed great popularity throughout the nation. The people remembered him as the selfless leader of the Continental Army, and even before the states had ratified the Constitution, everyone assumed he would be chosen president of the United States. He received the unanimous support of the electoral college, an achievement that no subsequent president has duplicated. Adams, a respected Massachusetts lawyer who championed national independence in 1776, was selected vice president. As Washington left his beloved Virginia plantation, Mount Vernon, for New York City, he recognized that the people—now so vocal in their support—could be fickle. "I fear," he explained with mature insight, "if the issue of public measures should not correspond with their sanguine expectations, they will turn the extravagant . . . praise . . . into equally extravagant . . . censures."

Washington bore great responsibility. The political stability of the young republic depended in large measure on how he handled himself in office. In the eyes of his compatriots, he had been transformed into a living symbol of the new government, and during his presidency (1789–1797), he carried himself with studied dignity and reserve—never ostentatious, he was the embodiment of classical republican values. Contemporaries persuaded themselves that although Washington put himself forward for elective office, he somehow stood above the hurly-burly of routine politics. A French diplomat who witnessed Washington's first inauguration in New York City reported in awe: "He has the soul, look, and figure of a hero united in him." But the adulation of Washington—however well meant—seriously affected the conduct of public affairs, for criticism of his administration was regarded as an attack on the president and, by extension, on the republic itself. During the earliest years of Washington's presidency, therefore, American public opinion discouraged partisan politics.

Washington created a strong, independent presidency. He had long advocated a strong federal government. Indeed, unlike some of his contemporaries, Washington rejected shrill states' rights claims, fearing that local political loyalties might compromise the integrity of the struggling republic, leaving it vulnerable to the predatory ambitions of European empires. While he discussed pressing issues with the members of his cabinet, he left no doubt that he alone made policy. Moreover, the first president resisted congressional efforts to restrict executive authority, especially in foreign affairs.

The first Congress quickly established executive departments. Some congressmen wanted to prohibit presidents from dismissing cabinet-level appointees without Senate approval, but James Madison—still a voice for a strong, independent executive—led a successful fight against this restriction on presidential authority. Madison recognized that the chief executive could not function unless he had personal confidence in the people with whom he worked. In 1789, Congress created the Departments of War, State, and the Treasury, and as secretaries, Washington nominated Henry Knox, Thomas Jefferson, and Alexander Hamilton, respectively. Edmund Randolph served as part-time attorney general, a position that ranked slightly lower in prestige than the head of a department. Since the secretary of the treasury oversaw the collection of customs and other future federal taxes, Hamilton could anticipate having several thousand jobs to dispense, an obvious source of political patronage.

To modern Americans accustomed to a huge federal bureaucracy, the size of Washington's government seems amazingly small. When Jefferson arrived in New York to take over the State Department, for example, he found two chief clerks, two assistants, and a part-time translator. With this tiny staff, he not only maintained contacts with the representatives of foreign governments, collected information about world affairs, and communicated with U.S. officials living overseas, but also organized the entire federal census! Since the Constitution tied congressional representation to state population, it was extremely important to count the number of inhabitants fairly and efficiently, a task that strained the resources of the new administration. In 1790, at a cost of only $44,377.28, hundreds of federal enumerators were dispatched to obtain an accurate tally of the nation's inhabitants. Anxious to impress predatory European monarchies with the rapid growth of the United States, Washington hoped the number would be large. The final figure of 3,929,214 people, of which some 700,000 were African American slaves, disappointed the president.

Jefferson immediately recognized that his new job would allow him little leisure for personal interests. The situation in other departments was similar. Overworked clerks scribbled madly just to keep up with the press of correspondence. John Adams, reviewing a bundle of letters and memos, grumbled that "often the handwriting is almost illegible." Considering these working conditions, it is not surprising that the president had difficulty persuading able people to accept positions in the new government. It is even more astonishing that Hamilton and

This unfinished portrait of George Washington was done by the portrait painter Gilbert Stuart in 1796. Because of the large popular demand for images of the first president, Stuart developed a good business copying his original painting. The image of Washington that appears on the U.S. dollar bill is based on this "Athenaeum" portrait. ❖

Jefferson were able to accomplish as much as they did with so little assistance.

Congress also provided for a federal court system. The Judiciary Act of 1789, the work primarily of Connecticut Congressman Oliver Ellsworth, created a Supreme Court staffed by a chief justice and five associate justices. In addition, the statute set up thirteen district courts authorized to review the decisions of the state courts. John Jay, a leading figure in New York politics, agreed to serve as chief justice, but since federal judges in the 1790s were expected to travel hundreds of miles over terrible roads to attend sessions of the inferior courts, few persons of outstanding talent and training joined Jay on the federal bench. One who did, Judge James Iredell, complained that service on the Supreme Court had transformed him into a "travelling postboy."

Remembering the financial insecurity of the old Confederation government, the newly elected congressmen passed the tariff of 1789, a tax of approximately 5 percent on imports. The new levy generated considerable revenue for the young republic. Even before it went into effect, however, the act sparked controversy. Southern planters, who relied heavily on European imports and the northern shippers who could control the flow of imports into the South,

*A view of the west front of George Washington's Virginia mansion, Mount Vernon, here depicted by an unknown artist in the 1790s. The house was the site of the first cabinet meetings of the new government of the United States.* ❖

claimed that the tariff discriminated against southern interests in favor of those of northern merchants.

## CONFLICTING VISIONS: JEFFERSON AND HAMILTON

Washington's first cabinet included two extraordinary personalities, Alexander Hamilton and Thomas Jefferson. Both had served the country with distinction during the Revolution, were recognized by contemporaries as men of special genius as well as high ambition, and brought to public office a powerful vision of how the American people could achieve greatness. The story of their opposing views during the decade of the 1790s provides insight into the birth and development of political parties. It also reveals how a common political ideology, republicanism, (see Chapter 6) could be interpreted in such vastly different ways that decisions about government policy turned friends into adversaries. Indeed, the falling out of Hamilton and Jefferson reflected deep, potentially explosive political divisions within American society.

Hamilton was a brilliant, dynamic young lawyer who had distinguished himself as Washington's aide-de-camp during the Revolution. Born in the West Indies, the child of an adulterous relationship, Hamilton employed charm, courage, and intellect to fulfill his inexhaustible ambition. He strove not for wealth but for reputation. Men and women who fell under his spell found him almost irresistible, but to enemies, Hamilton appeared a dark, calculating, even evil, genius. He advocated a strong central government

and refused to be bound by the strict wording of the Constitution, a document Hamilton once called "a shilly shally thing." While he had fought for American independence, he admired British culture, and during the 1790s, he advocated closer commercial and diplomatic ties with the former mother country, with whom, he said, "we have a similarity of tastes, language, and general manners."

Jefferson possessed a profoundly different temperament. This tall Virginian was more reflective and shone less brightly in society than Hamilton. Contemporaries sometimes interpreted his retiring manner as lack of ambition. They misread Jefferson. He thirsted not for power or wealth but for an opportunity to advance the democratic principles that he had stated so eloquently in the Declaration of Independence. When Jefferson became secretary of state in January 1790, he had just returned from Paris where he witnessed the first exhilarating moments of the French Revolution. These earthshaking events, he believed, marked the beginning of a worldwide republican assault on absolute monarchy and aristocratic privilege. His European experiences biased Jefferson in favor of France over Great Britain when the two nations clashed.

The contrast between these two powerful figures during the early years of Washington's administration should not be exaggerated. They shared many fundamental beliefs. Indeed, both Hamilton and Jefferson insisted they were working for the creation of a strong, prosperous republic, one in which commerce would play an important role. Hamilton was publicly accused of being a secret monarchist, but he never repudiated the ideals of the American Revolution. Rather than being spokespersons for competing ideologies, Hamilton and Jefferson were different kinds of republicans who, during the 1790s, attempted as best they could to cope with unprecedented political challenges.

However much these two men had in common, serious differences emerged. Washington's secretaries disagreed on precisely how the United States should fulfill its destiny. As head of the Treasury Department, Hamilton urged his fellow citizens to think in terms of bold commercial development, of farms and factories embedded within a complex financial network that would reduce the nation's reliance on foreign trade. Because Great Britain had already established an elaborate system of banking and credit, the secretary looked to that country for economic models that might be reproduced on this side of the Atlantic.

Hamilton also voiced concerns about the role of the people in shaping public policy. His view of human nature caused him to fear democratic excess. He assumed that in a republican society, the gravest threat to political stability was anarchy rather than monarchy. "The truth," he claimed, "unquestionably is, that the only path to a subversion of the republican system of the Country is, by flattering the prejudices of the people, and exciting their jealousies and apprehensions, to throw affairs into confusion and bring on civil commotion." The best hope for the survival of the republic, Hamilton believed, lay with the country's monied classes. If the wealthiest people could be persuaded their economic self-interest could be advanced—or at least made less insecure—by the central

government, then they would work to strengthen it, and by so doing, bring a greater measure of prosperity to the common people. From Hamilton's perspective, there was no conflict between private greed and public good; one was the source of the other.

On almost every detail, Jefferson challenged Hamilton's analysis. The secretary of state assumed that the strength of the American economy lay not in its industrial potential but in its agricultural productivity. The "immensity of land" represented the country's major economic resource. Contrary to the claims of some critics, Jefferson did not advocate agrarian self-sufficiency or look back nostalgically to a golden age dominated by simple yeomen. He recognized the necessity of change, and while he thought that persons who worked the soil were more responsible citizens than were those who labored in factories for wages, he encouraged the nation's farmers to participate in an expanding international market. Americans could exchange raw materials "for finer manufactures than they are able to execute themselves."

Unlike Hamilton, Jefferson expressed faith in the ability of the American people to shape policy. Throughout this troubled decade, even when the very survival of constitutional government seemed in doubt, Jefferson maintained a boundless optimism in the judgment of the common folk. He instinctively trusted the people, feared that uncontrolled government power might destroy their liberties, and insisted public officials follow the letter of the Constitution, a frame of government he described as "the wisest ever presented to men." The greatest threat to the young

*During the first years of Washington's administration, neither Hamilton (left) nor Jefferson (right) recognized the full extent of their differences. But as events forced the federal government to make decisions on economic and foreign affairs, the two secretaries increasingly came into open conflict.* ❖

republic, he argued, came from the corrupt activities of pseudoaristocrats, persons who placed the protection of "property" and "civil order" above the preservation of "liberty." To tie the nation's future to the selfish interests of a privileged class—bankers, manufacturers, and speculators—seemed cynical as well as dangerous. He despised speculators who encouraged "the rage of getting rich in a day," since such "gaming" activities inevitably promoted the kinds of public vice that threatened republican government. To mortgage the future of the common people by creating a large national debt struck Jefferson as particularly insane. But the responsibility for shaping the economy of the new nation fell mainly to Alexander Hamilton as the first secretary of the treasury.

## HAMILTON'S PLAN FOR PROSPERITY AND SECURITY

The unsettled state of the nation's finances presented the new government with a staggering challenge. In August 1789, the House of Representatives announced that "adequate provision for the support of public credit [is] a matter of high importance to the national honor and prosperity." However pressing the problem appeared, no one was prepared to advance a solution, and the House asked the secretary of the treasury to make suggestions.

Congress may have received more than it bargained for. Hamilton threw himself into the task. He read deeply in abstruse economic literature. He even developed a questionnaire designed to find out how the U.S. economy really worked and sent it to scores of commercial and political leaders throughout the country. But when Hamilton's three major reports—on public credit, on banking, and on manufacturers—were complete, they bore the unmistakable stamp of his own creative genius. The secretary synthesized a vast amount of information into an economic blueprint so complex, so innovative that even his allies were slightly baffled. Theodore Sedgwick, a congressman who supported Hamilton's program, explained weakly that the secretary's ideas were "difficult to understand . . . while we are in our infancy in the knowledge of Finance." Certainly, Washington never fully grasped the subtleties of Hamilton's plan.

The secretary presented his *Report on the Public Credit* to Congress on January 14, 1790. His research revealed that the nation's outstanding debt stood at approximately $54 million. This sum represented various obligations that the U.S. government had incurred during the Revolutionary War. In addition to foreign loans, the figure included loan certificates the government had issued to its own citizens and soldiers. But

that was not all. The states still owed creditors approximately $25 million. During the 1780s, Americans desperate for cash had been forced to sell government certificates to speculators at greatly discounted prices, and it was estimated that approximately $40 million of the nation's debt was owed to twenty thousand people, only 20 percent of whom were the original creditors.

### Funding and Assumption

Hamilton's *Report on the Public Credit* contained two major recommendations covering the areas of funding and assumption. First, under his plan, the United States promised to fund its foreign and domestic obligations at full face value. Current holders of loan certificates, whoever they were and no matter how they obtained them, could exchange the old certificates for new government bonds bearing a moderate rate of interest. Second, the secretary urged the federal government to assume responsibility for paying the remaining state debts.

Hamilton reasoned that his credit system would accomplish several desirable goals. It would significantly reduce the power of the individual states in shaping national economic policy, something Hamilton regarded as essential in maintaining a strong federal government. Moreover, the creation of a fully funded national debt signaled to investors throughout the world that the United States was now solvent, that its bonds represented a good risk. Hamilton argued that investment capital, which might otherwise flow to Europe, would remain in this country, providing a source of money for commercial and industrial investment. In short, Hamilton invited the country's wealthiest citizens to invest in the future of the United States. Critics claimed that the only people who stood to profit from the scheme were Hamilton's friends—some of whom sat in Congress and who had purchased great numbers of public securities at very low prices.

To Hamilton's great surprise, Madison—his friend and collaborator in writing *The Federalist*—attacked the funding scheme in the House of Representatives. The Virginia congressman agreed that the United States should honor its debts. He worried, however, about the citizens and soldiers who, because of personal financial hardship, had been compelled to sell their certificates at prices far below face value. Why should wealthy speculators now profit from their hardship? If the government treated the current holders of certificates less generously, Madison declared, then there might be sufficient funds to provide equitable treatment for the distressed patriots. Whatever the moral justification for Madison's plan may have been, it proved unworkable on the national level. Far too many records had been lost since the Revolution for the Treasury Department to be able to identify all the original holders. In February 1790, Congress soundly defeated Madison's proposal.

The assumption portion of Hamilton's plan unleashed even greater criticism. Some states had already paid their revolutionary debts, and Hamilton's program seemed designed to reward certain states—Massachusetts and South Carolina, for example—simply because they had failed to put their finances in order. In addition, the secretary's opponents in Congress became suspicious that assumption was merely a ploy to increase the power and wealth of Hamilton's immediate friends. "The Secretary's people scarce disguise their design," observed William Maclay, a crusty Scots-Irish senator from Pennsylvania, "which is to create a mass of debts which will justify them in seizing all the sources of government."

No doubt, Maclay and others expressed genuine fears. Some of those who protested, however, were simply looking after their own speculative schemes. These men had contracted to purchase huge tracts of vacant western lands from the state and federal governments. They anticipated that when settlers finally arrived in these areas, the price of land would skyrocket. In the meantime, the speculators had paid for the land with revolutionary certificates, often purchased on the open market at fifteen cents on the dollar. This meant that one could obtain 1000 acres for only $150. Hamilton's assumption proposal threatened to destroy these lucrative transactions by cutting off the supply of cut-rate securities. On April 12, a rebellious House led by Madison defeated assumption.

The victory was short-lived. Hamilton and congressional supporters resorted to legislative horse trading to revive his foundering program. In exchange for locating the new federal capital on the Potomac River, a move that would stimulate the depressed economy of northern Virginia, several key congressmen who shared Madison's political philosophy changed their votes on assumption. Hamilton may also have offered to give the state of Virginia more federal money than it actually deserved. Whatever the details of these negotiations may have been, in August, Washington signed assumption and funding into law. The first element of Hamilton's design was now securely in place.

## Interpreting the Constitution: The Bank Controversy

The persistent Hamilton submitted his second report to Congress in January 1791. He proposed that the U.S. government charter a national bank. This privately owned institution would be funded in part by the federal government. Indeed, since the **Bank of the United States** would own millions of dollars of new U.S. bonds, its financial stability would be tied directly to the strength of the federal government and, of course, to the success of Hamilton's program. The secretary of the treasury argued that a growing financial community required a central bank to facilitate increasingly complex commercial transactions. The institution not only would serve as the main depository of the U.S. government but also would issue currency acceptable in payment of federal taxes. Because of that guarantee, the money would maintain its value while in circulation.

Madison and others in Congress immediately raised a howl of protest. While they were not oblivious to the many important services a national bank might provide for a growing country, they suspected that banks—especially those modeled on British institutions—might "perpetuate a large monied interest" in the United States. And how was one to interpret the Constitution? That document said nothing specifically

## ❖ A Look at the Past ❖

### Eagle Decoration

Following the American Revolution, patriotic symbols and themes became common in decorative arts. Eagles, a traditional symbol of strength, enjoyed especial popularity. English manufacturers printed eagles on ceramics and textiles. Women embroidered eagles and appliquéd them onto quilts and coverlets like the one pictured here. Even fine furniture displayed eagles. Such objects reflected pride in a new, untested republic. Why would consumers want patriotic emblems on their fine fabric and furniture? Were all Americans encouraged to celebrate the spirit of nationalism?

about chartering financial corporations, and critics warned that if Hamilton and his supporters were allowed to stretch fundamental law on this occasion, they could not be held back in the future. Popular liberties would be at the mercy of whoever happened to be in office. "To take a single step," Jefferson warned, "beyond the boundaries thus specifically drawn around the powers of Congress is to take possession of a boundless field of power, no longer susceptible to definition." On this issue, Hamilton stubbornly refused to compromise, announcing angrily, "This is the first symptom of a spirit which must either be killed or will kill the constitution of the United States."

This intense controversy involving his closest advisers worried the president. Even though the bank bill passed Congress (February 8), Washington seriously considered vetoing the legislation on constitutional grounds. Before doing so, however, he requested written opinions from the members of his cabinet. Jefferson's rambling, wholly predictable attack on the Bank of the United States was not one of his more persuasive performances. By contrast, in only a few days, Hamilton prepared a masterful essay titled "Defense of the Constitutionality of the Bank." He assured the president that Article I, Section 8 of the Constitution— "The Congress shall have Power . . . To make all Laws which shall be necessary and proper for carrying into Execution the foregoing Powers"—justified issuing charters to national banks. The "foregoing Powers" on which Hamilton placed so much weight were taxation, regulation of commerce, and making war. He boldly articulated a doctrine of *implied powers*, an interpretation of the Constitution that neither Madison nor Jefferson had anticipated. Hamilton's "loose construction" carried the day, and on February 25, 1791, Washington signed the bank act into law.

Hamilton triumphed in Congress, but the general public looked on his actions with growing fear and hostility. Many persons associated huge national debts and privileged banks with the decay of public virtue. Men of Jefferson's temperament believed that Great Britain—a country Hamilton held in high regard— had compromised the purity of its ancient constitution by allowing speculators to worm their way into positions of political power.

Hamilton seemed intent on reproducing this corrupt system in the United States. When news of his proposal to fund the national debt at full face value leaked out, for example, urban speculators rushed to rural areas, where they purchased loan certificates from unsuspecting citizens at bargain prices. To backcountry farmers, making money without actually engaging in physical labor appeared immoral, unrepublican, and, certainly, un-American. When the greed of a former Treasury Department official led to

several serious bankruptcies in 1792, ordinary citizens began to listen more closely to what Madison, Jefferson, and their associates were saying about growing corruption in high places.

## Setback for Hamilton

In his third major report, *Report on Manufactures,* submitted to Congress in December 1791, Hamilton revealed the final details of his grand design for the economic future of the United States. This lengthy document suggested ways by which the federal government might stimulate manufacturing. If the country wanted to free itself from dependence on European imports, Hamilton observed, then it had to develop its own industry, textile mills for example. Without direct government intervention, however, the process would take decades. Americans would continue to invest in agriculture. But, according to the secretary of the treasury, protective tariffs and special industrial bounties would greatly accelerate the growth of a balanced economy, and with proper planning, the United States would soon hold its own with England and France.

In Congress, the battle lines were clearly drawn. Hamilton's opponents—not yet a disciplined party but a loose coalition of men who shared Madison's and Jefferson's misgivings about the secretary's program—ignored his economic arguments. Instead, they engaged him on moral and political grounds. Madison railed against the dangers of "consolidation," a process that threatened to concentrate all power in the federal government, leaving the states defenseless. Under the Confederation, of course, Madison had stood with the nationalists against the advocates of extreme states' rights. His disagreements with Hamilton over economic policy, coupled with the necessity of pleasing the voters of his Virginia congressional district every two years, transformed Madison into a spokesman for the states, echoing the substance of Antifederalist arguments he had once hotly rejected (see Chapter 6).

Jefferson attacked the *Report on Manufactures* from a different angle. He assumed—largely because he had been horrified by Europe's urban poverty—that cities breed vice. The government, Jefferson argued, should do nothing to promote their development. He believed that Hamilton's proposal guaranteed that American workers would leave the countryside and crowd into urban centers. "I think our government will remain virtuous for many centuries," Jefferson explained, "as long as they [the people] are chiefly agricultural. . . . When they get piled upon one another in large cities, as in Europe, they will become corrupt as in Europe." And southern congressmen saw tariffs and bounties as vehicles for enriching Hamilton's northern friends at the planters' expense. The recommendations in the *Report on Manufactures* were soundly defeated in the House of Representatives.

Washington detested political squabbling. The president, of course, could see that the members of his cabinet disagreed on many issues, but in 1792, he still believed that Hamilton and Jefferson—and the people who looked to them for advice—could be reconciled. In August, he personally begged them to rise above the "internal dissensions [that are] . . . harrowing and tearing at our vitals." The appeal came too late. By the conclusion of Washington's first term, neither secretary trusted the other's judgment. Their sparring had produced congressional factions, but as yet no real political parties with permanent organizations that engaged in campaigning had come into existence. At this point, Hamilton and Jefferson only dimly appreciated the force of public opinion in shaping federal policy.

# CHARGES OF TREASON: THE BATTLE OVER FOREIGN AFFAIRS

During Washington's second term (1793–1797), war in Europe dramatically thrust foreign affairs into the forefront of American life. The impact of this development on the conduct of domestic politics was devastating. Officials who had formerly disagreed on economic policy now began to identify their interests with either Britain or France, Europe's most powerful nations. Differences of political opinion, however trivial, were suddenly cited as evidence that one group or the other had entered into treasonous correspondence with external enemies eager to compromise the independence and prosperity of the United States. As Jefferson observed during the troubled summer of 1793, European conflict "kindled and brought forward the two parties with an ardour which our own interests merely, could never excite." The spirit of nationalism even spilled over into scientific debate. The normally dispassionate Jefferson reacted very badly when a French writer claimed, among other things, that North American animals were smaller than those found in Europe. (See the Feature Essay, "Defense of Superiority: Science in the Service of Nationalism in the Early Republic," pp. 200–201.)

Formal political organizations—the Federalists and Republicans—were born in this poisonous atmosphere. The clash between the groups developed over how best to preserve the new republic. The Republicans (Jeffersonians) advocated states' rights, strict interpretation of the Constitution, friendship with France, and vigilance against "the avaricious, monopolizing Spirit of Commerce and Commercial Men." The Federalists urged a strong national government, central economic planning, closer ties with Great Britain, and maintenance of public order, even if that meant calling out federal troops.

## The Peril of Neutrality

Great Britain treated the United States with arrogance. The colonists had defeated the redcoats on land, but on the high seas, the Americans were no match for the British navy, the strongest in the world. Indeed, the young republic could not even compel its old adversary to comply with the Treaty of 1783, in which the British had agreed to vacate military posts in the Northwest Territory. In 1794, approximately a thousand British soldiers still occupied American land, an obstruction that Governor George Clinton of New York claimed had excluded U.S. citizens "from a very valuable trade to which their situation would naturally have invited them." Moreover, even though 75 percent of American imports came from Great Britain, that country refused to grant the United States full commercial reciprocity. Among other provocations, it barred American shipping from the lucrative West Indian trade.

France presented a very different challenge. In May 1789, Louis XVI, desperate for revenue, authorized a meeting of a representative assembly known as the Estates General. By so doing, the king unleashed explosive revolutionary forces that toppled the monarchy and cost him his life (January 1793). The men who seized power—and they came and went rapidly—were militant republicans, ideologues eager to liberate all Europe from feudal institutions. In the early years of the **French Revolution,** France drew on the American experience, and Thomas Paine and the Marquis de Lafayette enjoyed great popularity. But the French found they could not stop the violence of revolution. Constitutional reform turned into bloody purges, and one radical group, the Jacobins, guillotined thousands of people who were suspected of monarchist sympathies during the so-called Reign of Terror (October 1793–July 1794). These horrific events left Americans confused. While those who shared Jefferson's views cheered the spread of republicanism, others who sided with Hamilton condemned French expansionism and political excess.

In the face of growing international tension, neutrality seemed the most prudent course for the United States. But that policy was easier for a weak country to proclaim than to defend. In February 1793, France declared war on Great Britain—what the leaders of revolutionary France called the "war of all peoples against all kings"—and these powerful European rivals immediately challenged the official American position on

# DEFENSE OF SUPERIORITY

## Science in the Service of Nationalism in the Early Republic

Nationalism promotes patriotism. Sometimes, however, expressions of pride turn malicious, belittling outsiders as inferior. When claims of superiority seem to have scientific justification, the rhetoric of nationalism can become dangerous, often outright racist. Such a situation developed during the earliest years of the American republic.

Even before the Revolution, respected scientists such as Benjamin Franklin resented disparaging remarks about American inferiority. Europeans accepted as fact the notion that New World animals and humans were smaller, slower, and less clever than those found in the Old World. Franklin dismissed the theory as nonsense, and at a dinner party in Paris he took the opportunity to demonstrate that if size really mattered, then the Americans were bigger. When the abbe Raynal, a French naturalist, announced that everything American was substandard compared to European experience, Franklin challenged his host to a test. All the Americans at the table stood; so did the French. Franklin noted with satisfaction that the Americans had the "finest stature and form." Raynal, he observed, was a "mere shrimp."

Although Franklin may have won the battle of the dinner table, other Americans still worried that New World creatures fell short of Europe standards. The seeds of doubt could be traced to a widely read scientific treatise entitled *Histoire naturelle*, the first volumes of which appeared in 1749. The author, French philosopher Comte de Buffon, argued that the climate of North America produced animals of smaller size than those encountered in the Old World. As evidence, Buffon cited the absence of elephants, lions, and other large beasts in the New World. He scoffed that the Brazilian tapir was no bigger than "the six month-old calf" of an African elephant. The only New World creatures that exceeded their Old World counterparts in size, he declared, were the toads and snakes that thrived in North America's abundant swamps. Worse yet, Buffon asserted that America's climate caused animals found in Europe to "shrink and diminish" when transported to the New World.

For Buffon, Native Americans were a case in point. On the basis of superficial reports of Indian weakness, Buffon announced that conditions in the New World were "pernicious to men, who are degenerated, debilitated, and vitiated in a surprising manner in all parts of their organization." The implications of this idea were not lost on people such as Franklin. If the American environment sapped the Indians of vitality, it was only a matter of time until European settlers who breathed the same air, drank the same water, and cultivated the same land succumbed to sloth. One of Buffon's followers counseled those colonists condemned to live in such an unpromising environment "to know how to make themselves happy . . . with mediocrity," leaving intellectual greatness to those who had wisely remained in the Old World.

After simmering for thirty years, American anger over Buffon's theory came to a boil following the American Revolution. The new nation had its honor to defend. If, as the French scientist had maintained, the North American climate caused the physical, mental, and moral abilities of humans to decline, then the republican experiment of the young United States seemed destined to fail. Having already asserted that "all men are created equal" in the Declaration of Independence, Thomas Jefferson set out to prove American equality through science. An uncompromising patriot, he devoted himself almost entirely to the defense of the fledgling republic, spending much of the 1780s poring over accounts of American animals in search of holes in Buffon's theory.

Jefferson published his results in 1785. In *Notes on the State of Virginia* he countered Buffon with a lengthy series of tables comparing the weight of European and American animals. Not surprisingly, Jefferson always tipped the scale in favor of the New World. While

### A COMPARATIVE VIEW OF THE QUADRUPEDS OF EUROPE AND AMERICA

|  | Europe lb. | America lb. |
|---|---|---|
| Bear | 153.7 | 410.0 |
| Red deer | 288.8 | 273.0 |
| Beaver | 18.5 | 45.0 |
| Otter | 8.9 | 12.0 |
| Cow | 763.0 | 2500.0 |

**Source:** Adapted from Thomas Jefferson, *Notes on the State of Virginia* (1787).

Europe's puny flying squirrels weighed only 2.2 pounds, America could boast of impressive 4-pound squirrels. American bears were three times fatter than Old World bears. And most telling, America had once been the home of huge Ice Age animals called woolly mammoths. They looked a lot like elephants, and one recently unearthed in Kentucky matched the best Old World elephants in terms of size. In terms of size, Americans apparently had nothing to fear.

Jefferson did not stop there. Determined to use science to improve the international reputation of the United States, Jefferson commissioned the governor of New Hampshire to kill a giant moose, which was then shipped to Paris as a present for Buffon. The plan miscarried. While hunters managed to shoot the moose and drag it from the forest, the unrefrigerated voyage to France made for an extremely foul-smelling gift. For Jefferson, the unlucky moose's decay was a minor problem, since by his own reasoning, he had put to rest misguided European ideas about animal deficiency in the new American republic.

Turning from moose to men, Jefferson took a step that transformed a harmless squabble over the weight of squirrels into something much more alarming. Using the latest scientific research, Jefferson claimed that climate had almost no effect on human beings. Instead, a person's race determined his or her size, vitality, and intelligence. In this scheme, European Americans and Native Americans were equal. And, according to Jefferson, both were vastly superior to Africans. A celebration of national pride had now become a defense of racism.

To make his case, Jefferson first defended Native Americans against Buffon's assertions of climate-induced inferiority. Buffon had suggested that Indians' beardless faces and "lack of ardour for their female" demonstrated their physical inadequacy in comparison to manly Europeans. In response, Jefferson outlined the practice of face plucking. "With them it is disgraceful to be hairy," he claimed of Native Americans, because many believed "it likens them to hogs." Moreover, the Indians did not value French-style

womanizing. Jefferson explained that "Their soul is wholly bent upon war," a trait that "procures them glory among men, and makes them the admiration of women." Differences between whites and Indians could be attributed not to the environment, but to culture. Indeed, he saw the two groups as a single race, so closely related that he recommended letting them "intermix, and become one people."

Jefferson rejected completely any notion that Africans in America could be part of this "one people." An unbridgeable biological gulf separated whites and Indians— groups that Jefferson lumped together as "Homo Sapiens Europaeus"—from blacks. Jefferson argued that while Europeans and Native Americans produced fine arts and engaged in brilliant oratory, African slaves exhibited no skill in painting or sculpture, and never "uttered a thought above the level of plain narration." With only anecdotal evidence to support his claims, Jefferson concluded that blacks were "inferior to the whites in the endowments of both body and mind." According to Jefferson, the harsh truth was that whether found in Africa, on Carolina rice plantations, or on the streets of Boston, Africans were a "different species of the same genus." They were a separate race, unworthy of genuine political and social equality.

During the late eighteenth and early nineteenth centuries, American nationalists seized upon Jefferson's ideas, seeing *Notes on the State of Virginia* as a blueprint for a republican society, grounded in rational science and dedicated to racial inequality. In a world still dominated by powerful monarchies and Old World cultures,

Illustration of frogs from Comte de Buffon's *Histoire Naturelle*, 1749. Buffon declared that in the damp American climate only cold-blooded animals such as snakes and frogs flourished and grew larger than their European counterparts. ❖

Americans of all European backgrounds took comfort in being equal to each other and superior to African Americans. In an atmosphere of strident nationalism, few were willing to explain differences between whites and blacks as cultural or environmental. There existed, in Jefferson's words, a "real distinction which nature has made." White Americans were destined to be free, while enslaved blacks, whose labor formed the backbone of the whites' economy, must accept their lesser place in the nation's future. Jefferson's scientific thinking about race—inspired by national insecurity and a Frenchman's musing on New World toads—promoted a divisiveness in American society that continues to trouble the nation.

*The execution of Louis XVI by French revolutionaries served to deepen the growing political division in America. Although they deplored the excesses of the Reign of Terror, Jeffersonian Republicans continued to support the French people. Federalists feared that the violence and lawlessness would spread to the United States.* ❖

shipping: "free ships make free goods," meaning that belligerents should not interfere with the shipping of neutral carriers. To make matters worse, no one was certain whether the Franco-American treaties of 1778 (see Chapter 5) legally bound the United States to support its old ally against Great Britain.

Both Hamilton and Jefferson wanted to avoid war. The secretary of state, however, believed that nations desiring American goods should be forced to honor American neutrality and, therefore, that if Britain treated the United States as a colonial possession, if the Royal Navy stopped American ships on the high seas and forced seamen to serve the king—in other words, if it impressed American sailors—then the United States should award France special commercial advantages. Hamilton thought Jefferson's scheme insane. He pointed out that Britain possessed the largest navy in the world and was not likely to be coerced by American threats. The United States, he counseled, should appease the former mother country even if that meant swallowing national pride.

A newly appointed French minister to the United States, Edmond Genêt, precipitated the first major diplomatic crisis. This incompetent young man ar-

rived in Charleston, South Carolina, in April 1793. He found considerable popular enthusiasm for the French Revolution, and, buoyed by this reception, he authorized privately owned American vessels to seize British ships in the name of France. Such actions clearly violated U.S. neutrality and invited British retaliation. When U.S. government officials warned Genêt to desist, he threatened to take his appeal directly to the American people, who presumably loved France more than did members of Washington's administration.

This confrontation particularly embarrassed Jefferson, the most outspoken pro-French member of the cabinet. He described Genêt as "hot headed, all imagination, no judgment, passionate, disrespectful and even indecent towards the President." Washington did not wait to discover whether the treaties of 1778 were still in force. Before he had formally received the impudent French minister, the president issued a Proclamation of Neutrality (April 22). Ironically, after Genêt learned that the Jacobins intended to cut off his head if he returned to France, he requested asylum, married into an extremely wealthy family, and spent the remainder of his life in New York.

## Jay's Treaty Sparks Domestic Unrest

Great Britain failed to take advantage of Genêt's insolence. Instead, it pushed the United States to the brink of war. British forts in the Northwest Territory remained a constant source of tension. In June 1793, a new element was added. The London government blockaded French ports to neutral shipping, and in November, its navy captured several hundred American vessels trading in the French West Indies. The British had not even bothered to give the United States advance warning of a change in policy. Outraged members of Congress, especially those who identified with Jefferson and Madison, demanded retaliation, an embargo, a stoppage of debt payment, even war.

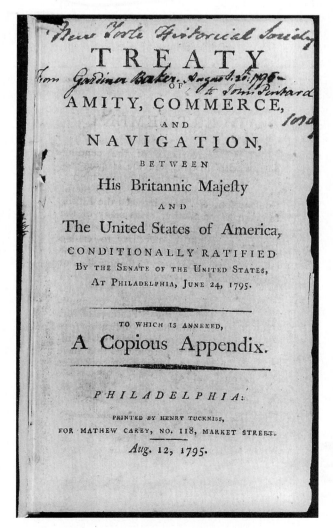

Printer Matthew Carey helped fire the protest over Jay's Treaty by printing the terms of the agreement and adding a series of partisan comments to the appendix. ✦

Before this rhetoric produced armed struggle, Washington made one final effort to preserve peace. In May 1794, he sent Chief Justice John Jay to London to negotiate a formidable list of grievances. The effort resulted in a political humiliation known simply as **Jay's Treaty.** Jay's main objectives were removal of the British forts on U.S. territory, payment for ships taken in the West Indies, improved commercial relations, and acceptance of the American definition of neutral rights.

Jefferson's supporters—by now openly called the Republican interest—anticipated a treaty favorable to the United States. After all, they explained, the war with France had not gone well for Great Britain, and the British people were surely desperate for American foodstuffs. Even before Jay departed, however, his mission stood little chance of success. Hamilton, anxious as ever to placate the British, had already secretly informed British officials that the United States would compromise on most issues.

Not surprisingly, when Jay reached London, he encountered polite but firm resistance. The chief justice did persuade the British to abandon their frontier posts and to allow small American ships to trade in the British West Indies, but they rejected out of hand the U.S. position on neutral rights. The Royal Navy would continue to search American vessels on the high seas for contraband and to impress sailors suspected of being British citizens. Moreover, there would be no compensation for the ships seized in 1793 until the Americans paid British merchants for debts contracted before the Revolution. And to the particular annoyance of Southerners, not a word was said about the slaves the British army had carried off at the conclusion of the war. While Jay salvaged the peace, he appeared to have betrayed the national interest.

News of Jay's Treaty—perhaps more correctly called Hamilton's Treaty—produced an angry outcry in the nation's capital. Even Washington was apprehensive. He submitted the document to the Senate without recommending ratification, a sign that the president was not entirely happy with the results of Jay's mission. After an extremely bitter debate, the upper house, controlled by Federalists, accepted a revised version of the treaty (June 1795). The vote was 20 to 10, a bare two-thirds majority.

The details of the Jay agreement soon leaked to the press. This was an important moment in American political history. The popular journals sparked a firestorm of objection. Throughout the country, people who had generally been apathetic about national politics were swept up in a wave of protest. Urban mobs condemned Jay's alleged sellout; rural settlers burned him in effigy. Jay jokingly told friends he could find his way across the country simply by following the light of those fires. Southerners announced they would not pay prerevolutionary debts to British merchants. The Virginia legislature proposed a constitutional amendment reducing the Senate's role in the treaty-making process. As Fisher Ames, a Federalist congressman, noted darkly, "These little whirlwinds of dry leaves and dirt portend a hurricane."

His prediction proved accurate. The storm broke in the House of Representatives. Republican congressmen, led by Madison, thought they could stop Jay's Treaty by refusing to appropriate funds for its implementation. As part of their plan, they demanded that Washington show the House state papers relating to Jay's mission. The challenge raised complex issues of constitutional law. The House, for example, was claiming a voice in treaty ratification, a power explicitly reserved to the Senate. Second, there was the question of executive secrecy in the interest of national security. Could the president withhold information from the public? According to Washington—as well as all subsequent presidents—the answer was yes. He took the occasion to lecture the rebellious representatives that "the nature of foreign negotiations requires caution; and their success must often depend on secrecy."

The president still had a trump card to play. He raised the possibility that the House was really contemplating his impeachment. Such an action was, of course, unthinkable. Even criticizing Washington in public was politically dangerous, and as soon as he redefined the issue before Congress, petitions supporting the president flooded into the nation's capital. The Maryland legislature, for example, declared its "unabated reliance on the integrity, judgment, and patriotism of the President of the United States," a statement that clearly called into question the patriotism of certain Republican congressmen. The Federalists won a stunning tactical victory over the opposition. Had a less popular man than Washington occupied the presidency, however, they would not have fared so well. The division between the two parties was beyond repair. The Republicans labeled the Federalists "the British

party"; the Federalists believed that the Republicans were in league with the French.

By the time Jay's Treaty became law (June 14, 1795), the two giants of Washington's first cabinet had retired. Late in 1793, Jefferson returned to his Virginia plantation, Monticello, where, despite his separation from day-to-day political affairs, he remained the chief spokesman for the Republican party. His rival, Hamilton, left the Treasury in January 1795 to practice law in New York City. He maintained close ties with important Federalist officials, and even more than Jefferson, Hamilton concerned himself with the details of party organization.

## Pushing the Native Americans Aside

Before Great Britain finally withdrew its troops from the Great Lakes and Northwest Territory, its military officers encouraged local Indian groups—the Shawnees, Chippewas, and Miamis—to attack settlers and traders from the United States. The Indians, who even without British encouragement fully appreciated that the newcomers intended to seize their land, won several impressive victories over federal troops in the area that would become western Ohio and Indiana. In 1790, General Josiah Harmar led his soldiers into an ambush. The following year, an army under General Arthur St. Clair suffered more than nine hundred casualties near the Wabash River. But the Indians were militarily more vulnerable than they realized, for when confronted with a major U.S. army under the command of General Anthony Wayne, they received no support from their former British allies. At the battle of Fallen Timbers (August 20, 1794), Wayne's forces crushed Indian resistance in the Northwest Territory, and the native peoples were compelled to sign the Treaty of Greenville, formally ceding to the U.S. government the land that became Ohio. In 1796, the last British soldiers departed for Canada.

Shrewd negotiations mixed with pure luck helped secure the nation's southwestern frontier. For complex

*At the Treaty of Greenville in 1795, negotiators shared this calumet, or peace pipe, a spiritually symbolic act for Native Americans. This superficial recognition of the legitimacy of Native American cultures barely disguised the Indians' crushing loss of sovereignty.* ❖

**CONQUEST OF THE WEST**  *Withdrawal of the British, defeat of Native Americans, and negotiations with Spain secured the nation's frontiers.* ❖

reasons having to do with the state of European diplomacy, Spanish officials in 1795 encouraged the U.S. representative in Madrid to discuss the navigation of the Mississippi River. Before this initiative, the Spanish government not only had closed the river to American commerce but also had incited the Indians of the region to harass settlers from the United States (see Chapter 6). Relations between the two countries probably would have deteriorated further had the United States not signed Jay's Treaty. The Spanish assumed—quite erroneously—that Great Britain and the United States had formed an alliance to strip Spain of its North American possessions.

To avoid this imagined disaster, officials in Madrid offered the American envoy, Thomas Pinckney, extraordinary concessions: the opening of the Mississippi, the right to deposit goods in New Orleans without paying duties, a secure southern boundary on the 31st parallel (a line roughly parallel to the northern boundary of Florida and running west to the Mississippi), and a promise to stay out of Indian affairs. An amazed Pinckney signed the Treaty of San Lorenzo (also called

Pinckney's Treaty) on October 27, 1795, and in March the Senate ratified the document without a single dissenting vote. Pinckney, who came from a prominent South Carolina family, instantly became the hero of the Federalist party.

## POPULAR POLITICAL CULTURE

More than any other event during Washington's administration, ratification of Jay's Treaty generated intense political strife. Even as members of Congress voted as Republicans or Federalists, they condemned the rising partisan spirit as a grave threat to the stability of the United States. Popular writers equated "party" with "faction" and "faction" with "conspiracy to overthrow legitimate authority." Party conflict also suggested that Americans had lost the sense of common purpose that had united them during the Revolution. Contemporaries did not appreciate the beneficial role that parties could play by presenting alternative solutions to foreign and domestic problems. Organized opposition smacked of disloyalty and therefore had to be eliminated by any means—fair or foul. These intellectual currents coupled with the existence of two parties created an atmosphere that bred suspicion. In the name of national unity, Federalists as well as Republicans advocated the destruction of political adversaries.

## Informing the Public: News and Politics

More than any other single element, newspapers transformed the political culture of the United States. Americans were voracious readers. In 1789, a foreign visitor observed, "The common people [here] are on a footing, in point of literature, with the middle ranks of Europe. They all read and write, and understand arithmetic; almost every little town now furnishes a circulating library."

A rapidly expanding number of newspapers appealed to this large literate audience. John Fenno established the *Gazette of the United States* (1789), a journal that supported Hamilton's political philosophy. The Republicans responded in October 1790 with Philip Freneau's influential *National Gazette*. While the format of the publications was similar to that of the colonial papers, their tone was quite different. These fiercely partisan journals presented rumor and opinion as fact. Public officials were regularly dragged through the rhetorical mud. Jefferson, for example, was accused of cowardice; Hamilton, vilified as an adulterer. As party competition became more bitter, editors showed less restraint. One Republican paper even suggested that George Washington had been a British agent during the Revolution. No wonder Fisher

*The front page of Benjamin Franklin Bache's fiercely partisan* Aurora General Advertiser, *February 22, 1798, includes several advertisements. However shrill their coverage of political news, newspapers required the solid financial support of advertisers to survive.* ❖

Ames announced in 1801, "The newspapers are an overmatch for any government."

Even poets and essayists were caught up in the political fray. The better writers—and this was not a period of outstanding artistic achievement in the United States—often produced party propaganda. However much Freneau aspired to fame as a poet, he is remembered today chiefly as a champion of the Republican cause. Noah Webster, who later published *An American Dictionary of the English Language* (1828), spent the 1790s editing a strident Federalist journal, *American Minerva*, in New York City. And Joel Barlow, a Connecticut poet of modest talent, celebrated the French Revolution in verse, thus identifying himself with the party of Jefferson. American writers sometimes complained that the culture of the young republic was too materialistic, too unappreciative of the subtler forms of art then popular in Europe. But it was clear that poets who ignored patriotism and politics simply did not sell well in the United States.

This decade also witnessed the birth of political clubs. These "Democratic" or "Republican" associations, as they were called, first appeared in 1793 and were modeled on the political debating societies that sprang up in France during the early years of the French Revolution. Perhaps because of the French connection, Federalists assumed that the American clubs represented the interests of the Republican party. Their purpose was clearly political indoctrination. The Philadelphia Society announced it would "cultivate a just knowledge of rational liberty." A Democratic club in New York City asked each member to declare himself a "firm and steadfast friend of the EQUAL RIGHTS OF MAN."

By 1794, at least twenty-four clubs were holding regular meetings. How many Americans actually attended their debates is not known, but regardless of the number, the clubs obviously complemented the newspapers in providing the common people with highly partisan political information.

## Whiskey Rebellion: Charges of Republican Conspiracy

Political tensions became explosive in 1794. The Federalists convinced themselves that the Republicans were actually prepared to employ violence against the U.S. government. Although the charge was without foundation, it took on plausibility in the context of growing party strife.

The crisis developed when a group of farmers living in western Pennsylvania protested a federal excise tax on distilled whiskey that Congress had originally passed in 1791. These men did not relish paying any taxes, but this tax struck them as particularly unfair.

*Tarring and feathering federal officials was one way in which western Pennsylvanians protested the tax on whiskey in 1794. Washington's call for troops to put down the insurrection drew more volunteers than he had been able to raise during most of the Revolution.* ❖

They made a good deal of money distilling their grain into whiskey, and the excise threatened to put them out of business.

Largely because the Republican governor of Pennsylvania refused to suppress the angry farmers, Washington and other leading Federalists assumed that the insurrection represented a direct political challenge. The president called out fifteen thousand militiamen, and, accompanied by Hamilton, he marched against the rebels. The expedition was an embarrassing fiasco. The distillers disappeared, and predictably enough, no one living in the Pittsburgh region seemed to know where the troublemakers had gone. Two supposed rebels were convicted of high crimes against the United States; one was reportedly a "simpleton" and the other insane. Washington eventually pardoned both men. As peace returned to the frontier, Republicans gained much electoral support from voters the Federalists had alienated.

In the national political forum, however, the **Whiskey Rebellion** had just begun. Spokesmen for both parties offered sinister explanations for the seemingly innocuous affair. Washington blamed the Republican clubs for promoting civil unrest. He apparently believed that the opposition party had dispatched French agents to western Pennsylvania to undermine the authority of the federal government. In November 1794, Washington informed Congress that these "self-created societies"—in other words, the Republican political clubs—had inspired "a spirit inimical to all order." Indeed, the Whiskey Rebellion had

been "fomented by combinations of men who . . . have disseminated, from an ignorance or perversion of facts, suspicions, jealousies, and accusations of the whole Government."

The president's interpretation of this rural tax revolt was no less charitable than the conspiratorial explanation offered by the Republicans. Jefferson labeled the entire episode a Hamiltonian device to create an army for the purpose of intimidating Republicans. How else could one explain the administration's gross overreaction to a few disgruntled farmers? "An insurrection was announced and proclaimed and armed against," Jefferson noted, "but could never be found." The response of both parties reveals a pervasive fear of some secret evil design to destroy the republic. The clubs and newspapers—as yet unfamiliar tools for mobilizing public opinion—fanned these anxieties, convincing many government officials that the First Amendment should not be interpreted as protecting political dissent.

## Washington's Farewell

In September 1796, Washington published his famed **Farewell Address,** formally declaring his intention to retire from the presidency. In the address, which was printed in newspapers throughout the country, Washington warned against all political factions. Written in large part by Hamilton, who drew on a draft prepared several years earlier by Madison, the address served narrowly partisan ends. The product of growing political strife, it sought to advance the Federalist cause in the forthcoming election. By waiting until September to announce his retirement, Washington denied the Republicans valuable time to organize an effective campaign. There was an element of irony in this initiative. Washington had always maintained he stood above party. While he may have done so in the early years of his presidency, events such as the signing of Jay's Treaty and the suppression of the Whiskey Rebellion transformed him in the eyes of many Americans into a spokesman solely for Hamilton's Federalist party.

Washington also spoke to foreign policy matters in the address. He counseled the United States to avoid making any permanent alliances with distant nations that had no real interest in promoting American security. This statement guided foreign relations for many years and became the credo of later American isolationists, who argued that the United States should steer clear of foreign entanglements.

## THE ADAMS PRESIDENCY

The election of 1796 took place in an atmosphere of mutual distrust. Jefferson, soon to be the vice president, informed a friend that "an Anglican and aristocratic party has sprung up, whose avowed object is to draw over us the substance, as they have already done the forms, of British government." On their part, the Federalists were convinced their Republican opponents wanted to hand the government over to French radicals. By modern standards, the structures of both political parties were primitive. Leaders of national stature, such as Madison and Hamilton, wrote letters encouraging local gentlemen around the country to support a certain candidate, but no one attempted to canvass the voters in advance of the election.

During the campaign, the Federalists sowed the seeds of their eventual destruction. Party stalwarts agreed that John Adams should stand against the Republican candidate, Thomas Jefferson. Hamilton,

John Adams in the suit and sword he wore for his 1797 inauguration. The portrait is by English artist William Winstanley, 1798. Throughout his presidency, Adams was plagued by political extremists, Federalist as well as Republican. ❖

### THE ELECTION OF 1796

| Candidate | Party | Electoral Vote |
|---|---|---|
| J. Adams | Federalist | 71 |
| Jefferson | Republican | 68 |
| T. Pinckney | Federalist | 59 |
| Burr | Republican | 30 |

however, could not leave well enough alone. From his law office in New York City, he schemed to deprive Adams of the presidency. His motives were obscure. He apparently feared that an independent-minded Adams would be difficult to manipulate. He was correct.

Hamilton exploited an awkward feature of the electoral college. In accordance with the Constitution, each elector cast two ballots, and the person who gained the most votes became president. The runner-up, regardless of party affiliation, served as vice president. Ordinarily the Federalist electors would have cast one vote for Adams and one for Thomas Pinckney, the hero of the negotiations with Spain and the party's choice for vice president. Everyone hoped, of course, there would be no tie. Hamilton secretly urged southern Federalists to support only Pinckney, even if that meant throwing away an elector's second vote. If everything had gone according to plan, Pinckney would have received more votes than Adams, but when New Englanders loyal to Adams heard of Hamilton's maneuvering, they dropped Pinckney. When the votes were counted, Adams had 71, Jefferson 68, and Pinckney 59. Hamilton's treachery not only angered the new president but also heightened tensions within the Federalist party.

Adams assumed the presidency under intolerable conditions. He found himself saddled with the members of Washington's old cabinet, a group of second-raters who regularly consulted with Hamilton behind Adams's back. The two most offensive were Timothy Pickering, secretary of state, and James McHenry, secretary of war. But to have dismissed them summarily would have called Washington's judgment into question, and Adams was not prepared to take that risk publicly.

Adams also had to work with a Republican vice president. Adams hoped that he and Jefferson could cooperate as they had during the Revolution—they had served together on the committee that drafted the Declaration of Independence—but partisan pressures soon overwhelmed the president's good intentions. Jefferson recorded their final attempt at reconciliation. Strolling home one night after dinner, Jefferson and Adams reached a place "where our road separated, his being down Market Street, mine along Fifth, and we took leave; and he [Adams] never after that . . . consulted me as to any measure of the government."

## The XYZ Affair and Domestic Politics

Foreign affairs immediately occupied Adams's full attention. The French government regarded Jay's Treaty as an affront. By allowing Great Britain to define the conditions for neutrality, the United States had in effect sided with that nation against the interests of France.

Relations between the two countries had steadily deteriorated. The French refused to receive Charles Cotesworth Pinckney, the U.S. representative in Paris. Pierre Adet, the French minister in Philadelphia, openly tried to influence the 1796 election in favor of the Republicans. His meddling in domestic politics not only embarrassed Jefferson, it also offended the American people. The situation then took a violent turn. In 1797, French privateers began seizing American ships. Since neither the United States nor France officially declared war, the hostilities came to be known as the Quasi-War.

Hamilton and his friends welcomed a popular outpouring of anti-French sentiment. The High Federalists—as members of Hamilton's wing of the party were called—counseled the president to prepare for all-out war, hoping that war would purge the United States of French influence. Adams was not persuaded to escalate the conflict. He dispatched a special commission in a final attempt to remove the sources of antagonism. This famous negotiating team consisted of Charles Pinckney, John Marshall, and Elbridge Gerry. They were instructed to obtain compensation for the ships seized by French privateers as well as release from the treaties of 1778. Federalists still worried that this old agreement might oblige the United States to defend French colonies in the Caribbean against British attack, something they were extremely reluctant to do. In exchange, the commission offered France the same commercial privileges granted to Great Britain in Jay's Treaty. While the diplomats negotiated for peace, Adams talked of strengthening American defenses, rhetoric that pleased the militant members of his own party.

The commission was shocked by the outrageous treatment it received in France. Instead of dealing directly with Talleyrand, the minister of foreign relations, they met with obscure intermediaries who demanded a huge bribe. The commission reported that Talleyrand would not open negotiations unless he was given $250,000. In addition, the French government expected a "loan" of millions of dollars. The Americans refused to play this insulting game. Pinckney angrily sputtered,

This cartoon, **Property Protected, à la Françoise** *(1798), captures the anti-French sentiment many Americans felt after President Adams disclosed the papers of the XYZ Affair. America—depicted as a young maiden—is being plundered by five Frenchmen, who represent the five directors of the French government.* ❖

"No, no, not a sixpence," and with Marshall he returned to the United States. When they arrived home, Marshall offered his much-quoted toast: "Millions for defense, but not one cent for tribute."

Diplomatic humiliation set off a domestic political explosion. When Adams presented the commission's official correspondence before Congress—the names of Talleyrand's lackeys were labeled X, Y, and Z—the Federalists burst out with a war cry. At last, they would be able to even old scores with the Republicans. In April 1798, a Federalist newspaper in New York City announced ominously that any American who refused to censure France "must have a soul black enough to be *fit for treasons, strategems, and spoils.*" Rumors of conspiracy, referred to as the **XYZ Affair,** spread throughout the country. Personal friendships between Republicans and Federalists were shattered. Jefferson described the tense political atmosphere in a letter to an old colleague: "You and I have formerly seen warm debates and high political passions. But gentlemen of different politics would then speak to each other, and separate the business of the Senate from that of society. It is not so now. Men who have been intimate all their lives, cross the streets to avoid meeting, and turn their heads another way, lest they should be obliged to touch their hats."

## Crushing Political Dissent

In the spring of 1798, High Federalists assumed that it was just a matter of time until Adams asked Congress for a formal declaration of war. In the meantime, they pushed for a general rearmament, new fighting ships, additional harbor fortifications, and most important, a greatly expanded U.S. Army. About the need for land forces, Adams remained understandably skeptical. He saw no likelihood of French invasion.

The president missed the political point. The army the Federalists wanted was intended not to thwart French aggression but to stifle internal opposition. Indeed, militant Federalists used the XYZ Affair as the occasion to institute what Jefferson termed the "reign of witches." The threat to the Republicans was not simply a figment of the vice president's overwrought imagination. When Theodore Sedgwick, now a Federalist senator from Massachusetts, first learned of the commission's failure, he observed in words that capture the High Federalists' vindictiveness, "It will afford a glorious opportunity to destroy faction. Improve it."

During the summer of 1798, a provisional army gradually came into existence. George Washington agreed to lead the troops, but he would do so only on condition that Adams appoint Hamilton as second in command. This demand placed the president in a terrible dilemma. Several revolutionary veterans—Henry

Knox, for example—outranked Hamilton. Moreover, the former secretary of the treasury had consistently undermined Adams's authority, and to give Hamilton a position of real power in the government seemed awkward at best. When Washington insisted, however, Adams was forced to support Hamilton.

The chief of the High Federalists threw himself into the task of recruiting and supplying the troops. No detail escaped his attention. He and Secretary of War McHenry made certain that in this political army, only loyal Federalists received commissions. They even denied Adams's son-in-law a post. The entire enterprise took on an air of unreality. Hamilton longed for military glory, and he may have contemplated attacking Spain's Latin American colonies. His driving obsession, however, was the restoration of political order. No doubt, he agreed with a Federalist senator from Connecticut who predicted that the Republicans "never will yield till violence is introduced; we must have a partial civil war . . . and the bayonet must convince some, who are beyond the reach of other arguments."

Hamilton should not have treated Adams with such open contempt. After all, the Massachusetts statesman was still the president, and without presidential cooperation, Hamilton could not fulfill his grand military ambitions. Yet whenever pressing questions concerning the army arose, Adams was nowhere to be found. He let commissions lie on his desk unsigned; he took overlong vacations to New England. He made it quite clear his first love was the navy. In May 1798, the president persuaded Congress to establish the Navy Department. For this new cabinet position, he selected Benjamin Stoddert, a person who did not take orders from Hamilton. Moreover, Adams further infuriated the High Federalists by refusing to ask Congress for a formal declaration of war. When they pressed him, Adams threatened to resign, making Jefferson president. As the weeks passed, the American people increasingly regarded the idle army as an expensive extravagance.

## Silencing Political Opposition: The Alien and Sedition Acts

The Federalists did not rely solely on the army to crush political dissent. During the summer of 1798, the party's majority in Congress passed a group of bills known collectively as the **Alien and Sedition Acts.** This legislation authorized the use of federal courts and the powers of the presidency to silence the Republicans. The acts were born of fear and vindictiveness, and in their efforts to punish the followers of Jefferson, the Federalists created the nation's first major crisis over civil liberties.

Congress drew up three separate Alien Acts. The first, the Alien Enemies Law, vested the president with extraordinary wartime powers. On his own authority, he could detain or deport citizens of nations with which the United States was at war and who behaved in a manner he thought suspicious. Since Adams refused to ask for a declaration of war, this legislation never went into effect. A second act, the Alien Law, empowered the president to expel any foreigner from the United States simply by executive decree. Congress limited the acts to two years, and while Adams did not attempt to enforce them, the mere threat of arrest caused some Frenchmen to flee the country. The third act, the Naturalization Law, was the most flagrantly political of the group. The act established a fourteen-year probationary period before foreigners could apply for full U.S. citizenship. Federalists recognized that recent immigrants, especially the Irish, tended to vote Republican. The Naturalization Law, therefore, was designed to keep "hordes of wild Irishmen" away from the polls for as long as possible.

The Sedition Law struck at the heart of free political exchange. It defined criticism of the U.S. government as criminal libel; citizens found guilty by a jury were subject to fines and imprisonment. Congress entrusted enforcement of the act to the federal courts. Republicans were justly worried that the Sedition Law undermined rights guaranteed by the First Amendment. When they protested, however, the High Federalists dismissed their complaints. The Constitution, they declared, did not condone "the most groundless and malignant lies, striking at the safety and existence of the nation." They were determined to shut down the opposition press and were willing to give the government what seemed almost dic-tatorial powers to achieve that end. The Jeffersonians also expressed concern over the federal judiciary's expanded role in punishing sedition. They believed such matters were best left to state officials.

Americans living in widely scattered regions of the country soon witnessed political repression firsthand. District courts staffed by Federalist appointees indicted seventeen people for criticizing the government. Several cases were absurd. In Newark, New Jersey, for example, a drunkard staggered out of a tavern to watch a sixteen-gun salute fired in honor of President Adams. When the man expressed the hope a cannonball might lodge in Adams's ample posterior, he was arrested. No wonder a New York City journal declared that "joking may be very dangerous even to a free country."

The most celebrated trial occurred in Vermont. A Republican congressman, Matthew Lyon, who was running for reelection, publicly accused the Adams administration of mishandling the Quasi-War. This was not the first time this Irish immigrant had angered the Federalists. On the floor of the House of Representatives, Lyon once spit in the eye of a Federalist congressman from Connecticut. Lyon was immediately labeled the "Spitting Lyon," and one Bostonian declared, "I feel grieved that the saliva of an Irishman should be felt upon the face of an American & he, a New Englandman." A Federalist court was pleased to have the opportunity to convict him of libel. But Lyon enjoyed the last laugh. While he sat in jail, his constituents reelected him to Congress.

As this and other cases demonstrated, the federal courts had become political tools. While the fumbling efforts at enforcement of the Sedition Law did not

*In the early years of the republic, political dissent sometimes escalated to physical violence. This fistfight took place on the floor of Congress, February 15, 1798. The combatants are Republican Matthew Lyon and Federalist Roger Griswold.* ❖

silence opposition—indeed, they sparked even greater criticism and created martyrs—the actions of the administration persuaded Republicans that the survival of free government was at stake. Time was running out. "There is no event," Jefferson warned, " . . . however atrocious, which may not be expected."

## Kentucky and Virginia Resolutions

By the fall of 1798, Jefferson and Madison were convinced that the Federalists envisioned the creation of a police state. According to Madison, the Sedition Law "ought to produce universal alarm." It threatened the free communication of ideas that he "deemed the only effectual guardian of every other right." Some extreme Republicans such as John Taylor of Virginia recommended secession from the Union; others advocated armed resistance. But Jefferson wisely counseled against such extreme strategies. "This is not the kind of opposition the American people will permit," he reminded his desperate supporters. The last best hope for American freedom lay in the state legislatures.

As the crisis deepened, Jefferson and Madison drafted separate protests known as the **Kentucky and Virginia Resolutions.** Both statements vigorously defended the right of individual state assemblies to interpret the constitutionality of federal law. Jefferson wrote the Kentucky Resolutions in November 1798, and in an outburst of partisan anger, he flirted with a doctrine of nullification as dangerous to the survival of the United States as anything advanced by Hamilton and his High Federalist friends.

In the Kentucky Resolutions, Jefferson described the federal union as a compact. The states transferred certain explicit powers to the national government, but, in his opinion, they retained full authority over all matters not specifically mentioned in the Constitution. Jefferson rejected Hamilton's broad interpretation of the "general welfare" clause. "Every state," Jefferson argued, "has a natural right in cases not within the compact . . . to nullify of their own authority all assumptions of power by others within their limits." Carried to an extreme, this logic could have led to the breakup of the federal government, and in 1798, Kentucky legislators were not prepared to take such a radical stance. While they diluted Jefferson's prose, they fully accepted his belief that the Alien and Sedition Acts were unconstitutional and ought to be repealed.

When Madison drafted the Virginia Resolutions in December, he took a stand more temperate than Jefferson's. Madison urged the states to defend the rights of the American people, but he resisted the notion that a single state legislature could or should have the authority to overthrow federal law.

The Virginia and Kentucky Resolutions must be viewed in proper historical context. They were not intended as statements of abstract principles and most certainly not as a justification for southern secession. They were pure political party propaganda. Jefferson and Madison dramatically reminded American voters during a period of severe domestic tension that the Republicans offered a clear alternative to Federalist rule. No other state legislatures passed the Resolutions, and even in Virginia, where the Republicans enjoyed broad support, several important figures such as John Marshall and George Washington censured the states' rights argument.

## Adams's Finest Hour

In February 1799, President Adams belatedly declared his independence from the Hamiltonian wing of the Federalist party. Throughout the confrontation with France, Adams had shown little enthusiasm for war. Following the XYZ debacle, he began to receive informal reports that Talleyrand had changed his tune. The French foreign minister told Elbridge Gerry and other Americans that the bribery episode had been an unfortunate misunderstanding and that if the United States sent new representatives, he was prepared to negotiate in good faith. The High Federalists ridiculed this report. But Adams, still brooding over Hamilton's appointment to the army, decided to throw his own waning prestige behind peace. In February, he suddenly asked the Senate to confirm William Vans Murray as U.S. representative to France.

The move caught the High Federalists totally by surprise. They sputtered with outrage. "It is solely the President's act," Pickering cried, "and we were all thunderstruck when we heard of it." Adams was just warming to the task. In May, he fired Pickering and McHenry, an action he should have taken months earlier. With peace in the offing, American taxpayers complained more and more about the cost of maintaining an unnecessary army. The president was only too happy to dismantle Hamilton's dream.

When the new negotiators—Oliver Ellsworth and William Davie joined Murray—finally arrived in France in November 1799, they discovered that yet another group had come to power there. This government, headed by Napoleon Bonaparte, cooperated in drawing up an agreement known as the Convention of Mortefontaine. The French refused to compensate the Americans for vessels taken during the Quasi-War, but they did declare the treaties of 1778 null and void. Moreover, the convention removed annoying French restrictions on U.S. commerce. Not only had Adams avoided war, but he had also created an atmosphere of mutual trust that paved the way for the purchase of the Louisiana Territory. The president declared with considerable justification that the second French mission was "the most disinterested, the most determined and the most successful [act] of my whole life." It also cost him reelection.

## THE PEACEFUL REVOLUTION: THE ELECTION OF 1800

On the eve of the election of 1800, the Federalists were fatally divided. Adams enjoyed wide popularity among the Federalist rank and file, especially in New England, but articulate party leaders such as Hamilton vowed to punish the president for his betrayal of their militant policies. Hamilton even composed a scathing pamphlet titled *Letter Concerning the Public Conduct and Character of John Adams,* an essay that questioned Adams's ability to hold high office.

Once again the former secretary of the treasury attempted to rig the voting in the electoral college so that the party's vice presidential candidate, Charles Cotesworth Pinckney, would receive more ballots than Adams and America would be saved from "the fangs of Jefferson." As in 1796, the conspiracy backfired. The Republicans gained 73 votes while the Federalists trailed with 65.

### THE ELECTION OF 1800

| Candidate | Party | Electoral Vote |
|-----------|-------|----------------|
| Jefferson | Republican | 73 |
| Burr | Republican | 73 |
| J. Adams | Federalist | 65 |
| C. Pinckney | Federalist | 64 |

To everyone's surprise, however, the election was not resolved in the electoral college. When the ballots were counted, Jefferson and his running mate, Aaron Burr, had tied. This accident—a Republican elector should have thrown away his second vote—sent the selection of the next president to the House of Representatives, a lame-duck body still controlled by members of the Federalist party.

As the House began its work on February 27, 1801, excitement ran high. Each state delegation cast a single vote, with nine votes needed for election. On the first ballot, Jefferson received the support of eight states, Burr six, and two states divided evenly. People predicted a quick victory for Jefferson, but after dozens of ballots, the House had still not selected a president. "The scene was now ludicrous," observed one witness. "Many had sent home for night-caps and pillows, and wrapped in shawls and great-coats, lay about the floor of the committee-rooms, or sat sleeping in their seats."

*The cast of ballots by presidential electors in December 1800 resulted in a tie between Thomas Jefferson and Aaron Burr, who each received 73 votes. The election was finally decided in February 1801 when the House of Representatives, on the thirty-sixth ballot, chose Jefferson by a vote of 10 to 4. This flag commemorates Jefferson's victory in the election.* ❖

The drama dragged on for days. To add to the confusion, Burr unaccountably refused to withdraw. Contemporaries thought his ambition had overcome his good sense.

The logjam finally broke when leading Federalists decided that Jefferson, whatever his faults, would make a more responsible president than would the shifty Burr. Even Hamilton labeled Burr "the most dangerous man of the community." On the thirty-sixth ballot, Representative James A. Bayard of Delaware announced he no longer supported Burr. This decision, coupled with Burr's inaction, gave Jefferson the presidency, ten states to four.

The Twelfth Amendment, ratified in 1804, saved the American people from repeating this potentially dangerous turn of events. Henceforth, the electoral college cast separate ballots for president and vice president.

During the final days of his presidency, Adams appointed as many Federalists as possible to the federal bench. Jefferson protested the hasty manner in which these "midnight judges" were selected. One of them, John Marshall, became chief justice of the United States, a post he held with distinction for thirty-four years. But behind the last-minute flurry of activity lay bitterness and disappointment. Adams never forgave Hamilton. "No party," the Federalist president wrote, "that ever existed knew itself so little or so vainly overrated its own influence and popularity as ours. None ever understood so ill the causes of its own power, or so wantonly destroyed them." On the morning of Jefferson's inauguration, Adams slipped away from the capital—now located in Washington, D.C.—unnoticed and unappreciated.

In the address that Adams missed, Jefferson attempted to quiet partisan fears. "We are all republicans; we are all federalists," the new president declared. By this statement, he did not mean to suggest that party differences were no longer important. Jefferson reminded his audience that whatever the politicians might say, the people shared a deep commitment to a federal union based on republican ideals set forth during the American Revolution. Indeed, the president interpreted the election of 1800 as a revolutionary episode, as the fulfillment of the principles of 1776.

Recent battles, of course, colored Jefferson's judgment. The contests of the 1790s had been hard fought, the outcome often in doubt. Jefferson looked back at this period as a confrontation between the "advocates of republican and those of kingly government," and he believed that only the vigilance of his own party had saved the country from Federalist "liberticide."

The Federalists were thoroughly dispirited by the entire experience. In the end, it had not been

## CHRONOLOGY

| | |
|---|---|
| 1787 | Constitution of the United States signed (September) |
| 1789 | George Washington inaugurated (April) ❖ Louis XVI of France calls meeting of the Estates General (May) |
| 1790 | Congress approves Hamilton's plan for funding and assumption (July) |
| 1791 | Bank of the United States is chartered (February) ❖ Hamilton's *Report on Manufactures* rejected by Congress (December) |
| 1793 | France's revolutionary government announces a "war of all people against all kings" (February) ❖ Genêt affair strains relations with France (April) ❖ Washington issues Proclamation of Neutrality (April) ❖ Spread of "Democratic" clubs alarms Federalists ❖ Jefferson resigns as secretary of state (December) |
| 1794 | Whiskey Rebellion put down by U.S. Army (July–November) ❖ General Anthony Wayne defeats Indians at battle of Fallen Timbers (August) |
| 1795 | Hamilton resigns as secretary of the treasury (January) ❖ Jay's Treaty divides the nation (June) ❖ Pinckney's Treaty with Spain is a welcome surprise (October) |
| 1796 | Washington publishes Farewell Address (September) ❖ John Adams elected president (December) |
| 1797 | XYZ Affair poisons U.S. relations with France (October) |
| 1798–1800 | Quasi-War with France |
| 1798 | Congress passes the Alien and Sedition Acts (June and July) ❖ Provisional army is formed ❖ Virginia and Kentucky Resolutions protest the Alien and Sedition Acts (November and December) |
| 1799 | George Washington dies (December) |
| 1800 | Convention of Mortefontaine is signed with France, ending Quasi-War (September) |
| 1801 | House of Representatives elects Thomas Jefferson president (February) |

Hamilton's foolish electoral schemes that destroyed the party's chances in 1800. Rather, the Federalists had lost touch with a majority of the American people. In office, Adams and Hamilton—whatever their own differences may have been—betrayed their doubts about popular sovereignty too often, and when it came time to marshal broad support, to mobilize public opinion in favor of the party of wealth and privilege, few responded. As Secretary of War Oliver Wolcott observed on hearing of Jefferson's victory, "Have our party shown that they possess the necessary skill and courage to deserve . . . to govern? What have they done? . . . They write private letters. To whom? To each other, but they do nothing to give a proper direction to the public mind."

## CONCLUSION: DANGER OF POLITICAL EXTREMISM

From a broader historical perspective, the election of 1800 seems noteworthy for what did not occur. There were no riots in the streets, no attempted coup by military officers, no secession from the Union, nothing ex-cept the peaceful transfer of government from the leaders of one political party to those of the opposition.

Americans had weathered the Alien and Sedition Acts, the meddling by predatory foreign powers in domestic affairs, the shrilly partisan rhetoric of hack journalists, and now, at the start of a new century, they were impressed with their own achievement. As one woman who attended Jefferson's inauguration noted, "The changes of administration which in every government and in every age have most generally been epochs of confusion, villainy and bloodshed, in this our happy country take place without any species of distraction, or disorder." But as she well understood—indeed, as modern Americans must constantly relearn—extremism in the name of partisan political truth can easily unravel the delicate fabric of representative democracy and leave the republic at the mercy of those who would manipulate the public for private benefit.

## RECOMMENDED READING

The sudden development of deeply partisan politics on the national level dominated public life during the 1790s. Several recent accounts capture the sense of anger and disappointment that informed the political culture: Joanne B. Freeman, *Affairs of Honor: National Politics in the New Republic* (2001) and Joseph J. Ellis, *Founding Brothers: The Revolutionary Generation* (2000). Joyce Appleby provides useful insights into the ideological tensions that divided former allies in *Liberalism and Republicanism in the Historical Imagination* (1992). Jack N. Rakove offers a fine short introduction to James Madison's political thought in *James Madison and the Creation of the American Republic* (1990). An excellent discussion of the conflicting economic visions put forward by Hamilton and Jefferson can be found in Drew McCoy, *The Elusive Republic: The Political Economy in Jeffersonian America* (1980). Anyone curious about the controversial rise of political parties should consult Richard Hofstadter, *The Idea of a Party System: The Rise of Legitimate Opposition in the United States, 1780–1840* (1997) and Stanley Elkins and Eric McKitrick, *The Age of Federalism: The Early Republic* (1993). One can obtain many useful and readable biographies of the dominant leaders of the period. Two more analytic studies are Peter Onuf, ed., *Jeffersonian Legacies* (1993) and Paul K. Longmore, *The Invention of George Washington* (1999). How Americans constructed a convincing sense of national identity is examined in David Waldstreicher, *In the Midst of Perpetual Fetes: The Making of American Nationalism, 1776–1820* (1997). Two regional studies suggest how republican values worked themselves out among ordinary people: Alan Taylor, *Liberty Men and Great Proprietors: The Revolutionary Settlement of the Maine Frontier, 1760–1820* (1990) and Andrew Cayton, *Frontier Republic: Ideology and Politics in Ohio Country, 1780–1825* (1986). Conor Cruise O'Brien helps explain why foreign affairs, especially with the leaders of the French Revolution, disrupted domestic politics: *The Long Affair: Thomas Jefferson and the French Revolution, 1785–1800* (1996). A scientific debate driven by nationalism is the subject of Gordon S. Wood, "The Bigger the Beast the Better," *American History Illustrated*, Vol. 17 (1982), 30–37.

**For a list of additional titles related to this chapter's topics, please see** http://www.ablongman.com/divine.

## SUGGESTED WEB SITES

**Temple of Liberty—Building the Capitol for a New Nation**

http://www.lcweb.loc.gov/exhibits/us.capitol/s0.html
Compiled from holdings in the Library of Congress, this site contains detailed information on the design and early construction of the Capitol building in Washington, D.C.

**U.S. Electoral College**

http://www.nara.gov/fedreg/elctcoll/index.html
This National Archives and Records Administration site explains how the electoral college works.

### George Washington Papers

http://www.virginia.edu/gwpapers/
Information on the publishing project, with selected documents, essays, and an index of the published volumes.

### George Washington's Mount Vernon

http://www.mountvernon.org/
Pictures and documents of Mount Vernon, the home of the first president, George Washington.

### George Washington Papers at the Library of Congress, 1741–1799

http://memory.loc.gov/ammem/gwhtml/gwhome.html
This site is "the complete George Washington Papers from the Manuscript Division at the Library of Congress and consists of approximately 65,000 documents. This is the largest collection of original Washington documents in the world."

### Archiving Early America

http://earlyamerica.com/
Old newspapers are excellent windows into the issues of the past. This site includes the Keigwin and Matthews collection of historic newspapers.

### John Adams

http://www.ipl.org/div/potus/jadams.html
This Internet Public Library page contains biographical information about the second president, his inaugural address, and links to more information.

William Birch's illustration of the partially-constructed United States capitol building in Washington, D.C, in 1800. When Jefferson first took office, the nation's new capital was little more than a swampy and isolated village. ❖

# Republican Ascendancy: The Jeffersonian Vision

## *Limits of Equality*

British visitors often expressed contempt for Jeffersonian society. Wherever they traveled in the young republic, they met ill-mannered people inspired with a ruling passion for liberty and equality. Charles William Janson, an Englishman who lived in the United States for thirteen years, recounted an exchange he found particularly unsettling that had occurred at the home of an American acquaintance. "On knocking at the door," he reported, "it was opened by a servant maid, whom I had never before seen." The woman's behavior astonished Janson. "The following is the dialogue, word for word, which took place on this occasion:—'Is your master at home?'—'I have no master.'—'Don't you live here?'—'I stay here.'—'And who are you then?'—'Why, I am Mr. ——'s *help*. I'd have you know, *man*, that I am no *sarvant* [sic]; none but *negers* [sic] are *sarvants*.'"

Standing on his friend's doorstep, Janson encountered the authentic voice of Jeffersonian republicanism—self-confident, assertive, blatantly racist, and having no intention of being relegated to low social status. The maid who answered the door believed she was her employer's equal, perhaps not in wealth but surely in character. She may have even dreamed of someday owning a house staffed with "*help*." American society fostered such ambition. In the early nineteenth century, thousands of settlers poured across the Appalachian Mountains or moved to cities in search of opportunity. Thomas Jefferson and individuals who stood for public office under the banner of the Republican party claimed to speak for these people.

The limits of the Jeffersonian vision were obvious even to contemporaries. The people who spoke most eloquently about equal opportunity often owned slaves. As early as the 1770s, the famed English essayist Samuel Johnson had chided Americans for their hypocrisy. "How is it," he asked the indignant rebels, "that we hear the loudest yelps for liberty from the drivers of Negroes?" Little had changed since the Revolution. African Americans, who represented one-fifth of the population of the United States, were totally excluded from the new opportunities opening up in the cities and the West. Indeed, the maid in the incident just described insisted—with no apparent sense of inconsistency—that her position was superior to that of blacks, who were brought involuntarily to lifelong servitude.

IT IS NOT SURPRISING THAT in this highly charged racial climate leaders of the Federalist party accused the Republicans, especially those who lived in the South, of disingenuousness, and in 1804, one Massachusetts Federalist sarcastically defined "Jeffersonian" as "an Indian word, signifying '*a great tobacco planter, who had herds of black slaves.*'" The race issue was always just beneath the surface of political maneuvering. Indeed, the acquisition of the Louisiana Territory and the War of 1812 fanned fundamental disagreement about the spread of slavery to the western territories.

In other areas, the Jeffersonians did not fulfill even their own high expectations. As members of an opposition party during the presidency of John Adams, they insisted on a strict interpretation of the Constitution, peaceful foreign relations, and a reduction of the role of the federal government in the lives of the average citizens. But following the election of 1800, Jefferson and his supporters discovered that unanticipated pressures, foreign and domestic, forced them to moderate these goals. Before he retired from public office, Jefferson interpreted the Constitution in a way that permitted the government to purchase the Louisiana Territory when the opportunity arose; he regulated the national economy with a rigor that would have surprised Alexander Hamilton; and he led the country to the brink of war. Some Americans praised the president's pragmatism; others felt betrayed. For a man who played a leading role in the revolt against George III, it must have been shocking in 1807 to find himself labeled a "despot" in a popular New England newspaper. "Give ear no longer to the siren voice of democracy and Jeffersonian liberty," the editor shrieked. "It is a cursed delusion, adopted by traitors, and recommended by sycophants."

## REGIONAL IDENTITIES IN A NEW REPUBLIC

During the early decades of the nineteenth century, the population of the United States experienced substantial growth. The 1810 census counted 7,240,000 Americans, a jump of almost 2 million in just ten years. Of this total, approximately 20 percent were black slaves, the majority of whom lived in the South. The large population increase in the nation was the result primarily of natural reproduction, since during Jefferson's presidency few immigrants moved to the New World. The largest single group in this society was children under the age of sixteen, boys and girls who were born after Washington's election and who defined their own futures at a time when the nation's boundaries were rapidly expanding. For white Americans, it was a time of heightened optimism, and many people possessing entrepreneurial skills or engineering capabilities aggressively made their way in a society that seemed to rate personal merit higher than family background.

Even as Americans defended the rights of individual states, they were forming strong regional identifi-

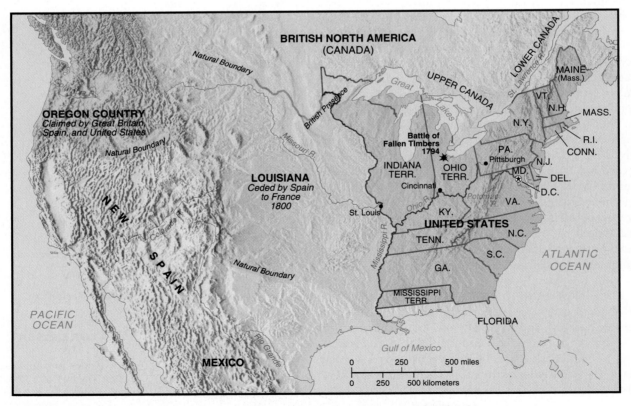

**NORTH AMERICA IN 1800** *In the 1790s, diplomatic agreements with Britain and Spain and defeat of the Native Americans at the battle of Fallen Timbers opened the way to U.S. settlement of the land beyond the Appalachian Mountains.* ❖

cations. In commerce and politics, they perceived themselves as representatives of distinct subcultures— as Southerners, New Englanders, or Westerners. No doubt, the broadening geographic horizons reflected improved transportation links that enabled people to travel more easily within the various sections. But the growing regional mentality was also the product of defensiveness. While local writers celebrated New England's cultural distinctiveness, for example, they were clearly uneasy about the region's rejection of the democratic values that were sweeping the rest of the nation. Moreover, during this period people living south of the Potomac River began describing themselves as Southerners, not as citizens of the Chesapeake or the Carolinas as they had done in colonial times.

This shifting focus of attention resulted not only from an awareness of shared economic interests but also from a sensitivity to outside attacks on slavery. Several times during the first fifteen years of the nineteenth century, conspirators actually advocated secession, and though the schemes failed, they revealed the powerful sectional loyalties that threatened national unity.

## Westward the Course of Empire

The most striking changes occurred in the West. Before the end of the American Revolution, only Indian traders and a few hardy settlers had ventured across the Appalachians. After 1790, however, a flood of people rushed west to stake out farms on the rich soil. Many settlers followed the so-called northern route across Pennsylvania or New York into the old Northwest Territory. Pittsburgh and Cincinnati, both strategically located on the Ohio River, became important commercial ports. In 1803, Ohio joined the Union, and territorial governments were formed in Indiana (1800), Louisiana (1805), Michigan (1805), Illinois (1809), and Missouri (1812). Southerners poured into the new states of Kentucky (1792) and Tennessee (1796). Wherever they located, Westerners depended on water transportation. Because of the extraordinarily high cost of hauling goods overland, riverboats represented the only economical means of carrying agricultural products to distant markets. The Mississippi River was the crucial commercial link for the entire region, and Westerners did not feel secure so long as New Orleans, the southern gate to the Mississippi, remained under Spanish control.

Families that moved west attempted to transplant familiar eastern customs to the frontier. In some areas such as the Western Reserve, a narrow strip of land along Lake Erie in northern Ohio, the influence of New England remained strong. In general, however, a creative mixing of peoples of different backgrounds in a strange environment generated distinctive folkways. Westerners developed their own heroes, such as Mike

View of the City of Pittsburgh in 1817, *painted by a Mrs. Gibson while on her honeymoon. As the frontier moved west, Pittsburgh became an important trade and manufacturing center.* ❖

Fink, the legendary keelboatman of the Mississippi River; Daniel Boone, the famed trapper and Indian fighter; and the eye-gouging "alligatormen" of Kentucky and Tennessee. Americans who crossed the mountains were ambitious and self-confident, excited by the challenge of almost unlimited geographic mobility. A French traveler observed in 1802 that throughout the region he visited, there was not a single farm "where one cannot with confidence ask the owner from whence he had emigrated, or, according to the light manners of the Americans, 'What part of the world do you come from?'" These rootless people, he explained, "incline perpetually toward the most distant fringes of American settlement."

## Native American Resistance

At the beginning of the nineteenth century, a substantial number of Native Americans lived in the greater Ohio Valley; the land belonged to them. The tragedy was that the Indians, many dependent on trade with the white people and ravaged by disease, lacked unity. Small groups of Native Americans, allegedly representing the interests of an entire tribe, sold off huge pieces of land, often for whiskey and trinkets.

Such fraudulent transactions disgusted the Shawnee leaders Tenskwatawa (known as the Prophet) and his brother Tecumseh. Tecumseh rejected classification as a Shawnee and may have been the first native leader to identify himself self-consciously as "Indian." These men desperately attempted to revitalize native cultures, and against overwhelming odds, they briefly persuaded Native Americans living in the Indiana Territory to avoid contact with whites, to resist alcohol, and, most important, to hold on to their land. White intruders saw Tecumseh as a threat to progress, and during the War of 1812, they shattered the Indians' dream of cultural renaissance. The populous Creek nation, located in the modern states of Alabama and Mississippi, also resisted the settlers' advance, but its warriors were crushed by Andrew Jackson's Tennessee militia at the battle of Horseshoe Bend (March 1814).

Well-meaning Jeffersonians disclaimed any intention to destroy the Indians. The president talked of creating a vast reservation beyond the Mississippi River, just as the British had talked before the Revolution of a sanctuary beyond the Appalachian Mountains. He sent federal agents to "civilize" the Indians, to transform them into yeoman farmers. But even the most enlightened white thinkers of the day did not believe the Indians possessed cultures worth preserving. In fact, in 1835, the Democratic national convention selected a vice presidential candidate whose major qualification for high office seemed to be

*Tenskwatawa, known as the Prophet, provided spiritual leadership for the union of the native peoples he and his brother Tecumseh organized to resist white encroachment on Native American lands.* ❖

that he had killed Tecumseh. And as early as 1780, Jefferson himself—then serving as the governor of Virginia—instructed a military leader on the frontier, "If we are to wage a campaign against these Indians the end proposed should be their extermination, or their removal beyond the lakes of the Illinois river. The same world will scarcely do for them and us."

## Commercial Life in the Cities

Before 1820, the prosperity of the United States depended primarily on its agriculture and trade. Jeffersonian America was by no stretch of the imagination an industrial economy. The overwhelming majority of the population—84 percent in 1810—was directly involved in agriculture. Southerners concentrated on the staple crops of tobacco, rice, and cotton, which they sold on the European market. In the North, people generally produced livestock and cereal crops. Regardless of location, however, the nation's farmers followed a backbreaking work routine that did not differ substantially from that of their parents and grandparents. Except for the cotton gin, important chemical and mechanical inventions did not appear in the fields for another generation. Probably the major innovation of this period was the agricultural fair, an idea first advanced in 1809 by a Massachusetts farmer, Elkanah Watson. In hopes of improving animal breeding, he offered prizes for the best livestock in the country. The experiment was a great success, for as Watson reported, "Many farmers, and even women, were excited by curiosity to attend this first novel, and humble exhibition."

The merchant marine represented an equally important element in America's preindustrial economy. At the turn of the century, ships flying the Stars and Stripes transported a large share of the world's trade. Merchants in Boston, New York, and Philadelphia received handsome profits from such commerce. Their vessels provided essential links between European countries and their Caribbean colonies. France, for example, relied heavily on American transport for its sugar. These lucrative transactions, coupled with the export of domestic staples, especially cotton, generated impressive fortunes. Between 1793 and 1807, the year Jefferson imposed the embargo against Britain and France, American commerce enjoyed a more than 300 percent increase in the value of exports and in net earnings. Unfortunately, the boom did not last. The success of the "carrying trade" depended in large measure on friendly relations between the United States and the major European powers. When England and France began seizing American ships—as they both did after 1805—national prosperity suffered.

The cities of Jeffersonian America functioned chiefly as depots for international trade. Only about 7 percent of the nation's population lived in urban centers, and most of these people owed their livelihoods either directly or indirectly to the carrying trade. Recent studies revealed that several major port cities of the early republic—New York, Philadelphia, and Baltimore, for example—had some of the highest population densities ever recorded in this country's history. In 1800, more than 40,000 New Yorkers crowded into an area of only 1.5 square miles; in Philadelphia, some 46,000 people were packed into less than one square mile. As one historian explained, "The cities contained disproportionate numbers of young white males, free black men and women, and white widows. These people had below-average incomes and also an increasing propensity to live on their own rather than as dependents." As is common today, many city dwellers rented living space, and since the demand for housing exceeded the supply, the rents were high.

Within these densely crowded urban centers, artisans maintained the fleet; skilled workers produced new ships; laborers loaded cargoes. And as some merchant families became wealthy, they demanded luxury items such as fine furniture. This specialized market drew a small, but highly visible, group of master craftspeople, and their extraordinarily beautiful and intricate pieces—New England tall clocks, for example—were perhaps the highest artistic achievement of the period.

Despite these accomplishments, American cities exercised only a marginal influence on the nation's vast hinterland. Because of the high cost of land transportation, urban merchants seldom purchased goods

*Before the Industrial Revolution, national prosperity depended on commercial capitalism. Jonathan Budington's painting of* Cannon House and Wharf *(1792), the busy dock area of lower Manhattan, reflects the robust maritime trade of the new republic.* ❖

*Although cotton was an important trade item in the early nineteenth century, technological advances in textile production were slow to take hold. Some spinning mills, such as the one pictured here, were built in New England, but what historians call the "Industrial Revolution" did not begin for several more decades.* ❖

fuel would eventually transform the character of the American economy.

Ordinary workers often felt threatened by the new machines. Skilled artisans who had spent years mastering a trade and who took pride in producing an object that expressed their own personalities found the industrial workplace alienating. Moreover, they rightly feared that innovative technology designed to achieve greater efficiency might throw traditional craftspeople out of work or, if not that, transform independent entrepreneurs into dependent wage laborers. One New Yorker, for example, writing in the *Gazette and General Advertiser* in 1801, warned tradespeople to be on guard against those who "will screw down the wages to the last thread . . . [and destroy] the independent spirit, so distinguished at present in our mechanics, and so useful in republics."

for export—flour, for example—from a distance of more than 150 miles. The separation between rural and urban Americans was far more pronounced during Jefferson's presidency than it was after the development of canals and railroads a few decades later.

The booming carrying trade may actually have retarded the industrialization of the United States. The lure of large profits drew investment capital—a scarce resource in a developing society—into commerce. By contrast, manufacturing seemed too risky. One contemporary complained, "The brilliant prospects held out by commerce, caused our citizens to neglect the mechanical and manufacturing branches of industry."

This man may have exaggerated slightly to make his point. Samuel Slater, an English-born designer of textile machinery, did establish several cotton-spinning mills in New England, but until the 1820s these plants employed only a small number of workers. In fact, during this period far more cloth was produced in individual households than in factories. Another farsighted inventor, Robert Fulton, sailed the first American steamship up the Hudson River in 1807. In time, this marvelous innovation opened new markets for domestic manufacturers, especially in the West. At the end of the War of 1812, however, few people anticipated how greatly power generated by fossil

## JEFFERSON AS PRESIDENT

The District of Columbia seemed an appropriate capital for a Republican president. At the time of Jefferson's first inauguration, Washington was still an isolated rural village, a far cry from the crowded centers of Philadelphia and New York. Jefferson fit comfortably into Washington society. He despised formal ceremony and sometimes shocked foreign dignitaries by meeting them in his slippers or a threadbare jacket. He spent as much time as his official duties allowed in reading and reflection. Isaac, one of Jefferson's slaves, recounted, "Old master had abundance of books: sometimes would have twenty of 'em down on the floor at once; read fust one then tother."

The president was a poor public speaker. He wisely refused to deliver annual addresses before Congress. In personal conversation, however, Jefferson exuded considerable charm. His dinner parties were major intellectual as well as social events, and in this forum, the president regaled politicians with his knowledge of literature, philosophy, and science.

According to Margaret Bayard Smith, the wife of a congressman, the president "has more ease than grace—all the winning softness of politeness, without the artificial polish of courts."

Notwithstanding his commitment to the life of the mind, Jefferson was a politician to the core. He ran for the presidency in order to achieve specific goals: the reduction of the size and cost of federal government, the repeal of obnoxious Federalist legislation such as the Alien Acts, and the maintenance of international peace. To accomplish his program, Jefferson realized he needed the full cooperation of congressional Republicans, some of whom were fiercely independent men. Over such figures Jefferson exercised political mastery. He established close ties with the leaders of both houses of Congress, and while he seldom announced his plans in public, he made certain his legislative lieutenants knew exactly what he desired. Contemporaries who described Jefferson as a weak president—and some Federalists did just that—did not read the scores of memoranda he sent to political friends or witness the informal meetings he held at the executive mansion with important Republicans. In two terms as president, Jefferson never had to veto a single act of Congress.

Jefferson carefully selected the members of his cabinet. During Washington's administration, he had witnessed—even provoked—severe infighting; as president, he nominated only those who enthusiastically supported his programs. James Madison, the leading figure at the Constitutional Convention, became secretary of state. For the Treasury, Jefferson chose Albert Gallatin, a Swiss-born financier who understood the complexities of the federal budget. "If I had the universe to choose from," the president announced, "I could not change one of my associates to my better satisfaction."

## Jeffersonian Reforms

A top priority of the new government was cutting the national debt. Throughout American history, presidents have advocated such reductions, but such rhetoric has seldom yielded tangible results. Jefferson succeeded. He and Gallatin regarded a large federal deficit as dangerous to the health of republican institutions. In fact, both men associated debt with Alexander Hamilton's Federalist financial programs, measures they considered harmful to republicanism. Jefferson claimed that legislators elected by the current generation did not have the right to mortgage the future of unborn Americans.

Jefferson also wanted to diminish the activities of the federal government. He urged Congress to repeal all direct taxes, including the tax that had sparked the Whiskey Rebellion in 1794. Secretary Gallatin linked federal income to the carrying trade. He calculated that the entire cost of national government could be borne by customs receipts. As long as commerce flourished, revenues provided sufficient sums. When international war closed foreign markets, however, the flow of funds dried up.

To help pay the debt inherited from the Adams administration, Jefferson ordered substantial cuts in the national budget. The president closed several American embassies in Europe. He also slashed military spending. In his first term, Jefferson reduced the size of the U.S. Army by 50 percent. This decision left only three thousand soldiers to guard the entire frontier. In addition, he retired a majority of the navy's warships. When New Englanders claimed the cuts left the country defenseless, Jefferson countered with a glib argument. As ships of the U.S. Navy sailed the world's oceans, he claimed, they were liable to provoke hostilities, perhaps even war; hence, by reducing the size of the fleet, he promoted peace.

More than budgetary considerations prompted Jefferson's military reductions. He was deeply suspicious of standing armies. In the event of foreign attack, he reasoned, the militia would rise in defense of the republic. No doubt, his experiences during the Revolution influenced his thinking on military affairs, for in 1776, an aroused populace had taken up arms against the British. To ensure that the citizen soldiers would receive professional leadership in battle, Jefferson created the Army Corps of Engineers and the military academy at West Point in 1802.

Political patronage was a great burden to the new president. Loyal Republicans throughout the United States had worked hard for Jefferson's victory, and as soon as he took office, they stormed the executive mansion seeking federal employment. While the president controlled several hundred jobs, he refused to dismiss all the Federalists. To be sure, he acted quickly to remove the so-called midnight appointees, highly partisan selections that Adams had made after learning of Jefferson's election. But to transform federal hiring into an undisciplined spoils system, especially at the highest levels of the federal bureaucracy, seemed to Jefferson to be shortsighted. Moderate Federalists might be converted to the Republican party, and, in any case, there was a good chance they possessed the expertise needed to run the government. At the end of his first term, half of the people holding office were appointees of Washington and Adams.

Jefferson's political moderation helped hasten the demise of the Federalist party. This loose organization had nearly destroyed itself during the election of 1800, and following Adams's defeat, prominent Federalist spokesmen such as Fisher Ames and John Jay withdrew from national affairs. They refused to adopt the popular forms of campaigning that the Republicans had developed so successfully during the late 1790s. The mere prospect of flattering the common people was odious enough to drive some Federalists into political retirement.

Many of them also sensed that national expansion worked against their interests. The creation of new states and congressional reapportionment inevitably seemed to increase the number of Republican representatives in Washington. By 1805, the Federalists retained only a few seats in New England and Delaware. "The power of the [Jefferson] Administration," confessed John Quincy Adams in 1802, "rests upon the support of a much stronger majority of the people throughout the Union than the former administrations ever possessed since the first establishment of the Constitution."

After 1804, a group of younger Federalists belatedly attempted to pump life into the dying party. They experimented with popular election techniques. In some states, they tightened party organization, held nominating conventions, and campaigned energetically for office. These were essential reforms, but with the exception of a brief Federalist revival in the Northeast between 1807 and 1814, the results of these activities were disappointing. Even the younger Federalists thought it demeaning to appeal for votes. Diehards such as Timothy Pickering promoted wild secessionist schemes in New England, while the most promising moderates—John Quincy Adams, for example—joined the Republicans.

## The Louisiana Purchase

When Jefferson first took office, he was confident that Louisiana as well as Florida would eventually become part of the United States. After all, Spain owned the territory, and Jefferson assumed he could persuade the rulers of that notoriously weak nation to sell their colonies. If that peaceful strategy failed, the president was prepared to threaten forcible occupation.

In May 1801, however, prospects for the easy or inevitable acquisition of Louisiana suddenly darkened. Jefferson learned that Spain had secretly transferred title to the entire region to France, its powerful northern neighbor. To make matters worse, the French leader Napoleon seemed intent on reestablishing an empire in North America. Even as Jefferson sought additional information concerning the details of the transfer, Napoleon was dispatching a large army to put down a rebellion in France's sugar-rich Caribbean colony, Haiti. From that island stronghold in the West Indies, French troops could occupy New Orleans and close the Mississippi River to American trade.

A sense of crisis enveloped Washington. Some congressmen urged Jefferson to prepare for war against France. Tensions increased when the Spanish officials who still governed New Orleans announced the closing of that port to American commerce (October 1802). Jefferson and his advisers assumed that the Spanish had acted on orders from France, but despite this serious provocation, the president preferred negotiations to war. In January 1803, he asked James Monroe, a loyal Republican from Virginia, to join the American minister, Robert Livingston, in Paris. The president instructed the two men to explore the possibility of purchasing the city of New Orleans. Lest they underestimate the importance of their diplomatic mission, Jefferson reminded them, "There is on the globe one single spot, the possessor of which is our natural and habitual enemy. It is New Orleans." If Livingston and Monroe failed, Jefferson realized he would be forced to turn to Great Britain for military assistance. Dependence on that country seemed repellent, but he recognized that as soon as French troops moved into Louisiana, "we must marry ourselves to the British fleet and nation."

By the time Monroe joined Livingston in France, Napoleon had lost interest in establishing an American empire. The army he sent to Haiti succumbed to tropical diseases. By the end of 1802, more than thirty thousand veteran troops had died. In a fit of disgust, Napoleon announced, "Damn sugar, damn coffee, damn colonies . . . I renounce Louisiana." The diplomats from the United States knew nothing of these developments. They were taken by complete surprise, therefore, when they learned that Talleyrand, the French minister for foreign relations, had offered to sell the entire Louisiana Territory in April 1803. For only $15 million, the Americans doubled the size of the United States with the **Louisiana Purchase.** In fact, Livingston and Monroe were not certain how much land they had actually purchased. When they asked Talleyrand whether the deal included Florida, he responded ambiguously, "You have made a noble bargain for yourselves, and I suppose you will make the most of it." Even at that moment, Livingston realized that the transaction would alter the course of American history. "From this day," he wrote, "the United States take their place among the powers of first rank."

The American people responded enthusiastically to news of the Louisiana Purchase. The only criticism came from a few disgruntled Federalists in New England who thought the United States was already too large. Jefferson, of course, was immensely relieved. The nation had avoided war with France. Nevertheless, he worried that the purchase might be unconstitutional. The president pointed out that the Constitution did

UNDER MY WINGS EVERY THING PROSPERS

*President Jefferson recognized the strategic location of New Orleans and determined to buy it from the French. By 1803, when this view was painted, New Orleans was already a thriving port and an important outlet for exports produced by new communities along the Ohio and Mississippi Valleys. ❖*

not specifically authorize the acquisition of vast new territories and the incorporation of thousands of foreign citizens. To escape this apparent legal dilemma, Jefferson proposed an amendment to the Constitution. Few persons, even his closest advisers, shared the president's scruples. Events in France soon forced Jefferson to adopt a more pragmatic course. When he heard that Napoleon had become impatient for his money, Jefferson rushed the papers to a Senate eager to ratify the agreement, and nothing more was said about amending the Constitution.

Jefferson's fears about the incorporation of this new territory were not unwarranted. The area that eventually became the state of Louisiana (1812) contained many people of French and Spanish background who possessed no familiarity with representative institutions. Their laws had been autocratic, their local government corrupt. To allow such persons to elect a representative assembly struck the president as dangerous. He did not even know whether the population of Louisiana would remain loyal to the United States. Jefferson, therefore, recommended to Congress a transitional government consisting entirely of appointed officials. In March 1804, the Louisiana Government Bill narrowly passed the House of Representatives. Members of the president's own party attacked the plan. After all, it imposed taxes on the citizens of Louisiana without their consent. According to one outspoken Tennessee congressman, the bill "establishes a complete despotism." Most troubling perhaps was the fact that the legisla-

tion ran counter to Jefferson's well-known republican principles.

## The Lewis and Clark Expedition

In the midst of the Louisiana controversy, Jefferson dispatched a secret message to Congress requesting $2500 for the exploration of the Far West (January 1803). How closely this decision was connected to the Paris negotiations is not clear. Whatever the case may have been, the president asked his talented private secretary, Meriwether Lewis, to discover whether the Missouri River "may offer the most direct & practicable water communication across this continent for the purposes of commerce." The president also regarded the expedition as a wonderful opportunity to collect precise data about flora and fauna. He personally instructed Lewis in the latest techniques of scientific observation. While preparing for this great adventure, Lewis's second in command, William Clark, assumed such a prominent role that the effort became known as the **Lewis and Clark Expedition.** The effort owed much of its success to a young Shoshoni woman known as Sacagawea. She served as a translator and helped persuade suspicious Native Americans that the explorers meant no harm. As Clark explained, "A woman with a party of men is a token of peace."

The exploring party set out from St. Louis in May 1804, and after barely surviving crossing the snow-covered Rocky Mountains, with their food supply running dangerously low, the Americans reached the Pacific

**THE LOUISIANA PURCHASE AND THE ROUTE OF LEWIS AND CLARK** *Not until Lewis and Clark had explored the Far West did citizens of the United States realize just how much territory Jefferson had acquired through the Louisiana Purchase.* ❖

Ocean in November 1805. The group returned safely the following September. The results of the expedition not only fulfilled Jefferson's scientific expectations but also reaffirmed his faith in the future economic prosperity of the United States.

## Conflict with the Barbary States

During this period, Jefferson dealt with another problem. For several decades, the North African states of Tangier, Algiers, Tripoli, and Tunis—the Barbary States—had preyed on commercial shipping. (See the Feature Essay, "Barbary Pirates and American Captives: The Nation's First Hostage Crisis," pp. 230–231.) Most European nations paid the pirates tribute, hoping thereby to protect merchants trading in the Mediterranean. In 1801, Jefferson, responding to Tripoli's increased demand for tribute, decided the extortion had become intolerable and dispatched a small fleet to the Barbary Coast, where, according to one commander, the Americans intended to negotiate "through the mouth of a cannon." Tripoli put up stiff resistance, however, and in one mismanaged engagement it captured the

U.S. frigate *Philadelphia.* Ransoming the crew cost Jefferson's government another $60,000. An American land assault across the Libyan desert provided inspiration for the words of the "Marines' Hymn"—"to the shores of Tripoli"—but no smashing victory.

Despite a generally unimpressive American military record, a vigorous naval blockade brought hostilities to a conclusion. In 1805, the president signed a treaty formally ending the **Barbary War.** One diplomat crowed, "It must be mortifying to some of the neighboring European powers to see that the Barbary States have been taught their first lessons of humiliation from the Western World."

Jefferson concluded his first term on a wave of popularity. He had maintained the peace, reduced taxes, and expanded the boundaries of the United

### THE ELECTION OF 1804

| Candidate | Party | Electoral Vote |
| --- | --- | --- |
| Jefferson | Republican | 162 |
| C. Pinckney | Federalist | 14 |

## ❖ A Look at the Past ❖

### Buffalo Robe

Lewis and Clark collected Native American artifacts, including this Mandan buffalo robe. They sent the robe to Jefferson following a winter spent with the Mandans. Why would the Mandans give Lewis and Clark a robe that depicted a recent battle with their traditional enemies, the Sioux? Why would Lewis and Clark send the robe to Jefferson?

States. Not surprisingly, he overwhelmed his Federalist opponent in the presidential election of 1804. In the electoral college, Jefferson received 162 votes to Charles Cotesworth Pinckney's 14. Republicans controlled Congress. John Randolph, the most articulate member of the House of Representatives, exclaimed, "Never was there an administration more brilliant than that of Mr. Jefferson up to this period. We were indeed in 'the full tide of successful experiment!'"

## JEFFERSON'S CRITICS

At the moment of Jefferson's greatest electoral victory, a perceptive person might have seen signs of serious division within the Republican party and within the country. The president's heavy-handed attempts to reform the federal courts stirred deep animosities. Republicans had begun sniping at other Republicans, and one leading member of the party, Aaron Burr, became involved in a bizarre plot to separate the West from the rest of the nation. Congressional debates over the future of the slave trade revealed the existence of powerful sectional loyalties and profound disagreement on the issue.

### Attack on the Judges

Jefferson's controversy with the federal bench commenced the moment he became president. The Federalists, realizing they would soon lose control over the executive branch, had passed the Judiciary Act of 1801. This bill created several circuit courts

**THE BARBARY STATES**    *In 1801, President Jefferson refused to continue paying the tribute that pirates of the Barbary States had received for decades.* ❖

# BARBARY PIRATES AND AMERICAN CAPTIVES

## The Nation's First Hostage Crisis

For more than a quarter-century after Independence, terror haunted American sailors and challenged the new republic's influence throughout the world. Pirates from North Africa preyed on commercial vessels in the Mediterranean Sea and along the European Coast. Those unlucky enough to be captured faced enslavement or death. Although such piracy had been going on for a very long time, American entrepreneurs were always willing to risk the dangers to make a profit. The crew of one ship, the *Polly*, left a record of the horrors awaiting those who encountered the Barbary pirates, North African Muslims based in Algiers, Morocco, Tunis, and Tripoli.

Sailing out of Baltimore in autumn 1793, the *Polly* was on its way to a Spanish port when a sailor on watch reported a "strange sail". No one seems to have anticipated trouble.

They were in for a dreadful surprise. When the strange vessel drew alongside the *Polly,* someone "dressed in the Christian habit" hailed the Americans from the deck. Then, without warning, "a great number" of men "dressed in the Turkish habit" poured over the railings brandishing "scimitars and pistols . . . pikes, spears, lances, and knives." The Americans had no defense. The pirates plundered the ship then stripped the Americans of all clothing except "a shirt and a pair of drawers" and chained them in

preparation for the voyage to Algiers, reputed to be the cruelest "of any state in all Barbary."

The *Polly*'s crew had become casualties of the young republic's first prolonged hostage crisis involving Muslim states. By the end of the year, Barbary pirates had seized the crews of at least ten other vessels. The captives were thrown into prisons, where they labored in terrible conditions alongside sailors who had been in Algiers for as long as a decade. Algerian guards beat their captives. The enslaved Americans were driven in chains each day to a quarry outside the city of Algiers. Their masters forced them to drag twenty-ton rocks to construction sites. Anyone who attempted escape faced execution. Overcrowded prisons invited epidemic disease.

News of the captives' ordeal offended American pride. Outraged American citizens organized charitable societies pledged to oppose the pirates, send relief to the captives, and lobby Congress to take effective action for their release. In Baltimore, sailors resolved "not to proceed to sea, until they can do so without apprehension of insult and robbery." Some Americans advocated paying ransom to liberate the prisoners, but others pointed out that such a policy would only encourage more attacks on the nation's merchant marine.

The outpouring of private action and nationalist sentiment forced the U. S. government, which had championed a policy of free trade throughout the world, to adjust to the changing realities of international relations. If

Print depicting the bombardment of Tripoli by U.S. naval vessels in 1804. ❖

Images of American captives enduring various forms of torture at the hands of their Barbary captors. ❖

the United States allowed itself to be humiliated by the Barbary states— places where "bribery, treachery, rapine, murder, and all the hideous offspring of accursed tyranny, have often drenched the streets with blood"— then it could not expect other, more powerful states to respect its hard-won independence.

U.S. military power frightened no one, especially the rulers of Barbary states. Neither the French nor the British showed interest in helping the Americans. After all, they viewed them as commercial competitors in the region. In 1795, the federal government finally recognized the seriousness of the problem. President Washington ordered U.S. envoy Joseph Donaldson, Jr., to negotiate release of the captives and to sign treaties ensuring that Algiers would no longer molest American shipping. For these alleged favors, the United States had to promise a humiliating sum totaling nearly $1 million. The combination of debt payments and annual tribute represented about one-sixth of each year's federal budget. Treaties with Tripoli and Tunis also included yearly payments for peace, raising the total even higher.

A policy that essentially condoned blackmail continued until Thomas Jefferson won election as president in 1800. Hoping to extort a larger share of the annual ransom monies, the Pasha of Tripoli forced Jefferson's hand by declaring war on the United States. This preemptive move confirmed belief that attempts to buy off extortionists only generated further greed. It also compelled the United States to back up its world commerce with military might, a decision congressional budget-cutters had tried to avoid.

Vowing not to pay "one penny in tribute," Jefferson dispatched U.S. naval vessels to blockade Tripoli's harbor. Despite brave talk, American intervention proved a failure, at least initially. One battleship went aground and had to be destroyed by marines. Eventually, Commodore Edward Preble and Captain Stephen Decatur showed fighting spirit sufficient to turn defeat into a draw. The American consul at Tunis, William Eaton, even attempted an early form of "regime change," leading a company of Mediterranean mercenaries in an unauthorized effort to depose the Pasha and install his brother. Eaton's mission "to the shores of Tripoli" failed. In 1805 the Pasha, whose power was unshaken, decided that war was becoming too expensive, and he negotiated a peace with the United States that in-

cluded a payment of $60,000 to ransom the last prisoners.

During the long ordeal with the Barbary pirates, American nationalists portrayed North African states as the opposite of their free republic. Survivors of captivity published narratives containing lurid descriptions of the despotism and cruelty they had endured under their Muslim masters. The popular press castigated Muslims as enemies of civilized society and devoid of human compassion. Several so-called Algerian plays became audience favorites by creating innocent, but heroic American characters who embodied liberty and courage against a backdrop of Islamic tyranny.

Propaganda against Muslim pirates generated its own embarrassing backlash. Shrill nationalist rhetoric reminded many Americans of the uncomfortable similarities between the white slavery of the Barbary states and the African slavery that flourished throughout the southern United States. The African American abolitionist Absalom Jones could discern no real difference between "the unconstitutional bondage in which multitudes of our fellows in complexion are held" and "the deplorable . . . situation of citizens of the United States captured and enslaved . . . in Algiers."

America's first hostage crisis produced a complex legacy. It forced ordinary citizens of the new republic to take stock of themselves within a larger international framework. The war in Tripoli encouraged Jefferson, who had always disfavored a permanent military establishment, to accept a professional navy. Preparedness, he concluded, was the price of maintaining free trade throughout the world. War provided a stark contrast between liberty and tyranny and stimulated the loud celebration of American freedom. In doing so, it also intensified debate over the republic's most glaring domestic contradiction, the persistence of slavery within a nation that was prepared to fight in distant places in the name of liberty.

and sixteen new judgeships. Through his "midnight" appointments, Adams had quickly filled these positions with stalwarts of the Federalist party. Such blatantly partisan behavior angered Jefferson. In the courts, he explained, the Federalists hoped to preserve their political influence, and "from that battery all the works of Republicanism are to be beaten down and erased." Even more infuriating was Adams's appointment of John Marshall as the new chief justice. This shrewd, largely self-educated Virginian of Federalist background, whose training in the law consisted of a series of lectures he attended at the College of William and Mary in 1780, was clearly a man who could hold his own against the new president.

In January 1802, Jefferson's congressional allies called for repeal of the Judiciary Act. In public debate, they studiously avoided the obvious political issue. The new circuit courts should be closed not only because they were staffed by Federalists but also, as they argued, because they were needlessly expensive. The judges did not hear enough cases to warrant continuance. The Federalists mounted an able defense. The Constitution, they observed, provided for the removal of federal judges only when they were found guilty of high crimes and misdemeanors. By repealing the Judiciary Act, the legislative branch would in effect be dismissing judges without a trial, a clear violation of their constitutional rights. This argument made little impression on the Republican party. In March, the House, following the Senate, voted for repeal.

While Congress debated the Judiciary Act, another battle erupted. One of Adams's "midnight" appointees, William Marbury, complained that the new administration would not give him his commission for the office of justice of the peace for the District of Columbia. He sought redress before the Supreme Court, demanding that the federal justices compel James Madison, the secretary of state, to deliver the necessary papers. When they learned that Marshall had agreed to hear this case, the Republicans were furious. Apparently the chief justice wanted to provoke a confrontation with the executive branch.

Marshall was too clever to jeopardize the independence of the Supreme Court over such a relatively minor issue. In his celebrated *Marbury v. Madison* decision (February 1803), Marshall berated the secretary of state for withholding Marbury's commission. Nevertheless, he concluded that the Supreme Court did not possess jurisdiction over such matters. Poor Marbury was out of luck. The Republicans proclaimed victory. In fact, they were so pleased with the outcome that they failed to examine the logic of Marshall's decision. He had ruled that part of the earlier act of Congress, the one on which Marbury based his appeal, was unconstitutional. This was the first time the Supreme Court asserted its right to judge the constitutionality of congressional acts, and while contemporaries did not fully appreciate the significance of Marshall's doctrine, *Marbury v. Madison* later served as an important precedent for judicial review of federal statutes.

Neither Marbury's defeat nor repeal of the Judiciary Act placated extreme Republicans. They insisted that federal judges should be made more responsive to the will of the people. One solution, short of electing federal judges, was impeachment. This clumsy device provided the legislature with a way of removing particularly offensive individuals. Early in 1803, John Pickering, an incompetent judge from New Hampshire, presented the Republicans with a curious test case. This Federalist appointee suffered from alcoholism as well as insanity. While his outrageous behavior on the bench embarrassed everyone, Pickering had not committed any high crimes against the U.S. government. Ignoring such legal niceties, Jefferson's congressional allies pushed for impeachment. Although the Senate convicted Pickering (March 1804), many senators refused to compromise the letter of the Constitution and were conspicuously absent on the day of the final vote.

Jefferson was apparently so eager to purge the courts of Federalists that he failed to heed these warnings. By the spring of 1803, he had set his sights on a target far more important than John Pickering. In a Baltimore newspaper, the president stumbled on the transcript of a speech allegedly delivered before a federal grand jury. The words seemed almost treasonous. The person responsible was Samuel Chase, a justice of the Supreme Court, who had frequently attacked Republican policies. Jefferson leapt at the chance to remove Chase from office. Indeed, the moment he learned of Chase's actions, the president wrote to a leading Republican congressman, asking, "Ought the seditious and official attack on the principles of our Constitution . . . go unpunished?" The congressman took the hint. In a matter of weeks, the Republican-controlled House of Representatives indicted Chase.

Even at this early stage of the impeachment, some members of Congress expressed uneasiness. The charges drawn up against the judge were purely political. There was no doubt that the judge's speech had been indiscreet. He had told the Baltimore jurors that "our late reformers"—in other words, the Republicans—threatened "peace and order, freedom and property." But while Chase lacked good judgment, his attack on the Jefferson administration hardly seemed criminal. Nathaniel Macon, a powerful Republican congressman from North Carolina, wondered aloud, "Is error of opinion to be dreaded where enquiry is free?" This was the sort of question that Jefferson himself had asked the Federalists following passage of the Alien and Sedition Acts, but in 1804, Macon went unanswered. It

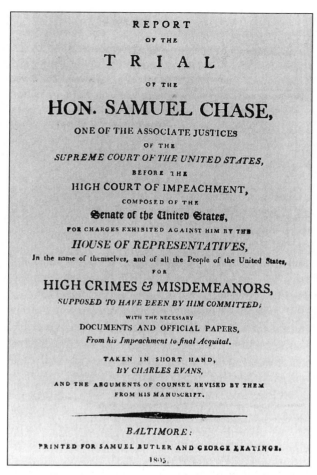

REPORT
OF THE
**T R I A L**
OF THE
## HON. SAMUEL CHASE,
ONE OF THE ASSOCIATE JUSTICES
OF THE
*SUPREME COURT OF THE UNITED STATES,*
BEFORE THE
HIGH COURT OF IMPEACHMENT,
COMPOSED OF THE
𝔖enate of the United 𝔖tates,
FOR CHARGES EXHIBITED AGAINST HIM BY THE
*HOUSE OF REPRESENTATIVES,*
In the name of themselves, and of all the People of the United States,
FOR
## HIGH CRIMES & MISDEMEANORS,
*SUPPOSED TO HAVE BEEN BY HIM COMMITTED;*
WITH THE NECESSARY
DOCUMENTS AND OFFICIAL PAPERS,
*From his Impeachment to final Acquital.*
TAKEN IN SHORT HAND,
BY CHARLES EVANS,
AND THE ARGUMENTS OF COUNSEL REVISED BY THEM
FROM HIS MANUSCRIPT.

*BALTIMORE:*
PRINTED FOR SAMUEL BUTLER AND GEORGE KEATINGE.
1805.

*Presiding officer Aaron Burr ordered extra seating installed in the Senate chamber to accommodate the spectators who attended Justice Chase's impeachment trial.* ❖

was clear that if the Senate convicted Chase, every member of the Supreme Court, including Marshall, might also be dismissed.

Chase's trial before the U.S. Senate was one of the most dramatic events in American legal history. Aaron Burr, the vice president, organized the proceedings. For reasons known only to himself, Burr redecorated the Senate chamber so that it looked more like the British House of Lords than the meeting place of a republican legislature. In this luxurious setting, Chase and his lawyers conducted a masterful defense. By contrast, John Randolph, the congressman who served as chief prosecutor, behaved in an erratic manner, betraying repeatedly his ignorance of relevant points of law. While most Republican senators personally disliked the arrogant Chase, they refused to expand the constitutional definition of impeachable offenses to suit Randolph's argument, and on March 1, 1805, the Senate acquitted the justice of all charges. The experience apparently convinced Chase of the need for greater moderation. After returning to the federal bench, he refrained from attacking Republican policies. His Jeffersonian opponents also learned something important. American politicians did not like tampering with the Constitution in order to get rid of specific judges, even an imprudent one like Chase.

## Politics of Desperation

The collapse of the Federalists on the national level encouraged dissension within the Republican party. Extremists in Congress insisted on monopolizing the president's ear, and when he listened to political moderates, they rebelled. The members of the most vociferous faction called themselves "the *good old republicans*"; the newspapers labeled them the "Tertium Quids," loosely translated as "nothings" or "no accounts." During Jefferson's second term, the Quids argued that the president's policies, foreign and domestic, sacrificed virtue for pragmatism. Their chief spokesmen were two members from Virginia, John Randolph and John Taylor of Caroline (the name of his plantation), both of whom were convinced that Jefferson had betrayed the republican purity of the Founders. They both despised commercial capitalism. Taylor urged Americans to return to a simple agrarian way of life. Randolph's attacks were particularly shrill. He saved his sharpest barbs for Gallatin and Madison, Republican moderates who failed to appreciate the congressman's self-righteous posturing.

The Yazoo controversy raised the Quids from political obscurity. This complex legal battle began in 1795 when a thoroughly corrupt Georgia assembly sold 35 million acres of western land, known as the Yazoo claims, to private companies at bargain prices. It soon became apparent that every member of the legislature had been bribed, and in 1796, state lawmakers rescinded the entire agreement. Unfortunately, some land had already changed hands. When Jefferson became president, a specially appointed federal commission attempted to clean up the mess. It recommended that Congress set aside 5 million acres for buyers who had unwittingly purchased land from the discredited companies.

Randolph immediately cried foul. Such a compromise, however well-meaning, condoned fraud. Republican virtue hung in the balance. For months, the Quids harangued Congress about the Yazoo business, but in the end, their impassioned oratory accomplished nothing. The Marshall Supreme Court upheld the rights of the original purchasers in *Fletcher* v. *Peck* (1810). The justices unanimously declared that legislative fraud did not impair private contracts and that the Georgia assembly of 1796 did not have authority to take away lands already sold to innocent buyers. This important case upheld the Supreme Court's authority to rule on the constitutionality of state laws.

## Murder and Conspiracy: The Curious Career of Aaron Burr

Vice President Aaron Burr created far more serious difficulties for the president. The two men had never been close. Burr's strange behavior during the election of 1800 raised suspicions that he had conspired to deprive Jefferson of the presidency. Whatever the truth may have been, the vice president entered the new administration under a cloud. He played only a marginal role in shaping policy, a situation extremely frustrating for a person as ambitious as Burr.

In the spring of 1804, Burr decided to run for the governorship of New York. Although he was a Republican, he entered into political negotiations with High Federalists who were plotting the secession of New England and New York from the Union. In a particularly scurrilous contest—and New York politics were always abusive—Alexander Hamilton described Burr as " . . . a dangerous man . . . who ought not to be trusted with the reins of government" and urged Federalists in the state to vote for another candidate.

Whether Hamilton's appeals influenced the voters is not clear. Burr, however, blamed Hamilton for his

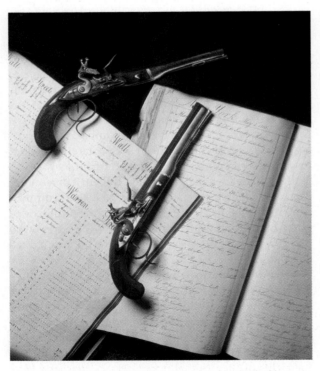

*Large caliber, smoothbore flintlock pistols used in the duel between Aaron Burr and Alexander Hamilton on July 11, 1804. Burr was not hit, but Hamilton was mortally wounded and died the next day. Though many condemned the practice of dueling, it was a fairly common means of resolving grievances in America until the time of the Civil War.* ❖

subsequent defeat and challenged him to a duel. Even though Hamilton condemned this form of violence— his own son had recently been killed in a duel—he accepted Burr's "invitation," describing the foolishness as a matter of personal honor. On July 11, 1804, at Weehawken, New Jersey, the vice president shot and killed the former secretary of the treasury. Both New York and New Jersey indicted Burr for murder. If he returned to either state, he would immediately be arrested. His political career lay in shambles.

In his final weeks as vice president, Burr hatched a scheme so audacious that the people with whom he dealt could not decide whether he was a genius or a madman. On a trip down the Ohio River in April 1805, after his term as vice president was over, he hinted broadly that he was planning a private military adventure against a Spanish colony, perhaps Mexico. Burr also suggested that he envisioned separating the western states and territories from the Union. The region certainly seemed ripe for secession. The citizens of New Orleans acted as if they wanted no part of the United States. Burr covered his tracks well. No two contacts ever heard the same story. Wherever Burr traveled, he recruited adventurers; he mingled with the leading politicians of Kentucky, Ohio, and Tennessee. James Wilkinson, commander of the U.S. Army in the Mississippi Valley, accepted an important role in this vaguely defined conspiracy. The general was a thoroughly corrupt opportunist. Randolph described him as "the only man that I ever saw who was from bark to the very core a villain."

In the late summer of 1806, Burr put his ill-defined plan into action. A small group of volunteers constructed riverboats on a small island in the Ohio River owned by Harman Blennerhassett, an Irish immigrant who, like so many contemporaries, found Burr's charm irresistible. By the time this armed band set out to join Wilkinson's forces, however, the general had experienced a change of heart. He frantically dispatched letters to Jefferson denouncing Burr. Wilkinson's betrayal destroyed any chance of success, and conspirators throughout the West rushed pellmell to save their own skins. Facing certain defeat, Burr tried to escape to Spanish Florida. It was already too late. Federal authorities arrested Burr in February 1807 and took him to Richmond to stand trial for treason. The prospect of humiliating his old rival was hardly displeasing to the president. Even before a jury had been called, Jefferson announced publicly that Burr's guilt "is placed beyond all question."

Jefferson spoke prematurely. John Adams wisely observed, if Burr's "guilt is as clear as the Noon day Sun, the first Magistrate ought not to have pronounced it so before a Jury had tryed him." The trial judge was John Marshall, a strong Federalist not likely to do the Republican administration any favors. During the entire proceedings, Marshall insisted on a narrow constitutional definition of treason. He refused to hear testimony regarding Burr's supposed intentions. "Troops must be embodied," Marshall thundered, "men must be actually assembled." He demanded two witnesses to each overt act of treason.

Burr, of course, had been too clever to leave this sort of evidence. While Jefferson complained bitterly about the miscarriage of justice, the jurors declared on September 1, 1807, that the defendant was "not proved guilty by any evidence submitted to us." The public was outraged, and Burr prudently went into exile in Europe. The president threatened to introduce an amendment to the Constitution calling for the election of federal judges. Nothing came of his proposal. And Marshall, who behaved in an undeniably partisan manner, inadvertently helped protect the civil rights of all Americans. If the chief justice had allowed circumstantial evidence into the Richmond courtroom, if he had listened to rumor and hearsay, he would have made it much easier for later presidents to use trumped-up conspiracy charges to silence legitimate political opposition.

## The Slave Trade

Slavery sparked angry debate at the Constitutional Convention of 1787 (see Chapter 6). If delegates from the northern states had refused to compromise on this issue, Southerners would not have supported the new government. The slave states demanded a great deal in return for cooperation. According to an agreement that determined the size of a state's congressional delegation, a slave counted as three-fifths of a free white male. This political formula meant that while blacks did not vote, they helped increase the number of southern representatives. The South in turn gave up very little, agreeing only that after 1808 Congress *might consider* banning the importation of slaves into the United States. Slaves even influenced the outcome of national elections. Had the three-fifths rule not been in effect in 1800, for example,

Adams would surely have had the votes to defeat Jefferson in the electoral college.

In an annual message sent to Congress in December 1806, Jefferson urged the representatives to prepare legislation outlawing the slave trade. During the early months of 1807, congressmen debated various ways of ending the embarrassing commerce. It was clear that the issue cut across party lines. Northern representatives generally favored a strong bill; some even wanted to make smuggling slaves into the country a capital offense. But there was a serious problem. The northern congressmen could not figure out what to do with black people captured by the customs agents who would enforce the legislation. To sell these Africans would involve the federal government in slavery, which many Northerners found morally repugnant. Nor was there much sympathy for freeing them. Ignorant of the English language and lacking personal possessions, these blacks seemed unlikely to long survive free in the American South.

Southern congressmen responded with threats and ridicule. They explained to their northern colleagues that no one in the South regarded slavery as evil. It appeared naive, therefore, to expect local planters to enforce a ban on the slave trade or to inform federal agents when they spotted a smuggler. The notion that these culprits deserved capital punishment seemed viciously inappropriate. At one point in the debate, Peter Early, a congressman from Georgia, announced that the South wanted "no civil wars, no rebellions, no insurrections, no resistance to

*Although the external slave trade was officially outlawed in 1808, the commerce in humans persisted. An estimated 250,000 African slaves were brought illicitly to the United States between 1808 and 1860. The internal slave trade continued as well. Folk artist Lewis Miller sketched this slave coffle marching from Virginia to new owners in Tennessee under the watchful eyes of mounted white overseers.* ❖

the authority of government." All he demanded, in fact, was to let the states regulate slavery. To this, a Republican congressman from western Pennsylvania retorted that Americans who hated slavery would not be "terrified by the threat of civil war."

The bill that Jefferson finally signed in March 1807 probably pleased no one. The law prohibited the importation of slaves into the United States after the new year. Whenever customs officials captured a smuggler, the slaves were to be turned over to state authorities and disposed of according to local custom. Southerners did not cooperate, and for many years African slaves continued to pour into southern ports. Even more blacks would have been imported had Great Britain not outlawed the slave trade in 1807. As part of their ban of the slave trade, ships of the Royal Navy captured American slave smugglers off the coast of Africa, and when anyone complained, the British explained that they were merely enforcing the laws of the United States.

## EMBARRASSMENTS OVERSEAS

During Jefferson's second term (1805–1809), the United States found itself in the midst of a world at war. A brief peace in Europe ended abruptly in 1803, and the two military giants of the age, France and Great Britain, fought for supremacy on land and sea. This was a kind of total war unknown in the eighteenth century. Napoleon's armies carried the ideology of the French Revolution across the Continent. The emperor—as Napoleon Bonaparte called himself after December 1804—transformed conquered nations into French satellites. Only Britain offered effective resistance. On October 21, 1805, Admiral Horatio Nelson destroyed the main French fleet at the battle of Trafalgar, demonstrating decisively the absolute supremacy of the Royal Navy. But only a few weeks later (December 2, 1805), Napoleon crushed Britain's allies, Austria and Russia, at the battle of Austerlitz and confirmed his clear superiority on land.

During the early stages of the war, the United States profited from European adversity. As "neutral carriers," American ships transported goods to any port in the world where they could find a buyer, and American merchants grew wealthy serving Britain and France. Since the Royal Navy did not allow direct trade between France and its colonies, American captains conducted "broken voyages." American vessels sailing out of French ports in the Caribbean would put in briefly in the United States, pay nominal customs, and then leave for France. For several years, the British did little to halt this obvious subterfuge.

Napoleon's successes on the battlefield, however, quickly strained Britain's economic resources. In July 1805, a British admiralty court announced in the *Essex* decision that henceforth "broken voyages" were illegal. The Royal Navy began seizing American ships in record number. Moreover, as the war continued, the British stepped up the impressment of sailors on ships flying the U.S. flag. Estimates of the number of men impressed ranged as high as nine thousand.

Beginning in 1806, the British government issued a series of trade regulations known as the Orders in Council. These proclamations forbade neutral commerce with the Continent and threatened seizure of any ship that violated these orders. The declarations created what were in effect "paper blockades," for even the powerful British navy could not monitor the activities of every Continental port.

Napoleon responded to Britain's commercial regulations with his own paper blockade called the Continental System. In the Berlin Decree of November 1806 and the Milan Decree of December 1807, he announced the closing of all continental ports to British trade. Since French armies occupied most of the territory between Spain and Germany, the decrees obviously cut the British out of a large market. The French emperor also declared that neutral vessels carrying British goods were liable to seizure. For the Americans there was no escape. They were caught between two conflicting systems. The British ordered American ships to stop off to pay duties and secure clearances in England on the way to the Continent; Napoleon was determined to seize any vessel that obeyed the British.

This unhappy turn of international events baffled Jefferson. He had assumed that civilized countries would respect neutral rights; justice obliged them to do so. Appeals to reason, however, made little impression on states at war. "As for France and England," the president growled, " . . . the one is a den of robbers, the other of pirates." In a desperate attempt to avoid hostilities for which the United States was ill prepared, Jefferson ordered James Monroe and William Pinckney to negotiate a commercial treaty with Great Britain. The document they signed on December 31, 1806, said nothing about impressment, and an angry president refused to submit the treaty to the Senate for ratification.

The United States soon suffered an even greater humiliation. A ship of the Royal Navy, the *Leopard,* sailing off the coast of Virginia, commanded an American warship to submit to a search for deserters (June 22, 1807). When the captain of the *Chesapeake* refused to cooperate, the *Leopard* opened fire, killing three men and wounding eighteen. The attack clearly violated the sovereignty of the United States. Official protests received only a perfunctory apology from the British government, and the American people demanded revenge.

Despite the pressure of public opinion, however, Jefferson played for time. He recognized that the

United States was unprepared for war against a powerful nation such as Great Britain. The president worried that an expensive conflict with Great Britain would quickly undo the fiscal reforms of his first term. As Gallatin explained, in the event of war, the United States "will be poorer, both as a nation and as a government, our debt and taxes will increase, and our progress in every respect be interrupted."

## Embargo Divides the Nation

Jefferson found what he regarded as a satisfactory way to deal with European predators with a policy he called "peaceable coercion." If Britain and France refused to respect the rights of neutral carriers, then the United States would keep its ships at home. Not only would this action protect them from seizure, but it would also deprive the European powers of much needed American goods, especially food. The president predicted that a total embargo of American commerce would soon force Britain and France to negotiate with the United States in good faith. "Our commerce is so valuable to them," he declared, "that they will be glad to purchase it when the only price we ask is to do us justice." Congress passed the **Embargo Act** by large majorities, and it became law on December 22, 1807.

"Peaceable coercion" turned into a Jeffersonian nightmare. The president apparently believed the American people would enthusiastically support the embargo. That was a naive assumption. Compliance required a series of enforcement acts that over fourteen months became increasingly harsh.

By the middle of 1808, Jefferson and Gallatin were involved in the regulation of the smallest details of American economic life. Indeed, in the words of one of Jefferson's biographers, the president assumed the role of "commissar of the nation's economy." The federal government supervised the coastal trade, lest a ship sailing between two states slip away to Europe or the West Indies. Overland trade with Canada was proscribed. When violations still occurred, Congress gave customs collectors the right to seize a vessel merely on suspicion of wrongdoing. A final desperate act, passed in January 1809, prohibited the loading of any U.S. vessel, regardless of size, without authorization from a customs officer who was supported by the army, navy, and local militia. Jefferson's eagerness to pursue a reasonable foreign policy blinded him to the fact that he and a Republican Congress would have had to establish a police state to make it work.

Northerners hated the embargo. Persons living near Lake Champlain in upper New York State simply ignored the regulations, and they roughed up collectors who interfered with the Canadian trade. The administration was determined to stop the smugglers. Jefferson

The *Ograbme* (embargo *spelled backward) snapping turtle, created by cartoonist Alexander Anderson, is shown here biting an American tobacco smuggler who is breaking the embargo.* ❖

urged the governor of New York to call out the militia. "I think it so important," the president explained in August 1808, " . . . to crush these audacious proceedings, and to make the offenders feel the consequences of individuals daring to oppose a law by force, that no effort should be spared to compass the object." In a decision that Hamilton might have applauded, Jefferson dispatched federal troops—led by the conspiratorial General Wilkinson—to overawe the citizens of New York.

New Englanders regarded the embargo as lunacy. Merchants of the region were willing to take their chances on the high seas, but for reasons that few people understood, the president insisted that it was better to preserve ships from possible seizure than to make profits. Sailors and artisans were thrown out of work. The popular press maintained a constant howl of protest. One writer observed that embargo in reverse spelled "O grab me!" A poem published in July 1808 captured the growing frustration:

> Our ships, all in motion,
> Once whitened the ocean,
>     They sail'd and returned with a cargo;
> Now doom'd to decay
> They have fallen a prey
>     To Jefferson, worms, and Embargo.

Not surprisingly, the Federalist party experienced a brief revival in New England, and a few extremists suggested the possibility of state assemblies nullifying federal law.

By 1809, the bankruptcy of Jefferson's foreign policy was obvious. The embargo never seriously damaged the British economy. In fact, British merchants rushed to take over the lucrative markets that the Americans had been forced to abandon. Napoleon liked the embargo, since it seemed to harm Great Britain more than it did France. Faced with growing popular opposition, the Republicans in Congress panicked. One newly elected representative declared that "peaceful coercion" was a "miserable and mischievous failure" and joined his colleagues in repealing the embargo a few days before James Madison's inauguration. Relations between the United States and the great European powers were much worse in 1809 than they had been in 1805. During his second term, the pressures of office weighed heavily on Jefferson, and after so many years of public service, he welcomed retirement to Monticello.

## A New Administration Goes to War

As president, James Madison suffered from several personal and political handicaps. Although his intellectual abilities were great, he lacked the qualities necessary for effective leadership. In public gatherings, he impressed people as being "exceedingly modest," and one foreign visitor claimed that the new president " . . . always seems to grant that the one with whom he talks is his superior in mind and training." Critics argued that Madison's humility revealed a weak, vacillating character.

During the election of 1808, Randolph and the Quids tried unsuccessfully to persuade James Monroe to challenge Madison's candidacy. Jefferson favored his old friend Madison. In the end, a caucus of Republican congressmen gave the official nod to Madison, the first time in American history that such a congressional group controlled a presidential nomination. The former secretary of state defeated his Federalist rival, Charles Cotesworth Pinckney, in the electoral college by a vote of 122 to 47, with New Yorker George Clinton receiving 6 ballots. The margin of victory was substantially lower than Jefferson's had been in 1804, a warning of political troubles ahead. The Federalists also made impressive gains in the House of Representatives, raising their delegation from 24 to 48.

The new president confronted the same foreign policy problems that had occupied his predecessor. Neither Britain nor France showed the slightest interest in respecting American neutral rights. Threats against either nation rang hollow so long as the United States failed to develop its military strength. Out of weakness, therefore, Madison was compelled to put the Non-Intercourse Act into effect. Congress passed this clumsy piece of legislation at the same time as it repealed the embargo (March 1, 1809). The new bill authorized the resumption of trade between the United States and all nations of the world *except* Britain and France. Either of these countries could restore full commercial relations simply by promising to observe the rights of neutral carriers.

The British immediately took advantage of this offer. Their minister to the United States, David M.

## THE ELECTION OF 1808

| Candidate | Party | Electoral Vote |
|---|---|---|
| Madison | Republican | 122 |
| C. Pinckney | Federalist | 47 |

Erskine, informed Madison that the British government had modified its position on a number of sensitive commercial issues. The president was so encouraged by these talks that he publicly announced that trade with Great Britain could resume in June 1809. Unfortunately, Erskine had not conferred with his superiors on the details of these negotiations. George Canning, the British foreign secretary, rejected the agreement out of hand, and while an embarrassed Madison fumed in Washington, the Royal Navy seized the American ships that had already put to sea.

Canning's apparent betrayal led the artless Madison straight into a French trap. In May 1810, Congress passed Macon's Bill Number Two, an act sponsored by Nathaniel Macon of North Carolina. In a complete reversal of strategy, this poorly drafted legislation reestablished trade with *both* England and France. It also contained a curious carrot-and-stick provision. As soon as either of these European states repealed restrictions upon neutral shipping, the U.S. government promised to halt all commerce with the other.

Napoleon spotted a rare opportunity. He informed the U.S. minister in Paris that France would no longer enforce the hated Berlin and Milan Decrees. Again, Madison acted impulsively. Without waiting for further information from Paris, he announced that unless Britain repealed the Orders in Council by November, the United States would cut off commercial relations. Only later did the president learn that Napoleon had no intention of living up to his side of the bargain; his agents continued to seize American ships. Madison, who had been humiliated by the Erskine experience, decided to ignore the French provocations, to pretend the emperor was behaving in an honest manner. The British could not explain why the United States tolerated such obvious deception. No one in London would have suspected that the president really had no other options left.

Events unrelated to international commerce fueled anti-British sentiment in the newly conquered parts of the United States. Westerners believed—incorrectly, as it turned out—that British agents operating out of Canada had persuaded Tecumseh's warriors to resist the spread of American settlement. According to the rumors that ran through the region, the British dreamed of monopolizing the fur trade. In any case, General William Henry Harrison, governor of the Indiana Territory, marched an army to the edge of a large Shawnee village at the mouth of Tippecanoe Creek near

*Dolley Madison, in a portrait by Gilbert Stuart, 1804, hosted popular informal entertainments at the White House.* ❖

the banks of the Wabash River. On the morning of November 7, 1811, the American troops routed the Indians at the battle of Tippecanoe. Harrison immediately became a national hero, and several decades later the American people rewarded "Tippecanoe" by electing him president. This incident forced Tecumseh—a brilliant leader who was trying to restore the confidence and revitalize tribal cultures of the Indians of the Indiana Territory—to seek British military assistance in battling the Americans, something he probably would not have done had Harrison left him alone.

## Fumbling Toward Conflict

In 1811, the anti-British mood of Congress intensified. A group of militant representatives, some of them elected to Congress for the first time in the election of 1810, announced they would no longer tolerate national humiliation. They called for action, for resistance to Great Britain, for any course that promised to achieve respect for the United States and security for its republican institutions. These aggressive nationalists, many of them elected in the South and West, have sometimes been labeled the **War Hawks.** The group included Henry Clay, an earthy Kentucky congressman who served as speaker of the House, and John C. Calhoun, a brilliant South Carolinian. These fiery orators spoke of honor and pride, as if foreign relations were a sort of duel between gentlemen. While the War

Hawks were Republicans, they repudiated Jefferson's policy of peaceful coercion.

Madison surrendered to the War Hawks. On June 1, 1812, he sent Congress a declaration of war against Great Britain. The timing of his action was peculiar. Over the preceding months, tensions between the two nations had relaxed. No new attacks had occurred. Indeed, at the very moment Madison called for war, the British government was suspending the Orders in Council, a conciliatory gesture that in all likelihood would have preserved the peace.

However inadequately Madison communicated his goals, he did seem to have had a plan. His major aim was to force the British to respect American maritime rights, especially in Caribbean waters. The president's problem was to figure out how a small, militarily weak nation like the United States could bring effective pressure on Great Britain. Madison's answer seemed to be Canada. This colony supplied Britain's Caribbean possessions with much needed foodstuffs. The president reasoned, therefore, that by threatening to seize Canada, the Americans might compel the British to make concessions on maritime issues. It was this logic that Secretary of State James Monroe had in mind when he explained in June 1812 that "it might be necessary to invade Canada, not as an object of the war but as a means to bring it to a satisfactory conclusion."

Congressional War Hawks, of course, may have had other goals in mind. Some expansionists were probably more concerned about conquering Canada than they were about the impressment of American seamen. For others, the whole affair may have truly been a matter of national pride. Andrew Jackson wrote, "*For what are we going to fight? . . . we are going to fight for the reestablishment of our national character, misunderstood and vilified at home and abroad.*" New Englanders in whose commercial interests the war would supposedly be waged ridiculed such chauvinism. The vote in Congress was close, 79 to 49 in the House, 19 to 13 in the Senate. With this doubtful mandate, the country marched to war against the most powerful maritime nation in Europe. Division over the war question was reflected in the election of 1812. A faction of antiwar Republicans nominated De Witt Clinton of New York, who was endorsed by the Federalists. Nevertheless Madison, the Republican, won narrowly, gaining 128 electoral votes to Clinton's 89.

### THE ELECTION OF 1812

| Candidate | Party | Electoral Vote |
|-----------|-------|----------------|
| Madison | Republican | 128 |
| Clinton | Republican* (antiwar faction) | 89 |

*Clinton was nominated by a convention of antiwar Republicans and endorsed by the Federalists.

# THE STRANGE WAR OF 1812

Optimism for the **War of 1812** ran high. The War Hawks apparently believed that even though the United States possessed only a small army and navy, it could easily sweep the British out of Canada. Such predictions flew in the face of political and military realities. Not only did the Republicans fail to appreciate how unprepared the country was for war, but they also refused to mobilize needed resources. The House rejected proposals for direct taxes and authorized naval appropriations only with the greatest reluctance. Indeed, even as they planned for battle, the Republican members of Congress were haunted by the consequences of their political and economic convictions. They did not seem to understand that a weak, highly decentralized government—the one that Jeffersonians championed—was incapable of waging an expensive war against the world's greatest sea power.

## ❖ A Look at the Past ❖

**"We Owe Allegiance to No Crown"**

Patriotic symbols abound in this print by John Archibald Woodside, Jr. Miss Liberty, carrying a liberty cap on a pole, crowns an American sailor with a laurel wreath, signifying that American liberty is victorious. The sentiment expressed visually and emphatically, "We Owe Allegiance to No Crown," seems appropriate for the revolutionary era, but in fact this print dates much later, to the early nineteenth century, when the War of 1812 sparked nationalism. What does this print suggest about American confidence at that time? Does it raise questions about United States–British relations following the American Revolution?

New Englanders refused to cooperate with the war effort. In July 1812, one clergyman in Massachusetts urged the people of the region to "proclaim an honourable neutrality." Many persons did just that. New Englanders carried on a lucrative, though illegal, commerce with the enemy. When the U.S. Treasury appealed for loans to finance the war, wealthy northern merchants failed to respond. The British government apparently believed the New England states might negotiate a separate peace, and during the first year of war, the Royal Navy did not bother to blockade the major northern ports.

American military operations focused initially on the western forts. The results were discouraging. On August 16, 1812, Major General William Hull surrendered an entire army to a smaller British force at Detroit. Michilimackinac was lost. Poorly coordinated marches against the enemy at Niagara and Montreal achieved nothing. These experiences demonstrated that the militia, led by aging officers with little military aptitude, no matter how enthusiastic, was no match for well-trained European veterans. On the sea, the United States did much better. In August, Captain Isaac Hull's *Constitution* defeated the HMS *Guerrière* in a fierce battle, and American privateers destroyed or captured a number of British merchant ships. These successes were somewhat deceptive, however. So long as Napoleon threatened the Continent, Great Britain could spare few warships for service in America. As soon as peace returned to Europe in the spring of 1814, Britain redeployed its fleet and easily blockaded the tiny U.S. Navy.

The campaigns of 1813 revealed that conquering Canada would be more difficult than the War Hawks ever imagined. Both sides in this war recognized that whoever controlled the Great Lakes controlled the West. On Lake Erie, the Americans won the race for naval superiority. On September 10, 1813, Oliver Hazard Perry destroyed a British fleet at Put-in-Bay, and in a much quoted letter written immediately after the battle, Perry exclaimed, "We have met the enemy; and they are ours." On October 5, General Harrison overran an army of British troops and Indian warriors at the battle of Thames River. During this engagement, Tecumseh was killed. On the other fronts, however, the war went badly for the Americans. General Wilkinson suffered an embarrassing defeat near Montreal (battle of Chrysler's Farm, November 11), and the British navy held its own on Lake Ontario.

In 1814, the British took the offensive. Following their victory over Napoleon, British strategists planned to increase pressure on three separate American fronts: the Canadian frontier, Chesapeake coastal settlements, and New Orleans. Sir George Prevost, commander of the British forces in Canada,

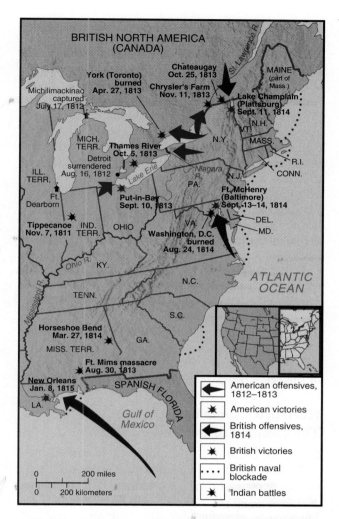

**THE WAR OF 1812**   *Major battles of the War of 1812 brought few lasting gains to either the British or the Americans.* ❖

marched his army south into upper New York State. A hastily assembled American fleet led by Captain Thomas Macdonough turned back a British flotilla off Plattsburg on Lake Champlain (September 11, 1814). When Prevost learned of this setback, he retreated quickly into Canada. Although the Americans did not realize the full significance of this battle, the triumph accelerated peace negotiations, for after news of Plattsburg reached London, the British government concluded that major land operations along the Canadian border were futile.

Throughout the year, British warships harassed the Chesapeake coast. To their surprise, the British found the region almost totally undefended, and on August 24, 1814, in retaliation for the Americans' destruction of the capital of Upper Canada (York, Ontario), a small force of British marines burned the American capital, a victory more symbolic than strategic. Encouraged by their easy success and contemptuous of America's ragtag soldiers, the British launched a full-scale attack on Baltimore (September 13–14). To everyone's surprise, the fort guarding the harbor held out against a heavy naval bombardment, and the British gave up the operation. The survival of Fort McHenry inspired Francis Scott Key to write "The Star-Spangled Banner."

The battle of New Orleans should never have occurred. The British landed a large assault force under General Edward Pakenham at precisely the same time as diplomats in Europe were preparing the final drafts of a peace treaty. The combatants, of course, knew nothing of these distant developments, and on January 8, 1815, Pakenham foolishly ordered a frontal attack against General Andrew Jackson's well-defended positions. In a short time, the entire British force had been destroyed. The Americans suffered only light casualties. The victory not only transformed Jackson into a national folk hero, but it also provided the people of the United States with a much needed source of pride. Even in military terms, the battle was significant, for if the British had managed to occupy New Orleans, they would have been difficult to dislodge regardless of the specific provisions of the peace treaty.

## Hartford Convention: The Demise of the Federalists

In the fall of 1814, a group of leading New England politicians, most of them moderate Federalists, gathered in Hartford to discuss relations between the people of their region and the federal government. The **Hartford Convention** delegates were angry and hurt by the Madison administration's seeming insensitivity to the economic interests of the New England states. The embargo had soured New Englanders on Republican foreign policy, but the events of the War of 1812 added insult to injury. When British troops occupied the coastal villages of Maine, then part of Massachusetts, the president did nothing to drive out the enemy. Of course, the self-righteous complaints of convention organizers overlooked New England's tepid support for the war effort.

The men who met at Hartford on December 15 did not advocate secession from the Union. Although people living in other sections of the country cried treason, the convention delegates only recommended changes in the Constitution. They drafted a number of amendments that reflected the New Englanders' growing frustration. One proposal suggested that congressional representation be calculated on the basis of the number of white males living in a state. New England congressmen were tired of the three-fifths rule that gave southern slaveholders a disproportionately large voice in the House. The convention also wanted to

## CHRONOLOGY

| | |
|---|---|
| **1800** | Thomas Jefferson elected president |
| **1801** | Adams makes "midnight" appointments of federal judges |
| **1802** | Judiciary Act is repealed (March) |
| **1803** | Chief Justice John Marshall rules on *Marbury v. Madison* (February); sets precedent for judicial review ❖ Louisiana Purchase concluded with France (May) |
| **1803–1806** | Lewis and Clark explore the Northwest |
| **1804** | Aaron Burr kills Alexander Hamilton in a duel (July) ❖ Jefferson elected to second term |
| **1805** | Justice Samuel Chase acquitted by Senate (March) |
| **1807** | Burr is tried for conspiracy (August–September) ❖ Embargo Act passed (December) |
| **1808** | Slave trade is ended (January) ❖ Madison elected president |
| **1809** | Embargo is repealed; Non-Intercourse Act passed (March) |
| **1811** | Harrison defeats Indians at Tippecanoe (November) |
| **1812** | Declaration of war against Great Britain (June) ❖ Madison elected to second term, defeating De Witt Clinton of New York |
| **1813** | Perry destroys British fleet at battle of Put-in-Bay (September) |
| **1814** | Jackson crushes Creek Indians at Horseshoe Bend (March) ❖ British marines burn Washington, D.C. (August) ❖ Hartford Convention meets to recommend constitutional changes (December) ❖ Treaty of Ghent ends War of 1812 (December) |
| **1815** | Jackson routs British at battle of New Orleans (January) |

limit each president to a single term in office, a reform that New Englanders hoped might end Virginia's monopoly of the executive mansion. And finally, the delegates insisted that a two-thirds majority was necessary before Congress could declare war, pass commercial regulations, or admit new states to the Union. The moderate Federalists of New England were confident these changes would protect their region from the tyranny of southern Republicans.

The convention dispatched its resolutions to Washington, but soon after an official delegation reached the federal capital, the situation became extremely awkward. Everyone was celebrating the victory of New Orleans and the announcement of peace. Republican leaders in Congress accused the hapless New Englanders of disloyalty, and people throughout the country were persuaded that a group of wild secessionists had attempted to destroy the Union. The Hartford Convention accelerated the final demise of the Federalist party.

## Treaty of Ghent Ends the War

In August 1814, the United States dispatched a distinguished negotiating team to Ghent, a Belgian city where the Americans opened talks with their British counterparts. During the early weeks of discussion, the British made impossible demands. They insisted on territorial concessions from the United States, the right to navigate the Mississippi River, and the creation of a large Indian buffer state in the Northwest Territory. The Americans listened to this presentation, more or less politely, and then rejected the entire package. In turn, they lectured their British counterparts about maritime rights and impressment.

Fatigue finally broke the diplomatic deadlock. The British government realized that no amount of military force could significantly alter the outcome of hostilities in the United States. Weary negotiators signed the Treaty of Ghent on Christmas Eve 1814. The document dealt with virtually none of the topics contained in Madison's original war message. Neither side surrendered territory; Great Britain refused even to discuss the topic of impressment. In fact, after more than two years of hostilities, the adversaries merely agreed to end the fighting, postponing the vexing issues of neutral rights until a later date. The Senate apparently concluded that stalemate was preferable to continued conflict and ratified the treaty 35 to 0.

Most Americans—except perhaps the diehard Federalists of New England—viewed the War of 1812 as an important success. Even though the country's military accomplishments had been unimpressive, the people of the United States had been swept up in a contagion of nationalism. The Hartford debacle served to discredit secessionist fantasies for several decades. Americans had waged a "second war of independence" and in the process transformed the Union into a symbol

*This engraving by Joseph Yeager (ca. 1815) depicts the Battle of New Orleans and the death of British Major General Edward Packenham. The death of the British commander was a turning point in the battle in which over 2,000 British soldiers died at the hands of General Andrew Jackson and the American army.* ❖

of national destiny. "The war," reflected Gallatin, had made Americans "feel and act more as a nation; and I hope that the permanency of the Union is thereby better secured." That nationalism had flourished in times of war was an irony that Gallatin's contemporaries did not fully appreciate. After the Treaty of Ghent, however, Americans came gradually to realize they had nothing further to fear from Europe, and in an era of peace, the process of sectional divergence began to quicken, threatening to destroy the republic that Jefferson and Madison had worked so hard to preserve.

## CONCLUSION: REPUBLICAN LEGACY

During the 1820s, it became fashionable to visit retired presidents. These were not, of course, ordinary leaders. Jefferson, Adams, and Madison linked a generation of younger men and women to the heroic moments of the early republic. When they spoke about the Declaration of Independence or the Constitution of the United States, their opinions carried symbolic weight for a burgeoning society anxious about its political future.

A remarkable coincidence occurred on July 4, 1826, the fiftieth anniversary of the Declaration of Independence. On that day, Thomas Jefferson died at Monticello. His last words were, "Is it the Fourth?" On the same day, several hundred miles to the north, John Adams also passed his last day on earth. His mind was

on his old friend and sometimes adversary, and during his final moments, Adams found comfort in the assurance that "Thomas Jefferson still survives."

James Madison lived on at his Virginia plantation, the last of the Founders. Throughout a long and productive career, he had fought for republican values. He championed a Jeffersonian vision of a prosperous nation in which virtuous, independent citizens pursued their own economic interests. He tolerated no aristocratic pretensions. Leaders of a Jeffersonian persuasion—and during his last years, that probably included John Adams—brought forth a democratic, egalitarian society. Although they sometimes worried that the obsessive grubbing for wealth might destroy public virtue, they were justly proud of the republic they had helped to create.

But many visitors who journeyed to Madison's home at Montpelier before he died in 1836 were worried about another legacy of the founding generation. Why, they asked the aging president, had the early leaders of this nation allowed slavery to endure? How did African Americans fit into the republican scheme? Try as they would, neither Madison nor the politicians who claimed the Jeffersonian mantle could provide satisfactory answers. In an open, egalitarian society, there seemed no place for slaves, and a few months before Madison died, a visitor reported sadly, "With regard to slavery, he owned himself almost to be in despair."

## RECOMMENDED READING

A challenge for historians of this period is explaining how Thomas Jefferson and his followers managed to reconcile Republican theories of government with the practical responsibilities of the presidency. The fullest account of his administration can be found in Merrill D. Peterson, *Thomas Jefferson and the New Nation: A Biography* (1970). Three more recent books examine Jefferson's complex character as well as the impact of Republican policies on the larger society: Peter S. Onuf, *Jeffersonian America* (2001); Joseph J. Ellis, *American Sphinx: The Character of Thomas Jefferson* (1997); and James Horn, et al., eds., *The Revolution of 1800: Democracy, Race, and the New Republic* (2002). The tensions that made this political culture so explosive are treated in Roger Sharp, *American Politics in the Early Republic: The New Nation in Crisis* (1993) and Bernard A. Weisberger, *America Afire: Jefferson, Adams, and the Revolutionary Election of 1800* (2000). The controversies over how best to interpret the Constitution and the politics of the Supreme Court are explored in Jean Edward Smith, *John Marshall: Definer of a Nation* (1996). Also valuable for understanding difficult legal issues are Richard E. Ellis, *The Jeffersonian Crisis: Courts and Politics in the Young Republic* (1971); Leonard W. Levy, *Emergence of a Free Press* (1985); and Morton J. Horowitz, *The Transformation of American Law, 1780–1860* (1977). The Louisiana Purchase is the subject of

Alexander DeConde, *The Affair of Louisiana* (1976). On the Lewis and Clark Expedition, see James P. Ronda, *Lewis and Clark Among the Indians* (1984) and Donald Jackson, *Thomas Jefferson and the Stony Mountains: Exploring the West from Monticello* (1981). Several fine studies chronicle the politics of slavery and Jefferson's own problems with freeing African Americans; Henry Wiencek tells how Washington confronted the problem in *An Imperfect God: George Washington, His Slaves, and the Creation of America* (2003). On foreign relations, see Peter S. Onuf, ed., *America and the World: Diplomacy, Politics, and War* (1991); J. C. A. Stagg, *Mr. Madison's War: Politics, Diplomacy, and Warfare in the Early American Republic* (1983); James E. Lewis, Jr., *The American Union and the Problem of Neighborhood: The United States and the Collapse of the Spanish Empire, 1783–1829* (1998); and Paul Baepler, ed., *White Slaves, African Masters: An Anthology of American Barbary Captivity Narratives* (1999). Two splendid works demonstrate how Evangelical Protestantism shaped early nineteenth-century public culture: Nathan O. Hatch, *The Democratization of American Christianity* (1989) and Mark A. Noll, *America's God: From Jonathan Edwards to Abraham Lincoln* (2002).

**For a list of additional titles related to this chapter's topics, please see** http://www.ablongman.com/divine.

# SUGGESTED WEB SITES

### Thomas Jefferson

http://www.pbs.org/jefferson/

A companion site to the Public Broadcasting Service series on Jefferson, especially important because it contains a fine collection of other people's view of Jefferson.

### White House Historical Association

http://www.whitehousehistory.org/

This site contains a timeline of the history of the White House and several interesting photos and links.

### Thomas Jefferson Digital Archive at the University of Virginia

http://etext.virginia.edu/jefferson/

Mr. Jefferson's University—the University of Virginia—houses this site with numerous on-line resources about Jefferson and his times, including electronic versions of texts by Jefferson, a page of selected quotations, and a comprehensive annotated bibliography of works on Jefferson from 1826 to 1997.

### Lewis and Clark: The Maps of Exploration 1507–1814

http://www.lib.virginia.edu/speccol/exhibits/lewis_clark/home.html

Maps and charts reveal knowledge and conceptions about the known and the unknown. This site includes a number of eighteenth-century maps.

### PBS Online—Lewis and Clark

http://www.pbs.org/lewisandclark/

This is a companion site to Ken Burns's documentary on Lewis and Clark containing a timeline of the expedition, a collection of related links, a bibliography, and more than 800 minutes of unedited, full-length RealPlayer interviews with seven experts featured in the film.

### The War of 1812

http://members.tripod.com/~war1812/index.html

In-depth and varied information about the War of 1812.

*An exuberant crowd celebrates in the square outside Independence Hall in this painting* Election Day in Philadelphia *(1815) by German American artist John Lewis Krimmel.* ❖

# Nation Building and Nationalism

## *A Revolutionary War Hero Revisits America in 1824*

When the Marquis de Lafayette returned to the United States in 1824 he found a peaceful and prosperous nation. For more than a year, the great French hero of the American Revolution toured the country that he had helped to bring into being, and he marveled at how much had changed since he had fought beside George Washington more than forty years before. He was greeted by adoring crowds in places that had been unsettled or beyond the nation's borders four decades earlier. Besides covering the eastern seaboard, Lafayette went west to New Orleans, then up the Mississippi and the Ohio by steamboat. He thus sampled a new mode of transportation that was helping to bring the far-flung outposts and settlements of a much enlarged nation into regular contact with each other. Such travel was still hazardous. Lafayette had to be rescued from a sinking steamboat on the Ohio before he could complete his journey to Cincinnati, hub city of the newly settled trans-Appalachian West.

Everywhere Lafayette was greeted with patriotic oratory celebrating the liberty, prosperity, and progress of the new nation. Speaking before a joint session of both houses of Congress, the old hero responded in kind, telling his hosts exactly what they wanted to hear. He hailed "the immense improvements" and "admirable communications" that he had witnessed and declared himself deeply moved by "all the grandeur and prosperity of these happy United States, which . . . reflect on every part of the world the light of a far superior political civilization."

Americans had good reasons to make Lafayette's return the occasion for patriotic celebration and reaffirmation. Since the War of 1812, the nation had been free from serious foreign threats to its independence and way of life. It was growing rapidly in population, size, and wealth. Its republican form of government, which many had considered a risky experiment at the time of its origin, was apparently working well. James Monroe, the current president, had proclaimed in his first inaugural address that "the United States have flourished beyond example. Their citizens individually have been happy and the nation prosperous." Expansion "to the Great Lakes and beyond the sources of the great rivers which communicate through our whole interior" meant that "no country was ever happier with respect to its domain." As for the government, it was so near to perfection that "in respect to it we have no essential improvement to make."

BENEATH THE OPTIMISM AND SELF-CONFIDENCE, however, lay undercurrents of doubt and anxiety about the future. The visit of the aged Lafayette signified the passing of the Founders. Less than a year after his departure, Jefferson and Adams, except for Madison the last of the great Founders, died within hours of each other on the fiftieth anniversary of the Declaration of Independence. Most Americans saw the coincidence as a good omen for the nation. But, some asked, could their example of republican virtue and self-sacrifice be maintained in an increasingly prosperous and materialistic society? Many in fact believed public virtue had declined since the heroic age of the Revolution. And what about the place of black slavery in a "perfect" democratic republic? Lafayette himself noted with disappointment that the United States had not yet extended freedom to southern slaves.

But the peace following the War of 1812 did open the way for a great surge of nation building. As new lands were acquired or opened up for settlement, hordes of pioneers often rushed in. Improvements in transportation soon gave many of them access to distant markets, and advances in the processing of raw materials led to the first stirrings of industrialization. Politicians looked for ways to encourage the process of growth and expansion, and an active judiciary handed down decisions that served to promote economic development and assert the priority of national over state and local interests. To guarantee the peace and security essential for internal progress, statesmen proclaimed a foreign policy designed to insulate America from external involvements. A new nation of great potential wealth and power was emerging.

Sheet music of a "grand march and quick step" to welcome the Marquis de Lafayette to the United States in 1824. ❖

## EXPANSION AND MIGRATION

The peace concluded with Great Britain in 1815 allowed Americans to shift their attention from Europe and the Atlantic to the vast lands of North America. Two treaties negotiated with Great Britain dealt with northern borders. The Rush-Bagot Agreement (1817) limited U.S. and British naval forces on the Great Lakes and Lake Champlain and guaranteed that the British would never try to invade the United States from Canada and that the United States would never try to take Canada from the British. The Anglo-American Convention of 1818 set the border between the lands of the Louisiana Purchase and Canada at the 49th parallel and provided for joint U.S. and British occupation of Oregon.

Between the Appalachians and the Mississippi, settlement had already begun, especially in the new states of Ohio, Kentucky, and Tennessee. In the lower Mississippi Valley, the former French colony of Louisiana had been admitted as a state in 1812, and a thriving settlement existed around Natchez in the Mississippi Territory. Elsewhere in the trans-Appalachian west white settlement was sparse and much land remained in Indian hands. Diplomacy, military action (or at least the threat of it) and massive

westward migration and settlement were needed before the continent would yield up its wealth to its white inhabitants.

### Extending the Boundaries

Postwar expansionists turned their attention first to Spanish holdings, which included Florida and much of the present-day American West. The first goal of postwar expansionists was to obtain Florida from Spain. In the eyes of the Spanish, their possession extended along the Gulf Coast to the Mississippi. Between 1810 and 1812, however, the United States had annexed the area between the Mississippi and the Perdido River in what became Alabama, claiming that it was part of the Louisiana Purchase. The remainder, known as East Florida, became a prime object of territorial ambition for President James Monroe and his energetic secretary of state, John Quincy Adams. Adams had a grand design for continental expansion that required nullifying or reducing Spanish claims west of the Mississippi as well as east of it; he eagerly awaited an opportunity to apply pressure for that purpose.

General Andrew Jackson provided such an opportunity. In 1816, U.S. troops first crossed into East Florida in pursuit of hostile Seminole Indians. This

**NORTH AMERICA, 1819**
*Treaties with Britain following the War of 1812 setting the border between the United States and Canada (British North America) made this border the longest unfortified boundary line in the world.* ❖

raid touched off a wider conflict, and after taking command in late 1817, Jackson went beyond his official orders and occupied East Florida in April and May of 1818. Except for Adams, all the members of Monroe's cabinet privately condemned this aggressive action; so did a report of the House of Representatives. But no disciplinary action was taken, mainly because public opinion rallied behind the hero of New Orleans.

In November 1818, Secretary Adams informed the Spanish government that the United States had acted in self-defense and that further conflict would be avoided only if East Florida was ceded to the United States. The Madrid government, weakened by Latin American revolutions and the breaking up of its empire, was in no position to resist American bullying. As part of the **Adams-Onís Treaty,** signed on February 22, 1819, Spain relinquished Florida to the United States. In return, the United States assumed $5 million of the financial claims of American citizens against Spain.

A strong believer that the United States had a continental destiny, Adams also used the confrontation over Florida to make Spain give up its claim to the

Pacific Coast north of California, thus opening a path for future American expansion. Taking advantage of Spain's desire to keep its title to Texas—a portion of which the United States had previously claimed as part of the Louisiana Purchase—Adams induced the Spanish minister Luis de Onís to agree to the creation of a new boundary between American and Spanish territory that ran north of Texas but extended all the way to the Pacific. Great Britain and Russia still had competing claims to the Pacific Northwest, but the United States was now in a better position to acquire frontage on a second ocean.

Interest in exploitation of the Far West continued to grow during the second and third decades of the nineteenth century. In 1811, a New York merchant, John Jacob Astor, founded the fur-trading post of Astoria at the mouth of the Columbia River in the Oregon Country. Astor's American Fur Company operated out of St. Louis in the 1820s and 1830s, with fur traders working their way up the Missouri to the northern Rockies and beyond. First they limited themselves to trading for furs with the Indians, but later, businesses such as the Rocky Mountain Fur Company, founded in 1822, relied on trappers or "mountain men" who went after game on their own and sold the furs to agents of the company at an annual meeting or "rendezvous."

These colorful characters, who included such legendary figures as Jedediah Smith, Jim Bridger, Kit Carson, and Jim Beckwourth (one of the many African Americans who contributed to the opening of the West as fur traders, scouts, or settlers), accomplished prodigious feats of survival under harsh natural conditions. Following Indian trails, they explored many parts of the Rockies and the Great Basin. Many of them married Indian women and assimilated much of the culture and technology of the Native Americans. Although they actually depleted the animal resources on which the Indians depended, the mountain men were portrayed in American literature and popular mythology as exemplars of a romantic ideal of lonely self-reliance in harmony with unspoiled nature.

Reports of military expeditions provided better documented information about the Far West than did the tales of illiterate mountain men. The most notable of the postwar expeditions was mounted by Major Stephen S. Long in 1819–1820. Long surveyed parts of the Great Plains and Rocky Mountains, but his reports encouraged the misleading view that the Plains were a "great American desert" unfit for cultivation or settlement. For the time being, the Far West remained beyond American dreams of agrarian expansion. The real focus of attention between 1815 and the 1840s was the nearer West, the rich agricultural lands between the Appalachians and the Mississippi that were being opened up for settlement.

## Settlement to the Mississippi

To completely occupy and exploit the trans-Appalachian interior, white Americans generally believed they had to displace the Indian communities still inhabiting that region in 1815. In the Ohio Valley and the Northwest Territory, military defeat had already made Native Americans only a minor obstacle to the ambitions of white settlers and land speculators. When the British withdrew from the Old Northwest in 1815, they left their former Indian allies virtually defenseless before the tide of whites who rushed into the region. Consigned by treaty to reservations outside the main lines of white advance, most of the tribes were eventually forced west of the Mississippi. The last stand of the Indians in this region occurred in 1831–1832, when a faction of the confederated Sac and Fox Indians under Chief Black Hawk refused to abandon their lands east of the Mississippi. Federal troops and Illinois state militia pursued Black Hawk's band and drove the Indians back to the river, where they were almost exterminated while attempting to cross to the western bank.

Uprooting once populous Indian communities of the Old Northwest was part of a national program for removing Indians of the eastern part of the country to an area beyond the Mississippi. Whites of the time viewed Indian society and culture as radically inferior to their own and doomed by the march of "progress." Furthermore, the fact that Indians based property rights to land on use rather than absolute ownership was regarded as an insuperable obstacle to economic development. As originally conceived by Thomas Jefferson, removal would have allowed those Indians who became "civilized" to remain behind on individually owned farms and qualify for American citizenship. This policy would reduce Indian holdings without appearing to violate American standards of justice. Not everyone agreed with Thomas Jefferson's belief that Indians, unlike blacks, had the natural ability to adopt white ways and become useful citizens of the republic. People living on the frontier who coveted Indian land and risked violent retaliation for trying to take it were more likely to think of Native Americans as irredeemable savages, or even as vermin to be exterminated if necessary. During the Monroe era, it became clear that white settlers wanted nothing less than the removal of all Indians, "civilized" or not. The issue was particularly pressing in the South. Greed combined with racism as land-grabbing state governments pressed for the total extinction of Indian land titles within their borders.

In the South, as in the Old Northwest, a series of treaties negotiated between 1815 and 1830 reduced tribal holdings and provided for the eventual removal of most Indians to the trans-Mississippi West. But some southern tribes held on tenaciously to their homelands. Many members of the so-called five civilized tribes—the Cherokee, Creek, Seminole, Choctaw, and Chickasaw—had become settled agriculturists. It was no easy task to induce the civilized tribes to give up the substantial and relatively prosperous enclaves in Georgia, Florida, Alabama, and Mississippi that they still held in the 1820s. But the pressure continued to mount. The federal government used a combination of deception, bribery, and threats to induce land cessions. When federal action did not yield results fast enough to suit southern whites who coveted Indian land for mining, speculation, and cotton production, state governments began to act on their own, proclaiming state jurisdiction over lands still allotted by federal treaty to Indians within the state's borders. The stage was thus set for the forced removal of the five civilized tribes to Oklahoma during the administration of Andrew Jackson. (See the Feature Essay,

*Mountain men such as Jim Beckwourth (left) and Native Americans met at a rendezvous to trade their furs to company agents in exchange for food, ammunition, and other goods. Feasting, drinking, gambling, and sharing exploits were also part of the annual event. Moccasins trimmed with trade beads (right), worn by both Native Americans and trappers, show how trade influenced both cultures. (Bottom) The painting* Rendezvous *(ca. 1837) by Alfred Jacob Miller.* ❖

"Confronting New Land," pp. 252–253. Jackson's Indian Removal policy is discussed in further detail in Chapter 10).

While Indians were being hustled or driven beyond the Mississippi, settlers poured across the Appalachians and filled the agricultural heartland of the United States. In 1810, only about one-seventh of the American population lived beyond the Appalachians; by 1840, more than one-third did. During that period, Illinois grew from a territory with 12,282 inhabitants to a state with 476,183; Mississippi's population of about 40,000 increased tenfold; and Michigan grew from a remote frontier area with fewer than 5,000 people into a state with more than 200,000. Eight new western states were added to the Union during this period. Because of the government's removal policies, few settlers actually had to fight Indians. But they did have to obtain possession of land and derive a livelihood from it. For many, this was no easy task.

Much of the vast acreage opened up by the westward movement passed through the hands of land speculators before it reached farmers and planters. Government lands in the western territories were first surveyed and then sold at auction. In the prosperous period following the War of 1812, and again during the boom of the early to mid-1830s, speculation in public lands proceeded at a massive and feverish rate. After a financial panic in 1819 brought ruin to many who had purchased tracts on credit, the minimum price was lowered from $2.00 to $1.25 an acre, but full payment was required in cash. Since few settlers could

# *Feature Essay*

# CONFRONTING NEW LAND

Relocating Indians to make room for white settlers was U.S. government policy from the presidency of Thomas Jefferson until the end of the nineteenth century when Indians were last placed on reservations. Persuasion and the promise of compensation were the preferred methods for inducing Indians to move. But if these methods failed, force could be applied. In his address to Congress on December 6, 1830, President Andrew Jackson celebrated the progress of his vigorous Indian removal policy, and chided those being removed for their ingratitude:

> Our [white] children by thousands yearly leave the land of their birth to seek new homes in distant re-

gions. Does Humanity weep at these painful separations from every thing, animate and inanimate, with which the young heart has become entwined? Far from it. It is rather a source of joy that our country affords scope where our young population may range unconstrained. . . .

Indeed there were two westward migrations in the antebellum era—one by European American settlers, one by Native Americans. During the same decades that hundreds of thousands of white farmers moved to Illinois and Missouri, tens of thousands of Indians were removed to present-day Kansas and Oklahoma. Despite obvious differences, these two streams of migration had something in common. Both groups of migrants had to adapt to the same unfamiliar prairie environment.

European Americans and Eastern Indians were woodland people. They lived at the tail end of the "Age of Wood" when forests provided the primary material for building, fencing, and heating, not to mention habitat for game that supplemented their diets. The ideal landscape was a clearing for a farm or small village

surrounded by thick forest. In the prairie, emigrants confronted an opposite landscape: huge openings—"barrens"—fringed by trees. "To one unaccustomed to it, there is something inexpressibly lonely in the solitude of a prairie," wrote Washington Irving. "The loneliness of the forest seems nothing to it." Settlers clustered at the prairie's edge, and only partly for the timber. The grassland had a reputation for fire, dryness, and infertility. James Madison, writing to Thomas Jefferson, expressed the conviction that Illinois was a "miserably poor" country that would never bear "a single bush." Unsurprisingly, therefore, most of the early setters to the prairie states gravitated to the relatively rare hilly and wooded areas that reminded them from where they had come.

At the time, most Americans believed that vegetation revealed its soil's fertility: the bigger the greenery, the richer the earth. Soil that produced no trees seemed mighty poor indeed. People eventually tried farming the prairie, of course, and discovered the truth: The soil was, in fact, so immensely fertile it supported a thick shield of tangled roots. "Sod-busting" required oxen, tools, and muscle; before the John Deere iron plow became readily available in the mid-nineteenth century, most early settlers were not up to the difficult task.

If Illinois initially seemed barren, the lands of present-day Kansas-Oklahoma seemed positively sterile. In 1820, a government surveyor gave an exaggerated but well-publicized name to this swath of the continent: "The Great American Desert." It was here that a diverse assemblage of Indian refugees tried their best to set up new homes in the removal era. In addition to the well-known Five Civilized Tribes from the South, the newcomers included groups from the Northeast

A KANSAS HOUSE.

A pioneer family's sod house on the Kansas plains. Unlike the eastern woodlands, the prairie offered little timber for building log cabins and settlers there often built houses of sod bricks. ❖

This 1839 satire on western emigration depicts a battered wagon of half-starved pioneers returning to New England after suffering hardships in Illinois, while an optimistic traveler is on his way there. ❖

and Old Northwest, including the Chippewa, Kickapoo, Miami, Ottawa, Potawatomi, Sac-Fox, Seneca, and Winnebago, among others.

For these woodland peoples, the sea of grass came as a shock. No wonder that many of the relocated Indians complained to the "Great Father"—the federal government. Writing to Indian agent William Clark (of Lewis and Clark fame), Shawnee leaders related that they "traveled three days through prairies and thought we were in the land of the great spirit, for we could see nothing but what was above us and the earth we walked upon." The Wyandot Nation of Ohio decided to send an "unbiased, unprejudiced" exploring expedition to see their promised land on the Missouri-Kansas border. The report was discouraging: "[T]here is but little timber and what there is, is of a low scrubby, knotty and twisted kind and fit for nothing but firewood. . . . [T]here is not good timber sufficient for the purposes of a people that wish to pursue agriculture."

From its inception, federal Indian policy meant to turn natives into sedentary farmers, as European-style agriculture was assumed to be the mark of "civilization." In fact, Eastern Indians like the Wyandot had extensive experience with various forms of agriculture. But old methods could not be easily replicated on the prairie, where the soil was too hard to be easily cultivated, and water was scarce. A few

Indian groups, such as the Cherokees, had learned to grow marketable crops in their traditional homelands and continued to do so in the new lands after removal. Nonetheless, some Cherokees chose to become seasonal bison hunters on the Southern Plains. Even with changes in their farming and hunting methods, it took decades for the Cherokee to recover from the dispossession of their towns and farms in Georgia. Adaptation was made more difficult by the staggering human losses they suffered on their forced march to the West.

The sickness and death on the Cherokee Trail of Tears—nearly a third of the migrants died on the way—was an extreme form of an experience that European American settlers also faced. For whites and natives alike, moving west meant growing ill; the body became unsettled in its new environment. A spokesperson for tribes removed from upstate New York to Kansas called it "a poor barren unhealthy country where many families have lost all their children in a course of a few years." For both races, catching the "ague" was an inevitable part of "seasoning" in this new country, which had a reputation for sickliness. Now understood as malaria, the ague commonly presented itself in cycles of shaking. Indeed, the experience was so common that there were essentially two types of settlers: veterans of the "pioneer shakes" and greenhorns.

Likewise, it was impossible to completely avoid "the chills" because it could arrive on the very air that permeated wooden cabins.

Antebellum settlers attributed many of their maladies to "miasma." Noah Webster defined it as "infecting substances floating in the air; the effluvia of any putrefying bodies, rising and floating in the atmosphere." According to popular belief, miasma came from rot in humus-rich forests, fertile bottomlands, and well-watered prairie. When settlers broke the prairie in order to "improve" the land, they released foul airs. People attempted to fight miasma by purging the air with coal smoke or wearing strong-smelling bags of herbs around the neck. But the land got sicker before it got healthier. The irony was not lost on settlers. Timothy Flint, who published an influential western guidebook in 1831, wrote that "there appears to be in the great plan of Providence a scale, in which the advantages and disadvantages of human condition are balanced. Where the lands are extremely fertile, it seems to be appended to them, as a drawback to that advantage, that they are generally sickly."

In the antebellum period, many Americans believed that land, like bodies, had intrinsic constitutions or states of health. Ideally, individuals and races could be matched to their "proper" environment (an idea used to defend slavery). Many Northerners and Indians from the North feared for their health when migrating to the hot, humid Mississippi basin. Billy Caldwell, a half-Irish, half-Indian chief from the Great Lakes region declared that Kansas was "unhealthy for people from a cold climate." There was always the hope that the new Indian homelands would prove unsuitable to white settlers. In 1836, en route to their new home, the Sac and Fox Indians said with bitter sarcasm that "the south side of the Missouri River is intended by the great spirit for the Red skins and for this reason he made so much prairie, that it would not suit . . . the white man, and if this had not been the case the red man would in short time have been without a home." In a matter of time, though, the "white man" would find the prairie suitable and would claim this homeland, too.

**View of the Great Treaty Held at Prairie du Chien** *(1825). Representatives of eight Native American tribes met with government agents at Prairie du Chien, Wisconsin, in 1825 to define the boundaries of their respective land claims. The United States claimed the right to make "an amicable and final adjustment" of the claims. Within twenty-five years, most of the tribes present at Prairie du Chien had ceded their land to the government.* ❖

afford the necessary outlays, wealthy speculators continued to acquire most good land.

Eventually, most of the land did find its way into the hands of actual cultivators. In some areas, squatters arrived before the official survey and formed claims associations that policed land auctions to prevent "outsiders" from bidding up the price and buying their farms out from under them. Squatters also agitated for formal right of first purchase or **preemption** from the government. Between 1799 and 1830, Congress passed a number of special acts that granted squatters in specific areas the right to purchase at the minimum price the land that they had already improved. In 1841, Congress formally acknowledged the right to farm on public lands with the assurance of a *future* preemption right.

Settlers who arrived after speculators had secured title had to deal with land barons. Fortunately for the settlers, most speculators operated on credit and needed a quick return on their investment. They did this by selling land at a profit to settlers who had some capital, by renting out farms until tenants had earned enough to buy them, or by loaning money to squatters who would later pay for the land in installments. As a result, the family farm or owner-operated plantation became the characteristic unit of western agriculture.

Since the pioneer family was likely to be saddled with debt of one kind or another, it was often forced from the beginning to do more than simply raise enough food to subsist. Farmers also had to produce something for market. Not surprisingly, most of the earliest settlement was along rivers that provided a natural means of transportation for flatboats loaded with corn, wheat, cotton, or cured meat. From more remote areas, farmers drove livestock over primitive trails and roads to eastern markets. To turn bulky grain, especially corn, into a more easily transportable commodity, farmers in remote regions often distilled grain into whiskey. To meet the needs of farmers, local marketing centers quickly sprang up, usually at river junctions. Some of these grew into small cities virtually overnight. In the Midwest especially, the rapid rise of towns and cities serving surrounding farming areas greatly accelerated regional development.

Most frontier people welcomed the opportunity to sell some of their crops in order to acquire the consumer goods they could not produce for themselves. Women especially benefited from the chance to buy some household necessities that they had previously made at home, such as soap, candles, and some articles of clothing. But many of them also valued self-sufficiency and tried to produce enough of the necessities of life to survive when cash crops failed or prices were low.

## The People and Culture of the Frontier

Most of the settlers who populated the West were farmers from the seaboard states. Rising land prices and declining fertility of the soil in the older regions often motivated their migration. Few sought to escape or repudiate the "civilized" and settled way of life they had known in the East. Most moved in family units and tried to re-create their former ways of life as soon as possible. Women were often reluctant to migrate in the first place, and when they arrived in new areas, they strove valiantly to recapture the comfort and stability they had left behind.

New Englanders moving to western New York or northern Ohio, Indiana, and Illinois brought with them their churches, schools, notions of community uplift, Puritan ideals of hard work and self-denial, and respect for law and government. The Southerners who emigrated from Virginia, the Carolinas, and Georgia to Kentucky, Tennessee, Alabama, and Mississippi, as well as the lower part of the Midwest, were more devoted to the defense of personal or family honor and independence. They therefore tended to be less committed to the development of public authority and institutions.

In general, pioneers sought out the kind of terrain and soil with which they were already familiar. People from eastern uplands favored western hill country. Piedmont and Tidewater farmers or planters usually made for the lower and flatter areas. Early settlers avoided the fertile prairies of the Midwest preferring instead river bottoms or wooded sections because they were more like home and could be farmed by tried-and-true methods. Rather than being the bold and deliberate innovators pictured in American mythology, typical agricultural pioneers were deeply averse to changing their habits.

Yet adjustments were necessary simply to survive under frontier conditions. Initially, at least, isolated homesteads required a high degree of self-sufficiency. Men usually cut down trees, built cabins, broke the soil, and put in crops. Besides cooking, keeping house, and caring for children, women made clothes, manufactured soap and other household necessities, churned butter, preserved food for the winter, and

worked in the fields at busy times; at one time or another, women performed virtually all the tasks required by frontier farming. Crops had to be planted, harvested, and readied for home consumption with simple tools brought in wagons from the East—often little more than an axe, a plow, and a spinning wheel.

But this picture of frontier self-reliance is not the whole story. Most settlers in fact found it extremely difficult to accomplish all the tasks using only family labor. A more common practice was the sharing of work by a number of pioneer families. Except in parts of the South, where frontier planters had taken slaves with them, the normal way to get heavy labor done in newly settled regions was through mutual aid. Assembling the neighbors to raise a house, burn the woods, roll logs, harvest wheat, husk corn, pull flax, or make quilts helped turn collective work into a festive social occasion. Passing the jug was a normal feature of these "bees," and an uproarious good time often resulted from the various contests or competitions that speeded the work along. These communal events represented a creative response to the shortage of labor and at the same time provided a source for community solidarity. They probably tell us more about the "spirit of the frontier" than the conventional image of the pioneer as a lonely individualist.

While some settlers remained in one place and "grew up with the country," many others moved on after a relatively short time. The wandering of young Abraham Lincoln's family from Kentucky to Indiana and finally to Illinois between 1816 and 1830 was fairly typical. The physical mobility characteristic of nineteenth-century Americans in general was particularly pronounced in frontier regions. Improved land could be sold at a profit and the proceeds used to buy new acreage beyond the horizon where the soil was reportedly richer. The temptations of small-scale land speculation and the lure of new land farther west induced a large proportion of new settlers to pull up stakes and move on after only a few years. Few early nineteenth-century American farmers developed the kind of attachment to the land that often characterized rural populations in other parts of the world.

Americans who remained in the East often ignored the frontier farmers and imagined

*Dwellings on the frontier could be rough and unfinished like the log cabin depicted in this 1832 watercolor of an Indiana farmstead by Swiss artist Carl Bodmer.* ❖

the West as an untamed American wilderness inhabited by Indians and solitary white "pathfinders" who turned their backs on civilization and learned to live in harmony with nature. James Fenimore Cooper, the first great American novelist, fostered this mythic view of the West in his stories of the frontier. He began in 1823 to publish a series of novels featuring Natty Bumppo, or "Leatherstocking"—a character who became the prototype for the western hero of popular fiction. Natty Bumppo was a hunter and scout who preferred the freedom of living in the forest to the constraints of civilization. Through Natty Bumppo, Cooper engendered a main theme of American romanticism—the superiority of a solitary life in the wilderness to the kind of settled existence among the families, schools, and churches to which most real pioneers aspired.

## A REVOLUTION IN TRANSPORTATION

It took more than the spread of settlements to bring prosperity to new areas and ensure that they would identify with older regions or with the country as a whole. Along the eastern seaboard, land transportation was so primitive that in 1813 it took seventy-five days for one wagon of goods drawn by four horses to make a trip of about a thousand miles from Worcester, Massachusetts, to Charleston, South Carolina. Coastal shipping eased the problem to some extent in the East and stimulated the growth of port cities. Traveling west over the mountains, however, meant months on the trail.

After the War of 1812, political leaders realized that national security, economic progress, and political unity were all more or less dependent on a greatly improved transportation network. Accordingly, President Madison called for a federally supported program of "internal improvements" in 1815. Recommending such a program in Congress, Representative John C. Calhoun described it as a great nationalizing enterprise: "Let us, then, bind the nation together with a perfect system of roads and canals. Let us conquer space." In ensuing decades, Calhoun's vision of a transportation revolution was realized to a considerable extent, although the direct role of the federal government proved to be less important than anticipated.

### Roads and Steamboats

Americans who wanted to get from place to place rapidly and cheaply needed, at a bare minimum, new and improved roads. The first great federal transportation project was the building of the National Road between Cumberland, Maryland, on the Potomac and Wheeling, Virginia, on the Ohio (1811–1818). This impressive toll road had a crushed stone surface and immense stone bridges. It was subsequently extended to reach Vandalia, Illinois, in 1838. Another thoroughfare to the West completed during this period was the Lancaster Turnpike connecting Philadelphia and Pittsburgh. Other major cities were also linked by turnpikes—privately owned toll roads chartered by the states. By about 1825, thousands of miles of turnpikes crisscrossed southern New England, upstate New York, much of Pennsylvania, and northern New Jersey.

By themselves, however, the toll roads failed to meet the demand for low-cost transportation over long distances. For the most part, travelers benefited more than transporters of bulky freight. The latter usually found that total expenses—toll plus the cost and maintenance of heavy wagons and great teams of horses—were too high to guarantee a satisfactory profit from haulage. Hence traffic was less than anticipated, and the tolls collected were often insufficient to provide an adequate return to investors.

Even the National Road itself had severe limitations. Although it was able to carry a substantial east-west traffic of settler parties and wagonloads of manufactured goods, as well as a reverse flow of livestock being driven to market, it could not offer the low freight costs required for the long-distance hauling of wheat, flour, and the other bulky agricultural products of the Ohio Valley. For these commodities, water transportation of some sort was required.

The United States' natural system of river transportation was one of the most significant reasons for its rapid economic development. The Ohio-Mississippi system in particular provided ready access to the rich agricultural areas of the interior and a natural outlet for their products. By 1815, large numbers of flatboats loaded with wheat, flour, and salt pork were making a part of the 2000-mile trip from Pittsburgh to New Orleans. On the lower Mississippi and its main tributaries, cotton could be loaded from plantation or town wharves onto rivercraft or small seagoing vessels and carried to the same destination. Even after the coming of the steamboat, flatboats continued to carry a major share of the downriver trade.

The flatboat trade, however, was necessarily one-way. A farmer from Ohio or Illinois, or someone hired to do the job, could float down to New Orleans easily enough, but there was generally no way to get back except by walking overland through rough country. Until the problem of upriver navigation was solved, the Ohio-Mississippi could not carry the manufactured goods that farmers desired in exchange for their crops.

Fortunately, a solution was readily at hand: the use of steam power. Late in the eighteenth century, a num-

The Clermont on the Hudson *(1830–1835) by Charles Pensee. Although some called his* Clermont *"Fulton's Folly," Robert Fulton immediately turned a profit from his fleet of steamboats, which reduced the cost and increased the speed of river transport.* ❖

ber of American inventors had experimented with steam-driven riverboats. John Fitch even exhibited an early model to delegates at the Constitutional Convention. But making a commercially successful craft required further refinement. In 1807, inventor Robert Fulton, backed by Robert R. Livingston—a New Yorker of great wealth and political prominence—demonstrated the full potential of the steamboat by successfully propelling the *Clermont* 150 miles up the Hudson River. The first steamboat launched in the West was the *New Orleans,* which made the long trip from Pittsburgh to New Orleans in 1811–1812. Besides becoming a principal means of passenger travel on the inland waterways of the East, the river steamboat revolutionized western commerce. In 1815, the *Enterprise* made the first return trip from New Orleans to Pittsburgh. Within five years, sixty-nine steamboats with a total capacity of 13,890 tons were plying western waters.

Steam transport was a great boon for farmers and merchants. It reduced costs, increased the speed of moving goods and people, and allowed a two-way commerce on the Mississippi and Ohio. Eastern manufacturers and merchants now had a better way to reach interior markets than the old method of hauling everything over the Appalachians by road.

The steamboat quickly captured the American imagination. Great paddle wheelers became luxurious floating hotels, the natural habitats of gamblers, confidence men, and mysterious women. For the pleasure of passengers and onlookers, steamboats sometimes raced against each other, and their more skillful pilots became folk heroes. But the boats also had a lamentable safety record, frequently running aground, colliding, or blowing up. The most publicized disasters of antebellum America were spectacular boiler explosions that claimed the lives of hundreds of passengers. As a result of such accidents, the federal government began in 1838 to attempt to regulate steamboats and monitor their construction and operation. The legislation, which failed to create an agency capable of enforcing minimum safety standards, stands as virtually the only federal effort in the pre–Civil War period to regulate domestic transportation.

## The Canal Boom

A transportation system based solely on rivers and roads had one enormous gap—it did not provide an economical way to ship western farm produce directly east to ports engaged in transatlantic trade or to the growing urban market of the seaboard states. The solution offered by the politicians and merchants of the Middle Atlantic and midwestern states was to build a system of canals that linked seaboard cities directly to the Great Lakes, the Ohio, and ultimately the Mississippi.

The best natural location for a canal connecting a river flowing into the Atlantic with one of the Great Lakes was between Albany and Buffalo, a relatively flat stretch of 364 miles. The potential value of such a project had long been recognized, but when it was actually approved by the New York legislature in 1817, it was justly hailed as an enterprise of breathtaking boldness. At that time, no more than about 100 miles of canal existed in the entire United States, and the longest single canal extended only 26 miles. Credit for the project belongs mainly to New York's vigorous and farsighted governor, De Witt Clinton. He persuaded the New York state legislature to underwrite the project by issuing bonds, and construction began in 1818. In less than two years, 75 miles were already finished and the first tolls were being collected. In 1825, the entire canal was opened with great public acclaim and celebration.

At 364 miles long, 40 feet wide, and 4 feet deep, and containing 84 locks, the Erie Canal was the most spectacular engineering achievement of the young republic. Furthermore, it was a great economic success. It reduced the cost of moving goods from Buffalo to Albany to one-twelfth the previous rate. It not only lowered the cost of western products in the East but caused an even sharper decline in the price of goods imported from the East by Westerners. It also helped to make New York City the commercial capital of the nation.

The great success of the Erie Canal inspired other states to extend public credit for canal building. Between 1826 and 1834, Pennsylvania constructed an even longer and more elaborate canal, covering the 395 miles from Philadelphia to Pittsburgh and requir-

ing twice as many locks as its New York competitor. But the Pennsylvania Main Line Canal did not do as well as the Erie, partly because of a bottleneck at the crest of the Alleghenies where an inclined-plane railroad had to haul canalboats over a high ridge. Ohio also embarked on an ambitious program of canal construction, completing an artificial waterway from the Ohio River to Cleveland on Lake Erie in 1833. Shorter canals were built in many other states, connecting navigable rivers with sea or lake ports. The last of these was the Illinois and Michigan Canal, completed in 1848. It linked Chicago and the Great Lakes with the Illinois River and the Mississippi.

The canal boom ended when it became apparent in the 1830s and 1840s that most of the waterways were unprofitable. State credit had been overextended, and the panic and depression of the late 1830s and early 1840s forced retrenchment. Moreover, by this time railroads were beginning to compete successfully for the same traffic, and a new phase in the transportation revolution was beginning.

But canals should not be written off as economic failures that contributed little to the improvement of transportation. Some of them continued to be important arteries up to the time of the Civil War and well beyond. Furthermore, the "failure" of many of the canals was due solely to their inability to yield an adequate return on the money invested in them. Concerning one failing canal, a contemporary argued

*Illustration of a lock on the Erie Canal at Lockport, New York, 1838. The successful canal facilitated trade by linking the Great Lakes regions to the eastern seaports.* ❖

that it "has been more useful to the public, than to the owners." Had the canals been thought of as providing a service rather than yielding a profit—in the manner, for example, of modern interstate highways—their vital contribution to the nation's economic development would have been better appreciated.

## EMERGENCE OF A MARKET ECONOMY

The desire to reduce the costs and increase the speed of shipping heavy freight over great distances laid the groundwork for a new economic system. Canals made it less expensive and more profitable for western farmers to ship wheat and flour to New York and Philadelphia and also gave manufacturers in the East ready access to an interior market. Steamboats reduced shipping costs on the Ohio and Mississippi and put farmers in the enviable position of receiving more for their crops and paying less for the goods they needed to import. Hence improved transport increased farm income and stimulated commercial agriculture.

### The Beginning of Commercial Agriculture

At the beginning of the nineteenth century, the typical farming household consumed most of what it produced and sold only a small surplus in nearby markets. Most manufactured articles were produced at home. Easier and cheaper access to distant markets caused a decisive change in this pattern. Between 1800 and 1840, agricultural output increased at an annual rate of approximately 3 percent, and a rapidly growing portion of this production consisted of commodities grown for sale rather than consumed at home. The rise in productivity was partly due to technological advances. Iron or steel plows proved better than wooden ones, the grain cradle displaced the scythe for harvesting, and better varieties or strains of crops, grasses, and livestock were introduced. But the availability of good land and the revolution in marketing were the most important spurs to profitable commercial farming. Good land made for high yields, at least for a time, and when excessive planting wore out the soil, a farmer could migrate to more fertile lands farther west. The existence or extension of transportation facilities made distant markets available and plugged farmers into a commercial network that provided credit and relieved them of the need to do their own selling.

The emerging exchange network encouraged movement away from diversified farming and toward regional concentration on staple crops. Wheat was the

## ❖ A Look at the Past ❖

### Merino Sheep

Increasing commercialism and industrialism affected both urban and rural dwellers during the early nineteenth century. Farmers could choose to participate in the changing economy in several ways. Supplying factories with raw materials and workers with food numbered among their options. Successful agriculture required farmers to alter their strategies. Some farmers intensified production, experimented with scientific methods, increased their herd sizes, and imported improved livestock breeds such as these very woolly merino sheep. Importing livestock, breeding improved varieties, and increasing production required money. What kind of a risk did a farmer take by enthusiastically producing for factories? What do the changes farmers made reveal about economic attitudes?

main cash crop of the North, and the center of its cultivation moved westward as soil depletion, pests, and plant diseases lowered yields in older regions. In 1815, the heart of the wheat belt was New York and Pennsylvania. By 1839, Ohio was the leading producer and Indiana and Illinois were beginning to come into their own. On the rocky hillsides of New England, sheep raising was displacing the mixed farming of an earlier era. But the prime examples of successful staple production in this era were in the South. Tobacco continued to be a major cash crop of the upper South (despite declining fertility and a shift to wheat in some areas), rice was important in coastal South Carolina, and sugar was a staple of southern Louisiana. Cotton, however, was the "king" crop in the lower South as a whole. In the course of becoming the nation's principal export commodity, it brought wealth and prosperity to a belt of states running from South Carolina to Louisiana.

A number of factors made the Deep South the world's greatest producer of cotton. First was the great demand generated by the rise of textile manufacturing in England and, to a lesser extent, in New England. Second was the effect of the cotton gin on processing. Invented by Eli Whitney in 1793, this simple device cut the labor costs involved in cleaning short-staple cotton, thus making it an easily marketable commodity.

A third reason for the rise of cotton was the availability of good land in the Southwest. As yields fell in original areas of cultivation—mainly South Carolina and Georgia—the opening of the rich and fertile plantation areas or "black belts" of Alabama, Mississippi, and Louisiana shifted the Cotton Kingdom westward and resulted in a vast increase in total production. In 1816, New Orleans, the great marketing center for western crops, received 37,000 bales; in 1830, 428,000 arrived; in 1840, the annual number had reached 923,000. Between 1817 and 1840, the amount of cotton produced in the South tripled from 461,000 to 1,350,000 bales.

A fourth factor—the existence of slavery, which provided a flexible system of forced labor—permitted operations on a scale impossible for the family labor system of the agricultural North. Finally, the cotton economy benefited from the South's splendid natural transportation system—its great network of navigable rivers extending deep into the interior from the cotton ports of Charleston, Savannah, Mobile, and, of course, New Orleans. The South had less need than other agricultural regions for artificial internal improvements such as canals and good roads. Planters could simply establish themselves on or near a river and ship their crops to market via natural waterways.

## Commerce and Banking

As regions specialized in growing commercial crops, a new system of marketing emerged. During the early stages in many areas, farmers did their marketing personally, even when it required long journeys overland or by flatboat. With the growth of country towns, local merchants took charge of the crops near their sources, bartering clothing and other manufactured goods for produce. These intermediaries shipped the farmers' crops to larger local markets such as Pittsburgh, Cincinnati, and St. Louis. From there the commodities could be sent on to Philadelphia, New York, or New Orleans. Cotton growers in the South were more likely to deal directly with factors or agents in the port cities from which their crop was exported. But even in the South, commission merchants in such inland towns as Macon, Atlanta, Montgomery, Shreveport, and Nashville became increasingly important as intermediaries.

Credit was a crucial element in the whole system. Farmers borrowed from local merchants, who received an advance of their own when they consigned crops to a commission house or factor. The commission agents relied on credit from merchants or manufacturers at the ultimate destination, which might be Liverpool or New York City. The intermediaries all charged fees and interest, but the net cost to the farmers was less than when they had handled their own marketing. The need for credit encouraged the growth of money and banking.

Before the revolutions in transportation and marketing, small-scale local economies could survive to a considerable extent on barter. Farmers could give grain to blacksmiths who could in turn exchange grain for iron from a local forge. But long-distance transactions involving credit and deferred payment required money and lots of it. Under the Constitution, the U.S. government is the only agency authorized to coin money and regulate its value. But in the early to mid-nineteenth century, the government printed no paper money and produced gold and silver coins in such small quantities that it utterly failed to meet the expanding economy's need for a circulating currency.

Private or state banking institutions filled the void by issuing banknotes, promises to redeem their paper in specie—gold or silver—on the bearer's demand. After Congress failed to recharter the Bank of the United States in 1811, existing state-chartered banks took up the slack. Many of them, however, lacked adequate reserves and were forced to suspend specie payments during the War of 1812. The demand for money and credit during the immediate postwar boom led to a vast increase in the number of state banks—from 88 to 208 within two years. The resulting flood of state banknotes caused this form of currency to depreciate well below its face value and threatened a runaway inflation. In an effort to stabilize the currency, Congress established a second Bank of the United States in 1816. The Bank was expected to serve as a check on the state banks by forcing them to resume specie payments.

But it did not perform this task well in its early years. In fact, its own free lending policies contributed to the overextension of credit that led to financial panic and depression in 1819. When the economy collapsed, as it would do again in 1837, many Americans questioned whether the new system of banking and credit was as desirable as it had seemed to be in times of prosperity. As a result, hostility to banks became a prominent feature of American politics.

## Early Industrialism

The growth of a market economy also created new opportunities for industrialists. In 1815, most manufacturing in the United States was carried on in households, in the workshops of skilled artisans, or in small mills, which used waterpower to turn wheat into flour or timber into boards. The factory form of production, in which supervised workers tended or operated machines under one roof, was rare. It was found mainly in southern New England, where a number of small spinning mills, relying heavily on the labor of women and children, accomplished one step in the manufacture of cotton textiles. But most spinning of thread, as well as the weaving, cutting, and sewing of cloth, was still done by women working at home.

As late as 1820, about two-thirds of the clothing worn by Americans was made entirely in households by female family members—wives and daughters. A growing proportion, however, was produced for market rather than direct home consumption. Under the "putting-out" system of manufacturing, merchant capitalists provided raw material to people in their own homes, picked up finished or semifinished products, paid the workers, and took charge of distribution. Items such as simple shoes and hats were also made under the putting-out system. Home manufacturing of this type was centered in the Northeast and often involved farm families making profitable use of their slack seasons. It did not usually present a direct challenge to the economic preeminence of agriculture, nor did it seriously disrupt the rural pattern of life.

The making of articles that required greater skill—such as high-quality shoes and boots, carriages or wagons, mill wheels, and barrels or kegs—was mostly carried on by artisans working in small shops in towns. But in the decades after 1815, shops expanded in size, masters tended to become entrepreneurs rather than working artisans, and journeymen often became wage earners rather than aspiring masters. At the same time, the growing market for low-priced goods led to a stress on speed, quantity, and standardization in the methods of production. Even where no substantial mechanization was involved, shops dealing in handmade goods for a local clientele tended to become small factories turning out cheaper items for a wider public.

A fully developed factory system emerged first in textile manufacturing. The establishment of the first cotton mills utilizing the power loom as well as spinning

*Lowell, Massachusetts, became America's model industrial town in the first half of the nineteenth century. In this painting of the town in 1814, (when it was still called East Chelmsford), a multi-story brick mill is prominent on the river. Textile mills sprang up throughout Lowell in the 1820s and 1830s, employing thousands of workers, mostly women. At right, Lowell mill workers are shown holding shuttles they used in their work at the looms.* ❖

machinery—thus making it possible to turn fiber into cloth in a single factory—resulted from the efforts of a trio of Boston merchants: Francis Cabot Lowell, Nathan Appleton, and Patrick Tracy Jackson. On a visit to England in 1810–1811, Lowell succeeded in memorizing the closely guarded industrial secret of how a power loom was constructed. Returning to Boston, he joined with Appleton and Jackson to acquire a water site at nearby Waltham and to obtain a corporate charter for textile manufacturing on a new and expanded scale.

Under the name of the Boston Manufacturing Company, the associates began their Waltham operation in 1813. Its phenomenal success led to the erection of a larger and even more profitable mill at Lowell, Massachusetts, in 1822 and another at Chicopee in 1823. Lowell became the great showplace for early American industrialization. Its large and seemingly contented workforce of unmarried young women residing in supervised dormitories, its unprecedented scale of operation, its successful mechanization of almost every stage of the production process—all captured the American middle-class imagination in the 1820s and 1830s. But in the late 1830s and 1840s conditions in the mills changed for the worse as the owners began to require more work for lower pay, and some of the mill girls became militant labor activists. One of these was Sarah Bagley, who helped found the Lowell Female Labor Reform Association in 1844. She subsequently led a series of protests against long hours and changes in the work routine that required more work from each operative. Other mills using similar harbor systems sprang up throughout New England, and the region became the first important manufacturing area in the United States.

The shift in textile manufacture from domestic to factory production shifted the locus of women's economic activity. As the New England textile industry grew, the putting-out system rapidly declined. Between 1824 and 1832, household production of textiles dropped from 90 to 50 percent in most parts of New England. The shift to factory production changed the course of capitalist activity in the region. Before the 1820s, New England merchants concentrated mainly on international trade, and Boston mercantile houses made great profits. A major source of capital was the lucrative China trade carried on by fast, well-built New England vessels. When the success of Waltham and Lowell became clear, many merchants shifted their capital away from oceanic trade and into manufacturing. This change had important political consequences, as leading politicians such as Daniel Webster no longer advocated a low tariff that favored importers over exporters. They now became leading proponents of a high duty designed to protect manufacturers from foreign competition.

The development of other "infant industries" of the postwar period was less dramatic and would not come to fruition until the 1840s and 1850s. Technology to improve the rolling and refining of iron was imported from England; it gradually encouraged a domestic iron industry centered in Pennsylvania. The use of interchangeable parts in the manufacture of small arms, pioneered by Eli Whitney and Simeon North, helped to modernize the weapons industry while also contributing to the growth of new forms of mass production.

Although most manufacturing was centered in the Northeast, the West also experienced modest industrial progress. Increasing rapidly in number and size were facilities for processing farm products, such as gristmills, slaughterhouses, and tanneries. Distilleries in Kentucky and Ohio began during the 1820s to produce vast quantities of corn whiskey for a seemingly insatiable public.

One should not assume, however, that America had already experienced an industrial revolution by 1840. In that year, 63.4 percent of the nation's labor force was still employed in agriculture. Only 8.8 percent of workers were directly involved in factory production (others were employed in trade, transportation, and the professions). Although this represented a significant shift since 1810, when the figures were 83.7 and 3.2 percent, the numbers would have to change a good deal more before it could be said that industrialization had really arrived. The revolution that did occur during these years was essentially one of distribution rather than production. The growth of a market economy of national scope—still based mainly on agriculture but involving a rapid flow of capital, commodities, and services from region to region—was the major economic development of this period. And it was one that had vast repercussions for all aspects of American life.

For those who benefited from it most directly, the market economy provided firm evidence of progress and improvement. But many of those who suffered from its periodic panics and depressions regretted the loss of the individual independence and security that had existed in a localized economy of small producers. These victims of boom and bust were receptive to politicians and reformers who attacked corporations and "the money power."

# THE POLITICS OF NATION BUILDING AFTER THE WAR OF 1812

Geographic expansion, economic growth, and the changes in American life that accompanied them were bound to generate political controversy. Farmers, merchants, manufacturers, and laborers were affected by the changes in different ways. So were Northerners, Southerners, and Westerners. Federal and state policies that were meant to encourage or control growth and expansion did not benefit all these groups or sections equally, and unavoidable conflicts of interest and ideology occurred.

But, for a time, these conflicts were not prominently reflected in the national political arena. During the period following the War of 1812, a single party dominated politics. Without a party system in place, politicians did not have to band together to offer the voters a choice of programs and ideologies. A myth of national harmony prevailed, culminating in the **"era of good feeling"** during James Monroe's two terms as president. Behind this facade, individuals and groups fought for advantage, as always, but without the public accountability and need for broad popular approval that a party system would have required. As a result, popular interest in national politics fell.

The absence of party discipline and programs did not completely immobilize the federal government. Congress did manage to legislate on some matters of national concern. Although the president had little control over congressional action, he could still take important initiatives in foreign policy. The third branch of government—the Supreme Court—was in a position to make far-reaching decisions affecting the relationship between the federal government and the states. The common theme of the public policies that emerged between the War of 1812 and the age of Andrew Jackson, which began in the late 1820s, was an awakening nationalism—a sense of American pride and purpose that reflected the expansionism and material progress of the period.

## The Republicans in Power

By the end of the War of 1812, the Federalist party was no longer capable of winning a national election. The party of Jefferson, now known simply as the Republicans, was so completely dominant that it no longer had to distinguish itself from its opponents. Retreating from their original philosophy of states' rights and limited government, party leaders now openly embraced some of the programs of their former Federalist rivals—policies that seemed dictated by postwar conditions. In December 1815, President Madison proposed to Congress that it consider such measures as the reestablishment of a national bank, a mildly protective tariff for industry, and a program of federally financed internal improvements to bind "more closely together the various parts of our extended confederacy." Thus did Jefferson's successor endorse parts of a program enunciated by Alexander Hamilton.

In Congress, Henry Clay of Kentucky took the lead in advocating that the government take action to promote economic development. The keystone of what Clay called the **American System** was a high protective tariff to stimulate industrial growth and provide a "home market" for the farmers of the West, making the nation economically self-sufficient and free from a dangerous dependence on Europe.

In 1816, Congress took the first step toward establishing a neo-Federalist American System. It enacted a tariff raising import duties an average of 25 percent. The legislation was deemed necessary because a flood of British manufactured goods was beginning to threaten the infant industries that had sprung up during the period when imports had been shut off by the embargo and the war. The tariff had substantial support in all parts of the country, both from a large majority of congressmen from New England and the Middle Atlantic states and from a respectable minority of the southern delegation. In 1816, manufacturing was not so much a powerful interest as a patriotic concern. Many Americans believed the preservation of political independence and victory in future wars required industrial independence for the nation. Furthermore, important sectors of the agricultural economy also felt the need of protection—especially hemp growers of Kentucky, sugar planters of Louisiana, and wool producers of New England.

Later the same year, Congress voted to establish the second Bank of the United States. The new national bank had a twenty-year charter, an authorized capital of $35 million, and the right to establish branches throughout the country as needed. Organized much like the first bank, it was a mixed public-private institution, with the federal government owning one-fifth of its stock and appointing five of its twenty-five directors. The Bank served the government by providing a depository for its funds, an outlet for marketing its securities, and a source of redeemable banknotes that could be used to pay taxes or purchase public lands. State banking interests and strict constructionists opposed the bank bill, but the majority of Congress found it a necessary and proper means for promoting financial stability and meeting the federal government's constitutional responsibility to raise money from taxation and loans.

Legislation dealing with internal improvements made less headway in Congress because it aroused stronger constitutional objections and invited disagreements among sectional groups over who would benefit from specific projects. Except for the National Road, the federal government undertook no major transportation projects during the Madison and Monroe administrations. Both presidents believed that internal improvements were desirable but that a constitutional amendment was required before federal monies could legally be used for the building of roads and canals within individual states. In 1817, just before leaving office, Madison vetoed a bill that would have distributed $1.5 million among the states for local transportation projects.

The following year, the House of Representatives held a lengthy debate on the question of whether Congress had the authority to make appropriations for internal improvements. Although a preliminary vote approved the principle, further discussion led to its rejection. In 1822, Monroe vetoed legislation for the repair and administration of the National Road, arguing that even this modest activity was beyond the constitutional powers of Congress. Consequently, public aid for the building of roads and canals continued to come mainly from state and local governments.

## Monroe as President

As did Jefferson before him, President Madison chose his own successor in 1816. James Monroe thus became the third successive Virginian to occupy the White House. He served two full terms and was virtually uncontested in his election to each. Monroe was well qualified in terms of experience, having been an officer in the Revolution, governor of Virginia, a special emissary to France, and secretary of state. He was reliable, dignified, and high principled, as well as stolid and unimaginative, lacking the intellectual depth and agility of his predecessors. He projected an image of a disinterested statesman in the tradition of the Founders. (He even dressed in the outmoded fashions of the revolutionary era.) Nominated, as was the custom of the time, by a caucus of Republicans in the House of Representatives, Monroe faced only nominal Federalist opposition in the general election.

Monroe avoided controversy in his effort to maintain the national harmony that was the keynote of his presidency. His first inaugural address expressed the complacency and optimism of the time, and he followed it up with a goodwill tour of the country, the first made by a president since Washington. A local newspaper was so impressed with Monroe's warm reception in Federalist Boston that it announced that party strife was a thing of the past and that an "era of good feeling" had begun.

A principal aim of Monroe's administrations was to encourage the good feelings. He hoped to accommodate or conciliate all the sectional or economic interests of the country and devote his main attention to the task of asserting American power and influence on the world stage.

The first challenge to Monroe's hopes for domestic peace and prosperity was the Panic of 1819, which

### THE ELECTION OF 1816

| Candidate | Party | Electoral Vote |
|-----------|-----------|----------------|
| Monroe | Republican | 183 |
| King | Federalist | 34 |

brought an abrupt end to the postwar boom. After a period of rampant inflation, easy credit, and massive land speculation, the Bank of the United States pricked the bubble by calling in loans and demanding the immediate redemption in specie of the state banknotes in its possession. This retrenchment brought a drastic downturn in the economy, as prices fell sharply, businesses failed, and land bought on credit was foreclosed.

In 1821, Congress responded weakly to the resulting depression by passing a relief act that eased the terms for paying debts owed on public land. Monroe himself had no program to relieve the economic crisis because he did not feel called on to exert that kind of leadership, and the voters did not seem to have expected it of him. The one-party system then prevailing left the president without the ability to work through an organized majority party in Congress; one-party rule had in fact degenerated into a chaotic "no-party" system. Unlike later presidents, Monroe could retain his popularity during a depression that began during his watch.

Monroe prized national harmony even more than economic prosperity. But during his first administration, a bitter controversy developed between the North and the South over the admission of Missouri to the Union. Once again Monroe remained above the battle and suffered little damage to his own prestige. It was left entirely to the legislative branch of the government to deal with the nation's most serious domestic political crisis between the War of 1812 and the late 1840s.

## The Missouri Compromise

In 1817, the Missouri territorial assembly applied for statehood. Since there were two to three thousand slaves already in the territory and the petition made no provision for their emancipation or for curbing further introduction of slaves, it was clear that Missouri would enter the Union as a slave state unless Congress took special action. Missouri was slated to be the first state, other than Louisiana, to be carved out of the Louisiana Purchase, and resolution of the status of slavery there would have implications for the rest of the trans-Mississippi West.

When the question came before Congress in early 1819, sectional fears and anxieties bubbled to the surface. Many Northerners resented southern control of the presidency and the fact that the three-fifths clause

## THE ELECTION OF 1820

| Candidate | Party | Electoral Vote |
|-----------|-------|----------------|
| Monroe | Republican | 231 |
| J. Q. Adams | No party designation | 1 |

of the Constitution, by which every five slaves were counted as three persons in figuring the state's population, gave the South's free population added weight in the House of Representatives and the electoral college. The South, on the other hand, feared for the future of what it regarded as a necessary balance of power between the sections. Up until 1819, a strict equality had been maintained by alternately admitting slave and free states; in that year, there were eleven of each. But northern population was growing more rapidly than southern, and the North had built up a decisive majority in the House of Representatives. Hence the South saw its equal vote in the Senate as essential for preservation of the balance.

In February 1819, Congressman James Tallmadge of New York introduced an amendment to the statehood bill, banning further introduction of slaves into Missouri and requiring steps toward the gradual elimination of slavery within the state. After a heated debate, the House approved the Tallmadge amendment

by a narrow margin. The Senate, however, voted it down. The issue remained unresolved until a new Congress convened in December 1819. In the great debate that ensued in the Senate, Federalist leader Rufus King of New York argued that Congress was within its rights to require restriction of slavery before Missouri could become a state. Southern senators protested that denying Missouri's freedom in this matter was an attack on the principle of equality among the states and showed that Northerners were conspiring to upset the balance of power between the sections. They were also concerned about the future of African American slavery and the white racial privilege that went with it.

A statehood petition from the people of Maine, who were seeking to be separated from Massachusetts, suggested a way out of the impasse. In February 1820, the Senate passed the **Missouri Compromise,** voting to couple the admission of Missouri as a slave state with the admission of Maine as a free state. A further amendment was also passed prohibiting slavery in the rest of the Louisiana Purchase north of the southern border of Missouri, or above the latitude of 36°30', and allowing it below that line. The Senate's compromise then went to the House, where it was initially rejected. Through the adroit maneuvering of Henry Clay—who broke the proposal into three separate bills—it eventually won House approval. The measure authorizing

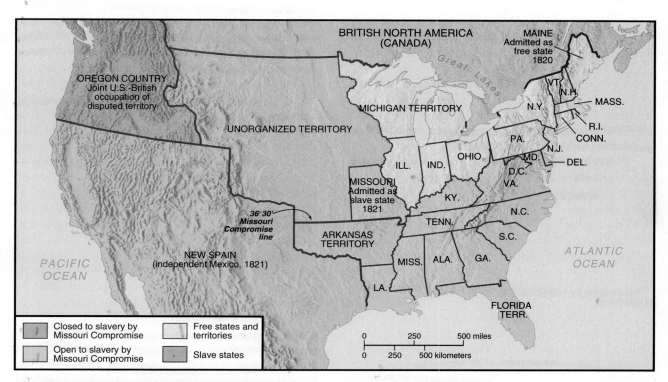

**THE MISSOURI COMPROMISE, 1820–1821**    *The Missouri Compromise kept the balance of power in the Senate by admitting Missouri as a slave state and Maine as a free state. The agreement temporarily settled the argument over slavery in the territories.* ❖

Missouri to frame a constitution and apply for admission as a slave state passed by a razor-thin margin of 90 to 87, with most northern representatives remaining opposed.

A major sectional crisis had been resolved. But the Missouri affair had ominous overtones for the future of North-South relations. Thomas Jefferson described the controversy as "a fire bell in the night," threatening the peace of the Union. In 1821, he wrote prophetically of future dangers: "All, I fear, do not see the speck on our horizon which is to burst on us as a tornado, sooner or later. The line of division lately marked out between the different portions of our confederacy is such as will never, I fear, be obliterated." The congressional furor had shown that when the issue of slavery or its extension came directly before the people's representatives, regional loyalties took precedence over party or other considerations. An emotional rhetoric of morality and fundamental rights issued from both sides, and votes followed sectional lines much more closely than on any other issue. If the United States were to acquire any new territories in which the status of slavery had to be determined by Congress, renewed sectional strife would be unavoidable.

## Postwar Nationalism and the Supreme Court

While the Monroe administration was proclaiming national harmony and congressional leaders were struggling to reconcile sectional differences, the third branch of government—the Supreme Court—was making a more substantial and enduring contribution to the growth of nationalism and a strong federal government. Much of this achievement was due to the firm leadership and fine legal mind of the chief justice of the United States, John Marshall.

A Virginian, a Federalist, and the devoted disciple and biographer of George Washington, Marshall served as chief justice from 1801 to 1835, and during that entire period he dominated the Court as no other chief justice has ever done. Discouraging dissent and seeking to hammer out a single opinion on almost every case that came before the Court, he played a role that has been compared to that of a symphony conductor who is also composer of the music and principal soloist.

As the author of most of the major opinions issued by the Supreme Court during its formative period, Marshall gave shape to the Constitution and clarified the crucial role of the Court in the American system of government. He placed the protection of individual liberty, especially the right to acquire property, above the attainment of political, social, or economic equal-

*Chief Justice John Marshall affirmed the Supreme Court's authority to overrule state laws and congressional legislation that it held to be in conflict with the Constitution. The portrait is by Chester Harding, ca. 1829.* ❖

ity. Ultimately he was a nationalist, believing that the strength, security, and happiness of the American people depended mainly on economic growth and the creation of new wealth.

The role of the Supreme Court, in Marshall's view, was to interpret and enforce the Constitution in a way that encouraged economic development, especially against efforts of state legislatures to interfere with the constitutionally protected rights of individuals or combinations of individuals to acquire property through productive activity. To limit state action, he cited the contract clause of the Constitution that prohibited a state from passing a law "impairing the obligation of contracts." As the legal watchdog of an enterprising, capitalist society, the Court could also approve a liberal grant of power for the federal government so that the latter could fulfill its constitutional responsibility to promote the general welfare by encouraging economic growth and prosperity.

In a series of major decisions between 1819 and 1824, the Marshall Court enhanced judicial power and used the contract clause of the Constitution to limit the power of state legislatures. It also strengthened the federal government by sanctioning a broad or loose construction of its constitutional powers and by clearly affirming its supremacy over the states.

In ***Dartmouth College v. Woodward*** (1819), the Court was asked to rule whether the legislature of New Hampshire had the right to convert Dartmouth from a private college into a state university. Daniel Webster, arguing for the college and against the state, contended that Dartmouth's original charter of 1769 was a valid and irrevocable contract. The Court accepted his argument. Speaking for all the justices, Marshall made the far-reaching determination that any charter granted by a state to a private corporation was fully protected by the contract clause.

In practical terms, the Court's ruling in the Dartmouth case meant that the kinds of business enterprises then being incorporated by state governments—such as turnpike or canal companies and textile manufacturing firms—could hold on indefinitely to any privileges or favors that had been granted in their original charters. The decision therefore increased the power and independence of business corporations by weakening the ability of the states to regulate them or withdraw their privileges. The ruling helped foster the growth of the modern corporation as a profit-making enterprise with only limited public responsibilities.

About a month after the Dartmouth ruling, in March 1819, the Marshall Court handed down its most important decision. The case of **McCulloch v. Maryland** arose because the state of Maryland had levied a tax on the Baltimore branch of the Bank of the United States. The unanimous opinion of the Court, delivered by Marshall, was that the Maryland tax was unconstitutional. The two main issues were whether Congress had the right to establish a national bank and whether a state had the power to tax or regulate an agency or institution created by Congress.

In response to the first question, Marshall set forth his doctrine of "implied powers." Conceding that no specific authorization to charter a bank could be found in the Constitution, the chief justice argued that such a right could be deduced from more general powers and from an understanding of the "great objects" for which the federal government had been founded. Marshall thus struck a blow for loose construction of the Constitution and a broad grant of power to the federal government to encourage economic growth and stability.

In answer to the second question—the right of a state to tax or regulate a federal agency—Marshall held that the Bank was indeed such an agency and that giving a state the power to tax it would also give the state the power to destroy it. In an important assertion of the supremacy of the national government, Marshall argued that the American people "did not design to make their government dependent on the states." This opinion ran counter to the view of many Americans, particularly in the South, that the Constitution did not take away sovereignty from the states. The debate over federal-state relations was not resolved until the northern victory in the Civil War decisively affirmed the dominance of federal authority. But Marshall's decision gave great new weight to a nationalist constitutional philosophy.

The **Gibbons v. Ogden** decision of 1824 bolstered the power of Congress to regulate interstate commerce. A steamboat monopoly granted by the state of New York was challenged by a competing ferry service operating between New York and New Jersey. The Court declared the New York grant unconstitutional because it amounted to state interference with Congress's exclusive right to regulate interstate commerce. The Court's ruling went a long way toward freeing private interests engaged in furthering the transportation revolution from state interference.

This case clearly showed the dual effect of Marshall's decision making. It broadened the power of the federal government at the expense of the states while at the same time encouraging the growth of a national market economy. The actions of the Supreme Court provide the clearest and most consistent example of the main nationalistic trends of the postwar period—the acknowledgment of the federal government's major role in promoting the growth of a powerful and prosperous America and the rise of a nationwide capitalist economy.

## Nationalism in Foreign Policy: The Monroe Doctrine

The new spirit of nationalism was also reflected in foreign affairs. The main diplomatic challenge facing Monroe after his reelection in 1820 was how to respond to the successful revolt of most of Spain's Latin American colonies after the Napoleonic wars. In Congress, Henry Clay called for immediate recognition of the new republics. In doing so, he expressed the belief of many Americans that their neighbors to the south were simply following the example of the United States in its own struggle for independence.

Before 1822, the administration stuck to a policy of neutrality. Monroe and Secretary of State Adams feared that recognizing the revolutionary governments would antagonize Spain and impede negotiations to acquire Florida. But pressure for recognition grew in Congress; in 1821, the House of Representatives, responding to Clay's impassioned oratory, passed a resolution of sympathy for Latin American revolutionaries and made it clear to the president that he would have the support of Congress if and when he decided to accord recognition. After the Adams-Onís treaty ceding Florida to the United States had been formally ratified in 1821, Monroe agreed to recognition and the establishment of diplomatic ties with the Latin American republics. Mexico and Colombia were recognized in 1822, Chile and Argentina in 1823, Brazil (which had separated from Portugal) and the Federation of Central American States in 1824, and Peru in 1826.

Recognizing the republics put the United States on a possible collision course with the major European powers. Austria, Russia, and Prussia were committed to rolling back the tides of liberalism, self-government, and national self-determination that had arisen during the French Revolution and its Napoleonic aftermath. After Napoleon's first defeat in 1814, the monarchs of Europe had joined in a "Grand Alliance" to protect "legitimate" authoritarian governments from democratic challenges. Great Britain was originally a member of this concert of nations but withdrew when it found that its own interests conflicted with those of the other members. In 1822, the remaining alliance members, joined now by the restored French monarchy, gave France the green light to invade Spain and restore a Bourbon regime that might be disposed to reconquer the empire. Both Great Britain and the United States were alarmed by this prospect.

Particularly troubling to American policymakers was the role of Czar Alexander I of Russia in the maneuverings. Not only was the czar an outspoken and active opponent of Latin American independence, but he was attempting to extend Russian claims on the Pacific Coast of North America south to the 51st parallel—into the Oregon Country the United States wanted for itself.

The threat from the Grand Alliance pointed to a need for American cooperation with Great Britain, which had its own reasons for wanting to prevent a restoration of Spanish or French power in the New World. Independent nations offered better and more open markets for British manufactured goods than the colonies of other nations, and the spokesmen for burgeoning British industrial capitalism anticipated a profitable economic dominance over Latin America. In early 1823, the British foreign secretary, George Canning, tried to exact from the French a pledge that they would make no attempt to acquire territories in Spanish America. When that venture failed, he sought to involve the United States in a joint policy to prevent the Grand Alliance from intervening in Latin America.

In August 1823, Canning broached the possibility of joint Anglo-American action against the designs of the Alliance to Richard Rush, U.S. minister to Great Britain, and Rush referred the suggestion to the president. Monroe welcomed the British initiative because he believed the United States should take an active role in transatlantic affairs by playing one European power against another. When Monroe presented the question to his cabinet, however, he encountered the opposition of Secretary of State Adams, who favored a different approach. Adams distrusted the British and differed from the president in his general view of proper relations between the United States and Europe. Adams believed the national interest would best be served by avoiding all entanglements in European politics while at the same time discouraging European intervention in the Americas.

Political ambition also predisposed Adams against joint action with Great Britain; he hoped to be the next president and did not want to give his rivals the chance to label him as pro-British. He therefore advocated unilateral action by the United States rather than a joint declaration with the British. As he told the cabinet in November, "It would be more candid, as well as more dignified, to avow our principles explicitly to Russia and France, than to come in as a cock-boat of the British man-of-war."

In the end, Adams managed to swing Monroe and the cabinet around to his viewpoint. In his annual message to Congress on December 2, 1823, Monroe included a far-reaching statement on foreign policy that was actually written mainly by Adams. What came to be known as the **Monroe Doctrine** solemnly declared that the United States opposed any further colonization in the Americas or any effort by European nations to extend their political systems outside their own hemisphere. In return, the United States pledged not to involve itself in the internal affairs of Europe or to take part in European wars. The statement envisioned a North and South America composed entirely of independent republics—with the United States preeminent among them.

Although the Monroe Doctrine made little impression on the great powers of Europe at the time it was proclaimed, it signified the rise of a new sense of independence and self-confidence in American attitudes toward the Old World. The United States would now go its own way free of involvement in European conflicts and would energetically protect its own sphere of influence from European interference.

## The Troubled Presidency of John Quincy Adams

Monroe endorsed John Quincy Adams to succeed him as president. An intelligent and high-minded New Englander and the son of the second president, Adams seemed remarkably well qualified for the highest office in the land. More than anyone else, except perhaps Monroe himself, he seemed to stand for a nonpartisan nationalism that put the public good above special interests. Early in his career, Adams lost a seat in the Senate for supporting the foreign policies of Thomas Jefferson in defiance of the Federalist majority of his home state of Massachusetts. After becoming a National Republican, he served mainly in diplomatic posts, culminating in his tenure as secre-

*John Quincy Adams in an 1828 portrait by Gilbert Stuart, the outstanding American portrait painter. As secretary of state under James Monroe, Adams advocated a policy of national self-interest and freedom from entanglement in European affairs. Elected president in 1824, he served one term.* ❖

tary of state. In this office, he did more than negotiate treaties. Believing that the rising greatness of America should be reflected not only in economic development and territorial expansion but also in scientific and intellectual achievement, he single-handedly produced a monumental report prescribing a uniform system of weights and measures for the United States. For three years, he rose early every morning in order to put in several hours of research on the project before doing a full day's work conducting the nation's foreign policy. Uniformity of weights and measures, he argued, was essential to scientific and technological progress. Showing that his nationalism was not of a narrow and selfish kind, he called for an agreement with Great Britain and France to promote a single universal system.

Adams represented a type of leadership that could not survive the growth of the sectional and economic divisions foreshadowed by the Missouri controversy and the fallout from the Panic of 1819. Adams did be-

come president, but only after a hotly contested election that led to the revival of partisan political conflict. As the nation's chief executive, he tried to gain support for government-sponsored scientific research and higher education, only to find the nation was in no mood for public expenditures that offered nothing immediate and tangible to most voters. As a highly educated "gentleman," he projected an image that was out of harmony with a rising spirit of democracy and veneration of "the common man."

## CONCLUSION: THE END OF THE "ERA OF GOOD FEELING"

The consensus on national goals and leadership that Monroe had represented could not sustain itself. The "era of good feeling" turned out to be a passing phase and something of an illusion. Although the pursuit of national greatness would continue, there would be sharp divisions over how it should be achieved. A general commitment to settlement of the West and the development of agriculture, commerce, and industry would endure despite serious differences over what role government should play in the process; but the idea that an elite of nonpartisan statesmen could define common purposes and harmonize competing elements—the concept of leadership that Monroe and Adams had advanced—would no longer be viable in the more contentious and democratic America of the Jacksonian era.

# RECOMMENDED READING

The standard surveys of the period between the War of 1812 and the age of Jackson are two works by George Dangerfield: *The Era of Good Feelings* (1952) and *Awakening of American Nationalism, 1815–1828* (1965); but see also the early chapters of Charles Sellers, *The Market Revolution: Jacksonian America, 1815–1846* (1991). For a positive account of the venturesome, entrepreneurial spirit of the age, see Joyce Appleby, *Inheriting the Revolution: The First Generations of Americans* (2000). On westward expansion, see Richard White, *It's Your Misfortune and None of My Own* (1992) and Malcolm J. Rohrbough, *The Trans-Appalachian Frontier* (1978).

Outstanding studies of economic transformation and the rise of a market economy are George R. Taylor, *The Transportation Revolution, 1815–1860* (1951); Paul W. Gates, *The Farmer's Age: Agriculture, 1815–1860* (1960); Stuart Bruchey, *Growth of the Modern American Economy* (1975); and Douglas C. North, *The Economic Growth of the United States, 1790–1860* (1961). Early manufacturing is de-

scribed in David J. Jeremy, *Transatlantic Industrial Revolution* (1981) and Robert F. Dalzell, *The Boston Associates and the World They Made* (1987). On early mill workers, see Thomas Dublin, *Women at Work: The Transformation of Work and Community in Lowell, Massachusetts, 1826–1860* (1979).

On the Marshall Court's decisions see Robert K. Faulkner, *The Jurisprudence of John Marshall* (1968) and G. Edward White, *The Marshall Court and Cultural Change, 1815–1835* (1991). Samuel F. Bemis, *John Quincy Adams and the Foundations of American Policy* (1949) provides the classic account of the statesmanship that led to the Monroe Doctrine. But see also Ernest May, *The Making of the Monroe Doctrine* (1976), for a persuasive newer interpretation of how the doctrine originated.

**For a list of additional titles related to this chapter's topics, please see** http://www.ablongman.com/divine.

# SUGGESTED WEB SITES

### The Era of the Mountain Men

http://www.xmission.com/~drudy/amm.html
Private letters can speak volumes about the concerns and environment of the writers and recipients. Letters from early settlers west of the Mississippi River are offered on this site.

### Prairietown, Indiana

http://www.connerprairie.org/explore/prairietown.html
This fictional model of a town and its inhabitants on the early frontier says much about America's movement westward and the everyday lives of Americans.

### The Seminole Tribe of Florida

http://www.seminoletribe.com/
Before he was president, Andrew Jackson began a war against the Seminole Indians. This site presents information on their history and culture.

### Erie Canal On-line

http://www.syracuse.com/features/eriecanal
This site, built around the diary of a 14-year-old girl who traveled from Amsterdam to Syracuse, New York, in the early nineteenth century, explores the construction and importance of the Erie Canal.

### Whole Cloth: Discovering Science and Technology Through American Textile History

http://www.si.edu/lemelson/centerpieces/whole_cloth/
The Jerome and Dorothy Lemelson Center for the Study of Invention and Innovation/Society for the History of Technology put together this site which includes excellent activities and sources concerning early American manufacturing and industry.

### Road Through the Wilderness: The Making of the National Road

http://www.connerprairie.org/historyonline/ntlroad.html
The National Road was a hot political topic in the Early Republic and was part of the beginning of the development of America's infrastructure. This on-line essay by historian Timothy Crumrin discusses the making of the National Road.

In Richard Cruikshank's engraving, "All Creation Going to the White House," crowds of supporters pour into the White House to celebrate the victory of "common man" Andrew Jackson in the presidential election of 1828. ❖

# The Triumph of White Men's Democracy

## Democratic Space: The New Hotels

During the 1820s and 1830s the United States became a more democratic country for at least some of its population. The emerging spirit of popular democracy found expression in a new institution—the large hotel with several stories and hundreds of rooms. President-elect Andrew Jackson, the political figure who best represented the spirit of the age, stayed in the recently opened National Hotel when he arrived in Washington in 1829 to prepare for his administration. After a horde of well-wishers made a shambles of the White House during his inaugural reception, Jackson retreated to the hotel for a little peace and a chance to consult with his advisers. The National was only one of several large "first class" hotels that opened immediately before or during Jackson's presidency. Among the others were the Tremont House in Boston, the Baltimore City Hotel, and New York's Astor House.

The hotel boom responded to the increasing tendency of Americans in the 1820s and 1830s to move about the country. It was to service the rising tides of travelers, transients, and new arrivals that entrepreneurs erected these large places of accommodation. There they provided lodging, food, and drink on an unprecedented scale. These establishments were as different from the inns of the eighteenth century as the steamboat was from the flatboat.

According to historian Doris Elizabeth King, "the new hotels were so obviously 'public' and 'democratic' in their character that foreigners were often to describe them as a true reflection of American society." Their very existence showed that many people, white males in particular, were on the move geographically and socially. Among the hotels' patrons were traveling salesmen, ambitious young men seeking to establish themselves in a new city, and restless pursuers of "the main chance" (unexpected economic opportunities) who were not yet ready to put down roots.

Hotel managers shocked European visitors by failing to enforce traditional social distinctions among their clientele. Under the "American plan," guests were required to pay for their meals and to eat at a common "table d'hôte" with anyone who happened to be there, including servants traveling with their employers. Ability to pay was the only requirement for admission (unless one happened to be an unescorted woman or dark-skinned), and every white male patron, regardless of social background and occupation, enjoyed the kind of personal service previously available only to a privileged class. Many patrons experienced such amenities as gaslight, indoor plumbing, and steam heat for the first time in their lives. Because a large proportion of the American population stayed in hotels at one time or another—a privilege that was, in Europe, reserved for the elite—foreigners inferred that there was widespread prosperity and a much greater "equality of condition" than existed in Europe.

*New York's Astor House, completed in 1836, was one of the grandest of the new American hotels, offering fine accommodations to travelers who could afford to pay for them.* ❖

THE HOTEL CULTURE REVEALED some of the limitations of the new era of democratic ideals and aspirations. African Americans, Native Americans, and women were excluded or discriminated against, just as they were denied suffrage at a time when it was being extended to all white males. The genuinely poor—of whom there were more than met the eye of most European visitors—simply could not afford to patronize the hotels and were consigned to squalid rooming houses. If the social equality *within* the hotel reflected a decline in traditional status distinctions, the broad gulf between potential patrons and those who could not pay the rates signaled the growth of inequality based squarely on wealth rather than inherited status.

The hotel life also reflected the emergence of democratic politics. Professional politicians of a new breed, pursuing the votes of a mass electorate, spent much of their time in hotels as they traveled about. Those elected to Congress or a state legislature often stayed in hotels during the session, and the political deals and bargains required for effective party organization or legislative success were sometimes concluded in these establishments.

The hotel can thus be seen as a fitting symbol for the democratic spirit of the age, one that shows its limitations as well as its strengths. The new democracy was first of all political, involving the extension of suffrage to virtually all white males and the rise of modern political parties appealing to a mass electorate. It was also social in that it undermined the habit of deferring to people because of their birth or ancestry and offered a greater expectation that individuals born in relatively humble circumstances could climb the ladder of success. But the ideals of equal citizenship and opportunity did not extend across the lines of race and gender, which actually hardened to some degree during this period.

## DEMOCRACY IN THEORY AND PRACTICE

During the 1820s and 1830s, the term *democracy* first became a generally accepted term to describe how American institutions were supposed to work. The Founders had defined democracy as direct rule by the people; most of them rejected this concept of a democratic approach to government because it was at odds with their conception of a well-balanced republic led by a "natural aristocracy." For champions of popular government in the Jacksonian period, however, the people were truly sovereign and could do no wrong. "The voice of the people is the voice of God" was their clearest expression of this principle. Conservatives were less certain of the wisdom of the common folk. But even they were coming to recognize that public opinion had to be won over before major policy decisions could be made.

Besides evoking a heightened sense of "popular sovereignty," the democratic impulse seemed to stimulate a process of social leveling. Earlier Americans had usually assumed that the rich and wellborn should be treated with special respect and recognized as natural leaders of the community and guardians of its culture and values. By the 1830s, the disappearance of inherited social ranks and clearly defined aristocracies or privileged groups struck European visitors such as Alexis de Tocqueville as the most radical feature of democracy in America. Historians have described this development as a decline of the spirit of "deference."

The decline of deference meant that "self-made men" of lowly origins could now rise more readily to positions of power and influence and that exclusiveness and aristocratic pretensions were likely to provoke popular hostility or scorn. But economic equality, in the sense of an equitable sharing of wealth, was not part of the mainstream agenda of the Jacksonian period. This was, after all, a competitive capitalist society. The watchword was equality of *opportunity,* not equality of *reward.* Life was a race, and so long as white males appeared to have an equal start, there could be no reason for complaint if some were winners and some were losers. Historians now generally agree that economic inequality—the gap between rich and poor Americans—was actually increasing during this period of political and social democratization.

## Democracy and Society

Although some types of inequality persisted or even grew during the age of democracy, they did so in the face of a growing belief that equality was the governing principle of American society. What this meant in practice was that no one could expect special privileges because of family connections. The plain folk, who in an earlier period would have known their place and deferred to their betters, were now likely to greet claims for special treatment with indifference or scorn. High-status Europeans who traveled in America were constantly affronted by democratic attitudes and manners. One aristocrat was rudely rebuffed when he tried to hire an entire stagecoach for himself and his valet. On other occasions, such blue-blooded tourists were forced to eat at the same table as teamsters and stagecoach drivers or share rooms in country inns with rough characters of all kinds. Another irritation to European visitors was the absence of special first-class accommodations on steamboats and railroads.

With the exception of slaveholders, wealthy Americans could not depend on a distinctive social class for domestic service. Instead of keeping "servants," they hired "help"—household workers who refused to wear livery, agreed to work for only short periods of time, and sometimes insisted on eating at the same table as their employers. As noted in the maid's comments quoted at the beginning of Chapter 8, no true American was willing to be considered a member of a servant class, and those who engaged in domestic work regarded it as a temporary stopgap. Except as a euphemistic substitute for the word *slave*, the term *servant* virtually disappeared from the American vocabulary.

The decline of distinctive modes of dress for upper and lower classes conveyed the principle of equality in yet another way. The elaborate periwigs and knee breeches worn by eighteenth-century gentlemen gave way to short hair and pantaloons, a style that was adopted by men of all social classes. Fashionable dress among women also ceased to be a sure index of gentility; serving girls on their day off wore the same kind of finery as the wives and daughters of the wealthy. Those with a good eye for detail might detect subtle differences in taste or in quality of materials, but the casual observer of crowds in a large city could easily conclude that all Americans belonged to a single social class.

Of course Americans were not all of one social class. In fact, inequality based on control of productive resources was increasing during the Jacksonian period. A growing percentage of the population, especially in urban areas, possessed no real estate and little other property. The rise of industrialization was creating a permanent class of low-paid, unorganized wage earners. In rural areas, there was a significant division between successful commercial farmers and smallholders, or tenants who subsisted on marginal land, as well as

**Village Tavern** *(1814) by John Lewis Krimmel. In the early republic, people gathered in taverns to catch up on news—both the local news exchanged with their neighbors and the national news printed in newspapers and often read aloud to the patrons.* ❖

enormous inequality of status between southern planters and their black slaves. But most foreign observers overlooked the widening gap between the propertied middle class and the laboring population; their attention was riveted on the fact that all white males were equal before the law and at the polls, a situation that was genuinely radical by European standards.

Traditional forms of privilege and elitism were also under strong attack, as evidenced by changes in the organization and status of the learned professions. Under Jacksonian pressure, state legislatures abolished the licensing requirements for physicians, previously administered by local medical societies. As a result, practitioners of unorthodox modes of healing were permitted to compete freely with established medical doctors. One popular therapy was Thomsonianism, a form of treatment based entirely on the use of common herbs and roots. Thomsonians argued that their own form of medicine would "make every man his own physician." The democratic tide also struck the legal profession. Local bar associations continued to set the qualifications for practicing attorneys, but in many places they lowered standards and admitted persons with little or no formal training and only the most rudimentary knowledge of the law.

For the clergy, "popular sovereignty" meant being increasingly under the thumb of the laity. The growing dependence of ministers on the support and approval of their congregations forced them to develop a more popular and emotional style of preaching. Ministers had ceased to command respect merely because of their office. To succeed in their calling, they had to please their public, in much the same way as a politician had to satisfy the electorate.

In this atmosphere of democratic leveling, the popular press came to play an increasingly important role as a source of information and opinion. Written and read by common folk, hundreds of newspapers and magazines ushered the mass of white Americans into the political arena. New political views—which in a previous generation might have been silenced by those in power—could now find an audience. Reformers of all kinds could easily publicize their causes, and the press became the venue for the great national debates on issues such as the government's role in banking and the status of slavery in new states and territories. As a profession, journalism was open to those who were literate and thought they had something to say. The editors of newspapers with a large circulation were the most influential opinion makers of the age.

## Democratic Culture

The democratic spirit also found expression in the rise of new forms of literature and art directed at a mass audience. The intentions of individual artists and writers varied considerably. Some sought success by pandering to popular taste in defiance of traditional standards of high culture. Others tried to capture the spirit of the age by portraying the everyday life of ordinary Americans rather than the traditional subjects of "aristocratic" art. A notable few hoped to use literature and art as a way of improving popular taste and instilling deeper moral and spiritual values. But all of them were aware that their audience was the broad citizenry of a democratic nation rather than a refined elite.

The romantic movement in literature, which came to the fore in the early nineteenth century in both Europe and America, valued strong feeling and mystical intuition over the calm rationality and appeal to common experience that had prevailed in the writing of the eighteenth century. Romanticism was not necessarily connected with democracy; in Europe, it sometimes went along with a reaffirmation of feudalism and the right of a superior few to rule over the masses. In the American setting, however, romanticism often appealed to the feelings and intuitions of ordinary people: the innate love of goodness, truth, and beauty that all people were thought to possess. Writers in search of popularity and economic success, however, often deserted the high plane of romantic art for crass sentimentalism—a willingness to pull out all emotional stops to thrill readers or bring tears to their eyes.

A mass market for popular literature was made possible by a rise in literacy and a revolution in the technology of printing. An increase in the number of potential readers and a decrease in publishing costs led to a flood of lurid and sentimental novels, some of which became the first American best-sellers. By the 1840s and 1850s, writers such as George Lippard, Mrs. E. D. E. N. Southworth, and Augusta Jane Evans had perfected the formulas that led to commercial success. Gothic horror and the perils of virtuous heroines threatened by dastardly villains were among the ingredients that readers came to expect from popular fiction. Lippard's *Quaker City* (1844) is a sensational tale of vice and corruption in Philadelphia. Southworth's *Hidden Hand* (1859) features an heiress who must go to extraordinary lengths to fend off villainous suitors. In one scene, which was extremely popular in the stage version, she disposes of the villain by springing a trap door conveniently located in her bedroom. Many of the new sentimental novels were written by and for women. Some women writers implicitly protested against their situation by portraying men in general as tyrannical, unreliable, or vicious and the women they abandoned or failed to support as resourceful individualists capable of making their own way in a man's world. But the standard happy endings sustained the convention that a woman's place was in the home, for a virtuous and protective man usually turned up and saved the heroine from independence.

In the theater, melodrama became the dominant genre. Despite religious objections, theater-going was a popular recreation in the cities during the Jacksonian era. The standard fare involved the inevitable trio of beleaguered heroine, mustachioed villain, and a hero who asserted himself in the nick of time. Patriotic comedies extolling the common sense of the rustic Yankee who foiled the foppish European aristocrat were also popular and served to arouse the democratic sympathies of the audience. Men and women of all classes went to the theater, and those in the cheap seats often behaved raucously and even violently when they did not like what they saw. Unpopular actors or plays could even provoke serious riots. In an 1849 incident in New York, 23 people were killed in disorders stemming from hostility toward an English actor who was the rival of Edwin Forrest, the most popular American thespian of the time.

The spirit of "popular sovereignty" expressed itself less dramatically in the visual arts, but its influence was felt nonetheless. Beginning in the 1830s, painters turned from portraying great events and famous people to depicting scenes from everyday life. Democratic genre painters such as William Sidney Mount and George Caleb Bingham captured the lives of plain folk with great skill and understanding. Mount, who painted lively rural scenes, expressed the credo of the democratic artist: "Paint pictures that will take with the public—never paint for the few but the many." Bingham was noted for his graphic images of Americans voting, carrying goods on riverboats, and engaging in other everyday activities.

Architecture and sculpture reflected the democratic spirit in a different way; they were viewed as civic art forms meant to glorify the achievements of the republic. In the 1820s and 1830s, the Greek style with its columned facades not only predominated in the architecture of public buildings but was also favored for banks, hotels, and private dwellings. Besides symbolizing an identification of the United States with the democracy of ancient Greece, it achieved monumental impressiveness at a fairly low cost. Even in newly settled frontier communities, it was relatively easy and inexpensive to put up a functional square building and then add a classical facade. Not everyone could live in structures that looked like Greek temples, but almost everyone could admire them from the outside or conduct business within their walls.

Sculpture was intended strictly for public admiration or inspiration, and its principal subjects were the heroes of the republic. The sculptors who accepted public commissions had to make sure their work met the expectations of politicians and taxpayers, who favored stately, idealized images. Horatio Greenough, the greatest sculptor of the pre–Civil War era, got into trouble when he unveiled a seated George Washington, dressed in classical garb and nude from the waist up. Much more acceptable was the equestrian figure of Andrew Jackson executed for the federal government by Clark Mills and unveiled in 1853.

*William Sidney Mount,* Rustic Dance After a Sleigh Ride, *1830. Mount's portrayals of country people folk dancing, gambling, playing music, or horse trading were pieces that appealed strongly to contemporaries. Art historians have found much to praise in his use of architecture, particularly that of the common barn, to achieve striking compositional effects.* ❖

Kindred Spirits (1849) by Asher Durand, depicting William Cullen Bryant and Thomas Cole in Kaaterskill Clove. Durand was an artist of the Hudson River School, a group of landscape painters who worked mainly in the area of the Hudson River and Catskill Mountains. Although the artists were not a formally organized group, they did share a sense of wonder at the grandeur of the American landscape, and they devoted painstaking attention to the details of nature in their works. ❖

The great landscape painters of the period—Thomas Cole, Asher Durand, and Frederic Edwin Church—believed their representations of untamed nature would elevate popular taste and convey moral truths. The modern ideal of art for art's sake was utterly alien to the instructional spirit of mid-nineteenth-century American culture. The responsibility of the artist in a democratic society, it was generally assumed, was to contribute to the general welfare by encouraging virtue and proper sentiments. Only Edgar Allan Poe seemed to fit the European image of romantic genius, rebelling against middle-class pieties. But in his own way, Poe exploited the popular fascination with death in his verse and used the conventions of Gothic horror in his tales. The most original of the antebellum poets, Walt Whitman, sought to be a direct mouthpiece for the rising democratic spirit, but his abandonment of traditional verse forms and his freedom in dealing with the sexual side of human nature left him relatively isolated and unappreciated during his most creative years.

## Democratic Political Institutions

The supremacy of democracy was most obvious in the new politics of universal white manhood suffrage and mass political parties. By the 1820s, most states had removed the last remaining barriers to voting participation by all white males. This change was not as radical or controversial as it would be later in nineteenth-century Europe; ownership of land was so common in the United States that a general suffrage did not mean men without property became a voting majority.

Accompanying this broadening of the electorate was a rise in the proportion of public officials who were elected rather than appointed. More and more judges, as well as legislative and executive officeholders, were chosen by "the people." A new style of politicking developed. Politicians had to get out and campaign, demonstrating in their speeches on the stump that they could mirror the fears and concerns of the voters. Electoral politics began to assume a more festive and dramatic quality.

Skillful and farsighted politicians—such as Martin Van Buren in New York—began in the 1820s to build stable statewide political organizations out of what had been loosely organized factions. Before the rise of effective national parties, politicians created true party organizations on the state level by dispensing government jobs to friends and supporters, and by attacking rivals as enemies of popular aspirations. Earlier politicians had regarded parties as a threat to republican virtue and had embraced them only as a temporary expedient, but Van Buren regarded a permanent two-party system as essential to democratic government. In his opinion, parties were an effective check on the

What most impressed the public was that Mills had succeeded in balancing the horse on two legs.

Serious exponents of a higher culture and a more refined sensibility sought to reach the new public in the hope of enlightening or uplifting it. The "Brahmin poets" of New England—Henry Wadsworth Longfellow, James Russell Lowell, and Oliver Wendell Holmes—offered lofty sentiments and moral messages to a receptive middle class; Ralph Waldo Emerson carried his philosophy of spiritual self-reliance to lyceums and lecture halls across the country; and great novelists such as Nathaniel Hawthorne and Herman Melville experimented with the popular romantic genres. But Hawthorne and Melville failed to gain a large readership. The ironic and pessimistic view of life that pervaded their work clashed with the optimism of the age. For later generations of American critics, however, the works of Melville and Hawthorne became centerpieces of the American literary "renaissance" of the mid-nineteenth century. Hawthorne's The Scarlet Letter (1850) and Melville's Moby-Dick (1851) are now regarded as masterworks of American fiction.

temptation to abuse power, a tendency deeply planted in the human heart. The major breakthrough in American political thought during the 1820s and 1830s was the idea of a "loyal opposition," ready to capitalize politically on the mistakes or excesses of the "ins" without denying the right of the "ins" to act the same way when they became the "outs."

Changes in the method of nominating and electing a president fostered the growth of a two-party system on the national level. By 1828, presidential electors were chosen by popular vote rather than by state legislatures in all but two of the twenty-four states. The new need to mobilize grassroots voters behind particular candidates required national organization. Coalitions of state parties that could agree on a single standard-bearer gradually evolved into the great national parties of the Jacksonian era—the Democrats and the Whigs. When national nominating conventions made their appearance in 1831, candidate selection became a matter to be taken up by representative party assemblies, not congressional caucuses or ad hoc political alliances.

New political institutions and practices encouraged a great upsurge of popular interest and participation. In the presidential election of 1824, the proportion of adult white males voting was less than 27 percent. In 1828, it rose sharply to 55 percent; it held at that level for the elections of 1832 and 1836 and then shot up to 78 percent in 1840—the first election in which two fully organized national parties each nominated a single candidate and campaigned for their choices in every state in the Union.

## Economic Issues

Economic questions dominated the political controversies of the 1820s and 1830s. The Panic of 1819 and the subsequent depression heightened popular interest in government economic policy, first on the state and then on the national level. No one really knew how to solve the problems of a market economy that went through cycles of boom and bust, but many people thought they had the answer. Some, especially small farmers, favored a return to a simpler and more "honest" economy without banks, paper money, and the easy credit that encouraged speculation. Others, particularly emerging entrepreneurs, saw salvation in government aid and protection for venture capital. Entrepreneurs appealed to state governments for charters that granted special privileges to banks, transportation enterprises, and manufacturing corporations. Politicians attempted to respond to the conflicting views about the best way to restore and maintain prosperity. Out of the economic distress of the early 1820s came a rapid growth of state-level political activity and organization that foreshadowed the

rise of national parties, which would be organized around economic programs.

The party disputes that arose over corporations, tariffs, banks, and internal improvements involved more than the direct economic concerns of particular interest groups. The republican ideology of the revolutionary period survived in the form of widespread fears of conspiracy against American liberty and equality. Whenever any group appeared to be exerting decisive influence over public policy, people who did not identify with that group's aspirations were quick to charge its members with corruption and the unscrupulous pursuit of power.

The notion that the American experiment was a fragile one, constantly threatened by power-hungry conspirators, eventually took two principal forms. Jacksonians believed that "the money power" endangered the survival of republicanism; their opponents feared that populist politicians like Jackson himself—alleged "rabble-rousers"—would gull the electorate into ratifying high-handed and tyrannical actions contrary to the true interests of the nation.

An object of increasing concern for both sides was the role of the federal government. Should it take positive steps to foster economic growth, as the National Republicans and later the Whigs contended, or should it simply attempt to destroy what Jacksonians decried as "special privilege" or "corporate monopoly"? Almost everyone favored equality of opportunity, but there was serious disagreement over whether this goal could best be achieved by active government support of commerce and industry or by divorcing the government from the economy in the name of laissez-faire and free competition.

## Labor Radicalism and Equal Rights

For one group of dissenters, democracy took on a more radical meaning. Working men's parties and trade unions emerged in eastern cities during the late 1820s and early 1830s. Their leaders condemned the growing gap between the rich and the poor resulting from early industrialization and the growth of a market economy. They argued that an expansion of low-paying labor was putting working people under the dominance of their employers to such an extent that the American tradition of "equal rights" was in grave danger. Society, in their view, was divided between "producers"—laborers, artisans, farmers, and small-business owners who ran their own enterprises—and nonproducing "parasites"—bankers, speculators, and merchant capitalists. Working men's parties aimed to give the producers greater control over the fruits of their labor.

These radicals called for a number of reforms to achieve their goal of equal rights. Thomas Skidmore,

## A Voice from the People!

## Great Meeting in the Park!!

*Working men's parties of the late 1820s and 1830s sought to protect and defend workers and to improve working conditions. This poster called for workers to unite in protest over the conviction of union shoemakers for conspiracy.* ❖

a founder of the New York Working Men's party, advocated the abolition of inheritance and a redistribution of property. Champions of the rights of labor also demanded greatly extended and improved systems of public education. But education reform, however radical or extensive, could provide equal opportunities only to future generations. To relieve the plight of adult artisans and craftspeople at a time when their economic and social status was deteriorating, labor reformers and trade unionists experimented with cooperative production and called for a ten-hour workday, abolition of imprisonment for debt, and a currency system based exclusively on hard money so workers could no longer be paid in depreciated banknotes.

Philadelphia was an especially active center of labor politics and trade union activity. In 1827, the city's skilled artisans formed the Mechanics Union of Trade Associations, the nation's first metropolitan labor movement, and shortly thereafter launched the Working Men's party to compete in local elections. In 1834, fifty craft associations incorporated into the General Trades' Union of the City and County of Philadelphia, and within a year the union took the leading role in the first general strike in American history. The strike was successful in getting the ten-hour day accepted in most Philadelphia industries, but the

depression that began in 1837 destroyed the General Trades' Union and nullified most of its gains. The same pattern of temporary success and ultimate defeat was repeated in other major cities. Nevertheless, American labor had set a precedent for the use of mass action aimed at the achievement of better working conditions.

In the 1830s and 1840s, northern abolitionists and early proponents of women's rights made other efforts to extend the meaning and scope of democracy. But Jacksonian America was too permeated with racism and male chauvinism to give much heed to claims that the equal rights prescribed by the Declaration of Independence should be extended to blacks and women. Most of those who advocated democratization explicitly limited its application to white males, and in some ways, the civil and political status of blacks and women actually deteriorated during "the age of the common *man*." (See Chapter 12 for a discussion of these movements.)

## JACKSON AND THE POLITICS OF DEMOCRACY

The public figure who came to symbolize the triumph of democracy was Andrew Jackson, who came out a loser in the presidential election of 1824. His victory four years later, his actions as president, and the great political party that formed around him refashioned national politics in a more democratic mold. No wonder historians have called the spirit of the age **Jacksonian Democracy.**

### The Election of 1824 and J. Q. Adams's Administration

As Monroe's second term ended, the ruling Republican party was in disarray and could not agree on who should succeed to the presidency. The party's congressional caucus chose William Crawford of Georgia, an old-line Jeffersonian. But a majority of congressmen showed their disapproval of this outmoded method of nominating candidates by refusing to attend the caucus. Monroe himself favored John Quincy Adams of Massachusetts. This gave the New England statesman an important boost but did not discourage others from entering the contest. Supporters of Henry Clay and John C. Calhoun mounted campaigns for their favorites, and a group of local leaders in his home state of Tennessee tossed Jackson's hat into the ring.

Initially, Jackson was not given much of a chance. Unlike other aspirants, he had not played a conspicuous role in national politics; his sole claim to fame was as a military hero, and not even his original supporters believed this would be sufficient to catapult him into the White House. But after testing the waters, Calhoun withdrew and chose instead to run for vice president. Then Crawford suffered a debilitating stroke that weakened his chances. With one Southerner out of the race and another disabled, Jackson began to pick up support in slaveholding states. He also found favor among those in the North and West who were disenchanted with the economic nationalism of Clay and Adams.

In the election, Jackson won a plurality of the electoral votes, but he lacked the necessary majority. The contest was thrown into the House of Representatives, where the legislators were to choose from among the three top candidates. There Adams emerged victorious over Jackson and Crawford. Clay, who had just missed making the final three, provided the winning margin by persuading his supporters to vote for Adams. When Adams proceeded to appoint Clay as his secretary of state, the Jacksonians charged that a "corrupt bargain" had deprived their favorite of the presidency. Although there was no evidence that Clay had bartered votes for the promise of a high office, the charge was widely believed. As a result, Adams assumed office under a cloud of suspicion.

Adams had a difficult and frustrating presidency. The political winds were blowing against nationalistic programs, partly because the country was just recovering from a depression that many thought had been caused or exacerbated by federal banking and tariff policies. Adams refused to bow to public opinion and called for an expansion of federal activity.

## THE ELECTION OF 1824

| Candidate | Party | Popular Vote | Electoral Vote* |
|---|---|---|---|
| J. Q. Adams | No party designations | 113,122 | 84 |
| Jackson | | 151,271 | 99 |
| Clay | | 47,531 | 37 |
| Crawford | | 40,856 | 41 |

*No candidate received a majority of the electoral votes. Adams was elected by the House of Representatives.

Advocates of states' rights and a strict construction of the Constitution were aghast, and the opposition that developed in Congress turned the administration's domestic program into a pipe dream.

The new Congress elected in 1826 was clearly under the control of men hostile to the administration and favorable to the presidential aspirations of Andrew Jackson. The tariff issue was the main business on their agenda. Pressure for greater protection came not only from manufacturers but also from many farmers, especially wool and hemp growers, who would supply critical votes in the upcoming presidential election. The cotton-growing South—the only section where tariffs of all kinds were unpopular—was assumed to be safely in the general's camp regardless of his stand on the tariff. Therefore, promoters of Jackson's candidacy felt safe in supporting a high tariff to swing critical votes in Jackson's direction. Jackson himself had never categorically opposed protective tariffs so long as they were "judicious."

As it turned out, the resulting tariff law was anything but judicious. Congress had operated on a give-and-take principle, trying to provide something for everybody. Those favoring protection for farmers agreed to protection for manufacturers and vice versa. The substantial across-the-board increase in duties that resulted, however, angered southern free traders and became known as the **tariff of abominations.** Historians long erred in explaining the 1828 tariff as a complex Jacksonian plot that backfired; it was in fact an early example of how special-interest groups can achieve their goals in democratic politics by trading votes in the legislative bargaining process known as logrolling.

### Jackson Comes to Power

The campaign of 1828 actually began with Adams's election in 1824. Rallying around the charge of a corrupt bargain between Adams and Clay, Jackson's supporters began to organize on the state and local level with an eye to reversing the outcome of the election. By late 1827, a Jackson committee was functioning in virtually every county and important town or city in the

*When it was clear that he would not win the presidency in 1824, Henry Clay, shown here in an 1822 portrait by Charles Bird King, threw his support to John Quincy Adams.* ❖

## ❖ A Look at the Past ❖

### Portrait of Andrew Jackson

Andrew Jackson's presidency ushered in a more democratic era and his fashionable clothing reflects that spirit. By the early nineteenth century, plain, dark fabrics had become common for men's suits. No longer did wealthy men flaunt their financial success by wearing sumptuous, richly colored fabrics trimmed with gold and lace. As decent-quality, manufactured textiles and cheaper, ready-made clothing started to become available, fabric quality and fit became less likely to indicate expense. In short, distinctions in men's clothing lessened. The change from the elaborate and body-conscious fashions of the eighteenth century to the modest and somber styles of the nineteenth century suggests that other changes were underway in the culture as well. How do Jackson's clothes suggest an egalitarian society? Why did American men abandon elaborate, body-conscious fashions and adopt somber, concealing suits? In addition to becoming more democratic, in what other ways was the United States changing in the early nineteenth century, and how did changes in men's fashion reflect those changes?

nation. Influential state or regional leaders who had supported other candidates in 1824 now rallied behind the Tennessean to create a formidable coalition.

The most significant of these were Vice President Calhoun, who now spoke for the militant states' rights sentiment of the South; Senator Martin Van Buren, who dominated New York politics through the political machine known as the Albany Regency; and two Kentucky editors, Francis P. Blair and Amos Kendall, who worked

in the West to mobilize opposition to Henry Clay and his "American System," which advocated government encouragement of economic development through such measures as protective tariffs and federally funded internal improvements. As they prepared themselves for the canvass of 1828, these leaders and their many local followers laid the foundations for the first modern American political party—the Democrats. The fact that the Democratic party was founded to promote the cause of a particular presidential candidate revealed a central characteristic of the emerging two-party system. From this time on, according to historian Richard P. McCormick, national parties existed primarily "to engage in a contest for the presidency." Without this great prize, there would have been less incentive to create national organizations out of the parties and factions developing in the several states.

The election of 1828 saw the birth of a new era of mass democracy. The mighty effort on behalf of Jackson featured the widespread use of such electioneering techniques as huge public rallies, torchlight parades, and lavish barbecues or picnics paid for by the candidate's supporters. Many historians believe that the massive turnout at such events during much of the rest of the nineteenth century revealed a deeper popular engagement with politics than at other times in American history. But it is also possible, as others have argued, that it merely showed that politicians had learned that providing entertainment and treats could lure people to the polls. Personalities and mudslinging dominated the campaign of 1828. The Democratic party press and a legion of pamphleteers bombarded the public with vicious personal attacks on Adams and praise of "Old Hickory," as Jackson was called. The supporters of Adams responded in kind; they even sank to the level of accusing Jackson's wife, Rachel, of bigamy and adultery because she had unwittingly married Jackson before being officially divorced from her first husband. The Democrats then came up with the utterly false charge that Adams's wife was born out of wedlock!

What gave Jacksonians the edge was their success in portraying their candidate as an authentic man of the people, despite his substantial fortune in land and slaves. His backwoods upbringing, his record as a popular military hero and Indian fighter, and even his lack of education were touted as evidence that he was a true representative of the common people, especially the plain folk of the South and the West. In the words of one of his supporters, Jackson had "a judgment unclouded by the visionary speculations of the academician." Adams, according to Democratic propagandists, was the exact opposite—an overeducated aristocrat, more at home in the salon and the study than among plain people. Nature's nobleman was pitted against the aloof New England intellectual, and Adams never really had a chance.

Jackson won by a popular vote margin of 150,000 and by more than 2 to 1 in the electoral college. Clearly, Jackson's organization had been more effective and his popular appeal substantially greater. He had piled up massive majorities in the Deep South, but the voters elsewhere divided fairly evenly. Adams, in fact, won a majority of the electoral vote in the northern

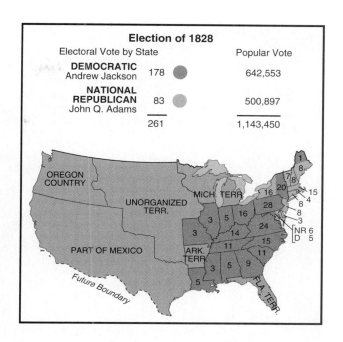

states. Furthermore, it was not clear what kind of mandate Jackson had won. Most of the politicians in his camp favored states' rights and limited government as against the nationalism of Adams and Clay, but the general himself had never taken a clear public stand on such issues as banks, tariffs, and internal improvements. He did, however, stand for the removal of Indians from the Gulf states, and this was a key to his immense popularity in that region.

Jackson turned out to be one of the most forceful and domineering of American presidents. His most striking character traits were an indomitable will, an intolerance of opposition, and a prickly pride that would not permit him to forgive or forget an insult or supposed act of betrayal. It is sometimes hard to determine whether his political actions were motivated by principle or personal spite. As a young man on his own in a frontier environment, he had learned to fight his own battles. Somewhat violent in temper and action, he fought a number of duels and served in wars against the British, the Spanish, and the Indians with a zeal his critics found excessive. His experiences had made him tough and resourceful but had also deprived him of the flexibility normally associated with successful politicians. Yet he generally got what he wanted.

Jackson's presidency commenced with his open endorsement of rotation of officeholders or what his critics called "the spoils system." Although he did not actually depart radically from his predecessors in the extent to which he removed federal officeholders and replaced them with his supporters, he was the first president to defend this practice as a legitimate application of democratic doctrine. He proclaimed in his

*Jackson's resigning cabinet members were, according to this cartoon, rats deserting a crumbling house as Jackson tries to sweep them away with a broom. Vice President John Calhoun is depicted as a terrier menacing the Secretary of State Van Buren rat, who is kept from climbing the "Ladder of Political Preferment" by an eagle.* ❖

When he raised the issue of Mrs. Eaton's social status at a cabinet meeting, only Secretary of State Van Buren, a widower, supported his stand. This seemingly trivial incident led to the resignation of all but one of the cabinet members, and the president was able to begin again with a fresh slate. Although Van Buren resigned with the rest to promote a thorough reorganization, his loyalty was rewarded by his appointment as minister to England and strong prospects of future favor.

## Indian Removal

The first major policy question facing the Jackson administration concerned the fate of Native Americans. Jackson had long favored removing eastern Indians to lands beyond the Mississippi. In his military service on the southern frontier, he had been directly involved in persuading and coercing tribal groups to emigrate. Jackson's support of removal was no different from the policy of previous administrations. The only real issues to be determined were how rapidly and thoroughly the process should be carried out and by what means. At the time of Jackson's election, the states of Georgia, Alabama, and Mississippi, distressed by the federal government's failure to eliminate the substantial Indian enclaves remaining within their boundaries, were clamoring for quick action. Since Adams seemed to have dragged his feet on the issue, voters in these states turned overwhelmingly to Jackson, who promised to expel the Indians without delay.

The greatest obstacle to voluntary relocation was the Cherokee nation, which held lands in Georgia, Alabama, North Carolina, and Tennessee. The Cherokees refused to move. They had instituted a republican form of government for themselves, achieved literacy in their own language, and made considerable progress toward adopting a settled agrarian way of life similar to that of southern whites. The professed aim of the government's Indian policy was the "civilization" of the Indians, and the official reason given for removal was that this aim could not be accomplished in areas surrounded by white settlements, subject to demoralizing frontier influences. Missionaries and northeastern philanthropists argued

first annual message that "the duties of all public officers are . . . so plain and simple that men of intelligence may readily qualify themselves for their performance" and that "no man has any more intrinsic claim to office than another."

Midway through his first administration, Jackson completely reorganized his cabinet, replacing almost all of his original appointees. At the root of this upheaval was a growing feud between Jackson and Vice President Calhoun, but the incident that brought it to a head was the Peggy Eaton affair. Peggy O'Neale Eaton, the daughter of a Washington tavern owner, married Secretary of War John Eaton in 1829. Because of gossip about her moral character, the wives of other cabinet members refused to receive her socially. Jackson became her fervent champion, partly because he found the charges against her reminiscent of the slanders against his late wife, who had died in 1828.

that the Cherokees were a major exception and should be allowed to remain where they were.

The southern states disagreed. Immediately after Jackson's election, Georgia extended its state laws over the Cherokees. Before his inauguration, Alabama and Mississippi took similar action by asserting state authority over the tribes in their own states. This legislation defied provisions of the Constitution giving the federal government exclusive jurisdiction over Indian affairs and also violated specific treaties. As anticipated, Jackson quickly gave his endorsement to the state actions. His own attitude toward Indians was that they were children when they did the white man's bidding and savage beasts when they resisted. He was also keenly aware of his political debt to the land-hungry states of the South. Consequently, in his December 1829 message to Congress, he advocated a new and more coercive removal policy. He denied Cherokee autonomy, asserted the primacy of states' rights over Indian rights, and called for the speedy and thorough removal of all eastern Indians to designated areas beyond the Mississippi.

Early in 1830, the president's congressional supporters introduced a bill to implement this policy. The ensuing debate was vigorous and heated. Opponents took up the cause of the Cherokees in particular and charged that the president had defied the Constitution by removing federal protection from the southeastern tribes. But Jackson and his supporters were determined to ride roughshod over humanitarian or constitutional objections to Indian dispossession. With strong support from the South and the western border states, the removal bill passed the Senate by a vote of 28 to 19 and the House by the narrow margin of 102 to 97.

Jackson then moved quickly to conclude the necessary treaties, using the threat of unilateral state action to bludgeon the tribes into submission. In 1832,

*Sequoyah's invention of the Cherokee alphabet enabled thousands of Cherokees to read and write primers and newspapers published in their own language.* ❖

he condoned Georgia's defiance of a Supreme Court decision (*Worcester* v. *Georgia*) that denied the right of a state to extend its jurisdiction over tribal lands. By 1833, all the southeastern tribes except the Cherokees had agreed to evacuate their ancestral homes. A stubbornly resisting majority faction of the Cherokees held out until 1838 when military pressure forced them to march to Oklahoma. This trek—known as the **Trail of Tears**—was made under such harsh conditions that almost four thousand of approximately thirteen thousand marchers died on the

*Robert Lindneux,* The Trail of Tears *(1942). Cherokees, carrying their few possessions, are prodded along by U.S. soldiers on the Trail of Tears. Several thousand Native Americans died on the ruthless forced march from their homelands in the East to the newly established Indian Territory in Oklahoma.* ❖

**INDIAN REMOVAL**    *Because so many Native Americans, uprooted from their lands in the East, died on the forced march to Oklahoma, the route they followed became known as the Trail of Tears.* ✦
*Treaty signed in 1835 by a minority faction was met with defiance from the majority, but removal was forced in 1838.

way. The Cherokee removal exposed the prejudiced and greedy side of Jacksonian democracy.

## The Nullification Crisis

During the 1820s, Southerners became increasingly fearful of federal encroachment on the rights of the states. Behind this concern, in South Carolina at least, was a strengthened commitment to the preservation of slavery and a resulting anxiety about possible uses of federal power to strike at the "peculiar institution." Hoping to keep the explosive slavery issue out of the political limelight, South Carolinians seized on another genuine grievance—the protective tariff—as the issue on which to take their stand in favor of a state veto power over federal actions they viewed as contrary to their interests. As a staple-producing and exporting region, the South had sound economic reasons for favor-

ing free trade. Tariffs increased the prices that southern agriculturists paid for manufactured goods and threatened to undermine their foreign markets by inciting counterprotection. An economic crisis in the South Carolina upcountry during the 1820s made that state particularly receptive to extreme positions on the tariff and states' rights.

Vice President John C. Calhoun emerged as the leader of the states' rights insurgency in South Carolina, abandoning his earlier support of nationalism and the American system. After the passage of the tariff of abominations in 1828, the state legislature declared the new duties unconstitutional and endorsed a lengthy statement—written anonymously by Calhoun—that affirmed **nullification,** or the right of an individual state to set aside federal law. Calhoun supported Jackson in 1828 and planned to serve amicably as his vice president, expecting Jackson to support his native

*Vice President John C. Calhoun emerged as a champion of states' rights during the nullification crisis, when cartoons such as this example depicted the emaciated South burdened by tariffs while the North grew fat at the southerners' expense.* ❖

region on questions involving the tariff and states' rights. He also entertained hopes of succeeding Jackson as president.

Early in his administration, Jackson appeared well attuned to the southern slaveholding position on state versus federal authority. Besides acquiescing in Georgia's de facto nullification of federal treaties upholding Indian tribal rights, he vetoed a major internal improvements bill in 1830, invoking a strict construction of the Constitution to deny federal funds for the building of the Maysville Road in Kentucky.

In the meantime, however, a bitter personal feud developed between Jackson and Calhoun. The vice president and his wife were viewed by Jackson as prime movers in the ostracism of Peggy Eaton. Furthermore, evidence came to light that Calhoun, as secretary of war in Monroe's cabinet in 1818, had privately advocated punishing Jackson for his incursion into Florida. As Calhoun lost favor with Jackson, it became clear that Van Buren rather than the vice president would be Jackson's designated successor. The personal breach between Jackson and Calhoun colored and intensified their confrontation over nullification and the tariff.

The two men differed on matters of principle as well. Although generally a defender of states' rights and strict construction of the Constitution, Jackson opposed the theory of nullification as a threat to the survival of the Union. In his view, federal power should be held in check, but this did not mean the states were truly sovereign. His nationalism was that of a military man who had fought for the United States against foreign enemies, and he was not about to permit the nation's disintegration at the hands of domestic dissidents. The differences between Jackson and Calhoun came into the open at the Jefferson Day dinner in 1830, when Jackson offered the toast "Our Union: It must be preserved," to which Calhoun responded, "The Union. Next to Liberty, the most dear. May we always remember that it can only be preserved by distributing equally the benefits and the burdens of the Union."

In 1830 and 1831, the movement against the tariff gained strength in South Carolina. Calhoun openly took the lead, elaborating further on his view that states had the right to set aside federal laws. In 1832, Congress passed a new tariff that lowered the rates slightly but retained the principle of protection. Supporters of nullification argued that the new law simply demonstrated that no genuine relief could be expected from Washington. They then succeeded in persuading the South Carolina state legislature to call a special convention. When the convention met in November 1832, the members voted overwhelmingly to nullify the tariffs of 1828 and 1832 and to forbid the collection of customs duties within the state.

Jackson reacted with characteristic decisiveness. He alerted the secretary of war to prepare for possible military action, issued a proclamation denouncing nullification as a treasonous attack on the Union, and asked Congress to vote him the authority to use the army to enforce the tariff. At the same time, he sought to pacify the nullifiers somewhat by recommending a lower tariff. Congress responded by enacting the Force Bill—which gave the president the military powers he sought—and the compromise tariff of 1833. The latter was primarily the work of Jackson's political enemy Henry Clay, but the president signed it anyway. Faced with Jackson's clear intention to use force if necessary and somewhat appeased by the prospect of a lower tariff, South Carolina suspended the nullification ordinance in late January 1833 and formally rescinded it in March, after the new tariff had been enacted. To demonstrate that they had not conceded their constitutional position, the convention delegates concluded their deliberations by nullifying the Force Bill.

The nullification crisis revealed that South Carolinians would not tolerate any federal action that seemed contrary to their interests or raised doubts about the institution of slavery. The nullifiers' philosophy implied the right of secession as well as the right to declare laws of Congress null and void. As subsequent events would show, a fear of northern meddling with slavery was the main spur to the growth of a militant doctrine of state sovereignty in the South. At the time of the nullification crisis, the other slave states had not yet developed such strong anxieties about the future of the "peculiar institution" and had not embraced South Carolina's radical conception of state sovereignty. Jackson was himself a Southerner and a slaveholder, a man who detested abolitionists and everything they stood for. In general, he was a proslavery president; later he would use his executive power to stop antislavery literature from being carried by the U.S. mails.

Some farsighted southern loyalists, however, were alarmed by the Unionist doctrines that Jackson propounded in his proclamation against nullification. More strongly than any previous president, he had asserted that the federal government was supreme over the states and that the Union was indivisible. What was more, he had justified the use of force against states that denied federal authority.

## THE BANK WAR AND THE SECOND PARTY SYSTEM

Jackson's most important and controversial use of executive power was his successful attack on the Bank of the United States. The **Bank war** revealed some of the deepest concerns of Jackson and his supporters and dramatically expressed their concept of democracy. It also aroused intense opposition to the president and his policies, an opposition that crystallized in a new national party—the Whigs. The destruction of the Bank and the economic disruption that followed brought to the forefront the issue of the government's relationship to the nation's financial system. Differences on this question helped to sustain and strengthen the new two-party system.

### Mr. Biddle's Bank

The Bank of the United States had long been embroiled in public controversy. Its role in precipitating the Panic of 1819 by first extending credit freely and then suddenly calling in its loans had led many, especially in the South and the West, to blame the Bank for the subsequent depression. But after Nicholas Biddle took over the Bank's presidency in 1823, the institution regained public confidence. Biddle was an able manager who probably understood the mysteries of banking and currency better than any other American of his generation. A Philadelphia gentleman of broad culture, extensive education, and some political experience, his major faults were his arrogance and his vanity. He was inclined to rely too much on his own judgment and refused to admit his mistakes until it was too late to correct them. But his record prior to the confrontation with Jackson was a good one. In 1825 and again in 1828, he acted decisively to curb an overextension of credit by state banks and helped avert a recurrence of the boom-and-bust cycle.

The actual performance of the Bank was not the only target of criticism about it. Old-line Jeffersonians had always opposed it on principle, both because they viewed its establishment as unconstitutional and because it placed too much power in the hands of a small, privileged group. The Bank was a chartered monopoly, an essentially private corporation that performed public services in return for exclusive economic rights. "In 1828," according to historian Robert Remini, "the Bank was a financial colossus, entrenched in the nation's economy, possessing the means of draining specie from state banks at will and regulating the currency according to its own estimate of the nation's needs."

Because of its great influence, the Bank tended to be blamed for anything that went wrong with the economy. For those who had misgivings about the rise of the national market, the Bank epitomized the forces threatening the independence and prosperity of small producers. In an era of rising white men's democracy, an obvious and telling objection to the Bank was simply that it possessed great power and privilege without being under popular control.

## The Bank Veto and the Election of 1832

Jackson came into office with strong reservations about banking and paper money in general—in part as a result of his own brushes with bankruptcy after accepting promissory notes that depreciated in value. He also harbored suspicions that branches of the Bank of the United States had illicitly used their influence on behalf of his opponent in the presidential election. In his annual messages in 1829 and 1830, Jackson called on Congress to begin discussing "possible modification of a system which cannot continue to exist in its present form without . . . perpetual apprehensions and discontent on the part of the States and the People."

Biddle began to worry about the fate of the Bank's charter when it came up for renewal in 1836. At the same time, Jackson was listening to the advice of close friends and unofficial advisers—members of his "Kitchen Cabinet"—especially Amos Kendall and Francis P. Blair, who thought an attack on the Bank would provide a good party issue for the election of 1832. Biddle then made a fateful blunder. Panicked by the presidential messages and the anti-Bank oratory of congressional Jacksonians such as Senator Thomas Hart Benton of Missouri, he determined to seek recharter by Congress in 1832, four years ahead of schedule. Senator Henry Clay, leader of the antiadministration forces on Capitol Hill, encouraged this move because he was convinced that Jackson had chosen the unpopular side of the issue and would be embarrassed or even discredited by a congressional endorsement of the Bank.

The bill to recharter, which was introduced in the House and Senate in early 1832, aroused Jackson and unified his administration and party against renewal. The bill found many supporters in Congress, however. A number of legislators had received loans from the Bank, and the economy seemed to be prospering under the Bank's guidance. As a result, the bill to recharter passed Congress with ease.

The next move was Jackson's, and he made the most of the opportunity. He vetoed the bill and de-

fended his action with ringing statements of principle. After repeating his opinion that the Bank was unconstitutional, notwithstanding the Supreme Court's ruling on the issue, he went on to argue that it violated the fundamental rights of the people in a democratic society: "In the full enjoyment of the gifts of Heaven and the fruits of superior industry, economy, and virtue, every man is equally entitled to protection by law; but when the laws undertake to add to those natural and just advantages artificial distinctions, to grant . . . exclusive privileges, the humble members of society—the farmers, mechanics, and laborers—who have neither the time nor the means of securing like favors to themselves, have a right to complain of the injustice of their government." Government, he added, should "confine itself to equal protection."

Jackson thus called on the common people to join him in fighting the "monster" corporation. His veto message was the first ever to use more than strictly constitutional arguments and to deal directly with social and economic issues. Congressional attempts to override the veto failed, and Jackson resolved to take the entire issue to the people in the upcoming presidential election.

The 1832 election, the first in which candidates were chosen by national nominating conventions, pitted Jackson against Henry Clay, standard-bearer of the National Republicans. Although the Democrats did not adopt a formal platform, the party stood firmly behind Jackson in his opposition to rechartering the Bank. Clay and the National Republicans attempted to marshal the pro-Bank sentiment that was strong in many parts of the country. But Jackson won a great personal triumph, garnering 219 electoral votes to 49 for Clay. His share of the popular vote was not quite as high as it had been in 1828, but it was substantial enough to be interpreted as a mandate for continuing the war against the Bank.

## Killing the Bank

Not content with preventing the Bank from getting a new charter, the victorious Jackson now resolved to attack it directly by removing federal deposits from Biddle's vaults. Jackson told Van Buren, "The bank . . . is trying to kill me, but I will kill it." The Bank had indeed used all the political influence it could muster in an attempt to prevent Jackson's reelection, in an act of self-defense. Old Hickory regarded Biddle's actions as a personal attack, part of a devious plot to destroy the president's reputation and deny him the popular approval he deserved. Although he presided over the first modern American political party, Jackson did not really share Van Buren's belief in the

### THE ELECTION OF 1832

| Candidate | Party | Popular Vote | Electoral Vote |
|---|---|---|---|
| Jackson | Democratic | 701,780 | 219 |
| Clay | National Republican | 484,205 | 49 |
| Wirt | Anti-Masonic | 100,715 | |
| Floyd | Independent Democratic | * | 11 |

*Delegates chosen by South Carolina legislature

*Aided by Van Buren (center), Jackson wields his veto rod against the Bank of the United States, whose heads represent the directors of the state branches. Bank president Nicholas Biddle is wearing the top hat.* ❖

legitimacy of a competitive party system. In his view, his opponents were not merely wrong; they were evil and deserved to be destroyed. Furthermore, the election results convinced him that he was the people's chosen instrument in the struggle against corruption and privilege, the only man who could save the pure republicanism of Jefferson and the Founders from the "monster bank."

In order to remove the deposits from the Bank, Jackson had to overcome strong resistance in his own cabinet. When one secretary of the treasury refused to support the policy, he was shifted to another cabinet post. When a second balked at carrying out removal, he was replaced by Roger B. Taney, a Jackson loyalist and dedicated opponent of the Bank. Beginning in late September 1833, Taney ceased depositing government money in the Bank of the United States and began to withdraw the funds already there. Although Jackson had earlier suggested that the government keep its money in some kind of public bank, he had never worked out the details or made a specific proposal to Congress. The problem of how to dispose of the funds was therefore resolved by an ill-advised decision to place them in selected state banks. By the end of 1833, twenty-three state banks had been chosen as depositories. Opponents charged that the banks had been selected for political rather than fiscal reasons and dubbed them Jackson's "pet banks." Since Congress refused to approve administration proposals to regulate

the credit policies of these banks, Jackson's effort to shift to a hard-money economy was quickly nullified by the use the state banks made of the new deposits. They extended credit more recklessly than before and increased the amount of paper money in circulation.

The Bank of the United States counterattacked by calling in outstanding loans and instituting a policy of credit contraction that helped bring on an economic recession. Biddle hoped to win support for recharter by demonstrating that weakening the Bank's position would be disastrous for the economy. With some justification, the president's supporters accused Biddle of deliberately and unnecessarily causing economic distress out of personal resentment and a desire to maintain his unchecked powers and privileges. The Bank never regained its charter.

Strong opposition to Jackson's fiscal policies developed in Congress. Henry Clay and his supporters contended that the president had violated the Bank's charter and exceeded his constitutional authority when he removed the deposits. They eventually persuaded the Senate to approve a motion of censure. Jacksonians in the House were able to block such action, but the president was further humiliated when the Senate refused to confirm Taney as secretary of the treasury. Not all of the criticism and obstructionism can be attributed to sour grapes on the part of pro-Bank politicians. Some congressmen who originally defended Jackson's veto now became disenchanted with the president because they thought he had gone too far in asserting the powers of his office.

## The Emergence of the Whigs

The coalition that passed the censure resolution in the Senate provided the nucleus for a new national party—the **Whigs.** The leadership of the new party and a majority of its support came from National Republicans associated with Clay and New England ex-Federalists led by Senator Daniel Webster of Massachusetts. The Whigs also picked up critical support from southern proponents of states' rights who had been upset by Jackson's stand on nullification and then saw an unconstitutional abuse of power in his withdrawal of federal deposits from the Bank of the United States. Even Calhoun and his nullifiers occasionally cooperated with the Whig camp. The initial rallying cry for this diverse anti-Jackson coalition was "executive usurpation." The Whig label was chosen because of its associations with both English and American revolutionary opposition to royal power and prerogatives. In their propaganda, the Whigs portrayed the tyrannical designs of "King Andrew" and his court.

The Whigs also gradually absorbed the Anti-Masonic party, a surprisingly strong political movement that had arisen in the northeastern states in the late 1820s and early 1830s. Capitalizing on the hysteria aroused by the 1826 disappearance and apparent murder of a New Yorker who had threatened to reveal the secrets of the Masonic order, the Anti-Masons exploited traditional American fears of secret societies and conspiracies. They also appealed successfully to the moral concerns of the northern middle class under the sway of an emerging evangelical Protestantism. Anti-Masons detested Jacksonianism mainly because it stood for a toleration of diverse lifestyles. Democrats did not think government should be concerned about people who drank, gambled, or found better things to do than go to church on Sundays. Their opponents from the Anti-Masonic tradition believed government should restrict such "sinful" behavior. This desire for moral and religious uniformity contributed an important cultural dimension to northern Whiggery.

As the election of 1836 approached, the government's fiscal policies also provoked a localized rebellion among the urban working-class elements of the Democratic coalition. In New York City, a dissident faction broke with the regular Democratic organization mainly over issues involving banking and currency. These radicals—called Loco-Focos after the matches they used for illumination when their opponents turned off the gaslights at a party meeting—favored a strict hard-money policy and condemned Jackson's transfer of federal deposits to the state banks

as inflationary. Because they wanted working people to be paid in specie rather than banknotes, the Loco-Focos went beyond opposition to the Bank of the United States and attacked state banks as well. Seeing no basis for cooperation with the Whigs, they established the independent Equal Rights party and nominated a separate state ticket for 1836.

Jackson himself had hard-money sentiments and regarded the "pet bank" solution as a stopgap measure rather than a final solution to the money problem. Somewhat reluctantly, he surrendered to congressional pressure in early 1836 and signed legislation allocating surplus federal revenues to the deposit banks, increasing their numbers, and weakening federal controls over them. The result was runaway inflation. State banks in the South and West responded to demands from land-speculating interests by issuing a new flood of paper money. Reacting somewhat belatedly to the speculative mania he had inadvertently helped to create, Jackson pricked the bubble on July 11, 1836. He issued his **specie circular,** requiring that after August 15 only gold and silver would be accepted in payment for public lands. The action served to curb inflation and land speculation but did so in such a sudden and drastic way that it helped precipitate the financial panic of 1837.

## The Rise and Fall of Van Buren

As his successor, Jackson chose Martin Van Buren, who had served him loyally as vice president during his second term. Van Buren was the greatest master of practical politics in the Democratic party, and the Democratic national convention of 1835 unanimously confirmed Jackson's choice. In accepting the nomination, Van Buren promised to "tread generally in the footsteps of General Jackson."

The newly created Whig party, reflecting the diversity of its constituency, did not try to decide on a single standard-bearer. Instead, each region chose candidates—Daniel Webster in the East, William Henry Harrison of Ohio (also the Anti-Masonic nominee) in the Old Northwest, and Hugh Lawson White of Tennessee (a former Jackson supporter) in the South. Whigs hoped to deprive Van Buren of enough electoral votes to throw the election into the House of Representatives where one of the Whigs might stand a chance.

The stratagem proved unsuccessful. Van Buren carried fifteen of the twenty-six states and won a clear majority in the electoral college. But the election foreshadowed future trouble for the Democrats, particularly in the South. There the Whigs ran virtually even, erasing the enormous majorities that Jackson had run up in 1828 and 1832. The emergence of a two-party system in the previously solid Deep South resulted

## THE ELECTION OF 1836

| Candidate | Party | Popular Vote | Electoral Vote |
|-----------|-------|-------------|---------------|
| Van Buren | Democratic | 764,176 | 170 |
| Harrison | Whig | 550,816 | 73 |
| White | Whig | 146,107 | 26 |
| Webster | Whig | 41,201 | 14 |
| Mangum | Independent Democratic | * | 11 |

*Delegates chosen by South Carolina legislature

from two factors—opposition to some of Jackson's policies and the image of Van Buren as an unreliable Yankee politician. The division did not reflect basic disagreement on the slavery issue. Southern Whigs and Democrats shared a commitment to protecting slavery, and each tried to persuade the electorate they could do the job better than the opposition.

As he took office, Van Buren was immediately faced with a catastrophic depression. The price of cotton fell by almost 50 percent, banks all over the nation suspended specie payments, many businesses went bankrupt, and unemployed persons demonstrated in several cities. The sale of public lands fell off so drastically that the federal surplus, earmarked in 1836 for distribution to the states, became a deficit.

The **Panic of 1837,** economic historians have concluded, was not exclusively, or even primarily, the result of government policies. It was in fact international in scope and reflected some complex changes in the world economy that were beyond the control of American policymakers. But the Whigs were quick to blame the state of the economy on Jacksonian finance, and the administration had to make a politically effective response. Since Van Buren and his party were committed to a policy of laissez-faire on the federal level, there was little or nothing they could do to relieve economic distress through subsidies or relief measures. But Van Buren could at least try to salvage the federal funds deposited in shaky state banks and devise a new system of public finance that would not contribute to future panics by fueling speculation and credit expansion.

Van Buren's solution was to establish a public depository for government funds with no connections whatsoever to commercial banking. His proposal for such an "independent subtreasury" aroused intense opposition from the congressional Whigs, who strongly favored the reestablishment of a national bank as the only way to restore economic stability. Whig resistance stalled the Independent Subtreasury Bill for three years; it was not until 1840 that it was enacted into law. In the meantime, the economy had temporarily revived in 1838, only to sink again into a deeper depression the following year.

Cartoon depicting the plight of tradesmen during the Panic of 1837, whose financial hardship the artist ascribes to Loco Foco politics supporting Van Buren's anti-federal bank policies and the effects of the specie circular, or "specie clause." The hungry children ask their unemployed and penniless father for some "specie claws" to eat. ❖

◆ A Look at the Past ◆

## Columbian Star Dishes

The election of 1840 set a new standard for political campaigns: exuberant and energetic. Rallies and parades awakened interest while a vast array of campaign paraphernalia maintained that interest. Whigs used log cabins to suggest that wealthy William Henry Harrison actually possessed a humble origin. Fabric, bandannas, sheet music, and ceramics came decorated with Whig campaign emblems. Dishes in the Columbian Star pattern, made in England, were available for purchase as individual pieces, entire sets, and even in miniature sizes. Why would consumers willingly, and sometimes eagerly, set their tables with pro-Whig dishes? What does that willingness reveal about the political culture of the time?

Van Buren's chances for reelection in 1840 were undoubtedly hurt by the state of the economy. The Whigs had the chance to offer alternative policies that promised to restore prosperity. In 1836, the Whigs had been disorganized and had not fully mastered the new democratic politics. But in 1840, they settled on a single nominee and matched the Democrats in grassroots organization and popular electioneering. The Whigs passed over the true leader of their party, Henry Clay. Instead they found their own Jackson in William Henry Harrison, a military hero of advanced age who was associated in the public mind with the battle of Tippecanoe and the winning of the West. To balance the ticket and increase its appeal in the South, they chose John Tyler of Virginia, a converted states' rights Democrat, to be Harrison's running mate.

Using the slogan "Tippecanoe and Tyler, too," the Whigs pulled out all stops in their bid for the White House. Rallies and parades were organized in every locality, complete with posters, placards, campaign hats and emblems, special songs, and even movable log cabins filled with coonskin caps and barrels of cider for the faithful. Imitating the Jacksonian propaganda

against Adams in 1828, they portrayed Van Buren as a luxury-loving aristocrat and compared him with their own homespun candidate. There was an enormous turnout on election day—78 percent of those eligible to vote. When it was over, Harrison had parlayed a narrow edge in the popular vote into a landslide in the electoral college. He carried 19 of the 26 states and won 234 electoral votes to 60 for Van Buren. Buoyed by the electorate's belief that their policies might revive the economy, the Whigs also won control of both houses of Congress.

Contrary to what most historians used to believe, personalities and hoopla did not decide the election of 1840. (See the Feature Essay, "Grassroots Democracy in Michigan," pp. 294–295.) The economy was in dire straits, and the Whigs, unlike the Democrats, had a program that seemed to offer hope for a solution—the latest version of Henry Clay's American System. Whigs proposed to revive the Bank of the United States in order to restore fiscal stability, raise tariffs to protect manufacturers and manufacturing jobs, and distribute federal revenues to the states for internal improvements that would stimulate

# GRASSROOTS DEMOCRACY IN MICHIGAN

The new popular politics of the Jacksonian era thrived on the local level. The electioneering and party competition found in Michigan was typical of the breadth and intensity of the democratic impulse. Democrats and Whigs alike could be deadly serious about their party affiliations, which rivaled their religious commitments as sources of identity and self-esteem.

In 1838, a Whig in western Michigan was invited to join the Democrats. "Sooner than vote the Democratic ticket," he reportedly replied, "I would crawl on my hands and knees from Battle Creek to Detroit, and be struck by lightning every other mile." A Democrat who confessed to having once voted the Whig ticket recalled that on the next day, goaded by his sins, he bought half a dozen candles and took them home "to light them and sit up and hate himself by them." Politics was very serious business for the common voter in the age of Jackson, full of important ritual; it was also the best show in town.

As did revivalist "camp meetings," political gatherings brought crowds and speakers into direct contact with the speakers working to entertain, inform, and convert the crowd. Between the first of July and the autumn election day, wandering political orators and local candidates would go from village to township, speaking to ready audiences on the topics of the day. An old tree stump or

Political candidates of the Jacksonian era traveled from town to town giving stump speeches. The political gatherings at which they spoke provided entertainment as well as an excellent source of political news. The sketch is by George Caleb Bingham, one of the most prolific of the democratic genre painters. ❖

"husting" would often be the only stage, leading citizens to call all small-town political orators "stump" speakers. These **hustings** visits would inform the voters of each party's stance on the issues of the day; before the era of the telegraph, stump speakers were the best source of political news.

Party workers organized parades and barbecues to boost the size and enthusiasm of the crowds. The parades would begin in the morning, at first informally as people arrived in groups from surrounding areas, and then with great pageantry, with brass bands and wagons full of farmers and artisans joining in. A Michigan college student in 1851 recalled a time eleven years earlier, in "those glorious days of Tippecanoe and Tyler, too," when a 9-year-old from Troy, Michigan, a boy who had earnestly declared himself a Whig, was seen "on the fourth of July of that eventful year, seated upon the reach of a double wagon 45 feet long, in company with some fifty others of his party, on his way to assist in the ceremonies of the day." The informant added that "our youthful politician, in his zeal, inflicted a severe castigation upon a young gentleman of about his age because he had the audacity to mar the solemnity of the occasion, by shouting for 'Young Hickory.'" The youthful Whig, it seems, had become "gloriously fuddled" by a combination of partisan spirit and hard cider.

Such festivities would lead into the speeches. Candidates for office would either speak on their own or debate their opponents. Before and after speaking, the politicians would mix with the crowd. A Michigan schoolteacher described a favorite politician "familiarly mingling among the

Democrats at their meetings, taking seat with them before the speaking began, and as one of them, talking freely on the subjects incident to the occasion. I used to think that here was where [he] got his power with the masses." That practice of elbow rubbing closed the distance between audience and speaker, between the leader and the led.

The audiences did their part to fill the gap, typically responding generously during the stump speech and filling the air with political songs between addresses. A conservative observer from Michigan noted in 1845 that prior to a typical political speech, the "miserable rabble" would greet the prospective speaker with "unmeaning and bacchanalian cries." The hurrahs of the audience (and songs with lyrics such as "Van, Van, he's a used-up man" and "The mustang colt has a killing pace / he's bound to win in the White House race") would inspire the orator. "It is well known that unless heartily cheered the 'stump orator' can do nothing," the sanctimonious onlooker continued. "It has therefore been supposed that in this kind of oratory the elements of eloquence are latently contained in cheers and are then conveyed through some unknown medium, perhaps animal magnetism, to the speaker."

Good stump speakers possessed a dramatic ability to communicate to the audience its own fears and concerns. The nearly mystic communication between speaker and hearer comes through in the following depiction of a Michigan Whig's eloquence and sincerity on the stump: "In whatever crowd or assembly he might be his mind would catch with marvelous facility the general tendency of the mind of the audience, and a chemical process, as it were, would take place within his mind. How could he fail then to force attention of those to whom he returned their own thoughts strengthened, broadened, and adorned with superb flights of eloquence."

In retrospect, these spectacular stump-speaking trips to where the voters lived helped to affirm the democratic nature of Jacksonian politics. Politicians in the era were typically far more educated and wealthy than their constituents, but they were supposed to represent faithfully the concerns of the common citizens. Mutual participation in the ritual of the hustings celebrated the people's significance in a manner that no far-away convention or latter-day press release could.

In a later era, popular politics would be less critical to a politician's election. The post–Civil War period was an era of stenography and the telegraph, of industrialism and class strife. Political speeches would be widely reported, and constituencies were more economically heterogeneous. Those conditions forced politicians to become far more cautious about what they would say, when, and to whom. To a large degree, the technology of the industrial age put an end to the stump speeches of Jacksonian America, and to a certain extent that same technology severed—for better or worse—the intimate bond between America's politicians and the rural electorate.

*County Election* by George Caleb Bingham portrays the variety of activities that occurred on election day. Some men cast their ballots, while others exchange their views or enjoy refreshments. Note the absence of women in the scene. ❖

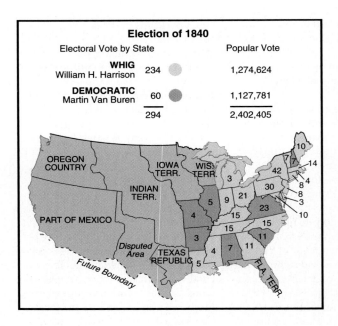

**Election of 1840**

| Electoral Vote by State | | Popular Vote |
| --- | --- | --- |
| **WHIG**<br>William H. Harrison | 234 | 1,274,624 |
| **DEMOCRATIC**<br>Martin Van Buren | 60 | 1,127,781 |
| | 294 | 2,402,405 |

commerce and employment. Whig victories in the state and local elections of 1840, many of which preceded the presidential vote, strongly suggest that voters were responding to the party and its program, not merely to the man who headed the ticket and to the Whigs' newfound skill at entertaining the electorate.

## HEYDAY OF THE SECOND PARTY SYSTEM

America's **second party system** came of age in the election of 1840. Unlike the earlier competition between Federalists and Jeffersonian Republicans, the rivalry of Democrats and Whigs made the two-party pattern a normal feature of electoral politics in the United States. During the 1840s, the two national parties competed on fairly equal terms for the support of the electorate. Allegiance to one party or the other became an important source of personal identity for many Americans and increased their interest and participation in politics.

In addition to drama and entertainment, the parties offered the voters a real choice of programs and ideologies. Whigs stood for a "positive liberal state"—which meant government had the right and duty to subsidize or protect enterprises that could contribute to general prosperity and economic growth. Democrats normally advocated a "negative liberal state." According to them, government should keep its hands off the economy; only by doing nothing could it avoid favoring special interests and interfering with free competition. They charged that granting subsidies

or special charters to any group would create pockets of privilege or monopoly and put ordinary citizens under the thumb of the rich and powerful.

Conflict over economic issues helped determine each party's base of support. In the Whig camp were industrialists who wanted tariff protection, merchants who favored internal improvements as a stimulus to commerce, and farmers and planters who had adapted successfully to a market economy. Democrats appealed mainly to smaller farmers, workers, declining gentry, and emerging entrepreneurs who were excluded from the established commercial groups that stood to benefit most from Whig programs. Democratic rhetoric about monopoly and privilege appealed to those who had mixed or negative feelings about the rise of a national market economy. To some extent, this division pitted richer, more privileged Americans against those who were poorer and less economically or socially secure. But it did not follow class lines in any simple or direct way. Many businessmen were Democrats, and large numbers of wage earners voted Whig. Merchants engaged in the import trade had no use for Whiggish high tariffs, whereas workers in industries clamoring for protection often concluded that their jobs depended on such duties.

Economic interest and ideology was not the only factor behind the choice of parties. Lifestyles and ethnic or religious identities strongly affected party loyalties during this period. In the northern states, one way to tell the typical Whig from the typical Democrat was to see what each did on Sunday. A person who went to one of the evangelical Protestant churches was very likely to be a Whig. On the other hand, the person who attended a ritualized service—Catholic, Lutheran, or Episcopalian—or did not go to church at all was most probably a Democrat.

The Democrats were the favored party of immigrants, Catholics, freethinkers, backwoods farmers, and those of all classes who enjoyed traditional amusements condemned by the new breed of moral reformers. One thing all these groups had in common was a desire to be left alone, free of restrictions on their freedom to think and behave as they liked. The Whigs enjoyed particularly strong support among Protestants of old stock living in smaller cities, towns, and prosperous rural areas devoted to market farming. In general, the Whigs welcomed a market economy but wanted to restrain the individualism and disorder it created by enforcing cultural and moral values derived from the Puritan tradition. Most of those who sought to be "their brothers' keepers" were Whigs. Some of the roots of party allegiance can be found in local divisions between old-stock Americans and immigrants over such matters as temperance, keeping the Sabbath, and reading the Protestant Bible in public schools.

## CHRONOLOGY

| 1824 | House of Representatives elects John Quincy Adams president |
| 1828 | Congress passes "tariff of abominations" ❖ Jackson elected president over J. Q. Adams |
| 1830 | Jackson vetoes the Maysville Road bill ❖ Congress passes Indian Removal Act |
| 1831 | Jackson reorganizes his cabinet ❖ First national nominating conventions meet |
| 1832 | Jackson vetoes the bill rechartering the Bank of the United States ❖ Jackson reelected, defeating Henry Clay (National Republican candidate) |
| 1832–1833 | Crisis erupts over South Carolina's attempt to nullify the tariff of 1832 |
| 1833 | Jackson removes federal deposits from the Bank of the United States |
| 1834 | Whig party comes into existence |
| 1836 | Jackson issues "specie circular" ❖ Martin Van Buren elected president |
| 1837 | Financial panic occurs, followed by depression lasting until 1843 |
| 1840 | Congress passes the Independent Sub-treasury Bill ❖ Harrison (Whig) defeats Van Buren (Democrat) for the presidency |

Nevertheless, party conflict in Congress continued to center on national economic policy. Whigs stood firm for a loose construction of the Constitution and federal support for business and economic development. The Democrats persisted in their defense of strict construction, states' rights, and laissez-faire. Debates over tariffs, banking, and internal improvements remained vital and vigorous during the 1840s.

True believers in both parties saw a deep ideological or moral meaning in the clash over economic issues. Whigs and Democrats had conflicting views of the good society, and their policy positions reflected these differences. The Democrats were the party of white male equality and personal liberty. They perceived the American people as a collection of independent and self-sufficient white men. The role of government was to see to it that the individual was not interfered with—in his economic activity, in his personal habits, and in his religion (or lack of it). Democrats were ambivalent about the rise of the market economy because of the ways it threatened individual independence. The Whigs, on the other hand, were the party of orderly progress under the guidance of an enlightened elite. They believed that the propertied, the well-educated, and the pi-

ous were responsible for guiding the masses toward the common good. Believing sincerely that a market economy would benefit everyone in the long run, they had no qualms about the rise of a commercial and industrial capitalism.

## CONCLUSION: TOCQUEVILLE'S WISDOM

The French traveler Alexis de Tocqueville, author of the most influential account ever written of the emergence of American democracy, visited the United States in 1831 and 1832. He departed well before the presidential election and had relatively little to say about national politics and the formation of political parties. For him, the essence of American democracy was local self-government, such as he observed in the town meetings of New England. The participation of ordinary citizens in the affairs of their communities impressed him greatly, and he praised Americans for not conceding their liberties to a centralized state, as he believed the French had done.

Despite his generally favorable view of the American experiment, Tocqueville was acutely aware of the limitations of American democracy. He knew that the kind of democracy men were practicing was not meant for women. Observing how women were strictly assigned to a separate domestic sphere, he concluded that Americans had never supposed "that democratic principles should undermine the husband's authority and make it doubtful who is in charge of the family." He also believed the nullification crisis foreshadowed destruction of the Union and predicted the problem of slavery would lead eventually to civil war and racial conflict. He noted the power of white supremacy, providing an unforgettable firsthand description of the sufferings of an Indian community in the course of forced migration to the West, as well as a graphic account of the way free blacks were segregated and driven from the polls in northern cities such as Philadelphia. White Americans, he believed, were deeply prejudiced against people of color, and he doubted it was possible "for a whole people to rise . . . above itself." Perhaps a despot could force the equality and mingling of the races, but "while American democracy remains at the head of affairs, no one would dare attempt any such thing, and it is possible to forsee that the freer the whites in America are, the more they will seek to isolate themselves." His observations have value because of their clear-sighted insistence that the democracy and equality of the Jacksonian era were meant for only some of the people. His belief that problems associated with slavery would endanger the union was keenly prophetic.

## RECOMMENDED READING

Arthur M. Schlesinger, Jr., *The Age of Jackson* (1945), sees Jacksonian democracy as a progressive protest against big business and stresses the participation of urban workers. Marvin Meyers, *The Jacksonian Persuasion: Politics and Belief* (1960), argues that Jacksonians appealed to nostalgia for an older America—"an idealized ancestral way" they believed was threatened by commercialization. Lee Benson, *The Concept of Jacksonian Democracy: New York as a Test Case* (1964), finds an ethnocultural basis for democratic allegiance. A sharply critical view of Jacksonian leadership— one that stresses opportunism, greed, and demagoguery— can be found in Edward Pessen, *Jacksonian America: Society, Personality, and Politics,* rev. ed. (1979). An excellent survey of Jacksonian politics is Harry L. Watson, *Liberty and Power* (1990), which stresses the crisis of "republicanism" at a time of "market revolution." Daniel Feller, *Jacksonian Promise: America, 1815–1840* (1995), focuses on the optimism that marked all sides of the political conflict and points to the similarities between the political parties. Development of the view that Jacksonianism was a negative reaction to the rise of market capitalism can be found in Charles Sellers, *The Market Revolution* (1991).

The classic study of the new party system is Richard P. McCormick, *The Second Party System: Party Formation in the Jacksonian Era* (1966). On who the anti-Jacksonians were, what they stood for, and what they accomplished, see Michael Holt's magisterial, *The Rise and Fall of the American Whig Party* (1999). James C. Curtis, *Andrew Jackson and the Search for Vindication* (1976), provides a good introduction to Jackson's career and personality. On Jackson's popular image, see John William Ward, *Andrew Jackson: Symbol for an Age* (1955). His Indian removal policy is the subject of Anthony F. C. Wallace, *The Long Bitter Trail: Andrew Jackson and the Indians* (1993). On the other towering political figures of the period, see Merrill D. Peterson, *The Great Triumvirate: Webster, Clay, and Calhoun* (1987). The culture of the period is well surveyed in Russel B. Nye, *Society and Culture in America, 1830–1860* (1960). Alexis de Tocqueville, *Democracy in America,* 2 vols. (1945), is a foreign visitor's wise and insightful analysis of American life in the 1830s.

On nullification, see William Freehling, *Prelude to Civil War: The Nullification Controversy in South Carolina, 1816–1836* (1966) and Richard B. Ellis, *The Union at Risk: Jacksonian Democracy, States' Rights, and the Nullification Crisis* (1987).

On the role of race in the formation of political parties and social divisions during this period, see David Roediger, *The Wages of Whiteness: Race and the Making of the American Working Class* (1991); Jean H. Baker, *Affairs of Party: The Political Culture of Northern Democrats in the Mid-Nineteenth Century* (1983); and Alexander Saxton, *The Rise and Fall of the White Republic: Class, Politics, and Mass Culture in Nineteenth-Century America* (1990).

**For a list of additional titles related to this chapter's topics, please see** http://www.ablongman.com/divine.

## SUGGESTED WEB SITES

### Indian Affairs: Laws and Treaties, compiled and edited by Charles J. Kappler (1904)

http://digital.library.okstate.edu/kappler
This digitized text at Oklahoma State University includes pre-removal treaties with the Five Civilized Tribes and other tribes.

### Medicine of Jacksonian America

http://www.connerprairie.org/historyonline/jmed.html
Survival was far from certain in the Jacksonian Era. This site discusses some of the reasons and some of the possible cures of the times.

### The University of Pennsylvania in 1830

http://www.archives.upenn.edu/histy/features/1830/
This "virtual tour" shows what a fairly typical campus looked like and what student life was like at one of the larger universities in the Antebellum Era.

### 19th Century Scientific American On-line

http://www.history.rochester.edu/Scientific_American/
Magazines and journals are windows through which we can view society. This site provides on-line editions of one of the more interesting nineteenth-century journals.

### National Museum of the American Indian

http://www.si.edu/nmai
The Smithsonian Institution maintains this site, providing information about the museum, which is dedicated to the history and culture of Native Americans.

### The Alexis de Tocqueville Tour: Exploring Democracy in America

http://www.tocqueville.org/
Text, images, and teaching suggestions are a part of this companion site to C-SPAN's programming on de Tocqueville.

A Ride for Liberty—The Fugitive Slaves *by Eastman Johnson depicts a slave family in flight to the North.* ❖

# Slaves and Masters

## *N*at Turner's Rebellion: A Turning Point in the Slave South

On August 22, 1831, the worst nightmare of southern slaveholders became reality. A group of slaves in Southampton County, Virginia, rose in open and bloody rebellion. Their leader was Nat Turner, a preacher and prophet who believed God had given him a sign that the time was ripe to strike for freedom; a vision of black and white angels wrestling in the sky had convinced him that divine wrath was about to be visited upon the white oppressor.

Beginning with a few followers and rallying others as he went along, Turner led his band from plantation to plantation and oversaw the killing of nearly sixty whites. The rebellion was short-lived; after only forty-eight hours, white forces dispersed the rampaging slaves. The rebels were then rounded up and executed, along with dozens of other slaves who were vaguely suspected of complicity. Nat Turner was the last to be captured, and he went to the gallows unrepentant, convinced he had acted in accordance with God's will.

After the initial panic and rumors of a wider insurrection had passed, white Southerners went about the grim business of making sure such an incident would never happen again. Their anxiety and determination were strengthened by the fact that 1831 also saw the emergence of a more militant northern abolitionism. Just two years after African American abolitionist David Walker published his *Appeal to the Colored Citizens of the World,* calling for blacks to take up arms against slavery, William Lloyd Garrison put out the first issue of his newspaper, *The Liberator,* the first publication by a white author to demand immediate abolition of slavery rather than gradual emancipation. Nat Turner and William Lloyd Garrison were viewed as two prongs of a revolutionary attack on the southern way of life. Although no evidence came to light that Turner was directly influenced by abolitionist propaganda, many whites believed that he must have been or that future rebels might be. Consequently, they launched a massive campaign to quarantine the slaves from possible exposure to antislavery ideas and attitudes.

A series of new laws severely restricted the rights of slaves to move about, assemble without white supervision, or learn to read and write. The wave of repression did not stop at the color line; laws and the threat of mob action prevented white dissenters from publicly criticizing or even questioning the institution of slavery. For the most part, the South became a closed society with a closed mind. Loyalty to the region was firmly identified with defense of it, and proslavery agitators sought to create a mood of crisis and danger requiring absolute unity and single-mindedness among the white population. This embattled attitude lay behind the growth of a more militant sectionalism and inspired threats to secede from the Union unless the South's peculiar institution could be made safe from northern or abolitionist attack.

THE CAMPAIGN FOR REPRESSION after the Nat Turner rebellion apparently achieved its original aim. Between 1831 and the Civil War, there were no further uprisings resulting in the mass killing of whites. This fact once led some historians to conclude that African American slaves were brainwashed into a state of docility. But

*This woodcut from 1831 titled* Horrid Massacre in Virginia *depicts scenes of Nat Turner's rebellion in Southampton County in which slaves who murdered white owners were driven by troops into hiding places in the woods. The slave revolt sparked a wave of repression against blacks in the South.* ❖

resistance to slavery simply took less dangerous forms than open revolt. The brute force employed in response to the Turner rebellion and the elaborate precautions taken against its recurrence provided slaves with a more realistic sense of the odds against direct confrontation with white power. As a result, they sought and perfected other methods of asserting their humanity and maintaining their self-esteem. The heroic effort to endure slavery without surrendering to it gave rise to an African American culture of lasting value.

This culture combined unique family arrangements, religious ideas of liberation, and creative responses to the oppression of servitude. Among white Southerners, the need to police and control the huge population of enslaved people influenced every aspect of daily life and produced an increasingly isolated, divided, and insecure society. While long-standing racial prejudice contributed to the divided society, the determination of whites to preserve the institution of slavery derived in large part from the important role slavery played in the southern economy.

## THE DIVIDED SOCIETY OF THE OLD SOUTH

Slavery would not have lasted as long as it did—and Southerners would not have reacted so strongly to real or imagined threats to its survival—if an influential class of whites had not had a vital and growing economic interest in this form of human exploitation. Since the early colonial period, forced labor had been considered essential to the South's plantation economy. In the period between the 1790s and the Civil

War, plantation agriculture expanded enormously, and so did dependence on slave labor; unfree blacks were the only workers readily available to landowners who sought to profit from expanding market opportunities by raising staple crops on a large scale. As slavery increased in its importance to the Southern economy and society, the divisions within that society grew increasingly apparent.

Most fundamentally, the fact that all whites were free and most blacks were slaves created a sharp cleavage between the races in Southern society.

Indeed, during the last decades before the Civil War, the racial divide grew ever more congruent with the split between free and unfree. Yet the overwhelming importance of race gives an impression of a basic equality within the "master race" that some would say is an illusion. The truth may lie somewhere in between. In the language of sociologists, inequality in the **Old South** was determined in two ways: by class (differences in status resulting from unequal access to wealth and productive resources) and by caste (inherited advantages or disadvantages associated with racial ancestry). Awareness of both systems of social ranking is necessary for an understanding of southern society.

White society was divided by class and by region; both were important for determining a white Southerner's relationship to the institution of slavery. More than any other factor, the ownership of slaves determined gradations of social prestige and influence among whites. The large planters were the dominant class, and nonslaveholders were of lower social rank. Planters (defined as those who owned twenty or more slaves) tended to live in the plantation areas of the "Cotton Belt" stretching from Georgia across Alabama, Mississippi, Louisiana, and Texas, as well as the low country of South Carolina. In upcountry and frontier areas lived yeoman farmers who owned few or no slaves.

In 1860, only one-quarter of all white Southerners belonged to families owning slaves. Even in the Cotton Belt, slaveholders were a minority of whites on the eve of the Civil War—about 40 percent. Planters were the minority of a minority, just 4 percent of the total white population of the South in 1860. Twenty percent of whites owned twenty slaves or less, and the remaining majority, three-fourths of all whites, owned no slaves at all. Thus, Southern society was dominated by a planter class that was a numerical and geographically isolated minority; inequalities of class became divisions of region as well.

There were also divisions within black society. Most African Americans in the South were slaves, but a small number, about 6 percent, were free. Even free blacks faced increasing restrictions on their rights during the antebellum era. Among slaves, the great majority lived on plantations and worked in agriculture, but a small number worked either in industrial jobs or in a variety of tasks in urban settings. Even on plantations, there were some differences in status and experience between field hands and servants who worked in the house or in skilled jobs such as carpentry or blacksmithing. Yet because all blacks, even those who were free, suffered under the yoke of racial prejudice and legal inequality, these diverse experiences did not translate into the kind of class divisions that caused rifts within white Southern society. Rather, most blacks shared the goal of ending slavery.

# THE WORLD OF SOUTHERN BLACKS

Most African Americans of the early to mid-nineteenth century experienced slavery on plantations; the majority of slaves lived on units owned by planters who had twenty or more slaves. On the other hand, only 2.4 percent lived on very large plantations of more than two-hundred slaves. Few slaves lived in all-black worlds like those of some Caribbean plantations, where it was possible to create autonomous black communities with little white intervention in daily life. In the South, most slaves lived in close contact with their masters and suffered their masters' strenuous efforts to maintain control over all aspects of their lives.

The masters of these agrarian communities sought to ensure their personal safety and the profitability of their enterprises by using all the means—physical and psychological—at their command to make slaves docile and obedient. By word and deed, they tried to convince the slaves that whites were superior and had a right to rule over blacks. Masters also drew constant attention to their awesome power and ability to deal harshly with rebels and malcontents. As increasing numbers of slaves were converted to Christianity and attended white-supervised services, they were forced to hear, over and over again, that God had commanded slaves to serve and obey their masters.

Despite these pressures, most African Americans managed to retain an inner sense of their own worth and dignity. When conditions were right, they openly asserted their desire for freedom and equality and showed their disdain for white claims that slavery was a positive good.

Some historians have argued that a stress on the strength of slave culture obscures the harshness and cruelty of the system and its damaging effect on the African American personality. Slavery was often a demoralizing and even brutalizing experience, and it provided little opportunity for learning about the world outside the plantation, developing mental skills, and exercising individual initiative. Compared with serfs in Russia or even with slaves on some of the large sugar plantations of the Caribbean, slaves on the relatively small southern plantations or farms, with their high turnover of personnel, had less chance to develop communal ties of the kind associated with peasant villages. Nevertheless, their sense of being part of a distinctive group with its own beliefs and ways of doing things, fragile and precarious though it may have been, made *psychic survival* possible and helped engender an

African American ethnicity that would be a source of strength in future struggles.

Although slave culture did not normally provoke violent resistance to the slaveholders' regime, the inner world that slaves made for themselves gave them the spiritual strength to thwart the masters' efforts to take over their hearts and minds. After emancipation, this resilient cultural heritage would combine with the tradition of open protest created by rebellious slaves and free black abolitionists to inspire and sustain new struggles for equality.

## Slaves' Daily Life and Labor

Slaves' daily life varied enormously depending on the region in which they lived and the type of plantation or farm on which they worked. By the time of the Civil War, 90 percent of the South's four million slaves worked on plantations or farms, with the remainder working in industry or in cities. Slaves were close to half of the total population in the "Black Belt" or "Cotton Belt" of the lower South—South Carolina, Georgia, Alabama, Mississippi, Louisiana, Arkansas, and Texas—and many lived in plantation regions with a slave majority. In the upper South—North Carolina, Virginia, Maryland, Delaware, Kentucky, Tennessee, and Missouri—whites outnumbered slaves by more than three to one, and slaves were far more likely to live on farms where they worked side by side with an owner.

On large plantations in the Cotton Belt, most slaves worked in "gangs" under an overseer. White overseers, sometimes helped by black "drivers," en-

*Although cotton cultivation required constant attention, many of the tasks involved were relatively simple. Thus on a plantation the majority of slaves, including women and children, were field hands who performed the same tasks. Here a slave family stands behind baskets of picked cotton in a Georgia cotton field.* ❖

forced a workday from sundown to sunup, six days a week. Cotton cultivation required year-round labor, so there was never a slack season under "King Cotton." Enslaved women and children were expected to work in the fields as well, often bringing babies and young children to the fields where they could be cared for by older children, and nursed by their mothers during brief breaks. Some older children worked in "trash gangs," doing lighter tasks such as weeding and yard cleaning. Life on the sugar plantations was even more harsh, sometimes entailing work well into the night during the harvest season. Mortality rates in some parts of sugar-growing Louisiana were very high.

Not all slaves in agriculture worked in gangs. In the low country of South Carolina and Georgia, slaves who cultivated rice worked under a "task system" that gave them more control over the pace of labor. With less supervision, many were able to complete their tasks within an eight-hour day. Likewise, slaves who lived on small farms often worked side by side with their masters rather than in large groups of slaves, although such intimacy did not necessarily mean a leveling of power relationships. Yet despite masters' efforts to control the pace of work, even under the gang system, slaves resisted working on "clock" time, enforcing customary rights to take breaks and especially to take Sunday off completely.

While about three-quarters of slaves were field workers, slaves performed many other kinds of labor. They dug ditches, built houses, worked on boats and in mills (often hired out by their masters for a year at a time), and labored as house servants, cooking, cleaning, and gardening. Some slaves also worked within the slave community as preachers, caretakers of children, and healers, especially women. While white masters sometimes treated domestic workers or other personal servants as having a special status, it would be a mistake to assume that their ranking system was shared by slaves. What evidence we have suggests that those with the highest status within slave communities were preachers and healers, people whose special skills and knowledge directly benefited their communities.

A small number of slaves, about 5 percent, worked in industry in the South. The closest thing to a factory in the Old South was the Tredegar Iron Works in Richmond, Virginia, staffed almost entirely by slaves. Slaves also built most of the railroads that existed in the Southern states, but these were few relative to the North before the Civil War. Overall, the South remained predominantly agricultural throughout the antebellum era, and most slaves worked in the fields.

Slaves in cities took on a wider range of jobs than plantation slaves, and in general enjoyed more autonomy. Some urban slaves even lived apart from their masters and hired out their own time, returning a por-

*The small number of slaves who were not employed in agriculture worked mainly in textile mills, ironworks, tobacco factories, and saltworks. In port cities, slaves might be dockworkers or longshoremen. The Tredegar Iron Works in Richmond, Virginia, was one of the South's largest industrial users of slave labor.* ❖

tion of their wages to their owners. They also worked in eating and drinking establishments, hotels, and as skilled laborers in tradesmen's shops.

In addition to the work they did for their masters in the fields or in other jobs, most slaves kept gardens or small farm plots for themselves to supplement their daily food rations. They also fished, hunted, and trapped animals. Many slaves also worked "overtime" for their own masters on Sundays or holidays in exchange for money or goods, or hired out their overtime hours to others. This "underground economy" suggests slaves' overpowering desire to provide for their families, sometimes even raising enough funds to purchase their freedom.

## Slave Families, Kinship, and Community

More than any other, the African American family was the institution that prevented slavery from becoming utterly demoralizing. Contrary to what historians and sociologists used to believe, slaves had a strong and abiding sense of family and kinship. But the nature of the families or households that predominated on particular plantations or farms varied according to local circumstances. On large plantations with relatively stable slave populations, a substantial majority of slave children lived in two-parent households, and many marriages lasted for as long as twenty to thirty years. They were more often broken up by the death or sale of one of the partners than by voluntary dissolution of the union. Here mothers, fathers, and children were

closely bonded, and parents shared child-rearing responsibilities (within the limits allowed by the masters). Marital fidelity was encouraged by masters who believed that stable unions produced more offspring and by Christian churches that viewed adultery and divorce as sinful.

But in areas where most slaves lived on farms or small plantations, and especially in areas of the upper South where the trading and hiring out of slaves was frequent, a different pattern seems to have prevailed. Under these circumstances, slaves frequently had spouses who resided on other plantations or farms, often some distance away, and ties between husbands and wives were looser and more fragile. The result was that female-headed families were the norm, and responsibility for child rearing was vested in mothers, assisted in most cases by female relatives and friends. Mother-centered families with weak conjugal ties were a natural response to the infrequent presence of fathers and to the prospect of their being moved or sold beyond visiting distance. Where the breakup of unions by sale or relocation could be expected at any time, it did not pay to invest all of one's emotions in a conjugal relationship. But whether the basic family form was nuclear or matrifocal (female-headed), the ties that it created were infinitely precious to its members. Masters acquired great leverage over the behavior of slaves by invoking the threat of family breakup through sale to enforce discipline.

The terrible anguish that usually accompanied the breakup of families through sale showed the depth of

*On large plantations, slave men and women formed stable monogamous unions that often lasted until the couple was broken up by the death or sale of one of the partners. This painting by Christian Mayr portrays a slave wedding celebrated in White Sulphur Springs, Virginia, in 1838. The wedding couple wears white attire.* ❖

kinship feelings. Masters knew that the first place to look for a fugitive was in the neighborhood of a family member who had been sold away. Indeed, many slaves tried to shape their own sales in order to be sold with family members or to the same neighborhood. These efforts were fraught with danger. As one ex-slave recalled, "The mistress asked her which she loved the best her mammy or her daddy and she thought it would please her daddy to say that she loved him the best so she said 'my daddy' but she regretted it very much when she found this caused her to be sold [along with her father] the next day."

After emancipation, thousands of freed slaves wandered about looking for spouses, children, or parents from whom they had been forcibly separated years before. Harriet Jacobs, an escaped slave famous for her published autobiography, hid in her grandmother's attic for seven years while attempting to secure her children's freedom. (For more on Harriet Jacobs, see the Feature Essay, "Harriet Jacobs and Maria Norcom: Women of Southern Households," pp. 314–315.) The famous spiritual "Sometimes I Feel Like a Motherless Child" was far more than an expression of religious need; it also reflected the family anxieties and personal tragedies of many slaves.

Feelings of kinship and mutual obligation extended beyond the primary family. Grandparents, uncles, aunts, and even cousins were often known to slaves through direct contact or family lore. A sense of family continuity over three or more generations was revealed in the names that slaves gave to their children or took for themselves. Infants were frequently named after grandparents, and those slaves who assumed surnames often chose that of an ancestor's owner rather than the family name of a current master.

Kinship ties were not limited to blood relations. When families were broken up by sale, individual members who found themselves on plantations far from home were likely to be "adopted" into new kinship networks. Orphans or children without responsible parents were quickly absorbed without prejudice into new families. Soon after the Civil War, one Reconstruction official faced an elderly ex-slave named Roger, who demanded land "to raise crop on" for his "family of sixty 'parents,' that is, relations, children included." A family with sixty parents made no sense to this official, but it made sense in a community in which families were defined by ties of affection and cooperation rather than "blood" relation.

What becomes apparent from studies of the slave family is that kinship provided a model for personal relationships and the basis for a sense of community. For some purposes, all the slaves on a plantation were in reality members of a single extended family, as their forms of address clearly reveal. Elderly slaves were addressed by everyone else as "uncle" and "aunty," and younger unrelated slaves commonly called each other "brother" or "sister." Slave culture was a family culture, and this was one of its greatest sources of strength and cohesion. Strong kinship ties, whether real or fictive, meant slaves

*Some slave families managed to stay together, as shown by the footnote to this 1835 bill of sale: "I did intend to leave Nancy['s] child but she made such a damned fuss I had to let her take it. . . ."* ❖

could depend on one another in times of trouble. The kinship network also provided a vehicle for the transmission of African American folk traditions from one generation to the next. Together with slave religion, kinship gave African Americans some sense that they were members of a community, not just a collection of individuals victimized by oppression.

## African American Religion

From the realm of culture and fundamental beliefs, African Americans drew the strength to hold their heads high and look beyond their immediate condition. Religion was the cornerstone of this emerging African American culture. Black Christianity may have owed its original existence to the efforts of white missionaries, but it was far from a mere imitation of white religious forms and beliefs. This distinctive variant of evangelical Protestantism incorporated elements of African religion and stressed those portions of the Bible that spoke to the aspirations of an enslaved people thirsting for freedom.

Most slaves did not encounter Christianity in a church setting. There were a few independent black churches in the antebellum South, which mainly served free blacks and urban slaves with indulgent masters. Free blacks who seceded from white congregations that discriminated against them formed a variety of

*Though many slave families were broken up by death or sale of members, some families, especially those on large, stable plantations, managed to stay together. This 1862 photograph by Timothy H. O'Sullivan shows five generations of a slave family, all born on the plantation of J. J. Smith in Beaufort, South Carolina.* ❖

autonomous Baptist groups as well as Southern branches of the highly successful **African Methodist Episcopal (AME) Church,** organized as a national denomination under the leadership of the Reverend Richard Allen of Philadelphia in 1816. But the mass of blacks did not have access to the independent churches.

Plantation slaves who were exposed to Christianity either attended the neighboring white churches or worshiped at home. On large estates, masters or white missionaries often conducted Sunday services. But the narratives and recollections of ex-slaves reveal that white-sanctioned religious activity was only a superficial part of the slaves' spiritual life. The true slave religion was practiced at night, often secretly, and was led by black preachers. Historian Albert J. Raboteau has described this underground black Christianity as "the invisible institution."

This covert slave religion was a highly emotional affair that featured singing, shouting, and dancing. In some ways, the atmosphere resembled a backwoods revival meeting. But much of what went on was actually an adaptation of African religious beliefs and customs. The chanting mode of preaching—with the congregation responding at regular intervals—and the expression of religious feelings through rhythmic movements, especially the counterclockwise movement known as the ring shout, were clearly African in origin. The black conversion experience was normally a state of ecstasy more akin to possession by spirits—a major form of African religious expression—than to the agony of those "struck down" at white revivals. The emphasis on sinfulness and fear of damnation that were core themes of white evangelicalism played a lesser role among blacks. For them, religion was more an affirmation of the joy of life than a rejection of worldly pleasures and temptations.

Slave sermons and religious songs spoke directly to the plight of a people in bondage and implicitly asserted their right to be free. The most popular of all biblical subjects was the deliverance of the children of Israel from slavery in Egypt. The book of Exodus provided more than its share of texts for sermons and images for songs. In one moving spiritual, God commands Moses to "tell Old Pharaoh" to "let my people Go." In another, Mary is told she can stop weeping and begin to rejoice because "Pharaoh's army got drownded" trying to cross the Red Sea. Many sermons and songs refer to the crossing of Jordan and the arrival in the Promised Land. "Oh Canaan, sweet Canaan, I am bound for the land of Canaan" and "Oh brothers, don't get weary. . . . We'll land on Canaan's shore" are typical of lines from spirituals known to have been sung by slaves. Other songs invoke the liberation theme in different ways. One recalls that Jesus had "set poor sinners free," and another prophesies, "We'll soon be free, when the Lord will call us home."

Most of the songs of freedom and deliverance can be interpreted as referring exclusively to religious salvation and the afterlife—and this was undoubtedly how slaves hoped their masters would understand them. But the slaves did not forget that God had once freed a people from slavery in this life and punished their masters. The Bible thus gave African Americans the hope that they, as a people, would repeat the experience of the Israelites and be delivered from bondage. During the Civil War, observers noted that freed slaves seemed to regard their emancipation as something that had been preordained, and some were inclined to view Lincoln as the reincarnation of Moses.

Besides being the basis for a deep-rooted hope for eventual freedom, religion helped the slaves endure bondage without losing their sense of inner

*John Antrobus,* Plantation Burial, *ca. 1860. The painting depicts slaves gathering in a forest to bury a fellow slave. Many spirituals sung by the slaves on such occasions portrayed death as a welcome release from bondage and created an image of an afterlife in which the trials and cares of this life were unknown.* ❖

worth. Unless their masters were unusually pious, religious slaves could regard themselves as superior to their owners. Some slaves even believed that all whites were damned because of their unjust treatment of blacks, while all slaves would be saved because any sins they committed were the involuntary result of their condition.

More important, the "invisible institution" of the church gave African Americans a chance to create and control a world of their own. Preachers, elders, and other leaders of slave congregations could acquire a sense of status within their own community that had not been conferred by whites; the singers who improvised the spirituals found an outlet for independent artistic expression. Although religion seldom inspired slaves to open rebellion, it must be regarded as a prime source of resistance to the dehumanizing effects of enslavement. It helped create a sense of community, solidarity, and self-esteem among slaves by giving them something of their own that they found infinitely precious.

## Resistance and Rebellion

Open rebellion, the bearing of arms against the oppressors by organized groups of slaves, was the most dramatic and clear-cut form of slave resistance. In the period between 1800 and 1831, a number of slaves participated in revolts that showed their willingness to risk their lives in a desperate bid for liberation. In 1800, a Virginia slave named Gabriel Prosser mobilized a large band of his fellows to march on Richmond. But a violent storm dispersed "Gabriel's army" and enabled whites to suppress the uprising without any loss of white life.

In 1811, several hundred Louisiana slaves marched on New Orleans brandishing guns, waving flags, and beating drums. It took three hundred soldiers of the U.S. Army, aided by armed planters and militiamen, to stop the advance and to end the rebellion. In 1822, whites in Charleston, South Carolina, uncovered an extensive and well-planned conspiracy, organized by a free black man named Denmark Vesey, to seize local armories, arm the slave population, and take possession of the city. Although the **Vesey conspiracy** was nipped in the bud, it convinced South Carolinians that blacks were "the Jacobins of the country [a reference to the militants of the French Revolution] against whom we should always be on guard."

Only a year after the Vesey affair, whites in Norfolk County, Virginia, complained of the activities of a marauding band of runaway slaves that had killed several whites. The militia was sent out and captured the alleged leader—a fugitive of several years' standing named Bob Ferebee. Groups of runaways, who hid for years in places such as the Great Dismal Swamp of Virginia, continued to raid plantations throughout the antebellum period and were inclined to fight to the death rather than be recaptured.

As we have already seen, the most bloody and terrifying of all slave revolts was the Nat Turner insurrection of 1831. Although it was the last slave rebellion of this kind during the pre–Civil War period, armed resistance had not ended. Indeed, the most sustained and successful effort of slaves to win their freedom by force of arms took place in Florida between 1835 and 1842, when hundreds of black fugitives fought in the Second Seminole War alongside the Indians who had given them a haven. The Seminoles were resisting removal to Oklahoma, but for the blacks who took part, the war was a struggle for their own freedom, and when it ended, most of them were allowed to accompany their Indian allies to the trans-Mississippi West.

Only a tiny fraction of all slaves ever took part in organized acts of violent resistance against white power. Most realized that the odds against a successful revolt were very high, and bitter experience had shown them that the usual outcome was death to the rebels. As a consequence, they characteristically devised safer or more ingenious ways to resist white dominance.

One way of protesting against slavery was to run away, and thousands of slaves showed their discontent and desire for freedom in this fashion. Most fugitives never got beyond the neighborhood of the plantation; after "lying out" for a time, they would return, often after negotiating immunity from punishment. But many escapees remained free for years by hiding in swamps or other remote areas, and a fraction made it to freedom in the North or Mexico. Some fugitives stowed away aboard ships heading to northern ports; others traveled overland for hundreds of miles, avoiding patrols and inquisitive whites by staying off the roads and moving only at night. Some were able to escape with the help of the **Underground Railroad,** an informal network of sympathetic free blacks (and a few whites) who helped fugitives make their way North. Light-skinned blacks sometimes made it to freedom by passing for white, and one resourceful slave even had himself packed in a box and shipped to the North.

The typical fugitive was a young, unmarried male from the upper South. For the majority of slaves, however, flight was not a real option. Either they lived too deep in the South to have any chance of reaching free soil, or they were reluctant to leave family and friends behind. Slaves who did not or could not leave the plantation had to register their opposition to the masters' regime while remaining under the yoke of bondage.

The normal way of expressing discontent was engaging in a kind of indirect or passive resistance. Many

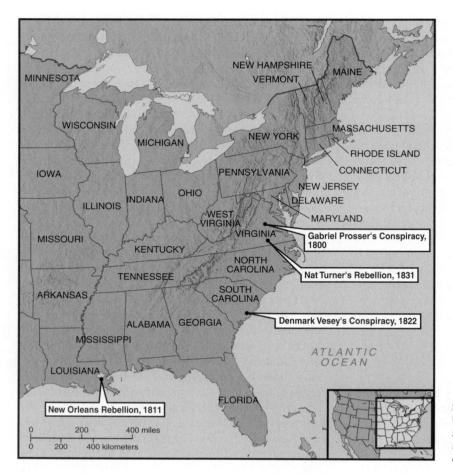

**SLAVE REBELLIONS AND UPRISINGS, 1800–1831**  *Although slave uprisings were infrequent, the fear that their slaves would rise up in rebellion was a constant worry for white slaveholders.* ❖

slaves worked slowly and inefficiently, not because they were naturally lazy (as whites supposed) but as a gesture of protest or alienation as conveyed in the words of a popular slave song, "You may think I'm working / But I ain't." Others withheld labor by feigning illness or injury. Stealing provisions—a very common activity on most plantations—was another way to show contempt for authority. According to the code of ethics prevailing in the slave quarters, theft from the master was no sin; it was simply a way for slaves to get a larger share of the fruits of their own labors.

Substantial numbers of slaves committed acts of sabotage. Tools and agricultural implements were deliberately broken, animals were willfully neglected or mistreated, and barns or other outbuildings were set afire. Often masters could not identify the culprits because slaves did not readily inform on one another. The ultimate act of clandestine resistance was poisoning the master's food. Some slaves, especially the "conjure" men and women who practiced a combination of folk medicine and witchcraft, knew how to mix rare, virtually untraceable poisons; and a suspiciously large num-

ber of plantation whites became suddenly and mysteriously ill. Sometimes whole families died from obscure "diseases" that did not infect the slave quarters.

The basic attitude behind such actions was revealed in the folktales that slaves passed down from generation to generation. The famous Brer Rabbit stories showed how a small, apparently defenseless animal could overcome a bigger and stronger one through cunning and deceit. Although these tales often had an African origin, they also served as an allegory for the black view of the master-slave relationship. Other stories—which were not told in front of whites—openly portrayed the slave as a clever trickster outwitting the master. In one such tale, a slave reports to his master that seven hogs have died of "malitis." Thinking this is a dread disease, the master agrees to let the slaves have all the meat. What really happened, so the story goes, was this: "One of the strongest Negroes got up early in the morning" and "skitted to the hog pen with a heavy mallet in his hand. When he tapped Mister Hog 'tween the eyes with that mallet, 'malitis' set in mighty quick."

*Henry "Box" Brown emerges from the crate in which he escaped from slavery in Richmond, Virginia, to freedom in Philadelphia.* ❖

## Free Blacks in the Old South

Southern society was shaped by the need to protect slavery. The attacks of abolitionists and the constant fear of slave revolt hardened the line that divided free whites from enslaved blacks. This intensification of the South into an even more sharply defined "slave society" threatened the status of all blacks who tried to live freely in the South.

Free blacks in the South were subject to a set of direct controls that tended to make them semi-slaves. Beginning in the 1830s, all of the Southern states passed a series of laws cracking down on free blacks, in part as a reaction to Nat Turner's rebellion. These laws forced free people of color to register or have white guardians who were responsible for their behavior. Invariably, free blacks were required to carry papers proving their free status, and in some states, they had to obtain official permission to move from one county to another. Licensing laws were invoked to exclude blacks from several occupations, and attempts by blacks to hold meetings or form organizations were frequently blocked by the authorities. Sometimes vagrancy and apprenticeship laws were used to force free blacks into a state of economic dependency barely distinguishable from outright slavery. Although beset by special problems of their own, most free blacks identified with the suffering of the slaves; when circumstances allowed, they protested against the peculiar institution and worked for its abolition. Many of them had once been slaves themselves or were the children of slaves; often

they had close relatives who were still in bondage. Furthermore, they knew that the discrimination from which they suffered was rooted in slavery and the racial attitudes that accompanied it. So long as slavery existed, their own rights were likely to be denied, and even their freedom was at risk; former slaves who could not prove they had been legally freed were subject to reenslavement. This threat existed even in the North: Under federal fugitive slave laws, escaped slaves could be returned to bondage. Even blacks who were born free were not perfectly safe. Kidnapping or fraudulent seizure by slave-catchers was always a possibility.

Because of the elaborate system of control and surveillance, free blacks in the South were in a relatively weak position to work against slavery. The case of Denmark Vesey showed that a prosperous and well-situated free black might make a stand in the struggle for freedom, but it also revealed the dangers of revolutionary activity and the odds against success. The wave of repression against the free black population that followed the Vesey conspiracy heightened the dangers and increased the odds. Consequently, most free blacks found that survival depended on creating the impression of loyalty to the planter regime. In some parts of the lower South, groups of relatively privileged free Negroes, mostly of racially mixed origin, were sometimes persuaded that it was to their advantage to preserve the status quo. As skilled artisans and small-business owners dependent on white favors and patronage, they had little incentive to risk everything by taking the side of the slaves. In southern Louisiana, there was even a small group of mulatto planters who lived in luxury, supported by the labor of other African Americans.

However, although some free blacks were able to create niches of relative freedom, their position in southern society became increasingly precarious in the late antebellum period. Beginning in the 1830s, Southern whites sought to draw the line between free and unfree more firmly as a line between black and white. Free blacks were an anomaly in this system; increasingly, the Southern answer was to exclude, degrade, and even enslave those free people of color who remained within their borders. Just before the outbreak of the Civil War, a campaign developed in some southern states to carry the pattern of repression and discrimination to its logical conclusion: Several state legislatures proposed laws giving free Negroes the choice of emigrating from the state or being enslaved.

# WHITE SOCIETY IN THE ANTEBELLUM SOUTH

Those who know the Old South only from modern novels, films, and television programs are likely to envision a land filled with majestic plantations. Pillared mansions behind oak-lined carriageways are portrayed as scenes of aristocratic splendor, where courtly gentlemen and elegant ladies, attended by hordes of uniformed black servants, lived in refined luxury. It is easy to conclude from such images that the typical white Southerner was an aristocrat who belonged to a family that owned large numbers of slaves.

The great houses existed—many of them can still be seen in places such as the low country of South Carolina and the lower Mississippi Valley—and some wealthy slaveholders did maintain as aristocratic a lifestyle as was ever seen in the United States. But census returns indicate that this was the world of only a small percentage of slaveowners and a minuscule portion of the total white population. The number of large planters who had the means to build great houses and entertain lavishly, those who owned at least fifty slaves, comprised fewer than 1 percent of all whites.

Most Southern whites were nonslaveholding yeoman farmers. Yet even those who owned no slaves grew to depend on slavery in other ways, whether economically, because they hired slaves, or psychologically, because having a degraded class of blacks below

them made them feel better about their own place in society. However, the class divisions between slaveholders and nonslaveholders did contribute to the political rifts that became increasingly apparent on the eve of the Civil War.

## The Planters' World

The great planters, although few in number, had a weighty influence on southern life. They set the tone and values for much of the rest of society, especially for the less wealthy slaveowners who sought to imitate the planters' style of living to the extent that resources allowed. Although many of them were too busy tending to their plantations to become openly involved in politics, wealthy planters held more than their share of high offices and often exerted a decisive influence on public policy. Within those regions of the South in which plantation agriculture predominated, they were a ruling class in every sense of the term. Contrary to legend, a majority of the great planters of the pre–Civil War period were self-made rather than descendants of the old colonial gentry. Some were ambitious young men who married planters' daughters. Others started as lawyers and used their fees and connections to acquire plantations.

As the Cotton Kingdom spread westward from South Carolina and Georgia to Alabama, Mississippi, and Louisiana, the men who became the largest slave-

*Painting by Adrien Persac depicting the back of a plantation house in Louisiana as seen from the bayou. Persac was commissioned to paint some of the great houses in the region, and in 1858 he published a map showing the plantations along the Mississippi River from Natchez to New Orleans.* ❖

holders were less and less likely to have come from old and well-established planter families. A large proportion of them began as hard-driving businessmen who built up capital from commerce, land speculation, banking, and even slave trading. They then used their profits to buy plantations. The highly competitive, boom-or-bust economy of the western Gulf states put a greater premium on sharp dealing and business skills than on genealogy. Stephen Duncan of Mississippi, probably the most prosperous cotton planter in the South during the 1850s (he owned eight plantations and 1018 slaves), had invested the profits from his banking operations. Among the largest sugar planters of southern Louisiana at this time were Maunsel White and John Burnside, Irish immigrants who had prospered as New Orleans merchants, and Isaac Franklin, former king of the slave traders.

To be successful, a planter had to be a shrewd entrepreneur who kept a careful eye on the market, the prices of slaves and land, and the extent of his indebtedness. Reliable "factors"—the agents who marketed the crop and provided advances against future sales—could assist him in making decisions, but a planter who failed to spend a good deal of time with his account books could end up in serious trouble. Managing the slaves and plantation production was also difficult and time-consuming, even when overseers were available to supervise day-to-day activities. Hence few planters could be the men of leisure featured in the popular image of the Old South.

Likewise, the responsibility of running an extended household that produced much of its own food and clothing kept plantation mistresses from being the idle ladies of legend. Despite typical images of women in the Old South—full hoop skirts and wide front porches, elaborate parties in plantation houses dripping with Spanish moss, elegant ladies gossiping over tea—few women fit the stereotype of the southern belle. Not only were plantation mistresses a tiny minority of the women who lived and worked in the slave states before the Civil War, but even those who were part of the planter elite rarely lived lives of leisure. (See the Feature Essay, "Harriet Jacobs and Maria Norcom: Women of Southern Households," pp. 314–315.) Some of the richest and most secure plantation families did aspire to live in the manner of a traditional landed aristocracy. A few were so successful that they were accepted as equals by visiting English nobility. Big houses, elegant carriages, fancy-dress balls, and excessive numbers of house servants all reflected aristocratic aspirations. The romantic cult of chivalry, described in the popular novels of Sir Walter Scott, was in vogue in some circles and even led to the nonviolent reenactment of medieval tournaments. Dueling, despite efforts to repress it, remained the standard way to settle "affairs of honor" among gen-

tlemen. Another sign of gentility was the tendency of planters' sons to avoid "trade" as a primary or secondary career in favor of law or the military. Planters' daughters were trained from girlhood to play the piano, speak French, dress in the latest fashions, and sparkle in the drawing room or on the dance floor. The aristocratic style originated among the older gentry of the seaboard slave states, but by the 1840s and 1850s it had spread southwest as a second generation of wealthy planters began to displace the rough-hewn pioneers of the Cotton Kingdom.

## Planters and Paternalism

No assessment of the planters' outlook or "worldview" can be made without considering their relations with their slaves. Planters, by the census definition, owned more than half of all the slaves in the South and set standards for treatment and management. It is clear from their private letters and journals, as well as from proslavery propaganda, that most planters liked to think of themselves as benevolent masters. Rather than seeing slavery as a brutal form of economic exploitation, they argued that blacks needed the slave system to ensure that they were cared for and protected. Often they referred to their slaves as if they were members of an extended patriarchal family—a favorite phrase was "our people." According to this ideology of paternalism, blacks were a race of perpetual children requiring constant care and supervision by superior whites. Paternalistic rhetoric increased greatly after abolitionists began to charge that most slaveholders were sadistic monsters.

While some historians have argued that paternalism was part of a social system that was organized like a family hierarchy rather than a brutal, profit-making arrangement, there was no inconsistency between planters' paternalism and capitalism. Slaves were themselves a form of capital; that is, they were both the main tools of production for a booming economy as well as an asset in themselves valuable for their rising prices, like shares in the stock market today. The ban on the transatlantic slave trade in 1808 was effective enough to make it economically necessary to the continuation of slavery for the slave population to reproduce itself. Rising slave prices also inhibited extreme physical abuse and deprivation. It was in the interest of masters to see that their slave property remained in good enough condition to work hard and produce large numbers of children. Furthermore, a good return on their investment enabled southern planters to spend more on slave maintenance than could masters in less prosperous plantation economies.

Much of the slaveholders' "paternalist" writing discussed "the coincidence of humanity and interest,"

# HARRIET JACOBS AND MARIA NORCOM

## Women of Southern Households

Harriet Jacobs, born enslaved in North Carolina in 1813, became a slave in James and Maria Norcom's household in 1825. James began to "whisper foul words" in Harriet's ears when she was a young teenager. Harriet had no one to whom she could turn, except for her free black grandmother, who lived in the town. Although her grandmother had been a slave, Harriet's master "dreaded her scorching rebukes" and furthermore "he did not wish to have his villainy made public." For a time, this wish to "keep up some outward show of decency" protected Harriet.

Harriet Jacobs's grandmother was an unusual woman, who had worked after hours for years to buy her children's freedom, only to be cheated out of her earnings at the end. Like most free black women, Harriet's grandmother was the unmarried head of her own household, separated long ago from the father of her children. Running their own households gave some free black women a measure of autonomy, but also left them with little support in the daily struggle against poverty and racism.

Maria Norcom, as the wife of a prominent doctor and large plantation owner, lived a life very different from Harriet's or her grandmother's. Yet it was not the life of carefree luxury sometimes portrayed in the magnolia-scented stereotypes of movies and books about the Old South. Compared to poorer women in the South, Maria had more access to education and periods of recreation and relaxation. But as a lady of the upper class, she was expected to master strict rules of womanhood that demanded moral purity and virtue. She also had to learn the personal and managerial skills necessary to oversee a household staffed by slaves.

Most southern white women worked hard to keep households and families together, and they all lived within a social system that denied them legal rights by placing them under the domination of husbands and fathers. James Norcom's behavior, while it certainly violated his vows of marriage, was not egregious enough to have won Maria a divorce under the laws of North Carolina.

Whether they were rich or poor, free or enslaved, women were, to a large degree, defined by their relationship to the head of the household, nearly always a white man. Although there were expectations that husbands would protect and care for their wives, women had little recourse against husbands who departed from those expectations. For example, Marion S.D. Converse, a woman from a prominent South Carolina family, dreaded her abusive second husband, Augustus. Through years of vicious beatings and jealous tirades, Marion was unable to escape the bonds of marriage because Augustus's deplorable conduct fell short of legal grounds for divorce in South Carolina (divorce was available only for abandonment or impotence). Yet Marion Converse was able to gain aid and protection from her prominent family, who shielded her from the worst consequences of an abusive marriage.

When Maria Norcom discovered her husband's overtures toward Harriet, she was distraught and took Harriet to sleep in her own room. Yet, as Harriet later described it, Maria "pitied herself as a martyr; but she was incapable of feeling for the condition of shame and misery in which her unfortunate, helpless slave was placed." Harriet often woke to find Maria bending over her, and came to fear for her safety around this "jealous mistress." Harriet Jacobs's and Maria Norcom's story illustrates that planters ruled their wives as well as their slaves. All southern women were embedded in a social system that gave authority over their lives and choices to men. Despite this commonality, few women were able to reach across the

## $100 REWARD

WILL be given for the apprehension and delivery of my Servant Girl HARRIET. She is a light mulatto, 21 years of age, about 5 feet 4 inches high, of a thick and corpulent habit, having on her head a thick covering of black hair that curls naturally, but which can be easily combed

Portion of a reward notice posted by James Norcom offering a reward for the return of runaway slave Harriet Jacobs. ❖

This 1836 engraving from an anti-slavery novel depicts a plantation mistress scolding a slave woman while the master looks on. Though white women were also subjugated to the authority of white men in southern society, the divide of race prevented plantation ladies and slaves from finding potential solidarity as women. ❖

ing a full day in the fields. Despite these brutal conditions, slave women organized communities and households, and tried to protect them against the worst excesses of the slave system. Harriet and her grandmother were involved in a complicated network of extended kin, and invested a great deal of energy in protecting brothers and sons from sale "up the river."

Harriet eventually escaped from the Norcoms in 1835, hiding in her grandmother's attic for seven years. Escaped from the bonds of slavery, Harriet eventually joined the battle to abolish it. Harriet's book, *Incidents in The Life of A Slave Girl, The Autobiography of Linda Brent*, was published in 1861, with the help of abolitionist novelist Lydia Maria Child. For many years, critics dismissed the narrative as either a work of fiction or the product of Child's own pen; but historians today have laid those charges to rest, recognizing Harriet Jacobs's important contribution to the struggle against slavery and to American literature.

We know much less about what happened to Maria Norcom, who neither kept a diary nor wrote her own story. All that we know is that she continued in her unhappy marriage to James Norcom. Her daughter Mary Matilda, when she came of age, pursued and attempted to reclaim Harriet as her slave under the Fugitive Slave Act. In order to thwart this effort, Harriet allowed an abolitionist friend to buy her and set her free.

In slaveholding households like that of the Norcoms, all the women, whether white or black, free or enslaved, were subject to the will of the master of the household. Most Southern women depended on white men legally and socially, giving them little recourse against men like James Norcom, who burst the bounds of "decency." Despite their shared submission to James, an impassable gulf separated Harriet and Maria, and its name was race. After the Civil War Southern women, white and black, reorganized their households in a changed society, but it would still be another century before they began to bridge that gulf.

divides of race and class to recognize these similarities. Tormented by jealousy and humiliation, Maria came to blame the slave rather than her husband for their intimacy, imagining that Harriet herself had seduced him.

Harriet managed to elude her master's advances, in part due to Maria's vigilance. Enslaved women such as Harriet Jacobs were the most vulnerable of Southern women. They were subject to a level of violence and sexual assault that was unknown to other women in the South; and when they were victims of violence they lacked even the limited legal defenses that were open to poor white women. Because black women were considered unable to give or withhold consent, it was not a crime to rape a black woman. And had Harriet fought back physically against her master's advances, she risked criminal prosecution and even death. For example, when the slave Celia killed the master who had been raping her for years, her court-appointed lawyer argued that she should not be crimi-

nally liable, based on a Georgia statute allowing women to use force to defend their "honor" against a rapist. The court, however, decreed that black women were not "women" within the meaning of the statute. Celia had no honor that the law recognized. She was thus convicted of murder, sentenced to death, and hanged.

Excluding black women from the laws of rape also reinforced common images of black women as either sexually aggressive "Jezebels" or sexless, nurturing "Mammies." The first stereotype justified the sexual exploitation of slave women and the second fed the slaveowners' fantasy that their slaves loved and cared for them. Of course, neither of these images corresponded to the realities and hardships of slave life. Enslaved women were often assigned backbreaking labor that paid little attention to common distinctions about "women's work." They were expected to do all of the normal tasks assigned to women—sewing, washing, child care—as well as work-

## ❖ A Look at the Past ❖

### Slave Clothing

Slaves typically received a yearly clothing allotment of one complete outfit and a pair of shoes. Slaves sometimes received cast-off clothing or lengths of decent fabric to make the year's new outfit, but generally they were given the cheapest fabric on the market, osnaburg, a coarse factory-woven cloth. While northern factories spun cotton and wove it into osnaburg for the southern market, men and women throughout New England earned extra money making brogans for slaves. Coarsely put together with soles pegged on rather than sewn, brogans were cheap and quick to make. How did slaves' clothing reinforce their position? What do northern fabric and shoes made especially for the slave market suggest about connections between slavery and the northern economy?

mate relationships with the mass of field slaves. The kind of affection and concern associated with a father figure appears to have been limited mainly to relationships with a few favored house servants or other elite slaves, such as drivers and highly skilled artisans. The field hands on large estates dealt mostly with overseers who were hired or fired because of their ability to meet production quotas.

The limits of paternalism were revealed in the slave market. Planters who looked down on slave traders as less than respectable gentlemen nevertheless broke apart families by selling slaves "down river" when they found themselves in need of money. Even slaveholders who claimed not to participate in the slave market themselves often mortgaged slaves to secure debts; as many as one-third of all slave sales in the South were court-ordered sheriff's auctions when such masters defaulted on their debts.

While paternalism may have moderated planters' behavior to some extent, especially when economic self-interest reinforced "humanity," it is important to remember that most departures from unremitting labor and harsh conditions were concessions wrested from owners through slaves' defiance and resistance, at great personal risk.

Furthermore, when they were being most realistic, planters conceded that the ultimate basis of their authority was the slaves' fear of force and intimidation, rather than the natural obedience resulting from a loving parent-child relationship. Scattered among their statements are admissions that they re-

by which they meant that treating slaves well (including firm discipline) was in their best economic interest. Thus, there was a grain of truth in the planters' claim that their slaves were relatively well provided for. Recent comparative studies have suggested that North American slaves of the pre–Civil War period enjoyed a somewhat higher standard of living than those in other New World slave societies, such as Brazil and the West Indian sugar islands. Their food, clothing, and shelter were normally sufficient to sustain life and labor at slightly above a bare subsistence level, and the rapid increase of the slave population in the Old South stands in sharp contrast to the usual failure of slave populations to reproduce themselves.

But some planters did not behave rationally. They failed to control their tempers or tried to work more slaves than they could afford to maintain. Consequently, there were more cases of physical abuse and undernourishment than a purely economic calculation would lead us to expect.

The testimony of slaves themselves and of some independent white observers suggests that masters of large plantations generally did not have close and inti-

*Not all slaves and masters had the benevolent relationship cited in defense of slavery. In fact, some masters devised various instruments of torture and punishment to control their slaves. For example, a slave fitted with this belled slave collar could not make a move without alerting the master.* ❖

lied on the "principle of fear," "more and more on the power of fear," or—most graphically—that it was necessary "to make them stand in fear." Devices for inspiring fear included whipping—a common practice on most plantations—and the threat of sale away from family and friends. Planters' manuals and instructions to overseers reveal that certain and swift punishment for any infraction of the rules or even for a surly attitude was the preferred method for maintaining order and productivity.

When some masters inevitably yielded to the temptations of power or to their bad tempers and tortured or killed their slaves or raped slave women, the slaves had little recourse. Slaves lacked legal protection against such abuse because their testimony was not accepted in court. Abolitionists were correct in condemning slavery on principle because it gave one human being nearly absolute power over another. This system was bound to result in atrocities and violence. Even Harriet Beecher Stowe acknowledged in *Uncle Tom's Cabin,* her celebrated antislavery novel of 1852, that most slaveholders were not as sadistic and brutish as Simon Legree. But—and this was her real point— there was something terribly wrong with an institution that made a Simon Legree possible.

## Small Slaveholders

As we have seen, 88 percent of all slaveholders in 1860 owned fewer than twenty slaves and thus were not planters in the usual sense of the term. Of these, the great majority had fewer than ten. Some of the small slaveholders were urban merchants or professional men who needed slaves only for domestic service, but more typical were farmers who used one or two slave families to ease the burden of their own labor. Relatively little is known about life on these small slaveholding farms; unlike the planters, the owners left few records behind. We do know that life was relatively spartan. Masters lived in log cabins or small frame cottages, and slaves lived in lofts or sheds that were not usually up to plantation housing standards.

For better or worse, relations between owners and their slaves were more intimate than on larger estates. Unlike planters, these farmers often worked in the fields alongside their slaves and sometimes ate at the same table or slept under the same roof. But such closeness did not necessarily result in better treatment. Slave testimony reveals that both the best and the worst of slavery could be found on these farms, depending on the character and disposition of the master. Given a choice, most slaves preferred to live on plantations because they offered the sociability, culture, and kinship of the slave quarters, as well as better prospects for adequate food, clothing, and

shelter. Marginal slaveholders often sank into poverty and were forced either to sell their slaves or give them short rations.

## Yeoman Farmers

Just below the small slaveholders on the social scale was a substantial class of **yeoman** farmers who owned land they worked themselves. Contrary to another myth about the Old South, most of these people did not fit the image of the degraded, shiftless poor white. Poor whites did exist, mainly as squatters on stretches of barren or sandy soil that no one else wanted. In parts of the South, a significant proportion of those working the land were tenants; some of these were "shiftless poor whites," but others were ambitious young men seeking to accumulate the capital to become landowners. The majority of the nonslaveholding rural population were proud, self-reliant farmers whose way of life did not differ markedly from that of family farmers in the Midwest during the early stages of settlement. If they were disadvantaged in comparison with farmers elsewhere in the United States, it was because the lack of economic development and urban growth perpetuated frontier conditions and denied them the opportunity to produce a substantial surplus for market.

The yeomen were mostly concentrated in the backcountry where slaves and plantations were rarely seen. In every southern state, there were hilly sections unsuitable for plantation agriculture. The foothills or interior valleys of the Appalachians and the Ozarks offered reasonably good soils for mixed farming, and long stretches of piney barrens along the Gulf Coast were suitable for raising livestock. In such regions slaveless farmers concentrated, giving rise to the "white counties" that complicated southern politics. A somewhat distinct group were the genuine mountaineers, who lived too high up to succeed at farming and relied heavily on hunting, lumbering, and distilling whiskey.

Yeoman women, much more than their wealthy counterparts, participated in every dimension of household labor. They worked in the garden, made handicrafts and clothing, and even labored in the fields when it was necessary. Women in the most dire economic circumstances even worked for wages in small businesses or on nearby farms. They also raised much larger families than their wealthier neighbors because having many children supplied a valuable labor pool for the family farm. Although yeoman farmers often recognized that their success was due to the help of their wives and daughters, they did not abandon the legal and cultural power they held as the heads of households.

*Carl G. Von Iwonski,* Block House, New Braunfels. *The majority of slaveholders in the South were not large plantation owners but small farmers of modest means who lived not in pillared mansions but in small, rough log cabins. Another substantial portion of Southerners were yeoman farmers who owned no slaves. Yet pervasive racism convinced most white Southerners they were entitled to own blacks, even if they had not yet acquired enough capital to afford slaves.* ❖

There were also a greater number of lower-class women who lived outside of male-headed households. Despite the pressures of respectability, there was a greater acceptance and sympathy in less affluent communities for women who bore illegitimate children or were abandoned by their husbands. Working women created a broader definition of "proper households" and navigated the challenges of holding families together in precarious economic conditions. The lack of transportation facilities, more than some failure of energy or character, limited the prosperity of the yeomen. A large part of their effort was devoted to growing subsistence crops, mainly corn. They raised a small percentage of the South's cotton and tobacco, but production was severely limited by the difficulty of marketing. Their main source of cash was livestock, especially hogs. Hogs could be walked to market over long distances, and massive droves from the back-country to urban markets were commonplace. But southern livestock, which was generally allowed to forage in the woods rather than being fattened on grain, was of poor quality and did not bring high prices or big profits to raisers.

Although they did not benefit directly from the peculiar institution, most yeomen and other nonslaveholders tolerated slavery and were fiercely opposed to abolitionism in any form. A few antislavery Southerners, most notably Hinton R. Helper of North Carolina, tried to convince the yeomen that they were victimized by planter dominance and should work for its overthrow. These dissenters presented a plausible set of arguments, emphasizing that slavery and the plantation system created a privileged class and severely limited the economic opportunities of the nonslaveholding white majority.

Most yeomen were staunch Jacksonians who resented aristocratic pretensions and feared concentrations of power and wealth in the hands of the few. When asked about the gentry, they commonly voiced their disdain of "cotton snobs" and rich planters generally. In state and local politics, they sometimes expressed such feelings by voting against planter interests on issues involving representation, banking, and internal improvements. Why, then, did they fail to respond to antislavery appeals that called on them to strike at the real source of planter power and privilege?

One reason was that some nonslaveholders hoped to get ahead in the world, and in the South this meant acquiring slaves of their own. Just enough of the more prosperous yeomen broke into the slaveholding classes to make this dream seem believable. Planters, anxious to ensure the loyalty of nonslaveholders, strenuously encouraged the notion that every white man was a potential master.

Even if they did not aspire to own slaves, white farmers often viewed black servitude as providing a guarantee of their own liberty and independence. A society that gave them the right to vote and the chance to be self-sufficient on land of their own encouraged the feeling they were fundamentally equal to the largest slaveholders. Although they had no natural love of planters and slavery, they believed—or could be induced to believe—that abolition would threaten their liberty and independence. In part, their anxieties were economic; freed slaves would compete with them for land or jobs. But an intense racism deepened their fears and made their opposition to black freedom implacable. "Now suppose they was free," a nonslaveholder told a northern traveler, "you see they'd think themselves just as good as we . . . just suppose you had a family of children, how would [you] like to hev a niggar feeling just as good as a white man? how'd you like to hev a niggar steppin' up to your darter?" Emancipation was unthinkable because it would remove the pride and status that automatically went along with a white skin in this acutely race-conscious society. Slavery, despite its drawbacks, served to keep blacks "in their place" and to make all whites, however poor and uneducated they might be, feel they were free and equal members of a master race.

## A Closed Mind and a Closed Society

Despite the tacit assent of most nonslaveholders, the dominant planters never lost their fear that lower-class whites would turn against slavery. They felt threatened from two sides: from the slave quarters where a new Nat Turner might be gathering his forces, and from the backcountry where yeomen and poor whites might heed the call of abolitionists and rise up against planter domination. Beginning in the 1830s, the ruling element tightened the screws of slavery and used their control of government and communications to create a mood of impending catastrophe designed to ensure that all southern whites were of a single mind on the slavery issue.

Before the 1830s, open discussion of the rights or wrongs of slavery had been possible in many parts of the South. Apologists commonly described the institution as "a necessary evil." In the upper South, as late as the 1820s, there had been significant support for the **American Colonization Society,** with its program of gradual voluntary emancipation accompanied by deportation of the freedmen. In 1831 and 1832—in the wake of the Nat Turner uprising—the Virginia state legislature debated a gradual emancipation plan. Major support for ensuring white safety by getting rid of both slavery and blacks came from representatives of the yeoman farmers living west of the Blue Ridge Mountains. But the defeat of the proposal effectively ended the discussion. The argument that slavery was "a positive good"—rather than an evil slated for gradual elimination—won the day.

The "positive good" defense of slavery was an answer to the abolitionist charge that the institution was inherently sinful. The message was carried in a host of books, pamphlets, and newspaper editorials published between the 1830s and the Civil War. Who, historians have asked, was it meant to persuade? Partly, the argument was aimed at the North, as a way of bolstering the strong current of antiabolitionist sentiment. But Southerners themselves were a prime target; the message was clearly calculated to resolve the kind of doubts and misgivings that had been freely expressed before the 1830s. Much of the message may have been over the heads of nonslaveholders, many of whom were semiliterate, but some of the arguments, in popularized form, were used to arouse racial anxieties that tended to neutralize antislavery sentiment among the lower classes.

The proslavery argument was based on three main propositions. The first and foremost was that enslavement was the natural and proper status for people of African descent. Blacks, it was alleged, were innately inferior to whites and suited only for slavery. Biased scientific and historical evidence was presented to support this claim. Second, slavery was held to be sanctioned by the Bible and Christianity—a position made necessary by the abolitionist appeal to Christian ethics. Ancient Hebrew slavery was held up as a divinely sanctioned model, and Saint Paul was quoted endlessly on the duty of servants to obey their masters. Southern churchmen took the lead in reconciling slavery with religion and also made renewed efforts to convert the slaves as a way of showing that enslavement could be a means for spreading the gospel.

Finally, efforts were made to show that slavery was consistent with the humanitarian spirit of the nineteenth century. The premise that blacks were naturally dependent led to the notion that they needed some kind of "family government" or special regime equivalent to the asylums that existed for the small numbers of whites who were also incapable of caring for themselves. The plantation allegedly provided such an environment, as benevolent masters guided and ruled this race of "perpetual children."

By the 1850s, the proslavery argument had gone beyond mere apology for the South and its peculiar institution and featured an ingenious attack on the free-labor system of the North. According to Virginian George Fitzhugh, the master-slave relationship was more humane than the one prevailing between employers and wage laborers in the North. Slaves had security against unemployment and a guarantee of care in old age, whereas free workers might face destitution and even starvation at any time. Worker insecurity in free societies led inevitably to strikes, bitter class conflicts, and the rise of socialism; slave societies, on the other hand, could more effectively protect property rights and maintain other traditional values because its laboring class was better treated and, at the same time, more firmly controlled.

In addition to arguing against the abolitionists, proslavery Southerners attempted to seal off their region from antislavery ideas and influences. Whites who were bold enough to criticize slavery publicly were mobbed or persecuted. One of the last and bravest of the southern abolitionists, Cassius M. Clay of Kentucky, armed himself with a brace of pistols when he gave speeches, until the threat of mob violence finally forced him across the Ohio River. In 1856, a University of North Carolina professor was fired because he admitted he would vote for the moderately antislavery Republican party if he had a chance. Clergymen who questioned the morality of slavery were driven from their pulpits, and northern travelers suspected of being abolitionist agents were tarred and feathered. When abolitionists tried to send their literature through the mails during the 1830s, it was seized in southern post offices and publicly burned.

Such flagrant denials of free speech and civil liberties were inspired in part by fears that nonslaveholding whites and slaves would get subversive ideas about slavery. Hinton R. Helper's book *The Impending Crisis*

*of the South,* an 1857 appeal to nonslaveholders to resist the planter regime, was suppressed with particular vigor; those found with copies were beaten up or even lynched. But the deepest fear was that slaves would hear the abolitionist talk or read antislavery literature and be inspired to rebel. Such anxieties rose to panic pitch after the Nat Turner rebellion. Consequently, new laws were passed making it a crime to teach slaves to read and write. Other repressive legislation aimed at slaves banned meetings unless a white man was present, severely restricted the activities of black preachers, and suppressed independent black churches. Free blacks, thought to be possible instigators of slave revolt, were denied basic civil liberties and were the object of growing surveillance and harassment.

All these efforts at thought control and internal security did not allay planters' fears of abolitionist subversion, lower-class white dissent, and, above all, slave revolt. The persistent barrage of proslavery propaganda and the course of national events in the 1850s created a mood of panic and desperation. By this time, an increasing number of Southerners had become

*This proslavery cartoon of 1841 contends that the slave in America had a better life than did the working-class white in England. Supposedly, the grateful slaves were clothed, fed, and cared for in their old age by kindly and sympathetic masters, while starving English workers were mercilessly exploited by factory owners.* ❖

convinced that safety from abolitionism and its associated terrors required a formal withdrawal from the Union—secession.

## SLAVERY AND THE SOUTHERN ECONOMY

Southern society transformed itself according to the needs of the slave system because slavery played such a crucial role in the economic life of the South. Despite the internal divisions of Southern society, white Southerners from all regions and classes came to perceive their interests tied up with slavery, whether because they owned slaves themselves or because they believed in slavery as essential to the "Southern way of life" or "white men's democracy." And because slavery was the cornerstone of the Southern economy, it affected white Southerners' attitudes toward landholding and toward industrialization.

For the most part, the expansion of slavery—the number of slaves in the South more than tripled between 1810 and 1860 to nearly 4 million—can be attributed to the rise of "King Cotton." The cotton-growing areas of the South were becoming more and more dependent on slavery, at the same time that agriculture in the upper South was actually moving away from the institution. Yet slavery continued to remain important to the economy of the upper South in a different way, through the slave trade. To understand Southern thought and behavior, it is necessary to bear in mind this major regional difference between a slave plantation society and a farming and slave-trading region.

### The Internal Slave Trade

Tobacco, the original plantation crop of the colonial period, continued to be the principal slave-cultivated commodity of the upper tier of southern states during the pre–Civil War era. But markets were often depressed, and profitable tobacco cultivation was hard to sustain for very long in one place because the crop rapidly depleted the soil. During the lengthy depression of the tobacco market that lasted from the 1820s to the 1850s, tobacco farmers in Virginia and Maryland experimented with fertilizer use, crop rotation, and diversified farming, all of which increased the need for capital but reduced the demand for labor.

As slave prices rose (because of high demand in the lower South) and demand for slaves in the upper South fell, the "internal" slave trade took off. Increasingly, the most profitable business for slaveholders in Virginia, Kentucky, Maryland, and the Carolinas was selling "surplus" slaves from the upper South to regions of the lower South, where staple crop production was more profitable. This interstate slave trade sent an estimated six- to seven-hundred-thousand slaves in a southwesterly direction between 1815 and 1860. Historian Michael Tadman estimates that the chances of a slave child in the Upper South in the 1820s to be "sold South" by 1860 was as high as 30 percent. Such sales were wrenching, not only splitting families, but making it especially unlikely that the slaves sold would ever see friends or family again.

Some economic historians have concluded that the most important crop produced in the tobacco kingdom was not the "stinking weed" but human beings cultivated for the auction block. Respectable planters did not like to think of themselves as raising slaves for market, but few would refuse to sell some of their "people" if they needed money to get out of debt or make expensive improvements. For the region as a whole, the slave trade provided a crucial source of capital in a period of transition and innovation.

**Lewis Miller,** Slave Sale, Virginia, *probably 1853. Slave auctions, such as the one depicted in this sketch from Lewis Miller's sketchbook, were an abomination and embarrassment to many Americans. To southern plantation owners dependent on slave labor, however, such activities were essential.* ❖

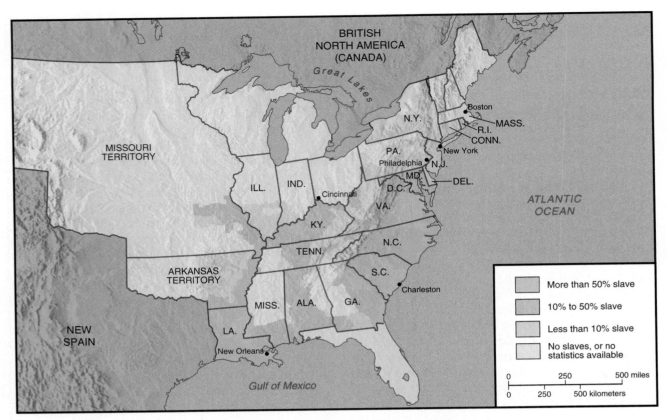

**SLAVE CONCENTRATION, 1820**   *In 1820, most slaves lived in the eastern seaboard states of Virginia and South Carolina and in Louisiana on the Gulf of Mexico.* ❖

Nevertheless, the fact that slave labor was declining in importance in the upper South meant the peculiar institution had a weaker hold on public loyalty there than in the cotton states. Diversification of agriculture was accompanied by a more rapid rate of urban and industrial development than was occurring elsewhere in the South. As a result, Virginians, Marylanders, and Kentuckians were seriously divided on whether their ultimate future lay with the Deep South's plantation economy or with the industrializing free-labor system that was flourishing just north of their borders.

## The Rise of the Cotton Kingdom

The warmer climate and good soils of the lower tier of southern states made it possible to raise crops more naturally suited than tobacco or cereals to the plantation form of agriculture and the heavy use of slave labor. Since the colonial or revolutionary periods, rice and a special long-staple variety of fine cotton had been grown profitably on vast estates along the coast of South Carolina and Georgia. In lower Louisiana, between New Orleans and Baton Rouge,

sugar was the cash crop. As in the West Indies, sugar production required a large investment and a great deal of backbreaking labor: in other words, large, well-financed plantations and small armies of slave laborers. Cultivation of rice, long-staple cotton, and sugar was limited by natural conditions to peripheral, semitropical areas. It was the rise of short-staple cotton as the South's major crop that strengthened the hold of slavery and the plantation on the southern economy.

Short-staple cotton differed from the long-staple variety in two important ways: Its bolls contained seeds that were much more difficult to extract by hand, and it could be grown almost anywhere south of Virginia and Kentucky—the main requirement was a guarantee of two hundred frost-free days. Before the 1790s, the seed extraction problem had prevented short-staple cotton from becoming a major market crop. The invention of the **cotton gin** in 1793 resolved that difficulty, however, and the subsequent westward expansion opened vast areas for cotton cultivation. Unlike rice and sugar, cotton could be grown on small farms as well as on plantations. But large planters enjoyed certain advantages that

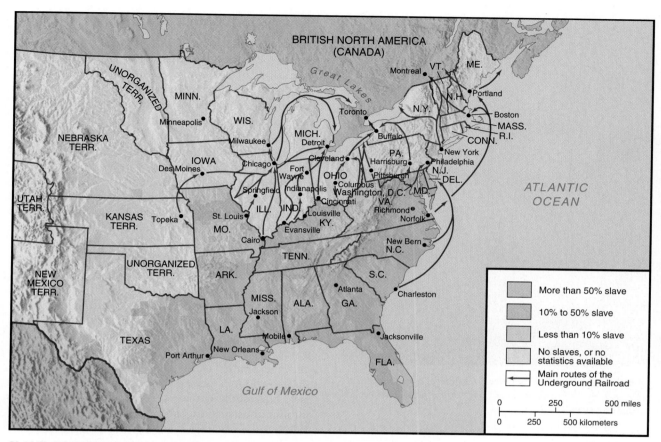

**SLAVE CONCENTRATION, 1860**   *In 1860, slavery had extended throughout the southern states, with the greatest concentrations of slaves in the states of the Deep South. There were also sizable slave populations in the new states of Missouri, Arkansas, Texas, and Florida.* ❖

made them the main producers. Only relatively large operators could afford their own gins or possessed the capital to acquire the fertile bottomlands that brought the highest yields. They also had lower transportation costs because they were able to monopolize land along rivers and streams that were the South's natural arteries of transportation.

The first major cotton-producing regions were inland areas of Georgia and South Carolina but the center of production shifted rapidly westward during the nineteenth century. By the 1830s, Alabama and Mississippi had surpassed Georgia and South Carolina as cotton-growing states. By the 1850s, Arkansas, northwest Louisiana, and east Texas were the most prosperous and rapidly growing plantation regions. The rise in total production that accompanied this geographic expansion was phenomenal. Between 1792 and 1817, the South's output of cotton rose from about 13,000 bales to 461,000; by 1840, it was 1.35 million; and in 1860, production peaked at the colossal figure of 4.8 million bales. Most of the cotton went to supply the booming textile industry of Great Britain. Lesser proportions went to the manu-

facturers of continental Europe and the northeastern United States.

"Cotton is king!" proclaimed a southern orator in the 1850s, and he was right. By that time, three-quarters of the world's supply of cotton came from the American South, and this single commodity accounted for more than half the total dollar value of American exports. Cotton growing and the network of commercial and industrial enterprises that marketed and processed the crop constituted the most important economic interest in the United States on the eve of the Civil War. Since slavery and cotton seemed inextricably linked, it appeared obvious to many Southerners that their peculiar institution was the keystone of national wealth and economic progress.

Despite its overall success, however, the rise of the Cotton Kingdom did not bring a uniform or steady prosperity to the lower South. Many planters worked the land until it was exhausted and then took their slaves westward to richer soils, leaving depressed and ravaged areas in their wake.

Planters were also beset and sometimes ruined by fluctuations in markets and prices. Boom periods and

A row of steamboats in New Orleans await bales of cotton for shipment. By 1860 production of "king" cotton in the south peaked at 4.8 million bales. ❖

flush times were followed by falling prices and waves of bankruptcies. The great periods of expansion and bonanza profits were 1815–1819, 1832–1837, and 1849–1860. The first two booms were deflated by a fall in cotton prices resulting from overproduction and depressed market conditions. During the eleven years of rising output and high prices preceding the Civil War, however, the planters gradually forgot their earlier troubles and began to imagine they were immune to future economic disasters.

Despite the insecurities associated with cotton production, most of the time the crop represented the Old South's best chance for profitable investment. Prudent planters who had not borrowed too heavily during flush times could survive periods of depression by cutting costs, making their plantations self-sufficient by shifting acreage away from cotton and planting subsistence crops. For those with worn-out land, two options existed: They could sell their land and move west, or they could sell their slaves to raise capital for fertilization, crop rotation, and other improvements that could help them survive where they were. Hence planters had little incentive to seek alternatives to slavery, the plantation, and dependence on a single cash crop. From a purely economic point of view, they had every reason to defend slavery and to insist on their right to expand it.

## Slavery and Industrialization

As the sectional quarrel with the North intensified, Southerners became increasingly alarmed by their region's lack of economic self-sufficiency. Dependence on the North for capital, marketing facilities, and manufactured goods was seen as evidence of a dangerous subservience to "external" economic interests. Southern nationalists such as J. D. B. DeBow, editor of the influential *DeBow's Review,* called during the 1850s for the South to develop its own industries, commerce, and shipping. As a fervent defender of slavery, DeBow did not believe such diversification would require a massive shift to free wage labor. He saw no reason for slaves not to be used as the main workforce in an industrial revolution. But his call for a diversified economy went unanswered. Men with capital were doing too well in plantation agriculture to risk their money in other ventures.

It is difficult to determine whether the main factor that kept most slaves working on plantations and farms was some inherent characteristic of slavery as a labor system or simply the strong market demand for cotton and the South's capacity to meet it. A minority of slaves—about 5 percent during the 1850s—were, in fact, successfully employed in industrial tasks such as mining, construction, and mill work. In the 1840s and 1850s, a debate raged among white capitalists over whether the South should use free whites or enslaved blacks as the labor supply for industry. William Gregg of South Carolina, the foremost promoter of cotton mills in the Old South, defended a white labor policy, arguing that factory work would provide new economic opportunities for a degraded class of poor whites. But other advocates of industrialization feared that the growth of a free working class would lead to social conflict among whites and preferred using slaves for all supervised manual labor. In practice, some factories employed slaves, others white workers, and a few even experimented with integrated workforces. It is clear, however, that the union of slavery and cotton that was central to the South's prosperity impeded industrialization and left the region dependent on a one-crop agriculture and on the North for capital and marketing.

## The "Profitability" Issue

Some Southerners were making money, and a great deal of it, using slave labor to raise cotton. The great mansions of the Alabama "black belt" and the lower Mississippi could not have been built if their owners had not been successful. But did slavery yield a good return for the great majority of slaveholders who were not large planters? Did it provide the basis for general prosperity and a relatively high standard of living for the southern population in general, or at least for the two-thirds of it who were white and free? These questions have been hotly debated by economic historians. Some knowledge of the main arguments regarding its "profitability" is helpful to an understanding of the South's attachment to slavery.

For many years, historians believed that slave-based agriculture was, on the average, not very lucrative. Planters' account books seemed to show at best a modest return on investment. In the 1850s, the price of slaves rose at a faster rate than the price of cotton, allegedly squeezing many operators. Some historians even concluded that slavery was a dying institution by the time of the Civil War. Profitability, they argued, depended on access to new and fertile land suitable for plantation agriculture, and virtually all such land within the limits of the United States had already been taken up by 1860. Hence slavery had allegedly reached its natural limits of expansion and was on the verge of becoming so unprofitable that it would fall of its own weight in the near future.

A more recent interpretation, based on modern economic theory, holds that slavery was in fact still an economically sound institution in 1860 and showed no signs of imminent decline. A reexamination of planters' records using modern accounting methods shows that during the 1850s, planters could normally expect an annual return of 8 to 10 percent on capital invested. This yield was roughly equivalent to the best that could then be obtained from the most lucrative sectors of northern industry and commerce.

Furthermore, it is no longer clear that plantation agriculture had reached its natural limits of expansion by 1860. Production in Texas had not yet peaked, and construction of railroads and levees was opening up new areas for cotton growing elsewhere in the South. With the advantage of hindsight, economic historians have pointed out that improvements in transportation and flood control would enable the post–Civil War South to double its cotton acreage. Those who now argue that slavery was profitable and had an expansive future have made a strong and convincing case.

But the larger question remains: What sort of economic development did a slave plantation system foster? The system may have made slaveholders wealthy, but did the benefits trickle down to the rest of the population—to the majority of whites who owned no slaves and to the slaves themselves? Did it promote efficiency and progressive change? Economists Robert Fogel and Stanley Engerman have argued that the plantation's success was due to an internally efficient enterprise with good managers and industrious, well-motivated workers. Other economic historians have

## CHRONOLOGY

| 1793 | Eli Whitney invents the cotton gin |
| 1800 | Gabriel Prosser leads abortive slave rebellion in Virginia |
| 1811 | Slaves revolt in Point Coupée section of Louisiana |
| 1822 | Denmark Vesey conspiracy uncovered in Charleston, South Carolina |
| 1829 | David Walker publishes *Appeal* calling for slave insurrection |
| 1830 | First National Negro Convention meets |
| 1831 | Slaves under Nat Turner rebel in Virginia, killing almost sixty whites |
| 1832 | Virginia legislature votes against gradual emancipation |
| 1835–1842 | Blacks fight alongside Indians in the Second Seminole War |
| 1837 | Panic of 1837 is followed by major depression of the cotton market |
| 1847 | Frederick Douglass publishes the *North Star*, a black antislavery newspaper |
| 1849 | Cotton prices rise, and a sustained boom commences |
| 1851 | Group of free blacks rescues escaped slave Shadrack from federal authorities in Boston |
| 1852 | Harriet Beecher Stowe's antislavery novel *Uncle Tom's Cabin* is published and becomes a best-seller |
| 1857 | Hinton R. Helper attacks slavery on economic grounds in *The Impending Crisis of the South*; the book is suppressed in the southern states |
| 1860 | Cotton prices and production reach all-time peak |

attributed the profitability almost exclusively to favorable market conditions.

Large plantation owners were the only segment of the population to enjoy the full benefits of the slave economy. Small slaveholders and nonslaveholders shared only to a very limited extent in the bonanza profits of the cotton economy. Because of various insecurities—lack of credit, high transportation costs, and a greater vulnerability to market fluctuations—they had to devote a larger share of their acreage to subsistence crops, especially corn and hogs, than did the planters. They were thus able to survive, but their standard of living was lower than that of most northern farmers. Slaves received sufficient food, clothing, and shelter for their subsistence and to make them capable of working well enough to keep the plantation afloat economically, but their living standard was below that of the poorest free people in the United States. It was proslavery propaganda rather than documented fact, to maintain that slaves were better off than northern wage laborers.

The South's economic development was skewed in favor of a single route to wealth, open only to the minority possessing both a white skin and access to capital. The concentration of capital and business energies on cotton production foreclosed the kind of diversified industrial and commercial growth that would have provided wider opportunities. Thus, in comparison to the industrializing North, the South was an underdeveloped region in which much of the population had little incentive to work hard. A lack of public education for whites and the denial of even minimal literacy to slaves represented a critical failure to develop human resources. The South's economy was probably condemned so long as it was based on slavery.

## CONCLUSION: WORLDS IN CONFLICT

If slaves lived to some extent in a separate and distinctive world of their own, so did planters, less afflu-ent whites, and even free blacks. The Old South was thus a deeply divided society. The northern traveler Frederick Law Olmsted, who made three journeys through the slave states in the 1850s, provided a vivid sense of how diverse in outlook and circumstances southern people could be. Visiting a great plantation, he watched the slaves stop working as soon as the overseer turned away; on a small farm, he saw a slave and his owner working in the fields together. Treatment of slaves, he found, ranged from humane paternalism to flagrant cruelty. Olmsted heard non-slaveholding whites damn the planters as "cotton snobs" but also talk about blacks as "niggers" and express fear of interracial marriages if slaves were freed. He received hospitality from poor whites living in crowded one-room cabins as well as from fabulously wealthy planters in pillared mansions, and he found life in the backcountry radically different from that in the plantation belts.

In short, he showed that the South was a kaleidoscope of groups divided by class, race, culture, and geography. What held it together and provided some measure of unity were a booming plantation economy and a web of customary relationships and loyalties that could obscure the underlying cleavages and antagonisms. The fractured and fragile nature of this society would soon become apparent when it was subjected to the pressures of civil war.

## RECOMMENDED READING

Major works that take a broad view of slavery are Kenneth M. Stampp, *The Peculiar Institution: Slavery in the Antebellum South* (1956), which stresses its coercive features; John W. Blassingame, *The Slave Community: Plantation Life in the Antebellum South* (1972), which focuses on slave culture and psychology; and Eugene D. Genovese, *Roll, Jordan, Roll: The World the Slaves Made* (1974), which probes the paternalistic character of the institution and the way in which slaves made a world for themselves within its bounds. An insightful interpretation of antebellum southern society is James Oakes, *Slavery and Freedom: An Interpretation of the Old South* (1990). For an overview of the history of slavery, see Peter Kolchin, *American Slavery, 1619–1877* (1993).

On the economics of slavery, see Gavin Wright, *The Political Economy of the Cotton South: Households, Markets, and Wealth in the Nineteenth Century* (1978). On women in the Old South, see Laura F. Edwards, *Scarlett Doesn't Live Here Anymore: Southern Women in the Civil War Era* (2000) and Deborah Gray White, *Ar'n't I a Woman: Female Slaves in the Plantation South* (1985). On the slave trade, see two excellent studies: Michael Tadman, *Speculators and Slaves: Masters, Traders, and Slaves in the Old South* (1989) and Walter

Johnson, *Soul by Soul: Life Inside the Antebellum Slave Market* (1999). For the history of the slave family, see Herbert Gutman, *The Black Family in Slavery and Freedom, 1750-1925* (1976); Brenda Stevenson, *Life in Black and White: Family and Community in the Slave South* (1996); and Marie Jenkins Schwartz, *Born in Bondage: Growing Up Enslaved in the Antebellum South* (2000). For Southern law and slavery, see Thomas D. Morris, *Southern Slavery and the Law, 1619-1860* (1996) and Ariela J. Gross, *Double Character: Slavery and Mastery in the Antebellum Southern Courtroom* (2000).

Black resistance to slavery is described in Vincent Harding, *There Is a River: The Black Struggle for Freedom in America* (1981). Slave culture is examined in Albert J. Raboteau, *Slave Religion: The "Invisible Institution" in the Antebellum South* (1978); Lawrence W. Levine, *Black Culture and Consciousness: Afro-American Folk Thought from Slavery to Freedom* (1977); Sterling Stuckey, *Slave Culture: Nationalist Theory and the Foundations of Black America* (1987); and Sharla M. Fett, *Healing, Health, and Power on Southern Slave Plantations* (2002).

**For a list of additional titles related to this chapter's topics, please see** http://www.ablongman.com/divine.

# Suggested Web Sites

### "Been Here So Long": Selections from the WPA American Slave Narratives

http://newdeal.feri.org/asn/index.htm
Slave narratives are some of the more interesting primary sources about slavery.

### Exploring Amistad

http://amistad.mysticseaport.org/main/welcome.html
Mystic Seaport runs this site that includes extensive collections of historical resources relating to the revolt and subsequent trial of enslaved Africans.

### Africans in America: America's Journey Through Slavery

http://www.pbs.org/wgbh/aia/home.html
This PBS site contains images and documents recounting slavery in America.

### Amistad Trials (1839–1840)

http://www.law.umkc.edu/faculty/projects/ftrials/amistad/AMISTD.HTM
Images, chronology, court and official documents comprise this site by Dr. Doug Linder at University of Missouri–Kansas City Law School.

### Slave Narratives

http://docsouth.unc.edu/neh/neh.html
This site presents the telling narratives of several slaves housed at the Documents of the American South collection and the University of North Carolina.

### The Settlement of African Americans in Liberia

http://www.loc.gov/exhibits/african/perstor.html
This site contains images and text relating to the colonization movement to return African Americans to Africa.

### Images of African Americans from the Nineteenth Century

http://digital.nypl.org/schomburg/images_aa19/
The New York Public Library–Schomburg Center for Research in Black Culture site contains numerous visuals.

### Images of African American Slavery and Freedom

http://lcweb.loc.gov/rr/print/082_slave.html
This site contains numerous photographs and other images of slaves and free blacks from the Library of Congress.

### St. Louis Circuit Court Historical Records Project

http://stlcourtrecords.wustl.edu/resources.cfm
This site contains links to full-text reproductions of slaves' freedom suits in Missouri, including Dred Scott's case, and many other African American history links.

## Chapter 12

Jeremiah Paul, Revival Meeting ❖

# The Pursuit of Perfection

## *Redeeming the Middle Class*

In the winter of 1830 to 1831, a wave of religious revivals swept the northern states. The most dramatic and successful took place in Rochester, New York. Large audiences, composed mostly of respectable and prosperous citizens, heard Presbyterian evangelist Charles G. Finney preach that every man or woman had the power to choose Christ and a godly life. Finney broke with his church's traditional belief that it was God's inscrutable will that decided who would be saved when he preached that "sinners ought to be made to feel that they have something to do, and that something is to repent. That is something that no other being can do for them, neither God nor man, and something they can do and do now."

For six months, Finney held prayer meetings almost daily, putting intense pressure on those who had not experienced salvation. Hundreds came forth to declare their faith, and church membership doubled during his stay. The newly awakened Christians of Rochester were urged to convert relatives, neighbors, and employees. If enough people enlisted in the evangelical crusade, Finney proclaimed, the millennium would be achieved within months.

Finney's call for religious and moral renewal fell on fertile ground in Rochester. The bustling boomtown on the Erie Canal was suffering from severe growing pains and tensions arising from rapid economic development. Leading families were divided into quarreling factions, and workers were threatening to break free from the control their employers had previously exerted over their daily lives. Most of the early converts were from the middle class. Businessmen who had been heavy drinkers and irregular churchgoers now abstained from alcohol and went to church at least twice a week. They also pressured the employees in their workshops, mills, and stores to do likewise. More rigorous standards of proper behavior and religious conformity unified Rochester's elite and increased its ability to control the rest of the community. As in other cities swept by the revival, evangelical Protestantism provided the middle class with a stronger sense of identity and purpose.

BUT THE WAR ON SIN was not always so unifying. Among those converted in Rochester and elsewhere were some who could not rest easy until the nation as a whole conformed to the pure Christianity of the Sermon on the Mount. Finney expressed such a hope himself, but he concentrated on religious conversion and moral uplift of the individual, trusting that the purification of American society and politics would automatically follow. Other religious and moral reformers were inspired to crusade against those social and political institutions that failed to measure up to the standards of Christian perfection. They proceeded to attack such collective "sins" as the liquor traffic, war, slavery, and even government.

Religiously inspired reformism cut two ways. On the one hand, it imposed a new order and cultural unity to previously divided and troubled communities like Rochester. But it also inspired a variety of more radical movements or experiments that threatened to undermine established institutions that failed to live up to the principles of the more idealistic reformers. One of these movements—abolitionism—challenged the central social and economic institution of the southern states and helped trigger political upheaval and civil war.

# THE RISE OF EVANGELICALISM

American Protestantism was in a state of constant ferment during the early nineteenth century. The separation of church and state, a process that began during the Revolution, was now complete. Government sponsorship and funding had ended, or would soon end, for the established churches of the colonial era, such as the Congregationalists of New England and the Episcopalians of the South. Dissenting groups, such as Baptists and Methodists, welcomed full religious freedom because it offered a better chance to win new converts. All pious Protestants, however, were concerned about the spread of "infidelity"—a term they applied to Catholics, freethinkers, Unitarians, Mormons, and anyone else who was not an evangelical Christian. But they faced opposition to their effort to make the nation officially Protestant. Some of the Founders of the nation had set a troubling example by their casual or even unfriendly attitude toward religious orthodoxy. Secular ideas drawn from the Enlightenment of the late eighteenth century had achieved wide acceptance as a basis for the establishment of a democratic republic, and opposition to mixing religion with public life remained strong during the age of Jackson. As deism—the belief in a God who expressed himself through natural laws accessible to human reason—declined in popularity in the early to mid-nineteenth century, Catholic immigration increased, and the spread of "Popery" became the main focus of evangelical concern. Both Catholics and Unitarians (who quietly carried forward the rationalistic traditions of the eighteenth century) resented and resisted the evangelicals' efforts to convert them to "the Christianity of the heart." Most of those who accepted Christ as their personal savior in revival meetings previously had been indifferent to religion rather than adhering to an alternative set of beliefs.

Revivalism proved to be a very effective means to extend religious values and build up church membership. The Great Awakening of the mid-eighteenth century had shown the wonders that evangelists could accomplish, and new revivalists repeated this success by greatly increasing the proportion of the population that belonged to Protestant churches. They also capitalized on the growing willingness of Americans to form voluntary organizations. Spiritual renewals were often followed by mobilization of the faithful into associations to spread the gospel and reform American morals.

According to some historians, evangelical revival and the reform movements it inspired reflected the same spirit as the new democratic politics. In a sense this is true: Jacksonian politicians and evangelists both sought popular favor and assumed that individuals were free agents capable of self-direction and self-improvement. But leaders of the two types of movements made different kinds of demands on ordinary people. Jacksonians idealized common folk pretty much as they found them and saw no danger to the community if individuals pursued their worldly interests. Evangelical reformers, who tended to support the Whigs or to reject both parties, believed that the common people, and not just the elite, needed to be redeemed and uplifted—committed to a higher goal than self-interest. They did not trust a democracy of unbelievers and sinners. The republic would be safe, they insisted, only if a right-minded minority preached, taught, and agitated until the mass of ordinary citizens was reborn into a higher life.

## The Second Great Awakening: The Frontier Phase

The **Second Great Awakening** began in earnest on the southern frontier around the turn of the century. In 1801, a crowd estimated at nearly fifty thousand gathered at Cane Ridge, Kentucky. According to a contemporary observer:

> The noise was like the roar of Niagara. The vast sea of human beings seemed to be agitated as if by a storm. I counted seven ministers all preaching at once. . . . Some of the people were singing, others praying, some crying for mercy . . . while others were shouting most vociferously. . . . At one time I saw at least five hundred swept down in a moment, as if a battery of a thousand guns had been opened upon them, and then followed immediately shrieks and shouts that rent the heavens.

Highly emotional camp meetings, organized usually by Methodists or Baptists but sometimes by Presbyterians, became a regular feature of religious life in the South and the lower Midwest. On the frontier, the camp meeting met social as well as religious needs. In the sparsely settled southern backcountry, it was difficult to sustain local churches with regular ministers. Methodists solved part of the problem by sending out circuit riders. Baptists licensed uneducated farmers to preach to their neighbors. But for many people, the only way to get baptized or married or to have a communal religious experience was to attend a camp meeting.

Rowdies and scoffers also attended, drinking whiskey, carousing, and fornicating on the fringes of the small city of tents and wagons. Sometimes they were "struck down" by a mighty blast from the pulpit. Evangelists loved to tell stories of such conversions or near conversions. According to Methodist preacher Peter Cartwright, one scoffer was seized by the "jerks"—a set of involuntary bodily movements often observed at camp meetings. Normally such an exercise would lead to conversion, but this particular sinner was so hardhearted that he refused to surrender to God. The result was that he kept jerking until his neck was broken.

Camp meetings obviously provided an emotional outlet for rural people whose everyday lives were often lonely and tedious. They could also promote a sense

Lithograph depicting a camp meeting. Religious revival meetings on the frontier attracted hundreds of people who camped for days to listen to the preacher and to share with their neighbors in a communal religious experience. Notice that the men and women are seated in separate sections. ❖

of community and social discipline. Conversion at a camp meeting could be a rite of passage, signifying that a young man or woman had outgrown wild or antisocial behavior and was now ready to become a respectable member of the community.

In the southern states, Baptists and Presbyterians eventually deemphasized camp meetings in favor of "protracted meetings" in local churches, which featured guest preachers holding forth day after day for up to two weeks. Southern evangelical churches, especially Baptist and Methodist, grew rapidly in membership and influence during the first half of the nineteenth century and became the focus of community life in rural areas. Although they fostered societies to improve morals—to encourage temperance and discourage dueling, for example—they generally shied away from social reform. The conservatism of a slaveholding society discouraged radical efforts to change the world.

## The Second Great Awakening in the North

Reformist tendencies were more evident in the distinctive kind of revivalism that originated in New England and western New York. Northern evangelists were mostly Congregationalists and Presbyterians, strongly influenced by New England Puritan traditions. Their greatest successes were not in rural or frontier areas but in small- to medium-sized towns and cities. Their revivals could be stirring affairs but were less extravagantly emotional than the camp meetings of the South. The northern brand of evangelism resulted in formation of societies devoted to the redemption of the human race in general and American society in particular.

The reform movement in New England began as an effort to defend Calvinism against the liberal views of religion fostered by the Enlightenment. The Reverend Timothy Dwight, who became president of Yale College in 1795, was alarmed by the younger generation's growing acceptance of the belief that the Deity was the benevolent master architect of a rational universe rather than an all-powerful, mysterious God. Dwight was particularly disturbed by those religious liberals whose rationalism reached the point of denying the doctrine of the Trinity and who proclaimed themselves to be "Unitarians."

To Dwight's horror, Unitarians captured some fashionable and sophisticated New England congregations and even won control of the Harvard Divinity School. He fought back by preaching to Yale undergraduates that they were "dead in sin" and succeeded in provoking a series of campus revivals. But the harshness and pessimism of orthodox Calvinist doctrine, with its stress on original sin and predestination, had limited appeal in a republic committed to human freedom and progress.

A younger generation of Congregational ministers reshaped New England Puritanism to increase its appeal to people who shared the prevailing optimism about human capabilities. The main theologian of early-nineteenth-century neo-Calvinism was Nathaniel Taylor, a disciple of Dwight, who also held forth at Yale. Taylor softened the doctrine of predestination almost out of existence by contending that every individual was a free agent who had the ability to overcome a natural inclination to sin.

The first great practitioner of the new evangelical Calvinism was Lyman Beecher, another of Dwight's pupils. In the period just before and after the War of 1812, Beecher helped promote a series of revivals in the Congregational churches of New England. Using his own homespun version of Taylor's doctrine of free agency, Beecher induced thousands—in his home church in Litchfield, Connecticut, and in other churches that offered him their pulpits—to acknowledge their sinfulness and surrender to God.

During the late 1820s, Beecher was forced to confront the new and more radical form of revivalism being practiced in western New York by Charles G. Finney. Upstate New York was a seedbed for religious enthusiasms of various kinds. A majority of its population were transplanted New Englanders who had left behind their close-knit village communities and ancestral churches but not their Puritan consciences. Troubled by rapid economic changes and the social dislocations that went with them, they were ripe for a new faith and a fresh moral direction.

Although he worked within Congregational and Presbyterian churches (which were then cooperating under a plan of union established in 1804), Finney departed radically from Calvinist doctrines. In his hands, free agency became unqualified free will. One of his sermons was titled "Sinners Bound to Change Their Own Hearts." Finney was relatively indifferent to theological issues. His appeal was to emotion or to the heart rather than to doctrine or reason. He wanted converts to feel the power of Christ and become new men and women. He eventually adopted the extreme view that redeemed Christians could be totally free of sin—as perfect as their Father in Heaven.

Beginning in 1823, Finney conducted a series of highly successful revivals in towns and cities of western New York, culminating in the aforementioned triumph in Rochester in 1830–1831. Even more controversial than his freewheeling approach to theology were the means he used to win converts. Finney sought instantaneous conversions through a variety of new methods. These included holding protracted meetings that lasted all night or several days in a row, placing an "anxious bench" in front of the congregation where those in the process of repentance could receive special attention, and encouraging women to pray publicly for the souls of male relatives.

The results could be dramatic. Sometimes listeners fell to the floor in fits of excitement. "If I had had a sword in my hand," Finney recalled, "I could not have cut them off as fast as they fell." Although he appealed to emotion, Finney had a practical, almost manipulative, attitude toward the conversion process: it "is not a miracle or dependent on a miracle in any sense. . . . It is purely a philosophical result of the right use of constituted means."

Lyman Beecher and eastern evangelicals were disturbed by Finney's new methods and by the emotionalism that accompanied them. They were also upset

*The Beecher family, shown here in a photograph by Mathew Brady, contributed four influential members to the reform movement. Lyman Beecher (seated center) was a successful preacher and a master strategist in the organized campaign against sin and "infidelity." His eldest daughter, Catharine (on his right), was a leader in the movement supporting higher education for women. Another daughter, Harriet (seated far right), wrote the novel* Uncle Tom's Cabin. *Lyman's son, Henry Ward Beecher (standing far right), was an ardent antislavery advocate and later became one of the most celebrated preachers of the post–Civil War era. He also became involved in a notorious scandal and trial.* ❖

because he violated long-standing Christian tradition by allowing women to pray aloud in church. An evangelical summit meeting between Beecher and Finney, held at New Lebanon, New York, in 1827, failed to reach agreement on this and other issues. Beecher even threatened to stand on the state line if Finney attempted to bring his crusade into Connecticut. But it soon became clear that Finney was not merely stirring people to temporary peaks of excitement; he also was leaving strong and active churches behind him, and eastern opposition gradually weakened. Finney eventually founded a tabernacle in New York City that became a rallying point for evangelical efforts to reach the urban masses.

## From Revivalism to Reform

The northern wing of the Second Great Awakening, unlike the southern, inspired a great movement for social reform. Converts were organized into voluntary associations that sought to stamp out sin and social evil and win the world for Christ. An activist and outgoing Christianity was being advanced, not one that called for withdrawal from a sinful world. Most of the converts of northern revivalism were middle-class citizens already active in the lives of their communities. They were seeking to adjust to the bustling world of the market revolution in ways that would not violate their traditional moral and social values. Their generally optimistic and forward-looking attitudes led to hopes that a wave of conversions would save the nation and the world.

In New England, Beecher and his evangelical associates were behind the establishment of a great network of missionary and benevolent societies. In 1810, Presbyterians and Congregationalists founded a Board of Commissioners for Foreign Missions and soon dispatched two missionaries to India. In 1816, the Reverend Samuel John Mills took the leading role in organizing the American Bible Society. By 1821, the society had distributed 140,000 Bibles, mostly in parts of the West where churches and clergymen were scarce.

Another major effort went into publication and distribution of religious tracts, mainly by the American Tract Society, founded in 1825. Special societies targeted groups beyond the reach of regular churches, such as seamen, Native Americans, and the urban poor. In 1816 to 1817, middle-class women in New York, Philadelphia, Charleston, and Boston formed societies to spread the gospel in lower-class wards—where, as one of their missionaries put it, there was "a great mass of people beyond the restraints of religion."

Evangelicals founded moral reform societies as well as missions. Some of these aimed at curbing irreligious activity on the Sabbath; others sought to stamp out dueling, gambling, and prostitution. In New York in 1831, a zealous young clergyman published a sensational report claiming there were ten

THE DRUNKARD'S PROGRESS.

*Temperance propaganda warned that the drinker who began with "a glass with a friend" would inevitably follow the direct path to poverty, despair, and death.* ❖

thousand prostitutes in the city laying their snares for innocent young men. As a result of this exposé, an asylum was established for the redemption of "abandoned women." When middle-class women became involved in this crusade, they shifted its focus to the men who patronized prostitutes, and they proposed that teams of observers record and publish the names of men seen entering brothels. The plan was abandoned because it offended those who thought the cause of virtue would be better served by suppressing public discussion and investigation of sexual vices.

Beecher was especially influential in the **temperance movement,** the most successful of the reform crusades; his published sermons against drink were the most important and widely distributed of the early tracts calling for total abstinence from "demon rum." The temperance movement was directed at a real social evil. Since the Revolution, whiskey had become the most popular American beverage. Made from corn by individual farmers or, by the 1820s, in commercial distilleries, it was cheaper than milk or beer and safer than water (which was often contaminated). In some parts of the country, rum and brandy were also popular. Hard liquor was frequently consumed with food as a table beverage, even at breakfast, and children sometimes imbibed along with adults. Per capita annual consumption of distilled beverages in the 1820s was almost triple what it is today, and alcoholism had reached epidemic proportions.

The temperance reformers viewed indulgence in alcohol as a threat to public morality. Drunkenness was seen as a loss of self-control and moral responsibility that spawned crime, vice, and disorder. Above all, it threatened the family. Drinking was mainly a male vice, and the main target of temperance propaganda was the husband and father who abused, neglected, or abandoned his wife and children because he was a slave to the bottle. Women played a vital role in the movement and were instrumental in making it a crusade for the protection of the home. The drinking habits of the poor or laboring classes also aroused great concern. Particularly in urban areas, the "respectable" and properted elements lived in fear that lower-class mobs, crazed with drink, would attack private property and create social chaos.

Many evangelical reformers regarded intemperance as the greatest single obstacle to a republic of God-fearing, self-disciplined citizens. In 1826, a group of clergymen previously active in mission work organized the American Temperance Society to coordinate and extend the work already begun by local churches and moral reform societies. The original aim was to encourage abstinence from "ardent spirits" or hard liquor; there was no agreement on the evils of beer and wine. The society sent out lecturers, issued a flood of literature, and sponsored essay contests. Its agents organized revival meetings and called on those in attendance to sign a pledge promising abstinence from spirits.

The campaign was enormously effective. By 1834, there were five thousand local branches with more than a million members, a large proportion of them women. Although it may be doubted whether huge numbers of confirmed drunkards were cured, the movement did succeed in altering the drinking habits of middle-class American males by making temperance a mark of respectability. Per capita consumption of hard liquor declined more than 50 percent during the 1830s.

Cooperating missionary and reform societies—collectively known as "the benevolent empire"—were a major force in American culture by the early 1830s. Efforts to modify American attitudes and institutions seemed to be bearing fruit. The middle class was embracing a new ethic of self-control and self-discipline, equipping individuals to confront a new world of economic growth and social mobility without losing their cultural and moral bearings.

## DOMESTICITY AND CHANGES IN THE AMERICAN FAMILY

The evangelical culture of the 1820s and 1830s influenced the family as an institution and inspired new conceptions of its role in American society. Many parents viewed children's rearing as essential preparation for self-disciplined Christian life and performed their nurturing duties with great seriousness and self-consciousness. Women—regarded as particularly susceptible to religious and moral influences—were increasingly confined to the domestic circle, but they assumed a greater importance within it.

### Marriage for Love

The white middle-class American family underwent major changes in the decades between the Revolution and the mid-nineteenth century. One was the triumph of marriage for love. Parents now exercised even less control over their children's selection of mates than they had in the colonial period. The desire to protect family property and maintain social status remained strong, but mutual affection was now considered absolutely essential to a proper union. Beginning in the late eighteenth century, romantic novels popularized the idea that marriage should be based exclusively on the promptings of the heart. It became easier for sons to marry while their fathers were still alive and for younger daughters to wed before their oldest sisters—trends that reflected a weakening of the traditional parental role.

Wives now began to behave more like the companions of their husbands and less like their servants or children. In the main, eighteenth-century correspondence between spouses had been formal and distant in tone. The husband often assumed a patriarchal role, even using such salutations as "my dear child" and rarely confessing that he missed his wife or craved her company. Letters from women to their husbands were highly deferential and did not usually give advice or express disapproval.

By the early nineteenth century, first names, pet names, and terms of endearment such as "honey" or "darling" were increasingly used by both sexes, and absent husbands frequently confessed they felt lost without their mates. In their replies, wives assumed a more egalitarian tone and offered counsel on a wide range of subjects. One wrote to a husband who had admitted to flirting with pretty women that she was more than "a little jealous." She asked him angrily how he would feel if she made a similar confession: "Would it be more immoral in me than in you?"

The change in middle- and upper-class marriage should not be exaggerated or romanticized. In law, and in cases of conflict between spouses, the husband remained the unchallenged head of the household. True independence or equality for women was impossible at a time when men held exclusive legal authority over a couple's property and children. Divorce was difficult for everyone, but the double standard made it easier for husbands than wives to dissolve a marriage on grounds of adultery.

## The Cult of Domesticity

Such power as women exerted within the home came from their ability to affect the decisions of men who had learned to respect their moral qualities and good sense. The evangelical movement encouraged this quiet expression of feminine influence. The revivals not only gave women a role in converting men but presented as the main object of worship a Christ with stereotypical feminine characteristics. A nurturing, loving, merciful savior, mediating between a stern father and his erring children, provided the model for woman's new role as spiritual head of the home. Membership in evangelical church–based associations inspired and prepared women for new roles as civilizers of men and guardians of domestic culture and morality. Female reform societies taught women the strict ethical code they were to instill in other family members; organized mothers' groups gave instruction in how to build character and encourage piety in children.

Historians have described the new conception of woman's role as the **Cult of Domesticity** or the "Cult of True Womanhood." In the view of most men, a woman's place was in the home and on a pedestal. The ideal wife and mother was "an angel in the house," a model of piety and virtue who exerted a wholesome moral and religious influence over members of the coarser sex. A poem published in 1846 expressed a masculine view of the true woman:

> I would have her as pure as the snow on the mount—
> As true as the smile that to infancy's given—
> As pure as the wave of the crystalline fount,
> Yet as warm in the heart as the sunlight of heaven.

The sociological reality behind the Cult of True Womanhood was an increasing division between the working lives of men and women. In the eighteenth century and earlier, most economic activity had been centered in and near the home, and husbands and wives often worked together in a common enterprise. By the early to mid-nineteenth century this way of life was declining, especially in the Northeast. In towns and cities, the rise of factories and countinghouses severed the home from the workplace. Men went forth every morning to their places of labor, leaving their wives at home to tend the house and the children. Married women were therefore increasingly deprived of a productive economic role. The cult of domesticity made a virtue of the fact that men were solely responsible for running the affairs of the world and building up the economy.

A new conception of gender roles justified and glorified this pattern. The "doctrine of two spheres"—as set forth in novels, advice literature, and the new women's magazines—sentimentalized the woman who kept a spotless house, nurtured her children, and offered her husband a refuge from the heartless world of commerce and industry. From a modern point of view, it is easy to condemn the cult of domesticity as a rationalization for male dominance; to a considerable extent, it was. But many women of the early to mid-nineteenth century do not seem to have felt oppressed or degraded by the new arrangement. The earlier pattern of cooperation had not implied sexual equality—normally, men had been very much in charge of farms or home industries and had often treated their wives more like servants than partners. The new norm of confinement to the home did not necessarily imply that women were inferior. By the standards of evangelical culture, women in the domestic sphere could be viewed as superior to men, since women were in a good position to cultivate the "feminine" virtues of love and self-sacrifice and thus act as official guardians of religious and moral values.

The domestic ideology had real meaning only for relatively affluent women. Working-class wives were not usually employed outside the home during this period, but they labored long and hard within the household.

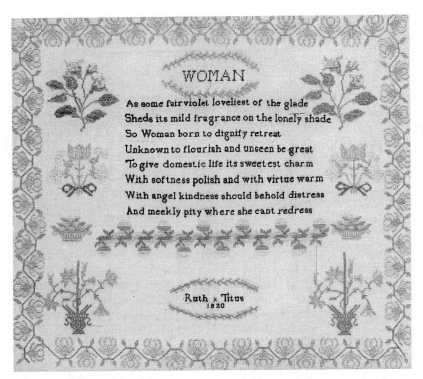

*The sentiment on this sampler, stitched in 1820 by Ruth Titus, typifies beliefs about woman's proper role, according to the Cult of True Womanhood.* ❖

Besides cleaning, cooking, and taking care of large numbers of children, they often took in washing or piecework to supplement a meager family income. Their endless domestic drudgery made a sham of the notion that women had the time and energy for the "higher things of life." Life was especially hard for African American women. Most of those who were "free Negroes" rather than slaves did not have husbands who made enough to support them, and they were obliged to serve in white households or work long hours at home doing other people's washing and sewing.

In urban areas, unmarried working-class women often lived on their own and toiled as household servants, in the sweatshops of the garment industry, and in factories. Barely able to support themselves and at the mercy of male sexual predators, they were in no position to identify with the middle-class ideal of elevated, protected womanhood. For some of them, the relatively well-paid and gregarious life of the successful prostitute seemed to offer an attractive alternative to a life of loneliness and privation.

For middle-class women whose husbands or fathers earned a good income, freedom from industrial or farm labor offered some tangible benefits. They now had the leisure to read extensively the new literature directed primarily at housewives, to participate in female-dominated charitable activities, and to culti-

vate deep and lasting friendships with other women. The result was a distinctively feminine subculture emphasizing "sisterhood" or "sorority." This growing sense of solidarity with other women and of the importance of sexual identity could transcend the private home and even the barriers of social class. Beginning in the 1820s, urban women of the middle and upper classes organized societies for the relief and rehabilitation of poor or "fallen" women. The aim of the organizations was not economic and political equality with men but the elevation of all women to true womanhood.

For some women, the domestic ideal even sanctioned efforts to extend their sphere until it conquered the masculine world outside the home. This domestic feminism was reflected in women's involvement in crusades to stamp out such masculine sins as intemperance, gambling, and sexual vice.

In the benevolent societies and reform movements of the Jacksonian era, especially those designated as women's organizations, women handled money, organized meetings and public appeals, made contracts, and sometimes even gave orders to male subordinates—activities they could not usually perform in their own households. The desire to extend the feminine sphere was the motivating force behind Catharine Beecher's campaign to make schoolteaching a woman's occupation. A prolific and influential writer on the theory and practice of domesticity, this unmarried daughter of Lyman Beecher saw the spinster-teacher as equivalent to a mother. By instilling in young males the virtues that only women could teach, the schoolmarm could help liberate America from corruption and materialism.

But Beecher and other domestic feminists continued to emphasize the role of married women who stayed home and did their part simply by being wives and mothers. Reforming husbands was difficult: They were away much of the time and tended to be preoccupied with business. But this very fact gave women primary responsibility for the rearing of children—an activity to which nineteenth-century Americans attached almost cosmic significance. Since women were considered particularly well qualified to transmit piety and morality to future citizens of the republic, the cult of domesticity exalted motherhood and encouraged a new concern with childhood as the time of life when "character" was formed.

## Gothic Revival Cottage

Sentimentality and romanticism strengthened their hold on American culture after 1820. At the same time, a cult of domesticity arose, which promoted family life as critical to a person's moral regeneration. Evangelism and a wide variety of reform movements swept the nation as well. Middle-class Americans engaged enthusiastically in these social and cultural developments, spending money or hours buying or making materials that revealed their participation. New houses provided clean, neat spaces—and more of them—for family members to pursue their interests together. Styles such as the Gothic Revival embodied the romantic and spiritual sentiments of the age. Gothic Revival presented home as more than a haven; home became a spiritual sanctuary. What does this house remind you of? If homes became sanctuaries, what role did women play in creating and maintaining that sanctuary?

## The Discovery of Childhood

The nineteenth century has been called "the century of the child." More than before, childhood was seen as a distinct stage of life requiring the special and sustained attention of adults. The family now became "child-centered," which meant that the care, nurture, and rearing of children was viewed as the family's main function. In earlier times, adults treated children in a more casual way, often sending them away from home for education or apprenticeship at a very early age. Among the well-to-do, children spent more time with servants or tutors than with their parents.

By the early decades of the nineteenth century, however, children were staying at home longer and receiving much more attention from parents, especially mothers. Much less common was the colonial custom—nearly inconceivable today—of naming a child after a sibling who had died in infancy. Each child was now looked on as a unique and irreplaceable individual.

New customs and fashions heralded the "discovery" of childhood. Books aimed specifically at juveniles began to roll off the presses. Parents became more self-conscious about their responsibilities and sought help from a new literature providing expert advice on child rearing. One early-nineteenth-century mother wrote, "There is scarcely any subject concerning which I feel more anxiety than the proper education of my children. It is a difficult and delicate subject, the more I feel how much is to be learnt by myself."

The new concern for children resulted in more intimate relations between parents and children. The ideal family described in the advice manuals and sentimental literature was bound together by affection rather than authority. Firm discipline remained at the core of "family government," but there was a change in the preferred method of enforcing good behavior. Corporal punishment declined, partially displaced by shaming or withholding of affection. Disobedient middle-class children were now more likely to be confined to their rooms to reflect on their sins than to receive a good thrashing. Discipline could no longer be justified as the constant application of physical force over naturally wayward beings. In an age of moral perfectionism, the role of discipline was to induce repentance and change basic attitudes. The intended result was often described as "self-government"; to achieve it, parents used guilt, rather than fear, as their main source of leverage. A mother's sorrow or a father's stern and prolonged silence was deemed more effective in forming character than were blows or angry words.

Child-centered families also meant smaller families. If nineteenth-century families had remained as large as those of earlier times, it would have been impossible to lavish so much care and attention on individual offspring. For reasons that are still not completely understood, the average number of children born to each woman during her fertile years dropped from 7.04 in 1800 to 5.42 in 1850. As a result, the average number of children per family declined about 25 percent, beginning a long-range trend lasting to the present day.

## ❖ A Look at the Past ❖

### Manufactured Toy

Manufactured toys, such as this pull toy, became common during the early nineteenth century and suggest dramatic changes in family life and consumer behavior. Before toys were manufactured in the United States, most parents or children themselves had to make toys or games from available materials, or if they were wealthy enough, they might purchase wood, tin, or cast iron toys imported from Europe. The availability of cheap manufactured goods gave mothers the opportunity to lavish attention on their children, without the toil. What does the emergence of a toy manufacturing industry reveal about attitudes toward children?

competitive world that demanded special talents and training, they were a financial liability.

## INSTITUTIONAL REFORM

The family could not carry the whole burden of socializing and reforming individuals. Children needed schooling as well as parental nurturing, and many were thought to lack a proper home environment. Some adults, too, seemed to require special kinds of attention and treatment. Seeking to extend the advantages of "family government" beyond the domestic circle, reformers worked to establish or improve public institutions that were designed to shape individual character and instill a capacity for self-discipline.

### The Extension of Education

The period from 1820 to 1850 saw an enormous expansion of free public schools. The new resolve to put more children in school for longer periods reflected many of the same values that exalted the child-centered family. Up to a certain age, children could be effectively nurtured and educated in the home. But after that they needed formal training at a character-molding institution that would prepare them to make a living and bear the burdens of republican citizenship. Intellectual training at school was regarded as less important than moral indoctrination.

Sometimes more than just an extension of the family, the school served as a substitute for it. Educational reformers were alarmed at the masses of poor and immigrant children who allegedly failed to get proper nurturing at home. It was up to schools to make up for this disadvantage. Otherwise, the republic would be in danger from masses of people "incapable of self-government."

Before the 1820s, schooling in the United States was a haphazard affair. The wealthy sent their children to private schools, and some of the poor sent their children to charity or "pauper" schools that were usually financed in part by local governments. Public education was most highly developed in the New England states, where towns were required by law to support elementary schools. It was weakest in the South, where almost all education was private.

Agitation for expanded public education began in the 1820s and early 1830s as a central demand of the workingmen's movements in eastern cities. These hard-pressed artisans viewed free schools open to all as a way of countering the growing gap between rich and poor. Initially, strong opposition came from more affluent taxpayers who did not see why they should pay for the education of other people's children. But middle-class reformers soon seized the initiative, shaped

The practice of various forms of birth control undoubtedly contributed to this demographic revolution. Ancestors of the modern condom and diaphragm were openly advertised and sold during the pre–Civil War period, but it is likely that most couples controlled family size by practicing the withdrawal method or limiting the frequency of intercourse. Abortion was also surprisingly common and was on the rise. One historian has estimated that by 1850 there was one abortion for every five or six live births.

Parents seemed to understand that having fewer children meant they could provide their offspring with a better start in life. Such attitudes were appropriate in a society that was beginning to shift from agriculture to commerce and industry. For rural households short of labor, large families were an economic asset. For urban couples who hoped to send their children into a educational reform to their own end of social discipline, and provided the momentum needed for legislative success.

The most influential supporter of the common school movement was Horace Mann of Massachusetts. As a lawyer and member of the state legislature, Mann worked tirelessly to establish a state board of education and adequate tax support for local schools. In 1837, he persuaded the legislature to enact his proposals, and he subsequently resigned his seat to become the first secretary of the new board, an office he held with great distinction until 1848. He believed children were clay in the hands of teachers and school officials and could be molded to a state of perfection. Like advocates of child rearing through moral influence rather than physical force, he discouraged corporal punishment except as a last resort. His position on this issue led to a bitter controversy with Boston schoolmasters who retained a Calvinist sense of original sin and favored a freer use of the rod.

Against those who argued that school taxes violated property rights, Mann contended that private property was actually held in trust for the good of the community. "The property of this commonwealth," he wrote, "is pledged for the education of all its youth up to such a point as will save them from poverty and vice, and prepare them for the adequate performance of their social and civil duties." Mann's conception of public education as a means of social discipline converted the middle and upper classes to the cause. By teaching middle-class morality and respect for order, the schools could turn potential rowdies and revolutionaries into law-abiding citizens. They could also encourage social mobility by opening doors for lower-class children who were determined to do better than their parents.

In practice, new or improved public schools often alienated working-class pupils and their families rather than reforming them. Compulsory attendance laws in Massachusetts and other states deprived poor families of needed wage earners without guaranteeing new occupational opportunities for those with an elementary education. As the laboring class became increasingly immigrant and Catholic in the 1840s and 1850s, dissatisfaction arose over the evangelical Protestant tone of "moral instruction" in the schools. Quite consciously, Mann and his disciples were trying to impose a uniform culture on people who valued differing traditions.

In addition to the "three Rs" ("reading, 'riting, and 'rithmetic"), the public schools of the mid-nineteenth century taught the "Protestant ethic"—industry, punctuality, sobriety, and frugality. These were the virtues stressed in the famous *McGuffey's Eclectic Readers,* which first appeared in 1836. Millions of children

> ### THE ECLECTIC SERIES.    77
>
> ## LESSON XXI.
>
> 1. IN′DO-LENT; *adj.* lazy; idle.
> 2. COM-MER′CIAL; *adj.* trading.
> 3. COM′IC-AL; *adj.* amusing.
> 3. DRONE; *n.* an idler.
> 4. NAV′I-GA-BLE; *adj.* in which boats can sail.
>
> ### THE IDLE SCHOOL-BOY.
>
> PRONOUNCE correctly. Do not say *indorlunt* for in-do-lent; *creepin* for creep-ing; *sylubble* for syl-la-ble; *colud* for col-ored; *scarlit* for scar-let; *ignerunt* for ig-no-rant.
>
> 1. I WILL tell you about the †laziest boy you ever heard of. He was indolent about every thing. When he played, the boys said he played as if the teacher told him to. When he went to school, he went creep-ing along like a snail. The boy had sense enough; but he was too lazy to learn any thing.
>
> 2. When he spelled a word, he †drawled out one syllable after another, as if he were afraid the †syllables would quarrel, if he did not keep them a great way apart.
>
> 3. Once when he was †reciting, the teacher asked him, "What is said of †Hartford?" He answered, "Hartford is a †flourishing *comical* town." He meant that it was a "flourishing *commercial* town;" but he was such a drone, that he never knew what he was about.
>
> 4. When asked how far the River †Kennebec was navigable, he said, "it was navigable for *boots* as far as †Waterville." The boys all laughed, and the teacher could not help laughing, too. The idle boy †colored like scarlet.
>
> 5. "I say it is so in my book," said he. When one of the boys showed him the book, and pointed to the

*The lessons and examples in* McGuffey's Eclectic Readers *upheld the basic virtues of thrift, honesty, and charity, and taught that evil deeds never went unpunished.* ❖

learned to read by digesting McGuffey's parables about the terrible fate of those who gave in to sloth, drunkenness, or wastefulness. Such moral indoctrination helped produce generations of Americans with personalities and beliefs adapted to the needs of an industrializing society—people who could be depended on to adjust to the precise and regular routines of the factory or the office. But as an education for self-government—in the sense of learning to think for oneself—it left much to be desired.

Fortunately, however, education was not limited to the schools nor devoted solely to children. Every city and almost every town or village had a lyceum, debating society, or mechanics' institute where adults of all social classes could broaden their intellectual horizons. Lyceums featured discourses on such subjects as "self-reliance" or "the conduct of life" by creative thinkers such as Ralph Waldo Emerson, explanations and demonstrations of the latest scientific discoveries, and debates among members on controversial issues.

Young Abraham Lincoln, who had received less than two years of formal schooling as a child in backwoods Indiana, sharpened his intellect in the early 1830s as a member of the New Salem (Illinois) debating society. In 1838, after moving to Springfield, he set forth his political principles when he spoke at the local lyceum on "The Perpetuation of Our Political Institutions." More than the public schools, the lyceums and debating societies fostered independent thought and encouraged new ideas.

## Discovering the Asylum

Some segments of the population were obviously beyond the reach of family government and character training provided in homes and schools. In the 1820s and 1830s, reformers became acutely aware of the danger to society posed by an apparently increasing number of criminals, lunatics, and paupers. Their answer was to establish special institutions to house those deemed incapable of self-discipline. Their goals were humanitarian; they believed reform and rehabilitation were possible in a carefully controlled environment.

In earlier times, the existence of paupers, lawbreakers, and insane persons had been taken for granted. Their presence was viewed as the consequence of divine judgment or original sin. For the most part, these people were dealt with in ways that did not isolate them from local communities. The insane were allowed to wander about if harmless and were confined at home if they were dangerous; the poor were supported by private charity or the dole provided by towns or counties; convicted criminals were whipped, held for limited periods in local jails, or—in the case of very serious offenses—executed.

By the early nineteenth century, these traditional methods had come to seem both inadequate and inhumane. Dealing with deviants in a neighborly way broke down as economic development and urbanization made communities less cohesive.

At the same time, reformers were concluding that all defects of mind and character were correctable—the insane could be cured, criminals reformed, and paupers taught to pull themselves out of destitution. The result was what historian David Rothman termed "the discovery of the asylum"—the invention and establishment of special institutions for the confinement and reformation of deviants.

The 1820s and 1830s saw the emergence of state-supported prisons, insane asylums, and poorhouses. New York and Pennsylvania led the way in prison reform. Institutions at Auburn, New York, and Philadelphia attracted international attention as model penitentiaries, mainly because of their experiments in isolating inmates from one another. Solitary confinement was viewed as a humanitarian and therapeutic policy because it gave inmates a chance to reflect on their sins, free from the corrupting influence of other convicts. In theory, prisons and asylums substituted for the family. Custodians were meant to act as parents, providing moral advice and training.

In practice, the institutions were far different from the affectionate families idealized by the cult of domesticity. Most accommodated only a single sex or maintained a strict segregation of male and female inmates. Their most prominent feature was the imposition of a rigid daily routine. The early superintendents and wardens believed the enforcement of a rigorous set of rules and procedures would encour-

*The Eastern State Penitentiary in Philadelphia followed the Pennsylvania system of prison design. Prisoners were kept in solitary confinement in individual cells, and seven long cellblocks radiated out from a central rotunda. Each cell had two front doors—one of wood and the other of metal equipped with a trap through which meals were passed to the inmate. The cell also had a back door that opened to a small exercise yard. A strict regimen of silence was meant to encourage prisoners to reflect on their crimes.* ✦

*Dorothea Dix (1802–1887). Her efforts on behalf of the mentally ill led to the building of more than thirty institutions in the United States and the reform and restaffing—with well-trained personnel—of existing hospitals. She died in Trenton, New Jersey, in 1887, in a hospital that she had founded.* ❖

age self-discipline. The French observers Alexis de Tocqueville and Gustave de Beaumont summed up these practical expectations after a tour of American prisons in 1831 and 1832: "The habits or order to which the prisoner is subjected for several years . . . the obedience of every moment to inflexible rules, the regularity of a uniform life . . . are calculated to produce a deep impression upon his mind. Perhaps, leaving the prison he is not an honest man, but he has contracted honest habits."

Prisons, asylums, and poorhouses did not achieve the aims of their founders. Public support was inadequate to meet the needs of a growing inmate population, and the personnel of the institutions often lacked the training needed to help the incarcerated. The results were overcrowding and the use of brutality to keep order. For the most part, prisons failed to reform hardened criminals, and the primitive psychotherapy known as "moral treatment" failed to cure most asylum patients. Poorhouses rapidly degenerated into sinkholes of despair. A combination of naive theories and poor performance doomed the institutions to a custodial rather than a reformatory role.

Conditions would have been even worse had it not been for Dorothea Dix. Between 1838 and the Civil War, this remarkable woman devoted her energies and skills to publicizing the inhumane treatment prevailing in prisons, almshouses, and insane asylums and to lobbying for corrective action. As a direct result of her activities, fifteen states opened new hospitals for the insane and others improved their supervision of penitentiaries, asylums, and poorhouses. Dix ranks as one of the most practical and effective of all the reformers of the pre–Civil War era.

# REFORM TURNS RADICAL

During the 1830s, internal dissension split the great reform movement spawned by the Second Great Awakening. Efforts to promote evangelical piety, improve personal and public morality, and shape character through familial or institutional discipline continued and even flourished. But bolder spirits went beyond such goals and set their sights on the total liberation and perfection of the individual.

## Divisions in the Benevolent Empire

Early-nineteenth-century reformers were, for the most part, committed to changing existing attitudes and practices gradually and in ways that would not invite conflict or disrupt society. But by the mid-1830s, a new mood of impatience and perfectionism surfaced within the benevolent societies. In 1836, for example, the Temperance Society split over two issues— whether the abstinence pledge should be extended to include beer and wine and whether pressure should be applied to producers and sellers of alcoholic beverages as well as to consumers. Radicals insisted on a total commitment to "cold water" and were prepared to clash head-on with an important economic interest. Moderates held back from such goals and tactics because they wanted to avoid hostility from prominent citizens who drank wine or had money invested in the liquor industry.

A similar rift occurred in the American Peace Society, an antiwar organization founded in 1828 by clergymen seeking to promote Christian concern for world peace. Most of the founders admitted the propriety of "defensive wars" and were shocked when some members of the society began to denounce all use of force as a violation of the Sermon on the Mount. Dissidents, who called themselves "nonresistants," withdrew from the organization in 1838. Led by Henry C. Wright, they formed the New England Non-Resistance Society to promote an absolute pacifism, which denied the right of self-defense to nations or individuals and repudiated all forms of government coercion.

The new perfectionism realized its most dramatic and important success within the antislavery movement. Before the 1830s, most people who expressed religious and moral concern over slavery were affiliated with the **American Colonization Society,** a benevolent organization founded in 1817. Most colonizationists admitted that slavery was an evil, but they also viewed it as a deeply rooted social and economic institution that could be eliminated only very gradually and with the cooperation of slaveholders. Reflecting the power of racial prejudice, they proposed to provide transportation to Africa for free blacks who chose to go, or were emancipated for the purpose, as a way of relieving southern fears that a race war would erupt if slaves were simply released from bondage and allowed to remain in America. In 1821, the society established the colony of Liberia in West Africa, and during the next decade a few thousand African Americans were settled there.

Colonization proved to be grossly inadequate as a step toward the elimination of slavery. Many of the blacks transported to Africa were already free, and those liberated by masters influenced by the movement represented only a tiny percentage of the natural increase of the southern slave population. Northern blacks denounced the enterprise because it denied the prospect of racial equality in America. Black opposition to colonizationism helped persuade William Lloyd Garrison and other white abolitionists to repudiate the Colonization Society and support immediate emancipation without emigration.

Garrison launched a new and more radical antislavery movement in 1831 in Boston, when he began to publish a journal called the *Liberator*. Besides calling for immediate and unconditional emancipation, Garrison denounced colonization as a slaveholder's plot to remove troublesome free blacks and as an ignoble surrender to un-Christian prejudices. His rhetoric was as severe as his proposals were radical. As he wrote

*In the inaugural issue of his antislavery weekly, the* Liberator, *William Lloyd Garrison announced that he was launching a militant battle against the evil and sin of slavery. The stirring words that appeared in that first issue are repeated on the* Liberator's *banner.* ❖

in the first issue of the *Liberator*, "I will be as harsh as truth and as uncompromising as justice. . . . I am in earnest—I will not equivocate—I will not excuse—I will not retreat a single inch—And I WILL BE HEARD!" Heard he was. In 1833, Garrison and other abolitionists founded the American Anti-Slavery Society. "We shall send forth agents to lift up the voice of remonstrance, of warning, of entreaty, and of rebuke," its Declaration of Sentiments proclaimed. The colonization movement was placed on the defensive, and during the 1830s, many of its most active northern supporters became abolitionists.

## The Abolitionist Enterprise

The abolitionist movement, like the temperance crusade, was a direct outgrowth of the Second Great Awakening. Many leading abolitionists had undergone conversion experiences in the 1820s and were already committed to a life of Christian activism before they dedicated themselves to freeing the slaves. Several were ministers or divinity students seeking a mission in life that would fulfill spiritual and professional ambitions.

The career of Theodore Dwight Weld exemplified the connection between revivalism and abolitionism. Weld came from a long line of New England ministers. After dropping out of divinity school because of a combination of physical and spiritual ailments, he migrated to western New York. There he fell under the influence of Charles G. Finney and, after a long struggle, underwent a conversion experience in 1826. He then became an itinerant lecturer for various reform causes. By the early 1830s, he focused his attention on the moral issues raised by the institution of slavery. After a brief flirtation with the colonization movement, Weld was converted to abolitionism in 1832, recognizing that colonizationists did not really accept blacks as equals or "brothers-in-Christ." In 1834, he instigated what amounted to a series of abolitionist revivals at Lane Theological Seminary in Cincinnati. When the trustees of the seminary attempted to suppress further discussion of the case for immediate emancipation, Weld led a mass walkout of most students. The "Lane rebels" subsequently founded Oberlin College as a center for abolitionist activity.

In 1835 and 1836, Weld toured Ohio and western New York preaching abolitionism. He also supervised and trained other agents and orators as part of a campaign to convert the entire region to immediate emancipation. The tried-and-true methods of the revival—fervent preaching, protracted meetings, and the call for individuals to come forth and announce their redemption—were put at the service of the antislavery movement. Weld and his associates often had to face angry mobs, but they left behind them tens of thousands of new abolitionists and hundreds of local antislavery societies. As a result of their efforts, northern Ohio and western New York became hotbeds of abolitionist sentiment.

Antislavery orators and organizers tended to have their greatest successes in the small- to medium-sized towns of the upper North. The typical convert came from an upwardly mobile family engaged in small business, the skilled trades, or market farming. In larger towns and cities, or when they ventured close to the Mason-Dixon line, abolitionists were more likely to encounter fierce and effective opposition. In 1835, Garrison was mobbed in the streets of Boston and almost lynched. In New York City, the Tappan brothers—Lewis and Arthur—were frequent objects of threats and violence. These two successful merchants were key figures in the movement because they used their substantial wealth to finance antislavery activities. In 1835–1836, they supported a massive effort to print antislavery pamphlets and distribute them through the U.S. mails. But they made relatively few converts in their own city; most New Yorkers regarded them as dangerous radicals.

Abolitionists who thought of taking their message to the fringes of the South had reason to pause, given the fate of the antislavery editor Elijah Lovejoy. In 1837, while attempting to defend himself and his printing press from a mob in Alton, Illinois, just across the Mississippi River from slaveholding Missouri, Lovejoy was shot and killed.

Racism was a major cause of antiabolitionist violence in the North. Rumors that abolitionists advocated or practiced interracial marriage could easily incite an urban crowd. If it could not find white abolitionists, the mob was likely to turn on local blacks. Working-class whites tended to fear that economic and social competition with blacks would increase if abolitionists succeeded in freeing slaves and making them citizens. But a striking feature of many of the mobs was that they were dominated by "gentlemen of property and standing." Solid citizens resorted to violence, it would appear, because abolitionism threatened their conservative notions of social order and hierarchy.

By the end of the 1830s, the abolitionist movement was under great stress. Besides the burden of external repression, there was dissension within the movement. Becoming an abolitionist required an exacting conscience and an unwillingness to compromise on matters of principle. These character traits also made it difficult for abolitionists to work together and maintain a united front. During the late 1830s, Garrison, the most visible proponent of the cause, began to adopt positions that some other abolitionists found extreme and divisive. He embraced the nonresistant or "no-government" philosophy of Henry C. Wright and urged abolitionists to abstain from voting or otherwise participating in a corrupt political system. He also attacked the clergy and the churches for refusing to take a strong antislavery stand and encouraged his followers to "come out" of the established denominations rather than continuing to work within them.

These positions alienated those members of the Anti-Slavery Society who continued to hope that organized religion and the existing political system could be influenced or even taken over by abolitionists. But it was Garrison's stand on women's rights that led to an open break at the national convention of the American Anti-Slavery Society in 1840. Following their leader's principle that women should be equal partners in the crusade, a Garrison-led majority elected a woman abolitionist to the society's executive committee. A minority, led by Lewis Tappan, then withdrew to form a competing organization—the American and Foreign Anti-Slavery Society.

The new organization never amounted to much, but the schism did weaken Garrison's influence within the movement. When he later repudiated the U.S. Constitution as a proslavery document and called for northern secession from the Union, few antislavery people in the Middle Atlantic or midwestern states went along. Outside New England, most abolitionists worked within the churches and avoided controversial side issues such as women's rights and nonresistant pacifism. Some antislavery advocates chose the path of political action. The **Liberty party,** organized in 1840, was their first attempt to enter the electoral arena under their own banner; it signaled a new effort to turn antislavery sentiment into political power.

## Black Abolitionists

From the beginning the abolitionist movement depended heavily on the support of the northern free black community. Most of the early subscribers to Garrison's *Liberator* were African Americans. Black orators, especially escaped slaves such as Frederick Douglass, made northern audiences aware of the realities of bondage. But relations between white and black abolitionists were often tense and uneasy. Blacks protested that they did not have their fair share of leadership positions or influence over policy. Eventually a black antislavery movement emerged that was largely independent of the white-led crusade. In addition to Douglass, prominent black male abolitionists were Charles Remond, William Wells Brown, Robert Purvis, and Henry Highland Garnet. Outspoken women such as Sojourner Truth, Maria Stewart, and Frances Harper also played a significant role in black antislavery activity. The Negro Convention movement, which sponsored national meetings of black leaders beginning in 1830, provided an important forum for independent black expression. Their most eloquent statement came in 1854, when black leaders met in Cleveland to declare their faith in a separate identity, proclaiming, "We pledge our integrity to use all honorable means, to unite us, as one people, on this continent."

*African American leaders in the abolitionist movement included Frederick Douglass (right) and William Whipper (left). Douglass, who escaped from slavery in 1838, became one of the most effective voices in the crusade against slavery. In 1837, twelve years before Thoreau's essay "Civil Disobedience," Whipper published an article titled "An Address on Non-Resistance to Offensive Aggression." Whipper was also one of the founders of the American Moral Reform Society, an African American abolitionist organization.* ❖

Black newspapers, such as *Freedom's Journal*, first published in 1827, and the *North Star*, founded by Douglass in 1847, gave black writers a chance to preach their gospel of liberation to black readers. African American authors also produced a stream of books and pamphlets attacking slavery, refuting racism, and advocating various forms of resistance. One of the most influential publications was David Walker's *Appeal . . . to the Colored Citizens of the World*, which appeared in 1829. Walker denounced slavery in the most vigorous language possible and called for a black revolt against white tyranny.

Free blacks in the North did more than make verbal protests against racial injustice. They were also the main conductors on the fabled Underground Railroad that opened a path for fugitives from slavery. It has been supposed that benevolent whites were primarily responsible for organized efforts to guide and assist fugitive slaves, but modern research has shown that the Underground Railroad was largely a black-operated enterprise. Courageous ex-slaves such as Harriet Tubman and Josiah Henson made regular forays into the slave states to lead other blacks to freedom, and many of the "stations" along the way were run by free blacks. In northern towns and cities, free blacks organized "vigilance committees" to protect fugitives and thwart the slave-catchers. Groups of blacks even used force to rescue recaptured fugitives from the authorities. In Boston in 1851, one such group seized a slave named Shadrack from a U.S. marshal who was in the process of returning him to bondage. In deeds as well as words, free blacks showed their unyielding hostility to slavery and racism.

Historians have debated the question of whether the abolitionist movement of the 1830s and early 1840s was a success or a failure. It obviously failed to convert a majority of Americans to its position that slavery was a sinful institution that should be abolished immediately. This position implied that blacks should be granted equality as American citizens, so it ran up against the powerful commitment to white supremacy prevailing in all parts of the country. In the South, abolitionism caused a strong counteraction and helped inspire a more militant and uncompromising defense of slavery. The belief that peaceful agitation, or what abolitionists called "moral suasion," would convert slaveholders and their northern sympathizers to abolition was obviously unrealistic.

But in another sense the crusade was successful. It brought the slavery issue to the forefront of public consciousness and convinced a substantial and growing segment of the northern population that the South's peculiar institution was morally wrong and potentially dangerous to the American way of life. The South helped the antislavery cause in the North by responding hysterically and repressively to abolitionist agitation. In 1836, Southerners in Congress forced

*Harriet Tubman, far left, is shown here with some of the slaves she helped escape on the Underground Railroad. Born a slave in Maryland, she escaped to Philadelphia in 1849. She is said to have helped as many as three-hundred African Americans flee slavery. She led many of them all the way to Canada, where they would be beyond the reach of the Fugitive Slave Law.* ❖

adoption of a "gag rule" requiring that abolitionist petitions be tabled without being read; at about the same time, the post office refused to carry antislavery literature into the slave states. Prominent Northerners who had not been moved to action by abolitionist depictions of slave suffering became more responsive to the movement when it appeared their own civil liberties might be threatened. The politicians who later mobilized the North against the expansion of slavery into the territories drew strength from the antislavery and antisouthern sentiments that abolitionists had already called forth.

## From Abolitionism to Women's Rights

Abolitionism also served as a catalyst for the women's rights movement. From the beginning, women were active participants in the abolitionist crusade. Between 1835 and 1838, the American Anti-Slavery Society bombarded Congress with petitions, mostly calling for abolition of slavery in the District of Columbia. More than half of the thousands of antislavery petitions sent to Washington had women's signatures on them.

Some antislavery women went further and defied conventional ideas of their proper sphere by becoming public speakers and demanding an equal role in the leadership of antislavery societies. The most famous of these were the Grimké sisters, Sarah and Angelina, who attracted enormous attention being the rebellious daughters of a South Carolina slaveholder. When some male abolitionists objected to their speaking in public to mixed audiences of men and women, Garrison

came to their defense and helped forge a link between blacks' and women's struggles for equality.

The battle to participate equally in the antislavery crusade made a number of women abolitionists acutely aware of male dominance and oppression. For them, the same principles that justified the liberation of the slaves also applied to the emancipation of women from all restrictions on their rights as citizens. In 1840, Garrison's American followers withdrew from the first World's Anti-Slavery Convention in London because the sponsors refused to seat the women in their delegation. Among the women thus excluded were Lucretia Mott and Elizabeth Cady Stanton.

Wounded by men's reluctance to extend the cause of emancipation to include women, Stanton and Mott began discussing plans for a women's rights convention. They returned to New York, where a campaign was already underway to reform the state's laws limiting the rights of married women, spearheaded by a young Jewish activist, Ernestine Rose, and Judge Thomas Herttell, the political radical and freethinker who had introduced the first bill to reform the state's marriage laws to the New York state legislature. (See the Law and Society essay, "The Legal Rights of Married Women: Reforming the Law of Coverture, pp. 354–357.) The campaign for women's rights came to a head at the famous **Seneca Falls Convention** Stanton and Mott organized in upstate New York in 1848. The Declaration of Sentiments issued by this first national gathering of feminists charged that "the history of mankind is a history of repeated injuries and usurpations on the part of man toward woman, having in direct object the establishment of an absolute tyranny over her." It went on to demand that all women be given the right to vote and that married women be freed from unjust laws giving husbands control of their property, persons, and children. Rejecting the cult of domesticity with its doctrine of separate spheres, these women and their male supporters launched the modern movement for gender equality.

## Radical Ideas and Experiments

Hopes for individual or social perfection were not limited to reformers inspired by evangelicalism. Between the 1820s and 1850s, a great variety of schemes for human redemption came from those who had rejected orthodox Protestantism. Some were secular humanists carrying on the freethinking tradition of the Enlightenment, but most were seekers of new paths to spiritual or religious fulfillment. A movement that achieved remarkable success or notoriety was

*Elizabeth Cady Stanton, a leader of the women's rights movement, reared seven children. In addition to her pioneering work, especially for woman suffrage, she also lectured frequently on family life and child care.* ❖

spiritualism—the belief that one could communicate with the dead. (See the Feature Essay, "Spiritualism: Religion or Entertainment?" pp. 348–349.) These philosophical and religious radicals attacked established institutions, prescribed new modes of living, and founded utopian communities to put their ideas into practice.

A radical movement of foreign origin that gained a toehold in Jacksonian America was utopian socialism. In 1825–1826, the British manufacturer and reformer Robert Owen visited the United States and founded a community based on common and equal ownership of property at New Harmony, Indiana. About the same time, Owen's associate Frances Wright gathered a group of slaves at Nashoba, Tennessee, and set them to work earning their freedom in an atmosphere of "rational cooperation." The rapid demise of both of these model communities suggested that utopian socialism did not easily take root in American soil.

But the impulse survived. In the 1840s, a number of Americans, including the prominent editor Horace Greeley, became interested in the ideas of the French utopian theorist Charles Fourier. Fourier called for cooperative communities in which everyone did a fair share of the work and tasks were allotted to make use of the natural abilities and instincts of the members. Between 1842 and 1852, about thirty Fourierist "phalanxes" were established in the northeastern and midwestern states, and approximately a hundred thousand people lived for a time in these communities or otherwise supported the movement. The phalanxes were not purely socialistic; in fact, they were organized as joint-stock companies. But they did give the members an opportunity to live and work in a communal atmosphere. Like the Owenite communities, they were short-lived, surviving for an average of only two years. The common complaint of the founders was that Americans were too individualistic to cooperate in the ways that Fourier's theories required.

Two of the most successful and long-lived manifestations of pre–Civil War **utopianism** were the Shakers and the Oneida community. The **Shakers**—officially known as the Millennial Church or the United Society of Believers—began as a religious movement in England. In 1774, a Shaker leader, Mother Ann Lee, brought their radical beliefs to the United States. Lee believed herself to be the feminine incarnation of Christ and advocated a new theology based squarely on the principle of sexual equality. The Shakers, named for their expressions of religious fervor through vigorous dancelike movements, believed in communal ownership and strict celibacy. They lived simply and minimized their contact with the outside world because they expected Christ's Second Coming to occur momentar-

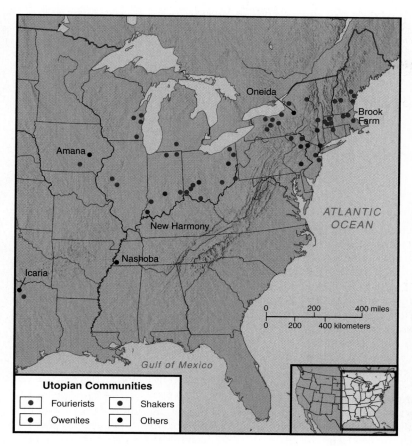

**UTOPIAN COMMUNITIES BEFORE THE CIVIL WAR**  *The search for new paths to spiritual or religious fulfillment attracted many to utopian communitarian societies. By far the largest of these societies during the period before the Civil War was the Shakers, who by the 1830s had established twenty settlements in seven states with a combined membership of approximately six thousand. Their rule of celibacy meant that Shaker communities gained members through adoption and conversion, rather than by natural reproduction.* ❖

ily. The **Oneida community** was established in 1848 at Oneida, New York, and was inspired by an unorthodox brand of Christian perfectionism. Its founder, John Humphrey Noyes, believed the Second Coming of Christ had already occurred; hence human beings were no longer obliged to follow the moral rules that their previously fallen state had required. At Oneida, traditional marriage was outlawed, and a carefully regulated form of "free love" was put into practice.

It was a literary and philosophical movement known as **transcendentalism** that inspired the era's most memorable experiments in thinking and living on a higher plane. The main idea was that the individual could transcend material reality and ordinary understanding, attaining through a higher form of reason—or intuition—a oneness with the universe as a whole and with the spiritual forces that lay behind it. Transcendentalism was the major American version of the romantic and idealist thought that emerged in the early nineteenth century. Throughout the Western world, and especially in Germany, romanticism was challenging the rationalism and materialism of the Enlightenment in the name of exalted feeling and cosmic spirituality. Most American transcendentalists

were Unitarians or ex-Unitarians who were dissatisfied with the sober rationalism of their denomination and sought a more intense kind of spiritual experience. Unable to embrace evangelical Christianity because of intellectual resistance to its doctrines, they sought inspiration from a philosophical and literary idealism of German origin.

Their prophet was Ralph Waldo Emerson, a brilliant essayist and lecturer who preached that each individual could commune directly with a benign spiritual force that animated nature and the universe, which he called the "oversoul." Emerson was a radical individualist committed to "self-culture" and "the sufficiency of the private man." He carefully avoided all involvement in organized movements or associations because he believed they limited the freedom of the individual to develop inner resources and find a personal path to spiritual illumination. In the vicinity of Emerson's home in Concord, Massachusetts, a group of like-minded seekers of truth and spiritual fulfillment gathered during the 1830s and 1840s. Among them for a time was Margaret Fuller, the leading woman intellectual of the age. In *Woman in*

# SPIRITUALISM

## Religion or Entertainment?

On November 26, 1855, George Templeton Strong, a prominent New York attorney, returned home from an elegant dinner. That night, he sat down to record in his diary the day's events, including a long conversation about how many of his friends and neighbors had embraced spiritualism—the belief that it was possible to communicate with the spirits of the dead. He asked his diary,

> What would I have said six years ago to anybody who predicted that before the enlightened nineteenth century was ended hundreds of thousands of people in this country would believe themselves able to communicate daily with the ghosts of their grandfathers? It is surely one of the most startling events that have occurred for centuries and one of the most significant. A New Revelation, hostile to that of Church and the Bible, finding acceptance on the authority of knocking ghosts . . . is a momentous fact in history, throwing light on the intellectual caliber and moral tone of the age in which multitudes adopt it.

Indeed, by the mid-1850s it seemed as if everyone in the country was talking about spirits. Most scholars have agreed that during the decade at least a million Americans were active believers in spiritualism. Many more were exposed to the belief through articles and editorials in popular magazines such as *Harper's* and *Atlantic Monthly*. Stories about hauntings and seances also appeared on the front pages of newspapers such as the *New York Times* and the *New York Tribune*. Hundreds of books and pamphlets described encounters with the world beyond and spiritualism was featured in popular plays, poems, and songs. Some notable Americans, including governors, clergymen, and scientists, publicly declared their belief in the ability to make contact with the spirit world. Spiritualist themes even found their way into the work of authors such as Nathaniel Hawthorne, Ralph Waldo Emerson, and Henry James.

Many Americans were shocked by the sudden popularity of talking to the dead. Some critics saw the passion for spiritualism as foolish or dangerous; they accused spiritualists of perpetrating a "humbug," a fraud that was less credible than the exhibits found at P. T. Barnum's American Museum. Others, however, thought that the belief in the spirits was a kind of witchcraft or even a sign of widespread insanity. Because of this opposition, some people who claimed that they talked to the spirits were thrown in jail or taken to insane asylums. Given these tensions, respected scientists investigated spiritualism in the hopes of explaining what caused the manifestations. In 1857, one committee, led by several professors from Harvard University, offered $500 to anyone who could provide proof of spiritualism. After a number of mediums failed to provide convincing evidence of their powers, the committee announced that spiritualism was a "contaminating influence."

Even spiritualists argued over what the manifestations meant. For some, contacting the spirits was mainly a form of entertainment. Others argued that the spirits provided the basis for a new philosophy—or even a new religion. The view of spiritualism as entertainment grew out of the experiences of two girls in Hydesville, a small village in upstate New York. On March 28, 1848, Kate and Margaret Fox reported hearing loud raps and poundings on the walls and floorboards of their bedroom. The girls assumed that the noises were spirits who were attempting to communicate and asked questions of the spirits, who allegedly rapped their answers in a code. Soon, curious onlookers filled the Fox house, and the girls' parents sent them to live with their sister Leah in Rochester, New York. The rapping spirits followed the girls, and their fame spread. Before long, the three girls were performing in New York City, where their demonstrations created a sensation. By the time the sisters left the city, hundreds of mediums were operating to the accompaniment of raps, spirit voices, and ghostly music. Many people gathered in parlors to hold séances or attended public displays of "spirit rapping" in hope of receiving proof of the existence of spirits. For many of the observers, spiritualism offered the thrill of a magic show or the solace of talking to a departed loved one.

The view of spiritualism as a philosophical system began in 1847 with the publication of Andrew Jackson Davis's book, *The Principles of*

The three Fox sisters, Margaret, Kate, and Leah, shown here in solemn pose, became professional mediums who thrilled audiences at their performances with loud rappings, tilting tables, and visions and materialization of spirits. ❖

*Nature.* In this long work, Davis described the world of spirits he visited while in a hypnotic trance. He argued that the spirits were trying to teach people a better way of life and interpreted his experiences with the spirit world as a call for a new philosophy, which he called Harmonialism. Davis, and spiritualists who shared his reforming dreams, saw spiritualism as an agent of universal reform—a way to use the knowledge of the spirit realm to revolutionize religion, medicine, and society and to make the human world more closely resemble the "summer land" of the spirits.

One crucial issue was the relationship between spiritualism and Christianity. Many people believed that it was possible to be a Christian and a spiritualist; after all, spiritualism proved the Bible's claim that spirits lived past death. Others believed that talking to spirits was evil and a form of heresy condemned by Christ. For the latter, spiritualism was

not a religion—it was a sin. Yet spiritualism definitely resembled a religion in some of the answers it provided believers. For example, it offered guidance about the best way to live and information about the world beyond death. Unlike most religions, however, it had no dogma that defined spiritualist beliefs, no special places to worship, and no established religious leaders. Individual spiritualists were left to determine for themselves what it meant to be talking to the spirits of the dead.

Although spiritualism answered some of the same questions as more mainstream religions, in some ways spiritualism operated in a very nonreligious fashion. Most religions required that certain beliefs, such as the existence of God, be taken on faith—people accepted those beliefs without proof. Spiritualists, however, could see and hear the spirits of the dead, which eliminated the need to trust in faith alone. For some believers, spiritualism

was a "scientific" religion that offered evidence of the existence of life after death. The séance parlor became a kind of religious laboratory where spiritualists sought scientific proof for religious hypotheses.

Spiritualism continued to be popular through the Civil War. Séances even were conducted in the Lincoln White House. Immediately following the war, spiritualism experienced a revival as a generation of Americans grappled with the death of more than 600,000 soldiers. As the memory of the war waned, the popularity of spiritualism declined, although its notoriety rose and fell throughout the rest of the nineteenth century. The interest in the spirit world spread into other pursuits, such as the scientific exploration of the paranormal by Harvard professor William James (brother of the novelist Henry James) and the founding of the American Society for Psychical Research in 1885.

*Ritualized dances were part of the Shakers' spiritual preparation for the Second Coming. The dancers in this nineteenth-century etching exemplify the mixed heritage of the Shaker community.* ❖

*the Nineteenth Century* (1845), she made a strong claim for the spiritual and artistic equality of women.

One group of transcendentalists, led by the Reverend George Ripley, rejected Emerson's radical individualism and founded a cooperative community at **Brook Farm,** near Roxbury, Massachusetts, in 1841. For the next four years, group members worked the land in common, conducted an excellent school on the principle that spontaneity rather than discipline was the key to education, and allowed ample time for conversation, meditation, communion with nature, and artistic activity of all kinds. Visitors and guest lecturers included such luminaries as Emerson, Margaret Fuller, and Theodore Parker, the Unitarian theologian and radical reformer. In 1845, Brook Farm was reconstituted as a Fourierist phalanx, but some of the original spirit persisted until its dissolution in 1849.

Another experiment in transcendental living adhered more closely to the in-dividualistic spirit of the movement. Between 1845 and 1847, Henry David Thoreau, a young disciple of Emerson, lived by himself in the woods along the shore of Walden Pond and carefully recorded his thoughts and impressions. In a sense, he pushed the ideal of self-culture to its logical outcome—a utopia of one. The result was *Walden* (published in 1854), one of the greatest achievements in American literature.

*Henry David Thoreau explained that he went to live in solitude in the woods because he wanted to "front only the essential facts of life." The sketch at right appeared on the title page of the first edition of* Walden *(1854), the remarkable record of his experiment in living.* ❖

## CHRONOLOGY

| | |
|---|---|
| **1801** | Massive revival held at Cane Ridge, Kentucky |
| **1826** | American Temperance Society organized |
| **1830–1831** | Charles G. Finney evangelizes Rochester, New York |
| **1831** | William Lloyd Garrison publishes first issue of the *Liberator* |
| **1833** | Abolitionists found American Anti-Slavery Society |
| **1835–1836** | Theodore Weld advocates abolition in Ohio and upstate New York |
| **1836** | American Temperance Society splits into factions |
| **1837** | Massachusetts establishes a state board of education  ❖  Abolitionist editor Elijah Lovejoy killed by a proslavery mob |
| **1840** | American Anti-Slavery Society splits over women's rights and other issues |
| **1841** | Transcendentalists organize a model community at Brook Farm |
| **1848** | Feminists gather at Seneca Falls, New York, and found the women's rights movement |
| **1854** | Henry David Thoreau's *Walden* published |

## CONCLUSION: COUNTERPOINT ON REFORM

One great American writer observed at close quarters the perfectionist ferment of the age but held himself aloof, suggesting in his novels and tales that pursuit of the ideal led to a distorted view of human nature and possibilities. Nathaniel Hawthorne lived in Concord, knew Emerson and Margaret Fuller, and even spent time at Brook Farm. But his sense of human frailty made him skeptical about the claims of transcendentalism and utopianism. He satirized transcendentalism as unworldly and overoptimistic in his allegorical tale "The Celestial Railroad" and gently lampooned the denizens of Brook Farm in his novel *The Blithedale Romance* (1852). His view of the dangers of pursuing perfection too avidly came out in his tale of a father who kills his beautiful daughter by trying to remove her one blemish, a birthmark. His greatest novels, *The Scarlet Letter* (1850) and *The House of the Seven Gables* (1851), imaginatively probed New England's Puritan past and the shadows it cast on the present. By dwelling on original sin as a psychological reality, Hawthorne told his contemporaries that their efforts to escape from guilt and evil were futile. One simply had to ac-

cept the world as an imperfect place. Although he did not engage in polemics against humanitarian reformers and cosmic optimists, Hawthorne wrote parables and allegories that implicitly questioned the fundamental assumptions of pre–Civil War reform.

One does not have to agree with Hawthorne's antiprogressive view of the human condition to acknowledge that the dreams of perfectionist reformers promised more than they could possibly deliver. Revivals could not make all men like Christ; temperance could not solve all social problems; abolitionist agitation could not bring a peaceful end to slavery; and transcendentalism (as Emerson himself sometimes conceded) could not fully emancipate people from the limitations and frustrations of daily life. The consequences of perfectionist efforts were often far different from what their proponents expected. In defense of the reformers, however, one could argue that Hawthorne's skepticism and

*Hester Prynne and her daughter Pearl in an illustration from* The Scarlet Letter *by Nathaniel Hawthorne. In the novel, which stands as one of the masterpieces of American literature, Hawthorne probes the dark side of human nature as he explores the effect of sin—actual and symbolic—on the characters.* ❖

fatalism were a prescription for doing nothing in the face of intolerable evils. If the reform impulse was long on inspirational rhetoric but somewhat short on durable, practical achievements, it did at least disturb the complacent and opportunistic surface of American life and open the way to necessary changes. Nothing could possibly change for the better unless people were willing to dream of improvement.

## RECOMMENDED READING

Alice Felt Tyler, *Freedom's Ferment: Phases of American Social History from the Colonial Period to the Outbreak of the Civil War* (1944), gives a lively overview of the varieties of pre–Civil War reform activity. Ronald G. Walters, *American Reformers, 1815–1860, rev. ed.* (1997), provides a modern interpretation of these movements. Steven Mintz, *Moralists and Modernizers: America's Pre–Civil War Reformers* (1995), provides another good overview of the reform activities during this period. A particularly useful collection of documents on reform movements and other aspects of antebellum culture is David Brion Davis, *Antebellum American Culture: An Interpretive Anthology* (1979).

The best general work on the revivalism of the Second Great Awakening is William G. McLoughlin, *Modern Revivalism* (1959). A general survey of the religious ferment of this period is Nathan O. Hatch, *The Democratization of American Christianity* (1989). Paul E. Johnson, *A Shopkeeper's Millennium: Society and Revivals in Rochester, New York, 1815–1837* (1978), incisively describes the impact of the revival on a single community. The connection between religion and reform is described in Robert H. Abzug, *Cosmos Crumbling: American Reform and the Religious Imagination* (1994).

A good introduction to the changing roles of women and the family in nineteenth-century America is Carl N.

Degler, *At Odds: Women and the Family in America from the Revolution to the Present* (1980). On the rise of the domestic ideology, see Nancy F. Cott, *The Bonds of Womanhood: "Woman's Sphere" in New England, 1780–1835* (1977). The condition of working-class women is incisively treated in Christine Stansell, *City of Women: Sex and Class in New York, 1789–1860* (1986). For an extended history of the *Cruger* case and an excellent legal history of marriage and divorce, see Hendrick Hartog, *Man and Wife in America: A History* (2000).

David J. Rothman, *The Discovery of the Asylum: Social Order and Disorder in the New Republic* (1971), provides a penetrating analysis of the movement for institutional reform. For good surveys of abolitionism, see James Brewer Stewart, *Holy Warriors: The Abolitionists and American Slavery* (1976) and Paul Goodman, *Of One Blood: Abolitionism and Racial Equality* (1998). On transcendentalism, see Charles Capper and Conrad E. Wright, *Transient and Permanent: The Transcendentalist Movement and Its Contexts* (1999).

**For a list of additional titles related to this chapter's topics, please see** http://www.ablongman.com/divine.

## SUGGESTED WEB SITES

### America's First Look into the Camera: Daguerreotype Portraits and Views, 1839–1862

http://memory.loc.gov/ammem/daghtml/daghome.html
The Library of Congress's daguerreotype collection consists of more than 650 photographs dating from 1839 to 1864. Portraits, architectural views, and some street scenes make up most of the collection.

### 1830s Clothing

http://www.connerprairie.org/historyonline/clothing.html
See how clothing worn in the Early Republic was quite different from what people wear today.

### Votes for Women: Selections from the National American Woman Suffrage Association Collection, 1848–1921

http://memory.loc.gov/ammem/naw/nawshome.html
This Library of Congress site contains 167 books, pamphlets, and other artifacts documenting the suffrage campaign.

### History of Women's Suffrage

http://www.rochester.edu/SBA/history.html
This site includes a chronology, important texts relating to women's suffrage, and biographical information about Susan B. Anthony and Elizabeth Cady Stanton.

**By Popular Demand: "Votes for Women" Suffrage Pictures, 1850–1920**

http://memory.loc.gov/ammem/vfwhtml/vfwhome.html
Portraits, suffrage parades, picketing suffragists, an antisuffrage display, and cartoons commenting on the movement make up this Library of Congress site.

**Women in America, 1820 to 1842**

http://xroads.virginia.edu/~HYPER/DETOC/FEM/home.htm
This University of Virginia site takes a look at women in antebellum America.

**Godey's Lady's Book On-line**

http://www.history.rochester.edu/godeys/
Here is on-line text of this interesting nineteenth-century journal.

**Influence of Prominent Abolitionists**

http://www.loc.gov/exhibits/african/afam006.html
An exhibit site from the Library of Congress, with pictures and text, which discusses some key African American abolitionists and their efforts to end slavery.

# The Legal Rights of Married Women

## Reforming the Law of Coverture

By the common law in effect in the United States in the early nineteenth century, women lost their legal personality when they married. The system of *coverture* governed the union of husband and wife; married women were under the "wing, protection, or *cover*" of their husbands.

Coverture was based on the English medieval feudal system in which lords and vassals owed allegiance to the king, and commoners to lords and vassals. Under the common law of England, husband and wife were referred to as "baron" and "feme." William Blackstone, the English jurist, professor of common law, and author of *Commentaries on the Law of England,* explained, "the word baron, or lord, attributes to the husband not a very courteous superiority . . . if the baron kills his feme, it is the same as if he had killed a stranger, or any other person; but if the feme kills her baron, it is regarded by the laws as a much more atrocious crime; as she not only breaks through the restraints of humanity and conjugal affection, but throws off all subjection to the authority of her husband. And therefore the law denominates her crime, a species of treason, and condemns her to the same punishment as if she had killed the king." As Blackstone explained, "By marriage, the husband and wife are one person in the law."

Coverture denied married women their rights to own and manage property, to form contracts, to sue and be sued, and to exercise legal control over children. Upon marriage, all of a wife's personal property became her husband's, which he could give or will to someone else if he chose. The husband could not sell his wife's real estate, but he could control and manage it, and any profits derived from the property belonged to him.

Coverture had a few benefits for women. Husbands took legal responsibility for any crimes their wives committed, and sometimes wives could avoid responsibility for unwise financial transactions because they had had no legal right to enter into them. A widow had a right to one-third of her husband's property (her "dower"), if he died without a will. And a husband had a limited obligation to provide for his wife's "necessaries." Blackstone concluded his chapter on husband and wife with the observation that "even the disabilities, which the wife lies under, are for the most part intended for her protection and benefit. So great a favourite is the female sex of the laws of England."

In practice, some women, especially wealthy women, were able to get around some of the laws of coverture by taking advantage of loopholes in the law. First of all, women could go to courts of "equity" or "chancery," in which a chancellor, rather than a jury, could decide the fair or just outcome based on the facts of the individual case, rather than applying rules of law. (These two court systems of law and equity are merged into one in most states today.) An equity court had the power not only to assign money damages but to require a contract to be carried out. For example, a couple might specify in a prenuptial contract—made before the marriage was entered into—that the wife could keep her own property from before the marriage in a "separate estate." It was also possible for a husband to assign some of his property to his wife after the marriage in a "marriage settlement." And often they arranged for the wife's separate estate to be held in "trust" and managed by a third-party trustee, usually a man.

It was the legal arrangement of coverture into which Harriet Douglas, a rich New York heiress, resisted entering. Harriet Douglas had very definite ideas about what she wanted in a husband. If she married, she intended to keep control over all of her property, "in obedience to, and conformity with the opinions and precepts of her parents," and she wanted her husband to renounce his own name, his home, and his profession, to devote himself to her and her family property. As historian Hendrik Hartog observed, according to the norms of early America, Harriet Douglas effectively wanted "her husband [to] become her wife." Henry Cruger, a young lawyer who came to New York from South Carolina and who courted Harriet Douglas, at first chafed at the restrictions she proposed for a marriage arrangement. Henry argued that "the husband ought always to possess an absolute control over the wife's property." But a few years later, Henry rethought his position, writing to Harriet in 1829 that he would accept her terms, "however derogatory to proper pride . . . and self-respect." After extensive negotiations, they finally married in 1833. Henry took "D" for his middle initial without changing his last name, and Harriet was to be known as "Mrs. Douglas Cruger." Harriet agreed to sign a property settlement agreement after rather than before the marriage ceremony, because Henry claimed that a premarital contract would become part of an embarrassing public record.

Harriet's and Henry's marriage fell almost immediately on hard times, largely over money matters. Henry repeatedly threatened to return to legal practice if Harriet did not give him more freedom to control their property, urging her, "Take away this poignard of ice from between us . . . I desire no interests separate from yours, for I love you, and we are married." On several occasions, Harriet drew up new "agency" agreements, giving Henry more control of her estate as her "agent." Her friends all urged her to "relieve" Henry "from a state of dependence" that could only be galling to a "man of honor." After years of Henry's haranguing and lobbying, in 1841 Harriet signed an order guaranteeing him one-half of her income for life. That same year, their marriage fell apart completely.

It took eight more years in New York courts to work out Henry's and Harriet's rights to her property. Henry argued that their marriage settlement was invalid because it came after rather than before the marriage. Harriet claimed the original settlement should be enforced, but the 1841 gift was invalid because Henry and his friends had coerced her into signing it. In 1848, the case ended up in the New York Supreme Court, where Judge Selah Strong decreed that the original marriage settlement was valid, giving Harriet control over her own property, but that the 1841 order was enforceable as well, giving control over half of it to Henry. Years later, Strong wrote, "She was mad and he was bad, and the legal muddle they brought about between them was very deep and formidable."

At the end of their legal muddle, Henry emerged victorious with control over half of Harriet's separate estate. Despite her strenuous efforts to be an independent married woman, she had failed. In disgust, she "had her marriage bed cut in two, transforming it into two 'slightly peculiar' sofas."

The New York Supreme Court made its final decision in *Cruger v. Cruger*, just one year after the New York Legislature passed its first Married Women's Property Act, allowing women for the first time to maintain ownership and control over property they had inherited before they married. Over the course of the middle decades of the nineteenth century, an increasingly vocal minority of women chafed against the laws of husband and wife that restricted the independence of women like Harriet Cruger. They demanded the reform of the laws of coverture, first through Married Women's Property Acts, and then through Earnings Laws. Nowhere were they more vocal and successful than in New York.

At first, women's rights reformers concentrated on changing people's hearts and minds, as had temperance reformers, abolitionists, and others who were part of the great wave of reform in the United States in the early nineteenth century. In their private writings, women's rights reformers were often more frank than in public discussion, about how marriage kept women subjugated to their husbands. They often compared the married woman to a slave—with no right to own property, sign a contract, sue another, or even keep her own name.

After 1840, as in so many of the reform movements sparked by the religious fervor of the Second Great Awakening, women's rights reformers began to turn to legal solutions. The first group of advocates for women's rights took particular aim at the laws of marriage and divorce. They also organized women's rights activity on a large scale for the first time. On July 19–20, 1848, the first women's rights convention in the world took place at Seneca Falls, New York. Elizabeth Cady Stanton, a women's rights activist and an organizer of the convention, delivered the "Declaration of Sentiments," modeled on the Declaration of Independence: "We hold these truths to be self-evident: that all men and women are created equal . . . " Stanton declared further that "The history of mankind is a history of repeated injuries and usurpations on the part of man toward woman, having in direct object the establishment of an absolute tyranny over her."

The declaration listed a series of wrongs, followed by twelve resolutions. While winning the right to vote was part of the women's aim, their chief focus was reforming the laws of marriage. Eleven resolutions passed unanimously; the twelfth, calling for the extension of the vote to women, passed narrowly only after abolitionist and former slave Frederick Douglass made a rousing speech in its favor. The Declaration of Sentiments quickly became famous around the world, sparking women's rights reform movements in England and across Europe.

New York's first Married Women's Property Act, passed in 1848, the same year as the Seneca Falls convention, was the product of a number of factors. The persistent petition campaigns of feminist reformers had some influence on the legislators, but several other forces were at work as well. There was a strong movement in New York to "codify" the common law into written codes, accessible to everyone, thereby minimizing the power of judges and lawyers to shape decisions as they pleased. The leaders of that movement especially took aim at equity courts, which they saw as undemocratic institutions whose individually tailored settlements benefited only the propertied elite. For these politicians, reform of the laws governing married women's property was a way to democratize property law, making available to everyone the "separate estates" that wealthy families had been able to arrange through equity courts. Finally, wealthy Dutch landowners in the Hudson Valley saw the acts as a way to protect family property. Thus, the Married Women's Property Acts, in New York and elsewhere, were a good example of the way that legal reform comes about as a result of reformers' efforts coming together with other circumstances and constituencies.

The 1848 act pronounced that "the real and personal property of any female who may hereafter marry, and which she shall own at the time of the marriage, and the rents issues and profits thereof, shall not be subject to the disposal of her husband, nor be liable for his debts, and shall continue her sole and separate property, as if she were a single female." It also provided that gifts to married women could remain their separate property, and that marriage settlements and prenuptial agreements would be enforced. The second act, in 1849, made it possible for women to sell or transfer their separate property under certain conditions, and for the trustees of their separate estates to deed property to them if a judge found them capable of managing it.

Despite the Married Women's Property Acts, women who did not have substantial property to inherit from their families still suffered severe legal constraints, most importantly because they still did not control their earnings. New Yorker Ernestine Rose, an early activist for women's rights, observed, "Here is some provision for the favored few; but for the laboring many, there is none. The mass of people commence life with no other capital than the union of heads, hearts and hands. To the benefit of this best of capital, the wife has no right. If they are unsuccessful in married life, who suffers more the bitter consequences of poverty than the wife? But if successful, she can not call a dollar her own."

In the summer of 1854, Elizabeth Cady Stanton rose to address the Joint Judiciary Committee of the New York State Legislature, the first time a woman had ever spoken before that body. She began: "The thinking minds of all nations call for change. There is a deep-lying struggle in the whole fabric of society; a boundless grinding collision of the New with the Old." Stanton asked the legislators to consider the "legal disabilities under which [women] labor."

On behalf of women, Stanton demanded the right to vote, the right to sit on juries, and the reform of the law of coverture. "Look at the position of woman as wife," she demanded. "The wife who inherits no property holds about the same legal position that does the slave on the Southern plantation. She can own nothing, sell nothing. She has no right even to the wages she earns; her person, her time, her services are the property of another. . . . But the wife who is so fortunate as to have inherited property, has, by the new law in this State, been redeemed from her lost condition." Stanton told the legislators that she spoke on behalf of the "daughters of the revolution-

New Jersey's 1852 Married Women's Property Act. Several states introduced married women's property acts in the years following New York's successful 1848 legislation. ❖

Women's rights activist Ernestine Rose began petitioning for married women's property rights in New York in 1836. ❖

and was therefore the property of the husband. Repeatedly, courts held that women's labor in the household belonged to the husband, so that only wages earned outside the home—although a minor part of most women's earnings—were covered by the act.

In the Iowa case of *Miller* v. *Miller,* a husband and wife attempted to create their own marriage contract, in which both spouses promised to "refrain from scolding, fault-finding and anger." Mr. Miller promised to provide for family necessaries as well as a sum of $16.66 per month for Mrs. Miller's individual use, and she promised to "keep her home and family in a comfortable and reasonably good condition." When Mrs. Miller sued her husband to enforce this contract, she was turned away by the court because she had promised to do only what she was already obligated to do, but he had promised far more than marriage required from a husband, which was only to provide "necessaries."

New York's 1860 Earnings Act was a limited victory for reformers—they won a change in the law, but courts limited its reach through narrow interpretation. Had courts interpreted the act more broadly to cover all forms of women's earnings, it would have gone a long way to making women independent legally and economically.

Although the 1860 Earnings Act gained some legal rights for women, it failed to resolve completely the inequities that women faced. In the later nineteenth century, women's rights advocates became convinced that political power was the way to secure civil rights, and they began to focus more specifically on winning the right to vote. Achieving that goal would take another sixty years.

ary heroes of '76," and exhorted them to be true to the goals of the Revolution, mocking their claims to republicanism: "How like feudal barons you freemen hold your women." At the same time that Stanton spoke before the legislature, she presented more than six thousand petitions from women across the state.

Six years later, in 1860, New York passed the first Earnings Act in the nation, providing that a married woman could "carry on any trade or business, and perform any labor or services on her sole and separate account, and the earnings of any married woman, from her trade, business, labor or services, shall be her sole and separate property, and may be used or invested by her in her own name." By the 1870s, most states had passed some version of married women's property acts, and many Northern states passed Earning Acts as well.

By and large, courts interpreted the Earnings Act narrowly. For example, in one 1876 case, the New York Supreme Court ruled that a wife who kept a boardinghouse and nursed a very ill man for several years could not control her earnings because work done in the home was considered to be on the "family account," rather than her "sole and separate account,"

## Discussion Questions

- What was the system of "coverture"? How could couples avoid some of the legal disabilities of coverture? Could they avoid all of them?

- What were the chief concerns of women's rights advocates in the mid-nineteenth century? How did their aims and tactics resemble those of other reform movements during this period?

- How did the Married Women's Property Acts and Earnings Act improve the legal status of married women, and in what ways did they fall short of reformers' aims? Why do you think these acts were passed?

St. Louis, Missouri, in the 1850s. Steamboat traffic on the Mississippi River helped develop this busy inland port. By 1850, St. Louis was one of the nation's largest cities. ❖

# An Age of Expansionism

## The Spirit of Young America

In the 1840s and early 1850s, politicians, writers, and entrepreneurs frequently proclaimed themselves champions of **Young America.** One of the first to use the phrase was Ralph Waldo Emerson, who told an audience of merchants and manufacturers in 1844 that the nation was entering a new era of commercial development, technological progress, and territorial expansion. Emerson suggested that a progressive new generation—the Young Americans—would lead this surge of physical development. More than a slogan and less than an organized movement, Young America stood for a positive attitude toward the market economy and industrial growth, a more aggressive and belligerent foreign policy, and a celebration of America's unique strengths and virtues.

Young Americans favored enlarging the national market by acquiring new territory. They called for the annexation of Texas, asserted an American claim to all of Oregon, and urged the appropriation of vast new territories from Mexico. They also celebrated the technological advances that would knit this new empire together, especially the telegraph and the railroad. Telegraphs, according to one writer, would "flash sensation and volition . . . to and from towns and provinces as if they were organs and limbs of a single organism"; railroads would provide "a vast system of iron muscles which, as it were, move the limbs of the mighty organism."

Young America was a cultural and intellectual movement as well as an economic and political one. In 1845, a Washington journal hailed the election of the 49-year-old James K. Polk, at that time the youngest man to have been elected president, as a sign that youth will "dare to take antiquity by the beard, and tear the cloak from hoary-headed hypocrisy. Too young to be corrupt . . . it is Young America, awakened to a sense of her own intellectual greatness by her soaring spirit. It stands in strength, the voice of the majority." During the Polk administration, Young American writers and critics—mostly based in New York City—called for a new and distinctive national literature, free of subservience to European themes or models and expressive of the democratic spirit. Their organ was the *Literary World*, founded in 1847, and its ideals influenced two of the greatest writers America has produced: Walt Whitman and Herman Melville.

Whitman captured much of the exuberance and expansionism of Young America in his "Song of the Open Road":

> From this hour I ordain myself loos'd of limits and imaginary lines,
> Going where I list, my own master total and absolute,
> . . . . . . . . . . . . . . . . . . . . . . . .
> I inhale great draughts of space,
> The east and the west are mine, and the north and the south are mine.
> I am larger, better than I thought.

In *Moby-Dick,* Herman Melville produced a novel sufficiently original in form and conception to more than fulfill the demand of Young Americans for "a New Literature to fit the New Man in the New Age." But Melville was too deep a thinker not to see the perils that underlay the soaring ambition and aggressiveness of the new

New York native Herman Melville, shown here in an 1870 portrait by Joseph Oriel Eaton, shaped the knowledge he gained as a merchant sailor into Moby-Dick, a cautionary saga about the dark side of human ambition. ❖

Walt Whitman in the "carpenter portrait" that appeared in the first edition of his great work, Leaves of Grass, in 1855. The poet's rough clothes and slouch hat signify his identification with the common people. ❖

age. The whaling captain Ahab, who brings destruction to himself and his ship by his relentless pursuit of the white whale, symbolized—among other things—the dangers facing a nation that was overreaching itself by indulging its pride and exalted sense of destiny with too little concern for the moral and practical consequences.

THE YOUNG AMERICAN IDEAL—the idea of a young country led by young men into new paths of prosperity and greatness—appealed to many people and found support across political party lines. But the attitude came to be identified primarily with young Democrats who wanted to move their party away from its traditional fear of the expansion of commerce and industry. Unlike old-line Jeffersonians and Jacksonians, Young Americans had no qualms about the market economy and the speculative, materialistic spirit it called forth.

Before 1848 the Young American impulse focused mainly on the great expanse of western lands that lay just beyond the nation's borders. After the Mexican-American War, when territorial gains extended the nation's boundaries from the Atlantic to the Pacific, attention shifted to internal development. New discoveries of gold in the nation's western territories fostered economic growth, technological advances spurred industrialization, and increased immigration brought more people to populate the lands newly acquired—by agreement or by force.

## MOVEMENT TO THE FAR WEST

In the 1830s and 1840s, the westward movement of population left the valley of the Mississippi behind and penetrated the Far West all the way to the Pacific. Pioneers pursued fertile land and economic opportunity beyond the existing boundaries of the United States and thus helped set the stage for the annexations and international crises of the 1840s. Some went for material gain, others went for adventure, and a significant minority sought freedom from religious persecu-

tion. Whatever their reasons, they brought American attitudes into regions that were already occupied or claimed by Mexico or Great Britain.

### Borderlands of the 1830s

U.S. expansionists directed their ambitions to the north, west, and southwest. For a time, it seemed that both Canada and Mexico might be frontiers for expansionism. Conflicts over the border between the United States and British North America led periodically to calls for diplomatic or military action to wrest the northern half of the continent from the British; similar conflicts in Mexican territory led ultimately to the United States' capture and acquisition of much of northern Mexico.

Since the birth of the republic, there had been a major dispute over the boundary between Maine and the Canadian province of New Brunswick. In 1839, fighting broke out between Canadian lumberjacks and the Maine militia. This long-festering controversy poisoned Anglo-American relations until 1842, when Secretary of State Daniel Webster concluded an agreement with the British government, represented by Lord Ashburton. The **Webster-Ashburton Treaty** gave over half of the disputed territory to the United States and established a definite northeastern boundary with Canada.

On the other side of the continent, the United States and Britain both laid claim to Oregon, a vast area that lay between the Rockies and the Pacific from the 42nd parallel (the northern boundary of California) to the latitude of 54°0' (the southern boundary of Alaska). In 1818, the two nations agreed to joint occupation for ten years, an agreement that was renewed indefinitely in 1827. Meanwhile, the Americans had strengthened their claim by acquiring Spain's rights to the Pacific Northwest in the Adams-Onís Treaty (see Chapter 9), and the British had

gained effective control of the northern portion of the Oregon Country through the activities of the Hudson's Bay Company, a well-financed fur-trading concern. Blocking an equitable division was the reluctance on both sides to surrender access to the Columbia River basin and the adjacent territory extending north to the 49th parallel (which later became the northern border of the state of Washington).

The Oregon Country was scarcely populated before 1840. The same could not be said of the Mexican borderlands that lay directly west of Jacksonian America. Spanish settlements in present-day New Mexico date from the late sixteenth century. By 1820, about forty thousand people of Spanish descent populated this province, engaging mainly in sheep raising and mining. In 1821, Spain granted independence to Mexico, which then embraced areas that currently make up the states of Texas, New Mexico, Arizona, California, Nevada, Utah, and much of Colorado. Spain's mercantilist policies had closed the region to outside traders, but the Republic of Mexico opted for a free-trade policy. Mexico in 1821 informed its northern neighbors of the changed laws encouraging trade. This action succeeded in stimulating commercial prosperity but also whetted expansionist appetites on the Anglo side of the border.

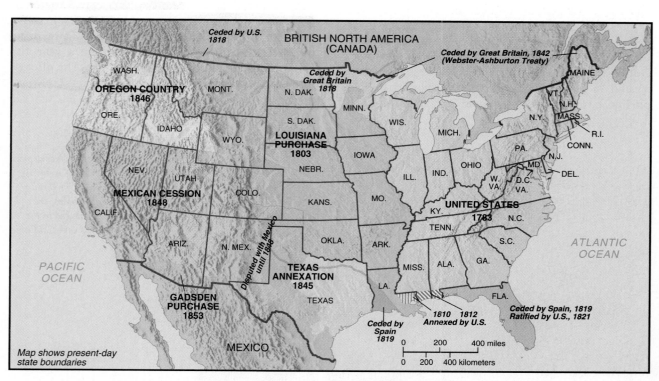

**TERRITORIAL EXPANSION BY THE MID-NINETEENTH CENTURY**   *Fervent nationalists identified the growth of America through territorial expansion as the divinely ordained "Manifest Destiny" of a chosen people.* ❖

California was the other major northward extension of Mexico. Spanish missionaries and soldiers had taken control of the region in the late eighteenth century. In the 1820s and 1830s, this land of huge estates and enormous cattle herds was far less populous than New Mexico—only about four thousand Mexicans of Spanish origin lived in California in 1827. The region's other inhabitants were the thirty thousand Indians, many of whom were forced to work on vast land tracts owned by Spanish missions. At the beginning of the 1830s, a chain of twenty-one mission stations, stretching from San Diego to north of San Francisco, controlled most of the province's land and wealth. Great as the Indian population may seem, the number represented only a small fraction of the original indigenous population; there had been a catastrophic decline in Indian population during the previous sixty years of Spanish rule. The stresses and strains of forced labor and exposure to European diseases had taken an enormous toll.

In 1833, the Mexican Congress's "secularization act" emancipated the Indians from church control and opened the mission lands to settlement. The government awarded immense tracts of the mission land to Mexican citizens and left the Indians landless. A new class of large landowners, or *rancheros,* replaced the *padres* as rulers of Old California and masters of the province's indigenous population. Seven hundred grantees took possession of *ranchos* ranging up to nearly 50,000 acres and proceeded to subject the Indians to a new and even harsher form of servitude. During the fifteen years they held sway, the rancheros created an American legend through their lavish hospitality, extravagant dress, superb horsemanship, and taste for violent and dangerous sports. Their flamboyant lifestyle and devotion to the pursuit of pleasure captured the fancy and aroused the secret envy of many American visitors and traders.

The Americans who saw California in the 1830s were mostly merchants and sailors involved in the oceanic trade between Boston and California ports. New England clipper ships sailed around Cape Horn at the southern tip of South America to barter manufactured goods for cowhides. One Boston firm came away with more than 500,000 hides in a twenty-year period. By the mid-1830s, several Yankee merchants had taken up permanent residence in towns such as Monterey and San Diego in order to conduct the California end of the business. The reports they sent back about the Golden West sparked interest in eastern business circles.

## The Texas Revolution

At the same time as some Americans were trading with California, others were taking possession of Texas. In the early 1820s, Mexican officials encouraged settlers from the United States to settle in Texas. Newly independent Mexico granted Stephen F. Austin, son of a onetime Spanish citizen, a huge piece of land in hopes he would help attract and settle new colonists from the United States. Some fifteen other Anglo-American *empresarios* received land grants in the 1820s. In 1823, three hundred families from the United States were settled on the Austin grant, and within a year, the colony's population had swelled to 2021. The offer of fertile and inexpensive land attracted many American immigrants.

*This painting by James Walker depicts ornately dressed rancheros rounding up a cattle herd. With their thrilling lifestyles and exotic costumes, the hacienda owners contributed to the vivid images associated with California in the 1830s.* ❖

Friction soon developed between the Mexican government and the Anglo-American colonists over the status of slavery and the authority of the Catholic Church. At its core, the dispute centered on the unwillingness of Anglo-American settlers to become Mexicans. Under the terms of settlement, all people living in Texas had to become Mexican citizens and adopt the Roman Catholic faith. Slavery presented another problem, for in 1829 Mexico freed all slaves under its jurisdiction. Slaveholders in Texas were given a special exemption that allowed them to emancipate their slaves and then sign them to lifelong contracts as indentured servants, but many refused to limit their ownership rights in any way. Settlers either converted to Catholicism only superficially or ignored the requirement entirely.

A Mexican government commission reported in 1829 that Americans were the great majority of the Texas population and were flagrantly violating Mexican law—refusing to emancipate their slaves, evading import duties on goods from the United States, and failing to convert to Catholicism. The following year, the Mexican Congress prohibited further American immigration and importation of slaves to Texas.

Enforcement of the new law was feeble, and the flow of settlers, slaves, and smuggled goods continued virtually unabated. A long-standing complaint of the Texans was the failure of the Mexican constitution to grant them local self-government. Under the Mexican federal system, Texas was joined to the state of Coahuila, and Texan representatives were outnumbered three to one in the state legislature. In 1832, the colonists showed their displeasure with Mexican rule by rioting in protest against the arrest of several Anglo-Americans by a Mexican commander.

Austin went to Mexico City in 1833 to present the Texans' grievances and seek concessions from the central government. He succeeded in having the ban against American immigration lifted, but he got only vague promises about tariff relief and failed to win agreement to the separation of Texas from Coahuila. As he was about to return to Texas, Austin was arrested and imprisoned for writing a letter recommending that Texans set up a state government without Mexico City's consent.

In 1835, some Texans revolted against Mexico's central government. The insurrectionists claimed they were fighting for freedom against a long experience of oppression. Actually, Mexican rule had not been harsh; the worst that can be said was that it was inefficient, inconsistent, and sometimes corrupt. Furthermore, the Texans' devotion to "liberty" did not prevent them from defending slavery against Mexico's attempt to abolish it. Texans had done pretty much what they

pleased, despite laws to the contrary and angry rumblings from south of the Rio Grande.

Developments in 1834 had threatened their status as "tolerated guests." In that year, General Antonio López de Santa Anna made himself dictator of Mexico and abolished the federal system of government. News of these developments reached Texas late in the year, accompanied by rumors of the impending disfranchisement and even expulsion of American immigrants. The rebels, already aroused by earlier restrictive policies, were influenced by the rumors and prepared to resist Santa Anna's effort to enforce tariff regulations by military force.

When he learned that Texans were resisting customs collections, Santa Anna sent reinforcements. On June 30, 1835, before any additional troops could arrive, a band of settlers led by William B. Travis captured the Mexican garrison at Anahuac without firing a shot. The settlers first engaged Mexican troops at Gonzales in October and forced the retreat of a cavalry detachment. Shortly thereafter, Austin laid siege to San Antonio with a force of five hundred men and after six weeks forced its surrender, thereby capturing most of the Mexican troops then in Texas.

## The Republic of Texas

While this early fighting was going on, delegates from the American communities in Texas convened and after

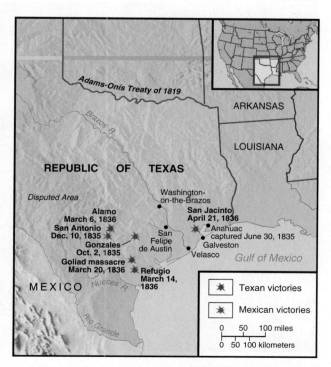

**TEXAS REVOLUTION**    *Major battles of the Texas Revolution. The Texans suffered severe losses at the Alamo and Goliad, but they scored a stunning victory at San Jacinto.* ❖

some hesitation voted overwhelmingly to declare their independence on March 2, 1836. A constitution, based closely on that of the United States, was adopted for the new Republic of Texas, and a temporary government was installed to carry on the military struggle. Although the ensuing conflict was largely one of Americans against Mexicans, some Texas Mexicans, or *Tejanos,* joined the fray on the side of the Anglo rebels. They too wanted to be free of Santa Anna's heavy-handed rule. (Most of the Tejanos would become victims of the same anti-Mexican prejudice that spurred the revolt. Tejano leader Juan Seguin, who served as a captain in the Texas army and became a hero of the independence struggle, was driven off his land by Anglo-Texans in 1841.)

Within days after Texas declared itself a republic, rebels and Mexican troops in San Antonio fought the famous battle of the **Alamo.** Myths about that battle have magnified the Anglo rebels' valor at the Mexicans' expense. The folklore is based on fact—only 187 rebels fought off a far larger number of Mexican soldiers for more than a week before eventually capitulating—but it is not true that all rebels, including the folk hero Davy Crockett, fought to the death. Crockett and seven other survivors were captured and then executed. Moreover, the rebels fought from inside a strong fortress with superior weapons against march-weary Mexican conscripts. Nevertheless, a tale that combined actual and mythical bravery inside the Alamo gave the insurrection new inspiration, moral sanction, outside support, and the rallying cry "Remember the Alamo."

The revolt ended with an exchange of slaughters. A few days after the Alamo battle, another Texas detachment was surrounded and captured in an open plain near the San Antonio River and was marched to the town of Goliad, where most of its 350 members were executed. The next month, on April 21, 1836, the main Texas army, under General Sam Houston, assaulted Santa Anna's troops at an encampment near the San Jacinto River during the siesta hour. The final count showed that 630 Mexicans and only a handful of Texans had been killed. Santa Anna was captured and marched to Velasco, the meeting place of the Texas government, where he was forced to sign treaties recognizing the independence of Texas and its claim to territory all the way to the Rio Grande. The Mexican Congress immediately repudiated the treaty, but their argument was in vain; although a strip of land between the Nueces River and the Rio Grande would be disputed during the next decade, Mexico failed to impose its authority on the victorious Texas rebels.

Sam Houston, the hero of San Jacinto, became the first president of Texas. His platform sought annexation to the United States, and one of his first acts in of-

Battle of San Jacinto *by H.A. McArdle. In this panorama of the Texas Revolution's decisive battle at San Jacinto, Sam Houston leads the charge against Santa Anna's forces.* ❖

fice was to send an emissary to Washington to test the waters. Houston's agent found much sympathy for Texas independence but was told by Andrew Jackson and others that domestic politics and fear of a war with Mexico made immediate annexation impossible. The most that he could win from Congress and the Jackson administration was formal recognition of Texas sovereignty.

In its ten-year existence as the Lone Star Republic, Texas drew settlers from the United States at an accelerating rate. The Panic of 1837 impelled many debt-ridden and land-hungry farmers to take advantage of the free grants of 1280 acres that Texas offered to immigrating heads of white families. In the decade after independence, the population of Texas soared from 30,000 to 142,000. Most of the newcomers assumed, as did the old settlers, that they would soon be annexed and restored to American citizenship.

## Trails of Trade and Settlement

After New Mexico opened its trade to American merchants, a thriving commerce developed along the trail that ran from Missouri to Santa Fe. The first of these merchants to reach the New Mexican capital was William Becknell, who arrived with his train of goods late in 1821. Others followed rapidly. To protect themselves from the hostile Indians whose territory they had to cross, the traders traveled in large caravans, one or two of which would arrive in Santa Fe every summer. The federal government assisted them by providing troops when necessary and by appropriating money to purchase rights of passage from various tribes. Even so, the trip across the Cimarron desert and the southern Rockies was often difficult and hazardous. But profits from the exchange of textiles and other manufactured goods for furs, mules, and precious metals were substantial enough to make the risk worth taking.

Relations between the United States and Mexico soured following the Texas revolution, and this had a devastating effect on the Santa Fe trade. Much of the ill feeling was caused by further Anglo-American aggressions. An expedition of Texas businessmen and soldiers to Santa Fe in 1841 alarmed the Mexican authorities, who arrested its members. In retaliation, a volunteer force of Texas avengers attacked Mexican troops along the Santa Fe Trail. The Mexican government then moved to curtail the Santa Fe trade. In April 1842, it passed a new tariff banning the importation of many of the goods sold by American merchants and prohibiting the export of gold and silver. Further restrictions in 1843 denied American traders full access to the Santa Fe market.

The famous Oregon Trail was the great overland route that brought the wagon trains of American migrants to the West Coast during the 1840s. Extending for two thousand miles, across the northern Great Plains and the mountains beyond, it crossed the Rockies at South Pass and then forked; the main northern route led to the Willamette Valley of Oregon, but alternative trails were opened during the decade for overlanders heading for California. The journey from Missouri to the West Coast took about six months; most parties departed in May, hoping to arrive in November before the great snows hit the last mountain barriers.

After small groups had made their way to both Oregon and California in 1841 and 1842, a mass migration—mostly to Oregon—began in 1843. Within two years, five thousand Americans, living in the Willamette Valley south of the Columbia River, were demanding the extension of full American sovereignty over the Oregon Country.

## The Mormon Trek

An important and distinctive group of pioneers followed the Oregon Trail as far as South Pass and then veered southwestward to establish a thriving colony in the region of the Great Salt Lake. These were Mormons, members of the largest religious denomination founded on American soil—the Church of Jesus Christ of Latter-day Saints.

The background of the Mormon trek was a history of persecution in the eastern states. Joseph Smith of Palmyra, New York, the founder of Mormonism, revealed in 1830 that he had received over many years a series of revelations that called upon him to establish Christ's pure church on earth. As the prophet of this faith, he published the *Book of Mormon,* a new scripture that he claimed to have discovered and translated with the aid of an angel. It was the record of a community of pious Jews who left the Holy Land six centuries before the birth of Christ and sailed to the American continent. After his crucifixion and resurrection, Christ appeared to this community and proclaimed the Gospel. Four hundred years later, a fratricidal war annihilated the believing Christians but not all of the descendents of the original Jewish migrants. Mormons held that the survivors had contributed to the ancestry of the American Indians. Smith and those he converted to his new faith were committed to restoring the pure religion that had once thrived on American soil by founding a western Zion where they could practice their faith unmolested and carry out their special mission to convert the Native Americans.

In the 1830s, the Mormons established communities in Ohio and Missouri, but the former went

*Carl Christian Anton Christensen, Handcart, ca. 1840. Instead of buying wagons and oxen, some groups of Mormon colonists made their trek to Deseret on foot, hauling their possessions in handcarts and working together as families to move their heavy loads.* ❖

bankrupt in the Panic of 1837 and the latter was the target of angry mobs and vigilante violence. After the Mormons lost the "war" they fought against the Missourians in 1839, Smith led his followers back across the Mississippi to Illinois, where he received a liberal charter from the state legislature to found a town at Nauvoo. Here the Mormons had a temporary measure of security and self-government, but Smith soon reported new revelations that engendered dissension among his followers and hostility from neighbor-

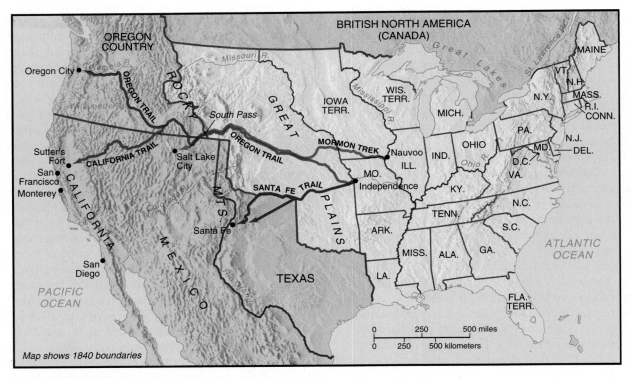

**WESTERN TRAILS**   *Among the greatest hazards faced by those migrating to the West was the rough and unfamiliar terrain over which their wagon trains traveled.* ❖

ing "gentiles." Most controversial was his authorization of polygamy, or plural marriage. In 1844, Smith was killed by a mob while being held in jail in Carthage, Illinois, on a charge stemming from his quarrels with dissident Mormons who objected to his new policies.

The death of Smith confirmed the growing conviction of the Mormon leadership that they needed to move beyond the borders of the United States to establish their Zion in the wilderness. In late 1845, Smith's successor, Brigham Young, decided to send a party of fifteen hundred men to assess the chances of a colony in the vicinity of the Great Salt Lake (then part of Mexico). Nauvoo was quickly depopulated as twelve thousand Mormons took to the trail in 1846. The following year, Young himself arrived in Utah and sent back word to the thousands encamped along the trail that he had found the promised land.

The Mormon community that Young established in Utah is one of the great success stories of western settlement. In contrast to the rugged individualism and disorder that often characterized mining camps and other new communities, "the state of Deseret" (the name the Mormons originally applied to Utah) was a model of discipline and cooperation. Because of its communitarian form of social organization, its centralized government, and the religious dedication of its inhabitants, this frontier society was able to expand settlement in a planned and efficient way and develop a system of irrigation that "made the desert bloom."

Utah's main problem was the determination of its political status. When the Mormons first arrived, they were encroaching illegally into Mexican territory. After Utah came under American sovereignty in 1848, the state of Deseret fought to maintain its autonomy and its custom of polygamy against the efforts of the federal government to extend American law and set up the usual type of territorial administration. In 1857, President Buchanan sent a military force to bring Utah to heel, and the Mormons prepared to repel this "invasion." But after a heavy snow prevented the army from crossing the Rockies, Buchanan offered an olive branch in the form of a general pardon for Mormons who had violated federal law but agreed to cooperate with U.S. authorities in the future. The Mormons accepted, and in return, Brigham Young called off his plan to resist the army by force and accepted the nominal authority of an appointed territorial governor.

# MANIFEST DESTINY AND THE MEXICAN-AMERICAN WAR

The rush of settlers beyond the nation's borders in the 1830s and 1840s inspired politicians and propagandists to call for annexation of those areas occu-

pied by migrants. Some went further and proclaimed it was the **Manifest Destiny** of the United States to expand until it had absorbed all of North America, including Canada and Mexico. Such ambitions—and the policies they inspired—led to a major diplomatic confrontation with Great Britain and a war with Mexico.

## Tyler and Texas

President John Tyler initiated the politics of Manifest Destiny. He was vice president when William Henry Harrison died in office in 1841 after serving scarcely a month. The first of America's "accidental presidents," Tyler was a states' rights, proslavery Virginian who had been picked as Harrison's running mate to broaden the appeal of the Whig ticket. Profoundly out of sympathy with the mainstream of his own party, he soon broke with the Whigs in Congress, who had united behind the latest version of Henry Clay's "American System." Although he lacked a base in either of the major parties, Tyler hoped to be elected president in his own right in 1844. To accomplish this difficult feat, he needed a new issue around which he could build a following that would cut across established party lines.

In 1843, Tyler decided to put the full weight of his administration behind the annexation of Texas. He anticipated that incorporation of the Lone Star Republic would be a popular move, especially in the South where it would feed the appetite for additional slave states. With the South solidly behind him, Tyler expected to have a good chance in the election of 1844.

To achieve his objective, Tyler enlisted the support of John C. Calhoun, the leading political defender of slavery and state sovereignty. Calhoun saw the annexation issue as a way of uniting the South and taking the offensive against the abolitionists. Success or failure in this effort would constitute a decisive test of whether the North was willing to give the southern states a fair share of national power and adequate assurances for the future of their way of life. If antislavery sentiment succeeded in blocking the acquisition of Texas, the Southerners would at least know where they stood and could begin to "calculate the value of the union."

To prepare the public for annexation, the Tyler administration launched a propaganda campaign in the summer of 1843 based on reports of British designs on Texas. According to information supplied by Duff Green, an unofficial American agent in England, the British were preparing to guarantee Texas independence and make a loan to the financially troubled republic in return for the abolition of slavery. It is doubtful the British had such intentions, but the stories were believed and used to give urgency to the annexation cause.

Secretary of State Abel Upshur, a proslavery Virginian and protégé of Calhoun, began negotiating an annexation treaty. After Upshur was killed in an accident, Calhoun replaced him and carried the negotiations to a successful conclusion. When the treaty was brought before the Senate in 1844, Calhoun denounced the British for attempting to subvert the South's essential system of labor and racial control by using Texas as a base for abolitionist operations. According to the supporters of Tyler and Calhoun, the South's security and well-being—and by extension that of the nation—required the immediate incorporation of Texas into the Union.

The strategy of linking annexation explicitly to the interests of the South and slavery led northern antislavery Whigs to charge that the whole scheme was a proslavery plot meant to advance the interest of one section of the nation against the other. Consequently, the Senate rejected the treaty by a decisive vote of 35 to 16 in June 1844. Tyler then attempted to bring Texas into the Union through an alternative means—a joint resolution of both houses of Congress admitting it as a state—but Congress adjourned before the issue came to a vote, and the whole question hung fire in anticipation of the election of 1844.

## The Triumph of Polk and Annexation

Tyler's initiative made the future of Texas the central issue in the 1844 campaign. But party lines held firm, and the president himself was unable to capitalize on the issue because his stand was not in line with the views of either party. Tyler tried to run as an independent, but his failure to gain significant support eventually forced him to withdraw from the race.

If the Democratic party convention had been held in 1843—as it was originally scheduled—ex-President Martin Van Buren would have won the nomination. But postponement of the Democratic conclave until May 1844 weakened his chances. In the meantime, the annexation question came to the fore, and Van Buren was forced to take a stand on it. He persisted in the view he had held as president—that incorporation of Texas would risk war with Mexico,

arouse sectional strife, and destroy the unity of the Democratic party. Fears of sectional and party division seemed confirmed in 1844 when the dominant party faction in Van Buren's home state of New York came out against Tyler's Texas policy. In an effort to keep the issue out of the campaign, Van Buren struck a gentleman's agreement with Henry Clay, the overwhelming favorite for the Whig nomination, that both of them would publicly oppose immediate annexation.

Van Buren's letter opposing annexation appeared shortly before the Democratic convention, and it cost him the nomination. Angry southern delegates, who secured a rule requiring approval by a two-thirds vote, blocked Van Buren's nomination. After several ballots, a dark horse candidate—James K. Polk of Tennessee—emerged triumphant. Polk, a protégé of Andrew Jackson, had been speaker of the House of Representatives and governor of Tennessee.

An avowed expansionist, Polk ran on a platform calling for the simultaneous annexation of Texas and assertion of American claims to all of Oregon. He identified himself and his party with the popular cause of turning the United States into a continental nation, an aspiration that attracted support from all parts of the country. His was a much more astute political strategy than the overtly prosouthern expansionism advocated by Tyler and Calhoun. The Whig nominee, Henry Clay, was basically antiexpansionist, but his sense of the growing popularity of Texas annexation among southern Whigs caused him to waffle on the issue during the campaign. This vacillation in turn cost Clay the support of a small but crucial group of northern antislavery Whigs, who defected to the abolitionist Liberty party.

Polk won the fall election by a relatively narrow popular margin. His triumph in the electoral college—170 votes to 105—was secured by victories in New York and Michigan, where the Liberty party candidate, James G. Birney, had taken away enough votes from Clay to affect the outcome. The closeness of the election meant the Democrats had something less than a clear mandate to implement their expansionist policies, but this did not prevent them from claiming that the people had backed an aggressive campaign to extend the borders of the United States.

## THE LIBERTY PARTY SWINGS AN ELECTION

| Candidate | Party | Actual Vote in New York | National Electoral Vote | If Liberty Voters had Voted Whig | Projected Electoral Vote |
|-----------|-------|-------------------------|-------------------------|----------------------------------|--------------------------|
| Polk | Democratic | 237,588 | 170 | 237,588 | 134 |
| Clay | Whig | 232,482 | 105 | 248,294 | 141 |
| Birney | Liberty | 15,812 | 0 | — | — |

## THE ELECTION OF 1844

| Candidate | Party | Popular Vote | Electoral Vote |
|-----------|-------|--------------|----------------|
| Polk | Democratic | 1,338,464 | 170 |
| Clay | Whig | 1,300,097 | 105 |
| Birney | Liberty | 62,300 | — |

After the election, Congress reconvened to consider the annexation of Texas. The mood had changed as a result of Polk's victory, and some leading senators from both parties who had initially opposed Tyler's scheme for annexation by joint resolution of Congress now changed their position. As a result, annexation was approved a few days before Polk took office.

### The Doctrine of Manifest Destiny

The expansionist mood that accompanied Polk's election and the annexation of Texas was given a name and a rationale in the summer of 1845. John L. O'Sullivan, a proponent of the Young America movement and editor of the influential *United States Magazine and Democratic Review,* charged that foreign governments were conspiring to block the annexation of Texas in an effort to thwart "the fulfillment of our manifest destiny to overspread the continent allotted by providence for the free development of our yearly multiplying millions."

Besides coining the phrase Manifest Destiny, O'Sullivan pointed to the three main ideas that lay behind it. One was that God was on the side of American expansionism. This notion came naturally out of the long tradition, going back to the New England Puritans, that identified the growth of America with the divinely ordained success of a chosen people. A second idea, implied in the phrase *free development,* was that the spread of American rule meant what other propagandists for expansion described as "extending the area of freedom." Democratic institutions and local self-government would follow the flag if areas claimed by autocratic foreign governments were annexed to the United States. O'Sullivan's third premise was that population growth required the outlet that territorial acquisitions would provide. Behind this notion lurked a fear that growing numbers would lead to diminished opportunity and a European-type polarization of social classes if the restless and the ambitious were not given new lands to settle and exploit.

In its most extreme form, the doctrine of Manifest Destiny meant that the United States would someday occupy the entire North American continent, that nothing less would appease its land-hungry population. "Make way, I say, for the young American

Buffalo," bellowed a Democratic orator in 1844, "—he has not yet got land enough. . . . I tell you we will give him Oregon for his summer shade, and the region of Texas as his winter pasture. (Applause) Like all of his race, he wants salt, too. Well, he shall have the use of two oceans—the mighty Pacific and the turbulent Atlantic. . . . He shall not stop his career until he slakes his thirst in the frozen ocean. (Cheers)"

### Polk and the Oregon Question

In 1845 and 1846, the United States came closer to armed conflict with Great Britain than at any time since the War of 1812. The willingness of some Americans to go to war over Oregon was expressed in the rallying cry "Fifty-four forty or fight" (referring to the latitude of the northern boundary of the desired territory). This slogan was actually coined by Whigs seeking to ridicule Democratic expansionists, but Democrats later took it over as a vivid expression of their demand for what is now British Columbia. Polk fed this expansionist fever by laying claim in his inaugural address to all of the Oregon Country, then jointly occupied by Britain and the United States. Privately, however, he was willing to accept the 49th parallel as a dividing line. What made the situation so tense was that Polk was dedicated to an aggressive diplomacy of bluff and bluster. As historian David M. Pletcher has put it, Polk "set forth on a foreign policy of strong stands, over-stated arguments, and menacing

**NORTHWEST BOUNDARY DISPUTE**   *President Polk's policy of bluff and bluster nearly involved the United States in a war with Great Britain over the disputed boundary in Oregon.* ❖

public announcements, not because he wanted war but because he felt that this was the only policy which his foreign adversaries would understand."

In July 1845, Polk authorized Secretary of State James Buchanan to reply to the latest British request for terms by offering a boundary along the 49th parallel. The offer did not meet the British demand for all of Vancouver Island and free navigation of the Columbia River, and the British ambassador rejected the proposal out of hand. This rebuff infuriated Polk who saw his offer as a generous and conciliatory retreat from his public position. He subsequently withdrew it and refused a British request of December 1845 that he renew the offer and submit the dispute to international arbitration. Instead he called on Congress to terminate the agreement for joint occupation of the Pacific Northwest. Congress complied in April 1846, and Polk submitted the required year's notice to the British on May 21.

Since abrogation of the joint agreement implied that the United States would attempt to extend its jurisdiction north to 54°40', the British government decided to take the diplomatic initiative in an effort to avert war, while at the same time dispatching warships to the Western Hemisphere in case conciliation failed.

This 1846 cartoon titled "This Is the House That Polk Built" shows President Polk sitting forlornly in a house of cards, which represents the delicately balanced issues facing him. ❖

Their new proposal accepted the 49th parallel as the border to a point where the boundary would veer south so that Britain could retain Vancouver Island. It also provided for British navigation rights on the Columbia River. When the draft treaty was received in June, Polk refused either to endorse or reject it and took the unusual step of submitting it directly to the Senate for advice. The Senate recommended the treaty be accepted with the single change that British rights to navigate the Columbia be made temporary. It was ratified in that form on June 15.

Polk was prompted to settle the Oregon question because he now had a war with Mexico on his hands. His reckless and aggressive diplomacy had brought the nation within an eyelash of being involved in two wars at the same time. American policymakers got what they wanted from the Oregon treaty, namely Puget Sound and the strait that led into it south of Vancouver Island. Acquisition of this splendid natural harbor gave the United States its first deepwater port on the Pacific. Polk's initial demand for all of Oregon was made partly for domestic political consumption and partly to bluff the British into making more concessions. It was a dangerous game on both fronts. When Polk finally agreed to the solution, he alienated expansionist advocates in the Old Northwest who had supported his call for "all of Oregon."

For many Northerners, the promise of new acquisitions in the Pacific Northwest was the only thing that made annexation of Texas palatable. They hoped new free states could be created to counterbalance the admission of slaveholding Texas to the Union. As this prospect receded, the charge of antislavery advocates that Texas annexation was a southern plot became more believable; to Northerners, Polk began to look more and more like a president concerned mainly with furthering the interests of his native region.

## War with Mexico

While the United States was avoiding a war with Great Britain, it was getting into one with Mexico. Although they had recognized Texas independence in 1845, the Mexicans rejected the Lone Star Republic's dubious claim to the unsettled territory between the Nueces River and the Rio Grande. When the United States annexed Texas and assumed its claim to the disputed area, Mexico broke off diplomatic relations and prepared for armed conflict.

Polk responded by placing troops in Louisiana on the alert and by dispatching John Slidell as an emissary to Mexico City in the hope he could resolve the boundary dispute and also persuade the Mexicans to sell New Mexico and California to the United States. The Mexican government refused to receive Slidell

*Handkerchief depicting Major General Zachary Taylor in battle scenes from the Mexican War. When the popular hero displeased President Polk with his actions in the capture of Monterrey, he was replaced by Winfield Scott. Scott carried out Polk's plan for the attack on the port city of Veracruz, which led to the capture of Mexico City.* ❖

May 13, American agents and an "exploring expedition" under John C. Frémont were already in California stirring up dissension against Mexican rule, and ships of the U.S. Navy lay waiting expectantly off the shore. Two days later, Polk ordered a force under Colonel Stephen Kearny to march to Santa Fe and take possession of New Mexico.

The **Mexican-American War** lasted much longer than expected because the Mexicans refused to make peace despite a succession of military defeats. In the first major campaign of the conflict, Taylor followed up his victory in two battles fought north of the Rio Grande by crossing the river, taking Matamoros, and marching on Monterrey. In September, his forces assaulted and captured this major city of northern Mexico after overcoming fierce resistance.

Taylor's controversial decision to allow the Mexican garrison to go free and his unwillingness or inability to advance farther into Mexico angered Polk and led him to adopt a new strategy for winning the war and a new commander to implement it. General Winfield Scott was ordered to prepare an amphibious attack on Veracruz with the aim of placing an American army within striking distance of Mexico City itself. With half his forces detached for the new invasion, Taylor was left to hold his position in northern Mexico. But this did not deprive him of a final moment of glory. At Buena Vista, in February 1847, he claimed victory over a sizable Mexican army sent northward to dislodge him. Despite his unpopularity with the administration, Taylor was hailed as a national hero and a possible candidate for president.

Meanwhile, the Kearny expedition captured Santa Fe, proclaimed the annexation of New Mexico by the United States, and set off for California. There they found that American settlers, in cooperation with John C. Frémont's exploring expedition, had revolted against Mexican authorities and declared their independence as the Bear Flag Republic. The navy had also captured the port of Monterey. With the addition of Kearny's troops, a relatively small number of Americans were able to take

because the nature of his appointment ignored the fact that regular diplomatic relations were suspended. While Slidell was cooling his heels in Mexico City in January 1846, Polk ordered General Zachary Taylor, commander of American forces in the Southwest, to advance well beyond the Nueces and proceed toward the Rio Grande, thus invading territory claimed by both sides.

By April, Taylor had taken up a position near Matamoros on the Rio Grande. On the opposite bank of the river, Mexican forces had assembled and erected a fort. On April 24, sixteen hundred Mexican soldiers crossed the river and the following day met and attacked a small American detachment, killing eleven and capturing the rest. After learning of the incident, Taylor sent word to the president: "Hostilities," he reported, "may now be considered as commenced."

The news was neither unexpected nor unwelcome. Polk in fact was already preparing his war message to Congress when he learned of the fighting on the Rio Grande. A short and decisive war, he had concluded, would force the cession of California and New Mexico to the United States. When Congress declared war on possession of California against scattered and disorganized Mexican opposition, a process that was completed by the beginning of 1847.

The decisive Veracruz campaign was slow to develop because of the massive and careful preparations required. But in March 1847, the main American army under General Scott finally landed near that crucial port city and laid siege to it. Veracruz fell after eighteen days, and then Scott began his advance on Mexico City. In the most important single battle of the war, Scott met forces under General Santa Anna at Cerro Gordo on April 17 and 18. The Mexicans occupied an apparently impregnable position on high ground blocking the way to Mexico City. A daring flanking maneuver that required soldiers to scramble up the mountainsides enabled Scott to win the decisive victory that opened the road to the Mexican capital. By August, American troops were drawn up in front of Mexico City. After a temporary armistice, a brief respite that the Mexicans used to regroup and improve their defenses, Scott ordered the massive assault that captured the city on September 14.

## Settlement of the Mexican-American War

Accompanying Scott's army was a diplomat, Nicholas P. Trist, who was authorized to negotiate a peace treaty whenever the Mexicans decided they had had enough. Despite a sequence of American victories and the imminent fall of Mexico City, Trist made little progress. No Mexican leader was willing to invite the wrath of an intensely proud and patriotic citizenry by agreeing to the kind of terms that Polk wanted to impose. Even after the United States had achieved an overwhelming military victory, Trist found it difficult to exact an acceptable treaty from the Mexican government. In November, Polk ordered Trist to return to Washington. Radical adherents of Manifest Destiny were now clamoring for the annexation of all Mexico, and Polk himself may have been momentarily tempted by the chance to move from military occupation to outright annexation.

Trist ignored Polk's instructions and lingered in Mexico City. On February 2, 1848, he signed a treaty that gained all the concessions he had been commissioned to obtain. The **Treaty of Guadalupe Hidalgo** ceded New Mexico and California to the United States for $15 million, established

the Rio Grande as the border between Texas and Mexico, and promised that the U.S. government would assume the substantial claims of American citizens against Mexico. The treaty also provided that the Mexican residents of the new territories would become U.S. citizens. When the agreement reached Washington, Polk censured Trist for disobeying orders but approved most of his treaty, which he sent to the Senate for ratification. Senate approval by a vote of 38 to 14 came on March 10.

As a result of the Mexican-American War, the United States gained 500,000 square miles of territory. The treaty of 1848 enlarged the size of the nation by about 20 percent, adding to its domain the present states of California, Utah, New Mexico, Nevada, and Arizona and parts of Colorado and Wyoming. Soon those interested in a southern route for a transcontinental railroad pressed for even more territory along the southern border of the cession. That pressure led in 1853 to the Gadsden Purchase, through which the United States acquired the southernmost parts of present-day Arizona and New

Richard Caton Woodville's, War News from Mexico, *suggests the role of the newspaper in keeping the public informed of developments in the expanding nation's quest for new territory.* ❖

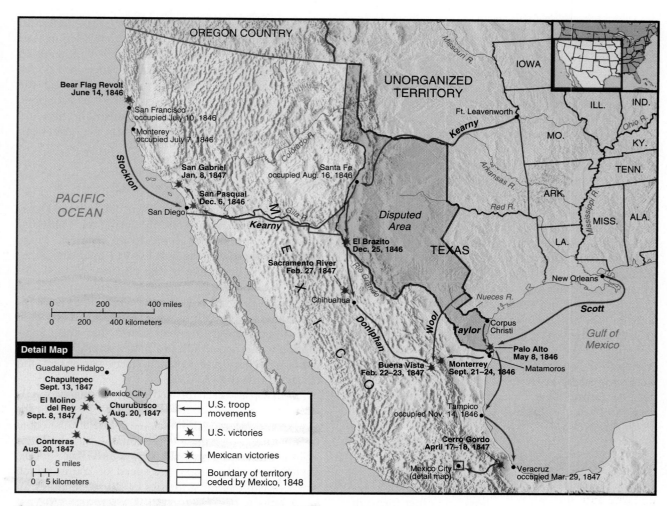

**THE MEXICAN-AMERICAN WAR**    *The Mexican-American War added half a million square miles of territory to the United States, but the cost was high: $100 million and 13,000 lives.* ❖

Mexico. But one intriguing question remains. Why, given the expansionist spirit of the age, did the campaign to acquire *all* of Mexico fail?

According to historian Frederick Merk, a major factor was the peculiar combination of racism and anticolonialism that dominated American opinion. It was one thing to acquire thinly populated areas that could be settled by "Anglo-Saxon" pioneers. It was something else again to incorporate a large population that was mainly of mixed Spanish and Indian origin. These "mongrels," charged racist opponents of the "All Mexico" movement, could never be fit citizens of a self-governing republic. They would have to be ruled in the way the British governed India, and the possession of colonial dependencies was contrary to American ideals and traditions.

Merk's thesis sheds light on why the general public had little appetite for swallowing all of Mexico, but those actually making policy had more mundane and

practical reasons for being satisfied with what was obtained at Guadalupe Hidalgo. What they had really wanted all along, historian Norman Graebner contended, were the great California harbors of San Francisco and San Diego. From these ports, Americans could trade directly with the Orient and dominate the commerce of the Pacific. Once acquisition of California had been assured, policymakers had little incentive to press for more Mexican territory.

The war with Mexico divided the American public and provoked political dissension. A majority of the Whig party opposed the war in principle, arguing that the United States had no valid claims to the area south of the Nueces. Whig congressmen voted for military appropriations while the conflict was going on, but they constantly criticized the president for starting it. More ominous was the charge of some Northerners from both parties that the real purpose of the war was to spread the institution of slavery and increase the political power of the southern states. While battles were being fought in Mexico, Congress was debating the Wilmot Proviso, a proposal to prohibit slavery in any territories that might be acquired from Mexico. A bitter sectional quarrel over the status of slavery in new areas was a major legacy of the Mexican-American War (see Chapter 14).

The domestic controversies aroused by the war and the propaganda of Manifest Destiny revealed the limits of mid-nineteenth-century American expansionism and put a damper on additional efforts to extend the nation's boundaries. Concerns about slavery and race impeded acquisition of new territory in Latin America and the Caribbean. Resolution of the Oregon dispute clearly indicated that the United States was not willing to go to war with a powerful adversary to obtain large chunks of British North America, and the old ambition of incorporating Canada faded. From 1848 until the revival of expansionism in the late nineteenth century, American growth usually took the form of populating and developing the vast territory already acquired. Although the rights of former inhabitants of Mexico were supposedly guaranteed by treaty, they in effect became second-class citizens of the United States. (See the Feature Essay, "Hispanic America After 1848," pp. 376–377.)

## INTERNAL EXPANSIONISM

Young American expansionists saw a clear link between acquisition of new territory and other forms of material growth and development. In 1844, Samuel F. B. Morse perfected and demonstrated his electric telegraph, a device that would make it possible to communicate rapidly over the expanse of a continental nation. Simultaneously, the railroad was becoming increasingly important as a means of moving people and goods over the same great distances. Improvements in manufacturing and agricultural methods led to an upsurge in the volume and range of internal trade, and the beginnings of mass immigration were providing human resources for the exploitation of new areas and economic opportunities.

After gold was discovered in newly acquired California in 1848, a flood of emigrants from the East and several foreign nations arrived by ship or wagon train, their appetites whetted by the thought of striking it rich. The gold they unearthed spurred the national economy, and the rapid growth of population centers on the Pacific Coast inspired projects for transcontinental telegraph lines and railroad tracks.

Despite the best efforts of the Young Americans, the spirit of Manifest Destiny and the thirst for acquir-

ing new territory waned after the Mexican-American War. The expansionist impulse was channeled instead into internal development. Although the nation ceased to grow in size, the technological advances and population increase of the 1840s continued during the 1850s. The result was an acceleration of economic growth, a substantial increase in industrialization and urbanization, and the emergence of a new American working class.

## The Triumph of the Railroad

More than anything else, the rise of the railroad transformed the American economy during the 1840s and 1850s. The technology came from England, where steam locomotives were first used to haul cars along tracks at the beginning of the century. In 1830 and 1831, two American railroads began commercial operation—the Charleston and Hamburg in South Carolina and the Baltimore and Ohio in Maryland. After these pioneer lines had shown that steam locomotion was practical and profitable, several other railroads were built and began to carry passengers and freight during the 1830s.

Canals, however, proved to be strong competitors, especially for the freight business. By 1840, railroads had 2818 miles of track—a figure almost equal to the combined length of all canals—but the latter still carried a much larger volume of goods. Passengers might prefer the speed of trains, which reached astonishing velocities of 20 to 30 miles an hour, but the lower unit cost of transporting freight on the canalboats prevented most shippers from changing their habits. Furthermore, states such as New York and Pennsylvania had invested heavily in canals and resisted chartering a competitive form of transportation. Most of the early railroads reached out from port cities, such as Boston and Baltimore, that did not have good canal routes to the interior. Steam locomotion provided them a chance to cut into the enormous commerce that flowed along the Erie Canal and gave New York an advantage in the scramble for western trade.

During the 1840s, rails extended beyond the northeastern and Middle Atlantic states, and mileage increased more than threefold, reaching a total of more than 9000 miles by 1850. Expansion, fueled by massive European investment, was even greater in the following decade, when about 20,000 miles of additional track were laid. By 1860, all the states east of the Mississippi had rail service, and a traveler could go by train from New York to Chicago and return by way of Memphis. Throughout the 1840s and 1850s, railroads cut deeply into the freight business of the canals and

BRITISH NORTH AMERICA
(CANADA)

Great Lakes

Boston

Detroit

Pittsburgh    New York

Chicago                Philadelphia

Washington, D.C.

St. Joseph    Cincinnati

St. Louis

ATLANTIC
OCEAN

Charleston

Railroads
in 1850

Railroads built
between 1850
and 1860

New Orleans

Houston

Gulf of Mexico

0          200          400 miles

0     200     400 kilometers

**RAILROADS, 1850 AND 1860**   *During the
1840s and 1850s, railroad lines moved rapidly
westward. By 1860, more than 30,000 miles of track
had been laid.* ❖

succeeded in driving many of them out of business. The cost of hauling goods by rail decreased dramatically because of improved track construction and the introduction of powerful locomotives that could haul more cars. New York and Pennsylvania were slow to encourage rail transportation because of their early commitment to canals, but by the 1850s, both states had accepted the inevitable and were promoting massive railroad building.

The development of railroads had an enormous effect on the economy as a whole. Although the burgeoning demand for iron rails was initially met mainly by importation from England, it eventually spurred development of the domestic iron industry. Since railroads required an enormous outlay of capital, their promoters pioneered new methods for financing business enterprise. At a time when most manufacturing and mercantile concerns were still owned by families or partnerships, the railroad companies sold stock to the general public and helped to set the pattern for the separation of ownership and control that characterizes the modern corporation. They also developed new types of securities, such as "preferred stock" (with no voting rights but the assurance of a fixed rate of return) and long-term bonds at a set rate of interest.

The gathering and control of private capital did not fully meet the desires of the early railroad barons.

State and local governments, convinced that railroads were the key to their future prosperity, loaned the railroads money, bought their stock, and guaranteed their bonds. Despite the dominant philosophy of laissez-faire (which meant that the government should keep its hands off the economy), the federal government became involved by surveying the routes of projected lines and providing land grants. In 1850, for example, several million acres of public land were granted to the Illinois Central. In all, forty companies received such aid before 1860, setting a precedent for the massive land grants of the post–Civil War era.

## The Industrial Revolution Takes Off

While railroads were initiating a revolution in transportation, American industry was entering a new phase of rapid and sustained growth. The factory mode of production, which had originated before 1840 in the cotton mills of New England, was extended to a variety of other products (see Chapter 9). The weaving and processing of wool, instead of being carried on in different locations, was concentrated in single production units beginning in the 1830s, and by 1860 some of the largest textile mills in the country were producing wool cloth. In the coal and iron regions of eastern Pennsylvania, iron was being forged and rolled in factories by 1850. Among the other

# Feature Essay

# HISPANIC AMERICA AFTER 1848

## A Case Study in Majority Rule

With the discovery of gold in 1848, more than one thousand Californians of Mexican ancestry joined the frenetic rush to the Sierras. Among them was Don Antonio Franco Coronel, a Los Angeles school teacher, who led a group of fellow *Californios* into the rich goldfields. Just months before the expedition, the United States and Mexico had concluded the Treaty of Guadalupe Hidalgo, which transformed Coronel and his companions from Mexicans to Americans. At the insistence of the Mexican government, the treaty stipulated that Mexicans living in the newly acquired territories would be granted "all the rights of citizens of the United

States . . . according to the principles of the Constitution." Coronel's gold-seeking enterprise would put that promise to the test. While panning rivers and staking claims, Coronel's company came into competitive contact with large numbers of Yankee miners. The interactions between the two ethnic communities suggested that a rough road lay ahead for Hispanic Americans.

Upon arriving in gold country, Coronel and his men immediately hit pay dirt. In the first day alone, Coronel pulled 45 ounces of gold from the ground; within eight days, one of his associates had amassed a pile of gold weighing a staggering 52 pounds. The

*Californios* seemed to have a head start in the race for gold. They understood the terrain, cooperated among themselves, and were familiar with the best mining techniques. Not surprisingly, their dramatic successes stirred the envy of their Anglo-American competitors. Though the Mexican-American War had technically made the Yankee and Hispanic miners compatriots, the tensions of gold fever exposed the shallowness of that new relationship.

After a year of relatively peaceful competition, Anglo miners began to express their resentments. Lumping *Californios* with all other "foreigners," they unleashed a barrage of physical and political attacks against their competitors. Lynch mobs, camp riots, and legal harassment were common forms of Yankee intimidation. Despite their entitlements to the rights of citizenship, the *Californios* were badgered and bullied into retreat. Fearing for his life, Coronel returned to Southern California, where Hispanics still outnumbered the newcomers. Earning prestige and prosperity in Los Angeles, Coronel went on to become mayor and state treasurer. But to the end of his life, he still painfully remembered his experiences in Northern California, where his rights as a U.S. citizen were so easily disregarded by his fellow Americans.

Coronel's experiences exemplify two truths about the effect U.S. expansion had on the lives of Mexicans who suddenly found themselves in American territory. First, in areas where Anglo-American settlement grew rapidly—such as Northern California—the Hispanic community

*Blessing of the Enrequita Mine,* 1860, by Alexander Edouart. Spaniards and Mexicans, men and women, surround the makeshift altar where the priest is saying the blessing to dedicate the Enrequita Mine in northern California. The idyllic scene does not hint at the violent and rough treatment Hispanic miners experienced during the California gold rush days. ✦

typically faced discrimination, intimidation, and a denial of the very civil rights that Guadalupe Hidalgo had supposedly guaranteed. Second, in areas where the Hispanic population remained a majority—such as Southern California—Spanish-speaking Americans were able to exercise the rights of republican citizenship, often wielding considerable political influence. Coronel had a taste of both experiences, going from intimidated miner to powerful politician. However, as Anglo settlers began to stream into Southern California, even that region ceased to be a safe haven for Hispanic rights.

By the mid-1840s Hispanics living in Texas, known as *Tejanos,* were outnumbered by Anglos at a ratio of twenty-to-one. True to the pattern described above, this decided minority faced intense prejudice. Among the most notable victims of this prejudice was Juan Sequin, a hero of the Texas war for independence (see p. 363). Perhaps no *Tejano* family fell further or faster than the posterity of Don Martin de Leon. The scion of an aristocratic family, de Leon had spearheaded Spanish efforts to colonize Texas and continued to organize settlements after Mexican independence. Establishing extensive cattle ranches, the de Leons enjoyed prominence and wealth on their holdings. As with most *Tejanos,* they fervently supported the struggle for Texan independence, fighting shoulder to shoulder with their Anglo neighbors. But when the war ended, the de Leon estate fell under siege from the surging wave of new settlers. Relying on the intricacies of Anglo-American law and the power of an electoral majority, the newcomers quickly encroached on de Leon's lands. With frightening rapidity, the de Leon family was reduced from its preeminent position to abject poverty.

The de Leons were not alone. A contemporary observed that many Anglo settlers worked "dark intrigues against the native families, whose only crime was that they owned large tracts of land and desirable property." Even after U.S. annexation of the Lone Star Republic, Hispanics continued to be pushed off their land. In 1856 a Texas

*West Side Main Plaza, San Antonio, Texas* by W. G. M. Samuel. San Antonio's religious and political history is reflected in this 1849 painting of the city's main plaza. The building at the center is San Fernando Cathedral; behind the cathedral an American flag flies over the nearby Military Plaza. The large house at the far right is the home of José Cassiano, a Mexican who sided with the Texans in the revolution against Mexico. ✦

newspaper reported that "The people of Matagorda county have held a meeting and ordered every Mexican to leave the county. To strangers this may seem wrong, but we hold it to be perfectly right and highly necessary." For many Mexican Americans, life on U.S. soil taught the cruelest lesson in white man's democracy.

Yet majority rule actually worked to the favor of Hispanics living in New Mexico, where they enjoyed numerical dominance. When U.S. troops entered Santa Fe in 1846, Albino Chacón, a prominent city judge, controlled his own future. Although he had been loyal to the Mexican government throughout the war, the U.S. Army offered him the opportunity to retain his judgeship. Given similar offers, other New Mexicans who had initially opposed the U.S. invasion accepted positions of prominence, such as Donanciano Vigil, who served as interim governor of the territory. But Chacón lived by a strict code of honor and could not switch loyalties so easily. Opting for exile, Chacón moved out of Santa Fe, left the practice of law, and took up farming. Aside from such self-imposed changes, however, American rule actually had little impact on most New Mexicans' lives.

Hispanics still formed the demographic and political backbone of the territory and often served their new nation with distinction. Chacón's own son, Rafael, served as a Union officer during the Civil War, winning acclaim in defending New Mexico against a Confederate invasion from Texas, and was eventually elected as territorial senator. Rafael's son studied law at Notre Dame and held several important positions in the Department of Justice. Majority status afforded New Mexican Hispanics opportunities in the American system that were denied their compatriots living in Anglo-dominated regions.

As settlement increased throughout the century, such Hispanic-controlled communities dwindled. The rise of the railroad acted as a funnel through which Anglo-Americans poured into western territories, and remaining pockets of Hispanic dominance rapidly disappeared. American majoritarianism and racism combined to place Hispanics in positions subordinate to those of the Anglo newcomers. Throughout the region the story was sadly similar; as Hispanic Americans lost their majority status, they also lost many of their basic rights.

industries that adopted the factory system during this period were those producing firearms, clocks, and sewing machines.

The essential features of the emerging mode of production were the gathering of a supervised workforce in a single place, the payment of cash wages to workers, the use of interchangeable parts, and manufacture by "continuous process." Within a factory setting, standardized parts, manufactured separately and in bulk, could be efficiently and rapidly assembled into a final product by an ordered sequence of continuously repeated operations. Mass production, which involved the division of labor into a series of relatively simple and repetitive tasks, contrasted sharply with the traditional craft mode of production, in which a single worker produced the entire product out of raw materials.

The bulk of American manufacturing of the 1840s and 1850s, however, was still carried on by traditional methods. Small workshops continued to predominate in most industries, and some relatively large factories were not yet mechanized. But mass production was clearly the wave of the future. The transformation of a craft into a modern industry is well illustrated by the evolution of shoemaking. The independent cobbler producing shoes for order was first challenged by a putting-out system involving the assignment of various tasks to physically separated workers and then was virtually displaced by the great shoe factories that by the 1860s were operating in cities such as Lynn, Massachusetts.

New technology often played an important role in the transition to mass production. Just as power looms and spinning machinery had made textile mills possible, the development of new and more reliable machines or industrial techniques revolutionized other industries. Elias Howe's invention of the sewing machine in 1846 laid the basis for the ready-to-wear clothing industry and also contributed to the mechanization of shoemaking. During the 1840s,

### ✦ A Look at the Past ✦

#### Steel Plow

In 1837, John Deere invented a plow with a smooth steel blade and successfully tested it on a farm in Illinois. Earlier plows had a blade made of cast iron. Deere's plow quickly became popular with pioneer farmers in the Midwest as an essential tool in cultivating the land. Why do you think Deere's new plow was necessary in the midwestern prairie? Why wouldn't a cast iron plow used in the East work equally well?

iron manufacturers adopted the British practice of using coal rather than charcoal for smelting and thus produced a metal better suited to industrial needs. Charles Goodyear's discovery in 1839 of the process for the vulcanization of rubber made a new range of manufactured items available to the American consumer, most notably the overshoe.

Perhaps the greatest triumph of American technology during the mid-nineteenth century was the development of the world's most sophisticated and

*A revolution in farming followed the introduction of new farm implements such as Cyrus McCormick's reaper, which could do ten times the work of a single person. The lithograph, by an anonymous artist, is titled* The Testing of the First Reaping Machine near Steele's Tavern, Virginia, 1831. ✦

## THE AGE OF PRACTICAL INVENTION

| Year* | Inventor | Contribution | Importance/Description |
|---|---|---|---|
| 1787 | John Fitch | Steamboat | First successful American steamboat |
| 1793 | Eli Whitney | Cotton gin | Simplified process of separating fiber from seeds; helped make cotton a profitable staple of southern agriculture |
| 1798 | Eli Whitney | Jig for guiding tools | Facilitated manufacture of interchangeable parts |
| 1802 | Oliver Evans | Steam engine | First American steam engine; led to manufacture of high-pressure engines used throughout eastern United States |
| 1813 | Richard B. Chenaworth | Cast-iron plow | First iron plow to be made in three separate pieces, thus making possible replacement of parts |
| 1830 | Peter Cooper | Railroad locomotive | First steam locomotive built in America |
| 1831 | Cyrus McCormick | Reaper | Mechanized harvesting; early model could cut six acres of grain a day |
| 1836 | Samuel Colt | Revolver | First successful repeating pistol |
| 1837 | John Deere | Steel plow | Steel surface kept soil from sticking; farming thus made easier on rich prairies of Midwest |
| 1839 | Charles Goodyear | Vulcanization of rubber | Made rubber much more useful by preventing it from sticking and melting in hot weather |
| 1842 | Crawford W. Long | First administered ether in surgery | Reduced pain and risk of shock in surgery during operations |
| 1844 | Samuel F. B. Morse | Telegraph | Made long-distance communication almost instantaneous |
| 1846 | Elias Howe | Sewing machine | First practical machine for automatic sewing |
| 1846 | Norbert Rillieux | Vacuum evaporator | Improved method of removing water from sugar cane; revolutionized sugar industry and was later applied to many other products |
| 1847 | Richard M. Hoe | Rotary printing press | Printed an entire sheet in one motion; vastly speeded up printing process |
| 1851 | William Kelly | "Air-boiling process" | Improved method of converting iron into steel (usually known as Bessemer process because English inventor Bessemer had more advantageous patent and financial arrangements) |
| 1853 | Elisha G. Otis | Passenger elevator | Improved movement in buildings; when later electrified, stimulated development of skyscrapers |
| 1859 | Edwin L. Drake | First American oil well | Initiated oil industry in the United States |
| 1859 | George M. Pullman | Pullman passenger car | First railroad sleeping car suitable for long-distance travel |

*Dates refer to patent or first successful use.

**Source:** From *Freedom and Crisis: An American History,* Third Edition, by Allen Weinstein and Frank Otto Gatell. Copyright © 1974, 1978, 1981 by Random House, Inc. Reprinted by permission of Random House, Inc.

reliable machine tools. Such advances as the invention of the extraordinarily accurate measuring device known as the vernier caliper in 1851 and the first production of turret lathes in 1854 were signs of a special American aptitude for the kind of precision toolmaking that was essential to efficient industrialization.

Progress in industrial technology and organization did not mean the United States had become an industrial society by 1860. Factory workers remained a small fraction of the workforce, and agriculture retained first place both as a source of livelihood for individuals and as a contributor to the gross national product. Nearly 60 percent of the gainfully employed still worked on the land. But farming itself, at least in the North, was undergoing a technological revolution of its own. John Deere's steel plow, invented in 1837 and mass produced by the 1850s, enabled midwestern farmers to cultivate the tough prairie soils that had resisted cast-iron implements. The mechanical reaper, patented by Cyrus McCormick in 1834, offered an enormous saving in the labor required for harvesting grain; by 1851, McCormick was producing more than a thousand reapers a year in his Chicago plant. Other new farm implements that came into widespread use before 1860 included seed drills, cultivators, and threshing machines.

A dynamic interaction between advances in transportation, industry, and agriculture gave great strength and resiliency to the economy of the northern states during the 1850s. Railroads offered western farmers better access to eastern markets. After Chicago and New York were linked by rail in 1853, the flow of most midwestern farm commodities shifted from the north-south direction based on riverborne traffic, which had still predominated in the 1830s and 1840s, to an east-west pattern.

The mechanization of agriculture did more than lead to more efficient and profitable commercial farming; it also provided an additional impetus to industrialization, and its laborsaving features released workers for other economic activities. The growth of industry and the modernization of agriculture can thus be seen as mutually reinforcing aspects of a single process of economic growth.

## Mass Immigration Begins

The original incentive to mechanize northern industry and agriculture came in part from a shortage of cheap labor. Compared with that of industrializing nations of Europe, the economy of the United States in the early nineteenth century was labor-scarce. Since it was difficult to attract able-bodied men to work for low wages in factories or on farms, women and children were used extensively in the early textile mills, and commercial farmers had to rely heavily on the labor of their family members. In the face of such limited and uncertain labor supplies, producers were greatly tempted to experiment with laborsaving machinery. By the 1840s and 1850s, however, even the newly industrialized operations were ready to absorb a new influx of unskilled workers. Factories required increasing numbers of operatives, and railroad builders needed construction gangs. The growth of industrial work opportunities helped attract a multitude of European immigrants during the two decades before the Civil War.

Between 1820 and 1840, an estimated 700,000 immigrants arrived in the United States, mainly from the British Isles and German-speaking areas of continental Europe. During the 1840s, this substantial flow suddenly became a flood. No fewer than 4.2 million people crossed the Atlantic between 1840 and 1860, and about 3 million of these arrived in the single decade between 1845 and 1855. This was the greatest influx in proportion to total population—then about 20 mil-

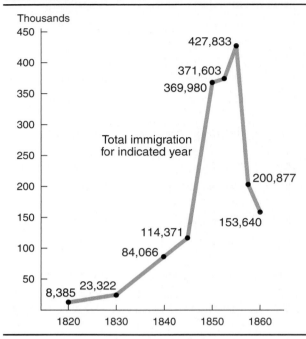

**IMMIGRATION TO THE UNITED STATES, 1820–1860**

Thousands

Total immigration for indicated year

8,385
23,322
84,066
114,371
369,980
371,603
427,833
200,877
153,640

1820    1830    1840    1850    1860

lion—that the nation has ever experienced. The largest single source of the new mass immigration was Ireland, but Germany was not far behind. Smaller contingents came from Switzerland, Norway, Sweden, and the Netherlands.

The massive transatlantic movement had many causes; some people were "pushed" out of their homes while others were "pulled" toward America. The great push factor that caused 1.5 million Irish to forsake the Emerald Isle between 1845 and 1854 was the great potato blight, which brought famine to a population that subsisted on this single crop. Escape to America was made possible by the low fares then prevailing on sailing ships bound from England to North America. Ships involved in the timber trade carried their bulky cargoes from Boston or Halifax to Liverpool; as an alternative to returning to America partly in ballast, they packed Irish immigrants into their holds. The squalor and misery in these steerage accommodations were almost beyond belief.

Because of the ports involved in the lumber trade—Boston, Halifax, Saint John's, and Saint Andrews—the Irish usually arrived in Canada or the northeastern states. Immobilized by poverty and a lack of the skills required for pioneering in the West, most of them remained in the Northeast. By the 1850s, they constituted a substantial portion of the total population of Boston, New York, Philadelphia, and many smaller cities of the New England and Middle Atlantic states. Forced to subsist on low-paid menial labor and crowded into festering urban slums, they were looked down on by most native-born Americans. Their devotion to Catholicism aroused Protestant resentment and mob violence (see Chapter 14 for a discussion of the growth of nativism and anti-Catholicism).

The million or so Germans who also came in the late 1840s and early 1850s were somewhat more fortunate. Most of them were also peasants, but they had fled hard times rather than outright catastrophe. Changes in German landholding patterns and a fluctuating market for grain crops put pressure on small operators. Those whose mortgages were foreclosed—or who could no longer make the regular payments to landlords that were the price of emancipation from feudal obligations—frequently opted for emigration to America. Unlike the Irish, they often escaped with a small amount of capital with which to make a fresh start in the New World.

Many German immigrants were artisans and sought to ply their trades in cities such as New York, St. Louis, Cincinnati, and Milwaukee—all of which became centers of German-American population. But a large portion of those with peasant backgrounds went back to the land. The possession of diversified agricultural skills and small amounts of capital enabled many Germans to become successful midwestern farmers. In general, they encountered less prejudice and discrimination than the Irish. For Germans who were Protestant, religious affinity with their American neighbors made for relative tolerance. But even Germans who were Catholic normally escaped the virulent scorn heaped on the Irish, perhaps because they were not so poverty stricken and did not carry the added burden of being members of an ethnic group Anglo-Americans had learned to despise from their English ancestors and cousins.

What attracted most of the Irish, German, and other European immigrants to America was the promise of economic opportunity. A minority, like some of the German revolutionaries of 1848, chose the United States because they admired its democratic political system. But most immigrants were more interested in the chance to make a decent living than in voting or running for office. The force of the economic motive can be seen in the fact that peak periods of immigration—1845 to 1854 is a prime example—coincided very closely with times of domestic prosperity and high demand for labor. During depressed periods, such as 1837 to 1842 and the mid-to-late 1850s, immigration dropped off significantly.

The arrival of large numbers of immigrants exacerbated the already serious problems of America's rapidly growing cities. The old "walking city" in which rich and poor lived in close proximity near the center of town was changing to a more segregated environment. The advent of railroads and horse-drawn streetcars enabled the affluent to move to the first American suburbs, while areas nearer commercial and industrial centers became the congested abode of newcomers from Europe. Emerging slums, such as the notorious Five Points district in New York City, were characterized by overcrowding, poverty, disease, and crime. Recognizing that these conditions created potential dangers for the entire urban population, middle-class reformers worked for the professionalization of police forces, introduction of sanitary water and sewage disposal systems, and the upgrading of housing standards.

They made some progress in these endeavors in the period before the Civil War, but the lot of the urban poor, mainly immigrants, was not dramatically improved. Except to the extent that their own communal activities—especially those sponsored by churches and mutual aid societies—provided a sense of security and solidarity, the existence of most urban immigrants remained unsafe, unhealthy, and unpleasant.

Despite the increasing segregation of the city into ethnic neighborhoods, the urban experience also produced a unifying effect on its mixed population. Individuals of all classes, occupations, and ethnicities met on the crowded streets and in the public squares of cities such as Boston and New York. Often, the entire population—or at least wide cross sections—came together in colorful parades, public celebrations, and political contests. Many city residents met other citizens as members of political parties, religious groups, and civic organizations. A single individual may have voted as a Democrat, worshiped as a Baptist, and served as a member of a volunteer fire department. These different affiliations created relationships that existed outside of ethnic identity. Antebellum cities showed the dark side of urbanization in their crowded slums and growing poverty, but they also became cauldrons of democracy in which different elements of nineteenth-century America met face-to-face to create a wider definition of what it meant to be an American.

## The New Working Class

A majority of immigrants ended up as wage workers in factories, mines, and construction camps or as casual day laborers doing the many unskilled tasks required for urban and commercial growth. By providing a vast pool of cheap labor, they fueled and accelerated the Industrial Revolution. During the 1850s, factory production in Boston and other port cities previously devoted to commerce grew—partly because thousands of recent Irish immigrants worked for the kind of low wages that almost guaranteed large profits for entrepreneurs.

In established industries and older mill towns of the Northeast, immigrants added to, or in some cases displaced, the native-born workers who had predominated in the 1830s and 1840s. The changing workforce of the textile mills in Lowell, Massachusetts, provided a striking example of this process. In 1836, only 3.7 percent of the workers in one Lowell mill were foreign born; most members of the labor force at that time were young unmarried women from New England farms. By 1860, immigrants constituted 61.7 percent of the workforce. Women still formed the majority, but there had been a great proportional increase in the number of men who tended machines in textile factories. Irish males, employers found, were willing to perform tasks that native-born men had generally regarded as women's work.

Sheet music cover for The Serious Family Polka. *In the 1840s and 1850s, the polka, a lively dance from central and eastern Europe, became a dance craze in the United States, where it remained especially popular among German, Polish, and Czech immigrants.* ❖

This trend reveals much about the changing character of the American working class. In the 1830s, most male workers were artisans, and factory work was still largely the province of women and children. Both groups were predominantly of American stock. In the 1840s, the proportion of men engaged in factory work increased, although the workforce in the textile industry remained predominantly female. During that decade, work conditions in many mills deteriorated. Workdays of twelve to fourteen hours were not new, but the paternalism that had earlier evoked a spirit of cooperation from workers was replaced by a more impersonal and cost-conscious form of management. During the depression that followed the Panic of 1837, bosses attempted to reduce expenses and increase productivity by cutting wages, increasing the speed of machinery, and "stretching out"—giving each worker more machinery to operate.

The result was a new upsurge of labor militancy involving female as well as male factory workers. Mill girls in Lowell, for example, formed a union of their own—the Female Labor Reform Association—and agitated for shorter working hours. On a broader front, workers' organizations petitioned state legislatures to pass laws limiting the workday to ten hours. Some such laws were actually passed, but they turned out to be ineffective because employers could still require a prospective worker to sign a special contract agreeing to longer hours.

The employment of immigrants in increasing numbers between the mid-1840s and the late 1850s made it more difficult to organize industrial workers. Impoverished fugitives from the Irish potato famine tended to have lower economic expectations and more conservative social attitudes than did native-born workers. Consequently, the Irish immigrants were initially willing to work for less and were not so prone to protest bad working conditions. Most industrial laborers remained unorganized and resisted appeals for solidarity along class lines.

But the new working class of former rural folk did not make the transition to industrial wage labor easily or without protesting in subtle and indirect ways. Tardiness, absenteeism, drunkenness, loafing on the job, and other forms of resistance to factory discipline reflected deep hostility to the unaccustomed and seemingly unnatural routines of industrial production. The adjustment to new styles and rhythms of work was painful and took time. Historians only now are beginning to examine the inner world of the early generations of industrial workers, and they are finding evidence of discontent rather than docility, cultural resistance rather than easy adaptation.

## CHRONOLOGY

| | |
|---|---|
| **1822** | Santa Fe opened to American traders |
| **1823** | Earliest American settlers arrive in Texas |
| **1830** | Mexico attempts to halt American migration to Texas |
| **1831** | American railroads begin commercial operation |
| **1834** | Cyrus McCormick patents mechanical reaper |
| **1835** | Revolution breaks out in Texas |
| **1836** | Texas becomes independent republic |
| **1837** | John Deere invents steel plow |
| **1841** | President John Tyler inaugurated |
| **1842** | Webster-Ashburton Treaty fixes border between Maine and New Brunswick |
| **1843** | Mass migration to Oregon begins ❖ Mexico closes Santa Fe trade to Americans |
| **1844** | Samuel F. B. Morse demonstrates electric telegraph ❖ James K. Polk elected president on platform of expansionism |
| **1845** | Mass immigration from Europe begins ❖ United States annexes Texas ❖ John L. O'Sullivan coins slogan "Manifest Destiny" |
| **1846** | War with Mexico breaks out ❖ United States and Great Britain resolve diplomatic crisis over Oregon |
| **1847** | American conquest of California completed ❖ Mormons settle Utah ❖ American forces under Zachary Taylor defeat Mexicans at Buena Vista ❖ Winfield Scott's army captures Veracruz and defeats Mexicans at Cerro Gordo ❖ Mexico City falls to American invaders |
| **1848** | Treaty of Guadalupe Hidalgo consigns California and New Mexico to United States ❖ Gold discovered in California |
| **1849** | "Forty-niners" rush to California to dig for gold |
| **1858** | War between Utah Mormons and U.S. forces averted |

## CONCLUSION: THE COSTS OF EXPANSION

By 1860, industrial expansion and immigration had created a working class of men and women who seemed destined for a life of low-paid wage labor. This reality stood in contrast to America's self-image as a land of opportunity and upward mobility. Wage labor was popularly viewed as a temporary condition from which workers were supposed to extricate themselves by hard work and frugality. According to Abraham Lincoln, speaking in 1859 of the North's "free-labor" society, "there is no such thing as a freeman being fatally fixed for life, in the condition of a hired laborer." This ideal still had some validity in rapidly developing regions of the western states, but it was mostly myth when applied to the increasingly foreign-born industrial workers of the Northeast.

Both internal and external expansion had come at a heavy cost. Tensions associated with class and ethnic rivalries were only one part of the price of rapid economic development. The acquisition of new territories became politically divisive and would soon lead to a catastrophic sectional controversy. The Young America wing of the Democratic party fought vainly to prevent this from happening. Its leader in the late 1840s and early 1850s was Senator Stephen A. Douglas of Illinois, called the Little Giant because of his small stature and large public presence. More than anyone else of this period, he sought political power for himself and his party by combining an expansionist foreign policy with the encouragement of economic development within the territories already acquired. His youthful dynamism made him seem the very embodiment of the Young America ideal. Recognizing that the slavery question was the main obstacle to his program, he sought to neutralize it through compromise and evasion (see Chapter 14). His failure to win the presidency or even the Democratic nomination before 1860 showed that the Young Americans' dream of a patriotic consensus supporting headlong expansion and economic development could not withstand the tensions and divisions that expansionist policies created or brought to light.

## RECOMMENDED READING

An overview of expansion to the Pacific is Ray A. Billington, *The Far Western Frontier, 1830–1860* (1956). The impulse behind Manifest Destiny has been variously interpreted. Albert K. Weinberg's classic *Manifest Destiny: A Study of National Expansionism in American History* (1935) describes and stresses the ideological rationale as does Anders Stephenson, *Manifest Destiny: American Expansion and the Empire of Right* (1995). Frederick Merk, *Manifest Destiny and Mission in American History* (1963), analyzes public opinion and shows how divided it was on the question of territorial acquisitions. Norman A. Graebner, *Empire on the Pacific: A Study in American Continental Expansionism*

(1956), highlights the desire for Pacific harbors as a motive for adding new territory. The most complete and authoritative account of the diplomatic side of expansionism in this period is David M. Pletcher, *The Diplomacy of Annexation: Texas, Oregon, and the Mexican War* (1973). Charles G. Sellers, *James K. Polk: Continentalist, 1843–1846* (1966), is the definitive work on Polk's election and the expansionist policies of his administration. A very good account of the Mexican-American War is John S. D. Eisenhower, *So Far from God: The U.S. War with Mexico* (1989). On gold rushes, see Malcolm J. Rohrbough, *Days of Gold: The California Gold Rush and the American Nation* (1997) and Elliott West, *The Contested Plains: Indians, Goldseekers, and the Rush to Colorado* (1998).

Economic developments of the 1840s and 1850s are well covered in George R. Taylor, *The Transportation Revolution, 1815–1960* (1952) and Albert Fishlow, *American Railroads and the Transformation of the Ante-Bellum Economy* (1965). For an overview of immigration in this period, see the early chapters of Roger Daniels, *Coming to America: Immigration and Ethnicity in American Life* (1990). On the Irish, see Kerby A. Miller, *Emigrants and Exiles: Ireland and the Irish Exodus to America* (1985). Oscar Handlin, *Boston Immigrants: A Study in Acculturation*, rev. ed. (1959), is a classic study of immigration to one city. A standard work on the antebellum working class is Sean Wilentz, *Chants Democratic: New York City and the Rise of the American Working Class, 1788–1850* (1984); for the new approach to labor history that emphasizes working-class culture, see Herbert G. Gutman, *Work, Culture, and Society in Industrializing America* (1976). For the rich public life of antebellum cities, see Mary P. Ryan, *Civic Wars: Democracy and Public Life in the American City During the Nineteenth Century* (1997). A pathbreaking and insightful study of workers in the textile industry is Thomas Dublin, *Women at Work: The Transformation of Work and Community in Lowell, Massachusetts, 1826–1860* (1979).

**For a list of additional titles related to this chapter's topics, please see** http://www.ablongman.com/divine.

## SUGGESTED WEB SITES

### Pioneering the Upper Midwest: Books from Michigan, Minnesota, and Wisconsin, ca. 1820–1910

http://memory.loc.gov/ammem/umhtml/umhome.html
This Library of Congress site looks at first-person accounts, biographies, promotional literature, local histories, ethnographic and antiquarian texts, colonial archival documents, and other works from the seventeenth to the early twentieth century. It covers many topics and issues that affected Americans in the settlement and development of the Upper Midwest.

### The Mexican-American War Memorial Homepage

http://sunsite.dcaa.unam.mx/revistas/1847/
Images and text explain the causes, courses, and outcomes of the Mexican-American War.

### On the Trail in Kansas

http://www.kancoll.org/galtrl.htm
This Kansas Collection site holds several good primary sources with images concerning the Oregon trail and America's early movement westward.

### Mountain Men and the Fur Trade

http://www.xmission.com/~drudy/amm.html
Private letters can speak volumes about the concerns and environment of the writers and recipients. Letters from early settlers west of the Mississippi River are offered on this site, along with other resources relating to explorers, trappers, and traders.

Henry Clay, shown here addressing the Senate, helped negotiate the Compromise of 1850 to settle the dispute over the extension of slavery in territories acquired as a result of the Mexican-American War. Daniel Webster, seated at left resting his head on his hand, supported Clay's proposed compromise. Ardent states' rightist John C. Calhoun, standing third from right, led the opposition. ❖

# The Sectional Crisis

## $\mathcal{B}$rooks Assaults Sumner in Congress

On May 22, 1856, Representative Preston Brooks of South Carolina erupted onto the floor of the Senate with a cane in his hand. He approached Charles Sumner, the antislavery senator from Massachusetts who had recently given a fiery oration condemning the South for plotting to extend slavery to the Kansas Territory. What was worse, the speech had included insulting references to Senator Andrew Butler of South Carolina, a kinsman of Brooks. When he found Sumner seated at his desk, Brooks proceeded to batter him over the head. Amazed and stunned, Sumner made a desperate effort to rise and ripped his bolted desk from the floor. He then collapsed under a continued torrent of blows.

Sumner was so badly injured by the assault that he did not return to the Senate for three years. But his home state reelected him in 1857 and kept his seat vacant as testimony against southern brutality and "barbarism." In parts of the North that were up in arms against the expansion of slavery, Sumner was hailed as a martyr to the cause of "free soil." Brooks, denounced in the North as a bully, was lionized by his fellow Southerners. When he resigned from the House after a vote of censure had narrowly failed because of solid southern opposition, his constituents reelected him unanimously.

These contrasting reactions show how bitter sectional antagonism had become by 1856. Sumner spoke for the radical wing of the new Republican party, which was making a bid for national power by mobilizing the North against the alleged aggressions of "the slave power." Southerners viewed the very existence of this party as an insult to their section of the country and a threat to its vital interests. Sumner came closer to being an abolitionist than any other member of Congress, and nothing created greater fear and anxiety among Southerners than their belief that antislavery forces were plotting against their way of life. To many Northerners, "bully Brooks" stood for all the arrogant and violent slaveholders who were allegedly conspiring to extend their barbaric labor system. By 1856, therefore, the sectional cleavage that would lead to the Civil War had already undermined the foundations of national unity.

THE CRISIS OF THE MID-1850S came only a few years after the elaborate compromise of 1850 had seemingly resolved the dispute over the future of slavery in the territories acquired as a result of the Mexican War. The renewed agitation over the extension of slavery that led to Brooks's attack on Sumner was set in motion by the Kansas-Nebraska Act of 1854. This legislation revived the sectional conflict and led to the emergence of the Republican party. From that point on, a dramatic series of events increased sectional confrontation and destroyed the prospects for a new compromise. The caning of Charles Sumner was one of these events, and violence on the Senate floor foreshadowed violence on the battlefield.

*After his constituents learned of Preston Brooks's caning of Senator Sumner, they sent Brooks a gold-handled cowhide whip to use on other antislavery advocates.* ❖

## THE COMPROMISE OF 1850

The "irrepressible conflict" over slavery in the territories began in the late 1840s. The positions taken on this issue between 1846 and 1850 established the range of options that would reemerge after 1854. But during this earlier phase of the sectional controversy, the leaders of two strong national parties, each with substantial followings in both the North and the South, had a vested interest in resolving the crisis. Efforts to create uncompromising sectional parties failed to disrupt what historians call the second party system—the vigorous competition between Whigs and Democrats that had characterized elections since the 1830s. Furthermore, the less tangible features of sectionalism—emotion and ideology—were not as divisive as they would later become. Hence a fragile compromise was achieved through a kind of give-and-take that would not be possible in the changed environment of the mid-1850s.

### The Problem of Slavery in the Mexican Cession

As the price of union between states committed to slavery and those in the process of abolishing it, the Founders had attempted to limit the role of the slavery issue in national politics. The Constitution gave the federal government the right to abolish the international slave trade but no definite authority to regulate or destroy the institution where it existed under state law. Although many of the Founders hoped for the eventual demise of slavery, they provided no direct means to achieve this end except voluntary state action. These ground rules limited the effect of northern attacks on the South's peculiar institution. It was easy to condemn slavery in principle but very difficult to develop a practical program to eliminate it without defying the Constitution.

Radical abolitionists saw this problem clearly and resolved it by rejecting the law of the land in favor of a "higher law" prohibiting human bondage. In 1844, William Lloyd Garrison publicly burned the Constitution, condemning it as "a Covenant with Death, an Agreement with Hell." But Garrison spoke for a small minority dedicated to freeing the North, at whatever cost, from the sin of condoning slavery.

During the 1840s, the majority of Northerners showed that while they disliked slavery, they also detested abolitionism. They were inclined to view slavery as a backward and unwholesome institution, much inferior to their own free-labor system, and could be persuaded that slaveholders were power-hungry aristocrats seeking more than their share of national political influence. But they regarded the Constitution as a binding contract between slave and free states and were likely to be prejudiced against blacks and reluctant to accept large numbers of them as free citizens. Consequently, they saw no legal or desirable way to bring about emancipation within the southern states.

But the Constitution had not predetermined the status of slavery in *future* states. Since Congress had the power to admit new states to the Union under any conditions it wished to impose, a majority arguably could require the abolition of slavery as the price of admission. An effort to use this power had led to the Missouri crisis of 1819–1820 (see Chapter 9). The resulting compromise was designed to decide future cases by drawing a line between slave and free states and extending it westward through the unsettled portions of what was then American soil. When specific territories were settled, organized, and prepared for statehood, slavery would be permitted south of the line and prohibited north of it.

The tradition of providing both the free North and the slave South with opportunities for expansion and the creation of new states broke down when new territories were wrested from Mexico in the 1840s. When Texas was admitted as a slave state, northern expansionists could still look forward to the admission of Oregon as a counterbalancing free state. But the Mexican War raised the prospect that California and New Mexico, both south of the Missouri Compromise line, would also be acquired. Since it was generally assumed in the North that Congress had the power to prohibit slavery in new territories, a movement developed in Congress to do just that.

### The Wilmot Proviso Launches the Free-Soil Movement

The Free-Soil crusade began in August 1846, only three months after the start of the Mexican-American War, when Congressman David Wilmot, a Pennsylvania

Democrat, proposed an amendment to the military appropriations bill that would ban slavery in any territory that might be acquired from Mexico.

Wilmot spoke for the large number of northern Democrats who felt neglected and betrayed by the party's choice of Polk over Van Buren in 1844 and by the "prosouthern" policies of the Polk administration. Pennsylvanians like Wilmot were upset because the tariff of 1846 reduced duties to a level unacceptable to the manufacturing interests of their state. Others, especially Midwesterners, were annoyed that Polk had vetoed a bill to provide federal funds for the improvement of rivers and harbors. Democratic expansionists also felt betrayed because Polk had gone back on his pledge to obtain "all of Oregon" up to 54°40' and then had proceeded to wage war to win all of Texas and the Southwest. This twist in the course of Manifest Destiny convinced them that the South and its interests were dominating the party and the administration. David Wilmot spoke for many when he wrote that he was "jealous of the power of the South."

The pioneer Free-Soilers had a genuine interest in the issue actually at hand—the question of who would control and settle the new territories. Combining an appeal to racial prejudice with opposition to slavery as an institution, Wilmot defined his cause as involving the "rights of white freemen" to go to areas where they could live "without the disgrace which association with negro slavery brings on white labor." Wilmot proposed that slavery as well as settlement by free African Americans be prohibited in the territory obtained in the Mexican cession, thus giving the common folk of the North a fair chance by preventing job competition from slaves and free blacks. By linking racism with resistance to the spread of slavery, Wilmot appealed to a broad spectrum of northern opinion.

Northern Whigs backed the Proviso because they shared Wilmot's concern about the outcome of an unregulated competition between slave and free labor in the territories. Furthermore, voting for the measure provided a good outlet for their frustration at being unable to halt the annexation of Texas and the Mexican-American War. The preferred position of some Whig leaders was no expansion at all, but when expansion could not be avoided, the northern wing of the party endorsed the view that acquisition of Mexican territory should not be used to increase the power of the slave states.

In the first House vote on the **Wilmot Proviso,** party lines crumbled and were replaced by a sharp sectional cleavage. Every northern congressman with the exception of two Democrats voted for the amendment, and every Southerner except two Whigs went on record against it. After passing the House, the Proviso was blocked in the Senate by a combination of southern influence and Democratic loyalty to the administration. When the appropriations bill went back to the House without the Proviso, the administration's arm-twisting succeeded in changing enough northern Democratic votes to pass the bill and thus send the Proviso down to defeat.

Reactions to the Proviso on the state and local level provided further evidence of the polarizing effect of the territorial issue. Northern state legislatures, with one exception, endorsed the Proviso, while southern orators proclaimed that its passage would insult their section and violate the principle of equality among the states by denying slaveholding citizens access to federal territories.

The end of the Mexican-American War, the formal acquisition of New Mexico and California, and the approaching election of 1848 gave new urgency to a search for politically feasible solutions to the crisis. The extreme alternatives—the Proviso policy of free soil and the radical southern response that slavery could be extended to any territory—threatened to destroy the national parties because there was no bisectional support for either of them.

## Squatter Sovereignty and the Election of 1848

After a futile attempt was made to extend the Missouri Compromise line to the Pacific—a proposal that was unacceptable to Northerners because most of the Mexican cession lay south of the line—a new approach was devised that appealed especially to Democrats. Its main proponent was Senator Lewis Cass of Michigan, an aspirant for the party's presidential nomination. Cass, who described his formula as "squatter sovereignty," would leave the determination of the status of slavery in a territory to the actual settlers. From the beginning, this proposal contained an ambiguity that allowed it to be interpreted differently in the North and the South. For northern Democrats, squatter sovereignty—or **popular sovereignty** as it was later called—meant the settlers could vote slavery up or down at the first meeting of a territorial legislature. For the southern wing of the party, it meant a decision would be made only at the time a convention drew up a constitution and applied for statehood. It was in the interest of national Democratic leaders to leave this ambiguity unresolved for as long as possible.

Congress failed to resolve the future of slavery in the Mexican cession in time for the election of 1848, and the issue entered the arena of presidential politics. The Democrats nominated Cass on a platform of squatter sovereignty. The Whigs evaded the question by running General Zachary Taylor—the hero of the battle of Buena Vista—without a platform. Taylor

## THE ELECTION OF 1848

| Candidate | Party | Popular Vote | Electoral Vote |
|-----------|-------|--------------|----------------|
| Taylor | Whig | 1,360,967 | 163 |
| Cass | Democratic | 1,222,342 | 127 |
| Van Buren | Free-Soil | 291,263 | — |

refused to commit himself on the status of slavery in the territories, but northern Whigs favoring restriction took heart from the general's promise not to veto any territorial legislation passed by Congress. Southern Whigs went along with Taylor mainly because he was a Southerner who owned slaves and would presumably defend the interests of his native region.

Northerners who strongly supported the Wilmot Proviso—and felt betrayed that neither the Whigs nor the Democrats were supporting it—were attracted by a third-party movement. In August, a tumultuous convention in Buffalo nominated former president Van Buren to carry the banner of the **Free-Soil party.** Support for the Free-Soilers came from antislavery Whigs dismayed by their party's nomination of a slaveholder and its evasiveness on the territorial issue, disgruntled Democrats who had backed the Proviso and resented southern influence in their party, and some of the former adherents of the abolitionist Liberty party. Van Buren himself was motivated less by antislavery zeal than by bitterness at being denied the Democratic nomination in 1844 because of southern obstructionism. The founding of the Free-Soil party was the first significant effort to create a broadly based sectional party addressing itself to voters' concerns about the extension of slavery.

After a noisy and confusing campaign, Taylor came out on top, winning a majority of the electoral votes in both the North and the South and a total of 1,360,967 popular votes to 1,222,342 for Cass and 291,263 for Van Buren. The Free-Soilers failed to carry a single state but did quite well in the North, coming in second behind Taylor in New York, Massachusetts, and Vermont.

### Taylor Takes Charge

Once in office, Taylor devised a bold plan to decide the fate of slavery in the Mexican cession. A brusque military man who disdained political give-and-take, he tried to engineer the immediate admission of California and New Mexico to the Union as states, thus bypassing the territorial stage entirely and avoiding a congressional debate on the status of slavery in the federal domain. Under the administration's urging, California, which was filling up rapidly with settlers drawn by the lust for gold, convened a constitutional convention and applied for admission to the Union as a free state.

Instead of resolving the crisis, President Taylor's initiative only worsened it. Once it was clear that California was going to be a free state, the administration's plan aroused intense opposition in the South. Fearing that New Mexico would also be free because Mexican law had prohibited slavery there, Southerners of both parties accused the president of trying to impose the Wilmot Proviso in a new form. The prospect that only free states would emerge from the entire Mexican cession inspired serious talk of secession.

In Congress, Senator John C. Calhoun of South Carolina saw a chance to achieve his long-standing

*In this cartoon, Democrats Lewis Cass and John C. Calhoun and antislavery radicals Horace Greeley, William Lloyd Garrison, and Abby Folsom look on as Martin Van Buren, the Free-Soil party candidate in the election of 1848, attempts to bridge the chasm between the Democratic platform and that of the antislavery Whigs. The Free-Soil influence was decisive in the election; it split the New York Democratic vote, thus allowing Whig candidate Zachary Taylor to win New York and the presidency.* ❖

goal of creating a southern voting bloc that would cut across regular party lines. State legislatures and conventions throughout the South denounced "northern aggression" against the rights of the slave states. As signs of southern fury increased, Calhoun rejoiced that the South had never been so "united . . . bold, and decided." In the fall and winter of 1849–1850, several southern states agreed to participate in a convention, to be held in Nashville in June, where grievances could be aired and demands made. For an increasing number of southern political leaders, the survival of the Union would depend on the North's response to the demands of the southern rights movement.

## Forging a Compromise

When it became clear that the president would not abandon or modify his plan in order to appease the South, independent efforts began in Congress to arrange a compromise. Hoping that he could again play the role of "great pacificator" as he had in the Missouri Compromise of 1820, Senator Henry Clay of Kentucky offered a series of resolutions meant to restore sectional harmony. He hoped to reduce tension by providing mutual concessions on a range of divisive issues. On the critical territorial question, his solution was to admit California as a free state and organize the rest of the Mexican cession with no explicit prohibition of slavery—in other words, without the Wilmot Proviso. Noting that Mexican law had already abolished slavery there, he also pointed to the arid climate of the New Mexico region, which made it unsuitable for cotton culture and slavery. He also sought to resolve a major boundary dispute between New Mexico and Texas by granting the disputed region to New Mexico while compensating Texas through federal assumption of its state debt. As a concession to the North on another issue—the existence of slavery in the District of Columbia—he recommended prohibiting the buying and selling of slaves at auction and permitting the abolition of slavery itself with the consent of the District's white inhabitants. He also called for a more effective Fugitive Slave Law.

These proposals provided the basis for the **Compromise of 1850.** Proposed in February 1850, it took several months for the Compromise to get through Congress. One obstacle was President Taylor's firm resistance to the proposal; another was the difficulty of getting congressmen to vote for it in the form of a single package or "omnibus bill." Few politicians from either section were willing to go on record as

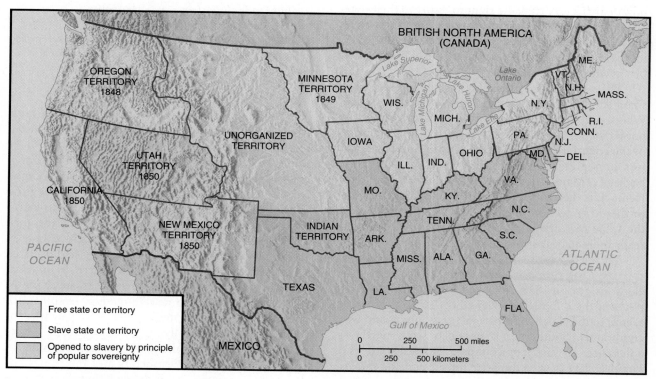

**THE COMPROMISE OF 1850**    *The "compromise" was actually a series of resolutions granting some concessions to the North—especially admission of California as a free state—and some to the South, such as a stricter Fugitive Slave Law.* ❖

supporting the key concessions to the *other* section. The logjam was broken in July by two crucial developments: President Taylor died and was succeeded by Millard Fillmore, who favored the compromise; and a decision was made to abandon the omnibus strategy in favor of a series of measures that could be voted on separately. After the breakup of the omnibus bill, Democrats replaced the original Whig sponsors as leaders of the compromise movement, and some of Clay's proposals were modified to make them more acceptable to the South and the Democrats. Senator Stephen A. Douglas, a Democrat from Illinois, was particularly influential in maneuvering the separate provisions of the plan through Congress.

As the price of Democratic support, the popular sovereignty principle was included in the bills organizing New Mexico and Utah. Territorial legislatures in the Mexican cession were explicitly granted power over "all rightful subjects of legislation," which might include slavery. Half of the compensation to Texas for giving up its claims to New Mexico was paid directly to holders of Texas bonds, a decision that reflected intense lobbying by interested parties.

Abolition of slave auctions and depots in the District of Columbia and a new **Fugitive Slave Law** were also enacted. The latter was a particularly outrageous piece of legislation. As the result of southern pressures and amendments, suspected fugitives were now denied a jury trial, the right to testify in their own behalf, and other basic constitutional rights. As a result, there were no effective safeguards against false identification by accusers or against the kidnapping of blacks who were legally free.

The compromise passed because its key measures were supported by northern Democrats, southern Whigs, and representatives of both parties from the border states. No single bill was backed by a majority of the congressmen from both sections, and few senators or representatives actually voted for the entire package. Many northern Whigs and southern Democrats thought the end result conceded too much to the other section. Doubts therefore persisted over the value of workability of a "compromise" that was really more like an armistice or a cease-fire.

Yet the Compromise of 1850 did serve for a short time as a basis for sectional peace. In southern state elections during 1850–1851, moderate coalitions won out over the radicals who viewed the compromise as a sellout to the North. But this emerging "unionism" was conditional. Southerners demanded strict northern adherence to the compromise, especially to the Fugitive Slave Law, as the price for suppressing threats of secession. In the North, the compromise was backed by virtually the entire Democratic party and by one faction of the Whigs.

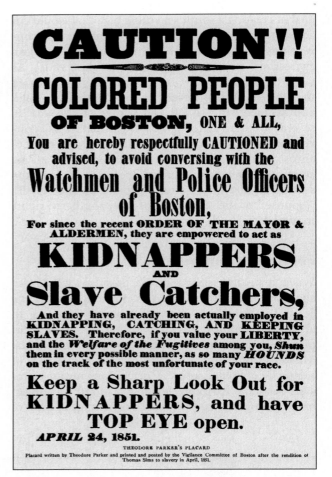

This abolitionist broadside was printed in response to a ruling that fugitive slave Thomas Sims must be returned to his master in Georgia. ❖

The Fugitive Slave Law was unpopular in areas where abolitionism was particularly strong because it required Northerners to enforce slavery, and there were a few sensational rescues or attempted rescues of escaped slaves. In Boston in 1854, an antislavery mob led by armed abolitionists tried to free fugitive Anthony Burns from the courthouse where his extradition hearing was to take place. One of the men guarding Burns was killed, but the fugitive himself could not be reached. After the hearing had declared Burns an escaped slave, he was escorted by units of the U.S. Army through a hissing and groaning crowd of twenty thousand to a waiting ship. Despite such abolitionist resistance, the Fugitive Slave Law was enforced fairly successfully in the early 1850s. Other parts of the compromise were less troublesome. In 1852, when both the Democrats and the Whigs endorsed the compromise in their platforms, it seemed that sharp differences on the slavery issue had once again been banished from national politics.

# POLITICAL UPHEAVAL, 1852–1856

The second party system—Democrats versus Whigs—survived the crisis over slavery in the Mexican cession, but in the long run the Compromise of 1850 may have weakened it. Although both national parties had been careful during the 1840s not to take stands on the slavery issue that would alienate their supporters in either section of the country, they had in fact offered voters alternative ways of dealing with the question. Democrats had endorsed headlong territorial expansion with the promise of a fair division of the spoils between slave and free states. Whigs had generally opposed annexations or acquisitions, because they were likely to bring the slavery question to the fore and threaten sectional harmony. With some shifts of emphasis and interpretation, each strategy could be presented to southern voters as a good way to protect slavery and to Northerners as a good way to contain it.

The consensus of 1852 meant the parties had to find other issues on which to base their distinctive appeals. Their failure to do so encouraged voter apathy and a disenchantment with the major parties. When the Democrats sought to revive the Manifest Destiny issue in 1854, they reopened the explosive issue of slavery in the territories. By this time, the Whigs were too weak and divided to respond with a policy of their own, and a purely sectional Free-Soil party—the Republicans—gained prominence. The collapse of the second party system released sectional agitation from the earlier constraints imposed by the competition of strong national parties.

## The Party System in Crisis

The presidential campaign of 1852 was singularly devoid of major issues. With the slavery question under wraps, some Whigs tried to revive interest in the nationalistic economic policies that were the traditional hallmarks of their party. But convincing arguments in favor of a protective tariff, a national bank, and internal improvements were hard to make in a period of sustained prosperity. Business was thriving under the Democratic program of virtual laissez-faire.

Another tempting issue was immigration. Many Whigs were upset by the massive influx from Europe, partly because most of the new arrivals were Catholics, and the Whig following was largely evangelical Protestant. For office-seeking Whig politicians, a more urgent problem was the fact that immigrants voted overwhelmingly for their Democratic opponents. The Whig leadership was divided on whether to compete with the Democrats for the immigrant vote or respond

## THE ELECTION OF 1852

| Candidate | Party | Popular Vote | Electoral Vote |
|-----------|-------|--------------|----------------|
| Pierce | Democratic | 1,601,117 | 254 |
| Scott | Whig | 1,385,453 | 42 |
| Hale | Free-Soil | 155,825 | — |

to the prejudices of the party rank and file by calling for restrictions on immigrant voting rights.

The Whigs nominated General Winfield Scott of Mexican-American War fame, who supported the faction that resisted nativism and sought to broaden the appeal of the party. The fact that Scott's daughters were being raised as Catholics was publicized to demonstrate his good intentions toward immigrant communities. This strategy backfired and contributed to disaster at the polls. For the most part, Catholic immigrants retained their Democratic allegiance, and some nativist Whigs apparently sat out the election to protest their party's disregard of their cultural prejudices.

But the main cause for Scott's crushing defeat was the support he lost in the South when he allied himself with the dominant northern antislavery wing of the party, led by Senator William Seward of New York. The Democratic candidate, Franklin Pierce of New Hampshire, was a colorless nonentity compared to his rival, but he ran up huge majorities in the Deep South, where Whigs stayed home in massive numbers. He also edged out Scott in most of the free states. In the most one-sided election since 1820, Pierce received 254 electoral votes from 27 states while Scott carried only 4 states with 42 electoral votes. This outcome revealed that the Whig party was in deep trouble because it lacked a program that would distinguish it from the Democrats and would appeal to voters in both sections of the country.

Despite their overwhelming victory in 1852, the Democrats had reasons for anxiety about the loyalty of their supporters. Because the major parties had ceased to offer clear-cut alternatives to the electorate, voter apathy or alienation was a growing trend in the early 1850s. The Democrats won majorities in both North and South in 1852 primarily because the public viewed them as the most reliable supporters of the Compromise of 1850, not because of firm party allegiance.

## The Kansas-Nebraska Act Raises a Storm

In January 1854, Senator Stephen A. Douglas proposed a bill to organize the territory west of Missouri and Iowa. Since this region fell within the area where slavery had been banned by the Missouri Compromise,

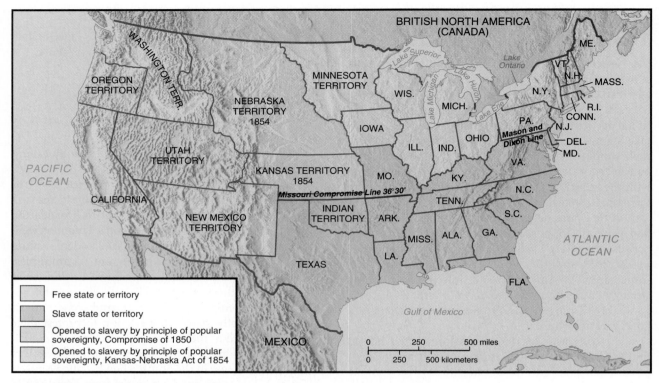

**THE KANSAS-NEBRASKA ACT OF 1854**    *The Kansas-Nebraska Act applied the principle of popular sovereignty to voters in the Kansas and Nebraska territories, allowing them to decide for themselves whether to permit slavery in their territories. The act repudiated the Missouri Compromise of 1820, which had prohibited slavery in the territory of the Louisiana Purchase north of 36°30' latitude.* ❖

Douglas anticipated objections from Southerners concerned about the creation of more free states. To head off this opposition and keep the Democratic party united, Douglas disregarded the compromise line and sought to set up the territorial government in Kansas and Nebraska on the basis of popular sovereignty, relying on the alleged precedent set in the Compromise of 1850.

Douglas wanted to organize the Kansas-Nebraska area quickly because he was a strong supporter of the expansion of settlement and commerce. Along with other midwestern promoters of the economic development of the frontier, he hoped a railroad would soon be built to the Pacific with Chicago (or another midwestern city) as its eastern terminus. A long controversy over the status of slavery in the new territory would slow down the process of organization and settlement and might hinder the building of the railroad. As a leader of the Democratic party, Douglas also hoped his Kansas-Nebraska bill would revive the spirit of Manifest Destiny that had given the party cohesion and electoral success in the mid-1840s (see Chapter 13). As the main advocate for a new expansionism, he expected to win the Democratic nomination and the presidency.

The price of southern support, Douglas soon discovered, was the addition of an amendment explicitly repealing the Missouri Compromise. Although he realized this would "raise a hell of a storm," he reluctantly agreed. In this more provocative form, the bill made its way through Congress, passing the Senate by a large margin and the House by a narrow one. The vote in the House showed that Douglas had split his party rather than uniting it; exactly half of the northern Democrats voted against the legislation.

The Democrats who broke ranks created the storm that Douglas had predicted but underestimated. A manifesto of "independent Democrats" denounced the bill as "a gross violation of a sacred pledge." A memorial from three thousand New England ministers described it as a craven and sinful surrender to the slave power. For many Northerners, probably a majority, the **Kansas-Nebraska Act** was an abomination because it permitted the possibility of slavery in an area where it had previously been prohibited. Except for an aggressive minority, Southerners had not pushed for such legislation or even shown much interest in it, but now they felt obligated to support it. Their support provided deadly ammunition to those who were seeking to convince the northern public that there was a conspiracy to extend slavery.

Douglas's bill had a catastrophic effect on sectional harmony. It repudiated a compromise that many in the North regarded as a binding sectional compact, almost as sacred and necessary to the survival of the Union as the Constitution itself. In defiance of the whole compromise tradition, it made a concession to the South on the issue of slavery extension without providing an equivalent concession to the North. It also shattered the fragile sectional accommodation of 1850 and made future compromises less likely. From then on, northern sectionalists would be fighting to regain what they had lost, while Southerners would battle to maintain rights already conceded.

The act also destroyed what was left of the second party system. The already weakened and tottering Whig party totally disintegrated when its congressional representation split cleanly along sectional lines on the Kansas-Nebraska issue. The Democratic party survived, but its ability to act as a unifying national force was seriously impaired. Northern desertions and southern gains (resulting from the recruitment of proslavery Whigs) combined to destroy the sectional balance within the party and place it under firm southern control.

The congressional elections of 1854 revealed the political chaos Douglas had created. In the North, "anti-Nebraska" coalitions of Whigs, dissident Democrats, and Free-Soilers swept regular Democrats out of office. Most congressmen who had voted for the act were decisively defeated, and sixty-six of the ninety-one House seats held by northern Democrats were lost to opponents running under various labels. In some states, these anti-Democratic coalitions would evolve directly into a new and stronger Free-Soil party—the **Republicans.** In the Deep South, however, the Democrats routed the remaining Whigs and came close to ending two-party competition on the state level.

The furor over Kansas-Nebraska also doomed the efforts of the Pierce administration to revive an expansionist foreign policy. Pierce and Secretary of State William Marcy were committed to acquiring Cuba from Spain. In October 1854, the American ministers to England, France, and Spain met in Ostend, Belgium, and drew up a memorandum for the administration urging acquisition of Cuba by any means necessary—including force—if Spain refused to sell the island. The **Ostend Manifesto** became public in the midst of the controversy resulting from the Kansas-Nebraska Act, and those Northerners who were convinced that the administration was trying to extend slavery to the Great Plains were enraged to discover it was also scheming to fulfill the southern expansionist dream of a "Caribbean slave empire." The resulting storm of protest forced Pierce and his cohorts to abandon their scheme.

## An Appeal to Nativism: The Know-Nothing Episode

The collapse of the Whigs created the opening for a new political party. The anti-Nebraska coalitions of 1854 suggested that such a party might be organized on the basis of northern opposition to the extension of slavery to the territories. Before such a prospect could be realized, however, an alternative emerged in the form of a major political movement based on hostility to immigrants. For a time, it appeared that the Whigs would be replaced by a nativist party rather than an antislavery one.

Massive immigration of Irish and Germans (see Chapter 13), most of whom were Catholic, led to increasing tension between ethnic groups during the 1840s and early 1850s. The fact that most of the new arrivals clustered in their own separate communities or neighborhoods helped arouse the suspicion and distrust of older-stock Americans. Native-born and even immigrant Protestants viewed the newcomers as bearers of alien cultures. They expressed their fears in bloody anti-Catholic riots, in church and convent burnings, and in a barrage of propaganda and lurid literature trumpeting the menace of "popery" to the American way of life. Nativist agitators charged that immigrants were agents of a foreign despotism, based in Rome, that was bent on overthrowing the American republic.

Political nativism first emerged during the 1840s in the form of local "American" parties protesting immigrant influence in cities such as New York and Philadelphia. In 1849, a secret fraternal organization, the Order of the Star-Spangled Banner, was founded in New York as a vehicle for anti-immigrant attitudes. When members were asked about the organization, they were instructed to reply, "I know nothing." The order grew rapidly in size, by 1854 reaching a membership of between 800,000 and 1,500,000. The political objective of the **Know-Nothing party** was to extend the period of naturalization in order to undercut immigrant voting strength and to keep aliens in their place.

From 1854 to 1855, the nativist movement surfaced as a major political force, the American party. Much of the party's backing came from Whigs looking for a new home, but the party also attracted some ex-Democrats. In addition, Know-Nothingism appealed to native-born workers who feared competition from low-paid immigrants. Many others supported the American party simply because it was an alternative for those who wanted to vote against the Democrats. In the North, Know-Nothing candidates

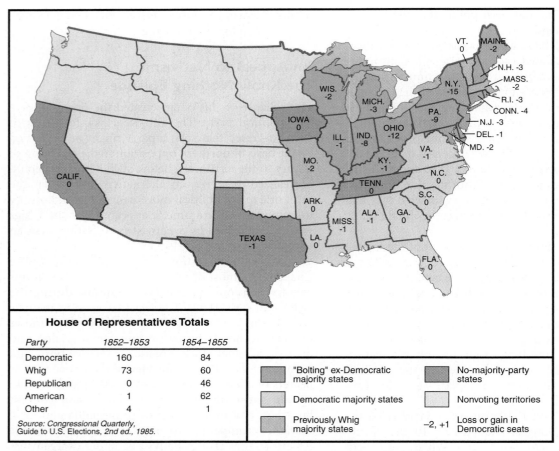

| House of Representatives Totals | | |
| --- | --- | --- |
| Party | 1852–1853 | 1854–1855 |
| Democratic | 160 | 84 |
| Whig | 73 | 60 |
| Republican | 0 | 46 |
| American | 1 | 62 |
| Other | 4 | 1 |

Source: Congressional Quarterly,
Guide to U.S. Elections, 2nd ed., 1985.

"Bolting" ex-Democratic majority states

Democratic majority states

Previously Whig majority states

No-majority-party states

Nonvoting territories

−2, +1    Loss or gain in Democratic seats

**CONGRESSIONAL ELECTION OF 1854**    The impact of the Kansas-Nebraska Act was immediately felt in the election of 1854. "Anti-Nebraska" coalitions and the fledgling Republican party made gains in the North; the Democrats remained dominant in the South. ❖

generally opposed the Kansas-Nebraska Act, and some of their support came from voters who were more anxious about the expansion of slavery than about the evils of immigration.

The success of the new party was so dramatic that it was compared to a hurricane. In 1854, it won complete control in Massachusetts, capturing the governorship, most of the seats in the legislature, and the entire congressional delegation. In 1855, the Know-Nothings took power in three more New England states; swept Maryland, Kentucky, and Texas; and emerged as the principal opposition to the Democrats everywhere else except in the Midwest. By late 1855, the Know-Nothings showed every sign of displacing the Whigs as the nation's second party.

Yet, almost as rapidly as it had risen, the Know-Nothing movement collapsed. Its demise in 1856 is one of the great mysteries of American political history. As an intersectional party, its failure is understandable enough. When the Know-Nothings attempted to hold a national convention in 1856, northern and southern delegates split on the question

of slavery in the territories, showing that former Whigs were still at odds over the same issue that had destroyed their old party.

Less clear is why the Know-Nothings failed to become the major opposition party to the Democrats in the North. The most persuasive explanation is that their Free-Soil Republican rivals, who were seeking to build a party committed to the containment of slavery, had an issue with wider appeal. In 1855 and 1856, the rate of immigration declined noticeably, and the conflict in Kansas heightened the concern about slavery. Consequently, voters who opposed both the expansion of slavery and unrestricted immigration were inclined to give priority to the former threat.

But the movement's peculiar "antipolitical" character also contributed to its rapid disintegration. Besides being a manifestation of real ethnic tensions, Know-Nothingism was a grassroots protest against the professional politicians who had led the Whig and Democratic parties. Concern about the effects of immigration on American culture and society would not have generated a mass political movement with the

*Know-Nothings often charged that immigrant voters were stealing American elections. In the cartoon above, German and Irish immigrants, represented by German beer and Irish whiskey, steal a ballot box. An anti–Know-Nothing cartoon (right) portrays the Know-Nothings as gun-wielding ruffians.* ❖

initial appeal of the Know-Nothings had it not been for the belief that political bosses were recruiting immigrant voters for their own corrupt purposes. As a result of the Know-Nothing party's distrust of conventional politics, most of its spokesmen and elected officials were neither professional politicians nor established community leaders. The very inexperience that was a major source of voter attraction to the party may have impeded development of organizational discipline. With inexperienced leaders and a lack of cohesion, the Know-Nothings were unable to make effective use of power once they had it. When voters discovered that the Know-Nothings also *did* nothing, or at least failed to do anything that a more conventional party could not do better, they looked for more competent and experienced leadership.

## Kansas and the Rise of the Republicans

The new Republican party was an outgrowth of the anti-Nebraska coalition of 1854. The Republican name was first used in midwestern states such as Wisconsin and Michigan where Know-Nothingism failed to win a mass following. A new political label was required because Free-Soil Democrats—who were an especially important element in the midwestern coalitions—refused to march under the Whig banner or even support any candidate for high office who called himself a Whig.

When the Know-Nothing party split over the Kansas-Nebraska issue in 1856, most of the northern nativists went over to the Republicans. The Republican argument that the "slave-power conspiracy" was a

greater threat to American liberty and equality than an alleged "popish plot" proved to be persuasive. But nativists did not have to abandon their ethnic and religious prejudices to become Republicans. Although Republican leaders generally avoided taking anti-immigrant positions—some out of strong principle and others with an eye to the votes of the foreign born—the party showed a clear commitment to the values of native-born evangelical Protestants. On the local level, Republicans generally supported causes that reflected an anti-immigrant or anti-Catholic bias—such as prohibition of the sale of alcoholic beverages, observance of the Sabbath, defense of Protestant Bible-reading in schools, and opposition to state aid for parochial education.

Unlike the Know-Nothings, the Republican party was led by seasoned professional politicians, men who had earlier been prominent Whigs or Democrats. Adept at organizing the grass roots, building coalitions, and employing all the techniques of popular campaigning, they built up an effective party apparatus in an amazingly short time. By late 1855, the party had won more than two-thirds of the anti-Nebraska congressmen elected in 1854. One of these, Nathaniel Banks of Massachusetts, was elected speaker of the House after a lengthy struggle. By early 1856, the new party was well established throughout the North and was preparing to make a serious bid for the presidency.

Underlying the rapid growth of the Republican party was the strong and growing appeal of its position on slavery in the territories. Republicans viewed the unsettled West as a land of opportunities, a place

*The bitter contest over popular sovereignty in Kansas erupted into violence between proslavery and antislavery groups. The skirmishes, including the one at Hickory Point, near Leavenworth, depicted here, resulted in two hundred deaths and heavy property destruction before federal troops were brought in to restore order.* ❖

Settlers favoring free soil, most of whom came from the Midwest, were already a majority of the actual residents of the territory when the fraudulently elected legislature denied them the right to agitate against slavery. To defend themselves and their convictions, they took up arms and established a rival territorial government under a constitution that outlawed slavery. The Pierce administration and its appointed local agents refused to recognize this "free-state" initiative, but Republicans in Congress defended it.

A small-scale civil war then broke out between the rival regimes, culminating in May 1856 when proslavery adherents raided the free-state capital at Lawrence. Portrayed in Republican propaganda as

to which the ambitious and hardworking could migrate in the hope of improving their social and economic position. Free soil would serve as a guarantee of free competition or "the right to rise." But if slavery was permitted to expand, the rights of "free labor" would be denied. Slaveholders would monopolize the best land, use their slaves to compete unfairly with free white workers, and block efforts at commercial and industrial development. They could also use their political control of new western states to dominate the federal government in the interest of the "slave power." Some Republicans also pandered to racial prejudice: They presented their policy as a way to keep African Americans out of the territories, thus preserving the new lands for exclusive white occupancy.

Although passage of the Kansas-Nebraska Act raised the territorial issue and gave birth to the Republican party, it was the turmoil associated with attempts to implement popular sovereignty in Kansas that kept the issue alive and enabled the Republicans to increase their following throughout the North. When Kansas was organized in the fall of 1854, a bitter contest began for control of the territorial government. New Englanders founded an Immigrant Aid Society to encourage antislavery settlement in Kansas, but the earliest arrivals came from slaveholding Missouri. In the first territorial elections, proslavery settlers were joined at the polls by thousands of Missouri residents who crossed the border to vote illegally. The result was a decisive victory for the slave-state forces. The legislature then proceeded to pass laws that not only legalized slavery but made it a crime to speak or act against it.

**"BLEEDING KANSAS"** *One result of the Kansas-Nebraska Act of 1854 was the border war that erupted between proslavery and antislavery forces in "bleeding" Kansas.* ❖

"the sack of Lawrence," this incursion resulted in substantial property damage but no loss of life. More bloody was the reprisal carried out by the antislavery zealot John Brown. Upon hearing of the attack on Lawrence, Brown and a few followers murdered five proslavery settlers in cold blood. During the next few months—until a truce was arranged by an effective territorial governor in the fall of 1856—a hit-and-run guerrilla war raged between free-state and slave-state factions. The national Republican press had a field day with the events in Kansas, exaggerating the extent of the violence but correctly pointing out that the federal government was favoring rule by a proslavery minority over a Free-Soil majority. Since the "sack of Lawrence" occurred at about the same time that Preston Brooks assaulted Charles Sumner on the Senate floor (see pp. 387–388), the Republicans launched their 1856 campaign under twin slogans "Bleeding Kansas" and "Bleeding Sumner." The image of an evil and aggressive "slave power," using violence to deny constitutional rights to its opponents, was a potent device for arousing northern sympathies and winning votes.

## Sectional Division in the Election of 1856

The Republican nominating convention revealed the strictly sectional nature of the new party. Only a handful of the delegates from the slave states attended, and all of these were from the upper South. The platform called for liberation of Kansas from the slave power and for congressional prohibition of slavery in all territories. The nominee was John C. Frémont, explorer of the West and participant in the conquest of California during the Mexican-American War.

The Democratic convention dumped the ineffectual Pierce, passed over Stephen A. Douglas, and nominated James Buchanan of Pennsylvania, who had a long career in public service. The Democrats' platform endorsed popular sovereignty in the territories. The American party, a Know-Nothing remnant that survived mainly as the rallying point for anti-Democratic conservatives in the border states and parts of the South, chose ex-President Millard Fillmore as its standard-bearer and received the backing of those northern Whigs who resisted the Republicans and hoped to revive the tradition of sectional compromise.

The election was really two separate races—one in the North, where the main contest was between Frémont and Buchanan, and the other in the South, which pitted Fillmore against Buchanan. The Pennsylvania Democrat emerged victorious because he outpolled Fillmore in all but one of the slave states (Maryland) and edged out Frémont in four crucial

### THE ELECTION OF 1856

| Candidate | Party | Popular Vote | Electoral Vote |
|---|---|---|---|
| Buchanan | Democratic | 1,832,955 | 174 |
| Frémont | Republican | 1,339,932 | 114 |
| Fillmore | American (Know-Nothing) | 871,731 | 8 |

*The Republican Party's presidential nominee in 1856 was John C. Frémont, explorer and Mexican-American War hero. Opposing the spread of slavery to the West, the Republican's call for "Free Speech! Free Men! Free Kansas," as shown on this campaign ribbon, stirred sectional tensions and revived talk of secession in the South.* ❖

northern states—Pennsylvania, New Jersey, Indiana, and Illinois. But the Republicans did remarkably well for a party that was scarcely more than a year old. Frémont won eleven of the sixteen free states, sweeping the upper North with substantial majorities and winning a larger proportion of the northern popular vote than either of his opponents. Since the free states had a substantial majority in the electoral college, a future Republican candidate could win the presidency simply by overcoming a slim Democratic edge in the lower North.

In the South, where the possibility of a Frémont victory had revived talk of secession, the results of the election brought a momentary sense of relief tinged with deep anxiety about the future. The very existence of a sectional party committed to restricting the expansion of slavery constituted an insult to the Southerners' way of life. That such a party was genuinely popular in the North was profoundly alarming and raised grave doubts about the security of slavery within the Union. The continued success of a unified Democratic party under southern control was widely viewed as the last hope for the maintenance of sectional balance and "southern rights."

## THE HOUSE DIVIDED, 1857–1860

The sectional quarrel deepened and became virtually "irreconcilable" in the years between Buchanan's election in 1856 and Lincoln's victory in 1860. A series of incidents provoked one side or the other, heightened the tension, and ultimately brought the crisis to a head. Behind the panicky reaction to public events lay a growing sense that the North and South were so different in culture and so opposed in basic interests that they could no longer coexist in the same nation.

### Cultural Sectionalism

Signs of cultural and intellectual cleavage had appeared well before the triumph of sectional politics. In the mid-1840s, the Methodist and Baptist churches split into northern and southern denominations because of differing attitudes toward slaveholding. Presbyterians remained formally united but had informal northern and southern factions that went their separate ways on the slavery issue. Instead of unifying Americans around a common Protestant faith, the churches became nurseries of sectional discord. Increasingly, northern preachers and congregations denounced slaveholding as a sin, while most southern church leaders rallied to a biblical defense of the peculiar institution and became influential apologists for the southern way of life. Prominent religious leaders—

such as Henry Ward Beecher, George B. Cheever, and Theodore Parker in the North and James H. Thornwell, Leonidas Polk, and Bishop Stephen Elliott in the South—were in the forefront of sectional mobilization. As men of God, they helped to turn political questions into moral issues and reduced the prospects for a compromise.

American literature also became sectionalized during the 1840s and 1850s. Southern men of letters, including such notable figures as novelist William Gilmore Simms and Edgar Allan Poe, wrote proslavery polemics. Popular novelists produced a flood of "plantation romances" that seemed to glorify southern civilization and sneer at that of the North. The notion that planter "cavaliers" were superior to money-grubbing Yankees was the message that most Southerners derived from the homegrown literature they read. In the North, prominent men of letters—Emerson, Thoreau, James Russell Lowell, and Herman Melville—expressed strong antislavery sentiments in prose and poetry, particularly after the outbreak of the Mexican-American War.

Literary abolitionism reached a climax in 1852 when Harriet Beecher Stowe published *Uncle Tom's Cabin*, an enormously successful novel (it sold more than 300,000 copies in a single year) that fixed in the

*Abolitionist writer Harriet Beecher Stowe is best known for her hugely successful antislavery novel* Uncle Tom's Cabin. ❖

## ❖ A Look at the Past ❖

**135,000 SETS, 270,000 VOLUMES SOLD.**

# UNCLE TOM'S CABIN

## FOR SALE HERE.

AN EDITION FOR THE MILLION, COMPLETE IN 1 Vol., PRICE 37 1-2 CENTS.
" " IN GERMAN, IN 1 Vol., PRICE 50 CENTS.
" " IN 2 Vols, CLOTH, 6 PLATES, PRICE $1.50.
SUPERB ILLUSTRATED EDITION, IN 1 Vol., WITH 153 ENGRAVINGS,
PRICES FROM $2.50 TO $5.00.

## The Greatest Book of the Age.

**Poster for *Uncle Tom's Cabin***

Three hundred thousand Americans purchased Harriet Beecher Stowe's *Uncle Tom's Cabin* in 1852, the year this poster appeared. While the poster might not have caused those sales, its design certainly appealed to middle-class readers. How does the scene depicted on the poster capture the ideal of domesticity? How does that ideal compare to the reality of slave life? Why would the scene have appealed to middle-class Americans?

northern mind the image of the slaveholder as a brutal Simon Legree. Much of its emotional impact came from the book's portrayal of slavery as a threat to the family and the cult of domesticity. When the saintly Uncle Tom was sold away from his adoring wife and children, Northerners shuddered with horror and some Southerners felt a painful twinge of conscience.

Southern defensiveness gradually hardened into cultural and economic nationalism. Northern textbooks were banished from southern schools in favor of those with a prosouthern slant; young men of the planter class were induced to stay in the South for higher education rather than going North (as had been the custom); and a movement developed to encourage southern industry and commerce as a way of reducing dependence on the North. Almost without exception, prominent southern educators and intellectuals of the late 1850s rallied behind southern sectionalism, and many even endorsed the idea of a southern nation.

### The Dred Scott Case

When James Buchanan was inaugurated on March 4, 1857, the dispute over the legal status of slavery in the territories was an open door through which sectional fears and hatreds could enter the political arena. Buchanan hoped to close that door by encouraging the Supreme Court to resolve the constitutional issue once and for all.

The Court was then about to render its decision in the case of *Dred Scott v. Sandford*. (See the Law and Society essay, "The Case of Dred and Harriet Scott," pp. 412–416.) The plaintiff in the case was a Missouri slave who sued for his freedom on the grounds that he had lived for many years in an area where slavery had been outlawed by the Missouri Compromise. The Supreme Court could have decided the issue on the narrow ground that a slave was not a citizen and therefore had no right to sue in federal courts. But President-elect Buchanan, in the days just before the inauguration, encouraged the Court to render a broader decision that would settle the slavery issue.

On March 6, Chief Justice Roger B. Taney announced that the majority had ruled against Scott. Taney argued that no African American—slave or free—could be a citizen of the United States. But the real bombshell in the decision was the ruling that Dred Scott would not have won his case even if he had been a legal plaintiff. His residence in the Wisconsin Territory established no right to freedom because Congress had no power to prohibit slavery there. The Missouri Compromise was thus declared unconstitutional and so, implicitly, was the main plank in the Republican platform.

If Buchanan expected the decision to reduce sectional tension, he was quickly proved wrong. In the North, and especially among Republicans, the Court's verdict was viewed as the latest diabolical act of the "slave-power conspiracy." The charge that the decision was a political maneuver rather than a disinterested interpretation of the Constitution was supported by strong circumstantial evidence. Five of the six judges who voted in the majority were proslavery Southerners, and their resolution of the territorial issue was close to the extreme southern rights position long advocated by John C. Calhoun.

Republicans denounced the decision as "a wicked and false judgment" and as "the greatest crime in the annals of the republic"; but they stopped short of openly defying the Court's authority. Instead, they argued on narrow technical grounds that the decision as written was not binding on Congress and that a ban on slavery in the territories could still be enacted. The decision actually helped the Republicans build support; it lent credence to their claim that an aggressive slave power was dominating all branches of the federal government and attempting to use the Constitution to achieve its own ends.

## The Lecompton Controversy

While the Dred Scott case was being decided, leaders of the proslavery faction in Kansas concluded that the time was ripe to draft a constitution and seek admission to the Union as a slave state. Since settlers with free-state views were now an overwhelming majority in the territory, the success of the plan required a rigged, gerrymandered election for convention delegates. When it became clear the election was fixed, the free-staters boycotted it, and the proslavery forces won complete control. The resulting constitution, drawn up at Lecompton, was certain to be voted

*Stephen Douglas, the "Little Giant" from Illinois, won election to Congress when he was just 30 years old. Four years later, he was elected to the Senate.* ✦

down if submitted to the voters in a fair election and sure to be rejected by Congress if no referendum of any kind was held.

To resolve the dilemma, supporters of the **Lecompton constitution** decided to permit a vote on the slavery provision alone, giving the electorate the narrow choice of allowing or forbidding the future importation of slaves. Since there was no way to vote for total abolition, the free-state majority again resorted to a boycott, thus allowing ratification of a constitution that protected existing slave property and placed no restriction on importations. Meanwhile, however, the free-staters had finally gained control of the territorial legislature, and they authorized a second referendum on the constitution as a whole. This time, the proslavery party boycotted the election, and the Lecompton constitution was overwhelmingly rejected.

The Lecompton constitution was such an obvious perversion of popular sovereignty that Stephen A. Douglas spoke out against it. But the Buchanan administration, bowing to southern pressure, tried to push it through Congress in early 1858, despite overwhelming evidence that the people of Kansas did not want to enter the Union as a slave state. The resulting debate in Congress became so bitter and impassioned that it provoked fistfights between northern and southern members. Buchanan, using all the political muscle he could command, scored a victory in the Senate, which voted to admit Kansas under the Lecompton constitution on March 23. But on April 1, a coalition of Republicans and Douglas Democrats defeated the bill in the House. A face-saving compromise was then devised. It allowed resubmission of the constitution to the Kansas voters on the pretext that a change in the provisions for a federal land grant was required. Finally, in August 1858, the people of Kansas killed the Lecompton constitution when they voted it down by a margin of 6 to 1.

The Lecompton controversy aggravated the sectional quarrel and made it truly "irreconcilable," if it had not been before. For Republicans, the administration's frantic efforts to admit Kansas as a slave state exposed southern dominance of the Democratic party and the lengths to which proslavery conspirators would go to achieve their ends. Among Democrats, the affair opened a deep rift between the followers of Douglas and the backers of the Buchanan administration. Because of his anti-Lecompton stand, Douglas gained popularity in the North, and some Republicans even flirted with the idea of joining forces with him against the "doughfaces"—prosouthern Democrats—who stood with Buchanan.

For Douglas himself, however, the affair was a disaster; it destroyed his hopes of uniting the Democratic party and defusing the slavery issue through the application of popular sovereignty. What had happened in Kansas suggested that popular sovereignty in practice was an invitation to civil war. Furthermore, the Dred Scott decision implied that the voters of a territory could not legally decide the fate of slavery at any time before the constitution-making stage. Hence, the interpretation of popular sovereignty favored in the North was undermined, and Southerners could insist on full protection of their right to own human property in all federal territories. For his stand against Lecompton, Douglas was denounced as a traitor in the South, and his hopes of being elected president were seriously diminished.

## Debating the Morality of Slavery

Douglas's more immediate problem was to win reelection to the Senate from Illinois in 1858. Here he faced surprisingly tough opposition from a Republican candidate who, in defiance of precedent, was nominated by a party convention. (At this time, senators were elected by state legislatures.) Douglas's rival, former Whig Congressman Abraham Lincoln, set out to convince the voters that Douglas could not be relied on to oppose the extension of slavery, even though he had opposed the admission of Kansas under a proslavery constitution.

In the famous speech that opened his campaign, Lincoln tried to distance himself from his opponent by taking a more radical position. He argued that the nation had reached the crisis point in the struggle between slavery and freedom: "'A house divided against itself cannot stand.' I believe this government cannot endure, permanently half *slave* and half *free*." Lincoln then described the chain of events between the Kansas-Nebraska Act and the Dred Scott decision as evidence of a plot to extend and nationalize slavery and called for defensive actions to stop the spread of slavery and place it "where the public mind shall rest in the belief that it is in the course of ultimate extinction." He tried to link Douglas to this proslavery conspiracy by pointing to his rival's unwillingness to take a stand on the morality of slavery, to his professed indifference about whether slavery was voted up or down in the territories. For Lincoln, the only security against the triumph of slavery and the slave power was moral opposition to human bondage. Neutrality on the moral issue would lull the public into accepting the expansion of slavery until it was legal everywhere.

In the subsequent series of debates that focused national attention on the Illinois senatorial contest, Lincoln hammered away at the theme that Douglas was a covert defender of slavery because he was not a principled opponent of it. Douglas responded by accusing Lincoln of endangering the Union by his talk of putting slavery on the path to extinction. Denying that

Abraham Lincoln, shown here in his first full-length portrait. Although Lincoln lost the contest for the Senate seat in 1858, the Lincoln-Douglas debates established his reputation as a rising star of the Republican party. ❖

he was an abolitionist, Lincoln made a distinction between tolerating slavery in the South, where it was protected by the Constitution, and allowing it to expand to places where it could legally be prohibited. Restriction of slavery, he argued, had been the policy of the Founders, and it was Douglas and the Democrats who had departed from the great tradition of containing an evil that could not be immediately eliminated.

In the debate at Freeport, Illinois, Lincoln questioned Douglas on how he could reconcile popular sovereignty with the Dred Scott decision. The Little Giant, as Douglas was called by his admirers, responded that slavery could not exist without supportive legislation to sustain it and that territorial legislatures could simply refrain from passing a slave code if they wanted to keep it out. Historians formerly believed that Douglas's "Freeport doctrine" suddenly alienated his southern supporters. In truth, Douglas's anti-Lecompton stand had already undermined his popularity in the slave states. But the Freeport speech undoubtedly hardened southern opposition to his presidential ambitions.

Douglas's most effective debating point was to charge that Lincoln's moral opposition to slavery implied a belief in racial equality. Lincoln, facing an intensely racist electorate, vigorously denied this charge and affirmed his commitment to white supremacy. He would grant blacks the right to the fruits of their own labor while denying them the "privileges" of citizenship. This was an inherently contradictory position, and Douglas made the most of it.

Although Republican candidates for the state legislature won a majority of the popular votes, the Democrats carried more counties and thus were able to send Douglas back to the Senate. Lincoln lost an office, but he won respect in Republican circles throughout the country. By stressing the moral dimension of the slavery question and undercutting any possibility of fusion between Republicans and Douglas Democrats, he had sharpened his party's ideological focus and had stiffened its backbone against any temptation to compromise its Free-Soil position.

## The South's Crisis of Fear

After Kansas became a free territory instead of a slave state in August 1858, the issue of slavery in the territories lost some of its immediacy, although it continued to carry great emotional and symbolic meaning. The remaining unorganized areas, which were in the Rockies and northern Great Plains, were unlikely to attract slaveholding settlers. Southern expansionists still dreamed of annexations in the Caribbean and Central America but had little hope of winning congressional approval. Nevertheless, Southerners continued to demand the "right" to take their slaves into the territories, and Republicans persisted in denying it to them. Although the Republicans repeatedly promised they would not interfere with slavery where it already existed, Southerners refused to believe them and interpreted their unyielding stand against the extension of slavery as a threat to southern rights and security.

A chain of events in late 1859 and early 1860 turned southern anxiety about northern attitudes and policies into a "crisis of fear." The events alarmed slaveholders because they appeared to threaten their safety and dominance in a new and direct way.

The first of these incidents was John Brown's raid on Harpers Ferry, Virginia, in October 1859. (See the Feature Essay, "The Enigma of John Brown," pp. 406–407.) Brown, who had the appearance and manner of an Old Testament prophet, thought of himself as God's chosen instrument "to purge this land with blood" and eradicate the sin of slaveholding. On October 16, he led eighteen men from his band of twenty-two (which included five free blacks) across the Potomac River from his base in Maryland and seized the federal arsenal and armory in Harpers Ferry.

Brown's aim was to commence from havens in the Appalachians a guerrilla war that would eventually extend to the plantation regions of the lower South. But the neighboring slaves did not rise up to join him, and Brown's raiders were driven out of the armory and arsenal by the local militia and forced to take refuge in a fire-engine house. There they held out until their bastion was stormed by a force of U.S. Marines commanded by Colonel Robert E. Lee. In the course of the fighting, ten of Brown's men were killed or mortally wounded, along with seven of the townspeople and soldiers who opposed them.

The wounded Brown and his remaining followers were put on trial for treason against the state of Virginia. The subsequent investigation produced evidence that several prominent northern abolitionists had approved of Brown's plan—to the extent they understood it—and had raised money for his preparations. This seemed to confirm southern fears that abolitionists were actively engaged in fomenting slave insurrection.

After Brown was sentenced to be hanged, Southerners were further stunned by the outpouring of sympathy and admiration that his impending fate aroused in the North. As Ralph Waldo Emerson expressed it, Brown "would make the gallows as glorious as the cross." His actual execution on December 2 completed Brown's elevation to the status of a martyred saint of the antislavery cause. The day of his death was marked in parts of the North by the tolling of bells, the firing of cannons, and the holding of memorial services.

Although Republican politicians were quick to denounce John Brown for his violent methods, Southerners interpreted the wave of northern sympathy as an expression of the majority opinion and the Republicans' "real" attitude. According to historian James McPherson, "They identified Brown with the abolitionists, the abolitionists with Republicans, and Republicans with the whole North." Within the South, the raid and its aftermath touched off a frenzy of fear, repression, and mobilization. Witch-hunts searched for the agents of a vast imagined conspiracy to stir up slave rebellion; vigilance committees were organized in many localities to resist subversion and ensure control of slaves; and orators pointed increasingly to secession as the only way to protect southern interests.

Brown was scarcely in his grave when another set of events put southern nerves on edge once more. Next to abolitionist-abetted rebellions, the slaveholding South's greatest fear was that the nonslaveholding majority would turn against the master class and the solidarity of southern whites behind the peculiar institution would crumble. When Congress met to elect a speaker of the House on December 5, Southerners bitterly denounced the Republican candidate—John Sherman of Ohio—because he had endorsed as a campaign document a condensed version of Hinton R. Helper's *Impending Crisis of the South.* Helper's book, which called on lower-class whites to resist planter dominance and abolish slavery in their own interest, was regarded by slaveholders as even more seditious than *Uncle Tom's Cabin,* and they feared the spread of "Helperism" among poor whites almost as much as they feared the effect of "John Brownism" on the slaves.

The ensuing contest over the speaker's office lasted almost two months. As the balloting went on, southern congressmen threatened secession if Sherman was elected, and feelings became so heated that some representatives began to carry weapons on the floor of the House. Since the Republicans did not have an absolute majority and needed the votes of a few members of the American party, it eventually became clear that Sherman could not be elected, and his name was withdrawn in favor of a moderate Republican who had refrained from endorsing Helper's book. The impasse over the speakership was thus resolved, but the contest helped persuade Southerners that the Republicans were committed to stirring up class conflict among southern whites.

*This painting,* The Last Moments of John Brown, *celebrates the passionate abolitionist as a hero and martyr to the antislavery cause. On his way to the gallows, he pauses to greet a slave mother and her child.* ❖

Republicans' identification with Helper's ideas may have been decisive in convincing many conservative planters that a Republican victory in the presidential election of 1860 would be intolerable. Anxiety about the future allegiance of nonslaveholding whites had been growing during the 1850s because of changes in the pattern of slave ownership. A dramatic rise in the price of slaves was undermining the ambition of slaveless farmers to join the slaveholding ranks. During the decade, the proportion of white heads of families owning slaves had shrunk from 30 to 25 percent in all the slave states and from 50 to 40 percent in the cotton belt of the lower South. Perceiving in this trend the seeds of class conflict, proslavery extremists had called for the reopening of the Atlantic slave trade as a way to reduce the price of slaves and make them more widely available. Although the interest of large owners in preserving the appreciated value of their human property had helped prevent the "proslavery crusade" from gaining broad support, many slaveholders were concerned about the social and political consequences of their status as a shrinking minority. Even those most strongly committed to the Union were terrified by the prospect that a Republican party in control of the federal government would use its power to foster "Helperism" among the South's nonslaveholding majority.

# Feature Essay

# THE ENIGMA OF JOHN BROWN

*O*n December 2, 1859, an old man with a thick white beard, who might have stepped out of the pages of the Old Testament, stood on a scaffold in Virginia awaiting execution for attempting to start a slave insurrection. He was unrepentant and without fear. Defiantly facing the assembled militiamen and other onlookers, he handed one of his attendants a prophetic message claiming that he had acted under divine inspiration and that it was God's will that "the crimes of this *guilty,* land: *will* never be purged *away;* but with Blood." His abortive raid on the federal arsenal at Harpers Ferry, Virginia, had sent a wave of fear through the slaveholding South, but the manner of his death and his strong antislavery sentiments made him a hero to many in the North. No single man did more to heighten the sectional crisis of the late 1850s and increase the probability of civil war.

But who was this man and how did he come to play such an important role in the sectional drama? Controversy surrounded him during his lifetime and has continued to do so ever since. Many African Americans have revered him as the rare example of a white man willing to give his life for black freedom. Unlike most white Americans, he seems to have been totally free of racial prejudice and at times identified with blacks so completely that he—and they—could almost forget that he was not one of them. But the means that he used to pursue his ends—his willingness to resort to violence, even to terrorism—has troubled many of those who find his objectives praiseworthy. The obvious impracticality of the plan for a massive slave uprising that he tried to put into effect at Harpers Ferry also has raised questions about his soundness of mind.

John Brown was born in Connecticut in 1800, the descendent of an old New England family that may have been represented on the Mayflower. He received little formal education and followed in his father's occupation as a tanner of leather. Lured westward like so many New Englanders of the time, he pursued the tanning business first in western Pennsylvania and then in Ohio. But unsuccessful land speculations and the hard times following the Panic of 1837 drove him into bankruptcy in 1842. He then became a wool dealer but faced ruin again in 1849 when his attempt to cut out the usual middlemen and make a direct sale of 200,000 pounds of American wool to buyers in England resulted in a huge loss. Such risk taking and the resulting ups and downs were normal experiences for the businessmen of the time. Brown may have been unluckier than some others, but the notion that his antislavery zeal was somehow a compensation for business failure makes little sense.

As early as 1834, at a time when his tannery was doing well, Brown proposed to raise a black boy in his own family as an experiment to show slaveholders that race was no obstacle to the building of character. He also considered opening a school for black children. By 1847, however, Brown had given up on the idea that education and example could end slavery. While still a successful wool merchant in Springfield, Massachusetts, he confided to the black abolitionist Frederick Douglass the germ of the plan he later tried to put into effect at Harpers Ferry: instigation of guerrilla war against slavery based in the mountains of the South. In 1851, Brown organized Springfield's blacks into a secret militia to resist enforcement of the Fugitive Slave Act of 1850. In 1854, he retired from the wool business with the intention of devoting the rest of his life to the cause of black freedom and equality. From a farm in North Elba, New York, he acted as patron of a struggling black agricultural colony

This is the earliest known photograph of John Brown, probably taken around 1846 in Springfield, Massachusetts. He pledges allegiance to an unknown flag, possibly an abolitionist banner. ❖

John Brown, shown here barricaded at Harpers Ferry with his followers and hostages, looked on his fight against slavery as a holy campaign ordained by God. In his last speech to the court before his execution for conviction of murder, promoting slave insurrection, and treason, Brown proclaimed, "Now, if it is deemed necessary that I should forfeit my life for the furtherance of the ends of justice and mingle my blood further with the blood of my children and with the blood of millions in this slave country whose rights are disregarded by wicked, cruel, and unjust enactments—I say, let it be done!" ❖

and also served as a conductor on the Underground Railroad when fugitives heading for Canada came his way.

By the fall of 1855 the frontline of the struggle against slavery was in Kansas (see p. 398). Following in the wake of his five sons, Brown went west to join the fray in September. After proslavery ruffians sacked the Free State capital of Lawrence in the spring of 1856, Brown led a retaliatory raid on proslavery settlers living along Pottawatamie Creek. In what can only be described as an act of terrorism, Brown and his men executed five defenseless men who had been rousted from their beds. His apparent objective was to instill fear and panic among the proslavery forces, possibly driving them to commit outrages of their own and thus further polarize the nation on the slavery question. Perhaps Brown already had concluded that a civil war, or something like it, was the only way to end slavery, and he appeared committed to bringing it about by any means necessary. For the next two years Brown operated as a guerrilla fighter in Kansas, raising money from eastern supporters who

were unaware of his role in the Pottawatamie massacre.

In May 1858, when the threat of the admission of Kansas to the Union as a slave state had been averted, Brown started organizing his raid on Harpers Ferry. He began by assembling a convention of black fugitives and abolitionists in Canada to draw up the constitution for the independent black state that he hoped to establish in the southern mountains as the base for a guerrilla war against the slaveholders. He then sought financial support from northern abolitionists and gathered a racially integrated force of twenty-two volunteers, eighteen of whom raided the federal arsenal. The plan was to seize the arms and distribute them to rebellious slaves. The raid turned into a debacle when the local militia trapped Brown and his men in a fire-engine house. Ten of Brown's men, including two of his sons, died as a result of the shooting that ensued. The survivors, including Brown himself, were captured by a force of U. S. Marines sent from Washington and commanded by Colonel Robert E. Lee. Local slaves did not, as Brown had

hoped, rise up spontaneously in rebellion once the violence had commenced.

If Brown was certain that his attempt to ignite a slave uprising and a guerrilla war would succeed, he was clearly deluded and possibly deranged. Frederick Douglass, whom Brown had invited to join the raiders, decided that the plan had no reasonable chance of success and refused to participate. But the fact that Brown seemed to welcome his martyrdom, almost rejoicing in it, raises another intriguing possibility. Brown may have realized that the odds were against him and that he would probably fail. But he may also have calculated, quite correctly as it turned out, that the panic that even an abortive raid would evoke from the South and the sympathy that the punishment of its perpetrators might arouse in the North would push the nation closer to the civil war that he had come to believe was the only way to end slavery. If the voice he heard in his head was indeed that of an angry God ready to punish the nation for the sin of slavery, his logic was irrefutable.

## The Election of 1860

The Republicans, sniffing victory and generally insensitive to the depth of southern feeling against them, met in Chicago on May 16 to nominate a presidential candidate. The initial front-runner, Senator William H. Seward of New York, had two strikes against him: He had a reputation for radicalism and a record of strong opposition to the nativist movement. What a majority of the delegates wanted was a less controversial nominee who could win two or three of the northern states that had been in the Democratic column in 1856. Abraham Lincoln met their specifications: He was from Illinois, a state the Republicans needed to win; he had a more moderate image than Seward; and he had kept his personal distaste for Know-Nothingism to himself. In addition, he was a self-made man, whose rise from frontier poverty to legal and political prominence embodied the Republican ideal of equal opportunity for all. After trailing Seward by a large margin on the first ballot, Lincoln picked up enough strength on the second to pull virtually even and was nominated on the third.

The platform, like the nominee, was meant to broaden the party's appeal in the North. Although a commitment to halt the expansion of slavery remained, economic matters received more attention than they had in 1856. With an eye on Pennsylvania, the delegates called for a high protective tariff; other planks included endorsement of free homesteads, which was popular in the Midwest and among working people, and federal aid for internal improvements,

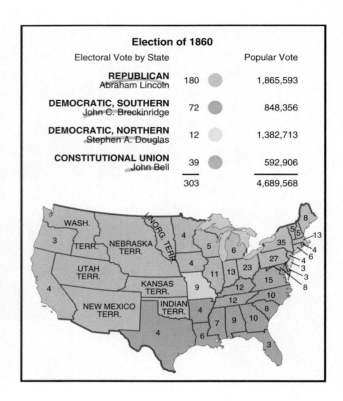

### Election of 1860

| Electoral Vote by State | | Popular Vote |
|---|---|---|
| **REPUBLICAN** Abraham Lincoln | 180 | 1,865,593 |
| **DEMOCRATIC, SOUTHERN** John C. Breckinridge | 72 | 848,356 |
| **DEMOCRATIC, NORTHERN** Stephen A. Douglas | 12 | 1,382,713 |
| **CONSTITUTIONAL UNION** John Bell | 39 | 592,906 |
| | 303 | 4,689,568 |

especially a transcontinental railroad. The platform was cleverly designed to bring most ex-Whigs into the Republican camp while also accommodating enough renegade Democrats to give the party a solid majority in the northern states.

The Democrats failed to present a united front against this formidable challenge. When the party first met in the sweltering heat of Charleston in late April, Douglas commanded a majority of the delegates but was unable to win the two-thirds required for nomination because of unyielding southern opposition. He did succeed in getting the convention to endorse popular sovereignty as its slavery platform, but the price was a walkout by Deep South delegates who favored a federal slave code for the territories.

Unable to agree on a nominee, the convention adjourned to reconvene in Baltimore in June. The next time around, a fight developed over whether to seat newly selected pro-Douglas delegations from some Deep South states in place of the bolters from the first convention. When the Douglas forces won most of the contested seats, another and more massive southern walkout took place. The result was a fracture of the Democratic party. The delegates who remained nominated Douglas and reaffirmed the party's commitment to popular sovereignty, while the bolters convened elsewhere to nominate John Breckinridge of Kentucky on a platform of federal protection for slavery in the territories.

In this cartoon from the 1860 election, candidates Lincoln and Douglas struggle for control of the country, while Breckinridge tears away the South. John Bell of the Constitutional Union party futilely attempts to repair the damage to the torn nation. ❖

## CHRONOLOGY

| | |
|---|---|
| **1846** | David Wilmot introduces Proviso banning slavery in the Mexican cession |
| **1848** | Free-Soil party is founded ❖ Zachary Taylor (Whig) elected president, defeating Lewis Cass (Democrat) and Martin Van Buren (Free-Soil) |
| **1849** | California seeks admission to the Union as a free state |
| **1850** | Congress debates sectional issues and enacts Compromise of 1850 |
| **1852** | Harriet Beecher Stowe publishes *Uncle Tom's Cabin* ❖ Franklin Pierce (Democrat) elected president by a large majority over Winfield Scott (Whig) |
| **1854** | Congress passes Kansas-Nebraska Act, repealing Missouri Compromise ❖ Republican party founded in several northern states ❖ Anti-Nebraska coalitions score victories in congressional elections in the North |
| **1854–1855** | Know-Nothing party achieves stunning successes in state politics |
| **1854–1856** | Free-state and slave-state forces struggle for control of Kansas Territory |
| **1856** | Preston Brooks assaults Charles Sumner on Senate floor ❖ James Buchanan wins presidency despite strong challenge in the North from John C. Frémont |
| **1857** | Supreme Court decides Dred Scott case and legalizes slavery in all territories |
| **1858** | Congress refuses to admit Kansas to Union under the proslavery Lecompton constitution ❖ Lincoln and Douglas debate slavery issue in Illinois |
| **1859** | John Brown raids Harpers Ferry, is captured and executed |
| **1859–1860** | Fierce struggle takes place over election of a Republican as speaker of the House (December–February) |
| **1860** | Republicans nominate Abraham Lincoln for presidency (May) ❖ Democratic party splits into northern and southern factions with separate candidates and platforms (June) ❖ Lincoln wins the presidency over Douglas, Breckinridge, and Bell |

By the time the campaign was under way, four parties were running presidential candidates. In addition to the Republicans, the Douglas Democrats, and the "Southern Rights" Democrats, a remnant of conservative Whigs and Know-Nothings nominated John Bell of Tennessee under the banner of the Constitutional Union party. Taking no explicit stand on the issue of slavery in the territories, the Constitutional Unionists tried to represent the spirit of sectional accommodation that had led to compromise in 1820 and 1850. In effect, the race became a separate two-party contest in each section: In the North, the real choice was between Lincoln and Douglas; in the South, the only candidates with a fighting chance were Breckinridge and Bell. Douglas alone tried to carry on a national campaign, gaining some support in every state, but actually winning only in Missouri.

When the results came in, the Republicans had achieved a stunning victory. By gaining the electoral votes of all the free states except those from three districts of New Jersey that voted for Douglas Lincoln won a decisive majority—180 to 123 over his combined opponents. In the North, his 54 percent of the popular vote annihilated Douglas. In the South, where Lincoln was not even on the ballot, Breckinridge triumphed everywhere except in Virginia, Kentucky, and Tennessee, which went for Bell and the Constitutional Unionists. The Republican strategy of seeking power by trying to win decisively in the majority section was brilliantly successful. Although fewer than 40 percent of those who went to the polls throughout the nation actually voted for Lincoln, his support in the North was so solid that he would have won in the electoral college even if his opponents had been unified behind a single candidate.

Most Southerners saw the result of the election as a catastrophe. A candidate and a party with no support in their own section had won the presidency on a platform viewed as insulting to southern honor and hostile to vital southern interests. Since the birth of the republic, Southerners had either sat in the White House or exerted considerable influence over those who did. Those days might now be gone forever. Rather than accepting permanent minority status in American politics and facing the resulting dangers to black slavery and white "liberty," the political leaders of the lower South launched a movement for immediate secession from the Union.

## CONCLUSION: EXPLAINING THE CRISIS

Generations of historians have searched for the underlying causes of the crisis leading to disruption of the Union but have failed to agree on exactly what they were. Some have stressed the clash of economic interests between agrarian and industrializing regions. But this interpretation does not reflect the way people at the time expressed their concerns. The main issues in the sectional debates of the 1850s were whether slavery was right or wrong and whether it should be extended or contained. Disagreements over protective tariffs and other economic measures benefiting one section or the other were clearly secondary. Furthermore, it has never been clear why the interests of northern industry and those of the South's commercial agriculture were irreconcilable. From a purely economic point of view, there was no necessity for producers of raw materials to go to war with those who marketed or processed those raw materials.

Another group of historians blame the crisis on "irresponsible" politicians and agitators on both sides of the Mason-Dixon line. Public opinion, they argue, was whipped into a frenzy over issues that competent statesmen could have resolved. But this viewpoint has been sharply criticized for failing to acknowledge the depths of feeling that could be aroused by the slavery question and for underestimating the obstacles to a peaceful solution.

The dominant modern view is that the crisis was rooted in profound ideological differences over the morality and utility of slavery as an institution. Most interpreters are now agreed that the roots of the conflict lay in the fact that the South was a slave society and determined to stay that way, while the North was equally committed to a free-labor system. In the words of historian David Potter, "slavery really had a polarizing effect, for the North had no slaveholders—at least not of resident slaves—and the South had virtually no abolitionists." No other differences divided the regions in this decisive way, and it is hard to imagine that secessionism would have developed if the South had followed the North's example and abolished slavery in the postrevolutionary period.

Nevertheless, the existence or nonexistence of slavery will not explain why the crisis came when it did and in the way that it did. Why did the conflict become "irreconcilable" in the 1850s and not earlier or later? Why did it take the form of a political struggle over the future of slavery in the territories? Adequate answers to both questions require an understanding of political developments that were not directly caused by tensions over slavery.

By the 1850s, the established Whig and Democratic parties were in trouble partly because they no longer offered the voters clear-cut alternatives on economic issues that had been the bread and butter of politics during the heyday of the second party system. This situation created an opening for new parties and issues. After the Know-Nothings failed to make attitudes toward immigrants the basis for a political realignment, the Republicans used the issue of slavery in the territories to build the first successful sectional party in American history. They called for "free soil" rather

than freedom for blacks because abolitionism conflicted with the northern majority's commitment to white supremacy and its respect for the original constitutional compromise that established a hands-off policy toward slavery in the southern states. For Southerners, the Republican party now became the main issue, and they fought against it from within the Democratic party until it ceased to function as a national organization in 1860.

If politicians seeking new ways to mobilize an apathetic electorate are seen as the main instigators of sectional crisis, the reasons that certain appeals were more effective than others must still be uncovered. Why did the slavery extension issue arouse such strong feelings in the two sections during the 1850s? The same issue had arisen earlier and had proved adjustable, even in 1820 when the second party system—with its vested interest in compromise—had not yet emerged. If the expansion of slavery had been as vital and emotional a question in 1820 as it was in the 1850s, the declining Federalist party presumably would have revived in the form of a northern sectional party adamantly opposed to the admission of slave states to the Union.

Ultimately, therefore, the crisis of the 1850s must be understood as having a deep social and cultural dimension as well as a purely political one. In *Uncle Tom's Cabin*, Harriet Beecher Stowe personified the cultural conflict in her depiction of two brothers with similar personalities, one of whom settled in Vermont "to rule over rocks and stones" and the other in Louisiana "to rule over men and women." The first became a deacon in the church, a member of the local abolition society, and, despite his natural authoritarianism, the adherent of "a democratic theory." The second became indifferent to religion, openly aristocratic, a staunch defender of slavery, and an extreme racist— "he considered the negro, through all possible gradations of color, as the intermediate link between man and animals." Stowe's comparison may have been biased, but she showed a good understanding of how the contrasting environments of slavery and freedom could lead very similar men to have sharply conflicting views of the world.

This divergence in basic beliefs and values had widened and become less manageable between the 1820s and the 1850s. Both sections continued to profess allegiance to the traditional "republican" ideals of individual liberty and independence, and both were strongly influenced by evangelical religion. But differences in the economic and social development of each region transformed a common culture into two conflicting cultures. In the North, a rising middle class adapted to the new market economy with the help of an evangelical Christianity that sanctioned self-discipline and social reform (see Chapter 12). The South, on the other hand, embraced slavery as a foundation for the liberty and independence of whites. Its evangelicalism encouraged personal piety but not social reform and gave only limited attention to building the kind of personal character that made for commercial success. The notion that white liberty and equality depended on resistance to social and economic change and—to get to the heart of the matter—on continuing to have enslaved blacks to do menial labor became more deeply entrenched.

When politicians appealed to sectionalism during the 1850s, therefore, they could evoke conflicting views of what constituted the good society. The South—with its allegedly idle masters, degraded unfree workers, and shiftless poor whites—seemed to a majority of Northerners to be in flagrant violation of the Protestant work ethic and the ideal of open competition in "the race of life." From the dominant southern point of view, the North was a land of hypocritical money-grubbers who denied the obvious fact that the virtue, independence, and liberty of free citizens was possible only when dependent laboring classes—especially racially inferior ones—were kept under the kind of rigid control that only slavery could provide. According to the ideology of northern Republicans, the freedom of the individual depended on equality of opportunity for everyone; in the minds of southern sectionalists, it required that part of the population be enslaved. Once these contrary views of the world had become the main themes of political discourse, sectional compromise was no longer possible.

## RECOMMENDED READING

The best general account of the politics of the sectional crisis is David M. Potter, *The Impending Crisis, 1848–1861* (1976). This well-written and authoritative work combines a vivid and detailed narrative of events with a shrewd and detailed interpretation of them. For a shorter overview, see Bruce C. Levine, *Half Slave and Half Free: The Roots of the Civil War* (1991). On the demise of the Whigs, see Michael F. Holt, *The Rise and Fall of the American Whig Party* (1999). The best treatment of the Know-Nothing movement is Tyler Anbinder, *Nativism and Slavery: The Northern Know-Nothings and the Politics of the 1850s* (1992). The most important studies of northern political sectionalism are Eric Foner, *Free Soil, Free Labor, Free Men: The Ideology of the Republican Party Before the Civil War* (1970), and William E.

Gienapp, *The Origins of the Republican Party, 1852–1856* (1987), on the Republican party generally; and Don E. Fehrenbacher, *Prelude to Greatness: Lincoln in the 1850s* (1962), on Lincoln's rise to prominence. On the climactic events of 1857, see Don E. Fehrenbacher, *The Dred Scott Case: Its Significance in American Law and Politics* (1978) and Kenneth M. Stampp, *America in 1857: A Nation on the Brink* (1990). On the background of southern separatism, see William W. Freehling, *The Road to Disunion: Secessionists at Bay, 1776–1854* (1990) and William L. Barney, *The Road to Secession: A New Perspective on the Old South* (1972).

**For a list of additional titles related to this chapter's topics, please see** http://www.ablongman.com/divine.

## SUGGESTED WEB SITES

### Secession Era Editorials Project

http://history.furman.edu/~benson/docs/
Furman University is digitizing editorials about the secession crisis and already includes scores of them on this site.

### John Brown Trial Links

http://www.law.umkc.edu/faculty/projects/ftrials/Brown.html
For information about the trial of John Brown, this site provides a list of excellent links.

### Abraham Lincoln and Slavery

http://odur.let.rug.nl/~usa/H/1990/ch5_p6.htm
This site discusses Lincoln's views and actions concerning slavery, especially the Lincoln-Douglas debate.

### Bleeding Kansas

http://www.kancoll.org/galbks.htm
Contemporary and later accounts of America's rehearsal for the Civil War comprise this University of Kansas site.

### The Compromise of 1850 and the Fugitive Slave Act

http://www.pbs.org/wgbh/aia/part4
From the series on Africans in America, an analysis of the Compromise of 1850 and of the effects of the Fugitive Slave Act on black Americans.

### The 1850s: An Increasingly Divided Union

http://www.thoughtfultech.com/MMTS/50essay.html
A tutorial skills development site focusing on the events in the 1850s leading to the Civil War; from MMTS, the Multi-Media Thinking Skills project.

### Words and Deeds in American History

http://lcweb2.loc.gov/ammem/mcchtml/corhome.html
A Library of Congress site containing links to Frederick Douglass; the Compromise of 1850; speeches by John C. Calhoun, Daniel Webster, and Henry Clay; and other topics from the Civil War era.

# The Case of Dred and Harriet Scott

## Blurring the Borders of Politics and Justice

The Missouri Compromise of 1820, which kept an even balance between the Union's slave states and free states by admitting Missouri as a slave state and Maine as a free state, was intended in part to answer the question of whether Congress had the authority to ban slavery in federal territories. That compromise, however, turned out to be only a temporary solution. Questions about the extension of slavery into new territories, the rights of slaveowners, and the status of slaves continued to plague Northerners and Southerners alike. Both the North and the South wanted to find a way to resolve these issues, but neither could agree on a compromise that would satisfy both sides. Finally, in 1857, a case came before the Supreme Court that seemed to address all these issues. To understand the Supreme Court's ruling in *Dred Scott* v. *Sandford*, it is necessary to go back to the year 1832, twenty-five years before the case reached the Court.

In the fall of 1832, with the Black Hawk War raging, a young physician named John Emerson accepted a temporary assignment as surgeon at Jefferson Barracks, an army post in Missouri. At this safe distance from any actual fighting, Dr. Emerson quickly became enamored of the life of a medical officer. As the war drew to a close, he sought and secured a full-time commission at Fort Armstrong, Illinois. Relieved to have obtained a permanent appointment, he headed north, setting the stage for the most controversial court decision in American history.

Emerson was accompanied on his journey by his sole slave, a pleasant looking man in his mid-thirties, known as Dred Scott. After arriving in Illinois, Scott continued to attend to Emerson's personal needs and performed most of the work on Emerson's land claims. For two years, Scott functioned as a contradiction in terms—a slave laboring in a free state. Scott's status grew even more complicated with Emerson's next transfer, which took the two men farther north. The pair traveled to Fort Snelling, in what was then Wisconsin Territory—an area where the Missouri Compromise explicitly forbade the practice of slavery. While in Wisconsin Territory, Scott met and married another transported slave, Harriet Robinson. Their union would last for the remainder of Dred Scott's life and produce four children, two of whom died in infancy. The surviving pair, Eliza and Lizzie, would join their parents in their famous fight for freedom.

When John Emerson died in December 1843, Dred and Harriet Scott found themselves back in Missouri and under the authority of Emerson's wife, Irene Sanford Emerson. Dred Scott attempted to purchase his family's freedom, but Mrs. Emerson refused his offer. Then, in the spring of 1846, the Scotts took Mrs. Emerson to court, claiming Dr. Emerson had forfeited all rights of ownership a decade earlier when he transported them into free territory. This relatively common maneuver by the Scotts initiated a series of legal struggles that would eventually wend all the way to the Supreme Court of the United States.

To avoid any direct challenge to the logic or legality of slavery, legal doctrine in Missouri required Dred and Harriet Scott to file a convoluted claim, which accused Mrs. Emerson of assault and false imprisonment. Such a claim did not directly argue the case for freedom, but in fact forced the court to decide on that very issue. If the Scotts were rightfully the slaves of Mrs. Emerson, her abusive behavior toward them would have been perfectly legitimate. If they were not her slaves, the claim of assault and false imprisonment would have been valid. Therefore, in order to consider the petitions of the Scotts, the court would first have to determine whether the Scotts were still slaves or whether their lengthy sojourn into free territory had automatically set them free. Such were the legal mazes made necessary by a slave regime.

One of the many myths that has developed about the Scott case claims that either the Scotts or their attorneys—who were paid for by white friends—had conceived of the suit as a test case, a chance to settle definitively some of the most perplexing questions posed by slavery. By all reliable accounts, however, Dred and Harriet Scott sought nothing more than freedom for themselves and their daughters. In fact, no one involved seems to have thought much about the possible political or legal implications of the particular case. Suits such as that filed by the Scotts were actually quite commonplace in the 1840s, and the typical outcome was freedom for the slave. Missouri courts had repeatedly held that slaves transported into free territory were thereby emancipated. A full decade before the Scotts' suit came to trial, a Missouri court had ruled in the slaves' favor in a case involving the specific issue of an army transfer. Given such precedents, the Scotts seemed to have a very strong case.

The Scotts also had the misfortune, however, of bringing their case to court at a time when public opinion in Missouri was experiencing a profound shift. As slavery came under increasing attack from the North and slaveholding became a fundamental element of Missourians' identity, judicial decisions grew steadily more hostile to the petitions of slaves. Missouri's precarious position as a border state intensified its preoccupation with any threat to the institution of slavery. As the premier student of the Scotts' case has commented, "the Scotts as suitors for freedom would become casualties of the sectional conflict."

When the trial finally began in June 1846, the Scotts' attorney brought a series of witnesses before the jury, all of whom testified that Dred Scott had indeed been at Forts Armstrong and Snelling. All that remained to secure the Scotts' freedom was the relatively simple task of proving what everyone already knew, that they were held as slaves by Mrs. Emerson. In a surprising legal move, Mrs. Emerson's lawyers raised doubts as to whether Mrs. Emerson, her brother, or her father actually claimed ownership of the Scotts. With bizarre logic, the jury returned the Scotts to Mrs. Emerson because the trial had failed to establish her as their rightful owner. The peculiar institution required a peculiar brand of law.

Undeterred, the Scotts moved for a retrial. After a series of complicated moves by both legal teams, the case came before the Missouri Supreme Court. The court handed down its decision in 1852, six years after

The case of Dred and Harriet Scott resulted in a Supreme Court ruling that has been called the "most overturned decision in history." ❖

the Scotts originally filed their petitions. During those six years, the slavery issue had reached a boiling point and no state felt its effects more than Missouri. Disputes over slavery had divided the state into two hostile factions.

Two of the Missouri supreme court justices stood squarely in the proslavery camp, and the third, a moderate, had neither the personality nor the inclination to oppose his colleagues on the Scott case. Relying heavily on a doctrine of states' rights, the court held that laws prohibiting slavery in Wisconsin Territory had no binding effect on the State of Missouri. Therefore, the court determined, the Scotts remained slaves. The decision explicitly referred to the deteriorating political climate, arguing that, "Times are not now as they were when the former decisions on this subject were made. Since then . . . States have been possessed with a dark and fell spirit in relation to slavery. . . . Under such circumstances it does not behoove the state of Missouri to show the least countenance to any measure which might gratify this spirit. . . ." Always closely related, law and politics had become indistinguishable in the Scott case.

Despite the ruling, neither the Scotts nor their supporters were prepared to give up the fight. The next step was to appeal to the nation's highest court, but such a move did not seem very promising. Not only did the United States Supreme Court have a majority of justices from slaves states, but one year earlier it had refused to hear a similar suit. In dismissing that case, Chief Justice Roger Taney followed the same logic that the Missouri Supreme Court had used in rejecting the Scotts' claims. Laws of federal territories, he reasoned, could have no effect on the policies of any state. Fearful of appealing to the court that had so recently issued an unfavorable ruling, the Scotts stalled.

Looking for a solution to the dilemma, the Scotts dropped the case of *Scott v. Emerson* and filed a new suit, *Scott v. Sandford*. (Somewhere along the way, Mrs. Emerson seems to have transferred her claim on the Scotts to her brother, John Sanford. In a misprint, the official court docket rendered his name as *Sandford*.) The terms of the new case would transform the Scotts' initially modest petition for freedom into a test case on the citizenship status of free African Americans and on the extent of federal prerogative in limiting the expansion of slavery. *Scott v. Sandford* thrust the Scotts immediately into a federal court and eventually into a national maelstrom. At this point, the two sides of the conflict seem to have lost sight of Dred and Harriet Scott, whose freedom could have easily been purchased by the resources that were devoted to the ensuing legal battle. They were being transformed from humble but determined slave petitioners into the icons of a national struggle.

*Scott v. Sandford* was tried in the small back room of a St. Louis store which served as the site of the United States Circuit Court for the District of Missouri. Neither side introduced new evidence or called witnesses; the case would be decided on the basis of evidence that had already been well established. The one new wrinkle was that by appealing to a federal court, the Scotts were making a claim for national citizenship, raising a controversial question that had yet to be resolved in American law: To what extent were free blacks entitled to the rights of citizens? The judge of the circuit court sidestepped this momentous issue to focus more narrowly on the specifics of the case. In May 1854, with the debate over the Kansas-Nebraska bill reaching a fevered pitch, a Missouri jury again refused to grant the Scotts their freedom. With no other recourse, the Scotts' attorney promptly made preparations to take their case to the U.S. Supreme Court.

Both sides pulled out the big guns for this final battle. Friends of the Scotts hired Montgomery Blair, a former U.S. solicitor general and a prominent figure in Washington society. Yet even a character as illustrious as Blair was outshone by Sanford's attorneys, among whom was Reverdy Johnson, a former U.S. attorney general, perhaps "the most respected constitutional lawyer in the country," and—even more importantly—the close personal friend of Chief Justice Taney. Dred and Harriet Scott were not in the courtroom as these eminent attorneys battled over their case; they remained in servitude in St. Louis. John Sanford also became a mere observer of the events. Battling mental illness throughout the period and finally seeking refuge in an asylum at the end of the year, Sanford grew increasingly irrelevant in a struggle that now overshadowed its original participants. Both legal teams pursued arguments that promoted their larger political objectives at the expense of their clients. Blair focused on the question of citizenship, which had already been *de facto* decided in Scott's favor by the lower court and could have been left alone. Instead of employing the proven strategy of claiming that territorial laws could not affect the policies of a given state, Sanford's attorneys used the more controversial but more consequential argument that federal antislavery laws were fundamentally unconstitutional.

After four days of such arguments, the Court surprisingly postponed the remainder of the trial until the next term, seven months away. During the lengthy recess, tensions in the country continued to rise at a frightening rate. In November, James Buchanan won a tight and acrimonious presidential race in which the extension of slavery had emerged as the preeminent political issue. The following month, with the nation still reeling from the bitter campaign, the trial resumed. The case was now more politicized than ever and the lawyers did not try to hide their respective agendas. Sanford's attorneys, in particular, frequently indulged in extensive defenses of the southern way of life. Not surprisingly, the debate grew hot and hostile. The Supreme Court had become the showcase for a nation coming apart at the seams.

Following the closing arguments, the justices gathered in early February to consider the Scott case. In addition to the specific question of the Scotts' freedom, the court debated the two weighty questions that had arisen from the trial: Were free African Americans citizens? Did Congress have the authority to prohibit slavery in the federal territories? The justices considered options that would have allowed them to decide on the Scotts' fate and still avoid the controversial issues, but there was immense public and political pressure for the Court to answer the broader questions once and for all. Chief Justice Taney was determined to do just that.

Roger Taney's presence on the bench loomed as the greatest single obstacle to the Scotts' freedom. In

Roger B. Taney, 1859 portrait by Emanuel Leutize. Taney's decision in the Dred Scott case evoked a variety of responses. Southern apologists for slavery applauded the ruling but abolitionists and opponents of slavery called the day of the decision one of the darkest in the history of the Republic. ❖

his late seventies when the Scott case was heard, Taney was a sickly man described by a colleague as "exceedingly feeble and broken." He had a stark courtroom demeanor and, despite his age and ill health, presided over the court with firmness. Taney spent most of his life in Maryland, and his views on slavery—and on just about everything else—were shaped by his experiences in that border state. A staunch Democrat and an unapologetic southerner, Taney doggedly defended states' rights against all federal encroachments. As the friction between North and South grew, the aged chief justice had become personally and emotionally embroiled in the issue. By the time the Scott case came before the Court, Taney was a "bitter sectionalist," anxious to put an end to "Northern insult and aggression."

On March 6, 1857, Taney addressed the packed courtroom and read the Court's official opinion, which he himself had composed. From start to Finish, Taney read for two full hours. As his tired voice concluded, the Scotts had lost their fight for freedom.

In rejecting the Scotts' claims, Taney tackled the issue of citizenship head on. The chief justice argued that the Constitution failed to afford blacks, slave or free, the rights of citizenship. Taney insisted that the framers of the Constitution considered people of African descent as a "subordinate and inferior class of beings, who had been subjugated by the dominant race, and, whether emancipated or not, yet remained subject to their authority, and had no rights or privileges but such as those who held the power . . . might chose to grant them." Emancipation, therefore, did not confer the rights of citizenship on blacks. Their race constituted a permanent mark of civil inferiority. In making the claim, Taney conspicuously failed to note that four New England states had already offered African Americans basic citizenship rights. Yet, despite this omission, the chief justice had actually been fairly accurate in gauging the era's prevailing mood. While Taney's racial doctrine seems extreme and even obscene by today's standards, it was representative of social attitudes of the time, even among many who opposed the institution of slavery. "Judge Taney's decision, infamous as it is," said Susan B. Anthony, "is but the reflection of the spirit and practice of the American people, North and South." It would take a war of unprecedented carnage before the nation was prepared to accept the citizenship of black Americans.

Having established that free blacks did not hold the rights of U.S. citizenship, Taney should have stopped. If Dred Scott was not entitled to bring a suit in federal court, the case was closed. But Taney was determined to issue an opinion on the second major question of the case, Congressional authority to prohibit slavery in the territories. The second half of Taney's ruling denied such Congressional authority and declared the Missouri Compromise unconstitutional. Taney relied on two highly questionable arguments to support this position: first, that the Constitution allowed Congress to legislate only on issues relating to the disposal of land, not on those affecting the legal status of the people living on that land, and second, that Congress only held such authority for land already claimed when the Constitution was drafted, excluding all territory acquired after 1787. Such arguments contradicted years of policy and precedent, including some of Taney's own rulings.

The Supreme Court's decision had four immediate effects. It outraged committed abolitionists, delighted apprehensive southerners, invalidated the principal plank of the new Republican party, and relieved worried moderates who believed the decision would lay the national controversy to rest. But despite the tremendous emotion the ruling evoked, many of its predicted effects proved illusory. It invited slavery to expand into the territories, but that never actually happened. It denied the Scotts their freedom, but they were shortly emancipated by new owners. And it claimed to answer fundamental questions of national importance, but those same questions continued to be debated until ultimately resolved by powder and shot.

The ruling's actual effects were quite different from those Taney expected. The emerging Republican Party, for instance, used the decision as a rallying point, decrying the slave power conspiracy that clearly controlled the highest court in the land. The party realized that it could overturn the decision only by changing the composition of the court and set its sights even more firmly on winning the presidency of 1860. By sparking intense political reactions and giving the Republican party a needed boost, the decision catalyzed sectional tensions, speeding the nation along the path to war.

Long after the Civil War had faded into history, *Scott* v. *Sandford* continued to leave its imprint on American law. The decision marked the first time the Supreme Court had actually struck down a major piece of federal legislation, paving the way for more aggressive judicial review in the future. It also signaled the development of a defining characteristic of American governance, a reliance on the courts to settle controversies that the normal processes of democracy cannot resolve. Ironically, *Scott* v. *Sandford* may have served as precedent for *Brown* v. *Board of Education*.

Although the legacy of the decision lives to this day, the major figures of this story did not long survive the momentous events. John Sanford died in an asylum two months after the Court handed down its decision. Dred and Harriet Scott remained in St. Louis after their emancipation where they worked as a hotel porter and a laundress; both died shortly before the onset of the Civil War. Roger Taney continued to serve as chief justice during the war. The southern octogenarian faced bitter animosity from the northern public, who considered him a traitor to the very government he claimed to serve. Taney died in 1864, not living to see the conclusion of the conflict he had

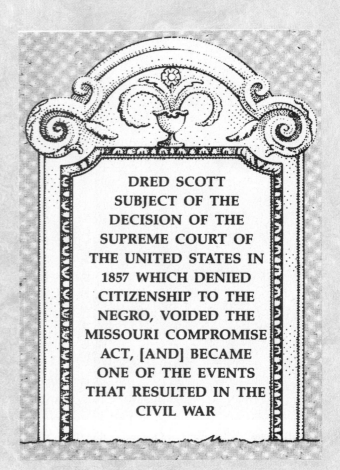

DRED SCOTT SUBJECT OF THE DECISION OF THE SUPREME COURT OF THE UNITED STATES IN 1857 WHICH DENIED CITIZENSHIP TO THE NEGRO, VOIDED THE MISSOURI COMPROMISE ACT, [AND] BECAME ONE OF THE EVENTS THAT RESULTED IN THE CIVIL WAR

helped start. As one sardonic contemporary noted, "The Hon. Old Roger B. Taney has earned the gratitude of his country by dying at last. Better late than never."

## Questions for Discussion

- What made the Dred Scott decision so important in American history?
- What does the decision tell us about the status of African Americans in the United States on the eve of the Civil War?

## Chapter 15

**Off to the Front,** *painted by an unknown artist ca. 1861. This scene of wartime departure captures the grief of loved ones as families were forced to separate. As a husband and wife embrace, a tiny child holding a flag sits alone on the floor.* ❖

# Secession and the Civil War

## *The Emergence of Lincoln*

The man elected to the White House in 1860 was striking in appearance—he was 6 feet 4 inches in height and seemed even taller because of his disproportionately long legs and his habit of wearing a high silk "stovepipe" hat. But Abraham Lincoln's previous career provided no guarantee he would tower over most of the other presidents in more than physical height. When Lincoln sketched the main events of his life for a campaign biographer in June 1860, he was modest almost to the point of self-deprecation. Especially regretting his "want of education," he assured the biographer that "he does what he can to supply the want."

Born to poor and illiterate parents on the Kentucky frontier in 1809, Lincoln received a few months of formal schooling in Indiana after the family moved there in 1816. But mostly he educated himself, reading and rereading a few treasured books by firelight. In 1831, when the family migrated to Illinois, he left home to make a living for himself in the struggling settlement of New Salem, where he worked as a surveyor, shopkeeper, and local postmaster. His brief career as a merchant was disastrous: He went bankrupt and was saddled with debt for years to come. But he eventually found a path to success in law and politics. While studying law on his own in New Salem, he managed to get elected to the state legislature. In 1837, he moved to Springfield, a growing town that offered bright prospects for a young lawyer-politician. Lincoln combined exceptional political and legal skills with a down-to-earth, humorous way of addressing jurors and voters. Consequently, he became a leader of the Whig party in Illinois and one of the most sought after of the lawyers who rode the central Illinois judicial circuit.

The high point of his political career as a Whig was one term in Congress (1847–1849). Lincoln did not seek reelection, but he would have faced certain defeat had he done so. His strong stand against the Mexican-American War alienated much of his constituency, and the voters expressed their disaffection in 1848 by electing a Democrat over the Whig who tried to succeed Lincoln. In 1849, President Zachary Taylor, for whom Lincoln had campaigned vigorously and effectively, failed to appoint him to a patronage job he coveted. Having been repudiated by the electorate and ignored by the national leadership of a party he had served loyally and well, Lincoln concentrated on building his law practice.

The Kansas-Nebraska Act of 1854, with its advocacy of popular sovereignty, provided Lincoln with a heaven-sent opportunity to return to politics with a stronger base of support. For the first time, his driving ambition for political success and his personal convictions about what was best for the country were easy to reconcile. Lincoln had long believed slavery was an unjust institution that should be tolerated only to the extent the Constitution and the tradition of sectional compromise required. He attacked Douglas's plan of popular sovereignty because it broke with precedents for federal containment or control of the growth of slavery. After trying in vain to rally Free-Soilers around the Whig standard, Lincoln threw in his lot with the Republicans, assumed leadership of the

419

*This campaign ribbon from the 1860 presidential election campaign depicts Republican candidate Abraham Lincoln as "the rail splitter of the West," a theme of the campaign intended to portray Lincoln as a figure with whom ordinary Americans could identify.* ❖

from Illinois up to the responsibilities he faced? Lincoln had less experience relevant to a wartime presidency than any previous chief executive; he had never been a governor, senator, cabinet officer, vice president, or high-ranking military officer. But some of his training as a prairie politician would prove extremely useful in the years ahead.

Another reason for Lincoln's effectiveness as a war leader was that he identified wholeheartedly with the northern cause and could inspire others to make sacrifices for it. In his view, the issue in the conflict was nothing less than the survival of the kind of political system that gave men like himself a chance for high office. In addressing a special session of Congress in 1861, Lincoln provided a powerful statement of what the war was all about:

> And this issue embraces more than the fate of these United States. It presents to the whole family of man, the question of whether a constitutional republic, or a democracy—a government of the people by the same people—can, or cannot, maintain its territorial integrity against its own domestic foes.

THE CIVIL WAR PUT ON TRIAL the very principle of democracy at a time when most European nations had rejected political liberalism and accepted the conservative view that popular government would inevitably collapse into anarchy. It also showed the shortcomings of a purely white man's democracy and brought the first hesitant steps toward black citizenship. As Lincoln put it in the Gettysburg Address, the only cause great enough to justify the enormous sacrifice of life on the battlefields was the struggle to preserve and extend the democratic ideal, or to ensure that "government of the people, by the people, for the people, shall not perish from the earth."

As he prepared to take office in 1861, Abraham Lincoln could scarcely anticipate the challenges he would face. The immediate problem was how to respond to the secession of the Deep South. But secession was just an expression of the larger question: Did the authority of the federal government outweigh the power of the individual states? No less important were questions about slavery: Was it morally acceptable for one person to "own" another? Could the Union continue to exist half-slave and half-free?

The sectionalism that had already led to a number of violent incidents—bloody fighting in Kansas, the assault on Charles Sumner, John Brown's raid on Harpers Ferry, his conviction on charges of treason against Virginia, and his eventual execution—continued to mount. Finally irreconcilable differences erupted into "total war" that left no part of society—North or South—untouched.

new party in Illinois, attracted national attention in his bid for Douglas's Senate seat in 1858, and turned out to have the right qualifications when the Republicans chose a presidential nominee in 1860. The fact that he had split rails as a young man was used in the campaign to show that he was a man of the people.

After Lincoln's election provoked southern secession and plunged the nation into the greatest crisis in its history, there was understandable skepticism about him in many quarters: Was the former rail-splitter

## THE STORM GATHERS

Lincoln's election provoked the secession of seven states of the Deep South but did not lead immediately to armed conflict. Before the sectional quarrel would turn from a cold war into a hot one, two things had to happen: A final effort to defuse the conflict by compromise and conciliation had to fail, and the North needed to develop a firm resolve to maintain the Union by military action. Both of these developments may seem inevitable in retrospect, but for most of those living at the time, it was not clear until the guns blazed at Fort Sumter that the sectional crisis would have to be resolved on the battlefield.

### The Deep South Secedes

South Carolina, which had long been in the forefront of southern rights and proslavery agitation, was the first state to secede. On December 20, 1860, a convention meeting in Charleston declared unanimously that "the union now subsisting between South Carolina and other states, under the name of the 'United States of America,' is hereby dissolved." The constitutional theory behind secession was that the Union was a "compact" among sovereign states, each of which could withdraw from the Union by the vote of a convention similar to the one that had ratified the Constitution in the first place. The South Carolinians justified seceding at that time by charging that "a sectional party" had elected a president "whose opinions and purposes are hostile to slavery."

In other states of the Cotton Kingdom, there was similar outrage at Lincoln's election but less certainty about how to respond to it. Those who advocated immediate secession by each state individually were opposed by the **cooperationists,** who believed the slave states should act as a unit. If the cooperationists had triumphed, secession would have been delayed until a southern convention had agreed on it. Some of these moderates hoped a delay would provide time to extort major concessions from the North and thus remove the need for dissolving the Union. But South Carolina's unilateral action set a precedent that weakened the cooperationists' cause.

Elections for delegates to secession conventions in six other Deep South states were hotly contested. Cooperationists did especially well in Georgia, Louisiana, and Texas. But nowhere did they stop secessionists from winning a majority. By February 1, seven states had removed themselves from the Union— South Carolina, Alabama, Mississippi, Florida, Georgia, Louisiana, and Texas. In the upper South, however, calls for immediate secession were unsuccessful; majority opinion in Virginia, North Carolina, Tennessee, and Arkansas did not subscribe to the view

A South Carolina newspaper announces the dissolution of the Union. South Carolina's secession was celebrated in the South with bonfires, parades, and fireworks. ❖

that Lincoln's election was a sufficient reason for breaking up the Union. In these states, a moderate Unionist element, deriving mainly from the old Whig party, had maintained its strength and cohesion despite the sectional crisis. Economic diversification had increased the importance of free labor and ties to the northern economy. Consequently, leaders in the border slave states were more willing than those in the lower South to seek a sectional compromise.

Without waiting for their sister slave states to the north, delegates from the Deep South met in Montgomery, Alabama, on February 4 to establish the Confederate States of America. The convention acted as a provisional government while at the same time

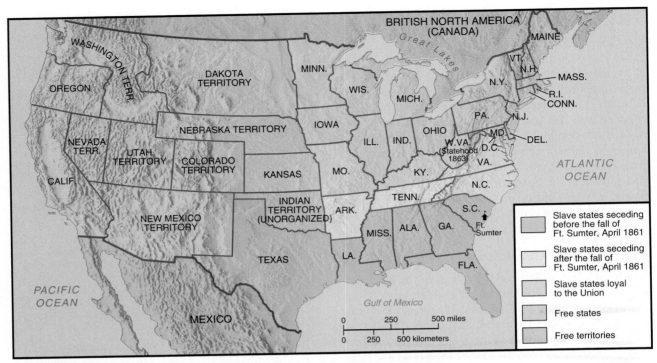

**SECESSION** *The fall of Fort Sumter was a watershed for the secessionist movement. With no room left for compromise, slave states of the upper South chose to join the Confederacy.* ✦

drafting a permanent constitution. Relatively moderate leaders, most of whom had not supported secession until *after* Lincoln's election, dominated the proceedings and defeated or modified some of the pet schemes of a radical faction composed of extreme southern nationalists. Voted down were proposals to reopen the Atlantic slave trade, to abolish the three-fifths clause (in favor of counting all slaves in determining congressional representation), and to prohibit the admission of free states to the new Confederacy.

The resulting constitution was surprisingly similar to that of the United States. Most of the differences merely spelled out traditional southern interpretations of the federal charter: The central government was denied the authority to impose protective tariffs, subsidize internal improvements, or interfere with slavery in the states and was required to pass laws protecting slavery in the territories. As provisional president and vice president, the convention chose Jefferson Davis of Mississippi and Alexander Stephens of Georgia, men who had resisted secessionist agitation. Stephens, in fact, had led the cooperationist forces in his home state. Radical "fire eaters" such as William Yancey of Alabama and Robert Barnwell Rhett of South Carolina were denied positions of authority in the new government.

The moderation shown in Montgomery resulted in part from a desire to win support for the cause of secessionism in the reluctant states of the upper South,

where such radical measures as reopening the slave trade were unpopular. But it also revealed something important about the nature of the separatist impulse even in the lower South. Proslavery reactionaries, who were totally lacking in reverence for the Union and wanted to found an aristocratic nation very different from the democratic United States, had never succeeded in getting a majority behind them. Most Southerners had been opposed to dissolving the Union and repudiating their traditional patriotic loyalties so long as there had been good reasons to believe slavery was safe from northern interference.

Lincoln's election and the panic that ensued gave Southerners cause to fear that Northerners would no longer keep their "hands off" southern slavery; but it was clear from the actions of the Montgomery convention that the goal of the new converts to secessionism was not to establish a slaveholder's reactionary utopia. What they really wanted was to re-create the Union as it had been before the rise of the new Republican party, and they opted for secession only when it seemed clear that separation was the only way to achieve their aim. The decision to allow free states to join the Confederacy reflected a hope that much of the old Union could be reconstituted under southern direction. Some optimists even predicted that all of the North except New England would eventually transfer its loyalty to the new government.

*Jefferson Davis, inaugurated as president of the Confederacy on February 18, 1861, was a West Point graduate and had served as secretary of war under President Franklin Pierce.* ❖

Secession and the formation of the Confederacy thus amounted to a very conservative and defensive kind of "revolution." The only justification for southern independence on which a majority could agree was the need for greater security for the "peculiar institution." Vice President Stephens spoke for all the founders of the Confederacy when he described the cornerstone of the new government as "the great truth that the negro is not equal to the white man—that slavery—subordination to the superior race—is his natural condition."

## The Failure of Compromise

While the Deep South was opting for independence, moderates in the North and border slave states were trying to devise a compromise that would stem the secessionist tide before it could engulf the entire South. When the lame-duck Congress reconvened in December 1860, strong sentiment existed, even among some Republicans, to seek an adjustment of sectional differences. Senator John Crittenden of Kentucky presented a plan that served as the focus for discussion. The proposed **Crittenden compromise,** which resembled Henry Clay's earlier compromises, advocated extending the Missouri Compromise line to the Pacific to guarantee the protection of slavery in the south-

western territories and in any territories south of the line that might be acquired in the future. It also recommended federal compensation to the owners of escaped slaves and a constitutional amendment that would forever prohibit the federal government from abolishing or regulating slavery in the states.

Initially, congressional Republicans showed some willingness to give ground and take the proposals seriously. At one point, William Seward of New York, the leading Republican in the Senate, leaned toward supporting a version of the Crittenden plan. Somewhat confused about how firmly they should support the party position that slavery must be banned in all territories, Republicans in Congress turned for guidance to the president-elect, who had remained in Springfield and was refusing to make public statements on the secession crisis. An emissary brought back word that Lincoln was adamantly opposed to the extension of the compromise line. In the words of one of his fellow Republicans, he stood "firm as an oak."

The resounding no to the central provision of the Crittenden plan and other similar compromise proposals stiffened the backbone of congressional Republicans, and they voted against compromise in committee. Also voting against it, and thereby ensuring its defeat, were the remaining senators and congressmen of the seceding states, who had vowed in advance to support no compromise unless the majority of Republicans also endorsed it. Their purpose in taking this stand was to obtain guarantees that the northern sectional party would end its attacks on "southern rights." The Republicans did in the end agree to support Crittenden's "un-amendable" amendment guaranteeing that slavery would be immune from future federal action. This action was not really a concession to the South, because Republicans had always acknowledged that the federal government had no constitutional authority to meddle with slavery in the states.

Some historians have blamed Lincoln and the Republicans for causing an unnecessary war by rejecting a compromise that would have appeased southern pride without providing any immediate practical opportunities for the expansion of slavery. But it is questionable whether approval of the compromise would have halted secession of the Deep South. If the secessionists are taken at their word, they would have been satisfied with nothing less than federal protection of slavery in all territories and the active suppression of antislavery agitation in the North.

Furthermore, Lincoln and those who took his advice had what they considered to be very good reasons for not making territorial concessions. One of these derived from the mistaken northern notion that the secession movement was a conspiracy that reflected the will of only a minority of white Southerners.

Concessions would allegedly demoralize southern Unionists and moderates by showing that the "rule-or-ruin" attitude of the radical sectionalists paid dividends. It is doubtful, however, that Lincoln and the dedicated Free-Soilers for whom he spoke would have given ground even if they had realized the secession movement was genuinely popular in the Deep South. In their view, extending the Missouri Compromise line of 36°30' to the Pacific would not halt agitation for extending slavery to new areas. South of the line were Cuba and Central America, long the target of southern expansionists who dreamed of a Caribbean slave empire. The only way to resolve the crisis over the future of slavery and to reunite "the house divided" was to remove any chance that slaveholders could enlarge their domain.

Lincoln was also convinced that backing down in the face of secessionist threats would fatally undermine the democratic principle of majority rule. In his inaugural address of March 4, 1861, he recalled that during the winter, many "patriotic men" had urged him to accept a compromise that would "shift the ground" on which he had been elected. But to do so would have signified that a victorious presidential candidate "cannot be inaugurated till he betrays those who elected him by breaking his pledges, and surrendering to those who tried and failed to defeat him at the polls." Making such a concession would mean that "this government and all popular government is already at an end."

### And the War Came

By the time of Lincoln's inauguration, seven states had seceded, formed an independent confederacy, and seized most federal forts and other installations in the Deep South without firing a shot. Lincoln's predecessor, James Buchanan, had denied the right of secession but had also refused to use "coercion" to maintain federal authority. In January, he sent an unarmed merchant ship, the *Star of the West*, to reinforce the federal garrison in Charleston Harbor, but the vessel turned back after being fired on. Buchanan's doubts about whether a Union held together by force was worth keeping were, for a time, widely shared in the North. Besides the business community, which was fearful of breaking commercial links with the cotton-producing South, some antislavery Republicans and abolitionists opposed coercive action because they thought the nation might be better off if "the erring sisters" of the Deep South were allowed "to depart in peace."

The collapse of compromise efforts eliminated the option of peaceful maintenance of the Union and narrowed the choices to peaceful separation or war between the sections. By early March, the tide of public opinion was beginning to shift in favor of strong action to preserve the Union. Once the business community realized conciliation would not keep the cotton states in the Union, it put most of its weight behind coercive measures, reasoning that a temporary disruption of commerce was better than the permanent loss of the South as a market and source of raw materials.

In his inaugural address, Lincoln called for a cautious and limited use of force. He would defend federal forts and installations not yet in Confederate hands but would not attempt to recapture the ones already taken. He thus tried to shift the burden for beginning hostilities to the Confederacy, which would have to attack before it would be attacked.

As Lincoln spoke, only four military installations within the seceded states were still held by U.S. forces. Two were in the remote Florida Keys and thus attracted

*This contemporary Currier and Ives lithograph depicts the bombardment of Fort Sumter on April 12–13, 1861. The soldiers are firing from Fort Moultrie in Charleston Harbor, which the Union garrison had evacuated the previous December in order to strengthen Fort Sumter.* ❖

little attention. The others were Fort Pickens in northern Florida, which was located in a defensible position on an island outside of the port of Pensacola, and Fort Sumter inside Charleston Harbor. Attention focused on Sumter because the Confederacy, egged on by South Carolina, was demanding the surrender of a garrison that was within easy reach of shore batteries and running low on supplies. Shortly after taking office, Lincoln was informed that Sumter could not hold out much longer and that he would have to decide whether to reinforce it or let it fall.

Initially, the majority of Lincoln's cabinet opposed efforts to reinforce or provision Sumter, on the grounds that it was indefensible anyway. Secretary of State Seward was so certain this would be the ultimate decision that he so advised representatives of the Confederacy. Lincoln kept his options open in regard to Sumter. On April 4, he ordered that an expedition be prepared to bring food and other provisions to the beleaguered troops in Charleston Harbor. Two days later, he discovered that his orders to reinforce Fort Pickens had not been carried out. Later that same day, he sent word to the governor of South Carolina that the relief expedition was being sent.

The expedition sailed on April 8 and 9, but before it arrived, Confederate authorities decided the sending of provisions was a hostile act and proceeded to attack the fort. Early on the morning of April 12, shore batteries opened fire; the bombardment continued for forty hours without loss of life but with heavy damage to the walls of the fort. Finally, on April 13, the Union forces under Major Robert Anderson surrendered, and the Confederate flag was raised over Fort Sumter. The South had won a victory but had also assumed responsibility for firing the first shot. Lincoln had taken pains to ensure that if the South was really determined to fight for its independence, it would have to begin by taking an aggressive action.

On April 15, Lincoln proclaimed that an insurrection against federal authority existed in the Deep South and called on the militia of the loyal states to provide 75,000 troops for short-term service to put it down. Two days later, a sitting Virginia convention, which had earlier rejected secession, reversed itself and voted to join the Confederacy. Within the next five weeks, Arkansas, Tennessee, and North Carolina followed suit. These slave states of the upper South had been unwilling to secede just because Lincoln was elected, but when he called on them to provide troops to "coerce" other southern states, they had to choose sides. Believing that secession was a constitutional right, they were quick to cut their ties with a government that opted for the use of force to maintain the Union and called on them to join in the effort.

In the North, the firing on Sumter evoked strong feelings of patriotism and dedication to the Union. "It seems as if we were never alive till now; never had a country till now," wrote a New Yorker; and a Bostonian noted, "I never before knew what a popular excitement can be." Stephen A. Douglas, Lincoln's former political rival, pledged his full support for the crusade against secession and literally worked himself to death rallying midwestern Democrats behind the government. By firing on the flag, the Confederacy united the North. Everyone assumed the war would be short and not very bloody. It remained to be seen whether Unionist fervor could be sustained through a long and costly struggle.

The entire Confederacy, which now moved its capital from Montgomery to Richmond, Virginia, contained only eleven of the fifteen states in which slavery was lawful. In the border slave states of Maryland, Delaware, Kentucky, and Missouri, a combination of local Unionism and federal intervention thwarted secession. Kentucky, the most crucial of these states, greeted the outbreak of war by proclaiming its neutrality. Kentucky eventually sided with the Union, mainly because Lincoln, who was careful to respect this tenuous neutrality, provoked the South into violating neutrality first by sending regular troops into the state. Maryland, which surrounded the nation's capital and provided it with access to the free states, was kept in the Union by more ruthless methods, which included the use of martial law to suppress Confederate sympathizers. In Missouri, the presence of regular troops, aided significantly by a staunchly pro-Union German immigrant population, stymied the secession movement. But pro-Union forces failed to establish order in this deeply divided frontier state. Brutal guerrilla fighting made wartime Missouri an unsafe and bloody place.

Hence the Civil War was not, strictly speaking, a struggle between slave and free states. Nor did it simply pit states that could not tolerate Lincoln's election against those that could. More than anything else, conflicting views on the right of secession determined the ultimate division of states and the choices of individuals in areas where sentiment was divided. General Robert E. Lee, for example, was neither a defender of slavery nor a southern nationalist. But he followed Virginia out of the Union because he was the loyal son of a "sovereign state." General George Thomas, another Virginian, chose the Union because he believed it was indissoluble. Although concern about the future of slavery had driven the Deep South to secede in the first place, the actual lineup of states and supporters meant the two sides would initially define the war less as a struggle over slavery than as a contest to determine whether the Union was indivisible.

## ADJUSTING TO TOTAL WAR

The Civil War was a "total war" involving every aspect of society because the North could achieve its aim of restoring the Union only by defeating the South so thoroughly that its separatist government would be overthrown. It was a long war because the Confederacy put up "a hell of a fight" before it would agree to be put to death. Total war is a test of societies, economies, and political systems, as well as a battle of wits between generals and military strategists—and the Civil War was no exception.

### Prospects, Plans, and Expectations

If the war was to be decided by sheer physical strength, then the North had an enormous edge in population, industrial capacity, and railroad mileage. Nevertheless, the South had some advantages that went a long way toward counterbalancing the North's demographic and industrial superiority. The South could do more with less, because its armies faced an easier task. To achieve its aim of independence, the Confederacy needed only to defend its own territory successfully. The North, on the other hand, had to invade and conquer the South. Consequently, the Confederacy faced a less serious supply problem, had a greater capacity to choose the time and place of combat, and could take advantage of familiar terrain and a friendly civilian population.

The nature of the war meant southern leaders could define their cause as defense of their homeland against an alien invader and thus appeal to the fervid patriotism of a white population that viewed Yankee domination as a form of slavery. The northern cause, however, was not nearly as clear-cut as that of the South. It seemed doubtful in 1861 that Northerners would be willing to give equally fervent support to a war fought for the seemingly abstract principle that the Union was sacred and perpetual.

Confederate optimism on the eve of the war was also fed by other—and more dubious—calculations. It was widely assumed that Southerners would make better fighting men than Yankees. Farm boys used to riding and shooting could allegedly whip several times their number among the clerks and factory workers (many of them immigrants) who, it was anticipated, would make up a large part of the Union army. (Actually, a majority of northern soldiers would also be farm boys.) When most of the large proportion of high-ranking officers in the U.S. Army who were of southern origin resigned to accept Confederate commands, Southerners confidently expected that their armies would be better led. If external help was needed, major foreign powers such as England and France might come to the aid of the Confederacy because the industrial economies of those European nations depended on southern cotton.

As they thought about strategy in the weeks and months after Fort Sumter, the leaders of both sides

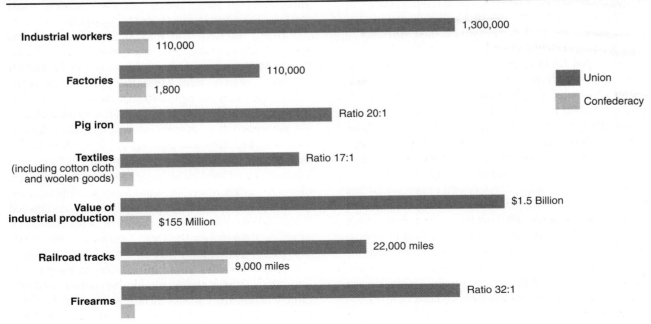

**RESOURCES OF THE UNION AND THE CONFEDERACY, 1861**

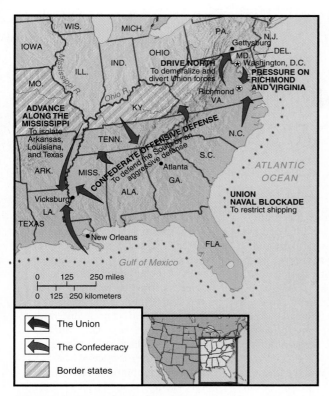

**OVERVIEW OF CIVIL WAR STRATEGY**    *Confederate military leaders were convinced the South could not be defended unless they took the initiative to determine where critical battles would be fought.* ❖

tried to find the best way to capitalize on their advantages and compensate for their limitations. The choice before President Davis, who assumed personal direction of the Confederate military effort, was whether to stay on the defensive or seek a sudden and dramatic victory by invading the North. He chose to wage a mainly defensive war in the hope he could make the Union pay so dearly for its incursions into the South that the northern populace would soon tire of the effort. But this plan did not preclude invading the North for psychological or military effect when good opportunities presented themselves. Nor did it inhibit Confederate aggressiveness against exposed northern forces within the South. Although their primary strategic orientation was defensive, it was an "offensive defense" that southern commanders put into effect.

Northern military planners had greater difficulty in working out a basic strategy, and it took a good deal of trial and error (mostly error) before there was a clear sense of what had to be done. Some optimists believed the war could be won quickly and easily by sending an army to capture the Confederate capital of Richmond, scarcely a hundred miles from Washington. The "On to Richmond" solution died on the battlefields of Virginia when it soon became clear that difficult terrain and an ably led, hard-fighting

Confederate army blocked the way. Aware of the costs of invading the South at points where its forces were concentrated, the aged General Winfield Scott—who commanded the Union army during the early months of the war—recommended an **anaconda policy.** Like a great boa constrictor, the North would squeeze the South into submission by blockading the southern coasts, seizing control of the Mississippi, and cutting off supplies of food and other essential commodities. This plan pointed to the West as the main locus of military operations.

Eventually Lincoln decided on a two-front war. He would keep the pressure on Virginia in the hope a breakthrough would occur there, while at the same time, he would authorize an advance down the Mississippi Valley with the aim of isolating Texas, Arkansas, and Louisiana. Lincoln also attached great importance to the coastal blockade and expected naval operations to seize the ports through which goods entered and left the Confederacy. His basic plan of applying pressure and probing for weaknesses at several points simultaneously was a good one because it took maximum advantage of the North's superiority in manpower and matériel. But it required better military leadership than the North possessed at the beginning of the war and took a painfully long time to put into effect.

## Mobilizing the Home Fronts

The North and South faced similar problems in trying to create the vast support systems needed by armies in the field. At the beginning of the conflict, both sides had more volunteers than could be armed and outfitted. The South was forced to reject about 200,000 men in the first year of the war, and the North could commit only a fraction of its forces to battle. Further confusion resulted from the fact that recruiting was done primarily by the states, which were reluctant to surrender control of the forces they had raised. Both Lincoln and Davis had to deal with governors who resisted centralized direction of the military effort.

As it became clear that hopes for a short and easy war were false, the pool of volunteers began to dry up. Many of the early recruits, who had been enrolled for short terms, showed a reluctance to reenlist. To resolve this problem, the Confederacy passed a conscription law in April 1862, and the Union edged toward a draft in July when Congress gave Lincoln the power to assign manpower quotas to each state and resort to conscription if they were not met. (See the Feature Essay, "Soldiering in the Civil War," pp. 428–429.)

To produce the materials of war, both governments relied mainly on private industry. In the North, especially, the system of contracting with private firms and individuals to supply the army resulted in much corruption and inefficiency. The government at times

# SOLDIERING IN THE CIVIL WAR

Early in the Civil War, William Tecumseh Sherman told an audience of fresh-faced recruits, "There's many a boy here today who looks on war as all glory, but, boys, it is all hell." Letters from Civil War soldiers reveal that Sherman's lesson was painfully learned by young men in both armies over the four years of conflict. At the outset, the firing on Fort Sumter infected both North and South with war fever. What later became a national nightmare began as a glorious defense of home and country. Young men rushed to join up in great numbers, taxing the ability of the authorities to process enlistments.

In contrast to the typical soldier of modern warfare, many of the early Civil War volunteers had well developed ideas of what the war was about. On both sides, such troops formed a core of stalwart soldiers who were committed to the ideological and political implications of the struggle. In the democratic atmosphere of the nineteenth century, when governments had little power to coerce citizen-soldiers, neither army could have sustained four years of brutal fighting if significant numbers of their troops did not genuinely believe in their side's cause. The ideologically motivated troops may have accounted for about half of the fighting force.

The other half was another matter. As with any large military force, the Union and Confederate armies struggled to motivate and discipline men who cared little for the principles at the root of the conflict. Such soldiers, who were typically drafted, cajoled, or bribed into service, found numerous ways to avoid the dangers of combat. Known as skulkers and sneaks, these reluctant troops could avoid combat by feigning sickness, hiding, hanging back, asking for "bomb-proof" assignments, or simply deserting in droves. The bad blood between such soldiers and those who fervently believed in the war effort could be intense.

But the skulker and the ideologue shared one thing in common: Neither was fully prepared for the rigors of war.

Early Union defeats and a strategic stalemate not only ended talk in both the North and the South of a "short engagement filled with glory" but also revealed how undisciplined the troops were. Of the more than three million Civil War servicemen, two-thirds were younger than 23 years of age and came from rural areas. They were not accustomed to the regimentation necessary to military life; as a young recruit from Illinois put it, "It comes rather hard at first to be deprived of liberty." Inadequate leadership, as well as the beginnings of war weariness and the arrival of letters from home pleading for help with the harvest, led to a degree of military anarchy. The early battles were contests between armed mobs that might break and run with little provocation. Moreover, the long casualty lists from the early battles discouraged new waves of enlistments.

Both governments hit on similar methods of recruiting and disciplining troops. Enlistment and reenlistment bounties were instituted, and the nation's first conscription laws were passed. The dual aim was to maintain the ranks of the original volunteers while at the same time stimulating more enlistments. Terms of service were lengthened, in most cases to three years, and all nonenlisted men of military age were registered and called on to either volunteer or be faced with the disgrace of being drafted. Although some Southerners were exempted to oversee their large numbers of slaves, and Northerners could escape military duty by paying a $300 fee, the laws did spur enlistments. Between 1861 and 1865, more than half of the nation's 5.5 million men of military age were mustered into service.

The solution to the problem of training the troops was the army training camp. With its "50,000 pup tents and wigwams," the camp was the volunteer's way station between home and battlefield. It was the place the raw recruit received his first bitter taste of the tedium, hardship, and deprivation of soldiering. "A soldier is not his own man," a Louisiana recruit wrote, astonished at how markedly camp routines differed from civilian life. "He has given up all claim on himself. . . . I will give you a little information concerning every day business. consider yourself a private soldier and in camp . . . the drum beats for drill. you fall in and start. you here feel youre inferirority. even the Sargeants is hollering at you close up; Ketch step. dress to the right, and sutch like."

Youthful idealism is still evident on the faces of these young Civil War soldiers who have not yet learned General Sherman's message that "war is hell." ❖

Professional noncommissioned officers from the peacetime army were used, more effectively by the Union, to turn men into soldiers who could fire a rifle and understand simple commands. The liberal use of the court-martial and the board of review enabled the professional soldiers to rid the army of its most incompetent officer-politicians and instill discipline in the ranks. Many recruits spent their entire terms of service within the tent cities, forming a reserve on which field commanders could call to replace casualties.

The camps were themselves the sites of hundreds of thousands of Civil War casualties. Fewer men died of battle wounds than of dysentery, typhoid fever, and other waterborne diseases contracted in the camps, which were often located on swampy land without adequate fresh water. The army food was always the butt of soldier humor—one soldier complained the beef issued to him must have been carved from a bull "too old for the conscript law"—but it was also the source of its own set of diseases, particularly scurvy. Men in the field were condemned to a diet of "hardtack and half-cooked beans," and no soldier could expect to receive fresh fruit or vegetables. But food became steadily more plentiful in the Union camps, and doctors, officers, and agents of the U.S. Sanitary Commission teamed up to improve camp cleanliness. "Johnny Reb," however, had to survive under steadily worsening conditions. The Confederate supply system did not improve significantly during the course of the war and grew worse wherever the North invaded or blockaded. Nevertheless, the battlefield performance of fighting men on the two sides remained roughly on a par throughout the war.

Camp lessons were often forgotten in the heat of battle, particularly by green troops who "saw the elephant" (went into battle for the first time) and ran from it. Like the youth in Stephen Crane's *The Red Badge of Courage,* a Mississippian anxiously admitted after his first fight that "though i did not run i mite have if i had thought of it in time." The Union's ability to call more new men into service may have guaranteed ultimate victory, but it meant that battle-hardened Confederate veterans faced large numbers of raw northern recruits in every major battle. Since experience often counted for more than basic training and equipment, southern troops could expect to engage the enemy on fairly equal terms.

The Civil War was the most costly and brutal struggle in which American soldiers have ever been engaged. More American servicemen died in that war (618,000) than in the two world wars and Vietnam combined. Contests were decided by deadly charges in which muskets were exploded at such close range as to sear the faces of the contestants. The survivors, in their letters home, attempted to describe the inhuman events, but, as a Maine soldier wrote to his parents after the battle of Gettysburg: "You can form no idea of a battlefield. . . . no pen can describe it. No tongue can tell its horror[.] I hope none of my brothers will ever have to go into a fight."

bought shoddy uniforms that disintegrated in a heavy rain, defective rifles, and broken-down horses unfit for service. But the North's economy was strong at the core, and by 1863 its factories and farms were producing more than enough to provision the troops without significantly lowering the living standards of the civilian population.

The southern economy was much less adaptable to the needs of a total war. Because of the weakness of its industrial base, the South of 1861 depended on the outside world for most of its manufactured goods. As the Union blockade became more effective, the Confederacy had to rely increasingly on a government-sponsored crash program to produce war materials. In addition to encouraging and promoting private initiative, the government built its own munitions plants, including a gigantic powder factory at Augusta, Georgia. Astonishingly, the Confederate Ordnance Bureau, under the able direction of General Josiah Gorgas, succeeded in producing or procuring sufficient armaments to keep southern armies well supplied throughout the conflict.

Southern agriculture, however, failed to meet the challenge. Planters were reluctant to shift from staples that could no longer be readily exported to foodstuffs that were urgently needed. But more significant was the inadequacy of the South's internal transportation system. Its limited rail network was designed to link plantation regions to port cities rather than to connect food-producing areas with centers of population, as was the pattern in the North. New railroad construction during the war did not resolve the problem; most of the new lines were aimed at facilitating the movement of troops rather than the distribution of food.

When northern forces penetrated parts of the South, they created new gaps in the system. As a result, much of the corn or livestock that was raised could not reach the people who needed it. Although well armed, Confederate soldiers were increasingly undernourished, and by 1863 civilians in urban areas were rioting to protest shortages of food. To supply the troops, the Confederate commissary resorted to the impressment of available agricultural produce at below the market price, a policy resisted so vigorously by farmers and local politicians that it eventually had to be abandoned.

Another challenge faced by both sides was how to finance an enormously costly struggle. Although special war taxes were imposed, neither side was willing to resort to the heavy taxation that was needed to maintain fiscal integrity. Americans, it seems, were more willing to die for their government than to pay for it. Besides floating loans and selling bonds, both treasuries deliberately inflated the currency by printing large quantities of paper money that could not be redeemed in gold and silver. In August 1861, the Confederacy issued $100 mil-

## ❖ A Look At the Past ❖

### Civil War Rations

Civil War soldiers depended upon hardtack, a saltless hard biscuit, as a food staple. Quinine, a remedy for malaria, also represented an essential supply for soldiers. Together the items testify to the hardships soldiers endured. If these were essential supplies, how common do you suppose were disease, hunger, and malnutrition?

lion of such currency. In early 1862, the Union followed suit by printing $150 million in Treasury notes, known as **greenbacks** because of their color. The presses rolled throughout the war, and runaway inflation was the inevitable result. The problem was much less severe in the North because of the overall strength of its economy.

War taxes on income were more readily collectable than in the South, and bond issues were more successful.

The Confederacy was hampered from the outset by a severe shortage of readily disposable wealth that could be tapped for public purposes. Land and cotton could not easily be turned into rifles and cannons, and the southern treasury had to accept payments "in kind." As a result, Confederate "assets" eventually consisted mainly of bales of cotton that were unexportable because of the blockade. As the Confederate government fell deeper and deeper into debt and printed more and more paper money, its rate of inflation soared out of sight. By August 1863, a Confederate dollar was worth only eight cents in gold. Late in the war, it could be said with little exaggeration that it took a wheelbarrow full of money to buy a purse full of goods.

## Political Leadership: Northern Success and Southern Failure

Total war also forced political adjustments, and both the Union and the Confederacy had to face the question of how much democracy and individual freedom could be permitted when military success required an unprecedented exercise of government authority. Since both constitutions made the president commander in chief of the army and navy, Lincoln and Davis took actions that would have been regarded as arbitrary or even tyrannical in peacetime. Nevertheless, "politics as usual"—in the form of free elections, public political controversy, and the maneuverings of parties, factions, and interest groups—persisted to a surprising degree.

Lincoln was especially bold in assuming new executive powers. After the fighting started at Fort Sumter, he expanded the regular army and advanced public money to private individuals without authorization by Congress. On April 27, 1861, he declared martial law, which enabled the military to arrest civilians suspected of aiding the enemy, and suspended the writ of habeas corpus in the area between Philadelphia and Washington, an action deemed necessary because of mob attacks on Union troops passing through Baltimore. Suspension of the writ enabled the government to arrest Confederate sympathizers and hold them without trial, and in September 1862 Lincoln extended this authority to all parts of the United States where "disloyal" elements were active. Such willingness to interfere with civil liberties was unprecedented and possibly unconstitutional, but Lincoln argued that "necessity" justified a flexible interpretation of his war powers. For critics of suspension, he had a question: "Are all the laws, *but one,* to go unexecuted, and the government itself to go to pieces, lest that one be violated?" In fact, however, most of the thousands of civilians arrested by military authorities were not exercising their right to criticize the government but were suspected deserters and draft dodgers, refugees, smugglers, or people who were simply found wandering in areas under military control.

For the most part, the Lincoln administration showed restraint and tolerated a broad spectrum of political dissent. Although the government closed down a few newspapers for brief periods when they allegedly published false information or military secrets, anti-administration journals were allowed to criticize the president and his party at will. A few politicians, including an Ohio Congressman, were arrested for pro-Confederate activity, but a large number of "Peace Democrats"—who called for restoration of the Union by negotiation rather than force—ran for office and sat in Congress and in state legislatures, and they thus had ample opportunity to present their views to the public. In fact, the persistence of vigorous two-party competition in the North during the Civil War strengthened Lincoln's hand. Since his war policies were also the platform of his party, he could usually rely on unified partisan backing for the most controversial of his decisions.

Lincoln was singularly adept at the art of party leadership; he was able to accommodate various factions and define party issues and principles in a way that would encourage unity and dedication to the cause. Since the Republican party served during the war as the main vehicle for mobilizing and maintaining devotion to the Union effort, these political skills assumed crucial importance. When a majority of the party came around to the view that freeing the slaves was necessary to the war effort, Lincoln found a way to comply with their wishes while minimizing the disenchantment of the conservative minority. Lincoln held the party together by persuasion, patronage, and flexible policymaking; this cohesiveness was essential to Lincoln's success in unifying the nation by force.

Jefferson Davis, most historians agree, was a less effective war leader than Lincoln. He defined his powers as commander in chief narrowly and literally, which meant he assumed personal direction of the armed forces but left policymaking for the mobilization and control of the civilian population primarily to the Confederate Congress. Unfortunately, he overestimated his capacities as a strategist and lacked the tact to handle field commanders who were as proud and testy as he was. Two of the South's best generals—Joseph E. Johnston and Pierre G. T. Beauregard—were denied the commands they deserved because they could not get along with Davis. One of the worst—Braxton E. Bragg—happened to be a personal favorite of the president and was allowed to keep a major

*Gaunt southern citizens stare unbelievingly at a poster announcing a day of fasting proclaimed by a horned Jefferson Davis. Davis's insistent demands for his army aroused the hard-pressed Southerners' anger.* ❖

command even after he had clearly demonstrated his incompetence.

Davis's greatest failing, however, was his lack of initiative and leadership in dealing with the problems of the home front. He devoted little attention to a deteriorating economic situation that caused great hardship and sapped Confederate morale. Although the South had a much more serious problem of internal division and disloyalty than the North, he refrained from declaring martial law on his own authority. The Confederate Congress grudgingly voted him such power when he asked for it but allowed it to be applied only in limited areas and for short periods.

As the war dragged on, Davis's political and popular support eroded. He was opposed and obstructed by state governors—such as Joseph E. Brown of Georgia and Zebulon Vance of North Carolina—who resisted conscription and other Confederate policies that violated the tradition of states' rights. The Confederate Congress served as a forum for bitter attacks on the administration's conduct of the war, and by 1863 a majority of southern newspapers were taking an anti-Davis stand. Even if he had been a more able and inspiring leader, Davis would have had difficulty maintaining his authority and credibility. Unlike Lincoln, he did not have an organized party behind him, for the Confederacy never developed a two-party system. As a result, it was difficult to mobilize the support required for hard decisions and controversial policies.

## Early Campaigns and Battles

The war's first major battle was a disaster for northern arms. Against his better judgment, General Winfield Scott responded to the "On to Richmond" clamor and ordered poorly trained Union troops under General Irvin McDowell to advance against the Confederate forces gathered at Manassas Junction, Virginia. They attacked the enemy position near Bull Run Creek on July 21, 1861, and seemed on their way to victory until Confederate reinforcements arrived from the Shenandoah Valley. After Confederate General Thomas J. Jackson had earned the nickname "Stonewall" for holding the line against the northern assault, the augmented southern army counterattacked and routed the invading force. As they retreated toward Washington, the raw Union troops gave in to panic and broke ranks in their stampede to safety.

The humiliating defeat at Bull Run led to a shake-up of the northern high command. The man of the hour was George McClellan, who first replaced McDowell as commander of troops in the Washington area and then became general in chief when Scott was eased into retirement. A cautious disciplinarian, McClellan spent the fall and winter drilling his troops and whipping them into shape. President Lincoln, who could not understand why McClellan was taking so long to go into the field, became increasingly impatient and finally tried to order the army into action.

Before McClellan made his move, Union forces in the West won some important victories. In February 1862, a joint military-naval operation, commanded by General Ulysses S. Grant, captured Fort Henry on the Tennessee River and Fort Donelson on the Cumberland. Fourteen thousand prisoners were taken at Donelson, and the Confederate army was forced to withdraw from Kentucky and middle Tennessee. Southern forces in the West then massed at Corinth, Mississippi, just across the border from Tennessee. When a slow-moving Union army arrived just north of the Mississippi state line, the South launched a surprise attack on April 6. In the battle of Shiloh, one of the bloodiest of the war, only the timely arrival of reinforcements prevented the annihilation of Union troops backed up against the Tennessee River. After a second day of fierce fighting, the Confederates retreated to Corinth, leaving the enemy forces battered and exhausted.

Although the Union's military effort to seize control of the Mississippi Valley was temporarily halted at Shiloh, the Union navy soon contributed dramatically to the pursuit of that objective. On April 26, a fleet under Flag Officer David Farragut, coming up from the Gulf, captured the port of New Orleans after boldly running past the forts below the city. The occupation of New Orleans, besides securing the mouth of the Mississippi, climaxed a series of naval and amphibious operations around the edges of the Confederacy that had already succeeded in capturing South Carolina's Sea Islands and North Carolina's

Roanoke Island. Strategically located bases were thus available to enforce a blockade of the southern coast. The last serious challenge to the North's naval supremacy ended on March 9, 1862, when the Confederate ironclad vessel *Virginia* (originally the USS *Merrimac*)—which had demolished wooden-hulled northern ships in the vicinity of Hampton Roads, Virginia—was repulsed by the *Monitor,* an armored and turreted Union gunship.

Successes around the edges of the Confederacy did not relieve northern frustration at the inactivity or failure of Union forces on the eastern front. Only after Lincoln had relieved him of supreme command and ordered him to take the offensive at the head of the Army of the Potomac did McClellan start campaigning. Spurning the treacherous overland route to Richmond, he moved his forces by water to the peninsula southeast of the Confederate capital. After landing at Fortress Monroe, which had remained in Union hands, McClellan began moving up the peninsula in early April 1862. For a month he was bogged down before Yorktown, which he chose to besiege rather than assault directly. After Yorktown fell on May 4, he pushed ahead to a point twenty miles from Richmond, where he awaited the additional troops that he expected Lincoln to send.

The reinforcements were not forthcoming. While McClellan was inching his way up the peninsula, a relatively small southern force under Stonewall Jackson was on the rampage in the Shenandoah Valley, where it succeeded in pinning down a much larger Union army and defeating its detached units in a series of lightning moves. When it appeared by late May that Jackson might be poised to march east and attack the Union capital, Lincoln decided to withhold troops from McClellan so they would be available to defend Washington.

If McClellan had moved more boldly and decisively, he probably could have captured Richmond with the forces he had. But a combination of faulty intelligence reports and his own natural caution led him to falter in the face of what he wrongly believed to be superior numbers. At the end of May, the Confederates under Joseph E. Johnston took the offensive when they discovered McClellan's army was divided into two segments by the Chickahominy River. In the battle of Seven Pines, McClellan was barely able to hold his ground on the side of the river under attack until a corps from the other side crossed over just in time to save the day. During the battle, General Johnston was severely wounded; succeeding him in command of the Confederate Army of Northern Virginia was native Virginian and West Point graduate Robert E. Lee.

Toward the end of June, Lee began an all-out effort to expel McClellan from the outskirts of Richmond. In a series of battles that lasted for seven days, the two armies clawed at each other indecisively. Although McClellan repulsed Lee's final assaults at Malvern Hill, the Union general decided to retreat down the peninsula to a more secure base. This backward step convinced Lincoln that the peninsula campaign was an exercise in futility.

On July 11, Lincoln appointed General Henry W. Halleck, who had been in overall command in the

*Mortar fire lights the sky in* Farragut's Fleet Passing Fort Jackson and Fort St. Philip *by artist J. Joffray. David G. Farragut went on to capture the port of New Orleans on April 24, 1862, then blockaded the Gulf of Mexico and controlled traffic on the lower Mississippi River. His activities helped secure control of the entire river for the Union. In 1866, the U.S. Congress created the rank of admiral especially for Farragut.* ❖

**CIVIL WAR, 1861–1862**  *Defeats on the battlefield forced a change in the Union's initial military campaign of capturing Richmond, the Confederate capital. The Union's targets in the West were the key cities of Vicksburg and New Orleans.* ❖

*After Antietam, Lincoln visited McClellan's headquarters to urge the general to take action. McClellan is on the left facing the president.* ❖

western theater, to be the new general in chief and through Halleck ordered McClellan to withdraw his army from the peninsula to join a force under General John Pope that was preparing to move on Richmond by the overland route. As usual, McClellan was slow in responding, and the Confederates got to Pope before he did. At the end of August, in the second battle fought near Bull Run, Lee established his reputation for brilliant generalship; he sent Stonewall Jackson to

Pope's rear, provoked the rash Union general to attack Jackson with full force, and then threw the main Confederate army against the Union's flank. Badly beaten, Pope retreated to the defenses of Washington, where he was stripped of command. Out of sheer desperation, Lincoln reappointed McClellan to head the Army of the Potomac.

Lee proceeded to lead his exuberant troops on an invasion of Maryland, in the hope of isolating Washington from the rest of the North. McClellan caught up with him near Sharpsburg, and the bloodiest one-day battle of the war ensued. When the smoke cleared at Antietam on September 17, almost five thousand men had been killed on the two sides and more than eighteen thousand were wounded. The result was a draw, but Lee was forced to fall back south of the Potomac to protect his dangerously extended supply lines. McClellan was slow in pursuit, and Lincoln blamed him for letting the enemy escape.

Convinced that McClellan was fatally infected with "the slows," Lincoln once again sought a more aggressive general and put

*Fresh recruits cannot avoid seeing battle casualties and field amputations as they wait to join the battle of Fredericksburg in this 1862 painting,* The Battle of Fredericksburg *by John Richards, based on an engraving that appeared in* Harper's *shortly after the battle.* ❖

Ambrose E. Burnside in command of the Army of the Potomac. Burnside was aggressive enough, but he was also rather dense. His limitations were disastrously revealed at the battle of Fredericksburg, Virginia, on December 13, 1862, when he launched a direct assault to try to capture an entrenched and elevated position. Throughout the Civil War such uphill charges almost invariably failed because of the range and deadly accuracy of small-arms fire when concentrated on exposed troops. The debacle at Fredericksburg, where Union forces suffered more than twice as many casualties as their opponents, ended a year of bitter failure for the North on the eastern front.

## The Diplomatic Struggle

The critical period of Civil War diplomacy was 1861 to 1862, when the South was making every effort to induce major foreign powers to recognize its independence and break the Union blockade. The hope that England and France could be persuaded to intervene on the Confederate side stemmed from the fact that these nations depended on the South for three-quarters of their cotton supply. In the case of Britain, the uninterrupted production of cotton textiles appeared essential to economic prosperity; an estimated 20 to 25 percent of its entire population was supported either directly or indirectly by this single industry.

The Confederate commissioners sent to England and France in May 1861 succeeded in gaining recognition of southern "belligerency," which meant the new government could claim some international rights of a nation at war. The North protested vigorously, but by declaring a blockade of southern ports, it had undermined its official position that the rebellion was merely a domestic insurrection. The main advantage of belligerent status was that it permitted the South to purchase and outfit privateers in neutral ports. As a result, Confederate raiders built and armed in British shipyards—such as the *Alabama,* which single-handedly sank sixty-two vessels—devastated northern shipping to such an extent that insurance costs eventually forced most of the American merchant marine off the high seas for the duration of the war.

In the fall of 1861, the Confederate government dispatched James M. Mason and John Slidell to be its permanent envoys to England and France, respectively, and instructed them to push for full recognition of the Confederacy. They took passage on the British steamer *Trent,* which was stopped and boarded in international waters by a U.S. warship. Mason and Slidell were taken into custody by the Union captain, causing a diplomatic crisis that nearly led to war between England and the United States. Refusing to tolerate this flagrant violation of its maritime rights, Britain threatened war

if the Confederate emissaries were not released. After a few weeks of ferocious posturing by both sides, Lincoln and Secretary of State Seward made the prudent decision to allow Mason and Slidell to proceed to their destinations.

These envoys may as well have stayed at home; they failed in their mission to obtain full recognition of the Confederacy from either England or France. The anticipated cotton shortage was slow to develop, for the bumper crop of 1860 had created a large surplus in British and French warehouses. Recognition did seem likely for a brief period in the fall of 1862. Napoleon III, the emperor of France, personally favored the southern cause, mainly because he was trying to set up a puppet government in Mexico and saw the chance to trade French support of the Confederacy for an acceptance of his regime south of the border. But he was unwilling to risk war with the United States unless the British would cosponsor his plan to offer European mediation of the American conflict and then recognize the Confederacy if—as expected—the North refused to go along.

British opinion, both official and public, was seriously divided on how to respond to the American conflict. In 1861 and 1862, Lord Palmerston, the prime minister, and Lord Russell, the foreign secretary, played a cautious waiting game. Their government was sympathetic to the South but wary of the danger of war with the United States if they acted in support of their preference. Northern diplomats knew how to play on these fears: Secretary of State Seward and Charles Francis Adams, the American minister to Great Britain, could be relied on to threaten war at any hint of British recognition or support of the Confederacy.

In September 1862, the British cabinet debated mediation and recognition as serious possibilities. Lord Russell pressed for a pro-Confederate policy because he was convinced the South was now strong enough to secure its independence. But when word arrived that Lee had failed to win a clear victory at Antietam and was retreating, Lord Palmerston overruled the foreign secretary and decided to maintain a hands-off policy. The British would intervene, his decision suggested, only if the South won decisively on the battlefield.

The cotton famine finally hit in late 1862, causing massive unemployment in the British textile industry. But, contrary to southern hopes, public opinion did not compel the government to abandon its neutrality and use force to break the Union blockade. Historians used to believe that unselfish pro-Union sympathy among the suffering mill workers was a main cause of restraint, but the British working class still lacked the right to vote and thus had relatively little influence over policy.

Influential interest groups that actually benefited from the famine provided the crucial support for continuing a policy of nonintervention. Among these groups were owners of large cotton mills, who had made bonanza profits on their existing stocks and were happy to see weaker competitors go under while they awaited new sources of supply. By early 1863, cotton from Egypt and India put the industry back on the track toward full production. Other obvious beneficiaries of nonintervention were manufacturers of wool and linen textiles, munitions makers who supplied both sides, and shipping interests that profited from the decline of American competition on the world's sea-lanes. Since the British economy as a whole gained more than it lost from neutrality, it is not surprising that there was little effective pressure for a change in policy.

By early 1863, when it was clear that "King Cotton diplomacy" had failed, the Confederacy broke off formal relations with Great Britain. Its hopes for foreign intervention came to nothing because the European powers acted out of self-interest and calculated that the advantages of getting involved were not worth the risk of a long and costly war with the United States. Only a decisive military victory would have gained recognition for southern independence, and if the Confederacy had actually won such a victory, it would not have needed foreign backing.

# FIGHT TO THE FINISH

The last two and a half years of the struggle saw the implementation of more radical war measures. The most dramatic and important of these was the North's effort to follow through on Lincoln's decision to free the slaves and bring the black population into the war on the Union side. The tide of battle turned in the summer of 1863, but the South continued to resist valiantly for two more years, until it was finally overcome by the sheer weight of the North's advantages in manpower and resources.

## The Coming of Emancipation

At the beginning of the war, when the North still hoped for a quick and easy victory, only dedicated abolitionists favored turning the struggle for the Union into a crusade against slavery. In the summer of 1861, Congress voted almost unanimously for a resolution affirming that the war was being fought only to preserve the Union and not to change the domestic institutions of any state. But as it became clear how hard it was going to be to subdue the "rebels," sentiment developed for striking a blow at the South's economic and social system by freeing its slaves. In a tentative move toward emancipation, Congress in July 1862 au-

thorized the government to confiscate the slaves of masters who supported the Confederacy. By this time, the actions of the slaves themselves were influencing policymaking. They were voting for freedom with their feet by deserting their plantations in areas where the Union forces were close enough to offer a haven. In this way, they put pressure on the government to determine their status and, in effect, offered themselves as a source of manpower to the Union on the condition that they be made free.

Although Lincoln favored freedom for blacks as an ultimate goal, he was reluctant to commit his administration to a policy of immediate emancipation. In the fall of 1861 and again in the spring of 1862, he had disallowed the orders of field commanders who sought to free slaves in areas occupied by their forces, thus angering abolitionists and the strongly antislavery Republicans known as Radicals. Lincoln's caution stemmed from a fear of alienating Unionist elements in the border slave states and from his own preference for a gradual, compensated form of emancipation. He hoped that such a plan could be put into effect in loyal slaveholding areas and then extended to the rebellious states as the basis for a voluntary restoration of the Union.

Lincoln was also aware that one of the main obstacles to any program leading to emancipation was the strong racial prejudice of most whites in both the North and the South. Although personally more tolerant than most white Americans, Lincoln was pessimistic about prospects of equality for blacks in the United States. He therefore coupled moderate proposals with a plea for government subsidies to support the voluntary "colonization" of freed blacks outside of the United States, and he actively sought places that would accept them.

But the slaveholding states that remained loyal to the Union refused to endorse Lincoln's gradual plan, and the failure of Union arms in the spring and summer of 1862 increased the public clamor for striking directly at the South's peculiar institution. The Lincoln administration also realized that emancipation would win sympathy for the Union cause in England and France and thus might counter the growing threat that these nations would come to the aid of the Confederacy. In July, Lincoln drafted an emancipation proclamation and read it to his cabinet, but he was persuaded by Secretary of State Seward not to issue it until the North had won a victory and could not be accused of acting out of desperation. Later in the summer, Lincoln responded publicly to critics of his cautious policy, indicating that he would take any action in regard to slavery that would further the Union cause.

Finally, on September 22, 1862, Lincoln issued his preliminary **Emancipation Proclamation.** McClellan's

In this allegorical painting, President Lincoln extends a copy of his Proclamation to the goddess of liberty who is driving her chariot, Emancipation. ✦

success in stopping Lee at Antietam provided the occasion, but the president was also responding to growing political pressures. Most Republican politicians were now firmly committed to an emancipation policy, and many were on the verge of repudiating the administration for its inaction. Had Lincoln failed to act, his party would have been badly split, and he would have been in the minority faction. The proclamation gave the Confederate states one hundred days to give up the struggle without losing their slaves. There was little chance they would do so, but in offering them the chance, Lincoln left the door open for a more conservative and peaceful way of ending slavery than sudden emancipation at the point of a gun. In December, Lincoln proposed to Congress that it approve a series of constitutional amendments providing for gradual, compensated emancipation and subsidized colonization.

Since there was no response from the South and little enthusiasm in Congress for Lincoln's gradual plan, the president went ahead on January 1, 1863, and declared that all slaves in those areas under Confederate control "shall be . . . thenceforward, and forever free." He justified the final proclamation as an act of "military necessity" sanctioned by the war powers of the president, and he authorized the enlistment of freed slaves in the Union army. The language and tone of the document—one historian has described it as having "all the moral grandeur of a bill of lading"—made it clear that blacks were being freed for reasons of state and not out of humanitarian conviction.

Despite its uninspiring origin and limited application—it did not extend to slave states loyal to the Union or to occupied areas and thus did not immedi-

ately free a single slave—the proclamation did commit the Union to the abolition of slavery as a war aim. It also accelerated the breakdown of slavery as a labor system, a process that was already well under way by early 1863. The blacks who had remained in captured areas or deserted their masters to cross Union lines before 1863 had been kept in a kind of way station between slavery and freedom, in accordance with the theory that they were "contraband of war." As word spread among the slaves that emancipation was now official policy, larger numbers of them were inspired to run off and seek the protection of approaching northern armies. One slave who crossed the Union lines summed up their motives: "I wants to be free. I came in from the plantation and don't want to go back; . . . I don't want to be a slave again." Approximately one-quarter of the slave population gained freedom during the war under the terms of the Emancipation Proclamation and thus deprived the South of an important part of its agricultural workforce.

## African Americans and the War

Almost 200,000 African Americans, most of them newly freed slaves, eventually served in the Union armed forces and made a vital contribution to the North's victory. Although they were enrolled in segregated units under white officers, were initially paid less than their white counterparts, and were used disproportionately for garrison duty or heavy labor behind the lines, "blacks in blue" fought heroically in several major battles during the last two years of the war. The assistant secretary of war observed them in action at Millikin's Bend on the Mississippi in June 1863 and reported that "the bravery of blacks in the battle . . . completely revolutionized the sentiment of the army with regard to the employment of Negro troops."

Those freed during the war who did not serve in the military were often conscripted to serve as contract wage laborers on cotton plantations owned or leased by "loyal" white planters within the occupied areas of the Deep South. Abolitionists protested that the coercion used by military authorities to get blacks back into the cotton fields amounted to slavery in a

This 1890 lithograph by Kurz and Allison commemorates the 54th Massachusetts Colored Regiment charging Fort Wagner, South Carolina, in July 1863. The 54th was the first African American unit recruited during the war. Charles and Lewis Douglass, sons of Frederick Douglass, served with this regiment. ❖

new form, but those in power argued that the necessities of war and the northern economy required such "temporary" arrangements. To some extent, regimentation of the freedmen within the South was a way of assuring racially prejudiced Northerners, especially in the Midwest, that emancipation would not result in a massive migration of black refugees to their region of the country.

The heroic performance of African American troops and the easing of northern fears of being swamped by black migrants led to a deepening commitment to emancipation as a permanent and comprehensive policy. Realizing that his proclamation had a shaky constitutional foundation and might apply only to slaves actually freed while the war was going on, Lincoln sought to organize and recognize loyal state governments in southern areas under Union control on condition that they abolish slavery in their constitutions. He also encouraged local campaigns to emancipate the slaves in the border states and saw these programs triumph in Maryland and Missouri in 1864.

Finally, Lincoln pressed for an amendment to the federal constitution outlawing involuntary servitude. After supporting its inclusion as a central plank in the Republican platform of 1864, Lincoln used all his influence to win congressional approval for the new Thirteenth Amendment. On January 31, 1865, the House approved the amendment by a narrow margin. There was an explosion of joy on the floor and in the galleries, and then the House voted to adjourn for the

rest of the day "in honor of this immortal and sublime event." The cause of freedom for blacks and the cause of the Union had at last become one and the same. Lincoln, despite his earlier hesitations and misgivings, had earned the right to go down in history as the Great Emancipator.

## The Tide Turns

By early 1863, the Confederate economy was in shambles and its diplomacy had collapsed. The social order of the South was also showing signs of severe strain. Masters were losing control of their slaves, and nonslaveholding whites were becoming disillusioned with the hardships of a war that some of them described as "a rich man's war and a poor man's fight." As slaves fled from the plantations, increasing numbers of lower-class whites deserted the army or refused to be drafted in the first place. Whole counties in the southern backcountry became "deserter havens," which Confederate officials could enter only at the risk of their lives. Appalachian mountaineers, who had remained loyal to the Union, resisted the Confederacy more directly by enlisting in the Union army or joining guerrilla units operating behind southern lines.

Yet the North was slow to capitalize on the South's internal weaknesses because it had its own serious morale problems. The long series of defeats on the eastern front had engendered war weariness, and the new policies that "military necessity" forced the government to adopt encountered fierce opposition.

Although popular with Republicans, emancipation was viewed by most Democrats as a betrayal of northern war aims. Racism was a main ingredient in their opposition to freeing blacks. According to one Democratic senator, "We mean that the United States . . . shall be the white man's home . . . and the nigger shall never be his equal." Riding a backlash against the preliminary proclamation, Democrats made significant gains in the congressional elections of 1862, especially in the Midwest, where they also captured several state legislatures.

The Enrollment Act of March 1863, which provided for outright conscription of white males but permitted men of wealth to hire substitutes or pay a fee to avoid military service, provoked a violent response from those unable to buy their way out of service and unwilling to "fight for the niggers." A series of antidraft riots broke out, culminating in one of the bloodiest domestic disorders in American history—the New York Riot of July 1863. The New York mob, composed mainly of Irish-American laborers, burned the draft offices, the homes of leading Republicans, and an orphanage for black children. They also lynched more than a dozen defenseless blacks who fell into their hands. At least 120 people died before federal troops restored order. Besides racial prejudice, the draft riots also reflected working-class anger at the wartime privileges and prosperity of the middle and upper classes; they showed how divided the North really was on the administration's conduct of the war.

To fight dissension and "disloyalty," the government used its martial law authority to arrest a few alleged ringleaders, including one prominent Democratic congressman—Clement Vallandigham of Ohio. Private patriotic organizations also issued a barrage of propaganda aimed at what they believed was a vast secret conspiracy to undermine the northern war effort. Historians disagree about the real extent of covert and illegal antiwar activity. No vast conspiracy existed, but militant advocates of "peace at any price"—popularly known as **Copperheads**—were certainly active in some areas, especially among the immigrant working classes of large cities and in southern Ohio, Indiana, and Illinois. Many Copperheads presented themselves as Jeffersonian believers in limited government who feared a war-induced growth of federal power. But it was opposition to emancipation on racial grounds rather than anxiety about big government that gave the movement most of its emotional force.

The only effective way to overcome the disillusionment that fed the peace movement was to start winning battles and thus convince the northern public that victory was assured. Before this could happen, the North suffered one more humiliating defeat on the eastern

THE RIOTS IN NEW YORK: THE MOB LYNCHING A NEGRO IN CLARKSON-STREET.—SEE PAGE 142.

*An 1863 draft call in New York provoked violence against African Americans, viewed by the rioters as the cause of an unnecessary war, and rage against the rich men who had been able to buy exemptions from the draft. This 1863 illustration from* Harper's Weekly *depicts a mob lynching a black man on Clarkson Street in New York City.* ❖

front. In early May 1863, Union forces under General Joseph Hooker were routed at Chancellorsville, Virginia, by a Confederate army less than half its size. Once again, Robert E. Lee demonstrated his superior generalship, this time by dividing his forces and sending Stonewall Jackson to make a devastating surprise attack on the Union right. The Confederacy prevailed, but it did suffer one major loss: Jackson himself died as a result of wounds he received in the battle.

In the West, however, a major Union triumph was taking shape. For more than a year, General Ulysses S. Grant had been trying to put his forces in position to capture Vicksburg, Mississippi, the almost inaccessible Confederate bastion that stood between the North and control of the Mississippi River. Finally, in late March 1863, he crossed to the west bank north of the city and moved his forces to a point south of it, where he joined up with naval forces that had run the Confederate batteries mounted on Vicksburg's high bluffs. In one of the boldest campaigns of the war, Grant crossed the river, deliberately cutting himself off from his sources of supply, and marched into the interior of Mississippi. Living off the land and out of communication with an anxious and perplexed Lincoln, his troops won a series of victories over two separate Confederate armies and advanced on Vicksburg from the east. After unsuccessfully assaulting the city's defenses, Grant settled down for a siege on May 22.

The Confederate government considered and rejected proposals to mount a major offensive into Tennessee and Kentucky in the hope of drawing Grant away from Vicksburg. Instead, President Davis approved Robert E. Lee's plan for an all-out invasion of the Northeast. Although this option provided no hope for relieving Vicksburg, it might lead to a dramatic victory that would more than compensate for the probable loss of the Mississippi stronghold. Lee's army crossed the Potomac in June and kept going until it reached Gettysburg, Pennsylvania. There Lee confronted a Union army that had taken up strong defensive positions on Cemetery Ridge and Culp's Hill. This was one of the few occasions in the war when the North could capitalize on the tactical advantage of choosing its ground and then defending it against an enemy whose supply lines were extended.

On July 2, a series of Confederate attacks failed to dislodge General George Meade's troops from the high ground they occupied. The following day, Lee faced the choice of retreating to protect his lines of communication or launching a final, desperate assault. With more boldness than wisdom, he chose to make a direct attack on the strongest part of the Union line. The resulting charge on Cemetery Ridge was disastrous; advancing Confederate soldiers dropped like flies under the barrage of Union artillery and rifle fire. Only a few made it to the top of the ridge, and they were killed or captured.

Retreat was now inevitable, and Lee withdrew his battered troops to the Potomac, only to find that the river was at flood stage and could not be crossed for several days. But Meade failed to follow up his victory with a vigorous pursuit, and Lee was allowed to escape a predicament that could have resulted in his annihilation. Vicksburg fell to Grant on July 4, the same day Lee began his withdrawal, and Northerners rejoiced at the simultaneous Independence Day victories that turned the tide of the war. The Union had secured control of the Mississippi and had at last won a major battle in the East. But Lincoln's joy turned to frustration when he learned his generals had missed the chance to capture Lee's army and bring a quick end to the war.

## Last Stages of the Conflict

Later in 1863, the North finally gained control of the middle South, an area where indecisive fighting had been going on since the beginning of the conflict. The main Union target was Chattanooga, "the gateway to the Southeast." In September, troops under General William Rosecrans managed to maneuver the Confederates out of the city, only to be outfought and driven back at Chickamauga. The Union army then retreated into Chattanooga, where it was surrounded and besieged by southern forces. After Grant arrived from Vicksburg to take command, the encirclement was broken by daring assaults on the Confederate positions on Lookout Mountain and Missionary Ridge. As a result of its success in the battle of Chattanooga, the North was poised for an invasion of Georgia.

Grant's victories in the West earned him promotion to general in chief of all the Union armies. After assuming that position in March 1864, he ordered a multipronged offensive to finish off the Confederacy. The offensive's main movements were a march on Richmond under Grant's personal command and a thrust by the western armies, now led by General William Tecumseh Sherman, to Atlanta and the heart of Georgia.

In May and early June, Grant and Lee fought a series of bloody battles in northern Virginia that tended to follow a set pattern. Lee would take up an entrenched position in the path of the invading force, and Grant would attack it, sustaining heavy losses but also inflicting casualties the shrinking Confederate army could ill afford. When his direct assault had failed, Grant would move to his left, hoping in vain to maneuver Lee into a less defensible position. In the battles of the Wilderness, Spotsylvania, and Cold Harbor, the Union lost about sixty thousand men—

**CIVIL WAR, 1863–1865**    *In the western theater of war, Grant's victories at Port Gibson, Jackson, and Champion's Hill cleared the way for his siege of Vicksburg. In the east, after the hard-won Union victory at Gettysburg, the South never again invaded the North. In 1864 and 1865, Union armies gradually closed in on Lee's Confederate forces in Virginia. Leaving Atlanta in flames, Sherman marched to the Georgia coast, took Savannah, then moved his troops north through the Carolinas. Grant's army, though suffering enormous losses, moved on toward Richmond, marching into the Confederate capital on April 3, 1865, and forcing surrender.* ❖

*Bold and decisive, Confederate General Robert E. Lee (left) often faced an enemy army that greatly outnumbered his own troops. Union General Ulysses S. Grant (right) demonstrated a relentless determination that eventually triumphed. ♦*

more than twice the number of Confederate casualties—without defeating Lee or opening the road to Richmond. After losing twelve thousand men in a single day at Cold Harbor, Grant decided to change his tactics and moved his army to the south of Richmond. There he drew up before Petersburg, a rail center that linked Richmond to the rest of the Confederacy; after failing to take it by assault, he settled down for a siege.

The siege of Petersburg was a long, drawn-out affair, and the resulting stalemate in the East caused northern morale to plummet during the summer of 1864. Lincoln was facing reelection, and his failure to end the war dimmed his prospects. Although nominated with ease in June—with Andrew Johnson, a proadministration Democrat from Tennessee, as his running mate—Lincoln confronted growing opposition within his own party, especially from Radicals who disagreed with his apparently lenient approach to the future restoration of seceded states to the Union. After Lincoln vetoed a Radical-supported congressional reconstruction plan in July, some Radicals began to call for a new convention to nominate another candidate.

The Democrats seemed to be in a good position to capitalize on Republican divisions and make a strong bid for the White House. Their platform appealed to war weariness by calling for a cease-fire followed by negotiations to reestablish the Union. The party's nominee, General George McClellan, announced he would not be bound by the peace plank and would pursue the war. But he promised to end the conflict sooner than Lincoln could because he would not insist on emancipation as a condition for reconstruction. By late summer, Lincoln confessed privately that he would probably be defeated.

But northern military successes changed the political outlook. Sherman's invasion of Georgia went well; between May and September, he employed a series of skillful flanking movements to force the Confederates to retreat to the outskirts of Atlanta. On September 2, the city fell, and northern forces occupied the hub of the Deep South. The news unified the Republican party behind Lincoln and improved his chances for defeating McClellan in November. The election itself was almost an anticlimax: Lincoln won 212 of a possible 233 electoral votes and 55 percent of the popular vote. The Republican cause of "liberty and Union" was secure.

The concluding military operations revealed the futility of further southern resistance. Cutting himself off from his supply lines and living off the land, Sherman marched unopposed through Georgia to the sea, destroying almost everything of possible military or economic value in a corridor three hundred miles long and sixty miles wide. The Confederate army that had opposed him at Atlanta, now under the command of General John B. Hood, moved northward into

## THE ELECTION OF 1864

| Candidate | Party | Popular Vote | Electoral Vote* |
|-----------|-------|-------------|-----------------|
| Lincoln | Republican | 2,218,388 | 212 |
| McClellan | Democratic | 1,812,807 | 21 |

*Out of a total of 233 electoral votes. The eleven secessionist states—Alabama, Arkansas, Florida, Georgia, Louisiana, Mississippi, North Carolina, South Carolina, Tennessee, Texas, and Virginia—did not vote.

Tennessee, where it was defeated and almost destroyed by Union forces under General George Thomas at Nashville in mid-December. Sherman captured Savannah on December 22 and presented the city to Lincoln as a Christmas present. He then turned north and carried his scorched-earth policy into South Carolina with the aim of continuing through North Carolina and eventually joining up with Grant at Petersburg near Richmond.

While Sherman was bringing the war to the Carolinas, Grant finally ended the stalemate at Petersburg. When Lee's starving and exhausted army tried to break through the Union lines, Grant renewed his attack and forced the Confederates to abandon Petersburg and Richmond on April 2, 1865. He then pursued them westward for a hundred miles, placing his forces in position to cut off their line of retreat to the south. Recognizing the hopelessness of further resistance, Lee surrendered his army at Appomattox Courthouse on April 9.

But the joy of the victorious North turned to sorrow and anger when John Wilkes Booth, a pro-Confederate actor, assassinated Abraham Lincoln as the president watched a play at Ford's Theater in Washington on April 14. Although Booth had a few accomplices—one of whom attempted to murder Secretary of State Seward—popular theories that the assassination was the result of a vast conspiracy involving Confederate leaders or (according to another version) Radical Republicans have never been substantiated.

The man who had spoken of the need to sacrifice for the Union cause at Gettysburg had himself given "the last full measure of devotion" to the cause of "government of the people, by the people, for the people." Four days after Lincoln's death, the only remaining Confederate force of any significance (the troops under Joseph E. Johnston, who had been opposing Sherman in North Carolina) laid down its arms. The Union was saved.

## Effects of the War

The nation that emerged from four years of total war was not the same America that had split apart in 1861. The 618,000 young men who were in their graves, victims of enemy fire or the diseases that spread rapidly in military encampments in this era before modern medicine and sanitation, would otherwise have married, raised families, and contributed their talents to building up the country. The widows and sweethearts they left behind temporarily increased the proportion of unmarried women in the population, and some members of this generation of involuntary "spinsters" sought new opportunities for making a living or serving the community that went beyond the purely domestic roles previously prescribed for women.

During the war, northern women pushed the boundaries of their traditional roles by participating on the home front as fund-raisers and in the rear lines as army nurses and members of the **Sanitary Commission.** The Sanitary Commission promoted health in the northern army's camps through attention to cleanliness, nutrition, and medical care. However,

**CASUALTIES OF WAR**

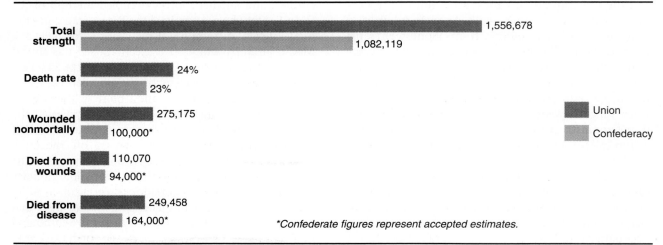

| | Union | Confederacy |
|---|---|---|
| Total strength | 1,556,678 | 1,082,119 |
| Death rate | 24% | 23% |
| Wounded nonmortally | 275,175 | 100,000* |
| Died from wounds | 110,070 | 94,000* |
| Died from disease | 249,458 | 164,000* |

*Confederate figures represent accepted estimates.

women were not limited to playing roles as nurses and "angels of mercy." Throughout the war, they also filled key positions in the administration and organization of patriotic organizations. Women in the North simultaneously utilized their traditional position as nurturers to participate in the war effort while they advanced new ideas about their role in society. The large number who had served as nurses or volunteer workers during the war were especially responsive to calls for broadening "the woman's sphere." Some of the northern women who were prominent in wartime service organizations—such as Louise Lee Schuyler, Josephine Shaw Lowell, and Mary Livermore—became leaders of postwar philanthropic and reform movements. The war did not destroy the barriers to sexual equality that had long existed in American society, but the efforts of women during the Civil War broadened beliefs about what women could accomplish outside of the home.

The effect on white women in the Confederacy was different from the effect of the war on women in the victorious North. Southern women had always been intimately involved in the administration of the farms and plantations of the South, but the coming of the war forced them to shoulder even greater burdens at home. This was true for wealthy plantation mistresses, who had to take over the administration and maintenance of huge plantations without the benefit of extensive training or the assistance of male relatives. The wives of small farmers found it hard to survive at all, especially at harvest time when they often had to do all the work themselves. The loss of fathers and brothers, the constant advance of Union troops, and the difficulty of controlling a slave labor force destroyed many southern women's allegiance to the Confederate cause. At the close of the conflict, southern women faced the challenge of rebuilding a society that had been permanently transformed by the experience of war. As in the North, the Civil War changed the situation of women in society. The devastation of the southern economy forced many women to play a more conspicuous public and economic role. These women responded by forming associations to assist returning soldiers, entering the workforce as educators, and establishing numerous benevolent and reform societies or temperance organizations. Although these changes created a more visible presence of southern women in public, the South remained more conservative in its views about women's "proper place" than did the North.

At enormous human and economic cost, the nation had emancipated four million African Americans from slavery, but it had not yet resolved that they would be equal citizens. At the time of Lincoln's assassination, most northern states still denied blacks equality under the law and the right to vote. Whether the North would extend more rights to southern

## CHRONOLOGY

| 1860 | South Carolina secedes from the Union (December) |
|---|---|
| 1861 | Rest of Deep South secedes: Confederacy is founded (January–February) ❖ Fort Sumter is fired upon and surrenders to Confederate forces (April) ❖ Upper South secedes (April–May) ❖ South wins first battle of Bull Run (July) |
| 1862 | Grant captures forts Henry and Donelson (February) ❖ Farragut captures New Orleans for the Union (April) ❖ McClellan leads unsuccessful campaign on the peninsula southeast of Richmond (March–July) ❖ South wins second battle of Bull Run (August) ❖ McClellan stops Lee at battle of Antietam (September) ❖ Lincoln issues preliminary Emancipation Proclamation (September) ❖ Lee defeats Union army at Fredericksburg (December) |
| 1863 | Lincoln issues final Emancipation Proclamation (January) ❖ Lee is victorious at Chancellorsville (May) ❖ North gains major victories at Gettysburg and Vicksburg (July) ❖ Grant defeats Confederate forces at Chattanooga (November) |
| 1864 | Grant and Lee battle in northern Virginia (May–June) ❖ Atlanta falls to Sherman (September) ❖ Lincoln is reelected president, defeating McClellan (November) ❖ Sherman marches through Georgia (November–December) |
| 1865 | Congress passes Thirteenth Amendment abolishing slavery (January) ❖ Grant captures Petersburg and Richmond; Lee surrenders at Appomattox (April) ❖ Lincoln assassinated by John Wilkes Booth (April) ❖ Remaining Confederate forces surrender (April–May) |

freedmen than it had granted to "free Negroes" was an open question.

The impact of the war on white working people was also unclear. Those in the industrializing parts of the North had suffered and lost ground economically because prices had risen much faster than wages during the conflict. But Republican rhetoric stressing "equal opportunity" and the "dignity of labor" raised hopes that the crusade against slavery could be broadened into a movement to improve the lot of working people in general. Foreign-born workers had additional reason to be optimistic; the fact that so many

*During the war, many northern women replaced skilled male workers in the manufacturing force. At left, women are shown filling cartridges in the U.S. Arsenal at Watertown, New York. In the South, women contributed to the war effort by producing materials such as bandages and performing services such as mending military clothing. They also worked to keep plantations and farms running, a task made even more difficult by the advance of Union troops and the proximity of battlefronts. This 1862 photograph by Timothy H. O'Sullivan shows a family on their property near Cedar Mountain, Virginia, in front of the house where Confederate General Charles S. Winder died of wounds suffered in a major battle nearby. ❖*

immigrants had fought and died for the Union cause had—for the moment—weakened nativist sentiment and encouraged ethnic tolerance.

What the war definitely decided was that the federal government was supreme over the states and had a broad grant of constitutional authority to act on matters affecting "the general welfare." The southern principle of state sovereignty and strict construction died at Appomattox, and the United States was on its way to becoming a true nation-state with an effective central government. But it retained a federal structure; although states could no longer claim the right to secede or nullify federal law, they still had primary responsibility for most functions of government. Everyone agreed that the Constitution placed limits on what the national government could do, and questions would continue to arise about where federal authority ended and states' rights began.

A broadened definition of federal powers had its greatest impact in the realm of economic policy. During the war, the Republican-dominated Congresses passed a rash of legislation designed to give stimulus and direction to the nation's economic development. Taking advantage of the absence of southern opposition, Republicans rejected the pre–Civil War tradition of virtual laissez-faire and enacted a Whiggish program of active support for business and agriculture. In 1862, Congress passed a high protective tariff, approved a homestead act intended to encourage settlement of the West by providing free land to settlers, granted huge tracts of public land to railroad companies to support the building of a transcontinental railroad, and gave the states land for the establishment of agricultural colleges. The following year, Congress set up a national banking system that required member banks to keep adequate reserves and invest one-third of their capital in government securities. The notes the national banks issued became the country's first standardized and reliable circulating currency.

These wartime achievements added up to a decisive shift in the relationship between the federal government and private enterprise. The Republicans took a limited government that did little more than seek to protect the marketplace from the threat of monopoly and changed it into an activist state that promoted and subsidized the efforts of the economically ambitious and industrious.

## CONCLUSION: AN ORGANIZATIONAL REVOLUTION

The most pervasive effect of the war on northern society was to encourage an "organizational revolution." Aided by government policies, venturesome businessmen took advantage of the new national market created by military procurement to build larger firms that could operate across state lines; some of the huge corporate enterprises of the post-war era began to take shape. Philanthropists also developed more effective national associations; the most notable of these were the Sanitary and Christian Commissions that ministered to the physical and spiritual needs of the troops. Efforts to care for the wounded influenced the development of the modern hospital and the rise of nursing as a female profession. Both the men who served in the army and those men and women who supported them on the home front or behind the lines became accustomed to working in large, bureaucratic organizations of a kind that had scarcely existed before the war.

Ralph Waldo Emerson, the era's most prominent man of letters, revealed in his Civil War writings that the conflict encouraged a dramatic shift in American thought about the relationship between the individual and society. Before the war, Emerson had generally championed "the transcendent individual," who stood apart from institutions and organizations and sought fulfillment in an inner world of imagination and cosmic intuition. During the conflict, he began to exalt the claims of organization, government, and "civilization" over the endeavors of "the private man" to find fulfillment through "self-culture." He even extolled

military discipline and became an official visitor to West Point. In 1837, he had said of young men who aspired to political office: "Wake them up and they shall quit the false good and leap to the true, and leave governments to clerks and desks." Now he affirmed almost the opposite: "Government must not be a parish clerk, a justice of the peace. It has, of necessity, in any crisis of the state, the absolute powers of a dictator." In purging his thoughts of extreme individualism and hailing the need to accept social discipline and participate in organized, cooperative activity, Emerson epitomized the way the war affected American thought and patterns of behavior.

The North won the war mainly because it had shown a greater capacity than the South to organize, innovate, and "modernize." Its victory meant the nation as a whole would now be ready to embrace the conception of progress that the North had affirmed in its war effort—not only its advances in science and technology, but also its success in bringing together and managing large numbers of men and women for economic and social goals. The Civil War was thus a catalyst for the great transformation of American society from an individualistic society of small producers into the more highly organized and "incorporated" America of the late nineteenth century.

## RECOMMENDED READING

The best one-volume history of the Civil War is James M. McPherson, *Battle Cry of Freedom: The Civil War Era* (1988). Other valuable surveys of the war and its aftermath are J. G. Randall and David Herbert Donald, *The Civil War and Reconstruction*, 2nd ed. (1969), and James M. McPherson, *Ordeal by Fire: The Civil War and Reconstruction* (1981). An excellent shorter account is David Herbert Donald, *Liberty and Union* (1978). The Confederate experience is covered in Clement Eaton, *A History of the Southern Confederacy* (1954), and Emory M. Thomas, *The Confederate Nation, 1861–1865* (1979). Eaton stresses internal problems and weaknesses; Thomas highlights achievements under adversity. Gary W. Gallagher, *The Confederate War* (1997) argues, contrary to a common view, that the South lost the war simply because it was overpowered and not because of low morale or lack of a will to win. On the North's war effort, see Phillip Paludan, *A People's Contest: The Union and the Civil War, 1861–1865* (1988). The best one-volume introduction to the military side of the conflict is still Bruce Catton, *This Hallowed Ground: The Story of the Union Side of the Civil War* (1956).

Lincoln's career and wartime leadership are well treated in David Herbert Donald, *Lincoln* (1995). Another competent biography is Stephen B. Oates, *With Malice Toward None: The Life of Abraham Lincoln* (1977). A penetrating analysis of events immediately preceding the fighting is

Kenneth M. Stampp, *And the War Came: The North and the Sectional Crisis* (1950). John Hope Franklin, *The Emancipation Proclamation* (1963), is a good short account of the North's decision to free the slaves. An incisive account of the transition from slavery to freedom is Barbara Jeanne Fields, *Slavery and Freedom on the Middle Ground: Maryland in the Nineteenth Century* (1985). The circumstances and activities of southern women during the war are covered in Drew Faust, *Mothers of Invention: Women of the Slaveholding States in the American Civil War* (1996) and in Laura F. Edwards, *Scarlett Doesn't Live Here Anymore: Southern Women in the Civil War Era* (2002). The experiences of northern women are described in Elizabeth D. Leonard, *Yankee Women: Gender Battles in the Civil War* (1994). Five leading historians offer conflicting interpretations in their attempts to explain the South's defeat in *Why the North Won the Civil War*, edited by David Donald (1960). A brilliant study of the writings of those who experienced the war is Edmund Wilson, *Patriotic Gore: Studies in the Literature of the American Civil War* (1962). On the intellectual impact of the war, see George M. Fredrickson, *The Inner Civil War: Northern Intellectuals and the Crisis of the Union*, 2nd ed. (1993).

**For a list of additional titles related to this chapter's topics, please see** http://www.ablongman.com/divine.

# SUGGESTED WEB SITES

### The American Civil War Homepage

http://sunsite.utk.edu/civil-war/warweb.html

This site has a great collection of hypertext links to the most useful identified electronic files about the American Civil War.

### The Valley of the Shadow: Living the Civil War in Pennsylvania and Virginia

http://jefferson.village.virginia.edu/vshadow/vshadow.html

This project tells the histories of two communities on either side of the Mason-Dixon line during the Civil War. It includes narrative and an electronic archive of sources.

### Civil War @ Charleston

http://www.awod.com/gallery/probono/cwchas/cwlayout.html

This site covers the history of the Civil War in and around Charleston, South Carolina.

### Abraham Lincoln Association

http://www.alincolnassoc.com/

This site allows the search of digital versions of Lincoln's papers.

### Crisis at Fort Sumter

http://www.tulane.edu/~latner/CrisisMain.html

This well-crafted use of hypermedia with assignments or problems explains and explores the events in and around the start of the Civil War.

### U.S. Civil War Center

http://www.cwc.lsu.edu/

This is a site whose mission is to "locate, index, and/or make available all appropriate private and public data regarding the Civil War and to promote the study of the Civil War from the perspectives of all professions, occupations, and academic disciplines."

### The Papers of Jefferson Davis Home Page

http://jeffersondavis.rice.edu

This site tells about the collection of Jefferson Davis papers and includes a chronology of his life, a family genealogy, some key Davis documents on-line, and a collection of related links.

### History of African Americans in the Civil War

http://www.itd.nps.gov/cwss/history/aa_history.htm

This National Park Service site explores the history of the United States Colored Troops.

### Civil War Women

http://scriptorium.lib.duke.edu/collections/civil-war-women.html

This site includes original documents, links, and biographical information about several women and their lives during the Civil War.

### Assassination of President Abraham Lincoln

http://memory.loc.gov/ammem/alhtml/alrintr.html

Part of the American Memory series with introduction, timeline, and gallery.

### Selected Civil War Photographs

http://memory.loc.gov/ammem/cwphtml/cwphome.html

Library of Congress site with more than one thousand photographs, many from Matthew Brady.

### A Timeline of the Civil War

http://www.historyplace.com/civilwar/index.html

A complete timeline of the Civil War, well illustrated with photographs.

### National Civil War Association

http://www.ncwa.org/info.html

One of the many Civil War reenactment organizations in the United States.

## Chapter 16

The First Vote, *drawn by A. H. Ward for Harper's Weekly, November 16, 1867.* ❖

# The Agony of Reconstruction

## *Robert Smalls and Black Politicians During Reconstruction*

During the Reconstruction period immediately following the Civil War, African Americans struggled to become equal citizens of a democratic republic. They produced a number of remarkable leaders who showed that blacks were as capable as other Americans of voting, holding office, and legislating for a complex and rapidly changing society. Among these leaders was Robert Smalls of South Carolina. Although virtually forgotten by the time of his death in 1915, Smalls was perhaps the most famous and widely respected southern black leader of the Civil War and Reconstruction era. His career reveals some of the main features of the African American experience during that crucial period.

Born a slave in 1839, Smalls had a white father whose identity has never been clearly established. But his white ancestry apparently gained him some advantages, and as a young man he was allowed to live and work independently, hiring his own time from a master who may have been his half brother. Smalls worked as a sailor and trained himself to be a pilot in Charleston Harbor.

When the Union navy blockaded Charleston in 1862, Smalls, who was then working on a Confederate steamship called the *Planter*, saw a chance to win his freedom in a particularly dramatic way. At three o'clock in the morning on May 13, 1862, when the white officers of the *Planter* were ashore, he took command of the vessel and its slave crew, sailed it out of the heavily fortified harbor, and surrendered it to the Union navy. Smalls immediately became a hero to those antislavery Northerners who were seeking evidence that the slaves were willing and able to serve the Union. The *Planter* was turned into a Union army transport, and Smalls was made its captain after being commissioned as an officer. During the remainder of the war, he rendered conspicuous and gallant service as captain and pilot of Union vessels off the coast of South Carolina.

Like a number of other African Americans who had fought valiantly for the Union, Smalls went on to a distinguished political career during Reconstruction, serving in the South Carolina constitutional convention, in the state legislature, and for several terms in the U.S. Congress. He was also a shrewd businessman and became the owner of extensive properties in Beaufort, South Carolina, and its vicinity. (His first purchase was the house of his former master, where he had spent his early years as a slave.) As the leading citizen of Beaufort during Reconstruction and for some years thereafter, he acted like many successful white Americans, combining the acquisition of wealth with the exercise of political power.

The electoral organization Smalls established resembled in some ways the well-oiled "machines" being established in northern towns and cities. It was so effective that he was able to control local government and get himself elected to Congress even after the election of 1876 had placed the state under the control of white conservatives bent on depriving blacks of political power. Organized mob violence defeated him in 1878, but he bounced back to win by decision of Congress a contested congressional election in 1880. He did not leave the House of Representatives for good until 1886, when he lost another contested election that had to be decided by Congress. It revealed the

*With the help of several black crewmen, Robert Smalls—then twenty-three years old—commandeered the* Planter, *a Confederate steamship used to transport guns and ammunition, and surrendered it to the Union vessel, U.S.S.* Onward. *Smalls provided distinguished service to the Union during the Civil War and after the war went on to become a successful politician and businessman.* ❖

changing mood of the country that his white challenger was seated despite evidence of violence and intimidation against black voters.

In their efforts to defeat him, Smalls's white opponents frequently charged that he had a hand in the corruption that was allegedly rampant in South Carolina during Reconstruction. But careful historical investigation shows that he was, by the standards of the time, an honest and responsible public servant. In the South Carolina convention of 1868 and later in the state legislature, he was a conspicuous champion of free and compulsory public education. In Congress, he fought for the enactment and enforcement of federal civil rights laws. Not especially radical on social questions, he sometimes bent over backward to accommodate what he regarded as the legitimate interests and

sensibilities of South Carolina whites. Like other middle-class black political leaders in Reconstruction-era South Carolina, he can perhaps be faulted in hindsight for not doing more to help poor blacks gain access to land of their own. But in 1875, he sponsored congressional legislation that opened for purchase at low prices the land in his own district that had been confiscated by the federal government during the war. As a result, blacks were able to buy most of it, and they soon owned three-fourths of the land in Beaufort and its vicinity.

Robert Smalls spent the later years of his life as U.S. collector of customs for the port of Beaufort, a beneficiary of the patronage that the Republican party continued to provide for a few loyal southern blacks. But the loss of real political clout for Smalls and men like him was one of the tragic consequences of the fall of Reconstruction.

FOR A BRIEF PERIOD OF YEARS, black politicians such as Robert Smalls exercised more power in the South than they would for another century. A series of political developments on the national and regional stage made Reconstruction "an unfinished revolution," promising but not delivering true equality for newly freed African Americans. National party politics, shifting priorities among Northern Republicans, white Southerners' commitment to white supremacy, backed by legal restrictions, as well as massive extra-legal violence against blacks, all combined to stifle the promise of Reconstruction.

Yet the Reconstruction Era also saw major transformations in American society in the wake of the Civil War—new ways of organizing labor and family life, new institutions within and outside of the government, and new ideologies regarding the role of institutions and government in social and economic life. Many of the changes begun during Reconstruction laid the groundwork for later revolutions in American life.

## THE PRESIDENT VERSUS CONGRESS

The problem of how to reconstruct the Union in the wake of the South's military defeat was one of the most difficult and perplexing challenges ever faced by American policymakers. The Constitution provided no firm guidelines, for the framers had not anticipated a division of the country into warring sections. After emancipation became a northern war aim, the problem was compounded by a new issue: How far should the federal government go to secure freedom and civil rights for four million former slaves?

The debate that evolved led to a major political crisis. Advocates of a minimal Reconstruction policy favored quick restoration of the Union with no protection for the freed slaves beyond the prohibition of slavery. Proponents of a more radical policy wanted readmission of the southern states to be dependent on guarantees that "loyal" men would displace the Confederate elite in positions of power and that blacks would acquire basic rights of American citizenship. The White House favored the minimal approach, whereas Congress came to endorse the more radical and thoroughgoing form of Reconstruction. The resulting struggle between Congress and the chief executive was the most serious clash between two branches of government in the nation's history.

## Wartime Reconstruction

Tension between the president and Congress over how to reconstruct the Union began during the war. Occupied mainly with achieving victory, Lincoln never set forth a final and comprehensive plan for bringing rebellious states back into the fold. But he did take initiatives that indicated he favored a lenient and conciliatory policy toward Southerners who would give up the struggle and repudiate slavery. In December 1863, he issued a Proclamation of Amnesty and Reconstruction, which offered a full pardon to all Southerners (with the exception of certain classes of Confederate leaders) who would take an oath of allegiance to the Union and acknowledge the legality of emancipation. This **Ten Percent Plan** provided that once 10 percent or more of the voting population of any occupied state had taken the oath, they were authorized to set up a loyal government. By 1864, Louisiana and Arkansas, states that were wholly or partially occupied by Union troops, had established Unionist governments. Lincoln's policy was meant to shorten the war. First, he hoped to weaken the southern cause by making it easy for disillusioned or lukewarm Confederates to switch sides. Second, he hoped to further his emancipation policy by insisting that the new governments abolish slavery

Congress was unhappy with the president's Reconstruction experiments and in 1864 refused to seat the Unionists elected to the House and Senate from Louisiana and Arkansas. A minority of congressional Republicans—the strongly antislavery **Radical Republicans**—favored protection for black rights (especially black male suffrage) as a precondition for the readmission of southern states. But a larger group of Congressional moderates opposed Lincoln's plan, not on the basis of black rights but because they did not trust the repentant Confederates who would play a major role in the new governments. They feared that the old ruling class would return to power and cheat the North of the full fruits of its impending victory.

Congress also believed the president was exceeding his authority by using executive powers to restore the Union. Lincoln operated on the theory that secession, being illegal, did not place the Confederate states outside the Union in a constitutional sense. Since individuals and not states had defied federal authority, the president could use his pardoning power to certify a loyal electorate, which could then function as the legitimate state government.

The dominant view in Congress, on the other hand, was that the southern states had forfeited their place in the Union and that it was up to Congress to decide when and how they would be readmitted. The most popular justification for congressional responsibility was based on the clause of the Constitution providing that "the United States shall guarantee to every State in this Union a Republican Form of Government." By seceding, Radicals argued, the Confederate states had ceased to be republican, and Congress had to set the conditions to be met before they could be readmitted.

After refusing to recognize Lincoln's 10 percent governments, Congress passed a Reconstruction bill of its own in July 1864. Known as the **Wade-Davis Bill,** this legislation required that 50 percent of the voters take an oath of future loyalty before the restoration process could begin. Once this had occurred, those who could swear they had never willingly supported the Confederacy could vote in an election for delegates to a constitutional convention. The bill in its final form did not require black suffrage, but it did give federal courts the power to enforce emancipation. Faced with this attempt to nullify his own program, Lincoln exercised a pocket veto by refusing to sign the bill before Congress adjourned. He justified his action by announcing that he did not want to be committed to any single Reconstruction plan. The sponsors of the bill responded with an angry manifesto, and Lincoln's relations with Congress reached their low.

Congress and the president remained stalemated on the Reconstruction issue for the rest of the war. During his last months in office, however, Lincoln showed some willingness to compromise. He persisted in his efforts to obtain full recognition for the governments he had nurtured in Louisiana and Arkansas but seemed receptive to the setting of other conditions—perhaps including black suffrage—for readmission of those states where wartime conditions had prevented execution of his plan. However, he died without clarifying his intentions, leaving historians to speculate whether his quarrel with Congress would have worsened or been resolved. Given Lincoln's past record of political flexibility, the best bet is that he would have come to terms with the majority of his party.

## Andrew Johnson at the Helm

Andrew Johnson, the man suddenly made president by an assassin's bullet, attempted to put the Union back together on his own authority in 1865. But his policies eventually set him at odds with Congress and the Republican party and provoked the most serious crisis in the history of relations between the executive and legislative branches of the federal government.

Johnson's background shaped his approach to Reconstruction. Born in dire poverty in North Carolina, he migrated as a young man to eastern Tennessee, where he made his living as a tailor. Lacking

In this cartoon, President Andrew Johnson (left) and Thaddeus Stevens, the Radical Republican Congressman from Pennsylvania, are depicted as train engineers in a deadlock on the tracks. Indeed, neither Johnson nor Stevens would give way on his plans for Reconstruction. ❖

formal schooling, he did not learn to read and write until adult life. Entering politics as a Jacksonian Democrat, he became known as an effective stump speaker. His railing against the planter aristocracy made him the spokesman for Tennessee's nonslaveholding whites and the most successful politician in the state. He advanced from state legislator to congressman to governor and in 1857 was elected to the U.S. Senate.

When Tennessee seceded in 1861, Johnson was the only senator from a Confederate state who remained loyal to the Union and continued to serve in Washington. But his Unionism and defense of the common people did not include antislavery sentiments. Nor was he friendly to blacks. While campaigning in Tennessee, he had objected only to the fact that slaveholding was the privilege of a wealthy minority. He revealed his attitude when he wished that "every head of family in the United States had one slave to take the drudgery and menial service off his family."

During the war, while acting as military governor of Tennessee, Johnson endorsed Lincoln's emancipation policy and carried it into effect. But he viewed it primarily as a means of destroying the power of the hated planter class rather than as a recognition of black humanity. He was chosen as Lincoln's running mate in 1864 because it was thought that a pro-administration Democrat, who was a southern Unionist in the bargain, would strengthen the ticket. No one expected Johnson to succeed to the presidency; it is one of the strange accidents of American history that a southern Democrat, a fervent white supremacist, came to preside over a Republican administration immediately after the Civil War.

Some Radical Republicans initially welcomed Johnson's ascent to the nation's highest office. Their hopes make sense in the light of Johnson's record of fierce loyalty to the Union and his apparent agreement with the Radicals that ex-Confederates should be severely treated. More than Lincoln, who had spoken of "malice toward none and charity for all," Johnson seemed likely to punish southern "traitors" and prevent them from regaining political influence. Only gradually did the deep disagreement between the president and the Republican Congressional majority become evident.

The Reconstruction policy that Johnson initiated on May 29, 1865, created some uneasiness among the Radicals, but most Republicans were willing to give it a chance. Johnson placed North Carolina and eventually other states under appointed provisional governors chosen mostly from among prominent southern politicians who had opposed the secession movement and had rendered no conspicuous service to the Confederacy. The governors were responsible for calling constitutional conventions and ensuring that only "loyal" whites were permitted to vote for delegates. Participation required taking the oath of allegiance that Lincoln had prescribed earlier. Once again, Confederate leaders and former officeholders who had participated in the rebellion were excluded. To regain their political and property rights, those in the exempted categories had to apply for individual presidential pardons. Johnson made one significant addition to the list of the excluded: all those possessing taxable property exceeding $20,000 in value. In this fashion, he sought to prevent his longtime adversaries—the wealthy planters—from participating in the Reconstruction of southern state governments.

Once the conventions met, Johnson urged them to do three things: Declare the ordinances of secession illegal, repudiate the Confederate debt, and ratify the **Thirteenth Amendment** abolishing slavery. After governments had been reestablished under constitutions meeting these conditions, the president assumed that the Reconstruction process would be complete and that the ex-Confederate states could regain their full rights under the Constitution.

The results of the conventions, which were dominated by prewar Unionists and representatives of backcountry yeoman farmers, were satisfactory to the president but troubling to many congressional Republicans. Rather than quickly accepting Johnson's recommendations, delegates in several states approved them begrudgingly or with qualifications. Furthermore, all the resulting constitutions limited suffrage to whites, disappointing the large number of Northerners who hoped, as Lincoln had, that at least some African Americans—perhaps those who were educated or had served in the Union army—would be given the vote. Johnson on the whole seemed eager to give southern white majorities a free hand in determining the civil and political status of the freed slaves.

Republican uneasiness turned to disillusionment and anger when the state legislatures elected under the new constitutions proceeded to pass **Black Codes** subjecting former slaves to a variety of special regulations and restrictions on their freedom. Especially troubling were vagrancy and apprenticeship laws that forced African Americans to work and denied them a free choice of employers. Blacks in some states were also prevented from testifying in court on the same basis as whites and were subject to a separate penal code. To Radicals, the Black Codes looked suspiciously like slavery under a new guise. More upsetting to northern public opinion in general, a number of prominent ex-Confederate leaders were elected to Congress in the fall of 1865.

Johnson himself was partly responsible for this turn of events. Despite his lifelong feud with the planter class, he was generous in granting pardons to members of the old elite who came to him, hat in hand, and asked for them. When former Confederate Vice President Alexander Stephens and other proscribed ex-rebels were elected to Congress although they had not been pardoned, Johnson granted them special amnesty so they could serve.

The growing rift between the president and Congress came into the open in December, when the House and Senate refused to seat the recently elected southern delegation. Instead of endorsing Johnson's work and recognizing the state governments he had called into being, Congress established a joint committee, chaired by Senator William Pitt Fessenden of

*"Slavery Is Dead?"* asks this 1866 cartoon by Thomas Nast. To the cartoonist, the Emancipation Proclamation of 1863 and the North's victory in the Civil War meant little difference to the treatment of the freed slaves in the South. Freed slaves convicted of crimes often endured the same punishments as had slaves—sale, as depicted in the left panel of the cartoon, or beatings, as shown on the right. ❖

Maine, to review Reconstruction policy and set further conditions for readmission of the seceded states.

## Congress Takes the Initiative

The struggle over how to reconstruct the Union ended with Congress doing the job of setting policy all over again. The clash between Johnson and Congress was a matter of principle and could not be reconciled. President Johnson, an heir of the Democratic states' rights tradition, wanted to restore the prewar federal system as quickly as possible and without change except that states would not have the right to legalize slavery or to secede.

Most Republicans wanted firm guarantees that the old southern ruling class would not regain regional power and national influence by devising new ways to subjugate blacks. They favored a Reconstruction policy that would give the federal government authority to limit the political role of ex-Confederates and provide some protection for black citizenship.

Republican leaders—with the exception of a few extreme Radicals such as Charles Sumner—lacked any firm conviction that blacks were inherently equal to whites. They did believe, however, that in a modern democratic state, all citizens must have the same basic rights and opportunities, regardless of natural abilities. Principle coincided easily with political expediency; southern blacks, whatever their alleged shortcomings, were likely to be loyal to the Republican party that had emancipated them. They could be used, if necessary, to counteract the influence of resurgent ex-Confederates, thus preventing the Democrats from returning to national dominance through control of the South.

The disagreement between the president and Congress became irreconcilable in early 1866, when Johnson vetoed two bills that had passed with overwhelming Republican support. The first extended the life of the **Freedmen's Bureau**—a temporary agency set up to aid the former slaves by providing relief, education, legal help, and assistance in obtaining land or employment. The second was a civil rights bill meant to nullify the Black Codes and guarantee to freedmen "full and equal benefit of all laws and proceedings for the security of person and property as is enjoyed by white citizens."

Johnson's vetoes shocked moderate Republicans who had expected the president to accept the relatively modest measures as a way of heading off more radical proposals, such as black suffrage and a prolonged denial of political rights to ex-Confederates. Presidential opposition to policies that represented the bare minimum of Republican demands on the South alienated moderates in the party and ensured a wide opposition to Johnson's plan of Reconstruction. Johnson suc-

ceeded in blocking the Freedmen's Bureau bill, although a modified version later passed. But the Civil Rights Act won the two-thirds majority necessary to override his veto, signifying that the president was now hopelessly at odds with most of the congressmen from what was supposed to be his own party. Never before had Congress overridden a presidential veto.

Johnson soon revealed that he intended to abandon the Republicans and place himself at the head of a new conservative party uniting the small minority of Republicans who supported him with a reviving Democratic party that was rallying behind his Reconstruction policy. In preparation for the elections of 1866, Johnson helped found the National Union movement to promote his plan to readmit the southern states to the Union without further qualifications. A National Union convention meeting in Philadelphia in August 1866 called for the election to Congress of men who endorsed the presidential plan for Reconstruction.

Meanwhile, the Republican majority on Capitol Hill, fearing that Johnson would not enforce civil rights legislation or that the courts would declare such federal laws unconstitutional, passed the **Fourteenth Amendment.** This, perhaps the most important of all the constitutional amendments, gave the federal government responsibility for guaranteeing equal rights under the law to all Americans. Section 1 defined national citizenship for the first time as extending to "all persons born or naturalized in the United States." The states were prohibited from abridging the rights of American citizens and could not "deprive any person of life, liberty, or property, without due process of law; nor deny to any person . . . equal protection of the laws."

The other sections of the amendment were important in the context of the time but had fewer long-term implications. Section 2 sought to penalize the South for denying voting rights to black men by reducing the congressional representation of any state that formally deprived a portion of its male citizens of the right to vote. Section 3 denied federal office to those who had taken an oath of office to support the U.S. Constitution and then had supported the Confederacy, and Section 4 repudiated the Confederate debt. The amendment was sent to the states with the understanding that Southerners would have no chance of being readmitted to Congress unless their states ratified it.

The congressional elections of 1866 served as a referendum on the Fourteenth Amendment. Johnson opposed the amendment on the grounds that it created a "centralized" government and denied states the right to manage their own affairs; he also counseled southern state legislatures to reject it, and all except Tennessee followed his advice. But the president's case for state autonomy was weakened by the publicity resulting from bloody race riots in New Orleans and Memphis. These and other reported atrocities against blacks made it clear that the existing southern state governments were failing abysmally to protect the "life, liberty, or property" of the ex-slaves.

Johnson further weakened his cause by taking the stump on behalf of candidates who supported his policies. In his notorious "swing around the circle," he toured the nation, slandering his opponents in crude language and engaging in undignified exchanges with hecklers. Enraged by southern inflexibility and the antics of a president who acted as if he were still campaigning in the backwoods of Tennessee, northern voters repudiated the administration. The Republican majority in Congress increased to a solid two-thirds in both houses, and the Radical wing of the party gained strength at the expense of moderates and conservatives.

## Congressional Reconstruction Plan Enacted

Congress was now in a position to implement its own plan of Reconstruction. In 1867 and 1868, it passed a series of acts that nullified the president's initiatives and reorganized the South on a new basis. Generally referred to as **Radical Reconstruction,** the measures actually represented a compromise between genuine Radicals and more moderate elements within the party.

Consistent Radicals such as Senator Charles Sumner of Massachusetts and Congressmen Thaddeus Stevens of Pennsylvania and George Julian of Indiana wanted to reshape southern society before readmitting ex-Confederates to the Union. Their program of "regeneration before Reconstruction" required an extended period of military rule, confiscation and redis-

Among the most influential of the Radical Republicans was Congressman Thaddeus Stevens of Pennsylvania. He advocated seizing land from southern planters and distributing it among the freed slaves. ✦

tribution of large landholdings among the freedmen, and federal aid for schools to educate blacks and whites for citizenship. But the majority of Republican congressmen found such a program unacceptable because it broke too sharply with American traditions of federalism and regard for property rights and might mean that decades would pass before the Union was back in working order.

The First Reconstruction Act, passed over Johnson's veto on March 2, 1867, did place the South under the rule of the army by reorganizing the region into five military districts. But military rule would last for only a short time. Subsequent acts of 1867 and 1868 opened the way for the quick readmission of any state that framed and ratified a new constitution providing for black suffrage. Ex-Confederates

## RECONSTRUCTION AMENDMENTS, 1865–1870

| Amendment | Main Provisions | Congressional Passage (2/3 majority in each house required) | Ratification Process (3/4 of all states required, including ex-Confederate states) |
|---|---|---|---|
| 13 | Slavery prohibited in United States | January 1865 | December 1865 (27 states, including 8 southern states) |
| 14 | National citizenship; State representation in Congress reduced proportionally to number of voters disfranchised; Former Confederates denied right to hold office; Confederate debt repudiated | June 1866 | Rejected by 12 southern and border states, February 1867; Radicals make readmission of southern states hinge on ratification; ratified July 1868 |
| 15 | Denial of franchise because of race, color, or past servitude explicitly prohibited | February 1869 | Ratification required for readmission of Virginia, Texas, Mississippi, Georgia; ratified March 1870 |

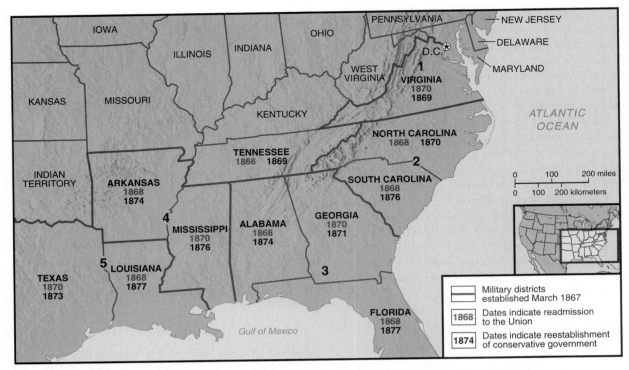

**RECONSTRUCTION**    *During the Reconstruction era, the southern state governments passed through three phases: control by white ex-Confederates; domination by Republican legislators, both white and black; and, finally, the regain of control by conservative white Democrats.* ❖

disqualified from holding federal office under the Fourteenth Amendment were prohibited from voting for delegates to the constitutional conventions or in the elections to ratify the conventions' work. Since blacks were allowed to participate in this process, Republicans thought they had found a way to ensure that "loyal" men would dominate the new governments. Radical Reconstruction was based on the dubious assumption that once blacks had the vote, they would have the power to protect themselves against white supremacists' efforts to deny them their rights. The Reconstruction Acts thus signaled a retreat from the true Radical position that a sustained use of federal authority was needed to complete the transition from slavery to freedom and prevent the resurgence of the South's old ruling class. (Troops were used in the South after 1868, but only in a very limited and sporadic way.) The majority of Republicans were unwilling to embrace centralized government and an extended period of military rule over civilians, and even Radicals such as Thaddeus Stevens supported the compromise as the best that could be achieved. Yet a genuine spirit of democratic idealism did give legitimacy and fervor to the cause of black male suffrage. Enabling people who were so poor and downtrodden to have access to the ballot box was a bold and innovative application of the principle of government by the consent of the governed. The problem was finding a way to enforce equal suffrage under conditions then existing in the postwar South.

## The Impeachment Crisis

The first obstacle to enforcement of congressional Reconstruction was resistance from the White House. Johnson thoroughly disapproved of the new policy and sought to thwart the will of Congress by administering the plan in his own obstructive fashion. He immediately began to dismiss officeholders who sympathized with Radical Reconstruction, and he countermanded the orders of generals in charge of southern military districts who were zealous in their enforcement of the new legislation. Some Radical generals were transferred and replaced by conservative Democrats. Congress responded by passing laws designed to limit presidential authority over Reconstruction matters. One of the measures was the Tenure of Office Act, requiring Senate approval for the removal of cabinet officers and other officials whose appointment had needed the consent of the Senate. Another measure—a rider to an army appropriations bill—sought to limit Johnson's authority to issue orders to military commanders.

Johnson objected vigorously to the restrictions on the grounds that they violated the constitutional doctrine of the separation of powers. When it became clear that the president was resolute in fighting for his powers and using them to resist the establishment of Radical regimes in the southern states, some congressmen began to call for his impeachment. A preliminary effort foundered in 1867, but when Johnson tried to discharge Secretary of War Edwin Stanton—the only Radical in the cabinet—and persisted in his efforts despite the disapproval of the Senate, the pro-impeachment forces gained in strength.

In January 1868, Johnson ordered General Grant, who already commanded the army, to replace Stanton as head of the War Department. But Grant had his eye on the Republican presidential nomination and refused to defy Congress. Johnson subsequently appointed General Lorenzo Thomas, who agreed to serve. Faced with this apparent violation of the Tenure of Office Act, the House voted overwhelmingly to impeach the president on February 24, and he was placed on trial before the Senate.

Because seven Republican senators broke with the party leadership and voted for acquittal, the effort to convict Johnson and remove him from office fell one vote short of the necessary two-thirds. This outcome resulted in part from a skillful defense. Attorneys for the president argued for a narrow interpretation of the constitutional provision that a president could be impeached only for "high crimes and misdemeanors," asserting that this referred only to indictable offenses. Responding to the charge that Johnson had deliberately violated the Tenure of Office Act, the defense contended that the law did not apply to the removal of Stanton because he had been appointed by Lincoln, not Johnson.

The prosecution countered with a different interpretation of the Tenure of Office Act, but the core of their case was that Johnson had abused the powers of his office in an effort to sabotage the congressional Reconstruction policy. Obstructing the will of the legislative branch, they claimed, was sufficient grounds for conviction even if no crime had been committed. The Republicans who broke ranks to vote for acquittal could not endorse such a broad view of the impeachment power. They feared that removal of a president for essentially political reasons would threaten the constitutional balance of powers and open the way to legislative supremacy over the executive. In addition, the man who would have succeeded Johnson— Senator Benjamin Wade of Ohio, the president pro tem of the Senate—was unpopular with conservative Republicans because of his radical position on labor and currency questions.

THE PAROQUET OF THE WH—E HO—E.

*Andrew Johnson's successful defense against conviction in his impeachment case centered on his invocation of the Constitution to defend his presidential rights and powers. Impeached in 1868, Johnson escaped conviction by a single vote.* ❖

Although Johnson's acquittal by the narrowest of margins protected the American presidency from congressional domination, the impeachment episode helped create an impression in the public mind that the Radicals were ready to turn the Constitution to their own use to gain their objectives. Conservatives were again alarmed when Congress took action in 1868 to deny the Supreme Court's appellate jurisdiction in cases involving the military arrest and imprisonment of anti-Reconstruction activists in the South. But the evidence of congressional ruthlessness and illegality is not as strong as most historians used to think. Modern legal scholars have found merit in the Radicals' claim that their actions did not violate the Constitution.

Failure to remove Johnson from office was an embarrassment to congressional Republicans, but the episode did ensure that Reconstruction in the South would proceed as the majority in Congress intended. During the trial, Johnson helped influence the verdict by pledging to enforce the Reconstruction Acts, and he held to this promise during his remaining months in office. Unable to depose the president, the Radicals had at least succeeded in neutralizing his opposition to their program.

# RECONSTRUCTING SOUTHERN SOCIETY

The Civil War left the South devastated, demoralized, and destitute. Slavery was dead, but what this meant for future relationships between whites and blacks was still in doubt. The overwhelming majority of southern whites wanted to keep blacks adrift between slavery and freedom—without rights, in a status resembling that of the "free Negroes" of the Old South. Blacks sought to be independent of their former masters and viewed the acquisition of land, education, and the vote as the best means of achieving this goal. The thousands of Northerners who went south after the war for materialistic or humanitarian reasons hoped to extend Yankee "civilization" to what they viewed as an unenlightened and barbarous region. For most of them, this reformation required the aid of the freedmen; not enough southern whites were willing to accept the new order and embrace northern middle-class values.

The struggle of these groups to achieve their conflicting goals bred chaos, violence, and instability. Unsettled conditions created many opportunities for corruption, crime, and terrorism. This was scarcely an ideal setting for an experiment in interracial democracy, but one was attempted nonetheless. Its success depended on massive and sustained support from the federal government. To the extent that this was forthcoming, progressive reform could be achieved. When it faltered, the forces of reaction and white supremacy were unleashed.

## Reorganizing Land and Labor

The Civil War scarred the southern landscape and wrecked its economy. One devastated area—central South Carolina—looked to an 1865 observer "like a broad black streak of ruin and desolation—the fences are gone; lonesome smokestacks, surrounded by dark heaps of ashes and cinders, marking the spots where human habitations had stood; the fields all along the roads widely overgrown with weeds, with here and there a sickly patch of cotton or corn cultivated by negro squatters." Other areas through which the armies had passed were similarly ravaged. Several major cities—including Atlanta, Columbia, and Richmond—were gutted by fire. Most factories were dismantled or destroyed, and long stretches of railroad were torn up.

Physical ruin would not have been so disastrous if investment capital had been available for rebuilding. But the substantial wealth represented by Confederate currency and bonds had melted away, and emancipation of the slaves had divested the propertied classes of their most valuable and productive assets. According to some estimates, the South's per capita wealth in 1865 was only about half what it had been in 1860.

Recovery could not even begin until a new labor system replaced slavery. It was widely assumed in both the North and the South that southern prosperity would continue to depend on cotton and that the plantation was the most efficient unit for producing the crop. Hindering efforts to rebuild the plantation economy were lack of capital, the deep-rooted belief of southern whites that blacks would work only under compulsion, and the freedmen's resistance to labor conditions that recalled slavery.

Blacks strongly preferred to determine their own economic relationships, and for a time they had reason to hope the federal government would support their ambitions. The freed slaves were placed in a precarious position and were, in effect, fighting a two-front war. Although they were grateful for the federal aid in ending slavery, freed slaves often had ideas about freedom that contradicted the plans of their northern allies. Many ex-slaves wanted to hold on to the family-based communal work methods that they utilized during slavery. Freed slaves in areas of South Carolina, for example, attempted to maintain the family task system rather than adopting the individual piecework system pushed by northern capitalists. Many ex-slaves opposed plans to turn them into wage laborers who produced exclusively for a market. Finally, freed slaves often wanted to stay on the land their families had spent generations farming rather than move elsewhere to assume plots of land as individual farmers.

While not guaranteeing all of the freed slaves' hopes for economic self-determination, the northern military attempted to establish a new economic base for the freed men and women. General Sherman, hampered by the huge numbers of black fugitives that followed his army on its famous march, issued an order in January 1865 that set aside the islands and coastal areas of Georgia and South Carolina for exclusive black occupancy on 40-acre plots. Furthermore, the Freedmen's Bureau, as one of its many responsibilities, was given control of hundreds of thousands of acres of abandoned or confiscated land and was authorized to make 40-acre grants to black settlers for three-year periods, after which they would have the option to buy at low prices. By June 1865, forty thousand black farmers were at work on 300,000 acres of what they thought would be their own land.

But for most of them the dream of "forty acres and a mule," or some other arrangement that would give them control of their land and labor, was not to be realized. President Johnson pardoned the owners of most of the land consigned to the ex-slaves by Sherman and the Freedmen's Bureau, and proposals for an effective program of land confiscation and redistribution failed to get through Congress. Among the considerations prompting most congressmen to oppose land reform were a tenderness for property rights, fear of sapping the freedmen's initiative by giving them something they allegedly had not earned, and the desire to restore cotton production as quickly as possible to increase agricultural exports and stabilize the economy. Consequently, most blacks in physical possession of small farms failed to acquire title, and the mass of freedmen were left with little or no prospect of becoming landowners. Recalling the plight of southern blacks in 1865, an ex-slave later wrote that "they were set free without a dollar, without a foot of land, and without the wherewithal to get the next meal even."

Despite their poverty and landlessness, ex-slaves were reluctant to settle down and commit themselves to wage labor for their former masters. Many took to the road, hoping to find something better. Some were still expecting grants of land, but others were simply trying to increase their bargaining power. One freedman later recalled that an important part of being free was that, "we could move around [and] change bosses." As the end of 1865 approached, many freedmen had still not signed up for the coming season; anxious planters feared that blacks were plotting to seize land by force. Within a few weeks, however, most holdouts signed for the best terms they could get.

One common form of agricultural employment in 1866 was a contract labor system. Under this system, workers committed themselves for a year in return for fixed wages, a substantial portion of which was withheld until after the harvest. Since many planters were inclined to drive hard bargains, abuse their workers, or cheat them at the end of the year, the Freedmen's Bureau assumed the role of reviewing the contracts and enforcing them. But bureau officials had differing notions of what it meant to protect African Americans from exploitation. Some stood up strongly for the rights of the freedmen; others served as allies of the planters, rounding up available workers, coercing them to sign contracts for low wages, and then helping keep them in line.

The bureau's influence waned after 1867 (it was phased out completely by 1869), and the experiment with contract wage labor was abandoned. Growing up

alongside the contract system and eventually displacing it was an alternative capital-labor relationship—**sharecropping.** First in small groups known as "squads" and later as individual families, blacks worked a piece of land independently for a fixed share of the crop, usually one-half. The advantage of this arrangement for credit-starved landlords was that it did not require much expenditure in advance of the harvest. The system also forced the tenant to share the risks of crop failure or a fall in cotton prices. These considerations loomed larger after disastrous harvests in 1866 and 1867.

African Americans initially viewed sharecropping as a step up from wage labor in the direction of landownership. But during the 1870s, this form of tenancy evolved into a new kind of servitude. Croppers had to live on credit until their cotton was sold, and planters or merchants seized the chance to "provision" them at high prices and exorbitant rates of interest. Creditors were entitled to deduct what was owed to them out of the tenant's share of the crop, and this left most sharecroppers with no net profit at the end of the year—more often than not with a debt that had to be worked off in subsequent years. Various methods, legal

*The Civil War brought emancipation to slaves, but the sharecropping system kept many of them economically bound to their employers. At the end of a year the sharecropper tenants might owe most—or all—of what they had made to their landlord. Here a sharecropping family poses in front of their cabin. Ex-slaves often built their living quarters near woods in order to have a ready supply of fuel for heating and cooking. The cabin's chimney lists away from the house so that it can be easily pushed away from the living quarters should it catch fire.* ❖

and extralegal, were eventually devised in an effort to bind indebted tenants to a single landlord for extended periods, but considerable movement was still possible.

## Black Codes: A New Name for Slavery?

While landless African Americans in the countryside were being reduced to economic dependence, those in towns and cities found themselves living in an increasingly segregated society. The Black Codes of 1865 attempted to require separation of the races in public places and facilities; when most of the codes were overturned by federal authorities as violations of the Civil Rights Act of 1866, the same end was often achieved through private initiative and community pressure. In some cities, blacks successfully resisted being consigned to separate streetcars by appealing to the military during the period when it exercised authority or by organizing boycotts. But they found it almost impossible to gain admittance to most hotels, restaurants, and other privately owned establishments catering to whites. Although separate black, or "Jim Crow," cars were not yet the rule on railroads, African Americans were often denied first-class accommodations. After 1868, black-supported Republican governments passed civil rights acts requiring equal access to public facilities, but little effort was made to enforce the legislation.

The Black Codes had other onerous provisions meant to control African Americans and return them to quasi-slavery. Most codes even made black unemployment a crime, which meant blacks had to make long-term contracts with white employers or be arrested for vagrancy. Others limited the rights of African Americans to own property or engage in occupations other than those of servant or laborer. The codes were set aside by the actions of Congress, the military, and the Freedmen's Bureau, but vagrancy laws remained in force across the South.

Furthermore, private violence and discrimination against blacks continued on a massive scale unchecked by state authorities. Hundreds, perhaps thousands, of blacks were murdered by whites in 1865–1866, and few of the perpetrators were brought to justice. The imposition of military rule in 1867 was designed in part to protect former slaves from such violence and intimidation, but the task was beyond the capacity of the few thousand troops stationed in the South. When new constitutions were approved and states readmitted to the Union under the congressional plan in 1868, the problem became more severe. White opponents of Radical Reconstruction adopted systematic terrorism and organized mob violence to keep blacks away from the polls.

The freed slaves, in the face of opposition from both their Democratic enemies and some of their Republican allies, tried to defend themselves by organizing their own militia groups for protection and to assert their political rights. However, the militia groups were not powerful enough to overcome the growing power of the anti-Republican forces. Also, the military presence was progressively reduced, leaving the new Republican regimes to fight a losing battle against armed white supremacists. In the words of historian William Gillette, "there was simply no federal force large enough to give heart to black Republicans or to bridle southern white violence."

## Republican Rule in the South

Hastily organized in 1867, the southern Republican party dominated the constitution making of 1868 and the regimes that came out of it. The party was an attempted coalition of three social groups (which varied in their relative strength from state to state). One was the same class that was becoming the backbone of the Republican party in the North—businessmen with an interest in enlisting government aid for private enterprise. Many Republicans of this stripe were recent arrivals from the North—the so-called **carpetbaggers**—but some were scalawags, former Whig planters or merchants who were born in the South or had immigrated to the region before the war and now saw a chance to realize their dreams for commercial and industrial development.

Poor white farmers, especially those from upland areas where Unionist sentiment had been strong during the Civil War, were a second element in the original coalition. These owners of small farms expected the party to favor their interests at the expense of the wealthy landowners and to come to their aid with special legislation when—as was often the case in this period of economic upheaval—they faced the loss of their homesteads to creditors. Newly enfranchised blacks were the third group to which the Republicans appealed. Blacks formed the vast majority of the Republican rank and file in most states and were concerned mainly with education, civil rights, and landownership.

Under the best of conditions, these coalitions would have been difficult to maintain. Each group had its own distinct goals and did not fully support the aims of the other segments. White yeomen, for example, had a deeply rooted resistance to black equality. And for how long could one expect essentially conservative businessmen to support costly measures for the elevation or relief of the lower classes of either race? In some states, astute Democratic politicians exploited these divisions by appealing to disaffected white Republicans.

But during the relatively brief period when they were in power in the South—varying from one to nine years depending on the state—the Republicans chalked up some notable achievements. They established (on paper at least) the South's first adequate systems of public education, democratized state and local government, and appropriated funds for an enormous expansion of public services and responsibilities.

As important as these social and political reforms were, they took second place to the Republicans' major effort—to foster economic development and restore southern prosperity by subsidizing the construction of railroads and other internal improvements. But the policy of aiding railroads turned out to be disastrous, even though it addressed the region's real economic needs and was initially very popular. Extravagance, corruption, and routes laid out in response to local political pressure rather than on sound economic grounds made for an increasing burden of public debt and taxation.

The policy did not produce the promised payoff of efficient, cheap transportation. Subsidized railroads frequently went bankrupt, leaving the taxpayers holding the bag. When the Panic of 1873 brought many southern state governments to the verge of bankruptcy, and railroad building came to an end, it was clear the Republicans' "gospel of prosperity" through state aid to private enterprise had failed miserably. Their political opponents, many of whom had originally favored such policies, now saw an opportunity to take advantage of the situation by charging that Republicans had ruined the southern economy.

In general, the Radical regimes failed to conduct public business honestly and efficiently. Embezzlement of public funds and bribery of state lawmakers or officials were common occurrences. State debts and tax burdens rose enormously, mainly because governments had undertaken heavy new responsibilities, but partly because of waste and graft. The situation varied from state to state; ruling cliques in Louisiana and South Carolina were guilty of much wrongdoing, yet Mississippi had a relatively honest and frugal regime.

Furthermore, southern corruption was not exceptional, nor was it a special result of the extension of suffrage to uneducated African Americans, as critics of Radical Reconstruction have claimed. It was part of a national pattern during an era when private interests considered buying government favors to be a part of the cost of doing business, and many politicians expected to profit by obliging them.

Blacks bore only a limited responsibility for the dishonesty of the Radical governments. Although sixteen African Americans served in Congress—two in the Senate—between 1869 and 1880, only in South Carolina did blacks constitute a majority of even one house of the state legislature. Furthermore, no black governors were elected during Reconstruction (although Pinkney B. S. Pinchback served for a time as acting governor of Louisiana). The biggest grafters were opportunistic whites. Some of the most notorious were carpetbaggers, but others were native Southerners. Businessmen offering bribes included members of the prewar gentry who were staunch opponents of Radical programs. Some black legislators went with the tide and accepted "loans" from those

*On either side of Frederick Douglass on this poster are two African American heroes of the Reconstruction era. Senator Blanche K. Bruce of Mississippi, on the left, was the first African American to be elected to a full term in the U.S. Senate. Senator Hiram R. Revels, also representing Mississippi, was elected to the U.S. Senate in 1870 to fill the seat previously occupied by Confederate President Jefferson Davis.* ❖

railroad lobbyists who would pay most for their votes, but the same men could usually be depended on to vote the will of their constituents on civil rights or educational issues.

If blacks served or supported corrupt and wasteful regimes, it was because the alternative was dire. Although the Democrats, or Conservatives as they called themselves in some states, made sporadic efforts to attract African American voters, it was clear that if they won control, they would attempt to strip blacks of their civil and political rights. But opponents of Radical Reconstruction were able to capitalize on racial prejudice and persuade many Americans that "good government" was synonymous with white supremacy.

Contrary to myth, the small number of African Americans elected to state or national office during Reconstruction demonstrated on the average more integrity and competence than their white counterparts. Most were fairly well educated, having been free Negroes or unusually privileged slaves before the war. Among the most capable were Robert Smalls (whose career was described earlier); Blanche K. Bruce of Mississippi, elected to the U.S. Senate in 1874 after rising to deserved prominence in the Republican party of his home state; Congressman Robert Brown Elliott of South Carolina, an adroit politician who was also a consistent champion of civil rights; and Congressman James T. Rapier of Alabama, who stirred Congress and the nation in 1873 with his eloquent appeals for federal aid to southern education and new laws to enforce equal rights for African Americans.

## Claiming Public and Private Rights

As important as party politics to the changing political culture of the Reconstruction South were the ways that freed slaves claimed rights for themselves. They did so not only in negotiations with employers and in public meetings and convention halls, but also through the institutions they created, and perhaps most important, the households they formed.

As one black corporal in the Union Army told an audience of ex-slaves, "The Marriage covenant is at the foundation of all our rights. In slavery we could not have *legalized* marriage: *now* we have it . . . and we shall be established as a people." Through marriage, historian Laura Edwards tells us, African Americans claimed citizenship. Freedmen hoped that marriage would allow them to take on the rights that accrued to the independent head of a household, not only political rights, but the right to control the labor of wives and children for the first time.

Many states' Black Codes included apprenticeship provisions, providing for freed children to be apprenticed by courts to some white person (with preference given to former masters) if their parents were paupers, unemployed, of "bad character," or even simply if it were found to be "better for the habits and comfort of a child." Ex-slaves struggled to win their children back from what often amounted to re-enslavement for arbitrary reasons. Freedpeople challenged the apprenticeship system in county courts, and through the Freedmen's Bureau. As one group of petitioners from Maryland asserted, "Our homes are invaded and our little ones seized at the family fireside."

While many former slaves lined up eagerly to formalize their marriages, many also retained their own definitions of marriage and defied the efforts of the Freedmen's Bureau to use the marriage relation as a disciplinary tool. Perhaps as many as 50 percent of ex-slaves chose not to marry legally, and whites criticized them heavily for it. African American leaders worried about this refusal to follow white norms. The Army cor-

*As slaves, many blacks attended white churches and listened to sermons preached by white ministers. After the Civil War and the end of slavery, African Americans joined or founded black churches, such as the Sixth Mount Zion Baptist Church of Richmond, Virginia. This postcard of the church's history includes a photograph of its founding pastor, John Jasper.* ❖

ORGANIZED SEPT. 1867

R. V. PEYTON, D.D.

1867

1925

The SIXTH MOUNT ZION CHURCH RICHMOND, VIRGINIA.

1887

1917

REV. JOHN JASPER

REV. A. W. BROWN

This church was founded in 1867 by Rev. John Jasper, who continued as pastor until death in 1901. Rev. R. V. Peyton served as pastor until 1924, and was succeeded by Rev. A. W. Brown, the present pastor.

*A Freedmen's school, one of the more successful endeavors supported by the Freedmen's Bureau. The bureau, working with teachers from northern abolitionist and missionary societies, founded thousands of schools for freed slaves and poor whites.* ❖

poral who had described marriage as "the foundation of all our rights" urged his audience: "Let us conduct ourselves worthy of such a blessing—and all the people will respect us." Yet many poor blacks continued to recognize as husband and wife people who cared for and supported one another without benefit of legal sanction. The new legal system punished couples who deviated from the legal norm through laws against bastardy, adultery, and fornication. Furthermore, the Freedmen's Bureau made the marriage of freedpeople a priority because, as historian Noralee Frankel explained, "The agency's overriding concern was keeping blacks from depending on the federal government for economic assistance." Once married, the husband became legally responsible for his family's support.

Some ex-slaves used institutions formerly closed to them like the courts to assert rights against white people as well as other blacks, suing over domestic violence, child support, assault, and debt. Freed women sued their husbands for desertion and alimony in order to enlist the Freedman's Bureau to help them claim property from men. Other ex-slaves mobilized kin networks and other community resources to make claims on property and family.

Immediately after the war, freedpeople flocked to create institutions that had been denied to them under slavery: churches, fraternal and benevolent associations, political organizations, and schools. Many joined all-black denominations such as the African Methodist Episcopal church, which provided freedom from white dominance and a more congenial style of worship. Black women formed all-black chapters of organizations such as the Women's Christian Temperance Union, and their own women's clubs to oppose lynching and work for "uplift" in the black community.

A top priority for most ex-slaves was the opportunity to educate their children; the first schools for freedpeople were all-black institutions established by the Freedmen's Bureau and various northern missionary societies. At the time, having been denied all education during the antebellum period, most blacks viewed separate schooling as an opportunity rather than as a form of discrimination. However, these schools were precursors to the segregated public school systems first instituted by Republican governments. Only in city schools of New Orleans and at the University of South Carolina were there serious attempts during Reconstruction to bring white and black students together in the same classrooms.

In a variety of ways, African American men and women during Reconstruction claimed freedom in the "private" realm as well as the public sphere, by claiming rights to their own families and building their own institutions. They did so in the face of the vigorous efforts of their former masters as well as the new government agencies to control their private lives and shape their new identities as husbands, wives, and citizens.

# RETREAT FROM RECONSTRUCTION

The era of Reconstruction began coming to an end almost before it got started. Although it was only a scant three years from the end of the Civil War, the impeachment crisis of 1868 represented the high point of popular interest in Reconstruction issues. That year, Ulysses S. Grant was elected president. Many historians blame Grant for the corruption of his administration and for the inconsistency and failure of his southern policy. He had neither the vision nor the sense of duty to tackle the difficult challenges the nation faced. From 1868 on, political issues other than southern Reconstruction moved to the forefront of national politics, and the plight of African Americans in the South receded in white consciousness.

## Rise of the Money Question

In the years immediately following the Civil War, another issue already competing for public attention was the money question: whether to allow "greenbacks"—paper money issued during the war—to continue to circulate or to return to "sound" or "hard" money, meaning gold or silver. Supporters of paper money, known as **greenbackers,** were strongest in the credit-hungry West and among expansion-minded manufacturers. Defenders of hard money were mostly the commercial and financial interests in the East; they received crucial support from intellectuals who regarded government-sponsored inflation as immoral or contrary to the natural laws of classical economics.

In 1868, the money question surged briefly to the forefront of national politics. Faced with a business recession blamed on the Johnson administration's policy of contracting the currency, Congress voted to stop the retirement of greenbacks. The Democratic party, responding to Midwestern pressure, included in its platform for the 1868 national election a plan calling for the redemption of much of the Civil War debt in greenbacks rather than gold. Yet they nominated for president a sound-money supporter, so that the greenback question never became an issue in the 1868 presidential campaign. Grant, already a popular general, won the election handily with the help of the Republican-dominated Southern states.

In 1869 and 1870, a Republican-controlled Congress passed laws that assured payment in gold to most bondholders but eased the burden of the huge Civil War debt by exchanging bonds that were soon coming due for those that would not be payable for ten, fifteen, or thirty years. In this way, the public credit was protected.

Still unresolved, however, was the problem of what to do about the $356 million in greenbacks that

### THE ELECTION OF 1868

| Candidate | Party | Popular Vote | Electoral Vote[*] |
|---|---|---|---|
| Grant | Republican | 3,013,421 | 214 |
| Seymour | Democratic | 2,706,829 | 80 |
| Not voted[*] | | | 23 |

[*]Unreconstructed states did not participate in the election.

remained in circulation. Hard-money proponents wanted to retire them quickly; inflationists thought more should be issued to stimulate the economy. The Grant administration followed the middle course of allowing the greenbacks to float until economic expansion would bring them to a par with gold, thus permitting a painless return to specie payments. But the Panic of 1873, which brought much of the economy to its knees, led to a revival of agitation to inflate the currency. Debt-ridden farmers, who would be the backbone of the greenback movement for years to come, now joined the soft-money clamor for the first time.

Responding to the money and credit crunch, Congress moved in 1874 to authorize a modest issue of new greenbacks. But Grant, influenced by the opinions of hard-money financiers, vetoed the bill. In 1875, Congress, led by Senator John Sherman of Ohio, enacted the Specie Resumption Act, which provided for a limited reduction of greenbacks leading to full resumption of specie payments by January 1, 1879. Its action was widely interpreted as deflation in the midst of depression. Farmers and workers, who were already suffering acutely from deflation, reacted with dismay and anger.

The Democratic Party could not capitalize adequately on these sentiments because of the influence of its own hard-money faction, and in 1876 an independent Greenback party entered the national political arena. The party's nominee for president, Peter Cooper, received an insignificant number of votes, but in 1878 the Greenback Labor party polled more than a million votes and elected fourteen congressmen. The Greenbackers were able to keep the money issue alive into the following decade.

## Final Efforts of Reconstruction

The Republican effort to make equal rights for blacks the law of the land culminated in the **Fifteenth Amendment.** Passed by Congress in 1869 and ratified by the states in 1870, the amendment prohibited any state from denying a male citizen the right to vote because of race, color, or previous condition of servitude. A more radical version, requiring universal manhood suffrage, was rejected partly because it departed too sharply from traditional views of federal-state rela-

*Shown seated at the table are feminist leaders Elizabeth Cady Stanton and Susan B. Anthony. They and their adherents split with Lucy Stone (right) and her followers over the Fifteenth Amendment and its failure to extend the vote to women.* ❖

tions. States therefore could still limit the suffrage by imposing literacy tests, property qualifications, or poll taxes allegedly applying to all racial groups; such devices would eventually be used to strip southern blacks of the right to vote. But the makers of the amendment did not foresee this result. They believed their action would prevent future Congresses or southern constitutional conventions from repealing or nullifying the provisions for black male suffrage included in the Reconstruction Acts. A secondary aim was to enfranchise African Americans in those northern states that still denied them the vote.

Many feminists were bitterly disappointed that the amendment did not extend the vote to women as well as freedmen. A militant wing of the women's rights movement, led by Elizabeth Cady Stanton and Susan B. Anthony, was so angered that the Constitution was being amended in a way that, in effect, made gender a qualification for voting that they campaigned against ratification of the Fifteenth Amendment. Another group of feminists led by Lucy Stone supported the amendment on the grounds that this was "the Negro's hour" and that women could afford to wait a few years for the vote. This disagreement divided the woman suffrage movement for a generation to come.

The Grant administration was charged with enforcing the amendment and protecting black men's voting rights in the reconstructed states. Since survival of the Republican regimes depended on African American support, political partisanship dictated federal action, even though the North's emotional and ideological commitment to black citizenship was waning.

## A Reign of Terror Against Blacks

Between 1868 and 1872, the main threat to southern Republican regimes came from the **Ku Klux Klan** and other secret societies bent on restoring white supremacy by intimidating blacks who sought to exercise their political rights. First organized in Tennessee in 1866, the Klan spread rapidly to other states, adopting increasingly lawless and brutal tactics. A grassroots vigilante movement and not a centralized conspiracy, the Klan thrived on local initiative and gained support from whites of all social classes. Its secrecy, decentralization, popular support, and utter ruthlessness made it very difficult to suppress. As soon as blacks had been granted the right to vote, hooded "night riders" began to visit the cabins of those who were known to be active Republicans; some victims were only threatened, but others were whipped or even murdered. One black Georgian related a typical incident: "They broke my door open, took me out of bed, took me to the woods and whipped me three hours or more and left me for dead. They said to me, 'Do you think you will vote for another damned radical ticket?'"

Such methods were first used effectively in the presidential election of 1868. Grant lost in Louisiana and Georgia mainly because the Klan—or the Knights of the White Camellia, as the Louisiana variant was called—launched a reign of terror to prevent prospective black voters from exercising their rights. In Louisiana, political violence claimed more than a thousand lives, and in Arkansas, which Grant managed to carry, more than two hundred Republicans, including a congressman, were assassinated.

Thereafter, Klan terrorism was directed mainly at Republican state governments. Virtual insurrections broke out in Arkansas, Tennessee, North Carolina, and parts of South Carolina. Republican governors called out the state militia to fight the Klan, but only the Arkansas militia succeeded in bringing it to heel. In Tennessee, North Carolina, and Georgia, Klan activities helped undermine Republican control, thus allowing the Democrats to come to power in all of these states by 1870.

This 1868 photograph shows typical regalia of members of the Ku Klux Klan, a secret white supremacist organization. Before elections, hooded Klansmen terrorized African Americans to discourage them from voting. ❖

Faced with the violent overthrow of the southern Republican Party, Congress and the Grant administration were forced to act. A series of laws passed in 1870–1871 sought to enforce the Fifteenth Amendment by providing federal protection for black suffrage and authorizing use of the army against the Klan. The **Force acts,** also known as the Ku Klux Klan acts, made interference with voting rights a federal crime and established provisions for government supervision of elections. In addition, the legislation empowered the president to call out troops and suspend the writ of habeas corpus to quell insurrection. In 1871–1872, thousands of suspected Klansmen were arrested by the military or U.S. marshals, and the writ was suspended in nine counties of South Carolina that had been virtually taken over by the secret order. Although most of the accused Klansmen were never brought to trial, were acquitted, or received suspended sentences, the enforcement effort was vigorous enough to put a damper on hooded terrorism and ensure relatively fair and peaceful elections in 1872.

A heavy black turnout in these elections enabled the Republicans to hold on to power in most states of the Deep South, despite efforts of the Democratic-Conservative opposition to cut into the Republican vote by taking moderate positions on racial and economic issues. This setback prompted the Democratic-Conservatives to make a significant change in their strategy and ideology. No longer did they try to take votes away from the Republicans by proclaiming support for black suffrage and government aid to business. Instead they began to appeal openly to white supremacy and to the traditional Democratic and agrarian hostility to government promotion of economic development. Consequently, they were able to bring back to the polls a portion of the white electorate, mostly small farmers, who had not been turning out because they were alienated by the leadership's apparent concessions to Yankee ideas.

This new and more effective electoral strategy dovetailed with a resurgence of violence meant to reduce Republican, especially black Republican, voting. The new reign of terror differed from the previously discussed Klan episode; its agents no longer wore masks but acted quite openly. They were effective because the northern public was increasingly disenchanted with federal intervention on behalf of what were widely viewed as corrupt and tottering Republican regimes. Grant used force in the South for the last time in 1874 when an overt paramilitary organization in Louisiana, known as the White League, tried to overthrow a Republican government accused of stealing an election. When another unofficial militia in Mississippi instigated a series of bloody race riots prior to the state elections of 1875, Grant refused the governor's request for federal troops. As a result, black

## ❖ A Look at the Past ❖

### Cartoon "Worse Than Slavery"

Political cartoonist Thomas Nast offered his commentary on and critique of contemporary events through his cartoons in *Harper's Weekly,* a popular magazine that had a circulation of over 100,000 readers. This Nast cartoon, "Worse Than Slavery," appeared in the magazine on October 24, 1874. Carefully examine the individuals and items depicted in the cartoon. Note that the phrase near the top of the drawing, "This is a white man's government," is a quotation from the 1868 Democratic Party platform. According to the cartoon, what conditions or events are "worse than slavery"? What view of Reconstruction policy does the cartoonist appear to be expressing?

voters were successfully intimidated—one county registered only seven Republican votes where there had been a black majority of two thousand—and Mississippi fell to the Democratic-Conservatives. According to one account, Grant decided to withhold troops because he had been warned that intervention might cost the Republicans the crucial state of Ohio in the same off-year elections.

By 1876, Republicans held on to only three southern states: South Carolina, Louisiana, and Florida. Partly because of Grant's hesitant and inconsistent use of presidential power, but mainly because the northern electorate would no longer tolerate military action to sustain Republican governments and black voting rights, Radical Reconstruction was falling into total eclipse.

### Spoilsmen Versus Reformers

One reason Grant found it increasingly difficult to take strong action to protect southern Republicans was the bad odor surrounding his stewardship of the federal government and the Republican Party. Reformers charged that a corrupt national administration was propping up bad governments in the South for personal and partisan advantage. An apparent case in point was Grant's intervention in Louisiana in 1872 on behalf of an ill-reputed Republican faction headed by his wife's brother-in-law, who controlled federal patronage as collector of customs in New Orleans.

The Republican party in the Grant era was losing the idealism and high purpose associated with the crusade against slavery. By the beginning of the 1870s, the men who had been the conscience of the party—old-line radicals such as Thaddeus Stevens, Charles Sumner, and Benjamin Wade—were either dead, out of office, or at odds with the administration. New leaders of a different stamp, whom historians have dubbed "spoilsmen" or "politicos," were taking their place. When he made common cause with hard-boiled manipulators such as senators Roscoe Conkling of New York and James G. Blaine of Maine, Grant lost credibility with reform-minded Republicans.

During Grant's first administration, an aura of scandal surrounded the White House but did not directly implicate the president. In 1869, the financial buccaneer Jay Gould enlisted the aid of a brother-in-law of Grant to further his fantastic scheme to corner the gold market. Gould failed in the attempt, but he did manage to save himself and come away with a huge profit.

Grant's first-term vice president, Schuyler Colfax of Indiana, was directly involved in the notorious Crédit Mobilier scandal. Crédit Mobilier was a construction company that actually served as a fraudulent device for siphoning off profits that should have gone to the stockholders of the Union Pacific Railroad, which was the beneficiary of massive federal land grants. In order to forestall government inquiry into this arrangement, Crédit Mobilier stock was distributed to influential congressmen, including Colfax (who was speaker of the House before he was elected vice president). The whole business came to light just before the campaign of 1872.

Republicans who could not tolerate such corruption or had other grievances against the administration broke with Grant in 1872 and formed a third party committed to "honest government" and "reconciliation" between the North and the South. Led initially by high-minded reformers such as Senator Carl Schurz of Missouri, the Liberal Republicans endorsed reform of the civil service to curb the corruption-breeding patronage system and advocated laissez-faire economic policies—which meant low tariffs, an end to government subsidies for railroads, and hard money. Despite their rhetoric of idealism

## THE ELECTION OF 1872

| Candidate | Party | Popular Vote | Electoral Vote[*] |
|---|---|---|---|
| Grant | Republican | 3,598,235 | 286 |
| Greeley | Democratic and Liberal Republican | 2,834,761 | Greeley died before the electoral college voted. |

[*]Out of a total of 366 electoral votes. Greeley's votes were divided among the four minor candidates.

and reform, the Liberal Republicans were extremely conservative in their notions of what government should do to assure justice for blacks and other underprivileged Americans.

The Liberal Republicans' national convention nominated Horace Greeley, editor of the respected New York *Tribune*. This was a curious and divisive choice, since Greeley was at odds with the founders of the movement on the tariff question and was indifferent to civil service reform. The Democrats also nominated Greeley, mainly because he promised to end Radical Reconstruction by restoring "self-government" to the South.

But the journalist turned out to be a poor campaigner who failed to inspire enthusiasm from life-long supporters of either party. Most Republicans stuck with Grant, despite the corruption issue, because they still could not stomach the idea of ex-rebels returning to power in the South. Many Democrats, recalling Greeley's previous record as a staunch Republican, simply stayed away from the polls. The result was a decisive victory for Grant, whose 56 percent of the popular vote was the highest percentage won by any candidate between Andrew Jackson and Theodore Roosevelt.

Grant's second administration seemed to bear out the reformers' worst suspicions about corruption in high places. In 1875, the public learned that federal revenue officials had conspired with distillers to defraud the government of millions of dollars in liquor taxes. Grant's private secretary, Orville E. Babcock, was indicted as a member of the "Whiskey Ring" and was saved from conviction only by the president's personal intercession. The next year, Grant's secretary of war, William E. Belknap, was impeached by the House after an investigation revealed he had taken bribes for the sale of Indian trading posts. He avoided conviction in the Senate only by resigning from office before his trial. Grant fought hard to protect Belknap, to the point of participating in what a later generation might call a cover-up.

There is no evidence that Grant profited personally from any of the misdeeds of his subordinates. Yet

*In this* Puck *cartoon, U. S. Grant clutches the Whiskey and Navy rings and supports an assortment of bosses, profiteers, and scandals associated with the Grant administration.* ❖

he is not entirely without blame for the corruption in his administration. He failed to take firm action against the malefactors, and, even after their guilt had been clearly established, he sometimes tried to shield them from justice. Ulysses S. Grant was the only president between Jackson and Wilson to serve two full and consecutive terms. But unlike other chief executives so favored by the electorate, Grant is commonly regarded as a failure. Although the problems he faced would have challenged any president, the shame of Grant's administration was that he made loyalty to old friends a higher priority than civil rights or sound economic principles.

# REUNION AND THE NEW SOUTH

Congressional Reconstruction prolonged the sense of sectional division and conflict for a dozen years after the guns had fallen silent. Its final liquidation in 1877 opened the way to a reconciliation of North and South. But the costs of reunion were high for less privileged groups in the South. The civil and political rights of African Americans, left unprotected, were progressively and relentlessly stripped away by white supremacist regimes. Lower-class whites saw their interests sacrificed to those of capitalists and landlords. Despite the rhetoric hailing a prosperous "New South," the region remained poor and open to exploitation by northern business interests.

## The Compromise of 1877

The election of 1876 pitted Rutherford B. Hayes of Ohio, a Republican governor untainted by the scandals of the Grant era, against Governor Samuel J. Tilden of New York, a Democratic reformer who had battled against Tammany Hall and the Tweed Ring. Honest government was apparently the electorate's highest priority. When the returns came in, Tilden had clearly won the popular vote and seemed likely to win a narrow victory in the electoral college. But the result was placed in doubt when the returns from the three southern states still controlled by the Republicans— South Carolina, Florida, and Louisiana—were contested. If Hayes were to be awarded these three states, plus one contested electoral vote in Oregon, Republican strategists realized, he would triumph in the electoral college by a single vote.

The outcome of the election remained undecided for months, plunging the nation into a major political crisis. To resolve the impasse, Congress appointed a special electoral commission of fifteen members to determine who would receive the votes of the disputed states. Originally composed of seven Democrats, seven Republicans, and an independent, the commission fell under Republican control when the independent member resigned to run for the Senate and a Republican was appointed to take his place. The commission split along party lines and voted eight to seven to award Hayes all of the disputed votes. But this decision still had to be ratified by both houses of Congress. The Republican-dominated Senate readily approved it, but the Democrats in the House planned a filibuster to delay the final counting of the electoral votes until after inauguration day. If the filibuster succeeded, neither candidate would have a majority and, as provided in the Constitution, the election would be decided by the House, where the Democrats controlled enough states to elect Tilden.

To ensure Hayes's election, Republican leaders negotiated secretly with conservative southern Democrats, some of whom seemed willing to abandon the filibuster if the last troops were withdrawn and home rule restored to the South. Eventually an informal bargain was struck, which historians have dubbed the **Compromise of 1877.** What precisely was agreed to and by whom remains a matter of dispute; but one

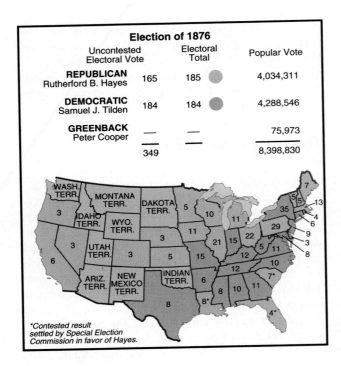

| Election of 1876 | | | |
|---|---|---|---|
| | Uncontested Electoral Vote | Electoral Total | Popular Vote |
| **REPUBLICAN** Rutherford B. Hayes | 165 | 185 | 4,034,311 |
| **DEMOCRATIC** Samuel J. Tilden | 184 | 184 | 4,288,546 |
| **GREENBACK** Peter Cooper | — | — | 75,973 |
| | | 349 | 8,398,830 |

*Contested result settled by Special Election Commission in favor of Hayes.

thing at least was understood by both sides: Hayes would be president and southern blacks would be abandoned to their fate. In a sense, Hayes did not concede anything, because he had already decided to end federal support for the crumbling Radical regimes. But southern negotiators were heartened by firm assurances that this would indeed be the policy. Some also were influenced by vaguer promises involving federal support for southern railroads and internal improvements.

With southern Democratic acquiescence, the filibuster was broken, and Hayes took the oath of office. He immediately ordered the army not to resist a Democratic takeover of state governments in South Carolina and Louisiana. Thus fell the last of the Radical governments, and the entire South was firmly under the control of white Democrats. The trauma of the war and Reconstruction had destroyed the chances for a renewal of two-party competition among white Southerners.

Northern Republicans soon reverted to denouncing the South for its suppression of black suffrage. But this "waving of the bloody shirt," which also served as a reminder of the war and northern casualties, quickly degenerated into a campaign ritual aimed at northern voters who could still be moved by sectional antagonism.

## "Redeeming" a New South

The men who came to power after Radical Reconstruction fell in one southern state after another are usually referred to as the **Redeemers.** They had differing backgrounds and previous loyalties. Some were members of the Old South's ruling planter class who had warmly supported secession and now sought to reestablish the old order with as few changes as possible. Others, of middle-class origin or outlook, favored commercial and industrial interests over agrarian groups and called for a New South committed to diversified economic development. A third group were professional politicians bending with the prevailing winds, such as Joseph E. Brown of Georgia, who had been a secessionist, a wartime governor, and a leading scalawag Republican before becoming a Democratic Redeemer.

Although historians have tried to assign the Redeemers a single coherent ideology or view of the world and have debated whether it was Old South agrarianism or New South industrialism they endorsed, these leaders can perhaps best be understood as power brokers mediating among the dominant interest groups of the South in ways that served their own political advantage. In many ways, the "rings" that they established on the state and county level were analogous to the political machines developing at the same time in northern cities. (See the Feature Essay, "Changing Views of Reconstruction," pp. 476–477.)

Redeemers did, however, agree on and endorse two basic principles: laissez-faire and white supremacy. Laissez-faire—the notion that government should be limited and should not intervene openly and directly in the economy—could unite planters, frustrated at seeing direct state support going to businessmen, and capitalist promoters who had come to realize that low taxes and freedom from government regulation were even more advantageous than state subsidies. It soon became clear that the Redeemers responded only to privileged and entrenched interest groups, especially landlords, merchants, and industrialists, and offered little or nothing to tenants, small farmers, and working people. As industrialization began to gather steam in the 1880s, Democratic regimes became increasingly accommodating to manufacturing interests and hospitable to agents of northern capital who were gaining control of the South's transportation system and its extractive industries.

White supremacy was the principal rallying cry that brought the Redeemers to power in the first place. Once in office, they found they could stay there by charging that opponents of ruling Democratic cliques were trying to divide "the white man's party" and open the way for a return to "black domination." Appeals to racism could also deflect attention from the economic grievances of groups without political clout.

The new governments were more economical than those of Reconstruction, mainly because they cut back

*The growing industrialization that was characteristic of the New South is evident in this photograph of a South Carolina cotton mill. Steam power and the abundance of cheap coal in the Appalachians helped shift the textile industry from the North to the South.* ❖

franchisement began as informal arrangements, they culminated in a legal regime of separation and exclusion that took firm hold in the 1890s.

The rise of Jim Crow in the political arena was especially bitter for Southern blacks who realized that only political power could ensure other rights. The Redeemers promised, as part of the understanding that led to the end of federal intervention in 1877, that they would respect the rights of blacks as set forth in the Fourteenth and Fifteenth Amendments. Governor Wade Hampton of South Carolina was especially vocal in pledging that African Americans would not be reduced to second-class citizenship by the new regimes. But when blacks tried to vote Republican in the "redeemed" states, they encountered renewed violence and intimidation. "Bulldozing" African American voters remained common practice in state elections during the late 1870s and early 1880s; those blacks who withstood the threat of losing their jobs or being evicted from tenant farms if they voted for the party of Lincoln were visited at night and literally whipped into line. The message was clear: Vote Democratic, or vote not at all.

Furthermore, white Democrats now controlled the electoral machinery and were able to manipulate the black vote by stuffing ballot boxes, discarding unwanted votes, or reporting fraudulent totals. Some states also imposed complicated new voting requirements to discourage black participation. Full-scale disfranchisement did not occur until literacy tests and other legalized obstacles to voting were imposed in the period from 1890 to 1910, but by that time, less formal and comprehensive methods had already made a mockery of the Fifteenth Amendment.

Nevertheless, blacks continued to vote freely in some localities until the 1890s; a few districts, like the one Robert Smalls represented, even elected black Republicans to Congress during the immediate post-Reconstruction period. The last of these, Representative George H. White of North Carolina, served until 1901. His farewell address eloquently conveyed the agony of southern blacks in the era of Jim Crow (strict segregation):

drastically on appropriations for schools and other needed public services. But they were scarcely more honest—embezzlement of funds and bribery of officials continued to occur to an alarming extent. Louisiana, for example, suffered for decades from the flagrant corruption associated with a state-chartered lottery.

The Redeemer regimes of the late 1870s and 1880s badly neglected the interests of small white farmers. Whites, as well as blacks, were suffering from the notorious crop lien system, which gave local merchants who advanced credit at high rates of interest during the growing season the right to take possession of the harvested crop on terms that buried farmers deeper and deeper in debt. As a result, increasing numbers of whites lost title to their homesteads and were reduced to tenancy. When a depression of world cotton prices added to the burden of a ruinous credit system, agrarian protesters began to challenge the ruling elite, first through the Southern Farmers' Alliance of the late 1880s and then by supporting its political descendant—the Populist party of the 1890s (see Chapter 20).

## The Rise of Jim Crow

African Americans bore the greatest hardships imposed by the new order. From 1876 through the first decade of the twentieth century, Southern states imposed a series of restrictions on black civil rights known as **Jim Crow laws.** While segregation and dis-

These parting words are in behalf of an outraged, heart-broken, bruised, and bleeding but God-fearing people, faithful, industrious, loyal people—rising people, full of potential force. . . . The only apology that I have to make for the earnestness with which I have spoken is that I am pleading for the life, the liberty, the future happiness, and manhood suffrage of one-eighth of the entire population of the United States.

The dark night of racism that fell on the South after Reconstruction seemed to unleash all the baser impulses of human nature. Between 1889 and 1899, an average of 187 blacks were lynched every year for alleged offenses against white supremacy. The protection of Southern white womanhood became the rally-

*Perhaps no event better expresses the cruel and barbaric nature of the racism and white supremacy that swept the South after Reconstruction than lynching. Although lynchings were not confined to the South, most occurred there and African American men were the most frequent victims. Here two men lean out of a barn window above a black man who is about to be hanged. Others below prepare to set on fire the pile of hay at the victim's feet. Lynchings were often public events, drawing huge crowds to watch the victim's agonizing death.* ✦

## CHRONOLOGY

| | |
|---|---|
| **1863** | Lincoln sets forth 10 percent Reconstruction plan |
| **1864** | Wade-Davis Bill passes Congress but is pocket vetoed by Lincoln |
| **1865** | Johnson moves to reconstruct the South on his own initiative ✦ Congress refuses to seat representatives and senators elected from states reestablished under presidential plan (December) |
| **1866** | Johnson vetoes Freedmen's Bureau Bill (February) ✦ Johnson vetoes Civil Rights Act; it passes over his veto (April) ✦ Congress passes Fourteenth Amendment (June) ✦ Republicans increase their congressional majority in the fall elections |
| **1867** | First Reconstruction Act is passed over Johnson's veto (March) |
| **1868** | Johnson is impeached; he avoids conviction by one vote (February–May) ✦ Southern blacks vote and serve in constitutional conventions ✦ Grant wins presidential election, defeating Horatio Seymour |
| **1869** | Congress passes Fifteenth Amendment, granting African Americans the right to vote |
| **1870–1871** | Congress passes Ku Klux Klan Acts to protect black voting rights in the South |
| **1872** | Grant reelected president, defeating Horace Greeley, candidate of Liberal Republicans and Democrats |
| **1873** | Financial panic plunges nation into depression |
| **1875** | Congress passes Specie Resumption Act ✦ "Whiskey Ring" scandal exposed |
| **1876–1877** | Disputed presidential election resolved in favor of Republican Hayes over Democrat Tilden |
| **1877** | Compromise of 1877 ends military intervention in the South and causes fall of the last Radical governments |

ing cry for many lynch mobs, as African American men were accused, often with little or no evidence, of raping white women.

Those convicted of petty crimes against property were often little better off; many were condemned to be leased out to private contractors whose brutality rivaled that of the most sadistic slaveholders. The convict-lease system enabled entrepreneurs, such as mine owners and extractors of forest products, to rent prisoners from the state and treat them as they saw fit. Unlike slaveowners, they suffered no loss when a

### SUPREME COURT DECISIONS AFFECTING BLACK CIVIL RIGHTS, 1875–1900

| Case | Effects of Court's Decisions |
| --- | --- |
| *Hall* v. *DeCuir* (1878) | Struck down Louisiana law prohibiting racial discrimination by "common carriers" (railroads, steamboats, buses). Declared the law a "burden" on interstate commerce, over which states had no authority. |
| *United States* v. *Harris* (1882) | Declared federal laws to punish crimes such as murder and assault unconstitutional. Declared such crimes to be the sole concern of local government. Ignored the frequent racial motivation behind such crimes in the South. |
| Civil Rights Cases (1883) | Struck down Civil Rights Act of 1875. Declared that Congress may not legislate on civil rights unless a state passes a discriminatory law. Declared the Fourteenth Amendment silent on racial discrimination by private citizens. |
| *Plessy* v. *Ferguson* (1896) | Upheld Louisiana statute requiring "separate but equal" accommodations on railroads. Declared that segregation is *not* necessarily discrimination. |
| *Williams* v. *Mississippi* (1898) | Upheld state law requiring a literacy test to qualify for voting. Refused to find any implication of racial discrimination in the law, although it permitted illiterate whites to vote if they "understood" the Constitution. Using such laws, southern states rapidly disfranchised blacks. |

forced laborer died from overwork. (Annual mortality rates in the convict camps ranged as high as 25 percent.) Even after convict leasing was banned in some states, blacks continued into the twentieth century to work on chain gangs and prison plantations such as the notorious Parchman Farm in Mississippi. Parchman Farm resembled a slave plantation more than a prison: Chained men picked cotton from sunup to sundown, constantly under the threat of being shot or whipped by "a leather strap, three feet long and six inches wide, known as 'Black Annie,' which hung from the driver's belt."

Finally, the dignity of blacks was cruelly affronted by the wave of segregation laws passed around the turn of the century, which served to remind them constantly that they were deemed unfit to associate with whites on any basis that implied equality. To some extent, the segregation laws were a white reaction to the refusal of many blacks to submit to voluntary segregation of railroads, streetcars, and other public facilities. On railroads, for example, elite free women of color had been accustomed to riding in the first-class ladies car; being relegated to the "smoking car" with men who were often drinking and gambling put them in physical danger of molestation.

The North and the federal government did little or nothing to stem the tide of racial oppression in the South. The high point of legislation came in 1875, when Congress passed a Civil Rights Act with far-reaching provisions to protect public and private discrimination on the basis of race. The Supreme Court invalidated the 1875 Act just eight years later, in an opinion that scolded the former slaves that "there must be some stage" when they "cease to be the special favorite of the laws." A series of Supreme Court decisions between 1878 and 1898

gutted the Reconstruction amendments and the legislation passed to enforce them, leaving blacks virtually defenseless against political and social discrimination.

## CONCLUSION: HENRY MCNEAL TURNER AND THE "UNFINISHED REVOLUTION"

The career of Henry McNeal Turner sums up the bitter side of the black experience in the South during and after Reconstruction. Born free in South Carolina in 1834, Turner became a minister of the African Methodist Episcopal (AME) Church just before the outbreak of the Civil War. During the war, he recruited African Americans for the Union army and later served as chaplain for black troops. After the fighting was over, he went to Georgia to work for the Freedmen's Bureau but encountered racial discrimination from white Bureau officers and left government service for church work and Reconstruction politics. Elected to the 1867 Georgia constitutional convention and to the state legislature in 1868, he was one of a number of black clergymen who assumed leadership roles among the freedmen. But whites won control of the Georgia legislature and expelled all the black members. Turner's reaction was an angry speech in which he proclaimed that white men were never to be trusted. As the inhabitant of a state in which blacks never gained the degree of power that they achieved in some other parts of the South, Turner was one of the first black leaders to see the failure of Reconstruction as the betrayal of African American hopes for citizenship.

Becoming a bishop of the AME Church in 1880, Turner emerged as the late nineteenth century's

# Feature Essay

# CHANGING VIEWS OF RECONSTRUCTION

A central issue of Reconstruction was the place of blacks in American life after slavery. Changing attitudes on this question strongly influenced later representations of the Reconstruction era, whether in historical writing or in the popular media. Indeed, what later generations imagined had happened in the South in the years immediately after the Civil War is a fairly reliable index of how they viewed black-white relations in their own time.

In the early twentieth century, when white supremacists were in control in the South and northern public opinion was learning to tolerate southern policies of rigid segregation and disfranchisement of blacks, historians played a major role in rationalizing the new order in southern race relations. According to historians such as Professor John W. Burgess of Columbia University, writing in 1902, Reconstruction governments represented an unholy alliance of corrupt northern carpetbaggers seeking to profit at the expense of the "prostrate South"; southern white opportunists of mean origins, known as "scalawags"; and black demagogues who sought power by putting false and dangerous aspirations for equality into the heads of newly freed slaves. What made this orgy of misrule possible, said Burgess, was the colossal blunder that Congress made when it extended the vote to "ignorant and vicious" blacks. In the eyes of Burgess and a whole school of historians, Reconstruction was "the most soul-sickening spectacle that Americans have ever been called upon to behold . . . here was government by the most ignorant and vicious part of the population for the vulgar, materialistic, brutal benefit of the governing set."

In 1915, the most ambitious film yet made by the fledgling American movie industry—D. W. Griffith's *Birth of a Nation*—popularized this image of Reconstruction and made its racism more lurid and explicit. To underscore the message of this technically brilliant film, words flashed on the screen describing Reconstruction as a callous attempt to "put the white South under the heel of the black South." In the film, leering blacks carry signs advocating interracial marriage. Mainly responsible for this state of affairs is a vengeful Congressman meant to represent Thaddeus Stevens, who hatches a devilish plot to oppress and humiliate the white South. One famous scene portrays the South Carolina state legislature as a mob of grinning barefoot blacks, carousing at the taxpayers' expense. The film's melodramatic plot features the suicide of one southern white maiden to escape the embraces of a black pursuer and the Ku Klux Klan's epic rescue of another damsel from a forced marriage to a mulatto politician.

*Birth of a Nation's* depiction of the Klan as saving white civilization from bestial blacks inspired vigorous protests from the recently founded National Association for the Advancement of Colored People (NAACP), and censors in a few northern cities deleted some of the more blatantly racist scenes. But President Woodrow Wilson endorsed the film. "My only regret is that it is all so terribly true," he is reported to have said. Most white moviegoers seemed to agree with the president rather than with the NAACP. Millions of Americans saw and applauded this cinematic triumph.

During the period between 1915 and the 1940s, most historians echoed the judgment of *Birth of a Nation* that efforts to enforce equal rights for blacks after the Civil War had been a grave mistake. One popular work of that era was *The Tragic Era,* and another summed up Reconstruction as "the blackout of honest government." The biases of mainstream historiography served to justify the Jim Crow system of the South by portraying blacks as unqualified for citizenship.

A few black historians of the 1920s and 1930s advanced the contrary view that Reconstruction was a noble effort to achieve a color-blind democracy, which failed because of the strength of white racism and conservative economic interests. The most powerful example of this early revisionism was W. E. B. DuBois's *Black Reconstruction in America* (1935).

During the 1950s and 1960s, another image of Reconstruction emerged. The majority of historians writing about the era finally rejected the exaggerations, distortions, and racist assumptions of the traditional view. The triumph of "revisionism" was evident in 1965 when Kenneth M. Stampp published his *Era of Reconstruction.* As influential northern opinion shifted from tolerance of segregation to support for the black struggle for equality in the South, a more favorable view of earlier efforts on behalf of civil rights became acceptable. White liberal historians like Stampp concentrated on rehabilitating the Radical Republicans by stressing their idealism, while black scholars like John Hope Franklin highlighted the constructive policies and positive achievements of the much maligned black leaders of the Reconstruction South. Previous moral judgments thus tended to be reversed; white and black Republicans became the heroes, and the southern whites who resisted and eventually overthrew Reconstruction became the villains. The analogy between these earlier adversaries and the civil rights activists and southern segregationists of the 1960s was clear.

During the 1970s and early 1980s, a "postrevisionism" began to develop. As it became apparent that the dream of equality for blacks was still unrealized, historians responded to the changing perceptions and complex crosscurrents of black-white relations in their own time by taking another look at Reconstruction. They found, among other things, that those in charge of efforts to make blacks equal citizens in the late 1860s had views that were quite moderate by the standards of the post–civil rights era of the 1970s and early 1980s. Radical Reconstruction no longer seemed very radical. The reputations of carpetbag-

gers and upper-class scalawags went down again as historians emphasized their opportunism and probusiness economic policies at the expense of social justice. Black politicians, too, came in for critical reassessment. It was argued that many worked more for their own interests as members of a black middle class than for the kinds of policies—such as land reform—that would have met the vital needs of their impoverished constituents.

Eric Foner's widely acclaimed *Reconstruction: America's Unfinished Revolution, 1863–1877* (1998) reemphasized some of the achievements of Radical rule in the South. Reflecting the new trend toward "history from the bottom up," its heroes were local black activists rather than white Radicals or even the black elite. But Foner and W. E. B. DuBois, historians who have argued that Reconstruction was a noble and inspiring effort to achieve racial democ-

racy, have had to acknowledge that it failed to prevent the restoration of a brutally oppressive form of white supremacy after the "Redemption" of the 1870s. Was that failure due primarily to the deep-seated racism that drove the white South to carry on a guerrilla war against black participation in politics and also prevented many white Republicans from identifying fully with the cause of black equality? Or did it result from the gulf between the economic interests of those in charge of implementing and managing Reconstruction and the poor people of the South who were supposed to be its beneficiaries? As historians debate this unresolved issue, they should be aware that policymakers and sociologists are currently engaged in similar debates about the relative significance of "race" and "class" as explanations for the persistence of black disadvantage in the United States.

leading proponent of black emigration to Africa. Because he believed that white Americans were so deeply prejudiced against blacks that they would never grant them equal rights, Turner became an early advocate of black nationalism and a total separation of the races. Emigration became a popular movement among southern blacks, who were especially hard hit by terror and oppression just after the end of Reconstruction. Still, a majority of blacks in the nation as a whole and even in Turner's own church refused to give up on the hope of eventual equality on American soil. But Bishop Turner's anger and despair were the understandable responses of a proud man to the way that he and his fellow African Americans had been treated in the post–Civil War period.

By the late 1880s, the wounds of the Civil War were healing, and white Americans were seized by the spirit of sectional reconciliation. Union and Confederate veterans were tenting together and celebrating their common Americanism. "Reunion" was becoming a cultural as well as political reality. But whites could come back together only because Northerners had tacitly agreed to give Southerners a free hand in their efforts to reduce blacks to a new form of servitude. The "outraged, heart-broken,

*Henry McNeal Turner, who was born in freedom, became a bishop of the African Methodist Episcopal Church and was elected to the Georgia legislature.* ❖

bruised, and bleeding" African Americans of the South paid the heaviest price for sectional reunion. Reconstruction remained, in the words of historian Eric Foner, an "unfinished revolution." It would be another century before African Americans rose up once more to demand full civil and political rights.

## RECOMMENDED READING

The best one-volume account of Reconstruction is Eric Foner, *Reconstruction: America's Unfinished Revolution* (1988). Two excellent short surveys are Kenneth M. Stampp, *The Era of Reconstruction, 1865–1877* (1965), and John Hope Franklin, *Reconstruction: After the Civil War* (1961). Both were early efforts to synthesize modern "revisionist" interpretations. W. E. B. DuBois, *Black Reconstruction in America, 1860–1880* (1935), remains brilliant and provocative. On the politics of Reconstruction, see Stephen David Kantrowitz, *Ben Tillman and the Reconstruction of White Supremacy* (2001), Laura F. Edwards, *Gendered Strife and Confusion: The Political Culture of Reconstruction* (1997), J. Morgan Kousser and James M. McPherson, eds., *Region, Race, and Reconstruction: Essays in Honor of C. Vann Woodward* (1982), and Eric Foner, *Nothing But Freedom: Emancipation and Its Legacy* (1983).

Leon F. Litwack, *Been in the Storm So Long: The Aftermath of Slavery* (1979), provides a moving portrayal of the black experience of emancipation. On changing society and family life during Reconstruction, see Noralee Frankel, *Freedom's Women: Black Women and Families in Reconstruction Era Mississippi* (1999), Dylan Penningroth, *Claiming Kin and Property: African American Life Before and After Emancipation* (2003), and Amy Dru Stanley, *From Bondage to Contract: Wage Labor, Marriage, and the Market in the Age of Slave Emancipation* (1998). On what freedom meant in economic terms, see Gerald David Jaynes, *Branches Without Roots: Genesis of the Black Working Class in the American South, 1862–1882* (1986). A work that focuses on ex-slaves' attempts to create their own economic order is Julie Saville, *The Work of Reconstruction: Free Slave to Wage Laborer in South Carolina, 1860–1870* (1994). The best overview of the postwar southern economy is Gavin Wright, *Old South, New South* (1986). On the end of Reconstruction, see David W. Blight, *Race and Reunion: The Civil War in American Memory* (2000). On the character of the post-Reconstruction South, see the classic work by C. Vann Woodward, *Origins of the New South, 1877–1913* (1951) and Edward Ayers, *The Promise of the New South* (1992).

**For a list of additional titles related to this chapter's topics, please see** http://www.ablongman.com/divine.

# SUGGESTED WEB SITES

### Diary and Letters of Rutherford B. Hayes

http://www.ohiohistory.org/onlinedoc/hayes/index.cfm

The Rutherford B. Hayes Presidential Center in Fremont, Ohio, maintains this searchable database of Hayes's writings.

### Images of African Americans from the Nineteenth Century

http://digital.nypl.org/schomburg/images_aa19/

The New York Public Library-Schomburg Center for Research in Black Culture site contains numerous visuals.

### Freedmen and Southern Society Project (University of Maryland-College Park)

http://www.inform.umd.edu/ARHU/Depts/History/Freedman/home.html

This site contains a chronology and sample documents from several print collections or primary sources about emancipation and freedom in the 1860s.

### Andrew Johnson

http://www.whitehouse.gov/WH/glimpse/presidents/html/aj17.html

White House history of Johnson.

### Ulysses S. Grant

http://www.whitehouse.gov/WH/glimpse/presidents/html/ug18.html

White House history of Grant.

### History of the Suffrage Movement

http://www.rochester.edu/SBA

This site includes a chronology, important texts relating to women's suffrage, and biographical information about Susan B. Anthony and Elizabeth Cady Stanton.

# Appendix

### The Declaration of Independence

### The Articles of Confederation

### The Constitution of the United States of America

### Amendments to the Constitution

### Presidential Elections

---

For additional reference material, go to
http://www.ablongman.com/divine/appendix
The on-line appendix includes the following:

---

# THE DECLARATION OF INDEPENDENCE

**In Congress, July 4, 1776**

## The Unanimous Declaration of the Thirteen United States of America,

When, in the course of human events, it becomes necessary for one people to dissolve the political bonds which have connected them with another, and to assume, among the powers of the earth, the separate and equal station to which the laws of nature and of nature's God entitle them, a decent respect to the opinions of mankind requires that they should declare the causes which impel them to the separation.

We hold these truths to be self-evident: That all men are created equal; that they are endowed by their Creator with certain unalienable rights; that among these are life, liberty, and the pursuit of happiness; that, to secure these rights, governments are instituted among men, deriving their just powers from the consent of the governed; that whenever any form of government becomes destructive of these ends, it is the right of the people to alter or to abolish it, and to institute new government, laying its foundation on such principles, and organizing its powers in such form, as to them shall seem most likely to effect their safety and happiness. Prudence, indeed, will dictate that governments long established should not be changed for light and transient causes; and accordingly all experience hath shown that mankind are more disposed to suffer, while evils are sufferable, than to right themselves by abolishing the forms to which they are accustomed. But when a long train of abuses and usurpations, pursuing invariably the same object, evinces a design to reduce them under absolute despotism, it is their right, it is their duty, to throw off such government, and to provide new guards for their future security. Such has been the patient sufferance of these colonies; and such is now the necessity which constrains them to alter their former systems of government. The history of the present King of Great Britain is a history of repeated injuries and usurpations, all having in direct object the establishment of an absolute tyranny over these states. To prove this, let facts be submitted to a candid world.

He has refused his assent to laws, the most wholesome and necessary for the public good.

He has forbidden his governors to pass laws of immediate and pressing importance, unless suspended in their operation till his assent should be obtained; and, when so suspended, he has utterly neglected to attend to them.

He has refused to pass other laws for the accommodation of large districts of people, unless those people would relinquish the right of representation in the legislature, a right inestimable to them, and formidable to tyrants only.

He has called together legislative bodies at places unusual, uncomfortable, and distant from the depository of their public records, for the sole purpose of fatiguing them into compliance with his measures.

He has dissolved representative houses repeatedly, for opposing, with manly firmness, his invasions on the rights of the people.

He has refused for a long time, after such dissolutions, to cause others to be elected; whereby the legislative powers, incapable of annihilation, have returned to the people at large for their exercise; the state remaining, in the mean time, exposed to all the dangers of invasions from without and convulsions within.

He has endeavored to prevent the population of these states; for that purpose obstructing the laws for naturalization of foreigners; refusing to pass others to encourage their migration hither, and raising the conditions of new appropriations of lands.

He has obstructed the administration of justice, by refusing his assent to laws for establishing judiciary powers.

He has made judges dependent on his will alone, for the tenure of their offices, and the amount and payment of their salaries.

He has erected a multitude of new offices, and sent hither swarms of officers to harass our people and eat out their substance.

He has kept among us, in times of peace, standing armies, without the consent of our legislatures.

He has affected to render the military independent of, and superior to, the civil power.

He has combined with others to subject us to a jurisdiction foreign to our constitution, and unacknowledged by our laws, giving his assent to their acts of pretended legislation:

For quartering large bodies of armed troops among us;

For protecting them, by a mock trial, from punishment for any murder which they should commit on the inhabitants of these states;

For cutting off our trade with all parts of the world;

For imposing taxes on us without our consent;

For depriving us, in many cases, of the benefits of trial by jury;

For transporting us beyond seas, to be tried for pretended offenses;

For abolishing the free system of English laws in a neighboring province, establishing therein an arbitrary government, and enlarging its boundaries, so as to render it at once an example and fit instrument for introducing the same absolute rule into these colonies;

For taking away our charters, abolishing our most valuable laws, and altering fundamentally the forms of our governments;

For suspending our own legislatures, and declaring themselves invested with power to legislate for us in all cases whatsoever.

He has abdicated government here, by declaring us out of his protection and waging war against us.

He has plundered our seas, ravaged our coasts, burned our towns, and destroyed the lives of our people.

He is at this time transporting large armies of foreign mercenaries to complete the works of death, desolation, and tyranny already begun with circumstances of cruelty and perfidy scarcely paralleled in the most barbarous ages, and totally unworthy the head of a civilized nation.

He has constrained our fellow-citizens, taken captive on the high seas, to bear arms against their country, to become the executioners of their friends and brethren, or to fall themselves by their hands.

He has excited domestic insurrection among us, and has endeavored to bring on the inhabitants of our frontiers the merciless Indian savages, whose known rule of warfare is an undistinguished destruction of all ages, sexes, and conditions.

In every stage of these oppressions we have petitioned for redress in the most humble terms; our repeated petitions have been answered only by repeated injury. A prince, whose character is thus marked by every act which may define a tyrant, is unfit to be the ruler of a free people.

Nor have we been wanting in our attentions to our British brethren. We have warned them, from time to time, of attempts by their legislature to extend an unwarrantable jurisdiction over us. We have reminded them of the circumstances of our emigration and settlement here. We have appealed to their native justice and magnanimity; and we have conjured them, by the ties of our common kindred, to disavow these usurpations, which would inevitably interrupt our connections and correspondence. They, too, have been deaf to the voice of justice and of consanguinity. We must, therefore, acquiesce in the necessity which denounces our separation, and hold them, as we hold the rest of mankind, enemies in war, in peace friends.

We, therefore, the representatives of the United States of America, in General Congress assembled, appealing to the Supreme Judge of the world for the rectitude of our intentions, do, in the name and by the authority of the good people of these colonies, solemnly publish and declare, that these United Colonies are, and of right ought to be, FREE AND INDEPENDENT STATES; that they are absolved from all allegiance to the British crown, and that all political connection between them and the state of Great Britain is, and ought to be, totally dissolved; and that, as free and independent states, they have full power to levy war, conclude peace, contract alliances, establish commerce, and do all other acts and things which independent states may of right do. And for the support of this declaration, with a firm reliance on the protection of Divine Providence, we mutually pledge to each other our lives, our fortunes, and our sacred honor.

### John Hancock

Button Gwinnett
Lyman Hall
Geo. Walton
Wm. Hooper
Joseph Hewes
John Penn
Edward Rutledge
Thos. Heyward, Junr.
Thomas Lynch, Junr.
Arthur Middleton
Samuel Chase
Wm. Paca
Thos. Stone
Charles Carroll of Carrollton
George Wythe
Richard Henry Lee
Th. Jefferson
Benj. Harrison
Thos. Nelson, Jr.

Francis Lightfoot Lee
Carter Braxton
Robt. Morris
Benjamin Rush
Benja. Franklin
John Morton
Geo. Clymer
Jas. Smith
Geo. Taylor
James Wilson
Geo. Ross
Caesar Rodney
Geo. Read
Tho. M'kean
Wm. Floyd
Phil. Livingston
Frans. Lewis
Lewis Morris
Richd. Stockton

Jno. Witherspoon
Fras. Hopkinson
John Hart
Abra. Clark
Josiah Bartlett
Wm. Whipple
Saml. Adams
John Adams
Robt. Treat Paine
Elbridge Gerry
Step. Hopkins
William Ellery
Roger Sherman
Sam'el Huntington
Wm. Williams
Oliver Wolcott
Matthew Thornton

# THE ARTICLES OF CONFEDERATION

Between the States of New Hampshire, Massachusetts Bay, Rhode Island and Providence Plantations, Connecticut, New York, New Jersey, Pennsylvania, Delaware, Maryland, Virginia, North Carolina, South Carolina, Georgia

## ARTICLE 1

The stile of this confederacy shall be "The United States of America."

## ARTICLE 2

Each State retains its sovereignty, freedom and independence, and every power, jurisdiction, and right, which is not by this confederation expressly delegated to the United States, in Congress assembled.

## ARTICLE 3

The said states hereby severally enter into a firm league of friendship with each other for their common defence, the security of their liberties and their mutual and general welfare; binding themselves to assist each other against all force offered to, or attacks made upon them, or any of them, on account of religion, sovereignty, trade, or any other pretence whatever.

## ARTICLE 4

The better to secure and perpetuate mutual friendship and intercourse among the people of the different states in this union, the free inhabitants of each of these states, paupers, vagabonds, and fugitives from justice excepted, shall be entitled to all privileges and immunities of free citizens in the several states; and the people of each State shall have free ingress and regress to and from any other State, and shall enjoy therein all the privileges of trade and commerce, subject to the same duties, impositions, and restrictions, as the inhabitants thereof respectively; provided, that such restrictions shall not extend so far as to prevent the removal of property, imported into any State, to any other State of which the owner is an inhabitant; provided also, that no imposition, duties, or restriction, shall be laid by any State on the property of the United States, or either of them.

If any person guilty of, or charged with treason, felony, or other high misdemeanor in any State, shall flee from justice and be found in any of the United States, he shall, upon demand of the governor or executive power of the State from which he fled, be delivered up and removed to the State having jurisdiction of his offence.

Full faith and credit shall be given in each of these states to the records, acts, and judicial proceedings of the courts and magistrates of every other State.

## ARTICLE 5

For the more convenient management of the general interests of the United States, delegates shall be annually appointed, in such manner as the legislature of each State shall direct, to meet in Congress, on the 1st Monday in November in every year, with a power reserved to each State to recall its delegates, or any of them, at any time within the year, and to send others in their stead for the remainder of the year.

No State shall be represented in Congress by less than two, nor by more than seven members; and no person shall be capable of being a delegate for more than three years in any term of six years; nor shall any person, being a delegate, be capable of holding any office under the United States, for which he, or any other for his benefit, receives any salary, fees, or emolument of any kind.

Each State shall maintain its own delegates in a meeting of the states, and while they act as members of the committee of the states.

In determining questions in the United States, in Congress assembled, each State shall have one vote.

Freedom of speech and debate in Congress shall not be impeached or questioned in any court or place out of Congress: and the members of Congress shall be protected in their persons from arrests and imprisonments, during the time of their going to and from, and attendance on Congress, except for treason, felony, or breach of the peace.

## ARTICLE 6

No State, without the consent of the United States, in Congress assembled, shall send any embassy to, or receive any embassy from, or enter into any conference, agreement, alliance, or treaty with any king, prince, or state; nor shall any person, holding any office of profit or trust under the United States, or any of them, accept of any present, emolument, office or title, of any kind whatever, from any king, prince, or foreign state; nor shall the United States, in Congress assembled, or any of them, grant any title of nobility.

No two or more statés shall enter into any treaty, confederation, or alliance, whatever, between them, without the consent of the United States, in Congress assembled, specifying accurately the purposes for which the same is to be entered into, and how long it shall continue.

No State shall lay any imposts or duties which may interfere with any stipulations in treaties entered into by the United States, in Congress assembled, with any king, prince, or state, in pursuance of any treaties already proposed by Congress to the courts of France and Spain.

No vessels of war shall be kept up in time of peace by any State, except such number only as shall be deemed necessary by the United States, in Congress assembled, for the defence of such State or its trade; nor shall any body of forces be kept up by any State, in time of peace, except such number only as, in the judgment of the United States, in Congress assembled, shall be deemed requisite to garrison the forts necessary for the defence of such State; but every State shall always keep up a well regulated and disciplined militia, sufficiently armed and accoutred, and shall provide, and constantly have ready for use, in public stores, a due number of field pieces and tents, and a proper quantity of arms, ammunition and camp equipage.

No State shall engage in any war without the consent of the United States, in Congress assembled, unless such State be actually invaded by enemies, or shall have received certain advice of a resolution being formed by some nation of Indians to invade such State, and the danger is so imminent as not to admit of a delay till the United States, in Congress assembled, can be consulted; nor shall any State grant commissions to any ships or vessels of war, nor letters of marque or reprisal, except it be after a declaration of war by the United States, in Congress assembled, and then only against the kingdom or state, and the subjects thereof, against which war has been so declared, and under such regulations as shall be established by the United States, in Congress assembled, unless such States be infested by pirates, in which case vessels of war may be fitted out for that occasion, and kept so long as the danger shall continue, or until the United States, in Congress assembled, shall determine otherwise.

## ARTICLE 7

When land forces are raised by any State for the common defence, all officers of or under the rank of colonel, shall be appointed by the legislature of each State respectively, by whom such forces shall be raised, or in such manner as such State shall direct; and all vacancies shall be filled up by the State which first made the appointment.

## ARTICLE 8

All charges of war and all other expences, that shall be incurred for the common defence or general welfare, and allowed by the United States, in Congress assembled, shall be defrayed out of a common treasury, which shall be supplied by the several states, in proportion to the value of all land within each State, granted to or surveyed for any person, as such land and the buildings and improvements thereon shall be estimated according to such mode as the United States, in Congress assembled, shall, from time to time, direct and appoint.

The taxes for paying that proportion shall be laid and levied by the authority and direction of the legislatures of the several states, within the time agreed upon by the United States, in Congress assembled.

## ARTICLE 9

The United States, in Congress assembled, shall have the sole and exclusive right and power of determining on peace and war, except in the cases mentioned in the 6th article; of sending and receiving ambassadors; entering into treaties and alliances, provided that no treaty of commerce shall be made, whereby the legislative power of the respective states shall be restrained from imposing such imposts and duties on foreigners as their own people are subjected to, or from prohibiting the exportation or importation of any species of goods or commodities whatsoever; of establishing rules for

deciding, in all cases, what captures on land or water shall be legal, and in what manner prizes, taken by land or naval forces in the service of the United States, shall be divided or appropriated; of granting letters of marque and reprisal in times of peace; appointing courts for the trial of piracies and felonies committed on the high seas, and establishing courts for receiving and determining, finally, appeals in all cases of captures; provided, that no member of Congress shall be appointed a judge of any of the said courts.

The United States, in Congress assembled, shall also be the last resort on appeal in all disputes and differences now subsisting, or that hereafter may arise between two or more states concerning boundary, jurisdiction or any other cause whatever; which authority shall always be exercised in the manner following: whenever the legislative or executive authority, or lawful agent of any State, in controversy with another, shall present a petition to Congress, stating the matter in question, and praying for a hearing, notice thereof shall be given, by order of Congress, to the legislative or executive authority of the other State in controversy, and a day assigned for the appearance of the parties by their lawful agents, who shall then be directed to appoint, by joint consent, commissioners or judges to constitute a court for hearing and determining the matter in question; but, if they cannot agree, Congress shall name three persons out of each of the United States, and from the list of such persons each party shall alternately strike out one, in the petitioners beginning, until the number shall be reduced to thirteen; and from that number not less than seven, nor more than nine names, as Congress shall direct, shall, in the presence of Congress, be drawn out by lot; and the persons whose names shall be drawn, or any five of them, shall be commissioners or judges to hear and finally determine the controversy, so always as a major part of the judges who shall hear the cause shall agree in the determination; and if either party shall neglect to attend at the day appointed, without shewing reasons which Congress shall judge sufficient, or, being present, shall refuse to strike, the Congress shall proceed to nominate three persons out of each State, and the secretary of Congress shall strike in behalf of such party absent or refusing; and the judgment and sentence of the court to be appointed, in the manner before prescribed, shall be final and conclusive; and if any of the parties shall refuse to submit to the authority of such court, or to appear or defend their claim or cause, the court shall nevertheless proceed to pronounce sentence or judgment, which shall, in like manner, be final and decisive, the judgment or sentence and other proceedings being, in either case, transmitted to Congress, and lodged among the acts of Congress for the security of the parties concerned: provided, that every commissioner, before he sits in judgment, shall take an oath, to be administered by one of the judges of the supreme or superior court of the State where the cause shall be tried, "well and truly to hear and determine the matter in question, according to the best of his judgment, without favour, affection, or hope of reward": provided, also, that no State shall be deprived of territory for the benefit of the United States.

All controversies concerning the private right of soil, claimed under different grants of two or more states, whose jurisdictions, as they may respect such lands and the states which passed such grants, are adjusted, the said grants, or either of them, being at the same time claimed to have originated antecedent to such settlement of jurisdiction, shall, on the petition of either party to the Congress of the United States, be finally determined, as near as may be, in the same manner as is before prescribed for deciding disputes respecting territorial jurisdiction between different states.

The United States, in Congress assembled, shall also have the sole and exclusive right and power of regulating the alloy and value of coin struck by their own authority, or by that of the respective states; fixing the standard of weights and measures throughout the United States; regulating the trade and managing all affairs with the Indians not members of any of the states; provided that the legislative right of any State within its own limits be not infringed or violated; establishing and regulating post offices from one State to another throughout all the United States, and exacting such postage on the papers passing through the same as may be requisite to defray the expences of the said office; appointing all officers of the land forces in the service of the United States, excepting regimental officers; appointing all the officers of the naval forces, and commissioning all officers whatever in the service of the United States; making rules for the government and regulation of the said land and naval forces, and directing their operations.

The United States, in Congress assembled, shall have authority to appoint a committee to sit in the recess of Congress, to be denominated "a Committee of the States," and to consist of one delegate from each State, and to appoint such other committees and civil officers as may be necessary for managing the general affairs of the United States, under their direction; to appoint one of their number to preside; provided that no person be allowed to serve in the office of president more than one year in any term of three years; to ascertain the necessary sums of money to be raised for the service of the United States, and to appropriate and apply the same for defraying the public expences; to borrow money or emit bills on the credit of the United States, transmitting, every half year, to the respective states, an account of the sums of money so borrowed or emitted; to build and equip a navy; to agree upon the number of land forces, and to make requisitions from each State for its quota, in proportion to the number of white inhabitants in such State; which requisitions shall be binding; and, thereupon, the legislature of each State shall appoint the regimental officers, raise the men, and cloathe, arm, and equip them in a soldier-like manner, at the expence of the United States; and the officers and men so cloathed, armed, and equipped, shall march to the place appointed and within the time agreed on by the United States, in Congress assembled; but if the United States, in Congress assembled, shall, on consideration of circumstances, judge proper that any State should not raise men, or should raise a smaller number than its quota, and that any other State should raise a greater number of men than the quota thereof, such extra number shall be raised, officered, cloathed, armed, and equipped in the same manner as the quota of such State, unless the legislature of such State shall judge that such extra number cannot be safely spared out of the same, in which case they shall raise, officer, cloathe, arm, and equip as many of such extra number as they judge can be safely spared. And the officers and men so cloathed, armed, and equipped, shall march to the place appointed and within the time agreed on by the United States, in Congress assembled.

The United States, in Congress assembled, shall never engage in a war, nor grant letters of marque and reprisal in time of peace, nor enter into any treaties or alliances, nor coin money, nor regulate the value thereof, nor ascertain the sums and expences necessary for the defence and welfare of the United States, or any of them: nor emit bills, nor borrow money on the credit of the United States, nor appropriate money, nor agree upon the number of vessels of war to be built or purchased, or the number of land or sea forces to be raised, nor appoint a commander in chief of the army or navy, unless nine states assent to the same; nor shall a question on any other point, except for adjourning from day to day, be determined, unless by the votes of a majority of the United States, in Congress assembled.

The Congress of the United States shall have power to adjourn to any time within the year, and to any place within the United States, so that no period of adjournment be for a longer duration than the space of six months, and shall publish the journal of their proceedings monthly, except such parts thereof, relating to treaties, alliances or military operations, as, in their judgment, require secrecy; and the yeas and nays of the delegates of each State on any question shall be entered on the journal, when it is desired by any delegate; and the delegates of a State, or any of them, at his, or their request, shall be furnished with a transcript of the said journal, except such parts as are above excepted, to lay before the legislatures of the several states.

## ARTICLE 10

The committee of the states, or any nine of them, shall be authorized to execute, in the recess of Congress, such of the powers of Congress as the United States, in Congress assembled, by the consent of nine states, shall, from time to time, think expedient to vest them with; provided, that no power be delegated to the said committee for the exercise of which, by the articles of confederation, the voice of nine states, in the Congress of the United States assembled, is requisite.

## ARTICLE 11

Canada acceding to this confederation, and joining in the measures of the United States, shall be admitted into and entitled to all the advantages of this union; but no other colony shall be admitted into the same, unless such admission be agreed to by nine states.

## ARTICLE 12

All bills of credit emitted, monies borrowed and debts contracted by, or under the authority of Congress before the assembling of the United States, in pursuance of the present confederation, shall be deemed and considered as a charge against the United States, for payment and satisfaction whereof the said United States and the public faith are hereby solemnly pledged.

## ARTICLE 13

Every State shall abide by the determinations of the United States, in Congress assembled, on all questions which, by this confederation, are submitted to them. And the articles of this confederation shall be inviolably observed by every State, and the union shall be perpetual; nor shall any alteration at any time hereafter be made in any of them, unless such alteration be agreed to in a Congress of the United States, and be afterwards confirmed by the legislatures of every State.

These articles shall be proposed to the legislatures of all the United States, to be considered, and if approved of by them, they are advised to authorize their delegates to ratify the same in the Congress of the United States; which being done, the same shall become conclusive.

# NSTITUTION OF THE UNITED STATES OF AMERICA

## PREAMBLE

We the People of the United States, in Order to form a more perfect Union, establish Justice, insure domestic Tranquility, provide for the common defence, promote the general Welfare, and secure the Blessings of Liberty to ourselves and our Posterity, do ordain and establish this Constitution for the United States of America.

## ARTICLE I

### Section 1

All legislative Powers herein granted shall be vested in a Congress of the United States, which shall consist of a Senate and House of Representatives.

### Section 2

The House of Representatives shall be composed of Members chosen every second Year by the People of the several States, and the Electors in each State shall have the Qualifications requisite for Electors of the most numerous Branch of the State Legislature.

No Person shall be a Representative who shall not have attained to the Age of twenty five Years, and been seven Years a Citizen of the United States, and who shall not, when elected, be an inhabitant of that State in which he shall be chosen.

Representatives and direct Taxes shall be apportioned among the several States which may be included within this Union, according to their respective Numbers, *which shall be determined by adding to the whole Number of free Persons, including those bound to Service for a Term of Years, and excluding Indians not taxed, three fifths of all other Persons.* The actual Enumeration shall be made within three Years after the first Meeting of the Congress of the United States, and within every subsequent Term of ten Years, in such Manner as they shall by Law direct. The Number of Representatives shall not exceed one for every thirty Thousand, but each State shall have at Least one Representative; *and until such enumeration shall be made, the State of New Hampshire shall be entitled to chuse three, Massachusetts eight, Rhode-Island and Providence Plantations one, Connecticut five, New York six, New Jersey four, Pennsylvania eight, Delaware one, Maryland six, Virginia ten, North Carolina five, South Carolina five, and Georgia three.*

When vacancies happen in the Representation from any State, the Executive Authority thereof shall issue Writs of Election to fill such Vacancies.

The House of Representatives shall chuse their Speaker and other Officers; and shall have the sole Power of Impeachment.

### Section 3

The Senate of the United States shall be composed of two Senators from each State, *chosen by the Legislature thereof,* for six Years; and each Senator shall have one Vote.

*Immediately after they shall be assembled in Consequence of the first Election, they shall be divided as equally as may be into three Classes. The Seats of the Senators of the first Class shall be vacated at the Expiration of the second Year, of the second Class at the Expiration of the fourth Year, and of the third Class at the Expiration of the sixth Year so that one third may be chosen every second Year; and if Vacancies happen by Resignation, or otherwise, during the Recess of the Legislature of any state, the Executive thereof may make temporary Appointments until the next Meeting of the Legislature, which shall then fill such Vacancies.*

No Person shall be a Senator who shall not have attained to the Age of thirty Years, and been nine Years a Citizen of the United States, and who shall not, when elected, be an Inhabitant of that State for which he shall be chosen.

The Vice President of the United States shall be President of the Senate, but shall have no Vote, unless they be equally divided.

The Senate shall chuse their other Officers, and also a President *pro tempore,* in the Absence of the Vice President, or when he shall exercise the Office of President of the United States.

The Senate shall have the sole Power to try all Impeachments. When sitting for that Purpose, they shall be on Oath or Affirmation. When the President of the United States is tried the Chief Justice shall preside: And no Person shall be convicted without the Concurrence of two thirds of the Members present.

Judgment in Cases of Impeachment shall not extend further than to removal from Office, and disqualification to hold and enjoy any Office of honor, Trust or Profit under the United States: but the Party convicted shall nevertheless be liable and subject to Indictment, Trial, Judgment and Punishment, according to Law.

### Section 4

The Times, Places and Manner of holding Elections for Senators and Representatives, shall be prescribed in each State by the Legislature thereof; but the Congress may at any time by Law make or alter such Regulations, except as to the Places of chusing Senators.

The Congress shall assemble at least once in every Year, *and such Meeting shall be on the first Monday in December, unless they shall by Law appoint a different Day.*

### Section 5

Each House shall be the Judge of the Elections, Returns and Qualifications of its own Members, and a Majority of each shall constitute a Quorum to do Business; but a smaller Number may adjourn from day to day, and may be

---

*Passages no longer in effect are printed in italic type.

authorized to compel the Attendance of absent Members, in such Manner, and under such Penalties as each House may provide.

Each House may determine the Rules of its Proceedings, punish its Members for disorderly Behaviour, and, with the Concurrence of two thirds, expel a Member.

Each House shall keep a Journal of its Proceedings, and from time to time publish the same, excepting such Parts as may in their Judgment require Secrecy; and the Yeas and Nays of the Members of either House on any question shall, at the Desire of one fifth of those Present, be entered on the Journal.

Neither House, during the Session of Congress, shall, without the Consent of the other, adjourn for more than three days, nor to any other Place than that in which the two Houses shall be sitting.

## Section 6

The Senators and Representatives shall receive a Compensation for their Services, to be ascertained by Law, and paid out of the Treasury of the United States. They shall in all Cases, except Treason, Felony and Breach of the Peace, be privileged from Arrest during their Attendance at the Session of their respective Houses, and in going to and returning from the same; and for any Speech or Debate in either House, they shall not be questioned in any other Place.

No Senator or Representative shall, during the Time for which he was elected, be appointed to any civil Office under the Authority of the United States, which shall have been created, or the Emoluments whereof shall have been encreased during such time, and no Person holding any Office under the United States, shall be a Member of either House during his Continuance in Office.

## Section 7

All Bills for raising Revenue shall originate in the House of Representatives; but the Senate may propose or concur with Amendments as on other Bills.

Every Bill which shall have passed the House of Representatives and the Senate, shall, before it become a Law, be presented to the President of the United States; If he approve he shall sign it, but if not he shall return it, with his Objections to the House in which it shall have originated, who shall enter the Objections at large on their Journal, and proceed to reconsider it. If after such Reconsideration two thirds of that House shall agree to pass the Bill, it shall be sent, together with the Objections, to the other House, by which it shall likewise be reconsidered, and if approved by two thirds of that House, it shall become a Law. But in all such Cases the Votes of both Houses shall be determined by yeas and Nays, and the Names of the Persons voting for and against the Bill shall be entered on the Journal of each House respectively. If any Bill shall not be returned by the President within ten Days (Sundays excepted) after it shall have been presented to him, the Same shall be a Law, in like Manner as if he had signed it, unless the Congress by their Adjournment prevent its Return, in which Case it shall not be a Law.

Every Order, Resolution, or Vote to which the Concurrence of the Senate and House of Representatives may be necessary (except on a question of Adjournment) shall be presented to the President of the United States; and before the Same shall take Effect, shall be approved by him, or being disapproved by him, shall be repassed by two thirds of the Senate and House of Representatives, according to the Rules and Limitations prescribed in the Case of a Bill.

## Section 8

The Congress shall have Power To lay and collect Taxes, Duties, Imposts and Excises, to pay the Debts and provide for the common Defence and general Welfare of the United States; but all Duties, Imposts and Excises shall be uniform throughout the United States;

To borrow Money on the credit of the United States;

To regulate Commerce with foreign Nations, and among the several States, and with the Indian Tribes;

To establish an uniform Rule of Naturalization, and uniform Laws on the subject of Bankruptcies throughout the United States;

To coin Money, regulate the Value thereof, and of foreign Coin, and fix the Standard of Weights and Measures;

To provide for the Punishment of counterfeiting the Securities and current Coin of the United States;

To establish Post Offices and post Roads;

To promote the Progress of Science and useful Arts, by securing for limited Times to Authors and Inventors the exclusive Right to their respective Writings and Discoveries;

To constitute Tribunals inferior to the supreme Court;

To define and punish Piracies and Felonies committed on the high Seas, and Offences against the Law of Nations;

To declare War, grant Letters of Marque and Reprisal, and make Rules concerning Captures on Land and Water;

To raise and support Armies, but no Appropriation of Money to that Use shall be for a longer Term than two Years;

To provide and maintain a Navy;

To make Rules for the Government and Regulation of the land and naval Forces;

To provide for calling forth the Militia to execute the Laws of the Union, suppress Insurrections and repel Invasions;

To provide for organizing, arming, and disciplining, the Militia, and for governing such Part of them as may be employed in the Service of the United States, reserving to the States respectively, the Appointment of the Officers, and the Authority of training the Militia according to the discipline prescribed by Congress;

To exercise exclusive Legislation in all Cases whatsoever, over such District (not exceeding ten Miles square) as may, by Cession of particular States, and the Acceptance of Congress, become the Seat of the Government of the United States, and to exercise like Authority over all Places purchased by the Consent of the Legislature of the State in which the Same shall be, for the Erection of Forts, Magazines, Arsenals, dock-Yards, and other needful Buildings;—And

To make all Laws which shall be necessary and proper for carrying into Execution the foregoing Powers, and all other Powers vested by this Constitution in the Government of the United States, or in any Department of Officer thereof.

## Section 9

*The Migration or Importation of such Persons as any of the States now existing shall think proper to admit, shall not be prohibited by the Congress prior to the Year one thousand eight hundred and eight, but a Tax or duty may be imposed on such Importation, not exceeding ten dollars for each Person.*

The Privilege of the Writ of Habeas Corpus shall not be suspended, unless when in Cases of Rebellion or Invasion the public Safety may require it.

No Bill of Attainder or ex post facto Law shall be passed.

No Capitation, or other direct, Tax shall be laid, unless in Proportion to the Census or Enumeration herein before directed to be taken.

No Tax or Duty shall be laid on Articles exported from any State.

No Preference shall be given by any Regulation of Commerce or Revenue to the Ports of one State over those of another: nor shall Vessels bound to, or from, one State, be obliged to enter, clear, or pay Duties in another.

No Money shall be drawn from the Treasury, but in Consequence of Appropriations made by Law; and a regular Statement and Account of the Receipts and Expenditures of all public Money shall be published from time to time.

No Title of Nobility shall be granted by the United States: And no Person holding any Office of Profit or Trust under them, shall, without the Consent of the Congress, accept of any present, Emolument, Office, or Title, of any kind whatever, from any King, Prince, or foreign State.

## Section 10

No State shall enter into any Treaty, Alliance, or Confederation; grant Letters of Marque and Reprisal; coin Money; emit Bills of Credit; make any Thing but gold and silver Coin a Tender in Payment of Debts; pass any Bill of Attainder, ex post facto Law, or Law impairing the obligation of Contracts, or grant any Title of Nobility.

No State shall, without the Consent of the Congress, lay any Imposts or Duties on Imports or Exports, except what may be absolutely necessary for executing its inspection Laws: and the net Produce of all Duties and Imposts, laid by any State on Imports or Exports, shall be for the Use of the Treasury of the United States; and all such Laws shall be subject to the Revision and Controul of the Congress.

No State shall, without the Consent of Congress, lay any Duty of Tonnage, keep Troops, or Ships of War in time of Peace, enter into any Agreement or Compact with another State, or with a foreign Power, or engage in War, unless actually invaded, or in such imminent Danger as will not admit of delay.

## ARTICLE II

### Section 1

The executive Power shall be vested in a President of the United States of America. He shall hold his Office during the Term of four Years, and, together with the Vice President, chosen for the same Term, be elected, as follows:

Each State shall appoint, in such Manner as the Legislature thereof may direct, a Number of Electors, equal to the whole Number of Senators and Representatives to which the State may be entitled in the Congress: but no Senator or Representative, or Person holding an Office of Trust or Profit under the United States, shall be appointed an Elector.

*The Electors shall meet in their respective States, and vote by Ballot for two Persons, of whom one at least shall not be an Inhabitant of the same State with themselves. And they shall make a List of all the Persons voted for, and of the Number of Votes for each; which List they shall sign and certify, and transmit sealed to the Seat of the Government of the United States, directed to the President of the Senate. The President of the Senate shall, in the Presence of the Senate and House of Representatives, open all the Certificates, and the Votes shall then be counted. The Person having the greatest Number of Votes shall be the President, if such Number be a Majority of the whole number of Electors appointed; and if there be more than one who have such Majority, and have an equal Number of Votes, then the House of Representatives shall immediately chuse by Ballot one of them for President; and if no Person have a Majority, then from the five highest on the List the said House shall in like Manner chuse the President. But in chusing the President, the Votes shall be taken by States, the Representation from each State having one Vote; A quorum for this Purpose shall consist of a Member or Members from two thirds of the States, and a Majority of all the States shall be necessary to a Choice. In every Case, after the Choice of the President, the Person having the greatest Number of Votes of the Electors shall be the Vice President. But if there should remain two or more who have equal Votes, the Senate shall chuse from them by Ballot the Vice President.*

The Congress may determine the time of chusing the Electors, and the Day on which they shall give their Votes; which Day shall be the same throughout the United States.

No person except a natural born Citizen, *or a Citizen of the United States, at the time of the Adoption of this Constitution,* shall be eligible to the Office of President; neither shall any Person be eligible to that Office who shall not have attained to the Age of thirty five Years, and been fourteen Years a Resident within the United States.

In Case of the Removal of the President from Office, or of his Death, Resignation, or Inability to discharge the Powers and Duties of the said Office, the Same shall devolve on the Vice President, and the Congress may by Law provide for the Case of Removal, Death, Resignation or Inability, both of the President and Vice President, declaring what Officer shall then act as President, and such Officer shall act accordingly, until the Disability be removed, or a President shall be elected.

The President shall, at stated Times, receive for his Services, a Compensation, which shall neither be encreased nor diminished during the Period for which he shall have been elected, and he shall not receive within that period any other Emolument from the United States, or any of them.

Before he enter on the Execution of his Office, he shall take the following Oath or Affirmation:—"I do solemnly swear (or affirm) that I will faithfully execute the Office of President of the United States, and will to the best of my Ability, preserve, protect and defend the Constitution of the United States."

## Section 2

The President shall be Commander in Chief of the Army and Navy of the United States, and of the Militia of the several States, when called into the actual Service of the United States; he may require the Opinion, in writing, of the principal Officer in each of the executive Departments, upon any Subject relating to the Duties of their respective Offices, and he shall have Power to grant Reprieves and Pardons for Offences against the United States, except in Cases of Impeachment.

He shall have Power, by and with the Advice and Consent of the Senate, to make Treaties, provided two thirds of the Senators present concur; and he shall nominate, and by and with the Advice and Consent of the Senate, shall appoint Ambassadors, other public Ministers and Consuls, Judges of the supreme Court, and all other Officers of the United States, whose Appointments are not herein otherwise provided for, and which shall be established by Law: but the Congress may by Law vest the Appointment of such inferior Officers, as they think proper in the President alone, in the Courts of Law, or in the Heads of Departments.

The President shall have Power to fill up all Vacancies that may happen during the Recess of the Senate, by granting Commissions which shall expire at the End of their next Session.

## Section 3

He shall from time to time give to the Congress Information of the State of the Union, and recommend to their Consideration such Measures as he shall judge necessary and expedient; he may, on extraordinary Occasions, convene both Houses, or either of them, and in Case of disagreement between them, with Respect to the Time of Adjournment, he may adjourn them to such Time as he shall think proper; he shall receive Ambassadors and other public Ministers; he shall take Care that the Laws be faithfully executed, and shall Commission all the officers of the United States.

## Section 4

The President, Vice President and all civil Officers of the United States, shall be removed from Office on Impeachment for, and Conviction of, Treason, Bribery or other high Crimes and Misdemeanors.

# ARTICLE III

## Section 1

The judicial Power of the United States, shall be vested in one supreme Court, and in such inferior Courts as the Congress may from time to time ordain and establish. The Judges, both of the supreme and inferior Courts, shall hold their offices during good Behaviour, and shall, at stated Times, receive for their Services, a Compensation, which shall not be diminished during their Continuance in Office.

## Section 2

The judicial Power shall extend to all Cases, in Law and Equity, arising under this Constitution, the Laws of the United States, and Treaties made, or which shall be made,

under their Authority;—to all Cases affecting Amb other public Ministers and Consuls;—to all Cases of ralty and maritime Jurisdiction;—to Controversies to wh the United States shall be a Party;—to Controversies be tween two or more States;—*between a State and Citizens of another State;*—between Citizens of different States;—between Citizens of the same State claiming Lands under Grants of different States, and between a State, or the Citizens thereof, and foreign States, Citizens or Subjects.

In all Cases affecting Ambassadors, other public Ministers and Consuls, and those in which a State shall be Party, the supreme Court shall have original Jurisdiction. In all the other Cases before mentioned, the supreme Court shall have appellate Jurisdiction, both as to Law and Fact, with such Exceptions, and under such Regulations as the Congress shall make.

The Trial of all Crimes, except in Cases of Impeachment, shall be by Jury; and such Trial shall be held in the State where the said Crimes shall have been committed, but when not committed within any State, the Trial shall be at such Place or Places as the Congress may by Law have directed.

## Section 3

Treason against the United States, shall consist only in levying War against them, or in adhering to their Enemies, giving them Aid and Comfort. No person shall be convicted of Treason unless on the Testimony of two Witnesses to the same overt Act, or on Confession in open Court.

The Congress shall have Power to declare the Punishment of Treason, but no Attainder of Treason shall work Corruption of Blood, or Forfeiture except during the Life of the Person attainted.

# ARTICLE IV

## Section 1

Full Faith and Credit shall be given in each State to the public Acts, Records, and judicial Proceedings of every other State. And the Congress may by general Laws prescribe the Manner in which such Acts, Records and Proceedings shall be proved, and the Effect thereof.

## Section 2

The Citizens of each State shall be entitled to all Privileges and Immunities of Citizens in the several States.

A Person charged in any State with Treason, Felony, or other Crime, who shall flee from Justice, and be found in another State, shall on Demand of the executive Authority of the State from which he fled, be delivered up, to be removed to the State having Jurisdiction of the Crime.

*No Person held to Service or Labour in one State, under the Laws thereof, escaping into another, shall, in Consequence of any Law or Regulation therein, be discharged from such Service or Labour, but shall be delivered up on Claim of the Party to whom such Service or Labour may be due.*

slavery

## Section 3

New States may be admitted by the Congress into this Union; but no new State shall be formed or erected within the Jurisdiction of any other State; nor any State be formed ore States, or Parts of States, Legislatures of the States con-ress.

Power to dispose of and make ions respecting the Territory or the United States; and nothing o construed as to Prejudice any or of any particular States.

## Section 4

The United States shall guarantee to every State in this Union a Republican Form of Government, and shall protect each of them against Invasion; and on Application of the Legislature, or of the Executive (when the Legislature cannot be convened) against domestic violence.

## ARTICLE V

The Congress, whenever two thirds of both Houses shall deem it necessary, shall propose Amendments to this Constitution, or, on the Application of the Legislatures of two thirds of the several States, shall call a Convention for proposing Amendments, which, in either Case, shall be valid to all Intents and Purposes, as Part of this Constitution, when ratified by the Legislatures of three fourths of the several States, or by Conventions in three fourths thereof, as the one or the other Mode of Ratification may be proposed by the Congress; Provided *that no Amendment which may be made prior to the Year One thousand eight hundred and eight shall in any Manner affect the first and fourth Clauses in the Ninth Section of the first Article;* and that no State, without its Consent, shall be deprived of its equal Suffrage in the Senate.

## ARTICLE VI

All Debts contracted and Engagements entered into, before the Adoption of this Constitution, shall be as valid against the United States under this Constitution, as under the Confederation.

This Constitution, and Laws of the United States which shall be made in Pursuance thereof; and all Treaties made, or which shall be made, under the Authority of the United States, shall be the supreme Law of the Land; and the Judges in every State shall be bound thereby, any Thing in the Constitution or Laws of any State to the Contrary notwithstanding.

The Senators and Representatives before mentioned, and the Members of the several State Legislatures, and all executive and Judicial Officers, both of the United States and of the several States, shall be bound by Oath or Affirmation, to support this Constitution; but no religious Test shall ever be required as a Qualification to any Office of public Trust under the United States.

## ARTICLE VII

The Ratification of the Conventions of nine States, shall be sufficient for the Establishment of this Constitution between the States so ratifying the Same.

Done in Convention by the Unanimous Consent of the States present the Seventeenth Day of September in the Year of our Lord one thousand seven hundred and Eighty seven and of the Independence of the United States of America the Twelfth* IN WITNESS whereof We have hereunto subscribed our Names,

**George Washington**
President and Deputy from Virginia

**Delaware**
George Read
Gunning Bedford, Jr.
John Dickinson
Richard Bassett
Jacob Broom

**Maryland**
James McHenry
Daniel of St. Thomas Jenifer
Daniel Carroll

**Virginia**
John Blair
James Madison, Jr.

**North Carolina**
William Blount
Richard Dobbs Spraight
Hugh Williamson

**South Carolina**
John Rutledge
Charles Cotesworth Pinckney
Charles Pinckney
Pierce Butler

**Georgia**
William Few
Abraham Baldwin

**New Hampshire**
John Langdon
Nicholas Gilman

**Massachusetts**
Nathaniel Gorham
Rufus King

**Connecticut**
William Samuel Johnson
Roger Sherman

**New York**
Alexander Hamilton

**New Jersey**
William Livingston
David Brearley
William Paterson
Jonathan Dayton

**Pennsylvania**
Benjamin Franklin
Thomas Mifflin
Robert Morris
George Clymer
Thomas FitzSimons
Jared Ingersoll
James Wilson
Gouverneur Morris

*The Constitution was submitted on September 17, 1787, by the Constitutional Convention, was ratified by the Convention of several states at various dates up to May 29, 1790, and became effective on March 4, 1789.

# AMENDMENTS TO THE CONSTITUTION

## AMENDMENT I

Congress shall make no law respecting an establishment of religion, or prohibiting the free exercise thereof; or abridging the freedom of speech, or of the press; or the right of the people peaceably to assemble, and to petition the Government for a redress of grievances.

## AMENDMENT II

A well regulated Militia being necessary to the security of a free State, the right of the people to keep and bear Arms, shall not be infringed.

## AMENDMENT III

No Soldier shall, in time of peace be quartered in any house, without the consent of the Owner, nor in time of war, but in a manner to be prescribed by law.

## AMENDMENT IV

The right of the people to be secure in their persons, houses, papers, and effects, against unreasonable searches and seizures, shall not be violated, and no Warrants shall issue, but upon probable cause, supported by Oath or affirmation, and particularly describing the place to be searched, and the persons or things to be seized.

## AMENDMENT V

No person shall be held to answer for a capital, or otherwise infamous crime, unless on a presentment or indictment of a Grand Jury, except in cases arising in the land or naval forces, or in the Militia, when in actual service in time of War or public danger; nor shall any person be subject for the same offense to be twice put in jeopardy of life or limb; nor shall be compelled in any criminal case to be a witness against himself, nor be deprived of life, liberty, or property, without due process of law; nor shall private property be taken for public use, without just compensation.

## AMENDMENT VI

In all criminal prosecutions, the accused shall enjoy the right to a speedy and public trial, by an impartial jury of the State and district wherein the crime shall have been committed, which district shall have been previously ascertained by law, and to be informed of the nature and cause of the accusation; to be confronted with the witnesses against him; to have compulsory process for obtaining witnesses in his favor, and to have the Assistance of Counsel for his defence.

## AMENDMENT VII

In Suits at common law, where the value in controversy shall exceed twenty dollars, the right of trial by jury shall be preserved, and no fact tried by a jury, shall be otherwise reexamined in any Court of the United States, than according to the rules of the common law.

## AMENDMENT VIII

Excessive bail shall not be required, nor excessive fines imposed, nor cruel and unusual punishments inflicted.

## AMENDMENT IX

The enumeration in the Constitution, of certain rights, shall not be construed to deny or disparage others retained by the people.

## AMENDMENT X*

The powers not delegated to the United States by the Constitution, nor prohibited by it to the States, are reserved to the States respectively, or to the people.

## AMENDMENT XI
## [ADOPTED 1798]

The Judicial power of the United States shall not be construed to extend to any suit in law or equity, commenced or prosecuted against one of the United States by Citizens of another State, or by Citizens or Subjects of any Foreign State.

## AMENDMENT XII
## [ADOPTED 1804]

The Electors shall meet in their respective states, and vote by ballot for President and Vice President, one of whom, at least, shall not be an inhabitant of the same state with themselves; they shall name in their ballots the person voted for as President, and in distinct ballots the person voted for as Vice President, and they shall make distinct lists of all persons voted for as President, and of all persons voted for as Vice President, and of the number of votes for each, which lists they shall sign and certify, and transmit sealed to the seat of the government of the United States, directed to the President of the Senate;—The President of the Senate shall, in the presence of the Senate and House of Representatives, open all the certificates and the votes shall then be counted;—The person having the greatest number of votes for President, shall be the President, if such number be a majority of the whole number of Electors appointed; and if no person have such majority, then from the persons having the highest numbers not exceeding three on the list of those voted for as President, the House of Representatives shall choose immediately, by ballot, the President. But in choosing the President, the votes shall be taken by states, the representation from each state having one vote; a quorum for this purpose shall consist of a member or members from two-thirds of the states, and a majority of all the states shall be necessary to a choice. And if the House of Representatives shall not choose a President whenever the

---

*The first ten amendments (the Bill of Rights) were ratified and their adoption was certified on December 15, 1791.

right of choice shall devolve upon them, before *the fourth day of March* next following, then the Vice President shall act as President, as in the case of the death or other constitutional disability of the President.—The person having the greatest number of votes as Vice President, shall be the Vice President, if such number be a majority of the whole number of Electors appointed, and if no person have a majority, then from the two highest numbers on the list, the Senate shall choose the Vice President; a quorum for the purpose shall consist of two-thirds of the whole number of Senators, and a majority of the whole number shall be necessary to a choice. But no person constitutionally ineligible to the office of President shall be eligible to that of Vice President of the United States.

## AMENDMENT XIII
## [ADOPTED 1865]

### Section 1
Neither slavery nor involuntary servitude, except as a punishment for crime whereof the party shall have been duly convicted, shall exist within the United States, or any place subject to their jurisdiction.

### Section 2
Congress shall have power to enforce this article by appropriate legislation.

## AMENDMENT XIV
## [ADOPTED 1868]

### Section 1
All persons born or naturalized in the United States, and subject to the jurisdiction thereof, are citizens of the United States and of the State wherein they reside. No State shall make or enforce any law which shall abridge the privileges or immunities of citizens of the United States; nor shall any State deprive any person of life, liberty, or property, without due process of law; nor deny to any person within its jurisdiction the equal protection of the laws.

### Section 2
Representatives shall be apportioned among the several States according to their respective numbers, counting the whole number of persons in each State, excluding Indians not taxed. But when the right to vote at any election for the choice of electors for President and Vice President of the United States, Representatives in Congress, the Executive and Judicial officers of a State, or the members of the Legislature thereof, is denied to any of the male inhabitants of such State, being twenty-one years of age, and citizens of the United States, or in any way abridged, except for participation in rebellion, or other crime, the basis of representation therein shall be reduced in the proportion which the number of such male citizens shall bear to the whole number of male citizens twenty-one years of age in such State.

### Section 3
No person shall be a Senator or Representative in Congress, or elector of President and Vice President, or hold any office, civil or military, under the United States, or under any State, who, having previously taken an oath, as a member of Congress, or as an officer of the United States, or as a member of any State legislature, or as an executive or judicial officer of any State, to support the Constitution of the United States, shall have engaged in insurrection or rebellion against the same, or given aid or comfort to the enemies thereof. But Congress may by a vote of two-thirds of each House, remove such disability.

### Section 4
The validity of the public debt of the United States, authorized by law, including debts incurred for payment of pensions and bounties for services in suppressing insurrection or rebellion, shall not be questioned. But neither the United States nor any State shall assume or pay any debt or obligation incurred in aid of insurrection or rebellion against the United States, or any claim for the loss or emancipation of any slave; but all such debts, obligations and claims shall be held illegal and void.

### Section 5
The Congress shall have power to enforce, by appropriate legislation, the provisions of this article.

## AMENDMENT XV
## [ADOPTED 1870]

### Section 1
The right of citizens of the United States to vote shall not be denied or abridged by the United States or by any State on account of race, color, or previous condition of servitude.

### Section 2
The Congress shall have power to enforce this article by appropriate legislation.

## AMENDMENT XVI
## [ADOPTED 1913]

The Congress shall have power to lay and collect taxes on incomes, from whatever source derived, without apportionment among the several States, and without regard to any census or enumeration.

## AMENDMENT XVII
## [ADOPTED 1913]

The Senate of the United States shall be composed of two Senators from each State, elected by the people thereof, for six years; and each Senator shall have one vote. The electors in each State shall have the qualifications requisite for electors of the most numerous branch of the State legislatures.

When vacancies happen in the representation of any State in the Senate, the executive authority of such State shall issue writs of election to fill such vacancies: *Provided,* That the legislature of any State may empower the executive thereof to make temporary appointments until the people fill the vacancies by election as the legislature may direct.

This amendment shall not be so construed as to affect the election or term of any Senator chosen before it becomes valid as part of the Constitution.

## AMENDMENT XVIII
## [ADOPTED 1919, REPEALED 1933]

### Section 1

*After one year from the ratification of this article the manufacture, sale, or transportation of intoxicating liquors within, the importation thereof into, or the exportation thereof from the United States and all territory subject to the jurisdiction thereof for beverage purposes is hereby prohibited.*

### Section 2

*The Congress and the several States shall have concurrent power to enforce this article by appropriate legislation.*

### Section 3

*This article shall be inoperative unless it shall have been ratified as an amendment to the Constitution by the legislatures of the several States, as provided in the Constitution, within seven years from the date of the submission hereof to the States by the Congress.*

## AMENDMENT XIX
## [ADOPTED 1920]

The right of citizens of the United States to vote shall not be denied or abridged by the United States or by any State on account of sex.

Congress shall have power to enforce this article by appropriate legislation.

## AMENDMENT XX
## [ADOPTED 1933]

### Section 1

The terms of the President and Vice President shall end at noon on the 20th day of January, and the terms of Senators and Representatives at noon on the 3d day of January, of the years in which such terms would have ended if this article had not been ratified and the terms of their successors shall then begin.

### Section 2

The Congress shall assemble at least once in every year, and such meeting shall begin at noon on the 3d day of January, unless they shall by law appoint a different day.

### Section 3

If, at the time fixed for the beginning of the term of the President, the President elect shall have died, the Vice President elect shall become President. If a President shall not have been chosen before the time fixed for the beginning of his term, or if the President elect shall have failed to qualify, then the Vice President elect shall act as President until a President shall have qualified; and the Congress may by law provide for the case wherein neither a President elect nor a Vice President elect shall have qualified, declaring who

shall then act as President, or the manner in which one who is to act shall be selected, and such person shall act accordingly until a President or Vice President shall have qualified.

### Section 4

The Congress may by law provide for the case of the death of any of the persons from whom the House of Representatives may choose a President whenever the right of choice shall have devolved upon them, and for the case of the death of any of the persons from whom the Senate may choose a Vice President whenever the right of choice shall have devolved upon them.

### Section 5

Sections 1 and 2 shall take effect on the 15th day of October following the ratification of this article.

### Section 6

This article shall be inoperative unless it shall have been ratified as an amendment to the Constitution by the legislatures of three fourths of the several States within seven years from the date of its submission.

## AMENDMENT XXI
## [ADOPTED 1933]

### Section 1

The eighteenth article of amendment to the Constitution of the United States is hereby repealed.

### Section 2

The transportation or importation into any State, Territory, or possession of the United States for delivery or use therein of intoxicating liquors in violation of the laws thereof, is hereby prohibited.

### Section 3

This article shall be inoperative unless it shall have been ratified as an amendment to the Constitution by conventions in the several States, as provided in the Constitution, within seven years from the date of the submission hereof to the States by the Congress.

## AMENDMENT XXII
## [ADOPTED 1951]

### Section 1

No person shall be elected to the office of the President more than twice, and no person who has held the office of President, or acted as President, for more than two years of a term to which some other person was elected President shall be elected to the office of the President more than once. But this Article shall not apply to any person holding the office of President when this Article was proposed by the Congress, and shall not prevent any person who may be holding the office of President, or acting as President, during the term within which this Article becomes operative from holding the office of President or acting as President during the remainder of such term.

## Section 2

This article shall be inoperative unless it shall have been ratified as an amendment to the Constitution by the legislatures of three-fourths of the several States within seven years from the date of its submission to the States by the Congress.

## AMENDMENT XXIII
## [ADOPTED 1961]

### Section 1

The District constituting the seat of Government of the United States shall appoint in such manner as the Congress shall direct:

A number of electors of President and Vice President equal to the whole number of Senators and Representatives in Congress to which the District would be entitled if it were a State, but in no event more than the least populous State; they shall be in addition to those appointed by the States, but they shall be considered, for the purposes of the election of President and Vice President, to be electors appointed by a State; and they shall meet in the District and perform such duties as provided by the twelfth article of amendment.

### Section 2

The Congress shall have power to enforce this article by appropriate legislation.

## AMENDMENT XXIV
## [ADOPTED 1964]

### Section 1

The right of citizens of the United States to vote in any primary or other election for President or Vice President, for electors for President or Vice President, or for Senator or Representative in Congress, shall not be denied or abridged by the United States or any state by reason of failure to pay any poll tax or other tax.

### Section 2

The Congress shall have the power to enforce this article by appropriate legislation.

## AMENDMENT XXV
## [ADOPTED 1967]

### Section 1

In case of the removal of the President from office or his death or resignation, the Vice President shall become President.

### Section 2

Whenever there is a vacancy in the office of the Vice President, the President shall nominate a Vice President who shall take the office upon confirmation by a majority vote of both houses of Congress.

### Section 3

Whenever the President transmits to the President pro tempore of the Senate and the Speaker of the House of Representatives his written declaration that he is unable to discharge the powers and duties of his office, and until he transmits to them a written declaration to the contrary, such powers and duties shall be discharged by the Vice President as Acting President.

### Section 4

Whenever the Vice President and a majority of either the principal officers of the executive departments or of such other body as Congress may by law provide, transmit to the President pro tempore of the Senate and the Speaker of the House of Representatives their written declaration that the President is unable to discharge the powers and duties of his office, the Vice President shall immediately assume the powers and duties of the office as Acting President.

Thereafter, when the President transmits to the President pro tempore of the Senate and the Speaker of the House of Representatives his written declaration that no inability exists, he shall resume the powers and duties of his office unless the Vice President and a majority of either the principal officers of the executive department or of such other body as Congress may by law provide, transmit within four days to the President pro tempore of the Senate and the Speaker of the House of Representatives their written declaration that the President is unable to discharge the powers and duties of his office. Thereupon Congress shall decide the issue, assembling within 48 hours for that purpose if not in session. If the Congress, within 21 days after receipt of the latter written declaration, or, if Congress is not in session, within 21 days after Congress is required to assemble, determines by two-thirds vote of both houses that the President is unable to discharge the powers and duties of his office, the Vice President shall continue to discharge the same as Acting President; otherwise, the President shall resume the powers and duties of his office.

## AMENDMENT XXVI
## [ADOPTED 1971]

### Section 1

The right of citizens of the United States, who are 18 years of age or older, to vote shall not be denied or abridged by the United States or any state on account of age.

### Section 2

The Congress shall have the power to enforce this article by appropriate legislation.

## AMENDMENT XXVII
## [ADOPTED 1992]

No law, varying the compensation for the services of the Senators and Representatives shall take effect, until an election of Representatives shall have intervened.

# PRESIDENTIAL ELECTIONS

| Year | Candidates | Parties | Popular Vote | Electoral Vote | Voter Participation |
|---|---|---|---|---|---|
| 1789 | **George Washington** | | * | 69 | |
| | John Adams | | | 34 | |
| | Others | | | 35 | |
| 1792 | **George Washington** | | * | 132 | |
| | John Adams | | | 77 | |
| | George Clinton | | | 50 | |
| | Others | | | 5 | |
| 1796 | **John Adams** | Federalist | * | 71 | |
| | Thomas Jefferson | Democratic-Republican | | 68 | |
| | Thomas Pinckney | Federalist | | 59 | |
| | Aaron Burr | Dem.-Rep. | | 30 | |
| | Others | | | 48 | |
| 1800 | **Thomas Jefferson** | Dem.-Rep. | * | 73 | |
| | Aaron Burr | Dem.-Rep. | | 73 | |
| | John Adams | Federalist | | 65 | |
| | C. C. Pinckney | Federalist | | 64 | |
| | John Jay | Federalist | | 1 | |
| 1804 | **Thomas Jefferson** | Dem.-Rep. | * | 162 | |
| | C. C. Pinckney | Federalist | | 14 | |
| 1808 | **James Madison** | Dem.-Rep. | * | 122 | |
| | C. C. Pinckney | Federalist | | 47 | |
| | George Clinton | Dem.-Rep. | | 6 | |
| 1812 | **James Madison** | Dem.-Rep. | * | 128 | |
| | De Witt Clinton | Federalist | | 89 | |
| 1816 | **James Monroe** | Dem.-Rep. | * | 183 | |
| | Rufus King | Federalist | | 34 | |
| 1820 | **James Monroe** | Dem.-Rep. | * | 231 | |
| | John Quincy Adams | Dem.-Rep. | | 1 | |
| 1824 | **John Quincy Adams** | Dem.-Rep. | 108,740 (30.5%) | 84 | 26.9% |
| | Andrew Jackson | Dem.-Rep. | 153,544 (43.1%) | 99 | |
| | William H. Crawford | Dem.-Rep. | 46,618 (13.1%) | 41 | |
| | Henry Clay | Dem.-Rep. | 47,136 (13.2%) | 37 | |
| 1828 | **Andrew Jackson** | Democratic | 647,286 (56.0%) | 178 | 57.6% |
| | John Quincy Adams | National Republican | 508,064 (44.0%) | 83 | |

*Electors selected by state legislatures.

| Year | Candidates | Parties | Popular Vote | Electoral Vote | Voter Participation |
|------|------------|---------|--------------|----------------|---------------------|
| 1832 | **Andrew Jackson** | Democratic | 687,502 (55.0%) | 219 | 55.4% |
|      | Henry Clay | National Republican | 530,189 (42.4%) | 49 | |
|      | John Floyd | Independent | | 11 | |
|      | William Wirt | Anti-Mason | 33,108 (2.6%) | 7 | |
| 1836 | **Martin Van Buren** | Democratic | 765,483 (50.9%) | 170 | 57.8% |
|      | William Henry Harrison | Whig | | 73 | |
|      | Hugh L. White | Whig | 739,795 (49.1%) | 26 | |
|      | Daniel Webster | Whig | | 14 | |
|      | W. P. Magnum | Independent | | 11 | |
| 1840 | **William Henry Harrison** | Whig | 1,274,624 (53.1%) | 234 | 80.2% |
|      | Martin Van Buren | Democratic | 1,127,781 (46.9%) | 60 | |
|      | J. G. Birney | Liberty | 7069 | — | |
| 1844 | **James K. Polk** | Democratic | 1,338,464 (49.6%) | 170 | 78.9% |
|      | Henry Clay | Whig | 1,300,097 (48.1%) | 105 | |
|      | J. G. Birney | Liberty | 62,300 (2.3%) | — | |
| 1848 | **Zachary Taylor** | Whig | 1,360,967 (47.4%) | 163 | 72.7% |
|      | Lewis Cass | Democratic | 1,222,342 (42.5%) | 127 | |
|      | Martin Van Buren | Free-Soil | 291,263 (10.1%) | — | |
| 1852 | **Franklin Pierce** | Democratic | 1,601,117 (50.9%) | 254 | 69.6% |
|      | Winfield Scott | Whig | 1,385,453 (44.1%) | 42 | |
|      | John P. Hale | Free-Soil | 155,825 (5.0%) | — | |
| 1856 | **James Buchanan** | Democratic | 1,832,955 (45.3%) | 174 | 78.9% |
|      | John C. Frémont | Republican | 1,339,932 (33.1%) | 114 | |
|      | Millard Fillmore | American | 871,731 (21.6%) | 8 | |
| 1860 | **Abraham Lincoln** | Republican | 1,865,593 (39.8%) | 180 | 81.2% |
|      | Stephen A. Douglas | Democratic | 1,382,713 (29.5%) | 12 | |
|      | John C. Breckinridge | Democratic | 848,356 (18.1%) | 72 | |
|      | John Bell | Union | 592,906 (12.6%) | 39 | |
| 1864 | **Abraham Lincoln** | Republican | 2,213,655 (55.0%) | 212* | 73.8% |
|      | George B. McClellan | Democratic | 1,805,237 (45.0%) | 21 | |
| 1868 | **Ulysses S. Grant** | Republican | 3,012,833 (52.7%) | 214 | 78.1% |
|      | Horatio Seymour | Democratic | 2,703,249 (47.3%) | 80 | |
| 1872 | **Ulysses S. Grant** | Republican | 3,597,132 (55.6%) | 286 | 71.3% |
|      | Horace Greeley | Dem.; Liberal Republican | 2,834,125 (43.9%) | 66† | |
| 1876 | **Rutherford B. Hayes‡** | Republican | 4,036,298 (48.0%) | 185 | 81.8% |
|      | Samuel J. Tilden | Democratic | 4,300,590 (51.0%) | 184 | |
| 1880 | **James A. Garfield** | Republican | 4,454,416 (48.5%) | 214 | 79.4% |
|      | Winfield S. Hancock | Democratic | 4,444,952 (48.1%) | 155 | |

*Eleven secessionist states did not participate.
†Greeley died before the electoral college met. His electoral votes were divided among the four minor candidates.
‡Contested result settled by special election.

| Year | Candidates | Parties | Popular Vote | Electoral Vote | Voter Participation |
|------|-----------|---------|--------------|----------------|---------------------|
| 1884 | **Grover Cleveland** | Democratic | 4,874,986 (48.5%) | 219 | 77.5% |
|      | James G. Blaine | Republican | 4,851,981 (48.2%) | 182 | |
| 1888 | **Benjamin Harrison** | Republican | 5,439,853 (47.9%) | 233 | 79.3% |
|      | Grover Cleveland | Democratic | 5,540,309 (48.6%) | 168 | |
| 1892 | **Grover Cleveland** | Democratic | 5,556,918 (46.1%) | 277 | 74.7% |
|      | Benjamin Harrison | Republican | 5,176,108 (43.0%) | 145 | |
|      | James B. Weaver | People's | 1,041,028 (8.5%) | 22 | |
| 1896 | **William McKinley** | Republican | 7,104,779 (51.1%) | 271 | 79.3% |
|      | William Jennings Bryan | Democratic People's | 6,502,925 (47.7%) | 176 | |
| 1900 | **William McKinley** | Republican | 7,207,923 (51.7%) | 292 | 73.2% |
|      | William Jennings Bryan | Dem.-Populist | 6,358,133 (45.5%) | 155 | |
| 1904 | **Theodore Roosevelt** | Republican | 7,623,486 (57.9%) | 336 | 65.2% |
|      | Alton B. Parker | Democratic | 5,077,911 (37.6%) | 140 | |
|      | Eugene V. Debs | Socialist | 402,283 (3.0%) | — | |
| 1908 | **William H. Taft** | Republican | 7,678,908 (51.6%) | 321 | 65.4% |
|      | William Jennings Bryan | Democratic | 6,409,104 (43.1%) | 162 | |
|      | Eugene V. Debs | Socialist | 420,793 (2.8%) | — | |
| 1912 | **Woodrow Wilson** | Democratic | 6,293,454 (41.9%) | 435 | 58.8% |
|      | Theodore Roosevelt | Progressive | 4,119,538 (27.4%) | 88 | |
|      | William H. Taft | Republican | 3,484,980 (23.2%) | 8 | |
|      | Eugene V. Debs | Socialist | 900,672 (6.0%) | — | |
| 1916 | **Woodrow Wilson** | Democratic | 9,129,606 (49.4%) | 277 | 61.6% |
|      | Charles E. Hughes | Republican | 8,538,221 (46.2%) | 254 | |
|      | A. L. Benson | Socialist | 585,113 (3.2%) | — | |
| 1920 | **Warren G. Harding** | Republican | 16,152,200 (60.4%) | 404 | 49.2% |
|      | James M. Cox | Democratic | 9,147,353 (34.2%) | 127 | |
|      | Eugene V. Debs | Socialist | 919,799 (3.4%) | — | |
| 1924 | **Calvin Coolidge** | Republican | 15,725,016 (54.0%) | 382 | 48.9% |
|      | John W. Davis | Democratic | 8,386,503 (28.8%) | 136 | |
|      | Robert M. La Follette | Progressive | 4,822,856 (16.6%) | 13 | |
| 1928 | **Herbert Hoover** | Republican | 21,391,381 (58.2%) | 444 | 56.9% |
|      | Alfred E. Smith | Democratic | 15,016,443 (40.9%) | 87 | |
|      | Norman Thomas | Socialist | 267,835 (0.7%) | — | |
| 1932 | **Franklin D. Roosevelt** | Democratic | 22,821,857 (57.4%) | 472 | 56.9% |
|      | Herbert Hoover | Republican | 15,761,841 (39.7%) | 59 | |
|      | Norman Thomas | Socialist | 881,951 (2.2%) | — | |
| 1936 | **Franklin D. Roosevelt** | Democratic | 27,751,597 (60.8%) | 523 | 61.0% |
|      | Alfred M. Landon | Republican | 16,679,583 (36.5%) | 8 | |
|      | William Lemke | Union | 882,479 (1.9%) | — | |
| 1940 | **Franklin D. Roosevelt** | Democratic | 27,244,160 (54.8%) | 449 | 62.5% |
|      | Wendell L. Willkie | Republican | 22,305,198 (44.8%) | 82 | |
| 1944 | **Franklin D. Roosevelt** | Democratic | 25,602,504 (53.5%) | 432 | 55.9% |
|      | Thomas E. Dewey | Republican | 22,006,285 (46.0%) | 99 | |

| Year | Candidates | Parties | Popular Vote | Electoral Vote | Voter Participation |
|------|-----------|---------|--------------|----------------|---------------------|
| 1948 | **Harry S Truman** | Democratic | 24,105,695 (49.5%) | 304 | 53.0% |
|      | Thomas E. Dewey | Republican | 21,969,170 (45.1%) | 189 | |
|      | J. Strom Thurmond | State-Rights Democratic | 1,169,021 (2.4%) | 38 | |
|      | Henry A. Wallace | Progressive | 1,156,103 (2.4%) | — | |
| 1952 | **Dwight D. Eisenhower** | Republican | 33,936,252 (55.1%) | 442 | 63.3% |
|      | Adlai E. Stevenson | Democratic | 27,314,992 (44.4%) | 89 | |
| 1956 | **Dwight D. Eisenhower** | Republican | 35,575,420 (57.6%) | 457 | 60.6% |
|      | Adlai E. Stevenson | Democratic | 26,033,066 (42.1%) | 73 | |
|      | Other | — | — | 1 | |
| 1960 | **John F. Kennedy** | Democratic | 34,227,096 (49.9%) | 303 | 62.8% |
|      | Richard M. Nixon | Republican | 34,108,546 (49.6%) | 219 | |
|      | Other | — | — | 15 | |
| 1964 | **Lyndon B. Johnson** | Democratic | 43,126,506 (61.1%) | 486 | 61.7% |
|      | Barry M. Goldwater | Republican | 27,176,799 (38.5%) | 52 | |
| 1968 | **Richard M. Nixon** | Republican | 31,770,237 (43.4%) | 301 | 60.6% |
|      | Hubert H. Humphrey | Democratic | 31,270,533 (42.7%) | 191 | |
|      | George Wallace | American Indep. | 9,906,141 (13.5%) | 46 | |
| 1972 | **Richard M. Nixon** | Republican | 47,169,911 (60.7%) | 520 | 55.2% |
|      | George S. McGovern | Democratic | 29,170,383 (37.5%) | 17 | |
|      | Other | — | — | 1 | |
| 1976 | **Jimmy Carter** | Democratic | 40,828,587 (50.0%) | 297 | 53.5% |
|      | Gerald R. Ford | Republican | 39,147,613 (47.9%) | 241 | |
|      | Other | — | 1,575,459 (2.1%) | — | |
| 1980 | **Ronald Reagan** | Republican | 43,901,812 (50.7%) | 489 | 52.6% |
|      | Jimmy Carter | Democratic | 35,483,820 (41.0%) | 49 | |
|      | John B. Anderson | Independent | 5,719,722 (6.6%) | — | |
|      | Ed Clark | Libertarian | 921,188 (1.1%) | — | |
| 1984 | **Ronald Reagan** | Republican | 54,455,075 (59.0%) | 525 | 53.3% |
|      | Walter Mondale | Democratic | 37,577,185 (41.0%) | 13 | |
| 1988 | **George H. W. Bush** | Republican | 48,886,000 (53.4%) | 426 | 57.4% |
|      | Michael S. Dukakis | Democratic | 41,809,000 (45.6%) | 111 | |
| 1992 | **William J. Clinton** | Democratic | 43,728,375 (43%) | 370 | 55.0% |
|      | George H. W. Bush | Republican | 38,167,416 (38%) | 168 | |
|      | H. Ross Perot | Independent | 19,237,247 (19%) | — | |
| 1996 | **William J. Clinton** | Democratic | 45,590,703 (50%) | 379 | 48.8% |
|      | Robert Dole | Republican | 37,816,307 (41%) | 159 | |
|      | Ross Perot | Reform | 7,866,284 | | |
| 2000 | **George W. Bush** | Republican | 50,456,167 (47.88%) | 271 | 51.2% |
|      | Al Gore | Democratic | 50,996,064 (48.39%) | 266* | |
|      | Ralph Nader | Green | 2,864,810 (2.72%) | — | |
|      | Other | | 834,774 (less than 1%) | — | |

*One District of Columbia Gore elector abstained.

# Maps

UNITED STATES

| | 6 | 7 | 8 |

**Legend**

— National boundary
--- State boundary
⍟ National capital
★ State capital
● Other city

Scale: 0 — 200 — 400 mi; 0 — 200 — 400 km

*Puerto Rico inset:* ATLANTIC OCEAN, San Juan, Bayamón, Carolina, Isla de Culebra, PUERTO RICO (U.S.), Ponce, Isla de Vieques, Caribbean Sea; 67°, 66°, 18°; 0 — 20 — 40 mi; 0 — 20 — 40 km

MINNESOTA
Lake Superior
MICHIGAN
Lake Huron
St. Lawrence R.
MAINE
Augusta
Portland
Montpelier
VERMONT
NEW HAMPSHIRE
Concord
NEW YORK
Boston
MASSACHUSETTS
Providence
RHODE ISLAND
CONNECTICUT
Albany
Hartford
Newark
New York City
Trenton
NEW JERSEY
Philadelphia
Dover
DELAWARE
L. Ontario
Syracuse
Buffalo
Lake Erie
PENNSYLVANIA
Harrisburg
Pittsburgh
Cleveland
Toledo
Detroit
Lansing
Grand Rapids
WISCONSIN
Madison
Milwaukee
Chicago
Gary
Lake Michigan
Minneapolis
St. Paul
Mississippi
IOWA
Davenport
Des Moines
Peoria
ILLINOIS
Springfield
Indianapolis
INDIANA
Cincinnati
Columbus
OHIO
Baltimore
Annapolis
Washington, D.C.
MARYLAND
WEST VIRGINIA
Charleston
Richmond
Newport News
VIRGINIA
Norfolk
Frankfort
Louisville
Lexington
KENTUCKY
Ohio R.
St. Louis
Kansas City
Jefferson City
MISSOURI
Tulsa
ARKANSAS
Little Rock
Memphis
Nashville
TENNESSEE
Knoxville
Chattanooga
Tennessee R.
APPALACHIAN MTS.
Raleigh
Charlotte
NORTH CAROLINA
Columbia
SOUTH CAROLINA
Charleston
Savannah
GEORGIA
Atlanta
Columbus
Huntsville
Birmingham
ALABAMA
Montgomery
MISSISSIPPI
Jackson
Mobile
Tallahassee
FLORIDA
Jacksonville
Orlando
Tampa
St. Petersburg
Lake Okeechobee
Fort Lauderdale
Miami
Key West
Florida Keys
Straits of Florida
BAHAMAS
CUBA
Shreveport
LOUISIANA
Baton Rouge
New Orleans
Houston
Gulf of Mexico
Corpus Christi
Dallas
Wichita
Oklahoma City
ATLANTIC OCEAN
Mississippi R.

95° 90° 85°
40° 35° 30° 25°

| 5 | 6 | 7 | 8 |

# PRESENT DAY WORLD

ARCTIC OCEAN

GREENLAND

Baffin Bay

C A N A D A

ICELAND

ALASKA (U.S.)

Beaufort Sea

Bering Sea

Gulf of Alaska

Hudson Bay

Labrador Sea

Great Lakes

UNITED STATES

ATLANTIC OCEAN

MOROCCO

WESTERN SAHARA

SEE CARIBBEAN INSET

MEXICO

Gulf of Mexico

CAPE VERDE

MAURITANIA

BURK. F

BELIZE

Hawaiian Islands (U.S.)

PACIFIC OCEAN

GUATEMALA
EL SALVADOR

Caribbean Sea

SENEGAL
THE GAMBIA
GUINEA-BISSAU

MA

GUINEA

SIERRA LEONE

COLOMBIA

LIBERIA

CÔTE D'IVOIRE

FRENCH GUIANA (FR.)

KIRIBATI

Galapagos Islands (EQ.)

ECUADOR

SURINAME

SÃO TOM
PRINC

GH

TOKELAU

SAMOA
AM.
SAMOA

COOK ISLANDS

PERU

B R A Z I L

TONGA

FRENCH POLYNESIA

BOLIVIA

PARAGUAY

ATLANTIC OCEAN

CHILE

URUGUAY

ARGENTINA

Falkland Islands (U.K.)

South Georgia (U.K.)

UNITED STATES

80°

70°

60°

BAHAMAS

0       300       600 mi

0       300       600 km

ATLANTIC OCEAN

Weddell Sea

CUBA

Turks & Caicos Is. (U.K.)

Cayman Is. (U.K.)

HAITI

DOMINICAN REPUBLIC

PUERTO RICO (U.S.)

Virgin Is.(U.S.)

ANTIGUA & BARBUDA

0       1500       3000

JAMAICA

ST. KITTS AND NEVIS

GUADALOUPE

0       1500       3000 km

HONDURAS

Caribbean Sea

DOMINICA

MARTINIQUE

ST. LUCIA

NICARAGUA

ST. VINCENT AND THE GRENADINES

CURACAO

BARBADOS

GRENADA

ANTARCTICA

COSTA RICA

PANAMA

COLOMBIA

VENEZUELA

TRINIDAD AND TOBAGO

GUYANA

1, 2, 6, 7
Row markers: A, B, C, D, E, F, G, H
1, 2, 3, 4, 5, 6, 7
Latitude/longitude labels: 160°, 140°, 120°, 60°, 40°, 20°, 80°, 60°, 40°, 20°, 0°, 20°, 40°

ARCTIC OCEAN

**Svalbard** (NOR.)

Novaya Zemlya

Kara Sea

Barents Sea

Laptev Sea

New Siberian Islands

East Siberian Sea

80°

A

R U S S I A

SEE EUROPE INSET

60°

B

Lake Baikal

Sea of Okhotsk

Sakhalin

KAZAKHSTAN

Lake Balkhash

MONGOLIA

40°

C

Aral Sea

UZBEKISTAN

Caspian Sea

Black Sea

TURKMENISTAN

KYRGYZSTAN

TAJIKISTAN

N. KOREA

S. KOREA

JAPAN

PACIFIC OCEAN

Mediterranean Sea

AFGHAN.

PEOPLE'S REPUBLIC OF CHINA

East China Sea

TUNISIA

ISRAEL

JORDAN

IRAQ

IRAN

KUWAIT

PAKISTAN

NEPAL

BHUTAN

MACAU

TAIWAN

D

ALGERIA

LIBYA

EGYPT

Red Sea

BAHRAIN

QATAR

U.A.E.

SAUDI ARABIA

OMAN

BANG.

INDIA

20°

NIGER

CHAD

SUDAN

ERITREA

YEMEN

DJIBOUTI

Arabian Sea

MYANMAR

LAOS

THAILAND

VIETNAM

South China Sea

Philippine Sea

NORTHERN MARIANA ISLANDS

MARSHALL ISLANDS

BENIN

NIGERIA

CONGO

CAMEROON

CENTRAL AFRICAN REP.

ETHIOPIA

SOMALIA

CAMBODIA

SRI LANKA

PHILIPPINES

FEDERATED STATES OF MICRONESIA

GABON

REP. OF CONGO

UGANDA

KENYA

RWAN.

MALDIVES

BRUNEI

MALAYSIA

PALAU

NAURU

0°

CABINDA

DEM. REP. OF CONGO

BURUNDI

TANZANIA

SINGAPORE

I N D O N E S I A

SOLOMON ISLANDS

TUVALU

E

ANGOLA

ZAMBIA

MALAWI

PAPUA NEW GUINEA

VANUATU

NAMIBIA

ZIMB.

MOZAMBIQUE

MADAGASCAR

MAURITIUS

Coral Sea

New Caledonia (FR.)

FIJI

20°

BOTSWANA

INDIAN OCEAN

A U S T R A L I A

SOUTH AFRICA

SWAZILAND

LESOTHO

Tasman Sea

NEW ZEALAND

F

NORWAY

SWEDEN

FINLAND

0    400    800 mi
0    400    800 km

60°

DENMARK

ESTONIA

LATVIA

Baltic Sea

G

North Sea

RUSSIA

LITHUANIA

UNITED KINGDOM

IRELAND

NETHERLANDS

GERMANY

POLAND

BELARUS

N

ATLANTIC OCEAN

BELGIUM

LUX.

LIECHT.

CZECH REPUBLIC

SLOVAKIA

UKRAINE

60°

SWITZ.

AUSTRIA

HUNGARY

MOLDOVA

FRANCE

SLOVENIA

CROATIA

BOSNIA & HERZ.

ROMANIA

SERBIA & MONTENEGRO

Caspian Sea

SPAIN

ANDORRA

ITALY

Adriatic Sea

ALBANIA

BULGARIA

MACEDONIA

Black Sea

GEORGIA

ARMENIA

ANTARCTICA

H

PORTUGAL

Mediterranean Sea

GREECE

TURKEY

AZERBAIJAN

40°

Aegean Sea

CYPRUS

SYRIA

LEBANON

# Glossary

**Adams-Onís Treaty** Signed by Secretary of State John Quincy Adams and Spanish minister Luis de Onís in 1819, this treaty allowed for U.S. annexation of Florida.

**African Methodist Episcopal (AME) Church** Richard Allen founded the African Methodist Episcopal Church in 1816 as the first independent black-run Protestant church in the United States. The AME Church was active in the promotion of abolition and the founding of educational institutions for free blacks.

**Agricultural Adjustment Administration (AAA)** Created by Congress in 1933 as part of the New Deal, this agency attempted to restrict agricultural production by paying farmers subsidies to take land out of production. The object was to raise farm prices, and it did, but the act did nothing for tenant farmers and sharecroppers. The Supreme Court declared it unconstitutional in 1936.

**Agricultural Revolution** The gradual shift from hunting and gathering to cultivating basic food crops that occurred worldwide from 7000 to 9000 years ago. This transition resulted in sedentary living, population growth, and establishment of permanent villages.

**AIDS** Acquired immune-deficiency syndrome (AIDS), a disease of the immune system transmitted through blood, especially by sexual contact or contaminated needles. AIDS reached epidemic proportions in the United States in the 1980s before it was gradually contained in the 1990s.

**Alamo** In 1835, Americans living in the Mexican state of Texas fomented a revolution. Mexico lost the conflict, but not before its troops defeated and killed a group of American rebels at the Alamo, a fort in San Antonio.

**Albany Plan** Plan of intercolonial cooperation proposed by prominent colonists including Benjamin Franklin at a conference in Albany, New York, in 1754. The plan envisioned the formation of a Grand Council of elected delegates from the colonies that would have powers to tax and provide for the common defense. It was rejected by the colonial and British governments, but was a prototype for colonial union.

**Alien and Sedition Acts** Collective name given to four laws passed in 1798 designed to suppress criticism of the federal government and to curb liberties of foreigners living in the United States.

**American Colonization Society** Founded in 1817, this abolitionist organization hoped to provide a mechanism by which slavery could gradually be eliminated. The society advocated the relocation of free blacks (followed by freed slaves) to the African colony of Monrovia, present day Liberia.

**American Federation of Labor (AFL)** Founded by Samuel Gompers in 1886, the AFL was a loose alliance of national craft unions that organized skilled workers by craft and worked for specific practical objectives such as higher wages, shorter hours, and better working conditions. The AFL avoided politics, and while it did not expressly forbid black and women workers from joining, it used exclusionary practices to keep them out.

**American system** A national economic strategy championed by Kentucky Senator Henry Clay, the American system stressed high tariffs and internal improvements.

**Americans with Disabilities Act (ADA)** Passed by Congress in 1991, this act banned discrimination against the disabled in employment and mandated easy access to all public and commercial buildings.

**anaconda policy** A key point in the Union's war strategy was encircling the South as an anaconda squeezes its prey. This plan entailed a naval blockade and the capture of the Mississippi River corridor.

**Antifederalists** Critics of the Constitution who expressed concern that it seemed to possess no specific provision for the protection of natural and civil rights. The antifederalists forced Congress to accept a number of amendments known as the **Bill of Rights.**

**Anti-Imperialist League** This organization was formed in November 1898 to fight against the **Treaty of Paris** ending the Spanish-American War. Members opposed the acquisition of overseas colonies by the United States, believing it would subvert American ideals and institutions. Membership centered in New England; the cause was less popular in the South and West.

**Antinomianism** Religious belief rejecting traditional moral law as unnecessary for Christians who possessed saving grace and affirming that an individual could experience divine revelation and salvation without the assistance of formally trained clergy.

**Articles of Confederation** Ratified in 1781, this document was the United States' first constitution, providing a framework for national government. The articles sharply limited central authority by denying the national government any taxation or coercive power.

**Ashcan School** This school of early twentieth-century realist painters took as their subjects the slums and streets of the nation's cities and the lives of ordinary urban dwellers. They often celebrated life in the city but also advocated political and social reform.

**Axis Powers** During World War II, the alliance between Italy, Germany, and Japan was known as the "Rome-Berlin-Tokyo axis," and the three members were called the Axis Powers. They fought against the Allied Powers, led by the United States, Britain, and the Soviet Union.

**baby boom** Post–World War II Americans idealized the family. The booming birth rate after the war led children born to this generation to be commonly referred to as "baby boomers."

**backcountry** In the eighteenth century, the edge of settlement extending from western Pennsylvania to Georgia. This region formed the second frontier as settlers moved westward from the Atlantic coast into the nation's interior.

**Bacon's Rebellion** An armed rebellion in Virginia (1675–1676) led by Nathaniel Bacon against the colony's royal governor Sir William Berkeley. Although some of his followers called for an end of special privilege in government, Bacon was chiefly interested in gaining a larger share of the lucrative Indian trade.

**Bank of the United States** National bank proposed by Secretary of the Treasury Alexander Hamilton and established in 1791. It served as a central depository for the U.S. government and had the authority to issue currency.

**Bank war** Between 1832–1836, Andrew Jackson used his presidential power to fight and ultimately destroy the second Bank of the United States.

**Barbary War** In response to constant attacks on trading vessels by pirates from the North African Barbary States, in 1801 President Thomas Jefferson sent a naval squadron to resolve the problem through military force. After failing to achieve most of its military objectives, the administration signed an 1805 treaty ending the war.

**Baruch Plan** In 1946, Bernard Baruch presented an American plan to control and eventually outlaw nuclear weapons. The plan called for United Nations control of nuclear weapons in three stages before the United States gave up its stockpile. Soviet insistence on immediate nuclear disarmament without inspection doomed the Baruch Plan and led to a nuclear arms race between the United States and the Soviet Union.

**Bay of Pigs** In April 1961, a group of Cuban exiles organized and supported by the U.S. Central Intelligence Agency (CIA) landed on the southern coast of Cuba in an effort to overthrow Fidel Castro. When the invasion ended in disaster, President Kennedy took full responsibility for the failure.

**beats** In the late 1950s, young poets and novelists such as Jack Kerouac became known as the beats or "beatniks" for their innovative writing and bizarre behavior. Calling themselves members of "the beat generation," they challenged the prevailing materialism of the consumer culture.

**Berlin airlift** In 1948, in response to a Soviet land blockade of Berlin, the United States carried out a massive effort to supply the two million Berlin citizens with food, fuel, and other goods by air for more than six months. The airlift forced the Soviets to end the blockade in 1949.

**Berlin Wall** In 1961, the Soviet Union built a high barrier to seal off their sector of Berlin in order to stop the flow of refugees out of the Soviet zone of Germany. The wall was torn down in 1989.

**Bill of Rights** The first ten amendments to the U.S. Constitution, adopted in 1791 to preserve the rights and liberties of individuals.

**birds of passage** Temporary migrants who came to the United States to work and save money and then returned home to their native countries during the slack season. World War I interrupted the practice, trapping thousands of migrant workers in the United States.

**Black Codes** Laws passed by southern states immediately after the Civil War in an effort to maintain the pre-war social order. The codes attempted to tie freedmen to field work and prevent them from becoming equal to white Southerners.

**Bland-Allison Silver Purchase Act** This act, a compromise between groups favoring the coinage of silver and those opposed to it, called for the partial coinage of silver. Those favoring silver coinage argued that it would add to the currency and help farmers and workers; those who opposed it pointed out that few other major countries accepted silver coinage. President Rutherford B. Hayes vetoed the Bland-Allison bill in 1878, but Congress overrode his veto.

**bonanza farms** Huge farms covering thousands of acres on the Great Plains. In relying on large size and new machinery, they represented a development in agriculture similar to that taking place in industry.

**bonus army** In June 1932, a group of twenty thousand World War I veterans marched on Washington, D.C., to demand immediate payment of their "adjusted compensation" bonuses voted by Congress in 1924. Congress rejected their demands, and President Hoover, fearing that their ranks were infested with criminals and radicals, had the bonus army forcibly removed from their encampment. It was a public relations disaster for Hoover.

**Boston Massacre** A violent confrontation between British troops and a Boston mob on March 5, 1770. Five citizens were killed when the troops fired into the crowd. The incident inflamed anti-British sentiment in Massachusetts.

**Brandeis brief** Filed by attorney Louis D. Brandeis in the Supreme Court case of *Muller* v. *Oregon,* this brief presented only two pages of legal precedents, but contained 115 pages of sociological evidence on the negative effects of long workdays on women's health and thus on women as mothers. The brief expanded the definition of legal evidence.

**Brook Farm** This transcendentalist commune, founded in Massachusetts in 1841, attracted many leading creative figures during its brief existence.

***Brown* v. *Board of Education of Topeka*** In 1954, the Supreme Court reversed the *Plessy* v. *Ferguson* decision (1896) that established the "separate but equal" doctrine. The *Brown* decision found segregation in schools inherently unequal and initiated a long and difficult effort to integrate the nation's public schools.

**Camp David accords** In 1978, President Carter mediated a peace agreement between the leaders of Egypt and Israel at Camp David, a presidential retreat near Washington, D.C. The next year, Israel and Egypt signed a peace treaty based on the Camp David accords.

**carpetbaggers** This term was applied to Northerners who moved to the South after the Civil War in order to aid in the reconstruction of the South or to invest in the southern economy. It derives from the claim that these Northerners carried everything they owned in one bag.

**Chinese Exclusion Act** Legislation passed in 1882 that excluded Chinese immigrant workers for ten years and denied U.S. citizenship to Chinese nationals living in the United States. It was the first U.S. exclusionary law that was aimed at a specific racial group.

**Civilian Conservation Corps (CCC)** One of the most popular **New Deal** programs, the CCC was created by Congress to provide young men between ages 18 and 25 with government jobs in reforestation and other conservation projects. It eventually employed over 300,000.

**Civil Rights Act of 1875** A federal law that forbade discrimination on public conveyances (transportation) and guaranteed African Americans "full and equal enjoyment" of such conveyances. It represented one of the last efforts on the part of the federal government to enforce civil rights.

***Civil Rights Cases*** A group of cases in 1883 in which the Supreme Court ruled that the **Fourteenth Amendment** barred state governments from discriminating on the basis of race but did not prevent private individuals or organizations from doing so. The ruling dealt a major blow to the Republican party's earlier efforts to provide protection for African Americans.

**Clayton Antitrust Act** An attempt to improve the **Sherman Anti-Trust Act** of 1890, this law outlawed interlocking directorates (companies in which the same people served as directors), forbade policies that created monopolies, and made corporate officers responsible for anti-trust violations. Benefiting labor, it declared that unions were not conspiracies in restraint of trade and outlawed the use of injunctions in labor disputes unless they were necessary to protect property.

**Coercive Acts** Also known as the Intolerable Acts, the four pieces of legislation passed by Parliament in 1774 in response to the Boston Tea Party were meant to punish the colonies.

**Columbian Exchange** The exchange of plants, animals, culture, and diseases between Europe and the Americas from first contact throughout the era of exploration.

**committee of correspondence** Vast communication network formed in Massachusetts and other colonies to communicate grievances and provide colonists with evidence of British oppression.

**Committee on Public Information (CPI)** Created in 1917 by President Wilson and headed by progressive journalist George Creel, this organization rallied support for American involvement in World War I through art, advertising, and film. Creel worked out a system of voluntary censorship with the press and distributed colorful posters and pamphlets. The CPI's Division of Industrial Relations rallied labor to help the war effort.

*Common Sense* Revolutionary tract written by Thomas Paine in January 1776. It called for independence and the establishment of a republican government in America.

**Compromise of 1850** This series of five congressional statutes temporarily calmed the sectional crisis. Among other things, the compromise made California a free state, ended the slave trade in the District of Columbia, and strengthened the Fugitive Slave Law.

**Compromise of 1877** Compromise struck during the contested Presidential election of 1876, in which Democrats accepted the election of Rutherford B. Hayes (Republican) in exchange for the withdrawal of federal troops from the South and the ending of Reconstruction.

**Comstock Lode** Discovered in 1859 near Virginia City, Nevada, this ore deposit was the richest discovery in the history of mining. Named after T. P. Comstock, a drifter who talked his way into partnership in the claim, between 1859 and 1879 the deposit produced silver and gold worth more than $306 million.

**conquistadores** Sixteenth-century Spanish adventurers, often of noble birth, who subdued the Native Americans and created the Spanish empire in the New World.

**conservation** As President, Theodore Roosevelt made this principle one of his administration's top goals. Conservation in his view aimed at protecting the nation's natural resources, but called for the wise use of them rather than locking them away. Roosevelt's policies were opposed by those who favored preservation of the wilderness over its development.

**containment** First proposed by George Kennan in 1947, containment became the basic strategy of the United States throughout the Cold War. Kennan argued that firm American resistance to Soviet expansion would eventually compel Moscow to adopt more peaceful policies.

**Contract with America** In the 1994 congressional elections, Congressman Newt Gingrich had Republican candidates sign a document in which they pledged their support for such things as a balanced budget amendment, term limits for members of Congress, and a middle-class tax cut.

**cooperationists** In late 1860, southern secessionists debated two strategies: unilateral secession by each state or "cooperative" secession by the South as a whole. The cooperationists lost the debate.

**Copperheads** Northern Democrats suspected of being indifferent or hostile to the Union cause in the Civil War.

**cotton gin** Invented by Eli Whitney in 1793, this device for separating the seeds from the fibers of short-staple cotton enabled a slave to clean fifty times more cotton as by hand, which reduced production costs and gave new life to slavery in the South.

**"court-packing" scheme** Concerned that the conservative Supreme Court might declare all his New Deal programs unconstitutional, President Franklin Delano Roosevelt asked Congress to allow him to appoint additional justices to the Court. Both Congress and the public rejected this "court-packing" scheme and it was defeated.

**Crittenden compromise** Faced with the specter of secession and war, Congress tried and failed to resolve the sectional crisis in the months between Lincoln's election and inauguration. The leading proposal, introduced by Kentucky Senator John Crittenden, would have extended the **Missouri Compromise** line west to the Pacific.

**Cuban missile crisis** In October 1962, the United States and the Soviet Union came close to nuclear war when President Kennedy insisted that Nikita Khrushchev remove the 42 missiles he had secretly deployed in Cuba. The Soviets eventually did so, nuclear war was averted, and the crisis ended.

**Cult of Domesticity** Term used by historians to characterize the dominant gender role for white women in the antebellum period. The ideology of domesticity stressed the virtue of women as guardians of the home, which was considered their proper sphere.

***Dartmouth College* v. *Woodward*** In this 1819 case, the Supreme Court ruled that the Constitution protected charters given to corporations by states.

**Dawes Severalty Act** Legislation passed by Congress in 1887 that aimed at breaking up traditional Indian life by promoting individual land ownership. It divided tribal lands into small plots that were distributed among members of each tribe. Provisions were made for Indian education and eventual citizenship. The law led to corruption, exploitation, and the weakening of Native American tribal culture.

**D-Day** D-Day (June 6, 1944) was the day Allied troops crossed the English Channel and opened a second front in western Europe during World War II. The "D" stands for "disembarkation": to leave a ship and go ashore.

**Dien Bien Phu** In 1954, Vietminh rebels besieged a French garrison at Dien Bien Phu, deep in the interior of northern Vietnam. In May, after the United States refused to intervene, Dien Bien Phu fell to the communists.

**Dixiecrats** In 1948, a group of southern Democrats known as the Dixiecrats bolted from their party and supported Governor Strom Thurmond of South Carolina as the presidential candidate of the States Rights party.

**deregulation** Ronald Reagan continued the deregulation process begun by Jimmy Carter, cutting back on the scope of federal agencies and relying instead on the free market to keep prices of consumer goods and services low and the quality high.

**Desert Storm** Desert Storm was the code name used by the United States and its coalition partners in waging war against Iraq in early 1991 to liberate Kuwait.

**détente** President Nixon and Henry Kissinger pursued a policy of détente, a French word meaning a relaxation of tension, with the Soviet Union as a way to lessen the possibility of nuclear war in the 1970s.

**"dollar diplomacy"** This policy, adopted by President William Howard Taft and Secretary of State Philander C. Knox, sought to promote U.S. financial and business interests abroad. It aimed to replace military alliances with economic ties, with the idea of increasing American influence and securing lasting peace. Under this policy, Taft worked in Latin America to replace European loans with American ones, assumed the debts of countries such as Honduras to fend off foreign bondholders, and helped Nicaragua secure a large loan in exchange for U.S. control of its national bank.

**dry farming** A farming technique developed to allow farming in the more arid parts of the West, where settlers had to deal with far less rainfall than they had east of the Mississippi. Furrows were plowed a foot or so deep and filled with a dust mulch to loosen soil and slow evaporation.

**Emancipation Proclamation** On January 1, 1863, President Lincoln proclaimed that the slaves of the Confederacy were free. Since the South had not yet been defeated, the proclamation did not immediately free anyone, but it made emancipation an explicit war aim of the North.

**Embargo Act** In response to a British attack on an American warship off the coast of Virginia, this 1807 law prohibited foreign commerce.

**encomienda** An exploitative labor system designed by Spanish rulers to reward **conquistadores** in the New World by granting them local villages and control over native labor.

**Enlightenment** Philosophical and intellectual movement that began in Europe during the eighteenth century. It stressed the application of reason to solve social and scientific problems.

**enumerated goods** Certain essential raw materials produced in the North American colonies, such as tobacco, sugar, and rice specified in the **Navigation Acts,** which stipulated that these goods could be shipped only to England or its colonies.

**Environmental Protection Agency** Congress created the Environmental Protection Agency (EPA) in 1970 as part of a broader effort to protect the environment and curb the pollution of the nation's air and water.

**Equal Rights Amendment (ERA)** In 1972, Congress approved the Equal Rights Amendment (ERA) to the Constitution, a measure designed to guarantee women equal treatment under the law. Despite a three-year extension in the time allowed for ratification, ERA supporters fell three states short of winning adoption.

**"era of good feeling"** A descriptive term for the era of President James Monroe, who served two terms from 1817-1823. During Monroe's administration, partisan conflict abated and bold federal initiatives suggested increased nationalism.

**Espionage Act** This law, passed after the United States entered World War I, imposed sentences of up to twenty years on anyone found guilty of aiding the enemy, obstructing recruitment of soldiers, or encouraging disloyalty. It allowed the postmaster general to remove from the mail any materials that incited treason or insurrection.

**Exodusters** A group of about six thousand African Americans who left their homes in Louisiana, Mississippi, and Texas in 1879, seeking freer lives in Kansas, where they worked as farmers or laborers.

**Fair Deal** A series of reform measures proposed by President Truman in 1949, including federal aid to education, civil rights measures, and national medical insurance. A bipartisan conservative coalition in Congress blocked this effort to move beyond the **New Deal** reforms of the 1930s.

**Farewell Address** In this 1796 speech, President George Washington announced his intention not to seek a third term in office. He also stressed federalist interests and warned the American people to avoid political factions and foreign entanglements that could sacrifice U.S. security.

**Federal Reserve Act** One of the most important laws in the history of the country, this act created a central banking system, consisting of twelve regional banks governed by the Federal Reserve Board. It was an attempt to provide the United States with a sound yet flexible currency. The Board it created still plays a vital role in the American economy today.

**The Federalist** A series of essays penned by Alexander Hamilton, James Madison, and John Jay that explained and defended the stronger national government created by the Constitutional Convention of 1787.

**Federalists** Supporters of the Constitution who advocated its ratification.

**Fifteenth Amendment** Ratified in 1870, this amendment prohibited the denial or abridgment of the right to vote by the federal government or state governments on the basis of race, color, or prior condition as a slave. It was intended to guarantee African Americans the right to vote in the South.

**First Continental Congress** A meeting of delegates from twelve colonies in Philadelphia in 1774, the Congress denied Parliament's authority to legislate for the colonies, condemned British actions toward the colonies, created the Continental Association, and endorsed a call to take up arms.

**flexible response** The Kennedy administration rejected the Eisenhower strategy of **massive retaliation** in favor of flexible response, which emphasized the use of conventional as well as nuclear weapons in meeting threats to American security.

**Food Administration** A wartime government agency that encouraged Americans to save food in order to supply the armies overseas. It fixed prices to boost production, asked people to observe "meatless" and "wheatless" days to conserve food, and promoted the planting of "victory gardens" behind homes, schools, and churches.

**Foraker Act** This act established Puerto Rico as an unorganized U.S. territory. Puerto Ricans were not given U.S. citizenship, but the U.S. president appointed the island's governor and governing council.

**Force acts** Congress attacked the Ku Klux Klan with three Enforcement or "Force" acts in 1870–1871. Designed to protect black voters in the South, these laws placed state elections under federal jurisdiction and imposed fines and imprisonment on those guilty of interfering with any citizen exercising his right to vote.

**Fourteen Points** In January 1918, President Wilson presented these terms for a far-reaching, nonpunitive settlement of World War I. He called, among other things, for removal of barriers to trade, open peace accords, reduction of armaments, and the establishment of a League of Nations. While generous and optimistic, the Points did not satisfy wartime hunger for revenge, and thus were largely rejected by European nations.

**Fourteenth Amendment** Ratified in 1868, this amendment provided citizenship to ex-slaves after the Civil War and constitutionally protected equal rights under the law for all citizens. Its provisions were used by **Radical Republicans** to enact a congressionally controlled Reconstruction policy of the former Confederate states.

**Freedmen's Bureau** Agency established by Congress in March 1865 to provide freedmen with shelter, food, and medical aid and to help them establish schools and find employment. The Bureau was dissolved in 1872.

**freedom ride** Bus trips taken by both black and white civil rights advocates in the 1960s. Sponsored by the Congress of Racial Equality (CORE), freedom rides in the South were designed to test the enforcement of federal regulations that prohibited segregation in interstate public transportation.

**French Revolution** A social and political revolution in France (1789–1799) that toppled the monarchy.

**Free-Soil party** Organized in 1848, this third party proposed to exclude slavery from federal territories and nominated former President Martin Van Buren in the presidential election of that year. Most Free Soilers eventually became Republicans.

**Fugitive Slave Law** Passed in 1850, this federal law made it easier for slaveowners to recapture runaway slaves; it also made it easier for kidnappers to take free blacks. The law became an object of hatred in the North.

**gay liberation movement** In the 1970s, homosexuals began an effort to win social and legal acceptance and to encourage gays to affirm their sexual identity. Despite some advances, the movement was slowed by the onset of the **AIDS** epidemic in the 1980s and the insistence of the military on banning openly gay individuals from the armed services.

**Ghost Dances** A religious movement that arose in the late nineteenth century under the prophet Wavoka, a Paiute Indian. It involved a set of dances and rites that its followers believed would cause white men to disappear and restore lands to the Native Americans. The Ghost Dance religion was outlawed by the U.S. government, and army intervention to stop it led to the **Wounded Knee Massacre.**

*Gibbons* v. *Ogden* In this 1824 case, the Supreme Court affirmed and expanded the power of the federal government to regulate interstate commerce.

**Glorious Revolution** Replacement of James II by William and Mary as English monarchs in 1688, marking the beginning of constitutional monarchy in Britain. American colonists celebrated this moment as a victory for the rule of law over despotism.

**Gold Rush of 1849** Individual prospectors made the first gold strikes along the Sierra Nevada Mountains in 1849, touching off a mining boom that helped shape the development of the West and set the pattern for subsequent strikes in other regions.

**Gold Standard Act** Passed by Congress in 1900, this law declared gold the nation's standard of currency, meaning that all currency in circulation had to be redeemable in gold. The United States remained on the gold standard until 1933.

**Good Neighbor policy** President Hoover's administration initiated a new approach to Western hemispheric relations. The Good Neighbor policy declared America's intention to use cooperation and friendship in place of threats and armed intervention in its dealings with Latin America. It was extended and elaborated by the administration of Franklin Roosevelt.

**Gramm-Rudman** The Gramm-Rudman-Hollings Balanced Budget Act of 1985, popularly known as Gramm-Rudman, revised federal budgeting procedures. It authorized the president to impose automatic spending reductions to meet annual deficit limits.

**Great Awakening** Widespread evangelical religious revival movement of the mid-1700s. The movement divided congregations and weakened the authority of established churches in the colonies.

**Great Society** President Johnson called his version of the Democratic reform program the Great Society. In 1965, Congress passed many Great Society measures, including **Medicare,** civil rights legislation, and federal aid to education.

**greenbackers** Members of the National Greenback Party, founded in 1874, who wanted to keep wartime paper money (**greenbacks**) in circulation. They believed that a floating currency, not tied to either gold or silver, would provide relief to debtors and impoverished farmers by increasing the money supply.

**greenbacks** Paper currency issued by the Union beginning in 1862.

**Gulf of Tonkin Resolution** After a North Vietnamese attack on an American destroyer in the Gulf of Tonkin in 1964, President Johnson persuaded Congress to pass a resolution giving him the authority to use armed force in Vietnam.

**Harlem Renaissance** An African American cultural, literary, and artistic movement centered in Harlem, an area in New York City, in the 1920s. Harlem, the largest black community in the world outside of Africa, was considered the cultural capital of African Americans.

**Hartford Convention** An assembly of New England federalists who met in Hartford, Connecticut, in December 1814 to protest Madison's foreign policy in the War of 1812, which had undermined commercial interests in the North. They proposed amending the Constitution to prevent future presidents from declaring war without a two-thirds majority in Congress.

**Hay-Bunau-Varilla Treaty** This 1903 treaty granted the United States control over a canal zone ten miles wide across the Isthmus of Panama.

In return, the United States guaranteed the independence of Panama and agreed to pay Colombia a onetime fee of $10 million and an annual rental of $250,000.

**Haymarket Riot** On May 4, 1886, a demonstration in Chicago's Haymarket Square to protest the slayings of two workers during a strike turned into a violent riot after a bomb explosion killed seven policemen. Although the bomb thrower was never found, the incident was blamed on labor "radicalism" and resulted in public condemnation of organized labor and contributed to the demise of the **Knights of Labor.**

**headright** System of land distribution in which settlers were granted a fifty-acre plot of land from the colonial government for each servant or dependent they transported to the New World. The system encouraged the recruitment of a large servile labor force.

**Hepburn Act** A law that strengthened the rate-making power of the **Interstate Commerce Commission,** again reflecting the era's desire to control the power of the railroads. It increased the ICC's membership from five to seven, empowered it to fix reasonable railroad rates, and broadened its jurisdiction. It also made ICC rulings binding pending court appeals.

**Highway Act of 1956** A significant legislative achievement of Eisenhower's presidency, the Highway Act created the interstate highway system. The system, built over twenty years, provided jobs in construction, shortened travel times, and increased dependence on the automobile while weakening the railroads.

**Homestead Act of 1862** Legislation granting 160 acres of land to anyone who paid a $10 fee and pledged to live on and cultivate the land for five years. Although there was a good deal of fraud, the act encouraged a large migration to the West. Between 1862 and 1900, nearly 600,000 families claimed homesteads under its provisions.

**Homestead Strike** In July 1892, wage-cutting at Andrew Carnegie's Homestead Steel Plant in Pittsburgh provoked a violent strike in which three company-hired detectives and ten workers died. Using ruthless force and strikebreakers, company officials effectively broke the strike and destroyed the union.

**House of Burgesses** An elective representative assembly in colonial Virginia. It was the first example of representative government in the English colonies.

**House Un-American Activities Committee (HUAC)** This congressional committee played a prominent role in attempting to uncover and punish those suspected of aiding the communist cause in the early years of the Cold War.

**hustings** Using tree stumps as podiums, traveling orators in America gave speeches on behalf of political parties. These visits were called "hustings" after a word for stump.

**imperialism** The policy of extending a nation's power through military conquest, economic domination, or annexation.

**indentured servants** Individuals who agreed to serve a master for a set number of years in exchange for the cost of boat transport to America. Indentured servitude was the dominant form of labor in the Chesapeake colonies before slavery.

**Industrial Workers of the World (IWW).** Founded in 1905, this radical union, also known as the Wobblies, aimed to unite the American working class into one union to promote labor's interests. It worked to organize unskilled and foreign-born laborers, advocated social revolution, and led several major strikes. Stressing solidarity, the IWW took as its slogan, "An injury to one is an injury to all."

**Intermediate Nuclear Forces agreement** Signed by President Reagan and Soviet President Gorbachev in Washington in late 1987, this agreement provided for the destruction of all intermediate-range nuclear missiles and permitted on-site inspection for the first time during the Cold War.

**Interstate Commerce Commission (ICC)** Created by Congress in 1887, this agency was authorized to investigate and oversee railroad activities. It also outlawed rebates and pooling agreements. An early attempt to remove certain issues from politics and turn them over to experts, the ICC became a prototype for the federal commissions that regulate many parts of the American economy today.

**Iran-Contra affair** The Iran-Contra affair involved officials high in the Reagan administration secretly selling arms to Iran and using the proceeds to finance the Contra rebels in Nicaragua. This illegal transaction usurped the congressional power of the purse.

**Iranian hostage crisis** In 1979, Iranian fundamentalists seized the American embassy in Tehran and held fifty-three American diplomats hostage for over a year. The Iranian hostage crisis weakened the Carter presidency; the hostages were finally released on January 20, 1981, the day Ronald Reagan became president.

**Iron Curtain** British Prime Minister Winston Churchill coined the phrase "Iron Curtain" to refer to the boundary in Europe that divided Soviet-dominated eastern and central Europe from western Europe, which was free from Soviet control.

**isolationism** A belief that the United States should stay out of entanglements with other nations. Isolationism was widespread after the Spanish-American War in the late 1890s and influenced later U.S. foreign policy.

**itinerant preachers** Traveling revivalist ministers of the **Great Awakening** movement. These charismatic preachers spread revivalism throughout America.

**Jacksonian Democracy** A historian's term for the political culture of white male citizens in the 1820s and 1830s. It celebrated the "self-made man" and rejected the idea that leaders should be drawn from the intellectual and economic elite. Andrew Jackson, the first "people's president," exemplified the spirit of the age.

**Jay's Treaty** Controversial treaty with Britain negotiated by Chief Justice John Jay in 1794 to settle American grievances and avert war. Though the British agreed to surrender forts on U.S. territory, the treaty failed to realize key diplomatic goals and provoked a storm of protest in America.

**Jim Crow laws** Laws enacted by states to segregate the population. They became widespread in the South after Reconstruction.

**joint-stock company** Business enterprise that enabled investors to pool money for commercial trading activity and funding for sustaining colonies.

**Kansas-Nebraska Act** This 1854 act repealed the Missouri Compromise, split the Louisiana Purchase into two territories, and allowed its settlers to accept or reject slavery by popular sovereignty. This act enflamed the slavery issue and led opponents to form the Republican party.

**Kellogg-Briand Pact** Also called the Pact of Paris, this 1929 agreement was the brainchild of U.S. Secretary of State Frank B. Kellogg and French premier Aristide Briand. It pledged its signatories, eventually including nearly all nations, to shun war as an instrument of policy. Derided as an "international kiss," it had little effect on the actual conduct of world affairs.

**Kentucky and Virginia Resolutions** Statements penned by Thomas Jefferson and James Madison to mobilize opposition to the Alien and Sedition Acts, which they argued were unconstitutional. Jefferson's statement (the Kentucky Resolution) suggested that states should have the right to declare null and void congressional acts they deemed unconstitutional. Madison produced a more temperate resolution, but most Americans rejected such an extreme defense of states' rights.

**Knights of Labor** Also known as the Noble and Holy Order of the Knights of Labor. Founded in 1869, this labor organization pursued broad-gauged reforms as much as practical issues like wages and hours. Unlike the **American Federation of Labor,** the Knights of Labor welcomed all laborers regardless of race, gender, or skill.

**Know-Nothing party** After the collapse of the Whig party in the 1850s, this anti-immigrant and anti-Catholic party rose to national prominence. Though the party enjoyed some success in local and state elections, it failed to sustain its existence and quickly disappeared.

**Ku Klux Klan** A secret terrorist society first organized in Tennessee in 1866. The original Klan's goals were to disfranchise Africa Americans, stop Reconstruction, and restore the pre-war social order of the South. The Ku Klux Klan re-formed after World War II to promote white supremacy in the wake of the "Second Reconstruction."

**Lecompton constitution** In 1857, a fraudulently-elected group of pro-slavery delegates met in Lecompton, Kansas, and drafted a state constitution. After bitter debate, Congress narrowly denied Kansas's entry into the Union under this constitution.

**Leisler's Rebellion** In the aftermath of England's **Glorious Revolution** in 1688, Jacob Leisler seized control of New York's government. Although Lesisler was executed as a traitor, his followers defended his memory against detractors well into the eighteenth century

**Lend-Lease** Arguing that aiding Britain would help America's own self-defense, President Roosevelt in 1941 asked Congress for a $7 billion Lend-Lease plan. This would allow the president to sell, lend, lease, or transfer war materials to any country whose defense he declared as vital to that of the United States.

**Levittown** In 1947, William Levitt used mass production techniques to build inexpensive homes in suburban New York to help relieve the postwar housing shortage. Levittown became a symbol of the movement to the suburbs in the years after World War II.

**Lewis and Clark Expedition** Overland expedition to the Pacific coast (1804–1806) led by Meriwether Lewis and William Clark. Commissioned by President Thomas Jefferson, the exploration of the Far West brought back a wealth of scientific data about the country and its resources.

**Liberty party** America's first antislavery political party, formed in 1840. When the party ran a presidential candidate in the 1844 election, it split the Republican vote and inadvertently tipped the 1844 election in favor of Democrat James Polk.

**Louisiana Purchase** U.S. acquisition of the Louisiana Territory from France in 1803 for $15 million. The purchase secured American control of the Mississippi River and doubled the size of the nation.

**Loyalists** Throughout the conflict with Great Britain, many colonists sided with the king and Parliament. Also called Tories, these people feared that American liberty might promote social anarchy.

**Manhattan Project** In early 1942, Franklin Roosevelt, alarmed by reports that German scientists were working on an atomic bomb, authorized a crash program to build the bomb first. The Manhattan Project, named for the Corps of Engineers district originally in charge, spent $2 billion dollars and produced the weapons that devastated Hiroshima and Nagasaki in 1945.

**Manifest Destiny** Coined in 1845, this term referred to a doctrine in support of territorial expansion based on the beliefs that population growth demanded territorial expansion, that God supported American expansion, and that national expansion equaled the expansion of freedom.

***Marbury* v. *Madison*** In this 1803 landmark decision, the Supreme Court first asserted the power of judicial review by declaring an act of Congress, the Judiciary Act of 1789, unconstitutional.

**March on Washington** In August 1963, civil rights leaders organized a massive rally in Washington to urge passage of President Kennedy's civil rights bill. The high point came when Martin Luther King, Jr. gave his "I Have a Dream" speech to more than 200,000 marchers in front of the Lincoln Memorial.

**Marshall Plan** In 1947, Secretary of State George Marshall proposed a massive economic aid program to rebuild the war-torn economies of western European nations. The plan was motivated by both humanitarian concern for the conditions of those nations' economies and fear that economic dislocation would promote communism in western Europe.

**massive retaliation** The "new look" defense policy of the Eisenhower administration in the 1950s was to threaten "massive retaliation" with nuclear weapons in response to any act of aggression by a potential enemy.

**Mayflower Compact** Agreement among the Pilgrims aboard the Mayflower in 1620 to create a civil government at Plymouth Colony.

**McCarthyism** In 1950, Senator Joseph R. McCarthy began a sensational campaign against communists in government that led to more than four years of charges and countercharges, ending when the Senate censured him in 1954. McCarthyism became the contemporary name for the red scare of the 1950s.

*McCulloch v. Maryland* Ruling on this banking case in 1819, the Supreme Court propped up the idea of "implied powers" meaning the Constitution could be broadly interpreted. This pivotal ruling also asserted the supremacy of federal power over state power.

**Medicare** The 1965 Medicare Act provided Social Security funding for hospitalization insurance for people over age 65 and a voluntary plan to cover doctor bills paid in part by the federal government.

**mercantilism** An economic theory that shaped imperial policy throughout the colonial period, mercantilism was built on the assumption that the world's wealth was a fixed supply. In order to increase its wealth, a nation needed to export more goods than it imported. Favorable trade and protective economic policies, as well as new colonial possessions rich in raw materials, were important in achieving this balance.

**Mexican-American War** Conflict (1846–1848) between the United States and Mexico after the U.S. annexation of Texas, which Mexico still considered its own. As victor, the United States acquired vast new territories from Mexico according to the terms of the **Treaty of Guadalupe Hidalgo.**

**military-industrial complex** In his farewell address in January 1961, President Eisenhower used the phrase "military-industrial complex" to warn about the danger of massive defense spending and the close relationship between the armed forces and industrial corporations that supplied their weapons.

**Missouri Compromise** A sectional compromise in Congress in 1820 that admitted Missouri to the Union as a slave state and Maine as a free state. It also banned slavery in the remainder of the Louisiana Purchase territory above the latitude of 36°30'.

**Modern Republicanism** President Eisenhower characterized his views as "Modern Republicanism." Claiming he was liberal toward people but conservative about spending public money, he helped balance the federal budget and lower taxes without destroying existing social programs.

**Monroe Doctrine** A key foreign policy made by President James Monroe in 1823, it declared the western hemisphere off limits to new European colonization; in return, the United States promised not to meddle in European affairs.

**Montgomery bus boycott** In late 1955, African Americans led by Martin Luther King, Jr., boycotted the buses in Montgomery, Alabama, after seamstress Rosa Parks was arrested for refusing to move to the back of a bus. The boycott, which ended when the Supreme Court ruled in favor of the protesters, marked the beginning of a new, activist phase of the civil rights movement.

**moral diplomacy** Policy adopted by President Woodrow Wilson that rejected the approach of **"dollar diplomacy."** Rather than focusing mainly on economic ties with other nations, Wilson's policy was designed to bring right principles to the world, preserve peace, and extend to other peoples the blessings of democracy. Wilson, however, often ended up pursuing policies much like those followed by Roosevelt and Taft.

**Moral Majority** In 1979, the Reverend Jerry Falwell founded the Moral Majority to combat "amoral liberals," drug abuse, "coddling" of criminals, homosexuality, communism, and abortion. The Moral Majority represented the rise of political activism among organized religion's radical right wing.

**muckrakers** Unflattering term coined by Theodore Roosevelt to describe the writers who made a practice of exposing the wrongdoings of public figures. Muckraking flourished from 1903 to 1909 in magazines such as *McClure's* and *Collier's*, exposing social and political problems and sparking reform.

**Mugwumps** Drawing their members mainly from among the educated and upper class, these reformers crusaded for lower tariffs, limited federal government, and civil service reform to end political corruption. They were best known for their role in helping to elect Grover Cleveland to the presidency in 1884.

*Muller v. Oregon* This Supreme Court decision established special protections for working women, upholding an Oregon law that limited women working in factories and laundries to a ten-hour work day. Louis D. Brandeis, attorney for the state of Oregon, argued that because of the importance of women's roles as mothers, they deserved special protection from labor abuses. The **Brandeis brief,** as it was called, was based largely on sociological data rather than legal evidence, and as a result, expanded the definition of legal evidence.

**National American Woman Suffrage Association** Founded by Susan B. Anthony in 1890, this organization worked to secure women the right to vote. While some suffragists urged militant action, it stressed careful organization and peaceful lobbying. By 1920 it had nearly two million members.

**National Association for the Advancement of Colored People (NAACP)** Created in 1909, this organization quickly became one of the most important civil rights organizations in the country. The NAACP pressured employers, labor unions, and the government on behalf of African Americans.

**National Defense Education Act (NDEA)** The 1958 National Defense Education Act (NDEA), passed in response to *Sputnik,* provided an opportunity and stimulus for college education for many Americans. It allocated funds for upgrading studies in the sciences, foreign languages, guidance services, and teaching innovation.

**National Farmers' Alliance and Industrial Union** One of the largest reform movements in American history, the Farmer's Alliance sought to organize farmers in the South and West to fight for reforms that would improve their lot, including measures to overcome low crop prices, burdensome mortgages, and high railroad rates. The Alliance ultimately organized a political party, the **People's (Populist) party.**

**National Grange of the Patrons of Husbandry** Founded by Oliver H. Kelly in 1867, the Grange sought to relieve the drabness of farm life by providing a social, educational, and cultural outlet for its members. It also set up grain elevators, cooperative stores, warehouses, insurance companies, and farm machinery factories. Although its constitution banned political involvement, the Grange often supported railroad regulation and other measures.

**National Organization for Women (NOW)** Founded in 1966, the National Organization for Women (NOW) called for equal employment opportunity and equal pay for women. NOW also championed the legalization of abortion and passage of an equal rights amendment to the Constitution.

**National Origins Quota Act** This 1924 law established a quota system to regulate the influx of immigrants to America. The system restricted the **new immigrants** from southern and eastern Europe and Asia. It also reduced the annual total of immigrants.

**National Reclamation Act (Newlands Act)** Passed in 1902, this legisaltion set aside the majority of the proceeds from the sale of public land in sixteen Western states to fund irrigation projects in the arid states.

**National Recovery Administration (NRA)** A keystone of the early **New Deal,** this federal agency was created in 1933 to promote economic recovery and revive industry during the Great Depression. It permitted manufacturers to establish industry-wide codes of "fair business practices" setting prices and production levels. It also provided for minimum wages and maximum working hours for labor and guaranteed labor the right to organize and bargain collectively (Section 7a). The Supreme Court declared it unconstitutional in 1935.

**National Security Act** Congress passed the National Security Act in 1947 in response to perceived threats from the Soviet Union after World War II. It established the Department of Defense and created the Central Intelligence Agency (CIA) and National Security Council.

**nationalists** Group of leaders who favored replacing the Articles of Confederation with a stronger national government.

**natural rights** Fundamental rights over which the government could exercise no control. An uncompromising belief in such rights energized the popular demand for a formal bill of rights in 1791.

**Navigation Acts** A series of commercial restrictions passed by Parliament intended to regulate colonial commerce in such a way as to favor England's accumulation of wealth.

**Neoconservatism** Former liberals who advocated a strong stand against communism abroad and free market capitalism at home became known as neoconservatives. These intellectuals stressed the positive values of American society in contrast to liberals who emphasized social ills.

**neutrality acts** Reacting to their disillusionment with World War I and absorbed in the domestic crisis of the Great Depression, Americans backed Congress's three neutrality acts in the 1930s. The 1935 and 1936 acts forbade selling munitions or lending money to belligerents in a war. The 1937 act required that all remaining trade be conducted on a cash-and-carry basis.

**New Deal** In accepting the nomination of the Democratic Party in 1932, Franklin Delano Roosevelt promised a "new deal" for the American people. After his election, the label was applied to his program of legislation passed to combat the Great Depression. The New Deal included measures aimed at relief, reform, and recovery. They achieved some relief and considerable reform but little recovery.

**New Freedom** Woodrow Wilson's program in his campaign for the presidency in 1912, the New Freedom emphasized business competition and small government. It sought to rein in federal authority, release individual energy, and restore competition. It echoed many of the progressive social-justice objectives while pushing for a free economy rather than a planned one.

**New Frontier** The New Frontier was the campaign program advocated by John F. Kennedy in the 1960 election. He promised to revitalize the stagnant economy and enact reform legislation in education, health care, and civil rights.

**new immigrants** Starting in the 1880s, immigration into the United States began to shift from northern and western Europe, its source for most of the nation's history, to southern and eastern Europe. These "new" immigrants tended to be poor, non-Protestant, and unskilled; they tended to stay in close-knit communities and retain their language,

customs, and religions. Between 1880 and 1910, approximately 8.4 million of these so-called "new" immigrants came to the United States.

**New Jersey Plan** Proposal of the New Jersey delegation at the Constitutional Convention that called for a strong national government with one house of Congress in which all states would have equal representation. This plan challenged the **Virginia Plan** and was the basis for a compromise in which one of the two houses of Congress, the Senate, was based on equal representation from each state regardless of size.

**New Nationalism** Theodore Roosevelt's program in his campaign for the presidency in 1912, the New Nationalism called for a national approach to the country's affairs and a strong president to deal with them. It also called for efficiency in government and society; it urged protection of children, women, and workers; accepted "good" trusts; and exalted the expert and the executive. Additionally, it encouraged large concentrations of capital and labor.

**Niagara Movement** A movement, led by W. E. B. Du Bois, that focused on equal rights and the education of African American youth. Rejecting the gradualist approach of Booker T. Washington, members kept alive a program of militant action and claimed for African Americans all the rights afforded to other Americans. It spawned later civil rights movements.

*Nixonomics* A word used by Democrats critical of President Richard Nixon's economic policies, in particular the inability to curb inflation at a time of high unemployment and recession.

**nonimportation** During their controversy with Britain over taxation, the colonists devised a strategy of political resistance in which they boycotted a wide range of British imported goods to put economic pressure on Britain. The cooperative effort promoted mutual trust among the colonists and strengthened their resistance to the British measures.

**North American Free Trade Agreement (NAFTA)** A free trade plan initiated in the Bush administration and enacted by a narrow vote in Congress in the early months of the Clinton administration. It established a common market without tariff barriers between the United States, Canada, and Mexico.

**North Atlantic Treaty Organization (NATO)** In 1949, the United States, Canada, and ten European nations formed this military mutual-defense pact. In 1955, the Soviet Union countered NATO with the formation of the Warsaw Pact, a military alliance among those nations within its own sphere of influence.

**Northwest Ordinance** Legislation that formulated plans for governments in America's northwestern territories, defined a procedure for the territories' admission to the Union as states, and prohibited slavery north of the Ohio River.

**NSC-68** National Security Council planning paper No. 68 redefined America's national defense policy. Adopted in 1950, it committed the United States to a massive military buildup to meet the challenge posed by the Soviet Union.

**nullification** The supposed right of any state to declare a federal law inoperative within its boundaries. In 1832, South Carolina created a firestorm when it attempted to nullify the federal tariff.

**Ocala Demands** Adopted by the Farmers' Alliance at an 1890 meeting in Ocala, Florida, these demands became the organization's main platform. They called for the creation of a sub-treasury system to allow farmers to store their crops until they could get the best price, the free coinage of silver, an end to protective tariffs and national banks, a federal income tax, the direct election of senators by voters, and tighter regulation of railroads.

**Old South** The term refers to the slaveholding states between 1830 and 1860, when slave labor and cotton production dominated the economies of the southern states. This period is also known as the "antebellum era."

**Oneida community** Founded in 1848 in Oneida, New York, this Christian utopian community earned notoriety for institutionalizing a form of "free love."

**Open Door policy** Established in a series of notes by Secretary of State John Hay in 1900, this policy established free trade between the United States and China and attempted to enlist major European and Asian nations in recognizing the territorial integrity of China. It marked a departure from the American tradition of **isolationism** and signaled the country's growing involvement in the world.

**Organization of Petroleum Exporting Countries (OPEC)** A cartel of oil-exporting nations. In late 1973, OPEC took advantage of the October War and an oil embargo by its Arab members to quadruple the price of oil. This huge increase had a devastating impact on the American economy.

**Ostend Manifesto** Written by American officials in 1854, this secret memo—later dubbed a "manifesto"—urged the acquisition of Cuba by any means necessary. When it became public, Northerners claimed it was a plot to extend slavery and the manifesto was disavowed.

**Overland Trail** The route taken by thousands of travelers from the Mississippi Valley to the Pacific Coast in the last half of the nineteenth century. It was extremely difficult, often taking six months or more to complete.

**Panic of 1837** A financial depression that lasted until the 1840s.

**parliamentary sovereignty** Principle that emphasized the power of Parliament to govern colonial affairs as the preeminent authority.

**Pearl Harbor** On December 7, 1941, Japanese warplanes attacked U.S. naval forces at Pearl Harbor, Hawaii, sinking several ships and killing more than 2400 American sailors. The event marked America's entrance into World War II.

**Pendleton Act** Passed by Congress in 1883 with the backing of President Chester A. Arthur, this act sought to lessen the involvement of politicians in the running of the government. It created a bipartisan Civil Service Commission to administer competitive exams to candidates for civil service jobs and to appoint officeholders based on merit. It also outlawed forcing political contributions from appointed officials. The measure served as the basis for later expansion of a professional civil service.

**Pentagon Papers** The Pentagon Papers was a secret Defense Department study of the Vietnam War. Publication of the papers in 1971 revealed how civilian and military leaders had misled the American people about the nation's role in Vietnam.

**People's (or Populist) party** This political party was organized in 1892 by farm, labor, and reform leaders, mainly from the Farmers' Alliance. It offered a broad-based reform platform reflecting the **Ocala Demands.** It nominated James B. Weaver of Iowa for president in 1892 and William Jennings Bryan of Nebraska in 1896. After 1896, it became identified as a one-issue party focused on free silver and gradually died away.

**Philippine-American War** A war fought from 1899 to 1903 to quell Filipino resistance to U.S. control of the Philippine Islands. Although often forgotten, it lasted longer than the Spanish-American War and resulted in more casualties. Filipino guerilla soldiers finally gave up when their leader, Emilio Aguinaldo, was captured.

**placer mining** A form of mining that required little technology or skill, placer mining techniques included using a shovel and a washing pan to separate gold from the ore in streams and riverbeds. An early phase of the mining industry, placer mining could be performed by miners working as individuals or in small groups.

**Platt Amendment** This amendment to the new Cuban constitution authorized U.S. intervention in Cuba to protect its interests. Cuba pledged not to make treaties with other countries that might compromise its independence, and it granted naval bases to the United States, the most notable being Guantanamo Bay.

***Plessy* v. *Ferguson*** A Supreme Court case in 1896 that established the doctrine of "separate but equal" and upheld a Louisiana law requiring that blacks and whites occupy separate rail cars. The Court applied it to schools in *Cumming* v. *County Board of Education* (1899). The doctrine was finally overturned in 1954, in **Brown v. Board of Education of Topeka.**

**popular sovereignty** The concept that the settlers of a newly organized territory have the right to decide (through voting) whether or not to accept slavery. Promoted as a solution to the slavery question, popular sovereignty became a fiasco in Kansas during the 1850s.

**Potsdam Conference** The final wartime meeting of the leaders of the United States, Great Britain, and the Soviet Union was held at Potsdam, outside Berlin, in July, 1945. Truman, Churchill, and Stalin discussed the future of Europe but their failure to reach meaningful agreements soon led to the onset of the Cold War.

**pragmatism** A doctrine that emerged in the early twentieth century, built largely on the ideas of Harvard psychologist and philosopher William James. Pragmatists were impatient with theories that held truth to be abstract; they believed that truth should work for the individual. They also believed that people were not only shaped by their environment but also helped to shape it. Ideas that worked, according to pragmatists, became truth.

**preemption** The right of first purchase of public land. Settlers enjoyed this right even if they squatted on the land in advance of government surveyors.

**progressivism** Movement for social change between the late 1890s and World War I. Its origins lay in a fear of big business and corrupt government and a desire to improve the lives of countless Americans. Progressives set out to cure the social ills brought about by industrialization and urbanization, social disorder, and political corruption.

**Progressive party** Also known as the "Bull Moose" party, this political party was formed by Theodore Roosevelt in an attempt to advance progressive ideas and unseat President William Howard Taft in the election of 1912. After Taft won the Republican party's nomination, Roosevelt ran on the Progressive party ticket.

**prohibition** The ban of the manufacture, sale, and transportation of alcoholic beverages in the United States. The Eighteenth Amendment, adopted in 1919, established prohibition. It was repealed by the Twenty-first Amendment in 1933. While prohibition was in effect, it reduced national consumption of alcohol, but it was inconsistently enforced and was often evaded, especially in the cities.

**Protestant Reformation** Sixteenth-century religious movement to reform and challenge the spiritual authority of the Roman Catholic Church, associated with figures such as Martin Luther and John Calvin.

**Pullman Strike** Beginning in May 1894, this strike of employees at the Pullman Palace Car Company near Chicago was one of the largest strikes in American history. Workers struck to protest wage cuts, high rents for company housing, and layoffs; the American Railway Union, led by Eugene V. Debs, joined the strike in June. Extending into twenty-seven states and territories, it effectively paralyzed the western half of the nation. President Grover Cleveland secured an injunction to break the strike on the grounds that it obstructed the mail and sent federal troops to enforce it. The Supreme Court upheld the use of the injunction in *In re Debs* (1895).

**Puritans** Members of a reformed Protestant sect in Europe and America that insisted on removing all vestiges of Catholicism from popular religious practice.

**Quakers** Members of a radical religious group, formally known as the Society of Friends, that rejected formal theology and stressed each person's "inner light," a spiritual guide to righteousness.

**Radical Reconstruction** The Reconstruction Acts of 1867 divided the South into five military districts. They required the states to guarantee black male suffrage and to ratify the **Fourteenth Amendment** as a condition of their readmission to the Union.

**Radical Republicans** The Radical Republicans in Congress, headed by Thaddeus Stevens and Charles Sumner, insisted on black suffrage and federal protection of civil rights of African Americans. They gained control of Reconstruction in 1867 and required the ratification of the **Fourteenth Amendment** as a condition of readmission for former Confederate states.

**Red Scare** A wave of anticommunist, antiforeign, and antilabor hysteria that swept over America at the end of World War I. It resulted in the deportation of many alien residents and the violation of the civil liberties of many of its victims.

**Redeemers** A loose coalition of prewar Democrats, Confederate Army veterans, and southern Whigs who took over southern state governments in the 1870s, supposedly "redeeming" them from the corruption of Reconstruction. They shared a commitment to white supremacy and laissez-faire economics.

**Renaissance** A cultural awakening that began in Italy and spread throughout Europe in the fifteenth and sixteenth centuries. This powerful humanistic movement encouraged creativity and a spirit of inquiry and brought forth new forms of artistic expression and political theory.

**republicanism** Concept that ultimate political authority is vested in the citizens of the nation. The character of republican government was dependent on the civic virtue of its citizens to preserve the nation from corruption and moral decay.

**Republicans** Members of the Republican party established following the enactment of the **Kansas-Nebraska Act** in 1854. Republicans were opposed to the extension of slavery into the western territories.

**Roe v. Wade** In 1973, the Supreme Court ruled in *Roe* v. *Wade* that women had a constitutional right to abortion during the early stages of pregnancy. The decision provoked a vigorous right-to-life movement that opposed abortion.

**Roosevelt Corollary** President Theodore Roosevelt's 1904 foreign policy statement, a corollary to the **Monroe Doctrine,** which asserted that the United States would intervene in Latin American affairs if the countries themselves could not keep their affairs in order. It effectively made the United States the policeman of the western hemisphere. The Roosevelt Corollary guided U.S. policy in Latin America until it was replaced by Franklin D. Roosevelt's **Good Neighbor policy** in the 1930s.

**Sanitary Commission** An association chartered by the Union government during the Civil War to promote health in the northern army's camps though attention to cleanliness, nutrition, and medical care.

**Scopes trial** Also called the "monkey trial," the 1924 Scopes trial was a contest between modern liberalism and religious fundamentalism. John T. Scopes was on trial for teaching Darwinian evolution in defiance of a Tennessee state law. He was found guilty and fined $100.

**Second Continental Congress** This meeting took place in Philadelphia in May 1775, in the midst of rapidly unfolding military events. It organized the Continental Army and commissioned George Washington to lead it, then began requisitioning men and supplies for the war effort.

**Second Great Awakening** A series of evangelical Protestant revivals that swept over America in the early nineteenth century.

**second party system** A historian's term for the national two-party rivalry between Democrats and **Whigs.** The second party system began in the 1830s and ended in the 1850s with the demise of the Whig party and the rise of the Republican party.

**Sedition Act** A wartime law that imposed harsh penalties on anyone using "disloyal, profane, scurrilous, or abusive language" about the U.S. government, flag, or armed forces.

**Selective Service Act** This 1917 law provided for the registration of all American men between the ages of 21 and 30 for a military draft. By the end of World War I, 24.2 million men had registered; 2.8 million had been inducted into the army. The age limits were later changed to 18 and 45.

**Seneca Falls Convention** The first women's rights convention held in 1848 in Seneca Falls, New York, and co-sponsored by Elizabeth Cady Stanton and Lucretia Mott. Delegates at the convention drafted a "declaration of sentiments," patterned on the Declaration of Independence, but which declared that "all men and women are created equal."

**settlement houses** Located in poor districts of major cities, these were community centers that tried to soften the impact of urban life for immigrant and other families. Often run by young, educated women, they provided social services and a political voice for their neighborhoods. Chicago's Hull House, founded by Jane Addams in 1889, became the most famous of the settlement houses.

**Seven Years' War** Worldwide conflict (1756–1763) that pitted Britain against France for control of North America. With help from the American colonists, the British won the war and eliminated France as a power on the North American continent. Also known in America as the French and Indian War.

**Shakers** A religious group, formally known as the United Society of believers, that advocated strict celibacy, gender equality, and communal ownership.

**sharecropping** After the Civil War, the southern states adopted a sharecropping system as a compromise between former slaves, who wanted land of their own, and former slave owners who needed labor. The landowners provided land, tools, and seed to a farming family, who in turn provided labor. The resulting crop was divided between them, with the farmers receiving a "share" of one-third to one-half of the crop.

**Shays's Rebellion** Armed insurrection of farmers in western Massachusetts led by Daniel Shays, a veteran of the Continental Army. Intended to prevent state courts from foreclosing on debtors unable to pay their taxes, the rebellion was put down by the state militia. Nationalists used the event to justify the calling of a constitutional convention to strengthen the national government.

**Sherman Antitrust Act** Passed by Congress in 1890, this act was the first major U.S. attempt to deal legislatively with the problem of the increasing size of business. It declared illegal "every contract, combination in the form of trust or otherwise, or conspiracy, in restraint of trade or commerce." Penalties for violations were strict, ranging from fines to imprisonment and even the dissolution of guilty trusts. The law was weakened when the Supreme Court, in *United States* v. *E. C. Knight and Co.* (1895), drew a sharp distinction between manufacturing and commerce and ruled that manufacturing was excluded from its coverage. Nonetheless, the law shaped all future antitrust legislation.

**Sherman Silver Purchase Act** An act that attempted to resolve the controversy over silver coinage. Under it, the U.S. Treasury would purchase 4.5 million ounces of silver each month and issue legal tender (in the form of Treasury notes) for it. The act pleased opponents of silver because it did not call for free coinage; it pleased proponents of silver because it bought up most of the nation's silver production.

**social Darwinism** Adapted by English social philosopher Herbert Spencer from Charles Darwin's theory of evolution, this theory held that the "laws" of evolution applied to human life, that change or reform therefore took centuries, and that the "fittest" would succeed in business and social relationships. It promoted the ideas of competition and individualism, saw as futile any intervention of government into human affairs, and was used by influential members of the economic and social elite to oppose reform.

**Social Gospel** Preached by a number of urban Protestant ministers, the Social Gospel focused as much on improving the conditions of life on earth as on saving souls for the hereafter. Its adherents worked for child-labor laws and measures to alleviate poverty.

**Social Security Act** The 1935 Social Security Act established a system of old age, unemployment, and survivors' insurance funded by wage and payroll taxes. It did not include health insurance and did not originally cover many of the most needy groups and individuals.

**social-justice movement** During the 1890s and after, this important movement attracted followers who sought to free people from the often devastating impact of urban life. It focused on the need for tenement house laws, more stringent child labor regulations, and better working conditions for women. Social-justice reformers also brought pressure on municipal agencies for better community services and facilities.

**Southern Christian Leadership Conference (SCLC)** An organization founded by Martin Luther King, Jr., to direct the crusade against segregation. Its weapon was passive resistance that stressed nonviolence and love, and its tactic direct, though peaceful, confrontation.

**specie circular** In 1836, President Andrew Jackson issued this executive order that required purchasers of public land to pay in "specie," gold or silver coin, rather than paper money.

**spectral evidence** In the Salem witch trials, the court allowed reports of dreams and visions in which the accused appeared as the devil's agent to be introduced as testimony. The accused had no defense against this kind of "evidence." When the judges later disallowed this testimony, the executions for witchcraft ended.

**Sputnik** In October 1957, the Soviet Union surprised the world by launching *Sputnik*, the first artificial satellite to orbit the earth. The resulting outcry in the United States, especially fears that the Soviets were ahead in both space exploration and military missiles, forced the Eisenhower administration to increase defense spending and accelerate America's space program.

**Stamp Act Congress** Meeting of colonial delegates in New York City in October 1765 to protest the Stamp Act, a law passed by Parliament to raise revenue in America. The delegates drafted petitions denouncing the Stamp Act and other taxes imposed on Americans without colonial consent.

**Strategic Arms Limitations Talks (SALT)** In 1972, the United States and the Soviet Union culminated four years of Strategic Arms Limitation Talks (SALT) by signing a treaty limiting the deployment of antiballistic missiles (ABM) and an agreement to freeze the number of offensive missiles for five years.

**Strategic Defense Initiative (SDI)** Popularly known as "Star Wars," President Ronald Reagan's Strategic Defense Initiative (SDI) proposed the construction of an elaborate computer-controlled, anti-missile defense system capable of destroying enemy missiles in outer space. Critics claimed that SDI could never be perfected.

**Student Nonviolent Coordinating Committee (SNCC)** A radical group advocating black power. The SNCC's leaders, scornful of integration and interracial cooperation, broke with Martin Luther King, Jr., to advocate greater militancy and acts of violence.

**Students for a Democratic Society (SDS)** Founded in 1962, the SDS was a popular college student organization that protested shortcomings in American life, notably racial injustice and the Vietnam War. It led thousands of campus protests before it split apart at the end of the 1960s.

**Suez crisis** Egyptian leader Gamal Abdel Nasser nationalized the Suez Canal in 1956 when the United States withdrew promised aid to build the Aswan Dam on the Nile River. Britain and France, dependent on Middle East oil that was transported through the Suez Canal, launched an armed attack to regain control. President Eisenhower protested the use of force and persuaded Britain and France to withdraw their troops.

**Sunbelt** This region consists of a broad band of states running across the South from Florida to Texas, extending west and north to include California and the Pacific Northwest. Beginning in the 1970s, this area has experienced rapid economic growth and major gains in population.

**supply-side economics** Advocates of supply-side economics claimed that tax cuts would stimulate the economy by giving individuals a greater incentive to earn more money, which would lead to greater investment and eventually larger tax revenues at a lower rate. Critics replied that supply-side economics would only burden the economy with larger government deficits.

**Taft-Hartley Act** This 1947 anti-union legislation outlawed the closed shop and secondary boycotts. It also authorized the president to seek injunctions to prevent strikes that posed a threat to national security.

**tariff of abominations** An 1828 protective tariff, or tax on imports, motivated by special interest groups. It resulted in a substantial increase in duties that angered many southern free traders.

**Teapot Dome scandal** A 1924 scandal in which Secretary of the Interior Albert Fall was convicted of accepting bribes in exchange for leasing government-owned oil lands in Wyoming (Teapot Dome) and California (Elks Hill) to private oil businessmen.

**Teller Amendment** In this amendment, sponsored by Senator Henry M. Teller of Colorado, the United States pledged that it did not intend to annex Cuba and that it would recognize Cuban independence from Spain after the Spanish-American War.

**temperance movement** Temperance—moderation or abstention in the use of alcoholic beverages—attracted many advocates in the early nineteenth century. Their crusade against alcohol, which grew out of the Second Great Awakening, became a powerful social and political force.

**Ten Percent Plan** Reconstruction plan proposed by President Abraham Lincoln as a quick way to readmit the former Confederate States. It called for full pardon of all Southerners except Confederate leaders, and readmission to the Union for any state after 10 percent of its voters in the 1860 election signed a loyalty oath and the state abolished slavery.

**Tennessee Valley Authority (TVA)** A **New Deal** effort at regional planning created by Congress in 1933, this agency built dams and power plants on the Tennessee River. Its programs for flood control, soil conservation, and reforestation helped raise the standard of living for millions in the Tennessee River valley.

**Tet offensive** In February 1968, the Viet Cong launched a major offensive in the cities of South Vietnam. Although caught by surprise, American and South Vietnam forces successfully quashed this attack, yet the Tet offensive was a blow to American public opinion and led President Johnson to end the escalation of the war and seek a negotiated peace.

**Thirteenth Amendment** Ratified in 1865, this amendment to the U.S. Constitution prohibited slavery and involuntary servitude.

**Trail of Tears** In the winter of 1838–1839, the Cherokee were forced to evacuate their lands in Georgia and travel under military guard to present-day Oklahoma. Due to exposure and disease, roughly one-quarter of the 16,000 forced migrants died en route.

**transcendentalism** An American version of the romantic and idealist thought that emerged in Europe in the early nineteenth century, this literary and philosophical movement held that individuals could rise above material reality and ordinary understanding.

**Treaty of Guadalupe Hidalgo** Signed in 1848, this treaty ended the Mexican-American War. Mexico relinquished its claims to Texas and ceded an additional 500,000 square miles to the United States for $15 million.

**Treaty of Paris** Signed by the United States and Spain in December 1898, this treaty ended the Spanish-American War. Under its terms, Spain recognized Cuba's independence and assumed the Cuban debt; it also ceded Puerto Rico and Guam to the United States. At the insistence of the U.S. representatives, Spain also ceded the Philippines. The Senate ratified the treaty on February 6, 1899.

**Treaty of Tordesillas** Treaty negotiated by the pope in 1494 to resolve competing land claims of Spain and Portugal in the New World. It divided the world along a north-south line in the middle of the Atlantic Ocean, granting to Spain all lands west of the line and to Portugal lands east of the line.

**Truman Doctrine** In 1947, President Truman asked Congress for money to aid the Greek and Turkish governments that were then threatened by communist rebels. Arguing for the appropriations, Truman asserted his doctrine that the United States was committed to support free people everywhere who were resisting subjugation by communist attack or rebellion.

**trunk lines** Four major railroad networks that emerged after the Civil War to connect the eastern seaports to the Great Lakes and western rivers. They reflected the growing integration of transportation across the country that helped spur large-scale industrialization.

**trust** A business-management device designed to centralize and make more efficient the management of diverse and far-flung business operations. It allowed stockholders to exchange their stock certificates for trust certificates, on which dividends were paid. John D. Rockefeller organized the first major trust, the Standard Oil Trust, in 1882.

**Turner's thesis** Put forth by historian Frederick Jackson Turner in his 1893 paper, "The Significance of the Frontier in American History," this thesis asserted that the existence of a frontier and its settlement had shaped American character; given rise to individualism, independence, and self-confidence; and fostered the American spirit of invention and adaptation. Later historians, especially a group of "new Western historians," modified the thesis by pointing out the environmental and other consequences of frontier settlement, the role of the federal government in peopling the arid West, and the clash of races and cultures that took place on the frontier.

**Underground Railroad** A network of safe houses organized by abolitionists (usually free blacks) to aid slaves in their attempts to escape slavery in the North or Canada.

**Underwood Tariff Act** An early accomplishment of the Wilson administration, this law reduced the tariff rates of the Payne-Aldrich law of 1909 by about 15 percent. It also levied a graduated income tax to make up for the lost revenue.

**undocumented aliens** Once derisively called "wetbacks," undocumented aliens are illegal immigrants, mainly from Mexico and Central America.

**unilateralism** A national policy of acting alone without consulting others.

**utopianism** Between the 1830s and 1850s, hopes for societal perfection—utopia—were widespread among evangelical Christians as well as secular humanists. These hopes found expression in various utopian communities and spiritual movements.

**vertical integration** A form of business organization in which a single firm owns and controls the entire process of production, from the procurement of raw materials to the manufacture and sale of the fin-ished product. In the 1880s and 1890s, many important companies, including Carnegie (later U.S.) Steel and Standard Oil, were vertically integrated.

**Vesey conspiracy** A plot to burn Charleston, South Carolina, and thereby initiate a general slave revolt, led by a free African American, Denmark Vesey, in 1822. The conspirators were betrayed before the plan was carried out, and Vesey and thirty-four others were hanged.

**Virginia Plan** Offered by James Madison and the Virginia delegation at the Constitutional Convention, this proposal called for a new government with a strong executive office and two houses of Congress, each with representation proportional to a state's population. Madison's plan also recommended giving the national government veto power over bills passed by the state legislatures. Smaller states countered with the **New Jersey Plan** that gave each state equal representation in Congress.

**virtual representation** Notion that although colonists had not elected members to Parliament, they were nonetheless represented by it. Espoused by British leaders, this claim countered colonists' argument that they had no voice in Parliament and therefore were being taxed without proper representation.

**Voting Rights Act of 1965** The 1965 Voting Rights Act effectively banned literacy tests for voting rights and provided for federal registrars to assure the franchise to minority voters. Within a few years, a majority of African Americans had become registered voters in the southern states.

**Wade-Davis Bill** In 1864, Congress passed the Wade-Davis bill to counter Lincoln's **Ten Percent Plan** for Reconstruction. The bill required that a majority of a former Confederate state's white male population take a loyalty oath and guarantee equality for African Americans. President Lincoln pocket-vetoed the bill.

**Wagner Act** The 1935 Wagner Act, formally known as the National Labor Relations Act, created the National Labor Relations Board to supervise union elections and designate winning unions as official bargaining agents. The board could also issue cease-and-desist orders to employers who dealt unfairly with their workers.

**War Hawks** Congressional leaders who, in 1811 and 1812, called for war against Britain to defend the national honor and force Britain to respect America's maritime rights.

**War Industries Board (WIB)** An example of the many boards and commissions created during World War I, this government agency oversaw the production of all American factories. It determined priorities, allocated raw materials, and fixed prices; it told manufacturers what they could and could not produce.

**War of 1812** War between Britain and the United States. U.S. justifications for war included British violations of American maritime rights, impressment of seamen, provocation of the Indians, and defense of national honor.

**war on poverty** Lyndon Johnson declared war on poverty in his 1964 State of the Union address. A new Office of Economic Opportunity (OEO) oversaw a variety of programs to help the poor, including the Job Corps and Head Start.

**war on terrorism** Initiated by President George W. Bush after the attacks of September 11, 2001, the broadly defined war on terrorism aimed to weed out terrorist operatives and their supporters throughout the world.

**Watergate scandal** A break-in at the Democratic National Committee offices in the Watergate complex in Washington was carried out under the direction of White House employees. Disclosure of the White House involvement in the break-in and subsequent cover-up forced President Richard Nixon to resign in 1974 to avoid impeachment.

**weapons of mass destruction (WMD)** Biological, chemical, and nuclear weapons capable of widespread destruction.

**Webster-Ashburton Treaty** This 1842 agreement with Britain resolved the boundary dispute between Maine and New Brunswick, Canada, setting the northeastern U.S. border.

**Whigs** In mid-eighteenth century Britain, the Whigs were a political faction that dominated Parliament. Generally they were opposed to royal influence in government and wanted to increase the control and influence of Parliament. In America, a Whig party—named for the British Whigs who opposed the king in the late seventeenth century—coalesced in the 1830s around opposition to Andrew Jackson. In general, the American Whigs supported federal power and internal improvements but not territorial expansion. The Whig party collapsed in the 1850s.

**Whiskey Rebellion** Protests in 1794 by western Pennsylvania farmers resisting payment of a federal tax on whiskey. The uprising was forcibly suppressed when President George Washington called an army of 15,000 troops to the area, where they encountered almost no resistance.

**Wilmot Proviso** In 1846, shortly after outbreak of the **Mexican-American War,** Congressman David Wilmot of Pennsylvania introduced this controversial amendment stating that any lands won from Mexico would be closed to slavery.

**Women's Christian Temperance Union (WCTU)** Founded by Frances E. Willard, this organization campaigned to end drunkenness and the social ills that accompanied it. The largest women's organization in the country, by 1898 it had 10,000 branches and 500,000 members. The WCTU illustrated the large role women played in politics and reform long before they won the right to vote.

**Women's Trade Union League (WTUL)** Founded in 1903, this group worked to organize women into trade unions. It also lobbied for laws to safeguard female workers and backed several successful strikes, especially in the garment industry. It accepted all women who worked, regardless of skill, and while it never attracted many members, its leaders were influential enough to give the union considerable power.

**Works Progress Administration (WPA)** Congress created this **New Deal** agency in 1935 to provide work relief for the unemployed. Federal works projects included building roads, bridges, and schools; the WPA also funded projects for artists, writers, and young people. It eventually spent $11 billion on projects and provided employment for 8.5 million people.

**World Trade Organization (WTO)** Global international organization that deals with rules of trade between nations. It became a target for demonstrations in the late 1990s by protesters claiming that global corporations exploited workers and damaged the environment.

**Wounded Knee Massacre** In December 1890, troopers of the Seventh Cavalry, under orders to stop the **Ghost Dance** religion among the Sioux, took Chief Big Foot and his followers to a camp on Wounded Knee Creek in South Dakota. It is uncertain who fired the first shot, but violence ensued and approximately two hundred Native American men, women, and children were killed.

**XYZ Affair** A diplomatic incident in which American peace commissioners sent to France by President John Adams in 1797 were insulted with bribe demands from their French counterparts, dubbed X, Y, and Z, in American newspapers. The incident heightened war fever against France.

**Yalta Conference** Yalta, a city in the Russian Crimea, hosted this wartime conference of the Allies in February 1945 in which the Allies agreed to final plans for the defeat of Germany and the terms of its occupation. The Soviets agreed to allow free elections in Poland, but the elections were never held.

**yellow journalism** In order to sell newspapers to the public before and during the Spanish-American War, publishers William Randolph Hearst and Joseph Pulitzer engaged in blatant sensationalization of the news, which became known as "yellow journalism." Although it did not cause the war with Spain, it helped turn U.S. public opinion against Spain's actions in Cuba.

**yeoman** Southern small landholders who owned no slaves, and who lived primarily in the foothills of the Appalachian and Ozark mountains. These farmers were self-reliant and grew mixed crops, although they usually did not produce a substantial amount to be sold on the market.

**Young America** In the 1840s and early 1850s, many public figures—especially younger members of the Democratic party—used this term to describe a movement that advocated territorial expansion and industrial growth in the name of patriotism.

# Credits

## CHAPTER 1

**2** Peter Newark's American Pictures **6** © David Muench Photography **7T** Courtesy of the National Museum of the American Indian, Smithsonian Institution [S2578 (5/2981) Photo by Carmelo Guadagno **7B** Art Resource, New York **12** The Granger Collection, New York **13T** AKG Images **13B** Courtesy of the Bancroft Library, University of California, Berkeley **15** Clement N'Taye/AP/Wide World Photos **16** © Parcs Canada **17** The Library of Congress **20** From Theodor de Bry, *America*, 1595 New York Public Library, Astor, Lenox and Tilden Foundations **21** Collection, the late Anthony Portago **22** North Wind Pictures **24** By permission of the Folger Shakespeare Library **27** © The British Museum

## CHAPTER 2

**30** The British Library **35T** Courtesy of the Association for the Preservation of Virginia Antiquities **35B** National Portrait Gallery, Smithsonian Institution/Art Resource, NY **36** Ashmolean Museum, Oxford **37** The Granger Collection, New York **38** Historic St. Mary's City **40** Photo courtesy of Maryland Department, Enoch Pratt Free Library **42** Courtesy, American Antiquarian Society **43** © Paul Skillings **44** Lee Snider Photo Images **46** Courtesy of the Massachusetts Historical Society **47** Stock Montage, Inc. **50** John E. Reinhardt, C & J Enterprises **52** The Library Company of Philadelphia **54** John Carter Brown Library

## CHAPTER 3

**60** *The Mason Children: David, Joanna, and Abigail*, 1670. Oil on canvas. Fine Arts Museums of San Francisco, Gift of Mr. and Mrs. John D. Rockefeller 3rd to The Fine Arts Museums of San Francisco, 1979.7.3 **63** Newport Historical Society **64** New York Public Library, Astor, Lenox and Tilden Foundations **66L** Worcester Art Museum, Worcester, Massachusetts, Sarah C. Garver Fund **66R** Worcester Art Museum, Worcester, Massachusetts, Gift of Mr. and Mrs. Albert W. Rice **67L** David Hiser/Photographers Aspen **67R** Phipps Street Burial Ground **70** The Maryland Historical Society **71** Abby Aldrich Rockeller Folk Art Museum, Colonial Williamsburg Foundation, Williamsburg, VA **73** National Maritime Museum, Greenwich, England **75** The Library of Congress **76** Courtesy, American Antiquarian Society **77** Abby Aldrich Rockefeller Folk Art Center, Williamsburg, VA **80** © Shelburne Museum, Shelburne, Vermont **81R & L** The National Portrait Gallery, London **82** New York Public Library, Astor, Lenox and Tilden Foundations **87–88** Jim McAllister

## CHAPTER 4

**92** New York Public Library/Art Resource, NY **94** Courtesy of Virginia Historical Society, Richmond **96** *Pennsylvania German Painted Wooden Box* by Elmer G. Anderson. Index of American Design, © 2005 Board of Trustees, National Gallery of Art, Washington, DC **97** The Historical Society of Pennsylvania **99T** The Historical Society of Pennsylvania/Atwater Kent Museum **99B** The Newberry Library **100** From the collections of the Henry Ford Museum & Greenfield Village **101** © Stephen M. Bailey **102** © Richard Cummins/Corbis **104** Courtesy of the Massachusetts Historical Society **105** Courtesy of Westover **106L**

The Historical Society of Pennsylvania/Atwater Kent Museum **106R** The Library Company of Philadelphia **108** From the collections of the Henry Ford Museum & Greenfield Village **110** The National Portrait Gallery, London **114** North Wind Pictures **116** Courtesy of the Trustees of the British Library **117** Anne S. K. Brown Military Collection, Brown University Library **119** Smithsonian Institution.

## CHAPTER 5

**124** *The Battle of Bunker Hill*, c. 1776–77; Winthrop Chandler. Oil on Panel; 34-7/8 x 53-5/8 inches. Gift of Mr. and Mrs. Gardner Richardson, 1982.281. Courtesy, Museum of Fine Arts, Boston. Reproduced with Permission. © 2005 Museum of Fine Arts, Boston. All Rights Reserved **126** Anne S. K. Brown Military Collection, Brown University Library **127** Colonial Williamsburg Foundation **128** Courtesy of the John Carter Brown Library at Brown University **133** *Stamp Act Repeal'd*, English, 1766. Cream colored earthenware, lead-glazed and hand painted. Photograph by Mark Sexton. Peabody Essex Museum **136** Collection of The New-York Historical Society. Negative number 49494 **137** New York Public Library, Astor, Lenox and Tilden Foundations **138** The Library of Congress **139** *Samuel Adams* by John Singleton Copley, c. 1772, oil on canvas, 49-1/2 x 39-1/2 inches. Courtesy, Museum of Fine Arts, Boston, Deposited by the City of Boston, 30.76c. Reproduced with Permission. © 2005 Museum of Fine Arts, Boston. All Rights Reserved **140L** The Library of Congress **140R** Courtesy, American Antiquarian Society **143** Chicago Historical Society, ICHi-20449 **144L** The Library of Congress **144R** The National Portrait Gallery, London **145** The Historical Society of Pennsylvania **148** The Historical Society of Pennsylvania/Atwater Kent Museum **150** Anne S. K. Brown Military Collection, Brown University Library **151** Charles Allen Munn Collection, Fordham University Library, Bronx, NY

## CHAPTER 6

**156** Collection of The New-York Historical Society. Negative number 6211, accession number 1907.32 **159** The Library Company of Philadelphia **160** *Preparations for the Enjoyment of a Fine Sunday Among the Blacks, Norfolk, VA.* by Benjamin Henry Latrobe. The Maryland Historical Society, Baltimore, Maryland **161** New York Public Library, Astor, Lenox and Tilden Foundations **163** *Abigail Adams*, by Benjamin Blyth, c. 1766. Courtesy of the Massachusetts Historical Society, MHS #73 **164** Museum of Art, Rhode Island School of Design. Museum Appropriation, (17.361) **166** The Historical Society of Pennsylvania/Atwater Kent Museum **172–173** Smithsonian Institution **175** The National Portrait Gallery, Smithsonian Institution/Art Resource, NY **179** The Historical Society of Pennsylvania **179** *James Madison* by Charles Willson Peale. From the Collection of Gilcrease Museum, Tulsa, Oklahoma (126.1006) **180** *Liberty Displaying the Arts and Sciences*, by Samuel Jennings. The Library Company of Philadelphia **184** The Colonial Williamsburg Foundation **184** *George Mason*, by Dominic W. Boudet, 1811, after a lost portrait by John Hesselius, ca. 1756. Oil on canvas. Virginia Museum of Fine Arts, Richmond. Gift of David K. E. Bruce. Photo: Ron Jennings. © Virginia Museum of Fine Arts **187** Courtesy of the Massachusetts Historical Society **189** *Elizabeth 'Mumbet' Freeman*, watercolor on ivory, by Susan Anne Livingston Ridley Sedgwick, 1842. MHS image #0028. Courtesy of the Massachusetts Historical Society

## CHAPTER 7

**190** Hulton|Archive/Getty Images **193** The National Portrait Gallery, Smithsonian Institution/Art Resource, NY **194** Detail from *A View of Mount Vernon*, Gift of Edgar William and Bernice Chrysler Garbisch, Photograph © 2001 Board of Trustees, National Gallery of Art, Washington **195R & L** Independence National Historical Park Collection **197** From the collections of the Henry Ford Museum & Greenfield Village **201** The Academy of Natural Sciences of Philadelphia **202** Bibliothéque Nationale/ Art Resource, NY **203** Collection of The New-York Historical Society. Negative number 19 **204** The Ohio Historical Society **206** Courtesy, American Antiquarian Society **208** Adams National Historical Park/US Department of the Interior, National Park Service **209** Courtesy Lilly Library, Indiana University, Bloomington, Ind. **211** The Library of Congress **213** National Museum of American History, Smithsonian Institution

## CHAPTER 8

**218** The Library of Congress **221** History Center of Western Pennsylvania **222** The Library of Congress **223** H. Richard Dietrich, Jr., The Dietrich American Foundation **224** The Library of Congress **227** The Chicago Historical Society, P & S-1932.0018 **229** Peabody Museum of Archaeology and Ethnology, Harvard University **230** The Granger Collection, New York **231** © Corbis **233** New York Public Library, Astor, Lenox and Tilden Foundations **234** Photo by Vincent Colabella Photography/Courtesy JP Morgan Chase Archives; **235** Abby Aldrich Rockefeller Folk Art Museum, Williamsburg, VA **237** Collection of The New-York Historical Society. Negative number 7278 **239** The White House Collection, © White House Historical Association **240** Collection of Davenport West, Jr. **243** Hulton|Archive/Getty Images

## CHAPTER 9

**246** Courtesy, Winterthur Museum **248** The Library of Congress **251** The Walters Art Museum, Baltimore **251L** Courtesy, National Museum of the American Indian, Smithsonian Institution, 15/4658. Photo by David Heald **251R** Courtesy, Colorado Historical Society, F17954A **252** North Wind Pictures **253–254** The Library of Congress **255** Joslyn Art Museum, Omaha, Nebraska. Gift of Enron Art Foundation **257** New York Public Library, Astor, Lenox and Tilden Foundations **258** The Granger Collection, New York **259** © John Eastcott/YVA Momatiuk/Photo Researchers, Inc. **261** American Textile History Museum, Lowell, Massachusetts **261L** Abby Aldrich Rockefeller Folk Art Museum, Colonial Williamsburg Foundation, Williamsburg, VA **266** *John Marshall* by Chester Harding, ca.1829. Washington & Lee University **269** Courtesy of the Harvard University Portrait Collection, Bequest of Ward Nicholas Boylston to Harvard College 1828. © President and Fellows of Harvard College

## CHAPTER 10

**272–274** The Granger Collection, New York **275** The Toledo Museum of Art; Purchased with funds from the Florence Scott Libbey Bequest in Memory of her Father, Maurice A. Scott **277** *Rustic Dance After a Sleigh Ride* by William Sidney Mount, 1830, oil on canvas, 22-1/8 x 27-1/8 inches. Museum of Fine Arts, Boston, Bequest of Martha C. Karolik for the M. and M. Karolik Collection of American Paintings, 1815–1865, 48.458. Reproduced with Permission. © 2005 Museum of Fine Arts, Boston. All Rights Reserved **278** © New York Public Library/Art Resource, NY **280** *The Union*, 1836. Courtesy, New York Public Library **281** *Charles Bird King*, 1822, Henry Clay. In the Collection of The Corcoran Gallery of Art **282** *General Andrew Jackson*, 1845, oil on canvas, 97 1/4 x 61 1/2 x inches. In the collection of The Corcoran Gallery of Art, Gift of William Wilson Corcoran **284** Fair Street Pictures **285** Courtesy of The Newberry Library, Chicago **285** Woolaroc Museum, Bartlesville, Oklahoma **287** The Library of Congress **290** Collection of The New-York Historical Society. Negative number 42459 **292** The Library of Congress **293R & L** Collection of David J. and Janice L. Frent

**294** Courtesy Mercantile Library Association, St. Louis **295** The Saint Louis Art Museum, Gift of Bank of America

## CHAPTER 11

**300** *A Ride for Liberty - The Fugitive Slaves* by Eastman Johnson, ca. 1862. Oil on paper board, 22 x 26 1/4 in. Brooklyn Museum of Art, Gift of Gwendolyn O.L. Conkling. 40.59a **302** Hulton|Archive/ Getty Images **304** The New-York Historical Society **305** The Library of Congress **306** North Carolina Museum of Art, Raleigh, Purchased with funds from the State of North Carolina **307T & B** The Library of Congress **308** The Historic New Orleans Collection **311** The Library of Congress **312** Collection of the Shadows-on-the-Teche. New Iberia, Louisiana. A National Trust Historic Site **314** Courtesy of the North Carolina Office of Archives and History, Raleigh, North Carolina **315** Fair Street Pictures **316B** From the collection of the Louisiana State Museum **316T** The Museum of the Confederacy, Richmond, Virginia. Photography by Katherine Wetzel **318** *Block House, New Braunfels* by Carl G. von Iwonski. Yanaguana Society Collection, Daughters of the Republic of Texas, CT96.8 **320** Collection of The New-York Historical Society. Negative number 3087 **323** Abby Aldrich Rockefeller Folk Art Center, Williamsburg, VA **324** The Library of Congress

## CHAPTER 12

**328** Laurie Platt Winfrey **331** Chicago Historical Society, ICHi-22019 **332** Harriet Beecher Stowe Center, Hartford, CT **333** Fruitlands Museums, Harvard, Massachusetts **336** Collection of The New-York Historical Society. Negative number 1941.910 **337** © Susan Oristaglio/Esto Photographics, Inc **338** Photograph Courtesy Peabody Essex Museum. Photo by Mark Sexton **339** Courtesy of The Newberry Library, Chicago **340** Archives of the American Corrections Association **341** © Bettmann/Corbis **342** Massachusetts Historical Society, MHS image #0031 **344L** Fenimore Art Museum, Cooperstown, New York **344R** National Portrait Gallery, Smithsonian Institution/Art Resource, NY **345** Sophia Smith Collection, Smith College, Northampton, Mass. **346** New York Public Library, Astor, Lenox and Tilden Foundations **350L & R** Courtesy, Concord Free Public Library **351** Culver Pictures **355** Acts of the Seventy-Sixth Legislature of the State of New Jersey, Somerville, 1852 page 407. Courtesy, Special Collections/University Archives, Rutgers University Libraries **357** Photo by permission: The Schlesinger Library, Radcliffe Institute, Harvard University

## CHAPTER 13

**358** Chicago Historical Society, ICHi-07197 **360L** Rare Book Divison/New York Public Library, Astor, Lenox and Tilden Foundations **360** right: By permission of The Houghton Library/Harvard University, Cambridge, Mass., Gift of the Houghton Library by Mrs. Henry K. Metcalf **362** Seaver Center for Western History Research, Natural History Museum of Los Angeles County **366** *Handcart Pioneers* by CCA Christensen. © by Intellectual Reserve, Inc. Courtesy of Museum of Church History and Art. Used by Permission **367** *Battle of San Jacinto* by H. A. McArdle. Photo by Eric Beggs. Texas State Library & Archives Commission **370** © Bettmann/Corbis **371** The New-York Historical Society, 1941.129 **372** *War News from Mexico* by Richard Caton Woodville, 1848. Courtesy of the National Gallery, Washington, DC **376** *Blessing of the Enrequita Mine* by Alexander Edouart, 1860. Bancroft Library, University of California, Berkely **377** Courtesy of Bexar County and the Witte Museum, San Antonio, Texas **378T** Agriculture Department, Smithsonian Institution **378B** Chicago Historical Society, ICHi-00013 **382** The Library of Congress.

## CHAPTER 14

**386** The Granger Collection, New York **388** New York Public Library, Astor, Lenox and Tilden Foundations **390** The Library of Congress **397L** New York Public Library, Astor, Lenox and Tilden Foundations **397R** Maryland Historical Society, Baltimore, Maryland **398** Anne S. K.

# Index

*Key terms and the text page on which the term is defined are highlighted in boldface type. Terms and definitions also appear in the Glossary, pp. G-1–G-13.*

## A

Abenaki Indians, 8
Abolition and abolitionism, 330; anti-Constitutionalism in, 388; black, 343–345; early, 344–345; in 1830s and 1840s, 280; Fugitive Slave Law and, 392; literary, 400–401; Nat Turner rebellion and, 301; proslavery argument and, 319; revivalism and, 342–343; after Revolution, 161; in South, 320; women's rights and, 345. *See also* Antislavery movement; Slaves and slavery
Abortion and abortion rights: in 19th century, 338
Act of Supremacy (England), 23
*Acts and Monuments* (Foxe). *See Book of Martyrs* (Foxe)
Adams, Abigail, 163, 163 (illus.), 186
Adams, Charles Francis, 436
Adams, John, 129, 130, 144, 145 (illus.), 208 (illus.), 234, 244, 247; Alien and Sedition Acts and, 210–212; on Boston Tea party, 140; Constitutional Convention and, 175; election of 1800 and, 213–214; at First Continental Congress, 142; France and, 212; Hamilton and, 214; Jeffersonians and, 220; Massachusetts constitution and, 165–166; midnight judicial appointees of, 225, 229–232; presidency of, 208–213; at Second Continental Congress, 143; on title of chief executive, 191; Treaty of Paris and, 153–154; as vice president, 192
Adams, John Quincy, 226, 269 (illus.); 1824 election and, 280–281; 1828 election and, 283, 283 (illus.); presidency of, 268–269, 281; as secretary of state, 248, 249, 267, 268
Adams, Samuel, 139, 139 (illus.), 141, 172; on republicanism, 158
**Adams-Onís Treaty, 249,** 267, 361
Adaptation, of Indians after removal, 253
"Address on Non-Resistance to Offensive Aggression, An" (Whipper), 344 (illus.)
Adet, Pierre, 209
Africa: black heritage from, 73–76; labor from, 11; Liberia colony in, 341; New World and, 4; slaves from, 71; trade routes in, 14 (map); trade with, 107. *See also* Slaves and slavery; West Africa
African Americans: as abolitionists, 343–345; in American painting, 70 (illus.); American Revolution and, 147; antidraft riots and, 440, 440 (illus.); Black Codes and, 455, 456, 462; churches of, 464 (illus.), 465; Civil War and, 438–438, 439 (illus.), 445; in Congress, 463, 463 (illus.), 464; contract labor system and, 461; convict-lease system and, 474–475; culture of, 77 (illus.), 302; *Dred Scott* case and, 401–402; Emancipation Proclamation and, 437–438; equality of, 162; Fifteenth

Amendment and, 466–467; Fourteenth Amendment and, 456; Great Awakening and, 111; heritage of, 73–76; identities of, 73–76; institutions of, 464–465; Jim Crow and, 473–475; Ku Klux Klan and, 467–469; lynchings of, 474, 474 (illus.); marriage and, 464–465; as mountain men, 250; newspapers for, 344; in Old South, 303; in political office, 463, 464, 473–474; popular democracy, hotel culture, and, 274; population of, 193, 219, 220; religion of, 307–309; Republican party and, 462; after Revolution, 160–162; share-cropping and, 461–462; Smalls, Robert, 451–452, 452 (illus.); Turner, Henry McNeal, and, 475–478, 478 (illus.); Underground Railroad and, 344; views of Reconstruction and, 476–477; voting and, 473–474; white families and, 63 (illus.); women workers and, 336. *See also* Africa; Civil rights; Free blacks; Freedmen; Segregation; Slaves and slavery; Voting and voting rights
**African Methodist Episcopal (AME) Church,** 111, 162, 162 (illus.), **308,** 465, 475
Africans: Jefferson on, 201; in Virginia, 71–72
Age, of colonial population, 126
Age of Reason, 104
"Age of Religious Wars," 25
Agricultural colleges, 446
Agricultural fair, 222–223
**Agricultural Revolution, 5**
Agriculture: Anasazi, 6; Aztec ritual killings and, 7; in Civil War, 430; commercial, 259–260; contract labor system in, 461; Jefferson and, 195, 198–199; mechanization of, 379–380; of Native Americans, 250; river transportation and, 256; tariffs and, 263; trade and, 131 (illus.); workforce in, 222, 379. *See also* Planters and plantations; Sharecropping
Air-boiling process, 379 (illus.)
Aix-la-Chapelle, Treaty of, 116
Alabama, 248; Indian removal and, 284, 285; Indians in, 250; secession of, 421
*Alabama* (ship), 436
**Alamo,** battle of, **364**
Albany, New York, 160; as Fort Orange, 49
Albany Congress, 117
**Albany Plan, 117,** 120
Albany Regency, 282
Albemarle region, 55
Alcohol and alcoholism: consumption by 1820s, 334; Native Americans and, 10. *See also* Temperance movement
Aldin, John, 87, 88
Alexander I (Russia), 269
Algiers, 228, 231
Algonquian Indians, 10–11, 28
Algonquian-speaking peoples, 8

**Alien and Sedition Acts** (1798), **210–212, 225,** 232
Alien Enemies Law (1798), 211
Alien Law (1798), 211
"All Creation Going to the White House" (Cruikshank), 272 (illus.)
Allen, Richard, 111, 162, 162 (illus.), 308
Alliances: with France, 149–150, 150 (illus.); with Indians, 98–99, 99 (illus.); Washington on, 208
"All Mexico" movement, 373
Alton, Illinois, antiabolitionist violence in, 343
Amendments: Bill of Rights as, 183–184, 184 (illus.). *See also* specific Amendments
American and Foreign Anti-Slavery Society, 343
American Anti-Slavery Society, 341, 345
American Bible Society, 333
American Board of Customs Commissioners, 134–135
**American Colonization Society,** 319, **341–342**
*American Crisis* (Paine), 148
*American Dictionary of the English Language, The* (Webster), 206
American Fur Company, 249
*American Minerva* (journal), 206
American Moral Reform Society, 344 (illus.)
American party, 395, 405
American Peace Society, 341
American Revolution, 145–152, 146 (illus.); army in, 147; British strategy in, 148–149; equality and, 125–136; French alliance in, 149–150, 150 (illus.); Loyalists in, 129, 147, 151, 152–153, 152 (illus.); popular resistance and, 136–137; social impact of, 159–164, 159 (illus.)
American Society (Philadelphia), 105
American Society for Psychical Research, 349
**American System** (Clay), **263,** 282, 286, 293–296, 367
American Temperance Society, 334
American Tract Society, 333
Americas: food, climate, and culture in, 5–6; marketing of, 28; naming of, 17, 18; routes of first Americans, 5 (map); Spanish conquests in, 18–20. *See also* New World
Ames, Fisher, 204, 206, 225
Amherst, Jeffrey, 119
Amity and Commerce, Treaty of, 150
**Anaconda policy, 427**
Anahuac, 363
Anasazi culture, 6
Anderson, Robert, 425
Andros, Edmund, 81
Anglican Church. *See* Church of England (Anglican Church)
Anglicization, of immigrants, 96
Anglo-American Convention (1818), 248
Anglo-Americans, in Texas, 362–363

# Primary Source Documents

# HOW TO ANALYZE PRIMARY SOURCE DOCUMENTS

Historians study sources to reconstruct the lifestyles and events of previous generations (what actually happened in the past), as well as to understand the past as the people who lived it did—to examine their ideas and thoughts about the world. By using sources, historians actually recreate history. They craft an understanding of the people, events, ideas, trends, and themes of the past based upon interpretation of those sources.

Primary sources are generally first-hand accounts or records. They may have been written or created during the time period under investigation, or perhaps were written by someone who lived then. Most crucially, they have not been interpreted by anyone else, though they may offer interpretations of the events they describe.

The primary source documents presented here give you the opportunity to put your investigative skills to the test by analyzing the sources yourself, rather than by reading others' interpretations.

## WHEN ANALYZING A PRIMARY SOURCE, YOU SHOULD ASK SEVEN KEY QUESTIONS.

1. **Who is the author?**

   Who wrote or created this? Is there a single or multiple authors? An author's identity sometimes helps you answer the later questions.

2. **What type of source is this?**

   All the sources here are documents, but what type? Is it a biography or a government document? This is a simple but crucial step because you must consider what you can expect to learn from the document.

3. **What is the message of this source?**

   What is the author describing? What is happening in the text? What is the story?

4. **Who is the intended audience?**

   Who is the author addressing? Was the source intended for private or public consumption? Identifying the audience will help you answer the next question.

5. **Why was this source created?**

   Does the author have an agenda, a larger purpose? Is the author trying to persuade the audience? Is the document or source simply a compilation of facts, or does it include opinion, inference, or interpretation?

6. **Is this source credible and accurate?**

   Historians must examine every source with a critical eye. What do you know about the author? Does the document make sense? Do the facts presented by the author or what you know about the time period support the thesis, statement, assertion, or story the author is conveying? Why should you trust, or distrust, this source?

7. **How is this source valuable to me?**

   How does the source relate to other sources from the time period or along the same issue or theme? Does it support or contradict them? Does it repeat information from other sources or add new information? How relevant is the source to your topic of inquiry? Does it extensively cover your topic, or only marginally or not at all? Remember, you should explore enough sources to obtain a variety of viewpoints.

Let's take a look at a portion of the document from chapter 16 to see how this process works. Reading the full document selection, of course, provides even more clues to understanding this source.

### DOCUMENT 16.1
### Carl Schurz, *Report on the Condition of the South* (1865)

*Carl Schurz was a German immigrant who rose to great political prominence in the United States. He was a leading member of the Republican Party from its founding and was a great supporter of Lincoln. During the Civil War he attained the rank of major general. After the war, Schurz continued to be active in politics, supporting many reform movements. In addition, he was writer and editor for several English- and German-language newspapers, and he wrote several books. In 1865 President Andrew Johnson sent Schurz to tour the South in order to report on its postwar status. An excerpt from Schurz's report appears below. The president was not pleased with the report.*

We ought to keep in view, above all, the nature of the problem which is to be solved. As to what is commonly termed "reconstruction," it is not only the political machinery of the States and their constitutional relations to the general government, but the whole organism of southern society that must be reconstructed, or rather constructed anew, so as to bring it in harmony with the rest of American society. The difficulties of this task are not to be considered overcome when the people of the south take the oath of allegiance and elect governors and legislatures and members of Congress, and militia captains. That this would be done had become certain as soon as the surrenders of the southern armies had made further resistance impossible, and nothing in the world was left, even to the most uncompromising rebel, but to submit or to emigrate. It was also natural that they should avail themselves of every chance offered them to resume control of their home affairs and to regain their influence in the Union. But this can hardly be called the first step towards the solution of the true problem, and it is a fair question to ask, whether the hasty gratification of their desire to resume such control would not create new embarrassments.

**1. Who is the author?**

From the head note, we know that Carl Schurz was a Republican politician, a Union officer in the Civil War, a German immigrant, and an author.

**2. What type of source is this?**

This is an official government report commissioned by President Johnson.

**3. What is the message of this source?**

In this first paragraph, Schurz is describing the potential difficulties of "reconstructing" the South after the Civil War. He is presenting what he perceives to be the goal of Reconstruction (to bring the South "in harmony with the rest of American society") as well as the potential pitfalls of quickly returning the southern states to the control of former Confederates ("creat[ing] new embarrassments").

**4. Who is the intended audience?**

Schurz's primary audience is President Johnson, who commissioned the tour and report. You should consider, however, that since it was commissioned by a government official, other members of the government may have had access to it as well. The head note does not tell us if it was published for the public at large. Some minimal additional research, however, would confirm that it was published as a U.S. Senate Executive Document for the 1st session of the 39th Congress.

**5. Why was this source created?**

In the very first sentence, Schurz presents Reconstruction as "the problem which is to be solved." From this statement we can infer that he felt his duty was not only to report on the "condition of the South," as described in the title, but to present his interpretation of the primary problems facing the nation as well as possible solutions.

**6. Is this source credible and accurate?**

Though this is a government document, we must remember that Schurz likely could not be considered an impartial observer. He was from the North, was a Republican (the head note identifies him as "a great supporter of Lincoln"), and had fought in the Civil War. The overall tone of this paragraph, however, is very matter-of-fact. This may be attributable to Schurz's experience as a writer and editor. But we also know, from answering question 5, that Schurz felt his job was to do more than simply report. He framed his report in the form of problems and solutions. You must decide if these factors affected Schurz's credibility and accuracy as an observer of the conditions of the South in 1865. Here is the opportunity to begin to craft your interpretation of Reconstruction.

**7. How is this source valuable to you?**

You must place the source within the context of your own research. Here are a few examples.

This source would be an invaluable central component if you were researching:
- first-hand accounts of the conditions in the South following the Civil War
- a biographical paper on Carl Schurz

It would be an important part of a paper on:
- the various stages of Reconstruction
- the disagreements between President Johnson and members of the Republican Party

It would be crucial background information if you were researching:
- Andrew Johnson's presidency
- the return of Democratic rule in the former Confederacy

You now have the basic tools to begin analyzing historical documents yourself. As you apply these skills to the documents contained here, you will likely find that your skill level will rapidly increase. You may even find yourself reading others' interpretations of primary source documents with a more critical eye.

## DOCUMENT 1.1
### Alvar Núñez Cabeza de Vaca, "Indians of the Rio Grande" (1528–1536)

*The story of Álvar Núñez Cabeza de Vaca is unique among the Spanish explorers and conquistadors who came to the New World. Cabeza de Vaca, along with half the crew of explorer Pánfilo de Navarez's ship, were stranded in present-day Florida and made their way across the Gulf of Mexico in search of help in 1528. When they arrived in Mexico, they were themselves enslaved by the native peoples. After six years of forced labor, Cabeza de Vaca and two others escaped and made their way through present-day Texas and into Mexico City. During his travels, Cabeza de Vaca kept an extensive journal of his experience. The following is an excerpt from that journal.*

They are so accustomed to running that, without resting or getting tired, they run from morning till night in pursuit of a deer, and kill a great many, because they follow until the game is worn out, sometimes catching it alive. Their huts are of matting placed over four arches. They carry them on their back and move every two or three days in quest of food; they plant nothing that would be of any use.

They are very merry people, and even when famished do not cease to dance and celebrate their feasts and ceremonials. Their best times are when "tunas" (prickly pears) are ripe, because then they have plenty to eat and spend the time in dancing and eating day and night. As long as these tunas last they squeeze and open them and set them to dry. When dried they are put in baskets like figs and kept to be eaten on the way. The peelings they grind and pulverize.

All over this country there are a great many deer, fowl and other animals which I have before enumerated. Here also they come up with cows; I have seen them thrice and have eaten their meat. They appear to me of the size of those in Spain. Their horns are small, like those of the Moorish cattle; the hair is very long, like fine wool and like a peajacket; some are brownish and others black, and to my taste they have better and more meat than those from here. Of the small hides the Indians make blankets to cover themselves with, and of the taller ones they make shoes and targets. These cows come from the north, across the country further on, to the coast of Florida, and are found all over the land for over four hundred leagues. On this whole stretch, through the valleys by which they come, people who live there descend to subsist upon their flesh. And a great quantity of hides are met with inland.

We remained with the Avavares Indians for eight months, according to our reckoning of the moons. During that time they came for us from many places and said that verily we were children of the sun. Until then Donates and the negro had not made any cures, but we found ourselves so pressed by the Indians coming from all sides, that all of us had to become medicine men. I was the most daring and reckless of all in undertaking cures. We never treated anyone that did not afterwards say he was well, and they had such confidence in our skill as to believe that none of them would die as long as we were among them. . . .

The women brought many mats, with which they built us houses, one for each of us and those attached to him. After this we would order them to boil all the game, and they did it quickly in ovens built by them for the purpose. We partook of everything a little, giving the rest to the principal man among those who had come with us for distribution among all. Every one then came with the share he had received for us to breathe on it and bless it, without which they left it untouched. Often we had with us three to four thousand persons. And it was very tiresome to have to breathe on and make the sign of the cross over every morsel they ate or drank. For many other things which they wanted to do they would come to ask our permission, so that it is easy to realize how greatly we were bothered. The women brought us tunas, spiders, worms, and whatever else they could find, for they would rather starve than partake of anything that had not first passed through our hands.

While traveling with those, we crossed a big river coming from the north and, traversing about thirty leagues of plains, met a number of people that came from afar to meet us on the trail, who treated us like the foregoing ones.

Thence on there was a change in the manner of reception, insofar as those who would meet us on the trail with gifts were no longer robbed by the Indians of our company, but after we had entered their homes they tendered us all they possessed, and the dwellings also. We turned over everything to the principals for distribution. Invariably those who had been deprived of their belongings would follow us, in order to repair their losses, so that our retinue became very large. They would tell them to be careful and not conceal anything of what they owned, as it could not be done without our knowledge, and then we would cause their death. So much did they frighten them that on the first few days after joining us they would be trembling all the time, and would not dare to speak or lift their eyes to Heaven.

Those guided us for more than fifty leagues through a desert of very rugged mountains, and so arid that there was no game. Consequently we suffered much from lack of food, and finally forded a very big river, with its water reaching to our chest. Thence on many of our people began to show the effects of the hunger and hardships they had undergone in those mountains, which were extremely barren and tiresome to travel.

The next morning all those who were strong enough came along, and at the end of three journeys we halted. Alonso del Castillo and Estevanico, the negro, left with the women as guides, and the woman who was a captive took them to a river that flows between mountains where there was a village in which her father lived, and these were the first adobes we saw that were like unto real houses. Castillo and Estevanico went to these and, after holding parley with the Indians, at the end of three days Castillo returned to where he had left us, bringing with him five or six of the Indians. He told how he had found permanent houses, inhabited, the people of which ate beans and squashes, and that he had also seen maize.

Of all things upon earth that caused us the greatest pleasure, and we gave endless thanks to our Lord for this news. Castillo also said that the negro was coming to meet us on the way, near by, with all the people of the houses. For that reason we started, and after going a league and a half met the negro and the people that came to receive us, who gave us beans and many squashes to eat, gourds to carry water in, robes of cowhide, and other things. As those people and the Indians of our company were enemies, and did not understand each other, we took leave of the latter, leaving them all that had been given to us, while we went on with the former and, six leagues beyond, when night was already approaching, reached their houses, where they received us with great ceremonies. Here we remained one day, and left on the next, taking them with us to other permanent houses, where they subsisted on the same food also, and thence on we found a new custom. . . .

Having seen positive traces of Christians and become satisfied they were very near, we gave many thanks to our Lord for redeeming us from our sad and gloomy condition. Anyone can imagine our delight when he reflects how long we had been in that land, and how many dangers and hardships we had suffered. That night I entreated one of my companions to go after the Christians, who were moving through the part of the country pacified and quieted by us, and who were three days ahead of where we were. They did not like my suggestion, and excused themselves from going, on the ground of being tired and worn out, although any of them might have done it far better than I, being younger and stronger.

Seeing their reluctance, in the morning I took with me the negro and eleven Indians and, following the trail, went in search of the Christians. On that day we made ten leagues, passing three places where they slept. The next morning I came upon four Christians on horseback, who, seeing me in such a strange attire, and in company with Indians, were greatly startled. They stared at me for quite awhile, speechless; so great was their surprise that they could not find words to ask me anything. I spoke first, and told them to lead me to their captain, and we went together to Diego de Alcaraz, their commander.

## DOCUMENT ANALYSIS

1. How does Cabeza de Vaca portray the Avavares Indians in his journal?

_____

_____

_____

2. What are the native peoples' opinions of de Vaca and his companions?

_____

_____

_____

## DOCUMENT 1.2
### William Penn, Description of Pennsylvania (1681)
From Albert Cook Myers, ed., *Narratives of Early Pennsylvania, West Jersey, and Delaware 1630–1707* (New York, 1912).

*In 1681, King Charles II awarded William Penn a charter for the North American territory that would become Pennsylvania. Penn named this colony after his father, who had served in the English Navy. Penn was a member of the Society of Friends, or Quakers, a Protestant denomination that faced persecution from more traditional Protestants, as well as others, in both England and the other colonies. As a result, freedom from persecution was a cornerstone of the government he established for the colony. Penn was the sole proprietor of the colony, and in order to turn a profit through the sale of land, he had to attract settlers. He did so through appeals to the English, Irish, and the inhabitants of the German states, such as the one excerpted below.*

Since (by the good providence of God) a Country in America is fallen to my lot, I thought it not less my Duty than my honest Interest to give some publick notice of it to the World, that those of our own, or other Nations, that are inclin'd to Transport themselves or Families beyond the Seas, may find another Country added to their choice, that if they happen to like the Place, Conditions and Constitutions, (so far as the present Infancy of things will allow us any prospect) they may, if they please, fix with me in the Province hereafter describ'd. . . .

1st. Those that go into a Foreign Plantation, their Industry there is worth more than if they stay'd at home, the Product of their Labour being in Commodities of a superiour Nature to those of this Country. For Instance; What is an improved Acre in Jamaica or Barbadoes worth to an improved Acre in England? We know 'tis threetimes the value, and the product of it comes for England, and is usually paid for in English Growth and Manufacture. Nay, Virginia shews that an ordinary Industry in one man produces Three thousand pound weight of Tobacco and Twenty Barrels of Corn yearly: He feeds himself, and brings as much of Commodity into England besides as being return'd in the Growth and Workmanship of this Countrey, is much more than he could have spent here: Let it also be remembered, that Three thousand weight of Tobacco brings in Three thousand Two-pences by way of Custom to the King, which makes Twenty five pounds; An extraordinary profit.

2dly. More being produc'd and imported than we can spend here, we Export it to other Countries in Europe, which brings in Money, or the growth of those Countries, which is the same thing; And this is the Advantage of the English-Merchants and Seamen.

3dly. Such as could not only not marry here, but hardly live and allow themselves Cloaths, do marry there, and bestow thrice more in all Necessaries and Conveniencies (and not a little in Ornamental things too) for themselves, their Wives and Children, both as to Apparel and Household-stuff; which coming out of England, I say 'tis impossible that England should not be a considerable Gainer.

## DOCUMENT ANALYSIS

1. How did Penn contrast life in Pennsylvania with life in Europe?

_____

_____

_____

2. What advantages could settlers in Pennsylvania enjoy that were unavailable in Europe?

_____

_____

_____

3. Would you have been convinced to leave your home and travel across the Atlantic to settle in Penn's colony? Why or why not?

_____

_____

_____

DOCUMENT 2.1

## Captain John Smith, President in Virginia, to the Treasurer and Council of the Virginia Company, from Smith's *The Generall Historie of Virginia* (1624)

*Virginia was the first and, for a time, the only English colony in the continental New World. Its boundaries spread as far to the north and west as its early explorers could imagine. In the document reproduced below, Virginia's president, John Smith, reports to the council of the underwriting Virginia Company to clarify some points and plead for a more rational approach to manpower and future shipments of provisions.*

Right Honorable, &c.

I received your letter, wherein you write, that our minds are so set upon faction, and idle conceits in dividing the country without your consents, and that we feed you but with ifs and ands, hopes, and some few proofs; as if we would keep the mystery of the business to ourselves: and that we must expressly follow your instructions sent by Captain Newport: the charge of whose voyage amounts to near two thousand pounds, the which if we cannot defray by the ships' return, we are like to remain as banished men. To these particulars I humbly entreat your pardons if I offend you with my rude answer.

For our factions, unless you would have me run away and leave the country, I cannot prevent them: because I do make many stay that would else fly any whither. For the idle letter sent to my Lord of Salisbury, by the President and his confederates, for dividing the country &c. What it was I know not, for you saw no hand of mine to it; nor ever dreamed I of any such matter. That we feed you with hopes, &c. Though I be no scholar, I am past a school-boy; and I desire but to know, what either you, and these here, do know but that I have learned to tell you by the continual hazard of my life. I have not concealed from you anything I know; but I fear some cause you to believe much more than is true. . .

For the charge of this voyage of two or three thousand pounds, we have not received the value of a hundred pounds. And for the quartered boat to be borne by the soldiers over the falls, Newport had 120 of the best men he could choose. If he had burnt her to ashes, one might have carried her in a bag; but as she is, five hundred cannot, to a navigable place above the falls. And for him at that time to find in the South Sea, a mine of gold, or any of them sent by Sir Walter Raleigh; at our consultation I told them was as likely as the rest. But during this great discovery of thirty miles, (which might as well have been done by one man, and much more, for the value of a pound of copper at a seasonable time) they had the pinnace and all the boats with them, but one that remained with me to serve the fort.

In their absence I followed the new begun works of pitch and tar, glass, soap ashes, and clapboard; whereof some small quantities we have sent you. But if you rightly consider, what an infinite toil it is in Russia and Swethland [Sweden], where the woods are proper for naught else, and though there by the help both of man and beast in those ancient commonwealths, which many a hundred years have used it; yet thousands of those poor people can scarce get necessaries to live, but from hand to mouth. And though your factors there can buy as much in a week as will fraught you a ship, or as much as you please; you must not expect from us any such matter, which are but a many of ignorant, miserable souls, that are scarce able to get wherewith to live, and defend ourselves against the inconstant savages: finding but here and there a tree fit for the purpose, and want all things else the Russians have.

. . . From your ship we have not provision in victuals worth twenty pound, and we are more than two hundred to live upon this: the one half sick, the other little better. For the sailors (I confess) they daily make good cheer, but our diet is a little meal and water, and not sufficient of that. Though there be fish in the sea, fowls in the air, and beasts in the woods, their bounds are so large, they so wild, and we so weak and ignorant, we cannot much trouble them. . .

Now that you should know, I have made you as great a discovery as [Captain Newport], for less charge than he spendeth you every meal; I have sent you this map of the bay and rivers, with an annexed relation of the countries and nations that inhabit them, as you may see at large. Also two barrels of stones, and such as I take to be good iron ore at the least; so divided, as by their notes you may see in what places I found them.

. . . When you send again I entreat you rather send but thirty carpenters, husbandmen, gardners, fishermen, blacksmiths, masons, and diggers up of trees, roots, well provided; than a thousand of such as we have: for except we be able both to lodge them, and feed them, the most will consume with want of necessaries before they can be made good for anything.

Thus if you please to consider this account, and of the unnecessary wages to Captain Newport, or his ships so long lingering and staying here (for notwithstanding his boasting to leave us victuals for 12 months; though we had 89 by this discovery lame and sick, and but a pint of corn a day for a man, we were constrained to give him three hogsheads of that to victual him homeward) or yet to send into Germany or Poland for glassmen and the rest, till we be able to sustain ourselves and relieve them when they come. It were better to give five hundred pound a ton for those gross commodities in Denmark, than send for them hither, till more necessary things be provided. For in over-toiling our weak and unskillful bodies, to satisfy this desire of present profit, we can scarce ever recover ourselves from one supply to another.

And I humbly entreat you hereafter, let us know what we should receive, and not stand to the sailors' courtesy to leave us what they please; else you may charge us with what you will, but we not you with anything.

These are the causes that have kept us in Virginia, from laying such a foundation, that ere this might have given much better content and satisfaction; but as yet you must not look for any profitable returns: so I humbly rest.

## DOCUMENT ANALYSIS

1. What was Smith's major complaint?

_____

_____

_____

2. Why were the colonists unable to fish and hunt for provisions?

_____

_____

_____

3. What general misconceptions did the treasury council seem to have concerning conditions in Virginia?

_____

_____

_____

## DOCUMENT 2.2
## John Winthrop, "A Model of Christian Charity" (1630)

*When the first settlers came to Virginia they were faced with numerous hardships that nearly devastated their entire venture. In contrast, when the Puritans settled in Massachusetts in 1630 they experienced few major difficulties and grew into a thriving community. The major difference between these two colonies was in their leadership and organization. Specifically, the strict religious beliefs and firm authority of the Puritans' leader, John Winthrop, and the established order he created before arriving in America enabled the Puritans to meet the challenges of colonization better than the Virginia colonists did.*

*On board the ship* Arabella, *Winthrop delivered the following sermon, entitled "A Model of Christian Charity." Notice how Winthrop portrayed their purpose in America as a divine mandate to serve as an example for the rest of the world.*

God almighty in His most holy and wise providence hath so disposed of the condition of mankind, as in all times some must be rich, some poor, some high and eminent in power and dignity, others mean and in subjection.

Reason: First, to hold conformity with the rest of His works, being delighted to show forth the glory of His wisdom in the variety and difference of the creatures and the glory of His power, in ordering all these differences for the preservation and good of the whole.

Reason: Secondly, that He might have the more occasion to manifest the work of His spirit. First, upon the wicked in moderating and restraining them, so that the rich and mighty should not eat up the poor, nor the poor and despised rise up against their superiors and shake off their yoke. Secondly, in the regenerate in exercising His graces in them, as in the great ones, their love, mercy, gentleness, temperance, etc., in the poor and inferior sort, their faith, patience, obedience, etc.

Reason: Thirdly, that every man might have need of other, and from hence they might all be knit more nearly together in the bond of brotherly affection. From hence it appears plainly that no man is made more honorable than another, or more wealthy, etc., out of any particular and singular respect to himself, but for the glory of his creator and the common good of the creature, man.

Thus stands the cause between God and us. We are entered into covenant with Him for this work, we have taken out a commission, the Lord hath given us leave to draw our own articles we have professed to enterprise these actions upon these and these ends, we have hereupon besought Him of favor and blessing. Now if the Lord shall please to hear us, and bring us in peace to the place we desire, then hath He ratified this covenant and sealed our commission, [and] will expect a strict performance of the articles contained in it, but if we shall neglect the observations

of these articles which are the ends we have propounded, and dissembling with our God, shall fall to embrace this present world and prosecute our carnal intentions seeking great things for ourselves and our posterity, the Lord will surely break out in wrath against us, be revenged of such a perjured people, and make us know the price of the breach of such a covenant.

Now the only way to avoid this shipwreck and to provide for our posterity is to follow the counsel of Micah, to do justly, to love mercy, to walk humbly with our God. For this end we must be knit together in this work as one man, we must entertain each other in brotherly affection, we must be willing to abridge ourselves of our superfluities for the supply of others' necessities, we must uphold a familiar commerce together in all meekness, gentleness, patience, and liberality, we must delight in each other, make others' conditions our own, rejoice together, mourn together, labor and suffer together, always having before our eyes our commission and community in the work, our community as members of the same body. So shall we keep the unity of the spirit in the bond of peace.

The Lord will be our God and delight in all our ways, so that we shall see much more of His wisdom, power, goodness, and truth than formerly we have been acquainted with. We shall find that the God of Israel is among us, when ten of us shall be able to resist a thousand of our enemies, when He shall make us a praise and glory, that men shall say of succeeding plantations, the Lord make it like that of New England. For we must consider that we shall be as a city upon a hill, the eyes of all people are upon us. So that if we shall deal falsely with our God in this work we have undertaken and so cause Him to withdraw His present help from us, we shall be made a story and byword throughout the world, we shall open the mouths of enemies to speak evil of the ways of God and all professors for God's sake, we shall shame the faces of many of God's worthy servants, and cause their prayers to be turned into curses upon us till we be consumed out of the good land whither we are going.

And to shut up this discourse with that exhortation of Moses, that faithful servant of the Lord in His last farewell to Israel, Deut. 30., Beloved there is now set before us life and good, death and evil, in that we are commanded this day to love the Lord our God, and to love one another, to walk in His ways and to keep His commandments and His ordinance, and His laws, and the articles of our covenant with Him that we may live and be multiplied, and that the Lord our God my bless us in the land whither we go to possess it. But if our hearts shall turn away so that we will not obey, but shall be seduced and worship other Gods, our pleasures, our profits, and serve them, it is propounded unto us this day we shall surely perish out of the good land whither we pass over this vast sea to possess it. Therefore let us choose life, that we, and our seed, may live, and by obeying His voice, and cleaving to Him, for He is our life and our prosperity.

## DOCUMENT ANALYSIS

1. To which biblical events did Winthrop compare the Puritan voyage? Why?

_____

_____

_____

2. What did Winthrop mean when he asserted that the new colony should be like a "city on a hill"? What, in his interpretation, was the duty of all the Puritan settlers?

_____

_____

_____

## DOCUMENT 3.1
### Alexander Falconbridge, The African Slave Trade (1788)

*Alexander Falconbridge served as ship's surgeon on slaving ships during the latter half of the 18th century. During his voyages across the Atlantic, Falconbridge had occasion to observe the abhorrent treatment of the slaves at the hands of the crews. During one such voyage, Falconbridge wrote this account of the conditions on the ship, including his own views on the practice of slavery.*

As soon as the wretched Africans, purchased at the fairs, fall into the hands of the black traders, they experience an earnest of those dreadful sufferings which they are doomed in future to undergo. And there is not the least room to doubt, but that even before they can reach the fairs, great numbers perish from cruel usage, want of food, travelling through inhospitable deserts, etc. They are brought from the places where they are purchased to Bonny, etc. in canoes; at the bottom of which they lie, having their hands tied with a kind of willow twigs, and a strict watch is kept over them. Their usage in other respects, during the time of passage, which generally lasts several days, is equally cruel. Their allowance of food is so scanty, that it is barely sufficient to support nature. They are, besides, much exposed to the violent rains which frequently fall here, being covered only with mats that afford but a slight defense; and as there is usually water at the bottom of the canoes, from their leaking, they are scarcely every dry.

Nor do these unhappying beings, after they become the property of the Europeans (from whom as a more civilized people, more humanity might naturally be expected), find their situation in the least amended. Their treatment is no less rigorous. The men Negroes, on being brought aboard the ship, are immediately fastened together, two and two, by handcuffs on their wrists, and irons riveted on their legs. They are then sent down between the decks, and placed in an apartment partitioned off for that purpose. The women likewise are placed in a separate room, on the same deck, but without being ironed. And an adjoining room, on the same deck is besides appointed for the boys. Thus are they placed in different apartments.

But at the same time, they are frequently stowed so close, as to admit of no other posture than lying on their sides. Neither will the height between decks, unless directly under the grating, permit them the indulgence of an erect posture; especially where there are platforms, which is generally the case. These platforms are a kind of shelf, about eight or nine feet in breadth, extending from the side of the ship towards the centre. They are placed nearly midway between the decks, at the distance of two or three feet from each deck. Upon these the Negroes are stowed in the same manner as they are on the deck underneath.

. . . About eight o'clock in the morning the Negroes are generally brought upon deck. Their irons being examined, a long chain, which is locked to a ring-bolt, fixed in the deck, is run through the rings of the shackles of the men, and then locked to another ring-bolt, fixed also in the deck. By this means fifty or sixty, and sometimes more, are fastened to one chain, in order to prevent them from rising, or endeavoring to escape. If the weather proves favorable, they are permitted to remain in that situation till four or five in the afternoon, when they are disengaged from the chain, and sent down.

. . . Upon the Negroes refusing to take sustenance, I have seen coals of fire, glowing hot, put on a shovel, and placed so near their lips, as to scorch and burn them. And this has been accompanied with threats, of forcing them to swallow the coals, if they any longer persisted in refusing to eat. These means have generally had the desired effect. I have also been credibly informed that a certain captain in the slave trade poured melted lead on such of the Negroes as obstinately refused their food.

Exercise being deemed necessary for the preservation of their health, they are sometimes obligated to dance, when the weather will permit their coming on deck. If they go about it reluctantly, or do not move with agility, they are flogged; a person standing by them all the time with at cat-o'-nine-tails in his hand for that purpose. Their music, upon these occasions, consists of a drum, sometimes with only one head; and when that is worn out, they do not scruple to make use of the bottom of one of the tubs before described. The poor wretches are frequently compelled to sing also; but when they do so, their songs are generally, as may naturally be expected, melancholy lamentations of their exile from their native country.

. . . On board some ships, the common sailors are allowed to have intercourse with such of the black women whose consent they can procure. And some of them have been known to take the inconstancy of their paramours so much to heart, as to leap overboard and drown themselves. The officers are permitted to indulge their passions among them at pleasure, and sometimes are guilty of such brutal excesses as disgrace human nature.

The hardships and inconveniences suffered by the Negroes during the passage are scarcely to be enumerated or conceived. They are far more violently affected by the seasickness than the Europeans. It frequently terminates in death, especially among the women. But the exclusion of the fresh air is among the most intolerable. For the purpose of admitting this needful refreshment, most of the ships in the slave trade are provided, between the decks, with five or six air-ports on each side of the ship, of about six inches in length, and four in breadth; in addition to which, some few ships, but not one in twenty, have what they denominate wind-sails. But whenever the sea is rough and the rain heavy, it becomes necessary to shut these, and every other conveyance by which the air is admitted. The fresh air being thus excluded, the Negroes' rooms very soon grow intolerably hot. The confined air, rendered noxious by the effluvia exhaled from their bodies, and by being repeatedly breathed, soon produces fevers and fluxes, which generally carries off great numbers of them.

. . . One morning, upon examining the place allotted for the sick Negroes, I perceived that one of them, who was so emaciated as scarcely to be able to walk, was missing, and was convinced that he must have gone overboard in the night, probably to put a more expeditious period to his sufferings. And, to conclude on this subject, I could not help being sensibly affected, on a former voyage, at observing with what apparent eagerness a black woman seized some dirt from off an African yam, and put it into her mouth, seeming to rejoice at the opportunity of possessing some of her native earth.

From these instances I think it may have been clearly deduced that the unhappy Africans are not bereft of the finer feelings, but have a strong attachment to their native country, together with a just sense of the value of liberty. And the situation of the miserable beings above described, more forcibly urges the necessity of abolishing a trade which is the source of such evils, than the most eloquent harangue, or persuasive arguments could do.

## DOCUMENT ANALYSIS

1. What information does Falconbridge's account provide us about how Africans were taken into slavery, who participated in the African slave trade, and what role commerce and trade played in the slave trade system?

_____

_____

_____

**2.** How would Falconbridge's descriptions of the slave trade be of assistance to opponents of slavery?

_____

_____

_____

_____

## DOCUMENT 3.2
### Gottlieb Mittelberger, On The Misfortune of Indentured Servants (1754)

_Gottlieb Mittelberger emigrated to Pennsylvania from Germany in 1750 on a ship filled with poorer immigrants who would become indentured servants in Philadelphia. Mittelberger's own fortunes were not so bleak: he served as a schoolmaster and organist in Philadelphia for three years. He returned to Germany in 1754._

Both in Rotterdam and in Amsterdam the people are packed densely, like herrings so to say, in the large sea-vessels. One person receives a place of scarcely 2 feet width and 6 feet length in the bedstead, while many a ship carries four to six hundred souls; not to mention the innumerable implements, tools, provisions, water-barrels and other things which likewise occupy such space.

On account of contrary winds it takes the ships sometimes 2, 3, and 4 weeks to make the trip from Holland to England. But when the wind is good, they get there in 8 days or even sooner. Everything is examined there and the custom-duties paid, whence it comes that the ships ride there 8, 10 or 14 days and even longer at anchor, till they have taken in their full cargoes. During that time every one is compelled to spend his last remaining money and to consume his little stock of provisions which had been reserved for the sea; so that most passengers, finding themselves on the ocean where they would be in greater need of them, must greatly suffer from hunger and want. Many suffer want already on the water between Holland and Old England.

When the ships have for the last time weighed their anchors near the city of Kaupp [Cowes] in Old England, the real misery begins with the long voyage. For from there the ships, unless they have good wind, must often sail 8, 9, 10 to 12 weeks before they reach Philadelphia. But even with the best wind the voyage lasts 7 weeks.

But during the voyage there is on board these ships terrible misery, stench, fumes, horror, vomiting, many kinds of sea-sickness, fever, dysentery, headache, heat, constipation, boils, scurvy, cancer, mouth rot, and the like, all of which come from old and sharply salted food and meat, also from very bad and foul water, so that many die miserably.

Add to this want of provisions, hunger, thirst, frost, heat, dampness, anxiety, want, afflictions and lamentations, together with other trouble, as the lice abound so frightfully, especially on sick people, that they can be scraped off the body. The misery reaches the climax when a gale rages for 2 or 3 nights and days, so that every one believes that the ship will go to the bottom with all human beings on board. In such a visitation the people cry and pray most piteously.

Children from 1 to 7 years rarely survive the voyage. I witnessed misery in no less than 32 children in our ship, all of whom were thrown into the sea. The parents grieve all the more since their children find no resting-place in the earth, but are devoured by the monsters of the sea.

That most of the people get sick is not surprising, because, in addition to all other trials and hardships, warm food is served only three times a week, the rations being very poor and very little. Such meals can hardly be eaten, on account of being so unclean. The water which is served out of the ships is often very black, thick and full of worms, so that one cannot drink it without loathing, even with the greatest thirst. Toward the end we were compelled to eat the ship's biscuit which had been spoiled long ago; though in a whole biscuit there was scarcely a piece the size of a dollar that had not been full of red worms and spiders' nests.

At length, when, after a long and tedious voyage, the ships come in sight of land, so that the promontories can be seen, which the people were so eager and anxious to see, all creep from below on deck to see the land from afar, and they weep for joy, and pray and sing, thanking and praising God. The sight of the land makes the people on board the ship, especially the sick and the half-dead, alive again, so that their hearts leap within them; they shout and rejoice, and are content to bear their misery in patience, in the hope that they may soon reach the land in safety. But alas!

When the ships have landed at Philadelphia after their long voyage, no one is permitted to leave them except those who pay for their passage or can give good security; the others, who cannot pay, must remain on board the ships till they are purchased, and are released from the ships by their purchasers. The sick always fare the worst, for the healthy are naturally preferred and purchased first; and so the sick and wretched must often remain on board in front of the city for 2 or 3 weeks, and frequently die, whereas many a one, if he could pay his debt and were permitted to leave the ship immediately, might recover and remain alive.

The sale of human beings in the market on board the ship is carried out thus: Every day Englishmen, Dutchmen and High-German people come from the city of Philadelphia and other places, in part from a great distance, say 20, 30, or 40 hours away, and go on board the newly arrived ship that has brought and offers for sale passengers from Europe, and select among the healthy persons such as they deem suitable for their business, and bargain with them how long they will serve for their passage money, which most of them are still in debt for. When they have come to an agreement, it happens that adult persons bind themselves in writing to serve 3, 4, 5 or 6 years for the amount due by them, according to their age and strength. But very young people, from 10 to 15 years, must serve till they are 21 years old.

Many parents must sell and trade away their children like so many head of cattle; for if their children take the debt upon themselves, the parents can leave the ship free and unrestrained; but as the parents often do not know where and to what people their children are going, it often happens that such parents and children, after leaving the ship, do not see each other again for many years, perhaps no more in all their lives.

It often happens that whole families: husband, wife and children, are separated by being sold to different purchasers, especially when they have not paid any part of their passage money.

When a husband or wife has died at sea, when the ship has made more than half of her trip, the survivor must pay or serve not only for himself or herself but also for the deceased.

When both parents have died over half-way at sea, their children, especially when they are young and have nothing to pawn or pay, must stand for their own and their parents' passage, and serve till they are 21 years old. When one has served his or her term, he or she is entitled to a new suit of clothes at parting; and if it has been so stipulated, a man gets in addition a horse, a woman, or a cow. When a serf has an opportunity to marry in this country, he or she must pay for each year which he or she would have yet to serve, 5 or 6 pounds.

## DOCUMENT ANALYSIS

1. What was indentured servitude like in the colonies? Was it much different from being a slave?

_____

_____

_____

**2.** How were the hardships of the sea compounded upon reaching land?

_____

_____

_____

**3.** What could have motivated people to take the journey described by Mittelberger?

_____

_____

_____

## DOCUMENT 3.3
### Testimony by Pedro Naranjo, Pueblo Indian, to Spanish Authorities (1681)
From Charles Wilson Hackett, ed., *Revolt of the Pueblo Indians of New Mexico and Otermin's Attempted Reconquest 1680–82*
(Albuquerque: U. of New Mexico Press, 1942), pp. 245–249.

*In 1680, a Pueblo leader named Popé led what would become the most successful Native American revolt in North American history. In 1675, the Spanish governor of present-day New Mexico began a campaign against Pueblo religious practices. In Santa Fe, four of the Pueblo were hanged and 43 others, including Popé, were whipped for practicing witchcraft. By 1680, Popé was able to coordinate more than 20 Native American settlements, many of whom spoke different languages, from a large area of New Mexico. His efforts generated an uprising, known as the Pueblo Revolt, that caused the deaths of 400 Spaniards, including 33 missionaries who were held responsible for the 1675 persecutions. The city of Santa Fe was burned, and the Spanish retreated to El Paso. Popé continued to rule the reclaimed area until his death in 1688. In 1692 the Spanish re-established control. The excerpt below describes events on the first day of the uprising.*

In the said Plaza de Armas on the said day, month, and year, for the prosecution of the judicial proceedings of this case his lordship caused to appear before him an Indian prisoner named Pedro Naranjo, a native of the Pueblo of San Felipe, of the Queres nation, who was captured in the advance and attack upon the Pueblo of La Isleta. He makes himself understood very well in the Castilian language and speaks his mother tongue and the Tegua. He took the oath in due legal form in the name of God, our Lord, and a sign of the cross, under charge of which he promised to tell the truth concerning what he knows and as he might be questioned, and having understood the seriousness of the oath and so signified through the interpreters, he spoke as indicated by the contents of the autos.

Asked whether he knew the reason or motives which the Indians of this kingdom had for rebelling, forsaking the law of God and obedience to his Majesty, and committing such grave and atrocious crimes, and who were the leaders and principal movers, and by whom and how it was ordered; and why they burned the images, temples, crosses, rosaries, and things of divine worship, committing such atrocities as killing priests, Spaniards, women, and children, and the rest that he might know touching the question, he said that since the government of Señor General Hernando Ugarte y la Concha they have planned to rebel on various occasions through conspiracies of the Indian sorcerers, and that although in some Pueblos the messages were accepted, in other parts they would not agree to it; and that it is true that during the government of the said Señor General seven or eight Indians were hanged for this same cause, whereupon the unrest subsided. Some time thereafter they [the conspirators] sent from the Pueblo of Los Taos through the Pueblos of the *custodia* two deerskins with some pictures on them signifying conspiracy after their manner, in order to convoke the people to a new rebellion, and the said deerskins passed to the province of Moqui, where they refused to accept them. The pact which had been forming ceased for the time, but they always kept in their hearts the desire to carry it out, so as to live as they are living today. Finally, in the past years, at the summons of an Indian named Popé who is said to have communication with the devil, it happened that in an *estufa* of the Pueblo of Los Taos there appeared to the said Popé three figures of Indians who never came out of the *estufa*. They gave the said Popé to understand that they were going underground to the Lake of Copala. He saw these figures emit fire from all the extremities of their bodies, and that one of them was called Caudi, another Tilini, and the other Tleume; and these three beings spoke to the said Popé, who was in hiding from the secretary, Francisco Xavier, who wished to punish him as a sorcerer. They told him to make a cord of *maguey* fiber and tie some knots in it which would signify the number of days that they must wait before the rebellion. He said that the cord was passed through all the Pueblos of the kingdom so that the ones which agreed to it [the rebellion] might untie one knot in sign of obedience, and by the other knots they would know the days which were lacking; and this was to be done on pain of death to those who refused to agree to it. As a sign of agreement and notice of having concurred in the treason and perfidy they were to send up smoke signals to that effect in each one of the Pueblos singly. The said cord was taken from Pueblo to Pueblo by the swiftest youths under the penalty of death if they revealed the secret. Everything being thus arranged, two days before the time set for its execution, because his lordship had learned of it and had imprisoned two Indian accomplices from the Pueblo of Tesuque, it was carried out prematurely that night, because it seemed to them that they were now discovered; and they killed religious Spaniards, women, and children. This being done, it was proclaimed in all the Pueblos that everyone in common should obey the commands of their father whom they did not know, which would be given through El Caydi or El Popé. This was heard by Alonso Catití, who came to the Pueblo of this declarant to say that everyone must unite to go to the villa to kill the governor and the Spaniards who had remained with him, and that he who did not obey would, on their return, be beheaded; and in fear of this they agreed to it. Finally the Señor Governor and those who were with him escaped from the siege, and later this declarant saw that as soon as the Spaniards had left the kingdom an order came from the said Indian, Popé, in which he commanded all the Indians to break the lands and enlarge their cultivated fields, saying that now they were as they had been in ancient times, free from the labor they had performed for the religious and the Spaniards, who could not now be alive. He said that this is the legitimate cause and the reason they had for rebelling, because they had always desired to live as they had when they came out of the Lake of Copala. Thus he replied to the question.

Asked for what reason they so blindly burned the images, temples, crosses, and other things of divine worship, he stated that the said Indian, Popé, came down in person, and with him El Saca and El Chato from the Pueblo of Los Taos, and other captains and leaders and many people who were in his train, and he ordered in all the Pueblos through which he passed that they instantly break up and burn the images of the Holy Christ, the Virgin Mary and the other saints, the crosses, and everything pertaining to Christianity, and that they burn the temples, break up the bells, and separate from the wives whom God had given them in marriage and take those whom they desired. In order to take away their baptismal names, the water, and the holy oils, they were to plunge into the rivers and wash themselves with *amole*, which is a root native to the country, washing even their clothing, with the understanding that there would thus be taken from them the character of the holy sacraments. They did this, and also many other things which he does not recall, given to understand that this mandate had come from the Caydi and the other two who emitted fire from their extremities in the said *estufa* of Taos, and that they thereby returned to the state of their antiquity, as when they came from the Lake of Copala; that this was the better life and the one they desired, because the God of the Spaniards was worth nothing and theirs was very strong, the Spaniard's God being rotten wood. These things were observed and obeyed by all except some who, moved by the zeal of Christians, opposed it, and such persons the said Popé caused to be killed immediately. He saw to it that they at once erected and rebuilt their houses of idolatry which they call *estufas*, and made very ugly masks in imitation of the devil in order to dance the dance of the *cacina*; and he said likewise that the devil had given them to understand that living thus in accordance with the law of their ancestors, they would harvest a great deal of maize, many beans, a great abundance of cotton, calabashes, and very large watermelons and cantaloupes; and that they could erect their houses and enjoy abundant health and leisure. As he has said, the people were very much pleased, living at their ease in this life of their antiquity, which was the chief cause of their falling into such laxity. Following what has already been stated, in order to terrorize them further and cause them to observe the diabolical commands, there came to them a pronouncement from the three demons already described, and from El Popé, to the effect that he who might still keep in his heart a regard for the priests, the governor, and the Spaniards would be known from his unclean face and clothes, and would be punished. And he stated that the said four persons stopped at nothing to have their commands obeyed. Thus he replied to the question.

Asked what arrangements and plans they had made for the contingency of the Spaniards' return, he said that what he knows concerning the question is that they were always saying they would have to fight to the death, for they do not wish to live in any other way than they are living at present; and the demons in the *estufa* of Taos had given them to understand that as soon as the Spaniards began to move toward this kingdom they would warn them so that they might unite, and none of them would be caught. He having been questioned further and repeatedly touching the case, he said that he has nothing more to say except that they should be always on the alert, because the said Indians were continually planning to follow the Spaniards and fight with them by night, in order to drive off the horses and catch them afoot, although they might have to follow them for many leagues. What he has said is the truth, and what happened, on the word of a Christian who confesses his guilt. He said that he had come to the Pueblos through fear to lead in idolatrous dances, in which he greatly feared in his heart that he may have offended God, and that now having been absolved and returned to the fold of the Church, he has spoken the truth in everything he has been asked.

## DOCUMENT ANALYSIS

1. How did the leader of the revolt organize the various settlements?

_____

_____

_____

2. Why would the Spanish authorities trust Pedro Naranjo's testimony?

_____

_____

_____

3. What actions did the Native Americans take to rid themselves of Christianity?

_____

_____

_____

## DOCUMENT 4.1
### Virginia Law on Indentured Servitude (1705)

*Enacted in 1705, this Virginia law defined the legal differences between slaves and indentured servants. The act was very detailed and included 39 sections that addressed the specific situations that might occur in the colony concerning slaves, indentured servants, "mulattos," and others. Section 18, reproduced below, addressed the various punishments for servant (not slave) women who might conceive a child while serving their indenture, that is, the years in which they were bound to service. Although the 1705 law is best known for its directive that the children of slave women would "follow the condition of the mother," meaning that they would be slaves for life, Section 18 describes the complications inherent in differentiating groups of people based on race.*

**An Act Concerning Servants and Slaves**

I. Be it enacted, by the governor, council, and burgesses, of this present general assembly, and it is hereby enacted, by the authority of the same, That all servants brought into this country without indenture, if the said servants be Christians, and of Christian parentage, and above nineteen years of age, shall serve but five years; and if under nineteen years of age, 'till they shall become twenty-four years of age, and no longer. . . .

XVIII. And if any woman servant shall be delivered of a bastard child within the time of her service aforesaid, Be it enacted, by the authority aforesaid, and it is hereby enacted, That in recompense of the loss and trouble occasioned her master or mistress thereby, she shall for every such offence, serve her said master or owner one whole year after her time by indenture, custom, and former order of court, shall be expired; or pay her said master or owner, one thousand pounds of tobacco; and the reputed father, if free, shall give security to the church-wardens of the parish where that child shall be, to maintain the child, and keep the parish indemnified; or be compelled thereto by order of the county court, upon the said church-warden complaint: But if a servant, he shall make satisfaction to the parish, for keeping the said child, after his time by indenture, custom, or order of court, to his then present master or owner shall be expired; or compelled thereto, by order of the county court, upon complaint of the church-wardens of the said parish, for the time being. And if any woman servant shall be got with child by her master, neither the said master, nor his executors administrators, nor assigns, shall have any claim of service against her, for or by reason of such child; but she shall, when her time due to her said master, by indenture, custom or order of court, shall be expired, be sold by the church-wardens, for the time being, of the parish wherein such child shall be born, for one year, or pay one thousand pounds of tobacco; and the said one thousand pounds of tobacco, or whatever she shall be sold for, shall be employed, by the vestry, to the use of the said parish. And if any woman servant shall have a bastard child by a negro, or mulatto, over and above the years service due to her master or owner, she shall immediately, upon the expiration of her time to her then present master or owner, pay down to the church-wardens of the parish wherein such child shall be born, for the use of the said parish, fifteen pounds current money of Virginia, or be by them sold for five years, to the use aforesaid: And if a free Christian white woman shall have a bastard child, by a negro, or mulatto, for every such offense, she shall, within one month after her delivery of such bastard child, pay to the church-wardens for the time being, of the parish wherein such child shall be born, for the use of the said parish fifteen pounds of current money of Virginia, or be by them sold for five years to the use aforesaid: And in both the said cases, the church-wardens shall bind the said child to be a servant, until it shall be of thirty one years of age. . . .

### DOCUMENT ANALYSIS

1. How many different ways might the father of an illegitimate child be classified according to this section?

_____

_____

_____

2. What were the different punishments a woman might receive for conceiving a child out of wedlock? Which punishments were the harshest?

_____

_____

_____

3. What role did the local church parish play in this system?

_____

_____

_____

## DOCUMENT 4.2
### Benjamin Franklin on George Whitefield (1771)

*Benjamin Franklin was one of America's foremost statesmen and scientists. A philosopher of the Enlightenment period, Franklin advocated the use of practical experimentation and reason in all areas of human existence. Despite this scientific orientation, Franklin found himself quite moved by the sermons of revivalist preacher George Whitefield, especially those that solicited funds for establishing an orphanage in the new colony of Georgia. This selection is excerpted from* The Autobiography of Benjamin Franklin (1771).

In 1739 arriv'd among us from England the Rev. Mr. Whitefield, who had made himself remarkable there as an itinerant preacher. . . . The Multitudes of all Sects and Denominations that attended his Sermons were enormous, and it was matter of Speculation to me who was one of the Number, to observe the extraordinary Influence of his Oratory on his Hearers, and how much they admir'd & respected him, notwithstanding his common Abuse of them, by assuring them they were naturally half Beasts and half Devils. It was wonderful to see the Change soon made in the Manners of our Inhabitants; from being thoughtless or indifferent about Religion, it seem'd as if all the World were growing Religious; so that one could not walk thro' the Town in an Evening without Hearing Psalms sung in different Families of every Street. . . .

Mr. Whitefield, in leaving us, went preaching all the Way thro' the Colonies to Georgia. The Settlement of that Province had lately been begun; but instead of being made with hardy industrious Husbandmen accustomed to Labor, the only People fit for such an Enterprise, it was with Families of broken Shopkeepers and other insolvent Debtors, many of indolent & idle habits, taken out of the jails, who being set down in the Woods, unqualified for clearing Land, & unable to endure the Hardships of a new Settlement, perished in Numbers, leaving many helpless Children unprovided for. The Sight of their miserable Situation inspired the benevolent Heart of Mr. Whitefield with the idea of building an Orphan House there. . . .

Returning northward he preached up this Charity, & made large Collections; for his Eloquence had a wonderful Power over the Hearts and Purses of his Hearers, of which I myself was an Instance. I did not disapprove of the Design, but as Georgia was then destitute of Materials &

Workmen, and it was propos'd to send them from Philadelphia at a great Expense, I thought it would have been better to have built the House here & Brought the Children to it. This I advis'd, but he was resolute in his first Project, and rejected my Counsel, and I thereupon refus'd to contribute. I happened soon after on one of his Sermons, in the Course of which I perceived he intended to finish with a Collection, & I silently resolved he should get nothing from me. I had in my Pocket a Handful of Copper Money, three or four silver Dollars, and five Pistoles in gold. As he proceeded I began to soften, and concluded to give the Coppers. Another Stroke of his Oratory made me asham'd of that, and determin'd me to give the Silver & he finished so admirably, that I empty'd my Pocket wholly into the Collector's Dish, Gold and all. At this Sermon there was also one of our Club, who being of my Sentiments respecting the Building in Georgia, and suspecting a Collection might be intended, had by Precaution emptied his Pockets before he came from home; towards the Conclusion of the Discourse, however, he felt a strong Desire to give, and apply'd to a Neighbor who stood near him to borrow some Money for the Purpose.

## DOCUMENT ANALYSIS

1. How does Franklin explain the great impact that Whitefield's sermons had on him? How does Franklin fit his rational Enlightenment beliefs with Whitefield's evangelical religion of the Great Awakening?

_____

_____

_____

2. What kind of attitude does Franklin betray in his opinions of the new colony of Georgia?

_____

_____

_____

## DOCUMENT 5.1
### *Boston Gazette,* Description of the Boston Massacre (1770)

*The Boston Massacre took place on March 5, 1770, and was covered in detail by the* Boston Gazette. *British troops had been stationed in the city since late 1768 to protect British customs officers and tensions between the soldiers and citizens of Boston had been building. The resulting clash between a group of citizens and soldiers on March 5 resulted in five civilian deaths, the removal of British troops from Boston, and trials for some of the soldiers involved. The Boston Massacre became a crucial element in anti-British propaganda in the colonies.*

. . . On the evening of Monday, being the fifth current, several soldiers of the 29th Regiment were seen parading the streets with their drawn cutlasses and bayonets, abusing and wounding numbers of the inhabitants.

A few minutes after nine o'clock four youths, named Edward Archbald, William Merchant, Francis Archbald, and John Leech, Jr., came down Cornhill together, and separating at Doctor Loring's corner, the two former were passing the narrow alley leading to Murray's barrack in which was a soldier brandishing a broad sword of an uncommon size against the walls, out of which he struck fire plentifully. A person of mean countenance armed with a large cudgel bore him company. Edward Archbald admonished Mr. Merchant to take care of the sword, on which the soldier turned round and struck Archbald on the arm, then pushed at Merchant and pierced through his clothes inside the arm close to the armpit and grazed the skin. Merchant then struck the soldier with a short stick he had; and the other person ran to the barrack and brought with him two soldiers, one armed with a pair of tongs, the other with a shovel. He with the tongs pursued Archbald back through the alley, collared and laid him over the head with the tongs. The noise brought people together; and John Hicks, a young lad, coming up, knocked the soldier down but let him get up again; and more lads gathering, drove them back to the barrack where the boys stood some time as it were to keep them in. In less than a minute ten or twelve of them came out with drawn cutlasses, clubs, and bayonets and set upon the unarmed boys and young folk who stood them a little while but, finding the inequality of their equipment, dis-

persed. On hearing the noise, one Samuel Atwood came up to see what was the matter; and entering the alley from dock square, heard the latter part of the combat; and when the boys had dispersed he met the ten or twelve soldiers aforesaid rushing down the alley towards the square and asked them if they intended to murder people? They answered "Yes, by God, root and branch!" With that one of them struck Mr. Atwood with a club which was repeated by another; and being unarmed, he turned to go off and received a wound on the left shoulder which reached the bone and gave him much pain. Retreating a few steps, Mr. Atwood met two officers and said, "Gentlemen, what is the matter?" They answered, "You'll see by and by." Immediately after, those heroes appeared in the square, asking "Where were the boogers? Where were the cowards?" But notwithstanding their fierceness to naked men, one of them advanced towards a youth who had a split of a raw stave in his hand and said, "Damn them, here is one of them." But the young man seeing a person near him with a drawn sword and good cane ready to support him, held up his stave in defiance; and they quietly passed by him up the little alley by Mr. Silsby's to King Street where they attacked single and unarmed persons till they raised much clamor, and then turned down Cornhill Street, insulting all they met in like manner and pursuing some to their very doors. Thirty or forty persons, mostly lads, being by this means gathered in King Street, Captain Preston with a party of men with charged bayonets, came from the main guard to the commissioner's house, the soldiers pushing their bayonets, crying, "Make way!" They took place by the custom house and, continuing to push to drive the people off, pricked some in several places, on which they were clamorous and, it is said, threw snowballs. On this, the Captain commanded them to fire; and more snowballs coming, he again said, "Damn you, fire, be the consequence what it will!" One soldier then fired, and a townsman with a cudgel struck him over the hands with such force that he dropped his firelock; and, rushing forward, aimed a blow at the Captain's head which grazed his hat and fell pretty heavy upon his arm. However, the soldiers continued the fire successively till seven or eight or, as some say, eleven guns were discharged.

## DOCUMENT ANALYSIS

1. How does the author of this account describe the soldiers and pro-British persons? What adjectives does he use?

_____

_____

_____

2. Who are the "lads" in this account? How are they portrayed? What terms does the author use to describe them?

_____

_____

_____

3. Is the author of this account biased? If so, do his words and descriptions indicate that he is pro-British or anti-British?

_____

_____

_____

## DOCUMENT 5.2
### Slave Petition to the General Assembly in Connecticut (1779)
From Gary B. Nash, *Race and Revolution* (Madison, WI: Madison House, 1990), pp. 174–176.

*The petition reproduced below was signed by two slaves, Prime and Prince, in Fairfield County, Connecticut, on behalf of all slaves in that county. Combining—as did other slave petitions—references to both the ongoing Revolutionary War and Christianity, their plea is representative of this particular era of U.S. history. The petition was denied, and Connecticut instead opted for a plan of gradual emancipation. In 1774 the legislature had outlawed the importation of slaves. In 1784 and 1797, the legislature passed additional laws that freed children born as slaves at ages 25 and 21, respectively. Slavery was not completely abolished in the state until 1848.*

To the Honorable General Assembly of the State of Connecticut to be held at Hartford on the Second Thursday of Instant May [1779]—The Petition of the Negroes in the Towns of Stratford and Fairfield in the County of Fairfield who are held in a State of Slavery humbly showeth—

That many of your Petitioners, were (as they verily believe) most unjustly torn, from the Bosom of their dear Parents, and Friends, and without any Crime, by them committed, doomed, and bound down, to perpetual Slavery; and as if the Perpetrators of this horrid Wickedness, were conscious (that we poor Ignorant Africans, upon the least Glimmering Sight, derived from a Knowledge of the Sense and Practice of civilized Nations) should Convince them of their Sin, they have added another dreadful Evil, that of holding us in gross Ignorance, so as to render Our Subjection more easy and tolerable. May it please your Honors, we are most grievously affected, under the Consideration of the flagrant Injustice; Your Honors who are nobly contending, in the Cause of Liberty, whose Conduct excites the Admiration, and Reverence, of all the great Empires of the World; will not resent, our thus freely animadverting, on this detestable Practice; although our Skins are different in Color, from those whom we serve, Yet Reason & Revelation join to declare, that we are the Creatures of that God, who made of one Blood, and Kindred, all the Nations of the Earth; we perceive by our own Reflection, that we are endowed with the same Faculties with our masters, and there is nothing that leads us to a Belief, or Suspicion, that we are any more obliged to serve them, than they us, and the more we Consider of this matter, the more we are Convinced of our Right (by the Laws of Nature and by the whole Tenor of the Christian Religion, so far as we have been taught) to be free; we have endeavored rightly to understand what is our Right, and what is our Duty, and can never be convinced that we were made to be Slaves. Although God almighty may justly lay this, and more upon us, yet we deserve it not, from the hands of Men, we are impatient under the grievous Yoke, but our Reason teaches us that it is not best for us to use violent measures, to cast it off; we are also convinced, that we are unable to extricate ourselves from our abject State; but we think we may with the greatest Propriety look up to your Honors, (who are the fathers of the People) for Relief. And we not only groan under our own burden, but with concern, & Horror, look forward, & contemplate, the miserable Condition of our Children, who are training up, and kept in Preparation, for a like State of Bondage, and Servitude. We beg leave to submit, to your Honors serious Consideration, whether it is consistent with the present Claims, of the united States, to hold so many Thousands, of the Race of Adam, our Common Father, in perpetual Slavery. Can human Nature endure the Shocking Idea? can your Honors any longer Suffer this great Evil to prevail under your Government: we entreat your Honors, let no considerations of Public Inconvenience deter your Honors from interposing in behalf of your Petitioners; we ask for nothing, but what we are fully persuaded is ours to Claim. We beseech your Honors to weigh this matter in the Scale of Justice, and in your great Wisdom and goodness, apply such Remedy as the Evil does require; and let your Petitioners rejoice with your Honors in the Participation with your Honors of that inestimable Blessing, Freedom and your Humble Petitioners, as in Duty bound shall ever pray &c.

dated in Fairfield the 11th Day of May A D 1779—

Prime—a Negro man

servant to Mr. Vam A. Sturge of Fairfield

his mark

Prince—a Negro man

his mark

servant of Capt. Stephen Jenings of Fairfield—

in Behalf of themselves and the other Petitioners

## DOCUMENT ANALYSIS

1.  What religious argument did the petitioners offer?

_____

_____

_____

2.  What did the petitioners describe as their greatest "horror" when contemplating the slave system?

_____

_____

_____

3.  How did the petitioners place their argument within a global perspective? Which of their arguments referenced the Revolutionary War?

_____

_____

_____

# DOCUMENT 5.3
## Thomas Jefferson, Excerpt from a Rough Draught of the American Declaration of Independence (1776)

*Perhaps the most famous document in U.S. history, the Declaration of Independence went through several revisions before being accepted by the Continental Congress. Delegates compressed the original statement, cutting large sections that Jefferson had written in anger and haste. Although the alterations produced a more concise and persuasive document, Jefferson lamented the deletions, which he was convinced had deleted the force of his rhetoric. Among the sections deleted was Jefferson's painful farewell to the British Empire that appears in the next-to-last paragraph.*

A Declaration of the Representatives of the United States of America, in General Congress Assembled.

When in the course of human events it becomes necessary for a people to advance from that subordination in which they have hitherto remained, & to assume among the powers of the earth the equal & independent station to which the laws of nature & of nature's god entitle them, a decent respect to the opinions of mankind requires that they should declare the causes which impel them to the change.

We hold these truths to be sacred & undeniable that all men are created equal & independent, that from that equal creation they derive rights inherent & inalienable, among which are the preservation of life, & liberty, & the pursuit of happiness; that to secure these ends, governments are instituted among men, deriving their just powers from the consent of the governed; that whenever any form of government shall become destructive of these ends, it is the right of the people to alter or to abolish it, & to institute new government, laying its foundation on such principles & organizing it's powers in such form, as to them shall seem most likely to effect their safety & happiness. Prudence indeed will dictate that governments long established should not be changed for light & transient causes: and accordingly all experience hath shown that mankind are more disposed to suffer while evils are sufferable, than to right themselves by abolishing the forms to which they are accustomed. But when a long train of abuses & usurpations, begun at a distinguished period, & pursuing invariably the same object, evinces a design to subject them to arbitrary power, it is their right, it is their duty, to throw off such government & to provide new guards for their future security. Such has been the patient sufferance of these colonies; & such is now the necessity which constrains them to expunge their former systems of government. The history of his present majesty, is a history of unremitting injuries and usurpations, among which no one fact stands single or solitary to contradict the uniform tenor of the rest, all of which have in direct object the establishment of an absolute tyranny over these states. To prove this, let facts be submitted to a candid world, for the truth of which we pledge a faith yet unsullied by falsehood.

He has refused his assent to laws the most wholesome and necessary for the public good:

He has forbidden his governors to pass laws of immediate & pressing importance, unless suspended in their operation till his assent should be obtained; and when so suspended, he has neglected utterly to attend to them.

He has refused to pass other laws for the accommodation of large districts of people unless those people would relinquish the right of representation, a right inestimable to them, & formidable to tyrants alone.

He has dissolved Representative houses repeatedly & continually, for opposing with manly firmness his invasions on the rights of the people:

He has refused for a long space of time to cause others to be elected, whereby the legislative powers, incapable of annihilation, have returned to the people at large for their exercise, the state remaining in the mean time exposed to all the dangers of invasion from without, & convulsions within:

He has endeavored to prevent the population of these states; for that purpose obstructing the laws for naturalization of foreigners; refusing to pass others to encourage their migrations hither; & raising the conditions of new appropriations of lands:

He has suffered the administration of justice totally to cease in some of these colonies, refusing his assent to laws for establishing judiciary powers:

He has made our judges dependent on his will alone, for the tenure of their offices, and amount of their salaries:

He has erected a multitude of new offices by a self-assumed power, & sent hither swarms of officers to harass our people & eat out their substance:

He has kept among us in times of peace standing armies & ships of war:

He has affected to render the military, independent of & superior to the civil power:

He has combined with others to subject us to a jurisdiction foreign to our constitutions and unacknowledged by our laws; giving his assent to their pretended acts of legislation, for quartering large bodies of armed troops among us;

For protecting them by a mock-trial from punishment for any murders they should commit on the inhabitants of these states;

For cutting off our trade with all parts of the world;

For imposing taxes on us without our consent;

For depriving us of the benefits of trial by jury;

For transporting us beyond seas to be tried for pretended offences:

For taking away our charters, & altering fundamentally the forms of our governments;

For suspending our own legislatures & declaring themselves invested with power to legislate for us in all cases whatsoever:

He has abdicated government here, withdrawing his governors, & declaring us out of his allegiance & protection:

He has plundered our seas, ravaged our coasts, burnt our towns & destroyed the lives of our people:

He is at this time transporting large armies of foreign mercenaries to complete the works of death, desolation & tyranny, already begun with circumstances of cruelty & perfidy unworthy the head of a civilized nation:

He has endeavored to bring on the inhabitants of our frontiers the merciless Indian savages, whose known rule of warfare is an undistinguished destruction of all ages, sexes, & conditions of existence:

He has incited treasonable insurrections in our fellow-subjects, with the allurements of forfeiture & confiscation of our property:

He has waged cruel war against human nature itself, violating it's most sacred rights of life & liberty in the persons of a distant people who never offended him, captivating & carrying them into slavery in another hemisphere, or to incur miserable death in their transportation thither. this piratical warfare, the opprobrium of infidel powers, is the warfare of the CHRISTIAN king of Great Britain. Determined to keep open a market where MEN should be bought & sold, he has prostituted his negative for suppressing every legislative attempt to prohibit or to restrain this execrable commerce: and that this assemblage of horrors might want no fact of distinguished die, he is now exciting those very people to rise in arms among us, and to purchase that liberty of which he has deprived them, by murdering the people upon whom he also obtruded them; thus paying off former crimes committed against the liberties of one people, with crimes which he urges them to commit against the lives of another.

In every stage of these oppressions we have petitioned for redress in the most humble terms; our repeated petitions have been answered by repeated injury. A prince whose character is thus marked by every act which may define a tyrant, is unfit to be the ruler of a people who mean to be free. Future ages will scarce believe that the hardiness of one man, adventured within the short compass of 12 years only, on so many acts of tyranny without a mask, over a people fostered & fixed in principles of liberty.

Nor have we been wanting in attentions to our British brethren. We have warned them from time to time of attempts by their legislature to extend a jurisdiction over these our states. We have reminded them of the circumstances of our emigration & settlement here, no one of which could warrant so strange a pretension: that these were effected at the expense of our own blood & treasure, unassisted by the wealth or the strength of Great Britain: that in constituting indeed our several forms of government, we had adopted one common king, thereby laying a foundation for perpetual league & amity with them: but that submission to their parliament was no part of our constitution, nor ever in idea, if history may be credited: and we appealed to their native justice & magnanimity, as well as to the ties of our common kindred to disavow these usurpations which were likely to interrupt our correspondence & connection. They too have been deaf to the voice of justice & of consanguinity, & when occasions have been given them, by the regular course of their laws, of removing from their councils the disturbers of our harmony, they have by their free election re-established them in power. At this very time too they are permitting their chief magistrate to send over not only soldiers of our common blood, but Scotch & foreign mercenaries to invade & deluge us in blood. These facts have given the last stab to agonizing affection, and manly spirit bids us to renounce for ever these unfeeling brethren. We must endeavor to forget our former love for them, and to hold them as we hold the rest of mankind, enemies in war, in peace friends, we might have been a free & a great people together; but a communication of grandeur & of freedom it seems is below their dignity. Be it so, since they will have it: the road to glory & happiness is open to us to; we will climb it in a separate state, and acquiesce in the necessity which pronounces our everlasting Adieu!

We therefore the representatives of the United States of America in General Congress assembled do, in the name & by authority of the good people of these states, reject and renounce all allegiance & subject to the kings of Great Britain & all others who may hereafter claim by, through, or under them; we utterly dissolve & break off all political connection which may have heretofore subsisted between us & the people or parliament of Great Britain; and finally we do assert and declare these colonies to be free and independent states, and that as free & independent states they shall hereafter have power to levy war, conclude peace, contract alliances, establish commerce, & to do all other acts and things which independent states may of right do. And for the support of this declaration we mutually pledge to each other our lives, our fortunes, & our sacred honor.

## DOCUMENT ANALYSIS

1. What is the purpose of the Declaration of Independence? How would the arguments presented in the document affect a person's decision either to support or to oppose independence?

_____

_____

_____

2. Would the inclusion of Jefferson's farewell to empire had added to or detracted from the force of document? Explain your answer.

_____

_____

_____

# DOCUMENT 6.1
## Thomas Jefferson, *Notes on the State of Virginia* (1787)

*In response to a request for information from a French diplomat, Thomas Jefferson, then governor of Virginia, put in writing his ideas about his state. After working on the manuscript for several years, Jefferson eventually published it as* Notes on the State of Virginia. *Jefferson covered more than just institutions and geography. He also examined what he considered the future of the nation and its primary strength—free, white landowners. Jefferson did not include African Americans in his vision of the new nation, at least not as citizens.*

In Europe the lands are either cultivated, or locked up against the cultivator. Manufacture must therefore be resorted to of necessity not of choice, to support the surplus of their people. But we have an immensity of land courting the industry of the husbandman. Is it best then that all our citizens should be employed in its improvement, or that one half should be called off from that to exercise manufactures and handicrafts arts for the other? Those who labor in the earth are the chosen people of God, if ever he had a chosen people, whose breasts he has made his peculiar deposit for substantial and genuine virtue. It is the focus in which he keeps alive that sacred fire, which otherwise might escape from the face of the earth. Corruption of morals in the mass of cultivators is a phenomenon of which no age nor nation has furnished an example. It is the mark set on those, who not looking up to heaven, to their own soil and industry, as does the husbandman, for their subsistence, depend for it on the casualties and caprice of customers. Dependence begets subservience and venality, suffocates the germ of virtue, and prepares fit tools for the designs of ambition. This, the natural progress and consequence of the arts, has sometimes perhaps been retarded by accidental circumstances: but generally speaking, the proportion which the aggregate of the other classes of citizens bears in any state to that of its husbandmen, is the proportion of its unsound to its healthy parts, and is a good-enough barometer whereby to measure its degree of corruption. While we have land to labor then, let us never wish to see our citizens occupied at a work-bench, or twirling a distaff. Carpenters, masons, smiths, are wanting in husbandry: but, for the general operations of manufacture, let our workshops remain in Europe. It is better to carry provisions and materials, and with them their manners and principles. The loss by the transportation of commodities across the Atlantic will be made up in happiness and permanence of government. The mobs of great cities add just so much to the support of pure government, as sores do to the strength of the human body. It is the manners and spirit of a people which preserve a republic in vigor. A degeneracy in these is a canker which soon eats to the heart of its laws and constitution.

It will probably be asked, Why not retain and incorporate the blacks into the state, and thus save the expense of supplying, by importation of white settlers, the vacancies they will leave? Deep rooted prejudices entertained by the whites; ten thousand recollections, by the blacks, of the injuries they have sustained; new provocations; the real distinctions which nature had made; and many other circumstances, will divide us into parties, and produce convulsions which will probably never end but in the extermination of the one or the other race. To these objections, which are political, may be added others, which are physical and moral. The first difference which strikes us is that of color. Whether the black of the negro resides in the reticular membrane between the skin and scarf-skin, or in the scarf-skin itself; whether it proceeds from the color of the blood, the color of the bile, or from that of some other secretion, the difference is fixed in nature, and is as real as if its seat and cause were better known to us. And is this difference of no importance? Is it not the foundation of a greater or less share of beauty in the two races? Are not the fine mixtures of red and white, the expressions of every passion by greater or less suffusions of color in the one, preferable to that eternal monotony, which reigns in the countenances, that immoveable veil of black which covers all the emotions of the other race? Add to these, flowing hair, a more elegant symmetry of form, their own judgment in favor of the whites, declared by their preference of them, as uniformly as is the preference of the Orangutan for

the black women over those of his own species. The circumstance of superior beauty, is thought worthy attention in the propagation of our horses, dogs, and other domestic animals; why not in that of man? Besides those of color, figure, and hair, there are other physical distinctions proving a difference of race. They have less hair on the face and body. They secrete less by the kidneys, and more by the glands of the skin, which gives them a very strong and disagreeable odor. This greater degree of transpiration renders them more tolerant of heat, and less so of cold, than the whites. Perhaps too a difference of structure in the pulmonary apparatus, which a late ingenious experimentalist has discovered to be the principal regulator of animal heat, may have disabled them from extricating, in the act of inspiration, so much of that fluid from the outer air, or obliged them in expiration, to part with more of it. They seem to require less sleep. A black, after hard labor through the day, will be induced by the slightest amusements to sit up till midnight, or later, though knowing he must be out with the first dawn of the morning. They are at least as brave, and more adventuresome. But this may perhaps proceed from a want of forethought, which prevents their seeing a danger till it be present. When present, they do not go through it with more coolness or steadiness than the whites. They are more ardent after their female: but love seems with them to be more an eager desire, than a tender delicate mixture of sentiment and sensation. Their griefs are transient. Those numberless afflictions, which render it doubtful whether heaven has given life to us in mercy or in wrath, are less felt, and sooner forgotten with them. In general, their existence appears to participate more of sensation than reflection. To this must be ascribed their disposition to sleep when abstracted from their diversions, and unemployed in labor. An animal whose body is at rest, and who does not reflect, must be disposed to sleep of course. Comparing them by their faculties of memory, reason, and imagination, it appears to me, that in memory they are equal to the whites; in reason much inferior, as I think one could scarcely be found capable of tracing and comprehending the investigations of Euclid; and that in imagination they are dull, tasteless, and anomalous. It would be unfair to follow them to Africa for this investigation. We will consider them here, on the same stage with the whites, and where the facts are not apocryphal on which a judgment is to be formed. It will be right to make great allowances for the difference of condition, of education, of conversation, of the sphere in which they move. Many millions of them have been brought to, and born in America. Most of them indeed have been confined to tillage, to their own homes, and their own society: yet many have been so situated, that they might have availed themselves of the conversation of their masters; many have been brought up to the handicraft arts, and from that circumstance have always been associated with the whites. Some have been liberally educated, and all have lived in countries where the arts and sciences are cultivated to a considerable degree, and have had before their eyes samples of the best works from abroad. The Indians, with no advantages of this kind, will often carve figures on their pipes not destitute of design and merit. They will crayon out an animal, a plant, or a country, so as to prove the existence of a germ in their minds which only wants cultivation. They astonish you with strokes of the most sublime oratory; such as prove their reason and sentiment strong, their imagination glowing and elevated. But never yet could I find that a black had uttered a thought above the level of plain narration; never see even an elementary trait of painting or sculpture. In music they are more generally gifted than the whites with accurate ears for tune and time, and they have been found capable of imagining a small catch. Whether they will be equal to the composition of a more extensive run of melody, or of complicated harmony, is yet to be proved.

The opinion, that they are inferior in the faculties of reason and imagination, must be hazarded with great diffidence. To justify a general conclusion, requires many observations, even where the subject may be submitted to the Anatomical knife, to Optical glasses, to analysis by fire, or by solvents. How much more then where it is a faculty, not a substance, we are examining; where it eludes the research of all the senses; where the conditions of its existence are various and variously combined;

where the effects of those which are present or absent bid defiance to calculation; let me add too, as a circumstance of great tenderness, where our conclusion would degrade a whole race of men from the rank in the scale of beings which their Creator may perhaps have given them. To our reproach it must be said, that though for a century and a half we have had under our eyes the races of black and of red men, they have never yet been viewed by us as subjects of natural history. I advance it therefore as a suspicion only, that the blacks, whether originally a distinct race, or made distinct by time and circumstances, are inferior to the whites in the endowments both of body and mind. It is not against experience to suppose, that different species of the same genus, or varieties of the same species, may possess different qualifications. Will not a lover of natural history then, one who views the gradations in all the races of animals with the eye of philosophy, excuse an effort to keep those in the department of man as distinct as nature has formed them? This unfortunate difference of color, and perhaps of faculty, is a powerful obstacle to the emancipation of these people. Many of their advocates, while they wish to vindicate the liberty of human nature, are anxious also to preserve its dignity and beauty. Some of these, embarrassed by the question "What further is to be done with them?" join themselves in opposition with those who are actuated by sordid avarice only. Among the Romans emancipation required but one effort. The slave, when made free, might mix with, without staining the blood of his master. But with us a second is necessary, unknown to history. When freed, he is to be removed beyond the reach of mixture.

## DOCUMENT ANALYSIS

1. Why does Jefferson argue that the strength of the new nation lay in the hands of the small farmers?

_____

_____

_____

2. How does Jefferson use the scientific ideas of his day to justify denying African Americans the rights of citizens?

_____

_____

_____

DOCUMENT 7.1
## George Washington, Sixth Annual Address to Congress (1794)

*The Whiskey Rebellion of 1794 took place in western Pennsylvania. The reason for the rebellion was a federal tax on distilled spirits that had been levied in 1791. Producers resisted the tax, claiming that only the state had the right to impose such taxes. In a show of federal strength, President George Washington called up a militia to suppress the insurrection. The event was significant because it was the first challenge to federal authority in the United States and the first time a U.S. president called up state militias to enforce federal law. In this address Washington describes the rebellion and his decision to suppress it.*

Fellow Citizens of the Senate and of the House of Representatives: When we call to mind the gracious indulgence of Heaven, by which the American People became a nation; when we survey the general prosperity of our country, and look forward to the riches, power, and happiness, to which it seems destined; with the deepest regret do I announce to you, that during your recess, some of the citizens of the United States have been found capable of an insurrection. It is due, however, to the character of our government, and to its stability, which cannot be shaken by the enemies of order, freely to unfold the course of this event.

During the session of the year one thousand seven hundred and ninety, it was expedient to exercise the legislative power, granted by the constitution of the United States, "to lay and collect excises." In a majority of the States, scarcely an objection was heard to this mode of taxation. In some, indeed, alarms were at first conceived, until they were banished by reason and patriotism. In the four western counties of Pennsylvania, a prejudice, fostered and embittered by the artifice of men, who labored for an ascendancy over the will of others, by the guidance of their passions, produced symptoms of riot and violence. It is well known, that Congress did not hesitate to examine the complaints which were presented, and to relieve them, as far as justice dictated, or general convenience would permit, but the impression, which this moderation made on the discontented, did not correspond, with what it deserved. The arts of delusion were no longer confined to the efforts of designing individuals.

The very forbearance to press prosecutions was misinterpreted into a fear of urging the execution of the laws; and associations of men began to denounce threats against the officers employed. From a belief, that by a more formal concert, their operation might be defeated, certain self-created societies assumed the tone of condemnation. Hence, while the greater part of Pennsylvania itself were conforming themselves to the acts of excise, a few counties were resolved to frustrate them. It was now perceived, that every expectation from the tenderness which had been hitherto pursued, was unavailing, and that further delay could only create an opinion of impotency or irresolution in the government. Legal process was, therefore, delivered to the marshal, against the rioters and delinquent distillers.

No sooner was he understood to be engaged in this duty, than the vengeance of armed men was aimed at his person, and the person and property of the inspector of the revenue. They fired upon the marshal, arrested him, and detained him for some time, as a prisoner. He was obliged, by the jeopardy of his life, to renounce the service of other process, on the west side of the Allegany mountain; and a deputation was afterwards sent to him to demand a surrender of that which he had served. A numerous body repeatedly attacked the house of the inspector, seized his papers of office, and finally destroyed by fire, his buildings, and whatsoever they contained. Both of these officers, from a just regard to their safety, fled to the seat of government; it being avowed, that the motives to such outrages were to compel the resignation of the inspector, to withstand by force of arms the authority of the United States, and thereby to extort a repeal of the laws of excise, and an alteration in the conduct of government.

Upon the testimony of these facts, an associate Justice of the Supreme Court of the United States notified to me, that "in the counties of Washington and Allegany, in Pennsylvania, laws of the United States were opposed, and the execution thereof obstructed by combinations, too powerful to be suppressed by the ordinary course of judicial proceedings, or by the powers vested in the marshal of that district." On this call, mo-

mentous in the extreme, I sought and weighed, what might best subdue the crisis. On the one hand, the judiciary was pronounced to be stripped of its capacity to enforce the laws; crimes, which reached the very existence of social order, were perpetrated without control, the friends of government were insulted, abused, and overawed into silence, or an apparent acquiescence; and the yield to the treasonable fury of so small a portion of the United States, would be to violate the fundamental principle of our constitution, which enjoins that the will of the majority shall prevail. On the other, to array citizen against citizen, to publish the dishonor of such excesses, to encounter the expense, and other embarrassments of so distant an expedition, were steps too delicate, too closely interwoven with many affecting considerations, to be lightly adopted. I postponed, therefore, the summoning of the militia immediately into the field. But I required them to be held in readiness, that if my anxious endeavors to reclaim the deluded, and to convince the malignant of their danger, should be fruitless, military force might be prepared to act, before the season should be too far advanced.

My Proclamation of the 7th of August last was accordingly issued, and accompanied by the appointment of Commissioners, who were charged to repair to the scene of insurrection. They were authorized to confer with any bodies of men, or individuals. They were instructed to be candid and explicit, in stating the sensations, which had been excited in the Executive, and his earnest wish to avoid a resort to coercion. To represent, however, that without submission, coercion must be the resort; but to invite them, at the same time, to return to the demeanor of faithful citizens, by such accommodations as lay within the sphere of the executive power. Pardon, too, was tendered to them by the government of the United States, and that of Pennsylvania, upon no other condition, than a satisfactory assurance of obedience to the laws.

Although the report of the commissioners marks their firmness and abilities, and must unite all virtuous men, by showing, that the means of conciliation have been exhausted, all of those who had committed or abetted the tumults, did not subscribe the mild form, which was proposed, as the atonement; and the indications of a peaceable temper were neither sufficiently general, nor conclusive, to recommend or warrant, a further suspension of the march of the militia.

Thus, the painful alternative could not be discarded. I ordered the militia to march, after once more admonishing the insurgents, in my proclamation of the 25th of September last. It was a task too difficult to ascertain with precision, the lowest degree of force, competent to the quelling of the insurrection. From a respect, indeed, to economy, and the ease of my fellow citizens belonging to the militia, it would have gratified me to accomplish such an estimate. My very reluctance to ascribe too much importance to the opposition, had its extent been accurately seen, would have been a decided inducement to the smallest efficient numbers.

In this uncertainty, therefore, I put in motion fifteen thousand men, as being an army, which according to all human calculation, would be prompt, and adequate in every view; and might perhaps, by rendering resistance desperate, prevent the effusion of blood. Quotas had been assigned to the states of New-Jersey, Pennsylvania, Maryland, and Virginia; the governor of Pennsylvania having declared on this occasion, an opinion which justified a requisition to the other states.

As commander in chief of the militia, when called into the actual service of the United States, I have visited the places of general rendezvous, to obtain more exact information, and to direct a plan for ulterior movements. Had there been room for a persuasion, that the laws were secure from obstruction; that the civil magistrate was able to bring to justice such of the most culpable, as have not embraced the proffered terms of amnesty, and may be deemed fit objects of example; that the friends to peace and good government were not in need of that aid and countenance, which they ought always to receive, and I trust, ever will receive, against the vicious and turbulent; I should have caught with avidity the opportunity of restoring the militia to their families and home. But succeeding intelligence has tended to manifest the necessity of what has been done; it being now confessed by those who were not inclined to exaggerate the ill-conduct of the insurgents, that their malevolence was not pointed merely to a particular law; but that a spirit, inimical to all order, has actuated many of the offenders. If the state of things had afforded reason for the continuance of my presence with the army, it would not have been denied.

But every appearance assuring such an issue, as will redound to the reputation and strength of the United States, I have judged it most proper, to resume my duties at the seat of government, leaving the chief command with the governor of Virginia. Still, however, as it is probable, that in a commotion like the present, whatsoever may be the pretence, the purposes of mischief and revenge may not be laid aside; the stationing of a small force for a certain period in the four western counties of Pennsylvania will be indispensable; whether we contemplate the situation of those, who are connected with the execution of the laws; or of others who may have exposed themselves by an honorable attachment to them. . . .

While there is cause to lament, that occurrences of this nature should have disgraced the name, or interrupted the tranquility of any part of our community, or should have diverted to a new application, any portion of the public resources, there are not wanting real and substantial consolations for the misfortune. It has demonstrated, that our prosperity rests on solid foundations; by furnishing an additional proof, that my fellow citizens understand the true principles of government and liberty: that they feel their inseparable union: that notwithstanding all the devices which have been used to sway them from their interest and duty, they are now as ready to maintain the authority of the laws against licentious invasions, as they were to defend their rights against usurpation. It has been a spectacle, displaying to the highest advantage, the value of Republican Government, to behold the most and least wealthy of our citizens standing in the same ranks as private soldiers; pre-eminently distinguished by being the army of the constitution; undeterred by a march of three hundred miles over rugged mountains, by the approach of an inclement season, or by any other discouragement. Nor ought I to omit to acknowledge the efficacious and patriotic co-operation, which I have experienced from the chief magistrates of the states, to which my requisitions have been addressed.

To every description, indeed, of citizens let praise be given. But let them persevere in their affectionate vigilance over that precious depository of American happiness, the constitution of the United States. Let them cherish it too, for the sake of those, who from every clime are daily seeking a dwelling in our land. And when in the calm moments of reflection, they shall have retraced the origin and progress of the insurrection, let them determine whether it has not been fomented by combinations of men, who, careless of consequences, and disregarding the unerring truth, that those who rouse, cannot always appease a civil convulsion, have disseminated, from an ignorance of perversion of facts, suspicions, jealousies, and accusations of the whole government.

Having thus fulfilled the engagement, which I took, when I entered this office, "to the best of my ability to preserve, protect, and defend the constitution of the United States," on you, Gentlemen, and the people by whom you are deputed, I rely for support. In the arrangements, to which the possibility of a similar contingency will naturally draw your attention, it ought not to be forgotten, that the militia laws have exhibited such striking defects, as could not have been supplied but by the zeal of our citizens. Besides the extraordinary expense and waste, which are not the least of the defects, every appeal to those laws is attended with a doubt of its success. The devising and establishing of a well regulated militia, would be a genuine source of legislative honor, and a perfect title to public gratitude. I, therefore, entertain a hope, that the present session will not pass, without carrying to its full energy the power of organizing, arming, and disciplining the militia; and thus providing, in the language of the constitution, for calling them forth to execute the laws of the union, suppress insurrections, and repel invasions. As auxiliary to the state of our defense, to which Congress can never too frequently recur, they will not omit to enquire whether the fortifications, which have been already licensed by law, be commensurate with our exigencies. . . .

An estimate of the necessary appropriations, including the expenditures into which we have been driven by the insurrection, will be submitted to Congress. Gentlemen of the Senate, and of the House of Representatives: The mint of the United States has entered upon the coinage of the precious metals; and considerable sums of defective coins and bullion have been lodged with the director by individuals. There is a pleasing prospect that the institution will, at no remote day, realize the expectation which was originally formed of its utility.

In subsequent communications, certain circumstances of our intercourse with foreign nations, will be transmitted to Congress. However, it may not be unseasonable to announce that my policy in our foreign transactions has been, to cultivate peace with all the world; to observe treaties with pure and absolute faith; to check every deviation from the line of impartiality; to explain what may have been misapprehended; and having thus acquired the right, to lose no time in acquiring the ability, to insist upon justice being done to ourselves.

Let us unite, therefore, in imploring the Supreme Ruler of nations, to spread his holy protection over these United States: to turn the machinations of the wicked to the confirming of our constitution: to enable us at all times to root out internal sedition, and put invasion to flight: to perpetuate to our country that prosperity, which his goodness has already conferred, and to verify the anticipations of this government being a safe guard to human rights.

## DOCUMENT ANALYSIS

1. How did Washington defend his actions? What did he cite as the basis of his power to suppress the rebellion?

_____

_____

_____

2. What did Washington ask Congress to do in this address?

_____

_____

_____

3. How did Washington describe those who participated in the rebellion? In your opinion, was this a fair assessment? Why or why not?

_____

_____

_____

*The Virginia and Kentucky Resolutions were drafted by the two states primarily in response to the Alien and Sedition Acts of 1798. The legislatures of the two states considered the acts to be grievous errors on the part of the federal government that violated the basic rights guaranteed by the Bill of Rights.*

*The Virginia Resolution was drafted to oppose what the state's legislature viewed as an "infraction of those principles which constitute the only basis of [the] Union." The legislature felt that the Alien and Sedition Acts not only undermined the rights of citizens, but also of the states.*

*The Kentucky Resolution was drafted just over a year after the Virginia Resolution, in 1799. Following the lead of Virginia's legislature, the Kentucky legislature affirmed their allegiance to the Union and cited it as the reason for their protest against the Alien and Sedition Acts.*

### Virginia Resolution (1798)

RESOLVED, That the General Assembly of Virginia, doth unequivocally express a firm resolution to maintain and defend the Constitution of the United States, and the Constitution of this State, against every aggression either foreign or domestic, and that they will support the government of the United States in all measures warranted by the former.

That this assembly most solemnly declares a warm attachment to the Union of the States, to maintain which it pledges all its powers; and that for this end, it is their duty to watch over and oppose every infraction of those principles which constitute the only basis of that Union, because a faithful observance of them, can alone secure it's existence and the public happiness.

That this Assembly doth explicitly and peremptorily declare, that it views the powers of the federal government, as resulting from the compact, to which the states are parties; as limited by the plain sense and intention of the instrument constituting the compact; as no further valid that they are authorized by the grants enumerated in that compact; and that in case of a deliberate, palpable, and dangerous exercise of other powers, not granted by the said compact, the states who are parties thereto, have the right, and are in duty bound, to interpose for arresting the progress of the evil, and for maintaining within their respective limits, the authorities, rights and liberties appertaining to them.

That the General Assembly doth also express its deep regret, that a spirit has in sundry instances, been manifested by the federal government, to enlarge its powers by forced constructions of the constitutional charter which defines them; and that implications have appeared of a design to expound certain general phrases (which having been copied from the very limited grant of power, in the former articles of confederation were the less liable to be misconstrued) so as to destroy the meaning and effect, of the particular enumeration which necessarily explains and limits the general phrases; and so as to consolidate the states by degrees, into one sovereignty, the obvious tendency and inevitable consequence of which would be, to transform the present republican system of the United States, into an absolute, or at best a mixed monarchy.

That the General Assembly doth particularly protest against the palpable and alarming infractions of the Constitution, in the two late cases of the "Alien and Sedition Acts" passed at the last session of Congress; the first of which exercises a power no where delegated to the federal government, and which by uniting legislative and judicial powers to those of executive, subverts the general principles of free government; as well as the particular organization, and positive provisions of the federal constitution; and the other of which acts, exercises in like manner, a power not delegated by the constitution, but on the contrary, expressly and positively forbidden by one of the amendments thereto; a power, which more than any other, ought to produce universal alarm, because it is leveled against that right of freely examining public characters and measures, and of free communication among the people thereon, which has ever been justly deemed, the only effectual guardian of every other right.

That this state having by its Convention, which ratified the federal Constitution, expressly declared, that among other essential rights, "the Liberty of Conscience and of the Press cannot be cancelled, abridged, restrained, or modified by any authority of the United States," and from its extreme anxiety to guard these rights from every possible attack of sophistry or ambition, having with other states, recommended an amendment for that purpose, which amendment was, in due time, annexed to the Constitution; it would mark a reproachable inconsistency, and criminal degeneracy, if an indifference were now shown, to the most palpable violation of one of the Rights, thus declared and secured; and to the establishment of a precedent which may be fatal to the other.

That the good people of this commonwealth, having ever felt, and continuing to feel, the most sincere affection for their brethren of the other states; the truest anxiety for establishing and perpetuating the union of all; and the most scrupulous fidelity to that constitution, which is the pledge of mutual friendship, and the instrument of mutual happiness; the General Assembly doth solemnly appeal to the like dispositions of the other states, in confidence that they will concur with this commonwealth in declaring, as it does hereby declare, that the acts aforesaid, are unconstitutional; and that the necessary and proper measures will be taken by each, for co-operating with this state, in maintaining the Authorities, Rights, and Liberties, referred to the States respectively, or to the people.

That the Governor be desired, to transmit a copy of the foregoing Resolutions to the executive authority of each of the other states, with a request that the same may be communicated to the Legislature thereof; and that a copy be furnished to each of the Senators and Representatives representing this state in the Congress of the United States.

Agreed to by the Senate, December 24, 1798.

### Kentucky Resolution (1799)

RESOLUTIONS IN GENERAL ASSEMBLY

THE representatives of the good people of this commonwealth in general assembly convened, having maturely considered the answers of sundry states in the Union, to their resolutions passed at the last session, respecting certain unconstitutional laws of Congress, commonly called the alien and sedition laws, would be faithless indeed to themselves, and to those they represent, were they silently to acquiesce in principles and doctrines attempted to be maintained in all those answers, that of Virginia only excepted. To again enter the field of argument, and attempt more fully or forcibly to expose the unconstitutionality of those obnoxious laws, would, it is apprehended be as unnecessary as unavailing.

We cannot however but lament, that in the discussion of those interesting subjects, by sundry of the legislatures of our sister states, unfounded suggestions, and uncandid insinuations, derogatory of the true character and principles of the good people of this commonwealth, have been substituted in place of fair reasoning and sound argument. Our opinions of those alarming measures of the general government, together with our reasons for those opinions, were detailed with decency and with temper, and submitted to the discussion and judgment of our fellow citizens throughout the Union. Whether the decency and temper have been observed in the answers of most of those states who have denied or attempted to obviate the great truths contained in those resolutions, we have now only to submit to a candid world. Faithful to the true principles of the federal union, unconscious of any designs to disturb the harmony of that Union, and anxious only to escape the fangs of despotism, the good people of this commonwealth are regardless of censure or calumniation.

Least however the silence of this commonwealth should be construed into an acquiescence in the doctrines and principles advanced and attempted to be maintained by the said answers, or least those of our fellow citizens throughout the Union, who so widely differ from us on those important subjects, should be deluded by the expectation, that we shall be deterred from what we conceive our duty; or shrink from the principles contained in those resolutions: therefore.

RESOLVED, That this commonwealth considers the federal union, upon the terms and for the purposes specified in the late compact, as conducive to the liberty and happiness of the several states: That it does now unequivocally declare its attachment to the Union, and to that compact, agreeable to its obvious and real intention, and will be among the last to seek its dissolution: That if those who administer the general government be permitted to transgress the limits fixed by that compact, by a total disregard to the special delegations of power therein contained, annihilation of the state governments, and the erection upon their ruins, of a general consolidated government, will be the inevitable consequence: That the principle and construction contended for by sundry of the state legislatures, that the general government is the exclusive judge of the extent of the powers delegated to it, stop nothing short of despotism; since the discretion of those who administer the government, and not the constitution, would be the measure of their powers:

That the several states who formed that instrument, being sovereign and independent, have the unquestionable right to judge of its infraction; and that a nullification, by those sovereignties, of all unauthorized acts done under color of that instrument, is the rightful remedy: That this commonwealth does upon the most deliberate reconsideration declare, that the said alien and sedition laws, are in their opinion, palpable violations of the said constitution; and however cheerfully it may be disposed to surrender its opinion to a majority of its sister states in matters of ordinary or doubtful policy; yet, in momentous regulations like the present, which so vitally wound the best rights of the citizen, it would consider a silent acquiescence as highly criminal: That although this commonwealth as a party to the federal compact; will bow to the laws of the Union, yet it does at the same time declare, that it will not now, nor ever hereafter, cease to oppose in a constitutional manner, every attempt from what quarter so ever offered, to violate that compact:

AND FINALLY, in order that no pretexts or arguments may be drawn from a supposed acquiescence on the part of this commonwealth in the constitutionality of those laws, and be thereby used as precedents for similar future violations of federal compact; this commonwealth does now enter against them, its SOLEMN PROTEST.

Approved December 3, 1799.

## DOCUMENT ANALYSIS

1. What was at the heart of the Republican arguments in the Kentucky and Virginia Resolutions?

_____

_____

_____

2. Thomas Jefferson wrote the Kentucky Resolution. Why was this unusual?

_____

_____

_____

## DOCUMENT 8.1
### Opinion of the Supreme Court for *Marbury v. Madison* (1803)

*Prior to leaving office, President Adams appointed several Federalist judges to the federal courts. Angered by these "midnight" appointments, Jefferson and his administration made several attempts to block the nominations and unseat the judges. The new administration failed to block any of the appointments except for that of William Marbury in the District of Columbia. Angered over the administration's actions, Marbury sued the new secretary of state, James Madison. This case,* Marbury v. Madison, *failed to win Marbury his seat, but it officially established the Supreme Court's right to judicial review.*

In the order in which the Court has viewed this subject, the following questions have been considered and decided: 1st. Has the applicant a right to the commission he demands? 2nd. If he has a right, and that right has been violated, do the laws of this country afford him a remedy? 3rd. If they do afford him a remedy, is it a mandamus issuing from this court?. . .

It is . . . the opinion of the Court: 1st. That by signing the commission of Mr. Marbury, the President of the United States appointed him a justice of the peace for the county of Washington, in the District of Columbia; and that the seal of the United States, affixed thereto by the secretary of state, is conclusive testimony of the verity of the signature, and of the completion of the appointment; and that the appointment conferred on him a legal right to the office of the space of five years. 2nd. That, having this legal title to the office, he has a consequent right to the commission; a refusal to deliver which is a plain violation of that right, for which the laws of his country afford him a remedy. 3rd. It remains to be inquired whether he is entitled to the remedy for which he applies?. . .

This . . . is a plain case of a mandamus, either to deliver the commission, or a copy of it from the record; and it only remains to be inquired, whether it can issue from this court?

The act to establish the judicial courts of the United States authorizes the Supreme Court, "to issue writs of mandamus, in cases warranted by the principles and usages of law, to any courts appointed or persons holding office, under the authority of the United States." The secretary of state, being a person holding an office under the authority of the United States, is precisely within the letter of this description; and if this court is not authorized to issue a writ of mandamus to such an office, it must be because the law is unconstitutional. . .

The Constitution vests the whole judicial power of the United States in one Supreme Court, and such inferior courts as Congress shall, from time to time, ordain and establish. . .

In the distribution of this power, it is declared that "the Supreme Court shall have original jurisdiction in all cases affecting ambassadors, other public ministers and consuls, and those in which a state shall be a party. In all other cases, the Supreme Court shall have appellate jurisdiction.". . .

If it had been intended to leave it in the discretion of the legislature to apportion the judicial power between the supreme and inferior courts according to the will of that body, it would certainly have been useless to have proceeded further than to have defined the judicial power, and the tribunals in which is should be vested. The subsequent part of the section is mere surplus, is entirely without meaning,. . .

It cannot be presumed that any clause in the Constitution is intended to be without effect. . .

To enable this court, then, to issue a mandamus, it must be shown to be an exercise of appellate jurisdiction. . .

The authority, therefore, given to the Supreme Court, by the Act establishing the judicial courts of the United States, to issue writs of mandamus to public officers, appears not to be warranted by the Constitution. . .

### DOCUMENT ANALYSIS

1. What role does Chief Justice Marshall hope the Supreme Court adopts in regards to the U.S. Constitution?

_____

_____

_____

2. Why was it important that the Chief Justice should be seen as speaking for all the members of the Supreme Court on this issue?

_____

_____

_____

## DOCUMENT 8.2
### Lewis and Clark Meet the Shoshone, August 17, 1805

*Meriwether Lewis and William Clark were chosen by President Thomas Jefferson to survey the area known as Louisiana, purchased from France in 1803. Here, Lewis describes their first meeting with the Shoshone and the reunion of their guide Sacagawea with her people.*

This morning I arose very early and dispatched Drewyer and the Indian down to the river. Sent Shields to hunt. I made McNeal cook the remainder of our meat which afforded a slight breakfast for ourselves and the chief. Drewyer had been gone about two hours when an Indian who had straggled some little distance down the river returned and reported that the white men were coming, that he had seen them just below. They all appeared transported with joy, and the chief repeated his fraternal hug. I felt quite as much gratified at this information as the Indians appeared to be. Shortly after Captain Clark arrived with the interpreter Charbono,

and the Indian woman, who proved to be a sister of the Chief Cameahwait. The meeting of those people was really affecting, particularly between Sah-cah-gar-we-ah [Sacagawea] and an Indian woman, who had been taken prisoner at the same time with her and who had afterwards escaped from the Minnetares and rejoined her nation. At noon the canoes arrived, and we had the satisfaction once more to find ourselves all together, with a flattering prospect of being able to obtain as many horses shortly as would enable us to prosecute our voyage by land should that by water be deemed unadvisable.

We now formed our camp just below the junction of the forks on the larboard side in a level smooth bottom covered with a fine turf of greensward. Here we unloaded our canoes and arranged our baggage on shore; formed a canopy of one of our large sails and planted some willow brush in the ground to form a shade for the Indians to set under while we spoke to them, which we thought it best to do this evening. Accordingly about 4 PM we called them together and through the medium of Labuish, Charbono and Sah-cah-gar-we-ah, we communicated to them fully the objects which had brought us into this distant part of the country, in which we took care to make them a conspicuous object of our own good wishes and the care of our government. We made them sensible of their dependence on the will of our government for every species of merchandise as well for their defense and comfort; and apprised them of the strength of our government and its friendly dispositions towards them. We also gave them as a reason why we wished to penetrate the country as far as the ocean to the west of them was to examine and find out a more direct way to bring merchandise to them. That as no trade could be carried on with them before our return to our homes that it was mutually advantageous to them as well as to ourselves, that they should render us such aids as they had it in their power to furnish in order to hasten our voyage and of course our return home, that such were their horses to transport our baggage without which we could not subsist, and that a pilot to conduct us through the mountains was also necessary if we could not descend the river by water, but that we did not ask either their horses or their services without giving a satisfactory compensation in return, that at present we wished them to collect as many horses as were necessary to transport our baggage to their village on the Columbia where we would then trade with them at our leisure for such horses as they could spare us.

They appeared well pleased with what had been said. The chief thanked us for friendship towards himself and nation and declared his wish to serve us in every respect, that he was sorry to find that it must yet be some time before they could be furnished with firearms but said they could live as they had done heretofore until we brought them as we had promised. He said they had not horses enough with them at present to remove our baggage to their village over the mountain, but that he would return to-morrow and encourage his people to come over with their horses and that he would bring his own and assist us. This was complying with all we wished at present. We next inquired who were chiefs among them. Cameahwait pointed out two others whom he said were chiefs. We gave him a medal of the small size with the likeness of Mr. Jefferson the President of the United States in relief on one side and clasp hands with a pipe and tomahawk on the other, to the other chiefs we gave each a small medal which were struck in the president of George Washington Esq. We also gave small medals of the last description to two young men whom the first chief informed us were good young men and much respected among them. We gave the first chief a uniform coat, shirt, a pair of scarlet leggings, a carrot of tobacco and some small articles. To each of the others we gave a shi[r]t, legging[s], handkerchief, a knife, some tobacco and a few small articles. We also distributed a good quantity paint, moccasins, awles, knives, beads, looking-glasses, &c. among the other Indians and gave them a plentiful meal of lyed corn which was the first they had ever eaten in their lives. They were much pleased with it. Every article about us appeared to excite astonishment in their minds; the appearance of the men, their arms, the canoes, our manner of working them, the black man York, and the sagacity of my dog were equally objects of admiration. I also shot my air-gun which was so perfectly incomprehensible that they immediately denominated it the great medicine. The idea which the Indians mean to convey by this appellation is something that emanates from or acts immediately by the influence or power of the Great Spirit; or that, in which, the power of God is manifest by its incomprehensible power of action. Our hunters killed four deer and an antelope this evening of which we also gave the Indians a good proportion. The ceremony of our council and smoking the pipe was in conformity of the custom of this nation performed barefoot. On those occasions points of etiquette are quite as much attended to by the Indians as among civilized nations. To keep Indians in a good humor you must not fatigue them with too much business at one time. Therefore after the council we gave them to eat and amused them a while by showing them such articles as we thought would be entertaining to them, and then renewed our inquiries with respect to the country. The information we derived was only a repetition of that they had given me before and in which they appeared to be so candid that I could not avoid yielding confidence to what they had said. Captain Clark and myself now concerted measures for our future operations, and it was mutually agreed that he should set out to-morrow morning with eleven men furnished with axes and other necessary tools for making canoes, their arms, accoutrements and as much of their baggage as they could carry; also to take the Indians, Charbono and the Indian woman with him; that on his arrival at the Shoshone camp he was to leave Charbono and the Indian woman to hasten the return of the Indians with their horses to this place, and to proceed himself with the eleven men down the Columbia in order to examine the river and if he found it navigable and could obtain timber to set about making canoes immediately. In the meantime I was to bring on the party and baggage to the Shoshone camp, calculating that by the time I should reach that place that he would have sufficiently informed himself with respect to the state of the river &c. as to determine us whether to prosecute our journey from thence by land or water. In the former case we should want all the horses which we could purchase, and in the latter only to hire the Indians to transport our baggage to the place at which we made the canoes. In order to inform me as early as possible of the state of the river he was to send back one of the men with the necessary information as soon as he should satisfy himself on this subject. This plan being settled we gave orders accordingly and the men prepared for an early march. The nights are very cold and the sun excessively hot in the day. We have no fuel here but a few dry willow brush and from the appearance of the country I am confident we shall not find game here to subsist us many days. These are additional reasons why I conceive it necessary to get under way as soon as possible. This morning Captain Clark had delayed until 7 A.M. before he set out just about which time Drewyer arrived with the Indian; he left the canoes to come on after him, and immediately set out and joined me as has been before mentioned. The spirits of the men were now much elated at the prospect of getting horses.

## DOCUMENT ANALYSIS

1. In this excerpt, Lewis asserts that he and Clark "communicated to them fully the objects which had brought us into this distant part of the country." What messages did they attempt to convey to the Shoshone concerning the nature of their mission? How did they portray their country and its government? How do you think the Shoshone received these messages?

_____

_____

_____

2. How would you characterize Lewis's attitude toward the Shoshone?

_____

_____

_____

## DOCUMENT 9.1
## Black Hawk, Excerpt from "The Life of Black Hawk" (1833)

*Sauk warrior Black Hawk led the Sauk and Fox peoples in their resistance against attempts by the U.S. government to take their lands. In 1804 a small group of tribal representatives supposedly conceded a vast amount of territory to the United States, much of it in present-day Illinois. Black Hawk eventually emerged as the leader of the Sauk and Fox peoples who refused to abandon these lands. This dispute culminated in the Black Hawk War of 1832 in which the Indians won a few initial battles but were ultimately defeated and lost their lands. Black Hawk was taken prisoner, and he wrote his autobiography the following year.*

We generally paid a visit to St. Louis every summer; but, in consequence of the protracted war in which we had been engaged, I had not been there for some years. Our difficulties having all been settled, I concluded to take a small party, that summer, and go down to see our Spanish father. We went—and on our arrival, put up our lodges where the market-house now stands. After painting and dressing, we called to see our Spanish father, and were well received. He gave us a variety of presents, and plenty of provisions. We danced through the town as usual, and its inhabitants all seemed to be well pleased. They appeared to us like brothers and always gave us good advice.

On my next, and last, visit to my Spanish father, I discovered, on landing, that all was not right: every countenance seemed sad and gloomy! I inquired the cause, and was informed that the Americans were coming to take possession of the town and country! And that we should then lose our Spanish father! This news made myself and band sad—because we had always heard bad accounts of the Americans from Indians who had lived near them!—and we were sorry to lose our Spanish father, who had always treated us with great friendship.

A few days afterwards, the Americans arrived. I took my band, and went to take leave, for the last time, of our father. The Americans came to see him also. Seeing them approach, we passed out at one door, as they entered another—and immediately started, in canoes, for our village on Rock river—not liking the change any more than our friends appeared to, at St. Louis.

On arriving at our village, we gave the news, that strange people had taken St. Louis—and that we should never see our Spanish father again! This information made all our people sorry!

Some time afterwards, a boat came up the river, with a young American chief, and a small party of soldiers. We heard of them, (by runners,) soon after he had passed Salt river. Some of our young braves watched him every day, to see what sort of people he had on board! The boat, at length, arrived at Rock river, and the young chief came on shore with his interpreter, made a speech, and gave us some presents! We, in return, presented him with meat, and such provisions as we could spare.

We were all well pleased with the speech of the young chief. He gave us good advice; said our American father would treat us well. He presented us an American flag, which was hoisted. He then requested us to pull down our British flags—and give him our British medals promising to send us others on his return to St. Louis. This we declined, as we wished to have two Fathers!

When the young chief started, we sent runners to the Fox village, some miles distant, to direct them to treat him well as he passed—which they did. He went to the head of the Mississippi, and then returned to St. Louis. We did not see any Americans again for some time, being supplied with goods by British traders.

We were fortunate in not giving up our medals, for we learned afterwards, from our traders, that the chiefs high up on the Mississippi, who gave theirs, never received any in exchange for them. But the fault was not with the young American chief. He was a good man, and a great brave—and died in his country's service.

Some moons after this young chief descended the Mississippi, one of our people killed an American—and was confined, in the prison at St. Louis, for the offence. We held a council at our village to see what could be done for him,—which determined that Quàsh-quà-me, Pà-she-pa-ho, Oú-che-quà-ka, and Hà-she-quar-hi-qua, should go down to St. Louis, see our American father, and do all they could to have our friend released: by paying for the person killed-thus covering the blood, and satisfying the relations of the man murdered! This being the only means with us of saving a person who had killed another—and we then thought it was the same way with the whites!

The party started with the good wishes of the whole nation—hoping they would accomplish the object of their mission. The relatives of the prisoner blacked their faces, and fasted—hoping the Great Spirit would take pity on them, and return the husband and father to his wife and children.

Quàsh-quà-me and party remained a long time absent. They at length returned, and encamped a short distance below the village—but did not come up that day—nor did any person approach their camp! They appeared to be dressed in fine coats, and had medals! From these circumstances, we were in hopes that they had brought good news. Early the next morning, the Council Lodge was crowded—Quàsh-quà-me and party came up, and gave us the following account of their mission:

"On their arrival at St. Louis, they met their American father, and explained to him their business, and urged the release of their friend. The American chief told them he wanted land—and they had agreed to give him some on the west side of the Mississippi, and some on the Illinois side opposite the Jeffreon. When the business was all arranged, they expected to have their friend released to come home with them. But about the time they were ready to start, their friend was let out of prison, who ran a short distance, and was shot dead! This is all they could recollect of what was said and done. They had been drunk the greater part of the time they were in St. Louis."

This is all myself or nation knew of the treaty of 1804. It has been explained to me since. I find, by that treaty, all our country, east of the Mississippi, and south of the Jeffreon, was ceded to the United States for one thousand dollars a year! I will leave it to the people of the United States to say, whether our nation was properly represented in this treaty? or whether we received a fair compensation for the extent of country ceded by those four individuals? I could say much about this treaty, but I will not, at this time. It has been the origin of all our difficulties.

## DOCUMENT ANALYSIS

1. What event did Black Hawk describe as "the origin of all our difficulties"?

_____

_____

_____

**2.** What were Black Hawk's initial impressions of the first Americans he encountered? Based on this account, could you have predicted his future conflicts with the United States?

_____

_____

_____

## DOCUMENT 9.2
### "A Week in the Mill," *The Lowell Offering,* Vol. V (1845): 217–218

The Lowell Offering *was a monthly literary magazine published (primarily between 1841 and 1845) by women factory workers in the textile mills of Lowell, Massachusetts. For many of the women and girls who worked in the factories, working at Lowell offered an opportunity to earn the highest wages of any women workers in America. Despite their long work hours, the Lowell workers could devote some of their time to attending evening classes and lectures, accessing Lowell's circulating library, or working on the magazine.*

Much has been said of the factory girl and her employment. By some she has been represented as dwelling in a sort of brick-and-mortar paradise, having little to occupy thought save the weaving of gay and romantic fancies, while the spindle or the wheel flies obediently beneath her glance. Others have deemed her a mere servile drudge, chained to her labor by almost as strong a power as that which holds a bondman in his fetters; and, indeed, some have already given her the title of "the white slave of the North." Her real situation approaches neither one nor the other of these extremes. Her occupation is as laborious as that of almost any female who earns her own living, while it has also its sunny spots and its cheerful intervals, which make her hard labor seem comparatively pleasant and easy.

Look at her as she commences her weekly task. The rest of the Sabbath has made her heart and her step light, and she is early at her accustomed place, awaiting the starting of the machinery. Every thing having been cleaned and neatly arranged on the Saturday night, she has less to occupy her on Monday than on other days; and you may see her leaning from the window to watch the glitter of the sunrise on the water, or looking away at the distant forests and fields, while memory wanders to her beloved country home; or, it may be that she is conversing with a sister-laborer near; returning at regular intervals to see that her work is in order.

Soon the breakfast bell rings; in a moment the whirling wheels are stopped, and she hastens to join the throng which is pouring through the open gate. At the table she mingles with a various group. Each dispatches the meal hurriedly, though not often in silence; and if, as is sometimes the case, the rules of politeness are not punctiliously observed by all, the excuse of some lively country girl would be, "They don't give us time for manners."

The short half-hour is soon over; the bell rings again; and now our factory girl feels that she has commenced her day's work in earnest. The time is often apt to drag heavily till the dinner hour arrives. Perhaps some part of the work becomes deranged and stops; the constant friction causes a belt of leather to burst into a flame; a stranger visits the room, and scans the features and dress of its inmates inquiringly; and there is little else to break the monotony. The afternoon passes in much the same manner. Now and then she mingles with a knot of busy talkers who have collected to discuss some new occurrence, or holds pleasant converse with some intelligent and agreeable friend, whose acquaintance she has formed since her factory life commenced; but much of the time she is left to her own thoughts. While at her work, the clattering and rumbling around her prevent any other noise from attracting her attention, and she must think, or her life would be dull indeed.

Thus the day passes on, and evening comes; the time which she feels to be exclusively her own. How much is done in the three short hours from seven to ten o'clock. She has a new dress to finish; a call to make on some distant corporation; a meeting to attend; there is a lecture or a concert at some one of the public halls, and the attendance will be thin if she and her associates are not present; or, if nothing more imperative demands her time, she takes a stroll through the street or to the river with some of her mates, or sits down at home to peruse a new book. At ten o'clock all is still for the night.

The clang of the early bell awakes her to another day, very nearly the counterpart of the one which preceded it. And so the week rolls on, in the same routine, till Saturday comes. Saturday! the welcome sound! She busies herself to remove every particle of cotton and dust from her frame or looms, cheering herself meanwhile with sweet thoughts of the coming Sabbath; and when, at an earlier hour than usual, the mill is stopped, it looks almost beautiful in its neatness.

### DOCUMENT ANALYSIS

**1.** Does this excerpt present an essentially positive or negative portrait of the Lowell factory system? Explain your answer.

_____

_____

_____

**2.** According to the excerpt, what resting period makes the balance of the working week endurable?

_____

_____

_____

**3.** Does the lifestyle of Lowell more clearly benefit the workers or the factory owners?

_____

_____

_____

# DOCUMENT 9.3
## Henry Clay, "Defense of the American System" (1832)

*Senator Henry Clay of Kentucky was the leading proponent of the American System, a series of proposals for the federal government to play a more active role in promoting economic development. These proposals included a national bank, federally financed internal improvements such as roads and canals, and a tariff on imported goods to protect emerging U.S. industries. In the speech excerpted below Clay defends these policies.*

I have now to perform the more pleasing task of exhibiting an imperfect sketch of the existing state of the unparalleled prosperity of the country. On a general survey, we behold cultivation extended, the arts flourishing, the face of the country improved; our people fully and profitably employed, and the public countenance exhibiting tranquility, contentment and happiness. And if we descend into particulars, we have the agreeable contemplation of a people out of debt, land rising slowly in value, but in a secure and salutary degree; a ready though not extravagant market for all the surplus productions of our industry; innumerable flocks and herds browsing and gamboling on ten thousand hills and plains, covered with rich and verdant grasses; our cities expanded, and whole villages springing up, as it were, by enchantment; our exports and imports increased and increasing; our tonnage, foreign and coastwise, swelling and fully occupied; the rivers of our interior animated by the perpetual thunder and lightning of countless steam-boats; the currency sound and abundant; the public debt of two wars nearly redeemed; and, to crown all, the public treasury overflowing, embarrassing Congress, not to find subjects of taxation, but to select the objects which shall be liberated from the impost. If the term of seven years were to be selected, of the greatest prosperity which this people have enjoyed since the establishment of their present constitution, it would be exactly that period of seven years which immediately followed the passage of the tariff of 1824.

This transformation of the condition of the country from gloom and distress to brightness and prosperity, has been mainly the work of American legislation, fostering American industry, instead of allowing it to be controlled by foreign legislation, cherishing foreign industry. The foes of the American System, in 1824, with great boldness and confidence, predicted, 1st. The ruin of the public revenue, and the creation of a necessity to resort to direct taxation. The gentleman from South Carolina, (General Hayne,) I believe, thought that the tariff of 1824 would operate a reduction of revenue to the large amount of eight millions of dollars. 2nd. The destruction of our navigation. 3rd. The desolation of commercial cities. And 4th. The augmentation of the price of objects of consumption, and further decline in that of the articles of our exports. Every prediction which they made has failed—utterly failed. Instead of the ruin of the public revenue, with which they then sought to deter us from the adoption of the American System, we are now threatened with its subversion, by the vast amount of the public revenue produced by that system. . . .

If the system of protection be founded on principles erroneous in theory, pernicious in practice-above all if it be unconstitutional, as is alleged, it ought to be forthwith abolished, and not a vestige of it suffered to remain.

But, before we sanction this sweeping denunciation, let us look a little at this system, its magnitude, its ramifications, its duration, and the high authorities which have sustained it. We shall see that its foes will have accomplished comparatively nothing, after having achieved their present aim of breaking down our iron-foundries, our woolen, cotton, and hemp manufactories, and our sugar plantations. The destruction of these would, undoubtedly, lead to the sacrifice of immense capital, the ruin of many thousands of our fellow citizens, and incalculable loss to the whole community. But their prostration would not disfigure, nor produce greater effect upon the whole system of protection, in all its branches, than the destruction of the beautiful domes upon the capitol would occasion to the magnificent edifice which they surmount. Why, sir, there is scarcely an interest, scarcely a vocation in society, which is not embraced by the beneficence of this system.

It comprehends our coasting tonnage and trade, from which all foreign tonnage is absolutely excluded.

It includes all our foreign tonnage, with the inconsiderable exception made by the treaties of reciprocity with a few foreign powers.

It embraces our fisheries, and all our hardy and enterprising fishermen.

It extends to almost every mechanic and: to tanners, cordwainers, tailors, cabinet-makers, hatters, tinners, brass-workers, clock-makers, coach-makers, tallow-chandlers, trace-makers, rope-makers, cork-cutters, tobacconists, whip-makers, paper-makers, umbrella-makers, glass-blowers, stocking-weavers, butter-makers, saddle and harness-makers, cutlers, brush-makers, book-binders, dairy-men, milk-farmers, black-smiths, type-founders, musical instrument-makers, basket-makers, milliners, potters, chocolate-makers, floor-cloth-makers, bonnet-makers, hair-cloth-makers, copper-smiths, pencil-makers, bellows-makers, pocket book-makers, card-makers, glue-makers, mustard-makers, lumber-sawyers, saw-makers, scale-beam-makers, scythe-makers, wood-saw-makers, and many others. The mechanics enumerated, enjoy a measure of protection adapted to their several conditions, varying from twenty to fifty per cent. The extent and importance of some of these artisans may be estimated by a few particulars. The tanners, curriers, boot and shoe-makers, and other workers in hides, skins and leather, produce an ultimate value per annum of forty millions of dollars; the manufacturers of hats and caps produce an annual value of fifteen millions; the cabinet-makers twelve millions; the manufacturers of bonnets and hats for the female sex, lace, artificial flowers, combs, &c. seven millions; and the manufacturers of glass, five millions.

It extends to all lower Louisiana, the Delta of which might as well be submerged again in the Gulf of Mexico, from which it has been a gradual conquest, as now to be deprived of the protecting duty upon is great staple.

It effects the cotton planter himself, and the tobacco planter, both of whom enjoy protection.

The total amount of the capital vested in sheep, the land to sustain them, wool, woolen manufacturers, and woolen fabrics, and the subsistence of the various persons directly or indirectly employed in the growth and manufacture of the article of wool, is estimated at one hundred and sixty-seven millions of dollars, and the number of persons at one hundred and fifty thousand.

The value of iron, considered as a raw material, and of its manufacturers, is estimated at twenty-six millions of dollars per annum. Cotton goods, exclusive of the capital vested in the manufacture, and of the cost of the raw material, are believed to amount annually, to about twenty millions of dollars.

These estimates have been carefully made, by practical men of undoubted character, who have brought together and embodied their information. Anxious to avoid the charge of exaggeration, they have sometimes placed their estimates below what was believed to be the actual amount of these interests. With regard to the quantity of bar and other iron annually produced, it is derived from the known works themselves; and I know some in western States which they have omitted in their calculations. . . .

When gentlemen have succeeded in their design of an immediate or gradual destruction of the American System, what is their substitute? Free trade? Free trade! The call for free trade is as unavailing as the cry of a spoiled child, in its nurse's arms, for the moon, or the stars that glitter in the firmament of heaven. It never has existed, it never will exist. Trade implies, at least two parties. To be free, it should be fair, equal and reciprocal. But if we throw our ports wide open to the admission of foreign productions, free of all duty, what ports of any other foreign nation shall we find open to the free admission of our surplus produce? We may break down all barriers to free trade on our part, but the work will not be complete until foreign powers shall have removed theirs. There would be freedom on one side, and restrictions, prohibitions and exclusions on the other. The bolts, and the bars, and the chains of all other nations will remain undisturbed. It is, indeed, possible, that our industry and commerce would accommodate themselves to this unequal and unjust, state of things; for, such is the flexibility of our nature, that it bends itself to all circumstances. The wretched prisoner incarcerated in a jail, after a long time becomes reconciled to his solitude, and regularly notches down the passing days of his confinement.

Gentlemen deceive themselves. It is not free trade that they are recommending to our acceptance. It is in effect, the British colonial system that we are invited to adopt; and, if their policy prevail, it will lead substantially to the re-colonization of these States, under the commercial dominion of Great Britain. . . .

Gentlemen are greatly deceived as to the hold which this system has in the affections of the people of the United States. They represent that it is the policy of New England, and that she is most benefited by it. If there be any part of this Union which has been most steady, most unanimous, and most determined in its support, it is Pennsylvania. Why is not that powerful State attacked? Why pass her over, and aim the blow at New England? New England came reluctantly into the policy. In 1824 a majority of her delegation was opposed to it. From the largest State of New England there was but a solitary vote in favor of the bill. That enterprising people can readily accommodate their industry to any policy, provided it be settled. They supposed this was fixed, and they submitted to the decrees of government. And the progress of public opinion has kept pace with the developments of the benefits of the system. Now, all New England, at least in this house (with the exception of one small still voice) is in favor of the system. In 1824 all Maryland was against it; now the majority is for it. Then, Louisiana, with one exception, was opposed to it; now, without any exception, she is in favor of it. The march of public sentiment is to the South. Virginia will be the next convert; and in less than seven years, if there be no obstacles from political causes, or prejudices industriously instilled, the majority of eastern Virginia will be, as the majority of western Virginia now is, in favor of the American System. North Carolina will follow later, but not less certainly. Eastern Tennessee is now in favor of the system. And finally, its doctrines will pervade the whole Union, and the wonder will be, that they ever should have been opposed.

## DOCUMENT ANALYSIS

1. To which policies does Clay attribute "this transformation of the condition of the country from gloom and distress to brightness and prosperity"?

_____

_____

_____

2. Is Clay optimistic about the future of the American System?

_____

_____

_____

## DOCUMENT 10.1
### Female Industry Association, from the *New York Herald* (1825)

*In 1825, female craft workers in the needle trades—shirt sewers, tailors, dressmakers, and so on—in New York formed the Female Industry Association, also known as the Ladies Industrial Association. Women had traditionally been excluded from male trade unions. Therefore, when female workers sought to protest wage cuts in the industry, they formed their own organization. The association lasted only 20 years, dissolving following an unsuccessful strike in 1845. Nevertheless, it provided an example for future women's unions. The excerpt below describes one of its first meetings.*

Seldom or never did the Superior Court of the City Hall contain such an array of beauty under suffering, together with common sense and good order, as it did yesterday, on the occasion of the meeting of the female industrial classes, in their endeavors to remedy the wrongs and oppressions under which they labor, and, for some time past, have labored. At the hour appointed for the adjourned meeting, four o'clock, about 700 females, generally of the most interesting age and appearance, were assembled; and, after a trifling delay, a young lady stepped forward, and in rather a low, diffident tone, moved that Miss Gray take the Chair, which, having been put and carried in the usual business-like way Miss Gray (a young woman, neatly dressed, of some 22 or 24 years of age, fair complexion, interesting, thoughtful and intelligent cast of countenance) came forward from the back part of the room.

She proceeded to make a few observations on the nature and objects of their movements and intentions, and stated that, finding the class she belonged to were unable to support themselves, honestly and respectably, by their industry, under the present prices they received for their work, had, therefore, come to the determination of endeavoring to obtain something better, by appealing to the public at large, and showing the amount of sufferings under which they at present labored. She then went on to give instances of what wages they were in the habit of receiving in different branches of the business in which she was engaged, and mentioned several employers by name who only paid them from $.10 to $.18 per day; others, who were proficient in the business, after 12 or 14 hours hard labor, could only get about $.25 per day; one employer offered them $.20 per day, and said that if they did not take it, he would obtain girls from Connecticut who would work for less even than what he offered. The only employer who had done them justice was Mr. Beck, of Fourteenth street, who only allowed his girls to be out about two hours, when he complied with their reasonable demands. He was a man who was worthy of the thanks of every girl present, and they wished him health, wealth, and happiness. How was it possible that on such an income they could support themselves decently and honestly, let alone supporting widowed mothers, and some two, three, or four helpless brothers and sisters, which many of them had. Pieces of work for which they last year got seven shillings, this year they could only get three shillings.

A female stepped forward . . . and enquired if the association was confined to any one branch of business, or was it open to all who were suffering under like privations and injustice? The Chairwoman observed that it was opened to all who were alike oppressed, and it was only by a firm cooperation they could accomplish what they were laboring for. Another female of equally interesting appearance (Mrs. Storms) then came forward and said that it was necessary the nature and objects of the

party should be distinctly understood, particularly by those who were immediately interested; their own position should be fully known. If the supply of labor in the market was greater than the demand, it followed as a matter of course that they could not control the prices; and, therefore, it would be well for those present to look around them and see into what other channels they could turn their industry with advantage. There were many branches of business in which men were employed that they could as well fill. Let them memorialize the merchants in the dry goods department, for instance, and show them this also. That there were hundreds of females in this city who were able to keep the books as well as any man in it. There were various other branches of business in which men were employed for which females alone were suitable and intended. Let these men go to the fields and seek their livelihood as men ought to do, and leave the females their legitimate employment. There were the drapers also, and a number of other branches of trade in which females could be as well if not better and more properly employed. By these means, some thousands would be afforded employment in branches much more valuable to themselves and the community generally. She then proceeded to recommend those present to be moderate in their demands, and not to ask for more than the circumstances of trade would warrant, for if they acted otherwise, it would tend to their more ultimate ruin. Under present circumstances, a very few years broke down their constitutions, and they had no other resource but the alms-house, and what could bring this about sooner than the bread and water diet and rough shelter, which many of them at present were obliged to put up with.

The proceedings of the previous meeting were then read and approved of. A number of delegates from the following trades entered their names to act as a Committee to regulate future proceedings: tailoresses, plain and coarse sewing, shirt makers, book-folders and stitchers, cap makers, straw workers, dress makers, crimpers, fringe and lace makers, &c.

The following preamble and resolutions were agreed to: Whereas, the young women attached to the different trades in the city of New York, having toiled a long time for a remuneration totally inadequate for the maintenance of life, and feeling the truth of the Gospel assertion, that "the laborer is worthy of his hire," have determined to take upon themselves the task of asserting their rights against unjust and mercenary employers. It must be remembered by those to whom we address ourselves, that our object is not extortion; our desire, not to reap advantages which will be denied to our employers. The boon we ask is founded upon right, alone! The high prices demanded by tradesmen for their goods renders them amply able to advance wages to a standard, which, while it obviates the present cause of complaint, will render laborers only the more cheerful at their work, and still more earnest and willing to serve their employers. The scarcity of employment, and the low rates of pay which have so long prevailed, have, undoubtedly driven many virtuous females to courses which might, otherwise, have been avoided. Many of the female operatives of this city have families dependent upon their exertions; aged fathers and mothers—young brothers—helpless sisters, who, but for their exertions, must inevitably starve, or betake themselves to that scarcely less horrible alternative: the poor house! Such a picture is enough to bestir the most inert to active exertion; the love of life is a passion inherent in us all, and we feel persuaded that we need no better excuse for the movement to which the glaring injustice of our employers has driven us!

## DOCUMENT ANALYSIS

1. Do you think the reporter would have remarked upon the "countenances" of male workers at a union meeting? What is the significance of this reference?

_____

_____

_____

**2.** What were the women's demands?

_____

_____

**3.** How and why did these women think a union would help them meet their demands?

_____

_____

_____

## DOCUMENT 10.2
### Ralph Waldo Emerson, "The Concord Hymn" (1837)

_The great resurgence of national pride that characterized Jackson's rise to the presidency touched every aspect of American life. One of the most evident manifestations of this national pride came in the form of a renewed interest in commemorating the accomplishments of the nation's forefathers, who liberated the nation and provided for the prosperity at the time. "The Concord Hymn" by Ralph Waldo Emerson is an excellent example of the nationalistic pride felt by many Americans in the early nineteenth century. Emerson describes in great detail the sacrifices made by the men who fought at Concord, a great testament to the strength and will of the American nation._

By the rude bridge that arched the flood,
Their flag to April's breeze unfurled,
Here once the embattled farmers stood,
And fired the shot heard round the world.

The foe long since in silence slept;
Alike the conqueror silent sleeps;
And Time the ruined bridge has swept
Down the dark stream which seaward creeps.

On this green bank, by this soft stream,
We set to-day a votive stone;
That memory may their deed redeem,
When, like our sires, our sons are gone.

Spirit, that made those heroes dare
To die, or leave their children free,
Bid Time and Nature gently spare
The shaft we raise to them and thee.

### DOCUMENT ANALYSIS

**1.** How do you think this poem was received by the American people? Would Americans from every part of the country have appreciated it for the same reasons? Why or why not?

_____

_____

_____

**2.** Why did Emerson describe the battle of Concord as "the shot heard round the world"?

_____

_____

_____

DOCUMENT 11.1

### Slave Narrative, "The History of Mary Prince, A West Indian Slave, Related by Herself" (1831)

From *Six Women's Slave Narratives,* The Schomburg Library of Nineteenth-Century Black Women Writers
(New York: Oxford U. Press, 1988), pp. 34–38.

*The story of Mary Prince's survival of her brutal life as a slave was first published in London in 1831 under the title given above. Born into slavery in Bermuda, Prince was sold several times, and in 1828 her owner took her to England. Dictated by Prince to a third party, her story met the same fate as many other slave narratives in the United States and abroad. These stories were obviously very useful to the abolitionist movement, which was strong in Britain in the 1830s, and there is persuasive evidence that they were edited for content. For example, Prince's narrative contains no references to sexual brutality or indeed to sexuality at all, although such brutality undoubtedly was part of her story. It is uncertain whether Prince or the editor of her story excluded such references. Nevertheless, their omission does not diminish the value of her account of West Indian slavery.* [NOTE: Slavery was abolished in the British Empire in 1833. St. Anthony's fire, referenced below, is another name for ergotism, a disease which results from ingesting toxic amounts of a fungus that grows on rye. Symptoms include burning in the extremities, gangrene, and possibly death. St. Anthony is the patron saint of the disease's victims.]

. . . I was several years the slave of Mr. D— after I returned to my native place. Here I worked in the grounds. My work was planting and hoeing sweet-potatoes, Indian corn, plantains, bananas, cabbages, pumpkins, onions, &c. I did all the household work, and attended upon a horse and cow besides,—going also upon all errands. I had to curry the horse—to clean and feed him—and sometimes to ride him a little. I had more than enough to do—but still it was not so very bad as Turk's Island.

My old master often got drunk, and then he would get in a fury with his daughter, and beat her till she was not fit to be seen. I remember on one occasion, I had gone to fetch water, and when I was coming up the hill I heard a great screaming; I ran as fast as I could to the house, put down the water, and went into the chamber, where I found my master beating Miss D— dreadfully. I strove with all my strength to get her away from him; for she was all black and blue with bruises. He had beat her with his fist, and almost killed her. The people gave me credit for getting her away. He turned round and began to lick me. Then I said, "Sir, this is not Turk's Island." I can't repeat his answer, the words were too wicked—too bad to say. He wanted to treat me the same in Bermuda as he had done in Turk's Island.

He had an ugly fashion of stripping himself quite naked, and ordering me then to wash him in a tub of water. This was worse to me than all the licks. Sometimes when he called me to wash him I would not come, my eyes were so full of shame. He would then come to beat me. One time I had plates and knives in my hand, and I dropped both plates and knives, and some of the plates were broken. He struck me so severely for this, that at last I defended myself, for I thought it was high time to do so. I then told him I would not live longer with him, for he was a very indecent man—very spiteful, and too indecent; with no shame for his servants, no shame for his own flesh. So I went away to a neighboring house and sat down and cried till the next morning, when I went home again, not knowing what else to do.

After that I was hired to work at Cedar Hills, and every Saturday night I paid the money to my master. I had plenty of work to do there—plenty of washing; but yet I made myself pretty comfortable. I earned two dollars and a quarter a week, which is twenty pence a day.

During the time I worked there, I heard that Mr. John Wood was going to Antigua. I felt a great wish to go there, and I went to Mr. D—, and asked him to let me go in Mr. Wood's service. Mr. Wood did not then want to purchase me; it was my own fault that I came under him, I was so anxious to go. It was ordained to be, I suppose; God led me there. The truth is, I did not wish to be any longer the slave of my indecent master.

Mr. Wood took me with him to Antigua, to the town of St. John's, where he lived. This was about fifteen years ago. He did not then know whether I was to be sold; but Mrs. Wood found that I could work, and she wanted to buy me. Her husband then wrote to my master to inquire whether I was to be sold? Mr. D— wrote in reply, "that I should not be sold to any one that would treat me ill." It was strange he should say this, when he had treated me so ill himself. So I was purchased by Mr. Wood for 300 dollars, (or £100 Bermuda currency.)

My work there was to attend the chambers and nurse the child, and to go down to the pond and wash clothes. But I soon fell ill of the rheumatism, and grew so very lame that I was forced to walk with a stick. I got the Saint Anthony's fire, also, in my left leg, and became quite a cripple. No one cared much to come near me, and I was ill a long long time; for several months I could not lift the limb. I had to lie in a little old out-house, that was swarming with bugs and other vermin, which tormented me greatly; but I had no other place to lie in. I got the rheumatism by catching cold at the pond side, from washing in the fresh water; in the salt water I never got cold. The person who lived in next yard, (a Mrs. Greene,) could not bear to hear my cries and groans. She was kind, and used to send an old slave woman to help me, who sometimes brought me a little soup. When the doctor found I was so ill, he said I must be put into a bath of hot water. The old slave got the bark of some bush that was good for the pains, which she boiled in the hot water, and every night she came and put me into the bath, and did what she could for me: I don't know what I should have done, or what would have become of me, had it not been for her.—My mistress, it is true, did send me a little food; but no one from our family came near me but the cook, who used to shove my food in at the door, and say, "Molly, Molly, there's your dinner." My mistress did not care to take any trouble about me; and if the Lord had not put it into the hearts of the neighbors to be kind to me, I must, I really think, have lain and died. . . .

. . . Some time after I began to attend the Moravian Church, I met with Daniel James, afterwards my dear husband. He was a carpenter and cooper to his trade; an honest, hard-working, decent black man, and a widower. He had purchased his freedom of his mistress, old Mrs. Baker, with money he had earned whilst a slave. When he asked me to marry him, I took time to consider the matter over with myself, and would not say yes till he went to church with me and joined the Moravians. He was very industrious after he bought his freedom; and he had hired a comfortable house, and had convenient things about him. We were joined in marriage, about Christmas 1826, in the Moravian Chapel at Spring Gardens, by the Rev. Mr. Olufsen. We could not be married in the English Church. English marriage is not allowed to slaves; and no free man can marry a slave woman.

When Mr. Wood heard of my marriage, he flew into a great rage, and sent for Daniel, who was helping to build a house for his old mistress. Mr. Wood asked him who gave him a right to marry a slave of his? My husband said, "Sir, I am a free man, and thought I had a right to choose a wife; but if I had known Molly was not allowed to have a husband, I should not have asked her to marry me." Mrs. Wood was more vexed about my marriage than her husband. She could not forgive me for getting married, but stirred up Mr. Wood to flog me dreadfully with the horsewhip. I thought it very hard to be whipped at my time of life for getting a husband—I told her so. She said that she would not have nigger men about the yards and premises, or allow a nigger man's clothes to be washed in the same tub where hers were washed. She was fearful, I think, that I should lose her time, in order to wash and do things for my husband: but I had then no time to wash for myself; I was obliged to put out my own clothes, though I was always at the wash-tub.

I had not much happiness in my marriage, owing to my being a slave. It made my husband sad to see me so ill-treated. Mrs. Wood was always abusing me about him. She did not lick me herself, but she got her husband to do it for her, whilst she fretted the flesh off my bones. Yet for all this she would not sell me. She sold five slaves whilst I was with her; but though she was always finding fault with me, she would not part with me. However, Mr. Wood afterwards allowed Daniel to have a place to live in our yard, which we were very thankful for.

After this, I fell ill again with the rheumatism, and was sick a long time; but whether sick or well, I had my work to do. About this time I asked my master and mistress to let me buy my own freedom. With the help of Mr. Burchell, I could have found the means to pay Mr. Wood; for it was agreed that I should afterwards serve Mr. Burchell a while, for the cash he was to advance for me. I was earnest in the request to my owners; but their hearts were hard—too hard to consent. Mrs. Wood was very angry—she grew quite outrageous—she called me a black devil, and asked me who had put freedom into my head. "To be free is very sweet," I said: but she took good care to keep me a slave. I saw her change color, and I left the room. . . .

## DOCUMENT ANALYSIS

1. Having purchased Prince as a slave, why did her owners not take better care of her while she was ill? Wouldn't it have made economic sense to do so?

_____

_____

_____

2. Why did Prince insist on marrying in the Moravian church? Why were her owners so upset by her marriage?

_____

_____

_____

3. Was it acceptable to exclude details about Prince's life, such as sexual abuse, that might have offended readers in 1831? Would including these details most likely have furthered or hindered the abolitionist cause?

_____

_____

_____

## DOCUMENT 12.1
## National Convention of Colored People, Report on Abolition (1847)

*The National Convention of Colored People's Committee on Abolition included many runaway slaves who had become abolitionists, such as Frederick Douglass. Douglass and other African Americans advocated reform both on their own and through participation in organizations led by whites such as William Lloyd Garrison.*

The Committee appointed to draft a Report respecting the best means of abolishing Slavery and destroying Caste in the United States, beg leave most respectfully to Report: That they have had the important subjects referred to them, under consideration, and have carefully endeavored to examine all their points and bearings to the best of their ability; and from every view they have been able to take they have arrived at the conclusion that the best means of abolishing slavery is proclamation of truth, and that the best means of destroying caste is the mental, moral and industrial improvement of our people.

First, as respects Slavery, Your Committee find this monstrous crime, this stupendous iniquity, closely interwoven with all the great interests, institutions and organizations of the country; pervading and influencing every class and grade of society, securing their support, obtaining their approbation, and commanding their homage. Availing itself of the advantage which age gives to crime, it has perverted the judgment, blunted the moral sense, blasted the sympathies, and created in the great mass,—the overwhelming majority of the people—a moral sentiment altogether favorable to its own character, and its own continuance. Press and pulpit are alike prostituted and made to serve the end of this infernal institution. The power of the government, and the sanctity of religion, church and state, are joined with the guilty oppressor against the oppressed-and the voice of this great nation is thundering in the ear of our enslaved fellow countrymen the terrible fiat, you shall be slaves or die!

The slave is in the minority, a small minority. The oppressors are an overwhelming majority. The oppressed are three millions, their oppressors are seventeen millions. The one is weak, the other is strong; the one is without arms, without means of concert, and without government; the other possess every advantage in these respects; and the deadly aim of their million of musketry, and loud-mouthed cannon tells the downtrodden slave in unmistakable language, he must be a slave or die.

In these circumstances, your committee are called upon to report as to the best means of abolishing slavery. And without pretending parties and factions, though did time permit, they would gladly do so, they beg at once to state their entire disapprobation of any plan of emancipation involving a resort to bloodshed. With the facts of our condition before us, it is impossible for us to contemplate any appeal to the slave to take vengeance on his guilty master, but with the utmost reprobation. Your Committee regards any counsel of this sort as the perfection of folly, suicidal in the extreme, and abominably wicked. We should utterly frown down and wholly discountenance any attempt to lead our people to confide in brute force as a reformatory instrumentality. All argument put forth in favor of insurrection and bloodshed, however well intended, is either the result of an unpardonable impatience or an atheistic want of faith in the power of truth as a means of regenerating and reforming the world.

Again we repeat, let us set our faces against all such absurd, unavailing, dangerous and mischievous ravings, emanating from what source they may. The voice of God and of common sense, equally point out a more excellent way, and that way is a faithful, earnest, and persevering enforcement of the great principles of justice and morality, religion and humanity. These are the only invincible and infallible means within our reach with which to overthrow this foul system of blood and ruin. Your Committee deem it susceptible of the clearest demonstration, that slavery exists in this country, because the people of this country WILL its existence. And they deem it equally clear, that no system or institution can exist for an hour against the earnestly-expressed WILL of the people. It were quite easy to bring to the support of the foregoing proposition powerful and conclusive illustrations from the history of reform in all ages, and especially in our own. But the palpable truths of the propositions, as well as the familiarity of the facts illustrating them, entirely obviate such a necessity.

Our age is an age of great discoveries; and one of the greatest is that which revealed that this world is to be ruled, shaped and guided by the marvelous might of mind. The human voice must supersede the roar of cannon. Truth alone is the legitimate antidote of falsehood. Liberty is always sufficient to grapple with tyranny. Free speech—free discussion—peaceful agitation, the foolishness of preaching these, under God, will subvert this giant crime, and send it reeling to its grave, as if smitten by a voice from the throne of God. Slavery exists because it is popular. It will cease to exist when it is made unpopular. Whatever therefore tends to make Slavery unpopular tends to its destruction. This every Slaveholder knows full well, and hence his opposition to all discussion of the subject. It is an evidence of intense feeling of alarm, when John C. Calhoun calls upon the North to put down what he is pleased to term "this plundering agitation." Let us give the Slaveholder what he most dislikes.

Let us expose his crimes and his foul abominations. He is reputable and must be made disreputable. He must be regarded as a moral leper—slummed as a loathsome wretch-outlawed from Christian communion, and from social respectability—an enemy of God and man, to be execrated by the community till he shall repent of his foul crimes, and give proof of his sincerity by breaking every chain and letting the oppressed go free. Let us invoke the Press and appeal to the pulpit to deal out the righteous denunciations of heaven against oppression, fraud and wrong, and the desire of our hearts will soon be given us in the triumph of Liberty throughout all the land. . .

## DOCUMENT ANALYSIS

1. What are the principal ways the committee believed abolitionists could resist and overcome slavery? What means should be avoided? Why?

_____

_____

_____

2. How successful do you think the committee's strategy to abolish slavery would have been if the Civil War had not intervened?

_____

_____

_____

## DOCUMENT 12.2
## Mathew Carey, "Rules for Husbands and Wives" (1830)

*Irish-born Mathew Carey eventually settled in Philadelphia, where he became a publisher, bookseller, and economist, with a special fondness for universal education. His* Miscellaneous Essays *included the excerpt below, which outlined what he believed to be proper behavior between married persons. The United States was changing in the early 1830s, as recorded by Alexis de Tocqueville in* Democracy in America. *This period was marked by economic growth, westward expansion, expanding international and domestic markets, and scientific progress. The anti-slavery movement was gaining momentum, and from within that movement would emerge the women's rights movement. Carey's essay is an early reconsideration of proper gender roles in American society.*

Having seen various sets of maxims for the conduct of married life, which have appeared to me to contain some very injudicious items, degrading to wives, sinking them below the rank they ought to occupy, and reducing them in some degree to the level of mere housekeepers, and believing them radically erroneous, I annex a set which appear more rational and just than most of those which I have seen:

1. A good husband will always regard his wife as his equal; treat her with kindness, respect and attention; and never address her with an air of authority, as if she were, as some husbands appear to regard their wives, a mere housekeeper.
2. He will never interfere in her domestic concerns, hiring servants, &c.
3. He will always keep her liberally supplied with money for furnishing his table in a style proportioned to his means, and for the purchase of dress suitable to her station in life.
4. He will cheerfully and promptly comply with all her reasonable requests, when it can be done, without loss, or great inconvenience.
5. He will never allow himself to lose his temper towards her, by indifferent cookery, or irregularity in the hours of meals, or any other mismanagement of her servants, knowing the difficulty of making them do their duty.
6. If she have prudence and good sense, he will consult her on all great operations, involving the risk of ruin, or serious injury in case of failure. Many a man has been rescued from destruction by the wise counsels of his wife. Many a foolish husband has most seriously injured himself and family by the rejection of the advice of his wife, fearing, lest, if he followed it, he would be regarded as ruled by her! A husband can never procure a counselor more deeply interested in his welfare than his wife.
7. If distressed, or embarrassed in his circumstances, he will communicate his situation to her with candor, that she may bear his difficulties in mind, in her expenditures. Women sometimes, believing their husband's circumstances to be far better than they really are, expend money which cannot well be afforded, and which, if they knew their real situation, they would shrink from expending.

1. A good wife will always receive her husband with smiles,—leave nothing undone to render home agreeable—and gratefully reciprocate his kindness and attention.
2. She will study to discover means to gratify his inclinations, in regard to food and cookery; in the management of her family; in her dress, manners and deportment.
3. She will never attempt to rule, or appear to rule her husband. Such conduct degrades husbands—and wives always partake largely of the degradation of their husbands.
4. She will, in every thing reasonable, comply with his wishes—and, as far as possible, anticipate them.
5. She will avoid all altercations or arguments leading to ill-humor—and more especially before company.
6. She will never attempt to interfere in his business, unless he ask her advice or counsel, and will never attempt to control him in the management of it.

Should differences arise between husband and wife, the contest ought to be, not who will display the most spirit, but who will make the first advances. There is scarcely a more prolific source of unhappiness in the married state, than this "spirit," the legitimate offspring of pride and want of feeling.

Perhaps the whole art of happiness in the married state, might be compressed into these two maxims—"Bear and forbear"—and "let the husband treat his wife, and the wife treat her husband with as much respect and attention, as he would a strange lady, and she a strange gentleman." And surely this is not an extravagant requisition.

## DOCUMENT ANALYSIS

1. Would any aspects of this essay have been considered radical in 1830? If so, then which ones?

_____

_____

_____

2. Why did Carey feel he is qualified to write such an essay? Upon what did he base his authority?

_____

_____

_____

3. In what ways did Carey's maxims challenge traditional gender roles, and in what ways did they reinforce them?

_____

_____

_____

## DOCUMENT 13.1
### Levi Coffin, Reminiscences of the Underground Railroad in the 1850s

*Levi Coffin and his wife, Catherine, are remembered for their tireless work in assisting slaves to reach the safety of Canada via the Underground Railroad, a series of safe havens between the South and Montreal. Though originally from North Carolina, the Coffins were Quakers who adamantly opposed slavery. After moving to Indiana, they began working with the Underground Railroad in 1826. They continued their efforts after moving to Cincinnati in the 1840s. Eventually they helped more than 3,000 slaves to escape the South. Levi and Catherine were ostensibly the models for the characters Simeon and Rachel Halliday in Harriet Beecher Stowe's classic novel, Uncle Tom's Cabin. Levi's memoirs were published in 1876.*

I was personally acquainted with all the active and reliable workers on the Underground Railroad in the city, both colored and white. There were a few wise and careful managers among the colored people, but it was not safe to trust all of them with the affairs of our work. Most of them were too careless, and a few were unworthy—they could be bribed by the slave hunters to betray the hiding places of the fugitives. We soon found it to be the best policy to confine our affairs to a few persons and to let the whereabouts of the slaves be known to as few people as possible.

When slave hunters were prowling around the city we found it necessary to use every precaution. We were soon fully initiated into the management of Underground Railroad matters in Cincinnati, and did not lack for work. Our willingness to aid the slaves was soon known, and hardly a fugitive came to the city without applying to us for assistance. There seemed to be a continual increase of runaways, and such was the vigilance of the pursuers that I was obliged to devote a large share of time from my business to making arrangements for their concealment and safe conveyance of the fugitives.

They sometimes came to our door frightened and panting and in a destitute condition, having fled in such haste and fear that they had no time to bring any clothing except what they had on, and that was often very scant. The expense of providing suitable clothing for them when it was necessary for them to go on immediately, or of feeding them when they were obliged to be concealed for days or weeks, was very heavy. . . .

Our house was large and well adapted for secreting fugitives. Very often slaves would lie concealed in upper chambers for weeks without the boarders or frequent visitors at the house knowing anything about it. My wife had a quiet unconcerned way of going about her work as if nothing unusual was on hand, which was calculated to lull every suspicion of those who might be watching, and who would have been at once aroused by any sign of secrecy or mystery. Even the intimate friends of the family did not know when there were slaves hidden in the house. . . .

The fugitives generally arrived in the night and were secreted among the friendly colored people or hidden in the upper room of our house. They came alone or in companies, and in a few instances had a white guide to direct them. . . .

### DOCUMENT ANALYSIS

1. According to Coffin, what precautions or tactics did the Coffins employ to conceal fugitive slaves?

_____

_____

_____

2. Why did Coffin feel that he and his wife were successful conductors on the Underground Railroad?

_____

_____

_____

3. How did Coffin describe the plight of the fugitive slaves who fled to Cincinnati?

_____

_____

_____

## DOCUMENT 13.2
### Horace Greeley, "An Overland Journey" (1860)

*Horace Greeley was the editor of the* New York Tribune *from 1841 to 1872. An outspoken reformer, Greeley championed such causes as temperance, public education, and abolition. Greeley is also associated with the westward migration of the nineteenth century and in this document argues in favor of a railroad connecting the Atlantic and Pacific coasts. The first transcontinental railroad was completed on May 10, 1869.*

The social, moral, and intellectual blessings of a Pacific railroad can hardly be glanced at within the limits of an article. Suffice it for the present that I merely suggest them.

1. Our mails are now carried to and from California by steamships, via Panama, in twenty to thirty days, starting once a fortnight. The average time of transit from writers throughout the Atlantic states to their correspondents on the Pacific exceeds thirty days. With a Pacific railroad, this would be reduced to ten; for the letters written in Illinois or Michigan would reach their destinations in the mining counties of California quicker than letters sent from New York or Philadelphia would reach San Francisco. With a daily mail by railroad from each of our Atlantic cities to and from California, it is hardly possible that the amount of both letters and printed matter transmitted, and consequently of postage, should not be speedily quadrupled.

2. The first need of California today is a large influx of intelligent, capable, virtuous women. With a railroad to the Pacific, avoiding the miseries and perils of six thousand miles of ocean transportation, and making the transit a pleasant and interesting overland journey of ten days, at a reduced cost, the migration of this class would be immensely accelerated

and increased. With wages for all kinds of women's work at least thrice as high on the Pacific as in this quarter, and with larger opportunities for honorable and fit settlement in life, I cannot doubt that tens of thousands would annually cross the Plains, to the signal benefit of California and of the whole country, as well as the improvement of their own fortunes and the profit of the railroad.

3. Thousands now staying in California, expecting to "go home" so soon as they shall have somewhat improved their circumstances, would send or come for their families and settle on the Pacific for life, if a railroad were opened. Tens of thousands who have been to California and come back, unwilling either to live away from their families or to expose them to the present hardships of migration thither, would return with all they have, prepared to spend their remaining days in the land of gold, if there were a Pacific railroad.

4. Education is the vital want of California, second to its need of true women. School-books, and all the material of education, are now scarce and dear there. Almost all books sell there twice as high as here, and many of the best are scarcely attainable at any rate. With the Pacific railroad, all this would be changed for the better. The proportion of school-houses to grogshops would rapidly increase. All the elements of moral and religious melioration would be multiplied. Tens of thousands of our best citizens would visit the Pacific coast, receiving novel ideas and impressions, to their own profit and that of the people thus visited. Civilization, intelligence, refinement, on both sides of the mountain-still more, in the Great Basin enclosed by them—would receive a new and immense impulse, and the Union would acquire a greater accession of strength, power, endurance, and true glory, than it would from the acquisition of the whole continent down to Cape Horn.

The only points of view in which a railroad from the Missouri to the Pacific remains to be considered are those of its practicability, cost, location, and the ways and means. Let us look at them:

As to practicability, there is no room for hesitation or doubt. The Massachusetts Western, the Erie, the Pennsylvania, and the Baltimore and Ohio, have each encountered difficulties as formidable as any to be overcome by a Pacific railroad this side of the Sierra Nevada. Were the railroad simply to follow the principal emigrant trail up the Platte and down the Snake and Columbia to Oregon, or south-westwardly from the South Pass to the foot of the Sierra, it would encounter no serious obstacle. . . .

But let that government simply resolve that the Pacific road shall be built—let Congress enact that sealed proposals for its construction shall be invited, and that whichever responsible company or corporation shall offer adequate security for that construction, to be completed within ten years, on the lowest terms, shall have public aid, provided the amount required do not exceed fifty millions of dollars, and the work will be done, certainly for fifty millions' bonus, probably for much less. The government on its part should concede to the company a mile in width, according to the section lines, of the public lands on either side of the road as built, with the right to take timber, stone and earth from any public lands without charge; and should require of said company that it carry a daily through-mail each way at the price paid other roads for conveying mails on first-class routes; and should moreover stipulate for the conveyance at all times of troops, arms, munitions, provisions, etc., for the public service, at the lowest rates, with a right to the exclusive possession and use of the road whenever a national exigency shall seem to require it. The government should leave the choice of route entirely to the company, only stipulating that it shall connect the navigable waters of the Mississippi with those of the Pacific Ocean, and that it shall be constructed wholly through our own territory. . . .

By adopting this plan, the rivalries of routes will be made to work for, instead of working against, the construction of the road. Strenuous efforts will be made by the friends of each to put themselves in position to bid low enough to secure the location; and the lowest rate at which the work can safely be undertaken will unquestionably be bid. The road will be the property of the company constructing it, subject only to the rights of use, stipulated and paid for by the government. And, even were it to cost the latter a bonus of fully fifty millions, I feel certain that every farthing of that large sum will have been reimbursed to the treasury within five years after the completion of the work in the proceeds of land sales, in increased postages, and in duties on goods imported, sold, and consumed because of this railroad—not to speak of the annual saving of millions in the cost of transporting and supplying troops.

Men and brethren! let us resolve to have a railroad to the Pacific—to have it soon. It will add more to the strength and wealth of our country than would the acquisition of a dozen Cubas. It will prove a bond of union not easily broken, and a new spring to our national industry, prosperity and wealth. It will call new manufactures into existence, and increase the demand for the products of those already existing. It will open new vistas to national and to individual aspiration, and crush out filibusterism by giving a new and wholesome direction to the public mind. My long, fatiguing journey was undertaken in the hope that I might do something toward the early construction of the Pacific Railroad; and I trust that it has not been made wholly in vain.

## DOCUMENT ANALYSIS

1. What were Greeley's major arguments in support of constructing a Pacific railroad?

_____

_____

_____

2. Greeley asserted that constructing a Pacific railroad would contribute more to the nation's prosperity "than would the acquisition of a dozen Cubas." What is the significance of this observation, especially considering the year in which Greeley composed this piece?

_____

_____

_____

## DOCUMENT 14.1
### Frederick Douglass, Independence Day Speech (1852)

*After escaping slavery, Frederick Douglass fought for African Americans with all the powers of his intellect. He was an excellent writer and speaker whose texts did much to shape northern thinking on abolitionism. By the 1850s, particularly after the passage of the strengthened Fugitive Slave Act, Douglass and other abolitionists increasingly despaired of ever seeing the end of slavery. In this speech, Douglass gave a voice to some of that desperation.*

Fellow citizens above your national, tumultuous joy, I hear the mournful wail of millions! whose chains, heave and grievous yesterday, are, today, rendered more intolerable by the jubilee shouts that reach them. If I do forget, if I do not faithfully remember those bleeding children of sorrow this day, "may my right hand forger her cunning, and may my tongue cleave to the roof of my mouth"! To forget them, to pass lightly over their wrongs, and to chime in with the popular theme would be treason most scandalous and shocking, and would make me a reproach before God and the world. My subject, them, fellow citizens, is American Slavery.

. . . I do not hesitate to declare with all my soul that the character and conduct of this nation never looked blacker to me than on this Fourth of July! Whether we turn to the declarations of the past or to the professions of the present, the conduct of the nation seems equally hideous and revolting. America is false to the past, false to the present, and solemnly binds herself to be false to the future. Standing with God and the crushed and bleeding slave on this occasion, I will, in the name of humanity which is outraged, in the name of liberty which is fettered, in the name of the Constitution and the Bible which are disregarded and trampled upon, All the emphasis I can command, everything that serves to perpetuate slavery the great sin and shame of America! "I will not equivocate, I will not excuse"; I will use the severest of language I can command; and yet not one word shall escape that any man, whose judgment is not blinded by prejudice, or who is not at heart a slaveholder, shall not confess to be right and just.

. . . Must I undertake to prove that the slave is a man? That point is conceded already. Nobody doubts it. The slaveholders themselves acknowledge it the enactment of laws for their government. They acknowledge it when they punish disobedience on the part of the slave. There are seventy-two crimes in the state of Virginia which, if committed by a black man (no matter how ignorant he be), subject him to the punishment of death, while only two of the same crimes will subject a white man to the like punishment. What is this but the acknowledgment that the slave is a moral, intellectual, and responsible being? The manhood of the slave is conceded.

It is admitted in the fact that the Southern statute books are covered with enactments forbidding, under severe fines and penalties, the teaching of the slave to read or to write. When you can point to any such laws in reference to the beasts of the field, then I may consent to argue the manhood of the slave. When the dogs in your streets, when the fowls of the air, when the cattle on your hills, when the fish of the sea and the reptiles that crawl shall be unable to distinguish the slave from a brute, then will I argue with you that the slave is a man!

For the present, it is enough to affirm the equal manhood of the Negro race. It is not astonishing that, while we are plowing, planting, and reaping, using all kinds of mechanical tools erecting houses, constructing bridges, building ships, working in metals of brass, iron, copper and silver, and gold; that, while we are reading, writing, and ciphering, acting as clerks, merchants and secretaries, having among us lawyers, doctors, ministers, poets, authors, editors, orators, and teachers; that, while we are engaged in all manner of enterprises common to other men, digging gold in California, capturing the whale in the Pacific, feeding sheep and cattle on the hillside, living, moving, acting, thinking, planning, living in families as husbands, wives, and children, and, above all, confessing and worshipping the Christian's God, and looking hopefully for life and immortality beyond the grave, we are called upon to prove that we are men!

Would you have me argue that man is entitled to liberty? That he is the rightful owner of his own body? You have already declared it. Must I argue the wrongfulness of slavery? Is that a question for republicans? Is it to be settled by the rules of logic and argumentation, as a matter beset with great difficulty, involving a doubtful application of the principle of justice, hard to be understood? How should I look today, in the presence of Americans, dividing and subdividing a discourse, to show that men have a natural right to freedom? speaking of it relatively and positively, negatively and affirmatively? To do so would be to make myself ridiculous and to offer an insult to your understanding. There is not a man beneath the canopy of heaven that does not know that slavery is wrong for him.

What, am I to argue that is wrong to make men brutes, to rob them of their liberty, to work them without wages, to keep them ignorant of their relations to their fellow men, to beat them with sticks, to flay their flesh with the last, to load their limbs with irons, to hunt them with dogs, to sell them at auction, to sunder their families, to knock out their teeth, to burn their flesh, to starve them into obedience and submission to their masters? Must I argue that a system them marked with blood, and stained with pollution, is wrong? No! I will not. I have better employment for my time and strength than such arguments would imply.

What, then remains to be argued? Is it that slavery is not divine; that God did not establish it; that our doctors of divinity are mistaken? There is blasphemy in the thought. That which is inhuman cannot be divine? Who can reason on such a proposition? They that can may; I cannot. The time for such argument is past.

. . . What, to the American slave is your Fourth of July? I answer: a day that reveals to him, more than all other days in the year, the gross injustice and cruelty to which he s the constant victim. To him, your celebration is a sham; your boasted liberty an unholy license; your national greatness, swelling vanity; your sound of rejoicing are empty and heartless; your denunciation of tyrants, brass-fronted impudence; your shouts of liberty and equality, hollow mockery; your prayers and hymns, your sermons and thanksgivings with all your religious parade and solemnity, are, to Him, mere bombast, fraud, deception, impiety, and hypocrisy a thin veil to cover up crimes which would disgrace a nation of savages. There is not a nation of savages. There is not a nation on earth guilty of practices more shocking and bloody than are the people of the United States at this very hour.

Go where you may, search where you will, roam through all the monarchies and despotisms of the Old World, travel through South America, search out every abuse, and when you have found the last, lay your facts by the side of the everyday practices of this nation, and you will say with that, for revolting barbarity and shameless hypocrisy, America reigns without a rival.

## DOCUMENT ANALYSIS

1. Why did Douglass draw on both the Bible and the U.S. Constitution to make his arguments?

_____

_____

_____

**2.** In 1852, Frederick Douglass pointed out that the promise of American democracy remained unfulfilled. Has this promise since been fulfilled? Why or why not?

_____

_____

_____

# DOCUMENT 14.2
## John C. Calhoun, Proposal to Preserve the Union (1850)

*In the antebellum period, Senator John C. Calhoun was an ardent advocate of states' rights. In the great debates of the Jacksonian era, Calhoun combated federal tariff legislation by arguing that the states enjoyed the right to nullify certain pieces of federal legislation. In the ensuing years, Calhoun became increasingly strident in his defense of southern particularity. In this 1850 speech, Calhoun summarized his views on the present condition of the Union and his fears for the future.*

I have, Senators, believed from the first that the agitation of the subject of slavery would, if not prevented by some timely and effective measure, end in disunion. . . . The agitation has been permitted to proceed, with almost no attempt to resist it, until it has reached a period when it can no longer be disguised or denied that the Union is in danger. You have thus had forced upon you the greatest and the gravest question that can ever come under your consideration: How can the Union be preserved?

. . . The first question, then, presented for consideration, in the investigation I propose to make, in order to obtain such knowledge, is: What is it that has endangered the Union?

To this question there can be but one answer: That the immediate cause is the almost universal discontent which pervades all the States composing the southern section of the Union. . . .

It is a great mistake to suppose, as is by some, that it originated with demagogues. . . . No; some cause, far deeper and more powerful than the one supposed must exist to account for discontent so wide and deep. The question, then, recurs: What is the cause of this discontent? It will be found in the belief of the people of the southern States, as prevalent as the discontent itself, that they cannot remain, as things now are, consistently with honor and safety, in the Union. The next question to be considered is: What has caused this belief?

One of the causes is, undoubtedly, to be traced to the long-continued agitation of the slave question on the part of the North, and the many aggressions which they have made on the rights of the South during the time. . . .

There is another, lying back of it, with which this is intimately connected, that may be regarded as the great and primary cause. That is to be found in the fact that the equilibrium between the two sections in the Government, as it stood when the Constitution was ratified and the Government put in action has been destroyed. At that time there was nearly a perfect equilibrium between the two, which afforded ample means to each to protect itself against the aggression of the other; but, as it now stands, one section has the exclusive power of controlling the Government, which leaves the other without any adequate means of protecting itself against its encroachment and oppression. . . .

[The] great increase of Senators, added to the great increase of the House of Representatives and the electoral college on the part of the North, which must take place under the next decade, will effectually and irretrievably destroy the equilibrium which existed when the Government commenced. . . .

What was once a constitutional federal republic is now converted, in reality, into one as absolute as that of the Autocrat of Russia, and as despotic in its tendency as any absolute Government that ever existed.

As, then, the North has the absolute control over the Government, it is manifest that on all questions between it and the South, where there is a diversity of interests, the interests of the latter will be sacrificed to the former, however oppressive the effects may be. . . . But if there was no question of vital importance to the South, in reference to which there was a diversity of views between the two sections, this state of things might be endured without the hazard of destruction to the South. But such is not the fact. . . .

I refer to the relation between the two races in the southern section, which constitutes a vital portion of her social organization. Every portion of the North entertains views and feelings more or less hostile to it. . . .

If the agitation goes on, the same force, acting with increased intensity, as has been shown, will finally snap every cord, when nothing will be left to bind the States together except force. . . .

How can the Union be saved? To this I answer, there is but one way by which it can be, and that is by adopting such measures as will satisfy the States belonging to the southern section that they can remain in the Union consistently with their honor and their safety.

## DOCUMENT ANALYSIS

**1.** What presumptions do you think underlay Calhoun's thinking?

_____

_____

_____

**2.** Judging by this document, was it likely that a peaceful solution could have been found to the nation's sectional crisis in the 1850s, or was war inevitable?

_____

_____

_____

*Fitzhugh was the descendant of an old southern family that had fallen on hard times. He practiced law and struggled as a small planter, but he ultimately made a reputation through his writings, which roused southerners to take a new and higher ground in defense of slavery. Fitzhugh insisted that all labor, not merely black, had to be enslaved, and that the world must become either all slave or all free. These views had become commonplace in the South by the 1850s, but his originality lay in the insight that slavery could survive only if the capitalist world markets were destroyed. Such views greatly alarmed northerners like Abraham Lincoln. Significantly, Fitzhugh opposed secession, arguing that a slaveholding Confederacy could not survive until the advanced capitalist countries (Europe) had themselves converted to a slave system. Economically, according to Fitzhugh, slave labor could not compete with wage labor.* [NOTE: This work was initially published as a pamphlet, and later included in another work published in 1854.]

Liberty and equality are new things under the sun. The free states of antiquity abounded with slaves. The feudal system that supplanted Roman institutions changed the form of slavery, but brought with it neither liberty nor equality. France and the Northern States of our Union have alone fully and fairly tried the experiment of a social organization founded upon universal liberty and equality of rights. England has only approximated to this condition in her commercial and manufacturing cities. The examples of small communities in Europe are not fit exponents of the working of the system. In France and in our Northern States the experiment has already failed, if we are to form our opinions from the discontent of the masses, or to believe the evidence of the Socialists, Communists, Anti-Renters, and a thousand other agrarian sects that have arisen in these countries, and threaten to subvert the whole social fabric. The leaders of these sects, at least in France, comprise within their ranks the greater number of the most cultivated and profound minds in the nation, who have made government their study. Add to the evidence of these social philosophers, who, watching closely the working of the system, have proclaimed to the world its total failure, the condition of the working classes, and we have conclusive proof that liberty and equality have not conduced to enhance the comfort or the happiness of the people. Crime and pauperism have increased. Riots, trades unions, strikes for higher wages, discontent breaking out into revolution, are things of daily occurrence, and show that the poor see and feel quite as clearly as the philosophers, that their condition is far worse under the new than under the old order of things. Radicalism and Chartism in England owe their birth to the free and equal institutions of her commercial and manufacturing districts, and are little heard of in the quiet farming districts, where remnants of feudalism still exist in the relation of landlord and tenant, and in the laws of entail and primogeniture.

So much for experiment. We will now endeavor to treat the subject theoretically, and to show that the system is on its face self-destructive and impracticable. When we look at the vegetable, animal and human kingdoms, we discover in them all a constant conflict, war, or race of competition, the result of which is, that the weaker or less healthy generation, species and individuals are continually displaced and exterminated by the stronger and more hardy. It is a means by which some contend Nature is perfecting her own work. We, however, witness the war, but do not see the improvement. Although from the earliest date of recorded history, one race of plants has been eating out and taking the place of another, the stronger or more cunning animals been destroying the feebler, and man exterminating and supplanting his fellow, still the plants, the animals and the men of to-day seem not at all superior, even in those qualities of strength and hardihood to which they owe their continued existence, to those of thousands of years ago. To this propensity of the strong to oppress and destroy the weak, government owes its existence. So strong is this propensity, and so destructive to human existence, that man has never yet been found so savage as to be without government. Forgetful of this important fact, which is the origin of all governments, the political economists and the advocates of liberty and equality propose to enhance the well being of man by trammeling his conduct as little as possible, and encouraging what they call FREE COMPETITION. Now, free competition is but another name for liberty and equality, and we must acquire precise and accurate notions about it in order to ascertain how free institutions will work. It is, then, the war or conflict to which Nature impels her creatures, and which government was intended to restrict. It is true, it is that war somewhat modified and restricted, for the warmest friends of freedom would have some government. The question is, whether the proposed restrictions are sufficient to neutralize the self-destructive tendencies which nature impresses on society. We proceed to show that the war of the wits, of mind with mind, which free competition or liberty and equality beget and encourage, is quite as oppressive, cruel and exterminating, as the war of the sword, of theft, robbery, and murder, which it forbids. It is only substituting strength of mind for strength of body. Men are told it is their duty to compete, to endeavor to get ahead of and supplant their fellow men, by the exercise of all the intellectual and moral strength with which nature and education have endowed them. "Might makes right," is the order of creation, and this law of nature, so far as mental might is concerned, is restored by liberty to man. The struggle to better one's condition, to pull others down or supplant them, is the great organic law of free society. All men being equal, all aspire to the highest honors and the largest possessions. Good men and bad men teach their children one and the same lesson—"Go ahead, push your way in the world." In such society, virtue, if virtue there be, loses all her loveliness because of her selfish aims. None but the selfish virtues are encouraged, because none other aid a man in the race of free competition. Good men and bad men have the same end in view, are in pursuit of the same object—self-promotion, self-elevation. The good man is prudent, cautious, and cunning of fence; he knows well the arts (the virtues, if you please,) which will advance his fortunes and enable him to press and supplant others; he bides his time, takes advantage of the follies, the improvidence, and vices of others, and makes his fortune out of the misfortunes of his fellow men. The bad man is rash, hasty, and unskillful. He is equally selfish, but not half so cunning. Selfishness is almost the only motive of human conduct with good and bad in free society, where every man is taught that he may change and better his condition. A vulgar adage, "Every man for himself, and devil take the hindmost," is the moral which liberty and free competition inculcate. Now, there are no more honors and wealth in proportion to numbers, in this generation, than in the one which preceded it; population fully keeps pace with the means of subsistence; hence, those who better their condition or rise to higher places in society, do so generally by pulling down others or pushing them from their places. Where men of strong minds, of strong wills, and of great self-control, come into free competition with the weak and improvident, the latter soon become the inmates of jails and penitentiaries.

The statistics of France, England and America show that pauperism and crime advance *pari passu* with liberty and equality. How can it be otherwise, when all society is combined to oppress the poor and weak minded? The rich man, however good he may be, employs the laborer who will work for the least wages. If he be a good man, his punctuality enables him to cheapen the wages of the poor man. The poor war with one another in the race of competition, in order to get employment, by underbidding; for laborers are more abundant than employers. Population increases faster than capital. Look to the situation of woman when she is thrown into this war of competition, and has to support herself by her daily wages. For the same or equally valuable services she gets not half the pay that man does, simply because the modesty of her sex prevents her from resorting to all the arts and means of competition which men employ. He who would emancipate woman, unless he could make her as coarse and strong in mind and body as man, would be her worst enemy; her subservience to and dependence on man, is necessary to her very existence. She is not a soldier fitted to enlist in the war of free competition. We do not set children and women free because they are not capable of taking care of themselves, not equal to the constant struggle of society. To set them free would be to give the lamb to the wolf to take care of. Society would quickly devour them. If the children of ten years of age were remitted to all the rights of person and property which men enjoy, all can perceive how soon ruin and penury would overtake them. But half of mankind are but grown-up children, and liberty is as fatal to them as it would be to children.

We will cite another familiar instance to prove and illustrate the destructive effects of liberty or free competition. It is that where two races of men of different capacity are brought into juxtaposition. It is the boast of the Anglo-Saxon, that by the arts of peace under the influence of free trade he can march to universal conquest. However true this may be, all know that if Englishmen or Americans settle among inferior races, they soon become the owners of the soil, and gradually extirpate or reduce to poverty the original owners. They are the wire-grass of nations. The same law of nature which enables and impels the stronger race to oppress and exterminate the weaker, is constantly at work in the bosom of every society, between its stronger and weaker members. Liberty and equality rather encourage than restrict this law in its deadly operation. A Northern gentleman, who was both statesman and philosopher, once told us, that his only objection to domestic slavery was, that it would perpetuate an inferior race, who, under the influence of free trade and free competition would otherwise disappear from the earth.

Domestic slavery in the Southern States has produced the same results in elevating the character of the master that it did in Greece and Rome. He is lofty and independent in his sentiments, generous, affectionate, brave and eloquent; he is superior to the Northerner, in every thing but the arts of thrift. . . .

But the chief and far most important enquiry is, how does slavery affect the condition of the slave? One of the wildest sects of Communists in France proposes not only to hold all property in common, but to divide the profits not according to each man's in-put and labor but according to each man's wants. Now this is precisely the system of domestic slavery with us. We provide for each slave, in old age and in infancy, in sickness and in health, not according to his labor, but according to his wants. The master's wants are most costly and refined, and he therefore gets a larger share of the profits. A Southern farm is the beau ideal of Communism; it is a joint concern, in which the slave consumes more than the master, of the coarse products, and is far happier, because although the concern may fail, he is always sure of a support; he is only transferred to another master to participate in the profits of another concern; he marries when he pleases, because he knows he will have to work no more with a family than without one, and whether he live or die, that family will be taken care of; he exhibits all the pride of ownership, despises a partner in a smaller concern, "a poor man's negro," boasts of "our crops, horses, fields and cattle;" and is as happy as a human being can be. And why should he not?—he enjoys as much of the fruits of the farm as he is capable of doing, and the wealthiest can do no more. Great wealth brings many additional cares, but few additional enjoyments. Our stomachs do not increase in capacity with our fortunes. We want no more clothing to keep us warm. We may create new wants, but we cannot create new pleasures. The intellectual enjoyments which wealth affords are probably balanced by the new cares it brings along with it.

There is no rivalry, no competition to get employment among slaves, as among free laborers. Nor is there a war between master and slave. The master's interest prevents his reducing the slave's allowance or wages in infancy or sickness, for he might lose the slave by so doing. His feeling for his slave never permits him to stint him in old age. The slaves are all well fed, well clad, have plenty of fuel, and are happy. They have no dread of the future—no fear of want. A state of dependence is the only condition in which reciprocal affection can exist among human beings—the only situation in which the war of competition ceases, and peace, amity and good will arise. A state of independence always begets more or less of jealous rivalry and hostility. A man loves his children because they are weak, helpless and dependent; he loves his wife for similar reasons. When his children grow up and assert their independence, he is apt to transfer his affection to his grand-children. He ceases to love his wife when she becomes masculine or rebellious; but slaves are always dependent, never the rivals of their master. Hence, though men are often found at variance with wife or children, we never saw one who did not like his slaves, and rarely a slave who was not devoted to his master. "I am thy servant!" disarms me of the power of master. Every man feels the beauty, force and truth of this sentiment of Sterne. But he who acknowledges its truth, tacitly admits that dependence is a tie of affection, that the relation of master and slave is one of mutual good will. Volumes written on the subject would not prove as much as this single sentiment. It has found its way to the heart of every reader, and carried conviction along with it. The slave-holder is like other men; he will not tread on the worm nor break the bruised reed. The ready submission of the slave, nine times out of ten, disarms his wrath even when the slave has offended. The habit of command may make him imperious and fit him for rule; but he is only imperious when thwarted or crossed by his equals; he would scorn to put on airs of command among blacks, whether slaves or free; he always speaks to them in a kind and subdued tone. We go farther, and say the slave-holder is better than others—because he has greater occasion for the exercise of the affections. His whole life is spent in providing for the minutest wants of others, in taking care of them in sickness and in health. Hence he is the least selfish of men. Is not the old bachelor who retires to seclusion, always selfish? Is not the head of a large family almost always kind and benevolent? And is not the slave-holder the head of the largest family? Nature compels master and slave to be friends; nature makes employers and free laborers enemies."

## DOCUMENT ANALYSIS

1. What did Fitzhugh consider to be the basic failures of the northern states and France?

_____

_____

_____

2. According to Fitzhugh, what was the proper status and role of women?

_____

_____

_____

3. List some examples that illustrate why Fitzhugh considered slavery to be superior to free labor.

_____

_____

_____

## DOCUMENT 15.1
### Letter from H. Ford Douglas to Frederick Douglass's *Monthly* (January 8, 1863)
From: Edwin S. Redkey, ed., *A Grand Army of Black Men* (1992), pp. 24–25.

*Edwin S. Redkey's book is a collection of more than 150 letters from African American soldiers to various newspapers and journals. The excerpt below was written just days after the Emancipation Proclamation was issued on January 1, 1863. At that point the Union decided to accept, and in fact encourage, black enlistment in the army and navy. Although enlistment was slow at first, black leaders such as Frederick Douglass openly encouraged enlistment because they believed it would help assure black citizenship when the war was over. By May 1863 the U.S. government had established the Bureau of Colored Troops. Eventually, 179,000 black men served in the army, and other 19,000 in the navy.*

My wife sent me this morning the *Monthly* for December containing your appeal to England to "hands off" in this fearful conflict for freedom. It was indeed gratifying to me who have always felt more than a friendly interest in you and yours to read your eloquent and manly words of admonition to the Old Saxon mother States to give no moral or legal countenance to the claims of the impious Confederate States of America in their attempt to set up a Government established upon the idea of the perpetual bondage of the Negro. England has wisely withstood every temptation to do so—Abraham Lincoln has crossed the Rubicon and by one simple act of Justice to the slave links his memory with immortality.

The slaves are free! How can I write these precious words? And yet it is so unless twenty millions of people cradled in Christianity and civilization for a thousand years commit the foulest perjury that ever blackened the pages of history. In anticipation of this result I enlisted six months ago in order to be better prepared to play my part in the great drama of the Negro's redemption. I wanted its drill, its practical details, for mere theory does not make a good soldier. I have learned something of war, for I

have seen war in its brightest as well as its bloodiest phase, and yet I have nothing to regret. For since the stern necessities of this struggle have laid bare the naked issue of freedom on one side and slavery on the other—freedom shall have, in the future of this conflict if necessary, my blood as it has had in the past my earnest and best words. It seems to me that you can have no good reason for withholding from the government your hearty cooperation. This war will educate Mr. Lincoln out of his idea of the deportation of the Negro quite as fast as it has some of his other pro-slavery ideas with respect to employing them as soldiers.

Hitherto they have been socially and politically ignored by this government, but now by the fortunes of war they are cast morally and mentally helpless (so to speak) into the broad sunlight of our Republican civilization there to be educated and lifted to a higher and nobler life. National duties and responsibilities are not to be colonized, they must be heroically met and religiously performed. This mighty waste of manhood resulting from the dehumanizing character of slave institutions of America is now to be given back to the world through the patient toil and self-denial of this proud and haughty race. They must now pay back the negro in Spiritual culture in opportunities for self-improvement what they have taken from him for two hundred years by the constant over-taxing of his physical nature. This law of supply and demand regulates itself. And so this question of the colonization of the negro; it will be settled by laws over which war has no control. Now is the time for you to finish the crowning work of your life. Go to work at once and raise a Regiment and offer your services to the government, and I am confident they will be accepted. They say we will not fight. I want to see it tried on. You are the one to me of all others, to demonstrate this fact.

I belong to company G, 95th Regiment Illinois Volunteers—Captain Eliot N. Bush—a Christian and a gentleman. . . .

### DOCUMENT ANALYSIS

1. Why did Douglas enlist in the army? What did he hope to gain from his enlistment?

_____
_____
_____

2. What was his opinion of the idea that African Americans should be colonized?

_____
_____
_____

3. What did he mean by the phrase "Abraham Lincoln has crossed the Rubicon"?

_____
_____
_____

## DOCUMENT 15.2
### Clara Barton, Memoirs of Medical Life at the Battlefield (1862)

*Clara Barton was one of many women who supported the war effort by nursing troops, raising funds, and making clothes and bandages. This selection from her memoirs describes her initial ambivalence about exposing herself to the horrors of combat and the nightmarish conditions she found on the battlefields at Cedar Mountain and Second Manassas (Bull Run) during the summer of 1862.*

I was strong and thought I might go to the rescue of the men who fell. . . What could I do but go with them, or work for them and my country? The patriot blood of my father was warm in my veins. The country which he had fought for, I might at least work for. . .

But I struggled long and hard with my sense of propriety—with the appalling fact that I was only a woman whispering in one ear, and thundering in the other the groans of suffering men dying like dogs—unfed and unsheltered, for the life of every institution which had protected and educated me!

I said that I struggled long and hard with my sense of propriety and I say it with humiliation and shame. I am ashamed that I thought of such a thing.

When our armies fought on Cedar Mountain, I broke the shackles and went to the field. . .

Five days and nights with three hours sleep—a narrow escape from capture—and some days of getting the wounded into hospitals at Washington, brought Saturday, August 30. And if you chance to feel, that the positions I occupied were rough and unseemly for a woman—I can only reply that they were rough and unseemly for men. But under all, lay the life of the nation. I had inherited the rich blessing of health and strength of constitution—such as are seldom given to woman—and I felt that some return was due from me and that I ought to be there. . .

. . .Our coaches were not elegant or commodious; they had no seats, no platforms, no steps, a slide door on the side the only entrance, and this higher than my head. For my man attaining my elevated position, I must beg of you to draw on your imaginations and spare me the labor of reproducing the boxes, boards, and rails, which in those days, seemed to help me up and down the world. We did not criticize the unsightly helpers and were thankful that the stiff springs did not quite jostle us out. This need not be limited to this particular trip or train, but will for all that I have known in Army life. This is the kind of conveyance which your tons of generous gifts have reached the field with the freights. These trains through day and night, sunshine and heat and cold, have thundered over heights, across plains, the ravines, and over hastily built army bridges 90 feet across the stream beneath.

At 10 o'clock Sunday (August 31) our train drew up at Fairfax Station. The ground, for acres, was a thinly wooded slope—and among the trees on the leaves and grass, were laid the wounded who pouring in by scores of wagon loads, as picked up on the field the flag of truce. All day they came and the whole hillside was red. Bales of hay were broken open and scattered over the ground littering of cattle, and the sore, famishing men were laid upon it.

And when the night shut in, in the midst and darkness about us, we knew that standing apart from the world of anxious hearts, throbbing over the whole country, we were a little band of almost empty handed workers literally by ourselves in the wild woods of Virginia, with 3,000 suffering men crowded upon the few acres within our reach.

After gathering up every available implement or convenience for our work, our domestic inventory stood 2 water buckets, 5 tin cups, 1 camp kettle, 1 stew pan, 2 lanterns, 4 bread knives, 3 plates, and a 2-quart tin dish, and 3,000 guest to serve.

You will perceive by this, that I had not yet learned to equip myself, for I was no Pallas, ready armed, but grew into my work by hard thinking and sad experience. It may serve to relieve your apprehension for the future of my labors if I assure you that I was never caught so again.

But the most fearful scene was reserved for the night. I have said that the ground was littered with dry hay and that we had only two lanterns, but there were plenty of candles. The wounded were laid so close that it was impossible to move about in the dark. The slightest misstep brought a torrent of groans from some poor mangled fellow in your path.

Consequently here were seen persons of all grades from the careful man of God who walked with a prayer upon his lips to the careless driver hunting for his lost whip—each wandering about among this hay with an open flaming candle in his hands.

The slightest accident, the mere dropping of a light could have enveloped in flames this whole mass of helpless men.

How we watched and pleaded and cautioned as we worked and wept that night! How we put socks and slippers upon their cold feet, wrapped your blankets and quilts about them, and when we no longer these to give, how we covered them in the hay and left them to their rest!. . .

The slight, naked chest of a fair-haired lad caught my eye. Dropping down beside him, I bent low to draw the remnant of his blouse about him, when with a quick cry he threw his left arm across my neck and, burying his face in the folds of my dress, wept like a child at his mother's knee. I took his head in my hands and held it until great burst of grief passed away. "And do you know me?" he asked at length, "I am Charley Hamilton, we used to carry your satchel home from school!" My faithful pupil, poor Charley. That mangled right hand would never carry a satchel again.

About three o'clock in the morning I observed a surgeon with a little flickering candle in hand approaching me with cautious step up in the wood. "Lady," he said as he drew near, "will you go with me? Out on the hills is a poor distressed lad, mortally wounded, and dying. His piteous cries for his sister have touched all our hearts none of us can relieve him but rather seem to distress him by presence."

By this time I was following him back over the bloody track, with great beseeching eyes of anguish on every side looking up into our faces, saying so plainly "Don't step on us."

## DOCUMENT ANALYSIS

1. What conditions did Barton face when she reached the hospital in Fairfax? How did she cope with them?

_____

_____

_____

2. Women traditionally did not serve as nurses at this time period. How did that reality affect Barton's efforts at helping the men? How did the soldiers react to her assistance?

_____

_____

_____

## DOCUMENT 16.1
### Carl Schurz, *Report on the Condition of the South* (1865)

*Carl Schurz was a German immigrant who rose to great political prominence in the United States. He was a leading member of the Republican Party and a great supporter of Lincoln. During the Civil War he attained the rank of major general. After the war, Schurz continued to be active in politics, supporting many reform movements. He was writer and editor for several English- and German-language newspapers, and he published several books. In 1865 President Andrew Johnson sent Schurz to tour the South and to report on its postwar status. An excerpt from Schurz's report appears below. The president was not pleased with the report.*

We ought to keep in view, above all, the nature of the problem which is to be solved. As to what is commonly termed "reconstruction," it is not only the political machinery of the States and their constitutional relations to the general government, but the whole organism of southern society that must be reconstructed, or rather constructed anew, so as to bring it in harmony with the rest of American society. The difficulties of this task are not to be considered overcome when the people of the south take the oath of allegiance and elect governors and legislatures and members of Congress, and militia captains. That this would be done had become certain as soon as the surrenders of the southern armies had made further resistance impossible, and nothing in the world was left, even to the most uncompromising rebel, but to submit or to emigrate. It was also natural that they should avail themselves of every chance offered them to resume control of their home affairs and to regain their influence in the Union. But this can hardly be called the first step towards the solution of the true problem, and it is a fair question to ask, whether the hasty gratification of their desire to resume such control would not create new embarrassments.

The true nature of the difficulties of the situation is this: The general government of the republic has, by proclaiming the emancipation of the slaves, commenced a great social revolution in the south, but has, as yet, not completed it. Only the negative part of it is accomplished. The slaves are emancipated in point of form, but free labor has not yet been put in the place of slavery in point of fact. And now, in the midst of this critical period of transition, the power which originated the revolution is expected to turn over its whole future development to another power which from the beginning was hostile to it and has never yet entered into its spirit, leaving the class in whose favor it was made completely without power to protect itself and to take an influential part in that development. The history of the world will be searched in vain for a proceeding similar to this which did not lead either to a rapid and violent reaction, or to the most serious trouble and civil disorder. It cannot be said that the conduct of the southern people since the close of the war has exhibited such extraordinary wisdom and self-abnegation as to make them an exception to the rule. In my dispatches from the south I repeatedly expressed the opinion that the people were not yet in a frame of mind to legislate calmly and understandingly upon the subject of free negro labor. And this I reported to be the opinion of some of our most prominent military commanders and other observing men.

It is, indeed, difficult to imagine circumstances more unfavorable for the development of a calm and unprejudiced public opinion than those under which the southern people are at present laboring. The war has not only defeated their political aspirations, but it has broken up their whole social organization. When the rebellion was put down they found themselves not only conquered in a political and military sense, but economically ruined. The planters, who represented the wealth of the southern country, are partly laboring under the severest embarrassments, partly reduced to absolute poverty. Many who are stripped of all available means, and have nothing but their land, cross their arms in gloomy despondency, incapable of rising to a manly resolution. Others, who still possess means, are at a loss how to use them, as their old way of doing things is, by the abolition of slavery, rendered impracticable, at least where the military arm of the government has enforced emancipation. Others are still trying to go on in the old way, and that old way is in fact the only one they understand, and in which they have any confidence. Only a minority is trying to adopt the new order of things. A large number of the plantations, probably a considerable majority of the more valuable estates, is under heavy mortgages, and the owners know that, unless they retrieve their fortunes in a comparatively short space of time, their property will pass out of their hands. Almost all are, to some extent, embarrassed.

The nervous anxiety which such a state of things produces extends also to those classes of society which, although not composed of planters, were always in close business connection with the planting interest, and there was hardly a branch of commerce or industry in the south which was not directly or indirectly so connected. Besides, the southern soldiers, when returning from the war, did not, like the northern soldiers, find a prosperous community which merely waited for their arrival to give them remunerative employment. They found, many of them, their homesteads destroyed, their farms devastated, their families in distress; and those that were less unfortunate found, at all events, an impoverished and exhausted community which had but little to offer them. Thus a great many have been thrown upon the world to shift as best they can. They must do something honest or dishonest, and must do it soon, to make a living, and their prospects are, at present, not very bright. Thus that nervous anxiety to hastily repair broken fortunes, and to prevent still greater ruin and distress, embraces nearly all classes, and imprints upon all the movements of the social body a morbid character. In which direction will these people be most apt to turn their eyes? Leaving the prejudice of race out of the question, from early youth they have been acquainted with but one system of labor, and with that one system they have been in the habit of identifying all their interests. They know of no way to help themselves but the one they are accustomed to. Another system of labor is presented to them, which, however, owing to circumstances which they do not appreciate, appears at first in an unpromising light. To try it they consider an experiment which they cannot afford to make while their wants are urgent. They have not reasoned calmly enough to convince themselves that the trial must be made. It is, indeed, not wonderful that, under such circumstances, they should study, not how to introduce and develop free labor, but how to avoid its introduction, and how to return as much and as quickly as possible to something like the old order of things. Nor is it wonderful that such studies should find an expression in their attempts at legislation. But the circumstance that this tendency is natural does not render it less dangerous and objectionable.

The practical question presents itself: Is the immediate restoration of the late rebel States to absolute self-control so necessary that it must be done even at the risk of endangering one of the great results of the war, and of bringing on in those States insurrection or anarchy, or would it not be better to postpone that restoration until such dangers are passed? If, as long as the change from slavery to free labor is known to the southern people only by its destructive results, these people must be expected to throw obstacles in its way, would it not seem necessary that the movement of social "reconstruction" be kept in the right channel by the hand of the power which originated the change, until that change can have disclosed some of its beneficial effects? It is certain that every success of free negro labor will augment the number of its friends, and disarm some of the prejudices and assumptions of its opponents. I am convinced one good harvest made by unadulterated free labor in the south would have a far better effect than all the oaths that have been taken, and all the ordinances that have as yet been passed by southern conventions. But how can such a result be attained?

The facts enumerated in this report, as well as the news we receive from the south from day to day, must make it evident to every unbiased observer that unadulterated free labor cannot be had at present, unless the national government holds its protective and controlling hand over it. It appears, also, that the more efficient this protection of free labor against all disturbing and reactionary influences, the sooner may such a satisfactory result be looked for. One reason why the southern people are so slow in accommodating themselves to the new order of things is, that they confidently expect soon to be permitted to regulate matters according to their own notions. Every concession made to them by the government has been taken as an encouragement to persevere in this hope, and, unfortunately for them, this hope is nourished by influences from other parts of the country. Hence their anxiety to have their State governments restored at once, to have the troops withdrawn, and the Freedmen's Bureau abolished, although a good many discerning men know well that, in view of the lawless spirit still prevailing, it would be far better for them to have the general order of society firmly maintained by the federal power until things have arrived at a final settlement. Had, from the beginning, the conviction been forced upon them that the adulteration of the new order of things by the admixture of elements belonging to the system of slavery would under no circumstances be permitted, a much larger number would have launched their energies into the new channel, and, seeing that they could do "no better," faithfully co-operated with the government. It is hope which fixes them in their perverse notions. That hope nourished or fully gratified, they will persevere in the same direction. That hope destroyed, a great many will, by the force of necessity, at once accommodate themselves to the logic of the change.

If, therefore, the national government firmly and unequivocally announces its policy not to give up the control of the free-labor reform until it is finally accomplished, the progress of that reform will undoubtedly be far more rapid and far less difficult than it will be if the attitude of the government is such as to permit contrary hopes to be indulged in. The machinery by which the government has so far exercised its protection of the negro and of free labor in the south—the Freedmen's Bureau—is very

unpopular in that part of the country, as every institution placed there as a barrier to reactionary aspirations would be. That abuses were committed with the management of freedmen's affairs; that some of the officers of the bureau were men of more enthusiasm than discretion, and in many cases went beyond their authority: all this is certainly true. But, while the southern people are always ready to expatiate upon the shortcomings of the Freedmen's Bureau, they are not so ready to recognize the services it has rendered. I feel warranted in saying that not half of the labor that has been done in the south this year, or will be done there next year, would have been or would be done but for the exertions of the Freedmen's Bureau. The confusion and disorder of the transition period would have been infinitely greater had not an agency interfered which possessed the confidence of the emancipated slaves; which could disabuse them of any extravagant notions and expectations and be trusted; which could administer to them good advice and be voluntarily obeyed. No other agency, except one placed there by the national government, could have wielded that moral power whose interposition was so necessary to prevent southern society from falling at once into the chaos of a general collision between its different elements. That the success achieved by the Freedmen's Bureau is as yet very incomplete cannot be disputed. A more perfect organization and a more carefully selected personnel may be desirable; but it is doubtful whether a more suitable machinery can be devised to secure to free labor in the south that protection against disturbing influences which the nature of the situation still imperatively demands.

## DOCUMENT ANALYSIS

1. Was Schurz hopeful about the situation in the South in 1865?

_____

_____

_____

_____

2. What did Schurz predict would happen in the South? Was he correct?

_____

_____

_____

3. What was Schurz's opinion of the Freedmen's Bureau? Did he recommend that it continue to operate?

_____

_____

_____

## DOCUMENT 16.2
### James T. Rapier, Testimony Before U.S. Senate Regarding the Agricultural Labor Force in the South (1880)

*James T. Rapier was a free black man who was born in Alabama during slavery. Educated in Alabama and Canada, he was a lawyer, newspaper correspondent, teacher, successful politician (Republican representative to Congress from 1873 to 1875), and cotton planter. During and after Reconstruction, which officially ended in 1877, there was national concern about the southern labor system known as sharecropping, which had replaced slavery. Sharecropping, combined with legal restrictions, served to keep black farmers—and some white farmers as well—in debt to landowners. Success was practically impossible. In his testimony before the U.S. Senate, Rapier describes conditions in Alabama in 1880.*

**The Witness:** Well, sir, there are several reasons why the colored people desire to emigrate from Alabama; one among them is the poverty of the South. On a large part of it a man cannot make a decent living. Another is their want of school privileges in the State: and there is a majority of the people who believe that they cannot any longer get justice in the courts; and another and the greatest reason is found in the local laws that we have, and which are very oppressive to that class of people in the black belt.

**Mr. Vance:** State what some of them are.

A. First, we have only schools about three months in the year, and I suppose I need not say anything more on that head. In reference to the poverty of the soil, 33 to 40 per cent of the lands in Alabama is about all on which a man can make a living.

Q. Do you mean the parts that are subdued?

A. Yes, sir; the arable land. The average is one-third of a bale of cotton to the acre, not making three bales to the hand; and a hundred bushels of corn to the hand, on an average. Then take the price of cotton for the last two years; it has not netted more than $45 to $47.50 to the bale; and I suppose it would not be amiss for me to state something of the plans of working the land in Alabama.